shakespearean criticism

"Thou art a Monument without a tomb,
And art alive still while thy Book doth live
And we have wits to read and praise to give."

Ben Jonson, from the preface to the First Folio, 1623.

Frontispiece to the First Folio (1623). By permission of the Folger Shakespeare Library.

ISSN 0883-9123

Volume 46

shakespearean criticism

Excerpts from the Criticism of
William Shakespeare's Plays and Poetry,
from the First Published Appraisals
to Current Evaluations

Michelle Lee
Editor

Kathy D. Darrow
Associate Editor

DETROIT • SAN FRANCISCO • LONDON • BOSTON • WOODBRIDGE, CT

STAFF

Michelle Lee, *Editor*
Kathy D. Darrow, *Assistant Editor*

Janet Witalec, *Managing Editor*

Maria Franklin, *Permissions Manager*
Kimberly F. Smilay, *Permissions Specialist*
Kelly A. Quin, *Permissions Associate*
Sandy Gore, *Permissions Assistant*

Victoria B. Cariappa, *Research Manager*
Patricia T. Ballard, Tamara C. Nott, Tracie A. Richardson,
Corrine Stocker, *Research Associates*
Timothy Lehnerer, *Research Assistant*

Dorothy Maki, *Manufacturing Manager*
Cindy Range, *Buyer*

Randy Bassett, *Image Database Supervisor*
Robert Duncan, Michael Logusz, *Imaging Specialists*
Pamela A. Reed, *Imaging Coordinator*

Since this page cannot legibly accommodate all copyright notices, the acknowledgments constitute an extension of the copyright notice.

While every effort has been made to ensure the reliability of the information presented in this publication, The Gale Group neither guarantees the accuracy of the data contained herein nor assumes any responsibility for errors, omissions or discrepancies. Gale accepts no payment for listing; and inclusion in the publication of any organization, agency, institution, publication, service, or individual does not imply endorsement of the editors or publisher. Errors brought to the attention of the publisher and verified to the satisfaction of the publisher will be corrected in future editions.

This publication is a creative work fully protected by all applicable copyright laws, as well as by misappropriation, trade secret, unfair competition, and other applicable laws. The authors and editors of this work have added value to the underlying factual material herein through one or more of the following: unique and original selection, coordination, expression, arrangement, and classification of the information.

All rights to this publication will be vigorously defended.

Copyright © 1999
The Gale Group
27500 Drake Rd.
Farmington Hills, MI 48331-3535

This book is printed on acid-free paper that meets the minimum requirements of American National Standard for Information Sciences—Permanence Paper for Printed Library Materials, ANSI Z39.48-1984.

Library of Congress Catalog Card Number 86-645085
ISBN 0-7876-2422-5
ISSN 0883-9123

Printed in the United States of America
Published simultaneously in the United Kingdom
by The Gale Group International Limited
(An affiliated company of The Gale Group)
10 9 8 7 6 5 4 3 2 1

The Gale Group

Contents

Preface vii

Acknowledgments ix

List of Plays and Poems Covered in *SC* xii

Shakespeare's Clowns and Fools

    Introduction 1

    Overviews 1

    Fools in the Histories and Historical Fools 33

    Fools in the Comedies 60

    Fools in the Tragedies 74

    Further Reading 85

As You Like It

    Introduction 87

    Overviews 88

    Touchstone 105

    Sexual Identity 127

    Time 156

    Further Reading 174

King Lear

    Introduction 176

    Overview 177

    Lear's Fool 191

    Cordelia 218

The Family	231
Lear	254
Politics and the Law	269
Further Reading	283

Twelfth Night

Introduction	285
Overviews	286
Feste	297
Characterization	324
Gender Issues	347
Further Reading	387

Guide to *Shakespearean Criticism* Series 391

Cumulative Character Index 393

Cumulative Critic Index 403

Cumulative Topic Index 441

Cumulative Topic Index, by Play 459

Preface

Shakespearean Criticism (SC) provides students, educators, theatergoers, and other interested readers with valuable insight into Shakespeare's drama and poetry. A multiplicity of viewpoints documenting the critical reaction of scholars and commentators from the seventeenth century to the present day derives from the hundreds of periodicals and books excerpted for the series. Students and teachers at all levels of study will benefit from *SC*, whether they seek information for class discussions and written assignments, new perspectives on traditional issues, or the most noteworthy analyses of Shakespeare's artistry.

Scope of the Series

Volumes 1 through 10 of the series present a unique historical overview of the critical response to each Shakespearean work, representing a broad range of interpretations. Volumes 11 through 26 recount the performance history of Shakespeare's plays on the stage and screen through eyewitness reviews and retrospective evaluations of individual productions, comparisons of major interpretations, and discussions of staging issues.

Beginning with Volume 27 in the series, *SC* focuses on criticism published after 1960, with a view to providing the reader with the most significant modern critical approaches. Each volume is ordered around a theme that is central to the study of Shakespeare, such as politics, religion, or sexuality. The topic entry that introduces the volume is comprised of general essays that discuss this theme with reference to all of Shakespeare's works. Following the topic entry are several entries devoted to individual works. Volume 46 is devoted to the topic of clowns and fools in Shakespeare's works, and provides commentary on that topic as well as the plays *As You Like It, King Lear,* and *Twelfth Night*.

SC also compiles an annual volume of the most noteworthy essays published on Shakespeare during the previous year. The essays, reprinted in their entirety, have been recommended to Gale by an international panel of distinguished scholars. The most recent volume, *SC Yearbook 1997,* Volume 42 in the series, was published in October 1998.

Organization of the Book

Each entry consists of the following elements: an introduction, critical essays, and an annotated bibliography of further reading.

- The **Introduction** outlines modern interpretations of individual Shakespearean topics, plays, and poems.

- The **Criticism** for each entry consists of essays that are arranged both thematically and chronologically. This provides an overview of the major areas of concern in the analysis of Shakespeare's works, as well as a useful perspective on changes in critical evaluation over recent decades. Footnotes that appear with previously published pieces of criticism are reprinted at the end of each essay or excerpt. In the case of excerpted criticism, only those footnotes that pertain to the excerpted text are included.

- All of the individual essays are preceded by **Explanatory Notes** as an additional aid to students using *SC*. The explanatory notes summarize the criticism that follows.

- A complete **Bibliographical Citation** providing publication information precedes each piece of criticism.

- Each volume includes such **Illustrations** as reproductions of images from the Shakespearean period, paintings and sketches of eighteenth- and nineteenth-century performers, photographs of modern productions, and stills from film adaptations.

- The annotated bibliography of **Further Reading** appearing at the end of each entry suggests additional sources of study for the reader. Explanatory notes summarize each essay or book listed here.

- Each volume of *SC* provides the following indices:

    Cumulative Character Index: Identifies the principal characters of discussion in the criticism of each play and non-dramatic poem.
    Cumulative Critic Index: Identifies each critic that has appeared in *SC*.
    Cumulative Topic Index: Identifies the principal topics in the criticism and stage history of each work. The topics are arranged alphabetically, by topic.
    Cumulative Topic Index, by Play: Identifies the principal topics in the criticism and stage history of each work. The topics are arranged alphabetically, by play.

Citing *Shakespearean Criticism*

Students who quote directly from any volume in the Literature Criticism Series in written assignments may use the following general forms to footnote reprinted criticism. The first example pertains to material drawn from periodicals, the second to material reprinted from books.

[1]Gordon Ross Smith, "Shakespeare's *Henry V*: Another Part of the Critical Forest," in *Journal of the History of Ideas,* XXXVII, No. 1 (January-March 1976), 3-26; excerpted and reprinted in *Shakespearean Criticism,* Vol. 30, ed. Marie Lazzari (Detroit: Gale Research, 1996), pp. 262-73.

[2]Katherine Eisaman Maus, *Inwardness and Theater in the English Renaissance* (The University of Chicago Press, 1995); excerpted and reprinted in *Shakespearean Criticism,* Vol. 33, ed. Dana Ramel Barnes and Marie Lazzari, (Detroit: Gale Research, 1997), pp. 112-17.

Suggestions Are Welcome

The editors encourage comments and suggestions from readers on any aspect of the *SC* series. In response to various recommendations, several features have been added to *SC* since the series began, including the topic index and the sample bibliographic citations noted above. Readers are cordially invited to write, call, or fax the editors: *Shakespearean Criticism,* Gale Research, 27500 Drake Rd., Farmington Hills, MI 48331-3535. Call toll-free at 1-800-347-GALE or fax to 1-248-699-8049.

Acknowledgments

The editors wish to thank the copyright holders of the excerpted criticism included in this volume and the permissions managers of many book and magazine publishing companies for assisting us in securing reproduction rights. We are also grateful to the staffs of the Detroit Public Library, the Library of Congress, the University of Detroit Mercy Library, Wayne State University Purdy/Kresge Library Complex, and the University of Michigan Libraries for making their resources available to us. Following is a list of the copyright holders who have granted us permission to reproduce material in this volume of *SC*. Every effort has been made to trace copyright, but if omissions have been made, please let us know.

COPYRIGHTED EXCERPTS IN *SC*, VOLUME 46, WERE REPRODUCED FROM THE FOLLOWING PERIODICALS:

The Centennial Review, v. XXIII, Fall, 1979 for "*King Lear*: The Lear Family Romance" by Harry Berger, Jr. © 1979 by *The Centennial Review*. Reproduced by permission of the publisher and the author.—***The Classical Journal***, v. XXV, September, 1981. Reproduced by permission of the publisher.—***The Critical Quarterly***, v. 10, Autumn, 1968; v. 13, Autumn, 1971. © Manchester University Press 1968, 1971. Both reproduced by permission of Basil Blackwell Limited.—***Costerus: Essays in English & American Language & Literature***, v. 5, 1972. © Editions Rodopi B. V. 1972. Reproduced by permission.—***The Dalhousie Review***, v. 50, Spring, 1970. Reproduced by permission of the publisher.—***The Durham University Journal***, v. LXXI, June, 1979. Reproduced by permission.—***ELH***, v. 40, Winter, 1973. © 1973 by The Johns Hopkins University Press. Reproduced by permission of The Johns Hopkins University Press.—***English Literary Renaissance***, v. 21, Winter, 1991. Copyright © 1991 by *English Literary Renaissance*. Reproduced by permission.—***Essays in Criticism***, v. XXXIX, October, 1989 for "Finding a Part for Parolles" by David Ellis. Reproduced by permission of Oxford University Press and the author.—***Hebrew University Studies in Literature***, v. 11, Spring, 1983. © 1983 by HSLA. All rights reserved. Reproduced by permission.—***Interpretation: A Journal of Political Philosophy***, v. 21, Spring, 1994 for *"King Lear"* by David Lowenthal. Copyright © 1994 *Interpretation*. Reproduced by permission of the publisher and the author.—***The Massachusetts Review***, v. XXII, Winter, 1981. © 1981. Reproduced from The Massachusetts Review, Inc. by permission.—***The Modern Review***, v. CXXIX, May, 1969 for "An Apology for Fools (—A Study of Shakespearean Fools)" by Shyam M. Asnani. Reproduced by permission of the author.—***New Theatre Quarterly***, v. 1, February, 1985 for "Playing the Fool: The Pragmatic Status of Shakespeare's Clowns" by Roberta Mullini. Reproduced by permission of the author.—***Renascence: Essays on Values in Literature***, v. XLIII, Summer, 1991. © copyright 1991, Marquette University Press. Reproduced by permission.—***Shakespeare Quarterly***, v. XXVI, Summer, 1975; v. XXVI, Winter, 1975; v. 39, Spring, 1988; v. 47, Fall, 1996. © The Folger Shakespeare Library, 1975, 1988, 1996. All reproduced by permission of *Shakespeare Quarterly*.—***Shakespeare Survey: An Annual Survey of Shakespeare Studies and Production***, v. 35, 1982 for "The Art of the Comic Duologue in Three Plays by Shakespeare" by Robert Wilcher; v. 44, 1992 for "Demystifying the Mystery of State: *King Lear* and the World Upside Down" by Margot Heinemann; v. 46, 1994 for "Malvolio and the Eunuchs: Text and Revels in *Twelfth Night*" by John Astington. © Cambridge University Press, 1982, 1992, 1994. All reproduced with the permission of Cambridge University Press and the respective authors.—***Stanford Literature Review***, v. 7, Spring-Fall, 1990 for "'Tis Not So Sweet as It Was Before': Orsino and Olivia in *Twelfth Night*," by René Girard. © 1990 by ANMA Libri & Co. All rights reserved. Reproduced by permission of the publisher and Department of French and Italian, Stanford University and the author.—***Texas Studies in Literature and Language***, v. 27, Winter, 1985. Copyright © 1985 by the University of Texas Press. All rights reserved. Reproduced by permission of the publisher.—***The University of Dayton Review***, v. 23, Spring, 1995. Reproduced by permission.

COPYRIGHTED EXCERPTS IN *SC*, VOLUME 46, WERE REPRODUCED FROM THE FOLLOWING BOOKS:

Alulis, Joseph. From "Fathers and Children: Matter, Mirth, and Melancholy in *As You Like It*" in ***Shakespeare's Political Pageant: Essays in Literature and Politics***. Edited by Joesph Allulis and Vickie Sullivan. Rowman and Littlefield Publishers, Inc., 1994. Copyright © 1994 by Rowman and Littlefield Publishers, Inc. All rights reserved. Reproduced by permission.—Berge, Mark. From "'My Poor Fool is Hanged': Cordelia, the Fool, Silence and Irresolution in *King Lear*" in ***Reclamations of Shakespeare***. Editions Rodopi B. V., 1994. © Editions Rodopi B. V. 1994. Reproduced by permission.—Bryant, Jr., J. A. From *Shakespeare and the Uses of Comedy*. The University Press of Kentucky, 1986. Copyright © 1986 by The University Press of Kentucky. Reproduced by permission.—Cox, Catherine I. From "'Horn Pypes and Funeralls': Suggestions of Hope in Shakespeare's Tragedies" in *The Work of Dissimilitude: Essays from the Sixth Citadel Conference on Medieval and Renaissance Literature*. Edited by David G. Allen and Robert A. White. University of Delaware Press, 1992. © 1992 by Associated University Presses, Inc. All rights reserved. Reproduced by permission.—Dash, Irene G. From *Women's Worlds in Shakespeare's Plays*. University of Delaware Press, 1997. © 1997 by Irene G. Dash. All rights reserved. Reproduced by permission.—Donno, Elizabeth Story. From "Critical Commentary" in *Twelfth Night or What You Will*. Edited by Elizabeth Story Donno. Cambridge University Press, 1985. © Cambridge University Press 1985. Reproduced with the permission of Cambridge University Press and the author.—Evans, Gareth Lloyd. From *Shakespearian Comedy*. Edward Arnold, 1972. © Edward Arnold (Publishers) Ltd 1972. All rights reserved. Reproduced by permission.—Green, Douglas E. From "Shakespeare's Violation: 'One Face, One Voice, One Habit, and Two Persons'" in *Reconsidering the Renaissance: Papers from the Twenty-First Annual Conference*. Edited by Mario A. Di Cesare. Medieval & Renaissance Texts & Studies, Vol. 95, 1992. © Copyright 1992 Arizona Board of Regents for Arizona State University. Reproduced by permission.—Hart, John A. From *"Starre of Poets": Discussions of Shakespeare*. Carnegie Institute of Technology, 1966. Copyright © 1966 by the Department of English Carnegie Institute of Technology. Reproduced by permission.—Kaiser, Walter. From *Praisers of Folly: Erasmus, Rabelais, and Shakespeare*. Harvard University Press, 1963. Copyright 1963 by the President and Fellows of Harvard College. All rights reserved. Reproduced by permission of the publishers.—Leggatt, Alexander. From *Harvester New Critical Introductions to Shakespeare: King Lear*. Harvester Wheatsheaf, 1998. © 1988 Alexander Leggatt. All rights reserved. Reproduced by permission of the author.—Malcolmson, Cristina. From "What You Will: Social Mobility and Gender in *Twelfth Night*" in *The Matter of Difference: Materialist Feminist Criticism of Shakespeare*. Edited by Valerie Wayne. Harvester Wheatsheaf, 1991. Chapter 1 © Cristina Malcolmson 1991. All rights reserved. Reproduced by permission of the author.—McFarland, Thomas. From "The Image of the Family in *King Lear*" in *On King Lear*. Edited by Lawrence Danson. Princeton University Press, 1981. Copyright © 1981 by Princeton University Press. All rights reserved. Reproduced by permission of Princeton University Press.—Skura, Meredith Anne. From "Shakespeare's Clowns and Fools" in *Shakespeare Set Free: Teaching Romeo and Juliet, Macbeth and A Midsummer Night's Dream*. Edited by Peggy O'Brien. Washington Square Press, 1993. Copyright © 1993 by The Folger Shakespeare Library. All rights reserved. Reproduced by permission of A Washington Square Press Publication of Pocket Books, a division of Simon & Schuster, Inc.—Turner, Frederick. From *Shakespeare and the Nature of Time: Moral and Philosophical Themes in Some Plays and Poems of William Shakespeare*. Oxford at the Clarendon Press, 1971. © Oxford University Press, 1971. Reproduced by permission of Oxford University Press.—Videbæk, Bente A. From *The Stage Clown in Shakespeare Theatre*. Greenwood Press, 1996. Copyright © 1996 by Bente A. Videbæk. All rights reserved. Reproduced by permission of Greenwood Publishing Group, Inc., Westport, CT.—Ward, John Powell. From *Harvester New Critical Introductions to Shakespeare: As You Like It*. Harvester Wheatsheaf, 1992. © 1992 John Powell Ward. All rights reserved. Reproduced by permission of the author.—Willeford, William. From *The Fool and His Scepter: A Study in Clowns and Jesters and Their Audience*. Northwestern University Press, 1969. Copyright © 1969 by Northwestern University Press. Reproduced by permission.

PHOTOGRAPHS AND ILLUSTRATIONS APPEARING IN *SC*, VOLUME 46, WERE RECEIVED FROM THE FOLLOWING SOURCES:

Act I, scene ii, from a production still of *A Midsummer Night's Dream,* by William Shakespeare with Michael Blakemore as Snout, Julian Glover as Snug, Peter Woodthrope as Flute, Donald Eccles as Starveling, Charles Laughton as Bottom, and Cyril Luckham as Quince, photograph by Angus McBean. Copyright the Harvard Theatre Collection, The Houghton Library, Fredric Woodbridge Wilson, Curator. Reproduced by permission.—Act II, Scene v, from William Shakespeare's *The Two Gentlemen of Verona,* from an illustration by C. Green, photograph. Originally appeared in Austin Brereton's book *Shakespearean Scenes and Characteres: With Descriptive Notes on the Plays, and the Principal Shakespearean Players, from Betterton to Irving,* London, New York, Cassell, 1886. The Department of Rare Books and Special Collections, The University of Michigan Library. Reproduced by permission.—From a movie still of *Twelfth Night or What You Will* by William Shakespeare, directed by Trevor Nunn, Act V, scene I, with Helena Bonham Carter as Olivia and Nigel Hawthorne as Malvolio, Fine Line/Renaissance, 1996, photograph by Alex Bailey. Fine Line/Renaissance. Courtesy of The Kobal Collection. Reproduced by permission.—From a movie still of *Twelfth Night or What You Will* by William Shakespeare, directed by Trevor Nunn, Act III, scene I, with Ben Kingsley as Feste, Fine Line/Renaissance,

1996, photograph by Alex Bailey. Fine Line/Renaissance. Courtesy of The Kobal Collection. Reproduced by permission.—From a movie still of *Twelfth Night or What You Will* by William Shakespeare, directed by Trevor Nunn, Act III, scene iv, (l-r) with Imogen Stubbs as Viola/Cesario, Peter Gunn as Fabian, Mel Smith as Sir Toby Belch and Richard E. Grant as Sir Andrew Aguecheek, Fine Line/Renaissance, 1996, photograph by Alex Bailey. Fine Line/Renaissance. Courtesy of The Kobal Collection. Reproduced by permission.—From a movie still of *Twelfth Night or What You Will* by William Shakespeare, directed by Trevor Nunn, Act I, scene v, with Imogen Stubbs as Viola/Cesario and Helena Bonham Carter as Olivia, Fine Line/Renaissance, 1996, photograph by Alex Bailey. Fine Line/Renaissance. Courtesy of The Kobal Collection. Reproduced by permission.—From a production still of *King Lear,* by William Shakespeare with John Gielgud as King Lear, Stephen Haggard as the Fool and Lewis Casson as Kent, 1940, photograph by Angus McBean. Copyright the Harvard Theatre Collection, The Houghton Library, Fredric Woodbridge Wilson, Curator. Reproduced by permission.—From a theatre production of William Shakespeare's *As You Like It,* directed by Paul Kassel, costume design by Dorothy Johnson, Meyer Jacobs Theatre, Bradley University, 1996/97 Season, Act I, scene iii, with Amy Elizabeth Clark as Rosalind/Ganymede and Julie Boesch as Celia, photograph by Duane Zehr. Bradley University Theatre. Reproduced by permission.—From a theatre production of William Shakespeare's *As You Like It,* directed by Paul Kassel, costume design by Dorothy Johnson, Meyer Jacobs Theatre, Bradley University, 1996/97 Season, Act 5, scene iv, the wedding dance, photograph by Duane Zehr. Bradley University Theatre. Reproduced by permission.—From a theatre production of William Shakespeare's *As You Like It,* directed by Paul Kassel, costume design by Dorothy Johnson, Meyer Jacobs Theatre, Bradley University, 1996/97 Season, with Aaron M. Tidball as Touchstone and Jillian Spear as Audrey, Jaques in background, photograph by Duane Zehr. Bradley University Theatre. Reproduced by permission.—From a theatre production of William Shakespeare's *As You Like It,* directed by Paul Kassel, costume design by Dorothy Johnson, Meyer Jacobs Theatre, Bradley University, 1996/97 Season, Amy Elizabeth Clark as Rosalind/Ganymede, photograph by Duane Zehr. Bradley University Theatre. Reproduced by permission.—From a theatre production of William Shakespeare's *King Lear,* directed by Richard Monette, with William Hutt as King Lear, Stratford Festival, Stratford, Ontario, Canada, May 6 - November 3, 1996, King Lear is sitting on his throne dressed in his Royal best, photograph by Cylla von Tiedemann. Courtesy of Stratford Festival Archives.—From a theatre production of William Shakespeare's *King Lear,* directed by Richard Monette, with (l-r) Xuan Fraser as Lear's Attendant, Martha Burns as Regan, William Hutt as King Lear, Andrew Croft as Lear's Attendant, Colombe Demers as Cordelia and Diane D'Aquila as Goneril, Stratford Festival, Stratford, Ontario, Canada, May 6 - November 3, 1996, King Lear is sitting upon his throne with his three daughters Regan, Cordelia and Goneril around him, photograph by Cylla von Tiedemann. Courtesy of Stratford Festival Archives.—From a theatre production of William Shakespeare's *King Lear* directed by Robin Phillips, with Ingrid Blekys as Cordelia and Peter Ustinov as King Lear, Stratford Festival, Stratford, Ontario, Canada, 1979, King Lear is kneeling beside the prone Cordelia, photograph by Robert C. Ragsdale. Courtesy of Stratford Festival Archives.

List of Plays and Poems Covered in *SC*

Volumes 1-10 present a critical overview of each play, including criticism from the seventeenth century to the present. Beginning with Volume 11, the series focuses on the history of Shakespeare's plays on the stage and in important films. The Yearbooks reprint the most important critical pieces of the year as suggested by an advisory board of Shakespearean scholars. Beginning with Volume 27, each volume is organized around a theme and focuses on criticism published after 1960.

Volume 1
The Comedy of Errors
Hamlet
Henry IV, Parts 1 and 2
Timon of Athens
Twelfth Night

Volume 2
Henry VIII
King Lear
Love's Labour's Lost
Measure for Measure
Pericles

Volume 3
Henry VI, Parts 1, 2, and 3
Macbeth
A Midsummer Night's Dream
Troilus and Cressida

Volume 4
Cymbeline
The Merchant of Venice
Othello
Titus Andronicus

Volume 5
As You Like It
Henry V
The Merry Wives of Windsor
Romeo and Juliet

Volume 6
Antony and Cleopatra
Richard II
The Two Gentlemen of Verona

Volume 7
All's Well That Ends Well
Julius Caesar
The Winter's Tale

Volume 8
Much Ado about Nothing
Richard III
The Tempest

Volume 9
Coriolanus
King John
The Taming of the Shrew
The Two Noble Kinsmen

Volume 10
The Phoenix and Turtle
The Rape of Lucrece
Sonnets
Venus and Adonis

Volume 11
King Lear
Othello
Romeo and Juliet

Volume 12
The Merchant of Venice
A Midsummer Night's Dream
The Taming of the Shrew
The Two Gentlemen of Verona

Volume 13
1989 Yearbook

Volume 14
Henry IV, Parts 1 and 2
Henry V
Richard III

Volume 15
Cymbeline
Pericles
The Tempest
The Winter's Tale

Volume 16
1990 Yearbook

Volume 17
Antony and Cleopatra
Coriolanus
Julius Caesar
Titus Andronicus

Volume 18
The Merry Wives of Windsor
Much Ado about Nothing
Troilus and Cressida

Volume 19
1991 Yearbook

Volume 20
Macbeth
Timon of Athens

Volume 21
Hamlet

Volume 22
1992 Yearbook

Volume 23
As You Like It
Love's Labour's Lost
Measure for Measure

Volume 24
Henry VI, Parts 1, 2, and 3
Henry VIII
King John
Richard II

Volume 25
1993 Yearbook

Volume 26
All's Well That Ends Well
The Comedy of Errors
Twelfth Night

Volume 27
Shakespeare and Classical Civilization
Antony and Cleopatra
Timon of Athens
Titus Andronicus
Troilus and Cressida

Volume 28
1994 Yearbook

Volume 29
Magic and the Supernatural
Macbeth
A Midsummer Night's Dream
The Tempest

Volume 30
Politics
Coriolanus
Henry V
Julius Caesar

Volume 31
Shakespeare's Representation of Women
Much Ado about Nothing
King Lear
The Taming of the Shrew

Volume 32
1995 Yearbook

Volume 33
Sexuality in Shakespeare
Measure for Measure
The Rape of Lucrece
Romeo and Juliet
Venus and Adonis

Volume 34
Appearance versus Reality
As You Like It
The Comedy of Errors
Twelfth Night

Volume 35
Madness
Hamlet
Othello

Volume 36
Fathers and Daughters
Cymbeline
Pericles
The Winter's Tale

Volume 37
1996 Yearbook

Volume 38
Desire
All's Well That Ends Well
Love's Labour's Lost
The Merry Wives of Windsor
The Phoenix and Turtle

Volume 39
Kingship
Henry IV, Parts 1 and 2
Henry VI, Parts 1, 2, and 3
Richard II
Richard III

Volume 40
Gender Identity
The Merchant of Venice
Sonnets
The Two Gentlemen of Verona

Volume 41
Authorship Controversy
Henry VIII
King John
The Two Noble Kinsmen

Volume 42
1997 Yearbook

Volume 43
Violence
The Rape of Lucrece
Titus Andronicus
Troilus and Cressida

Volume 44
Psychoanalytic Interpretations
Hamlet
Macbeth

Volume 45
Dreams
A Midsummer Night's Dream
The Tempest
The Winter's Tale

Volume 46
Clowns and Fools
As You Like It
King Lear
Twelfth Night

Future Volumes

Volume 47
Deception in Shakespeare
Antony and Cleopatra
Cymbeline
The Merry Wives of Windsor

Volume 48
1998 Yearbook

Volume 49
Law and Justice
Henry IV, Parts 1 and 2
Henry V
Measure for Measure

Shakespeare's Clowns and Fools

INTRODUCTION

Appearing in most of Shakespeare's dramas, the clown or fool figure remains one of the most intriguing stage characters in the Shakespearean oeuvre and has frequently captured the interest of contemporary critics and modern audiences. Taking many forms, Shakespearean fools may be generally divided into two categories: the clown, a general term that was originally intended to designate a rustic or otherwise uneducated individual whose dramatic purpose was to evoke laughter with his ignorance; and the courtly fool or jester, in whom wit and pointed satire accompany low comedy.

The dramatic sources of Shakespeare's simple-minded clowns are at least as old as classical antiquity. In the plays themselves, such figures as Bottom of *A Midsummer Night's Dream* and Dogberry of *Much Ado About Nothing* are typically classified as clowns, their principal function being to arouse the mirth of audiences. The history of the courtly fool or jester in England is somewhat briefer, with these fools making early appearances in the courts of medieval aristocracy during the twelfth century. By the time of Queen Elizabeth's reign, courtly fools were a common feature of English society, and were seen as one of two types: natural or artificial. The former could include misshapen or mentally-deficient individuals, or those afflicted with dwarfism. Such fools were often considered pets—though generally dearly loved by their masters—and appear infrequently in Shakespeare's writing. The artificial fool, in contrast, was possessed of a verbal wit and talent for intellectual repartee. Into this category critics place Shakespeare's intellectual or "wise-fools," notably Touchstone of *As You Like It*, Feste of *Twelfth Night*, and King Lear's unnamed Fool.

Critical analysis of Shakespearean clowns and fools has largely explored the thematic function of these peculiar individuals. Many commentators have observed the satirical potential of the fool. Considered an outcast to a degree, the fool was frequently given reign to comment on society and the actions of his social betters; thus, some Shakespearean fools demonstrate a subversive potential. They may present a radically different worldview than those held by the majority of a play's characters, as critic Roger Ellis (1968) has observed. Likewise, such figures can be construed as disrupting the traditional order of society and the meaning of conventional language, as Roberta Mullini (1985) has argued. As for so-called clowns—including the simple "mechanicals" of *A Midsummer Night's Dream*, Trinculo of *The Tempest*, and Launcelot Gobbo of *The Merchant of Venice*—most are thought to parody the actions of other characters in the main plots of their respective plays and to provide low humor for the entertainment of groundlings. Several critics, however, have acknowledged the deeper, thematic functions of Shakespeare's clowns, some of whom are said to possess a degree of wisdom within their apparent ignorance.

Other topics of critical inquiry concerning fools are varied. Several scholars have studied the significance of certain Elizabethan actors who were thought to have initially enacted the roles Shakespeare wrote. Preeminent among these is the comedic actor Robert Armin, for whom several critics have suggested Shakespeare created the witty, even philosophical, fool roles of Feste, Touchstone, and Lear's Fool. Still other critics have focused on Shakespeare's less easily categorized clowns. Walter Kaiser (1963) has examined Falstaff's multifaceted function in the *Henriad*, which he has argued bears similarities to those of Shakespeare's other "wise fools." William Willeford (1969) has focused on the darker side of folly by exploring the title character of *Hamlet* as a unique form of the Shakespearean fool. Additionally, Catherine I. Cox (1992) has investigated Shakespeare's characteristic blending of comedy and tragedy through the use of clowns and other purveyors of laughter in his tragic plays.

OVERVIEWS

Roger Ellis (essay date 1968)

SOURCE: "The Fool in Shakespeare: A Study in Alienation," in *The Critical Quarterly,* Vol. 10, No. 3, Autumn, 1968, pp. 245-268.

[*In the following essay, Ellis discusses Shakespeare's fools as figures who represent worldviews fundamentally different from those of the majority of society.*]

I

Of all the characters in literature, hardly any has a longer life, runs truer to type, and is of more lasting significance, than the fool. As ancient as Pandarus, he is yet as modern as the tramps in *Waiting for Godot.*

In him society's anxieties about itself find an outlet; yet the laughter which he arouses is at the same time a profound criticism of the forces which have made him what he is. The counterpart in his exaggerated non-involvement of the society of which he is a part, he is yet in his profound self-awareness and in his pity for those who suffer, its one hope of salvation.

Of course, most of the time we do not see him in this way. For us, he is a man slipping on the beliefs of society, one always at odds with the standards it maintains: a man, as it seems, imprisoned in a world of fantasy, and whose sole function is to excite the laughter that assures us of the solidity of our beliefs. So we laugh at Chaplin's agonized incomprehension of a world of umbrellas, hats and lamp-posts that never seem to give *us* any trouble; we roar at Buster Keaton's unawareness of the logic of existence, from which only benevolent nature rescues him. The fool is often presented to us in this way, as an object merely for scorn or amusement. Consider the fools in Restoration drama, for instance: fops wishing to affect the graces they do not possess, country bumpkins who want to ape the manners of civilized London—these serve only to assure us that society is, after all, in the right.

But this way of presenting the fool depends on the writer's having a fixed view about the nature of the world he is representing. At its simplest, as in the case of Restoration drama, it depends on his having taken on uncritically all the prejudices of his audience. The key to this presentation is that the fool is being studied from the outside. No attempt is made to see why he is a fool, or what it means to him to be a fool, and why he is the fool, rather than the characters who represent a different world-view. But literature which, like Restoration drama, is the embodiment only of the one world-view seems not to represent adequately the fullness of existence for which men long. It is of the essence that there will be many world-views, and literature which does not attempt to represent the totality of existence, but expounds the ethic only of a particular group, runs the risk of ceasing to be literature and becoming something else.

Shakespeare, at least, is not one to neglect the world in order to put forward a certain view. In *A Midsummer Night's Dream,* for example, he has Duke Theseus say:

> . . . I never may believe
> These antique fables, nor these fairy toys.
> Lovers and madmen have such seething brains,
> Such shaping fantasies, that apprehend
> More than cool reason ever comprehends.
> The lunatic, the lover and the poet
> Are of imagination all compact . . .
> (Act V, Sc. i, ll. 2-8)

This speech is an airy dismissal of the whole fantastic action we have been witnessing—the fond illusions of love which drive people out of their minds. And, no doubt, it is fitting for a man in whom all opposites have harmonised to dismiss with such a wave of the hand all the imperfections of mankind. I am not sure, however, that Shakespeare adopts the same attitude. Perfection is no doubt an admirable thing, but not every man can hope to reach it, and Shakespeare will not risk the narrowness that would follow too rigorous and exclusive a definition of virtue.

But there is a more important point to be drawn from Theseus' speech. Theseus is making an after-dinner joke about the way all imperfections are related, as springing from an incomplete way of viewing the world and as expressed in actions that are consequently rather silly. But Shakespeare, I think, sees another connection between 'the lunatic, the lover and the poet'. In a world where opposites have not harmonised, the poet is like 'the lunatic [and] the lover' because, like them, he is different from the majority of people. He is a trail-blazer, committed to probing the totality of existence, and unwilling to reject any of the views, however bizarre, that are a part of it. If we may borrow Laing's phrase, he interiorizes human existence.[1] Where Theseus can consider a whole race of men from the outside, secure in the knowledge of his own perfection, the writer will present all existence *from the inside.*

In this important respect he is like the fool, for the fool understands his own existence from the inside, as most other characters do not. Set in a world where he is early made aware that he is different and somehow unacceptable to the majority, he is forced to examine himself and the bases of his behaviour. This self-examination is foreign to the others, who have never needed to assess their own existence in this way, and for whom the source of behaviour is found in beliefs outside them and half-felt assumptions shared with everyone else. Consequently, they react to a person who acts on assumptions other than theirs, rooted in the logic of his own being, by dismissing him contemptuously as a fool—treating him as an outsider, and denying him all personality. This is how Goneril treats the fool in *King Lear;* it is what happens time and again to the tramps and beggars who erupt into the world of modern drama and who are the fool's spiritual descendants—for instance, the tramp in David Rudkin's *Afore Night Come.* But the fool is aware, as those who judge him are not, that their reaction, far from demonstrating rightness or wrongness, merely shows that they have never examined their own existence, and have no way of interpreting difference except by labelling it folly. They can hardly respond to another person when they have never taken themselves seriously.

Like the writer, then, the fool is aware of the complexities of social living in a way that most people are not. But there is a vital difference between him and the writer. The writer chooses to present sides of a problem; he creates this complexity, and is thus, however involved he may be in the viewpoints expressed, distant from the conflict, secure in the lordship of creation. The fool, on stage and in real life, lacks this security. He is in the thick of things. He is forced to a recognition of the double standard, his own and the world's, and to the knowledge that where he sees himself as a self, the rest of the world will mark his caperings solely as an excuse for laughter. This becomes his greatest agony. It reflects in his failure to act. As a man, he must act meaningfully in order to build community; as the outsider, he is deprived of the possibility of ever doing so, because he has no one with whom to share the vision which, expressed in action, has as its end the making of community. To remain where he is is to be cut off from community; but the price of his integration into that community is the abandonment of all that he knows, all that makes him a self. The dotty old woman in *The Whisperers*, for example, is integrated, willy-nilly, into society. But this means the exposing of her 'voices', the only thing she has, as a fantasy, as nothing at all. Like the character of the parable, she is worse off in the end than she was before. So, whichever way he turns, the fool is caught. This agony of indecision is the special mark of Beckett's characters. For them, 'the dreadful has already happened'; the world has passed them by, bound for destruction, and damnation is all about them. They cannot return to a world which they desperately need. And so they remain, waiting, standing at doors, unable to move out into the world. It is the same for Pinter's tramp in *The Caretaker*. Placed in a mad world, he cannot ever become a person without the papers that give him his identity. But they are at Sidcup, and we know he will never get them. The agony is the greater because the fool sees that the labels society has pinned upon him fit just as well upon society itself, and that it is all merely a matter of perspective. 'Handy-dandy', cries the mad Lear, 'which is the justice, which is the thief?' Where does real madness lie—in the 'voices', or in the sterile cleanliness of a friendless observation ward? In a world where real living is not understood save by a minority, the real agony for the fool is to see that the rest of the world is mad. As Vendice observes in *The Revenger's Tragedy:*

> Surely we're all mad people, and they
> Whom we think mad, are not; we mistake those;
> 'Tis we are mad in sense, they but in clothes.
> (Act III, Sc. v, ll. 79-81)

In art the finest expression of this agonizing dilemma is surely the work of Rouault. The clowns and prostitutes whom he so often makes his subjects embody a consciousness of life at odds with the rest of society: a world blindly self-seeking and hypocritical, summed up in the cruel judges and the helmeted soldier of the Miserere etchings. Fixed forever on the point of the world's rejection, they betray no individuality whatever. Even when they band together in community, as in *La Petite Famille,* they never seem to smile, as if they are only too well aware of the temporary nature of their refuge and the abiding reality of their rejection.

The isolation of the Rouault clown or the Beckett tramp, and his consequent failure to act, is in real life an impossible situation. There is only one way to escape from it. That is for the fool to cover his tracks and to pretend that he does not care. He covers his tracks by laughing at himself, by mocking the self-knowledge which is the reason of his existence, and by inviting our laughter along with his own. He has no other course of action open to him, for to see society committed to standards opposed to his own, and to fell his own powerlessness to change things, or to ever make people see him as a person, is for him to be given over to the despair that drives people mad. He must therefore take on the mask of folly, deny his individuality, and parade his logicality as the illogicality the rest of us reckon it to be. That is, he pretends to be uncommitted. For this reason we welcome him among us, and tolerate the sharp satire which he uses to relieve his feelings because we know he can do nothing about us. But this is merely a temporary refuge for him. His agony is still with him, for he knows that at any moment we may reject him if he comes too close to the truth or if he bores us; and he knows that he has sold himself and accomplished nothing. He has bought himself time, and that is all.

Other people also behave in this way. The cynic, for example, is a person who reacts to the misery of the world by retreating from it. Ivan in *The Brothers Karamazov* is just such a person. There is no doubt how strongly he feels about the inhumanity of the so-called enlightenment. As an illustration of the way in which enlightened man has failed to treat his neighbour any better than his 'backward Russian brother' does, he tells the story of a young man brought up like a beast and neglected by society until he has committed murder and is condemned to death. Then people come to visit him; but not with expressions of sympathy. No, their purpose is to convince him that the sole responsibility for his actions lies with himself, and that the society which tolerated the abomination in the first place is clear of any guilt. Man's complete indifference to the outsider, except as an object to be cajoled into subscribing to his own ideals, and his readiness to sacrifice the outsider to them rather than seriously examine them, strikes Ivan as loathsome Pharisaism. But, as he recognises, 'That's characteristic'. There seems to be nothing he can do. And so he retreats into a pose of non-involvement, assuming the detachment of a scholar reporting on insignificant facts in an abstruse journal. His cynicism, then, is merely a front for a deep despair. This means that he is where he was, powerless, able only to jest with the sufferings of the world. His only relief is to show it, beneath a cloak which it cannot penetrate, what it is really like. He is baying at the moon.

What if the fool lacks self-awareness, like the hero of Ivan's story? He will not suffer the agonies I have described, for he will never see how his existence is thwarted and his aims frustrated by the rest of the world. Yet, even so, his existence will have a kind of sadness about it—the sadness of a thwarted child—for he will almost certainly react subconsciously to the hostility of the world by the assumption of one rôle or another. The recent performance of Bottom in *A Midsummer Night's Dream* by Mr. Jim Dale is a good case in point. Where I have been tempted to see in Bottom the eternal extrovert, as much at home in the world of the fairies as in the court of Theseus, the sensitive performance of Mr. Dale was a reminder that Bottom is at home everywhere merely because he is at home nowhere; that he is not so much actor as acted upon; and that extroversion is usually a mask for a deep insecurity. Marcel Marceau's great comic creation, Bip, is another example of this kind of fool. Raised for our laughter, he yet points to a malaise in society which prompts a man to retreat from authentic communication into a world of fantasy, and his humour, like Bottom's, is not without a deep sadness.

The fool then is a person committed to a world-view at odds with that of society and powerless to effect acceptance by others of it. In the face of this powerlessness, he will, deliberately or subconsciously, assume the mask of folly in order to protect himself from the world. However it goes with him, he cannot be involved overtly, for that is to lay himself open to the rejection of the world. Nor can he act: he can only be acted upon.

The 'natural fool of fortune' and the cynic are, I suggest, two expressions of the fool distinguished only by the greater degree of awareness possessed by the latter. There is a third kind of fool which it may be worth mentioning here, as representing a yet greater degree of self-awareness still, though we shall not be studying its occurrence in Shakespeare's plays. I mean, of course, the lunatic. As Laing points out,[2] the lunatic is a man whom the sense of the impossible demands of the world, and of the equal impossibility of ever realising his own aims, has drawn into himself in a state of permanent inaction. For him, the world is as frighteningly topsy-turvey as it is for the fool:

> Through tatter'd rags small vices do appear;
> Robes and furr'd gowns hide all. Plate sin
>   with gold,
> And the strong lance of justice hurtless
>   breaks;
> Arm it in rags, a pygmy's straw doth pierce it.
> (*King Lear,* Act IV, Sc. vi, ll. 166-9)

But now he lacks all ability to come to terms with it. He sees the world destroying his ideals, and he hunches up into himself in terror. There is only this difference between him and the fool: the fool has bought time. Time has stopped for the madman.

II

This account of the fool is surely unexceptionable. We can use it, for example, to account for the source of that ambivalent tone, something between comedy and tragedy but never siding with either, that is the mark of so much modern drama, and especially the plays of Beckett. It is not so easy, however, to apply it to the fools in Shakespeare's plays. This is because, if we are to share the fool's existence from the inside, we must have some expression of his troubled self-awareness; and we cannot expect this in any play where the fool is placed in a social context as accessory to the actions of other people, for this would inhibit his self-expression and, by confining him to the poses which he has to make in order to protect himself, prevent us from ever seeing him as he really is. If the fool is to be at all central, action has to be done away with, and a firm social context cannot be stated, but must be merely inferred, to be the source of this conflict within him. This is why society never appears in the Beckett world, and why in Tom Stoppard's recent play almost the whole action of Shakespeare's *Hamlet* is represented off stage. Only when the world of action, the world of other men, is somewhere else, can Rosencrantz and Guildenstern show us the real agonies of the fool. In the plays of Shakespeare, however, where the action of protagonists who exist in a firmly detailed social structure is of primary importance, no such opportunity is given to the fool to reveal himself, except in *Hamlet*. (It is fair to point out that Mr. Stoppard is only doing for Rosencrantz and Guildenstern what Shakespeare himself did for Hamlet). Consequently, we can only interpret the significance of the fool through the understanding other characters have of him. But they will be able to see *only* that 'this is not altogether fool'; that the fool

> uses his folly like a stalking-horse, and under the presentation of that he shoots his wit
> (*As You Like It,* Act V, Sc. iv, ll. 103-4)

The secret agonies of the fool can thus only be brought to light by inference, or by a sensitive performance. But I do not see this as a bad thing, because I believe that, if we are not to rob literature of its power, we must allow it something of the range and implication we would allow to people in real life. We do not deal simply in words, but in a whole complex of nuances and half-guessed meanings.

III

Shakespeare's world is thronged with fools and madmen, and often a single play will treat of several levels of madness. The folly of Hamlet, the madness of Ophelia, the professional Yorick; the natural Touchstone, the melancholic Jaques; the mad Lear, the professional fool, the masquerading Bedlam; these, to choose a few only, present various aspects of the outsider's awareness of himself and a world at odds with him. With Shakespeare's fools we are at once in a world where moral certainties are being questioned: where the questioner proves fool by his question, and the fool proves a wise man by his answer: and where the insane alone seem to understand what the real world is like. In the early plays this uncertainty is used to express a comic rather than a tragic vision. Shakespeare came to the mature comedies with a deep conviction that man, for all his folly, was redeemable, and that sin was not so much destructive as laughable in its presumption. Consequently, the fool's part is not so important. He is permitted to reveal inconsistencies in human behaviour, especially the follies that men commit in love ('wise men, folly-fall'n, quite taint their wit') but he does not directly challenge the bases of social living.

Folly is, however, symptomatic of something deeper than itself, and it is clear even in the mature comedies that the corrupt world, as represented by Shylock or the usurping Duke Frederic, can only be done away with in the magic forests or by the perpetration on it of some holy deceit. In the event, Shakespeare does not turn again to the magic forest, after the mature comedies, until he has probed more deeply the implications of the fool's behaviour, and seen that the good, far from being the victors, are really fatally vulnerable; that, in a world given up to selfishness, they are the real outsiders: and that it is not sin, but goodness, that is the great folly. This is the world of the problem plays and the tragedies, where the implications of the earlier comic vision: 'Most friendship is feigning, most loving mere folly' are made terrifyingly manifest. And it is here, especially in *King Lear,* that the fool comes into his own as the agonized expositor of a disordered conscience, the figure who sees truly what the world is like and feels his powerlessness to change it.

But we begin a long time before that—before even the world of the mature comedies. We begin with a small boy who is servant to a foolish knight, the braggadochio Armado:

> *Armado:* I am all these three [three faces of love]
> *Moth:* And three times as much more, and yet nothing at all.
> *Armado:* Fetch hither the swain: he must carry a letter.
> *Moth:* A message well sympathised: a horse to be an ambassador for an ass.
> *Armado:* Ha ha! What sayest thou?
> *Moth:* Marry, sir, you must send the ass upon the horse, for he is very slow-gaited.
>
> (*Love's Labours Lost,* Act III, Sc. i, ll. 45-54)

Moth in *Love's Labours Lost* is not a true Shakespearean fool. But he has much in common with them. Like the fool in *King Lear,* he is yoked to a blind and partial authority, and is quite as likely to receive punishment as praise if he put a foot wrong. Like the fool, too, he knows very well what a fool his master is. But, as his servant, he can do nothing to make him aware of this, for he cannot confront him with his true self. He is therefore reduced to asides which Armado will not understand; and if he should happen to be caught out, he must instantly change the meaning so as to protect himself. Moth, then, is playing a part, pretending to be uninvolved, and taking upon himself, in order to protect himself, the guise of folly that he is ridiculing in his master. But this guise is no solution to the problem, for it merely encourages Armado and the others in their attitude towards him. When, for example, Holofernes is bested by Moth in quipping, he can still retort: 'thou disputest like an infant; go, whip thy gig'. It is a vicious circle. Moth reacts to people viewing him from the outside, as it were, as a 'pretty infant'; but the rôle that is forced upon him involves a perpetuation of this attitude, which means that his position is insecure, and that he can do nothing to expose the world to itself. This does not mean for a moment that he has the wider significance of Shakespeare's fools; it means merely that he is placed in the same position as they are, and like them must have recourse to trickery—especially verbal trickery—to conceal his tracks.

Likewise, the 'natural fools' of Shakespearean comedy—Launce and Speed, Lancelot Gobbo, Dogberry and Verges, Justice Shallow—do not have the wider implications of the fool. They are fools raised for laughter, not for any significance they may have as commentators on the action. They stumble across words, and break their shins on the conventions of the world, but without that sense of the world's hostility towards them that marks out the fool. They are so completely lacking in self-awareness that they do not even hear the laughter of the other characters. Yet we can see in them links at a number of points with the true Shakespearean fool. Consider, for instance, Launce and his dog in *The Two Gentlemen of Verona.* This dog is a perpetual cross to him. He has been obliged to suffer time and again for its misbehaviour in the hope that it will mend its ways. But, of course, it does not. Launce's folly is that, just as Moth expects Armado to be more than Armado, he expects his dog to be more than a dog. On his departure for Milan, he tells us, 'this cruel-hearted cur shed (not) one tear: he is a stone, a very pebble-stone, and has no more pity in him than a dog'. What does he expect? Relationship of the kind he looks for is clearly not to be found with a dog. Shakespeare is here presenting the fool from the outside, since Launce's position is absurd and foolish. But he does have other characteristics in common with the fools of the later plays. Like them, he has a vision simple almost to the point of fixation. He is like a child in the way he can become so absorbed in turning the grief of parting into a game that he hardly has any room for grief. Lancelot Gobbo similarly plays games both with himself and his father in *The Merchant of Venice,* and he reacts to the threats of Shylock in the same way as, earlier, Moth had done to Armado. But this is because, like Launce, he *is* a child.

The naturals are also children in their incomprehension of the complexities of language. They do not use the right words; or if they have the right words, they lack the ability to string them together into meaningful sentences. Poor Peter Quince's stuttering version of the prologue to the mechanicals' entertainment earns this rejoinder:

> Indeed, he hath played on his prologue like a
> child on a recorder: a sound, but not in
> government.
> His speech was like a tangled chain, nothing
> impaired, but all disordered.
> (Act V, Sc. i, ll. 122-5)

and it is not untypical of the reaction which the mechanicals provoke among the gentry. The court of Theseus, Leonato, the court of the Duke of Navarre—the sophisticated world brushes them contemptuously aside and views them only as subjects for laughter, as blocks, as children. The fool similarly uses language to confuse his hearers, deliberately masking the apparent connections in order to achieve startling results:

> A sentence is but a cheveril glove to a good
> wit:
> how quickly the wrong side may be turned
> outward!
> (*Twelfth Night,* Act III, Sc. i, ll. 11-13)

Unlike the fools, however, these naturals are without agony, because they are without self-awareness. Their childlike absorption in their own world-view is total. This is why Costard's impersonation of Pompey at the end of *Love's Labours Lost* is a success, whereas Holofernes and Sir Nathaniel, characters whose social sense is more developed, are terribly put out by the mockery of the court. Because he is not aware of the court's attitude, Costard can respond to their ironical 'Great thanks, great Pompey', with the modest

> 'Tis not so much: but I hope I was perfect:
> I made a little fault in the 'great'
> (Act V, Sc. ii, ll. 553-5)

Characters somewhat like them, but with considerably more self-awareness, are Gratiano in *The Merchant of Venice* and Mercutio in *Romeo and Juliet.* Gratiano reacts to Antonio's heavy cheer in the opening scene with the words:

> Let me play the Fool:
> With mirth and laughter let old wrinkles
>   come . . .
> Why should a man, whose blood is warm
>   within
> Sit like his grandsire cut in alabaster?
> (Act I, Sc. i, ll. 79-80, 83-4)

—which earn him Bassanio's tart: 'Gratiano speaks an infinite deal of nothing, more than any man in all Venice'. But if, as Antonio has said, the world is a stage where people must play a part (and this is an important image for our understanding of the fool) why should Gratiano not play the part of the fool? Like the naturals, he seems to the others to be talking a great deal of nonsense. For him, however, it is merely a pose, and he knows it. Mercutio similarly talks a great deal, and is rebuked by Romeo for wasting their time: 'Peace, peace, Mercutio peace! Thou talkst of nothing'. The nothing is Mercutio's Queen Mab speech, and it *is* a great deal of nothing, as Mercutio himself recognises:

> True, I talk of dreams
> Which are the children of an idle brain
> Begot of nothing but vain fantasy
> (Act I, Sc. v, ll. 96-8)

Mercutio's attitude to dreams and to fantasy is much the same as Theseus': like Theseus, he takes his stand on the world of reality, the same world where men kill each other for the sake of honour. Yet he is unable to resist chasing an idea to its conclusion, however preposterous, or tilting at inconsistency in himself or his friends. When Romeo has jumped over the wall, Mercutio calls him:

> Nay, I'll conjure too:
> Romeo! Humours! madman! Passion! Lover! . . .
> (Act II, Sc. i, ll. 6-7)

This is all great fun: lovers lay themselves open to this sort of treatment because 'all nature in love is mortal in folly'. But the fool is here a little late with his witticisms. Romeo is no longer conjuring 'Helen's beauty [out of] a brow of Egypt', but calling on the woman whom he loves to distraction. Like Mercutio, the fool has considerable verbal fluency, a device that stretches, as we have seen, all the way back to the early comedies: more important, like Mercutio, he comes too late to do anything. He is always that instant behind the main action. Gratiano and Mercutio adopt the pose of fool here for reasons we cannot fathom. It may be that in a world where misfortune is the common lot of man, and where the Shylocks and the Capulets are always out for revenge, it is simpler to whistle trouble away than to face it. The pose is, however, merely a pose. Gratiano shows his commitment when in the trial scene he reproaches Shylock for his monstrous inhumanity; likewise, Mercutio shows his loyalty by dying for family ties. Comedian to the end, he attempts to externalise his situation by resuming the mask of folly; but the bitterness wrung from him in 'A plague o' both your houses' shows how even the fool's playing must sometimes give way to the realities which it is attempting to put aside. Secure though he may be for the moment, the time will come when he must face the realities symbolised, later, by the skull of Yorick.

IV

And so, by this roundabout way, we come to the fools of the mature comedies—Bottom, Touchstone, Jaques, Feste.[3] The characters we have so far considered are not used by Shakespeare strictly as fools. The logic for their existence is little more than quirks of personality. They are expressions of the outsider introduced mainly for the sake of variety, and even if, like Mercutio, they jest about the world they find themselves in, they never compromise it by their wit, or express the sense of divided loyalties. Shakespeare's fools are of course descended from them. Both the natural folly of the mechanicals and the inspired wit of the courtiers have gone into their making. We might think of Bottom and Touchstone as descended from one side of the family, and Jaques and Feste from the other. But there are significant differences; they are all greater than their begetters. They crystallise for us the existence of different worlds, and reflect in the 'shivered mirror'[4] of their language the opposites which in themselves make for destruction and which only benevolent nature harmonises. Bottom and Touchstone may be very like the mechanicals in their misuse of language, and Feste and Jaques like the courtiers in the way they deliberately distort it; but they are rather more aware of their position vis-à-vis the world. It is an awareness that sits uneasily upon them.

This is especially true, I believe, of Bottom. As I suggested earlier, he is, for all his extroversion, a character extremely sensitive to criticism, easily hurt, and with a child's need for the approval of the others and fear of being left out in the cold. This is plain from his dealings with Peter Quince, a character who has more sense of what is required by the world and who, like Holofernes, is terribly ill at ease when he has to recite the prologue before the clever lords and ladies of the Athenian court. Peter Quince sees Bottom only as a nuisance, someone who will never keep quiet and leave the managing of the play to its producer, and who has no respect for rank or the fitness of the occasion. He resorts to all kinds of pressure—flat contradictions, flattery, and so on—to persuade Bottom to stay in line. In acting like this he does not see Bottom as the self he is, and treats him only as the mask he presents. Bottom is uneasily aware of all this. When the others flee from him in terror in the forest, he is convinced that they are playing a cruel game on him:

> I see their knavery: this is to make an ass of
> me: to fright me, if they could. But I will not
> stir from this place, do what they can: I will
> walk up and down, and I will sing, that they shall
> hear I am not afraid.
> (Act III, Sc. i, ll. 115-18)

In a world where his own childlike games are misinterpreted as tiresome stupidity, the games other people play are full of menace, as it is with the game Goldberg devises for Stanley in Pinter's *Birthday Party*. Bottom knows that in this situation it is best to put on a brave face, to jest away his fear. But he is not at home, all the same, and his position is very much that of the fool—acted upon, unsure how to act himself. It is worth noticing in this connection how largely he takes his cue from the attitudes of other people. When the fairy queen addresses him, he seems to be terrified of her and desperately jests his way through the encounter for fear of being transformed into a beast. Not until the fairies greet him does he regain his assurance: from then on, all becomes grist to his mill. But this acceptance of him as a person, which allows him to indulge in his whimsy without rebuke, happens only in a magic world of fairies, in 'the fierce vexation of a dream'. Everywhere else, he seems to be faced with the dilemma of the fool: how to act and be himself.

It may seem strange that a character who has so little to do in the play should bear the weight of such a detailed study. Yet it is clear that what Theseus does for the play symbolically, as it were, Bottom does for it by his participation in the various levels of the action. Where Theseus' non-involvement, as expressed, for example, in the opening speech of Act 5, is the symbolic expression of the unity to which all life aspires, Bottom's non-involvement represents dramatically the only feasible course of action a man can follow in a world where people are given over to the weakness and folly which Theseus condemns. Only once is he given the kind of speeches that point up the fool's function in the other plays:

> Methinks, mistress, you should have little
> reason for that: and yet, to say the truth,
> reason and love keep little company together

nowadays: the more the pity, that some honest neighbours will not make them friends.
(Act III, Sc. i, ll. 135-8)

and this comment is worth setting alongside Theseus' utterance about the lunatic and the lover, in its expression of the same awareness of the divided self which we find Theseus rejecting from his godlike position. Yet the mere fact of his presence in the play shows us the outsider at odds with his society, unsure how to come to terms with it, and assuming, for his own protection, the mask of the fool. He is the other polarity in a play which has as its ideal the godlike Theseus.

Touchstone is a more obvious instance of the Shakespearean fool. He possesses an awareness of the reality of existence not shared by the other characters. He sees life, for example, as a process of physical change:

And so from hour to hour we ripe and ripe,
And then from hour to hour we rot and rot
(Act II, Sc. vii, ll. 26-7)

He sees love and marriage as a mere expression of instinct; likewise, he sees how the elaborate patterns of social custom are designed to prevent the natural from ever occurring. Above all, he sees the real wisdom to lie in those who know themselves for fools: 'the fool doth think he is wise, but the wise man knows himself to be a fool'. He knows, moreover, that this awareness of his is ill-matched with the other characters in the play, and not merely the sluttish Audrey, who is unable to understand one of his classical allusions, and to whom he says

When a man's verses cannot be understood,
nor a man's good wit seconded with the
forward child,
Understanding, it strikes a man more dead
than a great reckoning in a little room.
(Act III, Sc. ii, ll. 10-13)

He knows that the others, similarly, will fail to see the understanding behind his wit, and will not see the 'great reckoning' in his 'little room'. Nor is it wise for him to be too eager in putting his views to a world on whose sufferance he depends, and which has brought him into the forest simply 'as a comfort to our travel'. When, for instance, he satirises a foolish knight whom Rosalind's father loved, Rosalind replies:

Enough! Speak no more of him; you'll be
whipped for taxation one of these days

his reply:

The more pity, that fools may not speak
wisely what wise men do foolishly.
(Act I, Sc. ii, ll. 79-82)

We are some way from the tone of *King Lear* here, but it is not so great a jump from this to the words of Lear: 'Take heed, Sirra, the whip!' and the Fool's rejoinder:

Truth's a dog must to kennel; he must be
whipped out, when Lady the brach may
stand by the fire and stink.
(Act I, Sc. iv, ll. 117-20)

In the same way, when Rosalind attacks him for his attempt to reduce the love exemplified in Orlando's romantic verse to the level of his own awareness, he is silenced, and can only reply: 'You have spoken; but whether wisely or no, let the forest judge'. Like Bottom, he is poised uneasily between his awareness of what the world requires and where his own self-awareness would lead. It is for this reason that he takes the mask of fool upon him, and is quick to disclaim any wit if they should sense it in him:

. . . I shall ne'er be ware of mine own wit
till
I break my shins against it.
(Act II, Sc. iv, ll. 56-7)

A man, as it seems, equally at home in court and country, he is really at home nowhere. Isolation seems to be an escape for him from the world of men, at least as Jaques reports him: 'who laid him down and bask'd him in the sun'. Here, at least, he can be himself. Yet this is no escape from his need for community, and in order to be in community with his betters he is obliged to cover his tracks, to play the fool.

Yet, in himself, he does not represent the ideal of the play. His part in the action is minimal. He participates in the wedding rites at the end of the play for completeness' sake only. The reason for this lies in his perpetuating in himself the attitudes others have to him. At the same time as being one of nature's naturals, he has a hankering to be a courtier. This shows up most clearly in the way he treats the country-folk, not with the true respect given to them by men of sense, but with the scornful condescension others have used on him. 'Holla, you clown!' he cries; or, like some gay sophisticate, 'It is meat and drink to me to see a clown'. Even in his dealings with the rustics, he does not have things all his own way. Corin, in his simplicity, is a match for him, and forces him to demonstrate that the illogicality which he parades before the court is the illogicality of a divided self; a self that likes the country but thinks the court better because it is more civilized—and yet fails to realise that the arguments he is advancing are only proving how like they are. If the play has a point, it is surely this: that a man's true self requires neither court nor country. But Touchstone gives only lip-service to the ideal. In his heart of hearts, he would rather be a courtier. That is why he barely belongs to the world of Hymen's rites at the end of the play. It is the others who, purified by the consistency of their inner vision, are incorporated into the marriage feast. Touchstone's consistency is, finally, only a mask. Yet, even as he is, he is acceptable, and accepted, in the magic forests. If he but knew it, it is only here that he can hope to become himself. But it is the lovers who become themselves, and leave him behind. He can never be one with the world because he has not learned to be one with himself.

Jaques is in something of the same position. In a world where we seem to fear no tyranny but that of the bad weather, the voice of Jaques is early heard insisting that if court and country are not the same, it is not because man is less corrupt in the one than in the other. Indeed, for Jaques there is no difference:

> Thus most invectively he pierceth through
> The body of the country, city, court,
> Yea, and of this our life: swearing that we
> Are mere usurpers, tyrants, and what's worse,
> To fright the animals and kill them up . . .
> (Act II, Sc. i, ll. 58-62)

This cynicism may be more than a pose, and may reflect a defensive reaction against a world which is all too prone to idealise its situation. When Jaques thinks himself alone, for instance, he is full of sententious moralising about the way of the world: perhaps he does really believe in what he is saying. Moreover, the others view him unsympathetically: not even his isolation is free from malicious report, just as later, Touchstone's situation is gleefully reported back to the others. Yet much of what he says is clearly a pose: he can 'suck melancholy out of a song as a weasel sucks eggs'. He is, then, a character whose awareness of life is at odds with that of the society he mixes with, and who has therefore found retreat in a pose of cynicism which he hardly ever drops. But he has vested interests in this pose. He enjoys the existence which it provides, and the rôle of the baffling intellectual which his violent wit makes him appear. We see this very clearly in his speech to the Duke: 'I am ambitious for a motley coat'. In it he talks of using his rôle of licensed fool in order to cleanse 'the foul body of the infected world'; it matters most to him, however, that the fool is free to speak his mind and that he has 'a charter large as the wind'. That is, Jaques is not interested in the freedom which comes when inner and outer man are harmonised and the whole world is purified—a process which we see the fool aware of and trying to effect in himself. Jaques is interested only in the freedom from restraint which would enable him to snipe at anyone without suffering the consequences of it. This shows us two things about him. It shows us, first, that he has no understanding of the fool, save as a pose like his own. He has not seen anything of the inner agonies of the fool. Second, if his pose is more than a pose, he has no awareness of what it signifies, for he has no awareness of himself based on anything stronger than Hedonism. Ultimately, he is committed only to his own rôle-playing, which he uses as end rather than as means. The pose of cleansing the foul sins of the world is thus the biggest pose of all. Yet the others tolerate him, except when he comes the self-righteous Pharisee, like Malvolio in *Twelfth Night;* then they round on him and remind him that he is no better than they are. So Jaques leaves the marriage feast, where he could have no place, and bequeaths to the others the community which he has implicitly denied.

It is interesting that both fools in this play express the conscience of a divided world, not by being the victims of its tensions, but by expressing those tensions in their own characters. Shakespeare usually represents his fools as the conscience of a divided world because his drama is, in the end, symbolic, and its characters assume greater significance than they have in themselves. But in *As You Like It* the world is clearly a harmony. People who love are made self-consistent, and come to stand for the redemption of a whole society. In such a world, the fool's commentary, presented for the sake of fuller understanding of the real world in which this vision must be lived out, must perforce be a reflection of his own incompleteness as a person. In *A Midsummer Night's Dream,* on the other hand, where community and redemption are not certain, Bottom has more place as the expositor of a consistency at odds with the world's.

Feste is in a different class again. Altogether more urbane than Jaques, he covers his tracks so completely that we never see what he stands for, but only the folly and affectation which he ridicules in all around him. He shapes his behaviour completely to the situation. He 'wears no motley in [his] brain' but what he does wear there we never find. His function is simply to expose, to laugh, to snipe. Malvolio's comment about him, while it tells us more about Malvolio, is thus important for us: 'I marvel your ladyship takes delight in such a barren fool'. Because he never lets us see what he is really like, he remains, throughout the play, a barren fool. He has no significant part to play in forwarding the action. The heroes and heroines work out their destiny without his help. Like all the fools, he is left behind. The world whose signs he professed to read so clearly perhaps had more to it, after all, than the folly he observed:

> Those wits, that think they have thee, do very oft prove fools; and I, that am sure I lack thee, may pass for a wise man.
> (Act I, Sc. v, ll. 32-4)

A concrete example of the way in which the world shows itself at odds with his interpretation of it is his confusing the newly-arrived Sebastian with his twin sister Viola. But then, how could it be otherwise? The fool deals in probables; he cannot be expected to know about miracles. He thinks he knows everything: but about the possibilities of redemption in the material order, like all the fools, he is uninstructed.

V

In the characters whom we have so far studied certain common features emerge—an awareness at odds with the rest of the world, failure to act, the assumption of a mask. How if the fool should choose to act, or should drop the mask? The result will be either his integration into a society to which he had no wish to belong, or his destruction by that society. For the fool to be other than overtly uncommitted is to bring about his own destruction. We see this in the relationship of Hal to Falstaff. It becomes the key to our understanding of the character of Hamlet, and perhaps also the fool in *Lear*.

When we talk of Falstaff as a fool, we must remember that from the beginning he has committed himself to a state of misrule, and by putting himself outside the category of fool, has lost the immunity which he might otherwise expect. Nevertheless, his relationship to Hal is based on the apparent uncommitment of the fool, which conceals a deep affection that would not have otherwise been accepted, and which leaves the Prince free to express his ambiguous feelings towards him as he chooses. But Hal knows all along, as Falstaff does not, that the King's son is made for better things:

> By this hand, thou thinkest me as far in the devil's book as thou and Falstaff . . . let the end try the man.
> (*I Henry IV,* Act II, Sc. ii, ll. 43-5)

When he becomes King, Falstaff decides to step outside the rôles they have both been playing until now. It is true that he sees his relationship with the Prince still in material terms, but this matters to him really only as a return of affection which he sees as his due. He will be now, he thinks, treated as butt no longer. His repudiation by the King is inevitable. The rules of a game like that played by Falstaff do not have wider currency than the game; in the real world there is an entirely different set of rules. Only a fool would expect it to be otherwise. To identify the childish vision of society with that society's vision of itself is to invite disaster. And so *Henry IV* ends with Falstaff made humiliatingly aware of his folly, and, flung back into the world of the fool, making a game of his expectations to con himself out of his grief, like Launce in *The Two Gentlemen:*

> Do not you grieve at this: I shall be sent for in private to him: look you, he must seem
> thus to the world. Fear not your advancement: I will be the man yet that shall make you great.
> (Act V, Sc. v, ll. 76-80)

The world of the comedies is a benevolent one, so that the fool can exist and, to some extent, be himself. But the world of *Henry IV* is a world where policy reigns, and where men are altogether more calculating. The fool's only hope in such a world is to play his part and never step out of it. This is the world of *Hamlet* and above all of *King Lear*. The fool is in a bad way; he must make himself ridiculous, or he is lost. And even then, as Hamlet sees from the skull of Yorick, lost:

> Where be your gibes now? your songs? your flashes of merriment. that were wont to set the table on a roar? Not one now, to mock your own grinning?
> (Act V, Sc. i, ll. 183-86)

Here the fool comes to the point where even self-mockery fails. The reality which his jests concealed is expressed now in the changeless, impartial grinning of a skull. This is a potent symbol for the play. In the same way that the skull in *The Revenger's Tragedy* serves as the central symbol of the play, so the skull here points to the world's end, whether the world of men or the fool. *Hamlet* is, above all, about a man who to be secure has to resort to the shifts of folly, and so puts himself in the agonizing position of the fool—a self-awareness that is powerless to act. When he does act, and throw aside the mask of fool, it is his destruction.

Many words have been written about the character of Hamlet, and I cannot pretend that this interpretation will satisfy everybody.[5] I take as the key to his character the opening speeches to the Queen and King. I read these as the open, bitter outbursts of a man heavy with grief:

> Seems, madam! Nay, it is; I know not 'seems'.
> 'Tis not alone my inky cloak, good mother,
> Nor customary suits of solemn black . . .
> That can denote me truly: these indeed seem,
> For they are actions which a man might play.
> But I have that within which passeth woe . . .
> (Act I, Sc. ii, ll. 76-8, 83-5)

In a world of changing customs and loyalties where 'the funeral baked meats / Did coldly furnish forth the marriage tables', Hamlet is certain only of his love for his father and his grief at his death. In terms of this certainty, he sees how the mourning of the others was merely a pose, an affectation: even his mother did not mourn for her husband longer than 'a beast that wants discourse of reason'. But he also sees how his behaviour, springing from his inmost self, must look like a pose 'a man might play' to those who cannot see beyond the forms to the things they signify, and in whom self-interest is the dominant force. He may be right or wrong in thinking this. Probably, Shakespeare means us to see Hamlet as more right than not, because the whole play is mediated to us through his tortured self-consciousness. But that is not in point. Right or wrong, he sees himself in the right: sees the rest given over to a folly that he cannot cure, at best degrading, at worst criminal: sees that other people do not see him as a person, but only as a mask. This sense of his own isolation brings him to the despair that drives people mad, or makes them kill themselves:

> O that this too too solid flesh would melt,
> Thaw and resolve itself into a dew!
> Or that the Everlasting had not fix'd
> His canon 'gainst self-slaughter. O God!
>   God!
> How weary, stale, flat and unprofitable
> Seem to me all the uses of this world . . .
>   (Act I, Sc. ii, ll. 129-134)

This awareness of the way the court regards him as a man playing a part also suggests to him, when he has vowed vengeance for his father's murder, the pose he is to adopt. As the world sees him, so he will be. He will play the fool and 'put an antic disposition on'. He is not mad, as Ophelia is mad, though his sudden putting on of the mask makes everyone else think that he is. But for him, as for her, to play the fool is to arrest himself in a state of inaction. He can only lie in wait and plot, revealing himself through a mask which even the obtuse Polonius senses to be concealing something deeper: 'though this be madness, yet there is method in it'. His situation is clearly intolerable. He cannot allay suspicion, and the mask of fool leaves him with only the bitterness of a knowledge that is powerless to effect its end. If he is to bring anything about, he must remove the mask.

In the event, he does lower the mask, when he attempts to confront his mother with herself in her chamber. By an unhappy chance, the appearance of the ghost, which only Hamlet sees, convinces her of his madness, so that all he has said to her is merely a further proof of his disordered mind. He disturbs her and perhaps even leads her to a greater awareness of him than she had before, but he does not bring about her repentance. Her treatment of him in the play may be read, as I think Hamlet reads it, as an attempt to salve her conscience in the face of his death's-head awareness; to treat the son more kindly for the father's sake. So she never sees him as a person and cannot do anything to help him.

His confrontation with her, then, is a failure, and his failure to kill the King, and accidental killing of Polonius, mean that he has lost the upper hand, and must now take his chance with the mask of folly firmly in place (IV. 3). His only safety, now that he has exposed himself, is flight. This, as he recognises bitterly, only worsens his situation:

> Witness this army [of Fortinbras] of such
>   mass and charge
> Led by a delicate and tender prince . . .
> How stand I then
> That have a father kill'd, a mother stain'd . . .
> And let all sleep? while to my shame I see
> The imminent death of twenty thousand men
> That . . . go to their graves like beds
>   (Act IV, Sc. iv, ll. 47-8, 56-7, 59-60, 62)

Therefore, he casts aside the mask of folly, and learns the logic of vengeance, the only language the world can understand. There can be no more hesitating; only the fool has time to make the idea of vengeance square with the commandments of God. Hamlet reluctantly takes to the ways of the world. By putting himself on the side of the devils he proclaims that the world leads irresistibly to the grave. And so, for him, it does.

The Lear world is very like the world of *Hamlet*. In it, self-interest is seen to be the driving force. But where the other characters in *Hamlet* mostly stand for a simple opposite to virtue in a worldview that does not admit of great complexity, and are consequently flat characters, given prominence only as the searing light of Hamlet's awareness falls upon them, the villains in *King Lear* are presented much more fully. They have reason for their actions in the self-interested behaviour of their elders, and in their fear of being outside the pale. Goneril and Regan see themselves as deprived both of the power to express themselves and the love which alone makes self-expression possible. They are made to feel outside the pale by their wayward, domineering father. Consequently, when Lear commits the unparalleled folly of removing both the symbol of power and the one prop to his age, they are free to take out all their frustrations on him. Lear's failure is a simple one. He has passed his life in what the others see as a world of make-believe, with the power to make this world pass for the real. Consequently, Cordelia's stepping outside the make-believe in the opening scene leads inevitably to the same reaction as Hal showed to Falstaff. But it also leads to Lear's stepping, himself, outside the game into the real world, where old age, no longer protected by the mask of royalty:

> (shaking) all cares and business from our age,
>   . . . while we
> Unburdened crawl toward death
>   (Act I, Sc. i, ll. 39-41)

can be seen for what it is: 'Idle old man', and 'O sir, you are old . . . You should be ruled and led / By some discretion'. By removing all defences Lear puts himself out on to the heath, beyond the pale. In doing this he learns to see beyond the game to what it ought to have signified, and to what in fact it does signify. To remove the mask is perforce to come to the fool's awareness of the inner man. But for Cordelia, Lear would remain transfixed by this painful awareness of a rottenness, alike within and without, incurable.

Parallel to Lear's removal of the mask, other characters are putting theirs on, notably the fool.[6] The fool has a stronger motive for his motley than any of Shakespeare's other fools, for he is devoted to Cordelia and desolated by her banishment, as Lear himself recognises. That is, he is flung back into the hazardous world of the outsider, from which only the love of Cordelia could have protected him. Lear's action has shown the fool all too clearly the ways of the world. He sees Lear much more clearly than Lear sees himself: how blind and self-seeking Lear was in his love, and how violently he reacted to anything that might disturb it, even the threat of Cordelia's openness. This behaviour is of a piece with the rest of the world, and it shows the fool the madness of Lear's expectations of humanity among a people as blind and self-seeking as he is:

> Shalt see thy other daughter will use thee kindly; for though she's as like this as a crab's like an apple, yet I can tell what I can tell . . . she will taste as like this as a crab does to a crab.
> (Act I, Sc. v, ll. 14-16)

His function is thus to remind Lear insistently of what he has lost by his own stupidity. But because Lear is erratic in his behaviour, affectionate and angry by turns, the fool cannot reveal this awareness fully to him. His only refuge is the perpetual movement from one proposition to another that we saw adumbrated in Moth's relationship with Armado—the distraction that soothes but cannot cure, because it cannot confront the king with himself. But it is not clear that the fool ever hopes for Lear's redemption. The way of the world is a vortex, and there is no escaping from it. Joined together in negation, the fool would reduce Lear to the same awareness of desolation that he has; but not, it seems, in order that he might lead him through it to an acceptance of his situation. Consequently, he cannot, any more than his master, be redeemed, for he rejects the openness that would exchange loss with loss and so build community—in the way, for example, that Behan's characters in *The Quare Fellow* build community by accepting each other's failure. He hugs his loss of Cordelia to himself as the source of his tormenting of the King which is his only relief. He seems almost to be in love with his own pain.

Both, then, are joined together, by a love and a pain which they will not or cannot share. Yet the bond between them deepens as, one by one, the doors are shut against them, and Lear is reduced to the desolation that the fool had foreseen and perhaps hoped for. It is Lear, however, who makes the advances. In the face of his master's great grief the fool 'labours to outjest / his heart-struck injuries'. But he has not the capacity to respond to Lear as a person. Lear, on the other hand, has. In the fool, on the heath, Lear has the first sight of the human person (Tom o' Bedlam is to be the second) which can alone bring salvation to his fettered self-interest:

> My wits begin to turn.
> Come on, my boy: how dost, my boy, art cold?
> I am cold myself . . .
> Poor fool and knave, I have one part in my heart
> That's sorry yet for thee.
> (Act III, Sc. ii, ll. 67-9, 72-3)

Like the characters in *The Quare Fellow,* Lear is opening his arms in the overwhelming sense of his own desolation to someone whom he dimly recognises as partner. It is Lear's inherent nobility that brought him to this point. The fool could never have done it, for his refusal to confront Lear openly with himself, or to share his own pain with him, were an insuperable barrier to his being an effective agent in Lear's redemption. In this simple gesture on the heath Lear has outstripped his teacher. The fool is still unable to share his loss, and unable to respond to another's pain, to which his own pain is not in any way commensurate. That is why he disappears. Like Hamlet's actions, the fool's words have all along proclaimed that the way of the world is damnation. He cannot be present when Lear learns at length that this is not the case.

This portrait of the fool is the most compelling and finely drawn of all the fools in Shakespeare. A character who combines piercing insight with the narrowness of despair and who is arrested in the futility of disbelief, he is the perfect embodiment of the ambiguous relationship of the outsider to a world at odds with him. His jesting conceals an agony that is, for all its intensity, shallow. In the end, he fails, because he has not learned to free himself from the toils of his own playing, or to see that the other person matters most in the making of community. The path the fool takes has come a great way from the world of the comedies. It has led him all the way to the blasted heath. There we leave him, forever outside the closed doors of a society which will admit him, if at all, only as far as the kennels.

VI

It remains to consider some of the imagery that Shakespeare uses to point up the fool's situation. The key image seems to me that of the player. It can hardly be accidental that in *A Midsummer Night's Dream* and *Hamlet* the play-within-the-play has such an important part. Indeed, we find in Antonio's speech and Gratiano's replay an indication of what the image meant for Shakespeare:

> *Antonio:* I hold the world but as . . . A
> stage where every man must play a part
> And mine a sad one.
> *Gratiano:* Let me play the fool . . .
> (Act I, Sc. 1, ll. 77-9)

Jaques' speech about the seven ages of man takes up the theme again. Human life is a pageant in which characters act out their destinies and disappear into the wings. The idea was a commonplace at the time: Raleigh uses it, for example, in the poem 'What is our Life?' But Shakespeare develops the idea of playing a part to the point where the actor becomes obscured in the character he is representing. That is why the image fits the fool so perfectly. He is playing a part, and we can never be sure what is really him and what the lines the situation has forced upon him. Strangely, the image is only once used with direct reference to the fool, in *Hamlet*. Hamlet sees that the players, with no other 'cue for passion' but the need to please their audience, are able to act out vengeance and disaster. Someone in his position, on the other hand, with far more motive for passion, remains unable to act, but

> [peaks] like John-a' dreams, unpregnant of
> [his] cause
> And can do nothing.
> (Act II, Sc. ii, ll. 571-2)

The illusion of action and emotion displayed by the actors is all that the fool in real life has. The image of the stage, then, points up the irony of the fool's position. The device of the theatrical entertainment is also used as a means of confronting various levels of society, especially nature's naturals and the courtly, and of commenting on the attitudes one level has to another. In the entertainment that concludes *Love's Labours Lost,* Costard amuses the court not simply because of the part he is playing but because of its unconsciously superior attitude which sees all behaviour different from its own merely as a curious part well played.[7]

Another important image is the dream. One play is built upon the idea; it is referred to in Mercutio's Queen Mab speech; Hamlet uses it in the speech quoted above; it is how Hal describes his changed feelings to Falstaff:

> I have long dream'd of such a kind of man,
> So surfeit-swell'd, so old, and so profane;
> But, being awak'd, I do despise my dream.
> (Act V, Sc. v, ll. 49-51)

The world of the fool is very like a dream, in which the normal is distorted or upended, and whose shifts and alternations the world of sense, unless it explain them with Hal as detestable folly, cannot interpret. Bottom says of his dream, 'man is but a patched fool if he will offer to say what methought I had': it is a good statement of the fool's activity. He is always attempting to pierce the world of fantasy, and yet his own behaviour has the everchanging quality of a dream.

VII

For the fool to have the prominence he is given by Shakespeare, it is necessary for there to be two or more world-views in opposition to each other. One world-view will often be held by a minority. Those in the majority will tend to treat the minority as fools, especially if they are following a course of action internally consistent and at odds with the rest. But Shakespeare's deliberate presentation of opposed views is not merely a device for forwarding the action: it also reminds us that this attitude by the majority cannot be maintained. The folly of the fool, the wisdom of the wise . . . it may be, after all, one. The sophistication of the court, the rusticity of the country—who shall arbitrate? The fool then has the function of pointing us to the unity of all existence in community. The ambiguities in his position are not so important when a kindly nature is able to bring man's folly to heel; when, however, as in Edmund's opening speech, nature is seen to be malignant, the fatal weaknesses in the fool bring about his downfall. Nevertheless, even in his downfall he is making the valid point that real community is found not behind the closed doors of princes, but in exposure to all the wild weathers, in *As You Like It* no less than *King Lear*. He cannot be the agent of redemption: to become that he would have to take off his mask and suffer for the world instead of suffering from it and retreating into himself. Rouault has, indeed, used him as a symbol of redemption, and seems to equate him with the redeeming folly of the cross. But, according to theology, Christ suffered for the sake of community, and the fool, as presented in the literature of all ages, is unable, through his own weakness and sense of inadequacy, to suffer on anybody's account but his own. Yet, in his self-awareness, he serves to direct us to the Rosalinds and the Cordelias, the people who are to save society: people who may in their openness be destroyed by it, but will yet hand on to others the fragile secret of the making of community.

Notes

[1] R. D. Laing, *The Politics of Experience,* 1967, p. 72; and *cf.* in the discussion that follows, *ibid.,* cc. 4, 5.

[2] *op. cit.,* p. 95.

[3] On the mature comedies, see Barber, *Shakespeare's Festive Comedy;* and for studies of Touchstone and Jaques, see Goldsmith, *Shakespeare's Wise Fools.* Dr. Goldsmith's approach, like that of Welsford, *The Fool,* is largely historical and is not followed here.

[4] J. F. Danby, *Shakespeare's Doctrine of Nature,* 1961, p. 102.

[5] An article by T. Greene, 'The Postures of Hamlet' in *Shakespeare Quarterly* II (1960) arrives at much the same conclusions about the meaning of *Hamlet* as this article.

[6] See especially J. F. Danby, *op. cit.,* pp. 102-114.

[7] cf. Anne Righter, *Shakespeare and the Idea of Play,* 1962.

Shyam M. Asnani (essay date 1969)

SOURCE: "An Apology for Fools (—A Study in Shakespearean Fools)," in *The Modern Review,* Vol. CXXIX, No. 5, May, 1969, pp. 335-40.

[*In the essay below, Asnani offers an overview of Shakespeare's fools, notably Touchstone, Feste, and Lear's Fool.*]

The meaning of the word Fool has undergone a considerable change since the time of Shakespeare. The word as we understand today, means a person "marked by folly: lacking in judgment, fit consideration or intelligence, as lacking in intellect: Idiotic, feeble minded, simple[1]. etc. But the Fool of Shakespeare instead of being idiotic, simple and feeble minded, is marked by the sharpness of his wit, spontaneity in fun and sometimes satire in his tone.

During the Elizabethan period, the kings, the noblemen and other wealthy persons used to employ fools in order to entertain themselves, and their friends either on certain ceremonial occasions or in the common parlour. The fool, or the clown, or the jester (to be taken as synonymous terms presently,) used to wear the conventional 'motley'—particoloured dress and also a conical cap, and carry in his hands a staff with some jingling-bells attached to one end of it, which the fool used to shake before his listeners whenever he used to speak something foolish or funny in order to excite laughter in them. Such a fool or a jester was usually drawn from the ranks of the cultured, for he had to be polished, cultured, well-read and possessed of both moral courage and intellectual tact. He was most privileged in the sense that he was permitted to speak any amount of sense and nonsense before any august assembly and sparing none of the august persons for the jokes, which were sometimes humorous, sometimes witty, sometimes farcical and even vulgar. He had also the movements of his body, some kind of gesture, which also was intended to provoke laughter. Richard Tarleton, Will-Kempe, and Robert Armin were among the leading professional fools during the Tudor Age, which gave food for pastime to the royal court and noble audience.

Moulton in his interesting study of Shakespeare[2]. believes that this institution of fools seems to rest upon three medieval and ancient notions. The first is the barbarism of enjoying personal defects, illustrated in large number of Roman names derived from bodily infirmities Varus, the bandy-legged, Balbus the stammerer, and the like; this led our ancestors to find fun in the incoherence of natural idiocy, and finally made the imitation of it a profession. A second notion underlying the institution of a jester is the connection to the ancient mind between madness and inspiration; the same Greek word etheos stands for both and to this day the idiot of a Scotch village is believed in some way to see further than sane folk. A third idea to be kept in mind is the medieval conception of wit. With us wit is weighed by its intrinsic worth; the old idea, appearing repeatedly in Shakespeare's scenes, was that wit was a mental game, a sort of battledore and shuttlecock, in which the jokes themselves might be indifferent since the point of game, lay in keeping it up as smartly and as long as possible. The fool, whose title and motley dress suggested the absence of ordinary sense or propriety, combines in his office all three notions; from the last he was bound to keep up the fire of badinage, even though it were with witless nonsense; from the second he was expected at times to give utterance to deep truths; and in virtue of the first he had licence to make hard hits under protection of the 'folly' which all were supposed to enjoy:

> He that a fool doth very wisely hit,
> Doth very foolishly, although he smart,
> Not to seem senseless of the bob . . .

It was the fashion of the time to call these comic characters all indifferently, clowns; but Gordon has technically classified them into two groups: "those who play with words, and those who are played with by them—those, who are sufficiently masters of the English language to make fun out of it; and those who are mastered by it as to give fun unconsciously"[3]. In the first class he has placed the professional fools headed by Touchstone, with Feste, and such court-bred attendants as Moth-that 'tender juvenal.' In the class, though touching on the second, come the men servants, the roguish valets, like Speed, and Launce, and Launcelot. The second class consists of rustics like Costard, artisans like Bottom and officials like Dogberry, Verges and Dull. The amusement they cause is at their own expense. They are complacent, vain, and adorably stupid. Sometimes they achieve pure nonsense, than which nothing is more difficult to explain. "There is nothing in Shakespeare more certainly the work of genius" says Gordon, although with a little exaggeration, "than the mettled nonsense, the complacent nonsense, the perfectly contented and ideal inanity which Shakespeare, in some of these characters has presented to us"[4].

The purpose of Shakespeare's introducing the fool into comedies as well as tragedies, historical plays as well as romances, is manifold. It is, of course, the general one of making the company or the audience laugh, of keeping the dialogue going on in the intervals of action, of providing the song and dance, whenever and wherever necessary (for example Dull in *Love's Labour Lost,* Touchstone in *As You Like It,* Feste in *Twelfth Night* and Autolycus in the *Winter's Tale*). Another contribution of the fool in Shakespeare's plays is to moralise or sermonise or philosophise over certain situations and incidents of the play or even upon the actions of certain characters; while at other times, his function is to explain certain things—either the behaviour of the hero or the heroine, or the trend of the action of the play which would otherwise remain unintelligible to the audience. Hence the Fool in Shakespeare is not necessarily a 'fool' in modern context, or an imbecile or a half-witted fellow, but quite the reverse, he is one of the wisest or the most learned characters in the play. More than a jester or a humorist, he very often assumes the role of a philosopher, a Greek Chorus, an interpreter and a critic. It would be no exaggeration to say that it is through the lips of the fool that sometimes Shakespeare speaks and expresses his own opinion on certain matters, for he has made him more wise and profound than most of the so called wise men.

A study of the fool in Shakespeare's Comedies, Tragedies and Romances may lead to some interesting results. Let us take, first of all, Touchstone.

Touchstone, the prince among Shakespearean fools has neither the vulgarity of Autolycus, nor the indecent jests and coarse witticism of Brown. His wit, though a bit sophisticated is apt and entertaining without being vulgar; his humour is never boisterous and infectious; it is always playful, hilarious and designedly foolish. The motive of his witticism is to unmark the follies and human absurdities. He has been called "a mixture of the ancient cynic philosopher with the modern buffoon." His solemn, bright, lovable and deceptive fooling anent the flight of time is a sort of parody of Jaques' sombre meditations.

John Palmer esteems him as a "loyal servant who without any illusions as to the sequel is ready at a word to 'go along over the wide world' with his mistress"[5]. And he knows which side the bread is to be buttered, for like a complete realist gifted with abundant common sense he aptly responds to the situation:

> Ay, now am I in Arden, the more fool I.
> When I was at home, I was in a better
> Place, but travellers must he content[6].

His special lecture to Corin on the rival claims of town and country, court and rustic life casts sufficient light on his sharp and intelligent wit. He gives a very balanced view of life. He is at pains to show to Corin how full of fraud and humbug the court life is. But at the same time, he has no predisposition to idealise the forest life and presents it with a most convincing innocence.

> Truly . . . in respect of itself, it is a good life, but in respect that it's a shepherd's life, it is naught. In respect it is solitary, I like it well, but in respect it is private, it is a very vile life. Now in respect it is in the fields, it pleaseth me well; but in respect it is not in the court, it is tedious . . .[7].

The incomparable Rosalind, whose tide of wit and flush of love set her above any need of correction by the comic spirit, is moved to commit: "Thou speakest wiser than thou art ware of" (II, iv, 52). Even a character like Jaques-steeped head over heels, in the desponding slough of melancholy and dejection, is enthralled and pays the greatest compliment to Touchstone's wit. (II, vii, 12-19). It is a testimony worth recollecting that Touchstone is able to communicate some sort of enthusiasm for living to a man like Jaques—a born pessimist. It, no doubt, amounts to the undying popularity of Touchstone, when Jaques more than once wants to be invested with the power of the fool:

1. O, that I were a fool . . .
   I am ambitious for motley coat[8].

2. . . . I must have liberty
   Withal as large a character as the wind,
   To blow on whom I please; for so fools have[9].

But it is the senior Duke, a keen student of human nature, who understands Touchstone best and gives the aptest appreciation of the function of all fools in Shakespeare's plays, when he says of Touchstone that:

> He uses his folly like a stalking horse; and
> under presentation of that he shoots his wit[10].

We then find him as a critic of poetry which expresses the mad passion of a lover. When Rosalind is naturally thrilled to read the poems, scattered and hung on the boughs of the trees in the Forest of Arden by her lover-Orlando, Touchstone comes along and pours cold water on such effusions. He says it is clumsy, unmusical and cheap poetry; nothing better than a doggerel:

> I'll rhyme you so, eight years together,
> dinners, suppers, and sleeping hours
>   excepted;
> it is the right butter-woman's rank to the
>   market[11].

And he is not a mere boaster; he can do what he says and indeed gives a sample of extempore rhymes in the mock-heroic style—

His very marriage, so grotesquely ill-assorted is the partner of his choice. It tends (in Hazlitt's words) to "throw a degree of ridicule on the state of wedlock itself" and consequently on the others over whom Hymen speak his blessing.

During the course of the play Touchstone has to draw fun on demand from such diverse topics as Courtiers' oaths, travellers' complaints, the course of Time the irregularities of Fortune, music, versification, and even his own intended wife—"a poor virgin, sir, an ill-favoured thing, sir, but mine own." In the final scene, to fill up a moment of waiting, Touchstone treats us to a superb piece of comic casuistry. He very shrewdly brings in his famous anatomy of the lie in its seven fold stages and shows himself a refined logician. The seven stages are the Retort Courteous, the Quip Modest, the Reply Churlish, the Reproof Valiant, the Countercheck Quarrelsome, the Lie with the Circumstance and the Lie Direct. The passage is important for the light it throws on his claim to be considered a courtier. The evidence he adduces is: "I have flattered a lady, I have been polite with my friends, and smooth with mine enemy; I have undone three tailors; I have had four quarrels and like to have fought one"[12]. But actually he did never fight it out, since he and his opponent discovered that the quarrel was upon the seventh cause. He then explains that the seventh stage "Lie Direct" can be avoided by the addition of the qualifying word 'If'. 'Your if' is the only peace-maker; much virtue in 'If' he declares.

It has been wittily said of Touchstone: "He is undoubtedly slightly cracked, but the very cracks in his brain are chinks which let in light"[13]. If we take into account the effectiveness of his fooling, the unvarying versatility with which it is suited to its subject, and the insight into character and life with his apposite arguments, we can only doubt the existence of these alleged 'cracks'.

Thoughout the Forest scenes, Touchstone furnishes ballast in the shape of shrewd and homely thrusts to counteract the rarefied atmosphere of romance, mystery and idealised love. In short what has been said of Feste in *Twelfth Night*, is equally true of Touchstone: "Is not this a rare fellow, my lord? he's as good as anything and yet a fool."[14]

Feste: Feste, one of the most interesting characters in *Twelfth Night* is a sort of the Master of Revels—the highest prudence and the lowest buffooner in the play. He is conscious of his superiority and knows that he does not carry motley in his brain when he very shrewdly observes: "Those wits that think they have thee do very oft prove fools; and I that am sure that I lack thee, may pass for a wise man."[15] This fellow who is "too wise to play the fool" quickly wins Viola's applause when he sees the disease of both Malvolio and the Duke and prescribes remedies to them. This indeed is the top of wisdom to philosophise yet not to appear to do so, and in mirth to do the same with those that are serious and seem in earnest. On being asked by Viola if he is not Lady Olivia's fool, he at once retorts, "No, indeed, sir, the Lady Olivia has no folly; she will keep no fool, sir, till she is married; and Fools are as like husbands as pilchards are to herrings, husbands the bigger. . ."[16].

Some of his remarks have passed for sayings and maxims, for instance; "Better a witty fool than a foolish wit," or. "God give wisdom to those that have it; those who have it not, let them use it."

Feste, the wise fool, who translates deep truths of human nature into the languge of laughter, to use A. C. Bradley's phrase "endears himself to us",[17] because he is witty, satirical, apt enough at repartee, merry, jovial; in short "for all waters."

Lear's Fool: He is the traditional royal retainer whose licensed profession is to entertain the king in such ways as the king finds entertaining. But he goes beyond his privilege and thus transgressing his usual professional role, he becomes the commentator on his master's doings. "He points his remarks". says Charlton[18] "on Lear's projects with a sting which pierces to the quick, and he knows how near the edge he is thrusting".

> Thou wast a pretty fellow when thou hadst no need
> to care for her frowning; now thou art an O without
> a figure; I am better than thou art now; I am a fool,
> thou art nothing.[19]

So far as his presence for the most part in the play; his foresight and voice of disembodied wisdom, and his sharp chidings on the King are concerned, he is like the Chorus in the Greek Tragedies with one essential difference. Unlike the chorus in Greek Tragedies, his prophetic utterances are not mystically inspired. They are "the cumulative product of mankind's human experiences."[20]

He speaks from the well of traditional wisdom of the ages—all the wisdom stored up in Lear which might have been the well-spring of his actions if he could have listened to it and valued it. The keynote of Lear's tragedy is, in fact, sounded in the words of the fool: "Though should'st not have been old until thou hadst been wise." (K. L. I,v,45). He scolds the king for giving away his land, and for resigning his crown: "Thou hadst little wit in thy half crown", he says, "when thou gavest thy golden one away." And further," I can tell why a snail has a house," he says, "to put his head in, not to give it away to his daughters and leave his horns without a case." It is again the sensible fool who very cryptically sums up the essence of the common tragedy of the plot and the sub plot;

> The hedge-sparrow fed the cuckoo so long
> That it had its head bit off by its young.[21]

Autolycus: Moving in the midst of rustic merriment, the agile figure of Autolycus is, as if, an incarnation of rascal knavery and vagabondage. He has in him the wit of Touchstone, tunefulness of Feste and mental agility and a ready tongue of Falstaff. He is a rogue, not so much from malice as from his joyous and sportive nature. He takes delight in thievery for its own sake rather than for its gains. He is aware of his misdeeds, and laughs at them. His life is folly, to be sure, but then he wants to enjoy his own folly. A brilliant scapegrace, a knave of many faculties; of sparkling versatility of parts; with wit equal to thievery; quick, sharp and changeable—he belongs to the class of consciously comic characters, who make fun and enact folly for themselves.

To him, life is a festival of gay adventures in which his own unfailing resourcefulness brings him both money and enjoyment. Adventurous as he is, he makes no pretence to courage and virtue; much as he loves crime, he dreads its consequences. "Gallows and knock are too powerful on the highway; beatings and hangings are terror to me".[22] At the same time, he finds "Honesty a fool, and Trust his sworn brother, a very simple gentleman."[23] Simplicity and Honesty are thus an infamy to him. Consummate in arts of lying, fraud and imposture, this merry rogue, the incarnation of fun and rascality, practises them with such a droll and brazen audacity, with such a keen sense of enjoyment and fun, that we are inclined to be indulgent to him.

Trinculo in *The Tempest* is a mean type of Shakespearean fools, because he lacks decent humour or intelligent wit, because he indulges mostly in plays upon words or in vulgarity, which is nothing but bufoonery, and because, at the top of all, he is a dammed coward and a confirmed addict to drinking. Even Caliban, a monster hates Trinculo and outwits him. The only one remark which Trinculo makes and which is worth noting is "Misery acquaints a man with strange bedfellows," otherwise, Trinculo is really one of the most degenerate forms of the Elizabethan fools.

There are other fools or clowns in Shakespeare's plays, but they are not as remarkable as the fools just studied, and yet some of them deserve mention. These are Launcelet Gobleo in *The Merchant of Venice,* Costard in *Love's Labour Lost;* the grave diggers in *Hamlet;* Bottom the weaver in the *Mid Summer Night's Dream,* clowns in *Measure for Measure* and *All is Well That Ends Well;* and jesters who appear in *Othello* and *Timon of Athens.*

These fools can also be classified according to the various types of humour which Shakespeare uses in his plays. We have seen that in most of the comedies Shakespeare uses either witty humour or farcical humour, grim humour or ironic humour, philosophic or romantic humour, bantering or refreshing humour. The variety of fools in Shakespeare plays indicates not only his own insight into the various types of persons, who are capable of expressing their humorous spirit in their own typical ways which can be clearly distinguished from one another. We can surely distinguish Falstaff from Touchstone, or Feste from the fool of King Lear.

Notes

[1] *Webster's Third new International Dictionary Unabridged* p. 884.

[2] P. G. Moulton *Shakespeare As a Dramatic Artist* pp. 219-220. Chapter X.

[3] G. Gordon: *Shakespearean Comedy.*

[4] G. Gordon: *Shakespearean Comedy.*

[5] John Palmer: *Political and Comic Character of Shakespeare.*

[6] *As You Like It* II, iv, 16-18.

[7] Ibid III, ii, 11-18.

[8] *As You Like It* II, vii, 42-43.

[9] Ibid II, vii, 47-49.

[10] Ibid V, iv, 106-107.

[11] Ibid III, ii, 86-88.

[12] *As You Like It* V. iv, 43-46.

[13] Leopard *Shakespeare* pp. Iv iii.

[14] *Twelfth Night*—V, iv, 100-101.

[15] *Twelfth Night*—I, v, 28-31.

[16] Ibid III, i, 28-31.

[17] A. C. Bradley: *A Homage to Shakespeare.*

[18] H. B. Charlton: *Shakespearean Tragedy* ch VII, pp- 224.

[19] *King Lear*—I, iv, 210.

[20] H. B. Charlton: *Shakespearean Tragedy* p. 225.

[21] *King Lear*—I, iv, 213-214.

[22] *The Winter's Tale* IV, iii, 27-28.

[23] Ibid—IV, iv, 583-84.

Glenys McMullen (essay date 1970)

SOURCE: "The Fool as Entertainer and Satirist, On Stage and in the World," in *The Dalhousie Review*, Vol. 50, No. 1, Spring, 1970, pp. 10-22.

[*In the essay that follows, McMullen examines the fool's role as a satirical voice in Shakespeare's plays.*]

As an entertainer, the fool has always been a prime target for laughter. But it is through the jester in man that the riddle of his nature is approached in the twentieth century; and possibly the fool may lead us to discover his true glory. Whether dancing in the *komos* of Attic comedy, leading the morris, jigging on the apron stage, conducting the singing at a children's pantomime, or just gazing vacantly into a television camera, the fool can always make his audience merry. They wait for his entrance so eagerly that sometimes they will burst out laughing before he has had time to do, say, or even look a joke. The laughter is often kindly, occasionally sympathetic, but usually tinged with derision; it goes with a delightful feeling of superiority which may well lie behind our love of the fool. Yet it is the experience of a complacent audience that suddenly its laughter turns back upon itself, forcing it to ponder for the moment just where the real fool is to be found.

The public have always liked to suppose some deeper significance to the fool, apart from his talent for making them laugh or look at themselves askance. He has been made to represent some of their basic assumptions about life. For instance, in the Middle Ages he symbolized the vanity of human pretension, whereas the lord he served represented divine perfection; it was a neat image of the antithesis within man's nature, as they conceived it, sublime and ridiculous together. The twentieth century, which refuses to see any tidy or unified order in life, has made the fool a symbol of meaninglessness, or else an enviable dropout from the pressures of a worried, over-involved and conformist society. Perhaps because of this, most modern fools have no voice; they make comments rather by what they are and through the crazy fun they have, turning the world's values on end. In fact, a cult of the crazy has swept the modern world off its feet, largely through the work of such artists as Charlie Chaplin, Harpo Marx, Jacques Tati, and Giulietta Massina, who make such magnificent global village idiots that they dominate the movies in which they have appeared. It would not be surprising if some theatrical tycoon were to re-name *Twelfth Night* "Feste the Jester", as Charles II called it "Malvolio" for another age.

Modern scholars are taking man's absurdity very seriously. Following the "proper study of mankind" they choose to place emphasis upon the second element of Pope's definition of human nature: "The glory, jest and riddle of the world." By examining the jester in man it is possible to understand the riddle of his nature, which in turn reveals his glory. That is what Arthur Koestler, for example, sets out to do in his study, *The Act of Creation*:[1] the first section of his book is entitled "The Jester" and he begins by analyzing the intellectual, emotional, and physiological processes involved in the making of a joke. By the placing of a familiar object in a new light, where two incompatible frames of reference intersect, tension is set up in the audience and suddenly triggered off through laughter. This process, which he calls bisociation, is the basis of all creativity[2] and he draws a fascinating paradigm to demonstrate how awareness of the absurd shades into scientific discovery on one hand and into artistic presentation on the other. To the student of Shakespeare's fools, this offers an interesting explanation of the way in which these chameleon figures slip so easily from nonsense and fantasy into acute satirical commentary or exquisite songs.

Taking a different field of study altogether, Johan Huizinga has also found that the fool is basic to human nature; as he sees it, the earliest significant function of man is play.[3] From his anthropological studies of primitive festivity, he remarks how the spirit of play moves between the poles of wanton frivolity and religious ecstasy in such a way that it is sometimes difficult to tell them apart. The ridiculous and the sublime are closer together than we realize. As he develops his thesis, Huizinga demonstrates that play has many features in common with art: each creates a world of its own, an interlude in everyday life, where the participants are completely absorbed in obeying a fixed set of conventions; the experience is more satisfying than in real life, partly because the rules provide a rhythmic pattern of repetition and alternation which allows the players' tensions to gather and be released in a controlled and happy manner. As children lose themselves in games and the magic world of make-believe, so men lose themselves in equally artificial "worlds", in order to pursue noble professions in philosophy, religion, poetry, law, sport, or the making of civilization itself. It seems that the experience of artificial conventions from time to time is essential to human achievement and very far from being a frivolous waste of time. Finally, as he surveys human history, Huizinga calls the Renaissance the play period par excellence, which puts Shakespeare's fools right in their element; but he finds that the twentieth century fails too often to appreciate the true value of play and is even in danger of destroying it by imposing upon it such standards of daily life as commercial success and efficiency. Man may yet save the world if he can learn from the fool how to play.

A man who is doing his best to resurrect the fool, in his own way, is Joachim Foikis, the Vancouver Jester. When he attended a happening in his honour at York University in Toronto, the *Globe and Mail* published an article with many interesting comments on the fool's vocation in the modern world.[4] The humblest of all professions, it includes features of many of the noblest: those of preacher, poet, entertainer, and counsellor. He has been guide, philosopher, and friend to the aristocracy of past ages and now he must try to reach the democracies. Mr. Foikis actually graduated in theology and intended to become a minister, "but decided one Billy Graham was enough—so I became a fool." With a nod and a wink, some of Shakespeare's fools could say the same: at any rate, they demonstrated enough knowledge of theology and homilectics to parody the preacher, which is no more than many true servants of the Church achieve in earnest. Lavatch, the coarsest of them all, is always quoting the scriptures and consciously assumes the role of devil's advocate in his conversations with his mistress.[5] Touchstone cleverly burlesques the art of exhortation, as he hectors Corin on the damnation of his soul, ironically reversing the traditional values of the shepherd's vocation, either ecclesiastical-pastoral or rustical-pastoral, and ending by upholding the foppery of the court as the noblest of them all.[6] But Feste is the fool who actually dresses up as a parson, his Sir Topas displaying all the failings traditional in ecclesiastical satire, like the French *sotties,* where priest and fool were identified with each other: bumbling clericalism, blanketed by a pompous parade of false learning, and barricaded in turn with showy rhetoric: "Bonos dies, Sir Toby: for as the old hermit of Prague, that never saw pen and ink, very wittily said to a niece of King Gorboduc, 'That that is, is': so I, being Master Parson, am Master Parson; for what is 'that' but that? and 'is' but is?"[7] On the surface it is nonsense, but the mask of absurdity only just conceals a shrewd and caustic observation of human snobbery and egotism. Like all fools, Feste under cover of fun, brings down the mighty to his own level.

To show that he professes folly, a fool wears distinctive clothes which reveal his nature and serve his vocation in various ways. The parti-coloured suit with cap and bells was worn by medieval court jesters, and the long coat of flecked homespun, which Leslie Hotson argues was the "motley" of Shakespeare's fools, was worn by naturals or idiots.[8] Mr. Foikis wears a version of the better-known parti-coloured suit when he goes on duty, three days a week, in Vancouver's Courthouse Square. He admits frankly that "It took a lot of guts to appear publicly like this"; but, after all, exposure to ridicule is the point of being a fool. As well as being a badge of his own humiliation, motley offers several opportunities for the fool to humiliate others; by offering them his cockscomb or bauble, he makes a graphic comment upon their folly. Besides humble associations, Hotson remarks a number of honourable ones for the motley wear, which once again suggests the fool's closeness to the nobler professions. The long coat could suggest the priest's cassock, the soldier's gaberdine, the woman's petticoat, or the clothes worn by small children. All these were signs of a privileged member of society, one who goes under a great lord's protection.

The most ancient parts of the fool's dress are his cap and bauble, which parody the king's crown and sceptre. The bauble belongs to the fool in the *komos* of Attic comedy and was much flourished in the morris of the later Middle Ages; as a phallic symbol, it inspires either superstitious awe or puritanical revulsion, being one of the ways in which the fool, so to speak, separates the men from the boys. The cock's comb, a tuft of hair on a shaven head or a crest surmounting the fool's cap, goes back like the animal figures in the comedies of Aristophanes, to primitive rites. From the beginning, three elements are associated in the fool's nature: fertility, satire, and making merry; the rest of this paper will be concerned with examining some of the ways in which Shakespeare's fools combine satire and merry-making, so that they occupy a special place in both comedy and tragedy.

Because they occupy the lowest position in the social scale, and because they are self-judged, fools make excellent satirists. Their licence allows them to tell truth to the great, but since after all they are only fools, they usually manage to do this without offence. All Shakespeare's fools correspond to the Erasmian sage-fools in their satirical function: "what word coming out of a wise man's mouth were an hanging matter, the same yet spoken by a fool shall much delight even him that is touched therewith."[9] The way in which the fool's satirical comments are received is the measure of their victim's characters. Feste's sharp tongue is called a bird-bolt by Olivia, as she defends her fool to Malvolio, who most certainly is not amused by the fool's taunts. Her gracious indulgence of the fool contrasts with Orsino's lordly ignoring of the fool's bolts; he does not even hear Feste's plain criticism, so lost in his dream is he. Viola is realistic and prevents the fool from "passing upon" her by paying him off; in any case, she has nothing to learn from him since she too is self-humiliated.[10]

Touchstone is constantly "flouting", as he says, and all the leading figures of society, both at court and in

Arden, suffer him gladly. They show that they may grow by what they learn from him and they can give back as good as they get; Rosalind, Orlando, and Corin in particular enjoy parrying the thrusts of his sharp tongue, while Duke Senior and Jaques commend his skill, the Duke remaining egotistically unaware of any personal implications. At the other end of the social scale, Touchstone's satire scourges the fools Sir Oliver and William, but passes over Audrey's head; she gazes in admiration and marvels at his great powers of speech, with an innocent stupidity which makes the satirist throw down his arms.[11]

Lavatch in *All's Well* has a more "foul and calumnious" tongue than Feste and Touchstone combined, but once again the truly noble characters enjoy his satire and rebuke him if he grows tiresome. Only Parolles cannot take it: being all words, as his name implies, he is quite blown down by the clown's rude breath and has to cry quits.[12]

The tongue being his only weapon, the fool always runs off from actual violence, decrying it over his shoulder. When Sir Toby draws his sword to attack the supposed Cesario, Feste slips away to fetch Olivia. Touchstone makes clear his views on violence when he speaks to le Beau about his lurid account of the wrestling at court: "It is the first time that ever I heard breaking of ribs was sport for ladies." Lear's poor fool runs off from Goneril's wrath, taunting her over his shoulder with his version of a fool's satire, couched in pitifully inept doggerel.

While they tell the truth about individual and social evils, the fools' satire is often pleasing because it is expressed with so much wit, or with an amusing display of innocence. Snatches of song, doggerel from the morality plays, old ballads, strategic innuendo, parody, impersonation, and ironic asides are devices frequently employed by Shakespeare's fools. Only the ignoble need to fear him. As Enid Welsford points out, the truly aristocratic characters delight in him and survive his satire while shallow fops and conceited hollow men can do neither.[13] Those who are too stupid to understand the fool's satire are forgiven and accepted at the end of the comedies. That is why Touchstone marries Audrey; of all the women in Arden he chooses her for the very reason that she is a foul and silly slut. Apart from the satisfaction of his bodily desires, all he can hope for from her is a perpetual whetstone for his wit; the first conversation between them sounds like many modern comic acts, where wit and stooge are married partners. Perhaps it is because a fool himself alternates between being a wit and the butt for others' ridicule that he has a basic sympathy for folly which makes him gentler than other satirists.

It was mainly from Roman comedy that Elizabethan fools inherited the standard objects for satirical comment: the arrogance of princes, the wantonness of women, ecclesiastical greed and hypocrisy, and any form of social affectation. As E. K. Chambers has pointed out, they followed the humanistic bias by setting up ethical rather than aesthetic standards.[14] But while pleasure and profit go together when Shakespeare's fools are being satirical, it seems doubtful that they really aspired, as Jaques did, to cure the ills of all the world. They were not social workers at heart; on the contrary, they seemed to delight in the gulls, fops, dupes, cowards, lechers, and upstarts who surrounded them. The genial, holiday spirit of acceptance is theirs; at the worst, they shrug their shoulders cynically as they invite their audience, on stage and in the auditorium, to join in the merrymaking.

As an entertainer, the fool must strike a balance, or seesaw motion, between folly and wisdom. At one moment the fool amuses by his witless remarks and zany falling about; the next, he must provide apt replies to any question put to him by the casual onlooker; furthermore, he is expected to have special talents, for singing or juggling or tumbling. Shakespeare had two brilliant men to play his fools, one famous for his jigging and the other for his music. He gave them ample opportunity to display their particular skills but in addition he made both of them resemble the Athenian sophist. These men walked in the public squares to engage in contests of wit with any challenger, which is exactly what Touchstone does in Arden, Feste in Illyria, or Lavatch in Rossillion and the French court. And as they wander about waiting to be encountered, they resemble in turn Mr. Foikis in Vancouver Courthouse Square.

The capacity of fools to be both wit and stooge is clearly demonstrated at Touchstone's first appearance. Celia and Rosalind are debating in set terms upon the rivalry between Nature and Fortune when he meets them; at once they use him to continue their debate by exercising their wit at his expense. Wisely he refuses to rise to their baiting, even when Celia puns on his name, but in turn he sets up his own comic butt, in the form of the knight who swore away his honour. It appears that he has a satirical comment to make behind the mask of fooling, concerning the court of Duke Frederick; at one point he goes too far and draws a rebuke from Celia, who is honest enough to admit that she agrees with him: "By my troth, thou sayest true, for since the little wit that fools have was silenced, the little foolery that wise men have makes a great show."[15] It is a beautifully balanced observation on the connexions between fools and wise men. Usually, wise men conceal their own folly by encouraging the fool to show off.

As a topsy-turvy scholar, the fool gained many successes as an entertainer. In an age where everyone was thoroughly schooled in logic, he would often be applauded for turning an argument inside out. Feste gives a clever performance in this kind to win back Olivia's favour when he appears first in the play. He begins with a mock syllogism, in which he reduces a moral quality to the absurd level of the concrete: "any thing that's mended is but patched: virtue that transgresses is but patched with sin, and sin that amends is but patched with virtue . . ." and he follows it with his famous catechism of the lady, by which, in a logical trap, he proves her a fool through her own answers. Such crazy logic, associated as it often is with obsessive images, brings the fools close to the madmen of the tragedies. Both express tangential thoughts in staccato phrases, flashing truth through the sudden juxtaposition of ideas. It is exciting for an audience, and produces a restless feeling, even an uneasy sense that the table of sanity is turning. Versatility remains the major characteristic of Shakespeare's fools as entertainers.

Feste is the least coarse of all the fools, having no trace of the bucolic or bawdy about his language; he personifies the values of an older, more elegant and courtly world, especially when he is with the Duke, Cesario, and his mistress Olivia. Yet he can suit himself to other company, when he happens to fall in with Sir Toby and Sir Andrew; he sings them a love song, by request, joins in a rollicking version of the latest catch and improvises lines to egg on Sir Toby in his confrontation with Malvolio. No intriguer, he takes no part in setting the trap for his old enemy, but once the steward is in prison, Feste joins in the fun of teasing him, taking subtle pleasure in suiting his styles of speech to the characters he impersonates, all the while making an ironic commentary on Malvolio's moral plight; the fool's doggerel from the morality play makes an excellent foil for Sir Topas's puritan rhetoric-of-the-devil.

The songs of Feste have a magical quality which belongs in the comedy of high romance and which the other fools do not emulate. As he says to Orsino, he takes pleasure in singing, but even when he is performing his most plangent songs we do well to look for irony. His final song is a strange one, being as Bradley says "at once cheerful and rueful, stoical and humorous",[16] like Feste himself. Throughout life, the wind and rain beat upon him, but just the same he goes on striving to entertain. Singing in the rain is one of the most important duties of the fool, whether in romantic comedy, high tragedy, or theatre of the absurd.

Part of the fool's ability to entertain depended upon his intimate knowledge of the household and the mood of those he was called upon to amuse. It is viola who points this out, recognizing the delicate judgment he must show, in order to be all things to all men:

> He must observe their mood on whom he
>   jests,
> The quality of persons, and the time;

> And like the haggard, check at every feather
> That comes before his eye. . . .

The fool's position in the household was a most peculiar one. In the plays in which they appear, all the fools are licensed by the fathers, and in each one it is pointed out that the father took much delight in the fool, which adds an antique sanction to his antic nature. Duke Frederick, we are told, used to laugh at the "roynish" Touchstone; and Curio says of Feste that he was "a fool the Lady Olivia's father took much delight in"; while the Countess explains Lavatch's position: "My Lord that's gone made himself much sport out of him; by his authority he remains here, which he thinks is a patent for his sauciness." In fact they are all like Will Sommers, the famous fool in whom Queen Elizabeth's father took much delight, and who was still celebrated towards the end of Elizabeth's reign by writers like Thomas Nashe and Samuel Rowley.

Royally protected and often beloved, the fool in a great household was something between a child and a favourite dog, indulged until he became wearisome and then bundled off, sometimes for a whipping. Like children, fools live to play; they show a flattering dependence upon adults, although they may be saucy towards them; and they are capable of making wise remarks ingenuously, which delights the adults and is often received by them as a message from the oracle. Adults enjoy participating in the games of children, or fools, in order to escape from their own world; this may be a total escape into fantasy or a partial escape through recreating it from the child's point of view. In this latter form, play involves satire in the mimicking of adult activities or the reversal of adult values, which can be a refreshing experience, provided that the adult is capable of being completely absorbed. Once the world of play has been fully entered, however, the adult world fades far away and the mysterious world of spontaneous make-believe fills the scene. Both children and fools love to create a land of their own, filled with people with strange-sounding names, around which they march in fantastic garb, singing, shouting and dancing, or strumming any musical instrument that lies handy. It is familiar territory to poets and such humorists as Thackeray, Edward Lear, Lewis Carroll, and James Thurber. It is most familiar to Shakespeare's fools, who seem to dwell much of the time in a land apart. Whether we call it escapism, wish-fulfilment or the release of tensions and anxieties, such behaviour is organically related to festivity and therefore of the essence of comedy; perhaps this is why the fool leads the way into the true enjoyment of both of these.

Like children and dogs, however much they are petted, the fool may fall into sudden disgrace. It has been noticed already how Celia rebukes Touchstone shortly after his first appearance on stage; both Feste and Lavatch make their first entrance in disgrace, the former for "truancy" and the latter for "complaints". All of them endure a scolding, as part of their introduction to the audience, and then bounce back with a cheeky, knavish charm, using their wits to win favour. It is as if Shakespeare desired to stress the fool's duty toward his mistress, which seems to have resembled his own toward the Queen, by making her discipline him and remind him of his duty to entertain her. Also, of course, it is a wonderful excuse to make the fool perform his best tricks. After all, it is the fool's work to make others play, and if he falls off in this vocation he must be brought back to it sharply.

Though they were employed by the fathers, Shakespeare's fools are more attached to the children of the family, whom they have known since infancy. Hamlet recalls the fun he used to have with Yorick, laughing at unsuitable jokes about women and death, kissing and riding on his back; in the graveyard scene he asks the fool's skull: "Where be your gibes now? your gambols? your songs? your flashes of merriment that were wont to set the table on a roar?" It evokes the powers of Yorick to entertain in a variety of ways, suggesting the acrobatic, witty, and musical talents that all the fools combine, and Hamlet proved an apt pupil when his turn came to "put an antic disposition on". In Lear's household, the fool attached himself naturally to Cordelia, so that he pined away when she went to France. There are a few hints in the comedies that the fools and the heroines are very close, through a familiarity reaching back to childhood. Feste's names for Olivia sound like the pet names one gives a little girl: "Madonna" or "good my mouse of virtue". And she treats him with a special intimacy; her reprimand to him for his teasing of Malvolio is a very gentle one: "Now you see, sir, how your fooling grows old and people dislike it." Touchstone's devotion to Celia is so great that she has complete confidence that he will accompany her to Arden, blithely saying: "He'll go along o'er the wide world with me." Loyalty to the romantic heroine is a special task of the fool in the comedies. He cannot defend her against violence but he can at least comfort her and attend her in her wanderings. His comments remind us of her virtue and suggest that she will overcome, in her resistance to the forces of tyranny and delusion.

To summarize what has been said so far about the fool's vocation: as satirist the fool forces society to make a critical re-appraisal of itself, but as entertainer he relieves the tension accompanying this uncomfortable experience through laughter. By his nature, he is an object of ridicule, yet he is a shrewd observer of human follies. A realist, with his eye always on the passage of time and the signs of mortality, he is a sympathetic companion to the romantic heroine, who redeems mortality. To some extent he is involved in the scene he observes from the satirist's standpoint; for instance, Lear's fool comments all the time on his master's errors of judgment, yet it is he who accompanies Lear through their consequences and on to the heath. He is the suffering side of Lear, out in the storm, complaining of the cold and the rain, while his master majestically commands them or ignores them altogether. Perhaps he may be compared to the Greek Chorus, in that he is a helpless, sympathetic observer of the protagonists, seeing their errors and watching the approach of fate but unable to help them; for all his inactivity, his fate is bound up with theirs.

All the romantic comedies react react ugly and sterile reality, the everyday world that people complain about, and the fool makes the perfect guide from the world of everyday to the magic circle, within which lies the land of romance. He too resists ugliness and sterility, yet he remains realistic; Touchstone is the only one who takes a watch with him to Arden, while Feste reminds the young that "Youth's a stuff will not endure". Both breathe reminders of winter into the sunny world of lovers, without actually freezing their rapture. Touchstone belongs in Arden, because only he can prove its gold against his stony roughness. It is in his conversations with Corin that the pastoral landscape becomes real to us, with all his talk of rams and bellwethers and butterwomen going to market. Besides making the golden world real and providing an earthy romantic element, Touchstone contributes a philosophy of his own to the play. It is a tolerant one, appreciating that human nature will always be "mortal in folly", even in love, and that human institutions, however solemnly celebrated, are but temporary affairs; one must be ready to compromise rather than adopt a rigid attitude. Just before Hymen appears, at the climax of Act V, he is saying to Duke Senior: "Your If is the only peacemaker. Much virtue in If. . . ." And it is Hymen who points out that he and Audrey belong with each other, "As the winter to foul weather". Indeed he is the rude breath of winter, the not altogether unkind wind, celebrated in Amiens' song early in the play.

In *Twelfth Night* the romantic escape is from a barren world of vapid voluptuousness and morbid self-deceiving sentiment to a saturnalia. Feste comments shrewdly on the sentimentality and does not hesitate to join in the revelry, adding his voice to those of the rollicking knights. He does his best to cheer his mourning mistress and to pander to the melancholy of Orsino, realizing they need to be brought back to life. As C. L. Barber remarks, "His part does not darken the bright colours of the play; but it gives them a dark outline, suggesting that the whole bright revel emerges from shadow".[17] If the romantic world is to be more than merely escapist it has to cure the diseases of the real world, educating those who enter it for their inevitable return, and this is Feste's function. At the end of the play he supervises the audience's return to reality as well, striking his own philosophical note and ending with his desire to please.

All's Well That Ends Well, on the other hand, is not an escapist romance; it explores the ugly and barren world itself. The court of Rossillion, as Mark van Doren says,[18] is full of "darkness, old age, disease, sadness and death", while the old king of France suffers with a fistula and his troops fighting in Italy are decimated as much by syphilis as by battle injuries. In a play which explores the fallen nature of man, the fool must become a parody of Jeremiah, decrying the sins of the world as a form of entertainment. To the countess's accusation that he is "a foul-mouth'd and caluminous knave", Lavatch replies "A prophet I, madam, and I speak the truth the next way".

When we turn to tragedy, the ambivalence of the fool is nowhere more poignant than in *King Lear,* where his twittering truisms are disregarded until it is too late. Lear is mad when he comes to appreciate his fool's wisdom. But the paradox about folly and wisdom comes close in this play to Christian teaching about humility and blessedness, as Saint Paul told the Corinthians: "Let no man deceive himself. If any man among you seemeth to be wise in this world, let him become a fool, that he may be wise. For the wisdom of this world is foolishness with God. . . ." When we consider Shakespeare's fools in this light, it is clear that they possess many of the Christian-Stoic virtues, such as loyalty, truth-telling, humility, love and fortitude under persecution, which makes them worthy of the tragic state. It has often been said that Lear's fool is very like Cordelia; both tell truth to the king, suffer humiliation and exile for doing so, follow him into the wilderness, the one as his companion and the other to effect his cure. In all these actions, they not only follow Saint Paul but resemble Christ.

But folly pervades the entire play. All the virtuous characters in turn play the fool in *King Lear,* in that they are mocked at by the worldly and assume the burden of ridicule and humiliation. Kent is laughed at in the stocks, Edgar is mocked as Poor Tom, and Albany is scorned by his wife, who underestimates his power of understanding what is going on, when she tells Edmund, "My fool usurps my body". The apotheosis of the fool occurs at Dover, where Gloucester attempts suicide, lovingly fooled by Edgar, and Lear himself becomes "the natural fool of Fortune" on "this great stage of fools", as he talks to Gloucester.[19] The fool and the blind man meet with Death in tragedy.

It is possible to find some of the noblest professions contributing part of their nature to the humble vocation of fool: doctor, teacher, poet, preacher, guru, philosopher, martyr, counsellor, and friend. How horrified Stephen Gosson would be to hear how twentieth-century people dignify those whom he labelled "the caterpillars of the commonwealth"[20] to the status of his own vocation of evangelist. But this is what the fool must be to the modern world: in his own unassuming way, he must combine the best of all vocations, their curative, recreative, and regenerative principles. The central point of his nature is the meeting-place for truth, nonsense, humour, fantasy, play, poetry, and religion. No wonder that in the medieval folk plays he triumphed over Death.

Mr. Foikis is well aware of all this, of course. In the *Globe and Mail* article already referred to he says that he became a fool after what he calls "a mystic experience" in which it was revealed to him that his role in life was to walk the stage of the world as the fool of joy, reviving in others the ability to laugh in the face of death. But rather than with Mr. Foikis, we should end with a comparison that Bradley made between the fool and Shakespeare himself,

> . . . who, looking down from an immeasurable height on the mind of the public and the noble had yet to be their servant and jester, and to depend upon their favour, not wholly uncorrupted by this dependence, but yet superior to it, and also determined, like Feste, to lay by the sixpences it brought him, until at last he could say the words, "Our revels now are ended", and could break—was it a magician's staff or a Fool's bauble?[21]

Notes

[1] Arthur Koestler, *The Act of Creation* (London: Hutchinson, 1964).

[2] Compare Wordsworth, "the perception of similitude in dissimilitude . . . is the great spring of the activity of our minds. . . ." (Preface to the Second Edition of *Lyrical Ballads*).

[3] Johan Huizinga, *Homo Ludens* (Boston: Beacon Press, 1955).

[4] *Globe and Mail,* Saturday, March 2, 1968, p. 22. "The motley career of an official town fool", by Paul King.

[5] *All's Well That Ends Well,* I, iii, and IV, v.

[6] *As You Like It,* III, ii.

[7] *Twelfth Night,* IV, ii, 13-17.

[8] Leslie Hotson, *Shakespeare's Motley* (London: Rupert Hart-Davies, 1952).

[9] Erasmus, *The Praise of Folly,* translated by Sir Thomas Chaloner, 1549.

[10] *Twelfth Night,* I, v, 94; II, iv, 73-78; III, i, 42.

[11] *As You Like It,* V, iv, 63, 106-107.

[12] *All's Well*, II, iv, 36-38; V, ii, 19-27.

[13] Enid Welsford, *The Fool, his Social and Literary History* (London: Faber and Faber, 1935), p. 254.

[14] E. K. Chambers, *The Elizabethan Stage,* Vol. I, p. 238.

[15] *As You Like It,* I, ii, 43-54, 85-87.

[16] A. C. Bradley, *A Miscellany* (London: Macmillan, 1929).

[17] C. L. Barber, *Shakespeare's Festive Comedy* (Cleveland: World Publishing Company, 1963), p. 259.

[18] Quoted by G. K. Hunter in the Introduction to the New Arden Edition, xxxvi n.

[19] *King Lear,* IV, vi. See the article by Carolyn S. French, "Shakespeare's Folly: *King Lear*", in *Shakespeare Quarterly,* Vol. X, 1959, 523-529.

[20] Stephen Gosson, *The School of Abuse,* 1579.

[21] Bradley, *op. cit.,* p. 217.

Roberta Mullini (essay date 1985)

SOURCE: "Playing the Fool: The Pragmatic Status of Shakespeare's Clowns," in *New Theatre Quarterly,* Vol. 1, No. 1, February, 1985, pp. 98-104.

[*In the following essay, Mullini investigates Shakespeare's use of fools to disrupt hierarchical order and the conventions of language.*]

The title of this paper suggests most of the dramatic and metadramatic features of the fool character. In the fictitious world the fool plays on various levels: the fool-actor reproduces on the stage his acting role, carrying into the dramatic world his heritage of social satire. At the same time he mirrors the historical figure of the court-fool from which he draws his line of behaviour: a player, a specialized one, heir to the ancient *mimus* and the medieval *histrio,* whose person is strictly linked to the world of dramatic illusion, plays himself in an illusory scene, creating a breach in the illusion itself. That scene being taken from the court, the actor-fool need not look very far either for a character to imitate—the court-fool—or for clues from both narrative and dramatic sources and historical accounts as to how he should be performed. There is, moreover, a religious and philosophical background which traces its origin back to the biblical *topoi* and to Erasmus' *Praise of Folly.*

The Shakespearian fool stands at a crossroads where all these elements come together, a point where the dramatic traditions of the Tudor Vice and the folk-drama fool are renewed and where European culture shows at its best the mixture of medieval and humanist concepts of folly. 'This fellow is wise enough to play the fool', says Viola after Feste's exit in *Twelfth Night* (III, i). She is also saying that Robert Armin is a good enough actor to impersonate a court-fool, having all the faculties necessary to reproduce the nimble and saucy jester—and in making this metadramatic comment, she is also underlining Feste's *qua*-character ability to unmask the wise men's folly.[1]

The Typology of Historical Fools

Juri Lotman's typology of culture draws a line between symbolic and syntagmatic models of society—the former, medieval society, being characterized by a strong sense of hierarchy according to which individuals are worthy only so far and so long as they occupy a position in the hierarchical scale; the latter, modern society, marked by greater consideration for the biological person whose social existence is no longer linked to hierarchical status.[2] Starting from this division, which of course has no pretension to being chronologically precise, we can try to define the position and the stature of the court-fool.

The fool arrives at the court when the king wants to be amused, or wants to divert the 'evil eye' from his sacred person—fools being chosen from the wretches of society already struck by some infirmity. The fool is thus called from the outer world into the inner world, from the land of darkness into the light, from a chaotic reality into *the* order. A person is asked to play a role: that of the king's jester. Those who come from the mobile world outside, from the popular culture of the anti-model, are asked to live in an immobile world, that of the model and of the static hierarchy.[3]

However, once inside the high space of the court, the fool's chaotic significance is subjected to the influence of the power of symbolic society: his freedom is a sign of the power which calls him to life; his liberty finds expression through and is limited by the licence given by authority. If this licence is withdrawn, the court-fool is no longer himself and has to go back to the world from which he came. He neither belongs to the symbolic model, nor has any place in the hierarchy: he is accepted by this same hierarchy because the king wants a sort of speaking and tumbling toy, and a comic double of his royal person. The bauble and the coxcomb are comic copies of the sceptre and the crown.

So the court-fool is at the same time at the top and the bottom of the social scale, yet cannot be considered part of it: when his licence is revoked, the fool is sent back to the world of prostitutes and petty crime, back to the roads and the market-place. It is not difficult to see Pompey in *Measure for Measure* and Autolycus in *The Winter's Tale* as such displaced fools.

It is almost impossible, then, to separate fools *natural* from fools *artificial*. Robert Armin himself writes that Will Sommers was 'the Kings naturall Iester',[4] but the episodes he narrates of Sommer's life reveal him as an artificial fool rather than a natural one. In practice many people put on the mask of folly in order to earn their living at court, thus creating a first level of simulation. And it is at this point that other cultural cross-currents meet in the figure of the court-fool, the tradition of carnival buffoons and of marketplace players being grafted onto the insane children of nature (or onto those who feigned a degree of lunacy).

The clerical condemnation of *histriones* and the exclusion of the insane from the Christian community combined to give definition to a figure who lived outside society, far from any norm, blamed and feared both because of his behaviour and possible connection with supernatural (and infranatural) powers. All this is summed up in the typical costume of court-fools—the 'disorder' of the motley colours; the bauble as the sceptre of a nowhere bordering on an everywhere, and as a reminder of a disordered sexuality (the sin of lechery); the pig's bladder as the icon of a foolish mind, and simultaneously of the sin of gluttony; the coxcomb or the cap with ass's ears as the parodic crown of the king of the feast, and, together, as a link to two animals recorded in the Gospel as being near Christ at the time respectively of his death and birth.[5]

The humanistic view of the fool—that of Erasmus' *Praise of Folly* rather than Brant's *Narrenschiff*—evaluates the figure as the mouthpiece of truth. Fools, says Erasmus,

> *can provide the very thing a Prince is looking for, jokes, laughter, merriment and fun. And, let me tell you, fools have a gift which is not to be despised. They're the only ones who speak frankly and tell the truth, and what is more, passionately the truth. . . . The fact is kings do dislike the truth, but the outcome of this is extraordinary for any fools. They can speak truth and even open insults and be heard with positive pleasure: indeed, the words which would cost a wise man his life are surprisingly enjoyable when uttered by a clown.*[6]

But it must be emphasized that hierarchical society permits the fool's truth precisely because it is told by someone who this same 'wise' society considers to be a fool. The truth of the fool's discourse cannot be utilized to change the situation: it belongs to the time-off period of games and the sender of the message is licensed only so long as his satirical comments do not intrude into the sphere of action.[7] The fool's power of judgment is there like a toy to be enjoyed, but the fool's self-awareness cannot be transferred to the society which gives him the licence. Fools laugh and make men laugh, but their strength is limited by their being considered as playthings rather than as living individuals.

Games have their own rules which do not affect the level of reality. When the game is over, the players resume their daily activities: the fool, however, who constantly signifies play, is not allowed a proper time for serious activity. He is allowed no activity at all outside the game, unless he steps out of it. But in this event the fool turns into a man, and is therefore useless to the court games. While playing the game, the fool enjoys his particular licence to address anybody, anywhere. His word is tolerated as a warped comment on reality. And it is exactly within the boundaries of his own licence—nearly always on the border-line of being whipped—that the fool has to make a profit from his discourse.

Shakespeare's Fools

Writing about the development of stage characters in French *soties* and *moralités*, Michel Foucault says that

> *The denunciation of madness [la folie] becomes the general form of criticism. In farces and soties, the character of the Madman, the Fool, or the Simpleton assumes more and more importance. . . . He stands centre stage as the guardian of truth. . . . If folly leads each man into a blindness where he is lost, the madman, on the contrary, reminds each man of his truth; in a comedy where each man deceives the other and dupes himself, the madman is comedy to the second degree: the deception of deception; he utters, in his simpleton's language which makes no show of reason, the words of reason that release, in the comic, the comedy.*[8]

Shakespeare's fools epitomize this tradition of European drama and prolong it. But the playwright is also (and mainly) drawing upon a dramatic convention already rich in Tudor and early Elizabethan theatre, that of the Vice. Nevertheless he *invents* his fools, because what is left in them of earlier medieval types is linked to the humanist and Renaissance views of folly, so that the convention is renewed by Shakespeare, who severs the two main aspects of the Vice (as sovereign of words and rhetoric on one side and as the arch-intriguer of the plot on the other), dismissing his villainy and retaining only his role as jester. Shakespeare's fools are denied the ability to further the action, and do not take part in the events that advance the plot.

In *The Two Gentlemen of Verona, The Merchant of Venice, As You Like It, Twelfth Night, All's Well that Ends Well*, and *King Lear* there are characters whose status is similar to that of the historical court-fool. Fools act as messengers—often failing in their tasks without, however, seriously damaging the proairetic chain of events.

Speed, in *The Two Gentlemen of Verona*, is sent away by Proteus because he has not been able to report Julia's answer to his master's letter:

> *Go, go, be gone, to save your ship from wrack,*
> *Which cannot perish having thee aboard,*
> *Being destin'd to a drier death on shore.*
> *I must go send some better messenger:*
> *I fear my Julia would not deign my lines*
> *Receiving them from such a worthless post.*[9]

In *As You Like It,* after their decision to flee from the court, Celia and Rosalind observe that Touchstone, the 'clownish fool', would 'be a comfort to our travel' (I, iii, 127). The fool's *playful* function in the dramatic world is stressed (he is not considered to be *useful*) through the importance of his presence in relieving the burden of the play ('our journey') with his comic and witty character.

Feste is declared unreliable when reading Malvolio's letter in *Twelfth Night* (V, i, 292-6), and Olivia orders Fabian to perform the task. The fool is thought of as disrupting the channels of communication, unable to transfer information from the written page to the lady.

In *All's Well,* Lavatch actually does serve as a messenger between the Countess and Helena; but his answers to Helena, who inquires about the lady's health, are so rhetorically complicated that pure information is muddled with riddles and mock-logic (II, iv). The behaviour of such fools shows that Shakespeare does not want to use his jesters simply as servants: they carry out orders *if* they like and *how* they like, disregarding the issues. And it is no wonder that Lear's Fool does not work as a messenger: he is never sent on errands, his primary task being that of helping the king out of his madness, or driving him towards self-awareness.

Touchstone gets married to Audrey, but his marriage is barely 'for two months victuall'd', as Jaques acknowledges at the end of the play (*As You Like It,* V, iv, 191). And Touchstone himself (III, iii, 81-5) declares in an aside that 'not being well married' would be better for him. His nuptials appear as a game, with rules which last only till the game itself is over, and his marriage acquires a clear metadramatic hint, in so far as it reflects the short life of the whole game—the *play*—and of all the fictitious marriages with which the comedy ends.

Feste plays the chief part in Malvolio's exorcism—or rather, two parts, his own and the exorcist's. But this episode does not affect the Viola-Orsino-Olivia plot, and, most important, the action operates as a play-within-the-play, a game whose victim is Malvolio. Feste says 'I was one, sir, in this interlude' (*Twelfth Night,* V, i, 371), thus confessing both his participation in

Launce and Speed in Act II, Scene v of The Two Gentlemen of Verona. *By C. Green.*

and the nature of the plot against Malvolio: it was only an old game, a fiction, an *interlude*—its relationship to the Tudor drama all the more evident in that Feste, at the end of the exorcism, sings a song recalling his recent ancestor, 'the Old Vice' (IV, ii, 127).

There they are, the fools—ubiquitous, able to speak both as characters and as voices outside the plays through their metadramatic glosses, spokesmen of the commonsense of the audience and, at the same time, of the utopian aspirations of the playwright. As the court-fool is a stranger in the court—an external element to which the court gives a limited licence but, paradoxically, a powerful voice—so the stage court-fool lives inside the main action ready to step out of its borders, as little involved as possible. The fool goes 'to bed at noon' when the fictional kingdom breaks down and the old hierarchy is destroyed.

But during the performance fools always work on the two dynamic levels of illusion and reality, between the stage and the audience. On the former level their word operates as a kind of litmus paper of the characters' folly, on the latter it shows and proclaims this folly in dialectical balance with the fool's wit. The fool's word, and not his action, interacts with the other characters, who judge him according to the cultural codes of Elizabethan society—or, as Duke Senior puts it, 'He uses his folly like a stalking-horse, and under the presentation of that he shoots his wit' (*As You Like It,* V, iv, 105-6).

The Corruption of Words

The fool's words can be qualified as a macro-speech act of challenge. By the various means of his pseudo-logic, the fool sets up a competition between his so-called foolish word and the 'wise' discourse of the others. The usual distinction between *sweet* and *bitter* becomes invalid, because the fool's discourse is always the eloquent weapon of the fool's challenge, through either 'sweet' behaviour or 'bitter' conversation.

Shakespeare endows his fools with extraordinary powers of speech. Following Elizabethan poetics, all his characters show specific rhetorical competence, but the fool's acute sense of the semantics and rhetoric of language enables him to play with the subtleties of the common code in order to subvert—for a magic moment—the hierarchical order of the speakers. It is in the pragmatics of the fool's discourse that Shakespeare moulds this character, whose life is the word and whose interaction effects the corruption of the others' words.

From this point of view, a character like Launcelot Gobbo in *The Merchant of Venice* shows a double nature, the rustic clown's and the fool's. Before serving Bassanio, he is the man of Shylock's household. His speech displays flaws such as comic malopropisms (for example in II, ii, 119-27) and he is conceived by Shylock as the prototype of most sins. He enters the stage in II, i, acting out the one-man moral show of the conflict between his conscience and the devil, like the old Vice. But once he has put on the 'livery / More guarded than his fellows" (II, ii, 147-8), he turns into a witty fool, skilful in undermining the solidity and the semantic denotation of the universe of discourse. Let's look, for an example, at the puns he constructs on Lorenzo's order, 'bid them prepare for dinner' (*a*):

LAUN. *That is done, sir, they have all stomachs!*

LOR. *Goodly Lord, what a wit-snapper are you! then bid them prepare dinner!*

LAUN. *That is done too sir, only 'cover' is the word.* (*b*)

LOR. *Will you cover then sir?*

LAUN. *Not so sir neither. I know my duty.*

LOR. *Yet more quarrelling with occasion! Wilt thou show the whole wealth of thy wit in an instant? I pray thee understand a plain man in his plain meaning: go to thy fellows, bid them cover the table, serve in the meat, and we will come in to dinner.*

LAUN. *For the table sir, it shall be serv'd in,—for the meat sir, it shall be cover'd,—for your coming in to dinner sir, why let it be as humours and conceits shall govern.* (III, v, 44-58)

In his response to Lorenzo's directive (*a*), Launcelot shifts the meaning from what would be usual in a servant/master context to an *inter pares* interpretation: the relationship between the two men has already become 'democratic', so to say, instead of the one-up/one-down balance existing on the ontological level.[10] The fool's answer to the other's reformulated order (*b*) is quite correct, but it adds also a metalinguistic comment on Lorenzo's semantic inappropriateness.

At this point the discursive hierarchy is subverted: the fool can teach the wise man how to use language, and, furthermore, the former compels the latter to re-word the directive, now split into the three original constituents which are at the basis of the present idiomatic usage. Besides this, Lorenzo cannot but pray Launcelot to 'understand a plain man in his plain meaning': the one-up character descends to the one-down position, so that he begs comprehension and puts questions. The order, then, is carried out only after this metalinguistic performance.

The discoursive hierarchy is turned upside down in a more striking example from *Twelfth Night* when Feste, using the medieval device of catechism (instruction and education through what we now call adjacency pairs or question-and-answer exchange) brings the lady Olivia to acknowledge herself as *the* fool of the house (I, v). After playing with his own discourse and highlighting his rhetorical and semantic competence (he uses syllogistic structures, antanaclasis, and activates more than one isotopy in 40-7), Feste repeats his challenging riddle which confuses 'the lady' and 'the fool' into a single character. Then he proclaims that he is not a fool, but only wears the fool's cap: in so doing he implicitly suggests that those who do not wear the coxcomb are the actual fools.

Eventually Olivia succumbs to the catechistic process, which is nothing but a mock syllogism whose *praemissae* are distributed between the speakers and whose *conclusio* 'Take away the fool' (69) coincides with the *propositio* 'Take away the lady' (37). Olivia is not only degraded from her one-up position to the one-down, but is also repeatedly given the title of fool, the one we are 'born with', as Lear's Fool maintains (I, iv, 147). With his rhetorical performance, Feste changes the referent of his lady's words: he succeeds in proving his lady the real fool, even if his victory is limited—as is Launcelot's—to this realm of words, so that Olivia says, a few lines later, 'There is no slander in an allowed fool' (84).

Lear's Fool is often threatened with the whip because he dares to remind the king of his folly. The Fool here, however, need not use any particular device to call Lear by the name of 'fool'. All the jester's interaction in Act I aims at pointing out Lear's foolish behaviour, while a recovery of judgement still seems possible. The king does not contest his Fool's word—although the jester is threatened—because he now understands the 'logic' and truth of his word.

The Fool is a fool, Lear is 'nothing': the king is the first to lose his place in society and therefore his ontological value, whereas he was at the hierarchical top of symbolic society. The Fool will follow him, as a true fool, but, not belonging to this order, he is free to leave this world to its decay. He loses his job in the court because medieval society is crumbling: when the king reaches the stage of definitive madness and no longer needs the Fool's mirror, the Fool can retire. And Shakespeare, in his later plays, does not use stage court-fools.

Lear's Fool can be considered as the epitome of all Shakespearian fools: he is no messenger, uses monologues and asides addressing the audience directly, speaks almost exclusively to his master, is given no possibility of intervention in the plot, but has powers of satirical and utopian prophecy. The active power of his speech, however, here more than in other plays, proves extremely limited: words cannot govern tragic issues and the Erasmian fool is not sufficient to stop the events from destroying the hero.

Thus Shakespeare seems to acknowledge that this figure from the Middle Ages who uses a fanciful wisdom cannot act against the epistemological crisis of his age: late and post-Elizabethan times require new energies to resist the disruption of the old order. And tragic madness seems to be the only cognitive answer.

The Fool's word is endowed with special prophetic values which link the play's society to the Elizabethan audience, to our own world, and backwards to myth: 'This prophecy Merlin shall make, for I live before his time' (III, ii, 95-6). The Fool speaks in the here and now of the scenic present and so talks to Jacobean society, but he shifts this present back to a legendary past, prior even to Merlin. All the long tradition of the fool appears to be epitomized in this prophecy: the character comes from far off in the past and projects forward into an indefinite future, ready to turn up whenever the fool society needs witty chastisement.

Conclusion

All Shakespearian fools, then, are largely artificial, and as such they 'with their wits lay waite / To make themselues fools, likeing their disguyes, / To feed their owne mindes, and the gazers eyes', according to Robert Armin's definition.[11] They are actors on the stage of life, and doubly players in the fictional world: the awareness they possess of their condition, of their playing the fool, contrasts with the other characters' blindness, which does not allow them to accept the truth of the fool's discourse.

The fool's licence, often obscene, always pungent in throwing attention onto the dynamics between seeming and being, appears then as a conscious invention of Shakespeare's in order to stress the utopian values of his fictional societies. The satirical power of the ancient folk-fool and of the more recent market-place player is transferred by Shakespeare into the figure of the fool in his fictitious courts, where a lucid word substitutes for the tumbling and jesting of the historical personages.

Shakespearian fools, dramatic signs of the power which allows the licence of the court-fool, operate to dismantle the conventional signs of language: they anatomize the others' *langue*—dividing words, splitting proverbs, commenting metalinguistically on the structure of language, often disguising their *parole* as a riddle. And their word is rhetorically rich, semantically ambiguous, ontologically disruptive of the order of the fictional world. Shakespeare's fools are, as Feste himself says, actually not his 'fools', but his 'corrupters of words'.

Notes

[1] I have dealt more extensively with these aspects of the fool in *Corruttore di parole: il fool nel teatro di Shakespeare* (Bologna: CLUEB, 1983).

[2] Cf. J. Lotman, 'Problema znaka i znakovoj sistemy i tipologija russkoj kul'tury XI-XIX vekov', in *Stat'i po tipologii kul'tury,* I (Tartu, 1970).

[3] Cf. M. Corti, 'Modelli e antimodelli nella cultura medievale', *Strumenti critici,* 35 (1978).

[4] Cf. R. Armin, *Foole upon Foole,* in *The Collected Works,* with introductions by J. P. Feather (New York; London: Johnson Reprint Corporation, 1972), E2-1.

[5] For a more detailed study of both court- and stage-fools, cf. E. Welsford, *The Fool: His Social and Literary History* (London: Faber, 1935); and W. Willeford, *The Fool and His Sceptre: a Study in Clowns and Jesters and their Audience* (London: Arnold, 1977). Among the many articles on the subject, see particularly G. L. Evans, 'Shakespeare's Fools: the Nature and the Substance of Drama', in D. Palmer and M.

Bradbury, eds., *Shakespearian Comedy* (London: Arnold, 1972), for its specific stress on the actor/character and stage/audience relationships.

[6] Erasmus, *Praise of Folly,* trans. Betty Radice, Chapter XXXVI (Harmondsworth: Penguin, 1971).

[7] Here I make use of the concepts of 'time-on' and 'time-off' activities as introduced by E. Goffman, in *Interaction Ritual* (Chicago: Aldine Press, 1967).

[8] *Madness and Civilization: a History of Insanity in the Age of Reason* (London: Tavistock Publications, 1977), abridged translation, pp. 30-31.

[9] This quotation and the following are taken from the Arden Editions of Shakespeare's plays.

[10] P. Watzlawick, J. H. Beavin, and D. D. Jackson, in *Pragmatics of Human Communication* (New York: Norton, 1967), underline the relationship between the speaker's social and/or contextual status and his actual discourse.

[11] Armin, op. cit., B2-2.

Meredith Anne Skura (essay date 1993)

SOURCE: "Shakespeare's Clowns and Fools," in *Shakespeare Set Free: Teaching Romeo and Juliet, Macbeth and A Midsummer Night's Dream,* edited by Peggy O'Brien, Washington Square Press, 1993, pp. 19-24.

[*Below, Skura surveys Shakespeare's use of clowns in his plays, and their popularity with both Elizabethan and modern audiences.*]

For a long while Shakespeare's clowns were an embarrassment to everybody, and they were censored from productions. Lear's fool, for example, was left out of every one of the many eighteenth-century performances of *King Lear.* Producers in the nineteenth century kept Macbeth's porter in the play, but they cut his lines to "Knock, knock, knock." Twentieth-century productions have at times imposed their own censorship on Shakespeare, invoking aesthetic if not moral justifications. The clowns in *Romeo and Juliet* and *Othello* are occasionally removed from modern productions, for example. On the whole, however, in our era clowns have been rescued. We find more than random "comic relief" in the clown scenes, and we now see them as part of each play's larger thematic and imagistic design. Macbeth's porter doesn't merely "relieve" us (by slipping comically on a banana peel, for example); he helps create the grotesquely hellish atmosphere created by Macbeth's crime. The rest of this essay explores the clown's function both in Renaissance drama at large and in Shakespeare.

In turning to the fool and the clown we are true to the spirit of the sixteenth and seventeenth centuries. "Everything is full of Fools," said Erasmus—or, as Robin Goodfellow put it in *A Midsummer Night's Dream,* "Lord, what fools these mortals be!" Along with the new sense of individual possibility and the expansion of human horizons in the Renaissance came the continual reminder of the lower side of experience, and the fascination with fools, clowns, and rogues who represent the pure animal existence beneath all our civilized aspirations. They embody the pure life force, as Susanne Langer said appreciatively: "tumbling and stumbling through one disaster and another, the clown shows a brainy opportunism in the face of an essentially dreadful universe."

The clown wasn't invented by dramatists. The fool had always had his role in communal rituals and festivals, the seasonal celebrations that calibrated the agricultural year. And all year round there were real fools or jesters who were permanent representatives of human folly at court and in the great houses; and there were fools in literature, too. Given that comedy in general was part of theater almost from its beginnings, it is no wonder that fools and clowns found their way into plays as well. Even the mystery plays that acted out stories of the Bible for illiterate crowds had their shrewish wives and comic shepherds. The morality plays often starred a comic Vice or Fool who served as master of ceremonies as Everyman made his way between the forces of Good and Evil. Not only was he important to the plot, but he commented on it and interpreted it for the audience, and he occasionally stopped the play to collect ticket money. In the traveling groups who went from town to town putting on outdoor performances, the company clown often had the job of gathering the crowd as well as collecting the money.

By the time Shakespeare started writing plays, clowns were in most of the plays—even when there were none in the sources for those plays and when none seemed to belong. Preston's *King Cambyses,* for example, was advertised as "a lamentable tragedy," but it was nonetheless "mixed full of pleasant mirth"—just like Bottom's production of *Pyramus and Thisbe* in *A Midsummer Night's Dream.* For the crowds, the clown was the most popular part of the performance. He was the only character identified by role in stage directions, which remained the same from play to play—and from author to author and company to company. Thus Shakespeare's original scripts apparently read "Enter clown"—not "Enter Touchstone"—even though modern editors sometimes substitute the character's name. Audiences knew what to expect from "Clown," just as we know what to expect when we see a Charlie Chaplin film. The clown was usually ugly, wore country clothes with loose pants (called slops), and carried simple instruments like a drum. The clown's role was scattered through the play, but he also had his own skit or jig after the play was over. The jigs were vaudeville routines, the traditional song-and-dance act that was reliably simple, repetitive, funny, and obscence. Even the people who couldn't or wouldn't pay to see the main play waited until the "gatherers" or ticket-takers left their posts at the theater doors, and then sneaked in to see the clowns' jigs. These jigs collected such large and unruly crowds that they were finally outlawed while Shakespeare was still writing.

Some authors actually welcomed the clown's contribution and provided him with stage directions or lines that were in effect temporary licenses to do what he wanted. One stage direction in *The History of the Trial of Chivalry* (1605), for example, reads "Enter Forrester, speak anything, and exit"; and Heywood in *Edward the Fourth* writes that the clown Jocki is to be "led to whipping over the stage, speaking words, but of no importance." But many other authors resisted the clowns. They scorned the "jigging fool," as Brutus called him when he thrust himself head and shoulders into the general's tent during the war in *Julius Caesar;* they looked down on the "jigging veins of rhyming mother wits," as Marlowe called the writing he associated with clowns, and they scorned the audience who called for the clown. They made fun of characters like Polonius, who needed a jig or a tale of bawdry to keep him awake during a performance. Even if the author refused to include any clowning in the main body of his play, often the clown-actor added it himself. The clown was irrepressible—much like the class clown at school, who fills the same needs. Hamlet's warning to the clown among the players who come to Elsinore is typical of many an anticlown playwright's position:

> And let those that play your clowns speak no more than is set down for them, for there be of them that will themselves laugh, to set on some quantity of barren spectators to laugh too, though in the meantime some necessary question of the play be then to be considered. That's villainous and shows a most pitiful ambition in the fool that uses it.
>
> (3.2.40-47)

From Hamlet's lines we can see that clowns often did speak more than was set down for them, and that not only did they speak, they also engaged in attention-getting stage business, like faking a laugh (actors still do this to steal a scene). We can also learn that clowns as characters were considered extra or un-"necessary," and that as actors they seemed "ambitious" to the playwright who was competing for the audience's attention. In the "bad" First Quarto (1603) text of *Hamlet*, Hamlet speaks more than is set down for him in the Folio (1623). Was this a clown's addition? Wherever it originated, this Quarto speech gives Hamlet himself a chance to mimic the popular clown act—probably not very difficult for someone who already has an attitude or, as Hamlet called it, "an antic disposition":

> And then you have some again that keeps one suit of jests, as a man is known by one suit of apparel, and gentlemen quotes his jests down in their tables, before they come to the play, as thus:
>
> "Cannot you stay till I eat my porridge?"
> and: "You owe me a quarter's wages!"
> and: "Your beer is sour!"
> and blabbering with his lips:
> and thus:
>
> —keeping in his cinque-pace of jests, when, God knows, the warm clown cannot make a jest unless by chance, as the blind man catcheth a hare.
>
> (3.2)

We can't reconstruct these skits, which Hamlet thinks weren't very funny anyway, but you get the picture.

Understandably, then, the first theater "stars" in England were the clown actors (or "clowns"), Richard Wilson and Robert Tarlton. Tarlton in particular won the hearts of Londoners. Few Elizabethans were as popular, or simply as well known, as Tarlton. On stage all he had to do was show his face or peep out from behind the curtains and people laughed. But his reputation spread far beyond the walls of the amphitheater. His name was adopted for taverns and for a fighting gamecock. Unlike even Shakespeare's name, Tarlton's name entered the vocabulary—"Tarltonizing" or fooling it; his ghost was resurrected to defend the stage in a pamphlet four years after his death, and collections of his "jests" were still appearing twenty years after he died. When he died, myths grew about a line of successors almost as sacred as the royal line itself. Will Kempe, who followed Tarlton, was known as his "Vice-gerent General," and there are stories of Tarlton adopting Robert Armin, the famous actor of Shakespeare's fools, who followed Kempe. Tarlton's successors were gifted artists in their own right—entertainers, ballad-makers—and were really more like collaborators than scripted actors. Kempe was a dancer, whose marathon nine-days' dance from London to Norwich drew a tremendous crowd and an outpouring of support, if the texts we have are any indication. In plays, Kempe must have improvised his own lines or elaborated on the playwright's text. Kempe was famous for his scenes in *A Knack to Know a Knave,* advertised on the first page as including "Kempe's applauded merriments of the men of Gotham." But the clown's role in that play—at least the part of it that has been recorded in the text—is neither particularly large nor very amusing. It must have depended on Kempe's "extemporal wit." Of course, if for some the clowns were the most popular part of the play, for others in the audience they were also the most mistrusted. The Puritan attack on drama often focused on precisely the sort of outrage the clown was accustomed to perpetrate: "bawdry, wanton shews and uncomely gestures."

Who was this clown, and what did he do that was so terrible—or so wonderful? He simply represented the lowest level of existence in his world. Socially he was an outcast, literally a "rustic" or countryman; "clown" is etymologically related to the words for "clod" or "lump," as in "clod of clay" or "lump of earth." He could also turn up in the form of coal miner, miller, constable, shoemaker, carpenter, or any other form of "rude mechanical," as Shakespeare called Bottom and his friends in *A Midsummer Night's Dream.* Hamlet's speech suggests that the typical clown was a servant, like Macbeth's porter or Capulet's servants. Mentally the clown lived on a lower level, too. While Hamlet might have had his head in the clouds, the "warm clown" had his feet on the ground and was interested in material realities—the bottom line, as we might say. (He was known as a "material fool.") We can also see in Hamlet's speech that the clown's routines included things like porridge and beer: eating and drinking and appetite. Hamlet's clown was above all a physical and passionate creature, and he depended on the kind of humor that Hamlet indicates: blabbering lips and some action even less describable, which Hamlet refers to as "thus." His emotional volatility generated many of his routines. Even as the other players were learning not to out-Herod Herod, the clown howled, yelled, and, in a well-known skit, wept copiously. He made scurvy faces, and he used props (sticks, shoes, animals—Launce comes on with a dog, Launcelot Gobbo's father with a dish of doves, and Cleopatra's servant with a basket of snakes).

Hamlet goes on to describe the clown by using imagery of incompetence—"a blind man catching a hare"—which captures the slapstick nature of many of the clown's familiar routines. Much of the clown's humor consisted of the practical jokes and aggression now relegated to cartoon animals. Also, as Hamlet's lines suggest, the clown, ignorant as he was, was not necessarily stupid; in fact, he was usually something of a trickster or sly fox who was always out for number one ("I pray you, remember the porter" [*Macbeth* 2.3.21]) and not afraid to push others around. The most famous of the three anecdotes about Tarlton's routines tells how, having been boxed on the ear, Tarlton passed the blow on to poor John Cobbler—and called him a "clown" for taking it. A second tells how he was beaten by his fellow actor, and a third how he played the youngest of three sons and insulted his dying father. No wonder that the playwright Fletcher complained, "Just because a player can abuse his fellow," he thinks he's "a first class clown." The rest of the clown's humor depended on scatology and sex, probably in that order. The clown dropped his "slops," farted, pissed, and threw up freely. Macbeth's porter tells us about "urine," "lechery," and having just thrown up; and one clown in Greene's *James IV* provides a graphic description of his diarrhea attack. While the Puritan critic Gosson complained that the players were "uncircumcized philistines," Tarlton told the audience about his troubles with his prepuce.

Finally, as the actual resident clowns in Hamlet's own Elsinore show us, the clown is at home with death as well as dirt. If not always a literal gravedigger, he could collect shoes from dead soldiers, joke about corpses, or pretend to be one himself, always seeming able to rebound into life. His durability is almost mythic. Falstaff, who has much of the clown in him and may have been played by a clown—by Will Kempe—famously revived after being "killed" on the battlefield, all the more remarkably for his great bulk. When Bottom plays the lover in *Pyramus and Thisbe* and kills himself, there is some speculation among the audience that he may "yet recover and prove an ass," that is, he will return to life and be his old self again—which of course he does. In *Merchant of Venice* the clown Launcelot Gobbo stages his own death and rebirth for his father, blind old Gobbo. Those much-ignored clowns in *Romeo and Juliet* are musicians who fiddle while Rome burns, as it were, making music while the tragic world falls apart around them—just as the gravediggers in *Hamlet* make jokes out of death.

Distinctive as all these traits made the clown, however, his attraction—and his uniqueness—came at least as much from his relation to the audience as from the country character he played. He was like a vaudeville act or like one of today's stand-up comedians. In particular his role was to mediate between the play and the audience, whether to gather the crowds and collect money as clowns had done for road shows, or to provide between-act diversions which appealed more directly than the play did to the crowd already gathered. Often he commented on or parodied the action, just the way a spectator might; or he made reference to himself as actor. The character Bubble, played by the clown-actor Greene, makes a point of telling us he is going to see Greene in a play. In this intimate relation to the audience the clown was just as abusive to them as he was to his fellow actors. One spectator recalls that when Tarlton came on stage to hear "no end of hissing" instead of being greeted with the "civil attention" he expected, he broke into "this sarcasticall taunt":

> I liv'd not in the Golden Age,
>   When Jason wonne the fleece,
> But now I am on Gotam's stage,
>   Where fooles do hisse like geese.

If the people threw apples at Tarlton, he rhymed insults back at them. When someone in the gallery pointed at him, Tarlton pretended to take it as an insult, gave the man the horns, and got so much the best of him in the ensuing exchange that "the poore fellow, plucking his hat over his eyes," left the theater. Shakespeare's clowns are not so direct, but both Bottom and the porter are left onstage alone for important speeches, and then their remarks are directed to the audience. When Quince runs away after Bottom is "translated," Bottom reassures *us* that he's not afraid; he assumes we're on his side even if his friends have deserted him:

> I see their knavery. This is to make an ass of me, to fright me. . . . But I will not stir from this place. . . . I will sing, that they shall hear I am not afraid.
>
> (3.1.122-26)

And after the knocking in *Macbeth,* it is the audience whose sympathy the sleepy porter asks for when he enters alone, muttering,

> Here's a knocking indeed! If a man were porter of hell gate, he should have old turning the key.
>
> (2.3.1-3)

He might even wink at us as he exaggerates, to let us in on the joke of saying to his unwelcome but important visitors, in effect, "To hell with you!"

Many observers have emphasized the clown's role as index of social tension outside the theater and even as an ingredient in it. Dario Fo, the Italian director who has made use of the modern clown's comedy for savage political satire, observes that "Clowns always speak of the same thing, they speak of hunger: hunger for food, hunger for sex, but also hunger for dignity, hunger for identity, hunger for power. In fact they introduce questions about who commands, who protests." Scholars of the Renaissance clown do not agree about whether the clown helped work out the social conflicts of the period or helped exacerbate them, but his prominence is important. In any case, Bottom and the rude mechanicals in the palace at "Athens" reflect a version of class structure in Elizabethan England.

Whether for or against the lower classes, Shakespeare seems to have taken to clowns like a duck to water. Some scholars have suggested that Shakespeare was heavily influenced by the clown-actors available to him. Early in his career the company clown was Will Kempe, a dancer and slapstick comedian, so Shakespeare created roles to make use of Kempe's special talents: Bottom, Peter, Dogberry. Then Kempe left and Armin came. Since Armin was a very different kind of actor, Shakespeare created a very different kind of clown: the "wise fool" like Lear's fool and Feste. This may well be true; Shakespeare is just the sort who would make use of the materials at hand. But I think it's also true that Shakespeare would have found his way to the clowns no matter what. His clowns' scenes, as Samuel Johnson said, "seem to be instinct." And even in the very earliest plays (before Kempe's contributions), where we can see signs of awkwardness in many scenes, the clowns (like Jack Cade in *2 Henry VI* or Launce in *Two Gentlemen of Verona*) are often the best part of their play. Then in the middle comedies we find the likes of Bottom, Launcelot Gobbo, and Dogberry (many of whom are much funnier than you'd think just from reading the play). These are the epitome of the Shakespearean clown—physical, fleshly, everything we mean by the bottom. And although they may be ignorant and gauche, they are also savvy, even wise. They know things that the aristocrats have to learn. In *A Midsummer Night's Dream,* for example, although he is silly, Bottom is not merely "a shallow, thick-witted fool." On the contrary, Bottom is deep. He knows that "wisdom and love keep little company" these days. He has something of that other forest actor, Rosalynd:

> O coz, coz, coz, my pretty little coz, that thou didst know how many fathom deep I am in love! But it cannot be sounded; my affection hath an unknown bottom, like the bay of Portugal.
>
> (*As You Like It,* 4.1.205-8)[1]

The clowns know, like Hamlet, that man is neither so noble in reason nor so "infinite in faculty" as he may think. They know that even the loveliest fairy queen has a hairy bottom. And that, in fact, it's not only our lower nature but our very aspirations that make us fools. After all, who is more foolish, Bottom in Titania's arms, or Titania who dotes on him? Shakespeare may have been a clown himself, even before he came to London. We have only one anecdote about Shakespeare's childhood, and—to the degree that one can trust such data at all—it may bear witness to certain tendencies in young William which, with enough hindsight, suggest what was to come later. John Aubrey, one of Shakespeare's earliest biographers, reports that Shakespeare could kill a calf in the high old style. This gave later biographers an interesting clue, and, after much speculation about whether or not Shakespeare had been apprenticed to a butcher, most now agree that "killing a calf" probably refers to playing a role in a comic street play that was still extant in the early twentieth century. The modern version involves several boys to play the butcher and the calf and to catch the calf's blood in a basin. The older version may have been a solo ventriloquist act. Otherwise we do not know much about the show except that it was considered fit entertainment for a five-year-old child—which might explain Hamlet's scornful reference to killing "so capital a calf" when he wants to insult that second-time child, Polonius. Thus Shakespeare, who is said to have played the parts of old men during his acting career, may well have begun—like Mercutio and Hamlet—by playing the fool.

Notes

[1] *The Riverside Shakespeare*, ed. G. Blakemore Evans (Boston: Houghton Mifflin Company, 1974).

FOOLS IN THE HISTORIES AND HISTORICAL FOOLS

Charles S. Felver (essay date 1961)

SOURCE: "Armin's Foolish Parts with Shakespeare's Company 1599-1607," in *Robert Armin, Shakespeare's Fool: A Biographical Essay,* Kent State University, 1961, pp. 39-68.

[*In the following essay, Felver describes the fool roles in the plays of Shakespeare's middle period (1599-1607) that were likely performed by the versatile comedic actor Robert Armin.*]

> This fellow is wise enough to play the fool,
> And to do that well craves a kind of wit.
> *Twelfth Night*

The only Shakespearean part which Armin directly alludes to as his in any of his works, as I have remarked earlier, is that of Constable Dogberry, and yet it is clear that this was a part fashioned originally not for Armin but for Kempe. In the Q1 edition of the play, which appeared in 1600, the names of Kempe and Cowley still occur in IV.ii in place of Dogberry and Verges. The evidence for Armin's appearance in this part comes from his dedication of the *Italian Taylor and his Boy* (1609) to the Viscount Haddington and his wife, Lady Elizabeth Fitswater. Armin asks pardon of the Lady for

> the boldnes of a Beggar, who hath been writ downe for an Asse in his time, & pleades under *forma pauperis* in it still, not-withstanding his constableship and Office.
>
> (A3r)

A note in the "Chamber Accounts" records that in 1612-3 *Much Ado* was still being played by the King's Men,[1] which suggests, along with Armin's reference, that the play enjoyed continuous popularity. Although there is no evidence to show whether Armin played this role as one of his first with the Chamberlain's Men, it could have been his first role and we do know from this reference that later in his career he achieved a considerable success in it.

Shakespeare's audience, then, found in the company a new comedian, who was capable of handling older roles in the Kempe tradition like Dogberry and Launcelot Gobbo, but who had at the same time demonstrated in his own play and in his own observations that he had some new ideas for clowns. If such a versatile clown were available, one cannot help but wonder why the Company should wait a full year before signing Armin, as T. W. Baldwin suggests they did, in the hope that Kempe would come back. A man who could play Dogberry, could easily toss off the comic bits in *Julius Caesar,* which Platter saw in September of 1599, apparently shortly after the opening of the new theater season. And in the meantime, Armin's fellow player, Shakespeare, who could be observing his abilities in older roles and perhaps saw him as the versatile Tutch, was probably writing *As You Like It* as a vehicle in part for the special talents of the new clown.

Now such a sequence of events is clearly not demonstrable. But it does nevertheless seem remarkable, as I have pointed out elsewhere (*SQ*, VII, 1956), that Shakespeare should name his first fullfledged Fool, Touchstone, shortly after Armin had appeared in his own play as Tutch, a name formed from a shortened form of the word Touchstone. The aptness of the name to Armin's vocations, both old and new, is equally remarkable. A close analysis of Touchstone should reveal some other evidences of Armin's influence on the character. But first a word about the date of this play, and others that are of interest in this study.

It did not seem to me that it was a concern of this study to rehearse the hundreds of discussions of the dating of Shakespeare's plays in order to arrive at what are, in many cases, only conjectural conclusions. So I have, instead, accepted the conjectural dating of the plays by James G. McManaway, which he arrives at by analyzing respectable recent scholarship on the subject.[2] The general consensus is that *As You Like It* dates from 1599-1600, at the earliest sometime after June of 1599.

Although the editors of *As You Like It* customarily assign Touchstone the clown's part which begins I.ii.44, it should be remembered that the name Touchstone is not mentioned until II.iv.21. Exactly why Touchstone's name is mentioned so late is not clear, though it is possible that the play had been written in part before Armin joined the company and was then changed a bit to accommodate the new clown. What is clear, however, is that this clown is not an unknown minor official like Dogberry, wasting the time of his betters, but a known and affectionately regarded servant who provokes wit in others so that they may hear his own witty ripostes. On his first appearance Touchstone stands quietly but no doubt expressively for some eleven lines of dialogue before rising to the challenge of Celia's assertion that Nature

> hath sent this
> Naturall for our whetstone for alwaies the dullnesse

of the foole, is the whetsone of the wits. How now Witte, whether wander you?

(I.ii.53-56)[3]

Celia's facetious mixing of the terms "Naturall" and "Witte" suggests that she is trying to stir him into jesting rather than describing him accurately, for Touchstone soon convinces her and the audience that his wit is not an accident, as with Armin's natural fools, but the product of an active intelligence. At first, however, he speaks straightforwardly, persuading one for a moment that he has a clownish incomprehension of difficult words:

> Clo. Mistresse, you must come away to your father.
> Cel. Were you made the messenger?
> Clo. No by mine honour, but I was bid to come for you.
>
> (I.ii.57-59)

But his wit soon shows itself upon further provocation, for when Rosalind questions his trivial use of an oath on his honor, he proves that his use is no more trivial than that of a knight's; and he proceeds to show his ability to follow a quibble to its ultimate end, which is, for a witty fool, a jest. Asked to prove that neither he nor the knight were forsworn, he asks the ladies to stand forth, stroke their beards, and swear by them that he is a knave:

> Cel. By our beards (if we had them) thou art.
> Clo. By my knaverie (if I had it) then I were; but if you sweare by that that is not, you are not forsworn.
>
> (I.ii.70-73)

Touchstone has succeeded, by the end of this colloquy, not only in making fun of the great roaring oaths of his betters, but also in making fools of the ladies. Indeed, his general keenness about the political climate, for example, becomes clear when he replies to Celia's query as to the identity of the foolish knight that he is one whom her father loved. Celia thereupon warns him away from further criticism:

> My Fathers love is enough to honor him enough; speake no more of him, you'l be whipt for taxation one of these daies.
>
> (I.ii.77-79)

That his privilege is not merely an occasional license exercised upon encouragement by a member of the family, but a general privilege to jest with his betters is shown when Touchstone joins the ladies in teasing Le Beau about the "sport" in wrestling. His sensitivity to the world about him comes out in his questioning, for he does not accept the view that any kind of wrestling is sport. He first wishes to test the qualities of things before he makes decisions about them. Therefore when Le Beau replies that the sport the ladies have missed is the brutal wrestling that he has already described, Touchstone answers for the ladies and himself:

> Thus men may grow wiser every day. It is the first time that I ever heard breaking of ribbes was sport for Ladies.
>
> (I.ii.130-132)

A rustic clown like Dogberry reacts to his betters by becoming even more the pompous ass than he was with his inferiors, or a Bottom reacts by being ignorantly at ease to the amusement of his betters, but Touchstone, unlike the rustics, is never out of countenance. He is haughty and elegant with William and Audrey, a superior in discussions with Corin, a privileged servant-equal with Rosaline and Celia, and the respectful professional fool with Jacques, who fails to recognize as he laughs at the fool that Touchstone has been laughing at him. Now some of this social ease is clearly discernible among Armin's fools, notably Jemy Camber and Will Summers, both fools of royalty, and some of the cheekiness of Touchstone is found in the character of Tutch; but the full development of this cheeky social ease as a dramatic quality of the fool must be accredited to Shakespeare.

A love of material comfort is another notable aspect of the fool. Self-denial comes hard to Touchstone and he is always a reluctant stoic, one who feels that when he was at home he "was in a better place" (II.iv.18), and knows that an empty pocketbook is only a prelude to poor fare. Later Lear's Fool will suggest with some seriousness that court holy water in a dry house is better than wandering about bareheaded in a storm. Armin's fools, too, show their love of good food and good drink, as some of the verses quoted earlier attest, and many other stories bear out: whether Jack Miller was climbing into a red-hot oven after pies, only to be badly burned, or Jack Oates was standing in the moat dipping his master's quince pie in the muddy water to cool before eating, Armin's fools were constantly concerned about belly comfort.

Less evident among Armin's fools is a tendency to be lecherous, although Jemy Camber got his last illness as a result of an attempt to seduce a young Scotch woman. The fools portrayed by Shakespeare, in contrast, are very much interested in sexual activity. Touchstone is burning to join the "country copulatives," as he so unromantically names them, by marrying Audrey; Feste speaks of his lady and is apparently in some difficulties about earlier dishonesty at the beginning of *Twelfth Night;* both Lavache and Pompey are burdened by temptations of the flesh. None of them believes that romantic love is anything other than a useful ethical disguise for the baser desire of every young man and woman to "do't if they come to't," or "to cart with Rosaline" (III.ii.107).

One thing about the fool seems fairly clear in *As You Like It:* Shakespeare as writer and Armin as player were accustoming their audience to a new kind of clownish garb. The rustic clown dressed in russet, a countrified style popularized by Tarlton and Kempe, was so familiar a sight that his costume alone was enough to remind an audience to smile in preparation for the laughter soon to follow. But if the Globe sharers were interested in effacing the name of Kempe from their customers' memories, as some of the evidence discussed elsewhere certainly implies,[4] the new clown must appear in different habiliments. In his "quip" on his own playing of the fool, Armin had remarked that he wore "antic" dress, suggesting a general fantasy of custume rather than a particular stock costume. In his discussion of fools in the three works investigated earlier, the range of costumes suggests antic variety rather than stock similarity, and only Jack Oates is referred to as a wearer of motley, yellow or green, with the additional note that a colored coat on him was seldom seen.

Now it is quite possible that in his first appearances in the play as the Duke's servant, Touchstone wore a household livery, the usual long coat, often of blue, with the Duke's arms embroidered on his breast or perhaps worn as a badge (cullison) on his arm. At any rate, nothing is said to indicate that his garb is unique until Jacques meets him in the forest and reports his encounter to the Duke. In preparation for their flight, Rosaline and Celia assume disguises as upper-class country youths, and it seems likely that when the three are first seen on their way to the forest, Armin as Touchstone would be dressed for the first time in a long motley coat like those worn by Jack Oates, yellow or else green. Certainly Jacques seems surprised to find a fool in motley, for in twenty-three lines of delighted report on Touchstone he calls him a motley fool thrice and concludes that "Motley's the onely weare" (II.vii.36). Shakespeare seems to be telling the audience that motley is as proper a garb for laughter as russet.

But Touchstone's motley coat is not the only thing that Jacques notes about this new kind of clown. He is impressed with the Fool's ability to rail in "good terms, / In good set termes, and yet a motley foole" (II.vii.18-19). Like Tutch in the *Two Maids*, the fool is literate and witty not by chance but by design, and Jacques laughs "That Fooles should be so deepe contemplative" (II.vii.33). Indeed in his rapturous description of Touchstone, Jacques devotes more words to developing the special qualities of his wear and fooling than any gentleman in all of Shakespeare, or in any other play of the period that I have encountered. For the first time, too, a gentleman is found feeling envious of the fool's freedom rather than superior to his predecessor-clown's coarse manners and ignorant speech. Jacques wishes to be invested in motley so that he too may have the privilege "To blow on whom I please" (II.vii.52), and he descries in the role possibilities for moral improvement; for given leave to speak his mind he "will through and through / Cleanse the foule bodie of th'infected world" (II.vii.62-3).

Although Jacques clearly recognizes the literate wit of the fool, he also recognizes that he is not altogether a wise man; for he speaks of Touchstone's brain as being dry as "remainder bisket" (II.vii.39), and of his venting his observations "In mangled forms" (II.vii.42). But the observations of a character, himself limited by his particular kind of blindness, cannot be depended upon as an accurate description of another character of a peculiarly complex sort. Celia and Rosaline called Touchstone "Nature's natural" not altogether seriously, perhaps chiefly out of an awareness of the decorum that the fool expected and that he was accustomed wittily to operate under. Nor does Jacques seem to recognize that Touchstone is letting fly witty shafts against him either in his first encounter, when he rejects his naming him fool by quipping, "Call me not foole, till heaven hath sent me fortune" (II.vii.21), or in a later encounter, when Touchstone delicately euphemizes the vulgar Jacques (jakes-privy) to "Master What ye call't" (III.iii.68), a much more courtly term. Perhaps Duke Senior is the most trustworthy observer of the quality of Touchstone's fooling, for having heard Jacques' description and seen Touchstone himself, he remarks that Touchstone "is very swift, and sententious" (V.iv.67), and that "He uses his folly like a stalking-horse, and under the presentation of that he shoots his wit" (V.iv.107-108).

Someone familiar with Armin's *Quips* readily sees a certain congruence between Jacques' description of his first meeting with the fool who "drew a diall from his poake,/And looking on it, with lack lustre eye" (II.vii.22-23), complains that heaven has not sent him fortune, and Armin's verses on "Whats a clocke":

> One askes me whats a clocke, thinking
>   indeede,
> That I am Iacke of clock-hous, and can tell:
> He is a Iacke to think so, or to feede
> His humor, as the clapper doth the bell.
>   I have a Hand, but not a Dioll, I,
>   Right it poyntes not, and tongues may lie
>   (C4v)

Armin's concluding quip states the point that Touchstone implies in discussing heaven-sent fortune and in recognizing and feeding Jacques' melancholy by moralizing on the time:

> How vaine it is then, to ask whats a clocke?
> Of one who for an answere, lendes a mocke.
>   (D1r)

A play-goer must remind himself, then, in deciding the extent to which Touchstone's wit is artificial or natural that dramatic characters have their own blindnesses, and that the informed playgoer is the final judge of a character rather than another character pronouncing a judgment within the play. To the play-goer, Touchstone is clearly an artificial fool, making everyone he meets a victim of his wit.

Armin's songs in his own play have already been discussed, and his talent is clearly taken advantage of by Shakespeare in *Twelfth Night;* but what should be made of the singing in *As You Like It?* At only one point in the play is Touchstone involved in a scene with songs, the brief V.iii, where are also found for the first and last time, except perhaps as a part of the *mise en scène* elsewhere, two Pages. When Touchstone urges them to sing, "By my troth well met: come, sit, sit, and a song" (V.iii.9), the second Page replies, "We are for you, sit i'th middle" (V.iii.10); and his invitation to Touchstone to sit in the middle, suggests, according to Roffe,[5] that the song was arranged as a trio in which Armin took a part. If Baldwin's contention that most of the sharers key apprentices may be trusted, perhaps one of these pages was a boy trained by Armin.

As Touchstone, Armin sings only a little, if at all, in *As You Like It*. There is, however, a sweet singer in the play, Amiens, and it is worthy of note that he arrives with the company at about the same time as Armin and is not given opportunity to sing as a separate character in the next few plays. Amiens has a speaking part on stage only when Touchstone is off stage, and Armin could have doubled in the part as easily as he did in his old dual part as Tutch and Blue John. Amiens has but sixteen lines of dialogue besides his two lovely songs: "Under the Greenwood Tree," and "Blow, Blow, Thou Winter Wind." Only in V.iv is he listed as appearing simultaneously with the fool, and he has nothing to say. Only once is the fool in a scene preceding Amiens' entrance, and Armin could have made a quick change during the thirty-five lines of dialogue that occur after his last words as the fool and his appearance as Amiens in hunting costume. It is not impossible therefore, that Armin might have doubled these two roles—a kind of *tour de force* celebrating his appearance in the first role tailored specifically to his talents. This is only a conjecture, however, any other possible explanations, such as the hiring of an outsider or the arrival of a skilled singer who may have gone unnoted by theatrical historians, are equally plausible.

When Touchstone is finally introduced to Duke Senior in the last scene of the play, enough has been seen of his protean abilities as jesting servant, loyal follower, witty commentator on love, superior gentleman to the countryfolk, and pastoral satirist to leave few doubts of his claim to be a courtier:

> I have trod a measure, I have flattered a Lady, I have bin politicke with my friend, smooth with mine enemie, I have undone three Tailors, I have had foure quarrels, and like to have fought one.
>
> (V.iv.48-52)

He understands courts and courtly ways only too well, as he illustrates with his quibbling on his reasons for marriage and with his disquisition on the degrees of the lie.

For the first time in any play by Shakespeare, or for that matter in any other play up until that time, a fool is found who is "artificial" in every respect. He searches out the qualities of things, whether it be the sport of Le Beau, the character of Jacques, his own discomfort in the "comforts" of Arden, or the "right Butter-woman's rank" of Orlando's jogging verse. The country, he reminds his mistresses is not as comfortable as the court; wooing is perhaps romantic in part but has a very practical end in view for the country copulatives. His words are pithy, reflecting his wide knowledge of proverbial lore, and he glances at different meanings of words and situations at every turn. He can never be fully understood if taken literally. Moreover, Touchstone is so conscious of the ambiguities of words and situations that he cannot resist verbal effects even when they are lost on the listener, as they are on Audrey, William, and occasionally Jacques.

Until the appearance of Touchstone, the clowns who survive in extant plays that had been performed by the Chamberlain's Men were either rustics attired in the stock garb of a Tarlton, like Costard, or servants in a gentleman's household who had perhaps a certain amount of privilege to jest, like Launcelot Gobbo, and whose privilege is indicated in their wearing of coats more guarded or fanciful than those of their fellows. The latter breed are servants first and jesters incidentally. Tutch of the *Two Maids* seems not to have had even this occasional privilege, however, for he was allowed to exercise his natural gifts for intrigue and facetious wit only when appropriate in his primary function as a kind of steward.

But in describing this new genus "Fool" of the great species "Clown" to the audience of *As You Like It,* Shakespeare takes more than ordinary pains to explain to his audience what is happening. He introduces the Fool as "Nature's naturall," relating him to a species already familiar to Elizabethans in proverbial lore and in villages, taverns and great households, and at the same time demonstrates that he is a clown with whom (not *on* whom) the witty Rosalind and Celia sharpen their wits. He gives him 320 lines of dialogue to speak,[6] making Touchstone's part rank third in the play. Shakespeare moreover uses one-third of the lines of the important character, the malcontent Jacques, to develop the role of the fool in considerable detail. In order to emphasize the uniqueness of this new character further, Shakespeare clothes him in motley—another new departure in drama so far as I have been able to discover. Indeed a glance at Bartlett's *Concordance* reveals that the word "motley" occurs only eleven times in Shakespeare, once connected to another word "motley-Minded," and of these eleven references, eight are made by Jacques. Elsewhere the word is used once in connection with Feste, once with Lear's Fool, and once indicating the absence of a Fool in the prologue to *Henry VIII*.[7]

Some critics have suggested that in *As You Like It* Shakespeare and Armin were attempting to establish, in their emphasis on motley, a new stock costume for the Fool, to replace the old russet costume that had served for years as the badge of the country Clown.[8] But this suggestion underestimates badly the real advance in the art of clowning accomplished by Armin and Shakespeare. If we remember that the critics of Shakespeare in the "Parnassus" plays as well as critics of dramatic spectacle in general like Sidney had said that a clown irrelevantly thrust into the midst of a play mars all, and remember too that Shakespeare himself, through Hamlet, is critical of clownish impromptus, it seems unlikely that an artist growing with each play as Shakespeare was would simply substitute a new stock part for an old. Nor would Armin, whose discriminating appreciation for the peculiar contributions of each fool he described is evident on every page of *Foole Upon Foole,* be very likely to concur in anything that might create a stock character. He had painstakingly described the special turns, tricks, and individualized dress of each of his fools, and as a virtuoso clown himself, able to do many things well, would want to be as different as possible in moving from one role to another. Certainly he would not want to remind his audience of Touchstone when playing Feste or Lear's Fool. One of the great contributions of Elizabethan drama, as contrasted with the continental *Commedia dell'Arte* tradition in which players improvised on a stock role, was that the Elizabethan drama was often a drama of characters simulating real life. Indeed in Shakespeare the characters tend to come to life too fully at times, and to interfere with more stylized and artificial comic devices in comedies like *Measure for Measure* and *All's Well*.

The "privilege" of Touchstone, which is his passport to social mobility and his license to satirize with only the whip as punishment, had long been among the stock appendages of the actual Elizabethan fool. Moreover, Shakespeare had shown his familiarity with the fool's privilege years before in *Love's Labour's Lost,* in the course of Berowne's sneering reference to Boyet's mockery of himself and his fellow wooers: "Go, you are alowd. / Die when you will, a smocke shall be your shrowd" (V.ii.478-9). But nowhere in the earlier plays is the concept of the fool's privilege so fully developed as it is in Jacques' description of the advantages of being a Fool, and the medicinal effects of fooling:

> I must have liberty
> Withall, as large a charter as the winde,
> To blow on whom I please, for so fooles have:
> And they that are most gauled with my folly,
> They most must laugh
>
> (II.vii.50-54)

> I will through and through
> Cleanse the foule bodie of th'infected world,
> If they will patiently receive my medecine.
>
> (II.vii.62-64)

This privilege remains a property of Shakespeare's fools hereafter, varying only to the extent that the fool is more or less professional or in a reputable position. So Lavache is more a jesting servant accorded privilege occasionally than a fully accoutered and privileged fool, and Pompey, because of his disreputable role as bawd-fool, can be facetious with some of his betters, but is careful to choose his targets wisely.

The fool's possession of this privilege, or in the case of the idiot-fool his assertion of a privileged position owing to his irresponsible innocence, is implied throughout Armin's studies of fools, and cannot be credited to either Armin or Shakespeare as in any sense a discovery except insofar as they recognized the dramatic potentialities of the privilege. The fool's purgative satirical properties as amender of "th'infected world" are perhaps more emphasized in Shakespeare and in Armin's *Quips*—moralized metamorphoses of changes—than elsewhere in Elizabethan literature. But again the emblematic nature of the Fool as a guide to wisdom for oneself is asserted in Ecclesiastes, Book of Proverbs, and much subsequent literature.

But despite the Elizabethans' familiarity with privileged fools, Shakespeare frequently finds it necessary to remind his contemporaries as well as the more solemn asses in his plays of the fool's privileged position when the fool seems to violate social decorum more than usual. When Malvolio attempts to restrain Feste's tongue before the Lady Olivia, for example, she reminds her steward that "There is no slander in an allow'd fool, though he do nothing but rail" (I.v.101-102). When Patroclus protests against Thersites' slanders and threatens to strike him, Achilles similarly interferes saying, "He is a privileg'd man" (II.iii.61). The humorless Goneril complains to Lear about his "all-licens'd Fool" (I.iv.220). Without his license or privilege the fool is naught, an "O" without a figure like the powerless Lear.

Shakespeare's Other Plays to 1606

In investigating the next eight plays that follow *As You Like It* I shall concentrate my attention on those five roles which are akin to the fool and might well have been played by Robert Armin: *Twelfth Night,* 1599-1600; *Hamlet,* 1600-1601; *The Merry Wives of Windsor,* 1600-1601 (private performance); *Troilus and Cressida,* 1601-1602 (private performance); *All's Well That Ends Well,* 1603-1604; *Measure for Measure,* 1604-1605; *Othello,* 1604-1605; *King Lear,* 1605-1606. But by concentrating on the fool roles, I do not mean to imply that Armin did not play, or was not capable of playing the First Gravedigger in *Hamlet,* for example, a part more in the Kempe line, which he could have mastered as easily as the part of Dogberry. I feel, however, that Hotson's speculation that he played Polonius (p. 104) interferes with what seems to be a development of such a line for another player—perhaps Heminges—in plays by Shakespeare and other dramatists for the Company. Baldwin suggests that Armin played Evans in *Merry Wives* (pp. 228-9 insertions), not implausible as a speculation since Armin had imitated Welsh dialect in his part of Welsh knight in *The Two Maids.* But I do not wish here to multiply difficulties by going beyond a consideration of the clearer professional role of Armin as fool, and therefore I will discuss only those parts which seem most clearly and unambiguously in his vein.

After Touchstone, Armin's next part was Feste, and Feste is clearly the most artificial and wisest of all the Fools, and, at the same time, he is perhaps more than any other figure in the play the master of the *Twelfth Night* revels. Certainly never again would the Fool have so many sweet airs to sing, and Armin's sweet music here, and perhaps in *As You Like It,* may have been a considerable help to the Chamberlain's Men in their competition with the musical little "eyasses" of Blackfriars, and Paul's Boys, who were attracting so much attention in upper-class playgoing circles. The fool's part is third in the play, ranking after the parts of Toby and Viola, and Shakespeare was never again to write so many lines (347) for a Fool or clown.

The part of dull clod in *Twelfth Night* is assigned to the obtuse Sir Andrew, and no one in the play has any delusions that he is anything other than a moderately rich gull to feed Toby's purse and palate and to be a butt for Maria's sharp wit. But the shrewd Maria has no reservations about Feste's wit, as she shows when the Fool enters the play for the first time, jesting familiarly with her:

> Ma. Nay, either tell me where thou hast bin, or I will not open my lippes so wide as a brissle may enter, in way of thy excuse: my Lady will hang thee for thy absence.
>
> Clo. Let her hang mee: hee that is well hang'de in this world, needs to feare no colours.[9]
>
> (I.v.3-8)

Feste seems to be making an obvious and vulgar pun on another sense of being "well hang'de" here. That more was involved in Feste's offence than being absent without leave is hinted at in the Lady Olivia's sharp words later: "Go too, y'are a dry foole: Ile no more of you: besides you grow dis-honest" (I.v.39-40). Similarly Tutch of Armin's own play was reprimanded by his master Sir William for acting dishonestly, becoming a go-between for Tabitha and Filbon. At the same time he was dismissed and warned not to come near the house at risk of being charged as a "fellone" (Dlv), which reminds Tutch of the penalty for felons, being well hanged:

> Gang is the word, and hang is the worst, wee are even, I owe you no service, and you owe me no wages, short tale to make, the sommers daie is long, the winter nights be short, and brickill beds dos hide our heds. As spitell fields report.
>
> (Dlv)

It is pleasant to be reminded by the fool and the servant that though the penalties for various crimes in Elizabethan times were severe, as often as not their very severity caused them not to be brought to action. Both men accept their fates—Feste's possible, Tutch's actual—in a lighthearted manner.

It seems fairly clear that Feste's garb is different from Touchstone's wear in Arden. As a household retainer he would no doubt wear his mistress's arms, and Maria's jest on his "two points," "That if one breake, the other will hold: or if both breake, your gaskins fall" (I.v.23-5), suggests that he is wearing wide slops, great breeches of some sort rather than tightfitting hose,[10] under his servant's coat. Hotson based his argument[11] that Feste carries a marotte or fool's double on Feste's invocation to wit and citation of Quinapalus, but it seems clear that as a professional singer Feste would carry the tabor noted by Viola ("Save thee Friend and thy Musick: dost thou live by thy Tabor?" [III.i.3-4]), which he would use as a rhythmical accompaniment to his voice, and he might even have concealed about his person the ubiquitous pipe for general music-making. When Feste appears at the opening of Act IV, importuning Sebastian, whom he mistakes for Viola-Cesario, to return to his mistress, Sebastian refers to him as a "foolish fellow" (IV.i.5) and as a "foolish greeke" (IV.i.19), which suggests that his garb is not so distinctive as his apparent role—Sebastian thinks he is a pander. In the final act when Feste and Fabian are asked by the Duke if they belong to the Lady Olivia, it becomes fairly certain that he is identifying them by the badges on their livery rather than any distinctive garb worn by Feste, and he does not identify Feste separately from Fabian until the Fool begins to jest: "I sir, we are some of her trappings" (V.i.11).

The most direct indication found in the play for assuming that Feste does wear a distinctive garb comes just after he has been warned by Maria of Lady Olivia's displeasure, and he begins to jest with Olivia in order to save his job. He greets her familiarly, perhaps as a subtle reminder of his privilege, "God blesse thee Lady" (I.v.36-7), and she responds, coldly, with an order to take the fool away, which Feste quickly turns about by suggesting that she is the fool:

> Misprision in the highest degree. Lady, Cucullus non facit monachum: that's as much as to say, as I weare not motley in my braine: good Madona, give mee leave to prove you a foole.
>
> (I.v.53-56)

If Feste wears motley, this is the only hint that he does, and it comes in a metaphor. Certainly no one else in the play identifies him as a fool by his motley wear. Perhaps his garb is somewhat fantastical, and he uses motley in that sense of the word, or perhaps he uses the words to refer to his position as privileged jester rather than to his motley garb. Indeed if one becomes too literal in interpreting the passage about the cowl not making the monk, one might even conclude that Feste wore a hood, a garment which seems not to have been worn by any real fool in this period.

Later in the play, when Orsino seeks the singer who formerly pleased him so well, Curio refers to Feste as the jester. The only other fool referred to as a jester by Shakespeare is Yorick, and the possibility must be considered that as a jester, Feste occupies a somewhat different status or is possibly recognized as a more talented and versatile performer than the fool. Benedick is called jester by Beatrice, and Prince Hal called Falstaff jester in rejecting him from service when king. That Feste clearly regards himself as superior to the ordinary fool becomes fairly evident in his uncharacteristic silence and rage when Malvolio compares him with another fool:

> I marvell your Ladyship takes delight in such a barren rascall: I saw him put down the other day, with an ordinary foole, that has no more braine then a stone. Looke you now, he's out of his gard already: unles you laugh and minister occasion to him, he is gag'd.
>
> (I.v.80-85)

But Olivia defends Feste by reminding Malvolio of his privilege ("There is no slander in an allow'd foole, though he do nothing but rayle" [I.v.89-91]), and by implication accepts the fool into her service once more. Moreover, it is this insult from Malvolio that persuades Feste to become Sir Topas in the plot to bring about the steward's downfall and make him the butt of the *Twelfth Night* celebrants.

When Feste is seen some time later joining Sir Andrew and Toby in their drinking bout, his wit is much more easy and informal than in this first encounter. Andrew pays the fool's singing and appearance high praise, while suggesting in a compliment to his "legge" that either his limbs are well proportioned and therefore visible or that he bows elegantly: "I had rather than forty shillings I had such a legge, and so sweet a breath to sing, as the foole has" (II.iii.22-24). Upon his entrance in the scene, we are reminded through a stage direction that though the species is changed, Feste belongs to the same genus as Costard and Launcelot Gobbo: "Enter Clowne" (II.iii.17). The climax of the celebration that the fool joins is reached when Malvolio enters to protest its noisiness, and Toby and the fool send him packing:

> To. Art any more then a Steward? Dost thou thinke because thou art vertuous, there shall be no more Cakes and Ale?
> Clo. Yes by S. Anne, and Ginger shall bee hotte y'th mouth too.
>
> (II.iii.112-116)

It is helpful to find a passage from the introduction to Armin's *Quips* which explains the relationship of Feste's "Ginger" to Toby's "Cakes and Ale" and suggests that Feste spoke of a favorite custom of Armin's:

> Use me with kindnesse, as you shall in the like commande me hereafter: whose Barke I will grate like Ginger, and carrouse it in Ale, and drink a full cuppe to thy curtesie.
>
> (A2v)

Although Feste may ordinarily have accompanied himself on a tabor, the musical accompaniment to his songs was occasionally quite formal. When the Duke Orsino asks for an old song that he had heard the night before, and Curio tells him the singer "Feste the Iester" is not at hand to sing it, the Duke commands that the tune be played "the while" Curio seeks him; and the text inserts the direction "Musick playes" (II.iv.13-17). The song that the Duke requests is the lugubrious "Come away, come away death," and Feste facetiously reminds the Duke when he rewards him for his pains, "No paines sir, I take pleasure in singing sir" (II.iv.73).

So far as I have been able to discover, the only lady who ever kept a fool in England was the Queen, and both Mary and Elizabeth supported fools in their ménages. Perhaps it was considered inappropriate for an ordinary noble lady to keep a fool because Shakespeare is at pains to explain through Curio that Feste is "a foole that the Ladie Oliviaes Father tooke much delight in" (II.iv.13-14), and he tells us with equally unnecessary care that Lavache of *All's Well* is retained by the Countess because:

> My lord that's gone made himself much sport out of him. By his authority he remains here, which he

thinks is a patent for his sauciness; and indeed he has no pace, but runs where he will.

(IV.v.67-71)

The subtle and sophisticated Feste's own definition of his role must not be ignored in an investigation of the nature of his fooling. After his discussion of his tabor with Viola, the quibbling conversation continues, Feste making words wanton, until Viola is driven to ask him if he is not the Lady Olivia's fool. He denies the title, suggesting that it would be more fitting to her husband, when she takes one, and concludes that he is "indeede not her foole, but hir corrupter of words" (III.i.36-37). When Viola suggests that she has seen him at Orsino's, he replies that fools are readily to be found there: "Foolery sir, does walke about the Orbe like the Sun, it shines everywhere" (III.i.39-40). Feste thus denies that he is a fool unless everyone else is willing to accept the name too. It is after this witty passage, in which Feste has carefully educated Viola on the role of fool, that she makes the following comment, a compressed version of Armin's description of himself in his *Quips*, quoted earlier:

> This fellow is wise enough to play the foole,
> And to do that well craves a kinde of wit:
> He must observe their mood on whom he
>   iests,
> The quality of persons, and the time:
> And like the Haggard, checke at every
>   Feather
> That comes before his eye. This is a practice,
> As full of labour as a Wise-mans Art:
> For folly that he wisely shewes, is fit;
> But Wisemens folly falne, quite taint their
>   wit.
>
> (III.i.60-68)

In the remainder of the play, Feste is at whiles the ordinary household servant, doing an errand for his mistress by importuning Sebastian-Viola to return to the house; the clever mimic who switches costumes to become Sir Topas, and changes voices to carry on a conversation with himself and baffle Malvolio; and, finally, the epilogue of the play, singing his bittersweet song, "When that I was and a little tine boy" (V.i.409). After the identities of Viola and Sebastian have been established and Malvolio returns to Olivia's mind, the fool is allowed the last word, and reminds the lady of Malvolio's earlier smugness and self-conceit which brought about their plot against him, quoting the gulling letter by Maria, "Why some are borne great," and concluding with Malvolio's mockery of himself:

> Do you remember, Madam, why laugh you at such a barren rascall, and you smile not he's gag'd: and thus the whirlegigge of time, brings in his revenges.
>
> (V.i.393-396)

As has been pointed out earlier, Armin's own play abounded in imagery suggesting his trade of goldsmith, but the only suggestive reference of this sort in *As You Like It* is the name Touchstone. The language of Feste in *Twelfth Night*, however, occasionally reflects in its imagery some aspects of the goldsmith's trade. For example, when Feste has sung his song "Come away, come away death," he mockingly blesses the Duke with an invocation to the God of melancholy, asking that "the Tailor make thy doublet of changeable Taffata, for thy minde is a very Opall" (II.iv.77-80). To a son and brother of a tailor and as a goldsmith and lapidarist, comparisons of this sort would naturally occur, whether or not Armin had any influence on their occurrence here. The appropriateness of the name Sir Topas to the lapidarist goldsmith is particularly evident, and Furness long ago suggested that Shakespeare chose the name for its appropriateness to the situation, citing Reginald Scot's *Discoverie of Witchcraft*, which says that "A topase healeth the lunaticke person of his passion of lunacie."[12] Certainly any members of Shakespeare's audience capable of appreciating the appropriateness of the compliment to Armin in being called Touchstone in his first important role, could not fail to appreciate the additional jest of Armin as Sir Topas, and a roar might very well greet Sir Toby's admiring words, "The knaue counterfets well," because goldsmiths were responsible for coining and Armin's first master had been Elizabeth's master of the mint. When Malvolio cries out in despair, "Sir Topas, sir Topas," and the delighted Toby picks up the refrain with "My most exquisite sir Topas," Feste replies somewhat smugly, "Nay I am for all waters" (IV.ii.63-67). Furness comments as follows on the word "waters" without knowledge of Armin's special appropriateness to the role:

> The word "water," as used by jewellers, denotes the colour and the lustre of diamonds and pearls, and from thence is applied, though with less propriety, to the colour and hue of other precious stones. I think that Shakespeare in this place alludes to this sense of the word "water." The Clown is complimented by Sir Toby for personating Sir Topaz so exquisitely, to which he replies that he can put on all colours.[13]

Another place in the play which suggests this peculiarly appropriate pattern of imagery occurs when the Fool replies to the Duke's query, "Belong you to the Lady Olivia, friends," with the pert retort, "I sir, we are some of her trappings" (V.i.10-11). Now "trappings" conveys a clear enough meaning without reference to a dictionary, but, remembering the Fool's predilections to play on words mockingly, one is always tempted to look beyond the immediate and in this case he is rewarded: "trapping, n., Jewelry. Cutting of a gem in the form called the trap, or step, cut, or the cutting of a trap brilliant." Feste-Armin then is obviously paying himself and Fabian a deft compliment.

In my discussion of the peculiar appropriateness of some of the imagery associated with Feste to Armin, I certainly do not wish to suggest that all of these associations were inserted deliberately to carry on a private joke or that Armin himself was responsible for any of them. There do seem to be enough references, however, to tempt one to believe that Shakespeare, who was always fascinated with words and their punning and other ambiguous possibilities in his plays, may have been enjoying a little private joke from time to time in *Twelfth Night*.

Twelfth Night ends with Feste alone on the stage singing his bitter-sweet epilogue song, which will become more poignant when it reappears under tragic circumstances in King Lear:

> Clowne sings.
> When that I was and a little tine boy,
>   with hey, ho, the winde and the raine:
> A foolish thing was but a toy,
>   for the raine it raineth every day.
>
> A great while ago the world began,
>   hey ho, &c.
> But that's all one, our Play is done,
>   and wee'l strive to please you every day.
>   (V.i.408-412, 425-428)

In contrast with Touchstone, whose status hovers between natural and artificial fool until the final act of *As You Like It* when Duke Senior finally gives a considered judgement on his wit, Feste is clearly the allowed fool from the very beginning of his part. Only when Feste himself reflects on the paradox of his position to Malvolio does he make any reference to himself as a born or natural fool. Nor is there any hint of the "roynish" or rustic fool in Feste, who is shown associating only with gentlemen and who says that he frequents only the best taverns. Touchstone, Lavache, and Pompey, in contrast, are equally at home in low society, and the first two fools court plain country wenches.

Like Armin in his *Quips,* Touchstone rhymes badly in doggerel vein, but Feste sings and mimes like Tutch. Both Touchstone and Feste are material fools; two successful variations on the fool character. Feste is an especially graceful beggar of gratuities, but each Fool makes use of proverbial wisdom, seems to be lettered, and has some knowledge of classical lore.

For his third variation on a fool, Shakespeare wrote the unpleasant character of Thersites into *Troilus and Cressida,* a play which may never have been shown at a public performance during Shakespeare's time. In most discussions of *Troilus,* Thersites is treated as a foul-mouthed malcontent rogue, which indeed he is but it should also be noted that Shakespeare describes him as a fool—a combination of Touchstone and Jacques might be the aptest comparison. In his quarrel with Ajax, however, Thersites makes it clear that he is not a hired servant, for he says that he serves him not and emphasizes this in the next line by stating, "I serve here voluntary" (II.i.102), a statement which Ajax does not deny. His privilege is explained by Archilles when Patroclus objects to this insult:

> Ther. Ile decline the whole question:
>   Agamemnon commands Achilles, Achilles is
>   my Lord, I am Patroclus knower, and
>   Patroclus is a foole.
>
> Patro. You rascall.
>
> Ther. Peace, foole, I have not done.
>
> Achil. He is a priviledg'd man, proceed
>   Thersites.
>
> Ther. Agamemnon is a foole, Achilles is a
>   foole, Thersites is a foole, and as aforesaid,
>   Patroclus is a foole.
>   (II.iii.55-65)

But the conclusive statements of Thersites' role as fool are made by Ulysses and Nestor as they discuss the anger of Ajax at Achilles:

> Nest. What mooves Aiax thus to bay at him?
>
> Uliss. Achillis hath invegled his foole from
>   him.
>
> Nest. Who Thersites? Ulis. He.
>
> . . . . .
>
> Nes. All the better, their fractiô is more our
>   wish then theit [r] faction, but it was a
>   strôg composure a foole could disunite.
>
> Ulis. The amity that wisdom knits not, folly
>   may easily unty.
>   (II.iii.98-100, 105-111)

Thersites differs from Touchstone and Feste in a number of respects. First, he serves voluntarily without any formal pay arrangement and contractual agreement such as a servant was likely to have. He seems to have assumed his role of privileged fool in order to liberate his tongue, yet he is the only fool in Shakespeare's plays who is actually beaten by his master, Ajax. Whereas Touchstone and Feste are more often witty at the expense of the foibles of society, such as courtly love, unseemly melancholy, and the excesses that develop from them, Thersites makes more fun of individuals directly; no one escapes his calumny and the greater the target the better he is pleased. Like the malcontent Jacques, lacking qualities of greatness in himself, he mocks them in others; but he is forced to admit a grudging admiration for the wisdom and policy of Ulysses and ancient Nestor.

Thersites' part in *Troilus* is an important one, for some 271 lines of dialogue are assigned to him in the Folio version. He supplies the commentary on the motives of the various contestants, and, along with Pandarus, by words and deeds develops the tawdry moral tone of the play. Unlike Pandarus, however, he is fully conscious at all times of his mean role, and in his concluding words weighs himself to the exact scruple of his worth: "I am bastard begot, bastard instructed, bastard in minde, bastard in valour, in everything illigitimate" (V.vii.18-20).

In the next two important parts which Shakespeare wrote for Armin's line, the fool suffers a decline in his social position, the size of his part, and his relative importance to the plot. The part of Lavatch in *All's Well* ranks seventh with 214 lines and that of Pompey in *Measure for Measure* ranks sixth with 185 lines. Parolles, who becomes LaFeu's fool at the end of *All's Well*, has the second part in the play with 415 lines. McManaway dates *All's Well*, as 1603-1604, and *Measure for Measure*, 1604-1605.[14]

Lavatch's position as fool in the Countess's household is semi-official only. He is also very obviously a serving-man, and a somewhat troublesome one at that, as the Countess's displeasure on his first appearance in the play makes clear:

> What doe's this knave heere? Get you gone sirra: the complaints that I have heard of you, I do not all beleeve, 'tis my slownesse that I doe not: For I know you lack not folly to commit them, & have abilitie enough to make such knaveries yours.
>
> (*AWTEW* I.iii.8-13)

Lavatch quickly detects mingled with the Countess's displeasure a willingness to listen to an excuse. There is no indication here or elsewhere that the fool is to be regarded as a lackwit. Feste in a similar situation invoked wit; Lavatch feigns a willingness to be discharged and manages in the process to put his kindly mistress off her guard:

> 'This not so well that I am poore, though manie of the rich are damn'd, but if I may have your Ladiships good will to goe to the world, Isbell the woman and w [sic] will doe as we may.
>
> (I.iii.18-21)

From the outset, Lavatch shows the somewhat theologically oriented moralism that comes out so clearly in a later exchange with Lord Lafew when he speaks of the broad way to hell, the narrow, winding way to heaven, and the Prince that he serves. When Lafew asks him the Prince's name, Lavatch replies: "The blacke prince sir, alias the prince of darkenesse, alias the divell, (IV.v.54-55).

Lavatch also jests in the customary way about cuckolds, delighting like Touchstone in the necessity of horns, and passes his sallies of wit on Parolles and Helena with impunity. So far as his costume is concerned, the text is silent, a fact which suggests that he was wearing the costume of an ordinary servant. When he answers Lafew's catechism as to whether he is knave or fool, however, he refers to his bauble; but he uses the term in its vulgar reference to the penis: "And I would give his wife my bauble sir to doe her service" (IV.v.31-32). But the ambiguous nature of Lavatch's role as privileged servant is not revealed fully until a discussion between the Countess and Lafew near the end of the play:

> Laf. A shrewd knave and an unhappie.
>
> Lady. So a is. My Lord that's gone made himselfe much sport out of him, by his authoritie hee remaines heere, which he thinkes is a pattent for his sawcinesse, and indeed he has no pace, but runnes where he will.
>
> (IV.v.59-61)

"Unhappie" probably refers to the moralistic nature of some of Lavatch's jesting.

With the arrival of Lavatch in Shakespeare's plays, the professional fool begins to merge for a time into a more ambiguous figure, the privileged servant, who appeared in Shakespeare's plays before the arrival of Armin. The exemplar of the privileged servant is Launcelot Gobbo. But Lavatch differs from Launcelot in that his language is more courtly, he is more at home in aristocratic circles, and he jests with more important people. Although he is less presumptuous in his familiarity with his betters than Feste or Touchstone, his jests are more vulgar and his moral is more bluntly stated.

Pompey of *Measure of Measure* is even less the professional fool than Lavatch. In fact the term "foole" is applied to Pompey only once, and then only in a general way rather than as a specific description: "Come: you are a tedious foole" (II.i.123). As tapster-pimp for Mrs. Overdone, the clown has no very central role in the play, but serves to indicate something of the moral tone of society, to relieve the occasional tedium of the main plot and to pass the time more merrily. Neither Lavatch nor Pompey rime (Lavatch does sing [I.iii.69-75]), and there is no hint as to how Pompey is garbed unless Escalus's reference to his large "bum" can be interpreted to mean that he wore doublet and hose rather than a long serving-man's coat.

With the appearance of *Othello* in 1604-5, the fool diminishes further and becomes a humble servant-clown with a part only seventeen lines long. His jokes are no funnier than those of generations of clowns before him, and he can be dropped from the play with no harm to its organic unity. The earlier tragedy of *Hamlet* similarly provided little scope for a fool, offering only the interlude-like part of the first gravedigger to the talents of Robert Armin.

Shakespeare's boldest and most poignant use of the fool, however, is in *King Lear* (1605-6). The Fool becomes an integral part of the play without any wrenching of decorum which would justify the older critical belief that the fool in the midst of tragic action mars all. In *Lear*, moreover, Shakespeare develops the apothegmatic wisdom of the fool and his paradoxical reflection on the general dilemma of mankind to its highest dramatic achievement. The Fool becomes a tragic interlocutor instead of a Touchstone or Feste, reminding Lear of the tragic consequences of his folly.

There is no hint of the existence of a fool in *King Lear* until the conversation between those two chillingly humorless characters, Goneril and the venal Oswald. Goneril seizes upon the privileged Fool's antics as an excuse to quarrel with her father:

> Did my father strike my gentleman for chiding
>   of his Fool?
> Oswald. Ay, madam.
> Gon. By day and night he wrongs me; every
>   hour
> He flashes into one gross crime or other, That
>   sets us all at odds.[15]
>
> (I.iii.1-6)

One of the aspects of this tragedy which the Fool brings out tellingly is the saving human grace of laughter—a grace which the party of Lear retains but which the parties of Goneril and Regan ignore. Indeed it is the denial of the dignity of the human condition and of the existence of love which brings about the downfall of the Goneril-Regan factions, for they fail to recognize the innate humanity of most human beings, including in Regan and Cornwall's case their own outraged servants.

Besides the Fool's prominence in the minds of Goneril and Oswald, he is also in the forefront of Lear's mind when he returns from hunting and calls for dinner and the Fool in the same breath:

> Dinner,
>   ho, dinner! Where's my knave? my Fool?—
>   Go you, and call my Fool hither.
>
> (I.iv.40-42)

But the Fool is not his old gay self, for a knight replies:

> Since my young lady's going into France, sir,
> the Fool hath much pined away.
> Lear. No more of that; I have noted it well.
>
> (I.iv.70-72)

Nothing further is said to develop this close relationship between the Fool and Cordelia, but it is clear from these lines that the Fool, besides his function as reminder to Lear of his folly in general, also is a constant reminder to Lear of his absent and beloved daughter. These lines also suggest a close family bond between the Fool, Lear, and Cordelia, like the faithful Touchstone's bond which made him willing to "go o'er the wide world" with Rosaline and Celia, or Yorick's with the young Hamlet, or William Summers' with the Tudor family.

After all these preparations for the Fool's entrance, he finally capers on the stage with a jest about the disguised Kent's folly in electing to serve a man whose fortunes are on the wane. He offers to give Kent his coxcomb in payment for his service (the only time this old-fashioned article of Fool's wear appears in Shakespeare as an article of apparel), and in return he receives from Lear a threat of the whip. The Fool continues to jest about Lear's folly in giving away his property, and simultaneously alienating two of his daughters who loved him for his property, until Lear is driven to call him a bitter fool. The Fool offers to teach Lear the difference between a bitter fool and a sweet one:

> That Lord that counsell'd thee
>   To give away thy land,
> Come place him here by me;
>   Do thou for him stand:
> The sweet and bitter fool
>   Will presently appear;
> The one in motley here,
>   The other found out there.
> Lear. Dost thou call me fool, boy?
> Fool. All thy other titles thou hast given
>   away; that thou wast born with.
>
> (I.iv.135-145)

It quickly becomes evident that in *Lear* the Fool is more the rimer and as much the singer as he is anywhere else in Shakespeare. The verse above suggests that in addition to his archaic coxcomb (possibly the term is used figuratively), he wore the motley garb of Touchstone, although his reference to Lear and himself as "Grace and a codpiece" may mean that he wore gaskins on which a codpiece would be visible. Like his Shakespearean and historic predecessors, the Fool is a material fool. Throughout the play he reminds Lear of his lack of power in terms of his loss of property. He also reminds him of his loss of love in the absence of Cordelia. Although Lear's Fool seems at times to be more natural, less "artificial," than Feste or Touchstone, Goneril, a careful observer in these matters, seems to have little doubt about his keenness, for after Lear departs enraged by her taunts, the Fool is prevented from lingering behind by this command from Goneril: "You, sir, more knave than fool, after your master" (I.iv.309).

But as Lear's plight worsens in his conflict with Goneril and Regan, the Fool's materialistic arguments undergo a subtle change. He continues to urge the materialistic point of view, not much differently from the way it is urged by Edmund, Goneril, and Regan, but at the same time he indicates that this is not the way for him. These verses spoken by the Fool after Lear's party has arrived at Gloucester's house, only to find Kent in the stocks outside, illustrate the Fool's way with respect to materialism:

> That sir which serves and seeks for gain,
>   And follows but for form,
> Will pack when it begins to rain,
>   And leave thee in the storm.
> But I will tarry; the Fool will stay,
>   And let the wise man fly;
> The knave turns fool that runs away;
>   The Fool no knave perdy.
>
> (II.iv.74-81)

For the first time in Shakespeare's development of the fool there is a hint that the improvident folly of the fool in following for love instead of gain shares a kinship with the Christian folly of doing what is unwise in the eyes of the world for the sake of righteousness rather than gain.

Enough has been said to indicate the artificiality of Lear's Fool. It seems to become more apparent as his master loses his wits; the Gentleman reports, for example, during the storm on the heath that no one is with Lear "but the Fool; who labours to out-jest / His heart-strook injuries" (III.i.16-17), a function hardly possible for a natural to perceive, let alone fulfill. Shortly after the poignant and terrible trial scene in which Lear in his madness appoints the Fool and the Bedlam as judges and arraigns Goneril and Regan, the Fool disappears wordlessly from the play. Despite his disappearance so early as Act III, however, the Fool has had some 253 lines to speak, ranking his part fourth among fools after Feste, Touchstone, and Thersites.

The daring of Shakespeare and Armin in creating the first and only high tragedy fool has been amply rewarded by the 250 years of critical praise that have followed. The Fool's humanity in the face of adversity, his love for his master, and his faithfulness have even caused sentimental critics to say that he disappears from the play because he is dying of grief. But a more objective approach is to ask what part a Fool could play with a master whose wits have gone. We should also remember that the Fool's irrelevant tag, "She that's a maid now, and laughs at my departure / Shall not be a maid long, unless things be cut shorter" (I.iv.55-56), and Merlin's prophecy at the end of III.ii suggest that Shakespeare and Armin were concerned lest their Fool be too different from his predecessors and introduced these jests, which now seem irrelevant, as sops to a conservative 17th century audience. However we explain occasional irrelevancies in the Fool, he nonetheless remains in our minds as a supremely bold artistic conception and as a poignant dramatic character—an apotheosis of the dramatic fool.

Although I conclude my discussion of Shakespeare's Fools with Lear's Fool, I by no means intend to convey the impression that Lear's Fool is the last of Shakespeare's fools. But the later fools contribute little or nothing new to the genre which reaches its supreme expression in the part of Lear's Fool. It is not necessarily true, however, that because fool parts become smaller and less frequent after 1605, that Armin the player's importance to the company was lessened. There was always the role of between-the-acts entertainer to be filled, and although little is known about the nature of this entertainment, Chambers and others show that such entertainment remained a part of the clown's role until the closing of the theatres. Moreover, John Shank, apparently Armin's successor with the King's Men, is mentioned in a contemporary bit of doggerel as singing "his rhimes," which he may have left off singing to join the King's Men between 1613-1619, where he apparently became very prosperous, despite having but few listed parts in later plays.[16]

It is not until 1610-12 that any significant roles in Armin's vein reappear in Shakespeare's plays; but when they do reappear, with the arrival of Autolycus in *The Winter's Tale* (1610-11) and Trinculo in *The Tempest* (1611-12),[17] these roles become quite large. Of all the fool's parts, Autolycus is third in size with 322 lines and Trinculo is tenth with 116 lines. It may be true, as Baldwin has suggested, that Armin had in the meantime played parts like Polonius and Cloten, and if so the range of his performances in the Company would have been much greater than anyone has supposed. Whether Armin played these parts, however, must remain pure conjecture. But it is clear from Baldwin's charts that Robert Armin was given fatter parts than his famed ad-libbing predecessor, William Kempe. As company clown, Robert Armin would of course also appear in similar parts in other plays than those of Shakespeare. Among the extant plays by other authors for the Shakespearean Company, three embody rhyming, singing, saucy clowns with fool-like parts: Marston's *The Malcontent* (1604),

Wilkins' *The Miseries of Enforced Marriage* (1605-07), and Tourneur's *The Atheist's Tragedy* (1607-11).[18]

In Wilkins' play the clown Robin is obviously a witty household servant, partaking of the nature of Tutch or Lavatch, and garbed in the ordinary household livery. His privilege, if any, is not mentioned in any of the repartee:

> Enter Clowne
>
> Ilf. But stay, here is a Scrape-trencher arrived:
>   How now blew bottle, are you of the
>   house?
>
> Clow. I have heard of many Black Iacks Sir,
>   but never of a blew bottle.
>
> Ilf. Well Sir, are you of the house?
>
> Clow. No Sir, I am twenty yardes without,
>   and the house stands without me.[19]
>
>   Miseries (A2r-A2v)

The clown's jest is similar to Feste's reply to Viola's question "Do thou live by thy Tabor?" (II.i.3-4). To Ilford's further question the clown provides further evasions which similarly echo earrimes and responses by Shakespearean fools:

> Ilf. Dos maister Scarberow lie heere.
> Clow. Ile give you a rime for that sir,
>   Sicke men may lie, and dead men in their
>   Graves, Few else do lie abed at noone, but
>   Drunkards, Punks, & knaves.
> Ilf. What am I the better for thy answer?
> Clow. What am I the better for thy
>   question?
> Ilf. Why nothing.
> Clow. Why then of nothing comes nothing.
>
>   Enter Scarborrow
>
> Went. Sblud this is a philosophicall foole.
> Clow. Then I that am a foole by Art, am
>   better then you that are fooles by nature.
>
>   (A2v)

This is the only indication given in the play that the clown is to be regarded as an artificial fool and that it is not to be taken very seriously is evident in the balance of the play.

Robin's part is a hodge-podge of apparently successful bits repeated from Shakespeare's fools, suggesting that perhaps this part was created with Armin's line in mind, as it was developed in several of his Shakespearean parts. The more intricate impression of Armin's brand of fooling is certainly present on the follow lines:

> Ilf. Whats your busines?
> Clow. My busines is this Sir, and this Sir.
> Ilf. The meaning of all this Sir.
>
>   (C2r)

When Ilford understands the clown's references and offers to take his letter, however, Robin refuses with the following explanation:

> Because as the learned have very well instructed me, *Qui supranos, nihil ad nos,* and tho many Gentlemen will have to doe with other mens business, yet from me know, the most part of them prove knaves for their labor.
>
>   (C2r)

Shortly after delivering this message, Robin disappears from the play with a merry bit of doggerel which he may have sung:

> From London am I come, tho not with pipe
>   and Drum,
> Yet I bring matter, in this poor paper,
> Will make my young mistris, delighting in
>   kisses,
> Do as all Maidens will, hearing of such an ill,
> As to have lost, the thing they wisht most,
> A Husband, a Husband, a pretty sweete
>   Husband,
> Cry, oh, oh, and alas, And at last ho, ho, ho,
>   as I do.
>
>   (C3v)

Wilkins incorporated so much of Armin's line of fooling in his play, using bits of business from earlier Armin parts, that he may have decided to use the familiar nickname for Robert, "Robin," as an additional compliment to the company clown.

The part of the clown Fresco in *The Atheist's Tragedy* also shows the influence of Armin's art. Like Pompey Bum, Fresco is servant to a bawd and just as ready as Pompey to make a vulgar jest. When Belforest asks him if he has been acting as pander to Lady Levidulcia Belforest, he replies:

> Fres. O yes!   (Speakes like a Crier)
>
> Belfo. Is not thy Mistresse a Bawde to my
>   wife?
>
> Fres. O yes!
>
> Belfo. And acquainted with her trickes, and
>   her plots, and her devises?
>
> Fres. O yes! If any man o' Court, Citie, or
>   Countrey has found my Lady Levidulcia in
>   bed by my Lord Belforest, it is Sebastian.

Belfo. What dost thou proclaime it? Dost thou
   crie it, thou villaine?[20]

(p. 125)

In the final act of the play he defends his mistress, Cataplasma, in Pompey's vein:

Good my lord her rent is great.
The good gentlewoman has not other thing
To live by but her lodgings. So she's forc'd
To let her foreroomes out to others, and
Herselfe contented to lie backwards.

(p. 140)

Fresco and his mistress are then sentenced and disappear from the play.

The parts of Robin and Fresco, however, although similar in some respects to Armin's comic turns in Shakespeare's plays, are not large enough or distinctive enough to warrant making any very useful assumptions about the impact of the player Armin on the clownish parts. One must ask himself the question, If I did not know these were plays from the repertory of Shakespeare's Company, would the clown parts strike me as inevitably Armin's? And the only answer can be a mildly qualified No. But an investigation of the history of the clown part in the augmented version of John Marston's *The Malcontent* as played by Shakespeare's Company provides, in contrast, an unqualified Yes.

The Malcontent, produced in 1604 at the height of the stage fool's popularity, was obtained by the King's Men from the repertory of the Children of Blackfriars in apparent retaliation for an earlier act of dramatic larceny by the Children. The history of the three different Quartos of the play need not be given here except to point out that Quarto "C" is apparently the copy of the play produced by the King's Men.[21] That the playing of the piece by the King's Men involved no quarrel with the author, however it is clear from the title page, which shows that Marston was responsible for a part of the rewriting job done to make the play suitable for an adult company:

The/ Malcontent/ Augmented by Marston./ With the Additions played by the Kings/ Maiesties servants. Written by Iohn Webster./ (ornament)/ 1604./ At London/ Printed by V. S. for William Aspley, and/ are to be sold/ at his shop in Paules/ Church-yard.

(p. xlii)

Stoll's analysis of the play, which concludes that only the induction to the play is by Webster and that the new work in the play itself is by Marston,[22] has been generally accepted by scholars.

Webster's "Induction" introduces the players Sly, Condell, Burbage, and Sincklow to the audience, explains that the play was taken from the Boys' company in retaliation for their unauthorized use of "Ieronimo," and suggests that the additions are "not greatly needefull, only as your sallet to your great feast, to entertaine a little more time, and to abridge the not received custome of musicke in our Theater" (p. 143). The purpose of comic interludes in a serious plays could be explained much more learnedly than this, but no more effectively.

Substantial additions are made in Quarto "C" to Burbage's part of Malevole, the Malcontent, to the part of Bilioso, a court official of the Polonius type, and to the part of Bianca, his wife. But the most interesting addition to the play is the completely new part of Passarello, fool to Bilioso. The only modern edition of Marston, H. Harvey Wood's, seriously errs in indicating that a brief passage between Malevole and Passarello occurs in quarto "A". A check of the first edition in The Folger Shakespeare Library[23] shows, however, that this passage does not occur in quarto "A". The part of Passarello is an entirely new addition by Marston, an extra ingredient of the "sallet to your great feast," spoken of in the Induction, as well as an indication that the important comic fool created by Robert Armin could not be ignored in 1604 by the King's Men any more than the boys' companies could "abridge" the "custome of musicke in" their "Theater."

The fool Passarello appears for the first time in I.vii with Malevole, and immediately reveals details of his profession and his costume:

Mal. Foole, most happily incountred, canst sing foole?

Passar. Yes I can sing foole, if youle beare the burden, and I can play upon instruments, scurvily, as gentlemen do. . . .

Malevole. You are in good case since you came to court foole; what garded, garded!

Passar. Yes faith, even as footemen and bawdes weare velvet, not for an ornament of Honour, but for a badge of drudgery.

(I.vii.pp.160-161)

Here is another variant costume for the fool, a long servant's gown ("in good case") perhaps of velvet (it is velvet in I, 177) with extra guards as a badge of his profession much like Launcelot Gobbo's gown, "more guarded than his fellows." When Malevole asks Passarello about his master, Bilioso, and the fool answers that he is a sorry figure, Malevole speaks of the wisdom of fools in terms which had become commonplace to Shakespeare by 1604: "O world most vilde, when thy loose vanities / Taught by this foole, do make the fooles seeme wise!" (I.vii.pp.161-162).

Although Armin's 116 lines in this play make the part he played smaller than those of Feste and Touchstone, and smaller even than those of Pompey and Lavatch, Passarello, like Pompey and Thersites, has an important function in the play in establishing the brooding atmosphere of corruption and lust that permeates it. He is a cynical fool who has no fondness for anyone and suspects everyone of baseness. He jests vulgarly with his master when Bilioso attempts to show his wife how he will entertain a beautiful lady, and he makes covert fun of him when asked to admire his leg in a long stocking, "An excellent calfe my Lord" (V.i. p.199). He also offers logical proofs in Touchstone's syllogistic vein when informed that a rival of his is very valiant and a quarreller:

> Pasa. O is he so great a quarreller? Why then hees an arrant coward.
>
> Bili. How proove you that?
>
> Pasa. Why thus, he that quarrels seekes to fight; and he that seekes to fight, seekes to dye; and he that seekes to dye, seekes never to fight more; and he that will quarrell and seekes meanes never to answer a man more, I thinke hees a coward.
>
> Bili. Thou canst proove any thing.
>
> Pasa. Any thing but a ritch knave, for I can flatter no man.
>
> (V.i.p.200)

Passarello appears for the last time in V.i in a drunken scene with Malevole and Maquerelle the bawd. After some vulgar jesting and some toast-drinking, the bawd feels more friendly toward the fool, who has been insulting her about her trade: "Now thou hast drunke my health; foole I am friends with thee" (V.i.p.201). But Passarello, not flattered by the offer, replies with a question and a snatch of a bawdy song:

> Art art
> When Griffon saw the reconciled queane,
>   offerring about his neck her armes to cast:
> He threw of sword and hartes malignant streame,
>   And lovely her below the loynes imbrast.
>
> (V.i. p.201)

He then disappears from the play.

It is clear that in adding to his play for the King's Men, John Marston kept, no doubt at the instance of the Company, three important dramatic lines in mind: Burbage's, the player of Bilioso (probably John Heminges), and Robert Armin's. We learn, moreover, that the play was lengthened in these comic parts chiefly because the King's Men could not provide musical interludes like the Boys' Company which first produced the play. Certainly if Marston kept the players of these parts in mind in writing his augmentations, it seems likely that Shakespeare followed the same practice in writing parts for his own Company. Passarello sings, rails, is wise, manipulates words skillfully, and conducts himself familiarly with everyone at the court much like Shakespeare's fools. His elegant velvet costume is his main distinguishing characteristic and suggests that Marston's version of the fool was no more to be considered stock clowning than the differently costumed versions of Shakespeare were.

As I hope I have shown in my discussion of fools in the plays of Shakespeare from 1599 to 1605 and in three other plays performed by Shakespeare's Company, the character of the fool—a kind of fool that was Armin's specialty—becomes an important part of the repertory of the company. Of the eight plays by Shakespeare during this period, only three, *Hamlet, Merry Wives,* and *Othello,* do not have important parts for fools, but even in these plays there are opportunities in other roles for Armin's brand of clowning in the older tradition. The evidence clearly suggests that William Shakespeare found in Robert Armin a clown versatile enough to fill the more traditional Kempe-like roles of servant-clown or rustic fellow, including the preeminent Kempe part of Dogberry, as well as an artful student of comedy who had some new ideas picked up in his travels with a provincial company which could be adapted to the theatre in the character of the fool. This new comic character could move freely among all classes of society because of his privilege as a fool, could reflect in his antics a more cultivated kind of entertainment, and could adapt himself comfortably in a sophisticated courtly environment. With the arrival of Robert Armin as a member of the Chamberlain's Men, the roynish natural clown of Shakespeare's earlier comedies becomes the witty artificial fool of his mature comedies and great tragedy, *King Lear.*

Notes

[1] Sir Edmund K. Chambers, The *Elizabethan Stage,* Vol. IV, (Oxford: The Clarendon Press, 1923), 180.

[2] "Recent Studies in Shakespeare's Chronology," *Shakespeare Survey,* ed. Allardyce Nicoll (London, 1950), III, 22-33. All dates used in my discussion of Shakespeare's plays follow McManaway's chronology.

[3] All citations of *AYLI* are from A New Variorum edition of Shakespeare, edited by Horace Howard Furness, Vol. VIII: *As You Like It* (Philadelphia, 1891).

[4] Leslie Hotson, Shakespeare's Motley (1952), p. 88, believes that Shakespeare and Armin were: "Faced with the necessity of weaning their public little by little from its fanatic addiction to the Tarlton-Kempe-Cowley

convention. A significant progression in the treatment of the role can be traced in the comedies . . . *As You Like It,* and *Twelfth Night.*"

[5] *New Variorum Shakespeare,* VIII, 262.

[6] All line counts given with the exception of those for Thersites and Passarello come from Thomos W. Baldwin, The *Organization and Personnel* of the Shakespearean Company (Princeton, 1927) Charts between pp. 228-229.

[7] I discuss the ambiguous use of the word "motley" as a specific description of a kind of cloth and as a general term meaning parti-colored in Appendix III of my unpubl. diss. "William Shakespeare and Robert Armin His Fool: A Working Partnership" (University of Michigan, 1955). E. W. Ives, "Tom Skelton—A Seventeenth-Century Jester," in *Shakespeare Survey 13,* ed. Allardyce Nicoll (Cambridge, 1960) conclusively demonstrates in his discussion of the word "motley" and in the woodcuts reproduced in the text along with the paintings of Tom Skelton in Plate V that Elizabethan and Stuart fools were variously dressed off the stage as well as on.

[8] See Hotson, *Shakespeare's Motley* and Robert H. Goldsmith, *Wise Fools,* of Shakespeare (1955).

[9] All citations of *TN* are from A New Variorum edition of Shakespeare, edited by Horace Howard Furness, Vol. XIII: *Twelfth Night* (Philadelphia, 1901).

[10] Suggested by Furness, *New Variorum Shakespeare,* XIII, 63.

[11] Leslie Hotson, *The First Night of Twelfth Night* (New York, 1954), p. 157.

[12] *New Variorum Shakespeare,* XIII, 258.

[13] *New Variorum Shakespeare,* XIII, 264-265.

[14] *Shakespeare Survey III,* 22-33.

[15] All citations of *KL* are from A New Variorum edition of Shakespeare, edited by Horace HowArd Furness Vol. V: *King Lear* (Philadelphia, 1880).

[16] *Elizabethan Stage,* II, 338-339.

[17] *Shakespeare Survey III,* 22-33.

[18] Dates derived from Alfred Harbage, *Annals of English Drama 975-1700* (Philadelphia, 1940), p. 78 and p. 80.

[19] George Wilkins, *The Miseries of Enforced Marriage 1607,* fac. ed. J. S. Farmer (London, 1913). All citations are from this volume.

[20] Cyril Tourneur, *The Plays and Poems of Cyril Tourneur,* ed. John Churton Collins (London, 1878), Vol. I. All citations are from this volume.

[21] John Marston, *The Plays of John Marston,* ed. H. Harvey Wood (Edinburgh and London, 1934), I, xlii-xliv. All citations are from this volume.

[22] E. E. Stoll, *John Webster* (Boston, 1905), p. 56

[23] John Marston, *The Malcontent,* Augmented by Marston, with the additions played by the Kings Majesties Servants written by Iohn Webster (London, 1604).

Walter Kaiser (essay date 1963)

SOURCE: "Falstaff the Fool," in *Praisers of Folly: Erasmus, Rabelais, and Shakespeare,* Harvard University Press, 1963, pp. 267-75.

[*In the following excerpt, Kaiser analyzes Falstaff's position as the "wise fool" of the* Henriad.]

"But Falstaff, unimitated, unimitable Falstaff, how shall I describe thee?" The frustration of Samuel Johnson's question has been shared by all who have ever tried to encompass the fat old fool. Embodying nothing less than nature itself, he is so enormous that, as Empson has said, "it is hard to get one's mind all round him."[1] Because he actually is, in a certain sense, "all the world," he contains within himself so much that one can never take account of it all, and most attempts to map out this globe of sinful continents have tended to display the partial and falsified perspective of medieval cartography. Yet the very nature of the fool is such that it could hardly be otherwise. Even Stultitia, who knew more about fools than anyone, could not describe herself, because her influence was so vast and her nature so comprehensive (ME 5-6). Falstaff contains all the contradictions of folly, and just as nature includes both summer and winter, good and bad, Falstaff the Martlemas cannot be said to be either wholly good or wholly bad. If, as Empson claims, one's feelings of distaste for all the false sentiment about Falstaff "should not send one in headlong flight to the opposite extreme," at the same time one must confess that "it is hard to defend this strange figure without doing it too much."[2] In compensation for the affinity he felt with the fat old man, Johnson himself was, in the end, probably too morally censorious of him. But he came perhaps as close as one can to describing Sir John when he addressed him as "thou compound of sense and vice; of sense which may be admired but not esteemed, of vice which may be despised, but hardly detested."[3]

In calling Falstaff a compound of sense and vice, Johnson points directly at the oxymoronic nature of the wise fool. As an isolated figure, Falstaff is as filled with contradictions as Stultitia: he acts like a young man though he is old, he talks like a Puritan though he is an Epicurean, he teaches by misleading, he pays by borrowing, he counterfeits in order not to counterfeit, he claims that vices are virtues. One could pile up such self-contradictions endlessly, but these are simple in comparison with the complexities he engenders whenever he is in the presence of someone else; for then our point of perspective is not merely dual, but multiple. The dramatic form in which Falstaff is presented multiplies the complexities even more than the mock-encomiastic form in which Stultitia was presented. And while it is easy for Falstaff to pretend he is resolving all the confusion by mendaciously asking "Is not the truth the truth?" the rest of us come to despair of ever knowing what the truth is.

As perhaps only Prince Hal is meant to see, the truth somehow comprehends all the different points of view that the drama presents. But Falstaff, in his own way, comes close to an understanding of this also. At least, he is the only other person in the drama who is able to understand a point of view opposite to his own; it is because he understands it so well that he realizes he must oppose it so strongly. Another way of looking at this capacity of his is to perceive that he could not operate so successfully as a liar if he did not know what the truth is. He demonstrates this clearly when he boasts that he is not only witty in himself, but the cause that wit is in other men. Boast though it is, it is also the truth, and it is a truth of greater dimensions than either of those facts alone. That he can say he is the butt of wit as well as the source of wit reveals that he is able to see himself as others see him. Despite all the bombastic, conceited, stultiloquent smokescreens that he puts out to conceal it (smokescreens which, at times, confuse even him), he knows very well that he is a fool—that, as Dryden put it, he is "a liar, and a coward, a glutton, and a buffoon."[4]

The ability to see the same fact from his and from the opposite point of view is the capacity of the ironic man, and in this Falstaff represents one of the great flowerings of that Socratic irony which Stultitia replanted in the soil of European literature. But if he is what Cicero called Socrates, an *eirôn*,[5] he is also what Aristophanes called Socrates, an *alazôn*.[6] When Falstaff admits that he is the butt of other men's wit, he is wearing the mask of the eirôn; when he boasts that he is the source of wit in himself, he is wearing the mask of the alazôn. The distinction between the two is most clearly set forth in the *Nicomachean Ethics* in the course of Aristotle's discussion of the mean to which I have already referred in connection with honor. The passage in which he discusses the characteristics of the eirôn and the alazôn is, however, even more illuminating for the character of Falstaff and must be quoted:

> There are also other means, which, though similar to each other, yet are different one from another. They are all connected with intercourse in words and deeds, but they differ in that one is concerned with truth in this intercourse and the others with its pleasure. Of these latter two, one is concerned with giving pleasure in all circumstances of life... With regard to truth, the moderate man is a truthful person (*alêthes*) and the mean is truthfulness: pretense, which exaggerates, is boastfulness and he who has pretenses is a boaster (*alazôn*); understatement is false modesty and he who understates is falsely modest (*eirôn*). With regard to pleasure in amusement, the moderate man is witty (*eutrapelos*) and the condition wit: excess is buffoonery and he who exceeds a buffoon (*bômolochos*); he who is defective is a boor (*agroikos*) and the condition boorishness. With regard to the other pleasure, that in the affairs of life, he who is properly pleasant is a friend (*philos*) and the moderation is friendship: he who exceeds is (if he has no ulterior motive) obsequious (*areskos*) or (if he is looking for gain) a flatterer (*kolax*); he who is defective and unpleasant in every circumstance is contentious (*dyseris*) and surly (*dyskolos*).[7]...

[The] application of this Aristotelian schematization to Falstaff can help us to understand some of his paradoxical complexity and may indeed even help us to make his defeat more comprehensible. For once we perceive that Falstaff plays the alazôn as well as the eirôn, we can better understand, it seems to me, not only his personality but also the role he plays in this cycle of history plays. Whatever the old fool is, he is never the man of mean. That role is reserved for Hal to play when he becomes Henry V; and one way of looking at the story of the reign of Henry IV is to see it as a kind of *Bildungsspiel*—an account of a prince's education. Hal's ultimate role, like that of Spenser's Prince Arthur, is to personify Aristotle's magnanimous man, and that goal is reached by way of the middle road upon which he is able to set out only after he has defeated Hotspur in *Part One* and Falstaff in *Part Two*.

While Hotspur himself may be seen as a kind of alazôn, it is really the old lad of the castle who usurps this role. When Falstaff gives his speech on honor, when he admits to being old and white-bearded, when he concedes that he is the butt of other men's jokes, he is the eirôn. At most other times, however, he is the alazôn; for generally we hear him boasting of his prowess in love and war, his friendship with the prince, his courage and virtue. We think of him more often as the buffoon than as the boor. The point is that he incorporates within himself both extremes, and the complexity of his character arises from just this fact. What is more, he confuses things even further because, in a certain sense, he plays his roles in the wrong places. From one point of view at least, the alazôn, the man who claims to be more than he is, may be thought properly to belong to the heroics of the battlefield; the eirôn, the man who claims to be less than he is, would belong to the antics of the tavern world. Yet Falstaff reverses this. It is in the tavern world that he plays the alazôn, "the man of war" (2:V.i.31), boasting that he is more than he actually is. It is in the world of battle that he plays the eirôn, pretending that he is less than he is, even to the extent of pretending that he is dead.

The way of excess is the winding mountain path to the battlefield of tragedy; the way of defect is the crooked back-alley to the tavern of comedy; the middle road is the Camino Real of history. Although history may lead to either comedy or tragedy, the moment of comedy and the moment of tragedy are essentially timeless and outside history. Since time, as we have seen, is the fool's mortal enemy, he can play a role in either of those timeless moments, that of comedy (like Feste) or that of tragedy (like Lear's fool), but he cannot survive in the time of history. Time and history destroyed the comic moment of Yorick's gibes and gambols, but when the moment of tragedy comes he has a role to play once more. Thus Falstaff can be the eirôn and mock at honor and death on the battlefield of tragedy, and he can also be the alazôn and boast of courage and youth in the tavern of comedy. The prince, on the other hand, though he is challenged onto the battlefield by Hotspur and misled into the tavern by Falstaff, has his destiny on the broad King's Highway that leads between them, and, when he finally passes down this highway, the fool must stand rejected at the side.

That highway is, as Aristotle says, the place of truth. Since eirôn and alazôn stand on either side, and since Falstaff plays both, in him we look on truth from both sides. And this is where the greatest complexity of his character lies. By spanning the distance between defect and excess, he also manages to take in the mean. Were he simply on one side or the other, the mean would be external to him; but since he is constantly moving from one extreme to the other, the implication is that he is constantly passing through the condition of the mean, the location of truth. To be sure, he does not stop there (for to stay would be suicide), but he does pass through. In an inexplicable, paradoxical sense that such imagery may or may not help to understand, he comprehends the truth of the mean within his advocacy of the two extremes. And just as he may be looked upon as the most faithful friend (philos) and the wittiest man (eutrapelos) in the play, so he may also be said to be in possession of truth (alêthes)—perhaps even of the greatest truth. Not only does he possess the truth that he is a fool, but also, with his synoptic, comprehensive view of all three conditions of defect, mean, and excess, he possesses the Stultitian truth that folly is truth.

Yet history—the middle road, the moderate position, Henry V—defeats him in the end, rejecting the Stultitian truth he stands for. It was preordained that it should, for otherwise Falstaff would have defeated history. He is, as a recent critic has said, "the fool of the history plays. He steps out of the way of English history, an intruder who announces himself in the face of the commonwealth; and in Falstaff the idea of order meets its most dangerous fact."[8] He had warned that to banish him would be to banish all the world. That is not strictly true, for the world of Henry V goes on. Yet it is true that in order to banish him the world has had to narrow its scope; it has had to shrink, as it were, to fill up the large void the corpulent fool leaves behind. It has had to forego that breadth which can include the opposite extremes of excess and defect and that expansiveness which gives *Lebensraum* to the laughter of irony. As the fool goes off, he takes part, if not all, of the world with him; and Falstaff is entitled to say with Donne, "since you would have none of mee, I bury some of you."[9]

Though we understand why he must be banished, rare is the man who has not been bothered by the rejection of Falstaff. It is easy to dismiss the distress of Bradley and others as maudlin sentimentality; yet it is, I think, much harder to accept the moral justification of the expulsion provided by Johnson. Moreover, that Johnson felt obliged to give a justification and that so many others have indulged in sentimentality betray the more important fact that somehow the rejection does fail to come off properly. Tragic though it is, no one "objects" to the death of Hamlet, and even the shock of Cordelia's death, which Johnson found hardest to bear, has not occasioned nearly so much discontent as this rejection of the fool. Explain it though we may, if we are really honest with ourselves, I think we must admit that we never feel quite right about it. Falstaff has presented his case too strongly to be put down quite so simply. The fool, as he always will if given half a chance, has run away with us.

C. L. Barber has given a valuable explanation of why, though the rejection is morally justified, it is not dramatically cogent, and his comments on this are as valuable as anything that has been written about the end of *Henry IV*. His examination of the problem begins with an analysis of the historical situation that is particularly germane to this study:

> But Falstaff proves extremely difficult to bring to book—more difficult than an ordinary mummery king—because his burlesque and mockery are developed to a point where the mood of a moment crystallizes as a settled attitude of scepticism. As we have observed before, in a static, monolithic society, a Lord of Misrule can be put back in his place after the revel with relative ease. The festive burlesque of solemn sanctities does not seriously threaten social values in a monolithic culture, because the license depends utterly upon what it mocks: liberty is unable to envisage any alternative to the accepted order except the standing of it on its head. But Shakespeare's culture was not

monolithic: though its moralists assumed a single order, scepticism was beginning to have ground to stand on and look about—especially in and around London. So a Lord of Misrule figure, brought up, so to speak, from the country to the city, or from the traditional past into the changing present, could become on the Bankside the mouthpiece not merely for the dependent holiday scepticism which is endemic in a traditional sociey, but also for a dangerously self-sufficient everyday scepticism. When such a figure is set in an environment of sober-blooded great men behaving as opportunistically as he, the effect is to raise radical questions about social sanctities. At the end of *Part Two,* the expulsion of Falstaff is presented by the dramatist as getting rid of this threat; Shakespeare has recourse to a primitive procedure to meet a modern challenge. We shall find reason to question whether this use of ritual entirely succeeds.[10]

Surely this is the case. An increasingly skeptical century must have found a voice in Falstaff as it had in the two earlier fools; in such remarks as his speech on honor he must have given formulation to the doubts of many who had lived through a century of war. And yet the final appeal of Falstaff involves more than his articulation of doubt. What Barber calls his settled attitude of skepticism does not actually end there. Like the skepticism of Stultitia and Pantagruel, his does not come to rest in the despair of pyrrhonism, but rather it manages to lead beyond that doubt to optimism, which is, as Empson puts it, "a greater trust in the natural man [and] pleasure in contemplating him."[11] Hamlet will be left holding the empty skull of Yorick to symbolize all his disillusionment, but Falstaff goes off displaying his great belly as a symbol of the virtues of the little kingdom of natural man. That is *his* answer to doubt.

If he left us in doubt, we could accept his rejection; it is because he expresses such a positive answer that we find it so intolerable. Unquestionably, Shakespeare invented him in order to create doubt, and the answer to that doubt was to be Henry V; but Falstaff got out of control, so to speak, and answered his own doubt. Fools, if we are not careful, always do. By their very nature, their tendency is to exceed the roles we assign to them, and because we suffer fools gladly we let them take us where we are not supposed to go. The problem can perhaps be seen most clearly as a technical one, and in this Stultitia once again helps to explain Falstaff. Both Erasmus and Shakespeare start out with the intention of attacking the accepted values of society—what Erasmus calls *sapientia mundana*. In order to depose these idols, they ironically praise the accepted vices of society—*stultitia*. The two are expected to destroy each other, leaving (as we know from the *Enchiridion* and the portrait of Henry V) the field free for the triumph of the reasonable man—*homo rationalis*. Now when you have folly challenge worldly wisdom, the advantages, to begin with, are all on the side of worldly wisdom; for that is what the world accepts as its values. Therefore, in order to make the combat equal (and it must be exactly equal, so that the two opponents will destroy each other), you must give folly all the ammunition you can. Since, that is, the spectators start out having all their sympathies with worldly wisdom, the author must do everything possible to transfer some of those sympathies to folly.

The problem, of course, is that the fool enlists too much of our sympathy. His gaiety and license are so appealing that we cannot keep ourselves from falling in with him completely. In terms of the sympathies of the spectators, it is as easy for the author to kill off the wordly wise as it is for him to kill off Hotspur; but the fool has a frustrating habit of staying alive, even when you think he has died. At the end of *Part One* the rational man stands triumphant over Hotspur and Falstaff, and everything has worked out as it should: reason has triumphed over both folly and the false wisdom of the world. But then the fool gets up and takes over again. Erasmus wanted to leave us with a picture of a man reasonable in worldly things and a Fool in Christ. In order to exalt the reasonable man, he had to destroy the man "wise" in earthly things, and he created the fool to destroy him. But the arguments he gives to the foolish man are so compelling that we forget about the reasonable man. Once we are made to see things from the perspective of the fool, the reasonable man bears much too close a resemblance to the wise man. Shakespeare is able to force the triumph of the reasonable man, in a way that Erasmus without the drama at his disposal could not, by having him visually crowned at the end. The audience follows his progress to the palace, but too many of its sympathies stay behind with the rejected fool. Only Rabelais seems to have managed to control the situation as he wanted to. His fool, Panurge, creates exactly the proper doubt to knock down the idols of the "wise." Yet Panurge is as much the victim of the wise as they are his: the result is the defeat of both parties. For though Panurge is made powerful enough to demonstrate that the answers of the wise are wrong, he is not powerful enough to get an answer himself. At this point, the rational man, who is also the Fool in Christ, triumphs over both fool and wise in the character of Pantagruel.

We accept Pantagruel's triumph over Panurge in a way that we never do Hal's over Falstaff. We know that Falstaff must go, for he is far in the devil's book. We also know that "the King is a good king." And yet we are obliged to add, with Nym, "but it must be as it may; he passes some humours and careers" (*Henry V,* II.i.125-6). It is Falstaff who has won our hearts, and we wish, with Queen Elizabeth, to have the old fool back again.

Notes

[1] Empson, "Falstaff and Mr. Dover Wilson," p. 221.

[2] Empson, "Falstaff," pp. 221, 256.

[3] *Johnson on Shakespeare,* ed. Raleigh, p. 125.

[4] John Dryden, "Preface to *Troilus and Cressida: or, Truth Found Too Late, A Tragedy,*" in *The Works of John Dryden,* ed. Sir Walter Scott and George Saintsbury, VI (Edinburgh, 1883), 269.

[5] Cicero, *De officiis,* I.xxx.109.

[6] Aristophanes, *Nubes,* 102.

[7] Aristotle, *Ethica Nicomachea,* 1108a.

[8] Geoffrey Bush, *Shakespeare and the Natural Condition* (Cambridge, Mass., 1956), p. 31.

[9] John Donne, "The Funerall."

[10] Barber, *Shakespeare's Festive Comedy,* pp. 213-4.

[11] Empson, "Falstaff," p. 245.

Gareth Lloyd Evans (essay date 1972)

SOURCE: "Shakespeare's Fools: The Shadow and the Substance of Drama," in *Shakespearian Comedy,* Edward Arnold, 1972, pp. 142-59.

[*In the essay below, Evans observes developments in Shakespeare's dramatic representation of the fool character as they coincide with the appearance of Robert Armin as a member of Shakespeare's acting company.*]

I

In recent years increased attention has been paid by criticism to Shakespeare's Fools. This increase was, doubtless, fired by the excellently detailed and imaginatively presented work of Enid Welsford[1] which showed the vast antecedents of the character both in art forms and in real life, and suggested its importance to a full understanding of the nature of Shakespeare's imagination. Later, Robert Goldsmith[2] dealt shrewdly with the contradictory nature of the Fool—the contrapuntal effects of his drollery and sage comment. One of the most recent books takes the study a stage further. William Willeford[3] discusses, in both philosophical and psychological terms, the nature of folly and the significance of the relationship of the Fool to the actor and his audience.

The scope of the area for research is well indicated by recalling Leslie Hotson's[4] intricately clever work on the meaning of the word 'motley' and what it implies about the dress of real Fools and their status in royal and noble households. Hotson provided valuable pointers to yet another aspect of study—the nature and status of real Fools in history. At the time of writing, no such study, on a comprehensive basis, has yet appeared. If and when it does far greater attention than hitherto will have to be paid to sources other than literary; the evidence capable of being supplied by the social historian and the art historian is likely to prove immensely valuable in attempting to establish the place of real Fools in their society and their relationships with the various forms of entertainment in the early and late medieval periods.

For, indeed, with this figure, the student of Shakespeare is faced with the intriguing fact that an apparently fictional type has an accredited reality. Any Shakespeare Fool has (and there is perhaps a touch of wry irony here) a far more clearly definable and recognizable source than, say, Lear, or any other of Shakespeare's great characters whose 'historical' reality is so shadowy. The student also confronts the unique fact that the realization of the Fool figures on the Elizabethan stage was entrusted to a man who had a unique knowledge of real Fools. Robert Armin, who played Touchstone, Feste, Lear's unnamed Fool and Lavache, knew far more about their typical antecedents than Burbage did of the originals of the parts he played—Lear, Macbeth, Othello and Hamlet. It might, in passing, also be timely to record that Armin knew the difference between true Fools and clown figures like Gobbo far more clearly than many modern directors of Shakespeare's plays who, following a passing mode, seem to wish to put every zany into motley.

Armin serves to remind us that the study of the relationship of the actor to his role has been a marked preoccupation of twentieth-century thinking and writing on theatre matters. What happens to Olivier when he is Macbeth, or to Gielgud become King Lear? Most actors (but strangely fewer actresses) of quality have, in the past few decades, questioned deeply into the nature of their own personalities. It should perhaps not be surprising in a century in which psychology has drifted and sprayed its effects into almost every corner of existence, to find actors particularly prone to be magnetized by the kind of anwers that a probing into the unconscious might reveal. After all, not only is psychology a wonderful boost to the ego but it must be very beguiling to consider the nature of a man whose professional function is not to be himself. Has a chameleon a personality?

The implications of this preoccupation are many, and an indication of the extent to which it can exercise not only the minds of actors but also the modes of directors is Peter Brook's much-hailed production of *A Midsummer Night's Dream* (Straford-upon-Avon 1970, London 1971). As is customary in an age of shifty and shifting values, the production's importance was overrated. Phrases more applicable to the plastic enormities of technological discovery like 'break-through' and 'new horizons' were used to evaluate what was an extremely competent display of directorial ingenuity. The truly remarkable fact about the production was, however, its adroit use of a Shakespeare play to illustrate the twentieth-century preoccupation with the nature of the relationship between actor and role. For example, all the actors quite deliberately stepped out of character when they were not required to be an integral part of the spoken or visual action and watched (in their own 'real' personalities as it were) what was happening. It was like the chinese box, and the whole affair very germane to the preoccupation under discussion—partly because the audience wondered how much the non-acting postures that were taken up were, indeed, yet another layer of illusion. Brook's procedure (a sort of anglicized version of alienation) would impose far less strain on an audience's credibilities when the play is a comedy than when it is in any other mode. For an actor, on stage, as himself, to laugh at the antics of his colleagues playing parts and then, in turn, to be laughed at himself, seems curiously right. Yet, for an actor, on stage, as himself, to watch, for example, the murder of Lady Macduff which he set in motion in his role of Macbeth, seems curiously wrong.

Comedy invokes less identification from an audience than does tragedy. In fact, comedy depends for its effects upon a certain distancing. It requires a barely realized mental posture of superiority so that there can be a full deployment of that element that causes us to laugh. If tragedy induces the feeling—'there but for the grace of God and art go I'—then comedy involves the response—'catch me doing or saying that'.

II

If a study of his plays did not convince us that Shakespeare was, in a very direct sense, concerned about the relationship between actor and role, then a reminder of the conditions in which he worked should smother any doubts. The very close involvement with actors in the imbroglio of both public and private theatres must have daily brought him face to face with a practical manifestation of the problems facing the playwright who is not just a visitant but a close working colleague of temperamental actors. Drama created while the eventual executants are breathing over the dramatist's shoulder has a complicated grain that differs from the polished results of the writer's solitary immunity from interference.

What may seem definitive, imperishable, even sacrosanct in the quiet of the study may well be the first element to be transmuted, altered, even replaced when subjected to the various expediencies and histrionic expertise of the rehearsal room. To be aware that Shakespeare's plays were deeply and inevitably subjected (given the nature of the acting companies) to the latter environment immediately raises questions which admit of no final answer but whose very fascination invites speculation. How much of Burbage went into Macbeth? How much of Armin informed the creation of Feste or Lear's Fool? Is there, indeed, any common denominator to roles known to have been played by the same actor in Shakespeare's company?

Some common denominators seem to spring out of the group of tragic heroes known to have been played by Burbage, despite the singular differences we can observe in them. Two examples seem obvious enough. First the actor who played the tragic heroes must have had (and still needs to have) an imagination and a mental and emotional sensibility of a very developed order. These roles are beyond the run-of-the-mill matinee idol; they demand more than technical skill. Second, the actor who played these roles needed (and still needs) to have a quite unusual sensitivity to the appreciation and communication of language. Your rodomontade player will pull off Henry V, your skilled technician and cold-voiced villain will conquer Angelo, and Romeo would be adequately served by one with a sense of music, soft lips and a disposition to sentimentality. But Lear, Hamlet and Macbeth, in particular, demand a huge poetic feeling and an ability to apprehend the implications of the intellectual content of the lines. This is not to ask for an actor of immense intellectual stature, but one of limitless mental and emotional intuitiveness. Such men are rare. It is not enough to say that because Shakespeare was a great poet it is natural that his characters should speak great poetry: a bad actor can make sow's ears out of any poet's silk purses.

It is very tempting to assume that Burbage was possessed of these rare qualities and that this gave Shakespeare a kind of confidence which put no restriction whatsoever on his own imaginative immensity and his verbal splendour. The characters were, so to speak, only possible in the terms in which they eventually came to exist because the actor was big enough to meet the terms—indeed, may well have suggested them.

These kinds of relationships, and others less inchoate and theoretical, might well be multiplied. For example, were the evidence firmer, it might with confidence be expected to apply to all of Shakespeare's major characters. At least it can be said that all the tenuous evidence available points unerringly towards the existence of far closer relationships between actor and role than has hitherto been admitted. One might, indeed, find certain quirks of certain actors being exploited (perhaps covertly) by Shakespeare in the creation of certain characters.

If it is objected that there is too much supposition in this, it should be recalled that the use of the idosyncrasies of players (Green Room raw material, as it were) is far from uncommon in theatre today and has distinguished confirmation for its past usage in the work of Congreve who seems, quite relentlessly and presumably undetectedly, to have caused some well-known actors and actresses of his time to reproduce their own habits in fictional characters without being aware of what they were doing. Shakespeare, the most assiduous picker-up of trifles in the history of drama, could hardly give second place to Congreve in the matter of source-hunting. Equally, it should be recalled that the consanguinity of actor and role is at least suggested by the intriguing substitution of the names of actors for their roles, possibly as a result of a prompter, in II. ii of *Much Ado About Nothing*. Cowley (i.e. Richard Cowley, a member of the Lord Chamberlain's Men) appears three times for Verges, but the entire contribution of Dogberry, which is a major one, appears under the name of Kemp (i.e. Will Kemp) twelve times.

Two points are worth stressing here. First, the scene is, in an obvious sense, a throwaway, barely necessary to forward the action, and its dialogue is almost entirely designed to promote comic business. Second, the comedy of the scene seems arranged to 'feed' Dogberry/Kemp and, moreover, seems deliberately to be leading up to giving him the opportunity for the last solo speech of the scene—ending with 'O that I had been writ down an ass'. In truth, we get very much the same impression from those pantomime and music-hall sketches where a stooge or stooges build up the verbal atmosphere to enable the star comic to explode into his big solo which often ends with a well-known catchphrase.

When the substitution of Kemp for Dogberry for the entirety of the scene is considered, when the nature of the scene is recalled, when its dramatic irrelevance is recorded, is it unreasonable to lean towards a belief either that Kemp wrote it or that Shakespeare did, but in absolute and well-judged servility to the known values of Kemp's comic, genius?

Discussion of Burbage and Kemp in these contexts admittedly runs the risk of bogging down in speculation. Where, however, the Fools and Robert Armin are concerned, there is much firmer ground.

We know, with a certainty equal to that applicable to Burbage and his roles, that Armin played Feste, Touchstone, Lear's Fool and probably Lavache. It has been suggested that he also played Dogberry. The evidence for this derives from a line in the dedication to Armin's play *The Italian Taylor and his Boy* (1609) which goes—'I pray you the boldness of a beggar who hath been writ down an Asse in his time'.[5] Faced with the Kemp/Dogberry substitution already referred to, the strong possibility that the Ass phrase was, or became, a popular catchphrase either deriving from, or popularized by, Kemp and, as it is hoped to show, the quite un-Armin qualities required to play Dogberry, the difficulty of accepting the suggestion is very great.

III

It is well known, and it is thoroughly documented by Enid Welsford, that the Court Fools of Shakespeare derive, in essentials, from the real Fools of history. These essentials were transmuted by Shakespeare for his own dramatic puposes but he capitalized very much on his sources. The most obvious of them are:

1) The Fools are conspicuously classless or, at very least, difficult to place with confidence in the social hierarchies. Although, like Feste, they may haunt the houses, mansions, palaces of the high and mighty, they are obviously neither of the upper class nor distinctly of any other. Jaques' reference to Touchstone that he is 'One who hath been a courtier' seems calculatedly vague. Touchstone gives no particular indication of being more than on jester/master terms with the highborn of the play. If he cannot be truly seen as a member of the upper class, neither does he seem to fit well with the lower orders. His marriage to Audrey seems, in every way, a monumental aberration—like is certainly not marrying like in any sense, least of all a social one. Lear's Fool is classless to the point where even to consider his place in the social hierarchy seems ridiculous. Lavache, though listened to, is presented as a confidant whose words are countenanced, not because of equality of social status, but for some other reason.

2) This other reason has much to do with the fact that the Fools are conspicuously a law unto themselves. They utilize (as, for example, in Feste's catechizing of Olivia or Lear's Fool's wisdom-shafted jibes) an accepted right to speak their minds. A marked and important feature of this acceptance of a right is, of course, the irony that is embedded in it. They do speak what they think, they are often expected even incited to do so, and yet they can, incontinently, at the whim of the piper's payer, be punished for doing so—'Sirrah, the whip'.

This ironic 'right' to speak is often referred to as a Fool's licence and it is usually assumed that it is a tradition and not a palpable reality—a wry ghost of something that itself has no substance. An example of the way in which the art and social historian may well guide future research into the history of Fools may be indicated by the fact that, in the many depictions of these creatures carved on the underside of choir-stall seats in so many of our cathedrals and medieval churches, there are some who are holding quite conspicuously in one hand what seems like a rolled-up parchment. Whether or not the artist's licence has created a Fool's 'licence'—depicting something that did not exist but was well-known as a tradition—or whether some Fools actually did possess a written licence, is not known, but the matter is amenable to much detailed research.

3) At certain times—and, in the case of Feste, Lear's Fool and Lavache, at most times—their 'comic' utterances, whether in dialogue or monologue, are embarrassingly unsimple. It is an area of theatre-experience worth commenting on that the status of Fools in an audience's experience is quite dissimilar to that of the plain comic folk who are sometimes found in the presence of the Fools. Martext and Audrey provide uncomplicated laughter; Touchstone does not; Aguecheek by the side of Feste is a funny simple droll. When Feste is being 'funny' in the dialogue with Olivia, Viola and as Sir Topas, we are well aware that 'this is not altogether Fool'. There is little in Lear's Fool that inclines us from a strong feeling that he is less a comic than a prophetic or even tragic figure; and Lavache is more cynic than jester.

It may be added that another element in the audience's experience of these creatures re-emphasizes the complexity of their status. How often, as members of an audience, do we watch and listen to the actor playing the Fool and react a little nervously as he seems to beg for our laughter at his quips about the Vapians and impeticosing gratillity. Our response is so often nervous not only because we recognize the difficulty the actor has in inducing comic responses from what seems intractable material but also because we are reluctant for our neighbours to know that we do not understand the joke. On the contrary, to laugh alone in these circumstances can either be a conceit or a form of desperate insincerity!

It is true, of course, that some of the quips which leave us darkling would have had an immediate response from an Elizabethan audience because of their contemporary allusiveness. It is equally true, however, that there remains an area of their verbal communications which seems opaque for other, mysterious reasons.

4) The Fools have (to use a modern catch-phrase that any good Fool would reduce to mincemeat) a conspicuous withdrawal syndrome. Their involvement in the action, incidents, tensions of the plays is peripheral. This posture is implicitly comprehended on a reading of the plays but becomes explicit when the plays are experienced in the theatre. Feste's withholding of any comment whatsoever and his withdrawal from the action at the sudden intervention of Malvolio in the drunken below-stairs scene is sudden in its impact. In the production at the then Shakespeare Memorial Theatre in 1959, Feste couched beneath a table quietly strumming on a musical instrument—he seemed light years away from Illyria. Even Touchstone, the most socially integrated (to use modern parlance again) of them all, is not at the heart of the play. Comments about him hint at a kind of alienation in his make-up. 'He uses his folly like a stalking-horse and under the presentation of that he shoots his wit' (*As You Like It,* V. iv. 100).

Lear's Fool is the most removed of all. He darts in and out of the play with his wry comments, his unremarked wisdom and warnings, his saws and jingles which seem to come from a time before clock-time began. When he is no longer dramatically needed he disappears from the action with utter finality.

These four characteristics alone entitle us to look closely at these Fools, for a mystery seems to hand here. No other Elizabethan dramatist exploits the real Fools of history in this way. The kind of character that has been described is unique to Shakespeare.

IV

It is suggested that this is partly due to the fact that Robert Armin was unique in Shakespeare's company and that Shakespeare and he had a certain affinity in the sense that each kindled the other's imagination. Armin sensed what Shakespeare wanted, Shakespeare sensed what Armin could give him. Moreover they came together in a working relationship at a time (1599) when the timbre of Shakespeare's dramatic imagination was changing, becoming more complicated. For the kind of comedy he was about to begin writing at this particular time he needed the kind of conception which, it is claimed, Armin instinctively and sensitively understood. Together, they created a figure unique in drama and, through that figure, revealed an attitude towards comedy, acting and drama which is as strange as it is singular.

We know practically nothing about Robert Armin except that he was probably a pot-boy in a tavern, that he was probably anti-puritan and that he wrote plays, tracts and a curious work, *Foole upon Foole,*[6] which is a remarkable if uneven commentary on real Fools and some speculation upon the nature of folly. Armin probably belonged for a time to the Lord Chandos' men but in 1599 or thereabouts he joined the Lord Chamberlain's, replacing the great custard-pie, physical comedian, Will Kemp. The entry of Armin into the company coincided with the appearance and development of the Fool in Shakespeare's plays and with the consequent diminishing in importance of broad physical comedy.

It is reasonable, surely, to believe that Armin brought with him an excited respect for Shakespeare's work.

There are a considerable number of both close and possible echoes of Shakespeare's plays in Armin's work—perhaps more in number than in any other Elizabethan writer. Surely only close acquaintance and an attendant admiration could recognize the beauty of the image in *Romeo and Juliet* which goes—'Earth-treading stars that make dark heaven light' and reproduce it as 'Earth's bright-treading stars' in his own play *The Two Maids of Moorclacke?*[7] Again, surely only an intimate acquaintance with a popular play by his colleague could lie behind a remark in the same play— 'there are, as Hamlet says, things called whips in store'. The fact that he has misquoted is no argument against intimacy. The modern scholar is only too well aware that familiarity often breeds this kind of carelessness.

Apart from such respect and admiration, it is further suggested that Armin delivered into Shakespeare's mind and greedy imagination a notion of comedy far different from any he had perpended before and, through it, a more complicated notion of the place and function of character in drama.

Some idea of the strength that may lie in the suppositious connections thus made between Armin and Shakespeare may be strikingly indicated by a passage in an epistle signed 'R.A.' but prefixed 'R. Armin' printed in 1590 with a tract entitled *A brief Resolution of the right Religion*. The probability that the actor Armin is one and the same man as R. Armin is strong, and although nine more years were to elapse between the publication of the tract and Armin's joining the Lord Chamberlain's men this is no argument against Shakespeare's having read the tract either before 1599 or indeed having been introduced to it by a new colleague eager to impress the well-known dramatist. The passage in question refers to Puritans and it reads:

> The other vicious and detestable sect are Martinets, who see so far into matters that they oversee themselves, wresting things from the right sense to the wrong, making show of zeal when it is mere folly.[8]

A more evocative general description of Malvolio's colouring it would be difficult to find. The start of recognition which such a passage invokes is frequently repeated in a close examination of *Foole upon Foole* and its companion publication *A Nest of Ninnies* which amplifies some of the comments Armin makes in the former study of Fools. Not only are there occasional sharp reminders of the unusual ambience which Shakespeare's Fools have about them (as in Armin's description of Will Sommers, Henry VIII's Fool: 'His melody was of a higher strain, and he looked as the noon broad waking'), but occasionally it is possible to catch something of the rhythms, the anticlimaxes, guile and shrewdness, and descent into quipping bathos so characteristic particularly of Feste and Touchstone:

> By the first merry emblem I reach at stars, how they fire themselves at the firmament; whether it be with sitting too near the sun in the day, or couching too near the moon in the night I know not, but the hair of their happiness often falls off, and shoots from a blazing comet to a fallen star, and carries no more light than is to be seen in the bottom of Plato's ink-horn, and when they should study in private with Diogenes, in his cell, they are with Cornelius in his tub.[9]

We recall, for example,

> bid the dishonest man mend himself: if he mend, he is no longer dishonest; if he cannot, let the butcher mend him. Anything that's mended is but patch'd; virtue that transgresses is but patch'd with sin, and sin that amends is but patch'd with virtue.
>
> (*Twelfth Night*, I. v. 40-44)

Armin's conception of the subtlety of true folly and his sensitivity to the language of fooling—one moment a broad quip, then a nerve-jolting pun, then a mordant comment, all interwoven with strands of strange verbiage and occasionally decorated with a sad lyricism—is of the same order as Shakespeare's. What is more, his sense of the wisdom in folly is absolutely in line with Shakespeare's, not merely in conception (for the idea of wise folly was not original, as both men would have known from a reading of Erasmus's *Moriae Encomium* (translated as *The Praise of Folie*, 1549), but in its form of expression. It is in this that the uniqueness of the two writers lies.

> Fools questions reach to mirth, leading wisdom by the hand as age leads children by one finger, and though it holds not fast in wisdom, yet it points at it.[10]

To read Armin's books and to recall Shakespeare's Fools is to be immediately aware that both men had come to inhabit a country of the imagination in which the notion of comedy as a mere laughter-maker had been put aside. To hear Feste mocking Malvolio about whirligig Time, and Touchstone gravely turning to Rosalind and saying, 'but as all is mortal in nature, so is all nature in love mortal in folly', to overhear Viola say, 'This fellow is wise enough to play the Fool', is to be made aware that we are in a different realm from that inhabited by Gobbo, Costard, Bottom and their like.

The Fool's comic function in contradistinction to theirs is well expressed by William Willeford:

> The Fool is a fact, and he is the only fact that cannot be governed by the comic dream. . . . He is the reminder that the moment of perfection realized by the comic dream is only pretending.[11]

This comment not only suggests something of a clue to the nature of the Fool's effect in deepening and maturing Shakespeare's conception of comedy, but also the figure's status as a new kind of *dramatis persona*.

V

Before the coming of Armin and the Fool, Shakespeare, we may say, had exulted in the comic dream. *Love's Labour's Lost, The Two Gentlemen of Verona, The Taming of the Shrew, The Comedy of Errors, A Midsummer Night's Dream* are territories of delight which Shakespeare, no doubt, inhabited with wise joy. The adjective is important because, admittedly, even the earliest comedies are not without dark hues. In them the young playwright's comic spirit occasionally stirs a little restlessly in perturbation about mutability, aware that the sunlight on the garden must harden and grow cold. More than this, even the gayest, most effervescent, most witty moods and modes in these early comedies are rarely self-indulgent. This early comedy looks outward from itself, is purposeful in the sense that it is never allowed to cheapen or minimize, for the sake of mindless laughter, Shakespeare's deep sense of values in the matter of love, fidelity, friendship.

The arrival of the Fool immediately heightened Shakespeare's awareness of the contrast between created dream and ever-incipient reality. In his green days comedy and high exciting romance was able always to hold back the shadows of reality, but now Shakespeare fully realized that the darkness cannot be banished. *Twelfth Night* and *As You Like It* are indeed more poignantly comic, and their sunlight the more welcome and subtle, simply because the Fools are so often reminding us that comic perfection is, in a way, only pretending:

> But that's all one, our play is done.
> (*Twelfth Night*, V. i. 393)

But the Fool does much more than to remind Shakespeare and ourselves about the pretence of the comic dream. Inside the Fool there lies a mystery about which all we can instinctively say, either in reading or seeing the plays, is that it has something to do with a knowledge and sometimes a purpose which is exclusive to the Fool. This knowledge is connected not with the comic dream per se, but seems, we feel, to lie outside it, and the purpose is curiously stern. It is brilliantly expressed in the speech of Jaques to the Duke and his assembled followers:

> O worthy fool! One that hath been a courtier,
> And says if ladies be but young and fair,
> They have the gift to know it; and in his brain,
> Which is as dry as the remainder biscuit
> After a voyage, he hath strange places cramm'd
> With observation, the which he vents
> In mangled forms. O that I were a fool!
> I am ambitious for a motley coat . . .
> . . . It is my only suit,
> Provided that you weed your better judgments
> Of all opinion that grows rank in them
> That I am wise. I must have liberty
> Withal, as large a charter as the wind,
> To blow on whom I please, for so fools have;
> And they that are most galled with my folly,
> They most must laugh. And why, sir, must they so?
> The why is plain as way to parish church:
> He that a fool doth very wisely hit
> Doth very foolishly, although he smart,
> Not to seem senseless of the bob; if not,
> The wiseman's folly is anatomiz'd
> Even by the squand'ring glances of the fool.
> Invest me in my motley; give me leave
> To speak my mind, and I will through and through
> Cleanse the foul body of th' infected world,
> If they will patiently receive my medicine.
> (*As You Like It*, II. vii. 36-61)

The knowledge and the purpose are implicit here. The Fool's knowledge is of the folly of mankind, the fool's ability is to exorcize that folly. It is as if Jaques is saying that the exercise of the kind of wise folly possessed by the true Fool can purge mankind's so-called wise men of their own kind of folly. It is Jaques' ambition to ascend to this status of high therapy.

Why should Jaques be so adamant that the Fool's brand of folly should be so efficacious? Why should wit burn out rage, why should fooling cauterize pretensions, why should jibes and saws in the mouth of a true Fool be capable of making the mentally blind see and those near to madness come nearer to sanity? Why should the folly of Lear's Fool be so much more a kind of wisdom than any words uttered by anyone else in the infected world of the King? We know his words are more wise because our instincts tell us so as we listen to them—but why?

Simply because no true Fool is completely committed to the world within which the actions of the plays are placed. The Fool, in a way, is an ideal 'us'; he represents that part of us which does not identify with characters or situations, but sits back and is able to see behind illusion. But it is the uncommitted part of us in an idealized form which the Fool represents. His is the wisdom we would like to have, and if we had it not only would we be able to deal clearly with the 'truth' that lies behind the actions of a great play but, perhaps more pertinently, we would be able to deal more certainly with our own real infected world, and purge ourselves of our own folly. It is often said that if you look in a glass you see a fool. What Shakespeare does is to make us look into the glass of the world of his play—but the Fool we see there wears not our motley in his brain. The Fool, then, is able to purge folly and be seen to do so because this is, ideally, what we would wish to be wise enough to do—'give *me* leave to prove a fool' is unconsciously echoed by every member of the audience.

The Fool is capable of this purging process also because his licence is always at hazard. Yet there is a paradox here. Although at hazard, he is still more free than anyone else to speak because he is relatively uncommitted to any close association with anything or anyone, as has been noted above. He is almost as free to speak about the world of the play as we are in the audience, but the best kind of critic, like the best kind of Fool, is always at hazard because both are more likely to speak a truth that no-one wishes to hear unless they speak it themselves.

VI

Yet a further question arises from this consideration of the wisdom and status of the Fool within the play. If he has these antecedents with the audience and this distance from the rest of the *dramatis personae*, what kind of dramatic figure is he? He simply refuses to be categorized as we can categorize the other characters in a Shakespeare play; and yet we know him to be based on reality.

The Fool, in effect, as he is developed in Shakespeare's plays—a brain-child shared, we have assumed, with Armin—is like any real actor; his professional function is not to be himself. Like any true actor, the Fool's job is to wear the mask of jester or folly. He is, in his function in the social environment of the play's world, a purveyor of illusion—yet we know that beneath whatever mask he is wearing something very far from illusion is being communicated to us. We are experiencing what seems to be the impossible process by which a dramatic character whose function in the very play itself is virtually that of shadow is, nevertheless, the repository of the most important truths that the play has to communicate; it is like that curious form of (to mutate the original meaning) negative capability by which an actor who, offstage, is completely negative, evanescent, lacking in personality can ascend into the highest embodiment of historic invention when he steps into the limelight on stage. As Willeford says 'the fool on stage strikes us as radiant with a life that transcends his stylized attributes and often inconsequential jokes'.

The Fool's sudden quips, one line jokes, odd staccato sentences, often hide or contain a significance beyond their apparent meaning, and their jingles, like nursery rhymes, reverberate in the head and heart:

The hedge-sparrow fed the cuckoo so long,
That it had its head bit off by its young.

There is an uncanny resemblance, although of course the form and usage is different, between the dramatic effect of the Fool's interpolations (for this is where the meaningful trivia often occur) and that employed by another poet of the theatre—Harold Pinter. Those famous pauses of his, sometimes sudden and unexpected, sometimes 'telegraphed', have an equivalent importance to the Fool's utterances. Like the words of the Fools, the pauses are often more important than what, verbally, lies on each side of them. In the case of the Fools what is entirely misunderstood or only partially understood by others is important; in Pinter's case, what is unsaid—significantly unsaid—between people is important. Somewhere, we may fancy, a Fool lurks inside a Pinter play giving silence a wise language; and, curiously, we may apprehend that inside a Fool's mouth, when he speaks, in Shakespeare, what only *he* really understands, there is an aspiration for silence.

> *Fool:* If a man's brains were in's heels, were't not in danger of kibes?
> *Lear:* Ay, boy.
> *Fool:* Then, I prithee, be merry; thy wit shall not go slipshod.
> *Lear:* Ha, ha, ha!
> *Fool:* Shalt see thy other daughter will use thee kindly; for though she's as like this as a crab's like an apple, yet I can tell what I can tell.
> *Lear:* What canst tell, boy?
> *Fool:* She will taste as like this as a crab does to a crab. Thou canst tell why one's nose stands i'th' middle on's face?
> *Lear:* No.
> *Fool:* Why to keep one's eyes of either side's nose, that what a man cannot smell out, he may spy into.
> *Lear:* I did her wrong.
> *Fool:* Canst tell how an oyster makes his shell?
> *Lear:* No.
> *Fool:* Nor I neither; but I can tell why a snail has a house.
> *Lear:* Why?
> *Fool:* Why, to put's head in; not to give it away to his daughters, and leave his horns without a case.
> *Lear:* I will forget my nature. So kind a father!—Be my horses ready?
> (*King Lear*, I. v. 7-32)

> *Mick:* I'm very impressed with what you've just said.
>   [Pause]
> Yes that's impressive, that is.
>   [Pause]
> I'm impressed, anyway.

Davies: You know what I'm talking about, then?

Mick: Yes, I know. I think we understand one another.

Davies: Uh? Well . . . I'll tell you . . . I'd . . . I'd like to think that.

You been playing me about, you know, I don't know why. I never done you no harm.

Mick: No, you know what it was? We just got off on the wrong foot. That's all it was.

Davies: Ay, we did.

Mick: Like a sandwich?

Davies: What?

Mick [taking a sandwich from his pocket]: Have one of these.

Davies: Don't you pull anything.

Mick: No, you're still not understanding me. I can't help being interested in any friend of my brother's. I mean, you're my brother's friend, aren't you?

Davies: Well, I . . . I wouldn't put it as far as that.

Mick: Don't you find him friendly, then?

Davies: Well, I wouldn't say we was all that friends. I mean, he done me no harm, but I wouldn't say he was any particular friend of mine. What's in that sandwich, then?

Mick: Cheese.

Davies: That'll do me.

Mick: Take one.

(*The Caretaker,* II. ii.)

The pauses (implied or stated) in each case, and the quips or terse comments, accrete, because of the way they are placed, and where they are placed in the text: a body of knowledge about matters behind the apparent, behind what is being actually said. But, even more, what gives the resemblance a particular *frisson* is the atmospheric quality and effect of the experts. What lies in both dramatists, whether it be comment, judgement, irony, satire, grief, seems to come from light years away from the immediate environment of the play. Deep inside Pinter's pauses and his carefully architected dialogue, there is a primitive, elemental source whose nature is telling us something of what man really is and what his condition is. Deep inside the Fool's language and in Shakespeare's carefully modelled use of it, there seems to lie an area of comprehension of what man is that reaches back to a kind of beginning—a time before time:

> This prophecy Merlin shall make, for I live before his time.
>
> (*King Lear,* III. ii. 95)

The arrival of Armin gave Shakespeare the opportunity, which he took, of inserting into his plays an agency quite different from those other created characters of his plays written up to this time. We may say that, before 1599 and indeed basically, Shakespeare's normal method of characterization is realistic—that is, his characters have a high degree of fidelity to the actualities of real life. The Fools do not. They are, so to say, wild cards in the pack, errant strange jokers. They are neither realistic nor, indeed, may they confidently be asserted to be symbolic. William Willeford comments that 'The Fool is neither the player nor the audience, but both and something else', and he adds that 'The Fool is, in a unique way, both the actor and the thing he enacts.'[12]

One can sense how the critics and scholars strain as they try to come to terms with this figure. At the moment when it appears that one has grasped it, it slips away. At times the Fool seems to represent us, the audience—through his eyes and in his mouth we see and hear intimations of what might be beneath the play's obvious activities. At other times the Fool can be identified with the actor, any actor, who plays him (this is particularly true of Feste) and there is a wry poignancy in observing a superb purveyor of illusions (like Max Adrian) wandering through Illyria not, so to say, as a character but as his lonely vulnerable self.

Yet, in the long run, perhaps, in a certain sense, the Fool-figure is Shakespeare himself. The Fool was entertainer—so was Shakespeare. The Fool, as part of his professional function, lived in and helped to sustain a world of illusion—so did Shakespeare. The Fool used the mask of folly to hide his lonely apprehension of the truth behind illusion—Shakespeare, as dramatist, is the highest exemplar of the way in which the artist uses illusion to communicate reality.

The new element that entered into Shakespeare's plays with the coming of Armin was a full realization that the conventions of characterization and of drama itself are not final forms. Through Armin and the Fool he learned that character does not have to depend on that impersonative factor which ties it to the appearances of so-called real life, and that there is another country of drama in which the metaphorical and the allusive are as effective for the communication of character and meaning as what is actual and explicit.

Notes

[1] Enid Welsford, *The Fool: His Social and Literary History* (London, 1935).

[2] Robert Hillis Goldsmith, *Wise Fools in Shakespeare* (Michigan, 1955; Liverpool, 1958).

[3] William Willeford, *The Fool and His Sceptre* (London, 1969).

[4] Leslie Hotson, *Shakespeare's Motley* (London, 1952).

[5] *Works,* edited by A. B. Grosart (London, 1880).

[6] *Works,* edited by A. B. Grosart (London, 1880).

[7] *Ibid.*

[8] *Works,* edited by A. B. Grosart (London, 1880).

[9] *Ibid.*

[10] *Works,* edited by A. B. Grosart (London, 1880).

[11] Willeford, *op. cit.,* p. 74.

[12] Willeford, *op. cit.,* p. 49.

FOOLS IN THE COMEDIES

John A. Hart (essay date 1966)

SOURCE: "Foolery Shines Everywhere: The Fool's Function in the Romantic Comedies," in *"Starre of Poets": Discussions of Shakespeare,* Carnegie Institute of Technology, 1966, pp. 31-48.

[*In the essay that follows, Hart probes Shakespeare's presentation of fools in his romantic comedies from* A Midsummer Night's Dream *to* Twelfth Night.]

The Romantic Comedies are carefully structured work, for all their appearance of casual gaiety. I would like to demonstrate the case for this by examining the way in which Shakespeare develops his clowns in five plays, giving emphasis not so much to the characters themselves as to their function. Though such special attention inevitably neglects many other important elements, I hope that the limited nature of the study will be seen as a partial way toward understanding the dramatic structure of the Romantic Comedies. The comedies under consideration are: *A Midsummer-Night's Dream, The Merchant of Venice, Much Ado About Nothing, As You Like It,* and *Twelfth Night.*

The earliest of the five I have chosen is clearly a balanced and carefully structured play. Duke Theseus rules in Athens by law and reason and, when necessary, by conquest; Oberon, king of the night creatures, rules in the wood outside Athens by imagination and impulse and magic. Their paths never cross; their ways of life, potentially so threatening to one another, never impinge on one another. Theseus enters the wood, but only in the morning after Oberon has withdrawn; Oberon enters Theseus' palace, but only after the Duke has retired for the night. Two other sets of characters, however, find themselves subjects of both rulers: the artisans (the clowns, in more general terms) and the young lovers. Both of these groups begin their adventures in Athens under the authority of the Duke, go into the wood where they are dominated by Oberon, and come back to Theseus' court at the end of the play. The lovers leave Athens either to escape Theseus' laws or to pursue persons they love. The artisans go to the wood not to run away from the Duke's world and its laws, but to rehearse a play which will, they hope, be offered at the Duke's wedding celebration. I call attention to the motives for leaving Theseus' world because I think they are significant: the lovers are rejecting the Duke; the artisans are honoring him.

The artisans are in this sense Theseus' loyal subjects. Their intention is to please the Duke and to profit themselves. What makes them funny and dear to us is their honesty, their enthusiasm, their determination, combined with the most abysmal ignorance of play presentation and of the courtiers for whom they plan to put on their play. The mighty lords and ladies of the court are mysterious, unpredictable presences who must be approached with caution and with fear. The actors must name themselves so there will be no misunderstanding and a prologue must describe the action so that when Pyramus draws his sword to kill himself the audience will know it is only make-believe; and most especially Snug the Joiner, who plays the Lion, must name his name, and half his face must be seen through the Lion's neck, and he must roar sweetly, for "if you should fright the ladies out of their wits, they would have no more discretion but to hang us" (I, ii, 81-83). The management of stage problems is equally innocent: Moonshine must be brought on in person with his lantern and bush of thorns and "Some man or other must present Wall; and let him have some plaster, or some loam, or some rough-cast about him, to signify wall; or let him hold his fingers thus, and through that cranny shall Pyramus and Thisby whisper" (III, i, 69-73). Thus we see in the clowns the common sense, the reasonableness of Theseus carried to absurd literal-mindedness, with imagination entirely eliminated and with tragedy reduced to tears of laughter.

But the greatest triumph of their ignorance may be seen in their admiration for Bottom the Weaver, whose enthusiasm and accomplishments dazzle his fellows, and without whom they are sure the play could not go on: "If he come not, then the play is marr'd. . . . he hath simply the best wit of any handicraft man in Athens" (IV, ii, 5, 9-10). And indeed, Bottom deserves *our* full admiration as well. He will play the lover as it has never been done before:

> That will ask some tears in the true performing of it. If I do it, let the audience look to their eyes. I will move storms, I will condole in some measure.
>
> (I, ii, 27-30)

Michael Blakemore as Snout, Julian Glover as Snug, Peter Woodthorpe as Flute, Donald Eccles as Starveling, Charles Laughton as Bottom, and Cyril Luckham as Quince in Act I, Scene ii of A Midsummer Night's Dream.

If given the chance, he would play the beloved too. But most of all the Lion's part strikes his fancy, either with a great roar "that I will do any man's heart good to hear me," or with a tiny roar to please the ladies: "I will aggravate my voice so that I will roar you as gently as any sucking dove; I will roar you an 'twere any nightingale" (I, ii, 72-73, 83-86).

His unawareness of others carries him triumphantly through the play. When he is given the ass's head by Puck, he will not let his new appearance and his friends' desertion frighten him:

> I see their knavery; this is to make an ass of me, to fright me, if they could. But I will not stir from this place, do what they can. I will walk up and down here, and I will sing, that they shall hear I am not afraid.
>
> (III, i, 123-127)

Bottom proves impervious to everything. Impervious to the ass's head—presumably he feels just as much at home with it as without it. Impervious to his new friends Titania and her night spirits who are ready to serve his every whim; his chief interests, however, are to be fed "a peck of provender" and to be left in quiet: "I have an exposition of sleep come upon me" (IV, i, 33, 41). Impervious too to the night's experiences:

> Methought I was,—and methought I had,—but man is but a patch'd fool, if he will offer to say what methought I had. The eye of man hath not heard, the ear of man hath not seen, man's hand is not able to taste, his tongue to conceive, nor his heart to report, what my dream was. I will get Peter Quince to write a ballad of this dream. It shall be called "Bottom's Dream," because it hath no bottom; and I will sing it in the latter end of a play, before the Duke.
>
> (IV, i, 213-222)

Impervious, finally, to the laughter and the satirical remarks of the courtiers as the clowns play their play.

Yet Bottom, totally unaware himself, most literal-minded extension of Theseus' world of reason, is yet the agent by which the night quarrel of Oberon and Titania is healed, his earthy stupidity and animal appearance revealing to Titania the mad folly of which that night world is capable. And Bottom and his fellows provide in their play of Pyramus and Thisbe a sobering commentary also on the whirlwind exchanges of the young lovers, for their story shows young love coming to disaster when it lacks approval of parents, which as we recall is the problem in the beginning of the play. Theseus, the reasonable man, must learn tolerance of love; this he does through the madcap lovers; Oberon and Titania, rulers of the world of impulse and imagination, must learn tolerance of reason; this they do, as I have suggested, through Bottom the Weaver. Indeed Bottom himself sounds the keynote of this theme when he says upon meeting Titania:

> . . . to say the truth, reason and love keep little company together now-a-days; the more the pity that some honest neighbours will not make them friends.

> (III, i, 146-149)

Thus, the dramatic function of Bottom and his fellows is clearly set forth. They are absurd extensions of Theseus' reasonableness; they are one of the specific agents along with the little Western flower for reconciling Oberon and Titania; they present a new perspective to the commitments to love expressed throughout by the young lovers. They are essential dramatic elements in the fundamental opposition of reason and love and, symbolically, they are among the "honest neighbours" who help make them friends.

In *The Merchant of Venice* the clown Launcelot Gobbo occupies no central position such as Bottom's. His part is relatively small, and his function seems limited first to delivering messages between the romantic young lovers Lorenzo and Jessica, second to suggesting the differences between Shylock's way of life and Bassanio's, and third, to lending gaiety to the Belmont scene during Portia's absence in Venice. Considered superficially, Launcelot's actions seem either insignificant or irrelevant buffoonery beside the romantic events in Belmont or the steadily growing tensions in Venice. Yet thematically Launcelot Gobbo stands for an attitude and behavior which helps in a major way to establish a contrast between Belmont and Venice. For two of the most romantic conditions of the Belmont world are: one, the complete intimacy between the Lady of Belmont and her companion Nerissa, so complete that Nerissa knows all Portia's secrets, so complete that her future happiness in marriage is bound up with her mistress's; and two, the total commitment of Portia to her dead father's request that she marry the man who chooses the proper casket. In humorous but real terms, Launcelot Gobbo stands in Venice for a denial of these same conditions. When we first meet him he is debating whether to honor his commitment to serve Shylock:

> Certainly my conscience will serve me to run from this Jew my master. The fiend is at mine elbow and tempts me. . . . Well, my conscience, hanging about the neck of my heart, says very wisely to me. . . . "Launcelot, budge not." "Budge," says the fiend. "Budge not," says my conscience. . . . The fiend gives the more friendly counsel. I will run, fiend; my heels are at your commandment.

> (II, ii, 1-3, 13-14, 18-19, 31-33)

Since Shylock makes it unnecessary for Gobbo to run away by releasing him from his servant's agreement into the hands of Bassanio, since, in other words, there is insufficient affection or need on the part of either servant or master, no harm arises from Gobbo's decision, but the relationship shows the primacy given material advantage over duty and love. Gobbo wants the full dinner and the rare liveries that Bassanio offers; Shylock although he is fond of the boy wants more output for his input:

> The patch is kind enough, but a huge feeder;
> Snail-slow in profit, and he sleeps by day
> More than the wild-cat. Drones hive not with me.

> (II, v, 46-48)

The relationship between Bassanio and Launcelot is no more personal. They meet only once, on which occasion Bassanio is amused by the clown and his old father, gives orders that his new servant be given "a livery More guarded than his fellows'" (II, ii, 163-164), and goes off on other business. In Venice there is no evidence of a relationship between master and servant such as that of Orlando and Adam in *As You Like It* in which protection and loyalty and service are ultimate considerations or such as the complete intimacy of Portia and Nerissa.

The relationship between father and child is also given dimension by Launcelot's behavior toward his old half-blind father. When Old Gobbo comes looking for his son, Launcelot first gives him confusing directions, then pretends that the youth has become a gentleman, then that he has died, and finally identifies himself and asks his father for his blessing but fools him still by pretending that the hair on the back of his head is his hairy chin. This instance is a comic anticipation of the more serious misunderstanding of Jessica and Shylock and lends generalizing force to the impression that family ties in Venice are either absent or extremely weak. Affection in Venice is expressed through friendship and romantic love but not family respect and loyalty.

These thematic functions are joined to an equally important thematic contrast between the worlds of Belmont and Venice. Briefly stated, Belmont relies on good will and an unspoken understanding of others' motives in official relationships. Thus Portia's agreement with her suitors is that she will be won by the man who chooses the proper casket. Their agreement with her is that they will never marry if they choose incorrectly. Both sides treat these words seriously and are prepared to honor what is after all only verbal commitment.

Venetians in their relations with outsiders, however, rely on the law and the contract to give assurance of intention. The single instance we find, it is true, is Shylock's bond made with Antonio. But that contract is a sign of the whole law of Venice, a phenomenon stated most clearly (but not for the only time) by Antonio himself:

> The Duke cannot deny the course of law;
> For the commodity that strangers have
> With us in Venice, if it be denied,
> Will much impeach the justice of the state,
> Since that the trade and profit of the city
> Consisteth of all nations.
>
> (III, iii, 26-31)

Launcelot Gobbo is a perfectly consistent comic extension of the risks incurred by words, spoken or written, in the play. He soliloquizes about whether to follow his conscience and serve Shylock or the fiend who urges him to run away; he misleads and deceives his father: he diverts the gift his father had intended for Shylock to his new master Bassanio. Later, in joking with Jessica he maintains that she is damned for being the Jew's daughter, or damned if she is not the Jew's daughter—"a kind of bastard hope" (III, v, 7); and finally he argues that Lorenzo is to be blamed for making her Christian, for "This making of Christians will raise the price of hogs" (III, v, 25-26). To Lorenzo's accusation that Launcelot has got the Moor with child, he replies with witty but irrelevant evasion. Lorenzo aptly identifies this tendency in Launcelot:

> Oh dear discretion, how his words are suited!
> The fool hath planted in his memory
> An army of good words; and I do know
> A many fools, that stand in better place,
> Garnish'd like him, that for a tricksy word
> Defy the matter.
>
> (III, v, 70-75)

And suddenly we see all the characters who fit the description: the Princes of Morocco and of Arragon, who are deceived by the tricksy word on the gold and silver caskets; Shylock, driven out of his humanity by a lifetime of loneliness and by the unexpected, final betrayal of his daughter, relying on the tricksy word of his bond for revenge; Portia garnish'd in her lawyer's disguise using the tricksy word to save Antonio and the state from that revenge. Clearly in a Venetian world where traditional human values have broken down, the word, the bond, the contract is no promise of humanity. What is needed is the reliance on inner worth asked for by Portia's father; the internal assurance of a Bassanio who is not to be deceived by words; the generous, human deed of a Portia. Words in themselves are without value, as Portia says in welcoming Antonio to Belmont:

> Sir, you are very welcome to our house.
> It must appear in other ways than words,
> Therefore I scant this breathing courtesy.
>
> (V, i, 139-141)

Launcelot lives in comic word games, and he provides through those games a light but consistent counterpoint to the serious activities of Venice which also hinge so heavily on the uses to which words are put. Launcelot serves in *The Merchant of Venice* not as agent of the plot but as comic and thematic counterpoint. Bottom, as I have tried to suggest, though unconscious himself of his contribution, is a positive force in *A Midsummer-Night's Dream;* Launcelot Gobbo, though he sees nothing beyond his own interests, is a symbol of the disruptive forces which bring *The Merchant of Venice* close to tragedy.

The unmatchable Dogberry of *Much Ado About Nothing* takes the best talents of both his predecessors and emerges as one of the most awesomely stupid figures in all literature. Bottom as a logician is a mere novice to him. For instance, as constable, his officious charge to his watch contains this sample of reasoning: "The most peaceable way for you, if you do take a thief, is to let him show himself what he is and steal out of your company" (III, iii, 60-63). But never did Launcelot Gobbo have more confidence in himself and in his own ability to outwit Shylock, to play tricks on his father, to jest with Lorenzo, than Dogberry does without any ability at all. When he and his side-kick Verges report to Leonato, Governor of Messina, their garbled introduction leads Leonato to say impatiently, "Neighbours, you are tedious." To which Dogberry:

> It pleases your worship to say so, but we are the poor Duke's officers; but truly, for mine own part, if I were as tedious as a king, I could find in my heart to bestow it all of your worship.
>
> (III, v, 20-25)

His condescension toward Leonato, consistent as it is throughout the play, is exceeded only by his patronising attitude toward his slightly less foolish neighbor Verges.

> A good old man, sir; he will be talking: as they say, When the age is in, the wit is out. . . . Well, God's a good man; an two men ride of a horse, one must ride behind.
>
> (III, v, 36-37, 39-40)

And Leonato says: "Indeed, neighbour, he comes too short of you." To which we have Dogberry's irrepressible reply, "Gifts that God gives" (III, v, 45-47).

Along with the gross stupidity and the grand conceit, there goes finally a great pride in his place and standing in the community. When the villainous Conrade, furious and frustrated at being apprehended and cross-examined by such dolts, cries out at Dogberry: "Away! you are an ass, you are an ass," the constable's immortal reply is:

> But, masters, remember that I am an ass; though it be not written down, yet forget not that I am an ass.... I am a wise fellow, and, which is more, an officer, and, which is more, a householder, and, which is more, as pretty a piece of flesh as any is in Messina, and one that knows the law, go to; and a rich fellow enough, go to; and a fellow that hath had losses, and one that hath two gowns and every thing handsome about him. Bring him away. O that I had been writ down an ass!
>
> (IV, ii, 75, 78-80, 82-90)

Yet, like Bottom and Launcelot, Dogberry makes his contribution to and his commentary on the action of the play.

He contributes to the action of the plot by obscuring the confession which would have saved Hero the pain of being accused publicly by Claudio. Later he conducts the "examination" in which the treachery of Borachio and Conrade is revealed to the transcribing Sexton, though Dogberry himself misinterprets all the actions taken. Finally, he brings the villains into the presence of Pedro and Claudio where Borachio openly confesses, a confession which includes a shrewd comparison between the obtuseness of Don Pedro and Claudio and the stupidity of Dogberry and his fellows: "What your wisdoms could not discover, these shallow fools have brought to light" (V, i, 238-240).

And indeed the comparison is apt. For Dogberry's very presence in the play acts as a devastating commentary on the world in which *Much Ado About Nothing* takes place and especially on the character of Don Pedro of Arragon, the victorious warrior to whom so much deference is paid. Dogberry's pride in place and his conceit and his ineptness are only a picture in little of the pride and conceit and hollowness of the mighty Prince, who prides himself on his generosity and perception and especially his wit when he no more than the pretentious constable can tell that he is being taken in. He and his young favorite Claudio allow the innocent Hero to be publicly slandered and disgraced and indeed to die (at least as far as it is reported to them) without an indication of remorse, a cessation of witty remarks, a change or even a sign of a change of heart. By comparison with Pedro, Dogberry looks worthwhile, lovable, even perceptive.

In their one confrontation in the play, we are reminded of the magnificent stupidity of the constable and the shallow nothingness of the prince. As Dogberry and his men come in with his prisoners Conrade and Borachio, Pedro stops them:

> Officers, what offence have these men done?
> DOG. Marry, sir, they have committed false report; moreover, they have spoken untruths; secondarily, they are slanders; sixth and lastly, they have belied a lady; thirdly, they have verified unjust things; and, to conclude, they are lying knaves.

Pedro's reply is:

> First, I ask thee what they have done; thirdly, I ask thee what's their offence; sixth and lastly, why they are committed; and, to conclude, what you lay to their charge.
>
> (V, i, 217-228)

The jest, so rich and appropriate for Dogberry to utter, dies on the lips of Pedro and becomes one more in a long series of affronts to our sensibilities. We look back with some regret to Duke Theseus and his tender concern and humanity for his simple-minded subjects when the courtiers debate whether to allow them to put on their play:

> ... never anything can be amiss,
> When simpleness and duty tender it. ...
> Our sport shall be to take what they mistake;
> And what poor duty cannot do, noble respect
> Takes it in might, not merit.
> (*A Midsummer-Night's Dream,*
> V, i, 82-83, 90-92)

Though the clowns make us laugh in each of these three plays, there is less to be cheerful about in values, in trustworthiness, as each of these worlds succeeds the other. Reason and imagination in *A Midsummer-Night's Dream* give way in *The Merchant of Venice* to a struggle between external show and the tricksy word on the one hand, and internal values and human deeds on the other, which with the help of garden and moonlight and music of the spheres and perceptive lovers turns out all right. But *Much Ado About Nothing* is a picture of a world where other types of external shows (the office of prince, the ceremony of a wedding) and other types of tricksy words (empty-hearted witticisms and eavesdropping scenes) completely dominate what is left of internal values and humane deeds. Beatrice alone can see what kind of men are in charge here:

> ... manhood is melted into courtesies, valour into compliment, and men are only turned into tongue, and trim ones too.
>
> (IV, i, 321-323)

Her forcefulness sways Benedick, but when the ruffled surface is smoothed over, even they, knowing better, defer to the *status quo*. When Beatrice protests mildly to Benedick: "There's not one wise man among twenty that will praise himself," Benedick enlightens her:

> An old, an old instance, Beatrice, that liv'd in the time of good neighbours. If a man do not erect in this age his own tomb ere he dies, he shall live no longer in monument than the bell rings and the widow weeps. . . . therefore is it most expedient for the wise, if Don Worm, his conscience, find no impediment to the contrary, to be the trumpet of his own virtues, as I am to myself.
>
> (V, ii, 75-82, 85-88)

In such a world Dogberry rightfully has office. Where clowns formerly were private citizens, or brash young servants on the make, now it is time, it is almost inevitable, that they speak with the voice of authority. Wisdom and conscience will no longer suit; stupidity alone will serve.

In *As You Like It* Shakespeare moves in another direction. First of all, an unliterary consideration but one of great importance to Shakespeare: the actors had changed. Kempe, master of buffoonery, of the broad gesture, of the pratfall and the raucous laugh, was gone; and his place was taken by Robert Armin, a highly skilled dancer and singer, a subtle comedian, and a well-known wit in his own right. Touchstone in *As You Like It* and Feste in *Twelfth Night* are fools by title and profession rather than by desert.

Second, and more important for our purposes, Shakespeare seemed to be glancing back at the Belmont which had triumphed in *The Merchant of Venice,* and presenting some second thoughts about it. For the Forest of Arden like Belmont is certainly a world removed from time and place and specific actions and tensions. There is no clock in the forest; it is winter and spring together. Its place is one of all trees, of all types of animal creatures, of bleak air and hot sun, of love's idleness and philosophical speculation, of hunting and love songs. Though Belmont is a garden world, a projection of Portia's orderly and luminous and beautiful personality, and the Forest of Arden is an image of Nature beyond and above any single figure in the play, both are ideal worlds to be aspired to but never achieved. Yet the point of *As You Like It,* it seems to me, is not that the Forest world cannot be achieved but that it would not be a good thing if it were. For those who are out of touch with time and place, for him "Who doth ambition shun, And loves to live i' th' sun" (II, v, 40-41), the Forest is eminently suitable. Corin the shepherd in this world is a true laborer: "I earn that I eat, get that I wear, owe no man hate, envy no man's happiness, glad of other men's good, content with my harm" (III, ii, 77-80); Silvius, the lover, in this world is a true lover:

> If thou rememb'rest not the slightest folly
> That ever love did make thee run into,
> Thou hast not lov'd;
> Or if thou hast not sat as I do now,
> Wearing thy hearer in thy mistress' praise,
> Thou hast not lov'd;
> Or if thou hast not broke from company
> Abruptly, as my passion now makes me,
> Thou hast not lov'd.
> O Phebe, Phebe, Phebe!
>
> (II,iv,34-43)

The melancholy Jaques in this world can moralize on the stricken deer deserted of the herd, and brag of how he could cleanse the foul body of the infected world, and anatomize the story of man.

But for some in the Forest this life will not suffice. Duke Senior cannot help regretting that he is not Duke, and is clearly willing to return to his home at the end of the play. Young Orlando can be content with banishment and idle wooing only for a time; then heroic action and family name and a real Rosalind to hold in his arms become more important than aimless drifting. And Rosalind too, though her charming deception as Ganymede fills us with wonder and delight, cannot escape for long some thoughts for her father and some for her child's father, dwelling by implication on the values of family relationship, the importance of position, and the rightfulness of possession, which are reasserted in this play. And Touchstone, too, to come to my point, belongs to this group whose essential happiness must lie outside the Forest.

The function of the clown is neither agent (as in *A Midsummer-Night's Dream*) nor comic dimension of limitations in more major characters (as in *The Merchant of Venice* and *Much Ado About Nothing*) but instead a perceptive attitude toward one set of characters in this play—the Forest "natives"—and indeed toward the prevailing views of the Forest world.

For he is a fool who has lost his job, who has followed his mistress to the Forest where he idles with the rest until Duke Senior restores him to his position. Early in the play, Touchstone tells Rosalind and Celia how a knight may swear by his honor to a lie and yet not be forsworn; that is, if he has no honor. But when he hints that the knight he means is a friend of the usurping Duke Frederick, Celia cuts him off: "You'll be whipp'd . . . one of these days." To which he replies: "The more pity, that fools may not speak wisely what wise men do foolishly" (I, ii, 90-93). The professional fool's job is to utter truth as wisely and as wittily as he can. Being a "motley fool", Jaques' term (II, vii, 17), "an allow'd fool", as Olivia is to say of Feste (*Twelfth Night,* I,v, 101), he can say what he likes to his master without fear of reprisal from any but that master, in this case Duke Frederick. But Frederick will no longer hear truth and Touchstone goes into banishment as readily as do Rosalind and Celia and Orlando. In the Forest he is still without a job. He whiles away his time being "deep-contemplative" (again Jaques' term) (II, vii, 31):

> "Thus we may see . . . how the world wags.
> 'Tis but an hour ago since it was nine;
> And after one hour more 'twill be eleven;
> And so, from hour to hour, we ripe and ripe,
> And then, from hour to hour, we rot and rot;
> And thereby hangs a tale."
>
> (II, vii, 23-28)

Or patronising Corin the shepherd and forest life in general:

> In respect that it is solitary, I like it very well; but in respect that it is private, it is a very vile life. Now, in respect it is in the fields, it pleaseth me well; but in respect it is not in the court, it is tedious.
>
> (III, ii, 15-19)

Or wooing the ill-favored Audrey or pretending marriage to her, or mocking her bumpkin suitor William. In these confrontations he is acting different roles: philosopher, courtier, lover, rival suitor. These are all games, all out of the fool's part. It is only when he comes into Duke Senior's presence that he finds himself again. When Jaques introduces him as one who has been a courtier, he reaffirms his fool-ship with relish:

> If any man doubt that, [that is, that he has been a courtier] let him put me to my purgation. I have trod a measure; I have flatt'red a lady; I have been politic with my friend, smooth with mine enemy; I have undone three tailors; I have had four quarrels, and like to have fought one.
>
> (V, iv, 44-49)

And the Duke encourages him. "I like him very well. . . . he is very swift and sententious. . . . He uses his folly like a stalking-horse and under the presentation of that he shoots his wit" (V, iv, 55, 65-66, 111-112).

So Touchstone, whose profession is Fool, helps like many others to assert the importance of place and time, of rank and standing without which flesh and blood cannot exist. Arden must be rejected; it is not an acceptable alternative to the failures of Venice or Messina. Bottom who lacks the wit to learn a new profession, and Launcelot Gobbo who does not have the will to practise the profession he has, are not any more deprived than Touchstone who, having wit and will, has not the opportunity to practices it seriously, either in Frederick's court or in the Forest of Arden.

His case is appropriately compared to Feste's in *Twelfth Night*. Feste is also a professional fool, also brilliant, also "allow'd." His function, like Touchstone's, is to perceive and comment on the world in which he lives. But whereas Touchstone is witty in behalf of his profession and is lost without it, Feste is witty in behalf of himself. He will sing for Orsino, he will be witty for Olivia, he will dance for Sir Toby and Sir Andrew, he will play a role to mock Malvolio.

But the motive is money, or some self-satisfaction. "I did impeticos thy gratillity" (II, iii, 27), he says, having received money from Sir Andrew; and when Orsino gives him gold, he pursues the matter: "But that it would be double-dealing, sir, I would you could make it another." And when the Duke gives him another, he continues: "Primo, secundo, tertio, is a good play; . . . the third pays for all" (V, i, 32-33, 39-40). And he is not beyond personal revenge nor beyond bragging of his wit; as he says to Malvolio:

> I was one, sir, in this interlude; one Sir Topas, sir; but that's all one. . . . But do you remember? "Madam, why laugh you at such a barren rascal? An you smile not, he's gagg'd." And thus the whirligig of time brings in his revenges.
>
> (V, i, 380-381, 382-385)

But if he is unlike Touchstone and will not follow his mistress "along o'er the wide world" (*As You Like It*, I, iii, 134) but is secretly scornful of them all, can we blame him? Orsino is hardly a practising duke, so much in love with Olivia is he. Yet not truly in love with her but with music and flowers and mooning and musing. Feste signs to him of love:

> Come away, come away, death,
>   And in sad cypress let me be laid.
> Fly away, fly away, breath;
>   I am slain by a fair cruel maid.
>
> (II, iv, 52-55)

Orsino calls it an "old and plain" song (II, iv, 44), one that "dallies with the innocence of love" (II, iv, 48); but the mockery in it is clear. Rosalind has already in *As You Like It* pronounced that "Men have died from time to time and worms have eaten them, but not for love" (IV, i, 107-108). No more does Orsino die from love; he simply gets a new girl when his "fair cruel maid" marries another.

And what shall Feste admire in Olivia? Though their affection for one another is clear, he mocks her extravagant mourning:

> CLO. Good madonna, why mournest thou?
> OLI. Good fool, for my brother's death.
> CLO. I think his soul is in hell, madonna.
> OLI. I know his soul is in heaven, fool.

CLO. The more fool, madonna, to mourn for
your brother's soul being in heaven. Take
away the fool, gentlemen.

(I, v, 72-78)

Surely he has no respect for Toby and Andrew. He sings to and milks those continuous toss-pots and speaks to them in their own tongue:

Present mirth hath present laughter;
  What's to come is still unsure.

(II, iii, 49-50)

Even more surely he has none for Malvolio, who has no sense of humor, is full of his own importance, and is an enemy to everything Feste stands for. The prisonhouse for him and darkness for him and mockery for him.

Only with Viola does Feste approach serious confrontation. She is deserving, alone and lonely, in her page's disguise, desperately in love with Orsino, who is sending her to woo Olivia, who is in turn desperately in love with Viola. But he has no chance to read correctly through the disguise and his talk though serious occasionally is riddling and jesting:

To see this age! A sentence is but a chev'ril
  glove to a good wit.
How quickly the wrong side may be turn'd
  outward!

(III, i, 12-15)

When Viola says to him, "I warrant thou art a merry fellow and car'st for nothing," he replies, "Not so, sir, I do care for something; but in my conscience, sir, I do not care for you" (III, i, 30-33). And adds later, to give a hint of what he cares for: "Foolery, sir, does walk about the orb like the sun, it shines everywhere" (III, i, 43-44). Foolery everywhere: a lovesick Orsino, a distracted Olivia, a sottish Toby, a blown-up Malvolio, a pretty young messenger who looks like a girl. Whatever the values of a Theseus, of a Portia, of a Beatrice, of an Orlando and Rosalind, they have emptied out of Illyria. The world has no substance; the clown has no master; he has no place, for everyone would take the position from him. Foolery shines everywhere. He has moved in this play away from the function of the other clowns; Bottom is agent of the plot; Launcelot Gobbo and Dogberry set off in comic dimension the limitations of their worlds; Touchstone with wit and perception casts light on one aspect of his world, the Forest; now Feste stands as the sane, perceptive mind in a world where laughter still rings but where healthy minds and hearts are hard to discover.

So at the end of *Twelfth Night* as the actors retire from the great aproned stage, one of them, our Fool, steps forward and sings to the still lingering audience:

When that I was and a little tiny boy,
  With hey, ho, the wind and the rain,
A foolish thing was but a toy,
  For the rain it raineth every day.
But when I came to man's estate . . .
'Gainst knaves and thieves men shut their
  gate. . . .

But when I came alas! to wive . . .
By swaggering could I never thrive. . . .

But when I came unto my beds . . .
With toss-pots still had drunken heads. . . .

A great while ago the world begun
  With hey, ho, the wind and the rain,
But that's all one, our play is done,
  And we'll strive to please you every day.

(V, i, 398-402, 404, 406, 408,
410, 412, 414-417)

It is a jesting and riddling song. But its general meaning is not hard to fathom. And its relevance is to the shadows of the *Twelfth Night* world he has just walked out of. Foolish things were but toys to the child; but now equally foolish things—possession, for instance, or love, or pleasure—are taken seriously by men who should know better. And its relevance is to the shadows in the audience in front of him. ". . . we'll strive to please you every day," he says, giving to himself and his fellow players the function and role Feste had maintained throughout the play. The foolishness of Orsino, Olivia, Toby, Malvolio is given, just for a moment, just with the softest glance imaginable, a wider, more universal application. Foolery, indeed, shines everywhere.

The clowns have moved closer to center stage as the romantic comedies have developed, until at this moment Feste sounds the death knell of the gaiety and romantic, happy love relationships. We pass from here to the cynicism of *Troilus and Cressida,* the corruption of *Measure for Measure,* the obsession with sex and death in *Hamlet,* the convulsive emotions of *Othello,* straight on to the inevitable, pitiful shaking reprise of the Fool standing beside his tottering master Lear out on the heath, amid sheets of fire and bursts of horrid thunder:

"He that has and a little tiny wit,—
  With heigh-ho, the wind and the rain,—
Must make content with his fortunes fit,
  For the rain it raineth every day."

(*King Lear,* III, ii, 74-77)

So the pageant of the romantic comedies is done. The early clowns, those innocent fun-makers who followed whither their masters and fortune directed, were, as the plays went on, either placed above their station like Dogberry or removed from their position like Touchstone, or left like Feste, with the knowing charm and the calculating brilliant wit and nothing difficult or worth achieving in man's estate. With *Twelfth Night* the romantic comedies come to an end. That particular form as form is now used up. The man who so triumphantly mastered that form must now in 1601, halfway through his career, abandon it utterly and strike out in new directions to present new and more complicated thoughts and feelings in new and more complicated ways.

David Ellis (essay date 1989)

SOURCE: "Finding a Part for Parolles," in *Essays in Criticism*, Vol. XXXIX, No. 4, October, 1989, pp. 289-304.

[*In the following essay, Ellis marks Parolles' progress from knave to fool in Shakespeare's* All's Well That Ends Well.]

Shakespeare's plays often include characters ready to save us the bother of seeing for ourselves. Generally speaking, the higher their social status, the more chance they have of being listened to. Maria's character-sketch of Malvolio in Act II, Scene iii of *Twelfth Night* would not have enjoyed so much success if her mistress hadn't already pronounced him 'sick of self-love'. When in Act III, Scene ii of *All's Well That Ends Well* the two French lords deliver Bertram's unpleasant letters to Rossillion, the Countess asks who is with him in Florence and, on hearing that it is Parolles, complains, 'A very tainted fellow, and full of wickedness; / My son corrupts a well-derived nature / With his inducement'. This interpretation receives some support from the Florentine ladies watching the soldiers go by in Act III, Scene v. Diana remarks that it is a pity such a good-looking young man as Bertram is not honest and adds, 'Yond's that same knave / That leads him to these places. Were I his lady / I would poison that vile rascal'. The context makes clear that she is shifting to Parolles some of the blame for Bertram's 'dishonesty' in paying court to her when he is already married. But much weightier confirmation of the Countess's belief that Bertram has been led astray comes from Lafew. With the war in Tuscany over and Helena supposed dead, Act IV, Scene v opens in Rossillion as Lafew is saying,

> No, no, no, your son was misled with a snipp'd-taffeta fellow there, whose villainous saffron would have made all the unbak'd and doughy youth of a nation in his colour. Your daughter-in-law had been alive at this hour, and your son here at home, more advanc'd by the king than by that red-tail'd humble-bee I speak of.

The notion of Parolles as a successful corrupter of youth has received wide critical approval despite the obvious vested interest of those figures in *All's Well* who propound it (Bertram's mother, a young girl physically attracted to him and an old friend of the family). One reason is that critics, unlike ordinary playgoers, have recognised in Parolles vestiges of the medieval Vice. A similar recognition, allied to a similar inclination to trust 'the quality', leads several of them to believe those at Henry IV's court who say that Hal has been corrupted by Falstaff. The interpretation is no more satisfactory in one case than it is in the other, but for different reasons. There is never a moment in the Henry IV plays when an audience feels that Hal is in any genuine danger from Falstaff. *All's Well* begins with a few half-hearted indications that we shall be shown a well-bred young man tempted from the straight and narrow by a flashy companion; but it quickly becomes the tale of a headstrong youth with all the natural gifts for going to the bad on his own.

Joseph Price claims that Parolles 'prompts the plan that leads to his young master's flight' and the editor of the Arden edition goes further when he says that Parolles 'ships (Bertram) off to the war'.[1] They can only refer to the one occasion in the play on which Parolles appears to initiate rather than merely encourage wrong-doing. This is in Act II, Scene i when Bertram is complaining of the King's refusal to allow him to go to the Tuscan wars and Parolles says, 'And thy mind stand to't, boy, steal away bravely'. Urging a fiery young man to defy authority is perhaps wrong but it is hardly criminal, and any discredit which attaches to the gesture is lessened by the support Parolles receives from the two French Lords. After Bertram has decided that he will indeed steal away, the first of the Lords says, 'There's honour in the theft'; and when Parolles interjects, 'Commit it, count', the second adds, 'I am your accessory'. If Parolles is a wicked corrupter, so too are they.

When the two Lords have left the stage, Parolles makes an absurdly affected speech in which he tells Bertram that he ought to have used 'a more spacious ceremony to the noble lords' and urges him to go after them to 'take a more dilated farewell' (II.i. 49 - 56). Bertram's 'And I will do so' is the last serious indication we have of his being under Parolles's influence. There is no suspicion that he is acting on any but his own headstrong authority when in Act II, Scene iii he responds with indignant, snobbish dismay to the idea of marrying Helena ('A poor physician's daughter my wife! Disdain / Rather corrupt me ever!'); and after the King has forced him to accept her, he takes no-one's advice before flatly announcing his intentions, 'I'll to the Tuscan wars and never bed her'. Parolles is enthusiastic in Bertram's support and clearly not averse to being the young Count's instrument in fobbing Helena off; but he is a means of bad behaviour not its cause. This remains true for the rest of the play and, as R. L. Smallwood has pointed out, that 'Parolles is not the wicked angel responsible for leading Bertram astray is vividly shown in the final scene where, long after he has been made to see his companion for what he is, Bertram goes on to show himself independently capable of his most objectionable behaviour, in that long demonstration of weakness, cowardice, and lying'.[2] The demonstration Smallwood refers to also militates against efforts to represent the exposure of Parolles as a necessary stage in Bertram's moral regeneration. 'The two scenes which conclude Act III', writes Joseph Price, 'prepare for the expulsion of Parolles's influence and the cure of Bertram' and he goes on to claim that, 'when Bertram realizes the folly of his model he will begin to understand his own faults'.[3] It is true that in Act IV, Scene iii the two French Lords succeed in convincing Bertram that Parolles is not the courageous captain he pretends to be; but the young Count is shown as far less disturbed by this discovery than by the realization (via the letter to Diana discovered in Parolles's pocket) that his messenger in his own double-dealings with women can't be trusted. His indignation reaches its height when he learns that Parolles has not only made a feeble effort to seduce Diana on his own behalf ('Men are to mell with, boys are not to kiss'), but also had the audacity to tell her that a man like Bertram tells lies and doesn't keep his promises.

The failure of Shakespeare's text to support the readings which the Countess, Diana and Lafew try to impose upon it has clearly led to strange goings-on in the theatre, some of which must be reflected in J. L. Styan's relatively recent commentary on Act II, Scene iv of *All's Well* in the 'Shakespeare in Performance' series. This is the scene in which Parolles comes to tell Helena that Bertram will be leaving Paris before consummating his marriage. According to Styan, Parolles 'takes his time before he breaks the news that Bertram is leaving (Helena), for us an intolerable delay'; he 'relishes his secret', 'teases Helena with the unaccustomed colourfulness of his notion that this obstacle in the way of her wedded love will make fulfilment all the sweeter when it comes', and ends the scene 'beside himself with triumph'.[4] Although they purport to be a statement of the theme on which variations could be played, these comments on Act II, Scene iv sound much more like the description of a specific performance. But if Parolles does not immediately deliver his message to Helena it is because he makes the mistake on his entrance of acknowledging the Clown, who happens to be present, 'Oh, my knave! How does my old lady?' Lavatch is never complimentary to anyone, but he is particularly scathing with Parolles, calling him a nothing, a knave and a fool in rapid succession. Of the 150 or so words in their exchange, Parolles only has 27. He is too patently the unwilling recipient of a stream of witty insults to be relishing any secret, and would clearly be only too glad to say what he has to say to Helena, if he could only get rid of the Clown.

When he is able to speak to her, his language is colourful; but it is difficult to make much of that in a figure who is continually shown priding himself on elaborate speech. There is no convincing evidence in the text that Parolles takes any *special* pleasure in doing dirty work which, as the following scene shows, Bertram is in any case always prepared to do for himself. Parolles has told Helena that her new husband wants her to take 'instant leave a' th' king' and in Act II, Scene v she comes to Bertram to report that she has done so. He assures her that his reasons for going away and not consummating the marriage are better than they seem, when they are in fact much worse (ll. 58-69); and after a series of painful exchanges meanly denies her a parting kiss. In productions from the 1950s which Styan describes, Parolles was made responsible for preventing a kiss which would otherwise have come about.[5] It is in the spirit of these productions, or of others like them, that Styan writes his commentary on Act II, Scene iv. To present Parolles as more enterprisingly and, above all, effectively wicked than any lines he is given suggest he should be, makes it easier to turn him into a scapegoat; and if directors often share the same interest as the Countess, Diana and Lafew in achieving that result it is because it lessens the unattractiveness of a Bertram to whom, as Dr. Johnson memorably complained, it is difficult to reconcile one's heart.[6]

Giving Parolles behaviour which exaggerates his effectiveness also has the advantages of making him seem more coherent. 'Character criticism' may be long out of fashion among academics but, in the theatre, actors and directors are still inclined to look for some centre around which they can organise the various manifestations of a Shakespearian role. To see Parolles as the corrupter of youth helps to impose order on what, in the first half of *All's Well,* is an unusually loose assemblage of comic types. As an addition to the faint indications of the corrupting Vice which he offers, Parolles is also—with varying but never complete conviction on his creator's part—the traditional boasting soldier, the parasite, the foppish would-be courtier, the traveller and, in the feature of his many-sidedness which arbitrarily determines his name, the man of many words. In other circumstances, this variety of constituents might have been a sign of satisfying complexity; but in *All's Well* it leaves an audience wondering what or who Parolles is supposed to be. Their puzzlement is only likely to be increased by the fact that no-one in *All's Well,* apart of course from Bertram, believes in any specific part he attempts to play. (So strikingly is this so that Bertram's failure to see through his companion comes to seem more and more of an obvious dramatic convenience.) Parolles moves forward via a series of mortifying encounters as first Helena, then Lavatch and Lafew successfully call his bluff and oblige him to fall back on lame expostulation or excuse. The ineffectuality of his efforts to impose upon the world, and his lack of success in trying to hold his own in any company other than Bertram's, make it impossible to credit him with the force to corrupt anybody, least of all a young nobleman capable of replying to his king as impudently as Bertram does in Act II, Scene iii (111 - 3).

Parolles has too many features for Helena's accusation of cowardice in Act I, Scene i (186-202) to fix him in the mind as the *miles gloriosus* and Lavatch's refusal to take him seriously as a gentleman (II.iv. 17-36) doesn't determine how he should be taken. In remarks which excite Parolles to unwise and untypical self-defence, Lafew casually assumes that Bertram must be his 'master' (II.iii. 84-230), but servant is too broad a category to be usefully defining. These bruising encounters are effective in demonstrating that Parolles is not what he pretends to be but they fail to make clear what he is. The illusion of what a Shakespearian character 'is' most frequently establishes itself through monologue or soliloquy. The various parts which Iago plays in *Othello*, for example, are put into perspective by the explanation of his intentions which he offers in private to the audience. It is not until Act IV, Scene i of *All's Well* that Parolles is found communing with himself and on that occasion the consequence is not the tardy discovery of some 'key' to his character but engaging confirmation of an audience's feeling that—*qua* Captain, in this instance—he is not much of an actor. 'They begin to smoke me, and disgraces have of late knock'd too often at my door' (27-8). With the First Lord and his associates listening in, Parolles curses his habit of talking himself into situations which he has no means of handling. Since Bertram's enterprise and his own general ineffectuality up to this point prevent Parolles from being perceived as a serious threat, it is hard not to feel some stirrings of sympathy for him in his dilemma: 'I must give myself some hurts, and say I got them in exploit; yet slight ones will not carry it. They will say, "Came you off with so little?" And great ones I dare not give' (37-40). This sympathy is important because of the fine balance Shakespeare achieves during the great scene (IV. iii) in which the blindfolded Parolles is interrogated in the presence of Bertram and the two Lords.

The comedy in Act IV, scene iii depends not only on the irrepressible fatuity of Parolles in a 'life-threatening' situation but also on the way the balance of power shifts towards him as the conditions of the joke oblige Bertram and the two Lords to stand by helpless whilst he insults them. As the scene progresses, a vital difference emerges, which is not merely comic, between the first Lord's amused tolerance of the outrageous lies Parolles tells about him and Bertram's anger at characterizations ('lascivious boy' etc.) which are broadly accurate. Like the great Boar's Head Tavern scene (II.iv) in *1 Henry IV*, Act IV, Scene iii of *All's Well* gets even better after the reader or spectator is persuaded it has reached its climax. The play is a long way from being Shakespeare's most successful work, but there are few *more* effective moments in his drama than when Parolles is 'unmuffled'. With a laughing audience on one side and the social superiors he has just been betraying and abusing on the other, no-one's situation could be more humiliating. His first reaction is to protest with some justice that anyone can be crushed with a plot. But after the officers have bid him their ironic farewells, and the interpreter has left him alone on the stage with the ominous, 'Fare ye well, sir. I am for France too; we shall speak of you there', what every reader or spectator of *All's Well* remembers is the first half of Parolles's full response to his plight,

> Yet am I thankful. If my heart were great
> 'Twould burst at this. Captain I'll be no
>   more,
> But I will eat and drink and sleep as soft
> As captain shall. Simply the thing I am
> Shall make me live.
>   (IV.iii. 319-323)

Every critic of the play refers to these famous lines, but there is considerable confusion and disagreement over what to make of them. This is partly because the most striking of them—'Simply the thing I am / Shall make me live'—depend for their full effect on everything that has gone before. But a further difficulty for many has been that the lines have to be reconciled with the strong moral disapproval of Parolles which has become part of the orthodox interpretation of this play, and which is usually sustained by adding to a sense of his egregious shortcomings much of the blame for Bertram's. How the reconciliation is effected can be traced back at least as far as H. B. Charlton who, in the tone of a superior officer criticising a disgraced subaltern for failing to blow his brains out, described Parolles's response to his final discomfiture as 'his ignominious acceptance of mere existence'.[7] The critical climate which this remark suggests was evident in Michael Hordern's Parolles at the Old Vic in 1953, or at least in Richard David's account of that performance.

> When Parolles is finally unblindfolded, and discovers his captors to be his own comrades, Hordern managed an immediate and breathtaking transition from farce to deadly earnest. At the discovery he closed his eyes and fell straight backward into the arms of his attendants; then, as with taunts they prepare to leave him, he slithered to the ground, becoming wizened and sly on the instant, and with 'simply the thing I am shall make me live' revealed an essential meanness not only in Parolles but in human nature as a whole.[8]

David's whole description is vivid enough for its essentials to have found their way into Robert Hapgood's

'The Life of Shame: Parolles and *All's Well*', a short piece, published in these pages in 1965, which usefully reminded its readers that Charlton had called Parolles, 'that shapeless lump of cloacine excrement'.[9] (At the height of his anger in Act IV, Scene iii, even Bertram could only manage, 'I could endure anything before but a cat, but now he's a cat to me').

At the beginning of Act IV, Scene iii the first Lord shakes his head over Bertram's conduct and complains, 'As we are ourselves, what things we are!'. His 'things' here are human beings who are spiritually degraded because they ignore the teachings of religion. It is unlikely that Parolles ever paid much attention to these teachings either, but it is hard to see why so many commentators have found his celebration of being a 'thing' memorable if the intended sense is the same as the first Lord's. Harder still to understand is how a good proportion of these commentators could find something exhilarating in the celebration if all it revealed was, 'an essential meanness not only in Parolles but in *human nature as a whole*'. Robert Hapgood was justified in refusing to believe that 'Shakespeare intended an effect simply of revulsion'. He attributes the positive way in which many people respond to Parolles's soliloquy to the character's comic vitality, describing as 'his most redeeming trait' 'a love of life so strong that it can make him welcome (all too easily, it's true) even the prospect of living safest in shame'. Like Falstaff, Parolles turns his back on the precept 'Death rather than dishonour' and celebrates not the meanness of human nature but its resilience and powerful instinct for survival—its 'all-surviving tensile-strength', as Hapgood puts it.[10]

His remarks are helpful but insufficiently specific—after all, many other comic figures, apart from Parolles, have a jack-in-the-box resistance to misfortune—and they don't do enough to counter Charlton's charge that Parolles's thankful acceptance of life, after being deprived of any respectable social identity, is 'ignominious'. The memorability of Parolles's soliloquy, and its exhilarating effect on some, cannot only be dependent on his delighted relief that all his desperate efforts to stay alive—'Let me live, sir, in a dungeon, i'th' stocks, or anywhere, so I may live' (IV.iii. 235-6)—have been successful. What they depend on more is implied in his witty recognition that escaping death would not have done him much good had he in fact been the great-hearted captain the joke was designed to prove he wasn't. 'If my heart were great / 'Twould burst at this'. One certainly responds to the instinct for survival in his words, but even more to the feeling of relief in having to throw off a social role which had become a burden. Being a captain was especially burdensome to Parolles because, as the audience recognized and he himself acknowledged in his first soliloquy, he was such a proor performer in the part; but the oppressiveness of a defined social position is something which everyone occasionally feels from captains to authors with bad reviews ('Author I'll be no more, / But I will eat and drink . . . etc.'). Shakespeare has already instructed us in these matters earlier in *All's Well*. The King of France has consulted all the best doctors as only Kings can and is so convinced he is dying that his first instinct is to refuse Helena's offer of a cure.

> I say we must not
> So stain our judgement or corrupt our hope,
> To prostitute our past-cure malady
> To empirics, or to dissever so
> Our great self and our credit, to esteem
> A senseless help, when help past sense we deem.
> (II.i. 118-123)

These lines are good enough to bring to mind the intolerable dilemma of someone in the last stages of a fatal illness who is trapped between 'What harm could it do?' on the one hand and 'Have I not the courage to face up to the truth?' on the other. The King believes that he owes it to himself as a rational creature to reject what would constitute—and what in fact turns out to be—'a miracle cure'. Impossible to disentangle in his lines (especially as they move from the first person singular to the first person plural) is what he expects from himself as the individual who happens to be King, and his awareness of the general responsibilities of his position; but his sense of the latter is plain enough in his reference to the dangers of separating his 'great self' from his 'credit', or reputation. What he might think of himself if he welcomed Helena's offer is inextricably bound up with his sense of what other people would think of a King who accepted 'A senseless help'. In his case, the oppressiveness of a defined social position comes near to having fatal effects and it is evident that, if he could have followed the example Parolles is later to give and said, 'King I'll be no more', his resistance to his good fortune would have disappeared more speedily.

Parolles offers a momentary glimpse of a world where people have to play, not Jaques's 'many parts', but no part at all. In the best Falstaffian tradition, he turns the tables on his recent captors, emerging triumphantly from his ordeal like a Brer Rabbit thrown into the briar patch of non-identity by those who failed to realise how far his previous experiences would incline him to welcome it as his natural habitat. He makes of necessity an exhilarating virtue as does also, one might reasonably say, the Shakespeare who, up until this point in *All's Well,* has given Parolles a number of different personae none of which has proved wholly satisfactory. Now he both explains and excuses the relative failure of Parolles as a 'character' by allowing the audience to share in a utopian escape from the necessity of having any character at all: 'Simply the thing I am / Shall make me live'. In general, Shakespeare is always inclined to be more interested in immediate dramatic effect than larger questions of consistency or coherence. It is as if he wrote his parts in the foreknowledge that there would one day be a Coleridge to lay the foundations of a method for filling in all gaps and explaining away all discrepancies. Here he can be taken as using Parolles to entertain very briefly the notion of a 'thingness' which would absolve the dramatist from the duty of giving his figures adequate social definition. There can of course be no such absolution just as, when 'dropping out' is always as firmly defining as social conformity, Parolles can have no realistic hope of living both off and free from society. Shakespeare is obliged to draw back from having a 'thing' on the stage and Parolles will have to re-integrate himself into social life. The two processes are simultaneous and have already begun in the second and less memorable half of Parolles's soliloquy.

> Who knows himself a braggart,
> Let him fear this; for it will come to pass
> That every braggart shall be found an ass.
> Rust, sword; cool, blushes; and Parolles live
> Safest in shame; being fool'd, by fool'ry thrive.
> There's place and means for every man alive.
> I'll after them.
>
> (IV.iii. 323-9)

The move here into a different and, for modern ears, more conventional idiom exemplifies the struggle between two different kinds of drama which goes on throughout *All's Well*. The conflict is easiest to locate in Helena and has given rise to much dispute as to whether the emphasis should fall on revelations of a delicately sensitive inner life (as in III.ii. 99-129, for example), or on the actions to which she is committed by Shakespeare's sources and which, when the point of view remains psychological, mark her out as a predatory schemer.[11] In Parolles's soliloquy the change of manner is evident in the appearance of couplets, but also in his reminder of one of the several stock types ('braggart') with which he has been loosely associated. Now all of these are no longer serviceable, either for himself or Shakespeare, there is a hint of what will replace them ('being fool'd, by fool'ry thrive'), but as yet no clear or obvious indication. His decision to follow his recent tormentors into France ('I'll after them') is nevertheless a plain enough sign that the release from association of any kind, which he has just been celebrating, is imaginary.

'Simply the thing I am / Shall make me live' may be a defiant assertion of freedom from social definition, but by the end of his soliloquy Parolles is already referring to the 'place' which exists for every man alive. It is significant that in his quest for a new 'place', and in Shakespeare's final efforts to place or characterise him, the first person Parolles should meet is Lavatch. In a play in which many figures are problematic, Lavatch is not the least puzzling. This is not because, like Parolles, the impression he initially makes is indeterminate. On the contrary, the dominant features of his composition are immediately apparent on his first entrance and only become more so with each subsequent appearance. The difficulty lies rather in trying to follow the by now well-established custom of thinking of him along with the other domestic fools Robert Armin is assumed to have played; Touchstone, Feste and the Fool in *King Lear*. When the Countess excuses Lavatch to Lafew by saying, 'My lord that's gone made himself much sport out of him' (IV.v. 61-2), she is paying a very considerable tribute to the sturdiness of her late husband's sense of humour. To an even greater extent than the other three Fools, Lavatch has his order's earthy cynicism, especially on sexual matters; and his Fool status is confirmed by the memories and threats of whipping in Act II, Scene ii. Several important similarities between the four figures can be established, but Lavatch is unlike the others in that at no point in *All's Well* does he offer the slightest hint of mental unbalance. Touchstone and Feste can lay claim to being the cleverest people in their respective plays: they are much more clearly than the Fool in *King Lear* 'artificial'. But neither of them abandons completely a protective colouring of madness without which their manner of talking to social superiors would become unacceptable. Lavatch is different in that he never appears to feel he needs folly as a stalking horse, and one consequence is that Lafew's question in Act IV, Scene v—'Whether dost thou profess thyself—a knave or a fool?'—becomes a highly pertinent enquiry. The knave/boy collocation found in *King Lear* is obviously irrelevant and the dialogue which follows Lafew's question—the one in which Lavatch expounds the bawdy implications of his claim to be a fool at a woman's service and a knave at a man's—makes it clear that the issue is not whether Lavatch is a domestic fool or an ordinary servant or menial. 'So you were a knave at (a man's) service indeed', says Lafew, after Lavatch has explained that he would give the man's wife his bauble 'to do her service'; and he has then to admit, 'I will subscribe for thee; thou art both knave and fool'.

In the official designations of *All's Well*, Lavatch is more Fool than knave and Parolles the opposite. Their second encounter (V.ii) temporarily justifies the old adage that fools and knaves divide the world. Lavatch is even more scathing to the ragged and dischevelled Parolles than he had been on their first meeting and Parolles is only saved from his scorn by the entry of Lafew. After first of all failing to recognize the former dandy, Lafew offers Parolles a symbolic handshake. Earlier in the play, he had asked Parolles to acknowledge that he had been detected as a fraud by shaking hands: 'So, my good window of lattice, fare thee well; thy casement I need not open, for I look through thee. Give me thy hand' (II.iii. 212-14). The offer had been indignantly rejected. There is now no reason for

Parolles not to acknowledge openly that all his disguises have been stripped away, but despite Lafew's 'though you are a fool and knave you shall eat', what if anything they will be replaced by is not yet clear. The process of clarification is interrupted by the entry of the King and the final scene of reconciliation between Bertram and Helena. Parolles's minor role in this includes humbly accepting the King's reference to Bertram as his 'master', and then talking himself of the tricks 'which gentlemen have' in a way which makes it obvious that he no longer aspires to be one of them (V.iii. 233-9). But it is only after Helena and Bertram have been finally brought together that his own fate is decided. 'Mine eyes smell onions; I shall weep anon,' says Lafew, and then to Parolles, 'Good Tom Drum, lend me a handkercher. So, I thank thee. Wait on me home, I'll make sport with thee. Let thy curtsies alone, they are scurvy ones' (314-318). That the Countess's husband enjoyed making sport with Lavatch strengthens the impression that Parolles is here being adopted as Lafew's household fool and confirms the appropriateness of his advice to himself in his great soliloquy: 'being fool'd, by fool'ry thrive'. Looking back over *All's Well* in the light of this conclusion, it becomes evident that Parolles has already shown several attributes of the Fool or Clown, the most easily identifiable being his opening discussion with Helena on virginity (I.i. 104-160). When this dialogue is compared with the one in Act I, Scene iii in which the Countess plays the straight-man for Lavatch and when the topic is also sexual (7-93), it is hard not to feel that, in comparison with the Countess, Lafew has arranged for himself the better or at least more comfortable deal. Now that there are two Fools, it is also hard not to conclude that the official account of who is more knave than fool will have to be reversed.

From experimenting with various roles—none of which, either singly or in combination, he is much good at—Parolles moves to an exhilarating shedding of all social categorization, and is then finally accounted for as a domestic fool. Like the recovery of Bertram, his reintegration into society is a sign of that 'tolerance' so often stressed in thematic accounts of *All's Well*: 'There's place and means for every man alive'. Yet the ending to his career is no more unambiguously happy than the one which in the final scene unites the two protagonists. The lesson it provides as to what it means to be social—the stress on our inevitable dependence on the social group—is sobering. Interiorized social norms are always more likely to govern our behaviour than the promptings of some putative essential self.

The progress of Parolles is also illustrative of a problem of casting which Shakespeare appears to be struggling with, or at least working on, throughout *All's Well*. In the first part of the play the figure is too unfixed and ineffectual to be capable of the serious knavery of corrupting Bertram, a task for which Shakespeare does not give him the necessary character. As he moves from one humiliating encounter to another, his efforts to find himself a place in a world of gentlemen are too unsuccessful to be seriously threatening. The decisive contribution to the problem of how Parolles should be regarded is probably made in Act IV, Scene iii by the First Lord. When the blindfolded Parolles first begins to talk about the First Lord and suggests he was whipped from Paris 'for getting the shrieve's fool with child, a dumb innocent that could not say him nay' (181-2), Bertram has to restrain his fellow officer from violent retaliation. But after Parolles has slipped into his comically abusive stride and made a long speech on the First Lord's 'honesty', the latter's response is, 'I begin to love him for this' (253). A few lines later the First Lord says of Parolles, 'He hath outvillain'd villainy so far that the rarity redeems him' but the truth is rather than his insults are so outrageously and ineptly wide of the mark that they are laughable. It is this ability to provoke laughter which, after Shakespeare's brief euphoric toying with a drama of 'things', marks Parolles out as a Fool or Clown.

In *As You Like It,* Jaques is 'ambitious for a motley coat' (II.vii. 43) and in *Twelfth Night* Malvolio is reduced to the status of a 'poor fool' (V.i. 368); but only at the end of *All's Well* is there a genuine doubling of the number of Fools.[12] In the traditional method for distinguishing one kind of fool from another, 'natural' refers to those who are mentally deranged and 'artificial' to those who only pretend to be. The distinction can also be extended to refer to Fools whose humour is either inadvertant or deliberate. Lavatch is very clearly 'artificial' in that he tells jokes and exercises full control over the comedy of the situations in which he is involved. Parolles has some control in his opening dialogue with Helena but, in general, he might well have said of his rival Lavatch's fooling what Sir Andrew Aguecheek says of Sir Toby's, 'Ay, he does well enough, if he be disposed, . . . but I do it more natural' (II.iii. 82-4). Perhaps the disapprovers of Parolles, and latter-day Johnsonians anxious for Shakespeare to demonstrate more clearly his antipathy to vice, can be comforted with the thought that his likely role in Lafew's household would be less to make his new master laugh than to be laughed at by him.

Notes

[1] Joseph G. Price, *The Unfortunate Comedy, A Study of 'All's Well That Ends Well' and its Critics* (Toronto, 1968), p. 143. My citations are all taken from the Arden edition of *All's Well* (1959), ed. G. K. Hunter. For the remark quoted here see p. xxxiii.

[2] R. G. Smallwood, 'The Design of *All's Well That Ends Well*' in *Aspects of Shakespeare's 'Problem Plays'. Articles reprinted from 'Shakespeare Survey'*, eds. Kenneth Muir and Stanley Wells (Cambridge, 1982), p.

30. Smallwood is in a minority of critics who are sceptical of Parolles's influence on Bertram yet shortly before the sentence I quote he refers to the two figures as 'the comic villain and his dupe' (p. 28). More unequivocal concordance with my own scepticism can be found in Russell Fraser's Introduction to the New Cambridge edition of *All's Well* (Cambridge, 1985), pp. 8 & 22.

[3] Price, pp. 162 & 165.

[4] J. L. Styan, *Shakespeare in Performance: 'All's Well That Ends Well'* (Manchester, 1984), pp. 69-70.

[5] Styan, p. 72.

[6] Arthur Sherbo (ed.), *Johnson on Shakespeare,* The Yale Edition of the Works of Samuel Johnson, vol. VII (New Haven and London, 1968), p. 404.

[7] H. B. Charlton, *Shakespearian Comedy* (1938), p. 262.

[8] *Shakespeare Survey,* vol. 8 (Cambridge, 1955), p. 135.

[9] Vol. XV, (1965), p. 274.

[10] ibid., pp. 269-274.

[11] Opposing views of Helena can be found in Ian Donaldson, 'All's Well That Ends Well: Shakespeare's Play of Endings', *E in C,* vol. 27 (1977), pp. 34-35 and Richard A. Levine, 'All's Well That Ends Well and "All seems Well" ', *Shakespeare Studies,* vol. XIII (1980), pp. 131-144.

[12] My references are to the Arden editions of *As You Like It* (ed. Agnes Latham) and *Twelfth Night* (eds. J. M. Lothian and T. W. Craik).

As David Wiles has shown in his *Shakespeare's Clown* (Cambridge, 1987) the words 'fool' and 'clown' could both in Shakespeare's time refer to a particular kind of comic actor. I have used a capital letter when I want this meaning to be predominant, but in plays where a Fool plays a fool any attempt to make it consistently exclusive is both difficult and a waste of useful ambiguities.

FOOLS IN THE TRAGEDIES

William Willeford (essay date 1969)

SOURCE: "The Tragic Dimension of Folly: *Hamlet*," in *The Fool and His Scepter: A Study in Clowns and Jesters and Their Audience,* Northwestern University Press, 1969, pp. 192-200.

[*Below, Willeford views the character of Hamlet as a tragic fool.*]

According to an anecdote, the cross-eyed Ben Turpin fell into his métier as a slapstick comedian in the silent films from the tragic heights of Hamlet, as he tried on the stage to play the role straight. Whether or not the story is true, the image of Turpin as Hamlet is horrible, funny, and somehow legitimate. Hamlet's "To be or not to be" soliloquy has been burlesqued by many comedians; if Turpin were to have done it as a gag, we might have seen Hamlet's consciousness, which Henry James called the widest in all of literature, reduced to the mindlessness of a frightened chicken and his traipsing about the stage sped up to become part of a frenzied chase.

The pathetic sublimity of Hamlet, like that of Romeo, invites the clown, the noble words and gestures that he apes suddenly seeming themselves clownish pretense. In openly or surreptitiously establishing his parity with the hero, the clown presents a vision of the clod that will survive all winters as the heroic consciousness rooted in the same soil will not. The clown assumes the heroic role in the service of folly; the parity between the clown and the hero is also a contrast that supplies the fool show with materials and energies.

The clown's attraction to the heroic role is partly based on the quality of greatness that the hero shares with the king; but in addition, the hero, freer to act than is the king, stationary at the center, provides a suitable alter ego for the clown in his mobility and his urge actively and concretely to explore the unknown. The image of Ben Turpin as Hamlet accommodates the clown to the role of the hero in an even more specific sense: the presence of the clown within the character of Hamlet is not only a general fact about the heroic nature but belongs to the uniqueness of his character and to the deepest truth of the over-all action of the piece.

Since the time of Dr. Johnson several writers have seen similarities of one kind or another between Hamlet and the fool. Coleridge remarked that in *Hamlet* the character of the fool is divided and dispersed throughout the play, an idea that has also been developed, among others, by Francis Fergusson, Geoffrey Bush, L. G. Salingar and Harry Levin, who have described the ways in which Hamlet for moments becomes a part-incarnation of the foolish presence that can be felt in the background of the action.[1] Bush writes: "There is no fool in *Hamlet;* Yorick [the jester of the late king, Hamlet's father] is dead; and it is Hamlet himself who . . . puts on an antic disposition. . . . With a 'crafty madness,' Hamlet 'keeps aloof.' Like the fool, he is both within and without his situation; it is not only his misfortune, but his tragic privilege, to stand at one remove from the world."[2] This description would fit Lear's Fool, the *punctum indifferens,* as Enid Welsford describes him, of the

Lear story. But the difference between Hamlet-as-jester and Lear's Fool parallels that between Hamlet the dispossessed young king (or king-to-be) and Lear the dispossessed old king. Hamlet is called upon to act, though he cannot find a metaphysical and moral basis for the action demanded of him; Lear (after his initial folly) is deprived of the basis he had for action. Thus, although Hamlet and Lear superficially share the fate of the dispossessed, there is an essential difference in the demands placed upon them by their dispossession.

Hamlet's dispossession has come through no fault of his own, but he is left with the imperative of an action that will affect the whole body politic. Lear is dispossessed partly through his own folly, though behind his treatment of his daughters and his division of the kingdom stands his senility as a natural fact; and the range of action that is left him is primarily personal, with little direct consequence in the affairs of state. Hamlet must search for a metaphysical and moral basis for his action, because that basis, as it is provided naturally in the primitive kingship, has failed and become the lie of the person of the king, Claudius, against his office. Hamlet must find his way from his own position, with its personal motivations, to one from which he can act for the general weal. Thus the purification of purpose he must undergo in a sense leads in an opposite direction from that of Lear—from the personal to the collective, rather than the reverse; and it is in this necessity that he adopts the ambiguous, helpful, and disruptive role of the fool.

The background against which Hamlet acts and clowns is the rottenness in the state of Denmark; more specifically, it is the corruption of the center, which is expressed (whether as cause or effect or both) in Claudius' killing of the rightful king and the "unseemly haste" with which Hamlet's mother entered into her union, in any case incestuous, with the usurper. What is at stake in the action is the kingdom itself; the concept of kingship that informs the play is alive with the mythical significance of the center with its ritual and magical overtones. Rosenkrantz' speech about "the cease of Majesty," for example, draws for its effect upon the primitive sense of the king as the embodiment of the cosmic center:

> It is a massy wheel,
> Fix'd on the summit of the highest mount,
> To whose huge spokes ten thousand lesser things
> Are mortis'd and adjoin'd; which when it falls,
> Each small annexment, petty consequence,
> Attends the boist'rous ruin. Never alone
> Did the king sigh, but with a general groan.
> (III. iii. 17-23)

As Fergusson writes (following Dover Wilson): "Hamlet has lost a throne, and he has lost thereby a social, publicly acceptable *persona*, a local habitation and a name. It is for this reason that he haunts the stage like the dispossessed of classical drama."[3] And this dispossession—quite apart from his melancholy and the other flaws critics have found in his character—maims his capacity for action, since in the archaic conception it is precisely the hero's relation to the throne that not only defines his actions but ultimately makes them possible. And the problem of the center upon which the movement of the play is based may be seen in part in the absence of the fool. Just as the kingdom lacks an adequate king, so it lacks anyone in whom folly assumes a redeeming form: the hero is not really abetted by his folly, and there is no helpful jester. The ambiguity in the person of the king is reflected in Hamlet's fluctuation between the possibilities of heroism and those of folly.

The action of the play, the killing of the false king, requires a hero; but the problem on which the action is based, the hidden malady of the state, is one with which the hero alone, without the blessing of his folly, cannot deal; a vicious circle ensues that draws Hamlet again and again into the "imposthume" that he should stand outside and lance as though it were a monster or human enemy outside the kingdom. The vicious circle comes from the fact that the integrity of the center needs to be restored, but the abscess at the center destroys the basis for the action needed. It is, of course, possible for a hero to set himself against a corrupt or failing monarch and to assume the throne himself: even the crime of regicide may be regarded as justifiable under certain circumstances, especially when there is confusion as to who is the rightful king. But for a hero legitimately to oppose the reigning king, he must have a clear and undivided allegiance to the ground of the kingdom, to the center prior to its embodiment in that king. Hamlet is caught in the uncertainties which permeate the whole kingdom, in which none of the main characters is sure of his relation to anyone else, as may be seen in the elaborate spying on one another that engages them. Moreover, Hamlet's allegiance is divided between his dead father and his living mother, who, he feels, might not be spared if he were to give his capacities for action free play. He must admonish himself:

> Let me be cruel, not unnatural:
> I will speak daggers to her, but use none;
> My tongue and soul in this be hypocrites.
> (III. ii. 413-15)

in the same moment in which he is fighting to overcome what he feels to be hypocrisy. And insofar as the Oedipus complex, following Ernest Jones's interpretation, is central to Hamlet's dilemma, he is in his personal feelings toward his mother caught in a variant of Claudius' incestuous relationship to her.

The whole kingdom needs to free itself of the murk and disease that envelops and covers the center and obscures the working of the cosmic principle; thus Hamlet must purify his motives in an affirmation of allegiance to the ground of the kingdom, the archaic level of the kingship that overrides considerations of personality, including that of the reigning king. The purgation of the kingdom is, as Fergusson demonstrates, to be achieved through what he calls the ritual and improvisational elements of the play. The ritual elements are in part formal actions, magical in intent, arising from the primitive basis of the kingship and affecting it in turn; they are like attempts at self-healing by a physical organism. He writes: "If one thinks over the succession of ritual scenes as they appear in the play, it is clear that they serve to focus attention on the Danish body politic and its hidden malady: they are ceremonious invocations of the well-being of society, and secular or religious devices for securing it."[4] The improvisational elements of the play consist most importantly of Hamlet's clowning and playing of the madman. By stepping outside the main course of the action, Hamlet taps the fool's ability to suspend and even dissolve personal feelings when they become too sticky: he gropes for the freedom found by the mourner who laughs at a funeral. The ritual and improvisational strands would ideally be united in the figure of the court jester; but the position of Yorick stands empty, except insofar as it is illegitimately filled by Hamlet—as does that of Yorick's royal master, except insofar as it is illegitimately filled by Claudius.

The role of the clown seems to Hamlet to provide him with the sought-for position of a *punctum indifferens* in the midst of the action, but the role is a trap from which he must fight to get out, though he fights in vain. The fool becomes the *punctum indifferens* through the renunciation of action; and to renounce action in face of the threat of raging chaos is to become a fool either in the sense of the failed hero or in that of Lear's jester. Lear can become interchangeable with his fool, because the fool in his incapacity for action and his humble and shrewd acceptance of that incapacity leads Lear toward the moral condition in which he may find whatever salvation is open to him, a state in which he must leave off posturing as the personal agent of a might he does not have. But for Hamlet the necessity is to become the personal agent of a power that he does not have but should have. It is the power of the hero only partly differentiated from the fool, a state in which the hero is open to the dispositions of unseen powers and to the unexpected possibilities in the present moment for action, in which he is free from the inertia of his personal feelings and deaf to the play of reason when it is not immediately relevant to the task at hand. As Hamlet assumes the role of the fool actor, he becomes dissociated from the kind of folly that would have furthered heroism. It is appropriate to the nature of Hamlet's dilemma that at the peripeteia of the action, the play within the play, he should retire to a position between the Danish audience and the players. It is appropriate because the crucial members of the audience are infected with the disease of the state and because the enacted killing of the king points both to the source of that disease in the past and to the task demanded of the hero in the future. If (from Hamlet's viewpoint) the essentials of the action can be reduced to drama, there is a chance that the real world, momentarily focused in the spectacle, will become irradiated with the relative clarity and consciousness of the playlet and that Hamlet will be jarred from his own dramatic role-playing to become an actor in the world.

Fergusson writes about the play within the play that it is

> a "ritual" in that it assembles the whole tribe for an act symbolic of their deepest welfare; it is false and ineffective, like the other public occasions, in that the Danes do not really understand or intend the enactment which they witness. It is, on the other hand, not a true ritual, but an improvisation—for here the role of Hamlet, as showman, as master of ceremonies, as clown, as night-club entertainer who lewdly jokes with the embarrassed patrons—Hamlet the ironist, in sharpest contact with the audience on-stage and audience off-stage, yet a bit outside the literal belief in the story: it is here that this aspect of Hamlet's role is clearest.[5]

Moreover, when the mousetrap springs, Hamlet, who has been the failed hero, emerges not as a hero but as a failed fool. And even if he is, as a result, moved to action, part of his energies must continue to leak into the role of the unsuccessful fool-as-mock-hero, to which he has unwittingly committed himself.

The play within the play is superficially like jokes that jesters have made about the weaknesses, vices, and even villainies of their masters, but those jokes could be permitted and laughed at because the king and the jester were each in his place according to a convention that supported, even while mocking, the king's pretense of power. That Hamlet in his complex reaction to the playlet is on the verge of laughter is in keeping with Freud's idea that a joke often contains some kind of illicit material (of a sexual or aggressive nature) and that the person telling the joke uses the reaction of the hearer as a justification for his reveling in that material.[6] But a good joke does provoke laughter. According to the plausible notion of Helmuth Plessner, laughter is an autonomous reaction to a situation to which there is no answer according to one's habitual ways of thought and feeling and which is at the same time unthreatening; Hamlet's play is threatening in the extreme. It is like a joke in which the malice of the teller toward the listener is splashed like acid, the grimacing teller caught without the jester's mask of innocence, inconsequence, and unrelatedness. It is also like a joke with an even more specifically sinister purpose, which the teller gratuitously and pointlessly reveals—as when one politician or businessman intends to cheat another, makes a joke about cheating him, and, instead of luring him into the belief that the possibility of his being cheated is only a joke, puts him into a panic. Like the joke in Freud's description of it, the play within the play can be seen as an attempt to objectify Hamlet's anxieties, to justify them, and at the same time to relieve them in a wish-fulfilling fantasy. If the point of such a loaded joke does not open into the impersonal freedom of folly and thus meet Plessner's criteria for what is laughable, the joke is no longer a joke but an act of aggression or of self-immolation or of both. Hamlet's entertainment is both; it goads the king, and its point spreads like poison, working from him to Gertrude to Polonius to Laertes to Ophelia. Hamlet's position at the edge of the stage is that of both the clown and the stage manager and master of dramatic illusion. Dramatic illusion, the clown's presence, and heroic purpose cancel one another out in the offense of a bad joke that makes the teller a marked man.

In Fergusson's summary, "The performance of Hamlet's play is both rite and entertainment, and shows the Prince as at once clown and ritual head of state."[7] But the reunion of the two separate figures of clown and ritual head of state in the larger pattern of the kingship is the culmination of a long process. In becoming the hero in a public sense, the hero divests himself of that folly until the moment of his full power, when at his accession that power is bound. Then his folly re-emerges embodied in the fool actor as jester, who will re-establish his connection to the foolish ground from which he has separated himself. Hamlet, wise much before his time in the way the old king should be and lacking both the king's position and a jester of his own, must stumble in and out of the folly which he tries simultaneously to divest himself of and to enact. His course from this moment leads as though inevitably to the scene in which, in Fergusson's words, "Hamlet jokes and moralizes with the Gravedigger and Horatio. He feels like the gag-man and royal victim in one."[8] The skull of Yorick, the late and rightful king's jester, is like a lodestone to which he is drawn throughout the action, while intending instead to earn his right to his father's throne. The death's-head and skeleton are traditional emblems of the fool in the sense that death makes a fool of life's joys and purposes, as may be seen in graphic representations by Dürer, Holbein, and others.[9] And even more in keeping with the fundamental action of the play, the hero-prince's familiarity with the cynical Gravedigger as they contemplate the skull of the jester is a final epiphany, outside the course of consequential events, of the disintegration of the social structure, the death of the body politic that now can only await renewal from without.

However, Yorick's skull is an emblem of Hamlet's folly in a more personal sense as well. James Kirsch is convincing in his suggestion that the death of Ophelia means symbolically the death of Hamlet's soul;[10] by the time Hamlet encounters the grave-digging clowns he is himself one of the living dead. Moreover, the fact that the skull is unearthed in the grave intended for her implies a relation between the jester and the girl as factors in Hamlet's fate. In this light the skull may be taken to represent a single ambiguous psychic content that has expressed itself in both Hamlet's clowning and Ophelia's madness. Through his clowning he has sought, as Yorick surely had before him, to sustain the value of his father's kingship and to accommodate it to the circumstances of the kingdom. But even if Hamlet could somehow have managed the illegitimate amalgamation of princely and foolish roles in which he was caught, his clowning would still have remained contaminated by the self-destructive actual madness of Ophelia, since he was bound to her by affective ties, and these, in turn, entailed projections of psychic determinants within himself.

The character of this amalgamation of roles, and its self-destructive motivation, may be seen in Hamlet's famous question, "To be, or not to be . . . ?" (III. i. 56). The ego has no right to ask such a question; asking it is a form of psychic self-mutilation—in psychoanalytic terms, of self-castration—the deliberate abandonment of any possible basis for action. If we draw ourselves up enough to reject Hamlet's pathos, we may see this question as an intellectual equivalent of a clown's attempt to take a step with one foot while standing on it with the other. Or we may treat Hamlet's pathos more respectfully by regarding the question as an intellectual equivalent of Ophelia's suicide. This crucial question of the dispossessed royal person will give way in *King Lear* to another: "Who is it that can tell me who I am?" (I. iv. 50). The Fool's answer there—"Lear's shadow" (l. 251)—means in part that *the jester,* facing death *with* his royal master, serving as *Psychopompos* or *Seelenführer,* as guide to the living soul, can tell him who he is. But here, in *Hamlet,* the dead jester seals the Prince's doom. Just as Hamlet has been unable to find his way through his personal entanglements to a living connection with the center, so he has failed to achieve a connection with folly as the play of life furthering heroic purpose. In Yorick's skull, joy is dead and laughter silenced. In Yorick's skull, too, the force is at last objectified that has blocked Hamlet from assuming his father's throne and marrying his destined bride. (This objectification takes place somewhat in the way that a feeling-toned unconscious complex of archetypal character is sometimes revealed in the course of psychotherapy.) Hamlet's encounter with the skull might thus have signaled a new and more adequate differentiation of his motives and purposes, if it were not too late. But death has already won—and death's accomplices and foes, the grave-digging clowns.

Notes

[1] Samuel Taylor Coleridge, in *Coleridge's Shakespearean Criticism,* ed. T. M. Raysor (Cambridge, Mass.:

Harvard University Press, 1931), II, 212; Francis Fergusson, *The Idea of a Theater* (Garden City, N.Y.: Doubleday Anchor, 1953); Geoffrey Bush, *Shakespeare and the Natural Condition* (Cambridge, Mass.: Harvard University Press, 1956); L. G. Salingar, "The Elizabethan Literary Renaissance," in Boris Ford (ed.), *The Age of Shakespeare* (Harmondsworth: Penguin Books, 1955), pp. 88-89; Harry Levin, *The Question of Hamlet* (New York: Oxford, 1959), pp. 121-28.

[2] Bush, *Shakespeare and the Natural Condition,* p. 100.

[3] *The Idea of a Theater,* p. 112.

[4] *Ibid.,* p. 125.

[5] *Ibid.,* p. 134.

[6] Sigmund Freud, "The Motives of Jokes—Jokes as a Social Process," in *Jokes and Their Relation to the Unconscious,* trans. James Strachey, *Complete Psychological Works* (London: Hogarth Press and the Institute of Psycho-Analysis, 1960), VIII, 140-58.

[7] *The Idea of a Theater,* p. 126.

[8] *Ibid.,* p. 127.

[9] Erica Tietze-Conrat, *Dwarfs and Jesters in Art* (New York: Phaidon, 1957), pp. 50 and 105. On the ambiguous interplay between death and the fool in literature before Shakespeare see Barbara Swain, *Fools and Folly* (New York: Columbia University Press, 1932), pp. 42 ff. Salingar sees Death as the "supreme 'antic'" in *Hamlet* (*The Age of Shakespeare,* pp. 88-89). William Empson turns his attention briefly to "the business of the macabre, where you make a clown out of death." He observes that "Death in the Holbein Dance of Death, a skeleton still skinny, is often an elegant and charming small figure whose wasp waist gives him a certain mixed-sex quality, and though we are to think otherwise he conceives himself as poking fun; he is seen at his best when piping to an idiot clown and leading him on, presumably to some precipice, treating this great coy figure with so gay and sympathetic an admiration that the picture stays in one's mind chiefly as a love scene" (*Some Versions of Pastoral* [Norfolk, Conn.: New Directions, 1950], p. 14).

[10] *Shakespeare's Royal Self* (New York: G. P. Putnam, 1966), p. 174.

Catherine I. Cox (essay date 1992)

SOURCE: "'Horn Pypes and Funeralls': Suggestions of Hope in Shakespeare's Tragedies," in *The Work of Dissimilitude: Essays from the Sixth Citadel Conference on Medieval and Renaissance Literature,* edited by David G. Allen and Robert A. White, University of Delaware Press, 1992, pp. 216-34.

[*In the following essay, Cox explores Shakespeare's blending of comedy and death, principally through the use of laughter and clowning, in his tragedies.*]

As death coverges with humor in Shakespeare's tragedies, our sense of the grotesque reaches its highest pitch. Death is now literal and ominous. It cannot be averted as in the comedies by a symbolic gesture of humility but must be confronted at its most hideous and awesome. As death becomes more terrifying, so its convergence with gaiety becomes increasingly discordant. Many critics, such as Susan Snyder in *The Comic Matrix of Shakespeare's Tragedies,* see in Shakespeare's mingling of "Kings and Clownes" intimations of tragic absurdity. Commenting on the gravemaker scene in *Hamlet* Snyder insists that the graveyard questions the grounds for all action; for death, which renders human remains indistinguishable, indicates a meaningless world.[1] Images of death, however, do not for the Renaissance Christian negate all meaning. The skull dissolves only temporal meanings and questions actions for temporal ends. The Antic Leveler points its bony finger not at the existence of an immortal soul, but at earthly fame, beauty, and knowledge.

That death's grimace often expresses scorn and mockery is indisputable. In George Wither's emblem "This Ragge of Death," for example, the poem explains the grim meaning of the skeleton's smile: ". . . and marke what ugliness / Stares through the sightlesse Eye-holes, from within: / Note those leane Craggs, and with what Gastlinesse, / That horrid Countenance doth seeme to grin."[2] Death's scoffing smile starkly underscores life's transience and our own foolishness when we trust in life's illusion of permanence. The meaning of death's smile is often more complex, however, evoking not only a sense of mockery, a stark reminder of our inescapable destiny, but one of gaiety and joy as well. Wither's "Death is no Losse" . . . provides an example of the skull that both jeers and celebrates. The scene places in the foreground a large skull poised upright on an hourglass. In its eye sockets, the crevices of its temples, and the corners of its mouth, long strands of wheat protrude as though they are growing from the head. As the hourglass supports the skull to indicate life's brevity, a glowing candle stands upon the skull, illuminating the entire scene with its brilliance. While the hourglass and the candle pull together the ideas of death and life, so too do the background vistas. The scene on the left shows a bleak city and a procession of mourners delivering a casket for burial. On the right, a pleasant country scene suggests life's simple joys. A cottage with smoke rising gently from its chimney sits comfortably on a hill. In front of the cottage, workers are shown busily harvesting wheat. The accompanying poem clarifies the meaning of this smiling death's head. Like the wheat, the poem explains, we must lie in the earth awhile, "But, from that *Wombe* receives another *Birth*, / And, with Additions, riseth from the Clay." The grave then becomes not a *"Place of Feare"* but rather a *"Bed of Rest."*[3] This *memento mori* thus serves as a reminder not only of death but also of the bliss that awaits beyond the grave.

Like this emblem's hopeful message, Shakespeare's plays often blend death with the comical so as to suggest an unquenchable life force whose energy either emerges at moments of intense tragic awareness or develops within a comic context into a transforming and creative power. This paradoxical union of death and life finds an analogue in the comedy of Christian redemption in medieval and Renaissance thought. For death not only provides a portal to eternal life and an agon to test sincerity of belief, but also, by showing people their own nature, death encourages the requisites of remorse, humility, and faith. Thus the medieval preoccupation with bodily decomposition reveals not merely morbid sensuality but a desire to reify spiritual awareness. An anonymous work entitled "A Sermon of the Misery of Mankind" explains that, for the faithful "bodily death is a door or entering unto Life, and therefore not so much dreadful (if it be rightly considered,) as it is comfortable; not a mischief but a Remedy for all mischief . . . not a Sorrow and Pain, but to Joy and Pleasure."[4] By thinking on the grave, the faithful realize the duality of their natures: for they share with beasts the inevitability of death and with angels the spirit that enables escape from death's confines. Recognition of this hybrid nature and of the precarious stance between death and life is cause for uneasy but hopeful laughter. Charlotte Spivack explains that "Endowed with a perspective of his own incongruity, man is afforded laughter as a means of reconciling the contrary aspects of his nature."[5] Thus humor's frequent convergence with death in medieval literature and art should not be surprising, for the terms *rationali, mortali,* and *risus capax* interlock in the medieval conception of humanity.[6]

As in Christian comedy, so too in Shakespeare's comedies and romances death functions as an instrument of self-knowledge and regeneration. Unlike the Christian emphasis on celestial affairs, however, Shakespeare centers on temporal renewal.[7] Feigned or imaginary deaths, like that of Hero in *Much Ado About Nothing,* imminent deaths, like that of Claudio in *Measure for Measure,* and real deaths occurring either off stage or before the play's action begins, such as the deaths of Mamillius and Antigonus in *A Winter's Tale,* provide frequent plot complications whose resolutions depend on the characters' capacity for human understanding. Initially frustrating happiness, death opens the way to remorse, repentance, and compassion. Sympathetic action thus surmounts death and the comic catastrophe ensues.

While Shakespeare's comedies and romances make explicit death's regenerative powers by providing happy endings, his tragedies suggest merely possibilities for communal reordering. Risible elements thus blend with moments of death to promote the audience's sense of freedom from destruction and hope for social restoration. Juliet's deathlike sleep amid servants who jest of her wedding night, Hamlet's encounter with the merry gravemakers who quibble and sing while unearthing skulls, Cleopatra's visit by the jovial clown who bears the "pretty worm of Nilus," and Macduff's greeting by the equivocating porter who bids him enter Hell-Gate point at once to the unceasing dialectic of death and life and to our potential for future rejuvenation. We realize the intimate relation between death and its victims while we simultaneously sense, through the jovial nonchalance of the clowns, a cyclical order extending beyond personal tragedy. Herbert Weisinger's theory of tragic structure and John Holloway's discussion of ritual pattern in Shakespeare tragedies provide a context for understanding the function of risible moments in Shakespeare's tragedies. Both Weisinger and Holloway agree that it is our engagement with the protagonist as he or she undergoes a journey towards death that accounts for our sense of the tragic. Holloway explains, "It is rather that we make contact very directly with the experience through which the protagonist passes in the course of the play. The issue is not, what kind of man Hamlet is; but what he does. Or rather, what he both does and undergoes; how one can describe the whole volume of the experience through which he passes, as one who both acts and suffers the actions of others."[8] For both Weisinger and Holloway, great tragedy awakens in us a paradoxical feeling of suffering and joy as it imitates the ritual of death and resurrection. Weisinger explains that "our response to tragedy is a response deeply rooted in the past of man, which tragedy has the power to evoke afresh."[9] The pleasure that we take in suffering is not a perverse desire for another's pain or for our own but comes from our awareness of "a rational order" that extends beyond an individual's death: "The tragic occurs when by the fall of a man of strong character we are made aware of something greater than that man or even man-king; we seem to have a new and truer vision of the universe. . . ."[10]

Although neither Weisinger nor Holloway addresses the issue of the comical in Shakespeare's tragedies, Weisinger offers numerous examples of the festivals, maskings, and orgies that in ancient primitive rituals played a part in the society's slaying of the god-king. The comical elements in Shakespeare's tragedies serve a similar function, allowing the audience an occasion to complete its identification with the sacrificial victim and then begin to release him or her. The medieval cycle plays lend support to this theory, for the death of Christ is almost always accompanied by games and farce. V. A. Kolve emphasizes the distancing effect of the *tortores'* games: "The horror of the Passion is controlled by constantly breaking the flow of its action. As the judges, scorners, tormentors, and executioners become totally absorbed in each new and limited game which they take up, so too is our attention diverted in turn: the Cornish making of the nails, and the premature Chester dicing are notable examples."[12] Kolve also recognizes the irony implicit in these games and its regenerative value. While the torturers feel that they control the game, we realize by Christ's composure amid all their noise and laughter that they are unwitting participants in a cosmic game: "The *tortores* play with Christ, but we must not forget that Christ is playing too—that He is in the game, by His own choice, to serve His larger purposes. And the game must go as God intends."[12]

Sir Philip Sidney's defense of tragic purity in *An Apologie for Poetry* may shed further light on the irony implicit in comic-tragic blending:

> But if we marke them [the ancients] we shall find that they never, or very daintily, match Horn-pypes and Funeralls. So falleth it out that, having indeed no right Comedy, in that comicall part of our Tragedy we have nothing but scurrility, unworthy of any chast eares, or some extreame shew of doltishness, indeed fit to lift vp a loude laughter, and nothing els: Where the whole tract of a Comedy shoulde be full of delight, as the Tragedy shoulde be still maintained in a well raised admiration.[13]

In this passage Sidney explains that the mistake playwrights often make is in confusing delight with laughter. Although laughter and delight may arise from a single incident, the two are in themselves opposed. Delight "has a joy in it" and springs from things proportioned and apt. Laughter, on the other hand, is "a scornful tickling," arising from things disproportioned and incongruous. Sidney here considers laughter as satiric, as *vituperatio*. Thus while they may appear simultaneously, Sidney explains, laughter does not spring from delight, as many believe. Illustrating his point, Sidney refers to the brawny, heavily bearded Hercules who, dressed in woman's clothes, spins the distaff of Omphale. Delight and laughter here arise at once, "For the representing of so strange a power in love procureth delight: and the scornfulness of the action stirrith laughter" (140). While censorious laughter and delight are often independent responses, as Sidney holds, there may at times exist a paradoxical affinity between the two. If we examine closely Sidney's image of Hercules' spinning the distaff, we find that laughter and delight are not merely simultaneous occurrences but are interrelated effects. While delight does not here induce laughter, laughter does increase our delight. It is our laughter, mocking though it is, that informs us of the intensity of Hercules' passion, of his willingness to sacrifice his identity and his dignity for the love of Iole.

Just as comic degradation is essential to delight in the case of Hercules, it is similarly important to tragic joy in the cases of Hamlet, Macbeth, Cleopatra, and Juliet. Through the clowns' foolishness and through their satirical jibes, we glimpse the frailty and the folly of the protagonists and this in turn heightens our awareness of their passions and their tragedies. In act 4, scene 3, of *Romeo and Juliet,* Juliet gives her imagination free reign to the horrors of premature burial and then lifts the dreaded vial to her lips with the pledge, "Romeo, Romeo, Romeo! Here's drink—I drink to thee" (58).[14] The potion, whose virtue she fears, recalls the Friar's earlier correlation of human qualities with natural elements:

> For nought so vile that on the earth doth live
> But to the earth some special good doth give;
> Nor aught so good but, strain'd from that fair use,
> Revolts from true birth, stumbling on abuse.
> Virtue itself turns vice, being misapplied,
> And vice sometime by action dignified.
> (2.3.17-22)

Juliet's dangerous and defiant action suggests this moral ambivalence where good may "stumbl[e] on abuse" and vice find dignity in action. Both perspectives collide when laughter permeates the scene of seeming death. Juliet's drinking of the potion visually suggests suicide and is an unwitting preparation for that final action. The echoing words of the Friar thus push on to their bitter conclusion: "And where the worser is predominant / Full soon the canker death eats up the plant" (29-30). As Juliet swallows the potion, we realize her physical and spiritual jeopardy as well as her desperation and pain. No sooner does she fall into a deathlike sleep, however, than we are propelled into the world of comedy. We enjoy the domestic hustle and bustle of the Capulet servants who are preparing for the day's wedding festivities. Old Capulet's officious ordering of the servants, Angelica's bawdy jests and exaggerated lamentations, and Peter and the musicians' farcical quarrel suggest something comical about Juliet's situation and about Juliet herself. The implied ridicule of these earthbound creatures allows us to feel more intensely Juliet's isolation and foolishness. Like Hercules, Juliet suffers comic degradation. But in proportion to their foolishness, her passion and commitment also touch the sublime. By refusing to honor her parents' wishes and marry Paris, Juliet has estranged herself from the compromising world of ordinary humanity. Her actions, though impudent and rash, demonstrate her willingness to risk defamation, madness, and death to be rejoined with Romeo.

The sacrificial victim, in this case Juliet, mingles the sacred with the profane, wisdom with foolishness. In ancient cultures, the distinction between king and god was constantly blurred. Since the god-king was associated with fertility and with the spiritual health of the land, it is understandable that in time he would become linked to a more humble symbol of fecundity and joy, the fool. Because he was associated with the earth's vital forces and perhaps because he was expendable and stupid enough to die willingly, the fool often became the surrogate king in ancient rituals of renewal.[15] Exalted for a period of time, until his identification with the king was complete, the fool would then be mocked, scourged, and slain. The victim's foolishness, as it indicates his humanity, provides the people with a bridge to the sacred. Realizing the interrelation of the absurd and the sublime, we should not be surprised to find a painting by one of the earliest followers of Christ representing the crucified lord with an ass's head.[16] In the Corpus Christi cycles, Christ suffers similar indignities. The Wakefield Caiaphas in the *Buffeting,* for example, calls Christ "Kyng Copyn in oure game"[17] while the *tortores* of the York cycle dress Jesus in white cloth, the dress of a fool, and make him the butt of their games and gibes.[18] Here, of course, the plays satirize the torturers who do not see Christ's divine nature and the spectators who daily reopen Christ's wounds by their sins. The association of Christ with a fool is not merely ironic, however, for it points to the paradox at the heart of sacrifice. To suffer humiliation and death willingly for the salvation of another defies our most fundamental instinct of self-preservation and thus seems the height of folly. The action, on the other hand, is life-affirming. Because it is the highest demonstration of love, it is paradoxically the wisest and most sacred of actions.[19] Unlike Christ, the tragic protagonist of Shakespeare's plays is not a deity who can carry the sins of the world and remain pure. He or she must fully absorb the evil to be purged. The term *foolish* thus bears a more sinister meaning when applied to the mortal scapegoats of Shakespeare's tragedies. Indeed, foolishness in the case of Macbeth is identical with the demonic.

The striking change in tone at the entry of the clowns in Shakespeare's tragedies suggests that we stand at an important juncture in the tragedy. We recall that comic interludes were sometimes used in medieval drama to separate distinctive movements of the plot. So, too, the comical intrusions in Shakespeare's tragedies may signal a directional change. In *Macbeth,* for example, the episode of the drunken porter separates the act of regicide from its necessary retribution. The porter, as his name implies, is a transitional figure. He stands between the starless night that seals Macbeth's murderous deed and the new dawn whose diffusive light directs Scotland to gaze upon bloody Duncan. As in *Macbeth,* so too in *Hamlet, Romeo and Juliet,* and *Antony and Cleopatra,* the impertinent clowns signal the protagonists' changed or changing position in the play. The clown's gaiety in the face of death suggests an inversion of roles, for the protagonist is now discomfited. Although formerly secure, the center of society, the hero or heroine, is now exceedingly vulnerable. He or she has assumed the passive role of the scapegoat. Hamlet's return to Denmark, Juliet's swallowing of the Friar's potion, and Cleopatra's acceptance of the asp are all submissive responses to the call of death. Although Macbeth never submits to his destiny as fully as do the other victims, he nonetheless becomes increasingly numb and inert. The active champion of Scotland in act 1 will become in the acts that follow reactionary and defensive. Macbeth's sole endeavor will consist of warding off the dual furies, conscience and discovery.

Thus the clowns presage both death and life. With the exception of the burlesque figures in *Romeo and Juliet,* the merry harbingers bear no proper names. They are undeveloped, anonymous characters who appear suddenly, electrify the grim milieu with their indecorous antics, and disappear to be heard from no more. The startling appearance of these mysterious characters recalls the alarming image of death in the medieval and Renaissance *Vado Mori* and in the Dance of Death. Holbein's engraving of the queen and death is particularly relevant, for here death wears the cap and bells of a medieval jester. . . .[20] The inversion of roles in Holbein's Dance is bitterly ironic, for the queen, who on a former day might have commanded her fool to perform, is now herself ordered to dance by antic death. A similar inversion occurs in Shakespeare's tragedies. But while Shakespeare's antics approach their "victims" with the amused detachment of Holbein's jester, they possess an element of childlike innocence that is absent from Holbein's figure of death. Unlike Holbein's high-spirited skeleton, Shakespeare's sportive commoners are not court jesters. The distinction is significant, for the court or household jester in Shakespeare's plays is a sophisticated professional who uses his wit like a "stalkinghorse" to pierce the pretensions and illusions of his patrons. While Shakespeare's merry reapers delight in the duplicity of words like the professional jesters, they do not seem fully aware of the import of their quibbles and gibes. They seem hybrid creatures, partaking of the wit of clever jesters, like Lear's fool, Touchstone, and Lavatch, and the innocent gaiety of bungling fools, such as Bottom, Dogberry, and Elbow. It is their affinity to these naturals, their capacity for childlike joy, that turns satiric inversion, like that of Holbein's dance, into festive topsy-turvydom.[21] Thus while "a scornful tickling" contributes to our laughter, our laughter also springs from a humane and generous delight. The function of Shakespeare's gay harbingers is then primarily saturnalian. And satire in these plays waits upon mirthful celebration.[22]

The porter scene of *Macbeth* illustrates the clown's affinity to death and life and his ability to bring us intimations of tragic joy. As the drowsy porter staggers to the gate to receive the early morning visitors, he brings to mind weary and disturbed Macbeth. We recall Macbeth's envy of the sleeping guards and of their innocent prayers. And we remember his chilling prophecy, "Cawdor / Shall sleep no more" (2.2.39-40). The thane and his lady's hasty change into nightclothes at the sound of knocking emphasizes the truth that Macbeth has killed sleep. As the porter underscores Macbeth's fatigue and regret, our sympathy rises for the already haunted thane. We realize too that Macbeth, having cut himself off from this life-nurturing balm, must soon die. The knocking's disturbance of the porter's sleep and its startling effect upon Macbeth tell us that retribution has wasted no time in pressing its claim. As the porter welcomes the imaginary reaper, "Come in time!" (2.3.5), he seems a genius of death, signaling Macbeth's irreversible movement towards destruction. The porter, however, with his humorous role-playing and indecent puns, is just as surely a figure of life. Macduff's persistent knocking and the porter's allusion to hell's gate bring to mind not only the sudden visitation of death upon sinners, a frequent motif in the literature of the age, but also, as Glynne Wickham has pointed out, the victory of Christ over hell in the apocryphal harrowing of hell.[23] Hell was often depicted in medieval plays and paintings as a castle, and Christ was shown to pound repeatedly upon the gate before bursting through and scattering the minions of hell. Macduff's entry into Inverness parallels Christ's entry into hell-castle and foreshadows Macduff's defeat of Macbeth and the resulting triumph of Scotland. The porter thus opens the door both to death and to life. The farmer, the equivocator, and the tailor whom the porter mentions must dance down the primrose path to the everlasting bonfire. We may imagine, countering their descent, the ascent of Adam and Eve, the prophets, and the patriarchs who are taken by the hand of Christ and escorted to Paradise.... [24] And as we watch Macbeth prepare to follow the lesser sinners to hell, we sense Scotland's future victory and our own release from death. Like the farcical episodes of Marlowe's *Dr. Faustus,* the porter's comical greeting of sinners to hell diminishes the grandeur of the fallen hero. And the allusion to Christ's harrowing adds to the irony of Macbeth's fall. Medieval and Renaissance painters often depict Jesus as a knight, like Saint George, thrusting a sword into the mouth of the dragon and pressing its head under foot. In the first act the sergeant describes Macbeth's defeat of the rebel Macdonwald in somewhat similar terms: ". . . he unseam'd him from the nave to th' chops, / And fix'd his head upon our battlements" (1.2.22-23). The porter now shatters this heroic image. Macbeth is no longer the victorious defender of righteousness but a small, despicable rebel destined, like the farmer, the equivocator, and the tailor, for defeat.[25] Macbeth's shrinkage underscores his role as mock-king. Macbeth is a foolish and expendable usurper of majesty. By first eliciting our sympathy for Macbeth, the porter encourages us to accept him as our substitute. By then drawing forth our disdain, he prepares us for Macbeth's final diminution and readies us to release the shrunken king to his death. In act 5 Angus describes the diminished ruler as he awaits Malcolm's forces: "Now does he feel his title / Hang loose about him, like a giant's robe / Upon a dwarfish thief" (2.20-22). Macbeth suffers an even more degrading death than Macdonwald. The tyrant's head is not merely "fixed . . . upon the battlement" but is severed from his body and held up in contempt before the armies. With the help of the sportive porter, we find hope in this grotesque emblem. For us, as for Scotland, "the time is free."

A chilling irony infuses such burlesque moments as that involving the porter, for the audience, more keenly than the protagonist, feels death's approach. Two sixteenth-century portraits utilizing the *memento mori* tradition may help to demonstrate the sympathy bred for the protagonist by the sudden entrance of Shakespeare's grosteque. In early illustrations accompanying *vado mori* lyrics and poems of the Dance of Death, representative figures such as kings, ladies, and knights are portrayed about their usual business. They do not seem to notice the grinning skeletons lurking behind them, weapons poised for attack. . . .[26] One moral poem reads,

> This day I satt full royally in a chayre.
> Tyll sotyll deth knokkid at my gate
> And unavised he said to me, "chekmate"![27]

The N Town *Death of Herod* explores the dramatic potential of this tradition. We first see Herod rejoicing at the death of the innocents. But as he boasts his preeminence and gormandizes at a sumptuous feast, the figure of death approaches, unnoticed to any but the audience. The irony mounts as death exclaims:

> Ow! Se how prowdely yon kaitiff sitt at mete!
> Of Deth hath he no dowte; he wenith to leve evyrmore.
> To him wil I go and geve him such an hete
> That all the lechis of the londe his life shul nevyr restore.
>
> (194-97)[28]

By substituting a specific biblical personage in the place of the generic king, the N Town modifies the tradition of sudden death. Herod, however, is much more a type than a flesh-and-blood individual, and so the emphasis remains homiletic. We find the convention radically altered, however, in Holbein's portrait of Sir Brian Tuke . . . and in a portrait of a young man painted in 1524 and signed H. F. (Hans Fries).[29] The victims are now highly individualized. The figure of death still glares menancingly over its victim's shoulder. Unlike Herod, these men are prepared for death. Sir Brian Tuke, for example, points to a passage from

Job, "Will not the small number of my days be soon ended?" Although the victims are pious, the irony in these paintings is nevertheless biting, for the distinctive personal quality of these gentlemen engages our sympathies. We pity these men as we cannot Herod, for Herod possesses no redeemable charcteristics. As we recognize the traditional *memento mori* context of these portraits, the finger of death turns towards us. Sir Brian Tuke and the young man painted by H. F. are not only Renaissance lords, but also Everyman. By modifying the convention of the unwary victim, the portraits pull together the personal and the homiletic. A similar irony penetrates Shakespeare's tragedies when the impish clowns come into view. As Hamlet asks the gravemaker for whom he digs the grave, we know, though Hamlet does not, that the grave is meant for Ophelia. We also realize that Ophelia's death has placed Hamlet in direst jeopardy, for it has doubled the ire of Laertes and his determination to take revenge. The gravemaker scene not only harbors irony, but it also overlays the specific and the general as in the portraits. The skulls of Ophelia, Yorick, and Alexander will mingle with that of "my Lord Such-a-one, that prais'd my / Lord Such-a-one's horse . . ." (5.1.84-85).[30] The scene thus allows us to experience a crucial moment in the story of Hamlet and at the same time provides us with a forceful reminder of our own mortality.

With an enhanced sense of mortal limitations, we begin to move beyond identification with those facing death toward a new identity. Self-knowledge, as the Renaissance typically perceived it, begins with an acceptance of mortality and culminates in understanding one's relation to God, people, and the cosmos. The mistaken choices of the heroes and heroines have made their premature deaths unavoidable. With the knowledge of their errors and a consciousness of our own limitations, however, we hold the opportunity to shape our own futures. After the initial shock of death's nearness subsides, we begin to enjoy the levity of the clowns who hint at the healing power of laughter and encourage us to enter their magical arena of play. Participating in their unconscious mockery, we begin to separate from those who must soon die. With this release comes a sense of freedom and hope. The clowns thus prepare us to realize and accept the unavoidable calamity that awaits the protagonist and simultaneously to anticipate the sense of freedom and reintegration that this death makes possible.

Notes

[1] Susan Snyder, *The Comic Matrix of Shakespeare's Tragedies: Romeo and Juliet, Hamlet, Othello and King Lear* (Princeton: Princeton University Press, 1979), 126.

[2] *A Collection of Emblemes, Ancient and Moderne (1635) by George Wither,* Book I, Illustr. 8 (Columbia: University of South Carolina Press, 1975); this facsimile by the Renaissance English Text Society reproduces the Newberry Library copy, Taunton imprint (STC 25900d; call number Case W 1025.98).

[3] *A Collection of Emblemes,* Book I, Illustr. 21. As numerous critics such as Barbara W. Tuchman and Johan Huizinga have discerned, the skeletons and death's heads were often expressions of the terrors of the Black Death.

[4] *Certain sermons of homilies, appointed to be read in churches; in the time of Queen Elizabeth . . .* (London: Printed for George Wells, 1687).

[5] Charlotte Spivack, *The Comedy of Evil on Shakespeare's Stage* (Madison, N.J.: Fairleigh-Dickinson University Press, 1978), 25.

[6] Ibid., 25. Also see V. A. Kolve's *The Play Called Corpus Christi* (Stanford Calif.: Stanford University Press, 1966), 133-34: *Diues et Pauper* asserts that mirth is among the major purposes of medieval religious drama. The anonymous author "holds (on scriptural authority) that to play *to* God and *for* God is to please Him, that human joy and such humility as chooses to express joy in play and game are acceptable to heaven."

[7] In *Shakespeare and Christian Doctrine* (Princeton: Princeton University Press, 1963), Roland Mushat Frye stresses the "need for a sane and informed secularism in the interpretation of the plays, because the plays are themselves primarily concerned with the secular realm." By "secular" Frye means "temporal and 'this worldly,' somewhat after the fashion of the Latin *saeculum,* referring to an age or a generation, rather than to the domain of the eternal" (7).

[8] John Holloway, *The Story of the Night: Studies in Shakespeare's Major Tragedies* (Lincoln: University of Nebraska Press, 1963), 22.

[9] Herbert Weisinger, *Tragedy and the Paradox of the Fortunate Fall* (East Lansing: Michigan State College Press, 1953), 228.

[10] Ibid., 226. In *Fools of Time: Studies in Shakespearean Tragedy* (Toronto: University of Toronto Press, 1967), Northrop Frye states that "The hero of tragedy ultimately includes the audience who form the *substance* of the hero . . . who participate in a ritual act of suffering in which the suffering is not real but the awareness of it is" (118).

[11] Kolve, *Play Called Corpus Christi,* 200.

[12] Ibid.

[13] Sir Philip Sidney, *An Apologie for Poetry,* in *English Literary Criticism: The Renaissance,* ed. O. B.

Hardison, Jr. (Englewood Cliffs, N.J.: Prentice-Hall, 1963), 139. Subsequent citations from this work will be given in the text.

[14] Quoted from *The Riverside Shakespeare,* ed. G. Blakemore Evans (Boston: Houghton Mifflin Co., 1974). All further citations and quotations of Shakespeare's plays come from this edition.

[15] Enid Welsford, *The Fool: His Social and Literary History* (London: Faber and Faber, 1968), 68-69.

[16] Harvey Cox, *The Feast of Fools* (Cambridge: Harvard University Press, 1969), 140.

[17] Cited from David Bevington, ed., *Medieval Drama* (Boston: Houghton Mifflin Co., 1975), 542. Kolve discusses the convergence of laughter and the image of Christ in *Play Called Corpus Christi,* 181.

[18] *The York Cycle of Mystery Plays: A Complete Version,* ed. J. S. Purvis (London: S.P.C.K., 1957), 245. See Kolve, *Play Called Corpus Christi,* 184.

[19] In *King Lear,* Cordelia exemplifies this selfless, Christlike love by risking her life to save the father who rejected her. Her death brings to Lear's lips the cry, "and my poor fool is hang'd!" (5.3.306). Although Lear uses the word "fool" as a term of endearment, it suggests the loyal jester who suffered with the King on the heath. And if indeed Lear's fool and Cordelia were played by the same actor in Shakespeare's day, as Sir John Gielgud believed, the relationship between folly and sacrifice becomes still more highly charged. In *The Masks of King Lear* (Berkeley and Los Angeles: University of California Press, 1972), 318, Marvin Rosenberg emphasizes the visual and verbal imagery linking Cordelia and the fool: "Lear's tenderness with Cordelia recalls Lear's sheltering of Fool, his cross-grained love of both. . . . The two are joined by motif as well as character design: Lear's fool is someone who loves him, stays with him, pities him, suffers with him—who has been 'fooled' into holding on to his downhill wheel." While Cordelia serves as an emblem of Christian sacrifice, she does not perform the role of scapegoat in the pattern of the tragedy. It is Lear, wearing the coxcomb for ignoble reasons, who must perform this task. Referring to the "resurrection pattern" of *King Lear,* Northrop Frye says that "in the tragedy of isolation the hero becomes a scapegoat, a person excluded from his society and thereby left to face the full weight of absurdity and anguish that isolated man feels in nature" (*Fools of Time,* 118).

[20] *The Dance of Death by Hans Holbein the Younger: A Complete Facsimile of the Original 1538 Edition of "Les Simulachres & Historiees Faces de la Mort"* (New York: Dover Publications, 1971), 26. My appreciation also extends to the Lessing J. Rosenwald Collection, Library of Congress, Washington, D.C.

[21] Robert Weimann, *Shakespeare and the Popular Tradition in Theater: Studies in the Social Dimension of Dramatic Form and Function,* ed. Robert Schwartz (Baltimore: Johns Hopkins University Press, 1978), 21. Weimann sees the connection between the idea of Utopia and topsy-turvydom as significant: "As early as the Roman Saturnalia such topsy-turvydom was associated with a Utopian dream of the Golden Age. The festive abolition of inequality and the playful exchange of roles between masters and servants defined the 'democratic character' of the Saturnalia, which ostensibly served to 'preserve the memory of the original state of nature where every man was equal.'" The sense of topsy-turvy inversion that pervades the comic-tragic moment of Shakespeare's tragedies hints at just such a return to equality and peace. Death, the great equalizer, ironically bears the seeds of a Utopian dream.

[22] C. L. Barber recognizes the interplay of abusive wit and high-spirited mirth as essential components of Shakespeare's early comedies. Stressing Shakespeare's affinity to Aristophanes, Barber refers to *The Origins of Attic Comedy* in which F. M. Cornford suggests "that invocation and abuse were the basic gestures of nature worship behind Aristophanes' union of poetry and railing." Through these "two gestures," the early comedies, explains Barber, move us "through release to clarification": "The clarification achieved by the festive comedies is concomitant to the release they dramatize: a heightened awareness of the relation between man and 'nature'—the nature celebrated on holiday"; *Shakespeare's Festive Comedy: A Study of Dramatic Form and Its Relation to Social Custom* (Princeton: Princeton University Press, 1959), 7, 8. More pointed than Barber in his remarks on the destructive-recreative power of folk humor is Mikhail Bakhtin in his introduction to *Rabelais and His World,* trans. Helene Iswolsky (Bloomington: Indiana University Press, 1984), 52-53. For Bakhtin the grotesque image that emerges from carnival suggests ambivalence: the image encompasses "simutaneously the two poles of becoming: that which is receding and dying, and that which is being born: they show two bodies in one, the budding and the division of the living cell. . . . Old age is pregnant, death is gestation, all that is limited, narrowly characterized, and completed is thrust into the lower stratum of the body for recasting and a new birth." Also see Peter Burke's *Popular Culture in Early Modern Europe* (New York: Harper & Row, 1978), 201.

[23] In poetry of the Middle Ages and the Renaissance, death was often personified as knocking at its victim's door or gate. John Webster Spargo gives a detailed look at the relationship between knocking and death

in his article, "The Knocking at the Gate in *Macbeth*: An Essay in Interpretation," in *Joseph Quincy Adams Memorial Studies,* ed. James G. McManaway, Giles E. Dawson, and Edwin E. Willoughby (Washington, D.C.: Folger Shakespeare Library, 1948), 269-77. Two excellent articles deal with the porter scene's allusion to the harrowing of hell: Glynne Wickham's "Hell-Castle and Its Door-Keeper," *Shakespeare Survey* 19 (1970): 68-74, and John B. Harcourt's "I Pray You, Remember the Porter," *Shakespeare Quarterly* 12 (1961): 393-402. Wickham explains that "On the medieval stage hell was represented as a castle, more particularly as a dungeon or cesspit within a castle, one entrance to which was often depicted as a dragon's mouth. Its gate was guarded by a janitor or porter. Christ, after his crucifixion, but before his resurrection, came to the castle of hell to demand of Lucifer the release of the souls of the patriarchs and prophets. . . . Christ's arrival was signalled by a tremendous knocking at this gate and a blast of trumpets" (68-69). Frederic B. Tromly, in "Macbeth and His Porter," *Shakespeare Quarterly* 26 (1975): 151-56, takes still another look at the scene. He argues against Harcourt's view that the scene functions to isolate Macbeth. For Harcourt, the scene works to humanize the tyrant by forcing us to recognize him in the ordinary porter. While critics tend to read the scene as either drawing us into sympathy with Macbeth or isolating us from him, they do not acknowledge that the scene in fact does both. The porter is the master equivocator, moving us to both pity and contempt.

[24] *The St. Albans Psalter,* ed. G. Big, Studies of the Warburg Institute, no. 25 (London: Warburg Institute, University of London, 1960). My gratitude also goes to St. Godehard in Hildesheim, the owners of the manuscript.

[25] Harcourt, "I Pray You," 395. I agree with Harcourt that the porter's reference to the petty sinners serves to "destroy the pseudoheroic illusion."

[26] "Vado Mori" (British Museum, MS. Additional 37049, fol. 36r), reproduced in Douglas Gray's *Themes and Images in the Medieval English Religious Lyric* (Boston: Routledge and Kegan Paul, 1972), pl. 10.

[27] Roman Dyboski, ed., *Songs, Carols, and Other Miscellaneous Poems,* EETS, e.s., no. 101 (London: Kegan Paul, Trench, Trubner and Co., 1907), 87-88.

[28] Cited from Bevington, *Medieval Drama,* 456.

[29] *Portrait of Sir Brian Tuke* by Hans Holbein. Alte Pinakothek, Munich. Reproduced in *Katalog der Gemalde-Sammlung der KGL. Alteren Pinakothek in Munchen* (Verlag von F. Bruckmann, A.-G., 1908), 213. See also Frederick Parkes Weber, *Aspects of Death and Correlated Aspects of Life in Art, Epigram, and Poetry: Contributions Towards an Anthology and an Iconography of the Subject,* 4th ed. (College Park, Md: McGrath Publishing Co., 1971), 137, 796.

[30] My treatment of the regenerative implications of the graveyard scene in Hamlet may be found in "Saturnalian Sacrifices: Comic-Tragic Blending in Shakespeare's *Hamlet,*" *Explorations in Renaissance Culture* 12 (1986): 87-104.

FURTHER READING

Battenhouse, Roy. "Falstaff as Parodist and Perhaps Holy Fool." *PMLA: Publications of the Modern Language Association of America* 90, No. 1 (January 1975): 32-52.

>Regards Falstaff of the *Henriad* as a devout Christian in the guise of a fool.

Brown, John Russell. "Laughter in the Last Plays." In *Later Shakespeare,* Stratford-Upon-Avon Studies, edited by John Russell Brown and Bernard Harris, No. 8, pp. 103-25. London: Edward Arnold Ltd., 1966.

>Includes a discussion of the clown performances in *Cymbeline, The Winter's Tale, Pericles,* and *The Tempest.*

Frye, Dean. "The Question of Shakespearean 'Parody.'" *Essays in Criticism: A Quarterly Journal of Literary Criticism* XV, No. 1 (January 1965): 22-26.

>Disputes the critical position that the comic subplots and characters in Shakespeare's plays parody the main plot and its protagonists.

Goldsmith, Robert Hillis. *Wise Fools in Shakespeare.* Liverpool: Liverpool University Press, 1955, 123 p.

>Offers background on the tradition of fools in literature and studies Shakespeare's witty clowns—Touchstone, Lavache, Feste, and Lear's Fool.

Leinwand, Theodore B. "Conservative Fools in James's Court and Shakespeare's Plays." *Shakespeare Studies: An Annual Gathering of Research, Criticism, and Reviews* XIX (1991): 219-37.

>Argues that Shakespeare's fools, like their historical counterparts in the late-Elizabethan and Jacobean eras, were much less likely to disrupt social order than many critics have suggested.

Levin, Richard. "Elizabethan 'Clown' Subplots." *Essays in Criticism: A Quarterly Journal of Literary Criticism* XVI, No. 1 (January 1966): 84-91.

>Builds upon Dean Frye's thesis (see above) by concentrating on the varied thematic functions of Shakespeare's clown subplots.

Mangan, Michael. "Fools, Clowns and Jesters," in *A Preface to Shakespeare's Comedies: 1594-1603,* Longman Group Limited, 1996, 50-73.

> Focuses on the function of fools, jesters, and clowns in Shakespearean drama and Elizabethan society.

Maslen, Elizabeth. "Yorick's Place in *Hamlet*." *Essays and Studies* 36 (1983): 1-13.

> Maintains that Hamlet's remembrance of Yorick the Fool in *Hamlet* figures as an opposing force to the prince's vision of his father's vengeful ghost.

Messenger, Ann P. "Shakespearean Fools—Alive and Well in Restoration Comedy." *Wascana Review* 12, No. 2 (Fall 1977): 77-87.

> Sees resonances of Shakespeare's "wise fools" in the comedies of Congreve, Shadwell, Dryden, Etherege, and Wycherley.

Neill, Michael. "The Play of Perspective: Enobarbus as Choric Fool." In *The Tragedy of Anthony and Cleopatra,* by William Shakespeare, edited by Michael Neill, pp. 89-94. Oxford: Clarendon Press, 1994.

> Observes that Enobarbus's function in *Anthony and Cleopatra* is to provide commentary "close to that of the satiric clowns of earlier tragedies."

Ross, Lawrence J. "Shakespeare's 'Dull Clown' and Symbolic Music." *Shakespeare Quarterly* XVII, No. 2 (Spring 1966): 107-28.

> Relates the Clown's two appearances in *Othello* to the play's motifs of love and "the music of universal harmony."

Somerset, J. A. B. "Shakespeare's Great Stage of Fools, 1599-1607." In *Mirror up to Shakespeare: Essays in Honour of G. R. Hibbard,* edited by J. C. Gray, pp. 68-81. Toronto: University of Toronto Press, 1984.

> Discusses the influence of actor Robert Armin on Shakespeare's clowns in his plays dating from 1599 to 1607.

Steele, Eugene. "Shakespeare, Goldoni, and the Clowns." *Comparative Drama* 11, No. 3 (Fall 1977): 209-26.

> Examines Shakespeare's clowns in light of the extemporizing tradition of the Italian *Commedia dell' Arte*.

Videbæk, Bente A. *The Stage Clown in Shakespeare's Theatre*. Westport, Conn.: Greenwood Press, 215 p.

> Extensive study of rustics, clowns, court jesters, and fools on Shakespeare's stage.

Wilcher, Robert. "The Fool and his Techniques in the Contemporary Theatre." *Theatre Research International* IV, No. 2 (February 1979): 117-33.

> Explores the enduring influence of Shakespearean fools in modern theater.

Wiles, David. *Shakespeare's Clown: Actor and Text in the Elizabethan Playhouse*. Cambridge: Cambridge University Press, 1987, 223 p.

> Traces the history of the Elizabethan clown, particularly focusing on the characters enacted by William Kemp.

As You Like It

For further information on the critical and stage history of *As You Like It*, see *SC* Volumes 5, 23, and 34.

INTRODUCTION

Although *As You Like It* received little or no critical recognition prior to the early eighteenth century, it has become one of Shakespeare's most-performed comedies. Adapted primarily from Thomas Lodge's pastoral romance *Rosalynde, As You Like It* was written and first performed between 1598 and 1600, perhaps for the opening of the Globe Theatre. Many commentators have criticized *As You Like It* for its minimal plot and limited action, while praising the play for its dynamic characterizations and energetic prose. Past critical commentary has addressed such thematic issues as Touchstone's comic role, Rosalind's sexual disguise, and the depiction of time in the Forest of Arden. These topics continue to garner the attention of contemporary critics as well.

Scholars consider Touchstone to be one of Shakespeare's most important additions to the original cast of characters he borrowed from Lodge's *Rosalynde*. Described as an intellectual fool, Touchstone was regarded as a new figure in English drama. In contrast to the assertion by some that the role of Touchstone was written expressly for jester Robert Armin, who joined the Lord Chamberlain's Men in 1599, Guy Butler (1983) has contended that the role was "originally intended for [Will] Kempe, an old style clown," who was replaced by Armin in 1600. According to Butler, Shakespeare adapted Touchstone's part to Armin's "new style witty fool" in a deliberate decision to merge "the rival styles of humour" found in the taverns and on the stage in Elizabethan times. The significance and dramatic function of Touchstone in *As You Like It* has been of enduring interest to many critics, who frequently see the clown as a mediator between the action onstage and the audience. As such, David Frail (1981) has pointed out that as the "wise fool," Touchstone's function is to blur the line between wisdom and folly. Through his "riddle-dissolving riddles," Touchstone prods the members of the audience into acknowledging their own paradoxical thoughts, actions, and beliefs, thus enabling them to see what "foolish humans" they truly are. In a similar vein, Bente Videbæk (1996) has asserted that Touchstone's purpose is to "lift the audience to a higher level" of awareness and enjoyment. The critic has claimed that Touchstone mirrors, mocks, and exposes the folly of those he encounters so that the audience can anticipate and "view the 'strange capers' on stage from the delightful distance this new transparency brings."

Rosalind's disguise as the youth Ganymede continues to intrigue modern scholars, particularly as it relates to the theme of sexual identity. Philip Traci (1981) has asserted that although the characters themselves are heterosexual, the dramatization of Rosalind's multiple identities reveals the homosexual side of *As You Like It,* especially when the role is performed by a boy actor, as it was in Elizabethan times. Analyzing the impact that homosexuality had on families, sex, and marriage in early modern England, Mario DiGangi (1996) has relied on the Ganymede myth, a narrative that recounts Jupiter's desire for his page Ganymede in lieu of his wife, Juno. DiGangi has contended the myth, used by Shakespeare as a "parable of conflict between husbands and wives," reflected the Renaissance culture's promotion of male homoeroticism and fear of female sexuality. Thus, Rosalind's male disguise permits her to "assay the sincerity of Orlando's love" and assuage her fears of postmarital sexual rejection.

The concept of time in *As You Like It* remains a focus of modern critics. Although the Forest of Arden has frequently been hailed as a timeless refuge where the inhabitants "fleet the time carelessly, as they did in the golden world" (I.i.118-19), recent criticism has focused on alternative views. Frederick Turner (1971) has suggested that time itself has not been eliminated, but that the "measurable, social time of clocks" has transmuted into diverse modes of time that reflect the characters' perceptions: the personal, subjective time that rules Rosalind and Orlando, the historical, objective time that Jacques embraces, and the natural, biological time that governs Touchstone. Arguing for the existence of "more than one 'time-sense'" in the play, Rawdon Wilson (1975) has examined the shift from objective to subjective time, noting that it marks not only the journey from the court to the forest, but the characters' attitudes toward change as well. Harry Morris (1975) has delved into the darker aspects related to the subject of time in *As You Like It*—death and decay. According to Morris, Touchstone is the initiator of the "death-in-Arcadia motif," the agent of time. His announcement, "Ay, now am I in Arden," echoes the expression, "Ay, now am I in Arcadia," the translated version of *et in Arcadia ego*. This phrase was inscribed on the tomb of a shepherd found in seventeenth-century pastoral paintings by both Guercino and Nicolas Poussin, nearly twenty-five years after

As You Like It was written. Morris nevertheless has speculated that perhaps an earlier source was available to Shakespeare, given the parallels between the death elements in the paintings—the skull, the dead shepherd, and all-devouring time—and those found in the Forest of Arden.

OVERVIEWS

D. J. Palmer (essay date 1971)

SOURCE: "*As You Like It* and the Idea of Play," in *Critical Quarterly*, Vol. 13, No. 3, Autumn, 1971, pp. 234-45.

[*In the following essay, Palmer analyzes the nature and purpose of play in* As You Like It, *and contends that "[t]he heart of the comedy might be described as a demonstration of man's natural propensity for play."*]

> Now in myth and ritual the great instinctive forces of civilized life have their origin: law and order, commerce and profit, craft and art, poetry, wisdom, and science. All are rooted in the primeval soil of play.
>
> (J. Huizinga, *Homo Ludens,* 1949)
>
> Here nowe I recke not much, to passe over untouched, how no maner acte, or noble deede was ever attempted, nor any arte or science invented, other, than of whiche I might fully be holden first author.
>
> (Erasmus, *The Praise of Folie,* translated by Sir Thomas Chaloner 1549)

There is only enough story in *As You Like It* to send the main characters to the Forest of Arden and finally to bring most of them out again. Once in the forest, the action virtually dispenses with narrative plot. Rosalind, for instance, no longer requires her disguise when she has found her father, whom she came to seek, and Orlando as well; but she delays the discovery of her identity for as long as she can. Like the other sojourners in Arden, she passes the time (although there seems nothing to wait for) by playing games. The heart of the comedy might be described as a demonstration of man's natural propensity for play.

We first hear of Arden in the opening scene, when Charles the wrestler describes how Duke Senior and his companions live in exile:

> They say he is already in the Forest of Arden, and a many merry men with him; and there they live like the old Robin Hood of England. They say many young gentlemen flock to him every day, and fleet the time carelessly, as they did in the golden world.

It seems as though life has become a pastime for the Duke and his followers, as though they have passed out of reality into a story-book world. A legend of Merry England is merged with the classical myth of the Golden Age, and even in the word 'flock' there is a hint of pastoral associations. Yet this is only by report, as the repetition of 'they say' reminds us. Hearsay distances reality, and is itself the way in which legends come into being. We are left uncertain, therefore, whether this idyllic picture of life in Arden is the creation of the Duke and his followers or of Charles and his informants.

As a world of make-believe, however, it certainly reflects a sharp contrast with the stern realities of court life, where instead of a society of 'merry men' there is the conflict of brother with brother. As Duke Frederick usurped his brother's throne, Oliver now plots against Orlando, and immediately after Charles' description of the pastimes pursued in Arden we hear talk of another kind of play: 'You wrestle tomorrow before the new Duke?' Wrestling makes sport out of conflict, yet Oliver has a sinister design to turn Charles' match with Orlando into a game to be played in deadly earnest.

The juxtaposition of these two images of play is followed in the second scene by Celia's persuasion of her cousin to shake off melancholy and 'be merry':

> *Rosalind:* From henceforth I will, coz, and devise sports. Let me see; what think you of falling in love?
>
> *Celia:* Marry, I prithee, do, to make sport withal; but love no man in good earnest, nor no further in sport neither than with safety of a pure blush thou mayst in honour come off again.
>
> *Rosalind:* What shall be our sport, then?
>
> *Celia:* Let us sit and mock the good housewife Fortune from her wheel, that her gifts may henceforth be bestowed equally.
>
> *Rosalind:* I would we could do so . . .
>
> (I. ii. 20-31)

Their sport is in devising sport, experimenting with the exhilarating possibilities of play, and casting around for some suitable object for their wit and mockery. At this point Touchstone joins them, and the advent of the professional fool adds another dimension to the treatment of life as a game. The fool's wit is intelligence at play, delighting in its own caprice, and extending by inverting them the contrary values of folly and wisdom.

Before we reach Arden, therefore, we are given some anticipation of the nature of play, and of the equivocal relations between fiction and reality, game and earnest, folly and wisdom. Each of the different kinds of pastimes presented in these first two scenes is a response to a society broken by violent enmities: Duke Senior and his companions turn their exile into a make-believe life of good fellowship; the wrestling match between Charles and Orlando is a projection of the hostility between the two brothers; while the games of wit that Celia and Rosalind play with Touchstone make sport out of adversity ('Nature hath given us wit to flout at Fortune', as Celia says). Play may be seen as a civilising impulse to create a better world, or as a way of releasing energies restrained by civilised life. Significantly, in a world that has been reduced to barbarism, where violence and cruelty are real enough, there is little use for play: the wrestling match turns into a murder-plot, and the fool is put to silence. Wrestling is a fairly primitive form of sport, in any case ('Is there yet another dotes upon rib-breaking?' says Rosalind, determined out of perverse humour to stay and watch a sport not fit for ladies). But while it reflects what has become of courtly tastes and values in the ascendancy of Duke Frederick, it also suggests by analogy the element of ritualised conflict that exists in wit-combats and games of mockery. Similarly, the pastoralism of Duke Senior's way of life in Arden, as Charles describes it, is both primitivist and civilizing.

If poetry and drama are themselves forms of play, Shakespeare is also playing games with his own art in *As You Like It*. His critical intelligence and creative imagination are held in perfect equilibrium as he sports with style through parody and burlesque, and finds in the pastimes of Arden primitive analogues to the spirit of comedy. The forest itself, as we are several times reminded, is both literally and figuratively 'this wide and universal theatre', the wooden circle into which we are drawn, like fools at the call of 'Ducdame', and the 'abandoned cave' that we leave when the comedy is over.

II

After Charles' picture of the exiled Duke and his 'merry men' fleeting the time carelessly, it comes as something of a surprise when we first encounter the Duke in Arden to find him indulging a vein of serious philosophising:

> Now, my co-mates and brothers in exile,
> Hath not old custom made this life more sweet
> Than that of painted pomp? Are not these woods
> More free from peril than the envious court?
> Here feel we not the penalty of Adam,
> The seasons' difference?—as the icy fang
> And churlish childing of the winter's wind,
> Which when it bites and blows upon my body,
> Even till I shrink with cold, I smile and say
> 'This is no flattery; these are counsellors
> That feelingly persuade me what I am'.
> Sweet are the uses of adversity . . .
>
> (II. i. 1-12)

The climate, too, is apparently less hospitable than Charles' comparison with the golden world led us to anticipate. But it is only the nature of the game that is different: this is just as much an exercise in make-believe as playing at Robin Hood. The Duke is using imagination to convert the harshness of existence in Arden into a blessing in disguise; the struggle for survival in a hostile world becomes a benevolent schooling in self-knowledge. It is not the philosophical truth of the Duke's propositions that require assent, but his willingness to look on the bright side. So Amiens responds, not with 'How wise, how true, how noble', but with

> Happy is your Grace,
> That can translate the stubbornness of fortune
> Into so quiet and so sweet a style.
>
> (18-20)

The only moralist in evidence is the winter's wind, whose 'churlish chiding' is in marked contrast with the 'sweet' style of the Duke. He speaks here as a poet, a maker of fictions, even necessary fictions.

But discarding this role for another, the Duke abruptly changes his tune by proposing another pastime, and one that matches the cruelty of nature which has just been his theme:

> Come, shall we go and kill us venison?

The victim of adversity would now reverse roles; but he recollects himself immediately and returns to his vein of fanciful reflection:

> And yet it irks me the poor dappled fools,
> Being native burghers of this desert city,
> Should, in their own confines, with forked heads
> Have their round haunches gor'd.
>
> (22-25)

By attributing rights of prior occupation to the deer, and conflating their 'forked heads' with those of the huntsmen's arrows, the Duke puts man and beast on the same level, and relates bloodsport to the barbarism of the world that has expelled him.

This is the attendant lord's cue to report Jaques' meditation on the 'poor sequestered stag'. It echoes the Duke's own sentimentalising of misfortune so well that we can recognise Jaques and the Duke as complementary figures, even though the Duke's 'sweet' style and his love of fellowship are antithetical to Jaques' bitter raillery and solitariness. The wounded deer was a commonplace emblem of affliction and melancholy retirement, and the familiar Elizabethan pun of hart/heart, which lies just below the threshold of this image, enables it to be extended to conceits about amorous suffering, as we shall see. For his part, by identifying with the forlorn beast Jaques dissociates himself from his comrades-in-exile:

> Thus most invectively he pierceth through
> The body of the country, city, court,
> Yea, and of this our life; swearing that we
> Are mere usurpers, tyrants, and what's worse,
> To fright the animals, and kill them up
> In their assign'd and native dwelling-place.
> (58-63)

Hunting now provides the metaphor for another pastime played between Jaques and the ducal party. His invective 'pierceth through/The body . . . of this our life' like a wounding arrow, but it causes amusement instead of pain, for the Duke and company treat Jaques as fair game for their mockery. The scene ends as the Duke goes to seek Jaques like a sportsman stalking his quarry:

> Show me the place;
> I love to cope him in these sullen fits,
> For then he's full of matter.

Again, in introducing Jaques through the attendant lord's account, the technique of report has been used to arouse anticipation and to present action at an ironic distance.

The first scene in Arden reflects the equivocal nature of play as a series of reversible roles: the victim of misfortune is also its agent, man and beast change places, the usurped become the usurpers, the hunters hunted, the critic a butt of his adversaries. Men are feelingly persuaded what they are, not by 'churlish chiding', but by the contrary parts they play in their games. And these games are a bitter-sweet mixture of whimsical sentiment and wanton cruelty.

III

Play in Arden takes the form of a series of encounters, seemingly at random, for the suspension of narrative progression produces a sense of timelessness. Scenes must follow each other in linear succession, but the effect created is also that of simultaneity as we are taken from 'one part of the forest' to 'another part of the forest', in the words that eighteenth-century editors used for their sceneheadings. Indeed within Arden there is no constant impression of different locations; although logically we must suppose that the Duke's encampment, Rosalind's cottage, and the trysting-place of Touchstone and Audrey lie at a distance from each other, the play as conceived for the Elizabethan stage calls only for a forest setting. The sense of meandering through the forest, of paths that cross by chance, and of a corresponding dislocation in the time scheme, is essential to the feeling of liberation in the free activity of play.

It is curious, therefore, that time occupies so much attention in Arden. In the original golden world of pastoralism, there was no time; spring was eternal. Arden, however, is subject to 'the penalty of Adam,/The seasons' difference', and characters are aware of the passing of time. But since 'there's no clock in the forest', as Orlando says, the sense of time is relative, and Rosalind replies, 'Time travels in divers paces with divers persons'. Despite Orlando's assertion, Touchstone has brought a timepiece with him, for Jaques describes the fool drawing 'a dial from his poke':

> And, looking on it with lack-lustre eye,
> Says very wisely 'It is ten o'clock;
> Thus we may see' quoth he 'how the world
>   wags;
> 'Tis but an hour ago since it was nine;
> And after one more hour 'twill be eleven;
> And so, from hour to hour, we ripe and ripe,
> And then, from hour to hour, we rot and rot;
> And thereby hangs a tale'.

If this melancholy rumination is an antecedent of Macbeth's despairing reflections on the 'petty pace' that creeps through 'tomorrow and tomorrow and tomorrow', it is also a tale told by an idiot. Touchstone is mocking the sense of futility produced not by time itself but by the way time is spent, in fruitless moralising. 'Pastime', on the other hand, is the way in which those who devise sports 'lose and neglect the creeping hours of time'. Rosalind, for instance, is well aware that love is subject to time: 'men are April when they woo, December when they wed; maids are May when they are maids, but the sky changes when they are wives'. But the purpose of play is to '*fleet* the time carelessly', to make time pass quickly, as in Marvell's response to 'time's winged chariot':

> Thus, though we cannot make our sun
> Stand still, yet we will make him run.

Since 'life is but a flower', in the words of the song, sweet lovers must 'therefore take the present time'. There is nothing leisurely about Rosalind's life in Arden; 'woman's thoughts run before her actions', and in addition to her impatience and restlessness, the headlong dash of the prose she speaks is that of a wit moving so fast that the tongue and breath can scarcely keep up with it:

> Good my complexion! dost thou think, though I am comparison'd like a man, I have a doublet and hose in my disposition? One inch of delay more is a South

Sea of discovery. I prithee tell me who is it quickly, and speak apace. I would thou could'st stammer, that thou might'st pour this conceal'd man out of thy mouth, as wine comes out of a narrowmouth'd bottle—either too much at once or none at all. I prithee take the cork out of thy mouth that I may drink thy tidings.

(III. ii. 180-189)

IV

The mating game is of course the comedy's principal pastime, and like the other encounters in Arden those between the lovers have a certain combative quality which recalls the wrestling at the beginning of the play. Indeed Orlando and Rosalind fall in love in wrestling terms. The conqueror of Charles confesses that 'my better parts are all thrown down' at his first meeting with Rosalind, and she acknowledges a similar defeat:

Sir, you have wrestled well, and overthrown
More than your enemies.

(I. ii. 233-234)

It is only one of the many perversities in love that losers are also winners (as in Juliet's paradox, 'learn me how to lose a winning match').

After this preliminary but decisive bout between Rosalind and Orlando, their mock-courtship in the forest is like a further series of rounds in which roles are again reversed. As Orlando was the unknown youth who overthrew Charles, he now finds himself outplayed by 'Ganymede'. Rosalind exploits the advantage of her disguise not only to take the initiative in wooing but to floor her partner in the lists of love (until she is herself literally floored by the sight of Orlando's bloody napkin). The analogy between love and fighting is continued in Rosalind's comparison of the encounter between Celia and Oliver with 'the fight of two rams and Caesar's thrasonical brag of "I came, saw, and overcame"'.

The wrestling match was a game played in deadly earnest, and the treatment of love as a contest between adversaries is a means of using play to explore the cruelties and antagonisms inherent in sexual relationships. Similarly the bawdiness of the comedy confronts aspects of sexuality denied by romantic or Petrarchan attitudes; as the hunting song puts it,

The horn, the horn, the lusty horn,
Is not a thing to laugh to scorn,

(IV. ii. 17-18)

but we do laugh at the old jest about cuckoldry, because we are inclined to joke about what is otherwise embarrassing. So Touchstone's impromptu jingle parodying Orlando's bad verses reflects in its indecent wordplay the use of game to release repressed realities:

If a hart do lack a hind,
Let him seek out Rosalinde.
If the cat will after kind,
So be sure will Rosalinde . . .
He that sweetest rose will find
Must find love's prick and Rosalinde.

(III. ii. 91-102)

The point of 'love's prick' is felt by Silvius as 'the wounds invisible/That love's keen arrows make', as he sublimates the pain of unrequited passion into extravagant conceits. Though Silvius the fictions of the Elizabethan sonneteers are taken to their furthest extreme and reduced to absurdity, in Shakespeare's own game with contemporary poetic fashions. But Silvius himself is not disabled by the wounds of mockery, embracing his folly and wallowing in Phebe's scorn. Their 'pageant truly played' is a sado-masochistic farce, another variation of that sexual conflict called love. Yet at the point of Phebe's greatest cruelty, when she would employ Silvius thanklessly in her own suit to 'Ganymede', the game ceases to be quite so funny, and Silvius' devotion becomes for one brief glorious moment entirely moving instead of merely silly:

So holy and so perfect is my love,
And I in such a poverty of grace,
That I shall think it a most plenteous crop
To glean the broken ears after the man
That the main harvest reaps.

But the poignancy topples over into absurdity again:

Loose now and then
A scatt'red smile, and that I'll live upon.

(III. v. 98-103)

Such a moment illustrates the precarious poise between playful and serious values in this comedy, and Shakespeare's ability to turn artifice inside out. 'The truest poetry is the most feigning'.

Of all the love-games played in the forest, Rosalind's counterfeiting with Orlando is the most sophisticated and double-edged. It is essentially equivocal because Rosalind has three *personae,* as herself, as 'Ganymede', and as 'Ganymede-playing-Rosalind', and we often cannot tell with which voice she is speaking. 'Ganymede' is an inversion of Rosalind's true identity both sexually and as an enemy of love:

Love is merely a madness; and, I tell you, deserves as well a dark house and a whip as madmen do; and the reason why they are not so punish'd and cured is that the lunacy is so ordinary that the whippers are in love too. Yet I profess curing it by counsel.

(III. ii. 368-372)

As the free play of a sportive disposition, assuming attitudes for their amusing possiblities rather than their truth, Rosalind's wit has something in common with the teasing disinterestedness of Touchstone's mockery, and her disguise is another version of the fool's motley. But at the same time, since we know 'how many fathom deep in love' she is, the constant scepticism directed towards love's young dream verges on the melancholy disillusion of Jaques. The distinguishing feature of her wit is that, unlike Jaques who is always in earnest and Touchstone who never is, Rosalind/Ganymede is poised in ambivalence:

> The poor world is almost six thousand years old, and in all this time there was not any men died in his own person, videlicet, in a love-cause. Troilus had his brains dash'd out with a Grecian club; yet he did what he could to die before, and he is one of the patterns of love. Leander, he would have liv'd many a fair year, though Hero had turn'd nun, if it had not been for a hot midsummer-night; for, good youth, he went but forth to wash him in the Hellespont, and, being taken with the cramp, was drown'd; and the foolish chroniclers of that age found it was—Hero of Sestos. But these are all lies: men have died from time to time, and worms have eaten them, but not for love.
>
> (IV. i. 9-95)

This is the literary game again, turning artifice against itself in mockery of poetic fictions. But if there is a joyful exuberance in the demolition of the 'foolish chroniclers', felt through the running-on of the clauses, the last sentence invites a pause and a slight change of tone. One can almost detect a certain wistfulness in the dying fall of the conclusion, 'but not for love', as though Rosalind sighs behind 'Ganymede's' back. Her enthusiasm for play reflects both security and insecurity in love:

> *Rosalind:* Now tell me how long you would have her, after you have possess'd her.
> *Orlando:* For ever and a day.
> *Rosalind:* Say 'a day' without the 'ever'. No, no, Orlando; men are April when they woo, December when they wed; maids are May when they are maids, but the sky changes when they are wives.
>
> (IV. i. 127-133)

At moments such as these, there is a precarious balance between wit and feeling, between the delightful make-believe and the uncomfortable reality.

As for Orlando, for most of the time in these scenes he is little more than Rosalind's 'feed' and the butt of her wit. Her treatment of her lover, whose charm hardly lies in his mental agility, betrays a latent sexual aggression which sometimes rises to the surface:

> *Rosalind:* Make fast the doors upon a woman's wit, and it will out at the casement; shut that, and 'twill out at the keyhole; stop that, 'twill fly with the smoke out at the chimney.
> *Orlando:* A man that had a wife with such a wit, he might say 'Wit, whither wilt?'
> *Rosalind:* Nay, you might keep that check for it, till you met your wife's wit going to your neighbour's bed.
> *Orlando:* And what wit could wit have to excuse that?
> *Rosalind:* Marry, to say she came to seek you there. You shall never take her without her answer, unless you take her without her tongue. O, that woman that cannot make her fault her husband's occasion, let her never nurse her child herself, for she will breed it like a fool!
>
> (IV. i. 144-157)

In those unenlightened days, before Women's Lib was afoot, such an attitude was accounted shrewishness. Rosalind was sufficiently peremptory when she encountered it in Phebe:

> Down on your knees,
> And thank heaven, fasting, for a good man's love,
>
> (III. v. 57-58)

but her own treatment of Orlando bears a close resemblance to that belligerence she falsely attributes to Phebe's style:

> Why, 'tis a boisterous and a cruel style;
> A style for challengers. Why, she defies me,
> Like Turk to Christian.
>
> (IV. iii. 31-33)

If Rosalind's wit frequently leaves us guessing how far she believes what she says, it also seems at times to run away with her: 'the wiser, the waywarder'. 'We that have good wits', says Touchstone, 'have much to answer for: we shall be flouting, we cannot hold'. Her disguise is not merely the assumption of another personality; it serves as a liberation and extension of her true self, licensing what feminine modesty and a sense of decorum would else inhibit. Her game with Orlando is a lesson in awareness for each of them, a rehearsal for encountering with resilience the adversities that lie ahead. Yet, if she is being cruel only to be kind, there is no doubt that she also enjoys the sport, and that she proves herself as capricious as 'that same wicked bastard of Venus, that was begot of thought, conceived of spleen, and born of madness, that blind rascally boy'. The truths that are spoken in jest flout not only at romantic illusions but at the painful realities as well. Nevertheless, if love has its limitations, so does the play-world of Rosalind's wit. She seems willing to prolong the game for ever, but when Orlando hears that his brother and Celia are betrothed without fussing about such preliminaries as courtship, he loses interest in make-believe, finding 'how bitter a thing it is to look into happiness through another man's eyes'. The game must come to an end when he 'can no longer live by thinking'.

V

As commentators on the world of play around them, Jaques and Touchstone are complementary figures, the one transparently foolish in his wisdom, the other opaquely wise in his fooling. In a comedy composed of mutually balancing elements, where the qualities of correspondence and antithesis are as evident in the encounters between the characters as in the disposition of the scenes or the characteristics of the prose style, Jaques and Touchstone are symmetrically related. Jaques himself recognises this kinship of opposites in his ambition for motley, though his description of his meeting with the fool is another example of the dramatic use of report to gain ironic distance:

> When I did hear
> The motley fool thus moral on the time,
> My lungs began to crow like chanticleer
> That fools should be so deep-contemplative.
>
> (II. vii. 28-31)

The encounter might have been staged, but instead the joke is enriched at Jaques' expense by having him relate what is patently a parody of his own 'deep-contemplative' moralising, while he himself remains oblivious to the irony: 'O that I were a fool!'

Jaques might be described as the one character in Arden who lacks the capacity for play, since he refuses to join any of the pastimes around him. In another sense, however, to this detached observer of the passing scene life has indeed become no more than a play, as he declares in his speech on the Seven Ages of Man. 'All the world's a stage', and he is its spectator. Yet nobody takes him at his own valuation, because there is a self-conscious preciosité about his melancholy that smacks of affectation:

> it is a melancholy of mine own, compounded of many simples, extracted from many objects, and, indeed, the sundry contemplation of my travels; in which my often rumination wraps me in a most humorous sadness.
>
> (IV. i. 14-18)

Jaques is suspected by his fellow-exiles of playing a game, and ironically he is made a subject for their sport; even Orlando gets the better of him. But Jaques comes into his own at the end of the comedy, by sustaining his part after they have abandoned theirs. He will remain in Arden while they return to court, and his consistency lends a certain authority to his wry benedictions. As he awaits the next party of 'convertites', Jaques the spectator is the only character who refuses to believe that the comedy is over.

If Jaques is paradoxically at home in exile, Touchstone is out of his element in Arden, wasting his sharpness on the desert air and the rustics, 'like Ovid among the Goths'. True to his name, his wit serves to bring out the nature of those he encounters, particularly through parody. He seems only to exist as a witty echo of those around him, turning all experience into a disinterested love of wordplay. His encounter with Corin is typical:

> *Corin:* And how like you this shepherd's life, Master Touchstone?
> *Touchstone:* Truly, shepherd, in respect of itself, it is a good life; but in respect that it is a shepherd's life, it is nought. In respect that it is solitary, I like it very well; but in respect that it is private, it is a very vile life. Now in respect that it is in the fields, it pleaseth me well, but in respect it is not in the court, it is tedious. As it is a spare life, look you, it fits my humour well; but as there is no more plenty in it, it goes much against my stomach.
>
> (III. ii. 11-20)

Touchstone's wit is evasive. He remains perfectly uncommitted, sceptical of every point of view. His motley is so impenetrable that we wonder whether there is any identity at all beneath it. And his relationship with Audrey especially brings out this opaqueness: it is impossible to be certain whether he is happy or cynical, infatuated or merely contemptuous in his intentions towards her:

> I press in here, sir, amongst the rest of the country copulatives, to swear and to forswear, according as marriage binds and blood breaks. A poor virgin, sir, an ill-favour'd thing, sir, but mine own; a poor humour of mine, sir, to take that that no man else will.
>
> (V. iv. 53-57)

One can understand Jaques' concern for Touchstone, and bafflement at intelligence seemingly wasting itself in this way: 'O knowledge ill-inhabited, worse than Jove in a thatched house!' Perhaps his function is no more than that of the professional fool, to expose others but not himself. Yet delightful as it is there remains a sense of limitation in Touchstone's inability to do anything except in play, forever hedging his bets.

Before the lovers are united in Hymen's bands (the ceremonials of the theatre doing service for those of the church), it is Touchstone who rounds off this comedy of pastimes with his account of how a quarrel may be translated into a courtly game:

> O, sir, we quarrel, in print by the book, as you have books for good manners. I will name you the degrees. The first, the Retort Courteous; the second, the Quip Modest; the third, the Reply Churlish; the fourth, the Reproof Valiant; the fifth, the Countercheck Quarrelsome; the sixth, the Lie with Circumstance; the seventh, the Lie Direct. All these you may avoid but the Lie Direct; and you may avoid that too with an If. I knew when seven justices could not take up a quarrel; but when the parties were met themselves, one of them thought but of an If, as: 'If you said so, then I said so'. And they shook hands, and swore brothers. Your If is the only peace-maker; much virtue in If.
>
> (V. iv. 85-97)

Like the Lie Direct, the confusions of make-believe are finally resolved with an If, as Rosalind reveals herself:

> *Duke Senior:* If there be truth in sight, you are my daughter.
> *Orlando:* If there be truth in sight, you are my Rosalind.
> *Phebe:* If sight and shape are true, Why then, my love adieu!
> *Rosalind:* I'll have no father, if you be not he;
> I'll have no husband, if you be not he;
> Nor ne'er wed woman, if you be not she.

And Hymen unites the lovers in similar style:

> Peace, ho! I bar confusion;
> 'Tis I must make conclusion
>   Of these most strange events.
> Here's eight that must take hands
> To join in Hymen's bands,
>   If truth holds true contents.

In the world that now lies before them, subject to time and the stubbornness of fortune, there is indeed much virtue in vows made with If. 'If' is the provisional assent that play requires of us.

Joseph Alulis (essay date 1994)

SOURCE: "Fathers and Children: Matter, Mirth, and Melancholy in *As You Like It*," in *Shakespeare's Political Pageant: Essays in Literature and Politics*, edited by Joesph Alulis and Vickie Sullivan, Rowman and Littlefield Publishers, Inc., 1994, pp. 37-60.

[*In the essay below, originally presented at the University of Chicago in 1994, Alulis argues that* As You Like It *is about the relation between differing social states—one of convention, represented by the fathers, and the other of nature, represented by the children—and examines issues of justice and dependence that occur in the play.*]

Midway through *As You Like It*, in act 3, scene 4, there occurs a passage that, taken in context, is very amusing and, as Duke Senior might say, "full of matter." Rosalind speaks to her "coz" and confidant, Celia, of a chance encounter with her father in the Forest of Arden. She brings her account to an abrupt close by saying, "But what talk we of fathers, when there is such a man as Orlando" (3.4.34-35).[1]

Part of what makes this line so attractive is that it captures the spirit of the comedy. We laugh because of the pleasure we take in the sight of young love. Granted, one might criticize Rosalind for a lack of filial piety. She seems inconsiderate of a father from whom she has been long separated.[2] But in her defense it might be said there is a natural justice in the daughter's neglect of the father for the sake of the lover: for every old father was once a young lover. This equation is made explicit just after Rosalind has fallen in love with Orlando. Celia, seeing her cousin absorbed in thought, asks her if she is thinking of her exiled father. Rosalind replies that that is only partly true; part of her thought is for her "child's father" (1.3.11).[3]

The significance of Rosalind's line in act 3, scene 4 is, first, that it reflects the structure of the play. The play literally begins with the children talking of the fathers; first, Orlando talking of his father, Sir Rowland de Boys, then Celia and Rosalind talking of their fathers, Dukes Frederick and Senior. The latter two fathers dominate acts 1 and 2 respectively. Then, in the center of the play, the fathers are forgotten. Through all of act 3, save a short first scene, the fathers are gone from the stage and this is true of all of act 4 as well and nearly all of act 5. It is only at the end, in the last scene of the play, that the fathers are recalled.

This structure, in turn, points to the play's "matter," that is, what the play is about.[4] The great division in the play is between the court and the Forest of Arden. This division, as has often been noted, is not one between a corrupt state of society and an idyllic state of nature but rather between two different social states or ways of life: one a way of wealth and brilliance, the other, of simplicity and freedom.[5] But the contrast between these two ways of life, by raising the question of which is better (cf. the conversation between Touchstone and Corin, 3.2.11-83) suggests the idea of nature, not as a possible human state distinct from society but as a standard by which different social states may be evaluated. In this way, the theme of the relation of nature and convention emerges. This theme is then readily associated with the relations of fathers and children. For it is the fathers who make the rules, thereby defining a way of life, and it is the children who encounter these rules as an alien imposition upon their own natural impulses. But nature in this sense is not a standard but the human given, which must be shaped to conform to the standard. Thus nature appears in two lights. If the fathers represent "the right way of life," then nature is both child and "super" or "first" father.[6] In the play, Rosalind personifies both senses, as teacher and lover, judge and daughter.

The argument of this chapter is that the matter of the play is the relation between nature and convention, the former understood as both standard and native impulse, the latter understood as a society's accepted ideas of right and wrong and the mechanisms by which such ideas are made to govern our lives. The play explores the different standards of justice supplied by nature and convention and the different ways in which the children, or nature, are dependent upon and independent of the fathers, or convention. What makes this play the delightful affair it is, is that while it affirms an essential goodness of nature, hence the deficiencies of convention that depart from nature's standard, it also shows the necessary role of convention in relation to natural impulses, both in curbing those that are harmful and in protecting and fostering those that are beneficial. It rejects the melancholy view, occasioned by the spectacle of human injustice, that both nature and convention are meaningless, respectively teaching and serving only the pursuit of selfish ends by the most powerful. Shakespeare invites us to see our condition in nature and the world rather as an occasion of mirth. Whether we wish to accept that invitation is another question.

Matter: Nature and Convention

The matter of a tension between nature and convention, that is, between what is simply good and what is so because it is our own, is presented most plainly in the scene that introduces Rosalind, in the conversation between her and Celia that opens the scene. Celia's father, Duke Frederick, has taken from Rosalind's father, Duke Senior, the dukedom to which the latter possesses conventional title as "senior." Celia complains that Rosalind's sadness at her father's exile proves that Rosalind does not love Celia as much as Celia loves her. Had their situations been reversed, Celia says, she would have taught herself to take Rosalind's father as her own (1.2.7-13). But while the two men are equally fathers, they are not equally worthy of love: Duke Frederick is an unjust man and Duke Senior, his brother, is not. Celia loves her father as her own, not as good, and so cannot expect another, lacking this motive, to love him as she does.

That Celia understands this, act 1 makes clear. In her initial conversation with Rosalind, she tacitly censures her father's usurpation by assuring Rosalind that when she, Celia, inherits the dukedom, she will restore it to Rosalind (1.1.16-19). The censure is merely tacit because of filial piety: Celia honors her father as good because he has been good to her.[7] This piety is reflected in her anger at Touchstone later in this scene when he makes an observation that reflects badly upon Duke Frederick (70-79). At the same time, Celia honors what is good simply, that is, what is just, even though counter to her father's will. This is expressed in her commitment to restore the dukedom to Rosalind. In one sense, here, too, the good is merely conventional: the dukedom belongs to Rosalind as heir of the conventionally sanctioned possessor. But Celia's commitment seems to spring primarily from her "affection" for Rosalind for her personal qualities and as such may be said to reflect a love of justice as determined by nature. Rosalind should have the dukedom because she can make the best use of the office.[8] For Celia's love for Rosalind is a tribute to Rosalind's superior merit (cf. 1.3.67-68). In fact, Celia does love Rosalind more than Rosalind loves Celia because Rosalind is more worthy of love.[9] Though it is "natural" for Celia to protest against this inequality, it also appears that she accepts it and this, too, may be described as natural. In this way Celia is to be distinguished from her father.

Before scene 2 ends Celia does explicitly express her distress at her father's actions. When Duke Frederick refuses to reward Orlando for his victory in the wrestling match, Celia comments to Rosalind: "My father's rough and envious disposition/Sticks me at heart" (1.2.230-31). Here, too, a dual loyalty is expressed. A natural love of justice binds Celia to condemn the action while the tie of blood makes this necessity painful. In the third scene of act 1, in which Duke Frederick commits his third act of injustice, banishing Rosalind, Celia breaks with her father. But she does not seek to undo his actions or even openly reproach him; she removes herself from his dominion. Celia freely renounces all the goods associated with her father's rule: "Let my father find another heir" (1.3.95). Even more to the point, making clear the real meaning of her first speeches in the play, Celia seeks Rosalind's father for her own. After Duke Frederick leaves, having pronounced his sentence of banishment, Celia says to Rosalind, "Wilt thou change fathers? I will give thee mine" (1.3.87). Then, when the two plan their course of action in banishment, it is Celia, not Rosalind, who suggests that they seek out Rosalind's father in the Forest of Arden (102-3). Children love and need their fathers, just as all human beings need and love some rule that orders their collective life. But while they honor their fathers, all children wish that their fathers might be good, just as human beings desire that their collective way of life may be one that most closely conforms to what is simply good for humankind.

In order to distract themselves from melancholy reflections, occasioned by the presence and absence of fathers, Celia makes the following suggestion: "Let us sit and mock the good hussif Fortune from her wheel, that her gifts may henceforth be bestowed equally" (1.2.30-32). Celia's chief complaint against fortune, it seems, is the accident of her birth, that she should have the father she has rather than another. But whether this is a complaint against fortune or nature remains a question.

The way in which Rosalind takes up Celia's invitation offers a further development on the relation between nature and convention: "I would we could [mock fortune into bestowing her gifts equally]; for her benefits are mightily misplaced, and the bountiful blind woman doth most mistake in her gifts to women" (33-35).[10] Unlike a comparison of particular individuals, like Duke Frederick and Duke Senior, Rosalind speaks of women as a class being unjustly treated by fortune. She cannot mean that the distribution of worldly goods among individual women is mistaken because there is no reason to think this is any more mistaken among women than among men. The context suggests why this thought should be present to her mind. Fortune has deprived her father of his dukedom and in so doing has imposed a burden upon her as well. But fortune's blow to Duke Senior is assuaged as hers is not. As Duke Senior tells us in his first speech in act 2, the forest, being free of the ills inescapably associated with the life of the court, offers some compensation for his loss of office (2.1.1-17). Rosalind, however, detained at court, is denied that compensation. Her detention by her uncle reflects the fact that generally women, as the weaker sex, are denied the freedom men enjoy. Rosalind's thought, then, is that, in general, because women are weaker than men, fortune treats them less well. But Rosalind does not make her complaint against nature for making women physically weaker. Nature, presumably, has supplied ample compensation for the difference in bodily strength. For Rosalind, what is at issue is not nature but how we respond to nature; that is, the conventional arrangements that govern the relations of men and women. The natural physical weakness of women does not dictate that they be accorded an inferior status: that is the work of convention, the will of the fathers. If "the good hussif Fortune" is especially unjust in her treatment of women, it is only because of the antecedent injustice of the fathers.[11]

In directing her complaint against fortune rather than the fathers, Rosalind may be understood as shielding Celia from a harsh truth. Indeed, Celia is herself engaged in a kind of salutary self-deception insofar as her complaint against fortune on account of her father is, in fact, a complaint against nature. By substituting fortune for nature she succeeds in redirecting her complaint away from a provident deity, as nature's author, and toward a goddess of notoriously unreliable character. Rosalind's superiority to Celia is evident in her clear-sighted recognition of what belongs to each, nature and "fortune," and her ability to bear with equanimity the spectacle of the unequal distribution of their gifts. In particular she is able to bear the injustice to which she as a woman is subject. This capacity for bearing results from a recognition of a kind of necessity: because men are physically stronger, they *can* impose rules that are more advantageous to themselves and so *will* do so.[12] But it seems also to be related to a recognition that the natural relations of men and women also serve to moderate the degree of injustice that the former naturally do the latter. When they are searching for some sport to make themselves merry, it is Celia who suggests that they sit and mock fortune. Rosalind makes a different suggestion: "What think you of falling in love?" (1.2.24). Love softens the harshness of the dictates of the fathers.[13] Further, if convention unfairly forecloses from us the enjoyment of some of the pleasures that nature affords us as human beings, it does not necessarily foreclose all. One measure of the degree to which the conventional idea of justice departs from a natural standard is the quantity and quality of the natural pleasures it leaves within the power of those capable of enjoying them. In turning her thoughts to love in the fullest sense of the idea, Rosalind turns to what is the preeminent good available to her and, perhaps, the preeminent good available to any human being as such.[14]

The next stage of the conversation confirms the idea that Rosalind's account of fortune directs our attention to the relation between conventional and natural goods. Celia agrees with Rosalind that fortune treats women unjustly but she apparently misunderstands Rosalind's meaning.

> *Celia:* 'Tis true, for those that she makes fair, she scarce makes honest; and those that she makes honest, she makes very ill-favouredly.
>
> *Rosalind:* Nay now thou goest from Fortune's office to Nature's; Fortune reigns in gifts of the world, not in the lineaments of Nature.
>
> (36-41)

Celia is, at least in part, making a little joke: the "fair," being the object of so much attention, have a greater need for chastity than the ill-favored, while it is precisely the lack of opportunity that makes the ill-favored "honest." (Hamlet, in a less playful way, also comments on the relation between beauty and honesty.[15]) By making beauty a gift of fortune, Celia again begs the question of what belongs to nature and what to fortune. Rosalind distinguishes between the gifts of nature, beauty and just parents, and those of the world, wealth and, apparently, honesty. Celia responds to

Rosalind by seeking to reassert fortune's rule even in nature's realm: "No? When Nature hath made a fair creature, may she not fall into the fire?" (42-43).

This idea of the power of accident, however, does not lessen the utility of Rosalind's distinction between nature and "the world." Rather it clarifies the relation between the two. Because the good things that nature gives us may, in a contingent universe, suffer harm, the fathers should arrange things in the world to protect them. The role of convention is to protect and foster nature's goods. The fathers are entrusted with the responsibility to take care of things in the world for the common good. They do this best when their ideas of justice and right and wrong conform most closely to what nature dictates in these matters.

An important way in which convention protects and fosters nature's goods is by education, especially moral education. When Celia speaks, in the context of beauty and chastity, of a fair creature's "fall into the fire," the primary significance of "fire" is not literal but metaphorical. Fire is a common Shakespearean usage for "sexual ardor" or lust and from this takes on the additional meaning of the burning of veneral disease.[16] In this sense, it is "honesty" that saves one from the "fire" and Rosalind, in reply to Celia, makes honesty a gift not of nature but of the world. Honesty is the product of the education ordained by the fathers for the protection of the children.[17] Here is a convention that conforms to nature's rule, an instance in which the fathers' will is simply benign.

If we now turn to the first scene of the play, we see that it concerns the issue of education as, in both a literal and legal sense, the dictate of a father's will. Moreover, the issue here is precisely the distribution of material goods so as to protect and cultivate nature's gifts. The play opens with Orlando lamenting the fact that his education or, rather, lack of it, "mines [his] gentility" (1.1.20). His father, Sir Rowland de Boys, upon his death, provided for Orlando's education but his eldest brother, Oliver, in whose hands it rests to execute Sir Rowland's will, has deprived Orlando of his due. The old father's will is frustrated by his successor, the new father. Such gentility as Orlando possesses is not a product of education but a gift of nature. He is "gentle, never schooled yet learned, full of noble device" (1.1.164-65). Insofar as "gentility" includes virtue (cf. Touchstone's play with the different meanings of "manners," 3.2.39-43), one sees another sign of it in Orlando's native sense of justice.

In complaining to Adam of his plight, he shows he is able to weigh carefully what is due himself and what is due others: "I will no longer endure it [the injustice Oliver does him], though yet I know no wise remedy how to avoid it" (1.1.23-25). Though the victim of injustice, Orlando will not be so unjust to others, or to himself, as to embrace a remedy that he cannot approve as wise. Orlando is, so to speak, naturally virtuous. And yet one may perhaps detect a slight weakening of his disposition in the desperate remarks he makes to Rosalind and Celia before the wrestling match. He claims to have no friends, which is unjust to Adam; declares himself willing to die in a frivolous cause, which is unjust to himself; and opines that the world will suffer no injury by his loss because he has no place in it, which is unjust to the world. For we already know from his brother how much he is "in the heart of the world" for the sake of his natural gifts (1.2.177-80, 1.1.165-67). In short, as he says to his brother, he is in danger of being "marred" by his fortune (1.1.31-34).

Like Duke Senior Orlando is the victim of injustice at the hands of his brother. But by a natural standard he is a victim of injustice at the hands of Sir Rowland as well. For Orlando clearly possesses greater natural gifts than his brother, Oliver, and therefore can be expected to make better use of the world's gifts. But convention, the will of the fathers, dictates that the eldest son be favored before the youngest. In Shakespeare's source, Thomas Lodge's *Rosalynde,* Orlando's counterpart, Rosader, though the youngest, is awarded by the father the largest share of the estate because of his natural virtue.[18] Shakespeare alters his source to place Orlando in a situation where he can be described as suffering injustice at the hands of convention. In scene 2, when Rosalind makes a gift to Orlando to compensate for Duke Frederick's poor treatment of him, she speaks of herself as "one out of suits with fortune" (1.2.236). We recognize this description as appropriate to both young people because of the particular injustices they have suffered. But, as Shakespeare has taken care to suggest, it fits them also as members of classes of persons who are disadvantaged by the fathers generally.[19]

To women and youngest sons we may add as a third class of persons who are "out of suits with fortune": those of mean birth, like Adam.[20] Though we see Adam only as an old man, he recalls a time when he was Orlando's age. He tells us he was seventeen when he began service to Orlando's father and shows us by his account of his prudence (his temperance and his savings) that he is not unintelligent (2.3.71-72, 38-39, 47-51). Nonetheless, fortune decreed that he should lead the life of an "ox" and in age, be treated like a "dog" (1.1.10, 81). And yet Adam accepts his position and we are invited to admire his loyalty to the master who treats him well within the limits of the relation in which fortune has placed them both.

Here then is the question of the relation of nature and convention in its most troubling form. We have considered three characters "out of suits with fortune," Rosalind, Orlando, and Adam. Each represents a class—

women, youngest sons, persons of mean birth—that suffers by convention or the will of the fathers. Each by reason of personal merit deserves better at the world's hands. But not one condemns the fathers or seeks to reverse the fathers' will by force or fraud, justifying such expedients by an appeal to a natural standard. Shakespeare dramatically endorses their self-restraint by portraying each favorably and then ratifies this endorsement by portraying unfavorably a similarly situated character who does violate convention's dictate. This is Duke Frederick, who, like Orlando, is a younger son. In the persons of Frederick and Orlando Shakespeare presents two contrasting understandings of nature and convention and the relation of the two.

Like Orlando, Frederick appears superior to his brother in certain natural gifts. Clearly Duke Senior is superior morally: lords follow him into exile in devotion to his character and we see him in the forest of Arden bearing his exile without bitterness (1.1.100-104; 2.1.1-17). But the very fact that he is in exile may be taken as a sign of his weakness as a ruler. He has been taken unawares by his brother and deprived of his dukedom. Moreover, unlike Prospero in *The Tempest,* Duke Senior does not recover his state by his own actions. This suggests that Frederick, at least in a kind of practical sagacity, is superior to his elder brother. But Orlando, occupying a similar position of superiority vis-à-vis his brother, does not even think of justifying usurpation on that ground. He is wary of acting too rashly even in advancing his strictly conventional claims (1.1.23-35). The ground of this wariness is suggested by the way he characterizes that conventional arrangement that accords the greater share to the eldest. Orlando calls it the "courtesy of nations" (1.1.46). By contrast, Frederick's disregard for the same convention bespeaks a view of it as the "curiosity of nations," an arbitrary arrangement not worthy of respect. Frederick, like Edmund, mocks courtesy; Orlando respects it.[21]

The rules of courtesy prescribe those practices by which human beings curb their egoism in their interactions with others so that society may be peaceable. The idea of the courtesy of nations reminds us of the constant danger of an appeal to force in human intercourse. In his first encounter with Duke Senior, when Orlando appears sword in hand to demand satisfaction of his needs, the older man asks him if he is "a rude despiser of good manners" (2.7.93). Of course, Orlando is just the opposite and, at the hands of one like himself, secures his needs by courtesy rather than force. In despising courtesy Frederick implicitly embraces an appeal to force to decide differences among egoistic human beings. He does so confident that his superior ability will reward him with success regardless of harm to others.

It is the most powerful, the fathers, who set down the rules of courtesy as a restraint upon themselves as well as the less powerful. But it is more than an egoistic desire for peace that prompts respect for the imperfect rules of justice they dictate. When Orlando confronts Oliver over the injustice Oliver does him within the limits of convention, he tells us twice in the space of fifty lines that he is prompted to do so by "the spirit of [his] father" (1.1.21-22, 70). The spirit of his father aims at justice even if the father's will is defective.[22] One submits to the will of the father, though it sometimes be unjust by nature's standard, because the spirit is true. That spirit is itself a gift of nature. It is that disposition to justice that we all have to a greater or lesser degree by nature. In the case of Orlando and Rosalind the formula "spirit of my father" applies literally. Sir Rowland de Boys and Duke Senior are both men who love justice, hence the tie of love between them (1.2.224; 1.3.27; 2.7.198-99).[23] But Celia, who we have noticed loves justice, is the daughter of a father who does not, just as Sir Rowland has a son, Oliver, who does not. Each case casts some light upon the other. As a just Sir Rowland had two sons, one just and one unjust, so one might imagine that Duke Senior and Duke Frederick had a father who was just.

The love of justice in Celia is the spirit of her father's father. The generational scheme Shakespeare presents us in the two families leads the (traditional) mind backward to the first father, Adam, whom God made in his image. The conversions of Oliver and Duke Frederick at the play's end depend ultimately upon the triumph in them of the spirit of the first father, a triumph the possibility of which is thus suggested in the opening scene of the play. By the same token, reliance upon God is a reliance upon the spirit God places in man. Thus, in venturing forth with Orlando, Adam, the old servant, trusts that "He that doth the ravens feed, / Yea providently caters for the sparrow, / [Will] be comfort to may age" (2.3.43-45). When Adam is saved from starvation in act 2, scene 7 by Duke Senior, we are invited to think his faith is rewarded.[24]

Frederick's scorn for courtesy, his appeal to force to attain his title and to secure it for his heirs, suggests a radically different vision of nature and convention. In this view nature ordains no good but personal advantage, the will of the fathers seeks no more than this, and the spirit of the father aims only at power. If convention only serves the advantage of the more powerful, why shouldn't Frederick scorn it when it is disadvantageous to him, especially if he has the force and wit enough to do so successfully?[25] In this view the world is a place of "stern alarums" rather than "delightful measures" and life is to be encountered with vigor as a bracing struggle to get to the top of the heap by fair means or foul.[26] To one who does not share this view, however, this vision is an unattractive one. It is the world described by Duke Senior and the lords who surround him in the forest of Arden, a world that the egoism of individuals fills with "peril" and "ingratitude," in which "most friendship is feigning, most loving mere folly" (2.1.4; 2.7.176, 181). Love in this view is not the preeminent good but a snare and a weakness (cf. 3.2.277-78).

Surely there is peril, ingratitude, and falseness in the world, but that these things are dominant is a vision of the world that Shakespeare encourages us to reject as false. By and large, the world appears very well in this play. The world loves Orlando for his natural virtue (1.1.162-69) and one surmises it is for the same reason that it loved his father (1.2.224-25). Each day men of power give their allegiance to Duke Senior in preference to his usurping brother (5.4.153-54). Moreover, though Frederick is temporarily successful, it is the very nature of the world that dooms his usurpation to ultimate failure. The people are devoted to Rosalind for her virtue, which raises the likelihood that they will support her restoration at the earliest opportunity. It is this natural bent of the world that Frederick attempts to counter by banishing Rosalind (1.3.76-78).[27] But we know that his effort to secure the title to his heirs is fruitless because Celia has already promised to restore the dukedom to her cousin.

Finally, Shakespeare portrays the ground of Frederick's view and action as ugly. His action arises from something like a resentment of nature's goodness—resentment that nature's goodness does not yield to his will. Duke Frederick treats Orlando unjustly at the wrestling match because Orlando's father, Sir Rowland de Boys, was his enemy (1.2.213-19). Sir Rowland's enmity presumably sprang from the fact of Duke Frederick's injustice. By means of that injustice Duke Frederick attained the power, in terms of the world's gifts, that he must have thought would make him esteemed. Yet nonetheless, "all the world" loved Sir Rowland for his goodness while even those who pay court to Duke Frederick do not respect him (1.2.224-25 and Le Beau's remarks to Orlando in the same scene, 256-57). Frederick hates Sir Rowland and thereby Orlando because of their goodness and because the world in esteeming them more highly for their goodness than him for his "worldly" success is not as craven as he is.[28]

If the world were really such as Frederick imagines it, that would be an occasion for melancholy for anyone who loved the idea of justice as something more than the egoism of the strongest. It is that thought which accounts for the presence in the play of one of Shakespeare's most memorable characters, Jaques. Nature looks to Jaques as it does to Frederick; it is the scene of a cruel struggle for power by selfish individuals. But while this spectacle fills Frederick with ambition and resolve, it fills Jaques with dismay. He is, in Orlando's phrase, "Monsieur Melancholy" (3.2.288-89). Jaques represents, by reflection, the idea of nature as incapable of recognizing a good understood as independent of human will for its being. Shakespeare's depiction of Jaques, then, constitutes a further exploration of the matter developed in the first act of the play and to that depiction I will now turn.

Melancholy

Jaques is not merely a memorable character; we tend to like him and Shakespeare gives us some good reasons for doing so. He belongs to the circle of Duke Senior, which puts him in the camp of the just. He is one of those Lords of whom Charles spoke who have sacrificed their property out of love for Duke Senior (1.1.99-104). Jaques, not present on Duke Senior's first appearance, is spoken of by the Duke and other lords with evident goodwill (2.1.25-69); his melancholy is treated as a harmless, even amusing, disposition. If he is somewhat excessive in his criticism, still there is much in the world of which to be critical. He does not appear to be depressing company. And who has not sometime or other sucked melancholy out of a song (2.5.11-13)?[29]

It remains, however, that Shakespeare censures Jaques. Successively, in acts 2, 3, and 4, Duke Senior, Orlando, and Rosalind respectively, rebuke, reject, and ridicule Jaques's melancholy. One must feel the full force of this repudiation to appreciate the play's meaning.

The occasion for Jaques's melancholy seems to be the wickedness of the world (cf. 2.1.25-63). But in his consciousness of this Jaques is not unique. All in Duke Senior's party comment upon the same theme. In the speech that opens act 2, Duke Senior describes the court as "envious" and favorably compares the "icy fang . . . of the winter's wind" to the "flattery" of "counsellors" (2.1.6-11).[30] The idea is echoed by the song the Lords sing in the last scene of this act, which concludes: "Heigh-ho, sing heigh-ho, unto the green holly, / Most friendship is feigning, most loving mere folly" (2.7.190-191).

But while the other lords observe and comment upon the injustice of humankind they do not take pleasure in the contemplation of it the way Jaques does. More important, for Jaques the wickedness men do suggests that nature is utterly corrupt. In describing his melancholy to Ganymede, he tells "him" that it results from "the sundry contemplations of my travels" (4.1.17-18). What prompted Jaques to travel and what he saw he does not say. But we can surmise the answers to these questions from what we already know about Jaques. From the first, Jaques is presented as a witness to the folly, misery, and wickedness of human beings. As the First Lord reports to Duke Senior, in his moralizing, Jaques "invectively" pierces through "The body of country, city, court" (2.1.58-59). The manners of men differ from one sphere to the other but are no less wicked. We are led to the thought that Jaques went abroad to see if there was any place where men were wise, happy, and just and discovered that no such place exists.[31]

The melancholy of Jaques suggests that the will of the father is hopelessly corrupt. Whatever good nature may be said to intend for humankind, convention does little to foster it and much to undermine it. But the fathers are themselves products of nature. If their wills are hopelessly corrupt, then so is nature. One conforms to the will of the fathers, adopts manners, to escape the brutality of unchecked egoism but does not thereby escape the more refined egoism of social life in which manners merely cloak our indifference to or even hatred of each other (cf. 3.2.249-54). The choice for the individual seems to be between the savagery of anarchy or the injustice of the fathers' rule. Jaques presents this melancholy view most fully in the last scene of act 2 and it is in the same scene that it is most effectively rebutted.

In the third scene of act 2 we see Orlando flee Oliver for fear of his life, accompanied by Adam. They have no clear destination. In scene 6 we see Adam on the verge of collapse from hunger. Orlando settles him in some shelter and goes in search of food. In the next scene he comes upon Duke Senior's group and attempts to extort food from them by the threat of force. He has recourse to force because he thinks he is no longer in the realm of the fathers but in a Hobbesian state of nature: "I thought that all things had been savage here" (2.7.107). Duke Senior responds in such a way as to make him doubt this judgment. Orlando then applies the following test to determine whether these strangers are civil rather than savage. Here is what he asks his unknown host:

> If ever you have look'd on better days;
> If ever been where bells have knoll'd to church;
> If ever sat at any good man's feast;
> If ever from your eyelids wip'd a tear,
> And know what 'tis to pity and be pitied,
> Let gentleness my strong enforcement be.
> (2.7.113-18)

To this Duke Senior replies in kind:

> True is it that we have seen better days,
> And have with holy bell been knoll'd to church,
> And sat at good men's feasts, and wip'd our eyes
> Of drops that sacred pity hath engender'd;
> And therefore sit you down in gentleness,
> And take upon command what help we have
> That to your wanting may be minister'd.
> (120-26)

The effect is a kind of litany, chanted by the new father and the old father, of the way of the fathers when that way is designed to foster and cultivate nature's goods. The first institution characteristic of this way is the family. When Orlando, surveying a group of men separate from women and children, asks them if they have seen "better days," he is inquiring if they have known the gentling experience of family life. The second institution is that of religion, that is, the means by which we express our love of God who alone is good. Beyond this, his speech describes mores that encourage liberality and compassion. These are the means to tame egoism and foster nature's goods.

Just before Orlando entered Jaques had described a different way to deal with the wickedness of humankind. Given his vision of our moral incorrigibility, the aim would not be to make us good so much as to hold wrongdoing in check. He addresses the Duke: "Give me leave / To speak my mind, and I will through and through / Cleanse the foul body of th' infected world" (58-61). Now around the time this play appeared satire was very much in fashion. In 1598 John Marston published a work in this genre entitled *The Scourge of Villainy*. This is exactly what Jaques is proposing: to scourge men, verbally by raillery and mockery, to curb their wrongdoing by calling attention to the ugliness of their wickedness.[32] This is a very different approach from that which Orlando describes and Duke Senior echoes. Shortly after Marston's book appeared, the Bishop of London banned all works of satire.[33] The thought behind this action may have been the same as that which prompts the Duke to reply to Jaques with a rebuke.

> Most mischievous foul sin, in chiding sin.
> For thou thyself hast been a libertine,
> As sensual as the brutish sting itself,
> And all th'embossed sores and headed evils
> That thou with license of free foot hast caught
> Wouldst thou disgorge into the general world.
> (64-69)

The result of Jaques's proposed railing would be the opposite of what he intended. One whose ability to expose wickedness to mockery depends upon his own intimate acquaintance with it may rather put ideas in the heads of the innocent than correct the erring.[34] More important, Jaques would corrupt because his scourging would be seen by many, especially the young, as a cynical portrait of the way men inescapably are. In the end, what Jaques would inculcate, to use one critic's description of Marston's view, is "a dark pessimistic weariness that falls little short of complete despair."[35]

When Orlando leaves to fetch Adam, Jaques delivers his "seven ages" of man speech (2.7.139-66). This is, probably, the most often noted speech of the play. But given the context, it is a mistake to read this as intended by Shakespeare as a simply true or complete picture of human experience. Rather, the speech perfectly expresses Jaques's melancholy by portraying its cause. It depicts life as low and meaningless, dominated by senseless passion and corrupt motives. James Smith likens it to Macbeth's more famous comparison of life to the part acted by "a poor player": "a tale / Told by an idiot, full of sound and fury, / Signifying nothing."[36]

Though he has just rebuked Jaques for his melancholy vision of humankind, the Duke does not object to this speech. He is silent, I think, because it is well for us to be reminded of our foibles as long as the reminder is offered in a manner that reduces the likelihood of corruption. Jaques's scourge of villainy here is not "as free as the wind" but is restricted to a small circle; it is a rebuke to the ruler, the Duke, not to forget himself.[37] In addition, as has been often noted, all who hear it see something contrary.[38] They see a young man, "the lover" of Jaques's "seven ages," moved by "sacred pity" to care for an old man whose known worth marks him as a venerable being not a "pantaloon" and these two greeted by a "justice" whose wisdom we known is not a matter of "saws" drawn from books but something "feelingly" acquired in the Forest of Arden.

What makes Jaques attractive to us is precisely his goodness. He is not simply hopeless. His travels may have shown him that most men are corrupt and yet he knows some who are not: himself and those friends of the Duke who sacrificed material goods out of loyalty to virtue. In act 2, scene 5 where he improvises his *"ducdame"* stanzo, he mocks those who leave "wealth and ease / A stubborn will to please" (49-50) meaning, surely, those he addresses with his "Greek invocation," the followers of the Duke. But he is one of their number. Here he is like the Fool in *King Lear,* noting what the wicked think wise without himself following their opinion.[39] But he is less wise than the Fool because too doubtful of his own goodness. By suggesting that his action springs less from decency than "a stubborn will" he does himself, and nature, an injustice.[40] By the same token, we can let our perception of the world's injustice distort our vision. There is reason to be more hopeful about nature than Jaques. This reason is suggested in the persons of Rosalind and Orlando, the children, and it is to them, especially Rosalind, that I turn for my discussion of mirth.

Mirth

The word mirth occurs only twice in the play, but these two instances frame the action of the drama. It occurs in the second scene of the play and in the last. In the first case Rosalind is the speaker; in the second, Hymen. But insofar as Rosalind controls Hymen, it is she who speaks both times (cf. 5.2.58-62). The first time she comments that she is without mirth; the second time, the scene of the weddings that conclude the play, there is mirth in abundance. Both usages suggest a single meaning: mirth is occasioned by a union of two things that belong together, fathers and children, men and women. In the first scene, Rosalind is without mirth because of the forced separation between her and her father (1.2.2-6). In the last scene, there is mirth because she has been united, not only with her father but with "her child's father." Here is what Rosalind gives Hymen to say on the latter occasion: "Then is there mirth in heaven, / When earthly things made even / Atone together" (5.4.107-109).[41] The proper relation of fathers and children, that is, when nurture looks to and accomplishes the good of nature, is an occasion for mirth. Mirth is the sentiment proper to the comedic resolution of the matter of the play; it is the state to which a comedy about fathers and children, nature and convention looks as its conclusion.

But Hymen adopts a heavenly perspective. There is another kind of mirth on earth occasioned by just the opposite phenomenon: discord between things that belong together. Much of the humor of the play involves this earthly mirth: discord between nature and convention and discord within nature itself. Hymen's speech in the last scene serves as our point of departure. The point of view in these lines is explicitly divine and the divine teaching of the Judeo-Christian tradition, the tradition the play evokes in the person of Adam and in the word "atone" in the above speech, is that nature is good, albeit fallen.[42] These two ideas, the essential goodness of nature and our fallen condition, underlie both kinds of mirth stirred in us by the events in the Forest of Arden.

If heavenly mirth is occasioned by the redemption of nature, earthly mirth is occasioned by the disjunction between its essential goodness and its fallen condition.

Fallen nature establishes conventions that do not nurture but mar nature's goodness. An earthly mirth is then occasioned by nature's escape from convention seen as something alien and inferior.[43] When the children are free of the fathers' discipline, seen now not as care but as constraint, the experience is mirthful. We experience this escape in contemplating Orlando free of his brother's tyrannic will but even more so in contemplating Rosalind in disguise. Given that it is Rosalind who raises the issue of the injustice convention does to women, it is not surprising that it is she who volunteers to adopt the role of the man in her flight with Celia from the court (1.3.110-12). For in pretending to be a young man she not only escapes the unjust constraint of convention but heartily mocks that convention. In her account of the natural weakness of women, as "changeable," "proud," "shallow," and the more witty, the more "wayward" (3.2.398-400 and

4.1.152-53), she presents the justification offered for the inferior status convention assigns to women. But she thinks this justification false since she thinks women are treated unjustly. In presenting it seriously now to Orlando, whom she loves and who she knows loves her, she accomplishes an important object. In drawing from Orlando a defense of women, or at least of his Rosalind (4.1.60-61), she educates the future father of her child, freeing him from the corruption of unjust convention.

But if nature is essentially good, it is also fallen and contemplation of our fallen condition may also be a source of mirth so long as no serious harm results.[44] Atonement is the act by which humankind is pardoned and spared the ultimate penalty of the fall, the penalty of death. But humankind continues to suffer the penalty that Aquinas likens to a demotion in social status in a hierarchical society, in which a person born to one rank is made subject to the laws of an inferior rank.[45] From the perspective of our birth rank as rational beings the control the body and human passion exercises over our judgment is very amusing: it is an occasion of mirth. Nowhere is this control more tyrannical than when we fall in love. It is funny to see Silvius's infatuation, still funnier to see Phoebe, who scorns him for it, herself smitten. But best of all, it is delightful to see Rosalind in love.

When Rosalind first encounters the poems written for her by Orlando, not knowing their author, she mocks them for their technical crudeness. To Celia, who reads her one of them, she replies "what tedious homily of love have you wearied your parishioners withal" (3.2.152-53). When Celia first hints of the identity of the author, however, Rosalind adopts a different tone. Up till now she had loved Orlando without knowing that he loved her as well. The possibility that he does has, by Celia's testimony, a physical impact: "Change you colour?" (179). Rosalind is, by her own description, powerfully moved: she begs Celia "with most petitionary vehemence," to tell her plainly who the author is (186-87). When Celia does so, Rosalind's pleasure at the news is such that she showers Celia with a multitude of questions she does not allow her to answer (215-47). Love, as Rosalind says, is a kind of "madness" (388) and the actions it compels, so long as they cause no harm, fill us the spectator with mirth just as the experience of love, on the same condition, occasions mirth in the lover.

But the experience of another pair of lovers in the play, Touchstone and Audrey, suggests that fallen nature uncorrected by convention may lead to harm. Touchstone's love for Audrey is utterly egoistical and in his intentions he is careless of any harm he may do her (3.3.81-85). For himself, he could not honestly echo Silvius's account of love, that it is "all made of faith and service" as do Orlando and, tacitly, Rosalind (5.2.88, 91-92). Fallen nature as manifest in Touchstone must be checked by convention. Appropriately enough, it is Jaques who discovers Touchstone's designs upon Audrey. Jaques, we may imagine, by reason on his own experience as a libertine, is well acquainted with such expedients as Touchstone's proposed "bush" marriage. In his self-assumed role of chastiser of human wickedness he prevents it: "Get you to church, and have a good priest that can tell you what marriage is" (3.3.75-77). For Jaques, love is little more than the "brutish sting itself" (2.7.66). It is a piece of folly, that is, a "fault," something to be mocked as he does in his "seven ages" speech, not enjoyed as it clearly is by Orlando and Rosalind (3.2.277-78; 4.1.195-98). Conventional arrangements like marriage check the fault or limit the damage. For the other pairs of lovers, however, love has a deeper meaning, it is as much made of "patience" as "impatience," of "duty and observance" as of "passion" and "of wishes" (5.2.94-96).

But for them, too, the conventional arrangement of marriage is necessary. Their love impels Rosalind and Orlando to marriage, first to the mock wedding of act 4 and then to the formal ceremony of act 5. For what Rosalind says of woman is characteristic of humankind's fallen state in general: passion has learned to reason and will outface reason itself.

> You shall never take her without her answer, unless you take her without her tongue. O that woman that cannot make her fault her husband's occasion, let her never nurse her child herself, for she will breed it like a fool.
>
> (4.1.162-67)

Rosalind here personifies nature as a beautiful woman who tells the truth about her own capacity for deceit so that convention, in the person of her child's father, may be better able to protect that beauty and the good it occasions from harm. The convention of wedlock protects what is good in nature from the harm nature might do itself. It may be seen as a check to something vicious but this is a one-sided view. It is as much an "honoured" crown to what is good in nature, a means by which that good may be brought to fruition (5.4.140-45).

This image of Rosalind as personifying nature, a nature that knows her own essential goodness as well as her fallen state, takes us back to the passage with which I began in act 3, scene 4: "But what talk we of fathers." Rosalind has mentioned to Celia an encounter with her father the day before. Her father did not recognize her in her disguise, which she took as an occasion for a joke. The Duke asked her what her parentage was and she replied it was as good as his at which, she reports, "he laughed and let me go" (3.4.33-34). Now both father and daughter laugh for a similar reason. Rosalind laughs because she knows the remark is true but also knows that it does not appear to be true to her father. The Duke laughs because he thinks he knows that the remark is not true but also thinks that it must appear to be true since he bears no marks of his noble birth. Though the joke is similar on both sides, it is the daughter who has the better laugh because she laughs twice: once at her father's failure to recognize who she is and a second time at his confidence that he understands the situation better than she does. The encounter is symbolic of the meaning of the play. Convention, seeing the waywardness of fallen nature, mistakenly thinks itself superior. Nature, however, as essentially good, knows its own worth; but it knows as well its debt to convention for protection and nurturing. Finally, however, insofar as convention is true, both nature and convention have a common author. To paraphrase Rosalind's laughing response to her father, Duke Senior's parentage is as good as hers.

Notes

This paper was originally prepared as a talk for the University of Chicago's Basic Program Spring Weekend, April 22-24, 1994. I am grateful to Chris Colmo and Vickie Sullivan and to the readers for Rowman & Littlefield for their comments on earlier drafts of this essay.

[1] All references to *As You Like It* are to the Arden edition, ed. Agnes Latham (London: Methuen, 1975; reprinted, London: Routledge, 1989).

[2] Coleridge comments on this scene that "Rosalind is not a very dutiful daughter." While he grants that her neglect of her father "though not quite proper, is natural enough," he concludes that "she might, at any rate, have shown more interest in her father's fortunes," *A New Variorum Edition of Shakespeare: As You Like It,* ed. Horace Howard Furness (Philadelphia: J. B. Lippincott Co., 1891), 195.

[3] Rowe in his second edition (1714) altered this to read "father's child" and while Theobald (1733) restored Shakespeare's language, Pope (1723), Johnson (1765), and other editors accepted Rowe's emendation. Coleridge comments of the unemended passage, "Who can doubt that this is a mistake . . . ?" (Furness, *New Variorum Edition,* 49).

[4] See the entry for "matter" in C. T. Onions, *A Shakespeare Glossary,* enlarged and revised by Robert D. Eagleson (Oxford: Oxford University Press, 1986).

[5] Cf. Alfred Harbage, *William Shakespeare: A Reader's Guide* (New York: Farrar, Straus and Co., 1963), 229; Michael Taylor, "*As You Like It:* The Penalty of Adam," *Critical Quarterly* 15 (1976): 76; Russell Fraser, "Shakespeare's Book of Genesis," *Comparative Drama* 25 (1991): 122.

[6] Cf. C. L. Barber on the dual attitude toward nature in Shakespeare's festive comedy: In these plays "the poetry about the pleasures of nature and the naturalness of pleasure serves to evoke beneficent natural impulses; and much of the wit, mocking the good housewife Fortune from her wheel, acts to free the spirit as does the ritual abuse of hostile spirits. A saturnalian attitude assumed by a clear-cut gesture toward liberty, brings mirth, an accession of wanton vitality." But at the same time the saturnalian attitude brings "the clarification of limits which comes from going beyond the limit." "The plays present a mockery of what is unnatural," that is, whatever restrains "wanton vitality" at the same time that "they include another, complementary mockery of what is merely natural" (*Shakespeare's Festive Comedy* [Princeton: Princeton University Press, 1959], 7, 13, 8). See also Barber's discussion of Rosalind in *Ibid.,* chap. 9, "The Alliance of Seriousness and Levity in *As You Like It.*"

[7] Cf. Aristotle *Nicomachean Ethics* 1162a5f.

[8] The classic statement of this view of what nature dictates as regards rule is the idea of the philosopher king, *Republic* 473a-e. The modern critique of this view is probably best expressed by Hobbes, *Leviathan,* chap. 10, section on "Worthinesse, Fitnesse."

[9] Cf. Aristotle *Ethics* 1158b23-28.

[10] Harbage fails to see much significance in this conversation: "The logic chopping about Nature and Fortune will do as a sample of small talk between lively and cultivated girls, but it seems to come from the top of their heads" (*Reader's Guide,* 225). John Shaw, on the other hand, sees in this conversation between Rosalind and Celia, 1.2.30-53, "on one level . . . the plot of *As You Like It* in epitome," "Fortune and Nature in *As You Like It,*" *Shakespeare Quarterly* 6 (1955): 46. He argues that "behind the gay romancing of the characters throughout *As You Like It* there is a basic philosophical strife between Fortune and Nature that would be obvious to the Renaissance" (45). In this reading Rosalind, Orlando, and the Forest of Arden are associated with nature understood as wisdom and virtue and Frederick, Oliver, and the court are associated with fortune and the use of "policy and cunning" to win her gifts (48).

[11] Cf. John Stuart Mill, "As for vicissitudes of fortune, and other disappointments connected with worldly circumstances, these are principally the effect either of gross imprudence, of ill-regulated desires, or of bad or imperfect social institutions," *Utilitarianism* in *On Liberty and Other Essays,* ed. John Gray (Oxford: Oxford University Press, 1991), 146.

[12] Cf. Plato *Republic* 458c-d.

[13] Cf. David Hume, *An Inquiry Concerning the Principles of Morals,* Library of Liberal Arts, ed. Charles W. Hendel (New York: Macmillan, 1957), 21-22.

[14] See the discussion of the observations of Aristotle and Tocqueville on the place of women in the polity in Mary Nichols, "The Good Life, Slavery, and Acquisition: Aristotle's Introduction to Politics," *Interpretation* 11 (1983): 28-54 and Delba Winthrop, "Tocqueville's American Woman and the True Conception of Democratic Progress," *Political Theory* 14(1986): 239-59. When I speak of love "in the fullest sense of the idea" I have in mind the notion of love as an ascent to the highest as expressed in its classic form by Socrates in the *Symposium.*

[15] *Hamlet,* 3.1.103-15. All references to other plays by Shakespeare are to *The Complete Works,* ed. Alfred Harbage (Baltimore: Penguin Books, 1969).

[16] Eric Partridge, *Shakespeare's Bawdy,* 3d ed. (London: Routledge, 1968), 106; cf. *Hamlet,* 3.4.83-86.

[17] Cf. Fraser's treatment of this passage where safety from the fire is the product of fortune understood as grace, "Shakespeare's Book of Genesis," 125-26.

[18] Geoffrey Bullough, *Narrative and Dramatic Sources of Shakespeare,* 8 vols. (London: Routledge & Kegan Paul; New York: Columbia University Press, 1957-1975), 2:161.

[19] In an excellent article, "'The Place of a Brother' in *As You Like It:* Social Process and Comic Form," *Shakespeare Quarterly* 32 (1981), Louis Montrose argues that Orlando's plight as a younger brother disadvantaged by primogeniture is the source of conflicts, generational and social, the resolution of which give the plays its comic form (29). He views the play through the lens of the social anthropologist as a dramatization of a successful "transition" from youth to manhood, from poverty to gentility and the reconciliation of classes of persons divided into superior and subordinate by a patriarchal social order. This transition is brought about not by dissolving that order but by translating it "into a quiet and sweet style" (29-30, 35, 41).

[20] It may be worth noting in passing that according to a tradition first recorded in the seventeenth century, Shakespeare played the part of Adam: Samuel Schoenbaum, *William Shakespeare: A Compact Documentary Life* (Oxford: Oxford University Press, 1967), 202. And like Adam, Shakespeare as a player was, at least technically, a servant of the Lord Chamberlain, obliged, in order to enjoy the law's protection, to "carry [his] patron's livery as [one of] his personal retainers," Andrew Gurr, *The Shakespearean Stage, 1574-1642* (London: Cambridge University Press, 1970), 20.

[21] *King Lear,* 1.2.4. I think Montrose errs in reading into Orlando's speech the sentiments of Edmund simply because their place is similar, namely, that of younger brother ("'The Place of a Brother,'" 30-31). For, first, Orlando's response to their similar plight is so different from Edmund's and second, Shakespeare has introduced Frederick, who does act as Edmund does, as a foil to Orlando. Cf. 41-42, 47-48. See my "Wisdom and Fortune: The Education of the Prince in Shakespeare's *King Lear,*" *Interpretation* 21 (1994): 373-90.

[22] Cf. Aristotle *Politics* 1269a1-2.

[23] It is noteworthy that three times it is said that Duke Senior loved Sir Rowland but nowhere is it said that Sir Rowland loved Duke Senior. Sir Rowland, it may be supposed from this, is the superior of the two, the goodness of Duke Senior being reflected in his love for the best man. It may be taken as a sign of Sir Rowland's superiority that, unlike Duke Senior, he was not dispossessed of his property and, moreover, that as subordinate in rank to Senior he did not himself attempt to usurp the latter's office. The idea of such a usurpation of duke by knight is suggested by Oliver's conduct. When in scene 1, Oliver asks Charles for news of "the new court" he specifically asks about Rosalind: "can you tell if Rosalind the Duke's daughter be banished with her father?" (1.1.105-6) It is significant that he here speaks of Rosalind's father as the Duke without qualification. Charles speaks of "the old Duke" and "the new Duke" and Oliver in his next two speeches also employs this language. But it remains that he has insinuated that the new Duke's claim to the title is less good than the old Duke's claim and thus Celia's claim as heir is less good than Rosalind's. Oliver's inquiry suggests a scheme to attain the Dukedom by marrying Rosalind and using her claim to unseat Frederick, not with a view to justice but to personal advantage.

[24] Cf. Aristotle *Ethics* 1165a21-24.

[25] Cf. *Hamlet,* 1.2.103-4. Arguing that Hamlet's grief at the loss of his father is excessive, Claudius says it is "To reason most absurd, whose common theme / Is death of fathers." Reason, indeed, questions the rules of the fathers and may see their deaths as an opportunity to reform; in the eyes of Claudius, however, one feels that reason's theme is less the death than the murder of "fathers" and that for strictly personal ends: Claudius is not himself a father.

[26] *Richard III,* 1.1.8. In the BBC production of *Richard III* the last image offered to the viewer is one of Richard, literally, "on top of the heap," the heap being a pile of corpses with Richard's corpse in the arms of a madly cackling Queen Margaret.

[27] Cf. *Pericles,* 4.3.28-39; see also, 4.Cho.5-40.

[28] Cf. *Othello*, 5.1.18-20; see also, 1.3.311-14.

[29] Latham offers a generally positive account of Jaques, which highlights his most attractive qualities and defends him from those critics who have seen him in the harshest light ("Introduction" to Arden Edition, xlvii and lxxvi).

[30] Cf. *King Lear*, 3.2.14-18.

[31] Though Harold Jenkins sees Jaques as expressing "a jaundiced view of life" and thinks it "strange that some earlier critics should have thought it might be Shakespeare's," nonetheless he links this view of life with what he takes to emerge from the conversation of Touchstone and Corin of act 3, scene 2: "In city or country, *all* ways of life are at bottom the same, and we recognize a conclusion that Jaques, by a different route, has helped us to reach before" (*"As You Like It," Shakespeare Survey* 8 [1955]: 45, 48). Speaking of Touchstone then as the author of this "realistic" view, he comments: "Whether he is wiser or more foolish than other men it is never possible to decide, but Touchstone is, as well as the most artificial wit, the most natural man of them all; and the most conscious of his corporal needs" (48). Cf. 50-51.

[32] Latham notes that a number of critics have commented on the way in which Marston may be seen as the model for Jaques ("Introduction," xlviii-li).

[33] Latham, "Introduction," xxvii; *The Poems of John Marston*, ed. Arnold Davenport (Liverpool, UK: Liverpool University Press, 1961), "Introduction," 3.

[34] Cf. Robert Pierce, "Moral Language of *Rosalynde* and *As You Like It*," *Studies in Philology* 68 (1971): 172.

[35] Davenport, "Introduction" to *The Poems of John Marston*, 17; cf. Helen Gardner, *"As You Like It,"* in *Shakespeare: The Comedies*, ed. Kenneth Muir (Englewood Cliffs, N.J.: Prentice-Hall, 1965), 70.

[36] *"As You Like It," Scrutiny* 9 (1940): 16; *Macbeth*, 5.5.24, 26-28. Cf. Barber, *Shakespeare's Festive Comedy*, 266, who describes it as a speech in "praise of the folly of living in time."

[37] For a different account of Duke Senior's silence see Harbage, *Reader's Guide*, 234.

[38] For example, see Jenkins, *"As You Like It,"* 49; Harbage, *Reader's Guide*, 235; Gardner, *"As You Like It,"* 67.

[39] 2.4.65-73.

[40] Cf. Davenport, "Introduction" to *The Poems of John Marston*, 18: "This corruption Marston sees as universal, and he certainly recognizes it in himself. Unlike Hall and the earlier satirists, . . . who took the standpoint of being right-minded, moral men righteously lashing the base wickedness in others, and applying in their judgments criteria of unquestionable soundness, Marston is not certain of his own criteria, and is clearly aware 'that he is part of what he is attacking. The position of superior and aloof satirist he leaves to Hall.'" Davenport here quotes Hallett Smith, *Elizabethan Poetry*.

[41] As regards Rosalind's authorship of this speech, note that she uses similar language in her own name: 5.4.18, 24-25.

[42] Cf. Gardner, *"As You Like It,"* 70-71.

[43] Clearly this view is not that of Calvinist Christianity, the view which Davenport attributes to Marston, that "fallen man is wholly corrupt and if he is virtuous it is solely by the grace of God" ("Introduction" to *The Poems of John Marston*, 20). By introducing Jaques into the play, Shakespeare underscores the difference between a Calvinist Christian vision of nature and the Christian vision implicit in the story of Rosalind in the Forest of Arden. Russell Fraser appears to opt for a Calvinist reading of the play: "The joker in the pack and a puzzle to modern readers, grace, an absolute despot, complicates the relation between cause and effect" ("Shakespeare's Book of Genesis," 125.) For another discussion of the role of grace in the play see Taylor, "The Penalty of Adam," *passim*.

[44] I wish to reserve the word mirth, both heavenly and earthly, for a positive emotion. But one might speak of a splenetic mirth that is indifferent to the harm caused by the disjunction between an original and fallen nature. Cf. *Measure for Measure*, 2.2.117-23.

[45] St. Thomas Aquinas, *Treatise on Law* (Chicago: Henry Regnery, 1970), 28.

TOUCHSTONE

David Frail (essay date 1981)

SOURCE: "To the Point of Folly: Touchstone's Function in *As You Like It*," in *The Massachusetts Review*, Vol. XXII, No. 4, Winter, 1981, pp. 695-717.

[*In the essay below, Frail asserts that Touchstone mirrors the "kaleidoscopic" nature of* As You Like It, *blurring the lines between wisdom and folly so that we may free our minds long enough to recognize ourselves as "the foolish humans we are."*]

Some recent critics of Shakespeare's comedies have emphasized the plays' dissonant undertones and somber forebodings of the later (and, it is implied, greater) tragedies and romances. Since *As You Like It* is the next-to-last of the comedies, it is particularly vulnerable to this meteorological approach, which spots the dust particles about which the thunderheads form. Ralph Berry, for example, finds that the "reality principle," not the "festive principle," is Shakespeare's criterion by which to judge the comedies. In this light, Berry sees *As You Like It* as a pastoral idyll, but a "fairly perturbed" one, in which the characters keep finding themselves reflected in one another and react to these mirrorings with undue hostility—a latent tragic motif, to be fulfilled in, say, Iago's hatred of Othello? (Berry doesn't specify a particular masterwork so much as detect a mood-swing in the canon.)[1]

Thomas McFarland goes further than Berry and finds the moodswing within *As You Like It* itself. "The situation at the start," he says, "could . . . as well serve for a tragedy as for a comedy." The play "labors to keep its comic balance" under the staggering burden of the theme of Cain and Abel; while it manages to exhibit "more humor" than the earlier pastoral comedies, it finally contains "much less happiness," as if it were too exhausted by such weighty matter to do more than a perfunctory dance at its close.[2]

Now, we certainly may wonder with Berry why Rosalind chides Phebe so harshly, but I think we do so only after the play. I find it quite amusing to watch Rosalind explode so suddenly, so unaware that she chastises her own cruelty to Orlando. And while McFarland accurately sees the tragic potential in the opening, he doesn't acknowledge the effect of the opening's texture, which holds that potential so firmly in suspension that it could only be manifested if the entire play were rewritten. *As You Like It* would simply no longer be itself.

Such anti-romantic readings as Berry's and McFarland's do make valuable contributions to our understanding of Shakespeare's plays, but we must beware their tendency to falsify our experience of the comedies—especially *As You Like It*. In it romance and anti-romance counterpoint each other effortlessly, balanced as neatly as the phrases of Touchstone's evaluation of court and country. Like his speech, the play holds reason at the mercy of pure desire—and catches desire in the forms of reason and rhetoric. *As You Like It* demands a radical subjectivity from us: we are "conjured" to "like as much of the play as please you" (Epilogue), and if we wish to like it *all,* we must dismiss our urge to choose reality over festivity, or vice versa. Critical judgement, as Touchstone says, is the forest's duty; ours is to let the forest do so, and thus become wiser than we are 'ware. We should laugh as Stephen Dedalus does, "to free his mind from his mind's bondage."[3] The criticism we commit after experiencing the play is possible only when we have fallen back into that bondage from which the play seeks to free us. We all are caught in Jaques' predicament, trying to relate our encounter with "a fool!" and in the attempt transforming ourselves into—or, rather, recognizing ourselves as—the foolish humans we are.

Let us proceed with that transformation, then. We would do better, I'd suggest, to focus on how *As You Like It* goes about "un-meaning," rather than trying to say what some of its meanings are. At the least, we can figure out why there seems to be such a dissonance between our experience of the play and what we make of it afterwards; at most we will affirm Enid Welsford's claim that "comedy is the expression of the spirit of the Fool."[4] For I hope to show here that the "kaleidoscopic" structure and language of *As You Like It* force us into the vertiginous freedom of a radical subjectivity, and that this kaleidoscopic nature is mirrored by—even mirrored from—its Fool, Touchstone.

Surprisingly few have taken Shakespeare at his word and regarded Touchstone as the touchstone of *As You Like It*. Even Harold Jenkins, the play's best critic, calls Rosalind, not the fool, "expert in those dark riddles which mean exactly what they say."[5] Rosalind does embody the answers to those riddles, but she is expert only in acting them out, not in articulating them; it is Touchstone who, if he gives no answers, is expert at propounding the questions. Rosalind acts out her play-within-a-play of the paradoxes of identity and disguise, fidelity and cuckoldry, faith and cynical mockery on Touchstone's terms. (Certainly she does so with such exuberance and vitality that we'd rather call her up on the phone than Shakespeare.) Touchstone, tagged along into Arden by Rosalind and Celia, seems to be a mildly diverting, even intrusive "comfort to our travel" (l. iii. 129).

But this very sense of his intrusiveness, our very doubts about the necessity of his presence, is precisely his most important quality, and leads us to recognize his function. If Rosalind is the center of the play, Touchstone is the counter-center essential to its structural and textual relativity. We can let Jenkins sum up the play's meaning as a paradox (one which holds for comedy in general):

> . . . longing to escape to our enchanted world, we are constantly brought up against reality . . . Yet in *As You Like It* ideals, thought always on the point of dissolving, are forever recreating themselves. They do not delude the eye of reason, yet faith in them is not extinguished in spite of all that reason can do.[6]

But we must also recognize that Touchstone offers us a counter-meaning—an undoing of meaning—by

Aaron M. Tidball as Touchstone and Jillian Spear as Audrey in the Bradley University Theatre's 1996 production of As You Like It.

snatching the play and us up to that point where paradoxes themselves dissolve into folly.

To better understand how Touchstone goes about propounding his riddle-dissolving riddles, I want to call on two very fine writers on fools, Enid Welsford and William Willeford. I shall discuss their studies at some length before turning to *As You Like It,* to show how completely the Fool's "mere presence," as Welsford claims, "dissolves events, evades issues, and throws doubt upon the finality of fact," be it physical, social, psychological, or linguistic fact.[7]

The conventional notion of the "wise fool," Willeford cautions us, reveals the nature of the Fool only to conceal it. Duke Senior's praise of Touchstone is typical:

> He uses his folly like a stalking horse,
> And under the presentation of that shoots his wit.
>
> (5. iv. 106-7)

But the shrewd control that the Duke attributes to Touchstone is actually his own: he unwittingly extracts the "wit" from the "folly" and treats the latter as mere verbal disguise. We must remember that the "whetstone of the wits" (1. ii. 53) is also the "cutter-off of Nature's wit" (1. ii. 47-8). In fact, only by cutting it off does a Fool whet wit, as Welsford asserts.

> The Fool does not lead a revolt against the Law physical, social, moral, he lures us into a region of the spirit where, as Lamb would put it, the writ does not run.[8]

The "wisdom" to be found in this region of "the spirit" is neither conventionally wise nor spiritual. Willeford more appropriately describes the Fool's luring as "a kind of play . . . in which the final ignorance of our natures is brought to expression."[9] Wisdom and folly, then, are synonymous here. If we are to preserve the phrase "wise fool," we must treat it with the respect due to paradoxes, and acknowledge its synergetic powers: its significance is greater and qualitatively different than the sum of its parts. If we can locate the phrase's accuracy, it lies at the point of semantic fusion of the two words into an oxymoron.

If such a thing as "semantic fusion" occurs, that is. Since we are speaking of a "writ-free" region of experience, we might just as accurately call our experience of paradox a semantic *diff*usion, a scattering of ordinary meaning into an *aporia*.[10] "Oxymoron," "paradox," with this uncharacterizable "point" contained within them, are the best terms in which to describe the nature of the Fool, though we must remain aware that it is the nature of folly to take us beyond such terms. We can rest somewhat comfortably with "oxymoron" and "paradox," however; for just as the Fool dissolves our habitual modes of thought, perception, and behavior, so a paradox exposes those modes as illusions by running us up against their limits. W. V. O. Quine has described how one paradox, expressed in Gödel's Theorem, reveals that the concept of proof in mathematics is founded upon only an assumption of certainty. Not even numbers are made of iron. Other paradoxes, according to Quine, have driven logicians to construct "a hierarchy of truth locutions," in which statements have a relative degree of truth—a paradox in itself.[11] The Fool has an analogous effect, driving us to describe a "writ-free" region in writing, and to relish the irony rather than despair over it.

The Fool derives his power of dissolution-through-paradox from his playing out, and playing upon, those contradictions within ourselves with which we rest complacently or simply ignore. Welsford and Willeford work with different pairs of conceptual oppositions, but both show how the Fool engages us in a perpetual see-saw game with these oppositions.

Welsford describes this "certain inner contradiction" in fairly general terms.[12] We have a sense of ourselves as compounds of "Nature," or the biological, and "Leviathan," the network of the mental and social through which we civilize ourselves. When we encounter a Fool, he tips both ends of our see-saw selves, as it were. We perceive him as "Nature's natural" (l. ii. 47), and recognize our own "naturalness" without the shame "Leviathan" imposes on us to preserve social order. At the same time, we also perceive him through the eyes of our "Leviathan" selves, and

> ... we laugh also because we are normal enough to know how very unnatural it is to be as natural as all that.[13]

"Normal" here means the rationality of our "Leviathan" selves. Welsford makes clear, however, that we all sense that "Nature" is as normal as the systems we build. When those logical and civil constructs threaten to crush the "original personality" within us, she says, the "natural" Fool leads us to escape and to feel "a birth of new joy and freedom."[14]

Despite Welsford's recognition of the mutual doubleness of Fool and human, she tends to treat the Fool as merely the "natural," or as an Ariel-like spiritual creature. By translating Welsford's general terms into the language of psychology, William Willeford offers a more complex and useful analysis of Fool and human. He defines the inner contradiction as the division of consciousness into the conscious, rational ego and the irrational unconscious. We necessarily, though mistakenly, assume that the conscious is all. But the "totality of the self" is a vast *Gestalt* composed of the unconscious, the rhythms of the body, "tuned-out" responses to external stimuli, all of which have "a dynamism and meaning that exceed our grasp . . . but that belong to the self nonetheless."[15] The Fool symbolizes this "essential self-division" of the self, a "violation of the human image," yet whole himself.[16] For Willeford, then, the Fool is not merely a "natural"; he embraces both Nature and Leviathan and yet is neither. Here we return to the Fool's place at the "point" of paradox: to Willeford, the Fool sits on the boundary between the unconscious part of the *Gestalt* and the conscious center, flickering back and forth across this line like a giddy electron. Willeford goes on to analogize from his model of boundary and center to describe how the Fool inhabits the point (or gap) at which several fundamental antinomies meet: Leviathan and Nature, wisdom and folly, order and chaos, form and formlessness, meaning and meaningless, stasis and change, reality and illusion.

What happens when we encounter a Fool? How does he lead us to this point? According to Willeford, he frees us from our ordinary modes of thought, behavior, and speech by imprisoning us in them:

> Any fool we see is demarcated from what we assume to be a non-foolish background . . . We see this fool here only by disregarding that fool or those fools there, including the fools that we are.[17]

That is, in order to recognize a Fool at all, we must employ our rational powers of perception and cognition. But that fool within us, whom we push to the boundaries of our consciousness so we can see that Fool without, escapes us and leaps to the center of our attention, projected on to "that" Fool. We face our own folly, and only if we deny that it's our own. The Fool compels our "immediate and total" recognition of him, as Willeford aptly puts it.[18] Only after our encounter can we recognize that folly as ours.

Since much of our encounter with a Fool consists of jokes, we would expect that his language has the same effect as his presence. And so it does. The significance of *Foolsprach* lies not so much in the "translations" into sense and wisdom that we make as in our experiencing "the shattering of our customary forms of ignorance (i.e., normal speech)."[19] Willeford describes three ways in which a Fool's jokes lead us to their point, at which sense and nonsense meet:

> ... when we 'get the point,' it strikes us as intelligent enough to seem unintelligent; it impinges upon meaning at least enough to be felt as a violation of meaning. The point of a joke may lie in a hidden meaning, and this, as it comes to light, may be what strikes us as funny. But the point may also lie in the fact that the joke issues into nonsense with only a few strips and tatters of sense or that it seems to have a sense that one cannot get at; one gets stuck in one's inability to deal with it meaningfully at all.[20]

Touchstone, we should note, is especially full of this last kind of joke, the hidden sense of which we instantly grasp and laugh at, but which requires the most delicate dissection to expose its logic (or pseudologic). Perhaps this is why so little has been written on his function in *As You Like It;* to explain a line like "Nay, I shall ne'er be ware of mine own wit / till I break my shins against it" (2. iv. 56-7), much less place it in context, can make one feel like an overly rational sort of fool.

Touchstone is also full of the first kind of joke, portentously intoned riddles which, as Jenkins says, "mean exactly what they say":

> The heathen philosopher, when he had a desire to eat a grape, would open his lips when he put it into his mouth, meaning thereby that grapes were made to eat and lips to open. (5. i. 31-4)

Of course we say that here Touchstone does in fact utter a profound comic truth: we are actual beings in an actual world. We must admit, however, that we formulate this statement after the fact of utterance, and as if to rescue our short-circuited expectations; Touchstone inflates us and then deflates us, and we re-inflate the deflation. We get stuck in the paradox of uttering abstractions that insist on the physicality of the world.

Once we have extracted this profound truth, as equally profound doubt presents itself: Is that all there is? Lips and grapes? Touchstone has provoked us into awareness of what William Lynch calls the "double longing" that makes comedy possible. On the one hand, we want the "maximum beauty and insight" of full, pure meaning (a perfected Leviathan); on the other hand, we also want the experience of "pure, unalloyed, concrete objects" (a perfected Nature).[21] As Father Lynch proposes:

> We want the unlimited and the dream, and we also want the earth. . . . The ideal solution would be that the world should 'signify' without becoming less actual in so doing.[22]

When we laugh—before we start rationalizing—we confront the comic, "ugly and strong," through which, Lynch argues, we achieve the "pure cognition" which satisfies our double longing.[23]

Lynch denies the Fool this comic function. I don't, since I define the comic not as satisfaction of these desires, but as the rendering irrelevant of such double binds. The Fool's comic power is his ability to get us *so* stuck in contradictions that the forms burst open, if only for a moment. We have discussed some of the mental, social, and linguistic oppositions that the Fool dissolves, and may now sum them up as the Fool does, in his physical appearance. Mikhail Bakhtin has brilliantly defined the grotesque as a mode of imagination and expression which celebrates change and renewal by fusing the death of one form and the birth of another into a single image.[24] The Fool is just such a grotesque figure, ugly and strong; the point between fragmentation and wholeness at which he sits is that grotesque point of transition. As Willeford says, the Fool is the image of *possibility:* the possibility of order, meaning, physical there-ness, of "ripeness" in all senses. Paradoxically, though, from hour to hour he rots and rots, stuck at the point of change. Yet if he never can fulfill any of his possibilities, he can unfix us from our rigid "fulfillments."

This sense of grotesque potential leads us to encounter the Fool with what Welsford describes as

> ... that strange twofold consciousness which makes each one of us realize ... that he is a mere bubble of temporary existence threatened each moment with extinction, and yet be quite unable to shake off the sensation of his being a stable entity existing eternal and invulnerable at the very centre of the flux of history, a kind of *punctum indifferens,* or point of rest.[25]

Here, in this see-sawing twofold consciousness, is the essence of the comic. Most theorists have argued that this essence is the "vital balance," the "pure sense of life," the "joy of life invincible," the "living," or the "ugly and strong . . . actual."[26] But Welsford and Willeford's emphasis on doubleness and contradiction, and Bakhtin's emphasis on the grotesque's celebration of transition, remind us that death and dead forms are as essential to comedy as vitality. We can know this experience of pure life and joy only after we are re-imprisoned in those "dead" forms of "normality." The "pure sense of life" can manifest itself only in impure forms.

It is the fusion into diffusive paradox, then, our resolution of one contradiction into another and yet another, that is the comic. And it is the Fool who leads us into this state of mental and physical freedom, that state of possibility. We immediately fall out of this state, but the possibility remains that we will immediately re-enter it by way of the Fool. And so his "show," as Willeford calls it, flickers us back and forth between present-mindedness and laughter, the security of paradox and its dizzying release, until we believe we can stand on an abyss—and laugh at the folly of such a belief.

Let us now apply this theory of the phenomenology of folly to Touchstone and watch how he cuts off the wit of *As You Like It*. In three crucial scenes he acts as "detached commentator upon the action,"[27] as Welsford describes the Fool's use of his license in drama, and carries the play to the point of folly.

As we noted above, Touchstone always seems to intrude upon the action of the play. It is as if he stands on the boundary of the stage and tries to claim its center whenever he can. Each time he succeeds, he involves the other characters (and the audience) in a "show" which diffuses the conventions of the preceding scene into "mangled forms" like those with which his brain is said to be crammed (2. vii. 42). Yet by convincing us that the matter at hand is a mere bubble of convention, Touchstone also reveals the *punctum indifferens* from which such conventions are generated: desire.

In Act l, Scene ii, Touchstone literally intrudes on Celia and Rosalind to deliver a message and cuts off their argument over Nature's and Fortune's gifts. His presence suspends the women's discussion in ambiguity: has Fortune exploited Nature's purest creation, her "natural," to defeat wit, the one gift of Nature which enables humankind to defeat Fortune? Or has Nature herself sent in Touchstone to strengthen her one weapon against Fortune, whetting wit with dullness? Just as Celia and Rosalind find it difficult to keep their philosophical categories distinct, so we find them fusing together in Touchstone's presence. For if he is Nature's weapon as whetstone, he "sharpens" wit by leading it into folly. And if his mere entrance pushes the women's argument to the verge of contradiction, Touchstone's own proof of the paradoxical nature of oaths and honor leads us through all contradictions to the point of folly.

This process begins as soon as Celia asks him, "Were you made the messenger?" and Touchstone replies, "No, by mine honor, but I was bid to come for you" (l. ii. 57-9). He apparently contradicts himself, and so forswears that honor; after all, someone who comes for you is a messenger. But from another point of view, Touchstone's contradiction confirms his honor. He asserts that he is a courtier forced to do a lowly messenger's job. By merely implying this in the polite, judicious rhetoric of a courtier, he "proves" that he is one. His ability to contradict himself—the diplomat making a "fine distinction"—proves that he hasn't contradicted himself. Now of course Touchstone isn't a courtier, but a Fool. As Willeford says, our recognition of him as such is "immediate and total," and we can perceive him only as a Fool trying to be something else. We all reply to him as Celia does: "Where learned you that oath, *fool?*" (l. ii. 60; my emphasis).

But while his dullness whets our wits by challenging us to pierce through an obvious deception, it has also led us to drop our guards. He has exposed a contradiction which isn't a contradiction. Although we quickly dismiss his word-play and call him "fool," we proceed to accept the very contradiction we dismiss. For Touchstone's explanation of where he learned that mere "oath" depends on an oath: namely, the conventions of logical discourse. No argument can proceed unless all parties accept its premises; these premises, then, are "oaths," sworn statements about the nature of reality. Touchstone, then, uses oaths to prove logically the illusory nature of oaths. Furthermore, since honor depends on one's keeping oaths, it follows that honor, too, is illusory.

If this description of Touchstone's methods is a bit dizzying, it is because Touchstone's method is to dizzy us into accepting his fallacies as valid—or to make us wonder if his truths are fallacious. Or both. To proceed: although we deny that he is a courtier, we allow him to engage us in the gentlemanly art of the duel:

Ros. Ay, marry, now unmuzzle your wisdom.
Touch. Stand you both forth now . . .
(l. ii. 68-9)

We have mocked him as dull, yet gleefully accept the premise that he is intelligent enough to formulate an argument. Who is the fool? He who proposes the fallacy that "If you swear by that that is not, you are not forsworn" (l. ii. 73-4), or we who not only accept this premise, but believe that such a cheaply made tool as the syllogism enables us to arrive at truth?

An oath is always a syllogism; one always swears by something. For example, when I swear to rescue the princess, I implicitly or explicitly swear by mine honor. I also assume that this conditional is true; therefore, it necessarily follows that I will rescue the princess. But all that I've done, really, is to will my intention to save her into a necessity. I intend to kill the dragon—but will I? If I fail, my fellow knights won't question the folly of assuming that wishes can be transformed into necessities. They'll simply assume that my conditional was false, that I had no honor, and thus preserve the convention so that Sir Next-Knight can sally forth.

Touchstone, however, explodes the conventions of oath-taking and argument by using nothing but fallacies to prove, or apparently prove, his case. For one thing, his premise ignores the point of oath-taking entirely. One wants to make his intentions come true, not figure out a way to preserve one's honor while evading the responsibilities of honor. And as for logic, consider how Touchstone leads up to his premise:

> Touch. Stroke your chins, and swear by your beards that I am a knave.
> Cel. By our beards, if we had them, thou art.
> Touch. By my knavery, if I had it, then I were . . .
>
> (l. ii. 69-72)

He knows full well, with a cunning beyond the merely human, that Rosalind and Celia will accept his consequent as true—indeed he is a knave; but he has manipulated them into accepting a false conditional—obviously they have no beards. They have accepted Touchstone's premise and sworn "by that that is not." Of course, this also means that they are not forsworn, which leaves open the possibility that Touchstone is a knave. But he turns this possibility against them by reducing it to a tautology: "If I had knavery, then I would be a knave." But since they are arguing according to Touchstone's premise, he does not have knavery. Therefore, his dishonorably swearing by that that is not, his knavery, proves that he is honorable. Celia's assertion that he is a knave is false, since she swore by her imaginary beard. Furthermore, his hypothetical knight, who swore by honor which he didn't have, didn't dishonor himself by praising the pancakes and damning the mustard. So Touchstone has logically proven an obvious falsehood, knavishly asserted his honor, shown his knight to be both honorable and knavish—and, according to his premise, nobody, including his opponents, is forsworn.

Further still, another paradox presents itself. If Touchstone has exposed the folly of oaths, he has done so by hoodwinking us into accepting his judgment that the knight mis-tasted the pancakes and mustard—and the taste of knights and fools is subjective indeed. Touchstone swears that the knight was wrong—but does he swear here, too, by that that is not? Rosalind and Celia, and we, have no way to verify this oath; yet we all trust a Fool's proof that there is no basis for proof, a Fool's promise which undermines the very nature of promises. We have shown how Touchstone reveals that an oath is a syllogism, and a syllogism a kind of oath; so logic, Touchstone reveals here, is a mode of rhetoric. Honor and argument are both mere bubbles of language, a film of immeasurable thinness "containing" nothing more substantial than the air out of which words are made. Yet something, in a sense, "inhabits" those bubbles. Touchstone does reveal the *punctum indifferens* which causes us to blow them: the desire to harmonize one's perceptions, one's taste of pancakes and mustard, with those of one's fellows.

Rhetoric is a mode of logic. Each of us makes implicit and explicit promises in order to maintain his place in the social order, and in doing so concedes that his senses might not tell the truth. For if we insist that we're right, we risk losing our portion of pancakes and mustard. We constantly and tacitly swear by that that is not in order to preserve the Leviathan which insures that Nature's various hungers will be satisfied. Our "great heap of knowledge," like Touchstone's, is an inverted pyramid, stacked on the point of our desire to eat.[28]

It may be objected that I have extracted this wisdom from Touchstone's own great heap, and contradict my own thesis about "wise fools." Yes, I have—to write about it all, one has to. Our *experience* of his argument in l.ii is probably like this: knowing that Touchstone wants to show that he is a courtier, we await a clever proof from this "dull" fool, confident that he will make fools of Rosalind and Celia. But Touchstone shifts his ground so quickly that perhaps even an Elizabethan audience grounded in the conventions of logic and rhetoric would have trouble following it on first hearing. In Willeford's terms, it "impinges on meaning at least enough to be felt as a violation of meaning."[29] It also impinges on nonsense just enough to feel like a violation of meaninglessness. We feel as if that fool within us understands Touchstone (as he should, since, according to Willeford's notion of projection, that fool within confronts us in the figure of Touchstone). We "ourselves," however, can't quite grasp the point; the sense remains a potential sense. The point grasps *us,* and we are caught up into folly.

We remain thus caught up throughout the argument, until suddenly an easily graspable meaning shoots forth. This occurs when Touchstone reveals that his hypothetical knight is apparently an actual person who, the fool plainly declares, had no honor to begin with. One could argue that the point of Touchstone's argument is not to diffuse conventional modes of thought, but to shoot this wise satirical bolt shot from under the stalking horse of folly. But compare his satire to other characters' invective against social corruption—say, Orlando's praise of Adam for preserving "the constant service of the antique world" (2. iv. 57), Duke Senior's praise of life in Arden (2. i. 1-17), or Jaques' wish to "cleanse the foul body of th'infected world" (2. vii. 60). The follyfull context out of which Touchstone's bolt flies makes that bolt seem too improvisatory, fortuitous, even uncanny to be so purposefully controlled as the satire of the non-fools. Furthermore, the non-fools would replace one iron network of laws with another, while Touchstone's very mode of speaking mangles the forms in which such beams and girders are cast. His aim isn't to reform the world, but to claim a place in it—the whole place, in fact. He wants to occupy our attention, not merely as courtier, but as king. And so he does, ruling the center of the stage and our consciousness. Yet his leap to the center *displaces* the very world and mind he would rule, substituting his no-place of folly. When he does momentarily enter the world of sense and satire, we suddenly realize what Touchstone is up to, and we drive him back to the boundary of consciousness, silencing him, like Celia, with the threat of whipping him with the instruments of Leviathan.

More important than this insult is the way that Touchstone's argument mirrors, funhouse-fashion, the scene preceding it, in which Celia cheers up Rosalind with arguments and oaths. Their mind-play is not about knights' breakfast, however, but about love.

> Cel. Herein I see thou lov'st me not with the full weight that I love thee. *If* my uncle, thy banished father, had banished thy uncle, the Duke my father, *so* thou hadst been still with me, I could have taught my love to take thy father for mine. So wouldst thou, *if* the truth of thy love to me were so righteously tempered as mine is to thee.
>
> (1. ii. 7-13)
>
> . . . for what my father hath taken away from thy father perforce, I will render thee again in affection. *By mine honor,* I will, and when I break that oath, let me turn monster. *Therefore,* my sweet Rose, my dear Rose, be merry.
>
> (1. ii. 18-22)
> (my emphasis)

Like Touchstone, Celia swears by that that is not, the hypothetical case that she would love Rosalind were she in her position. She concludes with an oath sworn on her honor, from which it "necessarily" follows that Rosalind agree with her—not on the grounds of logic, but of her desire for Rosalind's happiness. Like Touchstone's, Celia's argument is pseudo-logical, exploiting the syllogism's persuasive force. Unlike Touchstone, she finally urges her opponent to agree on the grounds of charity (the fool's pseudo-logic ends with a self-interested insult).

Rosalind, and we, easily accept Celia's oath—but enter Touchstone soon after, and such oaths and honor are exposed as illusions. In fact, Touchstone's exposure throws back at us what we dismiss out of charity when judging Rosalind and Celia: the fallacious nature of this reasoning, and its generation by a desire to reach a consensus. We allow Celia and Rosalind their logical errors, if we notice them at all, since they commit them in the name of love. Touchstone enters and reveals that reasoning itself is a fallacy committed in the name of love (even if, like Touchstone, we commit such love out of self-interest in our self-preservation). It's wonderful to watch the two young women resolve such a difficult situation so easily, and with such a fragile thing as adolescent love. Perhaps it's more wonderful to watch Touchstone ironically expose the fragility not only of their resolution, but of all such resolutions. In so doing, he shows us that such a mere bubble is also the *punctum indifferens* at the heart of all human relationships, the self-interested charity which transforms briars into burrs of "holiday foolery" (1. iii. 14).

Thus Touchstone intrudes upon the main action of the play and, by diffusing both that action and our ability to judge it, enables us to clarify our judgments. He does so again in Act 3, Scene iii, when he tries to attach himself to the action in Arden by courting and marrying Audrey. Once again he diffuses the action of the previous scene, in which Ganymede, Rosalind and Orlando agree to "cure" Orlando's love-sickness through a mock-courtship. And once again Touchstone's diffusion reveals the desire which underlies and generates our conventional forms of expression:

> As the ox hath his bow, sir, the horse his curb, and the falcon his bells, so man hath his desires; and as pigeons bill, so wedlock would be nibbling.
>
> (3. iii. 76-9)

Touchstone unexpectedly transposes desire and marriage in this double analogy, and in doing so sounds the keynote of *As You Like It*. Desires are "natural," "animal" forces, yet they also "curb" one in that they force one to act out certain forms. That is, desire "in itself" may have no shape, but we only know it as specifically formed urges. In this sense one's desires "curb" one's polymorphous energies, even if one seems to uncurb or unleash them when one expresses them or fulfills them. Marriage is the highest, most elaborate form of sexual desire (certainly in Shakespearean comedy). Yet marriage, even if it is a bubble of artifice, is blown out of desire. So, if desire domesticates us, wedlock drives us out to (and provides) pasture to nibble and nourish. If Touchstone's transposition confuses the natural and the artifical, he forces us to see that desire and marriage are fused. His lines may be as inarticulate as pigeons' billing, but like the birds' song, they signify a joyful resignation to the "curb" of love (Touchstone's patent insincerity appropriately enough, only serves to heighten the joy in his delivery).

Just before Touchstone's courtship scene, Rosalind and Orlando have managed just such a fusion of desire and form, though not in animal imagery. Orlando accepts Ganymede's offer to "cure" him of his love when he realizes that the proposed mock-courtship will preserve his "madness," rather than restore him to the sanity of lack-love. As Ganymede, Rosalind will cure her love for Orlando by mocking him without penalty. Just as Rosalind and Celia agree out of love to transform their sadness into self-consciously devised "sports" (1. ii. 23)—including falling in love—

so Orlando and Rosalind self-consciously transform their desire into the sport of courtship. Their wooing will be a game, an illusion.

Orlando, of course, is unaware just how far the sport goes. While he thinks that he is fooling a shepherd boy into thinking that the youngster is saving him from love, he doesn't realize that he's pretending that Rosalind is Rosalind. What Orlando thinks is illusion is true. He doesn't realize that when he swears to be rid of his love "by the faith of my love" (3. ii. 418), he wins in sport what he wants in life (here, for once, someone in the play swears by that that is—the consequent, not the conditional, is obviously false).

Enter Touchstone and Audrey, who virtually rewrite Rosalind's and Orlando's scene the way that Touchstone "re-reads" Orlando's love poem as a filthy ditty (3. ii. 100-14), and Rosalind "re-reads" Phebe's love poem as "meaning me a beast" (4. iii. 50). Every revision by the fool-couple strips the disguises beneath the disguises of Rosalind and Orlando to reveal that *punctum indifferens* of desire. With their witty debate on time, and their time-consuming arrangements of their "sport," Rosalind and Orlando prolong their courtship and so preserve and heighten their desire. They would foreplay forever. Touchstone travels to a counterpace: he tries to conflate the whole ritual into one brief scene, from wooing, winning, and wedding right through to the cheating (he even engages the priest before he engages the bride). It's as if he takes the idea of *carpe diem* literally, counting it "but time lost to hear such a foolish song" (5. iv. 39) as the one the pages sing—or the one that Rosalind and Orlando act out. His hurry exposes the folly of the lovers' elaboration and delay; if love is here one day and all's gone the next, then don't waste time singing about time, don't hold off fulfilling desire by describing it. Touchstone's rush through each step of the way catches up marriage into a Bergsonian flow of *duration,* ripening and rotting in one instant. If the fool-couple's speed seems grotesque, in Bakhtin's sense of fused forms, then so by comparison do the elegant measures of Rosalind and Orlando.

Even fools, though, can't roll their strength and sweetness into one ball. Their desires inevitably manifest themselves in the forms of courtship, but in such degraded form that they are diffused. As if in imitation of Rosalind, Touchstone tries to follow the shepherd's fashion and put on a "simple feature" (3. iii. 3). But he can only be a Fool. When he tries to be something else, he comes close to being nothing at all, as Audrey unwittingly reveals: "Your features, Lord warrant us! What features?" (Orlando, too, has none of the "marks" of the lover (3. ii. 362).

This inauspicious opening sets the pattern of this pattern-breaking rite. As Willeford observes, a Fool is often either "not enough there" or "too much there,"[30] and just so Touchstone's wooing see-saws from botch to botch. He tries using the lover's rhetoric of the pastoral idyll to address an impenetrable (in all senses) mistress. He doesn't compliment this mistress with this rhetoric, but insults her. Worst of all, his elegance doesn't conceal, but reveals, that his aim isn't marriage but seduction.

His statements about love and marriage similarly see-saw. He treats honesty and beauty, sluttishness and foulness, as two pairs of inseparably fused qualities, never admitting the possibility that a woman could be foul and honest or beautiful and sluttish. In the same way he couples courtship with fidelity, and marriage with "horns," excluding the middle of a constant marriage. Just as his motley breaks apart the colors of his clothes, so Touchstone breaks up love into a crazy quilt of its qualities.

The crucial dip of the see-saw comes with Touchstone's play on a famous and fundamental idea:

> Touch. I would the gods had made thee political.
> Aud. I do not know what poetical is. Is is honest in word and deed? Is it a true thing?
> Touch. No, truly; for the truest poetry is the most feigning, and lovers are given to poetry, and what they swear in poetry may be said as lovers they do feign.
>
> (3. iii. 15-21)

To see how Touchstone diffuses this idea, we should place it in historical context. Robert Jordan explains that the Renaissance humanists believed that poetry is "literally untrue," since the poet had to speak in

> . . . such terms as only the initiated could understand . . . the obscurity of the surface and the need to penetrate it enhanced the value of the hidden truths and preserved them from vulgarization.[31]

To paraphrase Dante, the more beautiful the lie, the more beautiful the truth. This poetics goes back at least to St. Augustine's explanation of the Bible's obscurities. As Robert Kellogg and Oliver Steele point out, it informed the sonneteers' insistence that they worshipped the ideal woman in their praise of their beloveds' less spiritual qualities.[32] The more elaborate the confession of love, the more intense was the love confessed; the more one "feigned" in verse, the more one "fained" in life. Orlando understands this principle when he eloquently insists that "neither rhyme nor reason" (3. ii. 389) can express his love. His rhyme adequately expresses his love by denying its own adequacy. Now, Orlando *could* be lying. After all, the eloquent surface of language conceals one's passion even as it expresses it. We must infer the nature of the depths from the nature of the surface. Poetry, then, is an intentional illusion through which we must penetrate, if we can, to the truth.

In one sense, Touchstone's poetry is relatively easy to crack, since the Fool himself breaks up its illusory surface to reveal the desire beneath, or within. The truth that his "feigning" hides, however, is not the sonneteer's "faining" for the ideal, but physical lust. His whole courtship is a lie pure and simple, as he himself emphasizes by prefixing "truly" to line after line. Yet he also speaks truly; none of us doubt that he wishes Audrey were merely feigning her "honesty." Audrey herself is both unpoetical and poetical. When Touchstone feigns that she is beautiful ("No, truly, unless thou wert hardfavored"), she insists that she *is* hard-favored. Yet she is poetical, if unwittingly so, in that she accepts the illusion of Touchstone's "faining"; she can't penetrate that illusion and see what he is truly after. Finally, though, Touchstone drops all his feigning and fains plainly: "Well, praised be the gods for thy foulness! Sluttishness may come hereafter" (3. iii. 38-9).

The fools, then, expose the "feigning" of Rosalind and Orlando's feigned courtship. They degrade the lovers' self-conscious construction of an illusion which enhances the hidden truth of their "faining," transforming eloquence into a sham poetry which exposes a sham "faining," lust. Yet Touchstone shows us how desire generates the rhetoric of courtship, the illusory surface within which desire is fulfilled. Even if the surface is illusion, if language is a tissue of lies, desire fulfills itself, and so makes the lies true. Like Ovid, Touchstone is capricious yet honest—not chaste, but candid about his capriciousness (well, inadvertently candid). He frees us to see professions of love as lies, and the lust beneath as noble, and to dismiss this inversion with a fit of laughter.

It is ironically appropriate that Jaques disrupts and dissolves the fool-couple's wedding ceremony. Jaques assumes that Touchstone wants to get married, and mocks the fool's ignobility in getting married "under a bush like a beggar" (3. iii. 81). The cynic merely dislikes the categories of existence; he can't destroy them. Jaques wants Touchstone to "re-form" and be decently married. In his mockery, as Touchstone's aside makes clear, Jaques misses the fool's de-forming point entirely. Desire is beyond the categories of beggar and noble, bush and church, and Jaques can't glimpse beyond them, and beyond ideals and cynicism, to that desire informing them all. This rational man is the most foolish guest at the fool's wedding.

In both Act 1, Scene ii and Act 3, Scene iii, we have seen Touchstone diffuse the resolutions of the preceding scenes into parodic, joyful nonsense by breaking up the social, logical, and linguistic conventions through which such resolutions are achieved. We have also seen how Touchstone's diffusions also offer us—or that Fool within each of us—a revelation of the impulse of desire underlying those conventions, which drives us to both generate and violate such forms. In each scene preceding Touchstone's, a pair of non-foolish characters charitably agree on the nature of their situation and apparently deny its reality. By assenting to such illusions, however, Rosalind and Celia and Rosalind and Orlando shape reality "as they like it." Such is the "liberty" (1. iii. 136) of the Forest of Arden: it is the place where "desire, set deep within the eye," in the words of Wallace Stevens, can perceive by its own lights.[33] If the "eye of reason" is not deluded in Arden, as Jenkins says, it is because its function is taken over by that deeper sight; wit in Arden is cut off and freed to play.

If we take the Dukedom as the "center" and Arden as the "boundary," we can say that this latter realm of folly claims the center of our attention just as the Fool does. Ironically, and happily, enough, this occurs because the usurping Duke Frederick interprets reality as *he* likes it, banishing Rosalind as a traitor, and, significantly, pronouncing his daughter Celia "a fool" (1. iii. 84). We may call the Duke an overly tyrannical ego, whose only way of maintaining an illegitimate rule over the self is to banish vital, if not so rational, elements of that self, such as charitable daughters, their friends, and their Fools. The Duke's willful attempt to shape reality fails, of course, as Celia reshapes reality as she likes it: "Now go in we content / To liberty, and not to banishment" (1. iii. 135-6). And so folly displaces rationality, tagging one Fool along and leaving a greater fool behind.

It's not fair to say that reason is utterly banished from Arden. As we know from watching Touchstone in action the poor faculty is exploited by desire in the service of folly. But if reason is exposed as a rhetorical mode, it is also celebrated as such. Appropriately enough, Touchstone delivers the eulogy, in his praise of "the only peacemaker" (5. iv. 102), the virtuous "If." We have noted how non-fools use obviously fallacious syllogisms, with veridically false "Ifs," to persuade each other of virtual, loving truths. This is precisely the plot of Touchstone's parable of the seven stages of a lie.

That is, almost precisely. Touchstone characteristically inverts and parodies this process of consensus-making. His "If" begins not as a peacemaker, but as a troublemaker. Like Duke Frederick with Rosalind and Celia, Touchstone insists on imposing, not proposing, his interpretation of reality upon another: "I did dislike the cut of a certain courtier's beard" (5. iv. 69-70). This courtier proceeds from this completely subjective premise, and he and Touchstone build their seven-link chain of enthymemes:

> He sent me word, if I said his beard was not cut well, he was in mind it was: this is called the Retort Courteous. If I sent him word again it was not well cut . . .
>
> (5. iv. 71-4)

The question of the truth value of their judgments never figures in the quarrel. (We'll never know if the courtier's beard was well cut or not.) The splendid conclusion of this debate is that the two avoid the Lie Direct, and the inevitable duel, by agreeing to drop this unstated question of truth and falsity entirely. Touchstone and the courtier agree, it seems, out of cowardice, not daring to do more than measure swords. When Touchstone goes "by the book" (5. iv. 90), for the pedant Jaques' benefit, he makes it clear that the question dissolves in the agreement that "If you said so," then it follows that "I said so" purely out of a desire to make peace, swear brothers, and preserve the social order. By veridical standards, such a proposition is a Lie Direct—but veridical standards don't apply, for that "If" suspends them and substitutes virtual ones. Neither party cares if he actually said "so," he simply wants to agree.

Compared to Jaques' lugubrious lock-stepping of man through his Seven Ages of discomfort, pain, and decay, Touchstone's life of the Lie is by far the more preferable description of how we all are "merely players" (2. vii. 140). According to Touchstone, merely playing with fictions is the one thing necessary to human freedom, harmony, and joy. His Fool's argument persuades us of the truth of Stevens' "Nudity at the Capital" (quoted here in full):

> But nakedness, woolen massa, concerns an innermost atom; If that remains concealed, what does the bottom matter.

Stevens' wry epigram on the impossibility—and irrelevance—of revealing that innermost atom of truth is the truth celebrated by *As You Like It*. The entire play is finally one vast Fool-show, a mere bubble of a marriage song, which feeds us with questioning until we ask "If truth hold true contents" (5. iv. 130). By the time we reach this point in the play, we have learned not to doubt according to reason but to dismiss reason and transform doubt into the wonder of faith (5. iv. 138-9).

Over and over again through the play this question of truth's contents, both its substance and its satisfactions, is rendered irrelevant. The dance and spectacle of the closing triple marriage is the final diffusion. It is appropriate that Hymen so abruptly appear to insist that she "make conclusion to these most strange events" (5. iv. 126-27). The goddess who presides over the shaping of our desire for love is herself compelled by her desire to perform her office (and she herself is a "shape" of desire, a fiction). And she who bars confusion does so not by clearing up the illusions of Rosalind's appearance, but by unwittingly preserving them (once again the arbitrary interpreter of reality is made to look willful and foolish). Rosalind's punning "cure" of Orlando's madness preserves it beyond the courtship into the marriage itself, as he lives on never knowing that his "if"Rosalind was his "true" Rosalind.

Thus the play, as if it were a Fool, concludes balanced on the point of possibility, the point at which desire takes the form of marriage. One might conclude that the play does return from folly to normality. After all, Hymen does bar the confusion, the merry company is about to return to the Dukedom, and we at least are undeceived by Rosalind's cure. We should, however, recall Northrop Frye's observation that comedies end happily because they conclude the action at the point where the potential for a good marriage and just society, not the accomplished fact, is affirmed.[34] The moment of the wedding is also the point of folly: we guests are freed from having to consider the couple's future in the light of reason.

As for our freedom from confusion over Rosalind, Shakespeare slyly shows us how deluded our clarity is. We spectators are like Orlando, who lives "by thinking" (5. ii. 20), that is, by imagining that Ganymede is Rosalind. He never realizes that this self-conscious fiction-making is also plain life. And so has our "thinking" been unwitting living: just as Rosalind dispels Orlando's illusions only to replace it with another, so Shakespeare diffuses his dramatic illusion into life, and suggests that life is yet another dramatic illusion. For the moment the play closes it opens again. "Rosalind" steps on stage to deliver an Epilogue, in which "she" reveals that this woman who played a shepherd boy is herself played by a boy—and who is "he" played by? We have sat outside the play, rational spectators enjoying our self-conscious, self-controlled "thinking" of this pack of fools, and now we discover that we, too, have been caught up into the Fool-show of *As You Like It*. The play moves from Dukedom to "Ducdame"; when we leave the theater, do we return to our own Dukedom, or to a "Ducdame"? Does it matter? By leading us to this point, the play has performed the Fool's essential function: to "break down the distinction both between wisdom and folly, and between life and art."[35]

Notes

[1] *Shakespeare's Comedies: Explorations in Form* (Princeton: Princeton U. Press, 1972), p. 14 and 21, and 175-195.

[2] *Shakespeare's Pastoral Comedy* (Chapel Hill, N.C.: U. of North Carolina Press, 1972), pp. 98ff.

[3] James Joyce, *Ulysses* (New York: Random House, 1961), p. 312.

[4] *The Fool: His Social and Literary History* (Gloucester, Mass.: Peter Smith, 1966), p. 324. "Kaleidoscopic" is her term for the structure of *As You Like It*. I try to elaborate her brilliant one-word description.

[5] *As You Like It,* in *Shakespeare: Modern Essays in Criticism,* ed. Leonard F. Dean (New York: Oxford U. Press, 1957), p. 132. I am much indebted to Jenkins' discussion of the play's joyful subjectivity. Berry, p. 187ff., also names Touchstone "the standard" by which to judge the play, but defines that standard differently than I do.

[6] Jenkins, p. 132.

[7] Welsford, p. 324.

[8] Welsford, p. 323.

[9] *The Fool and His Scepter: A Study in Clowns and Jesters and Their Audience* (Evanston, Ill.: Northwestern U. Press, 1969), p. 50.

[10] J. Hillis Miller's "The Critic as Host," in *Deconstruction and Criticism,* ed. Harold Bloom (New York: Seabury Press, 1979), came to my attention too late to inform my essay, but it is clear that Touchstone's power to de-center the play, and to suspend critical discussion between opposed terms such as "fusion" and "diffusion," makes the fool a precursor of deconstructive critics such as Miller. Inspired by Jacques Derrida's argument that language is a chain of tropes rather than a univocal set of meanings "carried by a single referential grammar" (Miller, p. 222), Miller urges us to acknowledge the "uncanny antithetical relation" (221) between conceptual oppositions, word pairs, and meanings within single words. By seeking out such relations in literary works, we should come to recognize the "undecidability" of the meaning of the work's meaning: ". . . the critic can never show decisively whether or not it is capable of being definitively interpreted" (248). To use Miller's own metaphor, Touchstone inhabits the "host" text like a parasite and, like the deconstructive critic, leads us to the point where we question which is host and which parasite until the opposition breaks down in "undecidability"—or folly.

[11] "Paradox," in *Scientific American* 4 (April 1962), pp. 84-96.

[12] Welsford, p. 322.

[13] Welsford, p. 322.

[14] Welsford, p. 323.

[15] Willeford, p. 173.

[16] Willeford, p. 23.

[17] Willeford, p. 31.

[18] Willeford, p. 31.

[19] Willeford, p. 29.

[20] Willeford, p. 51.

[21] *Christ and Apollo: The Dimensions of the Literary Imagination* (New York: Sheed and Ward, 1960), p. 15.

[22] Lynch, p. 19.

[23] Lynch, p. 106.

[24] *Rabelais and His World,* trans. Helene Iswolsky (Cambridge, Mass.: MIT Press, 1968), pp. 24-33.

[25] Welsford, p. 325.

[26] "Vital balance" and "the pure sense of life" are Susanne K. Langer's terms, in *Feeling and Form* (New York: Charles Scribner's Sons, 1953), pp. 330 and 327; "the joy of life invincible" is Joseph Campbell's, in *Hero with a Thousand Faces* (New York and Cleveland: World Publishing, 1956), p. 28; "the living" is Henri Bergson's, in "Laughter," in *Comedy* ed. Wylie Sypher (Garden City, N.Y.: Anchor Editions, 1963 *passim;* "the ugly and strong . . . actual" is Lynch's, p. 106.

[27] Welsford, p. 325.

[28] I am indebted here to Donald Howard's citation of Hannah Arendt's discussion of Nietzsche's thesis that promises are the foundation of the social order in Howard's introduction to his edition of *Twentieth Century Interpretations of Gawain and the Green Knight* (Englewood Cliffs, N.J., 1967).

[29] Willeford, p. 51.

[30] Willeford, p. 26.

[31] *Chaucer and the Shape of Creation: The Aesthetic Possibilities of Inorganic Structure* (Cambridge, Mass.: Harvard U. Press, 1967), p. 7.

[32] D. W. Robertson discusses St. Augustine's theory of figurative expression and its influence through to the Renaissance in *A Preface to Chaucer: Studies in Medieval Perspectives* (Princeton, N.J.: Princeton U. Press, 1962), pp. 52-64.

Kellogg and Steele's discussion of the sonneteers' aesthetic of elaboration and idealization is contained in their introduction to the *Amoretti* in their edition of *The Faery Queene: Books I and II* (Indianapolis and New York: Bobbs-Merrill, 1965), pp. 450-454.

[33] "An Ordinary Evening in New Haven," in *The Palm at the End of the Mind: Selected Poems and a Play,* ed. Holly Stevens (New York: Random House, 1972), p. 332.

[34] *Anatomy of Criticism: Four Essays* (Princeton, N.J.: Princeton U. Press, 1957), pp. 169-70.

[35] Welsford, p. 27.

Guy Butler (essay date 1983)

SOURCE: "Shakespeare and Two Jesters," in *Hebrew University Studies in Literature and the Arts,* Vol. 11, No. 2, Spring, 1983, pp. 161-79.

[*In the following excerpt, Butler describes the influence that rival jesters Robert Armin and John Stone (circa 1600) had on Touchstone's evolution into a "new-style" fool.*]

My two jesters are Robert Armin, who joined the Chamberlain's Men in ca. 1600, generally accepted as the first interpreter of Touchstone, Feste, and Lear's Fool; and John Stone, a great, but neglected, tavern fool. They were both well-known, and rivals, about the year 1600. I shall attempt to show their influence in one play only, *As You Like It,* and on Touchstone in particular.

Robert Armin is in some respects the most remarkable among the first actors of Shakespeare's plays. He was, like Jonson and Shakespeare, an actor-playwright. His literary legacy is considerably larger than that of the only other Elizabethan fool to commit himself to print, William Kempe, whom he succeeded as chief comic actor in the Chamberlain's Men. Not only did he play the fool on the stage, but set himself up as an expert on fools; his *Foole upon Foole*[1] appeared in the year he joined the Chamberlain's Men, (1600). Before Armin was engaged by the Chamberlain's Men, their chief playwright, Shakespeare, must have watched him in performance. He might have taken particular note of him in the star role of Tutch, in *The History of the Two Maids of More-clacke,*[2] a play written by Armin himself.

I have called both Armin and Stone jesters. I could also have called them fools, even, possibly, clowns. The terms were used very loosely by Shakespeare and his contemporaries, and this vagueness is no help when we have to decide what jesters, or fools, or clowns wore in plays in which costume and disguise are important. As our text is *AYLI* and our focus Touchstone, we have to grapple with Shakespeare's Motley once more.[3]

Touchstone has always presented critics with a problem. A very useful summary of their responses to the supposed inconsistencies in his characterisation will be found in the *New Variorum* edition of the play, (ed. R. Knowles, 1975). Bethell (1944) expresses the widely held view that Touchstone has "two irreconcilable 'characters'," but he thinks they are "held in parallel throughout the play"; Gordon (1922) thinks that "the forest of Arden simply brings out the best in him"; Goldsmith (1943) and several others think that any inconsistencies are due to alterations in a role originally intended for Kempe, an old style clown, and now adapted to Armin, a new style witty fool. Harold Jenkins (*Shakespeare Survey,* 8, p. 42) believes that the play, particularly Act I, shows signs of haste and lack of revision, and that Shakespeare "has not quite decided about the character of Touchstone."

But much of this critical confusion disappears if we can see these teasing incompatabilities as quite deliberate, indeed necessary, to achieve one of the dramatist's purposes. To do this we need to entertain the following propositions:

First: when Armin joined the Lord Chamberlain's Men in 1600 he was already well-known for a kind of witty foolery very different from that of the traditional rustic clown whose place he had taken (William Kempe). He helped to transform the stage fool, This has been well argued by Baldwin, Felver, Hotson, Bradbrook and others.[4] In his own play, *Two Maids of More-clacke,* Armin had created a clever character called Tutch, in whose guise he mimicked John o' th' Hospital, and other fools.[5] Second: in 1600 John Stone, a very well-known traditional tavern fool, was practising a very different kind of wit, and attacking the new style, earning the animus of Jonson, among others.[6]

The ordinary was a most colourful and democratic meeting place, the popular exchange of news and gossip in a society without newspapers or radio.[7] It provided an audience for fools and entertainers of various calibre, many of whom exploited the unsophisticated 'clowns' from the country by claiming to be experts in courtship, swearing, duelling, etc. Hostesses gave them free meals if they attracted gulls to their tables, or otherwise added to their custom. By the end of the century, however, the more discriminating found the quality of most of this tavern humour tedious.[8] A new species appeared, the wits, who appealed to the more sophisticated portion of the audience, who clashed in something like flytings with the old-style entertainers. This clash found its best-known echo on the stage, when William Kempe, a clownish fool, left the Chamberlain's Men, shortly to be replaced by Robert Armin. For some years (about two decades, I suspect) a running battle between the witty fool and the clownish fool was waged on the public and the private stages, in the taverns and ordinaries, and at select entertainments in great houses of the nobles and the wealthy.

Scholars accept that Armin played a crucial role in that battle, by acting Shakespeare's new-style fools—Touchstone, Feste and Lear's Fool. I believe that his main opponent was John Stone, who, I would argue from the evidence of Jonson alone, was the chief among the tavern fools, an indomitable opponent of the wits and of the new set fools, i.e. fools who spoke no more than the dramatist set down for them. The new fools did not have an easy victory. People like Malvolio regarded the wits who applauded him as no better than fools themselves,[9] and is delighted when an ordinary fool (Stone) puts down a set fool (Feste-Armin) in Iv. 77. The old style fool seems to have continued to flourish. The death of Stone, (1605) according to Jonson, was felt acutely.[10]

Third: If, then, London theatre audiences, actors and playwrights were thoroughly aware of both a stage character called Tutch and a tavern fool called Stone, would any dramatist create a fool called Touchstone in an absent-minded fit, or as a mere compliment to his new actor's erstwhile apprenticeship to a goldsmith? Surely not. Shakespeare is inviting his audience to witness a catalysis or symbiosis of rival styles of humour. By combining the names of representatives of these styles—Tutch, the new, Stone, the old—he arrived at the happy oxymoron Touchstone: a character who, I believe, incorporates qualities of both his antecedents. The word, of course, has other connotations, which Shakespeare did not fail to exploit.

If we can accept this proposition we shall find that obscure pieces of business and dialogue are transformed into delightful visual and verbal jokes. I shall pay particular attention to the visual aspect, which professors of literature tend to neglect, but which producers and actors cannot. Let us start by reminding ourselves, with the aid of contemporary illustrations, of what the very different costume characteristics of the three main types of fool were.

First the Jester, usually found in courts and great houses, distinguished by his coxcomb, bauble, and bells. . . . I incline to the view that his costume was parti-coloured.[11] Second, the Clown, a popular entertainer. When dancing a jig, he will have a pipe and tabor, and festive trimmings to his costume. . . . When playing the bumpkin, or clown proper, he will be dressed in ill-fitting clothes, with exaggeratedly large slops, as shown in Elizabethan caricature. . . . Third, the Innocent, or simpleton. . . . Dressed like a baby in long petticoats made of a cloth called motley, he was frequently a pensioner, in large establishments, or looked after by institutions like Christ's Hospital, London. Now, which of these very different costumes did Touchstone wear?

Leslie Hotson in *Shakespeare's Motley* has, I think, established the nature of the motley which Touchstone is wearing in Arden, and which so delights and surprises Jaques.[12] It is the long innocent's garment, which Tutch wore when impersonating John in the Hospital. It is *the* garment—rather than several others he wore in his play—that Armin chose to be remembered by when he had the block cut for *Two Maids of Moreclacke*. . . . What surprises Jaques is the incompatibility of the motley costume and the reasoned quality of the speech of this fool in the forest: he does not ramble nor babble, he uses good set terms. Where I part company with Hotson is in his assumption that this form of motley costume is Touchstone's normal wear. Is he dressed in motley in Duke Frederick's palace? In the stage directions he is called, quite unequivocally, clown, (not fool, as in *Lear*); and, more important, "clownish fool" by Rosalind (I.iii.130).

We know, from Armin's own *Two Maids,* that as Tutch the clown he wore Sir William's household livery. We also know that Shakespeare had transformed a clown to a gaily dressed servingman in *The Merchant of Venice*.[13] What is more, he gave Launcelot no more than fifteen lines in which to change.[14] This suggests the simple donning of a servant's coat "more guarded than his fellows" over his clown's russet outfit. We must insist on "clown", because Rosalind does. But it is possible that the "fool" portion of Rosalind's phrase "clownish fool", signifies "jester" as it does in *Lear*: in which case we would have the very curious combination of slops, servingman's household coat, and fool's cap. There are, however, English illustrations of this possibility. The oddity of the combination may have appealed to Shakespeare. . . . This, with a cockscomb and a shortened surtout over exaggerated slops, gives us a comic enough effect. . . . However he is dressed, I suggest Armin is got up to remind the audience of Stone, and that he imitates his mannerisms. He is doing one of his famous turns, taking-off a fellow fool: in this case, one whom he has already lampooned in song in his play, *Two Maids*.[15]

Rosalind and Celia prepare us for a somewhat thick-witted presence. These two cultured, witty young ladies refer to him as a natural (i.e. simple, but also uneducated), as "a cutter off of nature's wit," a phrase which would have considerably more point if applied to the tavern fool, Stone, already engaged in a war of words with the new type of witty fool. The visual takeoff of Stone is accompanied by Celia's double pun on whetstone.[16] " . . . Nature . . . hath sent this natural for our whetstone; for always the dullness of the fool is the whetstone of the wits." This "whetstone," twice, has been a puzzle, e.g. to 'Q'., who says "It is rather remarkable that Celia appears to be making no reference to Touchstone's name here. Indeed, the audience do not hear the name until II.iv.19."[17] Exactly, but if Shakespeare's concern is with Stone, whose likeness is on the stage, the puzzle ceases and becomes a joke at Stone's expense.

Celia cries ironically, to "whetstone," "How now, wit! Whither wander you?"[18] In his replies the "roynish clown" comes out with a gentleman's oath (By mine honour) which leads to an exchange that immediately places him, and his sense of humour, as "ordinary." To Rosalind's surprised question, "Where learned you that oath, fool?" he replies:

> "Of a certain knight that swore by his honour that they were poor pancakes, and swore by his honour the mustard was nought" [I.ii.59.]

Where, but in an ordinary, would a knight make such observations on the pancakes and mustard? He would certainly not do so in high society, least of all at a duke's table.

Yet this "clownish fool" is not quite as dim as the bright girls have suggested; and he is redeemed for his devotion to Celia, and her fondness for him. The scene ends with the plans of the two girls to fly into the forest of Arden in his company. They will travel incognito, of course, with assumed names. Some time is devoted to discussing their disguises.[19] But how will the clown (Stone) disguise himself? This is kept from us. My belief is that he dons innocent's motley *as a disguise*. We see him in it for the first time in the forest. The stage direction for their next appearance makes good sense if we accept that the fool has been transformed by his disguise of motley, and that he, too, has acquired an alias, Touchstone, as the others had done earlier. *Enter Rosalind for Ganymede, Celia for Aliena, and Clown alias Touchstone* (II.iv.). . . .

Of the three disguises, then, this will come as a surprise; and yet, not entirely so; for Armin has donned his own favourite garment—Tutch's motley—over 'Stone's' russet garb. Tutch and Stone have been synthesised. The first jokes will be visual. In addition to the *coup* of forcing the Stone fool to assume as disguise the garment of Tutch, we have Armin's movements. There is some evidence that the dwarfish Stone was clumsy on his feet, a fact to which Jonson drew attention in his satirical portrait of him as Amorphus in *Cynthias Revels* (1600).[20] Shakespeare gives Armin his brief for a similar telling bit of mime for his Arden entry. He enters, according to the stage direction, after the girls, no doubt limping laboriously.

> Rosalind: O Jupiter! how weary are my spirits.
> Touchstone: I care not for thy spirits, if my legs were not weary.
> [II.iv.1.]

A few lines later when Touchstone cries, "Ay, now am I in Arden, the more fool I," he may well be quibbling on 'fool': more fool, less clown. A twitch or swirl of the motley to reveal the russet beneath would make the point. The point made, at least the wits in the audience would enjoy Rosalind's slowly spoken first utterance of his fool/clown name:

> Touch: . . . but travellers must be content.
> Ros: Aye, be so, good Touchstone.

In making Rosalind give him this name, Shakespeare is articulating in one word what the audience is witnessing: the transformation of a clownish fool—who is twice called whetstone on his first appearance—into a touchstone of wit. Armin, the authority on Fools, and on quick changes of costume, is now wearing the costumes of two fools.

We all know that, however quick and precise the touch of this witty fool may be, he is more down to earth than his successors, Feste and Lear's Fool. Unlike them, his personal love-life is part of the action of the play. Blunt, like Stone, "he knows what he knows and why he must mate with Audrey."[21]

Corin and Silvius now enter, and discourse of the agonies and fantasies of lovers. The distraught Silvius departs, hallooing his beloved's name aloud to the reverberate hills,

> . . . O Phebe, Phebe, Phebe!

> Ros: Alas, poor shepherd: searching of thy wound I have by hard adventure found mine own.

This is Touchstone's cue for a comic debate of a well known variety, with himself. 'Tutch' and 'Stone' take turns:

> Touch: And I mine. I remember when I was in love, I broke my sword upon a stone, and bid him take that for coming a-night to Jane Smile.[22]

The *New Variorum* comments: "Obviously a joke is intended here, but wherein the joke consists is not transparently clear." Hudson (ed. 1880) says that 'him' is the imaginary rival for whose visits to Jane the stone was held vicariously responsible. No doubt, but why is the rival symbolised by a stone?[23]

But if my thesis is accepted the source of the joke becomes clear. We have seen that Armin had written a song (in *Two Maids*) which took a swipe at Stone for seducing an unknown Jane Smile; but as the stone was apparently insensate, the blow was ill-considered, and a waste of wit. As the laughter at Tutch's chivalrous attack with sword, like a true knight, subsides, hey presto, his green motley is swept back, and there, in his clown's russet, stands 'Stone' in his slops, who immediately gives his account of how 'fantasy' affected his wooing. It is low comedy stuff; with a dairymaid, cows, milking, butter making, and, once more, vegetables such as peascods, as props. When 'Stone's' wooing is done, the motley sweeps back once more but unbuttoned, so that the audience is aware of both green & russet, fool and clown, Touch-Stone; who now speaks for both of them. The change to the first person plural, while embracing Rosalind and Corin, can also be Touch-stone's royal "we."

> We that are true lovers run into strange capers; but as all is mortal in nature, so is all nature in love mortal in folly.
>
> [I. 52.]

Shortly after this speech, Corin, a countryman, enters, whose costume is, of course, clownish.

> Touchstone: Hallow; you, clown!
> Rosalind: Peace, fool, he's not thy kinsman.
>
> [II.iv.66.]

Touchstone is playing on one of the older meanings of the word clown: countryman, bumpkin; while Rosalind is playing on its more recent meaning of comic entertainer but of a different breed or kin to that of the innocent fool, which Touchstone is pretending to be. Without some such quibbling on both meaning and on costume there seems little point to the exchange. That Touchstone continues with some fool/clown by-play or mimicry may explain Rosalind's otherwise inexplicable "Peace, I say."

This is the lesser of Touchstone's two encounters with clowns, but it is sufficient, if played this way, to lend point to his expression of his dislike of the entire breed when his second target, William, approaches.

> Touchstone: It is meat and drink to me to see a clown. By my troth, we that have good wits have much to answer for; we shall be flouting; we cannot hold.
>
> [IV.iii.10.]

The visual joke is over; and we now have a display of wit at the expense of simplicity.[24] I also believe that Touchstone in his set passages and exchanges may be mockingly imitating and ironically refining the characteristic mode of speech of Stone the Jester.[25]

The climax of the play is the multiple wedding (V. iv. 104). Folio's bald stage direction—*Enter Hymen, Rosalind and Celia*—is expanded by Q. to read: *Enter, as in a masque, persons representing Hymen and his train, together with Rosalind and Celia in their proper habits*. What habit will Touchstone wear? With everyone else (except Jaques), returning to decorum, what will happen to his innocent's disguise? He cannot, as I see it, return to the clownish fool's garb of the first act without losing the entire point of the symbiosis in Arden. I suggest he wears his coxcomb with his innocent's motley, which is over the clown's garb. Armin is now clown, innocent and jester, all in one. . . . There is, in fact, a delightful cut of a female fool which shows us how these two items, Innocent's motley and Jester's coxcomb could have been combined. . . . This would have the merit of uniting visual element of his Act I costume with his Arden disguise. And, as Professor Bradbrook has suggested to me, the jester icon would help to reinforce the return of the exiled Duke to the formal rituals of his court.

Armin appears to have had a good voice, which, as Feste and Lear's Fool, he is allowed to use. Why is Touchstone songless? Is it not that Shakespeare, no doubt with his new quick-change actor's enthusiastic concurrence, is doubling him with Amiens?[26] Is there not a quibble on Armin and Amiens?[27] But Shakespeare was less interested in Armin as quick change artist or as master of gesture and voice than in his ability to project mercurial shifts of stance and mood within the same character. The electrifying volatility, which is to characterize Lear's Fool, starts in Touchstone:[28] and Touchstone's range and versatility is the result of Shakespeare's demand that Armin should combine his own light Tutch with the clodishness of Stone. Such a blend of extremes might provide a moral Touchstone, but I have never found him the unerring distinguisher between false and true, which the alchemical pun suggests. Touchstone refers, rather, to a wit which is discriminating, a wit like Tutch's, honed on whetstones, like Stone.

Notes

[1] *Foole upon Foole* (London, 1600). Armin's reissue of this in 1608 as *A Nest of Ninnies* is much expanded. The additions are some indication of how his experiences in the ambience of Shakespeare had expanded and deepened his view of foolery. Available in Armin, *Works* (ed. Grosart, 1800, rept. Johnson Reprint Company, 1972). The work seems to have been popular. Editions appeared in 1600, 1605, 1608 (enlarged).

[2] *The History of the two Maids of More-clacke, with the life and simple Maner of John in the Hospital.* (London, 1609, rept. in Robert Armin, *Works,* ed. A.B. Grosart, 1880). T.W. Baldwin, "Shakespeare's Jester," *MLN,* 39 (1924): 452 dates the first performance between June 1597 and winter 1598.

[3] The best starting point for this debate is Leslie Hotson, *Shakespeare's Motley* (London, 1952).

[4] T.W. Baldwin, "Shakespeare's Jester," p. 447; C.S. Felver, *Shakespeare Quarterly*, 7 (1956): 135-37; Leslie Hotson, *Shakespeare's Motley*, Ch. 7; M.C. Bradbrook, "The New Clown," *Shakespeare the Craftsman* (1969).

[5] "I would have again inacted John myself." Armin's Introduction to the *Two Maids of More-clacke*. Felver, on the evidence of Armin's introduction, says: "This opens up a new area of activity for the company clown, who presumably filled individual engagements in which he performed as a mimic of different fools he had observed in London and elsewhere." Robert Armin (Kent, Ohio: Kent State Univ., 1961), pp. 15-16. It is clear from this and from his miming of John o' th' Hospital, that he did not confine himself to stage fools.

[6] See Appendix B, p. 190.

[7] ". . . he found, that an Ordinary was the only Rendevouz for the moft ingenious, moft terfe, moft trauaild, and moft phantaftick gallant: the very Exchange for newes out of al countries: the only Bookfellers fhop for conference of the beft Editions, that if a woman (to be a Lady) would caft away herfelf upon a knight, there a man fhould heare a Catalogue of moft of the richeft London widowes: at leaft, that it was a fchoole where they were all fellowes of one Forme, and that a country gentleman was of as great coming as y proudeft Iuftice that fat there on y bench aboue him: for he that had the graine of the table with his trencher, payd no more than he had place'd himfelf beneath the falt. *The Non-dramatic Works of Thomas Dekker*, ed. A.B. Grosart (rpt N.Y.: Russell & Russell, 1963), III: 221.

[8]
    The lurcher Lollus at the Ordinarie,
    Will ieft of all mens manners in the Cittie,
    Another fot applaudes him fitting by
    Thus: Sir, by heau'ns, that was wondrous wittie:
    I ouwer-heard, and when I heard the beft,
    In faith t'was but an ordinarie ieft.

John Weever, *Epigrammes in the Oldest Cut & Newest Fashion* (London, 1599; rpt. Sidgwick & Jackson Ltd., 1911. Re-issued at Stratford-upon-Avon: The Shakespeare Head Press, 1922).

[9] "I protest I take these wise men that crow so at these set kind of fools no better than the fools' zanies." I.v.80.

[10] ". . . they do lack a tavern foole extremely," *Volpone*, II.i.54.

[11] Figures are on pp. 173-178. Figs. 3, 7, 9, 10, 12, 13 and 14 are by K. Robinson, Senior Lecturer in Theatre Arts, Dept. of Speech & Drama, Rhodes University, Grahamstown.

[12] II. vii. 12.

[13] II.ii. 138-43.

[14] He leaves Shylock's service in II. iii, and enters as Bassanio's servant in II. iv.

[15] See Appendix A, p. 181.

[16] For a good note on the punning possibilities see R. Knowles, *AYLI* (Variorum, 1975), on I.ii.55. "It is clear that Celia refers to the ordinary uses of the ordinary stone"—a nice unconscious pun on both ordinary and on stone. See also Jonson, *Cynthias Revels*, Induction 1. 37 and II.iii.85ff.

[17] *AYLI* (Cambridge, 1926), p. 115.

[18] This phrase occurs in several plays during this "moromanchia."

[19] Celia will be in "poor and mean attire" (I.iii.111), Rosalind will be suited in all points like a man: "A gallant curtle axe upon my thigh, A boar-spear in my hand." (*ibid.*, 117).

[20] *Cynthias Revels or The Fountain of Self-Love. A comical satyre. As it hath been sundry times privately acted in Black Friars by the Children of her Majesties Chappell* (London, 1601), entered S.R. 23 May 1601. The Folio tells us it was first acted in 1600. See Appendix B, p. 190.

[21] *AYLI*, p. xv.

[22] One hesitates to press for a profound quibble here: but as we are dealing with rival methods of pleasing the muse of mirth, may not Jane Smile be something more than the name for an easy wench?

[23] *AYLI* (Variorum ed. R. Knowles, 1973), p. 93.

[24] After reading an earlier version of this paper Dr. David Wiles suggested that Touchstone, played by the new style fool, Armin, is ridiculing an old style fool, William, so called by Shakespeare to remind his audience of William Kempe, the clown who had recently left the Lord Chamberlain's Men. This strikes me as highly probable.

[25] See Appendix B. Certain topics, which Touchstone treats of, bear a close similarity to topics treated by Amorphus, Johnson's satirical picture of a tavern fool in *Cynthias Revels*. I would argue that both characters owe much to Stone, not only for matter, but for manner.

[26] Suggested by C.S. Felver, *Robert Armin*, p. 45. "A *tour de force* celebrating his appearance in the first role tailored specifically to his talents."

[27] Suggested by D.C. Maclennan in conversation.

[28] Although we see its potential very clearly in Mercutio.

Bente A. Videbæk (essay date 1996)

SOURCE: "Touchstone in *As You Like It*," in *The Stage Clown in Shakespeare Theatre,* Greenwood Press, 1996, pp. 85-94.

[*In the essay below, Videbæk maintains that Touchstone's function is to serve "the interests of the audience," and thus mirrors, mocks, and exposes the folly of those he encounters in order to "lift the audience to a higher level" of awareness and enjoyment.*]

Touchstone of *As You Like It* is probably the clown who has had most attention from critics. He is so well integrated in the play that at times he can seem to be a real participant. His part is undoubtedly a large one, and he is on stage regularly throughout the play. Touchstone is indeed an interesting object of analysis, and at times we may feel that we know him well and intimately, but what we really know is the pattern of the clown's part, and such predictability may mislead us.

Rosalind and Celia first prepare us for Touchstone. Rosalind uses the term "Nature's natural" (I.ii.47), for as Touchstone enters the ladies have been sporting their own wit and skill at punning, playing with the word "nature." A term like this comes easily to Rosalind's nimble mind. Celia speaks of "the dullness of the fool [which] is the whetstone of the wits" (52-53), but neither remark describes Touchstone's abilities, and his very first mental capers are far from "dull":

> *Touchstone.* No, by mine honour, but I was bid to come for you.
> *Celia.* Where learned you that oath, fool?
> *Touchstone.* Of a certain knight, that swore by his honour they were good pancakes, and swore by his honour the mustard was nought. Now, I'll stand to it, the pancakes were naught and the mustard was good, and yet was not the knight forsworn. . . . Stand you both forth now: stroke your chins, and swear by your beards that I am a knave.
> *Celia.* By our beards, if we had them, thou art.
> *Touchstone.* By my knavery, if I had it, then I were. But if you swear by that that is not, you are not forsworn.
>
> (I.ii.57-71)

Touchstone takes his examples from two widely different worlds, the common man's table with its pancakes and mustard and the lofty spheres of knights and unreliable honor. We are reminded of our knowledge of the very court in which we stand with Touchstone. He needs no "transformation" from the lowly to the witty, his wit is ready, sharp, and to the point from the very beginning. He grasps the opportunity to rail at the two witty ladies, "The more pity that fools may not speak wisely what wisemen do foolishly," and now he is acknowledged by Celia, "By my troth, thou sayest true" (I.ii.80-82). Touchstone is far too involved in the court circles to be "Nature's natural," he is an allowed or artificial fool and can therefore be expected to have considerable intelligence. But first and foremost he is a brilliant stage clown, and his duty as such is in serving the interests of the audience.

Touchstone, more than any other of Shakespeare's jester clowns, works well paired off with another player. Our first experience of him in this capacity is at the opening of II.iv, the arrival of the disguised travellers in Arden, where Rosalind sparks his wit: "O Jupiter, how weary are my spirits!" and Touchstone replies, "I care not for my spirits, if my legs were not weary" (II.iv.1-2). The audience has already developed an affection for Rosalind. We know of her background, her sweetness and resolution, and with Touchstone we have seen her falling comically in love.[1] We have throughly enjoyed her worry during the wrestling match, her giving Orlando a favor, and her unwillingness to part from him. Now Touchstone reminds us of this scene as he comments on the unhappy love of Silivius the shepherd:

> *Rosalind.* Alas, poor shepherd, searching of thy wound, I have by hard adventure found my own.
> *Touchstone.* And I mine. I remember when I was in love I broke my sword upon a stone, and bid him take that for coming a-night to Jane Smile . . .
>
> (II.iv.41-45)

Silvius's lament is in conventional verse, and lovesick Rosalind echoes him. When Touchstone breaks in with his mock lament in prose, using the most down-to-earth examples, the audience is alerted to the empty ring of Silvius's conventional phrasing, but also made aware that Rosalind's love needs maturing if it is to become real and lasting. Touchstone uses a wonderful technique, taking the lofty and making it ridiculous by putting the conventions to lowly use. The challenge to a duel becomes a sword broken on a stone, so at this point Touchstone will be brandishing his wooden sword furiously.[2] The reason for the challenge is not romantic, it is a direct accusation of sexual congress, and moreover it is not delivered to the rival but, as if practicing, to a mere stone, which cannot come "a-night" to anyone. Still the stone proves to be his superior and breaks the sword. In the wording of this monologue there are innumerable suggestions to the actor on how to behave on stage. The prime purpose, though, whether or not props are involved, must be heavy underscoring of the sexual aspects of love and courtship, so different from Silvius's stilted nonsense. Touchstone's sword can serve excellently as a prop to embody each and every reference to the penis. It will be a good batler, a fine peascod, could even be milked and kissed like the udder, and naturally serves grandly for a sword. The whole idea of romantic love is summed up at the very end of the speech: "We that are true lovers run into strange capers;[3] but as all is mortal in nature, so is all nature in love mortal in folly" (II.iv.51-53), and Rosalind replies, "Thou speak'st wiser than thou art ware of." This point can and should be debated, Rosalind and Celia, and later Jaques, interact with Touchstone the court jester and treat him like the inferior he is supposed to be. His wit is expected to be brilliant, but as far as intelligence is concerned he is seen as belonging on a lower plane. To the audience there can be no question that Touchstone is constantly aware of and adjusting to the people he associates with, and he lays bare their every folly at such an early point in time that we can anticipate what our protagonists will be doing next. Touchstone lifts the audience to a higher level, from which they can view the "strange capers" on stage from the delightful distance this new transparency brings. After all, there is no joke quite as enjoyable as the one we have seen through beforehand.

But Touchstone does not even have to be present on stage for him to make his points and for us to enjoy his mirror of the world. In II.vii Jaques comes to the court of Duke Senior and reports a meeting with "a motley fool" in the forest Jaques, the self-established malcontent, who "[him]self [has] been a libertine" (II.vii.65), has been made "ambitious for a motley coat" (43); he exposes himself and his ulterior motives to the audience by quoting what Touchstone has said to him, and his own overjoyed reactions. In his delight he repeats Touchstone's by now familiar actions and style as best he can, but instead of becoming parallel to the fool, maybe even his successful rival, he is an abuser of the license to which he aspires. Touchstone's mirror shows us Jaques's distortion.

What Jaques has marked most clearly is the clown's opportunity for castigating comments. First of all there is the famous "dial speech" with all its punning, which is made unsavory by Jaques's approach;[4] moreover, Touchstone is said to have exposed the conceit of the young ladies at court (37-38), but we already know Touchstone's views. Jaques envies the freedom of expression of the court jester. In the speed of performance every aspect of the mirroring and distortion may not emerge clearly, but an audience does not have to be consciously aware of every little tool of Shakespeare's trade for it to work. Duke Senior speaks to a well-prepared house when he chastises Jaques (II.vii.64-69). To any audience Touchstone's mission, even when he is absent, is perfectly clear.

The Forest of Arden itself and its symbolic function as representative of a golden age is also utilized, mirrored, and mocked by Touchstone. It is interesting to note that the character of Touchstone is one of few additions Shakespeare made to Lodge's *Rosalynde,* the main source of this play, and that the idea of comic mirroring is Shakespeare's own. It serves to expose the reverse of life in Arden to any who might be romantically inclined, and later it will serve to castigate Rosalind and her romantic sentiments to the joy of the audience.[5] In III.ii, paired off with Corin, Touchstone describes life in Arden:

> [I]n respect of itself, it is a good life; but in respect that it is a shepherd's life, it is naught. In respect that it is solitary, I like it very well; but in respect that it is private, it is a very vile life. Now in respect that it is in the fields, it pleaseth me well; but in respect that it is not in the court, it is tedious. As it is a spare life, look you, it fits my humour well; but as there is no more plenty in it, it goes much against my stomach.
>
> (III.ii.13-21)

Touchstone even succeeds in cornering Corin and delivering the final blow to the innocence of a shepherd's life, and at the same time he prepares the audience for the love scenes to come:

> *Corin.* . . . the greatest of my pride is to see my ewes graze and my lambs suck.
> *Touchstone.* That is another simple sin in you, to bring the ewes and the rams together, and to offer to get your living by the copulation of cattle; to be a bawd to a bell-wether, and to betray a she-lamb of a twelvemonth to a crooked-pated old cuckoldly ram, out of all reasonable match.
>
> (III.ii.74-81)

Touchstone's railing against the conventionally pure and innocent life in an unspoilt setting invests even the ideal life of a shepherd with rampant sexuality. The comedy is delightful when Rosalind enters with one of Orlando's conventionally romantic verses, which is extremely badly written. To the modern-day audience her disguise lends extra comedy to the scene, and Shakespeare's audience had the added spice of knowing that they were watching a boy playing a girl dressed up as a boy, sexually a most confusing and amusing combination; but any actress delivering a rapt reading of this awful doggerel will provoke laughter:

> From the east to western Inde
> No jewel is like Rosalind.

> Her worth being mounted on the wind,
> Through all the world bears Rosalind.
>
> (III.ii.86-89)

Touchstone, never in the mood for this kind of nonsense, proceeds to demonstrate what these verses lack:

> If a hart do lack a hind,
> Let him seek out Rosalind.
> If the cat will after kind,
> So be sure will Rosalind.
>
> (II.ii.99-102)

The audience cannot help seeing Touchstone's point; amidst our laughter at this sheer nonsense, delivered partly to us, we realize that any healthy human union cannot thrive on airy nothings. Touchstone could be supported by Celia, who could give a scathing reading of the next Orlandian verse; but Rosalind still has her head buried in a pink cloud, and Touchstone leaves in disgust (157-159). Rosalind/Ganymede's scene with Orlando in III.ii certainly demonstrates how "all nature in love [is] mortal in folly."

Rosalind is about to have Orlando woo her in her boy's disguise, a most comic situation, but despite the fun the audience sees Rosalind's feelings mature during the courtship. Orlando's views are also expanding, and his perception of the female sex is becoming less romantic. The comedy of the wooing is delightful, and it is made even more so by the contrast provided by Touchstone's wooing of Audrey. The two share the remainder of Touchstone's scenes; he has been furnished with a living prop, not unlike Launce's dog Crab.

The very fact that Touchstone admits to having sexual feelings and is willing to act upon them sets him apart from most of his brother clowns, and only Costard goes further than Touchstone. They both use their own sexuality to teach the audience about the world of the play. In *Love's Labour's Lost,* Costard's admission comes early because the audience needs this pointer to bring home the futility of the king's decree. We are being guided into an interpretation, and the rest of the play will be seen and understood accordingly. Lavatch and Launce also demonstrate some interest in women. Lavatch claims to be "driven on by the flesh" (I.iii.26-27) and to want "issue of [his] body" (23), but his interest in "Isbel the woman" disappears soon enough. Launce of *The Two Gentlemen of Verona* reads us the catalogue of his milkmaid lady-love (III.i.263-360) to show us the role of calculated wooing in this play. But both Launce and Lavatch keep their sexuality within the accepted bounds for a clown; everything remains at the verbal stage, and the "lovers" are never seen together. Costard's and Touchstone's sexuality is more intricate, but specifically because their respective plays demand this. Shakespeare keeps the clown type unblemished, however, by never having a true love scene between Costard and Jaquenetta, and never letting Touchstone accomplish anything physical because of Audrey's prudishness. But the couples are together on stage, and this opens up the possibility for various forms of comic clown courtship, which could well become quite rowdy. Still, both Costard and Touchstone stay within tradition. Their sexuality—blatant indeed for a clown—serves to create understanding of and distance from the madness of a world which has willfully chosen celibacy, or where male and female are totally intermixed and indistinguishable to the lover both in appearance and behavior.

The lady loves of Lavatch and Launce can be seen on stage only at the discretion of a director. Jaquenetta is more substantial with a sizable part and a comic effect of her own, but Audrey is quite another matter. She can well be seen as Touchstone's comic partner after the pattern of Dogberry and Verges or Stephano and Trinculo. Audrey is the passive, Touchstone the active partner of the relationship, which serves as an ingenious mirroring of the Rosalind-Orlando courtship. Where Rosalind is in control of the maturing love between herself and Orlando, Audrey is in control of the static relationship between herself and Touchstone; and Touchstone is mirroring Rosalind who ought to remain passive, being beloved and female. The clownish lovers constantly remind the audience of the physical aspects of love, a purpose elegantly served by the Celia-Oliver union as well. Moreover, the more foolish aspects of the wooing and winning of Orlando are held up to ridicule.

The parallels between the Touchstone-Audrey and the Rosalind-Orlando unions are legion, for example the lovers' use of their mistresses' names. The first nine lines of the fifth act has Touchstone use the name "Audrey" no less than four times, and Orlando uses "Rosalind" constantly. Rosalind's name can be spoken in many ways, as we see from Orlando's and especially Touchstone's rhymes, but Audrey's, which is connected with goats and sheep in our consciousness, can be given a baa-ing or lowing sound which will suit her slovenly appearance, her occupation, and the affair generally.

In III.iii, Touchstone and Audrey discuss poetry, recalling Rosalind's reading of Orlando's verses:

> *Touchstone.* When a man's verses cannot be understood, nor a man's good wit seconded with the forward child, understanding, it strikes a man more dead than a great reckoning in a little room. Truly, I would the gods had made thee poetical.
>
> *Audrey.* I do not know what 'poetical' is. Is it honest in deed and word? Is it a true thing?

> *Touchstone.* No truly; for the truest poetry is the most feigning, and lovers are given to poetry; and what they swear in poetry may be said as lovers they do feign.
> *Audrey.* Do you wish then that the gods had made me poetical?
> *Touchstone.* I do truly. For thou swear'st to me thou art honest. Now if thou wert a poet, I might have some hope thou didst feign.
>
> (III.iii.9-23)

Where Orlando's poetry is written as an outlet for passion, Touchstone sees the medium as a route of ingress into the fortress of the female. Orlando innocently expresses his infatuation, Touchstone sees poetry itself as devious, as a means of subtle communication. Only once is Touchstone directly involved with poetry itself. In V.iii he may or may not join in the singing of "There Was a Lover and His Lass," but he is certainly listening with Audrey. The song has the usual *carpe diem* theme, which Audrey could have been expected to comment negatively upon, but she refrains. The word "poetry" is not included in even her passive vocabulary.

While there is no doubt that Rosalind is intended to be a beautiful and admirable specimen of womanhood, Audrey is her opposite. She admits to ugliness herself (III.iii.29), and Touchstone is by no means blinded by Cupid: "A poor virgin sir, an ill-favoured thing sir, but mine own; a poor humour of mine sir, to take that no man else will" (V.iv.57-60). This, however, is not quite true. In V.i, Audrey's professed lover William appears on stage. William is a country clod, totally devoid of wit and an unworthy rival of Touchstone's. Audrey, who is always keeping up her image of the pure and honest woman, denies any relationship with William; still she is flattered to have the attention of two males. The audience sees an amusing parallel to another lover's triangle in the forest, the one between Silvius, Phebe, and Rosalind/Ganymede (III.v), with Touchstone acting comically in Rosalind's part, that of the omniscient controller. The difference between Touchstone and the two rustics is just as great as the one between Rosalind and the shepherds, but where Rosalind uses her knowledge of the hopelessness of Phebe's infatuation to punish kindly, Touchstone becomes intimidating:

> *Touchstone.* . . . Now you are not *ipse,* for I am he.
> *William.* Which he sir?
> *Touchstone.* He sir that must marry this woman. Therefore you clown, abandon—which is in the vulgar leave—the society—which in the boorish is company—of this female—which in the common is woman. Which together is, abandon the society of this female, or clown thou perishest; or to thy better understanding, diest; or, to wit, I kill thee . . . Therefore tremble and depart.
> *Audrey.* Do, good William.
> *William.* God rest you merry, sir.
>
> (V.i.43-59)

There is wonderful opportunity for Touchstone to clown in this scene, and for Audrey to contribute her share. In close contact with the audience, Touchstone has gradually worked his way from feigned friendliness to equally feigned frenzy, and he delivers his challenge capering about William and brandishing his wooden sword, making himself as large and dangerous as possible. Touchstone often uses his "superior learning" to best an opponent or score a point, and he never hesitates to use his "courtly" ways against the inhabitants of the forest. We know from Jaques that Touchstone's dress is "motley."[6] Whatever a director chooses to dress Touchstone in, there should always be an element of the comic in his garb to set him apart. When he blows himself up with words, the ridiculousness will be underscored and magnified by his clothes. Whatever such a fellow claims to intend, he will never convince his audience of ill intentions, we know that such wordiness never produces action. William's polite leave-taking, cap in hand, makes Touchstone's victory almost ridiculous, but still we love him. Audrey, though proud of her lover's prowess, must show some concern for William's welfare, so she hastens his departure and may even shoo him along, for a duel would stain her reputation.

The placing of the comical lovers' triangle lays the foundation for the audience's perception of the confrontation with the shepherds (V.ii.76). The four voices repeating their refrain would be amusing even without a Touchstone, but after we have just seen the thoroughly comic lovers in action, this sighing and moaning becomes doubly ridiculous:

> *Phebe.* . . . tell this youth what 'tis to love.
> *Silvius.* It is to be all made of sighs and tears,
> And so am I for Phebe
> *Phebe.* And I for Ganymede.
> *Orlando.* And I for Rosalind.
> *Rosalind.* And I for no woman.
> *Silvius.* It is to be all made of faith and service,
> And so am I for Phebe.
> *Phebe.* And I for Ganymede.
> *Orlando.* And I for Rosalind.
> *Rosalind.* And I for no woman.
>
> (V.ii.82-92)

The rhythm of the repetitions may suggest a dancelike choreography, which would add to the comedy. Still, amidst our amusement, we can see that Rosalind is playing her tricks with greater and greater skill, not only exposing the conventionality of the shepherds but also her beloved Orlando, who joins in the sighing; she herself does not.

Throughout the last half of the play there is much talk about marriage. Marriage is always a part of Rosalind's and Orlando's wooing, but Touchstone's ideas are of another stamp. He knows that marriage is the only way to gain ground with Audrey, and because his intentions are far from honorable he tries to get around the conventions as best he can. His whole ploy is set up and fails in III.iii:

> *Touchstone.* . . . sluttishness may come hereafter. But be it as it may be, I will marry thee; and to that end I have been with Sir Oliver Martext, the vicar of the next village, who hath promised to meet me in this place of the forest and to couple us.
>
> . . . . .
>
> *Audrey.* Well, the gods give us joy!
>
> (III.iii.34-41)

Both Touchstone's choice of words and the vicar's name clearly indicate to the audience what his true intentions are, and he reveals as much a short while later in conversation with Jaques:

> *Touchstone.* As the ox has his bow sir, the horse his curb, and the falcon her bells, so man has his desires, and as pigeons bill, so wedlock would be nibbling.
>
> *Jaques.* . . . Get you to church and have a good priest that can tell you what marriage is. This fellow will but join you together as they join wainscot; then one of you will prove a shrunk panel, and like green timber, warp, warp.
>
> *Touchstone* [*aside*]. I am not in the mind but I were better to be married of him than of another, for he is not like to marry me well; and not being well married, it will be a good excuse for me hereafter to leave my wife. . . . Come, sweet Audrey,
>
> We must be married or we must live in bawdry.
>
> (III.iii.70-88)

Touchstone only seeks sexual gratification. The wife is not the bow, the curb, and the bells; his desires are. The woman he will deal with later if necessary. Sexual desire is present, unpleasant, and must be served. His feelings for Audrey are summed up well in the final rhyme on her name.

When next we see the couple, marriage is still under discussion (V.i). Apparently Touchstone has fled Sir Oliver in fear of being truly bound, for Audrey was willing enough to accept the vicar, "the priest was good enough, for all the old gentleman's saying" (3-4). Apparently Audrey's decision to remain chaste until marriage stands firm, for Touchstone repeatedly returns to the subject. In the scene with William it is, "I am he . . . that must marry this woman" (V.i.43-45), and the opening lines of V.iii are

> *Touchstone.* Tomorrow is the joyful day, Audrey, tomorrow will we be married.
> *Audrey.* I do desire it with all my heart; and I hope it is no dishonest desire, to desire to be a woman of the world.
>
> (V.iii.1-5)

Rosalind's plotting gradually solves problems and slowly imposes order on her self-created chaos, and likewise Touchstone is brought to order by Audrey; no mean feat, and a very comical one. Where before he was all for bawdry, now he seems to be all for Audrey, and in performance this comes out clearly. At the beginning he is the active partner in the relationship, wooing her in a mock-pastoral, mock-conventional manner by helping with her goats and sheep (III.iii). All the while the audience is well aware of his sexual innuendo and attempts at seduction; goats are notorious lechers as we all know. But in the fifth act Touchstone has given in, and more comedy is created. Audrey may even lead the way in this act. She can come in trailing him behind in her relentless pursuit of marriage and honesty, which now begins to sound like female blackmail. In other regards Touchstone seems himself to the very end. As the problem-solving marriage ceremony approaches, all the protagonists are assembled on stage and Touchstone delivers his famous speech on "[the] lie seven times removed" and "the degrees of the lie" to Jaques (V.iv.67-102). Touchstone in the forest was somewhat out of depth amidst fatigue and hardship and maneuvered about by a woman. Touchstone at the court is quite another matter. Here he may sport his wit and be understood and praised. He is in his element as a court jester. But even Touchstone is not allowed to escape from the sea-change Arden works upon everybody who enters, and he emerges saddled with a wife. Still, his last remark is in praise of the great "virtue of If" (102).

Touchstone is not allowed to escape the stage. He has to be present with his Audrey at both the wedding ceremony and the final dance, and he will make his mark on both. Hymen addresses Touchstone and his wife with "You and you are sure together/As the winter and foul weather" (V.iv.134-135); and Jaques says, "And you to wrangling, for thy loving voyage/ Is but for two months victuall'd" (190-191). Winter and foul weather may not promise the brightest of prospects, but they are suited to each other. Seeing

Touchstone and Audrey with the three other couples will demonstrate to the audience that the four unions are seriously joined, not just a two months' venture as Jaques suggests, and this makes the impression even more comical. Here is our sprightly Touchstone tamed by a female, and what a female! But so was Orlando and Oliver, and both Silvius and Phebe for that matter. Audrey gradually gains the upper hand in the battle between the sexes, and she can make a wonderful, comic contribution to the clown partnership in the process. Fortunately Touchstone is not diminished by his sexual defeat, and during the final dance if not during the marriage ceremony he and Audrey must stand for the purely physical aspect of marriage, where Silvius and Phebe represent the tensions of the power struggle, and Celia and Oliver the true accord, all of which are elements of Rosalind's and Orlando's ideal union.

Notes

[1] In I.ii Touchstone last speaks the lines 127-129, but he is given no exit. It is an excellent idea to let him remain with the two young women and let him underscore the comedy of Rosalind and Orlando's falling in love by parodying their gestures, looks, and sighs in intimate detail.

[2] There are many indications that the clown's sword was indeed made of wood, the most famous example being Shakespeare's own; he lets Feste sing of it in *Twelfth Night,* IV.ii.125-132. Why mention a "dagger of lath" if the clown was not brandishing one at the time?

[3] His "we" will not include Silvius, but will include Rosalind and himself and everybody in the audience.

[4] "And so from hour/whore to hour/whore we ripe/search, and ripe/search, /And then from hour/whore to hour/whore we rot and rot (from syphilis),/And thereby hangs a tale/tail/penis" (26-28). See H. Kökeritz, *Shakespeare's Pronunciation* (New Haven: Yale University Press, 1953), 58-59.

[5] Duke Senior himself is well aware of the hunger and cold this world may offer its people. Touchstone is wary, already on entering it: "now I am in Arden, the more fool I; when I was at home I was in a better place, but travellers must be content" (II.iv.13-15).

[6] For a competent discussion of what "motley" probably looked like, see Leslie Hotson, *Shakespeare's Motley* (London: Rupert Hart-Davis, 1952); and Guy Butler, "Shakespeare and Two Jesters" (*Hebrew University Studies in Literature and the Arts* 11 no. 2, 1983).

SEXUAL IDENTITY

Philip Traci (essay date 1981)

SOURCE: "*As You Like It*: Homosexuality in Shakespeare's Play," in *CLA Journal,* Vol. XXV, No. 1, September, 1981, pp. 91-105.

[*In the essay below, Traci discusses the intimations of homosexuality between Orlando and the Ganymede/boy actor found in the text of* As You Like It.]

The diversity of sexual preference in *As You Like It* has long been noted. "As its title declares," Dame Helen Gardner explains, "this is a play to please all tastes."[1] Agnes Latham, editor of the recent New Arden, is one who echoes this idea. She sees the title of the play as "particularly suited to the do-as-you-please atmosphere of Arden, a place where a very mixed collection of people very happily go their own various ways."[2] Harold Jenkins, in his well-known and penetrating article on the play, emphasizes that "the characters do not keep in step. When they *seem* to be doing the same thing they are really doing something quite different, and if they echo one another, they mean quite different things by what they say—as could easily be illustrated from the little quartet of lovers in the fifth act ("And so am I for Phebe—And I for Ganymede—And I for Rosalind.—And I for no woman."), where the similarity of the tune they sing conceals their different situations."[3]

Critics thus have commented on the diverse sexual preferences of both characters and audience. Miss Latham, for example, observes that in the quartet of lovers "the sides we take in such encounters, if we take sides at all, are to a great extent dictated by our own inclinations."[4] The diversity, moreover, has been seen to extend to other than the lovers. For example, both Jaques, the ex-libertine, who now loves both fools and melancholy, and the exiled Duke, finally are "for other than dancing measures" (V.iv. 192).[5]

Generally, nonetheless, extended comments about the preferences in the play have focused on the heterosexuality of the audience and characters. Such is also the chief focus of the play. It is precisely because Ganymede is really a woman that Phebe takes Silvious only because he is a man. Her attraction for Ganymede is a heterosexual lust. She notes that he is a "pretty youth" (III.v.113) and that "he'll make a proper man" (III.1.115). Touchstone's love for Audrey is transiently "victuall'd" (V.iv.191) because of his lust, which is also heterosexual. Orlando's love for Ganymede most of the time seems but an unrealized or immature heterosexuality. He can "no longer live by thinking," and the desire to consummate with Rosalind is evident even without the pun on "live." It never occurs to him to have sex with Ganymede. His world is as heterosexual as Phebe's. His attraction to the boy is occasioned only as a last resort, inadequate substitute, or even cure, for Rosalind. His attraction to the boy is caused by the fact that "the boy is fair/Of female favour, and bestows himself like a ripe sister" (IV.iii.85-87). Duke Senior agrees with Orlando that the boy looks like Rosalind (V.iv.26-29).

But to see only the heterosexual side of the preferences is, in the words of one of the major spokesmen, to be "damn'd, like an ill-roasted egg, all on one side" (III.ii.36-37). One of the diverse preferences in the play, the homosexual way, is dramatized largely through the audience's awareness of the multiple identities (boy actor, Rosalind, and Ganymede) of the play's central character.

Nor has this homosexual side of the play been ignored. Jan Kott, for example, with his focus on the androgyny in the play, informs us that Rosalind's choice of name of Ganymede is not chance.[6] The name, he underscores, "remained above all, as it had been in antiquity, the symbol of pederasty."[7] Kott's analysis demonstrates his awareness both of the homosexual aspects of the Ganymede-Orlando relationship and of the fact that this is but one side of the relationship. He tells us, for example, that "Orlando does not recognize Rosalind in the shape of Ganymede. Rosalind woos him with intensity, but she does it as a boy, or rather as a boy who in this relationship wants to be a girl for his lover."[8] And yet more deeply: "On the surface of the dialogue, on the higher level of a disguise, identical with that of *Twelfth Night*, two youths, Ganymede and Orlando, play a love game. On the intermediate level we have Rosalind and Orlando in love with each other. But the real Rosalind happens to be a disguised boy."[9]

Kott's insight is aided by his undoubtedly being able to see the production in his mind's eye. With the Restoration and the boys no longer taking women's roles, it has apparently become more difficult for some to picture the many identities Kott points to in the play. Marvin Rosenberg in his well-known study on Elizabethan acting correctly generalizes that "apparently the audience forgot the 'boys' were male."[10] Quite so, but not in this play where the audience is exhorted to remember even at a moment when we might have otherwise forgotten. Michael Jamieson in his article on "Shakespeare's Celibate Stage" is specific in referring to this suspension of disbelief in *As You Like It*. He states flatly that "the moment an audience accepts Ganymede *as a boy*, instead of as a credibly disguised woman, the drily romantic irony of Rosalind's scenes with Orlando evaporates."[11] He continues as he demonstrates that Shakespeare stresses Ganymede's "femininity" in three ways: (1) by making a "comic theatrical point of Rosalind's falling short of that pose," (2) by fully exploiting Celia as a confidante to whom Rosalind "constantly speaks of herself *as a woman*," and (3) by "cunningly" suggesting to his audience "the close association of boys and women."[12] It is only in the Epilogue that he sees any emergence of the boy actor. He observes correctly, I believe, that this Epilogue has "nothing comparable elsewhere in Shakespeare" or "in other plays of the period." It provides, he explains, "a daring break with tradition." He sees the end of the play merely as "the cue for the boy-actress, as star of this comedy to take a solo 'curtain.'"[13]

And yet we do not forget that, until the Epilogue, the boys were male. The idea peeks out with intermittent appeal to a double consciousness, as the play occasionally provides added humor with the hint. Jamieson himself supplies evidence that this manner of viewing boys playing girls and yet remembering them as both, is not simply a 20th century Brechtian effect as he describes it. Jamieson quotes Goethe as he watched boys play girls in Roman comedies. Goethe says, "Only a kind of self-conscious illusion was produced." The poet explained that "We experience a double charm from the fact that these people are not women, but play the part of women. We see a youth who has studied the idiosyncrasies of the female sex in their character and behaviour; he has learned to know them, and reproduce them as an artist; he plays not himself, but a third, and in truth, a foreign nature."[14] Jamieson analyzes Goethe's attitude in this way: "The performance *was* analogous to an Elizabethan one, but Goethe's attitude was sophisticated; he was over-conscious of 'the thought of art.' What he enjoyed was akin to the Brechtian alienation-effect. That 'initial strangeness' differentiates him from the Elizabethans. . . ."[15]

Clearly the Brechtian alienation-effect has existed long before even Goethe. Samuel Pepys experienced it while watching a performance of a play with multiple identities closer to *As You Like It* than to the Roman comedy Goethe viewed. The play was *Epicoene;* the actor was the famous Edward Kynaston, the only boy actor whose portrait survives.[16] In an entry dated January 7, 1660-61, Pepys speaks of Kynaston appearing "in three shapes: first, as a poor woman in ordinary clothes, to please Morose; then in fine clothes as a gallant, and in them was clearly the prettiest woman in the whole house, and lastly, as a man; and then likewise did appear the handsomest man in the house."[17]

An even earlier observation of boy actors, one Jamieson could hardly see as different from an Elizabethan one, makes clear a contemporary double consciousness of the boy actor and female part he played. The observation is that of Thomas Heywood in *An Apology for Actors*. "But to see our youths attired in the habit of women," he observes, "who knows not what their interests be? Who cannot distinguish them by their names

Amy Elizabeth Clark as Rosalind dressed as Ganymede in the Bradley University Theatre's 1996 production of As You Like It.

assuredly knowing they are but to represent such a lady at such a time appointed?"[18] If Heywood could make this generalization about *all* boys playing women's parts, is it not fair to assume that in a play that virtually asks us to, members of an Elizabethan audience *might* recognize by name the boy actor of a major repertory company who was playing the starring female role?

Heywood, moreover, makes this observation in order to defend the boy actors from a charge which itself would add strength to the case for homosexual implications in *As You Like It*. The lines that immediately precede Heywood's comment about the audience knowing the boys' names, moreover, makes clear that they are but a defense against charges of the boys' homosexuality. Even the defense reflects that it was aimed at many who felt that at least some of the boys were homosexual. If the particular sexual orientation of a particular boy actor were known, that might color the perspective of the play, especially in the Epilogue. I acknowledge the "if." Heywood protests that "to do as the Sodomites did, use preposterous lusts in preposterous habits, is in that [biblical] text flatly and severely forbidden, nor can I imagine any man that hath in him any taste or relish or christianity to be guilty of so abhorred a sin. . . . "[19] Heywood's comments make known not only that some contemporaries felt the boys might well be homosexual, but, in his phrase "in preposterous habits," that transvestism and homosexuality need not be mutually exclusive.

Rosenberg, moreover, makes it apparent that the charges were well known. He does so, while, like Heywood, defending the boys against charges of homosexuality. "In the 16th and 17th centuries," he speculates, "men who wanted to act like women must have seen the stage as a kind of natural home. I certainly do not mean to say here that most—or even many—of Shakespeare's 'boy actors' were homosexual; but there may well have been some grains of truth in Prynne's furious assaults upon the "Sodomiticall' theatre."[20] Gordon Lell, in his article entitled "'Ganymede' on the Elizabethan Stage: Homosexual Implications of the Use of Boy-Actors," offers detailed contemporary evidence to support the idea that "the stage convention was susceptible to such homosexual implications. [This] is suggested by attacks leveled against plays between 1579-1583."[21] The most developed study of the boy actor also briefly discusses the idea of their homosexuality. The issue is summarized with consummate taste: "It is not necessary to discuss at length the justice of the Puritan charges of homosexuality against the players and the boy actors; doubtless there were some grounds for them and certainly it was inevitable that boys brought up in an artistic and somewhat raffish atmosphere should fall as short of the Puritan level of conduct as they soared above the Puritan understanding of the very mixed business of living."[22] Neither is a prolonged discussion of the ultimately unanswerable question necessary here. What is worthy of our consideration, however, is the possibility that the boy actors, especially the ones who play Rosalind/Ganymede and Orlando, *might* be known by name and as homosexual. Whatever their sexuality, however, the possibility of homosexuality between Orlando and Ganymede/boy actor is suggested in the play.

Whether or not the boy actor who plays Rosalind/Ganymede is homosexual, the text of the play comically points to the potential homosexual relationship between boys. While it has been argued by Jamieson, as but one example, that Shakespeare makes us aware of the similarity between boys and women to encourage our suspended belief of the differences between them, we are encouraged to notice their sexual similarities as well. When Ganymede tells Orlando he will impersonate Rosalind, he develops an idea in Shakespeare's source: "At which time, would I," says Ganymede, "being but a moonish youth, grieve, by effeminate, changeable, longing and liking, proud, fantastical, apish, shallow, inconstant, full of tears, full of smiles, for every passion truly anything, as boys and women are, for the most part, cattle of this colour" (III.iii.396-402). The speech is, after all, not without a flirtatious quality such as that the boy actor utilizes in the Epilogue. Given the context, whether one stresses psychoanalytic or other revealing fantasies, the expressions "longing and liking" and "for every passion" are a bit coquettish for this lad whom Orlando agrees to woo. Even the comic "for the most part," that may well remind us of "la différence" between boys and women, is not without sexual implications. The fact that the boy's name is Ganymede, which Kott, we have noted, explains "remained above all, a symbol of pederasty," should also surely lend support to this reading. That Shakespeare felt the boy actor Rosalind's choice of the name was more than a perfunctory imitation of his source is attested to by his using the name or that of Ganymede's lover, Jupiter, six times in the play. At the last point the name is mentioned three times (I.iii.120-21; II.iv.1; III.ii.84; IV.iii.157-59). I say "the boy actor Rosalind" to reinforce the kind of thought Gordon Lell has when he notes, "It must be remembered too that since Lodge's Rosalynde is a prose tale rather than a drama, the possible Greek-love reference to the Jove-Ganymede tradition is based solely on the disguise of a real girl and has none of the additional suggestions that the boy-actor of drama would provide."[23]

The reason Clifford Williams' 1967 all-male National Theatre Company of Britain production failed to enlighten us to any homosexual implications in the play is that if boys and women share many similarities, men and women do not necessarily do so. If occasionally men played women's roles on the Shakespearean stage,[24] they certainly did not do so in *As You Like It*. The references to Rosalind as young are made by characters with as diverse perspectives toward Ganymede as Phebe and Jaques (III.v.113 and IV.i.1). Most important, Orlando repeatedly views Ganymede as a "youth" from their first meeting (III.iii.413,421). Nor is pederasty the specific point. Orlando is no Jove to Rosalind's Ganymede. Orlando is a *young* man (I.i.127; I.ii.149, 161, 162, 169, 188, 201, 210, 211, 218, 222, 226, for example).

Another reason Williams' all-male production threw little light on the homosexual preferences in the play, is that its aim was to avoid all physicality, whatever the orientation. The director's "Clockwork-Orange" focus on violence and 1970s unisex distorted the play. Williams' said he found at "the very heart of *As You Like It*," a "sexual purity that transcends sensuality in the search for poetic sexuality."[25] There was as little heterosexuality as homosexuality in his production.

Surely these homosexual overtones must be in the audience's consciousness during what has been dubbed the mock-marriage episode. Agnes Latham devotes an entire appendix to this interlude. The scene, you remember, begins with Ganymede "in a holiday humour," "like enough to consent," exhorting Orlando to "Come, woo me, woo me" (IV.i.65-66). Ganymede asks Orlando what he would do if he were his "very very Rosalind" (IV.1.67-68). Orlando replies he would kiss before he spoke. After a good deal of flirtation and love play, Orlando asks Celia to marry them (IV.1.120), but Celia "cannot say the words" (IV.1.121). Argues Latham in her appendix to the New Arden edition informs us why Celia cannot: "Harold Brooks has called my attention to the validity of the mock-marriage, which comes very near to being a real one, a fact of which Rosalind, Celia and the Elizabethan audience must all have been aware."[26] Maura Slattery Kuhn in a recent article in *Shakespeare Quarterly* also discusses the episode at length. Her conclusions, though not aimed at explicating homosexual implications in the play, do much toward that end. Mrs. Kuhn validates the First and Second Folio reading, usually emended, standing as is:

> That thought mightst ioyne *his* hand with *his*
> Whose heart within his bosome is.
> (V.iv.113-14; emphasis is mine)

"To allow the First and Second Folio pronouns to stand as first printed," Mrs. Kuhn explains, "permits a re-enactment of the mock-marriage between Ganymede and Orlando in which Ganymede has said: 'Give me your hand, Orlando' (IV.i.114). The final stage picture of these two boys holding hands should mirror the earlier scene.'"[27] Her evidence, including such textual evidence as the Folio reading above as well as the fact of stage timing that would not allow Ganymede to change into Rosalind's gowns, is convincingly developed. With the two boys in this final picture mirroring an earlier mock-marriage, the homosexual implications are clear.

It is long before this reenactment, however, and even before the mock-marriage that the text asks us again and again to have the kind of double or triple consciousness Goethe described while viewing another play—the kind of viewing Pepys and Heywood shared with him. The boy actor often peeks through Rosalind/Ganymede's identity. He does so, if not in being known personally to the audience as Heywood suggests, in the reminders we receive from the text: "Is it a man?" (II.ii.177). "Dost thou think though I am comparisoned like a man I have a doublet and hose in my disposition?" (III.ii.191-93). "Do you not know I am a woman?" (III.ii.245). "Am I not your Rosalind?" (IV.i.84). Can so many provocations to remember the well-known stage convention escape the audience?

The reminders never stop. "I thank God I am not a woman" (III.ii.339-40), says Rosalind. "Take a good heart and counterfeit to be a man" (IV.iii.173-74), says Oliver to Ganymede. Never one to drop a joke, Shakespeare repeats the line and the idea when Ganymede responds to Oliver, "I pray you commend my counterfeiting to him" (IV.iii.181-82). Given the mock-marriage of two boys, one named Ganymede, and the constant reminders of the boy actor as player, is it not clear that homosexuality forms part of the themes and stage business of *As You Like It?* That some of these puns lack the sexual purity that Williams found in his all-male production is perhaps made most blatant in such lines as "He that sweetest rose will find/Must find love's *prick* and Rosalind?" (The lack of subtlety in emphasis is mine.) The line reminds us how humorously Shakespeare dramatizes the theme of sexual role playing whether on stage or off.

This dramatization of multiple sexualities is made repeatedly evident to the audience through the use of the word "if." It reverberates throughout the text with a frequency[28] that rivals "do," "did," and "deed" in *Macbeth*. It sets a suppositional mood that reminds us of the power of poetry to feign even sexual roles. If these boys are playing women, they also *are* Rosalind, Celia, Phebe, and Audrey.

The suppositional mood of the play is set early with Touchstone's lengthy story of the knight swearing by his beard—if he had one. When Touchstone asks Celia and Rosalind to "stroke your chins, and swear by your beards," there is yet another reminder of the boys playing the roles. Flute, not wanting to play Thisbe, illuminates what the women share with young boys when he protests that he cannot play a woman because he has a beard coming. Rosalind and Celia, as well as the boy actors who play them, share Beatrice's pronouncement that "he that hath no beard, is less than a man . . ." (*Much Ado About Nothing*, II.i.37).[29] Since neither Rosalind nor the boy actor has a beard, Touchstone's line and the "key of If" in which the play is written,[30] help to set up the fact that Rosalind is also a boy *before* she becomes Ganymede and has a near marriage with Orlando.

This fanciful and suppositional frame of mind so important to the illusion of the play is often delivered with ritualic force when we least expect it. Orlando, for example, reflects the tone when he asks the banished Duke:

> If ever you have look'd on better days;
> If ever been where bells have knoll'd to church;
> If ever sat at any good man's feast;
> If ever from your eyelids wip'd a tear. . . .
> (II.vii.113-16)

It is precisely at this point that Jaques informs us that the play itself is an illusion, an "if" that includes the audience as well as the characters. If *As You Like It* was presented to commemorate the opening of the new Globe theatre with its Latin motto about the world as a stage,[31] Jaques' speech would underscore to the audience that their world, too, was but a stage. "All the world's a stage," he begins, "And all the men and women merely players" (11.139-40). If the "merely" here carries the additional Elizabethan force of "utterly," then the roles a man might play can include even that of woman. It is conceivable that this is hinted at in the shift in point of view from "all the men and women" to "one man." The shift is to "one man in his time plays many parts." Is one of those many roles a female one?

The "if" takes on incremental significance in the fugue-like repetitions of Silvius, Phebe, Orlando, and Rosalind, in the quartet which Jenkins observes reflects individuality rather than agreement. It is in this same quartet, as we have seen, that Miss Latham notes that "our own inclinations" play a part. After the many quartets: "And I for Phebe.—And I for Ganymede—And I for Rosalind.—And I for no woman" (V.ii.84-87; 89-92 and 98-101), Rosalind exits with a speech filled with "ifs":

> [*To Sil.*] I will help you if I can. [*To Phebe*] I would love you if I could. Tomorrow, meet me all together. [*To Phebe*] I will marry you, if ever I marry woman and I'll be married tomorrow. [*To Orl.*] I will satisfy you, if ever I satisfied man and you shall be married tomorrow. [*To Sil.*] I will content you, if what pleases you contents you, and you shall be married tomorrow
>
> (11.111-118).

In a play in which we are made repeatedly aware that Rosalind is acted by a boy (she is Ganymede when delivering the line), can we deny the homosexual implications in a boy saying to another boy, "If ever I marry woman," "I will satisfy you, if ever I satisfied man," and "I will content you, if what pleases you contents you"? Even such negatives as implied in "I would love you if I could," are comic in their homosexual overtones. The allusion to homosexuality is there when Hymen informs Phebe of an alternative. "Or have a woman to your lord" (V.iv.133), he says, and whether one interprets that as comic absurdity or alternative, the manner of Hymen's delivery may direct us more than "our own inclinations." In any case, Hymen does not explicitly rule out this marriage.

Although it is far-fetched to see homosexual intention in suggesting that Celia and Rosalind love as "never two ladies loved" (I.i.112), one has to be obtuse to a sustained joke if he misses the multiple sexualities of Rosalind/Ganymede/boy actor with Phebe/boy actor. This, too, has the support of "if." "You say you'll marry me, if I be willing?" (1.11), Rosalind playfully queries Phebe. The homosexual potential of the line gains even more support with the added Elizabethan force of sexual desire in the word "will." This additional meaning is sustained when Rosalind asks Silvius, "You say you'll have Phebe if she will?" (1.16). Although the primary joke is founded on the "fact" that Ganymede is really Rosalind, the play's thematic concern with multiple sexual identities and diversity in love makes us aware that not only Rosalind, but Phebe herself, are boys—just as both also *are* women.

In the same scene the suppositional tone is continued as Touchstone echoes his earlier speech with an "if" and a beard when he talks of the seven lies rhetorical. While the speech has never received the critical attention of the seven-ages-of-man speech, audiences have seen the artistic significance of the dazzling *tour de force*. I have rarely attended a performance of the play when the speech was either cut or unapplauded. Does the echo of seven help to remind us that just as life is a stage, so are both life and stage ultimately but lies? Touchstone has already told us that "the truest poetry is the most feigning." Are we asked again if feigning can include even sexual roles?

> All these you may avoid but the Lie Direct; and you may avoid that with an If. I knew when seven justices could not take up a quarrel, but when the parties were met themselves, one of them thought but of an If, as 'If you said so, then I said so.' And they shook hands and swore brothers. Your If is your only peacemaker: much virtue in If.
>
> (11.96-102)

Hymen, the god of marriage himself (even if played by Corin with an elevated language that reflects his transcendence of self) rests his case in the last scene on "if":

> Here's eight that must take hands
> To join in Hymen's bands,
> If truth holds true contents.
>
> (11.127-29)

It is in the epilogue, however, that the homosexual possibilities of "if" are most fully exploited in the play. Rosalind, still dressed as Ganymede,[32] and about to marry Orlando, confronts us now, Mrs. Kuhn informs us, as "the Lie Direct in person."[33] The boy actor/Ganymede/Rosalind overtly refers to his many sexual identities, and with them separately flirts with the diverse sexualities of the audience. These include not only the heterosexual men and women, I suggest, but the homosexual ones as well. With Rosalind dressed as Ganymede, Mrs. Kuhn tells us that "as a dividend, the Epilogue line 'If I were a woman' can be spoken without threat for the woman who plays Rosalind. But actresses are not the only ones affected: a boy actor portraying a woman dressed in boy's attire saying 'If I were a woman' can bring a delight that is part and parcel of the play's effect."[34]

Part of this parcel of delight in the Epilogue derives from the sexual overtones, some of them homosexual, that come fully into play only when a boy playing a girl dressed as a boy delivers them. While the complexity of the puns, given the ambiguity of such a speaker, make the direction and intention of individual puns debatable at best, the sexual and flirtatious nature of the entire Epilogue is hardly arguable. The boy/girl/boy "charges" the women for the love they bear to men, "to like as much of this play as please you." But who is it who turns to the men to charge them for the love they bear to women? Is it Rosalind? While the phrase "for the love you bear to women" implies the heterosexuality of the audience, it does not imply that either the boy actor or Ganymede shares that preference. The context of that phrase, moreover, may well suggest a homosexual reading:

And I charge you, o men, for the love you bear to women—as I perceive by your simpering none of you hates them—that between you and the women, the play may please.

While D. J. Palmer has aptly pointed out the bawdy heterosexual pun in "between you and the women the play may please,"[35] it should not be forgotten that the phrase "between you and the women" is, after all, the very land in which he/she dwells. He/she rather charges *them* for the love *they* bear to women.

Even when the boy actor emerges over the other selves in the line "If I were a woman," homosexuality provides some of the delight:

If I were a woman, I would kiss as many of you as had beards that pleased me, complexions that like me, and breaths that I defied not.

The boy does not explicitly say that since he is a boy he would *not* kiss them. The line is rather flirtatious even in the world of If. The details of the line, moreover, inform us that the boy actor is, though now out of character, still regarding other males as a woman might—that is, homosexually. The boy's progression in the criteria he gives for kissing the men, as I interpret the line, begins with the beard that connotes virility. It then proceeds to a comic touch of exclusiveness in the second clause, and finally, to an hilarious desperation, not unlike Phebe's (who is not for all markets), that includes any man who doesn't have halitosis! The word "defied" may even suggest that he means any man who fulfills the virility requirement of the beard, and doesn't reject him. This *exact* progression from beards to complexions to those whose breaths defy not is repeated in the equally flirtatious final line of the boy actor, who again makes "his kind offer" to the audience. The fact that the boy is this time appealing primarily to the men, is clear with the repetition of beard:[36]

And I am sure, as many as have good beards, or good faces, or sweet breaths, will for my kind offer, when I make curtsy,[37] bid me farewell.

The pun on "fare well" may signal the men that he has not given up on his hopes of his offer being accepted, as they applaud his performance and the show. The boy's offer, like the tone of the play, echoes the kind of tone Shakespeare found in the line in his source that is said to have inspired his own title aimed at all tastes, "If you like it, so."[38]

Notes

[1] "As You Like It," in *More Talking of Shakespeare*, ed. John Garrett (London: Longmans, Green and Company, Ltd., 1959), p. 17.

[2] Agnes Latham, Introd., *As You Like It*, New Arden edition (London: Methuen and Co., Ltd., 1975), p. lxix.

[3] Harold Jenkins, "As You Like It," in *Twentieth Century Interpretations of As You Like It*, ed. Jay L. Halio (Englewood Cliffs, New Jersey: Prentice Hall, Inc., 1968), p. 32. Cf. Agnes Latham, p. lxxxii.

[4] Latham, p. lxxxiv.

[5] All quotations from *As You Like It* in this paper are from the New Arden edition cited in footnote 2.

[6] Jan Kott, *Shakespeare: Our Contemporary*, trans. Boleslaw Taborski (Garden City, New York: Doubleday and Co., Inc., 1966), p. 319.

[7] Ibid., p. 318.

[8] Ibid., p. 319.

[9] Ibid., pp. 319-20.

[10] Marvin Rosenberg, "Elizabethan Actors: Men or Marionettes?" in *The Seventeenth-Century Stage*, ed. Gerald Eades Bentley (Chicago: The University of Chicago Press, 1968), p. 98n.

[11] In *The Seventeenth-Century Stage*, p. 86.

[12] Ibid., pp. 86-87, *et passim*.

[13] Ibid., p. 88.

[14] Quoted in Jamieson, p. 76.

[15] Jamieson, p. 76.

[16] See the picture of Edward Kynaston printed opposite the title page in W. Robertson Davies, *Shakespeare's Boy Actors* (1939; rept. New York: Russell and Russell 1964). The original is in the Gabrielle Enthoven Collection of the Victoria and Albert Museum.

[17] Quoted in Jamieson, pp. 77-78.

[18] Thomas Heywood, *An Apology for Actors*, quoted in Alfred Harbage, *Shakespeare and the Rival Traditions* (1952; rpt. Bloomington: Indiana University Press, 1970), p. 211.

[19] Ibid.

[20] Rosenberg, p. 98n.

[21] In *Aegis*, 1 (1973), 9.

[22] Davies, p. 26.

[23] Lell, p. 12.

[24] See Jamieson, p. 79. Cf. J. B. Street, "The Durability of Boy Actors," who argues that at least two Elizabethan actors played female roles for a span of more than fourteen years, *Notes and Queries,* n.s. 20, 461-65.

[25] Clifford Williams, "Production Note," in October 17-19, 1974, program for performance at The Music Hall, Detroit, Michigan.

[26] Latham, p. 133 (Appendix B).

[27] Maura Slattery Kuhn, "Much Virtue in *If,*" *Shakespeare Quarterly,* 28 (1977), 44.

[28] Mrs. Kuhn's article on the frequency and significance of "if" in the play was published after this article was written and delivered to my Department. Its conclusions are reassuring in their independent interpretation of the suppositional tone of the play, and especially in their penetration into the utilization of the word "to draw up a contract between players and the audience." "If you will suspend your disbelief," she says the play agrees, "you will be delighted by our play" (p. 49). The conclusions of my own section on "if" in the play offer a different perspective by the very nature of our differing topics.

[29] I cite the Signet edition by David L. Stevenson, II.i.37. N.B. It is *Beatrice's* observation, given her desires, that a boy and a woman are "less than a man."

[30] Kuhn, p. 50.

[31] See Latham, p. xxvii.

[32] Mrs. Kuhn offers convincing proof of this fact in her article. I'll have occasion to refer to the implications of this final costuming on more than one occasion.

[33] Kuhn, p. 42.

[34] Ibid., p. 43.

[35] Cited in Kuhn, p. 50.

[36] I say "primarily" to the men, although I am aware that a beard could allude to the female pubic hair (as cited in Eric Partridge's *Shakespeare's Bawdy* with a reference to *Twelfth Night,* III.i.46-54).

[37] Mrs. Kuhn cites evidence in the *OED* that it was "an act appropriate to both sexes" in Shakespeare's time.

[38] Thomas Lodge, Preface to "Rosalynde," in Geoffrey Bullough, *Narrative and Dramatic Sources of Shakespeare* (New York: Columbia University Press, 1968), II, 160. See Latham, p. lxix.

John Powell Ward (essay date 1992)

SOURCE: "Chapter 3," in *Harvester New Critical Introductions to Shakespeare: As You Like It,* Harvester Wheatsheaf, 1992, pp. 38-56.

[*In the following essay, Ward explores the androgenous dimensions of Rosalind and suggests that her sexual ambiguity heightens sexual intrigue and contributes to the play's sense of unity.*]

Disguise

At this point the discussion becomes more convoluted. When Rosalind disguises she compounds the fact that all acting is performance anyway, with the further complication that in our day Rosalind is normally played by a woman, whereas Shakespeare had to assume an adolescent male took the part, as indeed was the case for all his female parts. Furthermore, while women characters have already worn male disguise in *Twelfth Night, Two Gentlemen of Verona* and *The Merchant of Venice, As You Like It* is unique in that Rosalind also plays another part, the male youth Ganymede, who then plays or re-plays her own self, folding the matter back in upon itself while giving it an extra twist. Finally the diverse conceptions of disguise, crossdressing, androgyny and transvestitism break up the straightforward matter of gender concealment into a subgroup of yet further possibilities.

We disguise much of the time anyway, to look tough, rich, respectable, Westernised, poor or pathetic. There is also a continuum between the aim to conceal what we are and the aim to reveal it. Men in the 1960s didn't grow long hair in order to be mistaken for girls, but to suggest unisex identification, or emancipation more generally. It is curious today that while women have commonly adopted what was male clothing—trousers, caps, rugby shirts—you don't see men in skirts and stockings or lace blouses without assuming they are fully transvestite. Disguise would seem to be something more specific.

In Elizabethan England females disguised themselves as males, or were presented as doing so on stage, from a number of motives: a) to cover their female parts and avoid lascivious approach; b) to get male privileges; c) to express defiance at patriarchy; and d) to get an erotic kick. Rosalind and Celia—and Julia in *Two Gentlemen of Verona*—disguise for the first reason given here (*TGV* II, vii, 39-43; *AYLI* I, iii, 106-10). A number of feminist critics (Howard, 1988, *et al.*) also ascribe the second motive to Rosalind and Celia, in the sense that those two thereby become liberated to speak freely, as men may already. The third motive, not unconnected, was that of the gangs of male-dressed women who roamed London in the late sixteenth century, and were attacked by offended males for their turpitude, as in the now well-known pamphlet of 1620, *Hic Mulier* (anon., published 1973). The fourth motive was the gist of the Puritan attacks on the theatre itself, as result of which boys were used for acting instead of women, not that this prevented titillations of a more homosexual nature arising instead. But, even if we see (as suggested earlier) some degree of phallic envy in Rosalind, and some lesbianism in Celia, it is hardly more than latent. So the first two of these four motives for cross-dressings look the likely ones for Rosalind. But they are also the two in which full disguise, as concealment, is essential. The fourth does not need concealment, although it is normally likely, and the third positively demands display as a protest against female suppression.

So, if Rosalind is disguising her womanhood from Orlando—the very person in the long run she most wants to know it—what credence can we give to the androgyny theories that have been widely elaborated in recent years as deep in the substructure of Shakespeare's mature, full-heroine comedies? Are Rosalind and those like her at last enjoying being fully women, normally under wraps through the subordinate role they normally get? Or are they for once enjoying being men, by inwardly at least savouring associating with men on basis of gender-equality? It is often said now that Rosalind can be fully woman at last because this is re-routed round through Ganymede. But even if this is true, a level of subtlety in the play is surely lost if we aren't awakened to the inner mixture of gender role and experience Rosalind must be thought of as gaining by playing both female and male at once. The further question is raised, then, of how far gender is itself socially constructed, as the modern pro-androgyny faction normally suggests. If Rosalind's physical sex does not change, is her response merely political, merely a sense of rights? Is she not experiencing a bit of malehood in her doublet and hose, or at least some kind of gender neutrality for social equality to hold her allegiance as well? The extreme sorority of the feminist movement might argue an equal-but-different (or superior-but-different) position anyway, but they would hardly go along with Rosalind's yearning for Orlando in the first place. Added to this is the question of Shakespeare's own approach; whether he was supporting female emancipation or silently subverting it (by bringing the women back to marriage at each play's end).

The renewed attention to the boy actor in recent years makes for further difficulties. It is underlined that there are four layers: the boy-actor, Rosalind, Ganymede and 'Rosalind' to Orlando. In fact, there are only three layers of performance: the boy playing Rosalind, Rosalind playing Ganymede and Ganymede playing 'Rosalind'. More importantly, these actings appear on scrutiny to have quite different degrees in them of the 'disguise' element we have already considered.

There is a boy-actor. Let us call him Basil (Boy Actor Simulation In Love). Basil plays Rosalind, but everyone knows it is a boy, and indeed an actor; the 'disguise' is not a concealment. Rosalind, however, plays Ganymede, but within the different world of the play; and this is part concealment, part not. Within the play's world Celia and Touchstone know who she is, and who her 'sister Aliena' is. No one else does. Below that line, however, the layers of acting divide. For Ganymede now plays Orlando's original lady-love, whom we might call Moira (Male Orlando's Idealised 'Rosalind' Acted). So we have the four: Basil playing Rosalind playing Ganymede playing Moira. But Ganymede is still visible to Orlando as Ganymede as well, and still within the same level of reality, the play's world. A final component to the situation is added by Orlando's position at this stage. If Ganymede is acting Moira to Orlando's full knowledge (just as Basil is acting Rosalind to the audience's full knowledge) then Orlando is acting too; he is at least playing along, with his 'then love me Rosalind' and (to Celia) 'pray thee marry us' (IV, i, 109, 120).

At a political level furthermore, if the very presence of the boy-actor reminded the women in Shakespeare's Elizabethan audience of their own suppression more generally, then that dimension has now departed, to some degree at least, when we see the Vanessa Redgraves and Fiona Shaws play the role today. (From one point of view, no doubt frivolous, this seems sad. As Juliet Dusinberre says (1975, p. 253), boys make bewitching girls, girls make lumbering youths.) So we have to choose between these two periods for interpretation of political significance, or turn to a different approach. I don't myself doubt the interest and truth of the political dimension, though I do wonder what Shakespeare made from it. But it is not the only dimension on which these cross-dressing plays can be read. There is, for example, the Foucault dimension of the raising of sexuality into existence by the very act of the articulation of its suppression (see Foucault, 1979). This historical process seems to parallel the way our play brings the woman's body into prominence by the act of hiding it, by disguise, from male approaches. But it seems to me that the approach most likely to gather all these strands of disguise and its ramification into a manageable idea is the one which makes the theatre, and acting, central themselves. It takes Jaques literally.

All these aspects of disguise—cross-dressing, boy-actors, comic doublings (Rosalind as Ganymede's twin), concealment, role-playing and the rest—are performances, all part of the theatrical world. The idea that all the world's a stage is explicitly highlighted by disguise, role-playing and even dressing. Normally disguise itself is as inherently suspenseful a situation for the audience as is, for example, whether a burglar will be caught or a lover interrupted. The small tension between what the person is and what they pretend to be, keeps the watching mind in gear, at the ready, waiting for developments from a possible disclosure, even when nothing is happening. But with Rosalind it is different. When the disguised person merely plays her original self, that tension is suspended. It is kept; it doesn't dissolve, because the actor does re-route herself round through another part, unknown to the observer on stage. But the action is stopped by the blocking circle of actor imitating herself. There is a void at the heart of the action, awaiting movement which doesn't come until she is ready for it. After all, Rosalind could have acted another woman and then played her own bed-trick. But she didn't. And because she is not acting another, no other is implicated. This takes the event into the heart and very principle of acting. It is sheer acting, sheer role-playing; playing oneself. The response from others present is, as the audience knows, not what matters. Orlando can only take so much of this pretence, and Celia just waits for Rosalind to finish. It is Rosalind who stands or falls, arrests or grows.

What does Rosalind do in this arrested space of her own making? We can come to that, but I'll throw my cap and towel into the ring at this point. I think that Shakespeare loved Rosalind, as Dante is said to have loved Beatrice and as, in some way perhaps, Dickens loved Little Dorrit. Rosalind was at least the fourth woman he had dressed as a man in his work, and, as Virginia Woolf said, his was the prototype of the androgynous mind. His males are inadequate, his women dominant whether generous or wicked. Rosalind seemed, in Lodge, a chance for him to write her in with the action stopped so that he could look at her in a full way, the camera frames seized. He wanted to enter her with his whole self; but he could not be so ungallant as to proclaim such conquest, so he put a double disguise over her as defence against his own intrusions. As Jan Kott (1967) said, Orlando doesn't know Rosalind is there, but she *is* there. Whether there is a real heterosexual meeting between Orlando and Rosalind is an open question. After *Romeo and Juliet* Shakespeare did not write another full love-story. The political implications of either cross-dressing or subordination didn't concern Shakespeare except as material; what he revealed about his own ideologies is another matter.

Rosalind's body

She has none; but the wounded deer has. So have Orlando and the lioness who wounds him. Is Shakespeare remotely suggesting the body is to be ignored? Or that in a truly civilised and green world all wounding and all blood will have gone; no tooth and claw? Shakespeare loved minds, perhaps, or so expresses it.

Was Rosalind a virgin? The one place where we might find the answer is at v, ii, 116 when Rosalind makes her round of promises to Orlando, Silvius and Phebe. To Orlando she says 'I will satisfy you, if ever I satisfied man, and you shall be married tomorrow'. The past tense might imply, as one would say, former relationships. And broadly Rosalind's tone of confidence and competence in the wooing scenes might strongly suggest necessary experiences. Yet the imaginative realm of the play won't let us particularise as to what such a man would have been like, or—more significant—even allow the existence of any such particularisation. In real life, given such a situation, one might wonder what the bloke was like. But Rosalind exists in a closed play; you can't 'wonder what the bloke was like' for to do so would be to invent another character within the play's fabric, which is impossible. An enclosed, finished fictional world of the play can't entertain an extra person, inserted from another world. To that extent the ethereal quality of the play, much beloved of the Victorians, does seem to insist itself.

The only conceivable candidate, therefore, was and is William Shakespeare. If he thought of her as not a virgin, then she wasn't one, and he was responsible. Since he doesn't say, the question, so far as it presses, hangs forever in balance, and again surely we are free to delight, perhaps required to delight, that it can only have been the one person who had gone with her to Arden and known her there, playing many parts in such times.

Do we know what she looked like? He knew her, but hardly tells us. Even where he briefly does, it is contradictory. At I, iii, III she is 'more than common tall', but at I, ii, 262 we were told by Le Beau that 'the taller is his daughter', that is Duke Frederick's daughter Celia. Unless Celia was a giantess this is either a mistake in transcription (the view of most editors) or, as I perversely suggest, Shakespeare planting false clues, something he just may have done on the virginity question. This one really *is* as we like it, a phrase the play's commentators must normally labour to avoid, so temptingly does it repeatedly offer itself. We don't ask, as of the number of Lady Macbeth's children, whether Rosalind was a virgin, for it is open but not blank; tenuously half-way; and we don't want to know what she looked like.

This last is a matter of the language, which leads us always sinuously around avoiding any matter of lily-white breasts, lovely blue eyes, slender legs or anything else of the kind one sees in much of Spenser and in Marlowe's *Hero and Leander*. In both of those poets the verbal allure is less voiced than physically present, sumptuously erotic:

> Her goodly eyes lyke Saphyres shining bright,
> Her forehead yvory white,
> Her cheeks lyke apples which the sun hath rudded,

> Her lips lyke cherryes charming men to byte,
> Her brest lyke to a bowle of creame
>   uncrudded,
> Her paps lyke lyllies budded,
> Her snowie necke lyke to a marble towre,
> And all her bodie lyke to a pallace fayre
> (Spenser, *Epithalamion* 171-8)

—which on Rosalind would have been absurd whether 'heavenly' or not. Such standing-back regard by the poet is nowhere found in Shakespeare's play. Rather, Shakespeare gives Rosalind a general sexuality in various ways. There is the occasional bodily reference which comes through jocular dialogue to which Rosalind never directly responds:

> *Rosalind* . . . I prithee take the cork out of
>   thy mouth, that I may drink thy tidings.
> *Celia* So you may put a man in your belly.
> *Rosalind* Is he of God's making? What
>   manner of man? Is his head worth a hat?
>   Or his chin worth a beard?
> (III, ii, 199-203)

This is a good case of the extraordinary technique of indirection the play evinces (another is that Audrey of all people asks the big questions about poetry), for Rosalind's body is the one in question, in this scene most of all. But this passage is also the one where Rosalind is put before us with her own desire heightened, and a musk of sexual excitement gathers:

> *Celia* And a chain, that you once wore,
>   about his neck. Change you colour?
> *Rosalind* I prithee who?
> *Celia* O Lord, Lord! It is a hard matter
>   for friends to meet; but mountains may be
>   remov'd with earthquakes, and so
>   encounter.
> *Rosalind* Nay, but who is it?
> *Celia* Is it possible?
> *Rosalind* Nay, I prithee now, with most
>   petitionary vehemence, tell me who it is.
> *Celia* O wonderful, wonderful . . . !

And Rosalind pesters Celia for more and more information, but with almost panting volubility herself: 'One inch of delay more is a South Sea of discovery. I prithee tell me who it is quickly, and speak space. I would thou couldst stammer, that thou mightst pour this concealed man out of thy mouth, as wine comes out of a narrow-mouthed bottle . . .'

According to Barbara Everett (1990), Shakespeare's characters are forms not persons, but, however, being perceived by the author as, and somehow bodily, embodied. But the embodiment of Rosalind comes out of her own mouth, without the distance of Cleopatra's lustrous barge (an indirection for herself) or Pandarus's news of Cressida's state when she is just coming to meet Troilus:

> She does so blush, and fetches her wind so short,
> as if she were frayed with a spirit! I'll fetch her: It
> is the prettiest villain; she fetches her breath as
> short as a new-ta'en sparrow.
> (*Troilus and Cressida* III, ii, 29-33)

If the play is indeed riddled with puns and *doubles entendres,* both sexual and otherwise, it makes for a seamless verbal web by which sexuality, and perhaps androgyny, pervade without exact placing of unique bodily detail on to separate characters. It makes the play, and Rosalind herself, porous, X-rayed; we needn't stray about on the skin to know her that way. I think incidentally that this may account for the credibility we can easily allow in believing that Orlando never recognises Rosalind. It wasn't that Elizabethans, lacking the high-tech photographic experience we have now, didn't know who they were talking to. They were attentive enough to facial detail, as the friar in *Much Ado About Nothing* makes clear:

> Hear me a little;
> For I have only been silent so long,
> And given way unto this course of fortune,
> By noting of the lady. I have mark'd
> A thousand blushing apparitions
> To start into her face, a thousand innocent
>   shames
> In angel whiteness beat away those blushes,
> And in her eye there hath appear'd a fire,
> To burn the errors that these princes hold
> Against her maiden truth. Call me a fool;
> Trust not my reading nor my observations,
> Which with experimental seal doth warrant
> The tenor of my book; trust not my age,
> My reverence, calling, nor divinity,
> If this sweet lady lie not guiltless here
> Under some biting error.
> (*Much Ado About Nothing* IV, i, 155-69)

Elizabethan preoccupation with eye-darts, blushes and the rest seems unlikely to have gone along with literal misrecognition of the actual face of the individual so emoting. Rather the switch of role symbolically put on by disguise was accepted, or certainly is in this play where all is a stage, as more significant than the incidental bodily differences individuals might have inherited. In *As You Like It* it is words themselves that are androgynous, or gendered. The double meanings pass quickly over in bush, nest, hind, heart, cote, bestow, cattle, misuse, forest, doublet, ripe, sister, wine, part, prick, Ganymede and many others. They saturate our awareness of the human physical presence in general and, of the characters in some cases, their alerted feelings. They undermine myth, whose double meanings are not verbal but palpable, animal, symbolic.

Rosalind's wooing

Rosalind neither woos Orlando nor acts the part of Moira. Rosalind draws Orlando inward to a sexual play-acting he always treats as such (he returns an hour late and then politely leaves) but which for all we know is not even heterosexual; and she never pretends to be Moira at all. Rather she tells Orlando what he needs to do to win Moira. As Rubinstein points out (1984, p. 123), 'heavenly' has the implication of homosexual, in that Plato contrasted heavenly love with earthly as that between man-man and man-woman. One reading of Orlando's silence at the play's end is disappointment. He has found this youth Ganymede rather attractive, and Ganymede is gone. His romanticising with his verses was merely the correct 'young man' thing to do; his heart was hardly in it.

The wooing has two phases. In the first (III, ii, 292-423) Rosalind persuades Orlando to agree to let this 'Ganymede' before him teach him how to woo and win his desired lady. In the second phase (IV, i, 36-190) she actually does this, although there turns out to have been more and less to it. *The first phase is based on titillation, the second on language.* The technique throughout the first phase is to intrigue Orlando by indirection. She repeatedly says the opposite of the truth, knowing Orlando knows the truth, so that even to raise the opposite is to raise a contrast and so hold his attention, his tension. He is drawn in to the orbit of the language, of its affirmations, so that his mind and feelings can't escape them. Even when what she says is not strictly untrue, it is underlyingly sexual, yet in such a way as not to raise suspicion of direct approach. His enticement is purely erotic.

As soon as she has asked him the time and he has replied that there is no clock in the forest, her answer is an untruth, the truth of which she herself knows is known to Orlando. 'Then there is no true lover in the forest.' He is that lover, as she knows. She then offers to tell him about time, not just generally, but its four speeds, a rich fabric of potential information about human foibles. The next erotilla is her answer when, now thoroughly intrigued, Orlando asks where she lives. 'Where dwell you pretty youth?' 'In the skirts of the forest', she replies enticingly, 'like fringe upon a petticoat', but quickly adds 'thank God I am not a woman', a possibility Orlando may not have thought of but will immediately start incubating: ' . . . to be touched with so many giddy offences as he hath generally taxed their whole sex withal'. The next move is the extended pretence (III, ii, 349-74) that Orlando is *not* the lover pinning verses to trees, and the disdainful suggestion that he is hardly dressed for the part (368-71). She has thus raised the whole wooing subject while never seeming to do so herself, a technique used to far more sinister effect by Iago throughout the third act of *Othello,* to a point where the Moor is knotted up with a nightmare tangle of what he believes to be his own thoughts.

Rosalind ends on the sexually potent 'come' (415, 422—it recurs at IV, i, 65), the refrain more plangent from Juliet when her lover was not listening:

> Come night, come Romeo, come thou day in
>   night,
> For thou wilt lie upon the wings of night
> Whiter than new snow upon a raven's back.
> Come gentle night, come loving black-brow'd
>   night,
> Give me my Romeo . . .
>   (*Romeo and Juliet* III, ii, 17-21)

Orlando does 'come', but only 'within an hour of my promise', and that speech-act failure is cue to his ensuing entanglement, in the second 'wooing' phase (IV, i, 36-190), in every kind of talk. Again, he has already started at a disadvantage. Not to elaborate each, there is the broken promise (42), the 'slander' of his wife (59), the naming of 'Rosalind' (62-3), the demand that he woo (65) and the interchange about talking and kissing (66-9), the talk of orators (72-3), the suit pun (82-3), the affirmations of saying (87-8), the accusations of male lies (89-103, especially 101), the request for favours (108)—all leading to the culmination in the mock-marriage (117-31), itself a form wholly of words though one now moving dangerously close to irreversible intimacies. But Rosalind does not leave it there. Orlando must say how long he would have his wife (135), hear how she will clamour and laugh (143, 147); and the whole is then summarised by Rosalind herself in a self-knowing mockery of her own volubility: 'You shall never take her [your wife] without her answer, unless you take her without her tongue' (162-4). The conclusion is disarming in its success, as Rosalind preposterously declares that 'That flattering tongue of yours won me' and ends with a spate of speech-acts which lead Orlando into essential courteous withdrawal:

> *Rosalind* By my troth, and in good earnest,
>   and so God mend me, and by all pretty
>   oaths that are not dangerous, if you break
>   one jot of your promise, or come one
>   minute behind your hour, I will think you
>   the most pathetical break-promise, and the
>   most hollow lover, and the most unworthy
>   of her you call Rosalind, that may be
>   chosen out of the gross band of the
>   unfaithful: therefore beware my censure and
>   keep your promise.
> *Orlando* With no less religion than if thou
>   wert indeed my Rosalind. So adieu.
>   (IV, i, 178-88)

Sexual enticement and the traps of language: Orlando is not wooed but entangled. Yet the language is generous; one couldn't really imagine the scene ending other than agreeably, although the degrees between fall-about laughter (Celia included) and the wistfulness of Rosalind in her speeches about male unfaithfulness (IV, i, 89-103, 138-48) may vary considerably as to how we imagine them. This might depend on what we feel about Orlando's entanglement. Is he so fated? What does he think this youth Ganymede is after? Or is he himself enticed toward that relationship, his own Moira fading? The mock-marriage is a conclusion, the game can't really go on; yet nothing has happened. The marriage was a fantasy. From his clinical studies Winnicott observed (1974, p. 32) that, with fantasy unlike with imagination, when you return to reality, nothing has happened. The titillations were indirect and the language-games rolled around, but where are we? Nowhere but with the happy question of uncategoric, indistinct gender: a boy-playing-girl-playing-boy, a boy-playing-boy, and a boy-playing-girl; one talking his/her head off, one answering moderately, one silent.

According to the founder-sociologist Georg Simmel, the dyad or interaction between two is characterised by triviality and intimacy. If true, then wooing is entrapped in the character of the dyad—whether of wooers or not—and all interaction between two is a kind of wooing itself, unless formalities are observed and constructed. One couldn't ask for more comment on our sexually ambiguous natures and situations.

Rosalind the hetero

The silent one (now *there's* a girl one might pin poems to trees for) has taken a lot; a lot too much, some critics have argued, among them Ralph Berry, Bernard Evans and Dr Johnson himself. Few agree today (though many sympathise with Celia) but perhaps the question needs a look. For it is deeply germane to the gender question, or so I shall argue.

Here is the case against Rosalind:

1. She is self-pitying (I, iii, 88, III, iv, 1-4).

2. She is vain: useless and faint-hearted about going to Arden until the self-indulgence of dressing-up is suggested (I, iii, 104-27) (Leggatt, 1974, p. 194, is surely wrong).

3. She brings talk back to herself (II, iv, 57-8, III, ii, 215-16, 225-6).

4. She doesn't reveal herself to her father, despite the joy it would presumably have given him (III, iv, 31-5; in fact she seems disdainful of him (34).

5. As indeed of everyone else, apart from Orlando; she never praises, never thanks. On occasion she is down-right rude.

6. She never stops nattering (*passim*).

7. She is an interfering busybody (with Silvius and Phebe: III, iv, 55; then III, v, 34-63).

8. She betrays Celia's loyalty and friendship just when it suits her, despite that Celia's accompaniment of her to exile was voluntary.

9. She is a trickster and a cheat, with Oliver (IV, iii, 172) as well as Orlando.

10. She swoons at blood, despite all the manly boasts. When she gets desperate, it is unedifying (IV, iii, 161, v, ii, 25-6).

11. Not once, even at the end (unless v, ii, 70 is such an occasion), does she tell Orlando she loves him.

This is a formidable list. But—aside from its omissions (as well as being amusing, Rosalind is caring, it would seem: II, iv, 3-7; II, iv, 41-2, 67 and 89; III, v, 58; IV, i, 106)—it also omits the vital dimension of self-knowledge and self-monitoring one may imagine in her, which would throw quite a different light across all that is said. The play as self-knowing, as about coming to learn, is validly seen on that front if no other. But it is more than that, and at a qualitatively different level. For my list would presume a 'Rosalind' with a character and biography the play doesn't warrant. This 'Rosalind' is furthermore female in traditional mode, one which, insofar as we can impute intention to Shakespeare in this way at all (and in a play of this one's title), would entail a prior assumption of gender roles which the play, on at least some perfectly legitimate readings, constantly subverts. The difficulty, paradoxically, is brought out as much by those feminist critics who would try to qualify the degree of Shakespeare's pro-feminine stance. Thus Clara Claiborne Park (in Lenz *et al.,* 1983, pp. 100-16), acknowledging the power and autonomy in Shakespeare's main heroines, says that even so his—and perhaps other—young men are vulnerable to too much feminine assertiveness, so that a way had to be found to mitigate this. Portia therefore gives herself into wifely submission to Bassanio before she tricks him over the court scene and the rings; and Beatrice must 'stand condemn'd', as she herself says, before her pride and scorn may continue. Rosalind has more autonomy than any other heroine—it is uniquely *her* play—in the Elizabethan canon (Park does not mention *The Duchess of Malfi*). But, as Park's editors say as well (p. 5), even Rosalind's effect has to be muted. For Marilyn French (1983, p. 113) Rosalind must not offend her audience. These critics point to the wedding at the end. The games are over and Rosalind will submit to her lord.

Both these views, the suspiciously male-sounding anti-Rosalind view of the immediate post-war period and the feminist defence that Elizabethan mores couldn't allow such insubordination in 'shrews' or anyone else, postulate a traditional gender-role differentiation, with its domination and submission. So indeed does the earlier fond, male view (e.g. Dover Wilson) of Rosalind as 'capable', having everything in her control, and so on. What the 'marriages' at the end entail is a matter to which I want to return, but for the present I suggest that Rosalind is a little like Phebe, but with this difference, that 'Rosalind'—the Rosalind figure—transcends Phebe completely, to a point where she overflows the gender distinction altogether, within which Phebe is so firmly trapped.

Rosalind the spellbinder

As Dusinberre (1975) and Barber (1959) have underlined, the woman in disguise is a reveller in her own masque; mistress of misrule until marriage and rain (there is none in Arden) stop it.

Rosalind is banished; she is already a marked character. Duke Frederick ominously tells Celia: 'She is too subtle for thee, and her smoothness, / Her very silence, and her patience / Speak to the people and they pity her' (I, iii, 73-5). Rosalind has already placed a talisman, a gold chain, round Orlando's neck, binding him to her. In Arden she walks up to the men one by one, Corin, Orlando, Jaques; and when in between she approaches Phebe, that girl is mesmerised into love. Disguised, Rosalind draws Orlando into the intricacies of her inferential talk about love, and takes him into a marriage ceremony with curious implications, and possible legality (Lathem, 1975, Appendix B). When her swooning threatens to bring back the real world she tells Orlando of the 'magician, most profound in his art' (V, ii, 61) whom she knew in childhood and by whose skill she will make all things even in love. In a gentle, subdued chant she tells all this to the pairs of lovers; in another, the next day, she completes the spell's implications and demonstrates their culmination (V, ii, 111-22; V, iv, 115-16, 121-3). In the play's epilogue, she 'conjures' the women in the audience toward liking the play and to love in general.

In *A Midsummer Night's Dream* there was no disguised woman weaving spells; rather, the women were themselves under spells, and returned from the moonlight to growth of awareness when released from that state. The failure to see was not because of the object (disguised woman) but in the subject (the woman under the spell). The nature description in *A Midsummer Night's Dream* thus could be exact and colourful, for it goes direct to the audience: Ralegh was right. But Rosalind is no witch or woodland sprite. There is not a phrase in the play to suggest that option. On the contrary, *pretending* to magic is just one more of Rosalind's strategies. Furthermore she is doing nothing wrong, for she merely leads Orlando toward the very thing he incessantly says he wants—leading him forward yet preventing undue precipitousness too. Rather, her controlling actions reconcile good and evil, comic pairings, the sexes, the brothers, the country and the court. Beckman (1978) has discussed this *concordia discors* and sees it as essentially borne out through marriage. Traditional critics saw a Christian motif in the play too, and certainly there are traces; for instance, Silvius's rhapsody on love is a romanticised version of 1 Corinthians 13. But is it marriage that effects this reconcilement?

One may as easily see androgyny as reconciling the sexes. Howard (1988) suggests that an androgyny privileging males (women seen as merely lesser men) was at work in Elizabethan England, and that the challenge to this by women's defiant cross-dressing led to the authoritarian need for gender construction, the ideology by which it could be shown that women had subordinate roles justified by difference. As Dusinberre argues (1975, especially pp. 1-19), the humanistic strain of Erasmus and More, attesting to the equal capability of the woman's mind for educational expansion, led equally to this reaction. Today the androgynous argument is used to support the view that gender is normally socially constructed—in favour, of course, of males. True enough as far as it goes, but it makes androgyny into a support-argument in a political cause, whereas if any truth of human gender does lie in androgyny, then that is surely what is important, that is where the focus of our attention might be expected to go.

It is probably therefore more fruitful to see how the sexual and gender signs woven into Rosalind are presented, along with the several degrees to which they tie to herself personally and to people generally. It would be excessive to say *Rosalind* is androgynous; that argument would mean that she was hermaphrodite, epicene, bisexual. The race is androgynous, or otherwise, as the case may be. Many critics make a prior assumption of sex-gender as clear separation, leading to a subordination demanded of women. They then divide, insisting either that this is plain unjust (equal but different) or unjust because illogical (equal and same, equal because androgynous). Linda Bamber's stimulating and sympathetic book (1982) accords to Shakespeare not full feminism, but acknowledgement of women as 'Other' in a dialectic with feminism which is 'persistent, various, surprising and wholehearted' (p. 5). That is generous indeed, but what if Shakespeare did not see women as so 'other'?

The further complication of the boy-actors, already mentioned, is severally interpreted by several critics (e.g. Jardine, 1983; Greenblatt, 1988), again informatively but somewhat according to varying political disposition. Roughly speaking, if one sees the matter politically, then the playwrights used Basil to show that women are as good as men while still women. If one was more sexual in disposition, then the intertwining of the boy-actor with the woman-role (compounded in *As You Like It,* of course) attracts attention as to the degree of androgyny and bisexuality implied. The actress Juliet Stevenson—not alone in this—states that when Rosalind is dressed as Ganymede she can be most truly herself'. But that is ambiguous, it begs the question. Does it mean that, trapped in a women-subordinated world, she can only be truly woman when disguised as man, and only then can her non-male, fully female self—normally suppressed—emerge? Or does it mean the very opposite: that only when in male clothes can the male, or at least bisexual, figure deep down inside her fully and secretly live itself? It is these questions which the whole political, sexual, and political/sexual argument hangs round.

The evidence from within the play has to be listed briefly. Rubinstein (1984) states: 'in *As You Like It,* as the title itself may have been intended to communicate, a feeling of bisexuality pervades the whole play' (p. 358). Rosalind takes for herself the name 'Ganymede': catamite; male prostitute. She is 'more than common tall', comes to life at the thought of wearing men's clothes, more than once puns on 'suit', and, of course, does wear male attire for most of the play's duration. Finally there is the brief suggestion of her relationship with Celia as 'dearer than the natural bond of sisters' (I, ii, 266). According to the Northrop Frye theory, comedy regenerates because the women imply the power of nurture; yet Rosalind (like most Shakespearian characters, it must be said) has no mother, and is contemptuous of 'ill-favoured children', the only reference she makes in the play to children apart from the admittedly ambiguous joke about her 'child's father', i.e. Orlando, at I, iii, II. (Some traditional editors reversed those two words; Norman Holland (1964) cited but questioned the view that it was a Freudian slip.)

There is another curious line on androgyny because of the play's historical position. In the seventeenth century, when Ganymede was on stage, a boy played a boy. Rainolds thought this 'monstrous', but in fact our actor Basil could, if he liked, mentally leave the woman bit out and just do Ganymede. By contrast, when a contemporary actress plays Moira she too, if she chooses, can, in her inner sense of the part, omit the male dimension of Ganymede altogether. And yet it is still the same part! It is Shakespeare's Rosalind from *As You Like It.* One could hardly have a more comprehensive illustration of the seamless stretch from female to male and back which this part provides. It does so uniquely, of course, because in no other play does the woman disguised as male then play back herself as woman too.

My suggestion is not that Rosalind is bisexual, less still lesbian, in some crude direct sense. Rather, Shakespeare has written into her that androgynous dimension, those signals, at least to a degree, and this attractive etherealised part, person or character alone can thus give a male-female reconciliation as deep as that of sacramental marriage. The latter implies separate genders; the androgynous is already a unity. Dusinberre shows (1975, pp. 200, 243, 251) that Erasmus, George Meredith and Virginia Woolf all moved, if varyingly, toward the idea of the androgynous as prototype of the adult mind, which rises above gender difference. Rosalind's spells thus work to inculcate this sense of union to the point where marriage may be seen as one (though perfectly valid and satisfying) form of it. It comes at the end, if at all. And since her spells are poetry itself, this secret is the secret of the play's unity, its undifferentiated, even if unusual, harmonies.

Works Cited

Bamber, Linda, *Comic Women, Tragic Men: A study of gender and genre in Shakespeare,* Stanford: University of California Press, 1982.

Barber, C.L., *Shakespeare's Festive Comedy: A study of dramatic form and its relation to social custom,* New Jersey: Princeton University Press, 1959.

Beckman, Margaret Boemer, 'The figure of Rosalind in "As You Like It"' , *Shakespeare Quarterly* 29 (1978), pp. 44-51.

Dusinberre, Juliet, *Shakespeare and the Nature of Women,* Basingstoke: Macmillan, 1975.

Everett, Barbara, 'The fatness of Falstaff—Shakespeare's characters' (British Academy Shakespeare Lecture, 24 April 1990.

Foucault, Michel, *The History of Sexuality,* vol. 1 (trans. Robert Hurley), London: Allen Lane, 1979.

Frye, Northrop, 'The argument of comedy' in *Shakespeare: Modern essays in criticism,* ed. Leonard F. Dean, Oxford University Press, 1967, pp. 79-89.

Greenblatt, Stephen, *Shakespearian Negotiations: The circulation of social energy in Renaissance England,* Oxford: Clarendon Press, 1988.

Holland, Norman N., *Psychoanalysis and Shakespeare,* New York: McGraw-Hill, 1964.

Jardine, Lisa, *Still Harping on Daughters,* Brighton: Harvester, 1983.

Kott, Jan, *Shakespeare Our Contemporary,* London: Methuen, 1967.

Lenz, C.R.S., G. Greene and C.T. Neely, *The Woman's Part: Feminist criticism of Shakespeare,* Urbana and Chicago: University of Illinois Press, 1983.

Park, Clara Clairborne, 'As we like it: how a girl can be smart and still popular', in *The Woman's Part: Feminist criticism of Shakespeare,* ed. C.R. Swift Lenz, G. Greene and C.T. Neely, Urbana, IL: University of Illinois Press, 1983, pp. 100-16.

Ralegh, Walter, *Shakespeare,* London: Macmillan, Morley's Men of Letters Series, 1907.

Rubinstein, Frankie, *A Dictionary of Shakespeare's Sexual Puns and Their Significance,* Basingstoke: Macmillan, 1984.

Winnicott, D.W., *Playing and Reality,* Harmondsworth: Penguin Education, 1974.

Mario DiGangi (essay date 1996)

SOURCE: "Queering the Shakespearean Family," in *Shakespeare Quarterly,* Vol. 47, No. 3, Fall, 1996, pp. 269-90.

[*In the essay below, DiGangi analyzes homoeroticism in* As You Like It *as it relates to the early modern family and the mythological narrative that recounts Jupiter's desire for his page Ganymede.*]

Is there anything queer about the family in Shakespeare's England? Until the mid-1980s, scholarship on early modern marriage and domestic life had proceeded as if homoerotic desire were largely irrelevant to its concerns. An obviously significant example of this tendency is Lawrence Stone's influential *The Family, Sex and Marriage in England 1500-1800,* which, despite its monumental scope, has very little to say about the relation of homosexuality to the family, sex, or marriage throughout three hundred years of English history.[1] As gay, lesbian, feminist, and queer scholarship have demonstrated with increasing subtlety and cumulative force, however, to ignore the place of same-sex desire or nonreproductive sexuality in early modern domestic life is to provide a historically inaccurate portrait of Renaissance social structures. It is to project back onto the Renaissance particularly modern biases and ideologies, especially the notion that there are two distinct sexualities, heterosexuality and homosexuality, and that only the former has anything to do with the constitution and production of families.[2]

Given the centrality of Shakespeare to Renaissance studies and his dominance as the dramatist of romantic married love, queer scholarship on the family in early modern England faces a double task. One, it must insist on the homoerotic dimensions of courtship, marriage, and domestic experience inside the Shakespearean canon. Two, it must also look outside the canon to less familiar, even obscure texts that depict the homoerotic dimensions of these institutions and experiences more explicitly or, at least, differently than Shakespeare's. As the plays of Jonson, Chapman, Middleton, or Fletcher will show, Shakespeare simply does not exhaust the possibilities for representing the homoerotic practices of his society.[3] For instance, Shakespeare's contemporaries often present a fuller picture of the early modern household and the same-sex relations enabled by its particular functioning and composition.[4] Perhaps Shakespeare's status as the most familiar Renaissance playwright depends in part on his status as the most familial: the one who seemingly celebrates the affective heterosexual couple that we "recognize" as the source, both biologically and historically, of the modern family. Indeed, Lynda Boose's essay "The Family in Shakespeare Studies; or—Studies in the Family of Shakespeareans; or—The Politics of Politics" exerts much of its rhetorical power precisely by reinscribing a familiar, naturalized, notion of the family even as it critiques familiar/familial gender politics. Boose, writing in 1987, observes that scholarship *on* the family is repeating the power dynamics *of* the family: feminists write about female subjectivity, gender, and the domestic, while male new historicists write about male subjectivity, power, and the state, effectively marginalizing their female colleagues. While Boose rightly insists that the patriarchal nuclear family is a historical and ideological construction, her essay reconstructs this family as a trope, as the "natural" way to describe the political relations between male and female Shakespeare scholars and their metaphorically male and female methodologies.[5]

As You Like It has enjoyed an especially familiar place in studies of gender, sex, and marriage in Shakespearean comedy. But because its resonance for a queer critique of the early modern family remains underappreciated, I have chosen it as my focus here. For Catherine Belsey and Mary Beth Rose *As You Like It* serves to illustrate the ideological contradictions within late-sixteenth-century discourses of marriage. While both critics read the play as an index of transformation of gender definitions and sexual relations, neither discusses "sexuality" other than as it occurs between women and men.[6] A reading of *As You Like It* that accounts for homoerotic as well as heteroerotic relations can be found in the powerful work of Valerie Traub. Her analysis distinguishes between gender and eroticism and severs erotic identity from erotic desire—both strategies of queer theory—and concludes that the polymorphous desire traversing *As You Like It* finally "prevents the stable reinstitution of heterosexuality, upon which the marriage plot depends."[7] Her emphasis here on the affirmative quality of the play's homoeroticism is later qualified in an indispensable essay, "The (in)significance of 'lesbian' desire in early modern England," which argues that, because the plot of *As You Like It* moves toward heterosexual marriage and reproductivity, "an implicit power asymmetry" distinguishes the woman who enunciates and clings to homoerotic desire (Celia) from the woman who abandons it (Rosalind).[8] Traub's later reading, which still resists mapping erotic identity onto characters, moves closer to the position I take as my own—namely, that anxieties about homoeroticism in *As You Like It* are manifested and managed through the asymmetrical, shifting erotic roles taken by or imposed on characters.

In what follows, I want to pursue this more anxious assessment of *As You Like It* via the myth Rosalind summons when she takes the role of "Jove's own page" (1.3.120).[9] The explicit naming of mythological figures in the play, along with the representation of banishment, familial discord, and homoerotic desire, evokes a tale familiar to Shakespeare and his contemporaries: Jupiter's replacement of Hebe with Ganymede, a move that angers Juno and alienates her from the marriage bed. An analysis of this mythological subtext brings into sharp relief the discordant aspects of Rosalind's enactment of Ganymede, by means of which female homoerotic desire (Celia's for Rosalind) and male homoerotic desire (Orlando's for Ganymede) are both finally rejected. Rather than considering Shakespeare's characters as the stable embodiments of mythological identities (e.g., that Rosalind "is" Ganymede), I will follow Traub in arguing that certain characters occupy contingently the familial and erotic roles delineated by this mythological narrative. These roles and the erotic transformations they help to effect are crucial to our understanding of the marriages that conclude the play, because the marriages succeed to the extent that premarital female homoerotic desire and postmarital male homoerotic desire have been successfully banished.

Many critics have found Jupiter's desire for Ganymede of signal importance in describing the particular age- and status-inflected structure of male homoeroticism in early modern England. But the myth also exists in an extended version as a familial drama involving Jupiter's wife, Juno, and their daughter Hebe, who is Juno's favorite and the royal cupbearer. According to Thomas Cooper's influential classical dictionary, when Hebe one day "chaunsed to fall, and disclosed further of hir neather partes, then comlinesse woulde have to be shewen, Jupiter, to the great displeasure of his wyfe Juno, removed hir from that office, and appointed *Ganymedes* to serve hym at his cuppe."[10] What is the meaning of Hebe's downfall? Does the uncomeliness of her fault reside in the public disclosure of "neather partes" or in the fact that specifically female "neather partes" have been disclosed? The latter explanation is suggested by Marlowe's treatment of the myth in *Dido, Queene of Carthage*, where Jupiter has no qualms about risking the public display of Ganymede's nether parts. The play opens with Jupiter "*dandling* Ganimed *upon his knee*" and "playing" wantonly with him. When Juno later expresses her "hate of Troian *Ganimed,* / That was advanced by my *Hebes* shame," she reinforces the sense that it is the display of "shameful" female parts (the "pudendum") that provokes Jupiter's ire.[11] Jupiter not only rejects Hebe but openly declares his love for Ganymede, "say *Juno* what she will," and bestows on him the necklace that "*Juno* ware upon her marriage day."[12] The little familial drama of this myth reveals a great deal of anxiety about female sexuality.

In fact, the rejection of women and devaluation of female sexuality recur in Renaissance versions of the Ganymede myth. In John Lyly's *Gallathea* (1592) the virgin rejected as a sacrifice because she is "not the fairest" is appropriately named Hebe.[13] In John Mason's play *The Turk* (1607) the courtier Bordello cites Jupiter's substitution of Ganymede for Hebe as a precedent for his renunciation of all women:

> BORDELLO Pantofle.
> PANTOFLE At your pleasure sir?
> BORDELLO Thou hast bene at my pleasure indeed *Pantofle,* I will retreate into the country, hate this amourous, Court and betake my selfe to obscurity: I tel thee boye I wil returne by this *Circyan* Isle without transformation since *Hebe* hath discouered her secrets I will turne *Iupiter,* hate the whole sexe of women, and onely embrace thee my *Ganimede.*
>
> PANTOFLE Sfoot sir you are as passionate for the disloyalty of your Sempstresse, as some needy knight would be for the losse of some rich magnificos widdow: doe you not see how the supporters of the Court, the Lady of the labby gape after your good parts like so many grigges after fresh water, and can you withhold the dew of your moyster element?
>
> BORDELLO I tel thee should the Lady *Iulia* when she was aliue haue profered me her cheeke to kisse, I would not haue bowed to that painted image for her whole Dukedome: *Mercury* had no good aspect in the horoscope of my natiuity: women and lotium are reciprocall, their fauour is noysome.[14]

Betrayed by a woman who "discouered her secrets" like Hebe, Bordello transforms himself into a Jupiter who will have sexual relations only with his Ganymede, or page. In Marlowe's *Edward II* (1594) after Queen Isabella has been sexually rejected by her husband, she finds in the myth a model for her own grief: "Like frantick *Juno* will I fill the earth, / With gastlie murmure of my sighes and cries, / For never doted *Jove* on *Ganimed,* / So much as he on cursed *Gaveston.*"[15] The court favorite in Marston's *The Malcontent* (1604) is similarly blamed for precipitating a conjugal rupture: "Duke's Ganymede, Juno's jealous of thy long stockings."[16] As these examples indicate, playwrights of the early modern period readily allude to this familiar myth in order to convey disruptions in male-female sexual relations and marital harmony.

The discordant connotations of the Ganymede myth should therefore alert us to similar conflicts and anxieties that attend the comic marriage plot of *As You Like It*. Behind the disruption of familial bonds in Shakespeare's play lies the mythic disruption of Jupiter's family caused by his banishing Hebe and advancing Ganymede. Touchstone's claim to be exiled as was "Ovid . . . among the Goths" reminds us obliquely of the *Metamorphoses* as it pointedly recalls those forced into exile by the "most unnatural" behavior of Duke Frederick and Oliver (3.3.6; 4.3.122), the "tyrant Duke" and "tyrant brother" who destroy familial harmony (1.2.278). The poet William Barksted describes Jupiter's dismissal of Hebe as an act of destructive rage:

> With this he storm'd, that's Priests from altars flie streight banish'd *Heboe,* & the world did thinke
> To a second Chaos they should turned be, the clouds for feare wept out th' immortal drinke.[17]

Like Hebe in Barksted's poem, Rosalind is "streight banish'd" by a capricious patriarch. But Celia willingly appropriates Hebe's role when she insists that, by banishing Rosalind, Duke Frederick has actually banished his own daughter. Shakespeare does not establish a firm correspondence between an Ovidian figure and a single character; rather, the Ovidian myth provides a repertory of possible erotic/familial roles which the characters draw on in different ways. Hence Rosalind not only exchanges the disgraceful position of banished Hebe for the more exalted position of adopted Ganymede, "Jove's own page"; she further adopts the fluid erotic (though not the angry paternal) agency of Jupiter. Just as Jupiter transfers his affections from the female sex (Hebe and Juno) to the male sex (Ganymede), so Rosalind has begun to transfer her affections from Celia to Orlando.

In the triangular structure that will develop in Arden, then, Rosalind plays both Ganymede and Jupiter. She plays Ganymede to Orlando's Jupiter—a "fair youth" wooed by a man (3.2.375); she plays Jupiter to Celia's Hebe/Juno—a "man" who turns from female to male companionship (1.3.112). It is no wonder that Celia, given the Hebe/Juno role, delays telling Rosalind of Orlando's arrival in Arden, impugns the sincerity of his love for her, and hesitates when saying the words of the mock marriage between them. At precisely the moment Rosalind confidently adopts "no worse a name" than Ganymede, Celia names her own worsened state "Aliena" (ll. 120, 124). Whereas "Celia" suggests Hebe's divine birth and habitation, "Aliena" not only describes Celia's present alienation from her father's love but also foreshadows her increasing alienation from Rosalind's love.

Rosalind's desire for Orlando relegates Celia's desire for her to a safely distanced past.[18] For Celia this is an ideal past symbolized by Juno, the *"Lady of mariage, and gouernesse of child-birth"* by whom Roman women swore.[19] The wedding song that closes the play proclaims that "Wedding is great Juno's crown, / . . . blessed bond of board and bed" (5.4.140-41), and Celia figures her bond with Rosalind, in which they shared board and bed, as just such a marriage:

> We still have slept together,
> Rose at an instant, learn'd, play'd, eat together,
> And whereso'er we went, like Juno's swans,
> Still we went coupled and inseparable.
> (1.3.69-72)

Coupled like swans, Celia and Rosalind serve under Juno, the patron goddess of female sexuality. Swans, however, were the birds not of Juno but of Venus. In the contemporary play *The Maid's Metamorphosis* (1600) Juno herself makes much of this distinction, bitterly complaining that rival Venus's "Doues and Swannes, and Sparrowes" are prized above her own "starry Peacocks."[20] By assigning Venus's swans to Juno, Shakespeare has Celia peacefully "couple" these often combative goddesses of love and marriage, just as she couples herself to Rosalind. Hence she reminds Rosalind that "thou and I am one" (l. 93). Very soon after Celia evokes their seemingly permanent union, however, Rosalind takes on the role of Ganymede; during the time she plays this role, Juno is never mentioned. Instead, allusions to Jupiter proliferate, beginning with the first words Rosalind speaks as Ganymede: "O Jupiter, how weary are my spirits!" (2.4.1). Ganymede swears twice by his master and lover—"Jove, Jove!" (l. 57), "O most gentle Jupiter" (3.2.152)—and praises as "Jove's tree" the oak under which Orlando is found (l. 232). As the latter instance makes especially clear—not least to Celia—Ganymede's evocations of Jupiter signal the shift in Rosalind's affections from her childhood companion to the man she hopes to marry.

In conjunction with the substitution of Orlando for Celia (and of Jupiter for Juno), a more purely symbolic or emblematic substitution facilitates the courtship between Rosalind and Orlando. Even before Rosalind impersonates a boy, a role that allows her to couch her heteroerotic desire for Orlando as a homoerotic desire for Jupiter, wrestling, an unmistakably masculine activity otherwise unavailable to her except as a spectator, offers her a language of desire. The spectacle of vigorous male-male combat staged before Rosalind not only occasions heteroerotic desire but becomes a central metaphor for it. Witnessing Orlando's victory over Charles, Rosalind confesses that he has "overthrown / More than your enemies"; he, too, feels "overthrown" and "master[ed]" by "Charles, or something weaker" (1.2.244-45, 249-50). Orlando is mastered not by Charles, of course, but by the weaker young woman who must "wrestle" with her own new affections (1.3.20). Orlando's attribution of his erotically induced confusion to *Charles,* while comic, signals a transition from wrestling as a male-male sport conducted in the court to wrestling as a figure for the male-female sport pursued in the forest. In Arden, Celia confirms this transferral by describing Orlando to Rosalind as the person "that tripped up the wrestler's heels and your heart, both in an instant" (3.2.208-9). Rosalind, in turn, recalls the wrestling match as an erotic as well as a competitive event: "Looks he as freshly as he did the day he wrestled?" (ll. 226-27). The subsequent exchanges between Ganymede and Orlando constitute mental and emotional wrestling matches that substitute the friction of physical struggle between men with the friction of linguistic struggle. In short, once Charles is *"borne out"* of the play (1.2.209 SD), Ganymede emerges as Orlando's new wrestling partner. That this substitution requires the complete physical and verbal incapacitation of Charles illustrates emblematically the point made narratively by the alienation of Celia and analogically by the discordant aspects of the Ganymede myth: Rosalind and Orlando's movement toward marriage implies strife and loss as well as concord and pleasure.

With her discovery of Orlando's presence in Arden comes Rosalind's first intimation that her impersonation might involve loss or compromise. Yet despite her initial dismay—"Alas the day, what shall I do with my doublet and hose?" (3.2.215-16)—she soon realizes that the disguise provides certain opportunities. Playing an "effeminate" (l. 398) boy who can plausibly impersonate Rosalind allows her to carry on a flirtation with Orlando. At the same time, playing a "saucy lackey" allows her to test his qualifications as a lover and husband, to ascertain whether he will be like or unlike most men, who are "April when they woo, December when they wed" (ll. 290-91; 4.1.139-40). Ganymede initially questions the sincerity of Orlando's publicly declared passion: "you are rather point-device in your accoutrements, as loving yourself than seeming the lover of any other" (3.2.372-74). This skepticism about Orlando's effusiveness is understandable, considering that the only time Rosalind spoke to him in her own person, he neither thanked her for her gift of a chain nor reciprocated her compliments. Her plan to "cure" Orlando of his love-sickness seems actually designed to cure her own doubts about his sincerity and constancy: "I would cure you, if you would but call me Rosalind and come every day to my cote and woo me" (ll. 414-15). The plan instates a daily regimen in which Ganymede elicits and Orlando performs his love for Rosalind.

The problem, of course, is that it becomes extremely difficult under these circumstances to ascertain the meaning or sincerity of Orlando's performance. This is where the Ganymede role seems to work against Rosalind, producing the very uncertainties about Orlando's desire that it seems meant to resolve. For instance, when Orlando misses his appointment with Ganymede, Rosalind has trouble interpreting his failure: "But why did he swear he would come this morning and comes not?" (3.4.17-18). Has Orlando stood up Rosalind? Or has he merely stood up Ganymede? Would he behave more reliably with the actual Rosalind? How can she tell? Although the ambiguity of playing Ganymede-playing-Rosalind thwarts Rosalind's ability to interpret Orlando's neglect, the disguise does allow her safely to rebuff him for it. Ganymede's imperious dismissal of Orlando is a bluff that the "real" Rosalind could hardly afford to risk: "You a lover! And you serve me such another trick, never come in my sight more" (4.1.37-39). Playing multiply gendered roles enables Rosalind to test, observe, and correct the man she wants to marry; yet at the same time, it prevents her from determining whether or not he actually loves her.

To Rosalind's string of questions regarding Orlando's apparent neglect—"But have I not cause to weep?" "Do you think so?" "Not true in love?" (3.4.4, 20, 24)—Celia furnishes some rather discouraging answers. Repeatedly maintaining that Orlando is not in love, Celia observes that "the oath of a lover is no stronger than the word of a tapster. They are both the confirmer of false reckonings" (ll. 27-29). Celia's nonsequitur—"He attends here in the forest on the Duke your father" (ll. 29-30)—associates Orlando's falseness to Rosalind with his loyalty to Duke Senior and reminds Rosalind that she is competing with her father for Orlando's time and devotion. Enticing Orlando from her father's side is no small task, given how lovingly Duke Senior welcomes Orlando into his all-male forest community (note how Rowland de *Boys,* the "name of the father" that unites Duke Senior and Orlando, contains a bilingual pun uniting *boys* and *bois* [woods]). The wifeless Duke takes no women to Arden. He is initially accompanied by "three or four loving lords," his "co-mates and brothers in exile," and joined later by "many young gentlemen" who "flock to him every day, and fleet the time carelessly as they did in the golden world" (1.1.100-101; 2.1.1; 1.1.117-19). For Charles, who reports Duke Senior's situation in the play's opening scene, Arden replicates the golden world of Robin Hood and his "merry men" (l. 115). As I hope to show, however, Arden recalls as well another all-male golden world described in contemporary poems—that presided over by Orpheus.

Amy Elizabeth Clark as Rosalind and Julie Boesch as Celia in the Bradley University Theatre's 1996 production of As You Like It.

The male communities of Duke Senior and Orpheus are linked by way of Ganymede at the level of Ovidian allusion: Ganymede's story, so central to Shakespeare's play, is told in the *Metamorphoses* by Orpheus, who celebrates the "prettie boyes / That were the derlings of the Gods." Orpheus has an agenda for such celebration: he "did utterly eschew / The womankynd" and "taught the *Thracian* folke a stewes of Males too make / And of the flowring pryme of boayes the pleasure for too take."[21] The connection between the exclusion of women and the expression of male homoerotic desire in Orpheus's story points to a similar logic within Renaissance culture, a logic that was realized in the transvestite theater of Shakespeare's England. The work of Lisa Jardine and Stephen Orgel suggests that the English convention of having boy-actors play women's parts was meant not merely to arouse the homoerotic interest of male spectators but also to protect them from the anxieties associated with female sexuality and heteroerotic desire. For Jardine, boys who dressed and acted like women were particularly appealing to adult male sexual tastes; for Orgel, boys were less threatening than women as objects of male erotic desire. Both believe that misogynist Renaissance gender ideology could turn men away from women and toward the young boys who were their effeminate substitutes or analogues.[22] The Orpheus myth reveals a similar dynamic, and this myth's resonance with the male forest community of *As You Like It* contributes to Rosalind's uncertainty. Whom or what does Orlando really love: Rosalind? the idea of marrying Rosalind? the public pose of a Petrarchan lover? himself? Ganymede? Ganymede's impersonation of Rosalind? the company of other men? In order more fully to appreciate Rosalind's doubts, it is necessary to appreciate how sixteenth-century versions of the Orpheus myth establish the link between the rejection of women and the promotion of male homoerotic desire.

Because of the diversity of its classical sources and medieval explications, the Orpheus myth was subject to radically divergent interpretations by Renaissance writers. The traditional understanding of Orpheus as a great poet, orator, and musician runs throughout the period.[23] Another tradition stresses the erotic aspects of his story, although earlier sixteenth-century treatments tend not to be explicit about Orpheus's misogyny and homoeroticism. Thomas Cooper's dictionary entry of 1565 explains that Orpheus was murdered by women because, "for the sorow of his wyfe *Eurydice,* he did not onely himselfe refuse the love of many women, and lyved a sole lyfe, but also disswaded other from the company of women."[24] Cooper's Orpheus, that is, rejects not just women but love and companionship altogether. In the 1590s the flourishing of erotic satires and mythological narratives brings Orpheus's misogyny and homoeroticism more directly to the fore.[25] A discussion of female imperfection in John Dickenson's *Shepheardes Complaint* (1596) leads to a misreading (or deliberate alteration) of the myth in which Eurydice, not Orpheus, looks back to Hades:

> Euridice, which living could not bee accused of inconstancie, was after death blemished with unkindnesse, because forgetting the couenant of her returne from hell, she fondly looked backe. The silver-tongued Thracian, whom Apollo had endued with a double gift of musicke and poetrie, beeing mooued with this, hated and with hatefull disgrace disparadged the woorth of that sexe which before hee had honoured by his matchlesse Art.[26]

Although Dickenson's Orpheus rejects women entirely, he does not consequently turn to boys.

Orpheus's misogyny does produce homoerotic consequences in two verse treatments of the myth from the mid-1590s. Like the young men who flock to Duke Senior in Shakespeare's play, many husbands flock to Orpheus in R. B.'s *Orphevs His Iourney to Hell* (1595):

> And in inuectiue Ditties [Orpheus] daylie singes, th'uncertain pleasure of vnconstant Loue:
> How manie woes a womans beautie bringes, and into what extreames this ioy doth shoue
> Poore foolish men, that ere they be awarre
> Will rashlie ouershoot themselues so farre.
>
> There gins he sing of secrete Loues deceites, and womens fawning fickle companie.
> The outward golden shew of poysoned baytes, that drawes so many men to miserie.
> And for an instance sets himselfe to shew,
> One that had suffred all this pleasing woe.
>
> Whose songes did sort vnto such deepe effect, as draw mens fancies from thir former wiues:
> Womens vaine loue beginning to neglect, and in the fieldes with *Orpheus* spend their liues:
> With which sweet life they seem'd so well content,
> As made them curse the former time they spent.[27]

In itself, Opheus's misogynist lore is nothing extraordinary: it derives from the standard Renaissance gender ideology that considered female sexuality to be inherently dangerous and uncontrollable.[28] By drawing "mens fancies from thir former wiues," Orpheus merely brings misogynist rhetoric to the logical, if extreme, conclusion of male separatism. In *Of Loues complaint; with the legend of Orpheus and Euridice* (1597), Orpheus's rejection of women produces a more overtly sexual consequence, the sinful practice of sodomy:

> Now still he cryes to flye that weaker kinde,
> And addeth base dishonour to their name,
> And sayes that nature first hath them assign'd
> As plagues to kindle mens destructions flame:
>   whose heate once ruling in our inner parts,
>   Doth never die, but with our dying harts.
>
> But what, my chaster Muse doth blush to heare
> The onely fault and sinne of this his youth,
> It shames to tell unto anothers eare,
> Sometimes it profits to conceale the truth;
>   Better it were none knew the way to sinne,
>   For knowing none, then none would enter in.
>
> Hee in this path sette his defiled foote, which leades unto the tree of sinne and shame,
> Woe is his fruite, and wickednes his roote,
> Both these he tasted, and to both he came;
>   Such are the snares which craftie sinne doth lay,
>   That justest men doe stumble in theyr way.
>
> Now he doth teach the soule to sinne by Art,
> And breake the Law which Nature had ordaind,
> And from her auncient customs to depart, which still ere this were kept untoucht, unstaind,
>   Teaching to spoyle the flower of that kinde,
>   Whose flower never yet could any find.[29]

Orpheus's devilish inducements to sodomy, teaching "the soule to sinne by Art," are silenced only when the slandered Thracian women tear him apart. For the writer of this poem, who is courting a scornful mistress of his own, Orpheus's monstrous rejection of women deserves swift and violent retaliation.

Yet for other writers Orpheus's misogyny and homoeroticism do not always seem aberrant or reprehensible, and this is why the myth becomes important for a consideration of Rosalind's doubts about Orlando. R. B.'s *Orphevs His Iourney to Hell* sympathetically portrays Orpheus as the king of a homoerotic golden world tragically destroyed by female vengeance and vainglory. When Orpheus lures the local husbands to his retreat, the abandoned wives grieve for "their fading glorie" and plot revenge. Having put together their "busie head[s]," the women "flocke incontinent" to Orpheus,

> And finding him alone without his traine,
> Vpon him fall they all with might and maine.
>
> And with confused weapons beat him downe, quenching their angrie thirst with his warm blood:
> At whose vntimely death though heauens frowne, yet they defend their quarrell to be good,
> And for their massacre this reason render,
> He was an enemie vnto their gender.[30]

Ambushing their defenseless foe, these violently self-righteous women seem merely to confirm Orpheus's tales of the misery that women inflict on men.

R. B.'s polarity between a loving male community and an invasive, disorderly female sexuality suggests the obstacle that the all-male golden world of Duke Senior's court presents to Rosalind in her attempt to assay the sincerity of Orlando's love. At least one contemporary of Shakespeare believed that classical idealizations of male love could actually have the Orphic effect of dissuading English men from marriage. Translator Philemon Holland, reflecting on Plutarch's dialogue "Of Love" remarks:

> This Dialogue is more dangerous to be read by yoong men than any other Treatise of *Plutarch*, for that there be certeine glaunces heere and there against honest marriage, to upholde indirectly and underhand, the cursed and detestable filthinesse covertly couched under the name of the Love of yoong boyes.[31]

Holland worries that the misogynist promotion of male homoeroticism might well divert the sexual desires of impressionable young men away from wives and toward boys. Holland's fear is, I would suggest, Rosalind's own.

If Rosalind competes with her own father for Orlando's attention during their courtship, she also risks furthering the Orphic project of making a pretty young Ganymede seem erotically attractive to her future husband. By making herself into Ganymede and Orlando into Jupiter, as Stephen Orgel has noted, Rosalind ironically seems to choose the one name that would most inescapably suggest or promote her husband's pederastic desires.[32] According to James Saslow's sociological account of the Ganymede myth in the Renaissance,

> Jupiter's preferment of Ganymede over Hebe and Juno's consequent jealous resentment were often interpreted as a parable of two closely connected social phenomena: the subordinate status or worth of women and the potentially disruptive effect of a man's homosexual infidelities on the relations between husband and wife.[33]

Saslow relies mainly on visual and literary sources from sixteenth-century Italy. Shakespeare and his English contemporaries also translated and reproduced this myth as a parable of sexual conflict between husbands and wives. I mentioned earlier the appearance of the myth to signal conjugal rupture in Marlowe's *Edward II* and Marston's *The Malcontent*. Marston had already used the myth in his verse satire *The Scourge of Villainy* (1598) to signify female animosity toward the spread of pederasty in England: "Marry, the jealous queen of air doth frown, / That Ganymede is up, and Hebe down." Thomas Heywood explains that his depiction of Jupiter's same-sex adultery in *Pleasant Dialogues and Dramma's* (1637) actually condemns "base sordid lust in man." In one rather unpleasant dialogue, Juno complains, "Since this yong Trojan Swain to heav'n thou hast brought, / O *Jupiter*, thou set'st thy Wife at nought." She elaborates, "I wish in my place you had that Lad wedded, / With whom you ofter than with me have bedded / Since his arrive." Making an antithetical point about marital relations, Robert Greene illustrates proper wifely submission by observing that, when Juno hoped to placate her angry husband, she called upon her rival Ganymede to serve him nectar.[34]

If the Ganymede myth provided a vocabulary for articulating the early modern phenomenon of marital strife arising from male homoerotic desire, Ganymede himself had his early modern counterparts in the young male servants who populated the public and private worlds of Shakespeare's London.[35] Homoerotic desire for a male subordinate informs the early modern institution of personal service for which the myth provided a recognized classical analogue. Rosalind/Ganymede and Orlando are therefore legible as a sexually involved page and gallant—a familiar couple in the "street, the ordinary, and stage" of late-sixteenth-century London if we are to believe the satires contemporary with *As You Like It*.[36] This kinship of Rosalind/Ganymede with the London ganymede, or sexually available page, is further suggested by Adam's curious disappearance from the play. Why should Adam suddenly vanish only after Orlando has encountered the "pretty youth" in the forest (3.2.328)? A possible explanation for the disappearance of old servingmen appears in Marston's play *Histrio-Mastix* (1599, exactly contemporary with *As You Like It*), in which faithful old retainers blame their former masters' sons for replacing them with erotically alluring "rascall boyes."[37]

Rosalind therefore needs to insure that by playing Ganymede (the enticing page) when she woos, she will not play Juno (the rejected wife) when she weds. That is, she needs to reassure herself that her husband will not one day replace her with an actual boy. Immediately following their mock marriage, Rosalind tests Orlando's reaction to the threat of being outwitted and cuckolded by his wife. Yet, I want to argue, she simultaneously tries to determine if Orlando will express a homoerotic desire for Ganymede, whom he has just "married," or if he will remain constant to the absent Rosalind whom Ganymede portrays. Ganymede first warns Orlando that Rosalind will "laugh like a hyen" when he wants to sleep (4.1.147-48). Why is the laughing hyena an analogue for the wife who disturbs her husband's peace in bed? According to medieval and Renaissance animal lore, the hyena experienced an annual sex-change; for this reason, as John Boswell has shown, it was commonly viewed as the symbolic type of an adulterer or homosexual seducer.[38] This wonderful ability to transform itself earns the hyena a brief mention in Ovid's *Metamorphoses*: "interchaungeably it one whyle dooth remayne / A female, and another whyle becommeth male againe."[39] By comparing herself to the mocking, adulterous hyena, Rosalind can elicit Orlando's reaction to the possibility of being cuckolded. At the same time, mentioning the hermaphroditism and homosexual behavior commonly associated with the hyena could provoke Orlando into expressing his possible pleasure at finding a "hyena" in his bed. Like the hyena, Rosalind switches between female and male genders, between the forms of Rosalind and Ganymede: might Orlando be tempted to switch his wife for an actual "ganymede"—a page or household servant—in their marriage bed? Reassuringly, Orlando fails to respond with enthusiasm to the amorphous hyena as a figure for the possible homoerotic alternatives to marital (hetero)sexuality: "But will my Rosalind do so?" (l. 149).

Approaching the problem of Orlando's potential homoeroticism from a different angle, Rosalind next raises the threat of adulterous sexuality outside the household. Ganymede warns Orlando that he might find his wife "going to your neighbour's bed." When Orlando wonders what she could say to excuse her infidelity, Ganymede quips, "Marry to say she came to seek you there" (ll. 160, 162). Tellingly, Rosalind fails to specify the sex of the neighbor who occupies the bed. She appears to be alerting Orlando that what he might do with another wife, she might do with another husband. Yet her ambiguous phrasing also recognizes the possibility that Orlando as well as she might be caught in bed with the same neighbor—the *male* neighbor with whom she threatens to cuckold him. Ganymede's wit conveys Rosalind's warning: if you commit adultery with the man next door, she implies, you give me an occasion and an excuse to do the same.[40] Rosalind fights sodomy with shrewishness.

Ironically, Ganymede's insistence on the jealousy, inconstancy, and shrewishness of wives risks promoting the very misogyny that, in the Orphic model, turns husbands away from wives to the company of men or boys. Ganymede claims to have once performed an essentially Orphic role by curing a lover's passion for a woman—the same role he offers to play for Orlando. By means of a stereotypically misogynist impersonation of this man's mistress, Ganymede supposedly converted the former lover of women into an Orpheus-figure himself, a recluse who lived in "a nook merely monastic" (3.2.408-9). Orlando does not know that this is Rosalind's fabrication; from his perspective both the substance and the ultimate rhetorical effect of Ganymede's misogynist satire—turning Orlando's love-sick predecessor into a gender separatist—may seem credible enough. As Celia complains to Rosalind, "You have simply misused our sex in your love-prate" (4.1.191-92). As long as Rosalind continues to misuse her sex by playing a misogynist Ganymede, she will never achieve the kind of clarity about Orlando's desires that she so desperately requires.

Whereas Rosalind struggles continuously and anxiously to direct the course of Orlando's desire, even anticipating his possible marital infidelities, the play rechannels Celia's homoerotic desire with far less subtlety. Rosalind's unbelievably hyperbolic account of Celia's attraction to Oliver suggests how ideologically motivated is the play's need to match her with a marriageable partner. Late in the play, Ganymede informs Orlando that Celia and Oliver have fallen instantly in love: "And in these degrees have they made a pair of stairs to marriage, which they will climb incontinent, or else be incontinent before marriage. They are in the very wrath of love, and they will together" (5.2.36-40). Attributing to Celia and Oliver a sexual impropriety characteristic of rakish men and simple women (e.g., Touchstone and Audrey), Rosalind represents Celia not as her loving childhood companion or devoted "sister" but as a bride impatient for the pleasures of the wedding night. By so describing Celia, Rosalind not only marks the end of their homoerotic friendship, thereby positioning both Celia and herself as marriageable women; she also provides Orlando with a model of marriage based in vigorous (hetero)erotic desire.

Yet female homoeroticism has not been eliminated so much as transferred onto Phebe, who falls in love with Rosalind/Ganymede as immediately as Celia falls in love with Oliver. Phebe, of course, believes that she has fallen in love with a boy named Ganymede. Nevertheless, as Traub has convincingly argued, what Phebe finds alluring are the particularly "'feminine" features of Ganymede's physique.[41] Phebe's desires for Rosalind/Ganymede are at once homoerotic and heteroerotic. More to the point, her desires for this unavailable object are ridiculed and ultimately rejected. It is through this rejection that the role of Hebe formerly occupied by Aliena is transferred to Phebe, whose name incorporates Hebe's. Ganymede's initial admonishment of Phebe contains the only mention of a mother in a play that continually returns to fathers: "Who might be your mother, / That you insult, exult, and all at once, / Over the wretched? What though you have no beauty . . . ?" (3.5.35-37). The implication that Phebe derives her inflated pride from her mother recalls Hebe's status as the daughter of Juno, whose bird was the conventionally proud peacock. In the medieval poem "Ganymede and Hebe," Ganymede deflates Hebe's pride through a gendered and racialized discourse of ugliness—"a vile old woman with the hand of a Moor—/ A shrew like this"—much as Rosalind/Ganymede disparages Phebe's "inky brows," "black silk hair," "bugle eyeballs," and "Ethiop words" (ll. 46-47; 4.3.35).[42] Phebe is humiliated for her folly in pursuing a "boy" who does not love women (Ganymede) and who actually is a woman (Rosalind). Whereas female homoerotic desire had once been a source of strength for Celia in her union with Rosalind, it compromises Phebe's power to negotiate her own marriage. Barred from wedding Rosalind, Phebe is forced to accept Silvius: "You to his love must accord, / Or have a woman to your lord" (5.4.132-33).

When she discards Ganymede, Rosalind is simultaneously released from her promise to marry Phebe and enabled to marry Orlando. Rosalind banishes Ganymede, the boy who disrupts Juno's marriage, and re-enters with Hymen. The god of marriage presides over Rosalind's reunion with Orlando as if divine intervention were needed to guarantee the permanence of a marriage so precariously fashioned through courtship inflected by the discordant Ganymede myth. Significantly, when Juno's name returns for the second time in the play, the goddess is no longer linked with Venus as the patroness of women and protector of a female-female couple. She now appears as the goddess of marriage, linked with Hymen, who assures the fertility of male-female couples:

> Wedding is great Juno's crown,
> O blessed bond of board and bed.
> 'Tis Hymen peoples every town;
> High wedlock then be honoured.
>
> (ll. 140-43)

The banishment of Ganymede and Jupiter from the play seems to signal the banishment of the male homoeroticism instrumental in Rosalind's courtship of Orlando but potentially disruptive to their marital harmony. Moreover, with the official sanction of Celia's desire for Oliver and the displacement of Hebe's role to the humiliated Phebe, youthful female homoeroticism no longer obstructs noble maidens' placement within the reproductive marital economy.

Hymen's marital "bands" are further secured by the Epilogue, which disavows the homoerotic mobility that earlier served to orchestrate individual figures into marriageable couples (l. 128). It seems impossible to fix the speaker of the Epilogue as female or male, Rosalind or Ganymede, the "lady" of the play or the boy who played her. But while this fluidly gendered speaker disrupts what Catherine Belsey calls "sexual difference," he/she nevertheless conjures up a consistently heteroerotic model of sexual desire, directly addressing the audience as women who love men and men who love women:

> I charge you, O women, for the love you bear to men, to like as much of this play as please you. And I charge you, O men, for the love you bear to women—as I perceive by your simpering none of you hates them—that between you and the women the play may please.
>
> (ll. 209-14)

Not even an appeal to the collapse of gender difference (and thus of the distinction between homoerotic and heteroerotic relations) produced by the boy-actor/Rosalind/Ganymede can deny that these words not only clearly distinguish between actual men and women playgoers but direct them into heteroerotic exchanges. The Epilogue presents male heteroerotic desire in particular as a completely transparent and universal phenomenon: "I perceive by your simpering none of you [men] hates them [women]." There is simply no acknowledgment that desire among these men and women might also circulate homoerotically. Queer theory, however, allows us to recognize the Epilogue's conceptual division between gender identity (multiple and fluid, at least for the boy-actor) and erotic desire (singular and fixed, at least among the playgoers).

A note of contingency is seemingly injected into heteroerotic fixity when the boy-actor confesses to his male spectators, "If I were a woman, I would kiss as many of you as had beards that pleased me," for he at least acknowledges the possibility of erotic contact with these men (ll. 214-16). Moreover, we may assume that at the Globe the boy playing Rosalind/Ganymede would have been complemented by an adult actor (though one with "but a little beard" [3.2.208]) playing Orlando, thus replicating in the casting the homoerotic roles of the plot.[43] The Epilogue's metadramatic self-reflexiveness might well remind the audience that when Rosalind played a boy, she was perhaps not adding a layer of disguise so much as stripping one away, revealing the homoerotic foundations of the play's marital structure.

Yet despite the contemporary belief that boy-players, also known as ganymedes, erotically delighted adult men both onstage and off, this particular boy-player in effect refuses, in the Epilogue, to realize his homoerotic potential. He would have sexual contact with a man only "if" he were a woman, which he is not, even if he has just played one and even if boys are like women. The Epilogue's *if* serves not, like the earlier *if*s in the play, to promote "erotic contingency"—the sense that anything goes—but to relegate it to what has gone before.[44] Those *if*s were instrumental in arranging the various couplings between the "appropriate" partners. Once the marriages have transpired onstage, the virtue of the Epilogue's *if* is to suggest that homoerotic play has been left behind: in courtship, in adolescence, in Arden, in the theater itself. The Epilogue thus redirects attention from Rosalind's erotic play with the conditional to the erotic conditions of playing Rosalind. The actor's homoerotic flirtation is playful precisely because he is figuring homoeroticism *as* play, as dramatic device. His playing the alluring ganymede for male spectators constitutes a "kind offer" designed to solicit their applause (5.4.219); Rosalind likewise plays Ganymede for Orlando to accomplish her immediate (erotic) designs. But the actor reminds these men that he really is neither woman nor ganymede offstage. Just as Orlando must leave Arden without Ganymede, so these male spectators are encouraged to relinquish to the theater (and to the Arden still represented there at play's end) the fantasy of kissing an attractive ganymede.

In short, the Epilogue not only reveals the homoeroticism of the theater but attempts to establish the theatricality of homoeroticism. Having so openly staged male homoerotic courtship, the play discourages male spectators from identifying with the sodomitical marital role of Jupiter once offered to Orlando. Instead, male homoerotic desire is finally offered as a retrospective theatrical pleasure. This anxiety about appropriate marital sexuality and comic form explains the Epilogue's tendentious promotion of heteroerotic bonds among its spectators. Of course, what an actual audience makes of the gender/sexual ideology of the Epilogue might exceed the text's explicit attempt to reassert heteroerotic desire. Weren't there any ganymedes in the Globe audience, pages who had sexual relations primarily with men? Weren't there any Orlandos, whose simpering for women was indistinguishable from their simpering for boys? Could such a spectator, attuned to (or identified with) the kind of homoerotic desire represented in the play, assume that Orlando might indeed play adulterous Jupiter to Rosalind's rejected Juno?

These considerations lead to a materialist line of inquiry. If Orlando's homoerotic desire represents an actual threat to early modern marriage, as I have argued, then what were the "cruising grounds" in which a husband might have pursued his homoerotic desires? The representation of an all-male court of exiles in *As You Like It* and in the Orpheus poems suggests that the aristocratic court was a place in which men, separated from their wives, could freely consort socially, and perhaps sexually, with each other or with available ganymedes. Recent scholarship on literary and nonliterary texts leaves little doubt about the significance of homoerotic relations between courtier and courtier, patron and client, king and favorite in the Tudor and Stuart courts.[45] The court is not only a place, of course, but a mobile political community, as in *Much Ado About Nothing,* where Claudio offers to leave his new wife behind to accompany the unmarried Don Pedro. Don Pedro protests that this "would be as great a soil in the new gloss of your marriage as to show a child his new coat and forbid him to wear it" (3.2.5-7). Like Othello ("You must away to-night." "With all my heart." [1.3.277-78]), Claudio places male courtly service above whatever desire he might have to enjoy his new wife sexually. We might also recall how the sharing of beds by married soldiers in *Othello* gives Iago an opportunity to construct from the unproblematic fact of homoerotic intimacy a plausible narrative of Cassio's illicit sexual desire for Desdemona.

Aside from the court, there is evidence that male homoerotic activity also occurred in the more geographically and socially accessible spaces of brothels, alehouses, taverns, and public theaters, the latter significantly located in the unruly Liberties of London.[46] Much has been written on the public theater as a site of homoerotic titillation and assignation.[47] More recently, Joy Wiltenburg has examined popular ballads that admonish unthrifty husbands to avoid the lewd company of the alehouse. In one such ballad, "Lamentation of a new-married man," a wife scolds her frequently absent husband:

> Quoth she, "You do not love me,
>   To leave me all alone;
> You must goe a gadding,
>   And I must bide at home,
> While you, among your minions,
>   Spend more than is your owne."
> *This life leads a married man.*[48]

Although the term *minion* in Renaissance usage can refer to either gender, it is often applied to men in homoerotic contexts, as in *Twelfth Night,* where Orsino calls his beloved Cesario Olivia's "minion" (5.1.125), or in Marlowe's *Edward II,* where it denotes the king's favorite, Gaveston.[49] Having transferred his love to his minions, the husband in this ballad may be "spending" with other men what he should rightfully save for his wife—not only money but seed. In a similar ballad, "Robin and Kate; or, A bad husband converted by a good wife," Kate objects to her husband's visits to the alehouse: "Let not thy companions thus lewdly intice

/ Thy heart from thy Kate." Robin offers the dubious assurance that he seeks the company of men: "I seek not for wenches, but honest good fellowes: / A pipe of tobacco, a pot, or a jugg, / These are the sweet honies that I kisse and hugg."[50] Robin's sarcasm ("*These* are the sweet honies that I kisse"), even as it intends to deny one kind of erotic interest (in "wenches") may nevertheless reveal another (in "fellowes"). Of course, a husband could pursue homoerotic adultery closer to home, either in a "neighbour's bed," as Ganymede's quip to Orlando may acknowledge, or in his own. Sir Simonds D'Ewes wrote of Francis Bacon that he "desert[ed] the bed of his lady, which he accounted as the italians and turks do, a poor and mean pleasure in respect of the other." Bacon instead made "his servants his bedfellows."[51]

More research on the material conditions that facilitated homoerotic activity within marriage in early modern England is required. Here it suffices to observe that, for men at least, patriarchal privilege meant that marriage did not necessarily curtail homoerotic desire, especially since the constitution of the early modern household and the absence of a distinct ideology of heterosexuality allowed a wider range of (adulterous) sexual practices than an ahistorical notion of the family would admit. Bacon seems to have known this. Even if his erotic tastes resembled those of "italians and turks," Bacon, like most of his countrymen, married.

It is not possible to answer the question of just how common it was for husbands in Shakespeare's England to seek homoerotic pleasure outside the marriage bed. Nor have I chosen to address here the theoretically and historically distinct issue of female homoerotic desire within marriage. But I hope to have demonstrated that the contradictions within early modern gender/sexual ideologies open the space for a critique of the "naturalness" of the marital (hetero)sexuality that appears to coalesce at the end of Shakespeare's romantic comedy. Indeed, the successful comic conclusion of *As You Like It*'s final configuration of male-female couples largely depends on our assent to an ideological imperative, the Epilogue's "charge" that men love women, women love men, and that between men and women "the play may please." The Epilogue intimates that the play will please to the extent that heteroerotic play pleases its audience. For queer readers, then, such (a) play may not please. I would like to believe that my attempt to queer the Shakespearean family will prevent readers from responding uncritically to the Epilogue's heteroerotic interpellation. Such a queer disidentification would mean no longer accepting as simply natural, psychologically inevitable, or blithely comedic—for our time or Shakespeare's—the play's displacement of male and female homoeroticism from the scene of marriage and the formation of the "family."

Finally, more is at stake in my analysis of *As You Like It* than a queer distrust of "the family" and familial metaphors—although such a distrust is certainly justified by ongoing political and legal assaults against gays and lesbians undertaken in the name of "family values" and the "traditional family." In *The Anti-social Family*, Michèle Barrett and Mary McIntosh argue from a socialist-feminist perspective that familial ideology actually impairs other forms of communality and solidarity: "the stronger and more supportive families are expected to be, the weaker the other supportive institutions outside of them become."[52] As in Boose's essay on the "Family of Shakespeareans," recourse to familial language for describing social communities like academia not only erases the real disjuncture Barrett and McIntosh find between "the family" and "the community" but perpetuates, however unintentionally, a conservative and naturalizing definition of the heterosexual nuclear family. As gay historian Jeffrey Weeks observes, "the family is a potent trope even in the hands of those whose adherence to a traditional model is dubious. The language of the family pervades our thinking about private life."[53] To Weeks's insight, I would add that the language of the family also pervades—hence limits—our thinking about public life: not only the notion of professional life that we construct for ourselves as a community of Shakespeare scholars but also the notion of domestic life that we construct for early modern England, a construction in which Shakespeare's comedies for the public theater enjoy such a familiar place.

Notes

For their generous comments on earlier versions of this essay and the chapter from which it derives, I am grateful to Jean Howard, David Kastan, Jim Shapiro, Nick Radel, Bruce Smith, Valerie Traub, Jonathan Goldberg, and Greg Bredbeck, who helped clarify my thinking about queer theory. Barbara Mowat and anonymous readers for *Shakespeare Quarterly* provided valuable criticism and suggestions. Finally, I would like to thank Stephen Orgel for the opportunity to present parts of this essay in the session "Renaissance Outsiders" at the 1993 annual meeting of the Modern Language Association, Toronto.

[1] Lawrence Stone, *The Family, Sex and Marriage in England 1500-1800* (New York: Harper and Row, 1977). Other historical accounts that neglect the homoerotic as a category of early modern domestic experience include Ralph A. Houlbrooke, *The English Family 1450-1700* (London and New York: Longman, 1984); and Alice T. Friedman, *House and Household in Elizabethan England: Wollaton Hall and the Willoughby Family* (Chicago and London: U of Chicago P, 1989).

[2] Evidence of homoeroticism within the early modern domestic sphere has been provided by several method-

ologically diverse studies: Alan Bray, *Homosexuality in Renaissance England* (London: Gay Men's Press, 1982), 44-51; Bruce R. Smith, *Homosexual Desire in Shakespeare's England: A Cultural Poetics* (Chicago and London: U of Chicago P, 1991), 82-88; Gregory W. Bredbeck, *Sodomy and Interpretation: Marlowe to Milton* (Ithaca, NY, and London: Cornell UP, 1991), 115-34; Bredbeck, "Sodomesticity," lecture delivered at the 1992 annual meeting of the Modern Language Association, New York City; Richard Rambuss, "The Secretary's Study: The Secret Designs of *The Shepheardes Calender,*" *ELH* 59 (1992): 313-35, esp. 318-21; Jonathan Goldberg, *Sodometries: Renaissance Texts, Modern Sexualities* (Stanford, CA: Stanford UP, 1992), 123-43. See also the following essays in *Erotic Politics: Desire on the Renaissance stage,* Susan Zimmerman, ed. (New York and London: Routledge, 1992): Valerie Traub, "The (in)significance of 'lesbian' desire in early modern England," 150-69, esp. 158-65; Lisa Jardine, "Twins and travesties: Gender, dependency and sexual availability in *Twelfth Night,*" 27-38; and Jean E. Howard, "Sex and social conflict: The erotics of *The Roaring Girl,*" 170-90, esp. 174-79.

[3] One goal of the larger project from which this essay is taken, *The Homoerotics of Early Modern Drama,* is to reveal the significant variety of homoerotic relations found in the plays of Shakespeare's contemporaries.

[4] The early modern household, also known as a "family," was comprised not only of parents and children but also of "non-kin inmates, sojourners, boarders or lodgers . . . as well as indentured apprentices and resident servants" (Stone, 26-27). Bray observes that the practice of sharing beds within the household could facilitate sex between servants or between masters and servants (50-51).

Non-Shakespearean (indeed, un-Shakespearean) representations of homoerotic master-servant relations in the drama are discussed in my essay on Jonson and Chapman, "Asses and Wits: The Homoerotics of Mastery in Satiric Comedy" (*English Literary Renaissance* 25 [1995]: 179-208); and in Theodore B. Leinwand's essay on Middleton, "Redeeming Beggary/Buggery in *Michaelmas Term*" (*ELH* 61 [1994]: 53-70).

[5] Lynda E. Boose, "The Family in Shakespeare Studies; or—Studies in the Family of Shakespeareans; or—The Politics of Politics," *Renaissance Quarterly* 40 (1987): 707-51. Boose develops the metaphor of feminism as a liminal daughter and new historicism as a "legitimate son" (738).

[6] Catherine Belsey, "Disrupting sexual difference: meaning and gender in the comedies" in *Alternative Shakespeares,* John Drakakis, ed. (London and New York: Methuen, 1985), 166-90; Mary Beth Rose, *The Expense of Spirit: Love and Sexuality in English Renaissance Drama* (Ithaca, NY, and London: Cornell UP, 1988), 12-42. In a note, Belsey says only that she is "not entirely persuaded" by the argument that boy-actors had a homoerotic appeal (235). She says nothing, however, about the homoerotic valence of the name Ganymede in *As You Like It.*

[7] Valerie Traub, *Desire and Anxiety: Circulations of sexuality in Shakespearean drama* (London and New York: Routledge, 1992), 123.

[8] Traub in Zimmerman, ed., 158.

[9] Quotations of *As You Like It* in this essay follow the Arden text, ed. Anges Latham (London: Methuen, 1975). Quotations of Shakespeare plays other than *As You Like It* follow *The Riverside Shakespeare,* ed. G. Blakemore Evans (Boston: Houghton Mifflin, 1974).

[10] Thomas Cooper, *Dictionarivm Historicum & Poeticum . . .* in *Thesavrvs Lingvae Romanae & Brittanicae . . .* (London, 1565), J4r. On Shakespeare's probable use of this dictionary, see DeWitt T. Starnes and Ernest William Talbert, *Classical Myth and Legend in Renaissance Dictionaries: A Study of Renaissance Dictionaries in Their Relation to the Classical Learning of Contemporary English Writers* (Chapel Hill: U of North Carolina P, 1955), 111-34. Arthur Golding's 1567 translation of Ovid flatly states that Jupiter advances Ganymede to cupbearer "against Dame *Junos* will" (*Shakespeare's Ovid: Being Arthur Golding's Translation of the* Metamorphoses, ed. W.H.D. Rouse [London: Centaur Press, 1961], Bk. 10, l. 167).

[11] Christopher Marlowe, *Dido, Queene of Carthage* in Vol. 1 of *The Complete Works of Christopher Marlowe,* ed. Fredson Bowers, 2 vols. (Cambridge: Cambridge UP, 1973), 1.1 SD, 1.1.51, and 3.2.42-43.

Whatever the anatomical similarities between the sexes posited by the Galenic one-sex model, certain bodily functions particular to women or attributed to women by Renaissance gender discourses were considered "different" enough to evoke male anxiety and disgust. The sixteenth-century physician Thomas Raynalde feared that knowledge of women's unique reproductive processes might lead men "*the more* to abhorre and loath the companie of women" (quoted in Gail Kern Paster, *The Body Embarrassed: Drama and the Disciplines of Shame in Early Modern England* [Ithaca, NY: Cornell UP, 1993], 187). On the Galenic one-sex model, see Thomas Laqueur, *Making Sex: Body and Gender from the Greeks to Freud* (Cambridge, MA, and London: Harvard UP, 1990). Laqueur's account has been criticized for downplaying differences, namely the competing Aristotelian model of *sexual* difference and the construction of *gender* differences in early modern texts about women. This argument is advanced by Patricia Parker, "Gender Ideology, Gender Change: The Case of Marie Germain," *Critical Inquiry* 19 (1993): 337-64, esp. 339-40; and Sally Shuttleworth, review of Laqueur, *Journal of the History of Sexuality* 3 (1993): 633-35. Paster provides a convincing corrective to Laqueur regarding the physiological/ethical gender differences posited by Renaissance humoral theory (16-17 and passim).

[12] Marlowe in Bowers, ed., 1.1.2 and 43.

[13] John Lyly, *Gallathea* in *Gallathea and Midas,* ed. Anne Begor Lancashire, Regents Renaisance Drama (Lincoln: U of Nebraska P, 1969), 5.2.65.

[14] John Mason, *The Turk,* ed. Fernand Lagarde (Salzburg: Institut für Anglistik and Amerikanistik, 1979), 1.2.130-48. Mason's play was performed in 1607 by the King's Revels Children at Whitefriars.

[15] Marlowe, *Edward II* in Vol. 2 of Bowers, ed., 1.4.178-81.

[16] John Marston, *The Malcontent* in Vol. 1 of *The Works of John Marston,* ed. A. H. Bullen, 3 vols. (London: John C. Nimmo, 1887), 1.1.15-16.

[17] William Barksted, *Mirrha the Mother of Adonis: or Lustes Prodegies* (London, 1607), C7[r].

[18] On this dynamic, see James Holstun, "'Will You Rent Our Ancient Love Asunder?': Lesbian Elegy in Donne, Marvell, and Milton," *ELH* 54 (1987): 835-67. In the context of *As You Like It,* it is significant that Hebe was the goddess of youth (cf. Cooper, J4[r]). The abandonment of youthful female love is discussed by Traub in Zimmerman, ed.; and by Dorothea Kehler, "Shakespeare's Emilias and the Politics of Celibacy" in *In Another Country: Feminist Perspectives on Renaissance Drama,* Dorothea Kehler and Susan Baker, eds. (Metuchen, NJ, and London: Scarecrow Press, 1991), 157-78.

[19] Abraham Fraunce, *The Third part of the Countesse of Pembrokes Yuychurch: Entituled,* Amintas Dale (London, 1592), E[r]. Sir Robert Staplyton, glossing a line in Juvenal's *Second Satire,* explains, "A man used to make protestation by his *Genius,* a woman by her *Juno*" (*Juvenal's Sixteen Satyrs or, A Svrvey of the Manners and Actions of Mankind* [London, 1647], 28).

[20] *The Maid's Metamorphosis* (1600), ed. John S. Farmer, The Tudor Reprinted and Parallel Texts (London: Hazell, Watson and Viney, 1908), C[1][v].

[21] Ovid, Bk. 10, ll. 157-58, 88-89, and 91-92. Shakespeare had already alluded to the homoerotic dimensions of the Orpheus myth in *The Two Gentlemen of Verona,* where Proteus ironically advises his rival, Sir Thurio, to woo Silvia like Orpheus: "For Orpheus' lute was strung with poets' sinews, / Whose golden touch could soften steel and stones" (3.2.77-78). Proteus recalls Orpheus's homoerotic pastoral life in the image of a "golden" touch applied to male "sinews." These dismembered sinews also prefigure Orpheus's own destruction by the Maenads. The next scene of the play assigns an Orphic role to Valentine, who, banished from Silvia and the court, agrees to lead the band of forest outlaws. The Orpheus myth helps explain why the outlaws find their new commander a "proper man" who is "beautified / With goodly shape" and gifted as a "linguist" (4.1.10, 55-57). We can identify a characteristically Shakespearean associative cluster in both plays—Orpheus/golden world/homoeroticism/outlaws—a cluster fulfilled in *As You Like It* when Duke Senior and his lords enter in Act 2 *"like outlaws"* (2.7 SD).

[22] Jardine, *Still Harping on Daughters: Women and Drama in the Age of Shakespeare* (Sussex: Harvester Press; Totowa, NJ: Barnes and Noble, 1983), 9-36; Stephen Orgel, "Nobody's Perfect: Or Why Did the English Stage Take Boys for Women?" in *Displacing Homophobia: Gay Male Perspectives in Literature and Culture,* Ronald R. Butters, John M. Clum, and Michael Moon, eds. (Durham, NC, and London: Duke UP, 1989), 7-29.

[23] See Thomas H. Cain, "Spenser and the Renaissance Orpheus," *University of Toronto Quarterly* 41 (1971): 24-47. Peggy Muñoz Simonds attempts "to synthesize what Orpheus might have signified to the mature Shakespeare" of the tragicomedies. Although she cites many contemporary allusions to Orpheus as a figure of consolation, she bypasses entirely the homoerotic elements of the myth ("'Killing care and grief of heart': Orpheus and Shakespeare," *Renaissance Papers 1990,* Dale B. J. Randall and Joseph A. Porter, eds. [Durham, NC: Southeastern Renaissance Conference, 1990], 79-90, esp. 79).

[24] Cooper, N2[v].

[25] See Harry Berger Jr., "Orpheus, Pan, and the Poetics of Misogyny: Spenser's Critique of Pastoral Love and Art," *ELH* 50 (1983): 27-60.

[26] John Dickenson, *The Shepheardes Complaint* (London, 1596), C2[v].

[27] R. B., *Orphevs His Iourney to Hell, And his Musicke to the Ghosts, for the regaining of faire Euridice his Loue, and hew spoused Wife* (London, 1595), D4[r].

[28] See Orgel, 26; and Howard in Zimmerman, ed., 172. Bruce Smith discusses the Renaissance gender ideology that encouraged men to form intimate friendships (which, he argues, could accommodate homoerotic desire) and that regarded women as the moral and in-

tellectual inferiors of men (33-41 and 56-77). Whereas Smith believes that marriage successfully disrupted male friendship, Joseph Pequigney argues that Shakespeare's homoerotically inclined Antonios are incorporated into the marriages that conclude their plays ("The Two Antonios and Same-Sex Love in *Twelfth Night* and *The Merchant of Venice*," ELR 22 [1992]: 201-21).

[29] *Of Loues complaint; with the legend of Orpheus and Euridice* (London, 1597), E6ᵛ.

[30] R. B., *Orphevs His Iourney to Hell*, D4ᵛ.

[31] Holland is quoted and discussed by Smith (40), who shows that the translation of explicitly homoerotic Greek and Latin texts played an important role in the discursive construction of homoeroticism in Renaissance England. For Renaissance humanism as an anthropological encounter with another culture, specifically in regard to the Ganymede myth, see Leonard Barkan, *Transuming Passion: Ganymede and the Erotics of Humanism* (Stanford, CA: Stanford UP, 1991).

[32] Orgel, *Impersonations: The Performance of Gender in Shakespeare's England* (Cambridge: Cambridge UP, 1996), 57-58.

[33] James M. Saslow, *Ganymede in the Renaissance: Homosexuality in Art and Society* (New Haven, CT, and London: Yale UP, 1986), 116. Significantly, one of Saslow's Italian sources is a passage from Poliziano's 1480 drama *Orfeo* in which Orpheus sings:

> Great Jupiter bears witness to this creed
> Who, by the knot of sweet love held in thrall,
> Enjoys in heaven his fair boy Ganymede
> As Apollo on earth for Hyacinth does call.
> To this holy love did Hercules concede,
> He who felled giants till Hylas made him fall.
> I urge all husbands: seek divorce, and flee
> Each one away from female company.
> (quoted in Saslow, 122)

[34] John Marston, *The Scourge of Villainy* in Bullen, ed., 3:295-382, esp. 313. Thomas Heywood, *Pleasant Dialogves and Dramma's*, ed. W. Bang (Louvain: Uystpruyst, 1903), 101. See Robert Greene, *Penelopes Web* (1587) in *The Life and Complete Works in Prose and Verse of Robert Greene*, ed. Alexander B. Grosart, 15 vols. (London: Hazell, Watson, and Viney, 1881-86), 5:137-234, esp. 165.

Smith discusses the Jupiter-Juno-Ganymede myth as it appears in Heywood, Shakespeare, Marlowe, and an anonymous poem about James I (199-223).

[35] Jardine surveys historical accounts of the high proportion of adolescent male servants in early modern England (in Zimmerman, ed., 29).

[36] Michael Drayton, quoted in Bray, *Homosexuality in Renaissance England*, 33. For scholarship on the homoerotics of service in early modern England, see notes 2 and 4 above. Many of the studies cited there assert that the word *ganymede* was used colloquially to signify a dependent boy, whether a page, prostitute, or player. Ganymedes and catamites are stock characters in the verse satires that begin to appear in the late 1590s. See Bray, *Homosexuality in Renaissance England*, 33-57; Bredbeck, *Sodomy and Interpretation*, 10-18 and 33-39; and Smith, 159-87.

[37] Marston, *Histrio-Mastix* in *The Plays of John Marston*, ed. H. Harvey Wood, 3 vols. (Edinburgh and London: Oliver and Boyd, 1939), 3:243-302, esp. 271.

[38] John Boswell traces the hyena lore back to its early Christian and ancient sources (*Christianity, Social Tolerance, and Homosexuality: Gay People in Western Europe from the Beginning of the Christian Era to the Fourteenth Century* [Chicago and London: U of Chicago P, 1980], 137-43). The commonplace belief in the hyena's sex-change appears in the *Physiologus*, which Boswell characterizes as the "single most popular work of natural science of the Middle Ages, [and] one of the most widely read treatises of any sort prior to the seventeenth century" (141). Ann Rosalind Jones and Peter Stallybrass call the *Physiologus* "one of the most popular books of the early Renaissance" and cite its account of the hyena as an example of the Renaissance discourse of hermaphroditism: "'At one time it becomes a male, at another a female'" ("Fetishizing Gender: Constructing the Hermaphrodite in Renaissance Europe" in *Body Guards: The Cultural Politics of Gender Ambiguity*, Julia Epstein and Kristina Straub, eds. [New York and London: Routledge, 1991], 80-111, esp. 80-81).

[39] Ovid, Bk. 15, ll. 451-52.

[40] The term *adultery*, despite the modern inclination to read it straight, did not in early modern usage necessarily refer to male-female sexuality. William Perkins writes in *The Foundation of Christian Religion*: "To commit adultery, signifieth as much, as to doe any thing, what way soeuer, whereby the chastitie of our selues, or our neighbours may be stained." Perkins furnishes examples of heteroerotic, autoerotic, and homoerotic lust (*The Workes of that Famous and Worthy Minister of Christ in the Vniuersitie of Cambridge, Mr. William Perkins*, 3 vols. [London, 1616-18], 1:58).

[41] Traub, *Desire and Anxiety*, 125-26.

[42] "Ganymede and Hebe" (*Post aquile raptus*, twelfth or thirteenth century) is quoted in Boswell (392-98, esp. 395), who provides useful translations and interpretations of the Ganymede myth in medieval texts.

On gender and race in Renaissance discourses of beauty, see Kim F. Hall, "'I Rather Would Wish to Be a Black-Moor': Beauty, race, and rank in Lady Mary Wroth's *Urania*" in *Women, "Race," and Writing in the Early Modern Period,* Margo Hendricks and Patricia Parker, eds. (London and New York: Routledge, 1994), 178-94.

[43] See Smith, 147.

[44] On the "erotic contingency" produced by the *if,* see Traub, *Desire and Anxiety,* 128.

[45] See Smith, 176-79; Goldberg, 29-61; Simon Shepherd, "What's so funny about ladies' tailors? A survey of some male (homo)sexual types in the Renaissance," *Textual Practice* 6 (1992): 17-30, esp. 23-25; John Michael Archer, *Sovereignty and Intelligence: Spying and Court Culture in the English Renaissance* (Stanford, CA: Stanford UP, 1993), 76-78; and Bray, "Homosexuality and the Signs of Male Friendship in Elizabethan England" in *Queering the Renaissance,* Jonathan Goldberg, ed. (Durham, NC, and London: Duke UP, 1994), 40-61, esp. 46-56.

[46] See Steven Mullaney, *The Place of the Stage: License, Play, and Power in Renaissance England* (Chicago and London: U of Chicago P, 1988). Bray mentions the London tavern as a likely site of homosexual prostitution (*Homosexuality in Renaissance England,* 53-54), and Goldberg remarks on the sodomitical taint of Prince Hal's male tavern companions in the Henriad (*Sodometries,* 155-56).

[47] See, for instance, Bray, *Homosexuality in Renaissance England,* 54-55; Jardine, *Still Harping on Daughters,* 9-36; Susan Zimmerman, "Disruptive desire: Artifice and indeterminacy in Jacobean comedy" in Zimmerman, ed., 39-63; and Laura Levine, *Men in women's clothing: Anti-theatricality and effeminization, 1579-1642* (Cambridge: Cambridge UP, 1994), 10-25.

[48] See Joy Wiltenburg, *Disorderly Women and Female Power in the Street Literature of Early Modern England and Germany* (Charlottesville and London: UP of Virginia, 1992). "Lamentation of a new-married man," *The Roxburghe Ballads,* ed. William Chappell, 9 vols. (Hertford, UK: Stephen Austin and Sons, 1871-99), 2:33-40, esp. 34.

[49] Marlowe, *Edward II,* 1.4.30, 87, and 393. "Minion," according to Eric Partridge, is "a man's—especially a king's or a prince's—male favourite; not necessarily a homosexual" (*Shakespeare's Bawdy: A Literary & Psychological Essay and a Comprehensive Glossary* [London: Routledge, 1947], 148). On the roles of "master" and "minion" in *Edward II,* see Smith, 209-23.

[50] "Robin and Kate; or, A bad husband converted by a good wife" (1634) in Chappell, ed., 2:413-18, esp. 415-16.

[51] Quoted in Bray, "Homosexuality and the Signs of Male Friendship," 55. Bray cites the autobiography of Simonds D'Ewes (British Museum, Harleian MSS, 646/59-59^v), written between 1622 and 1624.

[52] Michèle Barrett and Mary McIntosh, *The Anti-social Family,* 2d ed. (London and New York: Verso, 1991), 171.

[53] Jeffrey Weeks, "Pretended family relationships" in *Marriage, domestic life and social change: Writings for Jacqueline Burgoyne (1944-88),* David Clark, ed. (London and New York: Routledge, 1991), 214-34, esp. 227. Weeks's title quotes Britain's antigay statute, Section 28 of the Local Government Act, 1988.

TIME

Frederick Turner (essay date 1971)

SOURCE: "*As You Like It*: 'Subjective', 'Objective', and 'Natural' Time," in *Shakespeare and the Nature of Time: Moral and Philosophical Themes in Some Plays and Poems of William Shakespeare,* Oxford at the Clarendon Press, 1971, pp. 28-44.

[*In the essay below, Turner describes the attitudes of Jaques, Touchstone, and Rosalind and Orlando toward time—historical, natural, and personal, respectively—and asserts that all three viewpoints are reconciled through marriage at the end of the play.*]

As You Like It opens with two characters who, in terms of the hierarchy of social power, are weak and inferior: Orlando, the younger brother, and Adam, the old man. One is denied his place in society; the other is past his usefulness. Orlando tellingly distinguishes between the 'gentle condition of blood' and the 'courtesy of nations';[1] between what is owed him as a member of society, and what is due to his status as a human being. Adam has 'lost' his 'teeth' 'in service',[2] and though his master's legal obligation to him has been fulfilled, Oliver refuses to honour his human obligations to look after the faithful servant in his old age.

Those who are weak in the power structure of society—children, old men, beggars, strangers, the insane—can possess the most potent moral power in the human community. But this moral power must be recognized, if it is to exist; Malvolio's crime, we shall see, is to deny the moral power of the Fool. Orlando's description of his 'keeping' as no different from the 'stalling of an ox',[3] and Oliver's characterizing Adam as an 'old dog',[4] suggest that the socially strong in this play consider those who are socially weak to be no better than beasts, outside the community of man, and therefore ineligible for the basic human rights. But piety (or pité), insists that such figures are the true representatives of the human community, that we should treat them with the respect due to common humanity, whose dignity transcends the evanescent privileges of rank, wealth, or birth. There is only one thing that Orlando and Adam can do: leave the society which has rejected them.

Outcast also are the Duke Senior and his friends, and Rosalind, Celia, and Touchstone. Where can they go? What region of Shakespeare's poetic, philosophical, and moral world is appropriate to them?

If one escapes from the ordinary routine of society, one is on holiday. Rosalind can see nothing but 'briers' in this 'workingday' world; on 'holiday' they are but 'burs'. If, says Celia, 'we walk not in the trodden paths'—if we do not conform to the routines of society—'our very petticoats will catch them'.[5] The holiday that the outcasts must take is partly a holiday of the mind. 'Briers' become 'burs' when their attitude changes from 'workingday' to 'holiday'. Rosalind and Celia come to accept their existence with patience, but without paying the price of a vitiating and stoic detachment. On holiday life is only a game, even when it is a game of life and death. Rosalind and Celia are delightful partly because of their holiday attitude to the world—an attitude which combines levity with involvement, wisdom with feeling. Rosalind can satirize love and be in love at the same time.

Orlando, Rosalind, and the Duke Senior are all victims of injustice. They reject and are rejected by the power-structure of their society; and this structure includes its laws. The 'courtesy of nations' has become a tyranny for Orlando; for the Duke Senior it has been overturned. The accusation of treachery levelled by Duke Frederick at Rosalind is a legality divested of its sanctifying ritual of evidence, fair play, and impartiality. Thus the exiles become outlaws: they live 'like the old Robin Hood of England'.[6] This brings to mind the connection of Robin Hood with the old holiday ritual of rural England, and the enormous popularity of his story among the common folk. He was the hero of the socially weak; the semi-pagan god of Holiday. The Puritans recognized this strain in his cult when they abolished it nearly fifty years later.

Time in the forest is not social time. The exiled nobles 'fleet the time carelessly, as they did in the golden world'.[7] They 'lose and neglect the creeping hours of time;[8] the human measurement of time has no meaning here. In Thomas Mann's *Magic Mountain,* holiday has a similar effect:

> Such is the purpose of our changes of air and scene, of all our sojourns at cures and bathing resorts; it is the secret of the healing power of change and incident. Our first days in a new place, time has a youthful, that is to say, a broad and sweeping flow, persisting for some six or eight days. Then, as one 'gets used to the place', a gradual shrinkage makes itself felt. He who clings or, better expressed, wishes to cling to life, will shudder to see how the days grow light and lighter, how they scurry by like dead leaves, until the last week, of some four, perhaps, is uncannily fugitive and fleet.[9]

Here Mann is more interested in the subjective changes in the rate of time occasioned by circumstances than in the nature of holiday itself; but one interest tends to suggest the other, and we will find Shakespeare himself fascinated with subjective time in turn.

Helen Gardner discusses this subject illuminatingly in the context of the romantic comedies in general: 'In Shakespeare's comedies time . . . is not so much a movement onward as a space in which to work things out: a midsummer night, a space too short for us to feel time's movement, or the unmeasured time of *As You Like It* or *Twelfth Night.*'[10] Of *Much Ado About Nothing* she says: 'A sense of holiday, of *time off from the world's business,* reigns in Messina.'[11]

Twice in *As You Like It* the absurdity of social, measurable time is suggested:

> And then he drew a dial from his poke,
> And, looking on it with lack-lustre eye,
> Says very wisely 'It is ten o'clock;
> Thus we may see' quoth he 'how the world wags;
> 'Tis but an hour ago since it was nine;
> And after one hour more 'twill be eleven; . . . '
>   . . . When I did hear
> The motley fool thus moral on the time,
> My lungs began to crow like chanticleer
> That fools should be so deep contemplative;
> And I did laugh sans intermission
> An hour by his dial.[12]

—Is it significant that Jaques compares his laughter to the sound of the chanticleer, the marker of natural time as opposed to the time of clocks?—

> *Ros:* I pray you, what is't o'clock?
> *Orl:* You should ask me what time o'day; there's no clock in the forest.[13]

This last is reminiscent of Falstaff's first words in *I Henry IV,* and Hal's reply:

> *Fal:* Now, Hal, what time of day is it, lad? . . . etc.[14]

The Boar's Head is similarly on holiday from ordinary time. It is interesting that what follows in each case is also similar. Rosalind asserts that

> 'Then there is no true lover in the forest, else sighing every minute and groaning every hour would detect the lazy foot of Time as well as a clock.'[15]

Hal says to Falstaff:

> What a devil hast thou to do with the time of the day? Unless hours were cups of sack, and minutes capons, and clocks the tongues of bawds . . . etc.[16]

Time in each case is transmuted from the measurable, social time of clocks into the subjective time of experience. Falstaff now introduces another element:

> . . . we that take purses go by the moon and the seven stars, and not by Phoebus, he 'that wand'ring knight so fair'.[17]

Falstaff operates, so he claims, according to the natural and mysterious time of the moon and the stars, rather than the tamed and social time of the sun—which he anthropomorphizes with impunity.

The Forest of Arden is a poetic region which contains, as well as holiday and outlawry, the forces of natural time, the time of the seasons, of the great rhythms of nature; 'time not our time',[18] as T. S. Eliot puts it.

> Under the greenwood tree
> Who loves to lie with me,
> And turn his merry note
> Unto the sweet bird's throat . . .
> . . . Here shall he see
> No enemy
> But winter and rough weather.[19]
>
> Here feel we but the penalty of Adam,
> The seasons' difference . . . [20]
>
> Blow, blow, thou winter wind,
> Thou are not so unkind
> As man's ingratitude . . . [21]

Shakespeare's Arden contains other seasons than a perpetual springtime. It can be 'melancholy',[22] 'uncouth',[23] a 'desert inaccessible';[24] it contains real, as well as conventional, shepherds. Most important of all, it works convincingly by natural time. It is a place one lives in, not an abstraction of the poet's mind; it has the obduracy and unconcern for human desires that we recognize as authentic in nature. People can get old here in the forest; time rules over man, but it is the time of the seasons and not the time of the clock.

The exiles carry with them into the forest many of their human attitudes and preconceptions. Jaques relentlessly anthropomorphizes the deer; the nobles are seen as 'usurpers' on the life of the forest, which is contrasted with the human domains of 'country, city, court'.[25] For our purposes one of the most significant importations into the forest is Jaques' attitude to time in human existence:

> All the world's stage,
> And all the men and women merely players;
> They have their exits and their entrances;
> And one man in his time plays many parts,
> His acts being seven ages . . .
> . . . Last scene of all,
> That ends this strange eventful history,
> Is second childishness and mere oblivion;
> Sans teeth, sans eyes, sans taste, sans everything.[26]

This passage resembles the conventional picture of the attitude of the philosopher. Jaques is above it all; he preserves a lofty detachment from the affairs of the common herd. But his detachment denies to him much of the truth about human existence. This celebrated passage is oddly hypermetropic: Jaques is longsighted, and cannot see the trees for the wood. The statistical studies of sociologists frequently give the same impression of selective blindness. The individual is devalued, exceptions are discounted, particulars yield to trends, freedom and significance are made to seem absurd or irrelevant.

Two elements of this speech are of particular interest: first, the life of man in time as a stage play; and, second, that life as a 'history', a succession of objectively observable characteristics of behaviour.

'All the world's a stage.' In a play, the actor is bound to the lines that the dramatist has written for him. He is not free to say or do what he likes; man, according to Jaques, is only reading off a preordained script. A play exists before it is performed; time is like a motion picture, every frame of which has already been prepared. Life is only the playing-out of a set sequence of events, the projection of a reel of scenes. Part of the irony of Jaques' speech is that it is, of course, delivered by an actor who is himself keeping to his part.

Walter Bagehot makes an interesting point about Jaques' speech in a passage which David Cecil quotes and discusses in his charming essay, 'Shakespearean Comedy', from *The Fine Art of Reading*.[27] Bagehot's treatment deserves repetition:

> There seems an unalterable contradiction between the human mind and its employments. How can a soul be a merchant? What relation to an immortal being have the price of linseed, the fall of butter,

the tare on tallow, or the brokerage on hemp? Can an undying creature debit 'petty expenses,' and charge for 'carriage paid'? All the world's a stage;— 'the satchel, and the shining morning face'—the 'strange oaths';—'the bubble reputation'—the

> Eyes severe and beard of formal cut,
> Full of wise saws and modern instances.

Can these things be real? Surely they are acting. What relation have they to the truth as we see it in theory? What connection with our certain hopes, 'in respect of itself, it is a good life; but in respect it is a Shepherd's life, it is nought'. The soul ties its shoes; the mind washes its hands in a basin. All is incongruous.

In a play the actors are not being themselves, but donning masks and acting a pretence. Jaques' vision of human life is essentially external. For him all there is is the pretence, the mask, the actor's part, the accidents. He describes behaviour, but not experience. Jaques is, perhaps, the first of those great satirical *personae* that Hugh Kenner discusses with such penetration and wit in his 'historical comedy', *The Counterfeiters*.[28] Like Gulliver describing the Yahoos, like the extraordinary counterfeit sociologist who seems to have written *A Modest Proposal*, like the bad poet Pope invents to write the *Art of Sinking in Poetry*, Jaques is concerned not with the inner nature of a person, but with his surface, not with another 'I' but with an 'it'.

The reader, abetted by many critics, is often deceived in this passage by its breadth, inclusiveness, and metaphysical pathos into feeling that this is Shakespeare's viewpoint on the world, that here is some kind of ultimate wisdom about human life. On the contrary, Jaques' description of the schoolboy, lover, soldier, is only a series of brilliantly evoked stereotypes. If in some respects Shakespeare is *creating* or *originating* stereotypes (like Chaucer in the Prologue to the *Canterbury Tales*), this does not alter the fact that we are not being told the whole story about human existence; the sample of human information Jaques has chosen is not a fair one, and whole areas have been suppressed. Equally as important as what Jaques says is the insight we get into Jaques' point of view, and indeed into the flaws and virtues of a whole way of looking at existence.

Jaques' speech contains a certain cynicism, a mood alien, in some respects, to Shakespeare's own, as far as we can judge from his poems and sonnets, as well as from his plays. The other passages we should bear in mind when we read or hear 'All the world's a stage' include not only Prospero's 'our revels now are ended', and 'as an unperfect actor on the stage'; but also Macbeth's 'poor player, That struts and frets his hour upon the stage', and Lear's 'great stage of fools'.

Jaques' vision of human life ends as it began: with second childishness, sans everything; nothing has been gained, life is meaningless, it's all only a play. As soon as Jaques has finished his speech, Orlando, the young man and the lover, enters carrying Adam, the old man who is almost in his 'last scene'; the two are united and ennobled by a sense of love and care which somehow transcends and contradicts the stereotypical categories that would divide and degrade them.

The other theme of Jaques' speech that concerns us here is that of man's life as a history. 'History' can have two meanings, both of which are relevant in this context: 'story', and 'history' in the modern sense. The essential element in both is their dialectic: time in both is something expressed in terms of 'before' and 'after' rather than 'past', 'present', and 'future'. Time for 'history' is something static. The most obvious characteristic of Jacques' speech is the way for him human life seems to go in stages, each of which is changeless and restrictingly self-consistent. We can all remember our sense of chagrin and frustration when we were told by our parents that we were 'just going through a stage'. Our individuality, the validity of our ideals and feelings, seemed threatened. When, we asked, would we be real people, when would we cease to be merely the result of a biological or social situation? Jaques would, it seems, reply 'never'.

'His acts being seven ages.' This ignores a fundamental characteristic of time—time as flux, time as dynamic process. Jaques' human actor develops in a curiously jerky fashion. We cannot for the life of us see how that particular kind of lover can become that particular kind of soldier or lawyer. How does the plump Justice become the 'lean and slipper'd pantaloon'? We have no sense of this man being one person. In our own lives we can look back and sometimes fail to recognize what we call 'I'; but usually beneath the affectations and obsessions, the attempts to be what we were not, we can see one person whom we greet with almost the delighted shock of meeting an old friend unexpectedly. There is none of this in Jaques' creed. Yet time is seamless. It has no stages. And it is in this intimate connection of each moment of time with the next that the possibility of being one person, not just an infinite sequence of stages, can exist. If one takes an individual out of his temporal context at various stages of his development, as Jaques does, one will inevitably falsify as well as omit much of what he is.

Jaques sees himself as an 'historian', chronicling the life of man. Now 'history' in this sense is concerned with events and states; it cannot afford to occupy itself with the subtle rhythms of gradual growth. The dialectic of 'historical' time, as I have pointed out in the Introduction, is based on terms like 'before', 'after', 'earlier', and 'later', not on 'past', 'present', and 'future'. But the rhythm of growth is the rhythm of continuous, imperceptible change; and the growing-point of a human life is the present moment which carries with it the concepts of 'past' and 'future' as indications of the direction of growth. To take temporal cross-sections is to ignore the *process* of growth, concentrating only on its effects and results.

'History' in Jaques' sense, moreover, like philosophy, is a map; a map cannot reproduce the whole landscape in its minute detail. Yet we can only really know the landscape ('known' as *connaître*, not *savoir*), if we have all its details about us. A work of art can give us a sense of this but the pre-rational and personal principles of selection which are available to the artist are denied to Jaques' 'historian', who is in pursuit of impersonal truth, whose satire 'like a wild-goose flies, Unclaim'd of any man',[29] and who professes a disillusioned rationality.

Part of the force of Falstaff, perhaps, is that he is a dynamic character who changes and evolves in an environment of static, 'historical' time—the time of events and states. Falstaff is a work of art, and in fact develops from a wildly inaccurate selection and exaggeration by Shakespeare of meagre details in his sources.

Jaques' 'historical' viewpoint has other characteristics. One is that it is objective, rather than subjective. Jaques does not take into account what is almost the most important feature of time—the peculiar sensation, common to the human race, and therefore taken for granted, of living in time. What does it feel like to live in time? Everything that comes under that question is absent from Jaques' point of view. Since values and meaning exist only in the subjective sphere.[30] Jaques is presenting a view of existence as valueless and meaningless. Since the sense of the living self exists only in the present moment (which is given no particular significance by Jaques), he is describing people who seem to have no self.

Jaques describes 'dead time'—time with no present moments. The advantage the dissector has when working with a dead body rather than a live one is that there is no change in the material being dissected: the body can get no deader. The vivisectionist, on the other hand, has always to beware of the fact that, like Heisenberg's electrons, his subject will be altered by the process of observation. Jaques is safe, working with dead time, and indeed his analytical method is appropriate to his subject. When we work with live time, however, we will find the present moment slipping away in an instant, and other methods of comprehension than Jaques' analytical and objective one must be found.

Finally, we may give attention to Jaques' use of generalization in this speech. 'In all cases, or at least in a good statistical majority, human beings will act in such and such a way' he seems to say. To generalize requires an initial comparison, or 'making equal', of those things about which one generalizes. If I use the generalizing word 'tree', I am assuming *a priori* that oaks, pines, elms, palms, etc., are all in some way basically the same. Indeed, generalization, like the historical dialectic, like objectivity, like the analytic method of thought itself, is essential in order to come at many kinds of truth. About human beings themselves we can and must generalize to a large extent in order to obtain the most primary understanding. But there seems to be something in every sane, undefeated human being that cries out for uniqueness, peerlessness, a sense of his own incomparability. Again, Jaques is not telling the whole story about human existence.

Both Jaques and Touchstone satirize the extravagant claims of love; but their points of view should not be confused. What Jaques says is 'see how absurd is the lover, with his sighs and ballads; for what is he, when his act is past? What a puny figure he cuts in the perspective of history! Does he not swiftly turn into something quite different? Surely his self-importance is misplaced. He is only a stage between schoolboy and soldier. His transports and agonies have no significance.' What Touchstone says is subtly different: 'What is love but Nature's mechanism for repeopling the earth? When it comes down to it, sex is what the whole thing amounts to after all. I myself, with all my wit, "press in" among the "country copulatives";[31] we are all part of the same natural rhythm, there is no qualitative difference between true lovers and the mating of beasts. The true significance of love is biological; the rest only icing on the cake.' Jaques sees the lover in the perspective of history; Touchstone, against the backdrop of brute nature; Jaques' ultimate reality is death, Touchstone's the natural cycle of reproduction; Jaques questions value, Touchstone's values are materialistic.

Posed against both viewpoints are the attitudes of the lovers. If Jaques in his great speech expresses the 'historical' view of time, Rosalind and Orlando are the representatives of 'personal' time. Time for them is dynamic:

> *Orl:* And why not the swift foot of Time?
> Had not that been as proper?
> *Ros:* By no means, sir. Time travels in divers
> paces with divers persons. I'll tell you who
> Time ambles withal, who Time trots withal,
> who Time gallops withal, and who he
> stands still withal.
>
> *Orl:* I prithee, who doth he trot withal?
> *Ros:* Marry, he trots hard with a young maid
> between the contract of her marriage and
> the day it is solemniz'd; if the interim be
> but a se'nnight, Time's pace is so hard that
> it seems the length of seven year.

Orl: Who ambles Time withal?
Ros: With a priest that lacks Latin and a rich man that hath not the gout; for the one sleeps easily because he cannot study, and the other lives merrily because he feels no pain; the one lacking the burden of lean and wasteful learning, the other knowing no burden of heavy tedious penury. These Time ambles withal.

Orl: Who doth he gallop withal?
Ros: With a thief to the gallows; for though he go as softly as foot can fall, he thinks himself too soon there.

Orl: Who stays it still withal?
Ros: With lawyers in the vacation; for they sleep between term and term, and they perceive not how Time moves.[32]

Here time is a pace or journey. At first glance this dialogue apears fairly simple: a witty expression of the commonplaces contained in such phrases as 'how time drags!' and 'time flies'. But in fact this passage is extravagantly difficult. Surely the conventional way of describing the young maid's suspense would be in terms of the slowness of time. Time 'crawls', we would imagine, for the waiting girl. But for Shakespeare it 'trots'. Why? Perhaps Shakespeare means that, for her, every moment is crowded with emotions, fancies, and anticipations. Clock time inches past; her own personal time is in a furious hurry. A week contains seven years' subjective events. The actual sense of motion is important here. When a horse trots, it throws one about a good deal more than when it gallops. One is not actually progressing as fast as at a gallop, but a half-hour's trot can leave as many unpleasant after-effects as a whole morning's gallop. Shakespeare is talking here as much about the *rhythm* of time as about anything else.

With the priest and the rich man the emphasis is different. Time 'ambles' for them because there is little in their lives of excitement, anticipation, or pain: but chiefly because an amble connotes indirection and a sense of 'let time take me where it will'. An ambling horse will stray off the path to munch at choice greenery; the rider does not care where he is going, or at any rate how soon he gets there. We are reminded of Tristram Shandy's method of telling his story.[33]

The thief's progress again implies a different temporal epistemology; this time it is quite easily understood. Time 'flies' for the condemned man in its conventional way.

The lawyers present interesting problems. If they 'sleep between term and term', surely for them clock time flits by instantaneously: but according to Shakespeare it 'stands still'. What Shakespeare means, perhaps, is that subjective time is composed of changes and becomingness: if there is no change or becoming, time stands still. The lawyers 'perceive not how Time moves'.

It is clear that the operative words one would use to describe time in this passage would be 'past', 'present', and 'future'. Time here *is* movement, pace, change; man's life as the journey, not the road. Equally important here is the subjectivity of the temporal viewpoint. Rosalind sees her young maid, priest, rich man, thief, and lawyers not from the point of view of an impartial objective observer, but from their own point of view. Each has his own individual way of existing, his own perception of time. Rosalind is concerned not with what they appear to be externally, but what they feel themselves to be inside. Time is not something laid out inevitably before one, but is the motion of the present moment on which one rides into the unknown and non-existent world of the future, making it first exist and then part of the past. Man's life from this viewpoint can be full of meanings and direction: the young maid and the thief on his way to the gallows both see all their lives in relation to one hoped-for or feared event, some central fact that gives everything significance.

Rosalind, as we have seen earlier, is not 'above it all'; although her philosophy is more profound, perhaps, than Jaques', she is not 'philosophical'; she herself is in a plight not much different from that of her 'young maid'.

Elsewhere in the play the lovers' view of time is enlarged and elucidated for us. One of the most important aspects of it is the true lover's insistence on punctuality:

Orl: My fair Rosalind, I come within an hour of my promise.
Ros: Break an hour's promise in love! He that will divide a minute into a thousand parts, and break but a part of the thousand part of a minute in the affairs of love, it may be said of him that Cupid hath clapp'd him o' th' shoulder, but I'll warrant him heart-whole.[34]

The true lover is concerned not with measurable and divisible time, but with moments. The punctuality Rosalind insists on can be explained in terms of the etymology of the word. The Latin *punctus* means 'point'; for 'punctual' Webster gives '1. of or like point'. The lovers' time is a series of points; a temporal approximation is not good enough. The present moment is not an infinitesimal portion of the minute in which we are (if it were, then Zeno's paradox would have no solution); it is like a point, it has no temporal thickness.

Modern manuals on sex have familiarized us with the virtues of timing in love-making. For Rosalind proper timing is all-important. One wonders whether there is not a pun in 'if you break one jot of your promise, *or come one minute behind your hour,* I will think you the most pathetical break-promise, and *the most hollow lover . . .* that may be chosen out of the gross band of the unfaithful'.[35] In one of the earliest slang dictionaries in the English language,[36] a 'coming-woman' is glossed as a woman who is 'free' of her 'flesh' or a 'breeding woman'. Elsewhere in Shakespeare the pun on 'come' would deepen and extend the meaning.[37] Whether or not this reading can be upheld, one of the important features of lovers' time is the idea of temporal appropriateness, of timing, of the significance of one moment as opposed to another.

The present is what is of importance to the Shakespearean lover:

> This carol they began that hour,
> With a hey, and a ho, and a hey nonino,
> How that a life was but a flower,
> In the spring time, etc.
>
> And therefore take the present time,
> With a hey, and a ho, and a hey nonino,
> For love is crowned with the prime,
> In the spring time, etc.[38]

This is living time, the only time we exist, the present moment.

The enemy and test of lovers' time is 'historical' time. 'Well,' says Rosalind, 'Time is the old justice that examines all such offenders, and let Time try.'[39] Teasingly she assumes the attitudes of Jaques or Touchstone in order to wring denials out of Orlando: 'Say "a day" without the "ever". No, no, Orlando; men are April when they woo, December when they are wed: maids are May when they are maids, but the sky changes when they are wives.'[40] This echoes Jaques' view in its generalization and assumed 'philosophical' detachment; and Touchstone's in its subordination of love to the natural cycle. True love must ultimately deny both 'historical' and 'natural' time; though it must also find some reconciliation or *modus vivendi* with them. (The tragedy of *Romeo and Juliet* is that the reconciliation is not made with 'historical' time, the time of the Montagues and Capulets; and it is snuffed out or smothered by it. The tragedy of *Troilus and Cressida* and *Othello,* on the other hand, is that there is a compromise with 'historical' and 'natural' time, and not a true reconciliation. See Chapter 6.)

In *As You Like It* such a reconciliation can and does take place. In the 'lover and his lass' song, love is reconciled with the natural cycle:

> It was a lover and his lass,
> With a hey, and a ho, and a hey nonino,
> That o'er the green corn-field did pass
> In the spring time, the only pretty ring time
> When birds do sing, hey ding a ding, ding.
> Sweet lovers love the spring.[41]

The great seasons allow a time for love: nature is not essentially opposed to the spiritual movements of man. This reconciliation is brought about thematically by the use of the idea of musical 'time': the rhythm and temporal order of a song can form a bridge between the great natural rhythms and the smaller human ones. The pages who sing the song indicate its significance: 'We kept time, we lost not our time.'[42] Touchstone, who has consistently reduced human significances to subhuman natural drives, cannot accept the musical reconciliation: 'I count it but time lost to hear such a foolish song';[43] applying the judgments of expediency to it. 'What use is it? It is only a waste of time.' The verdict of Jaques on Touchstone is that 'Time, the old justice that examines all such offenders', will find him wanting: ' . . . thy loving voyage Is but for two months victuall'd.'[44] It is significant that when Hymen characterizes the nature of Touchstone's alliance with Audrey, she uses a seasonal image: 'as the winter to foul weather'.[45] But Touchstone has served his purpose. He too is a test, an assay. His function, as his name implies, is to point out true love where it exists, to distinguish gold from base metal.

Touchstone rejects the song; Jaques rejects the dance. At the end of the play, we are shown another rhythmic reconciliation:

> . . . you brides and bridegrooms all,
> With measure heap'd in joy, to th' measures fall.[46]

Dancing is one of the ways we ritually reconcile the individual with society. The measures of the dance bring together moderation and joy; social, or 'historical' time is reconciled with individual or 'personal' time. Jaques cannot accept this. Though he recognizes Orlando's 'true faith,'[47] he states that he is 'for other than for dancing measures';[48] 'to see no pastime I'[49] he insists—a sentiment almost identical to Touchstone's when he reacts to the 'spring time' song.

Obviously the most important thing about the last scene of *As You Like It* is its marriages. Helen Gardner, in a penetrating discussion of the difference between comedy and tragedy, declares: "The great symbol of pure comedy is marriage by which the world is renewed, and its endings are always instinct with a sense of fresh beginnings. Its rhythm is the rhythm of the life of mankind, which goes on and renews itself as the life of nature does."[50] Marriage is the reconciliation of the subjective faith, love, and hope of the individual, the objectivity and commonsense of society, and the mighty forces of fertile nature:

You to a love that your true faith doth
  merit;
You to your land, and love, and great allies;
You to a long and well-deserved bed . . .[51]

Marriage can contain love, a legal contract, and sex in an extra-ordinary harmony. 'Personal', 'historical', and 'natural' time are reconciled in its sacrament, its 'blessed bond':[52]

Then is there mirth in heaven,
When earthly things made even
Atone together.[53]

What Jaques and Touchstone have to say is indeed valid, within limits. If their basilisk eye of satire and cynicism were not open in all of us, we should be very impractical creatures. More important, if their viewpoints were not represented in the play we should soon lose sympathy with the highfalutin' dialectics of romantic love. Jaques and Touchstone inoculate us: and they prepare us for the grand reconciliation that is to be performed by the other great comic character in the play, Rosalind herself.

Other themes in *As You Like It* which are connected with the theme of time, such as providence, false and true sight, and outward appearance and inner reality, may be better dealt with in the next chapter on *Twelfth Night*. The marvellous modulation by which Shakespeare makes every play an individual organism, based on its own characteristic symbolic and philosophical structure, may be clearly seen in the comparison of these two 'romantic comedies'.

Notes

[1] I. i. 40.

[2] I. i. 75.

[3] I. i. 8.

[4] I. i. 73.

[5] I. iii. 12 et seq.

[6] I. i. 106.

[7] I. i. 109

[8] II. vii. 112.

[9] *The Magic Mountain,* ch. iv, 'Excursus on the Sense of Time', trans. H. T. Lowe-Porter, New York, 1939.

[10] *As You Like It* by Helen Gardner, from *More Talking about Shakespeare,* ed. John Garrett, 1959.

[11] Op. cit. My italics.

[12] II. vii. 20 et seq.

[13] III. ii. 282 et seq.

[14] *1 Henry IV,* 1. ii. 1.

[15] III. ii. 285.

[16] *1 Henry IV,* I. ii. 5.

[17] Ibid., I. ii. 12.

[18] 'The Dry Salvages', l. 36.

[19] II. v. 1.

[20] II. i. 5. I prefer 'but' to 'not' here. There is justification for either, though the Folio has 'not'.

[21] II. vii. 174.

[22] II. vii. 111.

[23] II. vi. 5.

[24] II. vii. 110.

[25] II. i. 59.

[26] II. vii. 139 et seq.

[27] 1957.

[28] Indiana U.P., 1968.

[29] II. vii. 86.

[30] In using the word 'subjective' I am not attempting to undermine values and meanings; rather I am emphasizing the importance of subjectivity as a way of perceiving truth, and trying to redefine and revive the stronger senses of the word.

[31] V. iv. 54.

[32] III. ii. 288 et seq.

[33] See William Holtz, 'Time's Chariot and *Tristram Shandy', Michigan Quarterly Review,* vol. v. (Summer 1966), pp. 197-203.

[34] IV. i. 40 et seq.

[35] IV. i. 169. My italics.

[36] *A New Dictionary of the Terms Ancient and Modern of the Canting Crew* by 'B. E., Gent', 1690.

37 e.g. *Romeo and Juliet,* II. iv. 94, *Antony and Cleopatra,* V. ii. 285, etc.

38 V. iii. 24 et seq.

39 IV. i. 177. The same idea, of time as judge, can be found in *The Winter's Tale.* See Chapter 8.

40 IV. i. 130 et seq.

41 V. iii. 14 et seq.

42 V. iii. 35.

43 V. iii. 36.

44 V. iv. 186.

45 V. iv. 130.

46 V. iv. 172, 173.

47 V. iv. 182.

48 V. iv. 187.

49 V. iv. 189.

50 Op. cit.

51 V. iv. 182 et seq.

52 V. iv. 136.

53 V. iv. 102 et seq.

Harry Morris (essay date 1975)

SOURCE: "*As You Like It*: Et in Arcadia Ego," in *Shakespeare Quarterly,* Vol. XXVI, No. 3, Summer, 1975, pp. 269-75.

[*In the following essay, Morris observes the "presence of death" and other "dark ingredients" in* As You Like It, *and examines Shakespeares treatment of time in the play.*]

Some recent commentators have emphasized those features of *As You Like It* that stand as a healthy corrective to the too-readily, too-often applied adjectives of gay, bright, happy, or golden.[1] And yet it takes little critical acumen to remark that Jaques injects a note of melancholy, a forest gloom, into the sunshine glade of Arden, and that Touchstone, as his name warns, holds up measurable quantities of the real world. It now seems clear that it is against the views of Jaques and Touchstone that we must judge those yearned-after serenities in the play, those beatitudes of an Eden that man was believed to have forfeited, of a paradise not yet regained.

What is lacking in these views is an awareness of the degree to which Shakespeare carried the somber counterpoint that underlies the joyous vitality of the world's best garden. True it is that Shakespeare's "mature comedy . . . permits . . . criticism of his ideal world in the very centre of it."[2] And true it is that Shakespeare "dares to speak in Arcadia, where one can never grow old, of Time's inevitable processes of maturity and decay."[3] But the degree of that decay has not been perceived to go beyond a "description of man's final decrepitude."[4] To date, the view we have of *As You Like It* is a composite of two of the most famous pastoral lyrics of the sixteenth century, themselves correctives to each other, but each, by itself, a half view that Shakespeare is able to avoid in the balanced vision that he brings to *As You Like It*. I have in mind Marlowe's passionate shepherd who will all pleasures prove on an unending succession of May-mornings, and Ralegh's cautious nymph who knows that "flowers doe fade," youth does not last, love does not regenerate unfailingly, joys have their termination, and age has its need. Ralegh's nymph knows that "Time driues the flocks from field to fold."[5] But I would like to go one step further to observe the presence of death in the Forest of Arden.

It is pertinent here to recall that Harold Jenkins, like other writers, substitutes for Arden Arcadia—Shakespeare "dares to speak in Arcadia . . . of Time's . . . decay"[6]—for I am convinced that Shakespeare made the same substitution, and that it was especially in his mind when he gave to Touchstone his answer to the magical utterance of Rosalind: "Well, this is the Forest of Arden" (II.iv.11).[7] As her words cast spells about us—spells of shallow rivers, melodious birds, and a thousand fragrant posies—Touchstone, on the instant, sounds the counternote: "Ay, now am I in Arden" (II.iv.12). If we exchange Arcadia for Arden and read, "Ay, now am I in Arcadia," there comes to us the echo, the cadence of the translated words *et in Arcadia ego.*

We are reasonably familiar with shepherds and their Arcadian contentment, but perhaps less versed in the elegiac notes that sound in the motto *et in Arcadia ego.* Unfortunately, the phrase has not been discovered earlier than the 1620s when the painter Guercino used it in a canvas shown to be a forerunner of Nicolas Poussin's famous painting.[8] Shakespeare wrote *As You Like It* no later than 1600, leaving us with approximately a quarter-century in which we cannot prove the existence of the phrase. But for the words to find such ready employment in the sister art of painting as a piece of tombstone verse argues an earlier existence. At least we may hypothesize that many a tomb now crumbled carried the legend borrowed by both Guercino and Poussin within approximately ten years of each other.[9]

Present in the Poussin painting are shepherds stopped in their pastoral joys by coming upon the tomb of an earlier inhabitant, an experience that has cast them into somber contemplation; present is the phrase upon the tomb, *et in Arcadia ego;* and present surmounting that tomb is the *memento-mori* icon, a skull.[10] In the Guercino painting are all these elements plus one lacking in Poussin's: Erwin Panofsky calls our attention to a mouse gnawing the skull the shepherds come upon: "a time-honoured and very well-known symbol for all-devouring time."[11]

We have, then, in a painting coming some twenty-odd years after the composition of *As You Like It,* a pastoral setting of great loveliness, peopled by youths of great beauty; the youths may be presumed to be leading idyllic existences, yet they have been brought to a moment of harsh reality by a tomb, a skull, and a symbol of time which tells them that their youth, beauty, and love will not last forever, that underneath the stonepile lies a dead shepherd who was once also in Arcadia. To quote Panofsky, "Death himself . . . stops the shepherds and sets them thinking with the awful warning: 'I hold sway, even in Arcadia.'"[12] If we can believe that the *memento-mori* elements, as put together by Guercino and Poussin, were commonly available before 1623, in fact before 1599, and thereby ready to Shakespeare's hand, we can show a thread that runs through *As You Like It* enforcing the theme found both in the Italian painting and in the French.

"Ay, now am I in Arden." If in these words of Touchstone we hear echoed *et in Arcadia ego* and believe death consequently introduced into the pastoral landscape, we should expect to find thereafter the other elements of the Guercino and Poussin paintings: all-devouring time, the *memento-mori* image, the dead shepherd who once like the others lived in Arcadia, and finally the somber meditation that youth, beauty, and love must fade even as men themselves.

But to find these dark ingredients in *As You Like It* we must do more than rehearse well-known features of the play such as Jaques's role as a conventional Elizabethan stage-malcontent or as a classic case of the Burtonian melancholic; we must do more than point out the very real enemies to joy, such as the double attempt at fratricide in which Oliver tries to dispatch Orlando and then Duke Frederick marches upon Arden with a host "purposely to take / His brother here and put him to the sword" (V.iv.149-50). We must do more than show that not every Jack has his Jill in this bright, gay comedy which concludes with as many marriages as any play in Shakespeare. It is true, of course, that William does not get his Audrey, Phebe does not get her Ganymede; and I do recount these matters before moving on, for it is an important part of the argument that the *et-in-Arcadia-ego* theme includes distresses other than death in the lovely garden-world. Unreciprocated love such as William's and Phebe's is one of the chief of these.[13]

Since Touchstone initiates the death-in-Arcadia motif, it is appropriate that he be the agent of time, and he emerges as the contradiction to Orlando's claim that "There's no clock in the forest" (III. ii. 286-87). Although the "dial" he pulls "from his poke" may not be a clock, it is nevertheless a timepiece that gives the lie direct to all young lovers who would have time stand still in order that their love, youth, and beauty may remain always at the golden moment:

> "It is ten o'clock.
> Thus we may see . . . how the world wags.
> 'Tis but an hour ago since it was nine,
> And after one hour more 'twill be eleven;
> And so, from hour to hour, we ripe and ripe,
> And then, from hour to hour, we rot and rot;
> And thereby hangs a tale."
>
> (II. vii. 22-28)

The hours are those of mid-morning, approaching the maturation of the day; in a similar fashion, the lovers are in the morning of their lives, just prior to the high-noon maturation of marriage. But the clock will not stop, not even in Arden; and the real impact, the shock that brings us up short, is not the image of maturation, the riping and riping, but the image of decay, the rotting and rotting. We should begin to envisage the *memento-mori* image of the skull beneath the rotting flesh.

Jaques, who retells these musings of Touchstone, was so charmed by their wit and wisdom that he "did laugh sans intermission / An hour by his dial" (II. vii. 32-33), joining for once in the prevailing mood of Arden, or Arcadia, joining in the supposedly unbroken joy of the Golden Age. But Jaques records for us also the passing of one more hour, to show that merriment too eats up the minutes that haste man toward decay.

The playwright's concern with time is not limited to these speeches, but may be found throughout the play. The noun *time* appears on forty-three occasions in *As You Like It.* Only two other nouns occur more frequently. One of these is, quite significantly, *man* (80 times); the other noun is *Rosalind* (71 times). The 43 uses of *time* do not include such other nouns as *hour[s]* (18), *[o']clock* (7), *minute* (4), *day[s]* (21), *months* (1), *week* (1), and *year* (11), which are measurements of time and would swell the word-count by 63, for a total of 106.[14]

Jaques's laughter "sans intermission" provides a word-link (*sans*) with the next passage at which we need look, a passage which produces an unmistakable *memento-mori* image: Jaques's seven-ages-of-man speech. Time is the vehicle that carries man to his seventh

The wedding dance in Act V, scene iv of the Bradley University Theatre's 1996 production of As You Like It.

condition, for "one man *in his time* plays many parts" (my italics); and time carries man *out of his time* as well, for Jaques does not end this account with "second childishness":

> Last scene of all,
> That ends this strange eventful history,
> Is second childishness and mere oblivion,
> Sans teeth, sans eyes, sans taste, sans
>   everything.
>
> (II. vii. 162-65)

Glosses on this passage have always indicated that the final line is a description of advanced decrepitude,[15] the lack of teeth and taste to be regarded as literal, but the lack of eyes and everything to be regarded as metaphorical. But if we read the line as modifying "mere oblivion" rather than "second childishness," the description may be regarded as literal throughout. Lack of teeth, of taste, of eyes, of everything then presents the charnel-house skull. For clarification, Shakespeare's image may be compared to Skelton's *memento-mori* lyric, "Upon a Dead Man's Head," where we find

> Deth holow eyed,
> With synnewes wyderyd,
> With bonys shyderyd,
> With hys worme etyn maw,
> And his gastly jaw.[16]

Skelton emphasizes the missing eyes and teeth and gives the general impression that everything else is lacking, including a tongue with which to taste. Shakespeare's image is also like Southwell's:

> I often looke upon a face
>   Most ugly, grisly, bare, and thinne,
> I often view the hollow place,
>   Where eies, and nose, had sometimes bin.[17]

That Shakespeare was familiar with the *memento-mori* lyric has been demonstrated,[18] and that the *memento-mori* object, the skull, was much in his work about this time can be shown by reference to the plays which bracket *As You Like It*. Both parts of *Henry IV*, completed before *As You Like It*, contain *memento-mori* imagery, and both evoke the death's-head at moments when merriment or love-making otherwise dominate the action. In *1 Henry IV*, inserted in the general revelry of the Boar's Head Tavern, is Falstaff's ridicule of Bardolph's face: "I make as good use of it as many a man doth of a death's-head or a memento mori. I never see thy face but I think upon hellfire" (III. iii. 27-29). In *2 Henry IV*, amidst Falstaff's wheezing loveplay with Doll, she wonders when he will reform, and the fat old ruffian quiets her with "Peace, good Doll! Do not speak like a death's-head. Do not bid me remember mine end" (II. iv. 209-10). On the other side of *As You Like It* is *Hamlet*, in which the gravedigger scene may be regarded as an extended dramatic treatment of the *memento-mori* lyric with at least three skulls produced.[19]

To this point we have produced the elements of time and decay as well as the *memento-mori* images that Panofsky has shown to be the ingredients of the *et-in-Arcadia-ego* theme. It remains to discover the tomb and the dead shepherd who lies under it.

The question of the dead shepherd, because of the treatment accorded it by Panofsky, needs some clarification. Panofsky argues that a dead shepherd under the tombstone "could lead to considerations of almost opposite nature, depressing and melancholy on the one hand, comforting and assuaging on the other" (pp. 239-40). For a person to have lived and died in Arcadia "not only warns the readers of the merciless future, but also opens a vision of the beautiful past in that it evokes the thought of a former fellow being who enjoyed the pleasure of life in the same place and under similar conditions" (p. 239). Panofsky appears to accept a further view that interprets the dead shepherd as saying, "'You, who are now happy, are doomed to die' but also 'I, who am now dead, was happy in my day'" (p. 239). And, somewhat strangely in my view, he concludes, "The very idea of death could fade . . . [so that] 'Even in the jaws of death, there may be Arcadian happiness'" (p. 240).

Panofsky's logic (as well as that of his source, for he takes over these views directly from André Félibien [pp. 237-40], a biographer of Poussin) escapes me. I do not see the dead shepherd under the tomb as different in any way from the skull on top of it: mouldered body like bleached cranium says very simply, "Remember man thou art but dust." It is unnecessary to require the dead shepherd to authenticate the joy and happiness of Arcadia, which is evident in the idyllic surroundings and in the youth, beauty, and love of the shepherds who are alive. For a rotted corpse to proclaim that "Even in . . . death there may be Arcadian happiness" works against the whole purpose of the *memento-mori* object, which is to put its observer into a frame of mind which we might represent best through Southwell's concluding stanza:

> If none can scape deaths dreadfull dart,
>   If rich and poore his becke obey,
> If strong, if wise, if all do smart,
>   Then I to scape shall have no way.
> Oh grant me grace O God that I,
>   My life may mend sith I must die.[20]

Any suggestion that removal from Arcadia to Paradise is merely a transfer from one perfect place to another, no matter how true that may prove to be, defeats and thwarts the purpose of *memento-mori* art, which is to turn the mind away from earthly felicity to sober meditation on the possibility exactly opposite: the possibility that the unprepared sinner may find himself transported from pleasant meads to plains of horror.

For Shakespeare, then, to add a dead shepherd to the skull strongly suggests some link between *As You Like It* and the *et-in-Arcadia-ego* tradition, for both the skull and the shepherd are parts of the Guercino-Poussin pictorial iconography. And in choice of his dead shepherd, Shakespeare is perfect: "Dead shepherd, now I find thy saw of might, / Who ever lov'd that lov'd not at first sight?" (III. v. 80-81). By quoting from *Hero and Leander*, Shakespeare glances at Christopher Marlowe. This is a brilliant device, for Marlowe as pastoral poet lived in Arcadia, but Marlowe as murdered poet died in the real world; the playwright from Canterbury ties together all the themes of melancholy in the play. As Marlowe, Shakespeare's "dead shepherd" reminds us that shepherds, poets, and playwrights "all must, / As chimney-sweepers, come to dust." As pastoral poet he reminds us that all golden lads and girls, all famous lovers, rich in youth and beauty, will have only the briefest span of life.

It may still be difficult for some to accept the *et-in-Arcadia-ego* theme because of the failure of the formula to appear early enough in art, in letters, or on tombstones to provide a source for Shakespeare. But in at least two separate pictorial traditions material in plenty demonstrates the presence of a *memento-mori* aspect in the Arcadian dirge prior to Shakespeare. As early as 1490-1500 may be found a distinct variation of *memento-mori* iconography that Horst Janson has called "The Putto with the Death's Head."[21] Shown to be in wide imitation throughout the fifteenth and sixteenth centuries, the Putto with the Death's Head may be described broadly as a pictorial representation that has as its minimum components a childlike figure (the Putto, more often depicted without wings than with them, suggesting a human child rather than a cherub), a *memento-mori* skull, and an hourglass. Frequently an inscription of horrifying import is present, drawing the viewer into an awareness of the brevity of life and of his own imminent decay. A German woodcut dated guardedly by Janson at about 1520-1530 includes a sarcophagus which might prove intermediary in the development of the Guercino-Poussin scene, for the background of the Putto in this print from Saxony is quite bucolic or Arcadian, and the Putto is presented as unnaturally deep in contemplation just as are the shepherds of the death-in-Arcadia canvases.[22]

The significance of these materials for *As You Like It* may be discerned readily in the speeches of Jaques and Touchstone that are central to this essay. In the seven-ages-of-man declension we go from the Putto itself—rendered in Shakespeare's "infant, / . . . in the nurse's arms"—to the skull, Shakespeare's "mere oblivion." From Touchstone's dial we get the all-important infusion of time, dial being Shakespeare's substitution for hourglass. And from the fool's formulaic pronouncement—"from hour to hour, we rot"—we get a variation on all the inscriptions in the pictorial tradition which range from *"L'hora Passa"* in the earliest woodcut adduced by Janson through Latin and German inscriptions (*"Hodie mihi cras tibi," "Heite mir morgen dir"*) to relatively complex *memento-mori* statements such as a 1570 version in an Antwerp print: *"Vigilate quia nescitis diem neque horam."*[23]

An interesting addition to the conventional theme is the appearance in some versions of a young man about which Janson says, "Obviously suggested to the Northern mind by the figures of putto, youth and skull was the idea of the Three Ages of Man, childhood, adult age, and death, just as they had been represented since the late fifteenth century."[24] Shakespeare's expansion to seven ages ends nevertheless with death, for be it the third age or seventh, the last stage was never construed merely as old age or any part of mortal existence, but rather as that condition of man after death and always represented by the *memento-mori* skull.

A second pictorial tradition eminently available to Shakespeare was the emblem book. Again, if we cannot accept in *As You Like It* the full-fledged Arcadian death as it is ultimately manifested in Poussin, we must recognize the minimal *memento-mori* tradition symbolized by the skull alone. The final print in Geffrey Whitney's *A Choice of Emblemes* (1586) displays the skull underpropped by a single large bone. The emblematic tag that surmounts the block—*Ex maximo minimum*—is Whitney's variation for all the inscriptions that take man through a time sequence all the way to decay. But more to our aid are the verses appended:

> Where liuely once, Gods image was expreste,
> Wherin, sometime was sacred reason plac'de,
> The head, I meane, that is so ritchly bleste,
> With sighte, with smell, with hearinge, and
>   with taste.
> Lo, nowe a skull, both rotten, bare, and drye,
> A relike meete in charnell house to lye.[25]

The similarity between Shakespeare's lost teeth, eyes, taste, and everything and Whitney's lost sight, smell, hearing, and taste is clearly that closeness to be found in two writers in the same tradition, the second of whom engages in those variations that keep him from being a mere copyist. But we should note Whitney's series, each item prefaced by the English preposition *with,* which is altered in Shakespeare's to the French *without.*

With the reminders before them all, not only Jaques at play's end but all characters, actors, theatergoers, and readers should think upon last will and testament. "All lovers young, all lovers must / Consign to [death] and come to dust."

Notes

[1] Note especially Harold Jenkins, *"As You Like It,"* ShS, 8 (1955), 40-51; and Helen Gardner, *"As You Like It,"* in *More Talking of Shakespeare*, ed. John Garrett (London: Longmans, 1959), pp. 17-32.

[2] Jenkins, p. 45.

[3] Jenkins, p. 49.

[4] "As has often been observed . . . the seven ages speech ends with a description of man's final decrepitude—'sans teeth, sans eyes, sans taste, sans everything'" (Jenkins, p. 49). But in using this quotation to illustrate decrepitude Jenkins errs.

[5] *The Poems of Sir Walter Ralegh,* ed. Agnes Latham (London: Routledge and Kegan Paul, 1951), pp. 16-17.

[6] Jenkins, p. 49.

[7] My text for all Shakespeare quotations is the Kittredge/Ribner *Complete Works* (Waltham, Mass.: Ginn and Co., 1971).

[8] Erwin Panofsky, "Et in Arcadia Ego," in *Philosophy and History,* ed. R. Klibansky and H. J. Paton (Oxford: Oxford Univ. Press, 1936), p. 233.

[9] See Panofsky, pp. 224, 233, and 236 for the dates of the three canvases under discussion.

[10] There are two canvases by Poussin: one is in the Louvre, the other is in the collection of the Duke of Devonshire. Only the Devonshire painting exhibits the skull. The Guercino is in the Corsini Gallery, Rome. For easy reference the three paintings have been reproduced by Panofsky, facing pages 224, 232, and 233.

[11] Panofsky, p. 233. See also John Doebler, "The Play Within the Play: the *Muscipula Diaboli* in *Hamlet,*" SQ, 23 (1972), 166 n.

[12] Panofsky, pp. 233-34.

[13] See Panofsky, pp. 228-29.

[14] These figures come from the *Oxford Shakespeare Concordances: As You Like It* (Oxford: Oxford Univ. Press, 1969).

[15] See note 4 above.

[16] *The Poetical Works of John Skelton,* ed. Alexander Dyce (London, 1843), I, 18.

[17] *The Poems of Robert Southwell, S. J.,* ed. J. H. McDonald and Nancy P. Brown (Oxford: Oxford Univ. Press, 1967), p. 73. The editors maintain that Southwell is not the author of the poem. See pp. lxxxi-xxxii.

[18] Harry Morris, "*Hamlet* as a *memento mori* Poem," *PMLA,* 85 (1970), 1035-40.

[19] Morris, p. 1037 and *passim*.

[20] Southwell, p. 74.

[21] Horst Janson, "The Putto with the Death's Head," *The Art Bulletin,* 19 (1937), 423-49.

[22] Janson, pp. 434, 438.

[23] Janson, pp. 433-45.

[24] Janson, p. 443.

[25] Geffrey Whitney, *A Choice of Emblemes* (Leyden, 1586); facsimile edition (Amsterdam: Da Capo Press, 1969), p. 229. Subsequent to the submission of this essay, Anne Barton has called attention to the Poussin paintings in "*As You Like It* and *Twelfth Night*: Shakespeare's Sense of an Ending," in *Stratford-upon-Avon Studies 14; Shakespearian Comedy* (1972), pp. 164-65.

Rawdon Wilson (essay date 1975)

SOURCE: "The Way to Arden: Attitudes Toward Time in *As You Like It*," in *Shakespeare Quarterly,* Vol. XXVI, No. 1, Winter, 1975, pp. 16-24.

[*In the following essay, Wilson argues that the journey from Duke Frederick's court to the Forest of Arden, represented by a the shift from objective to subjective time, signifies a "shift in attitudes toward change" as well as the characters' abilities to adjust to the pastoral way of life.*]

In an essay on *As You Like It* published in 1940, James Smith argued that Celia's remark at the end of the first act, that Touchstone would "go along o'er the wide world" with her,[1] might have had "importance in an earlier version, but in that which has survived Shakespeare is no more concerned with how the characters arrive in Arden—whether under Touchstone's convoy or not—than how they are extricated from it."[2] More recently, J. L. Halio has clarified the distinction between "the timelessness of the forest world" and the "time-ridden preoccupations of court and city life" in order to stress the absolute distinction between the two localities.[3] Each of these studies, employing markedly different critical methods, lays an obsessive emphasis upon an obvious half-truth: *As You Like It* contains no mention of the journey from Duke Frederick's court to the Forest of Arden. Each exemplifies a common critical assumption that in *As You Like It* Shakespeare created a structure of contrast and juxtaposition in which a bare minimum of causal and sequential development is present. The most lucid presentation of this assumption is that advanced by Harold Jenkins in his analysis of the play, but it is implicit in most other studies.[4] Thus Harold Toliver's recent discussion of time in Shakespeare's plays, though disagreeing with Halio with respect to the nature of the time associated with Arden, takes for granted that this nonsequential contrast exists.[5]

I should like to argue that, to the contrary, there is an explicit development in the play from the urban polity of Duke Frederick's court and Oliver's household to the pastoral way of life in the forest of Arden, and that this development is marked by determinable transitional states. It is not, as Smith made clear, a geographical progress, but rather a shift in attitudes toward the characteristics of the public world. The public world may, I think, be equated with the polity, while the world of Arden, if not precisely private, is the condition of several private worlds which, freed from containment, find fulfillment there. Halio demonstrated that the characteristics of the public world are predominantly temporal, but he failed to note that the difference in attitude between the polity and the forest was marked by a real shift and not merely a leap. It is a shift, both gradual and sequential, in two respects. First, it is a shift in attitudes toward change. Second, because change is, in the conceptual referent which may be inferred from the play, the inseparable substratum of time, it is ultimately a shift in attitudes toward time. The importance of time in *As You Like It* can scarcely be overstated, but change is the first fact of the play's being.

There is more than one concept of time present in *As You Like It*—which, in dramatic terms, means that there is more than one "time-sense"—and they are not as distinctly opposed, nor as mutually exclusive, as critics have assumed. The first act of the play is pervaded by the concept of time as an objective process in which things come into being and cease. Against this there is a concept of "timelessness," to be sure, but the time-sense of Arden is only partially and misleadingly reducible to it. "Timelessness" here functions largely as an element in the borrowed pastoral tradition and makes its presence felt in the play more as an implicit ideal than as an actuality. Distinct from both of these concepts there is the relativity of time which is not a single concept but rather a series of concepts expressing the specific time-sense of individual characters. It is the interior, private time of individuals which is, primarily, opposed to the objective time of the public world. This, however, is a multiple, not a single or absolute, opposition.

The initial concept of time, as it is found in the play's first act, is essentially the Aristotelian one of time as a "kind of number"[6]—that is, the measurement of objective change. It is, for example, the notion of time which is operative in Book VII of *The Faerie Queene*. There, the Titanesse, in pleading her case before Jove, argues that "*Time* on all doth pray," but Jove (in a plain statement of Aristotelian doctrine) responds:

> But, who is it (to me tell)
> That *Time* himselfe doth mouse and still compell
> To keepe his course? Is not that namely wee
> Which poure that vertue from our heauenly cell,
> That moues them all, and makes them changed be?[7]

Although it is not possible here to reconstruct the whole of Aristotle's doctrine concerning time, certain points need to be made since they have a direct bearing upon the present discussion. In the Aristotelian system, time is not simply the measurement of motion, but also the "condition of destruction" in which being emerges into existence and passes away.[8] Further, it is, as a "kind of number," contingent upon a knowing mind.[9] The internal dialectic of Aristotle's position arises from the constant play between the objectivity of time (as the correlative of motion) and its relativity (as the correlative of a knowing mind). This dialectical balance has, I think, a great deal to do with the concept of time in *As You Like It*. Touchstone's comments upon the passage of time, as reported by Jaques (II. vii. 20-28), are both a statement of the nature of objective time, as it obtains in the world beyond Arden, and, in their quality of pathos and lament, an indication of his inability to adjust to the forest world. If, and when, the time of Arden is reached, it is through losing the concern for (if not the awareness of) change. Thus, Aristotle's argument that "if nothing but soul, or in soul reason, is qualified to count, there would not be time unless there were soul, but only that of which time is an attribute"[10] is of the utmost importance. The subjectivity of time, stressed by later philosophers in the Augustinian tradition, has a firm basis in Aristotle's analysis of time. And *As You Like It* may be looked upon as presenting, through dramatic concretions, both sets of implications in Aristotle's discussion.[11]

The sense of objective time in *As You Like It* gives way to the subjective, or interior, time-sense associated with Arden. This interior time is only partially equivalent to the pastoral concept of "timelessness" as exemplified, say, in the perennial May morning of Marlowe's famous lyric.[12] Consciousness of the interiority of time, however disconnected from the awareness of objective change, is not at all a sense of non-time. I should, in fact, like to go one step further and assert that the sense of interior time which becomes possible within Arden, precisely because it is not correlative to objective change, mirrors a state of mind. It can exist, as a particular reflection of consciousness, only when objective change loses its importance and is no longer marked—but it is abundantly real, as minds and thoughts are real. The time-sense in Arden works outward from the mind rather than inward from things which change, and, indeed, finds its chief external show in the mutual obligations of lovers who keep appointments as duties imposed on them by love. Between these two concepts there are transitional stages during which the characteristics of the world of the polity begin to lose significance and those of Arden to gain it. Hence I shall postulate a period of adjustment to Arden. But it is an adjustment which some characters, such as Touchstone and Jaques, never achieve, and others, like Orlando, do but slowly.

This interiority of time in Arden implies that, in comparison with the time-sense of the polity, Arden will *appear* as timeless and that, within the forest, time will appear as a relative factor, varying from mind to mind. The first judgment is clearly that which the polity makes of Arden, as for example when Charles remarks that the exiled court "fleet the time carelessly" (I. i. 124-25) or when Orlando, bursting peremptorily upon the forest gathering with his mind full of preoccupations belonging to the polity, refers to Duke Senior's court as those who "lose and neglect the creeping hours of time" (II. vii. 112). The apparent relativity of time within Arden has been frequently remarked. Indeed, given Rosalind's observation that "Time travels in divers paces, with divers persons" (III. ii. 226-27), it would be difficult to ignore. H. B. Charlton, for instance, observes that one man's hour "is another man's minute."[13] And Toliver has noted how the lovers "all seek different levels and different ways of adjusting to time."[14] The shift in attitudes toward time which occurs between the polity and Arden is, then, largely a shift from a public to a private standard of measurement in which the latter becomes possible only through the fading into unimportance of the former.

It is less often noted, at least within the same context, that neither Jaques nor Touchstone perceives time as relative. Touchstone's reported comments upon the passage of time (II. vii. 20-28) and his later statement that he counts it "but time lost" to have heard the song which is, in effect, a description of the nature of interior time in relation to love (V. iii. 17-41) are equally indications of his unbreakable commitment to the public world in which time is the conventional measurement of change. Jaques' reflections on the seven ages of man (II. vii. 139-66) indicate a similar bondage to the world of objective time. The fact that Jaques' speech arises out of Touchstone's and is, actually, the conclusion of the latter's hanging tale underscores the similarity of the bondage which they share. Like Touchstone, Jaques cannot lose his awareness of, and concern for, change. Hence his time-sense quickens only to the public standard of objective measurement. Further, the obsession with objective time is consistent with Jaques' character since, as Smith observed, "time hangs heavy on a sceptic's hands, for whom the world contains nothing that can take it off."[15] Jaques is defined, within his dramatic context, solely by his worldly experience—a "nurture" which has cultivated in him a fixed obsession with the sense of public time. Thus, since Jaques is the most articulate spokesman for that sense in Arden, complementing as well as concluding Touchstone's reflections, it is no accident that his speech on time has a complex function in the development of the play's theme.

On one level Jaques' speech is a simple reflection upon the passage of time, since it is within time that the change of growth and degeneration occurs and it is, of course, time which measures this change. Yet, on another level, the distinction between time and change is collapsed and time appears as the source of the objective change (as the Titaness argues to Jove). Traditionally, the distinction had not been a strictly kept one, but exfoliated into a cluster of associations largely related to the Aristotelian concept of time. Samuel Chew has pointed out the manner in which time was considered, in the Renaissance, to be a source (and not merely a measurement) of change:

> George Chapman speaks of the "violent wheels of Time and Fortune" as though they were to be differentiated, as indeed they are, for, properly speaking, Time turns not the Wheel of Fortune upon which kings rise and descend but the Wheel of Life on which revolve the Ages of Man. But the two instruments were easily confused and conflated; and furthermore the Wheel of Life suggests the wheels of a clock.[16]

Time often appears in Renaissance literature as the agent rather than the yardstick of change, as, for example, in *The Shepheardes Calendar* or in Shakespeare's sonnets, as well as in *As You Like It*. This "conflation" of a rigorous philosophical distinction was a part of the Renaissance literary tradition, but it also had its roots in the writings of Aristotle. It is related to the inseparability of a knowing mind from the measurement of motion. Aristotle, at one point, argues that "not only do we measure the movement by time, but also the time by the movement, because they define each other. The time marks the movement, since it is its number, and the movement the time."[17] Thus Jaques' speech exemplifies, in a rich and provocative manner, several aspects of the cluster of associations which composed the Renaissance meaning of time.

Jaques' bondage to objective time, like Touchstone's more elementary commitment, is the reason for, as well as the sign of, his failure to adjust to the world of Arden. The central problem, then, would seem to be that of the process through which certain characters do adjust to Arden and substitute an interior time-sense for the sense of public, objective time—the process, that is, which leads to the full significance of such lines as Orlando's that "there's no clock in the forest" (III. ii. 318-19). This is the problem of transitional stages which criticism, allied to the "Jenkinsian" model of a method of contrast and juxtaposition, has neglected.

The first act quickly and clearly establishes the mood of the urban polity. It is, to be sure, on all counts the "working-day world" of objective change, but it is especially a commercial world of exchange and transaction only somewhat less marked than that of *The Merchant of Venice*. Orlando's initial lines (I. i. 1-27) are strewn with references to types of change and exchange; and some of the same terminology is repeated in Celia's protestation of love to Rosalind in the second scene (I. ii. 17-25). Such words as "bequeathed," "will," "profit," "hired," and "gain" are particularly suggestive of this theme. A second thematic strand is indicated by the sequence of such words as "breed," "unkept," "birth," "stalling," "bred," "feeding," and "growth." This sequence contributes to the very significant theme of nature opposed to nurture which runs through the play—as, in fact, it does in all of Shakespeare's comedies from *The Comedy of Errors* to *The Tempest*. It is not a simplistic opposition equatable to the opposition between forest and urban polity. Nature is given an embodiment in the character of Orlando, and nurture finds its expression in the character of Jaques (about whom *nothing* is learned except what pertains to his education and experience). Hence the dramatic conflict between them goes beyond the clash between "Signior Love" and "Monsieur Melancholy" into a contrast of profound thematic import. When, for instance, Orlando appears as still violently under the sway of the urban polity (II. vii. 87-99), his reference to his "nurture" casts into an ironic relief the little of false nurture that, in fact, contaminates him. Similarly, Jaques' reference to his "humorous sadness" (IV. i. 20) sounds with an ironic twist since it follows straight upon his account of the "many simples" of experience which have gone into making him the malcontent that he is; that is, all the evidence of the play, including Jaques' own account, points to a disposition bred by a certain kind of nurture and not the result of a "humor" or nature. I wish, however, to treat this terminology, in both sequences, as part of the thematic distinction between the awareness of change in the polity and its lack in Arden.

The references to change, and especially mercantile exchange, indicate the degree to which Orlando is dominated by the very polity from which he must escape. Significantly, Orlando's first statement of a willingness to withdraw from the world of the polity is couched in approximately the same language of commercial exchange (I. ii. 194-206) as the speech in which he had lamented his state. The cumulative effect of the references to types of change in the first act is to present the mood of the polity in terms of a kind of bondage to the awareness of change, and, through this awareness, to time. The mood is also created, in part, by the various peripeties connected with the characters introduced in the first act. All the characters (except Le Beau) from the Duke Senior to Charles the wrestler undergo, or have undergone, some change in fortune. Chew has analyzed the intricate interpenetration of the concepts of Fortune, Occasion, and Time in the Renaissance,[18] and it would appear that this interpenetration is operative in *As You Like It,* contributing to the thematic distinction between polity and forest. The changes in Fortune—that "good housewife" about whom Celia and Rosalind argue so lengthily (I. ii. 34-57)—occur in time; that is, they are measurable, or numberable, according to the Aristotelian definition. Even more, perhaps, their very occurrence underscores the passage of time, and the sense that time, as Aristotle noted, is that in which things cease to be. Charles's remark to Oliver that the old Duke and his exiled court "fleet the time" (I. i. 124-25) in Arden serves as a point of contrast to the mood of the first act. It foreshadows Orlando's comment in the second act that the exiled court "lose and neglect the creeping hours of time" (II. vii. 112) and points the way out of the polity toward Arden. And it is pertinent, I think, to note that after Charles's comparison of the life of the exiled court to the "golden world," there follow nine references to the "world" in the first act and, except for Le Beau's "better world," they all refer to the "working-day world" of the polity (as, indeed, does Le Beau's expression by implication). Thus Charles is the first counterweight to the world of the polity, and, though less than a full member perhaps, he suffers his reversal of fortune through his involvement in it.

Once Arden has been presented, with Duke Senior's speech at the beginning of Act II, the case is reversed and the references to the world of change and objective time are always in contrast to the world of Arden. Both Touchstone and Jaques, through their bondage to the world of the polity, contrast to, and force into deep relief, the characters who *have* adjusted to Arden. Similarly, the return, in Act III, to the polity and the idea of forcible seizure of property (III. i. 16-18) contrasts not only the two dukes but also the two worlds. Further, when Phebe, although a native of Arden, shows that she cannot participate in the forest life through her unwillingness to respond to love, Rosalind, with deliberate irony, applies to her the harsh language of the alien commercial world (II. v. 60). But the most important contrasts between the two worlds are made in terms of Orlando. Unlike Touchstone and Jaques, Orlando does adjust to Arden, but he does not, like Celia, do so immediately. Even Celia's remark, "I like this place, and willingly could / Waste my time in it" (II. iv. 94-95), may only indicate that Celia's adjustment to Arden *begins* immediately. "Waste" suggests something of the mood of the polity, as well as an implication that Arden presents to her no more than a temporary way-station. In fact, only Rosalind appears to adjust naturally and at once. Her father, of course, expresses his adjustment to Arden in terms of "old custom" (II. i. 2), which clearly implies a period of transition from one world to the other. Orlando, then, contrasts not only to Jaques and Touchstone but also to Rosalind in the manner of his adjustment to Arden. In so doing, Orlando provides a focus for the consideration of the transition which all the characters, except Jaques and Touchstone, implicitly make.

The dialogue between Orlando and Adam in the second act (II. iii) marks one stage in the transition between the two worlds. Adam refers consistently to the transactions of the public world, but his service is grounded in duty—and hence is unspoiled by any merely covetous motive. It is his gold, the product of his "thrifty hire," which is the link between the false gold of the polity and the true gold of Arden. For not merely does Adam's gold allow Orlando to leave the one world for the other, but it shows him the possibility of duty grounded in love. Adam offers the first statement of what is the chief lesson of Arden and, conversely, the chief obstacle to adjustment to that world. This lesson is simply that duty ought to be founded in love, and perhaps nowhere else (certainly not in the legal, political, and economic terrors of the polity) can it have any true basis. When Rosalind chides Orlando for breaking "an hour's promise in love" (IV. i. 44), her point is that love entails obligations, and the failure to keep them must seem proof that the love is only apparent (the offender being still "heartwhole"). The time which Orlando has not kept is scarcely the objective time of the polity, of course, but rather the interior time of the lover's awareness. This interior form of time characterizes the time-sense of Arden.

A further stage in the transition to Arden is reached in Orlando's attack upon the exiled court, which shows both his sense of duty springing from his reciprocated love for Adam and also his almost total domination by the standards of the polity which he has left. When Orlando says, "I thought that all things had been savage here" (II. vii. 107), he shows, as he does in his reiterated use of "desert," that he fails to understand the nature of Arden. Sword drawn, he has charged in among the exiled court very much as Oliver or Duke Frederick might have done; and the gentle answer of the Duke surprises him. Things are neither savage nor desert in Arden; the fact that they are not is, to the polity-ridden newcomer, a cause of wonder. Orlando's expectations, based upon his experience of behavior within the urban polity, are reversed and shattered as, indeed, they must be if he is to acquire the free disposition which is inseparable from the mood of Arden. The lesson of duty based on love which he had learned from Adam had been a step but not the entire course.

The final stage in this transitional development is expressed in Amiens' song at the end of Act II (II. vii. 174-90). This is the stage of pastoral timelessness which Halio, and other critics before him, noted as the chief characteristic of Arden. But it is, as I have argued, misleading to reduce the time-sense of Arden to mere timelessness. The consciousness of time continues but is transferred to the interiority of the mind's apperception. What is lost—precisely that which makes readers think of Arden as timeless—is the concern for change and objective, public time. Duke Senior's remark that in Arden they do not feel the "penalty of Adam" suggests the nature of this loss. It is, at best, a perplexing remark, and the nearly four pages of commentary in the *Variorum* demonstrate fairly well that it is far from univocal in meaning.[19] I think, however, that it can be interpreted, without wrenching the context, as equivalent to *feeling* the passing of time. The "penalty of Adam" is, presumably, decay within time which, when it is no longer a concern (as it is not in Arden), need not be felt or, in the terms of this essay, perceived. The "seasons' difference" is objective and absolute, but given the attitudes proper to Arden it is not necessary to feel a concern for this change.[20] Thus, before Orlando can join the Duke in not feeling the penalty of seasonal change in time, he must lose his commitment to the world of change and time. This is achieved through Rosalind's playful strategem, and the final break in Orlando's weakening subservience to the world of the polity occurs when Rosalind qualifies his observation that "there's no clock in the forest." There is, she points out, a subjective time—the interior time-sense of an aware mind whose only external manifestation is, like all genuine duty (as Adam had shown), an obligation grounded in love. The lover keeps his appointments simply because he is in love, but in this case the external is brought about by the interior compulsion of the mind and not, as in the polity, the other way round. Ultimately, adjustment to Arden means an interior and relative sense of time, but this final stage implies a prior series of steps to be passed through: recognition of love and the duties which it entails, the breaking down of conventional expectations founded upon the experience of everyday court behavior, and a loss of the acute sense of change and public time which characterizes the polity.

There is, then, a way to Arden. It is not, surely, the kind of way which Smith had in mind, marked by dusty highroads, worn boots, and all the common perils of travel. But it is there nonetheless. It is the way of the mind's journey; a mental voyage of discovery which leads to the recognition of self and the importance of feelings. It leads away from property and *its* appropriate concerns to a new experience of the value of feeling. In some respects it is a process of stripping value from externals, such as property, that might recall the foreshortened voyage of Everyman to the same conclusion. Along the way to Arden, Time becomes not merely the measurement of motion and change, the necessary context of voyaging, but also the symbolic function of each stage of the journey. And, of course, all, save Jaques' return to the world of the polity when occasion allows. No one, I trust, except perhaps a Jan Kott, would find this return from Arcadia ironic. One leaves the play certain that life in the polity will never again be the same—convinced that the lessons of Arden have been real.

Notes

[1] I. iii. 134, *The Complete Works of Shakespeare,* ed. Hardin Craig (Glenview, Ill.: Scott, Foresman, 1961). All subsequent references will be to this edition and will hereafter be given parenthetically following the citation.

[2] James Smith, "As You Like It," *Scrutiny,* 9 (1940), 19-20.

[3] J. L. Halio, "No Clock in The Forest: Time in *As You Like It,*" *SEL,* 2 (1962), 204.

[4] Harold Jenkins, "As You Like It," *Shakespeare Survey,* 8 (1955), 40-51.

[5] Harold Toliver, "Shakespeare And The Abyss of Time," *JEGP,* 64 (1965), 234-54.

[6] Aristotle, *Physica,* trans. R. P. Hardie and R. K. Gaye, in *The Basic Works of Aristotle,* ed. Richard McKeon (New York: Random House, 1941), p. 292; hereafter all references will be to *Works*.

[7] VII. vii. 48, in *The Poetical Works of Edmund Spenser,* ed. H. C. Smith and E. De Sélincourt (London: Oxford Univ. Press, 1950).

[8] *Works,* p. 298.

[9] *Works,* pp. 298-99.

[10] *Works,* p. 299.

[11] It should go without saying that I am not suggesting an "Aristotelianism" in Shakespeare. It does seem, however, that, to the degree that it may be inferred, the concept of objective time in *As You Like It* corresponds to Aristotle's. Probably, the basic notions of Aristotelian physics had as much currency in Renaissance England as they had elsewhere in Europe from the time of Albert the Great—that is, while never incontrovertible, always known. Cf. St. Thomas Aquinas, *Summa Theologica,* Q. 10, art. 4.

[12] Halio, p. 197, believes that "timelessness as a convention of the Pastoral ideal" is the only time-sense attributable to Arden.

[13] H. B. Charlton, *Shakespearian Comedy* (London: Methuen, 1938), p. 294.

[14] Toliver, p. 240; cf. Hardin Craig, "Shakespeare and the Here and Now," *PMLA,* 67 (1952), where an unconvincing claim is made for a general concept of relativity throughout Shakespeare's drama.

[15] Smith, p. 14.

[16] Samuel Chew, "Time and Fortune," *ELH,* 6 (1939), 111.

[17] *Works,* p. 294.

[18] Chew, pp. 103-4.

[19] Horace Howard Furness, ed., *A New Variorum Edition of Shakespeare: As You Like It* (Philadelphia: J. B. Lippincott, 1918), pp. 61-65.

[20] Although Furness sees in the line, "the seasons difference," a further proof of his theory of Shakespeare's "two clocks," I think that this does not preclude the possibility that the line also refers to the objective flow of time (*Variorum,* p. 392). Chew has shown that time was conceived of, by the Renaissance mind, as both continuous—"Time's thievish progress"—and also as pulsating or rhythmical. In the latter case it was associated with the passing of the seasons, the alternation of night and day, the movement of the stars, etc. (Chew, pp. 109-10). Again, Aristotle appears to be the source not only of the relevant distinction but also of its conflation. Thus, Aristotle argues that "as movement can be one and the same again and again, so too can time, e.g., a year or a spring or an autumn" (*Works,* p. 294) and that "if one and the same motion sometimes recurs, it will be one and the same time, and if not, not" (*Works,* p. 297). Hence, while not denying the function of the line in the duration of the action or its relation to the "two clocks," I believe that it can be best read as a comment upon the nature of objective time associated with the world beyond Arden.

FURTHER READING

Alpers, Paul. "Mode and Genre." In *What Is Pastoral?* pp. 44-78. Chicago: University of Chicago Press, 1996.
Classifies pastoral as a literary mode and examines the pastoral characteristics of *As You Like It.*

Calvo, Clara. "In Defence of Celia: Discourse Analysis and Women's Discourse in *As You Like It.*" In *Essays and Studies* 47 (1994): 91-115.
Argues that Rosalind's centrality to *As You Like It* has been overblown and demonstrates Celia's significance in the play through an analysis of her linguistic behavior.

Elam, Keir. "As They Did in the Golden World: Romantic Rapture and Semantic Rupture in *As You Like It.*" In *Reading the Renaissance: Culture, Poetics and Drama,* edited by Jonathan Hart, pp. 163-176. New York: Garland Publishing, 1996.
Asserts that Shakespeare reinvented the pastoral romance mode in *As You Like It.*

Emck, Katy. "Female Transvestism and Male Self-Fashioning in *As You Like It* and *La vida es sueño.*" In *Reading the Renaissance: Culture, Poetics and Drama,* edited by Jonathan Hart, pp. 75-88. New York: Garland Publishing, 1996.
Recounts the similarities between *As You Like It* and *La vida es sueño,* contending that Rosalind and Rosaura, as the cross-dressed heroines in control of their own fates, mirror "the needs of their marginalised male counterparts" Orlando and Segismundo.

Faber, M. D. "On Jaques: Psychoanalytic Remarks." In *The University Review* XXXVI, No. 2 (December 1969): 89-96.
Analyzes Jaques' sarcasm from a psychological perspective, claiming it demonstrates a form of oral aggression.

——. "On Jaques: Psychoanalytic Remarks II." In *The University Review* XXXVI, No. 3 (March 1970): 179-82.
Offers a psychological analysis of Jaques' "ambivalence toward the human community," suggesting that it stems from his fears of being castrated by his father and "becoming regressively involved" with his mother.

Fendt, Gene. "Resolution, Catharsis, Culture: *As You Like It.*" In *Philosophy and Literature* 19, No. 2, (October 1995): 248-260.

Examines the various types of resolutions achieved in *As You Like It* and the different cathartic effects they produce in both the audience and society as a whole.

Grady, Hugh. "Reification and Utopia in *As You Like It*: Desire and Textuality in the Green World." In *Shakespeare's Universal Wolf: Studies in Early Modern Reification,* pp. 181-212, New York: Oxford University Press, 1996.

Contends that *As You Like It* serves as an example of a bifurcated society, one in which a seemingly utopian counter-culture is constructed as a response to the reified power of a public state.

Jefferds, Keith N. "Vidūsaka Versus Fool: A Functional Analysis." In *Journal of South Asian Literature* XVI, No. 1 (Winter, Spring 1981): 61-73.

Discusses the contrasting functions of the Vidūsaka in Sanskrit theater and Touchstone in *As You Like It.*

Kawachi, Yoshiko. "Transvestism in English and Japanese Theatre: a Comparative Study." In *Shakespeare's Universe: Renaissance Ideas and Conventions: Essays in Hounour of W. R. Elton,* pp. 108-120. Aldershot, Hants, England: Scolar Press, 1996.

Compares and contrasts the dynamics of transvestism in the English Renaissance, particularly in Shakespeare's *As You Like It,* and Japanese Kabuki theater traditions.

Mangan, Michael. "*As You Like It,*" in *A Preface to Shakespeare's Comedies: 1594-1603,* Longman Group Limited, 1996, 202-28.

Explores ideas and meanings in *As You Like It* that derive "from the discourses of pastoral, satirical and love poetry, as well as stage conventions themselves."

Maurer, Margaret. "Facing the Music in Arden: ''Twas I, but 'Tis Not I.'" In *As You Like It from 1600 to the Present: Critical Essays,* pp. 475-509. New York: Garland Publishing, 1997.

Discusses two 1763 renderings of *As You Like It*—Charles Johnson's adaptation entitled *Love in a Forest* and Alexander Pope's edition of the text—and their impact on later interpretations of the play.

Orkin, Martin. "Touchstone's Swiftness and Sententiousness." In *English Language Notes* XXVII, No. 1 (September 1989): 42-47.

Analyzes the linguistic factors that contribute to Touchstone's satiric wit.

Stirm, Jan. "'For solace a twinne-like sister': Teaching Themes of Sisterhood in *As You Like It* and Beyond." In *Shakespeare Quarterly* 47, No. 4 (Winter 1996): 374-86.

Examines Shakespeare's representation of sisterhood in *As You Like It* in order to "help us to use the concept of sisterhood in our own teaching, both to introduce texts by women writers and to better understand texts by men."

King Lear

For further information on the critical and stage history of *King Lear,* see *SC* Volumes 2, 11, and 31.

INTRODUCTION

Frequently described as the most tragic of Shakespeare's tragedies, *King Lear* relates the tale of a father and a ruler who loses his family and his kingdom. The play's ending in particular fascinates audiences and critics alike, who can reach no consensus on whether the final scene, in which Lear follows his daughter Cordelia in death, is meant to impart a sense of hopelessness, chaos, and despair, or affirm the existence of love and hope in the world. First performed in 1606 for the court of King James I, critics speculate that there were public performances of *King Lear* prior to this date. It was not performed again in London, in court or elsewhere, unlike many of Shakespeare's other tragedies. The reason for this lack of revival is unknown, although some scholars suggest that the play's depiction of a foolish king and its presentation of the poor as victims of the rich was viewed as too subversive. Although the play was popular enough to be published in 1608, it is also possible that the reason it was not performed again was that the wholly tragic and disheartening ending displeased audiences. In 1681, Nahum Tate wrote a new version of the play which included a romance between Cordelia and Edgar and a happy ending for King Lear. It was Tate's version of the play, not Shakespeare's, that was performed for more than 150 years. By the 1820s, however, Shakespeare's version was restored and in 1838, William Charles Macready reintroduced the character of Lear's Fool, which had been omitted from performances for years.

In fact, the role of Lear's Fool has been the subject of critical debate, especially in the twentieth-century. Unlike the fools and clowns in Shakespeare's other plays, the Fool in *Lear* is more clearly drawn, possessing an emotional depth foreign to Shakespeare's other fools. Bente A. Videbæk (1996) has observed that Shakespeare's other clowns mainly serve to indicate and illuminate a turning point in the play's action. In contrast, Lear's Fool not only serves as "truth-teller" but also is a truly and deeply sad clown. The critic has further characterized Lear's Fool as "a creature whose whole being is founded on understanding of the human condition and pity for those who cannot cope with the harsh realities of Lear's world." Other critics study the way in which the Fool enhances the tragic mood of the play, or his relationship with Lear. Glena D. Wood (1972) has observed the ironic juxtaposition between Lear's actions and the Fool's words. Wood has demonstrated that the Fool's words and actions precipitate Lear's growth and at the same time increase both the irony and the tragic-comic effect in the play. In analyzing the rhetoric of the Fool, Toshiko Oyama (1963) has maintained that through the Fool's use of logical argumentation in his conversations with Lear, the Fool increases the ambiguity of the play's events and thereby heightens the tragic atmosphere and tension.

Lear and Cordelia have also generated considerable criticism. Each have been studied individually, but critics are equally concerned with the relationship of Lear and Cordelia, as well as their relationships to other characters in the play. Alexander Leggatt (1988) and Phoebe S. Spinrad (1991) are, like many critics, particularly interested in Lear's death and how it should be interpreted. Leggatt has used Gloucester's experience as a way, through contrast, of understanding Lear's own situation. While demonstrating Lear's resistance throughout the play to new knowledge, Leggatt has observed that in the Folio edition of the play, Lear is centered on Cordelia as he dies, suggesting, perhaps, that Lear has indeed learned how much he loves his daughter. In contrast, Spinrad has found little evidence that Lear has learned or demonstrated growth. Despite this lack of evidence, Spinrad has argued, audiences grieve at the end of the play. After stressing that Lear's death defies explanation through traditional dramatic or philosophical theories, Spinrad has concluded that the emotional response of audiences to Lear's death is perhaps generated by compassion. Cordelia's role in the play is often examined in its relationship to the Fool's. Richard Abrams (1985) has examined the theory that Cordelia and the Fool were played by the same actor in early productions of *King Lear*. Abrams has cited the theatrical benefits of such a doubling of the parts, as the two characters both serve as Lear's "truth-tellers." Mark Berge (1994) also has linked Cordelia to the Fool, arguing that both characters illustrate the play's theme of dramatic irresolution. Lear and Cordelia, as well as Goneril and Regan, are also studied together in another manner—as a family. Harry Berger, Jr. (1979) has explored the psychological motivation behind the rivalry between the sisters and Lear's division of his kingdom and his subsequent treatment of his children. Similarly, Thomas McFarland (1981) has examined the dynamics of the Lear family. McFarland has noted that in contrast to the family situation in *Hamlet*, Lear's situation is not "flamboyant or unique." McFarland has argued that in many ways, Lear's emotional attitude toward his children is an amplified version of similar emotions other parents might at one time feel toward their offspring. Additionally, McFarland has maintained that the tragic situation is sparked by the tension Lear feels between his role as father and as king.

It is this dual dimension of Lear's character—the fact that he is a king as well as a father—that fuels another area of critical commentary. Margot Heinemann (1992) has stated that too often, *King Lear* is presented only as a personal, family drama. Heinemann has emphasized the political nature of the play, demonstrating that it is as much about a personal loss of power as it is about the fractured social and political affairs in Lear's kingdom. Janet M. Green (1995) also has focused on a more public, civil aspect of this play, discussing its references to legal issues and to judgement, both secular and divine. Green has observed that the repeated references to legal situations in the play tend to heighten the experiences of "heavenly wrath" and "human cruelty" rather than creating the hope for justice or mercy, thus reinforcing the themes of the play.

OVERVIEWS

David Lowenthal (essay date 1994)

SOURCE: "King Lear," in *Interpretation: A Journal of Political Philosophy,* Vol. 21, No. 3, Spring, 1994, pp. 391-417.

[*In the essay that follows, Lowenthal reviews the setting, plot, language, characterization, and themes of* King Lear, *maintaining that in the last scene, the "perfections of king, father, and man" are fused together in Lear.*]

King Lear may be the most tragic of Shakespeare's tragedies. Nothing exceeds in pathos the final spectacle of Lear bending over his dead Cordelia, looking for life in her and then expiring himself. But what should we think of Lear generally? Is he the vain, irascible and doddering old man his critics make him out to be—a view quite close to the one held by his two bad daughters? Why, then, at the end, do we not only pity but admire him as a man of very great soul, a much greater man than the loyal Earl of Gloucester, his lesser counterpart in the play? Is the play named after him only because he was in fact a king or because Shakespeare wanted us to think of him as a king par excellence, a true king, a natural king? Hamlet is called the Prince of Denmark in the title to that play, and Pericles the Prince of Tyre in another, but—apart from the history plays—Shakespeare names no other king but Lear in his titles. What did he mean by this?

And is the play, as often remarked about its ending, intended to convey a sense of hopeless despair in a universe devoid of purpose or meaning? How can we square this interpretation with the admiration we feel for Lear, Cordelia, Edgar and Kent: Do they not qualify the universe in the direction of meaning and goodness?

Along with *Hamlet* and *Macbeth, King Lear* is one of the three tragedies set in northern countries. All the other tragedies are set in the south of Europe: the four Roman, the two Italian (*Othello* and *Romeo*), and *Timon of Athens.* And of the northern tragedies, it alone, like most of the tragedies generally, is pre-Christian in its setting. It may also be the earliest play dealing with Shakespeare's own country, followed by *Cymbeline* and then the history plays themselves.

The Setting

Shakespeare tells us nothing about how Lear became king, about his parents, his wife and past accomplishments, or about events and conditions in other European powers at the time. Whether Britain is geographically the same or different from the later England is not made clear. It is a country at peace with all its neighbors, and of such repute that France and Burgundy have come to court Lear's youngest daughter. It is also without the slightest sign of internal commotion or even dissension—such is the respect Lear has won for his rule.

The religion Lear shares with his society is polytheistic and astral: he swears by the gods of pagan antiquity, like Jupiter and Apollo, and seems to associate them with heavenly bodies. Yet some of the states in the play—France, Burgundy—in actual history arose only after the coming of Christianity and the collapse of the Roman Empire. Similarly, the British aristocracy, with its titles, entailed estates and primogeniture, was linked historically during the feudal period with Christianity rather than with the paganism of the play. For reasons unknown to us, therefore, Shakespeare has mixed together unrelated historical elements, with the consequence that Lear's Britain seems both modern and ancient at one and the same time. As such a composite, it is much more the poet's own fabrication than the Roman plays or the English history plays.

As the play begins, the reader is struck by the parallel—and contrast—between the situations of the old king and young Edmund, Gloucester's bastard son. By law Edmund is Gloucester's second son and would not inherit his father's title and estate. By law he is also condemned, as a bastard, to ignominy, so that Gloucester sends him away for nine years at a stretch, despite claiming to love both his sons equally and, this time, bringing Edmund with him to the court. Edmund challenges these laws and customs keeping him down as merely conventional and against the dictates of nature. His bold soliloquy appeals to nature as superior to human laws and customs. By nature he is equally Gloucester's natural son. By nature, by his natural endowment, he is his brother Edgar's equal or superior. Edmund will therefore use deception, and later force, to remedy the artificial injustice of law and custom. He will scheme to get Edgar's lands: "I grow; I prosper. Now, gods, stand up for bastards!"

The play actually opens not with this raucous invocation but with quiet references by Kent and Gloucester to Lear's imminent division of the kingdom, switching to the subject of Edmund only after their brief introductory remarks on this subject. Subsequently, the actual division of the kingdom takes place, though hardly as Lear planned it, and only then does Shakespeare return us to Edmund and have him give the amazing soliloquy quoted above. In this way the play can be said to open with two related topics, the inheritance of Lear's daughters, and the inheritance of Gloucester's sons. But there are also striking differences between the two cases. Gloucester has two sons, one older and legitimate, the other younger and illegitimate. Lear has three legitimate daughters and no sons.

The play gives us no direct indication of how the succession to the throne would normally take place. Was the eldest son expected to inherit, paralleling Edgar's situation? Could a daughter inherit? And why was Lear able to divide the kingdom in three, as if it were his own to do with as he pleases? One gets the impression that law or custom governed the inheritance of Gloucester's land and titles much more definitely. For neither Kent nor Gloucester seems surprised at the kingdom's division, and when Kent later objects to Lear's actions, it is not to the division of the kingdom as such but to his treatment of Cordelia and his surrender of power to her sisters and their husbands. Even the daughters—all of them—express no shock whatsoever at the division. Goneril, for example, never says or hints that it should all be hers: not one of them ever takes Lear to task for violating law or custom in any part of what he did.

Perhaps Shakespeare wants us to understand Lear's situation, in contrast to Gloucester's, as one *not* bound by law, thus leaving his discretion regarding the succession well-nigh absolute. Does this mean Lear could have bestowed the kingdom on whomsoever he pleased? Could he have given it to someone outside his family, like Kent or Edgar? Yet his attention seems to be wholly and exclusively riveted on his daughters, as if there were no other alternative. Moreover, he treats the lands as dowries—i.e., as traditionally obligatory wedding gifts from parents to marrying daughters to bring into their marriage, and he plainly vests political power (after his original plan for a tripartite division breaks down) in the Dukes of Albany and Cornwall rather than in Goneril and Regan. This makes it unlikely that any one of the daughters, whether Goneril, the eldest, or Cordelia, the best loved, could have herself been designated queen of all Britain. It suggests a traditional opinion or unwritten custom favoring maleness in the ruler, thus qualifying the seeming absoluteness of Lear's discretion in arranging the succession. And the priority plainly given by the law to one of Gloucester's sons over the other shows that age usually was the ground of priority in inheritance. Could Lear therefore have given all to Goneril, his first-born, much as Gloucester was expected to give all to Edgar?

Let us piece together the plan for the succession that the aged Lear has formed. Having already divided the kingdom into three parts, he tells the assembled court that he intends to give each daughter a dowry consisting of a part of the kingdom proportionate in worth to the love she expresses for him in a speech. This idea makes Lear look exceedingly vain and not a little dotty. To show how mistaken this impression is—Harry Jaffa was the first to do it in *Shakespeare's Politics,* many years ago—we must take note of a few simple facts. First, as Lear begins to express what he calls "our darker purpose"—i.e., a concealed purpose—the map of Britain he brings in and employs has already been divided into three parts, just as he said. Second, he does not wait for all the daughters to speak before making his allocations but does so one at a time, after each has spoken. Third, it is Lear who sets the order of speaking by asking his eldest daughter to speak first—i.e., by using the order of seniority in which society would usually grant preference. This leads to his giving substantially equal portions to the two elder sisters, who follow one another, leaving what Lear calls "a third more opulent than your sisters" to his favorite, Cordelia. By the time Cordelia speaks, no other part is available to her: she *has* to get the best third. To this way of treating the elder daughters, Gloucester and Kent had both given testimony at the very beginning of the play. It seems they were shown the map by Lear and expressed surprise only at the equality with which he had treated the two dukes in his division of the kingdom, since they agreed that up to then "the King had more affected the Duke of Albany than Cornwall."

This means that, contrary to the standard interpretation, Lear did not devise the love speeches as a test of his daughters' desert: he had already decided upon the allocations before setting up the contest and hearing the speeches! We are not told where these territorial thirds lay, but it is very likely that the third given to Regan and Cornwall was in the south, near Cornwall itself, and the part given to Goneril and Albany near Albany in the north. The "more opulent" third reserved for Cordelia must therefore have lain in the center, between these two. In an earlier move, before the play's action begins, Lear had in a most unusual action postponed giving Goneril and Regan their dowries at the time of their marriages. This implies that he had devised this scheme for the succession, entailing a "darker purpose," some time before. But the scheme could not be brought to fruition until Cordelia also married—an event now at hand—thus enabling the eighty-year-old Lear to put into place his momentous and much-needed settlement.

Both the Duke of Burgundy and the King of France are there because both wish to marry Cordelia, but the evidence (again per Jaffa) indicates that Lear intended Burgundy, not France, to be her husband. Only Burgundy was told in advance what dowry to expect with Cordelia, and it is to Burgundy that Lear first turns in offering Cordelia's hand. Why should this be, if the King of France was obviously the better catch? Marriage to the more powerful France would have threatened to make Britain a dependent subordinate of France politically. Lear seems to have thought that the danger of placing Cordelia's third between those of her sisters would be sufficiently offset by her link to Burgundy. And he himself would aid Cordelia's cause by residing for the remainder of his life with her alone, rather than shuttling from one daughter to the other, as he ended up doing with two of them: "I lov'd her most, and thought to set my rest on her kind nursery."

The language used by Lear throughout leaves no doubt (here I depart from Jaffa) that what he had in mind was an actual division of the kingdom, and not a temporary or merely apparent division. He explicitly says that he is shaking "all care and business from our age," giving up all "rule, interest of territory and cares of state." He implies that something like a tripartite council of state would give unity to the rule of Britain. When Cordelia herself thwarts his purpose and he disowns her, he divides her intended portion between the other two and invests his sons-in-laws, the two dukes, jointly "with my power, preeminence and the large effects that troop with majesty," keeping little more than his title and a hundred knights for himself. To these "beloved sons" he gives the "sway, revenue and execution of the rest. . . ." It is unlikely that, in this emergency, Lear would give the two dukes more power than he had originally intended to give the three dukes together (including the Duke of Burgundy, whose place in Britain was symbolized by the coronet Lear had on hand for the occasion). We can only conclude that Lear's plan really envisioned the tripartite division of a Britain that under him was entirely united, and that these three parts, as he says, were intended for the perpetual possession of the dukes and their heirs.

What drove Lear to this peculiar scheme? In what way did it necessitate his having a "darker purpose?" What were the alternatives he faced? The evidence in the play seems to warrant four premises: (1) that there was in Britain a presumption in favor of hereditary monarchy or keeping the crown within the family; (2) that women would not have been wanted to take the helm directly; (3) that—as in the case of Gloucester's sons—there was a social presumption in favor of the rule of the eldest, though without any binding authority at the level of the crown itself; (4) that Britain was regarded as a possession of the king's which he could even divide up into separate dowries or inheritances. On the basis of these premises taken together, it would appear that the most socially consistent, if not expected, alternative was leaving all to Goneril, the eldest, or rather, through her, to her husband, Albany. This would mean disinheriting both Regan and Cordelia, just as was to occur in the case of Edmund and does occur, as a matter of course, in all hereditary monarchies. But what if Lear's "darker purpose" and his foremost objective was to pass on the greatest share of his power to Cordelia, whose conventional claim, as the youngest, was weakest of all? Perhaps this is why he chose to avoid the problem of succession directly and instead to couch all decisions in terms of giving dowries to all three daughters.

Lear had no personal craving for public expressions of affection from his daughters. As he himself announces, what he wants to do is extend his largest bounty (in distributing the parts of the kingdom) "where nature doth with merit challenge." Merit is his concern, and it is the challenge or claim to the crown posed by nature in the form of merit—i.e., natural merit—that seems to have moved Lear to the conclusions embodied in his divided map of Britain. It is Cordelia's merit that he wanted to find a way of acknowledging in the allocation, and the "love speeches" were the secret means he had devised to do so. They are set up in such a way that the two elder sisters first praise him effusively and thereby inadvertently commit themselves to the more favorable treatment of Cordelia that he saves for last.

This solution, however, is already a compromise with convention: if merit is the natural standard for choosing kings, why should the choice be confined to his offspring? The compromise Lear arranges is that, among his children, merit should receive its due. Those that have descended from his body (his wife, their mother, is never mentioned in the play) will be treated in accordance with their merit, ability to rule, or excellence of soul. Loving Cordelia, Lear thinks he has found in her a person of exemplary virtue like himself, and he wants her to have the largest and most decisive share in ruling Britain. Dividing the kingdom was the only way of achieving this objective.

This means that Lear preferred dividing the kingdom and giving the best third to Cordelia over keeping it intact and giving it all to Goneril—and this long before he began to think badly of Goneril. But why? Shakespeare seems to have him engage in this radical and highly improbable action in order to indicate the full impact a natural principle is likely to have on the social order. Making Goneril (or Albany) his successor would have had the advantage of strengthening the social presumption in favor of the eldest and thereby bolstering social reliability and stability in the succession generally. This would have been even more important to consolidate on the political level of the monarchy than on the level of the individual aristocratic family like Gloucester's. Historically, the practical alternatives facing monarchies are either hereditary rule or chaos, but Lear does not do what he can to shore up hereditary monarchy and instead undermines it in the name of the principle of merit.

It turns out, therefore, that both Lear and Edmund appeal to nature—to a natural as distinguished from a merely legal or conventional or manmade claim. In Edmund's case, the legal rule working against him is already firmly and formidably established: he tries to break it down. In Lear's case, the legal rule governing succession exists only in an inchoate form and hence is much more open to the impress of what a king of his stature actually decides to establish. Lear can help form the tradition guiding royal succession; Edmund must undo the effect of a tradition already established. Moreover, both appeal to a principle of natural desert rather than age, though with Edmund this principle is understood to be based on manly strength or power, with Lear, on moral virtue in the broad sense. Or—since age can itself be thought of as a natural rather than a conventional principle—we find two natural principles in conflict. Whatever the defects of age as a principle, it has the advantage, for society, of being definite and clear cut. Once cast aside, many more Edmunds will make self-interested claims than Lears. The result will be to encourage injustice and lose all dependability at one and the same time.

Thus, the great question animating this play is whether human justice and political life have a foundation in nature or are merely conventional, and it is this question—applied to the problem of succession—that Shakespeare introduces at the beginning of the play and resolves in the rest. Neither Lear nor Edmund had to invent the term "nature" in the play, for they found it already at hand in their society. But someone had to discover "nature" in this sense. When Edmund exclaims, "Thou, Nature, art my goddess," and ends by exhorting the gods to "stand up for bastards," it is unclear whether he really retains any of the polytheistic beliefs of his society, or is rather clothing his radically untraditional beliefs in the traditional garb of religion. For nature is not a goddess in the ordinary meaning of that term. Nature means the necessary working of things due to their own internal makeup or composition, and it can apply either to particular things, like the nature of men or horses, or to the sum of all such things in Nature. It is distinguished from what men artificially establish, but also from the external will of the gods—from both human making and divine making.

The independent force of nature, taken in this specific sense—and the very word "nature"—had to be discovered by someone at some point: nature is not known to men by nature. In his chapter "The Origin of the Idea of Natural Right" (in *Natural Right and History*), Leo Strauss describes how philosophy itself comes into existence through the discovery of nature, so that the first philosophers were all natural philosophers. Their innovation was to insist on using only man's natural capacities—his senses and his reason—to discover the ultimate causes of things: their nature. This could not occur without a radical rejection of the traditional authority of both religion and society—of their claim to supply the authoritative account of these causes already. Philosophy, when it arises, challenges all authority as such in the name of the truth it discovers about nature, and in the play Shakespeare actually has Lear recapitulate this radical break with the belief in the gods that is presupposed by the discovery of nature through philosophy.

In the play Lear is first shown believing in a combination of the traditional gods and nature. It is to nature that he appeals as he searches for political merit in his successors; it is by the gods that he swears when punishing his "untender" daughter, Cordelia, and then again it is to nature now understood as a goddess (just as in the case of Edmund) that he appeals to bring sterility to his thankless and cruel daughter, Goneril. He seems to be able to believe in both nature and the gods because, in keeping with the tradition of his society, he looks upon the gods as supporting human justice, particularly through their power of punishing injustice. Thus, the gods seem to be both the source of nature and its rulers, and are capable of interfering with its normal working for the sake of sustaining the cause of justice. This dual belief makes it possible for Lear to address Nature herself as a goddess who can interfere with her own natural effects. Edmund appeals to a goddess he calls by the same name but she is really very different. Lear thinks of the gods as making up for weaknesses or defects in human justice, punishing where human justice cannot reach. Edmund, on the other hand, wants to oppose human justice in the name of a natural order centering on his own interests. He believes justice itself to be an artificial or conventional idea, since its concern for others or for the common good goes against the selfishness natural to us all.

By depicting Britain as a place where there is already knowledge of nature and philosophy, and combining this with a religion based on the identification of the heavenly bodies with personal deities, Shakespeare creates a situation something like the combination of biblical and classical elements that characterized medieval society all the way through to his own day. What Shakespeare sets forth in *King Lear* is a continuous reflection, primarily occurring in Lear's own mind, on the relationship of justice to the gods and nature. As Lear goes mad under the impact of his elder daughters' ingratitude and injustice, Shakespeare shows him preoccupied with the subject of justice and following a course of philosophical reasoning. He reaches the radical conclusion that justice is lacking not only in support from the gods but in support from nature as well: it is entirely conventional. This agrees with the position taken by Edmund from the beginning, and the absence of cosmic justice that it teaches seems to receive its final demonstration in the deep pessimism of the final scene, where Cordelia is needlessly murdered and Lear dies over her. But is this what Shakespeare sought to convey in the play? Is it even what the last scene teaches? Does Shakespeare agree with Lear in thinking justice conventional? If not, on what basis can he think otherwise, and why does the play seem to reach a conventionalist conclusion?

Fathers, Gods and Kings

To compromise his brother, Edmund writes himself a letter, claiming it came from Edgar, in which he calls for the overthrow of their father's "aged tyranny." He tells his father that he has even heard Edgar maintain "that sons at perfect age and fathers declin'd, the father should be as ward to the son, and the son manage his revenue." In a parallel to this, shortly after Lear has begun his visit with Goneril, she determines to be severe with him:

> . . . Idle old man,
> That still would manage those authorities
> That he has given away! No, by my life,
> Old fools are babes again, and must be us'd
> With checks as flatteries, when they are seen abus'd.

Shortly afterward, the fool tells Lear that he has made his daughters his mothers by giving them the rod and pulling down his own breeches.

All these instances involve an overturning of what seems to be the most obvious order of nature, whereby parents raise and rule over their children and are owed grateful obedience. This overturning puts all of society at risk, since the family is the original seat of authority and perhaps the archetype of political authority as such. In the play, Edmund makes it seem that his brother Edgar wishes to end his father's rule and even his life, whereas it is really he who, beginning with an effort to get his brother's inheritance, betrays his father and makes possible his cruel blinding by Cornwall. Similarly, Lear, having rashly and wrongly disowned Cordelia, finds himself cruelly mistreated by his two elder daughters, using the power he has relinquished to them and their husbands. They shuttle him back and forth between them, reduce his company of knights from one hundred to none, humiliate him further by putting his man in the stocks, and, finally, shut him out in a terrible storm.

Filial disobedience and ingratitude have always existed, but as an unfortunate aberration in human affairs and without receiving justification from abstract views. Shakespeare has Edmund express such views, with Goneril and the fool contributing concrete variations of their own. The reason for this is that the coming of philosophy, with its distinction between nature and convention, represents a challenge to even the most sacred and most self-evident authorities, including that of the father. Once philosophy enters the picture, it must be demonstrated why it is that the gratitude and obedience traditionally owed by children to parents are deserved, and other possibilities—including the rule of mature children over aged parents—must be considered dispassionately. The philosophical conclusion may end up supporting tradition—in deep conservatism—but its ground must now be rational proof rather than traditional reverence.

Reverence for parents and reverence for the gods have a clear link to each other. Just as parents create and care for their offspring, the gods, by their operation—Lear calls them "orbs"—generally cause us to "exist and cease to be." They are the first causes of things, and the things they cause are intrinsically dependent on them. Together, parents and gods introduce into society a marked disposition to favor the old—not only older parents but old people, older generations, and old ways generally. Both Lear and Edmund challenge this domination of the old—challenge Lear's own authority as an old father, an old man and an old king—when they appeal to nature and natural merit as against tradition and convention. According to the principle of natural merit taken by itself, Lear's view of it would indicate that perhaps an intelligent young son *should* rule over his old and foolish father, just as Edgar does when he undertakes to guide the blind Gloucester. He should do so *for* his father's good, and Edgar does so far more wisely than Gloucester could have, left to himself. But by Edmund's view of nature and merit, the young should rule over the old for their own good, as he attempts to do throughout. In the play as a whole, the overall change that occurs in Britain from beginning to end is a change from the rule of the very old—Lear is an octagenarian—to the rule of Edgar, a young man of the highest quality, who can be expected to reign justly and wisely and who wisely begins his reign by paying apt tribute to the old: "The oldest hath borne most; we that are young shall never see so much, nor live so long."

Between the customary authority of fathers or parents and the authority of the gods stands the authority of kings or rulers. Lear's conception of kingship does not emerge all at once in the play, but his original plan for dividing the kingdom is designed to give as much authority as possible to merit—i.e., to Cordelia. This effort for Cordelia is in turn predicated on the notion that a ruler must, above all, be just and virtuous, and so she is, even if lacking somewhat in prudence. It presumes that political rule is for the benefit of the ruled, not of the ruler—in this respect resembling paternal power. It requires of the ruler a nature that commands respect and is capable of command generally, all directed toward the common good. This is why the play takes an interest in the question whether there are any kings by nature—i.e., whether human life is well provided for not only through punitive justice but through just rule and proper authority of all kinds. As part of this interest, Kent, in disguise, tells Lear that "you have that in your countenance which I would fain call master," and upon being asked by Lear what that is, replies "Authority." To him, Lear is a natural king and deserves to be not only obeyed but admired and served. As Lear's madness and his understanding simultaneously deepen, he pursues this question of natural kingship further, at one point affirming that he himself is "every inch a king," yet immediately contradicting this idea by denying that royal authority amounts to anything more than a farmer's dog barking at a beggar. Which view is true?

When Lear is mistreated by his elder daughters, his reactions vary in adopting the different perspectives of father and king. It is as their father ("So kind a father!") that he feels the greater sorrow and anger, unable to comprehend their cruel ingratitude after he treated them so well and had just given them all. But he is almost equally sensitive to derogations from his majesty, marks of disrespect, having to plead where before he could command. Over the issue of the conduct and number of his knights, he curses Goneril and sets out for Regan's, perhaps with less hope than he expresses. By the end of Act I, helped by the fool's bitter jests, he has already regretted surrendering his power to these daughters, and recognized that his disowning Cordelia was the originating point of this folly: "O' Lear, Lear, Lear! Beat at this gate, that let thy folly in and thy dear judgment out!" Already, so early in the play, he fears going mad and begs "sweet heaven" to keep him from going mad. By the end of Act II he has been confronted and humiliated by both daughters together in Gloucester's castle. Again he appeals to the gods: "O heavens, if you do love old men, if your sweet sway allow obedience, if yourselves are old, make it your cause; send down, and take my part!" Torn between wanting to be patient and wanting vengeance, he begs the gods as a "poor old man" for patience, yet also wonders if they have caused his daughters' ingratitude. He asks to be touched by "noble anger" and helped to avoid weeping. Refusing to weep, and threatening to avenge himself on these "unnatural hags," he again fears losing his sanity: "O, Fool! I shall go mad!"

By appealing to the gods as a poor old man and father, rather than as a king, Lear chooses what he must instinctively sense to be the firmer ground. Being an old father is a natural and enduring condition, whereas being a king is something that can happen and unhappen. While retaining the title of king, Lear had in fact given up his royal power, but he did not and could not give up his status as a father and what was owed to him by his daughters. And this, of course, is the bond that most affects the audience—one they have all experienced and sense to be both natural and of the greatest moment. Nevertheless, something of Lear's case is lost when he forgoes arguing as a king and even, at times, as a progenitor, for these functions liken him more fully to the gods than the "oldness" he stresses. Symbolically, however, the challenge to "oldness" mounted by Edmund, Goneril and Lear himself—a challenge to all old things, including custom and tradition—provides the setting for the philosophizing Lear himself soon engages in as he descends into madness. In short, something like the original birth of philosophy is enacted before our eyes, but in a disguise that keeps us from recognizing it as such. It is amazing to discover how much of the play parallels Strauss's account of how the idea of natural right originated.

By the beginning of the great storm scene in Act III, Lear has more than regained whatever moral ground he had lost at the beginning of his rash and cruel dismissal of Cordelia and Kent. The depth of his love for Cordelia has not yet shown itself full force, but he plainly regrets his injustice to her. We are impressed, moreover, by Kent's returning in disguise to serve his master, and all the more because of Kent's independence of mind: it is a deed that speaks as well of his master as of himself. We begin to cringe at the fool's almost merciless sarcasm at his master's expense, and cannot but wonder how Lear can tolerate it and preserve his attachment to the fool throughout. Of course we sympathize most strongly with Lear's suffering at the hands of his elder daughters and begin to appreciate the grandeur, as well as the confusion, of his soul. Thinking back, we realize that his explosion at Cordelia was not simply the result of egotism or even irascibility. It was caused by great love combined with sudden frustration at seeing his elaborate scheme—itself animated by preference for her—destroyed by her unanticipated obstinacy.

By the end of Act II, then, we are prepared to concede, from watching Lear in action, what the situation in Britain originally implied. Far from being a man of selfish vanity, feeble intelligence and uncontrollable anger, Lear is cast in the heroic mould. He is usually not impulsive, not even given to anger, and certainly not vain. Until then he has combined wisdom with power, and that is why he has no enemies at home, is so well loved and respected by all those who count, and enjoys such standing abroad. His misfortune stems as much from the artificial complication of his scheme and his misunderstanding of his daughters as it does from his inordinate anger at Cordelia. "He always lov'd our sister most," is all that Goneril and Regan can hold against him, but they do not complain of abuse or neglect. They concealed their vices so long as their father had gifts to give and power to awe; Cordelia, whose virtue he had recognized and loved, had perhaps not yet had occasion to show the contempt she had for her sisters and her inclination to push virtue itself to an imprudent extreme.

"Reason in Madness": The Storm Scene of Act III

Let us now follow Lear's words in the storm at night, as he thinks about his daughters' injustice and his own suffering. First he urges the wind, rain, lightning ("thought-executing fires"—i.e., lightning that executes the thought of Zeus) and thunder to put an end to "ingrateful man." Unlike his children, these elements owe nothing to him and so can subject him to what they will without doing injustice. Yet they seem also to be in alliance with his daughters against him, despite his age and weakness, and are therefore unjust, since the daughters, after all, are safe inside Gloucester's castle while he is made to feel the full brunt of the storm outside.

Lear calls upon himself to be patient, without complaining, and then finds another way of justifying the gods: they must be using this dreadful storm to terrorize undetected criminals and make them beg for mercy. But in that case Lear himself need not fear: "I am a man more sinn'd against than sinning." At this point he turns sympathetically to the fool—"my boy"—and worries about *his* feeling cold, showing this innate concern for others, just as Kent tries to get him to some shelter in a hovel, showing the same concern.

On approaching the hovel, Lear still hesitates to enter, claiming that the "tempest in my mind" over his daughters' ingratitude keeps him from feeling the tempest of the storm battering his body. "Filial ingratitude! Is it not as this mouth should tear this hand for lifting food to't?" He is struck by what an inversion of nature is to be found in such ingratitude, but he will "punish home," suggesting that their punishment lies in his own hands and not in those of the gods. Meanwhile, urged by Kent to enter the hovel, Lear makes sure the fool enters first and then utters a prayer, as he calls it, for the houseless and unfed poor "that bide the pelting of this pitiless storm." He himself, he confesses, had not thought enough of the sufferings of the poor. He goes so far as to command those in "pomp"—the wealthy and powerful—to expose themselves to what poor wretches feel and bestow their surplus on them in order to "show the Heavens more just." With this reflection, Lear has taken his mind off himself and ceased thinking of the storm as a divine means of detecting or punishing criminals and sinners. Storms cannot be conceived as moral instruments, since their victims are the innocent even more than the guilty. Those mainly hurts are the poor, best helped not by prayer to the gods but by pleas to the wealthy, who in helping the poor "show the heavens more just."

At this point the almost naked Edgar, disguised as Tom o' Bedlam, is discovered in the hovel. Raving like a devout man, he speaks as if the world is ruled not by a good god or gods but by the "foul fiend," and even gives his own counterpart of the Ten Commandments. He tells Lear he has led a life of sinful pleasure, but Lear seems not to hear and to be considering only Tom's uncovered body. At first he thought Tom's penury must have been caused by the ingratitude of unkind daughters, like his own misery: "Could thou save nothing? Wouldst thou give 'em all?" Perhaps it was even a "judicious punishment" (without saying by whom) for having begotten such "pelican" daughters. But now Lear is struck by the contrast between naked Tom and the "three of us" (Lear, Kent, and fool) who are clothed and therefore "sophisticated." "Thou," Lear says to Tom, "are the thing itself; unaccommodated man is no more but such a poor, bare, forked animal as thou art"—whereupon he starts to strip off his own clothing (these "lendings"), obviously to make himself like Tom.

Let us try to reconstruct the unspoken movement of Lear's thought here. Why am I suffering the ingratitude and injustice of my daughters? The storm is not an instrument of the gods for punishing the wicked. In fact, the cause of human wickedness is in men themselves, for they have departed from nature. Man is essentially, or by nature, a simple animal without clothing, possessions or power—unsophisticated—and hence without the possibility of having unkind daughters. The source of human unhappiness and evil is what man adds to his nature, complicating and corrupting it, and, of these inventions and conventions, clothing is the perfect symbol. Stripping himself of his clothing—for now Edgar's being close to nakedness is a sign not of poverty but of natural purity—is Lear's way of regaining nature and undoing the evil man himself has caused.

So after Edgar gabbles about assorted evils caused by the foul fiend, about the awful things he eats and about the prince of darkness—thus presenting a view of the world as dominated by evil rather than good powers—Lear responds to Kent's "How fares your Grace?" with "What's he?"—i.e., by dismissing "your Grace" as a merely conventional title that has no place among natural things. And when Gloucester, acting against Lear's daughters' commands, seeks to bring his king out of this "tyrannous night" to a place where food and shelter are ready, Lear speaks the most amazing lines in the play: "First let me talk with this philosopher. What is the cause of thunder?"

It is to Tom that Lear turns when he speaks these lines, for he has mistaken him for a philosopher. Why? And what does his question signify? Again we must seek the unspoken train of thought. Tom is natural man—man prior to the influence of inventions, conventions and traditions. Philosophy is the exercise of human reason, challenging all accepted beliefs as such and seeking knowledge of nature—of the nature of all things, and the causes of them all. What is more plausible than to believe that this natural man would be in touch with nature or have a natural understanding of nature? For it is nature that Lear himself has discovered in his question, since simply asking the cause of thunder is to doubt what he and his society have always believed—that Jupiter is the cause of thunder, that both lightning and thunder are the "thought-executing" effects of a god, or that beings mentally akin to human beings are the directing causes of all things. It is to attribute the cause of thunder to forces inherent in or natural to the material world. Thus, when a few moments later Lear says to Tom, "Let me ask you one word in private," we can guess what that word must be, and why the question must be private. In all likelihood, Lear will ask whether the gods exist or, better, just what the fundamental cause of things really is. It is a question that cannot be asked openly or publicly if religion is essential to ordinary human life. And to show that introducing the idea of philosophy at this point was hardly accidental, Shakespeare has Lear invoke its Greek origins by his references to Tom as "this learned Theban" and "good Athenian," and identifying him twice more as a philosopher.

If one had to choose a single place in Shakespeare's plays that proves he wrote more for the study than the stage, for serious private reflection than theater viewing, this is it. Here we find no dramatic interest whatsoever. Nothing happens, no action, passion or perception: the plot stands absolutely still. For this reason, the critics (apart from Harry Jaffa, the first to draw attention to this point) have produced practically no commentary on the lines, which simply baffle them. But if *King Lear* is a play about Lear's mind and soul, as everyone has to admit, a failure to note the importance of these lines, and what has been happening inside Lear to cause them, is to miss and misunderstand the heart of the play. By making Lear grow increasingly rational as he grows increasingly mad, Shakespeare has him reenact the coming into existence of philosophy in sixth-century Greece.

Earlier in the play Shakespeare had even pointed us back toward the earliest philosophy of nature by twice citing playfully the fundamental maxim of these pre-Socratic philosophers, as we call them. When Cordelia first tells Lear that she will say nothing to express her love for him, he replies: "Nothing will come of nothing," meaning, in the context, that she will receive no dowry if she speaks no words. Later in Act I, when the fool asks Lear whether any use can be made of nothing, he replies: "Why, no, boy; nothing can be made of nothing." If the Harvard Concordance is right, this principle is mentioned in no other play, so Shakespeare must have appreciated its unique importance to the rational search for the natural causes of things which was and is philosophy. As Empedocles put it at about 450 B.C.:

> From what in no wise exists, it is impossible for anything to come into being; and for Being to perish completely is incapable of fulfillment and unthinkable . . .

This basic idea—that something must come from something and not from nothing, and cannot in turn become nothing—has often been regarded, quite properly, as the premise of all natural investigation, whether we call it philosophy or science. Rational inquiry into the cause of thunder can only proceed after the idea of its originating with Zeus has been discarded. In the play, natural philosophy as an undertaking seems already to have been known in Britain, just as the word "nature" was known and had even become part of common parlance there. Gloucester actually refers to and rejects the "wisdom of nature" (meaning this very natural philosophy) that can "reason it thus and thus" about solar and lunar eclipses—a wisdom, in short, that refuses to believe them to be the omens of imminent human disorders that (as he thinks) they really are. Privately, Edmund makes fun of his father's superstitious belief that the heavenly bodies determine our character and fate, but in front of Edgar he acts as if their father's belief is also his own, drawing from Edgar the criticism implied in the question, "How long have you been a sectary astronomical?" (we would say "astrological").

So, while Lear was probably expressing the generally accepted religious view when he spoke of the "operation of the orbs from whom we exist and cease to be," it does not seem to have been customary at the time to extend this view, as Gloucester does, into an overall deterministic astrology. The gods were expected to influence and intervene into human affairs, but it did not necessarily follow that their role as heavenly bodies or orbs determined the whole course of every life. And it is Gloucester's credulously taking recent eclipses as omens of disorder and divisions in human life that makes him susceptible to Edmund's lies about his brother's hostility to him. Gloucester remains pious and credulous throughout, but Lear leaves his piety far behind.

Having entered the farmhouse provided by Gloucester, Lear is still preoccupied with his bad daughters: "To have a thousand with red burning spits come hissing in upon 'em. . . ." He is thinking of how he might bring about their suitable punishment, but he will now rely on armed men rather than on the gods, which seem to be the only recourse left to him. Then something must tell him that it would be unjust to punish his daughters without a trial, and his next words are: "It shall be done; I will arraign them straight." So, guided by what looks like an inherent or natural sense of justice, but relying on the conventional device men have invented to administer justice, Lear appoints a bank of judges consisting of Tom, the fool and Kent. He arraigns Goneril first, charging her with kicking the poor king, her father—an apt physical metaphor for her mistreatment of him and very similar to an action Aristophanes attributes to the influence of Socrates in *The Clouds*. But Lear imagines that Regan escapes, due to corruption in the court—i.e., to a weakness in human institutions for enforcing justice, and after this comes his pathetic reflection, "The little dogs and all, Tray, Blanch and Sweetheart—see, they bark at me." Not only do his daughters, failing to recognize him as their father and king, treat him with such cruelty, but even his own little dogs (he imagines) fail to recognize him as their old beloved master and bark at him, baring their fangs as they would at a stranger.

Lear's final remark in the farmhouse returns to the theme of natural philosophy: "Then let them anatomize Regan; see what breeds about her heart. Is there any cause in nature that make these hard hearts?" This presumes that Regan's hardness of heart has a physical cause not endemic to civilized life itself, as his pondering of the appearance of Edgar (as Tom) had led him to conclude before, but peculiar to her own body. Thus, in place of explanations given in moral or religious terms, Lear looks for a natural cause in the most physical sense. He seems to have replaced the notion of mind and soul, divine or human, with that of matter, dismissing the idea of a divine superintendence of the world for the sake of justice. On the other hand, he still seems to harbor the belief that "these hard hearts" are an exception to the general rule of nature, which favors softer hearts or justice.

Before proceeding further, we should comment on the connection between Lear's mental wanderings and the physical circumstances surrounding him. A great storm is taking place in nature, and amid this storm Lear is losing his mind: two similar occurrences, both showing a departure from the harmony of nature. Lear tries desperately not to go mad. He has always been in control of himself, patient in the face of sorrow and suffering. But the majesty of his character, combined with the magnitude of his mistreatment by his daughters (and perhaps with his own awareness of having mistreated Cordelia) derange his mind. The chaos of this storm of unparalleled proportions matches the chaos of his mind, or so it seems, and together they absorb us so completely as to make us forget that the normal human condition is one of sanity and the normal condition of nature one of good, or at least non-stormy, weather. The harmony of nature—this goodness of nature—seems difficult to upset and plunge into a great storm, and the human mind even more difficult to render irrational, its proper nature being to remain in control of itself. In this respect, philosophy, by its attainment of truth, may be said to bring the mind into its fullest and most stable possession of itself and thereby to provide its natural perfection or greatest health. It is, intrinsically, the very hallmark of sanity, not madness.

"Reason in Madness" at Dover: Act IV

As Lear is about to fall asleep in the farmhouse, Gloucester comes urging him to flee for his life and providing him with a litter to take him to Dover, where Cordelia's army has landed. "Oppressed nature sleeps," says Kent. "This rest might yet have balmed thy broken sinews. . . ." But Lear is permitted no rest, and, subjected to the further motion of flight, not only remains mad but extends his reason-in-madness when we see him at Dover. The first report of his presence there comes from Cordelia. Having evidently escaped from Kent and his litter-bearers, Lear has fashioned himself a crown of weeds to show he is a king by nature and not merely by convention, for unlike flowers or grains, weeds grow spontaneously without cultivation by man.

The scene in the storm outside Gloucester's castle had ended with Lear's giving up on the gods, turning to original nature as his principle, realizing that his wicked daughters must be brought before the bar of human justice to receive their punishment, and then wondering whether there are physical causes of evil itself. At Dover, conceiving of himself as a natural and not merely conventional king, Lear begins by saying: "No, they cannot touch me for coining; I am the king himself," adding "Nature's above art in that respect." What he means is something like this: wearing an ordinary crown makes a merely conventional king guilty of counterfeiting ("coining"), since he is counterfeiting being a king, but he, Lear, is a natural king, a real king, and hence superior to any artificial or conventional king whatsoever. Nature *is* above art in that respect!

His next series of disconnected remarks form a pattern by their reference to activities he associates with kingship, and, except for one, pertain to the practices, attitudes and skills of war. They take it for granted—so obvious must it have seemed to Lear—that the defense of society against attack is the first requirement of political life. This priority of the military also accounts for his symbolic attachment to his knights, his continuing to hunt, even at the age of eighty, and his proud claim toward the end of the play that were he younger he would have done more than kill Cordelia's executioner: "With his good biting falchion" he would have made him skip. The only break in the military pattern of these remarks comes with the mystifying "Look, look, a mouse! Peace, peace, this piece of toasted cheese will do't." Is this meant to show Lear's gentler side—perhaps reliving a child's surprise at seeing a mouse and wanting to lure it out—or are his quieting call of "Peace, peace" and the toasted cheese just clever ways of catching a mouse? We do not know, but this is the only context in which he mentions peace.

Next Lear dwells on the flattery to which a king is exposed, even from his youth. He now knows, he says, that he could not really have been wise when he was young (as they told him), that he has no control over nature's great events, and that he himself is not "ague-proof." He recognizes his limits, and of course is a better man—and king—for doing so. In this way Lear seems to be continuing his reflection on kingship: a true and wise king—a natural king—would have to be aware of his own limitations and realize he is not a god.

A moment later, when the blind Gloucester recognizes Lear's voice and asks, "Is't not the King?", Lear replies "Ay, every inch a king!" and goes on to picture the king in his domestic role as the fearful dispenser of criminal justice—of punishment and pardon. But the picture he now presents constitutes a radical break from the ordinary. He will not, he proclaims, have adulterers killed, since lechery and copulation are the rule of nature for all animals, and for women even more than men, despite their outward modesty: "Let copulation thrive." Let appetite be followed and pleasure sought!

Nor are some men truly just and others unjust: no, in the desire to commit crime there is no difference between the justice and the thief, the beadle and the whore. Moreover, the system of justice is always unjust in its application, allowing the wealthy and powerful to elude its net while wreaking full vengeance on the poor. This is why Lear can find in a beggar running away from a farmer's barking dog the "great image of authority": authority has its foundation in fear alone, not justice. And it is also why this natural king, crowned with weeds of his own picking, can draw the grand and most radical conclusion that "None does offend, none, I say, none; I'll able 'em." What better place to have Edgar characterize Lear's utterances as "matter and impertinency mix'd; Reason in madness"?

About this high point of Lear's thinking the commentators have nothing to say. His claim is stated in the most general form—i.e., philosophically: there are no offenses, no crimes, in the strict sense, no crimes by nature, and he himself will so testify in defense of those accused of crimes. But if all crimes are merely conventional, the laws against them must be devised not out of a devotion to justice but—as we may conjecture—because each individual has a selfish interest in protecting himself from crimes, even though his own natural inclination is to commit them if he could do so with impunity. The general teaching expressed here by Lear in this odd manner is so old that it is traceable to some of the earliest natural philosophers—the ones who discovered nature and relied on "ex nihilo" as their first principle.

Shakespeare has already alerted us to that background in the play. He may have known of an expression by Heracleitus to the effect that "To God, all things are beautiful, good and just; but men have assumed some things to be unjust, others just." Heracleitus means that the distinction between just and unjust acts is not in the nature of things but assumed or devised by men: justice is conventional. Almost immediately after this point in the text, Lear imagines a chimerical stratagem to steal upon his sons-in-law and "kill, kill, kill, etc.," presumably killing all in sight, including his daughters. But the stratagem raises two questions: Do his sons-in-law deserve to be killed, even if his daughters do? What about innocent members of their households? Would that be just? Is it not more than a conventional rule to refrain from punishing the innocent? And—so basic to the play—is not Lear's sense, and ours, of the guilt of his daughters an indication that some justice is indeed by nature and not simply conventional? Lear's theoretical understanding, in the manner of Heracleitus, seems curiously at odds with the facts of the play.

It was also Heracleitus who declared that all things are in flux, but Shakespeare distinguishes between harmony and chaos, rest and motion in the natural constitution of things. With rest, Lear's mind can recover its normalcy—while of course losing the unnatural ability with which Shakespeare endows it to philosophize in madness. But nature, and the nature of each thing, consists in the control of motion by rest, of matter by form, and, in men, of matter by mind. The world is a cosmos more than a chaos, and so are the natural beings in it. As Lear sleeps still, Cordelia calls upon the gods to cure this "great breach in his abused nature! The untun'd and jarring senses, O, wind up of this child-changed father!" More conventional than her disturbed father, Cordelia relies on the gods to restore the harmony inherent in our nature by which we are rendered normal and sane. Nevertheless, quite appropriately, it is to the harmonies of music that Lear awakens, restored, from his rest.

Let us see the consequences of mad Lear's having adopted the conventionalist view of justice. According to that view, all men have the same, essentially selfish desires bereft of any concern for others, and unrestrained by any natural sense or understanding of justice. But in that case there are no natural crimes, no natural punishments, no nature-based systems of justice, and—no natural kings! It makes no sense to think of a king as one devoted to the public good and acting justly in the public's behalf—i.e., as a king by nature—if there is no natural basis for his activity. What Lear has done, through his thinking, is to undermine entirely his thought about himself and his daughters. And what Shakespeare has done is to confront us with these philosophical alternatives. If justice is natural, there are natural crimes, natural punishments and rewards, perhaps natural kings as well, and the fundamental injustices and virtuous actions of the play are themselves rooted in nature. If justice is conventional, the distinction between the selfish and the unselfish will prove unfounded, and all apparent justice and virtue will dissolve into selfishness of one sort or another. In that case, the internal foundation of the play itself, and Lear's entire being as a man in pursuit of justice, will collapse and leave no mark. The good and bad characters will fade into each other, and there will be nothing glorious left. But is this what happens in the play?

The Last Act

In no other play of Shakespeare's are the good and bad characters so starkly distinguished as in this one. Goneril, Regan, Cornwall, Edmund (until the very end) and Oswald are rotten to the core. Lear, Edgar, Cordelia, Kent, Gloucester, Albany are essentially good, whatever their faults. Now it is obvious that Shakespeare does not stand neutrally between these two groups. He makes the good as lovable and admirable as he can, the bad as detestable as he can. But on what is this distinction based? Are the good more natural than the bad? Are the bad to be understood as a falling away from or corruption of the good, or the good as a falling away from or corruption of the bad?

For one thing, it is plain that the principle of selfishness, as it operates in the play, not only wantonly destroys others but destroys oneself. Edmund is directly responsible for his father's blinding, for the death of Cordelia, for his father's mortal pursuit of Edgar, for the mutual jealousy of Goneril and Regan, and, finally, for Goneril's poisoning of Regan. Selfishness is inconsistent with the love and loyalty required in social relationships. But this is far from all. Provoked by Shakespeare's presentations, we in the audience love the good characters and despise the bad: there is something in us to which the poet appeals, and which had already to be there in order for him to make such an appeal in the first place. We are angry with Lear for dismissing Cordelia and Kent, while remaining concerned about his future. We too feel how sharper than a serpent's tooth is filial ingratitude. We suffer with Gloucester when Cornwall sets his foot on his face. We love Kent for his selfless service to a worthy master. We ache with Lear as he painfully loses his mind, and delight in the touches of love and sympathy he expresses in the midst of his misery. And as his plight worsens, and his daughters grow more repulsive, we wonder desperately with him what support justice has in the world.

We have these reactions because there are natural experiences in life which we particularly identify with being human. Love, friendship, the recognition of human greatness, pity, reflection occur, to some degree, in us all. Despite the constant truggings of self-interest, good people do not surrender the distinctive content of these experiences. We admire the loyalty of Edgar, Kent and Gloucester, realizing not only that their loyalty is well directed but that it costs them much to be loyal. We recognize a fault in Gloucester when we learn of his having kept Edmund abroad and wince at his credulousness in swallowing Edmund's traducing of Edgar. We see that this weakness in his character should not be there. This judgment derives from the fact that our relationships place requirements on us from within themselves. It is a very warped human being who has no friend or does not love someone and who fails to realize that sacrifice will at times be required of him, even great sacrifice. Are we to abandon our friends and loved ones at an instant? Will it be easy to find friends and loved ones again? Will we think well of ourselves? Would we ourselves wish to be so abandoned? Something similar can be said of ingrates and especially of ungrateful children, who receive benefits without wanting to thank their benefactors and help them in turn, but instead give slights, contempts or harms in return for affection and assistance.

It is to these elementary relationships of parent and child, brother and brother, sister and sister, master and servant, ruler and ruled, husband and wife that Shakespeare turns in this play for his material. While exhibiting some of the complications of ordinary morality, he is anxious to demonstrate its dignity, ground and necessity. By showing both injustice and justice at work, he traces them to their source, and reveals their basis in human nature. In consequence, far from demonstrating the meaninglessness of the universe, and its resistance to justice, the play shows why justice must have a lasting and secure place in the minds and hearts of men. Founded in the social nature of man, justice is conventional only in its forms, while its substance remains fixed and universal. This principle is perfectly consistent with acknowledging that the actual accomplishment of justice is difficult and elusive. Injustice receives its power from the selfishness that resists and thwarts the call of our better natures. Keeping it down depends on the wisdom, justice and power of rulers, who preserve an order in which justice thrives and injustice weakens. When the wicked gain the upper hand, not the principle of justice but its enforcement suffers, with untold consequences for the just and the innocent.

In the last scene of Act IV, when Lear awakens to the strains of music, he cannot believe he is before Cordelia herself, and takes her to be a soul in bliss while he is bound, suffering, to a wheel of fire—for treating her so badly. He want to kneel to her, but she wants him to bless her. He will take poison if she desires him to. He thinks she does not love him, and admits she has some cause to do him wrong, unlike her sisters. To which, in what may sound like a contradiction of the root principle of natural philosophy, she says, "No cause, no cause"—meaning only that she has no cause to harm him. Lear asks her to forget and forgive. Obviously, he has forgotten and forgiven the obstinacy on her part that had occasioned his rage, and she, having forgiven his rage, only wishes for his blessing again. Forgiving the errors of otherwise good people seems, in fact, to be a general trait of good people in the play. Cordelia and Kent both forgive Lear; Lear forgives Cordelia; Edgar forgives Gloucester. This forbearance cements the good people to each other, and either prevents, softens or terminates the harms they sometimes do inadvertently, influenced by passion or error.

In the last Act both Lear and Cordelia are captured by the native forces of Edmund, Albany and Regan. Lear wants only to live in prison with Cordelia, blessing and kneeling to each other, praying, singing, discussing those at court and trying to penetrate their motives, "as if we were God's spies." Even in seclusion Lear cannot help thinking about politics, though now the rise and fall of "great ones" is of little direct importance to him, their fall being as apparent as their rise. His private relation to Cordelia, which he seems to regard as never-ending, has replaced political life in his mind. On being ordered by Edmund to prison, however, Lear's old fighting spirit reappears. As they are led off he tells Cordelia to wipe her eyes: "We'll see 'em starv'd first," before they shall make us weep.

In the interim, with the help of a letter from Edgar, Albany discovers Edmund's and Goneril's deceit, and Edmund is mortally wounded when challenged to personal combat by Edgar, whose identity is then unknown to him. In revealing himself to Edmund, Edgar tries to vindicate the justness of the gods, who "of our pleasant vices make instruments to plague us. The dark and vicious place where thee he (Gloucester) got cost him his eyes." But we may doubt whether this was Edgar's serious view, since he had tricked his father into believing, falsely, that it was the gods rather than himself who saved him from death at the cliffs of Dover. We are entitled, however, to infer from this combat that, without Edgar's success defeating Edmund, the whole story might have had a very different conclusion. Moral superiority is not enough: the good must also be physically more powerful than the wicked. Edgar goes on to tell Albany and Edmund of his and Gloucester's sufferings, and of how Gloucester died after Edgar reveals his true identity, whereupon his heart, "Twixt two extremes of passion, joy and grief, burst smilingly." Edgar also tells of learning from Kent "the piteous tale of Lear and him," and seeing the "strings of life" begin to crack in Kent just as he leaves to fight his brother.

A peculiarity of this part of the play concerns Edmund, who, dying but not dead, is unexpectedly moved by his brother's account of his own and Gloucester's travails to promise that some good will come out of it, but unaccountably waits to act until urged by Albany a considerable number of lines later. Only then, on declaring: "Some good I mean to do, despite of mine own nature," does he tell of his order to kill both Lear and Cordelia, the latter by hanging. "The gods defend her," exclaims Albany, but too late, as Lear enters with the limp Cordelia in his arms, calling upon them all to howl against the heavens to protest her death. "Is this the promised end?" Kent asks, as if there had been a divine promise of a good end to life here on earth. Albany simply exclaims, "Fall, and cease!"—wishing, it seems, that the heavens would fall, and all things come to an end. Kent tries to identify himself one last time to Lear, but his master can think only of Cordelia and himself. For he had just killed the man who was hanging Cordelia, and recalls the much greater military prowess of his earlier days. Not even Kent's news of his other two daughters' death disturbs Lear's concentration on Cordelia. He cannot understand why his "poor fool" should be dead while dogs, horses and rats live on. She'll come no more—never, never, never, never, never. "Pray you, undo this button"—Lear probably means on his own tunic, feeling pressure in his chest—and thanks a man (perhaps imaginary) for doing it. For a moment, he thinks there's some sign of life on Cordelia's lips, only to faint himself and finally expire. Edgar calls upon Lear to look up, but Kent wants him to leave "the rack of this tough world," and prepares to follow his master.

There is nothing so tragic in Shakespeare's tragedies as this scene. To no other hero are we so attached as to Lear—not to Hamlet, or Othello, not to Cleopatra and Antony, not even to Romeo and Juliet, to name only those who exercise the greatest attraction for us. In no other case is the protagonist so admired and beloved by the end of the play, his original fault forgotten, his sufferings so prolonged, and with so remarkable a final display of his virtue. Other good people in the play die too—Gloucester, Cordelia and Kent soon enough—so that the ending has the net effect of producing not only the single going down of an excellent man but a collective going down of the good, thus demonstrating the truth of Kent's calling this the tough world on the rack of which Lear must be spared further suffering. Such is the dramatic impact of the play, but is it its deeper philosophical message?

The picture at the end is bleak indeed, but not without promise, for the succession to the throne has been determined, and Edgar—wise and good Edgar—will be the next king, and of a reunited Britain. As the sole surviving son-in-law on whom Lear had bestowed his power, Albany, in the final moments of the play, returns this power to the shattered Lear for as long as he will live. But on Lear's death seconds later, Albany—without explanation—removes himself from consideration by directing Kent and Edgar together to "rule in this realm." Was it in recognition of their greater service and suffering or of the blemishes he himself bore from his connection with Goneril? In any case, Kent expresses his intention to follow his master into death soon, and Edgar is left to accept the "weight of this sad time" and have the last word, remembering the sufferings of the old: ". . . we that are young shall never see so much, nor live so long."

While it is true that Lear's own dying picture of the world is as bleak as can be, is it Shakespeare's too? Or is it meant to provoke in us a reaction in terms of the play as a whole that goes beyond what the dying Lear can feel and see? Lear accuses the world of injustice: his wonderful daughter, Cordelia, is dead, gone forever, never to return. He wants heaven's vault to be cracked by the howls of men—though without specifically mentioning the gods—and even calls everyone else murderers and traitors for not helping to save her. Why should dogs, horses and rats have life but not Cordelia? But is it against her being murdered or against her mortality itself that Lear rails? He obviously feels there is no moral superintendence of the world, whether divine or natural. Life seems irrational: it doesn't care about men as compared to rats, or good men as compared to bad. But Lear's complaint goes too far, for if the world deserves blame for not preserving the life of Cordelia, it must get credit for producing her in the first place. And if men must die while rats still live, it is nevertheless true that the statement itself assumes, and testifies to, the lasting superiority of men to rats. Even so, would the world be improved if all horses and rats were to die before or along with Cordelia? And while every being is unique, will there not be other Cordelias, just as the case of Edgar shows there can be other Lears?

Moreover, the very sense of injustice by which Lear and we are gripped at the end testifies to the goodness with which we are endowed by nature, for it is nature itself that cries out at those features of the world allowing injustice, or failing to sustain the good. Praise arises out of our very condemnation, for the world that kills a Cordelia unjustly has given us the means of recognizing this injustice, and sometimes of averting or punishing injustice, and must therefore be weighed accordingly. As for our mortality, and hence the perishability of all good things and bad, this sad fact is a condition of nature that we must learn to accept, for without it nature is impossible, and therewith all the good things nature produces, as well as its sad and often anguishing limitations. What makes it possible for Edgar to face the prospect of ruling Britain if not a reflection such as this? As he had said earlier to his life-weary father: "Men must endure their going hence even as their coming hither; ripeness is all" (V.2).

Edgar's final remarks in the play also seem designed to recognize the prejudice in favor of the old that wisdom must encourage, not because the old are necessarily wiser, but because that prejudice keeps us from experimenting—even in the name of nature—with elements of society that cannot be directly drawn from nature. For Lear had wrought an innovation in the name of natural justice in his original succession plan, hoping to favor Cordelia, even at the cost of dividing the kingdom, for the sake of merit. And what else does the play demonstrate but that there is such a natural principle, that Cordelia is far worthier of rule than her sisters, that Lear—in the completion of his powers—is indeed a natural king, just as Kent is the natural servant of such a king? Even so, the principle of merit, more fundamental than that of age or any other consideration, must—for the sake of justice itself—bow to other more conventional principles that guarantee continuity and stability.

The play calls forth our sense of natural justice particularly by the fate of innocent and good people in it, or of people whose faults are in no way commensurate with the sufferings they are forced to endure. It is fitting and just that Goneril and Regan suffer for the evil they do their father, and Edmund as well. Cornwall should suffer for having blinded Gloucester. But Gloucester's loyalty to Lear did not deserve such treatment; Edgar did not deserve to be traduced by his brother and hunted by his father; Cordelia did not deserve to die by hanging. The play does not try to explain what makes particular people wicked, except perhaps in the case of Edmund and his bastardy. Goneril and Regan seem not to have been abused or badly neglected—they themselves have no complaints on this score—and of Cornwall's background we learn nothing. From these examples—all the more frightening when they have no apparent explanation—wickedness, it seems, can show itself anywhere. The only lesson the good can draw is that they must be constantly on the alert against it and show an ability to outsmart or overpower it whenever it comes to light.

The world is certainly not the kind of place where justice triumphs automatically or independently of man's own effort to sustain it. Neither is it the domain of just gods or—as Tom would have it—of the foul fiend: while engendering virtue and justice, nature cannot help also engendering vice and injustice and an unending struggle between them. Nevertheless, nature generally is conceived in the play as a kind of harmony or rest that encourages the best elements in man in the midst of disharmonies, motions and conflicts it can never completely contain. Its essential character is shown more by good weather than by storm, by normalcy and rationality than madness, by health than by illness, by self-control than by anger or profligacy, by fellowship than by selfishness, by philosophical comprehension than by ignorance, by justice than by war. It is closer to the understanding of nature in Plato and Aristotle than in Heraclitus or the materialists.

We do not know why Edmund suddenly decides to do a good deed in his dying moments, and it is even harder to understand why Shakespeare has him wait so many lines before acting to save the lives of Lear and Cordelia from the death he has already ordered for them. Jaffa believes this has a political explanation—that Edmund's good deed consisted precisely in waiting and letting Cordelia be killed as the head of a French force invading Britain, thus preventing all similar foreign designs in the future. But does this correspond to our sense of retributive justice? And why have Edmund want to do any good at all? Why not simply have Cordelia killed without introducing this complication?

If Shakespeare means to use Edmund to show the redemptive powers of goodness, even in the wicked, he seems not to have prepared the way sufficiently. Nothing in Edmund's past (except, perhaps, his adherence to the standard of power) would indicate this possible improvement on his part, any more than on Goneril's or Regan's. As for his delay, he has already heard of Edgar's devotion to Gloucester and now hears Edgar continue about Kent and Lear, immediately after which we learn the fate of Cordelia's sisters. Plainly, Edmund understands that his father and Lear had both been beloved and envies them for it, thus being led himself to exclaim, on seeing the bodies of the sisters: "Yet Edmund was belov'd! The one the other poison'd for my sake, and after slew herself." Quite a tribute to love from one who before had abused it as he wished!

Less obscure than Edmund's reason for delaying is the advantage Shakespeare gains in the play by it. Once we realize all that is at stake in the delay, we wonder nervously whether the forces of good will be in time to prevent the death of Cordelia and Lear. The partly fatal effect of the delay forces us to admit the role of accident in human affairs, for to frustrate an evil already ordered, a good desire must be activated in time, otherwise it is almost useless. Minutes, seconds can make all the difference between success and failure, and, as they go ticking by, human lives hang in the balance. Neither god nor nature can intervene to save these good people: it all depends on human action and hence to some extent on chance, as does the efficacy of justice generally. This at least accounts for both the reader's dramatic experience in these passages and the meaning they take on within Shakespeare's reflections on justice as a whole.

Standing back, now, we can say that this play about justice tries in fact to demonstrate that it has a natural base in our social nature, and that, even when we perceive the delicate ways in which self-interest tends to intermingle with our love of others, this attachment is still real. It is a concern for others that lies at the bottom of justice—a wish to see them properly treated, and an abhorrence at their being mistreated. This concern normally and naturally shows itself in both paternal and filial love, friendship, admiration and sexual love, and broadens out from them to a general concern for all men of the kind the best men, like Shakespeare himself, have always felt. The good feel a special kinship for each other, and it is in the spirit of this fellowship of the good that Albany finally addresses Kent and Edgar as "friends of my soul" and relinquishes to them his own claim to the throne.

It can therefore be said that Shakespeare emphatically disagrees with Lear's conclusions—and Kent's—at the end of the play. The examples of love he sets before us are far more impressive than the examples of wickedness, and even at the end, when all seems bleak, Lear's heroism, the devotion of Kent, Gloucester and Edgar, Albany's self-abnegation stand out more luminously than the acts of the wicked and help to counteract the sufferings of their victims. In short, we are only capable of discerning and judging wickedness because of our prior understanding and love of justice and the good. The wicked may triumph, and the good perish, but the separate character of each is set in the nature of things. Injustice derives from an inability to love others, and this insufficiency of the social element in us constitutes a distortion or defect of our nature.

What is the connection between this social foundation of justice and the idea of natural kingship? Assuming that men are naturally inclined toward justice, are they also equipped with a natural power capable of bringing justice about? Just as the family must be subject to some parental authority, so groups of men, living in society, must obey some authority that will protect them militarily from external attackers and from their own criminals as well. They need a system of justice, wisely wrought and wisely guided at the helm. In the best case, this justice would be implemented by natural leaders of outstanding virtue and wisdom who love justice and can be entrusted with such responsibility. The idea of the natural king is an extension of the idea of natural justice. Shakespeare is under no illusions as to the difficulty of finding such a king. Lear begins by being a very good but hardly a perfect king. He does not understand his daughters. He is imprudently attracted by the claim of natural merit in choosing his successors. He flies into a rage at both Cordelia and Kent. Nevertheless, his love of virtue and his devotion to the common good are joined to a majesty of body and soul that stamps the presence of royal authority in him, winning the respect, admiration and loyal service of men like Kent and Gloucester. Under the impact of his daughters' ingratitude and the storm, he becomes juster and wiser still—more aware of the plight of the poor, the abuse to which systems of justice are prone, and the limitations of political life generally. In the final scene he seems to join together the perfections of king, father and man all at once: then he is *King* Lear in the fullest sense.

King Lear and *The Tempest* both borrow the theme of the wise and just king from Plato and Aristotle but deal with it from different points of view. Unlike Prospero, Lear is not a student of the liberal arts, not directly or naturally a philosopher, and he does not have an Ariel to obtain the effects he seeks to have on political life. Spiritedness is not something that comes naturally to Prospero, and his physical prowess is nothing like Lear's. Lear is a political man from the outset, forced to reflect and philosophize in his madness, whereas Prospero is a philosopher turned king by the necessity of having to return Miranda to society. The absolutely perfect king—even more unlikely than either Prospero or Lear taken separately—would unite the essential natures of the political and the philosophical man.

A word must be said, finally, about the role of philosophy in *King Lear*. In no play of Shakespeare is more explicit attention given to the origin and import of philosophy (remembering that the term is neither used about nor by Prospero in *The Tempest*), but in such a way as to conceal or minimize that very fact. Moreover, in no Shakespearean play is a course of philosophizing followed more relentlessly than in Lear's passage from belief in the justice of the gods to the conventionalism of the natural philosophers, yet almost invisibly. This must tell us something about Shakespeare's understanding of philosophy and its relation to his poetry. Philosophy occupies for Shakespeare the kind of place that it occupies for Plato and Aristotle. It is the most important of all human activities, the source of our natural understanding of nature and right, the guide of life in all respects, and the basis for a poetry that teaches as well as entertains in the highest sense of the term. But, while undoubtedly the peak and greatest glory of human nature, it must remain hidden from public view because it can easily do harm and be harmed.

What could have led Shakespeare to this conclusion? Clearly, philosophy can do harm by undermining the necessary opinions of society that philosophy necessarily questions—which must be the reason why Lear takes Edgar (as Tom) aside to ask him a question Shakespeare conceals from us. Making philosophy public can also bring harm to the philosopher (and his writings), as it did to Socrates. But it can also lead to the institutionalization and hence the ossification and dogmatization of philosophy itself, and therewith to its political abuse—as it had during the Middle Ages. It must be for reasons such as these that Shakespeare, unlike Plato and Aristotle, conceals philosophy and disguises his own philosophizing so skillfully in all his plays, only rarely permitting a direct glimpse of it. How ironic but consistent, then, that he should conceal Lear's philosophizing within the ravings of a madman! The play shows the depth of Shakespeare's philosophical penetration into the problem of justice, and the way in which he resolved it in favor of natural right and against conventionalism. This teaching, in its philosophical form, is for the studious and reflective few, while the dramatic impact of the play on the stage allows the poet to influence the public at large in behalf of the good.

LEAR'S FOOL

Glena D. Wood (essay date 1972)

SOURCE: "The Tragi-Comic Dimensions of Lear's Fool," in *Costerus: Essays in English and American Language and Literature,* Vol. 5, 1972, pp. 197-226.

[*Below, Wood examines the Fool's function in* King Lear, *demonstrating the relation of the Fool to Lear's personal development.*]

For a century and a half—1681-1838—Nahum Tate's version of *King Lear* pre-empted the stage in preference to Shakespeare's text. Tate's version restored Lear his throne, betrothed Edgar and Cordelia, and omitted the Fool as indecorous to tragedy. The rich texture and meaning of the drama suffered as much, perhaps, from blotting out the Fool's role as by superimposing the happy and false denouément.

Critics have noted the many ways in which the Gloucester subplot adds overtones and complexity to the main plot and theme. Some hold that Gloucester's story illustrates not so much a less subtle and more physical level of the Lear tale as another dimension of the Lear character and theme. The role of the Fool, too, though complex to unravel, may reveal still another dimension of the King.

Those attempting analyses of the function of the Fool in *King Lear* have expressed divergent, sometimes self-contradictory views, at times misrepresenting or misinterpreting both the Fool's character and function. Nor have I found a complete analysis. This failure to see clearly what the Fool contributes leaves unprobed a significant tragic depth; for to examine fully the

Fool's role is to go deep into the heart, mind, and soul of Lear and into the tragi-comic structure of the world's most complex tragedy.

One cannot, I think, dispose of the Fool by saying, "Here is a wise man acting the part of a fool." Nor does the inversion, "Surely, this is a fool acting the part of a wise man," explain his function. Both are over-simplifications. Hazlitt's contention that the Fool is essential for three apposite reasons—to serve as a "grotesque ornament" to the heathen setting, to provide comic relief in circumstances which might otherwise strain pity and fear to the breaking point, and to carry pathos to its highest possible level—is one sort of over-simplification. Rümelin's scoffing at the three fools on the heath—one really crazy (Lear), one pretending madness (Edgar), and one a professional fool (Lear's Fool)—satisfying the Elizabethan craving for the ridiculous and madness in the "finest style," is a grosser sort of over-simplification.

Diverging almost every direction on many levels of simplicity and complexity from those two opposite views are the most commonly held critical opinions, ranging from the contention that the Fool's constant jibes are mere trivia to which Lear pays not the slightest heed to the judgment of Franz Horn and Oechelhaüser that he is the grandest, the most intellectual, and the most tragic of Shakespeare's rich gallery of fools.[1] Indeed, Ernest Schick praised the Fool as the *chief person* in the tragedy.[2]

To add problematical complexity, the Fool's identity, like that of other characters in the tragedy (notably Lear's), is ambiguous. Some critics have identified the Fool and Cordelia, stressing Lear's deep love for both and the empathy between the two, illustrated by the Fool's pining away during the two days of Cordelia's absence from court. Such critics stress also the facts that only the Fool and Cordelia speak unvarnished Truth, that they never appear together on the stage, and that after the Fool goes "to bed at noon," Cordelia arrives shortly to finish the task the Fool had so bravely and foolhardily begun—that of restoring Lear to sanity and to an acceptable, livable sort of self-knowledge. If one accepts this identification of the Fool and Cordelia, Lear's pitiful cry at the end, "And my poor fool is hang'd" possesses ambivalent and representational significance, like almost every other line of dialogue and episode of this highly complex play.

At times, Lear has even been identified with his Fool, a particularly pertinent viewpoint if one accepts Maynard Mack's contention that folk and medieval versions of the archetypal theme of the "Abasement of the Proud King" are formative source materials. In the best-known version of the archetypal theme of humbling the proud and exalting the humble—that of "King Robert of Sicily"—the ruler who is debased is

John Gielgud as King Lear with Stephen Haggard as the Fool and Lewis Casson as Kent in a 1940 production of King Lear.

deprived neither palace nor kingdom but is made the *court Fool* and is forced to eat with the "palace dogs."[3]

Finally, the single identity of the Fool is multiplied by that of every other character; for before *King Lear* arrives at its conclusion, every character is called a fool (and acts like some sort of fool), either by the Fool himself or by some other character in the play.[4]

When the many views are juxtaposed, one is struck by the wide range of ideas regarding the character, function, age, ultimate fate, and identity of Lear's Fool. To unravel or piece together the puzzle promises new insights. I propose, therefore, to analyze the function of the Fool in the tragedy of *King Lear*. Simultaneously, I shall relate his role first to the growth in Lear's character and second to the ironic tone the Fool makes us aware of and to the tragicomic structure which results from the Fool's collision with characters responsible for the tragic events which ensue. I hope that such an analysis and approach will throw light on the Fool's identity and reveal a significant tragic theme.

Just as Lear takes the disguised Kent into his service, the Fool runs on the stage, ready and willing to serve Lear too. In almost the same breath Lear has ordered one attendant, "Go you, and tell my daughter I would speak with her" (I.iv.83 & 46) and another servant, "call hither my fool" (I.iv.46).[5] Lear's reply to the knight reminding (or informing) him that since Cordelia's departure his Fool has "much pined away," (I.iv.80) shows that he recognizes a close attachment between Cordelia and the Fool and shows also considerable irritation regarding some details of the division of his kingdom and his banishment of Kent and Cordelia, already too painful to discuss. "No more of that; I have noted it well," (I.iv.81) he remonstrates; and then calls for Goneril and his Fool, unaware of why he needs the Fool during the first interview with Goneril since the parceling out of his kingdom. But the knight's planting the suggestion of a "faint neglect of late," which Lear had attributed to his own "jealous curiosity," rather than to purposeful or willful neglect or ingratitude, indicates that he senses, at least subconsciously, why he needs the Fool. He may already see dimly the willfulness of his whim in dividing his kingdom on the basis of public protestations of love and the monstrousness of his banishing from his kingdom those who love him best—Kent and Cordelia. He has, of course, to date very little insight and has had no time to consider or to recognize that those acts were occasioned in part not only by the unexpected turn of dialogue and events, but also by many other factors, not the least of which is his own rash and adamant nature.

In some clever concentrated dialogue prior to Goneril's entrance, the Fool proceeds to label Kent, Lear, Goneril and Regan, and himself fools, and introduces an ironic tone. First, he proffers Kent his coxcomb, insisting he needs to hire him, too, and that if Kent chooses to follow Lear, he must wear coxcombs; for only a fool would follow a "great wheel" as it rolls down hill. Having called Kent a fool, he adds, thoughtfully, that he wishes he had two coxcombs and two daughters. Lear asks why, and he replies (labeling Lear a fool), "If I gave them all my living, I'd keep my coxcombs myself" (I.iv.120-121). Then throwing his coxcomb to Lear (rather than to Kent to whom he had first offered it), he audaciously says, "Beg another of thy daughters" (I.iv.121-122). And that statement takes in Goneril and Regan—as fools.

The ironic tone becomes increasingly apparent as Lear threatens to have the Fool whipped for overstepping his "unlicensed" license. "Truth's a dog, must to kennel" (I.iv.124) the Fool replies. Though Lear is not yet ready to listen to or to believe truth, the Fool forces it upon Kent by insisting that anyone who takes the part of someone out of favor is a fool immediately establishing an ironic tone, pervasive until the Fool vanishes from the tragedy and influencing the remaining action. We recognize the irony because Kent as faithful and true counsellor has chosen to cast his lot with Lear, who he knows will need his services, despite the King's scorning his advice and banishing his person. To make clear the tone, the Fool insists, "Why this fellow has banished two on's daughters and did the third a blessing against his will; if thou follow him thou must needs wear my coxcomb" (I.iv.114-116). The Fool perceives that Lear has banished Goneril and Regan and blessed Cordelia, both literally and metaphorically; for he knows the two older daughters will not live up to the trust Lear has placed in their hands. And Lear has saved Cordelia from the mercenary Duke of Burgundy, but such interpretation extends, rather than limits, the ironic tone.

The literal contrast between the Fool's words and Lear's acts distills the ironic tone. The Fool's assessment, moreover, precedes the first bitter scene between Lear and Goneril and demonstrates prophetic insight. Indeed, only protestations of enduring filial love have been expressed. Apparently, the Fool is aware of the previously expressed and potential hypocrisy of Goneril and Regan as is Cordelia. According to station he is a fool, but in reality he is not so great a fool (as the world views such matters) as is his master.

More concentrated than the way Shakespeare establishes tone is his method of creating an ironic tragicomic structure. Lear's command, "Tell my daughter I would speak with her" and "call hither my fool" initiates that structure by bringing Goneril and his Fool into collision. For Lear has begun the interweaving of events simultaneously both comic and tragic and has converted *King Lear* into both a *Commedia* and a *Purgatorio*.

In dialogue designed, in part at least, to give Lear additional insight before Goneril appears, Kent, Lear, and the Fool use the word "nothing" in literal, ironic, and tragic contexts. Kent's remark that the Fool's platitudes, "Have more than thou showest, / Speak less than thou knowest, / Lend less than thou owest / Ride more than thou goest," (I.iv.131-134) mean nothing elicits the Fool's clever retort that they are, then, like the breath of an "unfeed lawyer / You gave me nothing for't" (I.iv.142-143).[6] Kent's insistence that the Fool has said nothing and the Fool's conviction that Lear now possesses noting lead the Fool to ask Lear the tantalizing and pointed question, "Can you make no use of nothing, Uncle?" (I.iv.143-144). For the Fool is puzzled by Lear's mistakes and capriciousness and poignantly aware that much will come of Lear's "nothing."

In answer, Lear unwittingly repeats (except for change in tense) the devastatingly ironical condemnation of Cordelia in the first scene, "Nothing will come of nothing," when he falls into the Fool's trap by replying "Why, no boy; *nothing* can be made out of *noth-*

ing" (I.iv.145-146).[7] Part of the intense irony of the first "nothing" is that Cordelia's naivety and truth stand naked and bare before the cunning hypocrisy of her sisters; part of the irony of the second "nothing" is that Lear will shortly be stripped of all retainers and will stand naked and bare before the universe. But in neither case does Lear seem aware of the metaphorical, ironical, and tragic meanings he has attached to the word—"nothing." And he glimpses but faintly, if at all, the ironical circumstances in which he has placed himself. The fool, wishing Lear to define his situation clearly, now chooses to place the word in literal context, bidding Kent tell the King that the rent of all his lands now comes to precisely "nothing." For Lear will not "believe a fool," though he will listen to no one else.

Lear lashes out, "A bitter fool!"

Fool. Dost thou know the difference, my boy,
   between a bitter fool and a sweet one?

Lear. No, lad; teach me.

Fool. That lord that counsell'd thee
   To give away thy land,
   Come place him here by me,
   Do thou for him stand;
   The sweet and bitter fool
   Will presently appear;
   The one in motley here
      [pointing to himself]
   The other found out there.
      [pointing to Lear]

Lear. Dost thou call me fool, boy?
                                    (I.iv.150-161)

Apparently Lear has ignored (or failed to note) when the Fool has previously called him a fool. The clever ironical reply the Fool now makes—that all other titles Lear was born with he has given away—unites tone and structure in the Fool's recognition of the types of Fool he and Lear represent—the Fool "sweet," Lear "bitter." The Fool's antics and words are comic with tragic overtones and insight; Lear's are tragic, with comic undertones and blindness. Those facts are acutely dramatized by Lear's giving away his land and titles, reducing him to Fool in deed and position. Again, allusion to the medieval tale of Robert of Sicily may be pertinent. King Robert repents only after following the usurping angel's retinue to Rome where neither the Emperor nor Pope, though former fellow rulers, recognize him but call him a "mad fool."[8]

With his egg analogy, the Fool then points out to Lear the kind of crown he now wears and the sort of power he now exercises. Cut in two and the meat devoured, only two eggshells remain. The shells represent Lear's empty, impotent crown and power since he divided his kingdom and gave the "meat" to his elder daughters—Goneril and Regan. He has upset the order of privilege: the chain of being, the relative position of man and beast. Instead of majestically straddling his ass (as a king should), Lear has placed the ass on his own back and dragged it over the dirt. Lear totally lacked wit in his bald crown when he gave his golden one away.

So summarizes the Fool and sings out sadly the ironical humor of Lear's tragic predicament: when wise men lose their wits and act like fools, what can one expect of a mere fool? A king, reduced to nothing, reduces a Fool to less than nothing, unless the total order of the universe has been reverted. The Fool says that it has indeed been partly reverted (and by Lear himself), for he is better off than Lear. At least he knows what he is and where he stands and what kind of fool he is and what kind of fool Lear is. But Lear is "nothing," and by his own deeds, and unaware that he is nothing.

Sensing part of the truth of the Fool's bitter-sweet accusations and song, Lear asks the Fool how long he has been so full of songs. The Fool replies, I have been singing, sadly and ironically, ever since you made your daughters your mother. When you gave them rule, you put "down thy breeches" and

Then they for sudden joy did weep,
And I for sorrow sung,
That such a king should play bo-peep,
And go the fools among.
                                    (I.iv.191-194).

The paradox of each line—weeping for joy, singing for sorrow, a king, such as Lear, playing "bo-peep" and placing himself by his words and acts among fools—is related to the self-knowledge the Fool knows Lear must eventually gain and to the tragic episodes through which Lear will arrive at that knowledge.

The jibes of the Fool and the services of the disguised Kent constantly set before Lear truths which are very difficult for him to accept. The Fool wishes, given the situation he finds Lear and himself in, that he could lie. Truth is bitter, not sweet, in a realm upset by Lear's capriciousness, his unwillingness to rule, though king. "Thy truth shall be thy dower" (I.i.110), Lear had threatened Cordelia when she replied she loved him neither more nor less than a daughter should love her father. Ironically, Truth is all the dower Cordelia needs to reveal her worth, and Truth is all the dower Goneril and Regan need to reveal their hypocrisy and potential viciousness. And bitter Truth is the dower the "sweet Fool" gives. Lear and that which the "bitter Fool"—Lear himself—is forced to accept, having given everything else away.

Ironically, Lear does not realize that his rash acts have made Truth and Love the only dower for every character in the play. Ironically, too, "bitter Truth" ultimately sends the "bitter Fool" sanely mad.

At this early point in the play, truth is Lear's only possession; unlike crown and kingdom and Cordelia's love, he has never fully possessed it. Sweet lies, prior to Cordelia's bitter truth, have helped initiate a tragic situation for Lear, Cordelia, and her siters. Ironically, the first scene (probably unwittingly on Lear's part) had been a test of Truth and Love, with property, according to Lear's initial plan, to be apportioned on those bases. His plan had gone awry in his own royal court, and only sweet lies prevailed in an intensely realistic dramatic situation.

Lear's next admonition—that he will have no lying in his kingdom—is especially ironical. The Fool, in particular, he will have whipped, if he lies. The King can, however, but dimly distinguish truth from lies and is having much difficulty accepting the truth which the Fool constantly reminds him of.

The Fool wonders by what stretch of imagination the King and his elder daughters could be called "kin," (a matter which will soon cause Lear to marvel). Note, in particular, the Fool says, how Goneril and Regan will have him whipped for telling the truth, but how Lear threatens to have him whipped for lying, and sometimes he is whipped for holding his peace. He says he would rather be anything than a fool. "And yet I would not be thee, uncle; thou hast pared thy wit o' both sides, and left nothing i' the middle: here comes one o' the parings" (I.iv.199-206). Too subtly for Lear's present perception, the Fool has informed him that Goneril and Regan have lied in their protestations of love, that they will scourge those who tell the truth. At that moment Goneril—one of the "parings"—arrives and jolts Lear into the recognition that all is not well in the kingdom he has given away.

Lear as "nothing"—juxtaposed between the Fool (less than nothing but aware of what he is and how he arrived at his position) and Goneril (unaware that she is a "paring," rapidly to degenerate to "nought")—touches precariously every facet of life, ranging from sweetness to bitterness, from truth to falseness, from comedy to tragedy. That juxtaposition begins with Goneril's stunning Lear with bitter, vituperative words.

We are in part prepared for the Fool's multiple function when Goneril questions Oswald, "Did my father strike my gentleman for chiding of his fool? (I.iii.1-2) We know at that moment that antipathy exists between Goneril and the Fool, between Lear and Oswald, between Kent and Oswald, in fact among all characters as they line up in the two camps of Lear and Oswald, or, if you prefer, Lear and Goneril. For Oswald is a bitter, ironical, foolish counterpart of his mistress, as the Fool is a bitter, ironical, foolish counterpart of Lear, what Lear is when he put down his breeches to become child of his daughters, what he is when he put aside his scepter but hoped to retain the power which the scepter represents, what he is as the proud king humbled, what he is when he becomes a fool.

The Fool has entered the stage of this great tragedy, a smile at his lips, a quip on his tongue. Goneril enters, scene four, a frown on her face, bitter, unnatural words on her lips. Lear cares not, he says, for the "frontlet" Goneril puts on and observes that of late (the last two days) she has been too much "i' the frown."

The tragi-comic structure becomes intense when Goneril and the Fool collide with his words to Lear, "Thou was a pretty fellow when thou hadst no care for her frowning. Now thou art an O without a figure. I am better than thou art now. I am a fool, thou art nothing" (I. iv. 210-215). And from this point onward in the tragedy, both Goneril and the Fool help Lear to arrive at self-knowledge through bitterness and sweetness, evil disloyalty to kin and faithful loyalty to a former master, with the recurring frowns and smiles, quips and scathing words.

The Fool, despite what some have called his cynical social views, always has a firm faith and hold on reality, blended with the ideal. And he tries, with every word he utters, to help Lear gain a comparable hold; for he knows Lear will need it desperately throughout the tragedy he himself has initiated. Part of the Fool's knowledge of real life lies in his recognition that man is secure if he does not have to ingratiate himself with other men, if he is self-sufficient in goods, in love, in affection, and if he does not have to lean on others or court their favor. Those are the few advantages of being an absolute monarch, such as Lear must have been three days before this episode.

Shooting daggerous frowns at the Fool for his latest comment about his now being better off than Lear, Goneril bids the Fool hold his tongue—a thing the Fool simply cannot do when something needs to be said or when a situation becomes too tense. So, despite his promise, the Fool proceeds to sing another ditty.

"Mum, mum
He that keeps nor crust nor crumb,
Weary of all, shall want some."
(I, iv, 216-218)

In more innocuous form, he has sung the *jist* of what he has *just said*. Pointing to Lear, he adds, "That is a shealed peascod" (I. iv. 219), (a shelled peapod), not substantially different from the analogy of the two crowns of meat Lear had given away, but more direct and more "all-licensed." Clearly, Goneril has spoken a smattering of truth when she maintains that the Fool is entirely unrestricted as to what he may say.

The Fool's primary and most obvious function to this point in the tragedy is repeatedly to show Lear the willfulness of his whim in dividing his kingdom on the basis of public declarations of love and the monstrousness of his banishing Kent and Cordelia. While reminding Lear of those truths, the Fool constantly introduces an ironical tone, shifting between humor, satire, and cynicism, but remaining basically ironical. That tone and his quips and quirks in the most tragic situations place the comic and the tragic alongside until the climactic scene of the third act, at which point the Fool disappears from the tragedy. Thereafter, an ironical tone is interwoven with pathos and brutal tragedy. Both Edgar and Cordelia in their relations with their fathers add pathos to the irony, and that addition tends to soften the tragedy, as in the first three acts the Fool's humor and pathos and irony soften and concentrate it. Bitter irony, however, is dominant in the scene at the end in which Edgar and Albany become so preoccupied with the punishment of evil characters, specifically Edmund (but Goneril and Regan also) that they forget all about the good characters—Cordelia and Lear—causing Albany, when he remembers, to cry out, "Great thing of us forgot!" (V. iii. 237) That pre-occupation with the punishment of evil results in Cordelia's being hanged and Lear's dying of a broken heart, ironical happenings as in life itself. So is Lear's dying, just as he may think he has faint indication that Cordelia breaths and lives.

Hereafter I shall illustrate additional ways in which the Fool contributes to Lear's growth. In order to eliminate repetition of episodes and dialogue, I shall retain my original organizational pattern, and point out how almost everything the Fool does and says not only aids Lear's character development but also adds to the ironic tone and in increasingly excruciating intensity places the comic and tragic alongside, at times to a degree very nearly unbearable.

The Fool's initial function, we have seen, was to make Lear fully aware of what he has done, what the probable results of his actions will be, what kinds of daughters he truly has fathered, what sort of kingdom he now lives in but no longer rules over, and what kind of men and social order are found in that kingdom. In others words, his function as an "all-licensed" Fool is to tell truth, the dower which Lear, unwittingly and angrily, has bequeathed every character, including himself, and which is, moreover, the only dower which any character possesses from the first to the last scene of Shakespeare's greatest tragedy.

The Fool has held up before Lear's eyes a mirror of the crown he wears; the power his two eldest daughters wield; the social and economic order and disorder in his kingdom (in reality no longer his); the way a wise, but not necessarily good, man should treat a person out of favor. A good man, the Fool insists, should maintain a position which renders him immune to the buffetings of fate and above currying favor from daughters. A wise man should not follow a great man, rolling down hill. The Fool's ditties and platitudes often express expedient ways of getting along with a minimum of friction in a corrupt (or amoral) society. At the same time, he questions the ethics of his own axioms and even more profoundly, the ethics of his social world. So almost every assertion he makes contains double or triple-edged irony.

Angered at Goneril's sudden shift from smiles to frowns, from praise to blame, from fawning to fuming, Lear cries out that he has another daughter who will respect and honor him, as should a daughter to whom her old father has given his all. We recognize the irony of Lear's words, even before the humiliating scene with Regan is enacted our eyes, because of the tone the Fool has injected into the play We likewise recognize the irony of Goneril's contentions that Lear's retainers have proved unruly, that she fears Lear himself condones their actions, and that his retainers are rapidly converting her "graced palace" into a tavern, or a brothel. The double-edged irony is that neither Lear nor Goneril knows it is she who is fast converting her own palace into a brothel, but that we and the Fool realize Goneril has unwittingly spoken a partial truth. When Lear shrilly shouts that he has another daughter who will not reduce the number of his retainers, we suspect, and the Fool knows, that Regan will reduce them from fifty to twenty-five, and from twenty-five to *none*.

Goneril, moreover, has scarcely concluded her hypocritical, smooth-sounding, "gracious" insults when the Fool observes, "For you know nuncle, / The hedge sparrow fed the cuckoo so long, / That it had it head bit off by it young. / So out went the candle, and we were left darkling" (I. iv. 234-237). The second and third lines are an old adage, but so true of Lear's predicament: he is left "darkling," his head dangerously close to being bitten off by his own offspring. But the Fool stands in pure light, revealing to the King his ultimate fate and the fate of all old men, throughout all time who do too much for ungrateful and unloving children.

Between the two most tragic questions which Lear asks, questions saturated with pathos, lie the Fool's most flippant statements. Appalled at the audacity and hypocrisy and disrespect of Goneril, Lear doubts his paternity of such an "unnatural hag." He doubts, moreover, the evidence of his own senses, and his own identity. So the tortured questions, "Are you our daughter?" and "Doth any here know me . . . Who is it that can tell me who I am?" (I. iv. 238, 246, & 250) reveal a search for a legitimate explanation for Goneril's existence and, more importantly in this context, for Lear's own self-identity. Between those two soul-searching questions, emphasizing and complicating them, are the Fool's sardonic and flippant question and exclamation, "May not an ass know when the cart draws the horse?" and "Whoop, Jug! I love thee" (I. iv. 244-245). Obviously, from the Fool's point of view Lear has sunk below the level of a fool to that of an ass (as in archetypal tales), and again he reminds Lear how disastrously he has upset the usual and prevailing order of the universe by making his daughters his mother. The Fool, moreover, has an instant reply to Lear's probing for identity. The King is but "Lear's shadow."

With uncanny insight, the Fool anticipates both questions and answers: Lear thus is but a shadow, standing in utter darkness. Only the Fool attempts to answer Lear's question, and his answer strikes closer to the heart of the King's tragedy than any assertion yet made.

Goneril, as anxious to rid herself of the Fool as to rid herself of Lear and his hundred knights, sends him after the King who has left in great haste (and "heat") for Regan, his devoted daughter—(so he thinks), with the command, "After thy master . . . thou more *knave* than *fool*" (I. iv. 237-38).[9] Calling "Nuncle Lear, nuncle Lear," take thy Fool and folly with thee, the Fool runs after Lear, singing another ditty—ironical, amusing, and tragic in content—about a fox and a daughter, sure to go to slaughter if my cap (with coxcombs) "would buy a halter" (I. iv. 337-343). Thus ends the first collision of comic and tragic elements.

The second such collision begins with the Fool's being present when Lear confronts Regan for the first time since the division of his kingdom. First, however, the Fool must prepare Lear for this meeting with Regan, as he had tried to prepare him for what to expect from Goneril. Consequently, the Fool says that if Lear's brains were reverted to his heels (as Lear has reverted order and privilege), he would need no slippers to preserve his brains from chilblains. He simply has *no brains,* no perception.

In the former scene, the Fool had made Lear half aware of what he had forfeited. Goneril had made him but half afraid he could never regain it. As yet, he feels not totally impotent, for he has still another daughter whom he has not rejected and who he hopes has not rejected him. Whereas Lear has high hopes for a cordial reception of his hundred retainers and himself at Regan's, the Fool "can tell what he can tell: Regan is as much like Goneril as a "crab is to a crab" (I. v. 18-19) Lear needs to know that before he confronts Regan, and the Fool warns him; still the significance of the warning does not dawn upon Lear until he arrives at Gloucester's palace with but half his retinue (the other fifty—wise in the way of the world—have deserted him enroute) and finds Kent in the stock. Then the fact dawns but dimly.

The Fool feels impelled to forewarn Lear before each encounter with Goneril and Regan so that he will survive the shock. The fact that the Fool is present at both initial encounters illustrates again the tragi-comic structure. It is, of course, a moot question which of the "parings" ultimately proves more vicious. Goneril first tells Regan they must "do something i' the heat" (I. 1. 312), but it is Regan who wants to know why Lear needs even *one* retainer; it is she who says during the night of the awful storm that her father may enter Gloucester's palace, but without a single follower.[10]

The Fool does not, however, want Lear to endure more pain than he can bear: he is merely trying to prepare and help him to endure pain. So when the King alludes to his having done "her [Cordelia] wrong," the Fool deftly switches topics to how an oyster makes his shell and to the timely discovery that he knows why a snail has a house. When Lear would know why, he says, "Why to put's head in, not to give it away to his daughters and leave his horns without a case" (I. v. 33-34). As Lear grieves over the "Monster ingratitude" of Goneril, the Fool says if Lear were his fool, he would have him whipped for "being old before he was wise," indirectly telling Lear again the sort of reception Regan will give him.

To divert Lear's attention away from himself and his misery, the Fool startles him with the ridiculous remark, "The reason why the seven stars are no more than seven is a pretty reason." Lear's reply, "Because they are not eight" (I. v. 37-40) pleases the Fool, convinces him he has achieved his objective. He tells Lear he would make a good fool.

Arriving with his reduced retinue at Regan's, Lear is stunned, more than he was by Goneril's bitter words, to find Kent in the stocks. But the Fool is not surprised. He knows too much of life, of privilege and lack of privilege, of those who control purse strings, and of those who are penniless. He tries to jest about Kent's predicament, alludes to his "cruel garters"; but Lear is beginning to awaken from the daze he has been in and demands an explanation. The Fool is willing to provide one, long before Cornwall and Regan do. He attributes Lear's reversal in treatment to his reversal in fortune, "Fathers that wear rags / Do make their children blind; / But fathers that bear [money] bags / Shall see their children kind." (II. iv. 48-51). He who controls fortune controls the affections, he has found. And Lear's experience verifies the Fool's words.

When Kent asks why Lear comes with so few followers, the Fool characteristically remarks that had Kent been placed in the stocks for that question he had well deserved to be. Kent, as usual, would know why. And the Fool's reply is the most expedient advice he ever gives:

> We'll set thee to school to an ant, to teach thee there's no labouring i' the winter. All that follow their noses are led by their eyes but blind men; and there's not a nose among twenty but can smell him that's stinking. Let go thy hold when a great wheel runs down hill, lest it break thy neck with following it; but the great one that goes up the hill, let him draw thee after. When a wise man gives thee better counsel, give me mine again: I would have none but knaves follow it, since a fool gives it.
>
> (II. iv. 68-77).

To that metaphorical prose counsel the Fool adds still another ditty which sums up what he has just said:

> That sir which serves and seeks for gain,
> And follows but for form,
> Will pack when it begins to rain,
> And leave thee in the storm.
> But I will tarry; the fool will stay,
> And let the wise man fly:
> The knave turns fool that runs away;
> The fool no knave, perdy
>
> (II. iv. 79-86).

Both ditty and advice probe Lear's problems, the very basis of his society with its misplaced values. The Fool knows something must be wrong with a world in which a man is loved only so long as he has "money bags," only so long as he is on the uphill road, only so long as he possesses power. What more expedient advice could he give Kent and himself? He asks for his advice to be returned when a wise man supplies something better.

The Fool's experience has showed him that when a man is rapidly slipping, those who remain faithful and loyal to him are fools. Yet those who forsake him are knaves. The Fool confesses himself to be a fool of that sort, perhaps because he prefers being fool to knave.[11] One feels strongly that if the Fool were not in his position forced to follow Lear, he would still be one of the faithful disguised followers, as Kent is. Can it be that the Fool has already learned through suffering, through the scorn of the world, not just that inflicted by two ungrateful daughters, the lessons Lear is being forced now to learn about his kingdom, his daughters, and himself? Already, those followers, wise in the way of the world, have deserted Lear, but the Fool's insistence that those who follow the way of the world are knaves condemns the moral basis of that social world.

It is debatable which of the two scenes after the division of kingdom—the first with Goneril or the one with Regan—is more tragi-comic in structure. The second, however, possesses an ironic intenseness which compels the Fool to indulge in fewer amusing or satirical aphorisms and ditties. The first possesses an unexpectedness which causes Lear to exhaust the resources of language in cursing. The second scene, in which Goneril soon joins her sister in usurping the "meat" of Lear's crown, eclipses the Fool's attempts at sad humor or ironical satire and stops the curses in Lear's throat. There are fewer of the Fool's quips because Lear has exhausted the welcome of both un-rejected daughters. Humbled, Lear kneels before Regan begging for gratitude and love.

And the Fool's feeble attempts to stay Lear's passion with poorly timed jests of "cockney and eels and buttered hay" do not permit us to forget that the irony of the play is becoming increasingly bitter. Under the new glaring light of double ungratefulness, the Fool's humorous quips, fulfilled, have become fundamentally tragic.

Powerless to further entertain or distract and enlighten or disillusion his King, helpless to shield him longer from pain and suffering, unable to teach him further how to endure, aware of the futility of jesting or shielding Lear, the Fool stands silently by pitying his master, until Lear, utterly exhausted emotionally and spiritually, appeals to him with the agonizing cry, ". . . this heart / Shall break into a hundred thousand flaws / Or ere I'll weep. O *fool*, I shall go mad!"

And indeed, Lear does go mad in that climactic scene in which the three fools—the professional (Lear's Fool), the assumed (Edgar), and the real (Lear)—"figure away in fine style on the heath,"[12] while the very elements of the universe go mad. Every facet of life, as represented by the witless King and the witty Fool, the disguised beggar and the disguised friend, is uprooted and repositioned by rain, wind, thunder, and fire.

The Fool's function in relation to Lear also shifts. I have showed that after Lear's first willful whim he needed to become acutely aware of what he had done and of the inexorable results. And the Fool performs that function. Later, Lear needed both additional warning and comfort, but more especially he needed a silent participator in his grief. That service, too, the Fool provides. At the crisis, when Nature collaborates with two unnatural hags to scourge Lear, he must have comfort, protection, companionship and love. We are told that throughout the mad heath scene the Fool has tried in vain to "outjest Lear's heart-struck injuries." Even the companionship and love he provides prove inadequate.

Internal and external convulsion of man and cosmos is Shakespeare's most magnificent imaginative tragic conception. Nothing could be more painful than Lear's

> Blow, winds and crack your cheeks! Rage
>   Blow!
> You cataracts and hurricanoes, spout . . .
> You sulphurous and thought-executing fires, . . .
> Singe my white head! And thou, all-shaking
>   thunder,
> Smite flat the thick rotundity o' the world

juxtaposed to the Fool's "O Nuncle, Court holy water in a dry house is better than this rain water out o' door. Good Nuncle, in, and ask thy daughter's blessing. Here's a night pities neither wise man nor fool!" Nor does any dialogue illustrate more painfully the tragi-comic structure (III. ii. 1-13).

The elements of the universe continue "rumbling their bellyful," spitting fire, spouting rain. Meanwhile Lear rejects the Fool's suggestion that it is better to flatter those in high places, those with "money bags," than to suffer so, houseless and bareheaded. The King does not tax the raging elements with unkindness: he never gave *them* kingdom, called *them* daughter. Still, he accuses rain, wind, thunder, and fire of collaborating with "two pernicious daughters" in "high-engendered" battle against a head as old, and bare, and white as his, and concludes, "Oh, oh! 'Tis foul!" And, indeed, "'tis foul" (III. ii. 15-24).

Simultaneously trying both to entertain Lear (incapable now of being entertained) and to remind him why he faces the violent storm without a "good headpiece" (a house to put his head in), the Fool sings an indecent ditty about unmarried men who beget children before they have a home to put them in. Gloucester and Lear's predicaments are thus summed up. Lear had truly made "his toe / What his heart should make" (III, ii. 25-35) with the inevitable woe and sleepless nights.[13]

At the very height of the storm, in reply to Kent's question regarding the identity of Lear and him, the Fool asserts, "Grace and a codpiece—that's a wise man and a fool." But at that point, Lear is dangerously close to madness, and the Fool close to being a wise man; so which is "grace," which "codpiece" is ambiguous, like so much else in the tragedy. Shocked that his master whom he has never seen without a golden crown on his white head could have endured such a night bareheaded, Kent leads the King to a hovel.

Lear agrees to seek the shelter, not for himself, but for his Fool, "Poor fool and knave, I have one part in my heart / That's sorry yet for thee" (III. ii. 73-74). At the hovel entrance, Lear, who has probably never before given way for any one to pass, bids his Fool proceed before him out of the storm into shelter. The Fool apparently objects and remonstrates against his King's latest Christian reversion of privilege; but Lear insists, "In, boy, go first. You houseless poverty / Nay, get thee in. I'll pray, and then I'll sleep" (III. iv. 26-27).

The ingratitude of natural daughters, the scourging of the elements, but more than all else, Lear's Fool and Gloucester's son, disguised as fool—gradually teach the pagan Lear two fundamental Christian virtues—compassion and charity.

From the scourging of unnatural men (daughters) and natural elements (rain, wind, thunder, fire) in the presence of *the thing itself*—Edgar—unaccomodated man—Lear gains a virtue and sees a vision never seen nor possessed before, certainly not in the pre-tragic days as imperious absolute monarch. Looking beyond the blanket without which they would all have been shamed,[14] Lear perceives for the first time in more than eighty years—the *thing itself*—man reduced to the lowest and exalted to the highest levels. The almost completely mad Lear identifies himself and generic humanity with the assumed mad Edgar to answer the heart-rendering question he had asked in Act I—"Who is there who can tell me who I am?" Lear's probing tragic questions, together with the Fool's quip about Edgar's blanket saving them from shame, combine, as so often in the play, the height of comedy and depth of pathos. Clearly, the tragi-comic structure is becoming increasingly bitter. For Edgar's deceived father has forced him to use his madman's disguise.

Of all cries in the tragedy, the most ironic and penetrating is Lear's tragic acknowledgment, "Thou art the thing itself." Here at the climax his immediate reaction—"Off, off, you lendings! Come unbutton here" (III. iv. 112-113) corresponds to his very last beautiful, ironic, tragic words which release his life, "Pray you undo this button" (V. iii. 308). Self-identity here is basically a social gesture—an attempt to become one with the lowest forked animal—shedding all gowns and furr'd robes. The last "unbuttoning" unites self with the cosmos; but both involve and "undressing" to release and find the real self.

Lear's most profound discovery and the Fool's witty retort, "Prithee, Nuncle, be contented, 'tis a naughty night to swim in;" (III. iv. 114-115) juxtapose the tragic and the amusing to a degree almost too painful to endure. Kent has been shocked to find Lear in the storm—bareheaded. Despite the cleverness of his retort, the Fool would be shocked to see his King, customarily robed in furred gowns, swimming naked in the rain. The Fool adds another tone to the ironic when he says of Gloucester, coming toward them bearing a torch, "Now a little fire in a wild field were like a lecher's heart, a small spark, all the rest on's body cold. Look, here comes a walking fire" (III, iv. 115-119). In view of Gloucester's past lechery, his future blindness, and his present loyalty to Lear, the Fool's comment is comic, lewd, symbolic, and ironically prophetic.

More than any other character in the play, the Fool has helped Lear to arrive at self-discovery in Edgar—

the unaccomodated man, who borrows no silk from worms, no furs from beasts, no wool from sheep. "Robes and furr'd gowns" which "hide all" had in the past kept Lear from arriving at self-knowledge, self-fulfillment, self-identity; more tragically, they have kept him from learning compassion, charity, and love. Lear sees Cordelia in the mad Edgar—the rejected daughter, the rejected son—and he goes beyond that vision to self-knowledge: the reason for the rejected Lear.

From his very first appearance with quips and coxcomb, the Fool has been trying to help Lear strip away all falsity all superfluity to discover the *thing itself*. Lear has just discovered what the Fool apparently has known all along that on a literal level *natural* man is but a "poor bare forked animal"; but it is also unaccommodated man who embodies those virtues and qualities which make the human predicament livable or bearable. Edgar owes no commodity to Nature; the Fool owes nothing to Society. Lear has but recently discovered that the Fool is "houseless poverty," as Edgar is "poor, bare, forked." From those two "unaccommodated men" Lear learns some Christian virtues and perceives that which reduces man to the level of animals and exalts him to the level of the gods.

Part of the power of episodes which I have analyzed derives, as I have showed, from the juxtaposition of disparate elements: Nature "rumbling its bellyful," weak humanity, a King and a Fool, whose roles have been interchangeably interwoven, the highest and lowest of mankind—at its mercy. The tragic knowledge Lear is forced to accept alongside the bitter tragicomic jests of a motley clown: a witty Fool, and at this point in the tragedy, an almost witless King. The comic and the tragic, the amusingly ironic and the highly serious are interwoven so skillfully that one is scarcely aware of the many ambiguities and contradictions and complexities until he tries to isolate them for purposes of analysis.

Before following Kent into the hovel, the Fool makes a final comment about the nasty night which has tried to destroy both King and Fool and which has, indeed, helped destroy Lear's wits, making Fool and King intellectually equal as Lear's first act had placed them on equal social and economic levels. The Fool sings out that such a night will turn all men to fools and madmen, that it is indeed a "brave night to cool a courtesan," and that men with little wit must be contented with "fortune fit," for "the rain it raineth every day" (III. ii. 74-77). In his present madness with but little wit and less property and overabundant rain, Lear heartily grants the Fool's assertions. And he prays heaven never to have to suffer such violent contact with any of those elements again.

Nor can the Fool resist making one final prophecy before leaving the storm for the protection Lear is demanding that he accept. The first lines are ironical comments about hypocritical priests who preach endlessly but provide no spiritual uplift and about brewers who enrich themselves by adding water to their malt, thus decreasing its quality. The rest of the prophecy is so far removed from real-life situations, so idealistic that the Fool knows no such social and spiritual Utopia will ever be attained "in Albion." They are these:

> When nobles are their tailors' tutors,
> No heretics burned, but wenches suitors,
> When every case in law is right,
> No squire in debt, nor no poor knight,
> When slanders do not live in tongues,
> Nor cutpurses come not to throngs,
> When usurers tell their gold i' the field,
> And bawds and whores do churches build—
> Then shall the realm of Albion
> Come to great confusion.
>
> (III. ii. 79-92)

Since these lines sum up the Fool's social philosophy and are his final assessment of the world which has dealt such cruel blows to Lear, we need to examine them closely. The total view seems harmonious with the Fool's digs and quips to and about Goneril and Regan.

It is realistic, without biting cynicism; critical, without damning sarcasm. If the Fool is severe in his comments about every moral and social strata from whores, to cutpurses, to nobles, the episodes of the tragedy corroborate his views. Nor is he as severe as Lear in his assessment of the world, and he is more right. Wiser than a Fool has a right to be, he knows his proposals will never be realized: thus the prophetical statement. If Eden or Arcadia or Utopia existed, truly England would be in great confusion. If an old man could even trust the public expressions of love made by his own daughters, such devastating chaos and tragedy would not ensue. *King Lear* provides a penetrating criticism of Shakespeare's social world and of its hypocrisy, of the discrepancy between public declamations and private acts, of a world in which words are separated from acts. And Shakespeare's most succinct and ironical, at times most amusing, expression of those social evils are to be found in the Fool's dialogue.

I have already dealt with the climactic episode in which the Fool plays such a significant role: the point at which Lear arrives at self-identity. But the denouément, so far as the Fool's role is concerned, follows immediately thereafter and consists of the trial scene, conducted by the three great fools of the play, and arraigns Goneril and Regan before the final bar of judgment. In that Day-of-Doom scene, Edgar serves as judge, the Fool as jury, Lear as arraigner. The mad

Lear accuses Goneril of having "kicked the poor King her father" and anatomizes Regan to find the "cause in nature that makes these hard hearts" (III. vi. 49-50; 81-82). The Fool asks the defendant if she is Goneril; Lear insists she cannot deny it. The Fool's reply, "Cry you mercy, I took you [Goneril] for a joint stool" (III.vi.54-55) reaches the height of tragedy and depth of comedy in a single stroke. The more intense the situation, the more ludicrous are the Fool's comments. This trial in which all major participants are mad becomes the maddest tragi-comic scene ever enacted before men.[15]

In the storm the Fool had cried out that the cold stormy night would turn all men to fools and madmen. By the time of the simulated trial of Goneril and Regan, one is forced to concede the night has done its worst. Knowing Lear is mad but wanting him to recognize his own condition, the Fool asks, "Prithee, Nuncle, tell me whether a madman be a gentleman or a yeoman" to which Lear replies that a madman is "A king, a king!" (III. vi. 10-12).

The Fool has barely called Goneril "a joint stool" when Lear madly strikes out against Regan "whose warped looks proclaim" what her heart is made of. Lear cries for arms, sword, and fire to fight the corruption in this hall of justice, threatening the ultimate rendition of God's justice in the Day of Doom itself; and he calls Edgar a "false justicer" to permit the vile Regan to escape (III. vi. 56-59)

In vain Kent attempts to convince Lear to lie down to rest so that his frenzy may pass away, but Lear cannot rest until justice has been restored in his kingdom. Throughout the trial scene, Lear's comments to Edgar suggest mental empathy if not identification with his Fool. For example, he wishes to "entertain" Edgar as one of his hundred retainers but dislikes the "fashion of his garments. You will say they are Persian attire, but let them be changed" (III. vi. 84-86). The ludicrous statement reminds us of the Fool's comment that had Edgar not retained a blanket they would all have been shamed; it reminds us that all Lear's retainers have forsaken him; it reminds us that "rob'd and furr'd gowns hide all" but that Lear apparently still prefers them to a blanket.

Lear, at last induced to lie down, bids Kent "draw the curtains so, so," thus closing the curtain on the role of his Fool with the words, "We'll go to supper i' the morning," to which the Fool adds the contradiction, "And I'll go to bed at noon" (III. vi. 89-92). Kent tells us that the Fool must help bear his master to Dover and cannot, therefore, be left behind; but after saying he will go to bed at noon, Lear's Fool speaks not another word. With the reappearance of Cordelia, his services are not needed, and the tone shifts to the ironically pathetic. With the villainies of Goneril, Regan, and Edmund, the tone shifts to the ironically tragic. But irony is one of the dominant tones from beginning to end of the tragedy. And more than any other character, the Fool contributes that tone.

Before summarizing the total effect of the Fool's role in *King Lear*, I should like to suggest precisely how contagious it is, for it spreads to every character. First, the Fool calls Kent a fool for entering the service of Lear, who has banished two daughters and blessed the third against his will. Throughout the remainder of Acts I and II, he repeatedly calls Lear a fool, insisting that the King could easily get another coxcomb from Goneril and Regan, strongly labeling them fools. In the third act, Lear himself becomes a mad fool. Meanwhile, Edgar, disguised as madman, is added to the Fool's list of fools for being faithful to the deceived Gloucester, who had threatened Edgar's life. And he calls himself a fool for following Lear, a "great wheel going down hill." But he reminds us he would rather be that sort of fool than a knave.

Kent, moreover, upon arriving at Gloucester's palace, calls Oswald a vicious pompous ass—the worst of fools and knaves—and insolently adds Cornwall to the list with the words, "None of these rogues and cowards / But Ajax is their fool" (II. ii. 132-133).

Both Goneril and her husband, the Duke of Albany, call each other fools. Goneril's "My fool usurps my body" and "O vain fool" are mild alongside Albany's "See thyself, a devil / Proper deformity seems not in the fiend / So horrid as in woman / . . . Thou changèd and self-covered thing, for shame." (IV, ii, 28-64) Threatening in his disillusionment and fury, should he lose control, to tear Goneril's flesh from her bones, Albany's words are mild compared with Goneril's foolish evil acts.

Edmund, moreover, calls both Regan and Goneril fools and plays them, like fools, one against the other. He obviously considers every character but himself a fool, particularly his father, the Duke of Gloucester, whom he dupes, deceives, betrays, and causes to be blinded. In the trial by combat, however, Edgar proved Edmund to be the most villainous fool of all. And Lear himself calls his dearly beloved Cordelia "my poor fool."

So the entire tragedy is one in which the fools of this world enact their respective roles, not the least of which is the dominant role of court fool, often assigned a proud King when he is debased. One becomes poignantly aware in analyzing the Fool's role of the "emblematic and Morality-based dimension as a meditation or oration in the tradition of *De Contempu Mundi*," which concludes with its dramatic illustration of man's miseries, "We came crying hither . . . When we are born, we cry that we are come to this great stage of fools."[16] One also becomes very much aware of the psychic distance which separates individualized characters from their homiletic and morality functions and from their emblematic and symbolic roles.[17]

In this paper, I have not attempted to relate the Fool with homiletic or morality functions; I have not directly attempted to analyze his emblematic or symbolic roles. Primarily, I have analyzed the Fool's role as it affects the development of Lear's character and as it contributes to the ironical tone and the tragicomic structure. But it would be difficult to select a character in *King Lear* who touches more complexly and deeply the tone, the structure, and the emblematic quality than Lear's Fool.

Is the Fool a man or a symbol? Is he a fool or a wise man? Is he himself, or some one other than what he purports to be? Is he a wise man clothed in motley and coxcomb? Or is he a fool gifted with a wise man's words and insight? Is he significant in the tragedy, or can his role be dropped without altering the meaning? What is his purpose? Does it change in the different scenes in which he appears? Why does Shakespeare drop him from the *dramatis personae* at the end of the sixth scene of the third act? Precisely what does he contribute to Lear's growth, precisely what does he contribute to the tone and structure of the tragedy?

The most tangible and unambiguous of these questions is what the Fool contributes to Lear's development. Still, even that is just about as intangible and ambiguous as anything can be. As I have showed in my analysis, Lear's first act endows all characters with Truth and Love as their sole doweries, thus forcing each to cast aside his customary hypocrisy to become what he truly is. As constant companion to Lear, that forces the Fool to speak only Truth, as ugly as it may be to the King. Because he speaks Truth and expresses what may have been Lear's attitude and what must have been Shakespeare's, the Fool becomes perhaps in part a mirror of the King's pagan society which is in fact Shakespeare's Elizabethan world, universalized as the cosmos.

To tell truth is merely one of the Fool's offices. Besides pointing out to Lear the irrationality of his initial acts in a society resting on an amoral hypocritical basis and besides drawing out for Lear his many other blunders, the Fool must teach Lear some basic lessons in human sympathy and Christian charity, qualities which an autocratic pagan monarch should not be expected to have acquired. Certainly Lear had not.

At times the Fool's function is to offer understanding and sympathy and to alleviate, after he has warned Lear he must suffer and told him why, Lear's suffering. He has showed Lear that he must suffer; he has partly showed him how and why, though Goneril, Regan, and Cordelia have performed that task more thoroughly. Having done those things, the Fool must save Lear from suffering too intensely. In this function, the Fool is not entirely successful, fundamentally because Lear has set in motion certain wheels of fire over which neither the Fool, nor Lear, nor any other character exercises control. When Lear goes mad, there is little the Fool can do for him. When he regains sanity, and a degree of wisdom, and Cordelia, he no longer needs his Fool.

The Fool sets up a mirror in which Lear can see himself and his acts, can see his daughters and their words which contradict their acts. And he helps Lear to grow immensely in wisdom and humility and in human kindness Imagine the pre-tragic Lear pitying his Fool, "I have one part in my heart / That's sorry yet for thee" or bidding him go before his king to seek shelter. Probably the pre-tragic Lear had never once thought of his Fool as a human being.

More importantly, the Fool must help Lear arrive at self-understanding and at self-identity so that he may answer his own tragic questions. The Fool with the disguised Edgar helps Lear to see behind robed and furred gowns to discover *the thing itself*—Man—a poor, bare forked creature, a worm, an animal, but gifted with the words, aspirations, and ideals of the gods. Even the lowliest of men—Edgar, a madman, who owes nothing to Nature, and a Fool, who owes nothing to Society, have within them that paradoxical reality and potential. Finally, in the trial scene, the Fool, again with Edgar, must help Lear arrive at an acceptable workable sense of justice among men which comes short of the justice of God but which still makes the life experience bearable and, at times, noble.

Those, then, are perhaps the major ways the Fool helps Lear to arrive at insight and wisdom.

But the Fool has a larger function in the tragedy than pointing out to Lear his mistakes, than suggesting the mediums of his punishment, than alleviating Lear's suffering when it becomes too intense to endure. He has other functions than serving as a mirror for Lear and his daughters and than speaking as a mouthpiece of Truth. He has another function besides helping Lear arrive at a balanced sense of justice and at self-recognition and self-identity.

King Lear, more than Shakespeare's other tragedies, speaks with many voices about the total human experience, and one of its major voices is its social outcry. In *Triolus and Cressida* (and elsewhere), Shakespeare expresses the generally accepted view of his age that in the universe there is a "place for everything, and everything is in its place." In *King Lear,* he questions that view and seriously doubts that everything is in its place. Lear's Fool cogently expresses Shakespeare's views regarding the social world, a world, if not topsy-turvy, at least with many misplaced values, worse than that, a world with many evil social conditions. Indeed, the Fool is the chief medium of Shakespeare's social protest. And on one very significant level, *King Lear* is a social protest.

For example, why cannot Lear take his daughters at their word? Is it not because there are too many hypocritical office seekers and crown grabbers? There are so many squires in debt, so much slander in the tongues of men, too many cutpurses among human throngs, so few whores who build churches, so few cases in law which are just.[18] Should those conditions be righted, then indeed would confusion reign in Albion. For men in a world in which only righteousness and justice and truth prevailed would not know how to live. Note the havoc resulting from Lear's making just one of these virtues—Truth—prevail in his kingdom.

It is the Fool who calls our attention to the evils prevalent in our social world, to its conniving and hypocrisy, to its lust for place and position, and gold. It is he who says a man is a fool (in the eyes of the world) if he follows a man whom the world has rejected. But he, who does not, is a knave. Being more "all-licensed" than any other character, he is also more all-knowing. And he knows most about society to which he owes nothing and by which he is not even recognized as existing. He knows truly that primitive unsophisticated man suffers intensely if forced to live in a civilized hypocritical society.

Lastly, the Fool creates a pervasive ironic tone and a basic tragi-comic structure, dominant in the tragedy, until the putting out of Gloucester's eyes. That is not to say that the tragi-comic is the sole structure,[19] but it is very important; and it possibly enables Shakespeare to make more penetrating comments about the human predicament than any other he may have used. It also made possible Shakespeare's *Commedia* and *Purgatorio* in the same scene, using identical episodes and dialogue, as in life itself.

The Fool's first words make one aware of the ironic tone. Thereafter he injects, extends, and intensifies that tone. I have suggested that is one reason Cordelia must die. As we in life forget about rewarding the good in our overlasting pre-occupation with punishing the wicked, so Edgar and Albany forget about Lear and Cordelia. Ironically, too, Lear must die just as he may have faint hope that Cordelia lives. The ironic tone begins, then, with the Fool's throwing Kent his coxcomb and telling him about Lear's having banished two daughters and having done the third a blessing.[20] Thereafter irony pervades the dialogue and major episodes, even those in which the Fool does not directly participate and together with the tragi-comic structure reaches, at times, an almost unbearable intensity, and lends the tragedy multiple contradictions, both realistic and idealistic, innumerable ambiguities, and much of its power and grandeur.

In a literal sense, one must grant that the Fool is what he purports to be—Lear's court fool; but, emblematically, considerable evidence could be presented, though it would be beyond the scope of this paper, to show that he pre-figures every character in the play, particularly every character embodying the virtues of Truth and Love, but especially Cordelia, and more fundamentally and truthfully Lear himself.

I agree with Hazlitt that *King Lear* is Shakespeare's greatest tragedy. He thought it Shakespeare's greatest work because in it "he is the most serious." I think it Shakespeare's greatest work because in it he is the most comic and tragic at the same moment and from the same point of view. And no character in the tragedy is more tragi-comic than Lear's Fool.

Notes

[1] *King Lear,* in *The Variorum Shakespeare,* ed. Horace Howard Furness (Philadelphia, 1908), pp. 452, 464.

[2] Ibid., p. 453. (Throughout the long footnote which follows, I shall refer to the Variorum edition as VE.) Some critics have held that the chief function of the Fool is to serve, when all others save Kent have abandoned Lear, as his closest friend and wisest counselor. Hudson thinks it inconceivable that Shakespeare, without the Fool, could have effected the desired growth in Lear's character (VE, pp. 436-437). Hense thinks the Fool holds up a mirror in which Lear can see himself as he really is (VE, p. 460). Others think that the chief function of the Fool is to speak Truth which Lear will accept only from the mouth of his "all-licensed" Fool; others say his role is to divert Lear's attention from his own suffering, to stave off madness, while still others hold that both Edgar's assumed madness and the Fool's professional role actually contribute to Lear's sanity. Some note that he adds to the total confusion of the play or stress his satisfying the cravings of the Elizabethan age for madness and horror, others that he gives the play unity and balance. (See VE, pp. 430-464).

Contradictory as are those views of function, there is even less agreement as to the Fool's ultimate fate. His last words, "And I shall go to bed at noon" (III. vi. 92) have been, among others things, interpreted to mean that he recognizes approaching death and must "breathe out his life in a play of thought" (VE, p. 437) or that he vanishes from the stage as fools did in life, as mere objects, without claim to personal interest (VE, p. 464). Others say that he disappears "of causes mysterious." Frederick Warde likes to think that Lear's cry, "And my poor fool is hang'd" (V. iii. 304) literally refers to the Fool. See Frederick Warde, *The Fools of Shake-*

speare (New York, 1913), p. 189. See also other critical views in the Variorum Edition of *King Lear,* pp. 430-464; *The Tragedy of King Lear,* ed. Virginia Gildersleeve (New York, 1933), p. xv; *Shakespeare's Tragedy of King Lear,* ed. William J. Rolfe (New York, 1890), p. 23; "Introduction," *The Tragedy of King Lear,* ed. Kenneth Muir, 8th ed. (Cambridge, Massachusetts, 1952); John Leslie Palmer, *Comic Characters of Shakespeare* (London, 1946), pp. vii & xiii; John W. Velz, "Division, Confinement, and the Moral Structure of King Lear," *Rice University Studies,* LI (Winter, 1965), 97-108; Harriet Dye, "The Appearance-Reality Theme in *King Lear,*" *College English* XXV (April, 1966), 514-517; and Maynard Mack, *King Lear in Our Time* (Berkeley and Los Angeles, 1965), pp. 40-53 & 66-69.

Nor has there been agreement as to the Fool's age. He has been said to be anywhere from twelve to eighty (and all ages in between). In the Macready production (1838), the first after Tate to restore the Shakespeare text, the Fool was even a woman. See Huntington Brown, "Lear's Fool, a Boy, Not a Man," *Essays in Criticism,* XIII (April, 1963), 164-171; Warde, pp. 188-189; and *The Variorum Shakespeare,* p. 464.

[3] Mack, pp. 49-50. See also *Middle English Romances,* ed. W. H. French and C. B. Hale (New York, 1930), pp. 937 ff. I agree with Professor Mack that the archetypal theme is significant source material; and I think, moreover, that in many ways it accounts for the important role assigned the Fool.

[4] According to the Fool, we have a kingdom of Fools—Kent, Lear, Goneril and Regan, and the Fool himself. Lear will add Cordelia. And everyone knows how foolish it was, as the world views matters, for the King of France to accept Cordelia—dowerless—and what a fool the Duke of Burgundy was, as the gods view such matters, not to recognize Cordelia's worth, though dowerless.

[5] All references to *King Lear* are from *Shakespeare The Complete Works,* ed. G. B. Harrison (New York, 1952) and will be cited in the body of the essay.

[6] The Fool's words mean more than Kent grants. Taken as a whole, they constitute sound pragmatic advice and, if followed, would place a man in a safe, if not admirable, position in a dramatic situation reverberating with social implications, crossing and upsetting every social strata. Lear, of course, had violated all the maxims, Kent a good portion.

[7] Italics are mine. Ironical and multiple meanings of "nothing" combine with the Fool's role to establish more than other aspects of the tragedy, its tone and structure. Indeed, the entire tragic action grows out of Cordelia and Lear's "nothing." And, too, the Fool (as a human being) is nothing.

[8] *Middle English Romances,* pp. 937 ff.

[9] Italics are mine.

[10] Apparently Regan has left her own palace to show Lear how inconvenient it is for her to receive him. That Lear is forced into the storm from Gloucester's palace; that Gloucester is blinded by Lear's daughter and her husband in his own palace; that Regan wishes to usurp that palace in union with the bastard Edmund as queen and king of Lear's realm—all these are tragically ironical.

[11] As her last insult to the Fool, Goneril had called him more *knave* than *fool;* but note, how by his acts, he has given her the lie. The court fool needed, of course, to be a man of learning, wisdom, quick observation and understanding. But he must constantly entertain and do the bidding of his master. Accordingly, the jester's life was lonely and subject to the whims and caprices of his master, "contemned above the board, hated below it, yet feared by all." See Warde, p. 2.

[12] Rümelin's comment regarding the heath scene, a scene which he calls "horrible" but lacking "in the wonderful" and lacking magnificence. See *The Variorum Shakespeare,* p. 462.

[13] The Fool's ditty is somewhat cryptic, but he apparently is reminding Lear that he had entered Goneril and Regan in the regions of his heart, when he should have placed them at his toe and that he should have placed Cordelia in his heart instead of trodding underfoot and banishing.

[14] When Lear, noting the nakedness of "poor Tom" asks if his daughters have brought him to his pass, if he could save nothing, the Fool facetiously remarks, "Nay, he reserved a blanket, else we had been all shamed" (III. iv. 64-67).

[15] This great scene is Shakespeare's tragic version of the great comic scene between Prince Hal and Falstaff in *Henry IV, Part I.*

[16] Mack, p. 69.

[17] Indirectly, I have had to touch on the Fool's emblematic and symbolical roles though detailed analysis of those roles is beyond the scope of this paper.

[18] I'm roughly paraphrasing the Fool's soliloquy—his prophesy (see III. ii. 80-92). Shakespeare's social comment contains double-edged irony. For example, he does not condone Lear's foolish notion that he can retain the name but not the responsibilities of kingship.

[19] Mack points out (p. 70) that the dominant structure of the Gloucester sub-plot is homiletic. I find other

structural patterns also, but the dominant structural pattern of episodes in which the Fool appears is tragicomic.

[20] Actually, the ironic tone begins with the first scene between Kent, Gloucester, and Edmund and with Lear's division of his kingdom on the basis of public declarations of love. But an audience does not become aware of the ironic tone until the first words of the Fool.

Allan R. Shickman (essay date 1991)

SOURCE: "The Fool's Mirror in *King Lear*," in *English Literary Renaissance,* Vol. 21, No. 1, Winter, 1991, pp. 75-86.

[*In the following essay, Shickman maintains that Lear's Fool was most likely intended to carry a mirror on stage in order to reinforce such concepts as "folly, prudence, and self-knowledge," with which the play is concerned.*]

At the height of the storm in which King Lear finds himself drenched and humiliated, and during which he begins to learn of mortal limitation and human responsibility, the faithful Fool labors to outjest his heartstruck injuries. Soaked to the skin himself, he urges Lear to recant and beg of his daughters the blessing that children would ordinarily be expected to ask of their fathers: "in, ask thy daughters blessing. Here's a night pities neither wise men nor fools" (3.2.12-13).[1] He versifies on the value of a roof over one's head, and then utters a problematic line, problematic because it seems to start so wildly from the previous one: "For there was never yet fair woman but she made mouths in a glass" (3.2.35-36).

Although attempts have been made to explicate this sudden sally,[2] it strikes many readers with its abruptness and incongruity, which is best explained as the product of a fool's vacillating wit or else his imperfect mental processes, for such capricious turns of thought recur in his speeches. What he is saying is that women in their vanity practice smiling before a mirror; literally, that they make faces—"mouths"—in front of a looking-glass.[3] The outlandishness of this court image when delivered on a rain-swept heath is magnified by the likelihood that the Fool of Shakespeare's stage actually demonstrated what he was talking about by making a few "mouths" of his own, timed so that the audience would laugh in the face of Lear's grief and pain. Making mouths was a function of fools, and indeed an occasional source of complaint. Thomas Lodge, referring to an old tradition of the fool as devil incarnate, wrote around 1596:

giue him a little wine in his head, he is cōtinually flearing and making of mouthes: he laughes intemperately at euery little occasion, and dances about the house, leaps ouer tables, out-skips mens heads, trips vp his companions héeles, burns Sacke with a candle, and hath all the feats of a Lord of misrule in the countrie . . . it is a speciall marke of him at the table, he sits and makes faces.[4]

The Praeludium to Goffe's *Careless Shepherdess* records a different reaction to similar clownish propensities:

I'ave laughed
Untill I cry'd again to see what Faces
The Rogue will make: O it does me good
To see him hold out's chin, hang down his hands,
And twirle his Bauble.[5]

And *Pilgrimage to Parnassus* remarks on "fine scurvy faces," while Dromo advises the clown to "draw thy mouth awrye . . . I warrant thee theile laughe mightilie."[6]

Although Shakespeare does not rely heavily on such crude buffoonery for comic effect, it is highly unlikely that Lear's Fool or any fool would talk about funny faces without making some. Nor would a skillful fool require props to imitate a woman simpering at her reflection. The palm of his hand would suffice as a looking-glass, and Lear's tragedy could, for a moment, be turned to hilarity. But it is the purpose of this essay to demonstrate that Shakespeare's Fool, in all probability, actually is meant to carry a mirror on the stage, not only in this section, where it clearly would be useful, but in others as well. In so doing, he presents emblems of folly, prudence, and self-knowledge, consonant with the tragic polarities of the play.

II

That the Fool holds a glass in this and other passages is not mere speculation. The association of the fool and the looking-glass is thoroughly established in the iconography of the period. Sometimes it is raised up to the face of the fool, as is the case in an engraving of about 1450-1460 by Master E.S., where an allegorical *Luxuria* presents the blithesome sinner[7] with his own fool's face. . . . Sometimes the fool holds it for himself, as in Alexander Barclay's 1509 translation of *The Ship of Fools*[8] . . . , where he admires his reflection, and actually appears to be practicing "mouths." Or he might hold the mirror up to others, as an ass-eared jester does in another of Barclay's woodcuts . . . , so that a sinner might see his folly, in this instance the vanity of fashionable dress. The last of these illustrations is especially pertinent, as we shall see, for the Fool in *King Lear* holds his mirror to Lear's folly in much the same way, although for different reasons.

The fool of medieval and Renaissance art has a mirror because in the metaphorical sense *he* is one. This attitude is revealed in the literature of fools, which typically introduces an encyclopedic catalogue of folly and sin with a mirror metaphor or simile, as in James Locher's prologue of Barclay's publication: "Therfore let euery man beholde and ouerrede this boke: And than I doute nat but he shal se the errours of his lyfe of what condycyon that he be. in lyke wyse as he shal se in a Myrrour the fourme of his countenaunce and vysage."[9] Clearly the comparison is important, for it is repeated in Barclay's own introduction: "this our Boke representeth vnto the iyen of the redars the states and condicions of men: so that euery man may behold within the same the cours of his lyfe and his mys-gouerned maners, as he sholde beholde the shadowe of the fygure of his visage within a bright Myrrour."[10]

Nigellus Wireker's *Speculum stultorum,* or *Mirror of Fools,* a much older book (1160, but republished many times, as late as 1669), is introduced with a similar declaration:

> The title of this book is *Speculum stultorum*. It has been given this name in order that foolish men may observe as in a mirror the foolishness of others and may then correct their own folly, and that they may learn to censure in themselves those things which they find reprehensible in others. But even as a mirror reflects only the outward appearance and the form of those who look into it, but never holds the memory of a past image, so is it with fools. Seldom, and then only with difficulty, are they drawn away from their folly, no matter how much they may have been taught by the foolishness of others.[11]

The frontispiece of *Speculum stultorum* predictably illustrates a fool in cap and bells holding a mirror up to the hero of the story, Daun Burnel the Ass, whose reflection in it is clearly visible. . . .

Also, there is the example of the trickster-fool Eulenspiegel, known in England as Howleglas (owl-glass), whose very name declares his function. The frontispiece of the book of his adventures, written in 1500 by the anonymous N., shows him with an owl in one hand and a mirror in the other. . . .[12] The message is always the same: here is the glass wherein you may behold your own folly.

III

Yet the reasonable suggestion that Lear's Fool also carries a mirror has not been examined by Shakespeare scholars, perhaps because of a certain disagreeable redundancy in the conception. In other words, if the Fool is himself the King's mirror, the "glass" in which his follies are reflected, why should he need to hold one too? To the modern audience, the device might seem repetitious or naively obvious, although evidently it was acceptable to the original viewers precisely because it evoked a readily recognizable tradition. Playgoers were formerly much more comfortable with emblemata than we are today, and considerably more receptive to the signals they provided. But the Fool's mirror conveys to us, too, a potent purpose beyond its specific emblematic import. It is this object which sets him apart as an iconic and didactic presence in a play of elementary proverbial wisdom and instruction on the most fundamental of lessons. We are intended to share in Lear's education—"set to school to an ant"—that we might learn, as a child does, from what is familiar, very plain, and, if need be, often repeated. A mirror in the hand of Lear's Fool produces something of this naive instructional effect, although the perception would be altogether insufficient to make the case if the lines in *King Lear* did not also give evidence.

It is remarkable that there are several unnoticed sections that do provide such evidence, but before citing them, it is necessary to mention other meanings of the mirror well established by the time of Shakespeare. I do not refer here to the ubiquitous use of the metaphor so thoroughly outlined in Professor Grabes' *The Mutable Glass,*[13] where it means "model" or "exemplar," (as in *The Myrrour of Magistrates*), but to specific iconographic associations. It was also understood as the standard attribute of the personages of Truth and Prudence, and of self-knowledge. . . . These virtues (or the egregious lack of them) are immediately recognizable as basic themes of the tragedy,[14] so that one would hardly be surprised to see a modern production that somehow introduced an on-stage looking-glass for its symbolic value.

The hypothesis here is that Shakespeare intended Lear's Fool to carry this complex emblem, thus prompting a re-examination of the lines. A surprising number would seem to reward the examiner, for they do assume significance and resonance in the light of the hypothesis, and enrich the important themes just named. The most notable of these passages is the "sweet and bitter fool" rhyme:

> *Fool:* That lord that counsell'd thee
> To give away thy land,
> Come place him here by me,
> Do thou for him stand.
> The sweet and bitter fool
> Will presently appear:
> The one in motley here,
> The other found out there.
> *Lear:* Dost thou call me fool, boy?
> (1.4.140-48)

Textual footnotes almost always agree that upon his last verse the Fool points to King Lear; Lear is the "bitter fool."[15] The troubling weakness of this interpretation is that it is undramatic, not very funny, nor does it really make sense. Is it worth the effort for the jester to set Lear up elaborately as the foolish lord and then point to him as a fool? Lear's response, "Dost thou call me fool, boy?" seems a superfluous question considering the thinness of the disguise. It is also awkward and implausible to "place him here by me" and then immediately say that the bitter fool, Lear, is "found out there." But with the prop of a mirror, this very oddity reveals a significant meaning.

Consider this interpretation: The Fool gives his mirror to Lear, instructing him to "stand" for the counsellor, who, mirror in hand, becomes a mock-Prudence, ostensibly the opposite of Folly. The Fool declares himself the "sweet" fool and then points, not at King Lear, but *into the mirror.* The "bitter fool" will presently appear *within the looking-glass.* The old man credulously looks where the Fool points, and sees—himself. "Dost thou call me fool, boy?" he demands, perhaps still uncertain of the Fool's intent.

This explication of the rhyme surely makes more dramatic sense than the generally accepted interpretation. It is at once comic and painful when the King is led (as a child might be) to peer curiously into the glass, realizing after a brief but crucial moment that the joke is on him.[16] Moreover, in discovering that he is the bitter fool, Lear presents familiar emblems. First, holding the glass, he seems the prudent counsellor, taking on the iconography of Prudence herself (who, in addition to bearing a glass, often wears the mask of an old man behind her head to signify the wisdom of years with its ability to look both backward and forward . . .); but then we recognize the iconography of the fool shown his folly. . . . This is not Prudence after all. Lear's petulant response indicates that he is not yet ready to learn from his errors, that he lacks the Socratic self-knowledge symbolized in Ripa's *Iconologia* by a mirror in the hand of Instruction. . . . Although a venerable figure similar to Ripa's, King Lear—too foolish, too stubborn, too old to learn—becomes, in this vignette, a negative example of introspection and the anti-type of Instruction.

In the same scene, the Fool very likely makes didactic use of his mirror a second time when he interjects that Lear is "Lear's shadow" (1.4.231). The word is sometimes synonymous with "reflection," as in the quotation from Barclay cited above, with the usage occasionally found in Shakespeare, as in *Richard II:* "The shadow of your sorrow hath destroy'd / The shadow of your face" (4.1.292-93); or in *Richard III:* "Shine out, fair sun, till I have bought a glass, / That I may see my shadow as I pass" (1.2.262-63). Understanding "Lear's shadow" in this sense, it is reasonable to suppose that the Fool might augment the words with Lear's actual reflection by raising a mirror to his master's face.[17]

This seems the more likely if we consider that at that very moment the King has briefly *closed his eyes:*

Lear: Does any here know me? This is not Lear.
Does Lear walk thus? speak thus? Where are his eyes?
Either his notion weakens, his discernings
Are lethargied—Ha! waking? 'Tis not so.
Who is it that can tell me who I am?
Fool: Lear's shadow.

(1.4.226-31)

The enraged king can hardly believe that the insulting events of the scene are happening to him: he *must* be asleep. As he speaks his astonishment, he feigns a sleep-walker's lethargy. He shuts his eyes: "Where are his eyes?"; and opens them with the words "Ha! waking?" Thus the Fool has time to position himself while Lear staggers absurdly as a somnambulist about the stage.[18] The tragic "Who is it that can tell me who I am?" from one who so slenderly knows himself is *dramatically* answered not only by the Fool's words, "Lear's shadow," but by the presentation of the appropriate emblem of self-knowledge and of folly. Perhaps the jester has another purpose as well. According to Stoic theory well known to Shakespeare, an angry man—as Lear certainly is at this moment—might mitigate his rage, and avert its consequences, if confronted with his reflection in a mirror.[19]

IV

It becomes almost problematic to explain the absence of an on-stage mirror in *King Lear,* so well does this symbol accord with the fundamental themes already mentioned: truth, prudence, folly, instruction, and self-knowledge. Other factors also suggest its place in the iconography of the play. For example, although Lear's jester may be identified by his coxcomb and motley, which are mentioned several times, there is no reference at all to the characteristic "bauble," nor any evidence that he owns one. When he would confer on Caius the status of fool (for following one who is "out of favor"), he offers only his coxcomb. Could it be that he does not have a bauble to offer because he has a mirror in his hand instead?[20] Moreover, the looking-glass symbol operates with several glass and mirror images: "I shall not need spectacles," "glass-gazing," "Get thee glass eyes," "see thyself," "Lend me a looking-glass." Its very shape—round, convex, and globe-like in most of our illustrations—repeats the circular figures of the play: coronet, "operation of the orbs," "true blank of thine eye," "O without a figure," "wheel of fire," "wheel come full circle."[21] And, as the attribute of Prudence placed in the hand of a motley fool, it restates one of the most persistent motifs in *King Lear,* that of "the world turned upside-down," in which fathers beg blessing of daughters, "the cart draws the horse," "old fools are babes," one "goes to bed at noon," and an aged father outlives his children contrary to the way of nature.

But the Fool's mirror makes an appearance of another kind in Act 3, Scene 2 when, prior to his exit, he declares, "I'll speak a prophecy ere I go." His glass now becomes a *magic mirror* as he delivers a prophecy in "pseudo-Chaucerian"[22] lines:

> When priests are more in word than matter;
> When brewers mar their malt with water;
> When nobles are their tailors' tutors;
> No heretics burn'd, but wenches' suitors;
> Then shall the realm of Albion
> Come to great confusion.
> When every case in law is right;
> No squire in debt, nor no poor knight;
> When slanders do not live in tongues;
> Nor cutpurses come not to throngs;
> When usurers tell their gold i' th' field;
> And bawds and whores do churches build;
> Then comes the time, who lives to see't,
> That going shall be us'd with feet.
> This prophecy Merlin shall make; for I live
>   before his time.
>
> (80-96)

Although there is no definite indication of a glass here, the presence of one would change for the better the delivery of this long speech. Instead of facing the audience, the Fool would gaze prophet-like into his mirror, intoning the lines with appropriate antics.[23]

What makes this interpretation more likely is that the magic mirror is the usual tool of prognosticators in the art and literature of the period. Magic glasses are discussed in Reginald Scot's *Discouerie of Witchcraft* and in comparable literature.[24] One appears in Beaumont and Fletcher's *The Bloody Brother,* in Greene's *Frier Bacon,* and in Chaucer's "Squire's Tale":

> This mirour eek, that I have in myn hond,
> Hath swich a myght that men may in it see
> Whan ther shal fallen any adversitee
> Unto youre regne or to youreself also,
> And openly who is youre freend or foo.
>
> (132-36)[25]

Shakespeare himself refers to one who "like a prophet / Looks in a glass" (*Measure for Measure* 2.2.94-95), and he places a prophetic mirror in the hand of Banquo's eighth king to show Macbeth the future Stuart line. Most important, the magician Merlin employs an enchanted mirror in Spenser's *Faerie Queene* (a known source for *King Lear*) through which the whole world can be seen and the future foretold. The Fool's mention of Merlin at the close of his "prophecy" confirms the likelihood that a prognostic glass was intended in *Lear* also.[26] Indeed, the Fool fantastically declares that he is acting the part of Merlin "before his time."

V

The hypothesis that Lear's Fool was intended to carry a mirror on the stage is strengthened by accumulation. The supposition that the Fool makes mouths in an actual glass becomes more credible because he appears to have a mirror in three other instances ("Lear's shadow," "The other found out there," and "I'll speak a prophecy"). One naturally looks for other citations which would verify further, and some possibilities deserve mention in closing. For example, the Fool might be entertaining himself with his glass in this passage:

> *Fool:* Shalt see thy other daughter will use thee kindly, for though she's as like this as a crab's like an apple, yet I can tell what I can tell.
>
> *Lear:* What canst tell, boy?
>
> *Fool:* She will taste as like this as a crab does to a crab. Thou canst tell why one's nose stands i' th' middle on's face?
>
> (1.5.14-20)

The play on "crab" (meaning crab apple, but with the implication of a "crabby" face); the talk of exact likeness; the emphatic use of "this" in both lines 15 and 18, which may signal sour faces grimaced for the benefit of the audience; the "telling" of things to come; and the riddle about the location of one's nose together indicate, or at least strongly suggest, that the Fool is regarding himself in a mirror as he speaks.[27]

Finally, there is an instance at the end of the play which, although also uncertain, could dramatically modify our perception of that pitiful and terrible scene. Enter Lear with Cordelia in his arms. Frantically he calls for a looking-glass, hoping she might yet be alive: "If that her breath will mist or stain the stone, / Why then she lives" (5.3.263-64). The heart-rending sorrow of this scene replicates the ending of *The Rape of Lucrece,* for there, too, "children predecease progenitors" (1756), leaving a father to lament a daughter's death. In these strikingly similar denouments, the identical image, that of the mirror, is evoked. Lucrece becomes for her sorrowing father a "Poor broken glass" in which he sees reflected the face of death (1758-61).[28] Lear, lacking a glass, desperately tries a feather, which does not stir. Is the mirror ever brought as he commands?[29] No stage direction indicates that it is, but if it is, surely it would be the long-absent Fool's own mirror, cracked now to signify his death, but recognizable to all, and a pathetic reminder of a "great thing of us forgot." Perhaps it is the sight of this very object which suggests to King Lear the remarkably ambiguous "And my poor fool is hang'd" (5.3.306), for it would be as if the body of the Fool were carried onto the stage. At this insupportable moment, Fool and daughter actually seem confused in Lear's failing mind. Moreover, because the Fool apparently is played by the same actor that boys Cordelia, the Shakespearean audience would respond in a similar way to their gradually merging identities, associating both together at last with the same transcendent principles of truth and selfless love.[30] And then, the dead Fool mystically present, a new and final truth would be told. Held to the lifeless mouth of Cordelia, but clairvoyantly reflecting the forgotten Fool, the mirror would become in the hand of the expiring king a symbol of the ultimate truth of death and of the ultimate self-knowledge.

Notes

[1] Shakespeare quotations are taken from *The Riverside Shakespeare,* ed. G. Blakemore Evans (Boston, 1974).

[2] For an example, see C. Herbert Gilliland, "*King Lear* III.ii.25-36: The Fool's 'Codpiece' Song," *English Language Notes,* 22, no. 2 (1984), 16-19.

[3] Cf., *The Winter's Tale* (1.2.116-17): "making practic'd smiles, / As in a looking-glass"; or *A Midsummer Night's Dream* (3.2.238): "Make mouths upon me when I turn my back." A fair lady with a fool at her feet regards her visage in a glass in Brosamer's engraving, "Le Fou et la Femme," reproduced in Raimond van Marle, *Iconographie de l'art profane au moyen-age et a la renaissance* (New York, 1971), II, p. 453, fig. 485.

[4] "Wits Miserie, and the Worlds Madnesse," in *The Complete Works of Thomas Lodge,* ed. E. W. Grosse (New York, 1963), IV, p. 84.

[5] Quoted in Olive Mary Busby, *Studies in the Development of the Fool in the Elizabethan Drama* (London, 1923), p. 66.

[6] Busby, p. 41. Other complaints of "scurvey" and "Mimik" faces "match't with monarchs, and with mighty kings" are noted in Leslie Hotson, *Shakespeare's Motley* (New York, 1952), pp. 86-87.

[7] William R. Elton, *"King Lear" and the Gods* (San Marino, Calif., 1966), p. 303, notes: "The Renaissance secularization of folly increasingly transformed it from a context of sinfulness to one of imprudence."

[8] Sebastian Brant, *Shyp of Folys of the World,* trans. Alexander Barclay (1509); also see T. H. Jamieson's edition of Barclay's *The Ship of Fools* (Edinburg, 1874).

[9] Jamieson Vol. I, p. 10.

[10] Jamieson p. 17.

[11] Nigellus Wireker, *The Book of Daun Burnel the Ass: Nigellus Wireker's "Speculum stultorum,"* trans., intro. and notes by Graydon W. Regenos (Austin, Texas, 1959), p. 23.

[12] Although the owl is often associated with wisdom, it is also frequently used as a symbol of folly, stupidity, ignobility, and drunkenness. In *Troilus and Cressida* (2.1.90), Ajax calls Thersites a "vile owl." See Seymour Slive, "On the Meaning of Frans Hals' 'Malle Babbe,'" *Burlington,* 105 (1963), 432-36; also, Enid Welsford, *The Fool: His Social and Literary History* (London, 1935), p. 223 illustrates fools with their owl.

[13] Herbert Grabes, *The Mutable Glass: Mirror-imagery in Titles and Texts of the Middle Ages and English Renaissance,* trans. Gordon Collier (Cambridge, Eng., 1982).

[14] To expand on these themes, or to cite the scholarship, would prove a monumental task, far beyond the scope of this essay. Truth differs in appearance from Prudence in that the former is frequently nude and holds a balance. For an examination of the iconography of truth, see Ivan Gaskell, "Vermeer, judgment and truth," *Burlington,* 126, (1984), 557-61. The mirror of Prudence also signifies self-reflection. Socrates was remembered to have exhorted his pupils to "know" themselves, and indeed to view themselves each day in a looking-glass to reflect on their deportment. See Grabes, pp. 137-39, for the "Socratic" mirror as the way to self-knowledge and self-correction. The mirror symbolizes self-knowledge in *Julius Caesar* (1.2.51-70), e.g., "And since you know you cannot see yourself / So well as by reflection, I, your glass, / Will modestly discover to yourself / That of yourself which you yet know not of."

[15] E.g., *The Riverside Shakespeare,* p. 1262, n. 147; the Arden *King Lear,* ed. Kenneth Muir (London, 1972), contains a similar gloss.

[16] Perhaps "sweet fool" refers to the one who holds up the mirror, while "bitter fool" means the one who is obliged to see himself reflected there. The expression, "found out there," contains a clever play on words: "Found out" means "discovered," while "out there" refers to the world within the looking-glass.

[17] Marvin Rosenberg, *The Masks of King Lear* (Berkeley, 1972) p. 107, states parenthetically, "A mirror in Fool's hand would multiply ironies. He is Lear's looking-glass. Does Lear himself carry a mirror?" Elsewhere (pp. 118-19) Rosenberg suggests that the Fool may hold a mirror up to show Lear "who he is." In the Quartos, the words "Lear's shadow?" are spoken in the interrogative by Lear, not the fool, and although this is not the widely accepted version, it is possible that Lear himself utters these words in response to the mirror thrust before him.

[18] The crux of this interpretation is that "walk" means "sleepwalk." See Lawrence Rosinger, "Shakespeare's *King Lear,* I.iv.226-230," *Explicator,* 41, no. 4 (1983), 8; and *Macbeth,* 5.1.2-3: "When was it she last *walk'd?*" (my italics).

[19] Grabes, p. 139.

[20] In Renaissance illustrations of fools, their baubles sometimes are graced with a carved fool's face, so that the clownish holder might confront or converse with his own image. To replace this with a mirror is consistent and plausible.

[21] See Rolf Soellner, "*King Lear* and the Magic of the Wheel," *Shakespeare Quarterly,* 35 (1984), 274-89. He states, "The play of Shakespeare in which the figures of circle and wheel are most prominent is *King Lear,*" and notes that most of the circular images in *Lear* are vertical, like the Wheel of Fortune, rather than horizontal, like the coronet. Elton, pp. 135-36, discusses cyclic themes and wheel imagery. The Fool's advice to Kent about a great wheel rolling down a hill (2.4.71-77) could be demonstrated with the round mirror, another "vertical" circle, serving as the wheel. Imagine how he would use its handle to pantomime "lest it break thy neck."

[22] As glossed in the Arden edition, the style of the lines quoted "are a parody of some pseudo-Chaucerian verses to be found in Puttenham, *Arte of English Poesie.*" Busby, pp. 69-70, points out that mock prophecy speeches of this kind are not unusual for clowns, and cites examples. Cf. Regan's words, "Jesters do oft prove prophets" (5.3.71). The "prognostic fool" theme occurs earlier. Gulled into believing in Edgar's perfidy, Gloucester finds confirmation of astrological prophecies: "This villain of mine comes under the prediction" (1.2.109-10).

[23] For example, upon "Then shall the realm of Albion / Come to great confusion," the Fool might turn the glass upside-down, figuring the "topsy-turvy world," which his speech essentially describes.

[24] For a discussion of the magic mirror, see Grabes, pp. 125-30.

[25] *The Works of Geoffrey Chaucer,* ed. F. N. Robinson (Boston, 1957), p. 129.

[26] See Roland M. Smith, "King Lear and the Merlin Tradition," *Modern Language Quarterly,* 7 (1946), 153-74. The author notes that the many references to Merlin literature in *Lear* argue that the Fool's "prophecy" lines are authentically Shakespeare's (154).

[27] It is remarkable that in *The Taming of the Shrew* (2.1.225-33), "crab" is associated not only with a sour face, but with a fool's coxcomb and a mirror.

[28] The father's lament over his dead daughter at the end of *The Rape of Lucrece* (1751-76) bears other comparisons with *King Lear:* "If children predecease progenitors, / We are their offspring, and they none of ours" (1756-57) is a *monde renversé* idea comparable to many in *King Lear.* Lucretius "counterfeits to die with her" (1776), as Lear actually does with Cordelia. See also 1812-13 and 1819-20 for fool motifs resembling *King Lear.* Cf. Truth's mirror in plate 6, which also reflects "a bare-bon'd death by time outworn" (*Lucrece,* 1761).

[29] Rosenberg, pp. 313-14, calls this looking-glass "a grim metaphor for the whole search for identity," but believes that both feather and glass are figments of Lear's disordered imagination. In *Richard II* (4.1.265ff.), a king calls for a glass which is brought, and which he turns to a symbol of *vanitas* by dashing it to the ground.

[30] See Richard Abrams, "The Double Casting of Cordelia and Lear's Fool: A Theatrical View," *Texas Studies in Literature and Language,* 27 (1985), 354-68, which shows how audience awareness of double casting "heightens the play's pathos by inducing an ironic consciousness." E. A. J. Honigmann, *Shakespeare: Seven Tragedies: The Dramatist's Manipulation of Response* (London, 1976), p. 116, believes that at the end of the play, "Cordelia and the Fool have become one in Lear's mind."

Bente A. Videbæk (essay date 1996)

SOURCE: "Lear's Fool in *King Lear,*" in *The Stage Clown in Shakespeare's Theatre,* Greenwood Press, 1996, pp. 123-35.

[*In the essay below, Videbæk explores the dimensions of the Fool's character and states that the Fool understands the "human condition" and pities the characters in the play who suffer under the harsh conditions of Lear's world. Furthermore, Videbæk contends that the function of Lear's Fool is extended further than that of the clowns in Shakespeare's other plays.*]

In *Troilus and Cressida,* Thersites' continuous exertions to create and maintain distance between house and stage through caustic commentary shows us a clown whose lack of compassion and empathy makes the comedy work. The audience needs this distance not to become distracted from the main points of the play. In *King Lear,* the Fool's biting jests result from the very opposite. Lear's Fool is a creature whose whole being is founded on understanding of the human condition and pity for those who cannot cope with the harsh realities of Lear's world. Where Thersites willingly isolates himself from human contact and does his best to ensure that bonds are broken and illusions rent, Lear's Fool, though biting, is always loyal, caring, and compassionate.

Lear's Fool in is the only clown in a major part found in a tragedy, and this fact adds new dimensions to him. Apart from this instance, Shakespeare has employed clowns only in minor parts in tragedies, and mainly used them to illuminate a turning point in the action. Lear's Fool certainly helps focus our attention on crucial turning points, but he has a much more expanded function, if not easy to pinpoint. In the great comedies where we find the other court jester clowns, their function is straightforward and not far different from that of the minor clowns. The mere sight of the clown is a signal to the audience, and we are ready to laugh before we even know what the jest will be, or at whom it will be directed. The nimble tongues of these clowns never bring them trouble more serious than a remote threat of banishment. Their mobility is great and fascinating, and they are welcome and enjoyed anywhere.

Not so Lear's Fool. He is so glued to Lear that he becomes an added dimension of Lear himself, and both he and Lear seem aware that this is so, if only unconsciously. Nimble though the Fool may be in body and tongue, his is not an unproblematic existence, and he is repeatedly threatened with whipping.[1] On the background of these repeated threats and his worsening circumstances, our laughter becomes constricted and may even disappear. Indeed, the Fool more often than not has to labor to extract laughter even from his master. Yet there is no doubt of Lear's attachment to him and our need for his presence. Lear's Fool is a court jester, and his essential function is no different from that of the court jesters in the comedies; he too brings forth the aspect of human folly and holds it up to ridicule. In the comedies, however, the target is broad and includes general ideas, but in the tragedy of *King Lear* the King's folly is the main target, and our involvement with the King becomes so close that laughter at him will be perceived as directed at ourselves also. Growing old and being unable to sound the depths of our fellow human beings are both conditions common to us all. Our understanding of these plights, and our involvement in Lear's fate which stems from it, can easily make us incapable of objectivity. Though we may feel uncomfortable about the Fool, we need him to keep our perspective on King Lear. The Fool as mediator between stage and audience is not always welcome to us, and though he is loved, the Fool's comments are not always welcome to Lear either; but as the real world fades from Lear's view and his sight is directed inwards in madness we come to see the Fool in a different light.

It can be debated whether the Fool is present in the first scene of the play, where Lear divides his kingdom and banishes Cordelia. The Fool does have many periods of silent presence on stage throughout the play, and it may be argued that this whole scene is one of them; if so, the bond between Lear and his Fool can be forged from the very beginning. But the Fool can serve a better purpose as a voice of reason rather than as an outcropping of Lear only, and therefore should not come on stage until he is called for. In the first scene, Cordelia herself serves the purpose of distinguishing reasonable from unreasonable and truth from lies, a function the Fool will take over once she departs for France. The clown-as-truth-teller is no new thing with Shakespeare, but the genuinely and deeply sad clown is.

The Fool is mentioned before we meet him: "Did my father strike my gentleman for chiding of his Fool?" asks Goneril, and labels this as another "gross crime" of her father's (I.iii.1-2, 5). Again in I.iv the Fool is mentioned before he appears. He is called for no less than four times, and the link between him and Cordelia is strongly pointed out:

> *Lear.* But where's my Fool? I have not seen him this two days.
> *Knight.* Since my young Lady's going into France, Sir, the Fool hath much pined away.
> *Lear.* No more of that; I have noted it well.
> (I.iv.69-73)

Apparently the mention of dinner triggers Lear's wish to see his Fool, presumably to be entertained during the meal, but the skirmish between Kent and Oswald makes both him and us forget the Fool momentarily. Therefore the effect is one of great surprise once the Fool comes up and makes himself "visible." Lear praises Kent and makes a kingly gesture of bestowing his favors on him and hiring him, but the Fool puts things back in perspective:

> *Lear.* Now, my friendly knave, I thank thee: there's earnest of thy service.
> *Fool.* Let me hire him too: here's my coxcomb.
> *Lear.* How now, my pretty knave! how dost thou?
> *Fool.* Sirrah, you were best take my coxcomb.
> *Kent.* Why, Fool?
> *Fool.* Why? for taking one's part that's out of favour.
> (I.iv.91-97)

The Fool glides up unnoticed and, ignoring Lear and his friendly question, proceeds to demonstrate the lie of the land for Kent. Only when this is accomplished does he do the same for Lear:

> How now, Nuncle! Would I had two coxcombs and two daughters!
> *Lear.* Why, my boy?
> *Fool.* If I gave them all my living, I'd keep my coxcombs myself. There's mine; beg another of thy daughters.

Lear. Take heed, sirrah: the whip.
Fool. Truth is a dog must to kennel.

(I.iv.103-109)

The Fool implies, not untruthfully, that he has more to give away than Lear, if only his one coxcomb. Lear has decided to keep the outward show of kingship, but has given away the regal power to his daughters. The Fool offers to give away only the mark of his profession, his hood, and yet will keep his essence. The same sentiments are voiced later (189-191), when the Fool says: "[N]ow thou art an O without a figure. I am better than thou art now; I am a Fool, thou art nothing." He also keeps a firm grasp on the necessity to remain frugal in order to prosper, a piece of advice suited equally well to a pauper and a king:

> Have more than thou showest,
> Speak less than thou knowest,
> Lend less than thou owest,
> Ride more than thou goest,
> Learn more than thou trowest,
> Set less than thou throwest;
> Leave thy drink and thy whore,
> And keep in-a-door,
> And thou shalt have more
> Than two tens to a score.
> . . . Can you make no use of nothing, Nuncle?
> *Lear.* Why no, boy, nothing can be made out of nothing.

(I.iv.116-130)

These three uses of "nothing" clearly recall the exchange between Cordelia and Lear in I.i (85-89). The echoes of Cordelia's speech in the Fool's lines serves to forge a bond of continuity between the two. The truly loving daughter is no longer with her father; his Fool, whose love is also great, has taken it upon himself to try to save Lear. The Fool's advice comes belatedly, however, as Lear has already sinned against all the commandments of rationality set up therein.

During this whole scene the Fool, in spite of threats of the whip, continues to press up to the fine line of Lear's tolerance. He calls Lear "Nuncle" and "my boy" (134), the same terms of endearment Lear uses for him, but in the same breath he also indirectly calls him a fool in one of the jingling rhymes he uses to get his points across (137-144). There is no doubt that of the two, Lear is the bitter fool.

The Fool also implies that Lear has entered into second childhood. He has "mad[e his] daughters [his] mothers" (168-169), and in the parallel of the egg and its two crowns (152-162) the Fool equates Lear with the meat of the egg, that which would become the chicken, but which is eaten here before its fulfillment. Lear's "bald crown" which used to bear the golden one, is the home of nothing; he has "pared [his] wit o'both sides and left nothing in the middle" (183-184). This continual prodding of Lear apparently pains the Fool: "I had rather be any kind o'thing than a fool; and yet I would not be thee, Nuncle" (181-183).

When Goneril enters, the Fool waxes daring and exploits her comments to further stress his point. Goneril is "the cuckoo" (213) which bit off the hedge-sparrow's head when there was no more need of food, and she is the one who blew out the light and left them "darkling" (215). She is also "the ass" (221), who sees the cart draw the horse. And to Lear's question: "Who is it that can tell me who I am?" the Fool replies: "Lear's shadow" (227-228). None of these parallels are flattering ones, and by his prodding the Fool fans the tempers of both father and daughter. Lear, insulted, leaves her house, and he forgets his Fool, both when he storms from the stage and finds half his knights gone and when he finally leaves in anger. Goneril sends him away:

> You, sir, more knave than fool, after your master.
> *Fool.* Nuncle Lear, Nuncle Lear! tarry, take the Fool with thee.
>   A fox, when one has caught her,
>   And such a daughter,
>   Should sure to the slaughter,
>   If my cap would buy a halter;
>   So the Fool follows after.

(I.iv.312-320)

When present, the Fool easily dominates the business on stage, making himself the center of the audience's attention because of the truths he delivers, and certainly also because of his physical agility.[2] This is the only Shakespearean court fool who stays attached to one master, and it would be a mistake not to let him make use of the court fool's traditional acrobatics, at least while he is still at court. Many of his speeches, particularly the rhymed ones, can be underscored by nimble skipping and jumping, especially once Goneril comes on stage, when he can hide behind Lear or Kent and pop out for a quick verbal salvo. His power of repartee is strongly linked to this physical aspect of his stage presence. When Lear and Goneril have their thunderous confrontation, the Fool has a span of almost one hundred lines of silence before he is literally thrown out. He could make use of this time by gradually becoming immobile as the confrontation sharpens, finally to cower in real fear when Lear leaves him, and then regain his mobility when he exits.

The short doggerel he uses as his exit line is a theatrically interesting thing. The Fool makes the entire action freeze while he steps out of the play, but not of his role, and addresses the audience directly. He has a similar effect in III.ii, where he ends the scene alone with the audience and delivers Merlin's prophecy (81-96). In both instances he serves as a lull, an eye of the storm, and creates an instance of breathing space before the next onslaught. In the third act we are in the midst of the actual storm scenes, but the tempest of tempers in the first act is a necessary prelude, an end to the Fool's comfortable existence and the beginning of his efforts to keep together the tattered remnants of Lear's reason.

The Fool of the first act is still a court jester, but the storm Goneril and Lear create between them forges him so close to Lear as to make them almost one. William Willeford says of the court fool:

> The fool enriches the king as a symbol of the self by making a constant game of our tendency to take the symbol for granted. And when the king loses his power to symbolize an experience of the self, that experience is available by way of compensation through the fool and the dissolution of consciousness that he effects.[3]

Such is the expected relationship between king and jester, and that is what we encounter in *King Lear* when we first see the Fool in action. But after Lear's fortunes truly begin to slide, the change is obvious. This must be very clear from the Fool's bearing. His court jester nimbleness may surface from time to time, but the audience has to see the change between Lear the King and Lear the husk of the King, and one efficient way to make this come across is in the physical behavior of the Fool. The Fool will disappear from the play when the question of Lear's kingship is no longer as urgent as that of Lear's fundamental humanity, that is at the true turning point, the lowest point of Lear's fortunes, where he takes over from the Fool and begins to make fundamental discoveries about himself and his relationship to his world. Therefore the Fool may describe a downward curve like his master's, may dwindle before us like Lear's reason, and finally fade from the play when Lear's madness takes him over.

I.v is a short scene of transition. Lear is preoccupied and has begun to fear for his sanity. The Fool labors mightily to keep his attention fixed, but has so little success that he changes tactics, only to find Lear even less cooperative. At the beginning of the scene the daughters are still the focus of the Fool's jibes (14-24), and his first reference is directed at Goneril and Regan, but Lear does not rise to the bait; the second one is more subtle, but Lear does not even hear. It is as if his responses are triggered more by the Fool's tone of voice than his actual words. Lear should move about the stage in thought, and the Fool try to engage his attention by following close, sometimes even blocking his way only to be brushed absentmindedly aside. When he finally gets a true response from Lear, it is no credit to his fooling; the King steals the Fool's punch line from him:

> The reason why the seven stars are no mo
>   than seven is a pretty reason.
> *Lear.* Because they are not eight?
> *Fool.* Yes, indeed; thou would'st make a
>   good Fool.
>
> (I.v.34-36)

The Fool exits on another of his little vignettes to the audience: "She that's a maid now, and laughs at my departure, / Shall not be a maid long, unless things be cut shorter" (48-49). He reminds the audience forcibly that though he is still trying to wring a smile from Lear by his jesting, he is cruelly aware of the seriousness of the situation, and the tragic implications of Lear's journey. The Fool has few of these moments completely devoted to the audience. Though he is our teacher and the clown of the play, his teaching is much less pleasant than that of the other court jesters. He teaches us much as he teaches Lear, and that can be caustic at times.

When Lear and the Fool come upon Kent in the stocks (II.iv), we see the same pattern. The Fool again attempts to catch Lear's attention, but now he gets even less response. We see a declining curve; Lear hears the Fool's words subconsciously, and reacts with a comment about his daughters, then about his impending madness, and finally not at all:

> *Fool.* Ha, ha! he wears cruel garters.
>   Horses are tied by the heads, dogs and
>   bears by th'neck, monkeys by th'loins,
>   and man by th'legs: when a man's
>   overlusty at legs then he wears wooden
>   nether-stocks.
> *Lear.* What's he that hath so much thy place
>   mistook
> To set thee here?
> *Kent.*   It is both he and she,
>   Your son and daughter.
> *Lear.* No.
>
> . . . . .
>
> *Fool.* Fathers that wear rags
>   Do make their children blind,
> But fathers that bear bags
>   Shall see their children kind.
> Fortune, that errant whore,
> Ne'er turns the key to th'poor.
> But for all this thou shalt have as many
>   dolours for thy daughters as thou canst tell
>   in a year.
> *Lear.* O! how this mother swells up toward
>   my heart;
> *Hysterica passio!* down, thou
>   climbing sorrow!
> Thy element's below.

> *Lear.* O me! my heart, my rising heart! but, down!
>
> *Fool.* Cry to it, Nuncle, as the cockney did to the eels when she put 'em i'th'paste alive; she knapp'd 'em o'th'coxcombs with a stick, and cried 'Down, wantons, down!' 'Twas her brother that, in pure kindness to his horse, buttered his hay.
>
> (II.iv.8-14; 46-56; 118-123)

The Fool tries his best but never reaches his master, who probably does not even notice his presence. In all three cases the Fool makes use of traditional techniques: he equates man with animals; he delivers a bit of doggerel and puns; finally he ridicules human stupidity. But no matter how pointed the Fool's observations may be to the audience, Lear is oblivious to them. It should come as a relief to the Fool when Kent reacts to his joking in the expected manner and answers him in prose as a contrast to Lear's verse (61-83). But during Lear's absence and his bout with Kent, the Fool also manages to express his unswerving loyalty to Lear (79-82). It is to the Fool, all he has left, that Lear cries: "O Fool! I shall go mad" (284).

During Lear's confrontation first with Regan, then both daughters, we have another of the Fool's long periods of silent presence. He is given no *Exit* in the Folio, but Quarto Two gives him one with Lear between lines 284 and 285, leaving him on stage without speaking for about 160 lines. His behavior now should echo that of the first act, where he was in a similar situation. We have just seen him hard at work to reach Lear, and it has been a sad affair for the Fool. More than ever he is predisposed to shrink back behind the fighting giants and finally cower close to Lear, probably even cling to his robe, as the Folio's *Storm and Tempest* is heard at line 282. Shakespeare employs the traditional and moving image of the fool cowering under the mantle of the defiant king, which shows us, as it were, two aspects of the same thing simultaneously, but Lear and his Fool are no mere image. The mighty clashes between Lear and his daughters, and between Lear's inner and outer man, leave less and less room for the Fool as jester, even the Fool as critic. The Fool is becoming more a symbol than a clown; he always was a symbol of Lear's court that was, now he begins to signify Lear's dwindling powers of reasonable action and reaction.

There is little room for laughter in *King Lear,* and what there is, is different from our unrestrained response to the comedies. The nature of the tragic mode prevents us. In a comedy we are interested in the outcome, but we remain in a position from where we may regard the proceedings with some superiority. In tragedy, however, we easily lose such a perspective because of our great personal involvement in the target of the jokes, here Lear himself. The stage clown in the guise of the Fool does trigger some amused response in the audience periodically, but when he first comes on stage the tragedy has already advanced too far to allow him free play. Even his remarks directed to the audience alone are more moralistic than amusing. We have been prepared for such behavior in the Fool, who has "much pined away" and is not his true self even when we first meet him. From the beginning of our relationship with this clown, he comes to stand as a mirror for Lear's decline; but where Lear's outward show and just cause for anger may periodically divert us from the downward curve, the Fool's behavior helps refocus our attention. The mirroring becomes ever more significant as we move into the third act. While the storm is raging, we are prepared for our next encounter with Lear and his Fool. Lear is alone in the storm, striving "in his little world of man to out-storm / The to-and-fro-conflicting wind and rain," and with him is "None but the Fool, who labours to out-jest / His heart-strook injuries" (10-11, 16-17). The pattern we have become used to will continue.

Not until III.ii does the Fool truly begin harping on sexuality:

> The cod-piece that will house
>   Before the head has any,
> The head and he shall louse;
>   So beggars marry many.
> . . . For there was yet never fair woman but she made mouths in a glass.
>
> . . . . .
>
> *Kent.* Who's there?
> *Fool.* Marry, here's grace and a cod-piece, that's a wise man and a Fool.
>
> (III.ii.27-41)

Sexuality, indeed, becomes greatly important later in the play, when Lear in his madness confronts the blinded Gloucester:

> What was thy cause?
> Adultery?
> Thou shalt not die: die for adultery! No:
> The wren goes to't, and the small gilded fly
> Does lecher in my sight.
> Let copulation thrive;
>
> (IV.vi.109-114)

Sexuality and the resulting issue is the strongest link between Lear's and Gloucester's tragedies. Gloucester is first to draw attention to a sexual transgression. In I.i he presents his bastard son Edmund to Kent, and freely admits that he was begotten out of wedlock. Lear has committed no such violation, but his view of love is clearly warped; he accepts his daughters' professions that they love him above everything else, but Cordelia is aware that something is wrong: "Sure I shall never marry like my sisters, / To love my father all" (I.i.102-103). The Fool's sexual allusions are comparatively few; but like every remark the Fool makes, these comments reach out to encompass a large problem within the play and create echoes of things past and hints of things to come.

When Kent comes to offer Lear shelter in a hovel, Lear becomes truly aware of his Fool for the first time since I.iv, but as a fellow human being rather than his jester. The Fool answers with a song to fit them both:

> *Lear.* My wits begin to turn.
> Come on, my boy. How dost, my boy? Art
>   cold?
> I'm cold myself. . . .
> Poor Fool and knave, I have one part in my
>   heart
> That's sorry yet for thee.
> *Fool.* He that has and a little tiny wit,
> With hey, ho, the wind and the rain,
> Must make content with his fortunes fit,
> Though the rain it raineth every day.
>
>   (III.ii.68-77)

Lear's anguish in combination with the storm has finally opened his eyes to the misery of the Fool, the one being more miserable than himself because he is more aware of Lear's decline. Lear's wits are slowly becoming extinguished, and when we meet him again after the storm is over, he must make do with what fortune has left him, nothing.

Merlin's prophecy, with which the Fool ends the scene, points in the same direction. When the world is turned upside-down, England shall "[c]ome to great confusion" (92). There is much truth to this prophecy. Lear's England, as well as Lear the microcosm, are both in great confusion, and the cause is to be found within Lear himself. Lear's idea that the essence and the show of kingship can be divided is as absurd as most elements in the prophecy "Merlin shall make" when his time comes. Only for Lear there is no hope of an Arthur to put things to rights. Though the Fool has this moment alone with the audience, he does not make use of it to solicit our laughter. Much of the prophecy can be seen as ridiculous and amusing when separated from its context of the storm scenes, especially the bits of social criticism and the fantastically Utopian ideas presented. But though the Fool steps out of the play and plot proper and creates an anachronism by drawing in Merlin, the prophecy is so well related to Lear's condition and its conclusion so apt to become true that the effect is one of sadness rather than mirth.[4] The Fool may not be a bitter fool, but he is a miserable one, and his handling of his misery does him credit.

The Fool as an extension of Lear is even more an object of our pity in III.iv. His court jester image has undergone a complete change. Though his jokes were unsuccessful, he constantly tried to amuse Lear in the past, but in this scene we hear no word from him till line 39. Lear is still concerned for him above himself: "In, boy, go first. You houseless poverty,— / Nay, get thee in" (26-27), and it is a measure of the Fool's misery that he does go in first. What he meets is not shelter, however, but Edgar disguised as Poor Tom. Edgar already has created a close intimacy with the audience, who has witnessed his transformation into Poor Tom. Our closeness with him allows him to put on and use several of the clown's characteristics, though he is no clown himself.[5] In certain ways his antics as Poor Tom are not unlike the Fool's efforts, but the underlying tragedy, which provokes most of the attempts at clowning, is an overwhelming presence and turns possible laughter into deep pity.

The Fool's first reaction to Edgar is fright: "Come not in here, Nuncle; here's a spirit. / Help me! help me! . . . A spirit, a spirit: he says his name's Poor Tom" (39-42). Lear's first reaction to this "spirit," however, is identification, not fright:

> Dids't give all to thy daughters?
> And art thou come to this?
>
>   . . . . .
>
> What! has his daughters brought him to this
>   pass?
> Couldst thou save nothing? Wouldst thou give
>   them all?
>
>   (III.iv.48-63)

In Edgar-as-Poor-Tom, Lear sees a mirror image of himself, a being reduced to nothing except what he was born with, and his indentification will progress so far that he strips himself in order also to become "a poor, bare, forked animal" (105-106). But the Fool's courage and control rise for a moment as Lear's wane. When Lear sees Tom as another who has given his daughters "all," the Fool replies to Lear, but certainly more to the audience: "Nay, he reserv'd a blanket, else we had all been sham'd" (64-65), and shortly afterwards: "This cold night will turn us all to fools and madmen" (77). The first comment has an ironic distance, which the audience needs at this point not to become totally overwhelmed; we see a glimmer of the traditional stage clown in action. The second comment has great truth to it. The horror of the night has been created mainly by Lear's madness, which is pitifully real. Poor Tom's madness is an act put on to save life itself. Of the three, the Fool is the most rational-seeming creature, though he too has felt his world slipping away from under him. They are all three suspended in the storm with no well-known frame of reference; the storm itself has taken over the world as we know it, raging within Lear as well as outside of him. Neither Lear nor Edgar has anything left of what they formerly used to define themselves. The Fool, however, still has his coxcomb, though the rest of his old life is lost. The Fool's remnants of control surface again when Lear strips himself. The Fool gentles him as if he were a little child, a "fool": "Prithee, Nuncle, be contented; 'tis a naughty night to swim in. Now a little fire in a wild field were like an old lecher's heart; a small spark, all the rest on's body cold. Look! here comes a walking fire" (108-111). The Fool still does his best to help Lear and make his way smoother, but his misery is growing as can be seen from another of his long silences. His jester's function becomes suspended when Lear and he are not more or less alone together. When anything even remotely threatening occurs, he fades into the background and into his sorrow. When Lear walks off with Edgar he excludes the Fool, who feels it keenly. At this point in the action, where the Fool's role is almost played out, his physical action should be limited to an absolute minimum. There should be no sprightliness left; in its stead we should see the Fool shivering, hugging himself to regain a little of the warmth a house and friendship provides man with, except when he attempts to comfort Lear; then he should become almost protective. But by now he is his own greatest resource, and he is almost spent.

The Fool, however, does not represent the element of sanity the audience needs to cling to; Kent provides this point of stability and calm. All his attempts at comforting and calming Lear, however, come to nought. In III.vi, the Fool's last scene, Lear passes judgment on his daughters with the help of Tom and the Fool. In this company the Fool resumes his joking, but he is still more the commentator than the court jester, and his subject is still Lear's problematic kingship:

> Prithee, Nuncle, tell me whether a madman
>   be a gentleman or a yeoman?
> *Lear.* A King, a King!
> *Fool.* No; he's a yeoman that has a gentleman
>   to his son; for he's a mad yeoman that sees
>   his son a gentleman before him. . . . He's
>   mad that trusts in the tameness of a wolf, a
>   horse's health, a boy's love, or a whore's
>   oath.
>
>   (III.vi.9-19)

Even now, when the Fool gets Lear's full attention as he jokes, his jest goes awry. Lear, always afraid of madness, now readily sees it in himself. The true madman here is indeed a King, but that was not one of the original choices. Still the Fool, mostly to the benefit of the audience, goes through with first his joke, then his bit of moralizing. It seems as if the Fool gradually becomes separated from Lear after their meeting with Poor Tom; Lear in his present state identifies more readily with him. The Fool feels deeply that he is cut adrift. However, when the trial of Goneril and Regan is to commence, the Fool is probably the one Lear addresses as "most sapient sir" while Tom is the "most learned justicer" (22, 21). As the trial progresses, Tom is the one in close contact with the audience, and the one who diverts Lear when total breakdown threatens:

> [*Aside*] My tears begin to take his part so
>   much,
> They mar my counterfeiting.
> *Lear.* The little dogs and all,
> Tray, Blanch, and Sweetheart, see, they bark
>   at me.
> *Edgar.* Tom will throw his head at them.
>   Avaunt, you curs!
>
>   (III.vi.59-63)

During the whole trial Kent hovers in the background, but his attention is riveted on Lear, and he has none to spare for the audience. When Lear has reached a point of exhaustion he persuades him to rest, and Lear lies down:

> *Lear.* Make no noise, make no noise; draw
>   the curtains: so, so.
> We'll go to supper i'th'morning.
> *Fool.* And I'll go to bed at noon.
>
>   (III.vi.81-83)

This is the Fool's last remark before he leaves with the party bearing Lear from the stage. Poor Tom is left to address the audience. Seven more or less credible meanings have been read into this one line,[6] but when we consider how the Fool's role has developed in relation to Lear, the meaning must be very simple. Lear, in need of sleep more than food, decides to sleep now and eat Gloucester's promised supper later. In the Fool this sparks one last remark about his topsy-turvy world: if Lear can eat supper at breakfast, the Fool can end his day at high noon and go to bed.

Of course there must be connotations of ending and death connected with the Fool's idea of going to bed, especially since the Fool has dwindled so drastically before our very eyes, but at this point there has been no warning that this is his last appearance. Lear himself disappears from our sight for a long time, and when he reappears his conditions are so changed and so many things have happened to shake us fundamentally that we most likely will have forgotten about the Fool. The triangle of Lear, Tom, and the Fool in the storm is appropriate for its place in the play, but the Fool would have made an awkward third at Dover Cliff, where none of the connotations he must carry with him *qua* his stage clown status would be appropriate. Moreover, his counterpart Cordelia will shortly reappear at Lear's side and take the Fool's place as truth-teller and healer of her father.

There may be one more reference to the Fool in the play. In V.iii.304 Lear says: "And my poor fool is hang'd! No, no, no life!" We know from line 273 that Cordelia was hanged. Lear is desperately and unsuccessfully trying to find the tiniest sign of life in her, so it seems most likely that the "fool" referred to is Cordelia, not the Fool, even though Lear's thoughts may also encompass the other person who truly loved him. This is very appropriate. The Fool, the court jester, is an intrinsic part of Lear-the-King, and his main focus concerns issues of kingship and Lear's wrongful idea that its outward show can be divided from its substance. In this connection the Fool becomes almost symbolic, the way the King's crown is. The crown stands for the totality of kingship, but the only one Lear has left is bald (I.iv.159), the "meat" itself is gone. The Fool comes to represent the idea of rationality, that which binds society together and gives meaning to existence, and his voice is always harping on the foolishness of deviating from the accepted patterns of human life and organization. His bauble and coxcomb are, after all, a mocking copy of the king's scepter and crown. Once Lear has left these patterns completely, he enters another dimension of existence and proceeds to examine his inner man, and there is no more need for the Fool's voice. The Fool as symbol disappears when his purpose is served.

Lear's Fool is a creature apart from the ordinary stage clown we encounter in Shakespeare's plays. He is bound to one other character, and therefore bereft of the volatility, freedom, and mobility lent the others of his kind. In Shakespeare's source play, *King Leir,* there is no court fool, and the conclusion of the play is happily romantic. Shakespeare changed his source into a tragedy, and the addition of the character of the Fool makes a great contribution toward this transformation. The Fool as an aspect of Lear's own tragedy makes many restrictions on his clown character, but the gain is immense in terms of the audience's understanding of events and characters. Where the stage clown usually remains personally aloof and unaffected by the other characters in the play, Lear's Fool is deeply touched by Lear's tragedy and shares in it himself. The stage clown will usually appear with a certain unexpectedness and say and do surprising and delightful things, but here we are prepared for the arrival of Lear's Fool as well as for his sadness. Still he is the audience's teacher and interpreter, possibly to a degree that surpasses any other stage clown, but his teachings are single-minded. He may be seen as more critic than clown, and the amusement he provides is always tinged with sorrow.[7] The Fool is the only major clown's part in a Shakespearean tragedy, and his function is eminently fitting to his role.

Thersites and the Fool share the role of the critic in a noncomedy, and they have much to say about the shortcomings of their respective worlds, but the way in which they use the critic's tools is widely different. Thersites is aggressive to the point of disgusting the audience, and this makes us doubt his value as truth teller. We tend to believe in likable people and go along with their ideas more readily. He is still our interpreter, though, only we have to interpret him as well as his comments, and our final views of the play may well be colored by our doubt of Thersites. Lear's Fool, on the other hand, is a lovable creature, and the failure of his efforts in his court jesterly role only endears him to us further. We soon recognize that his caustic comments spring from his deep love of Lear, and so his critical attitude serves to convince us of his value as commentator. He is a true guide and interpreter, whom we readily trust, and we feel for him all the more because his actions often go against his comments. He sees Lear's shortcomings and is critical of him, but his love prompts his every action.

Thersites and the Fool are both bitter fools, and their environments are hostile to human life and human feelings and therefore inviting of criticism, even satire; but where Thersites creates distance, the Fool invites closeness; where Thersites' bitterness is all-encompassing and inimical, the Fool's serves to deepen our understanding of Lear, indeed, he creates sympathy and even love from bitterness. Still, both clown characters are eminently well suited for the play in which we find them, and in both cases the audience stands well served by their commentary.

Notes

[1] Marvin Rosenberg, in *The Masks of King Lear* (Berkeley: University of California Press, 1972), makes much of these threats.

[2] I am aware that the Fool has often been played by an old man. The effect desired is the creation of Lear's *Doppelgänger,* old and wise beyond Lear himself.

[3] William Willeford, *The Fool and His Scepter* (Chicago: Northwestern University Press, 1969), 173.

[4] "Albion" could well be used to mean Lear; in *Hamlet,* Claudius and the Elder Fortinbras are referred to as Denmark and Norway respectively.

[5] It is interesting to see that, in the facsimile of the Quarto, the title page of King Lear (page 663) mentions *"the unfortunate life of Edgar, sonne and heire to the Earle of Gloster, and his sullen and assumed humor of Tom of Bedlam..."* The Fool is not mentioned.

[6] See note to III.vi.83 in the Arden Edition of the play.

[7] The combined Quarto edition of *King Lear* has fewer lines for the Fool than the Folio; the Quarto play reads

as if the Fool is more of a clown and less of a critic, but he is certainly no fountain of laughter and merriment in the Quarto either.

CORDELIA

Richard Abrams (essay date 1985)

SOURCE: "The Double Casting of Cordelia and Lear's Fool: A Theatrical View," in *Texas Studies in Literature and Language,* Vol. 27, No. 4, Winter, 1985, pp. 354-68.

[*In the essay that follows, Abrams explores the hypothesis that in early productions of* King Lear, *the characters of Cordelia and Lear's Fool were played by the same actor. Abrams emphasizes the theatrical benefits of such "doubling," noting that Cordelia and the Fool both serve as Lear's "truth-tellers."*]

Proposed near the turn of the past century, the hypothesis that the actor playing Cordelia doubled as the Fool in early productions of *King Lear* accords with our best knowledge of Shakespeare's theatrical practice and has rarely been contested. Strictly speaking, of course, the theory remains unprovable without external evidence; yet it rests on two fairly firm supports: that the two characters never meet on stage and that during Cordelia's absence the Fool takes over her function of telling Lear the painful truth about himself. In addition, such a theory strengthens various line readings, for example, the play on "nothing," Lear's description of the Fool as a "houseless poverty" after driving Cordelia from her home, "And my poor fool is hanged." But though critics have noted verbal ironies produced by double casting, the sustained theatrical impact of this device on spectators cognizant of the actor's role shift has yet to be explored. Only recently have critics advanced beyond a naive conception of double casting as a necessary evil in small Elizabethan acting troupes, recognizing the potential production values of this technique which enabled Shakespeare "to inform, comment on, and, perhaps, augment the events enacted."[1] In this essay I discuss the theatrical benefits of doubling the parts of Lear's two "truthtellers," showing how audience awareness of the actor's change heightens the play's pathos by inducing an ironic consciousness.

Past work on doubling in *Lear* focuses on Cordelia's and the Fool's relationship to the protagonist. Here, however, I concentrate less on their relation to Lear than on their common relation to Lear's *third* truthteller, his servant Kent, also in disguise for most of the play, hence presenting an analogy with the actor of Cordelia/Fool in his doubled role. If we accept the double casting hypothesis, two scenes can be defined as reunions: the actual reunion of kent and Cordelia in act 4, scene 7; but also, and less obviously, the Fool's great scene (I.iv) which reunites the *actors* formerly playing Cordelia (now the Fool) and Kent (now Caius) soon after their initial exit. Viewed as a pseudoreunion, act 1, scene 4, resolves expectations set up by the play's first scene, to which we turn.

Twice in parallel actions in act 1, scene 1, Kent is presented as the befriender of outcast children. Mildly in the case of Edmund slighted by the callous Gloucester, and then more boldly in Cordelia's case, he succors underdogs aggrieved by parental tyranny. Yet while Edmund thanks Kent for his kindness and promises to "study deserving," Cordelia neglects to do so.[2] Needless to say, no blame attaches to this omission; her hands are full at the moment of Kent's departure. Still, the opening scene's parallel fatherchild disturbances obviously function to establish a behavioral norm which Cordelia, for all that is right in her position, fails to satisfy. This failure is emphasized on her eventual return from France in act 4. Reunited with kent, she makes immediate amends for her minor fault by expressing gratitude and a keen desire to repay service (IV.vii.1-3). But even earlier, if Cordelia returns recast as the Fool in act 1's pseudoreunion scene, s/he displays a sense of obligation. As the actor reenters, he ignores the king who has been calling for his fool and heads directly for Kent, his coxcomb extended in token of a greater payment.

Superficially, the Fool offers *pre*payment to hire Caius, who displays the folly of "taking one's part that's out of favor" (I.iv.94). Lear is currently out of Goneril's favor; therefore, Caius, volunteering to serve such a master, deserves to be costumed as a fool. But meanings proliferate in the Fool's first witticism. Having changed his appearance by shaving his beard (cf. Kent's "razed . . . likeness," 1.4), Kent himself is "out of" his old "favor" (face), yet essentially unchanged, still recognizable as the same principled fool who earlier took Cordelia's part when *she* was "out of favor" (disliked). By the same token, Kent-as-Caius, volunteering to resume his old service, seeks to take his own part—that is, the part of a man out of favor, since Kent, banished from his former master's presence, is now out of Lear's favor. All these meanings can be signaled in performance. A brief pause and nod of recognition before slow, knowing delivery of the phrase "out of favor" would indicate that the Fool recognizes Caius as the man who previously took Cordelia's part, and the audience would then read the Fool's act of extending his coxcomb as a gesture of gratitude on his former mistress's behalf. Moreover, in a double cast performance, the grateful gesture would be read as proceeding not just from Cordelia's representative but from Cordelia-reincarnate to Kent-reincarnate. What we see (that the actor-Cordelia has returned) colors what we hear (that the Fool wants to "hire" Kent). As Cordelia-*revenant*, the Fool pays Kent not only for services to come ("hire") but for services already rendered.[3]

Viewing the Fool's payment of Kent as an expression of the recostumed Cordelia's gratitude to a former benefactor, the audience can now see deeper meaning in the coin of that payment: an article of the actor's latest apparel. In his exit lines of act 1, scene 4, Lear speaks of resuming "the shape" he has apparently "cast off" forever (ll. 300-01). Shape, Maurice Charney reminds us, "is a theatrical term, meaning the whole make-up and appearance demanded by a specific role."[4] Hence, Lear's final phrase recalls the beginning of the scene in which the casting off of shapes figures prominently on levels of both story and staging. Kent opens act 1, scene 4, by calling attention to his razed appearance. Audiences know that the actor does not grow a beard between performances but simply removes a false beard, and on the Fool's entry, which is also the actor-Cordelia's reentry, this knowledge is activated by parallelism, for if one of Lear's truthtellers returns minus a prop beard, the other presumably reenters stripped of the item of theatrical disguise which most readily turns a man into a woman, a long-haired wig.[5] Indeed, because both have cast off their richer costumes, the Fool offers to dress Kent against the cold. Knowing what it is to feel cold himself (since he is played by the newly stripped actor-Cordelia), the Fool hands the shorn Kent, exposed for Cordelia's sake and in danger of "catch[ing] cold shortly" (ll. 95-96), his coxcomb.[6] Of course, a fool's cap barely covers the wearer. But that in effect is the Fool's point, carried forward in rich wordplay on a snail's shell as a "house" to "put's head in" (I.v.24-27, also III.ii.25) and on a hovel as "a good head-piece" in a storm (III.ii.25-26)—that the art of our necessities is strange and can make vile things precious. By giving his coxcomb, the Fool asserts that, for taking the disinherited Cordelia's part and now Lear's part, Kent deserves at least a fool's minimal protection against the cold, a cap "to put's head in"; and he asserts this in a manner alluding to his own recent costume change.

One passage of *Lear*'s much-studied clothing motif strongly foreshadows the actor-Cordelia's costume change. France protests to Lear, "This is most strange, / That she whom even but now was your best object . . .";

> should in this trice of time
> Commit a thing so monstrous to dismantle
> So many folds of favor
>
> (I.i.216-18)

—phrasing echoed by Cordelia in her exit lines when she indicts her "plighted" (Q: "pleated," heavily draped) sisters whose cunning time will "unfold" (I.i.280-81). The theme of stripping down will resonate, of course, both in dialogue (Poor Tom's change from court fin-

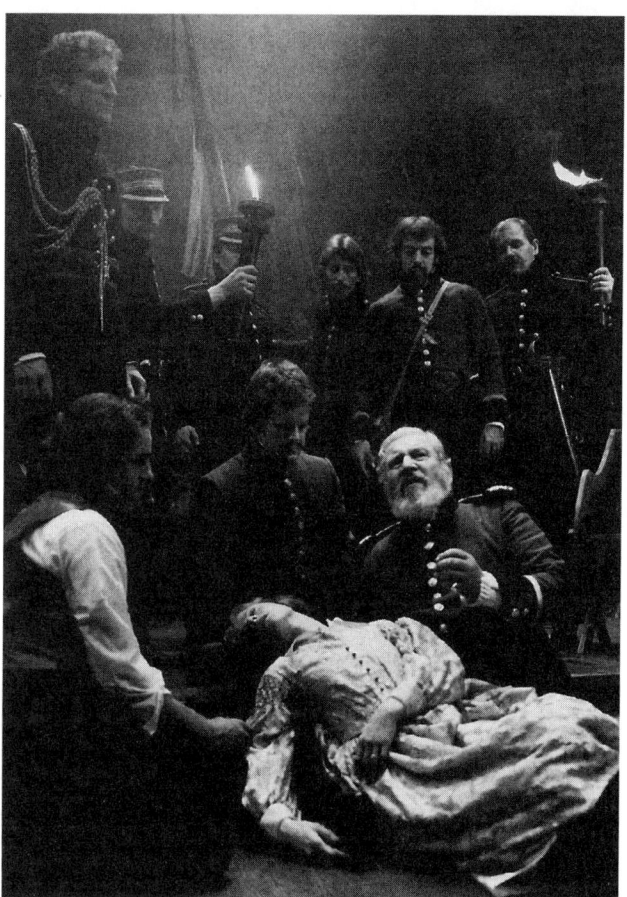

Ingrid Blekys as Cordelia and Peter Ustinov as King Lear in the Stratford Festival's 1979 production of King Lear.

ery) and stage imagery (Lear's unbuttoning), first recurring, after Cordelia's exit, in Kent's return in the rough, durable clothing of a country servingman. yet if France's metaphorical description of the dismantled Cordelia is ever visually applicable to Cordelia herself, it must be in the actor-Cordelia's return as the unaccommodated Fool, for when next we meet Cordelia *in propria persona* she is dressed presumably as a queen or general and tries to make a change for the better in Kent's costume (IV.vii.7-8) as well as re-outfitting her father in fresh raiment. But in act 1, scene 4, the audience can appreciate the literal propriety of France's metaphor of a stripped Cordelia when the actor reappears as the ill-clad Fool. Moreover, the recostumed Cordelia's (Fool's) sympathetic gesture of sharing "her" clothing to protect the exposed Kent can then prefigure Lear's charity on the health when, cold and wet, he sympathetically bids the drenched Fool enter the hovel before him.

Before I stray too far from a discussion of theatrical dynamics toward larger interpretive questions, let me try to distinguish the insights of the study from those of the playhouse, noting the different ways in which meaning is generated on page and stage. A passage in a text possesses potentially infinite resonance; interpretation must allow for its capacity to play off of any other passage in the mind of a hypothetical reader. But a theatrical event, such as the doubling of Cordelia and the Fool, is at the mercy of onrushing events. Reentering in a period of confused stage action when it is unclear "who is who, who is being sent for, and who answers,"[7] the recostumed actor-Cordelia sets off a shock of recognition. However, the tremors soon subside when fresher events such as the Fool's baiting of Lear and Lear's quarrel with Goneril compete for our attention. This is not to deny that spectators, tickled by suggestive dialogue, may flash back to the actor's role change at any moment. For instance (Stephen Booth's example, p. 164, n. 20), "If the actor who played Cordelia in I.i is a maid no longer—is now playing the Fool—then the Fool's exit speech, 'She that's a maid now, and laughs at my departure, / Shall not be a maid long, unless things be cut shorter' . . . reverberates in yet another extravagant direction." But very quickly the actor formerly playing Cordelia gains acceptance in his new role, so that by the end of a busy scene like act 1, scene 4, Lear's exit line about resuming his cast-off shape is presumably *glossed by* our recollection of the actor-Cordelia's role change rather than serving as a retrospective gloss on what we have already comfortably accepted.

But if the actor rapidly gains credibility in his new role, on another level the audience remains permanently shocked. When Cordelia returns transformed, the floodgates of bizarre possibility open, for nothing can be sacred in *King Lear* if Cordelia's person is not. Bradley's view of Lear's youngest daughter as "a thing enskied and sainted" could scarcely have survived a production in which Cordelia, leaving the stage with dignified forbearance in the first scene, comes back in an antic mode three scenes later. One knows that this silly chatterbox is not Cordelia, only her Fool; yet the feeling persists that it *is* Cordelia. Our two impressions vie for authenticity, like the teasing "natural perspective" of "is and is not" at the end of *Twelfth Night*. And more than shattering complacency, Cordelia's transformation conditions our expectations; it builds tension into the Fool's part from the beginning. Aware that the Fool's actor will eventually be needed to play a more important role, we sense that the character himself is living on borrowed time. Our first definite news of Cordelia's impending return comes in act 2 (II.ii.161 ff.); yet probably we guess we shall see her again even at her initial departure—an awareness that brings the Fool's exit speeches under morbid scrutiny. Although he is never seriously menaced onstage, the Fool's partings generally leave it uncertain whether this expendable character will return. For example, act 1 scene 4, features a running exit, while his exit lines in the next scene ominously conclude the act: "She that's a maid now, and laughs at my departure, / Shall not be a maid long, unless things be cut shorter" (I.v.45-46). If, as Booth recognized, the actor playing the Fool is himself "a maid no longer," then the double entendre in "unless things be cut shorter" underscores in a distressing manner the possibility of the actor changing back to Cordelia. The "thing" in danger of being cut shorter is both the Fool's traditionally outsized tool and his hour on the stage.[8] Indeed, these two meanings harmonize, since, according to the infantile fantasy of woman as a castrated man, the Fool's phallic truncation implies the curtailment of his present dramatic incarnation. Castration anxieties recur throughout the Fool's speeches, reminding us of his secret sharing in the identity of a character of opposite gender. If the Fool's "thing" is cut shorter, then the actor's stage life as a man will also come to an end. He will become a maid again, resuming Cordelia's cast-off shape.

Other passages play off our awareness that the Fool's character is unstable since his actor will be needed to play Cordelia again. The song on the heath, echoed from Feste, suggests that Lear's Fool is not specific to this time and place but floats through the King's Men's repertory—an impression heightened by Shakespeare's failure to provide a history for the Fool who mysteriously originates in Cordelia, so that her act 1 departure robs him of vital substance, causing him to pine away.[9] Then too, the Fool's odd scene-closing prophecy of Merlin prophesying ratifies our impression of his doubleness, since, as well as sharing his being with Cordelia, Lear's Fool exists both in the audience's present (hence confidently alluding to the historical Merlin) and in a distant past before Merlin was heard of.[10] And finally, of course, the exit line most powerfully intensified by our awareness of double casting is the Fool's actual last line of the play, "And I'll go to bed at noon" as a riposte to Lear's "We'll go to supper i'th' morning (III.vi. 82-83). By now the Fool's function has been drastically reduced by Lear's revival of conscience and by Poor Tom's usurpation of the Fool's place in Lear's counsel. So "I'll go to bed at noon" signals the disappearance we have long awaited, to which many dramatic signs are now pointing. In the recent Olivier television production of *King Lear*, the director, Michael Elliott, cut Kent's final remark which cues the Fool's exit ("Come, help to bear thy master. / Thou must not stay behind"), and the audience was then shown the shivering Fool stranded in the hovel. Everyone grasped that the Fool's end was at hand. But in a production doubling the roles of the Fool and Cordelia, the Fool's jeopardy need not be telegraphed in this obvious manner. The audience's awareness that Cordelia is returning to resume her cast-off role already creates an air of crisis in the Fool's part. Anticipating Cordelia's return, we read dark meaning into "And I'll go to bed at noon" at the moment of the line's delivery.

Cordelia returns in act 4 scene 4, accompanied by her retainers. Lear has been sighted, and Cordelia shows selfless concern for her father's welfare but fails as yet to reunite with her loved ones. Her next scene, however, features both reunion and *cognitio*. Cordelia enters speaking with Kent and is presently joined by Lear, brought in sleeping. Thus, act 4, scene 7, is a retake of the actors' reunion scene (I.iv), which brought Kent, Lear, and the actor-Cordelia together as a trio "out of favor"; the major antagonists of the play's opening are finally reconciled in their own persons. The two scenes (I.iv and IV.vii) are linked by significant echoes; we have already noted the parallelism of the Fool hiring Kent with a coxcomb and Cordelia "paying" gratitude for service. Similarly, in her first words of act 4, scene 7, Cordelia's short time remaining is foreshadowed in an ironic mode made familiar by the ever-departing Fool:

> *Cordelia:* O thou good Kent, how shall I live and work
> To match thy goodness? My life will be too short
> And every measure fail me.
> *Kent:* To be acknowledged, madam, is o'erpaid.
>
> (IV.vii.1-4)

Cordelia begins where her alter ego left off; she takes up the Fool's refrain of curtailment ("unless things be cut shorter," "And I'll go to bed at noon"), announcing her tragic fate in the same way that the Fool's prophecies announced his early departure. Then too, Cordelia introduces the subject of clothing—the Fool's topic ("coxcomb"), along with payment for hire, in his first exchange with Kent. "Be better suited," she begs Kent, "These weeds are memories of those worser hours. / I prithee put them off" (ll. 6-8). Her request goes unheeded and is the more curious in that, in all probability, we would never have noticed Kent's "failure" to change back to his former costume had not Shakespeare reminded us.[11] It appears, then, that Shakespeare is prodding us with various echoes to remember act 1's blurred reunion the better to appreciate act 4's satisfying resolution.

By firmly reestablishing Cordelia in her role before bringing in Lear, Shakespeare operates from the surest of theatrical instincts, safeguarding the tenderness of his great recognition scene. Identity already seems confused elsewhere in act 4, scene 7: Stanley Cavell shows that Lear probably takes the doctor accompanying Cordelia for the king of France,[12] and one tender moment is played perilously close to comedy (*Lear* [to Cordelia]: "You are a spirit, I know. Where did you die?"). A delicate balance could be upset if, even for a moment, Lear, wincing to make out his daughter ("Methinks I should know you"), was suspected of glimpsing her physical resemblance to the Fool. To clear a space for the returning Cordelia, then, the memories of Cordelia's "worser hours" in the Fool's role must be effaced. But once Lear has recognized Cordelia, the Fool may slip back in. "I am a very foolish fond old man" (l. 60), Lear confesses, preparing to enunciate what he fears is the derisible theory that the angelic lady standing before him is his favorite daughter. And again on exiting he tells Cordelia, "You must bear with me. / Pray you now, forget and forgive. I am old and foolish" (ll. 83-84). There is no likelihood here that Lear is thinking of his Fool, but Shakespeare no longer minds if *we* recall the Fool. "I am old and foolish" is what John Meagher, in connection with another line ("And my poor fool is hanged"), calls an "unrecognizing recognition,"[13] and as such it constitutes Lear's tribute to his most patient schoolmaster, acknowledging that the Fool's great lesson ("Dost thou call me fool, boy?") has finally penetrated. Thus, the scene that began with Cordelia repaying Kent appropriately ends (at least in the Folio version; Quarto follows Lear's and Cordelia's exit with a dozen lines of dialogue, presumably deleted in revision) with Lear's indirect payment of tribute to the Fool's wisdom. Already deeply moving if addressed only to Cordelia, Lear's admission of folly gains poignancy if directed also to the actor formerly playing the Fool's role. For then, in the mode of an "unrecognizing recognition," Lear attests that he himself is willing to undergo the low transformation he forced on his daughter. As the actor-Cordelia was obliged to play the Fool, so Lear as a "child-changed father" (IV.vii.17) is prepared to repay in kind: to be cast down, indeed, *re*-cast in the selfsame role he forced on his beloved.

Along with his two descriptions of himself as "foolish" in act 4, scene 7, Lear uses the noun "fool" three times near the end of the play, twice metaphorically ("great stage of fools," "natural fool of fortune") and the third time either metaphorically or in distant allusion to the absent Fool himself ("And my poor fool is hanged"). No one but Lear uses the word or a derivative in the latter part of the play, and all five of Lear's later uses are probing, compared to his earlier literal-minded usage of "fool" in direct address, response, and immediate reference to the Fool himself.[14] The shift from other characters' control of the word *fool*'s metaphorical extensions before Cordelia's return (e.g., Goneril's four applications of "fool" to Albany in IV.ii) to Lear's exclusive later control is revealing. Verbal distribution studies of individual Shakespearean plays such as S. L. Bethell's study of *Othello,* documenting the gradual transfer of the language of deviltry from Iago to Othello, reveal subterranean character resemblances.[15] Similarly, *Lear*'s shifting "fool" references suggest how deeply the Fool has marked his master. Though initially associated with, and in a sense emanating from, Cordelia, the Fool is finally absorbed back, not into Cordelia, but into Lear himself, who not only cherishes his companion's memory but strangely perpetuates his being. Lear's commemoration of the Fool is touching. The Fool's offstage pining convinces us of his genuine affection for Cordelia, but we question his feeling for Lear. We recall, for instance, that the Fool would have remained contentedly in Goneril's house if not driven thence, and we wonder why he continues to nag after Lear shows repentance. Yet despite our ambivalence, Lear asks no questions but returns pure for impure (or uncertain) love. Whereas in the opening scene he insisted that Cordelia provide verbal assurance of her love, he gives her alter ego the benefit of the doubt and finally reveals a revived paternal instinct by keeping the Fool alive with elegiac allusions after his mysterious disappearance.

In addition to evidencing moral growth, Lear's absorption of the Fool points to larger shifts in the play's ontological or representational premises. The king's relation to his Fool as a false other, a projection of conscience, is paradigmatic of his many ambiguous object-relations throughout the drama. Several critics comment on this aspect of *Lear;* for instance, Richard Fly discusses Lear's relation to his hundred knights on analogy with Talbot's shadow-substance bond with his army in *1 Henry VI,* observing that "in a manner that possibly defeats analysis much of *King Lear* exists as reflecting shadows of Lear's central experience."[16] However, these studies ignore the irony whereby Shakespeare's adaptation of the action to Lear's inner life follows from Lear's own early insistence that his daughters mirror his self-love. Again, the Fool's status is focal. "[A] screen on which Shakespeare flashes . . . readings from the psychic life of his protagonist,"[17] and by tradition a motley imitation of royalty, Lear's Fool becomes precisely what he calls Lear, "Lear's shadow" (I.iv.221), destined to be reabsorbed by his master—hence, going to sleep at noon like a shadow—when Lear has learned all that the Fool can teach. Indeed, Lear himself defines the Fool's pedagogic method vis-à-vis their overlapping identities. Just before the Fool's first appearance, Lear tells his Knight (the only one of the shadowy hundred we meet), "Thou but rememb'rest me of mine own conception" (I.iv.64). The remark's real thrust carries beyond its immediate circumstance, however; rather, it serves to introduce the Fool, who, as Lear's externalized conscience, can influence his master only by reminding him of what he already knows. Thus, the Fool lives the life of an echo, unlike Cordelia, who refuses to reflect in flattery her father's conception of how much love she owes him. But if Cordelia's initial refusal to be reduced to a mere reflector of Lear's self-love results in the advent of her mirrory or shadowlike alter ego, whose function is precisely to "rememb[er Lear] of [his] own conception," then the situation changes on her return to England. In act 1 Cordelia is stubbornly independent; yet in act 4 she returns compliant, Lear's satellite, never again recovering her former integrity. To put the case for this change provocatively, we may say that, on her return, Cordelia's role is remodeled on the part her actor has been playing ever since she went to France.

Let me step back to explore this proposition in a broader perspective. As often noted, events in *Lear* seem to occur in mocking fulfillment of Lear's fantasies. This is true not only of the appearance and disappearance of emanated "subcharacters" like Poor Tom and the Fool, but of the sudden blowing up of the storm and the behavior of otherwise realistically conceived major characters. The same pattern constantly repeats itself. First, a fantasy strikes Lear, *then* it is realized in the narrative, so that the event appears to owe its dramatic occurrence to Lear's anticipation of it. Take the way in which Lear's sorrow "holp the heavens to rain" (III.vii.62). If, in the self-characterizing phrase of Kent's anonymous Gentleman-interlocutor, Lear is a man "minded like the weather" (III.i.2), then by the same token the weather is minded like Lear; it owes its disorder, on an artistic level, to pathetic fallacy and, on a magical level, to the sacred bond uniting king and kingdom. But that bond has been severed—at least Lear himself fears it has been—so that what happens is inexplicable to him. "I'll not weep," he maintains (II.iv.278), and an instant later, pat on cue, nature weeps for him; stage directions call for sounds of *"Storm and tempest."* The whole sequence leaves him suspicious; "What is the cause of thunder?" (III.vi.146) is the first question he asks his "philosopher," Poor Tom. It is as though the character-Lear cannot rest complacently in the audience's overview of the storm as an instance of pathetic fallacy but, committed to the reality of the play-world, must wrestle with the paradox that these events nonetheless seem theatrically contrived.[18] Thus, the storm simultaneously shakes Lear's solipsism, making him feel small, and reinforces it by encouraging the delusion that he is the cruel gods' cynosure, that the weather centers on him. "They told me I was everything," he complains about his daughters, "'Tis a lie"; "When the thunder would not peace at my bidding; there I found 'em, there I smelt 'em out" (IV.vi.101-04). Yet the lie that he is everything contains a truth dramatically supported by the thunder's responsiveness to his bidding. Even when, exposed to violent nature on the heath, he ought to be learning the lesson of his own insignificance, Lear enjoys the illusion of solipsistic centrality, imagining that he matters enough for the gods to find and punish.

Other events follow Lear's fantasies; for example, Goneril's and Regan's murderous competition for Edmund's sexual favors gathers momentum soon after Lear's most cynical pronouncements on women's lust. But Lear's main fantasy-come-to-life is the returning Cordelia, who materializes in a form consistent with his desires and hovers dreamlike over her "scarce awake" father as he gradually regains consciousness

(IV.vii.51). A virtual personification of filial love, Cordelia on her return seems faded in verisimilitude, more idealized than before, much in the way that an initially assertive Desdemona, purged of attributes in the course of *Othello,* becomes the ideal sacrificial victim by shedding her particularity.[19] No new pressure to conform comes from Lear, who moderates his early insistence on obedience, prefers to kneel before his wronged daughter, and begs forgiveness. But Shakespeare remembers and grants Lear's original, now unstated desire for absolute love. Whereas initially Cordelia, refusing to flatter, stood alone on principle, the returned Cordelia, echoing Christ, defines herself entirely in relation to her father ("O dear father. / It is thy business that I go about," IV.iv.23-24). Led off to prison, she no longer cares to puncture Lear's pleasant fantasy of their quasi-connubial withdrawal ("We too alone will sing") by reminding him, merely for truth's sake, that she did not marry like her sisters to love her father all.

More a creature of her father's desires than her independent spirited act 1 prototype, the returning Cordelia paradoxically gains pathos by taking on a tinge of insubstantiality, even as the Fool gained pathos by our anticipating the actor's eventual abandonment of the Fool's role. Cordelia's prophetic comment to Kent, "My life will be too short," barely noticeable in the text registers with strange force on an audience theatrically rehearsed in watching the Fool's prophecies of a foreshortened life ripen to fulfillment. Alert for clues as to the direction the plot will take, "Oh no," we say in effect, "first the Fool; now her!" Indeed, the theatrical logic behind the killing off of Cordelia extends the logic of bringing her back in a form responsive to her father's wishes. For if Shakespeare fulfills Lear's unstated lingering desire for absolute love, he also recalls and fulfills Lear's unrealized parental threat to revoke his daughter's being. At the height of his anger, Lear intemperately spoke of reabsorbing the child who displeased him ("Better thou / Hadst not been born than not t'have pleased me better") in terms barely more civilized than "The barbarous Scythian, / Or he that makes his generations messes / To gorge his appetite" (I.i.116-18). This imagery recurs in the Fool's childlike obsession with being eaten (e.g., I.iv.206-08), which proves prophetically accurate; the fate of reabsorption into Lear, from whom he emanated as a voice of conscience, overtakes him in his noontime or midplay retirement when he goes to bed like Lear's shadow. But after the Fool's final exit, the threat of ingestion or reabsorption, from which Shakespeare spun out her surrogate's fate, is visited on Cordelia herself. Returning briefly, Cordelia vanishes again as though, from the time she reappeared to her half-sleeping father, she were only Lear's dream, "Too flattering-sweet to be substantial" (*Romeo and Juliet*, II.i.141). Thus, despite retracting his curse (or more precisely, superseding it with a blessing), Lear must at last endure the indecent horror of a parent outliving his own child. Initially reducing his daughters to flattering mirrors of his own vanity, he must ultimately stand alone, experiencing the pain of being "everything." Cordelia becomes unreal again, incapable of misting a looking glass, of sending forth new projections of her now-canceled being, as Lear pronounces over her corpse the words that bid simultaneous farewell to both his daughter and her double: "And my poor fool is hanged."

Theatrical doubling, as we have studied it in *Lear,* is more than an expedient permitting a small acting company to stage a large play, and finally even more than a means of commenting on the similar functions of two temperamentally dissimilar characters. By upstaging Cordelia's and the Fool's actions at key moments through the mobility of the double cast actor, Shakespeare exposes Lear's largely impenitent solipsism, his desire to be "everything," which entails other people becoming less real than himself. In a fine essay on the play, E. A. J. Honigmann writes of the overarching realness of King Lear's titanic protagonist vis-à-vis a host of necessarily dwarfed side characters:

> Lear seems to have a genetic relationship with almost everyone else. . . . Thus Cordelia, Kent and the Fool sympathise and obscurely communicate with one another, and in a sense melt into one another: Kent not only talks of Lear as one whom he has "lov'd as my father" . . . as the Fool calls him "nuncle," but we hear that since Cordelia's going into France, "the Fool hath much pined away". . . that Kent and Cordelia are secretly in touch and admire each other, and finally that Cordelia and the Fool have become one in Lear's mind ("And my poor fool is hang'd"). All three, Cordelia, Kent and the Fool, exist separately and yet partake of one another's identity, and all three are refracted images of Lear, or of his better nature.[20]

Honigmann then discusses the characters who reflect Lear's selfish nature but never mentions double casting which, along with the plot devices he does mention, controls an audience's impression that side characters "melt into one another" or "are secretly in touch [with] each other," finally disposing these characters to incorporation in the king. Viewing a double cast performance of *Lear,* an audience witnesses the dramatic illusion decomposing and reforming in rhythms intensifying our grasp of the action. Of course, other Shakespearean plays also feature double casting, and one wonders whether, in those plays too, illusions break up and reform in characteristic ways. In an interpretive era like the present when performance-centered criticism is flourishing, research into "Shakespeare's art of doubling," as Giorgio Melchiori has recently called it, offers a fascinating field for conjecture, potentially valuable both to theatrical and textual studies.

Notes

[1] Stephen Booth, *King Lear, Macbeth, Indefinition, and Tragedy* (New Haven: Yale University Press, 1983), p. 134. Booth's illuminating essay, "Speculations on Doubling in Shakespeare's Plays" (App. 2, pp. 127-55), questions the "hard scholarship" of such studies as that of William A. Ringler, Jr. ("The Number of Actors in Shakespeare's Early Plays," *The Seventeenth-Century Stage,* ed. Gerald Eades Bentley [Chicago: University of Chicago Press, 1968], pp. 110-34), sagely noting that "even the hard evidence on Renaissance doubling practices is soft." For specific discussion of Cordelia and the Fool, see Booth, pp. 33-34, 129, 134-46, 153-54, 163-64. Giorgio Melchiori ("Peter, Balthazar, and Shakespeare's Art of Doubling," *Modern Language Review* [1983], pp. 777-92) discusses "doubling by function" in *Romeo and Juliet,* a concept clearly relevant to Cordelia and the Fool.

The double casting hypothesis's first proponents are Alois Brandl, *Shakspere* (Berlin: Hoffman, 1894), p. 179, and Wilfred Perrett, *The Story of King Lear* (Berlin: Mayer & Muller, 1904). Thomas Stroup ("Cordelia and the Fool," *Shakespeare Quarterly,* 12 [1961], 127-32) makes some interesting points (e.g., Lear's reduction of Cordelia to a "houseless poverty" is his), but his article suffers from a strong textual bias masking as theatrical consciousness. Noting that the Fool appears 357 lines after Cordelia's first exit and that Cordelia reappears 356 lines after the Fool's final exit, Stroup argues, "Time [*sic*] is exactly meted out for some reason, probably for the change in costume and make-up" (p. 127). Even setting aside the possibility of an interlude between acts 3 and 4, the stage business surrounding Gloucester's blinding takes longer than the relatively uneventful action separating Cordelia's exit and the Fool's first entry; also, the costume change can be effected in a matter of moments, as Booth shows; it hardly requires the "exact measure" of some twenty minutes of performance time. Even less plausible, in my view, is H. L. Anshutz's argument that the character Cordelia herself, not just the actor playing her, returns disguised as the Fool, "Cordelia and the Fool," *Research Studies* (Washington State University), 32 (1964), 240-60.

[2] *King Lear,* I.i.28, 30; all Shakespearean citations are from *The Complete Works,* gen. ed. Alfred Harbage (Baltimore: Penguin, 1969). For a discussion of changes in the Fool's part in the apparent F revision of Q *Lear,* cf. John Kerrigan, "Revision, Adaptation, and the Fool in *King Lear,*" in *The Division of the Kingdoms: Shakespeare's Two Versions of* King Lear, ed. Gary Taylor and Michael Warren (Oxford: Clarendon Press, 1983), pp. 195-245. Kerrigan's essay, though excellent, fails to take up the question of double casting. Several F changes (the reattribution of "Lear's shadow," the inclusion of "And I'll go to sleep at noon," the deletion of the dialogue following Lear's and Cordelia's exit in IV.vii), discussed in my text, offer enrichment of the ironies associated with double casting; that would not mean, however, that the stage production reflected in the Q version separated the two roles. In the same volume Beth Goldring argues cogently that at I.i.162 Cordelia (rather than Cornwall) intervenes with Albany to prevent Lear's violence against Kent, "*Cor.*'s Rescue of Kent," *Division,* pp. 143-51; Cordelia's gesture does not change the fact, however, that the *ceremony* of thanking Kent remains unfulfilled.

[3] Hence the ambiguities of the Fool's gesture line up with Lear's overdetermined act of hiring Kent, which cues the Fool's entry. "There's earnest of thy service" (I.iv.88-89), Lear tells Caius, meaning that he definitely plans to hire him (removing the earlier condition of "If I like thee no worse after dinner") and simultaneously paying him for service already rendered in tripping Oswald. Compare Caius's double hiring by Lear and the Fool to the Fool's own double employment by Lear and Cordelia.

[4] Maurice Charney, "'We Put Fresh Garments on Him': Nakedness and Clothes in *King Lear,*" in *Some Facets of* King Lear: *Essays in Prismatic Criticism,* ed. Rosalie L. Colie and F. T. Flahiff (Toronto: University of Toronto Press, 1974), p. 80.

[5] No reference to Cordelia's or the Fool's relative hair lengths occurs in *KL;* for the routine strategem of a girl cutting her hair to look like a boy, see however *TGV,* II.vii.42-44. For the motif of "undressing the part" in *KL,* cf. James Black, "*King Lear:* Art Upside-Down," *Shakespeare Survey,* 33 (1980), 35-42, esp. 36-37. Regarding actual costume, there would perhaps not have been much change in length from Cordelia's robes to the Fool's petticoat, taken by Lear for the long robe of a man of justice in the hovel (cf. Leslie Hotson, *Shakespeare's Motley* [1952; rpt. New York: Haskell House, 1971], pp. 69-70).

[6] The usual gloss for "catch cold shortly," cited in the Variorum and Arden *Lear,* gives "be turned out of doors and be exposed to the inclemency of the weather." However, this meaning is read back into the line by editors familiar with Lear's and the Fool's fate of being driven into the cold; spectators viewing the play for the first time have not yet seen this happen. Cordelia, of course, was threatened with exposure (of sorts) yet found warm shelter in France (hence the Fool's immediate qualification about Lear doing his third daughter "a blessing against his will"). Thus it is the actor-Cordelia, more than the character-Cordelia, who illustrates the sense in which Kent is in danger of catching cold. The Fool's words look to the past and the future, but his stripped appearance makes an immediate visual statement about chilliness.

[7] Booth, p. 154; cf. Stroup, pp. 128-29; Anshutz, p. 244.

[8] Feste's "A foolish thing was but a toy" is verbally similar. For the priapic fool, cf. Leslie Hotson, *The First Night of* Twelfth Night (New York: Macmillan, 1955), chap. 7.

[9] If Robert Armin played both Feste and Lear's Fool, the song about the wind and the rain becomes still more haunting; cf. Julian Markels, "Shakespeare's Confluence of Tragedy and Comedy: *Twelfth Night* and *King Lear*," *Shakespeare Quarterly*, 15 (1964), 75-88; William A. Ringler, Jr. ("Shakespeare and His Actors: Some Remarks on *King Lear*," *Proceedings of the Comparative Literature Symposium*, 12 [1981], 183-94), challenges the traditional assumption that Armin played the Fool on the grounds that he would therefore have been too old to double as Cordelia. However, his strongest argument is undercut by Doris Adler, whose Ohio Shakespeare Conference paper on "Robert Armin: Cordelia and the Fool?" is abstracted in *Shakespeare Newsletter*, 27 (1977), 30.

[10] For the fool's doubleness of being, William Willeford, *The Fool and His Scepter* (Evanston: Northwestern University Press, 1969), chap. 3, "The Fool and Mimesis," also chap. 4; for the scattering of the seeds of folly, hence of the Fool's being, throughout the play, John Reibetanz, *The "Lear" World: A Study of* King Lear *in Its Dramatic Context* (Toronto: University of Toronto Press, 1977), pp. 80-107.

[11] The best discussion is Hugh MacLean, "Disguise in *King Lear*: Kent and Edgar," *Shakespeare Quarterly*, 11 (1964), 49-56. Rachel Massey points out to me that the principal "good" characters—Edgar/Poor Tom, Kent/Caius, Cordelia/Fool—all prove themselves by their willingness to undergo costume changes.

[12] Stanley Cavell, "The Avoidance of Love: A Reading of *King Lear*," in his *Must We Mean What We Say?* (Cambridge: Cambridge University Press, 1976), chap. 10.

[13] Cf. John C. Meagher, "Economy and Recognition: Thirteen Shakespearean Puzzles," *Shakespeare Quarterly*, 35 (1984), 18.

[14] Similarly, the first metaphorical use of "fool" in the main plot is Goneril's "Old fools are babes again" (I.iii.19), so if the Fool is absorbed into Lear, he may also be said to originate in Lear. As an instance of direct response to the Fool's accusations, Lear's "Dost thou call me fool, boy?" produces the delayed response in the same scene, "Beat at this gate that let thy folly in" (I.iv.262). This leaves only II.iv.270 (Lear's "fool me not so much") as a gratuitous use of "fool" early in the play, compared to Lear's five gratuitous allusions toward the end. The classic study of "Fool in *Lear*" is William Empson, *The Structure of Complex Words* (Norfolk, Conn.: New Directions, 1951), chap. 6. For another illustration of Lear's continuation of the Fool's role, cf. E. A. J. Honigmann, *Shakespeare: Seven Tragedies: The Dramatist's Manipulation of Response* (London: Macmillan, 1976), pp. 118-19: "The extraordinary oneness of the two [the Fool and Lear] continues after the Fool has dropped out of the play, for in IV.6 Lear echoes the Fool's voice and personality, continuing his riddling (e.g., 'your eyes are in a heavy case, your purse in a light'), his *Schadenfreude*, his sex obsession and, probably, his 'fantastic' general demeanour."

[15] S. L. Bethell, "Shakespeare's Imagery: The Diabolic Images in *Othello*," *Shakespeare Survey*, 5 (1952), 62-80.

[16] Richard Fly, *Shakespeare's Mediated World* (Amherst: University of Massachusetts Press, 1976), p. 113. Cf. text for n. 20, below.

[17] Maynard Mack, "The Jacobean Shakespeare: Some Observations on the Construction of the Tragedies," in *Essays in Shakespearean Criticism*, ed. James Calderwood and Harold Toliver (Englewood Cliffs, N.J.: Prentice-Hall, 1970), p. 33.

[18] Cf. Leontes's "unrecognizing recognition" of the theatrical falseness of the "real" world in *WT*, I.ii.291 ff.: "Is this nothing? / Why, then the world and all that's in't is nothing," etc.

[19] I owe this view of Desdemona to Irving Massey's brilliant unpublished essay, "The Ethics of Particularity: Leibniz and Literature." Massey writes, "Like all sacrificial victims, Desdemona must be pure; but, as the special kind of sacrificial victim she is, what she must be pure of is attributes, other than the attribute of innocence itself."

[20] Honigmann, p. 116.

Mark Berge (essay date 1992)

SOURCE: "'My Poor Fool is Hanged': Cordelia, the Fool, Silence and Irresolution in *King Lear*," in *Reclamations of Shakespeare*, Editions Rodopi B. V., 1994, pp. 211-22.

[*In the following essay, originally written in 1992, Berge maintains that the theme of dramatic irresolution is represented in the play first by Cordelia, then by the Fool, and finally by Lear himself. Berge observes that Cordelia serves as Lear's model of truth and self-knowledge.*]

In the chaotic world of *King Lear,* resolution of character seems remote and veiled from an aged king bent on denying the unspoken truth. Dramatically speaking, his enemies fare conventionally better. Philip McGuire concludes that when the mortally wounded Edmund declares that "The wheel is come full circle", his words serve as an explicit statement of dramatic fulfilment.[1] Accordingly, Edmund, Goneril, and Regan move towards a dramatic consummation in which their deaths bond them in malevolence. However, Lear, Cordelia and the Fool seem divided, separated, and never allowed a mode of completion like their three counterparts. Lear's hopes of union with Cordelia are never realized, and are portrayed as unnatural: "We two alone", as the king puts it, "will sing like birds i'th'cage" (5.3.9). Cordelia's final line, "Shall we not see these daughters and these sisters?" (5.3.7), echoes Lear's wish for dramatic union, but she is silenced before it can be fulfilled. In the Folio addition to the play, the Fool reiterates this attitude on union when he utters, in despair of common sense, a contradictory disunity: "And I'll go to bed at noon" (3.6.41); John Kerrigan aptly stresses that this line "expresses the Fool's determination to leave *King Lear* with its course half run".[2] The Fool's intentional silence marks the end of his usefulness to the king in madness, and Cordelia's silence would appear to function in a similar way. Their removal from speech deprives Lear of their supporting influence and drives him farther into self-examination. However, fulfilment remains elusive for Lear. McGuire's argument that the play's final scene presents silences which deny our certainty of a single "promised end" seems to point directly to the dramatic elusiveness Shakespeare tried to cultivate.

Shakespeare portrays this theme of irresolution through Cordelia, the Fool, and finally of Lear. When Shakespeare imposes a silence on Cordelia and the Fool, effectively halting their fulfilment, he denies Lear the chance to gain the dramatic completion which Regan, Goneril, and Edmund enjoy. The Fool's disappearance leads to a shift towards Lear's madness, and Cordelia's speechlessness allows Lear to deny the reality of their imprisonment. Lear imagines a captivity of companionship:

> So we'll live,
> And pray, and sing, and tell old tales and laugh
> At gilded butterflies, and hear poor rogues
> Talk of court news, and we'll talk with them too.
>
> (5.3.11-14)

Lear is dependent on Cordelia and the Fool for support. Questions of stability and independence are raised by the need of these characters. For this reason, it is necessary to examine exactly how the Fool and Cordelia influence Lear, and what they take with them when they are removed from speech and action.

The question of Cordelia's character has been an issue of criticism for some time. Samuel Johnson could not bear the treatment of Cordelia and the painful ending of *King Lear*. John Danby explains Johnson's reaction as a product of the prevalent attitude towards Cordelia at the time: "It was intolerable to the moral optimism of the eighteenth century that such transcendent goodness should not be taken care of in the human universe."[3] Harley Granville-Barker stated the contrary in his conception of Cordelia: "It will be a fatal error to present Cordelia as a meek saint."[4] William Elton conceptualizes Cordelia as the model of self-sacrificing and healing virtue: "Cordelia is devoted to curing division. Strife between North and South [. . .] has its antithesis in Cordelia's healing and restoring forgiveness."[5] What all three critics acknowledge concerning Cordelia is her strength of character and silent resolve. Her courage in standing up to Lear and his demands while wrapped in the mantle of his power emanates from what Elton describes as her "argumentum ex silentio" (Elton, 25), and what Granville-Barker sees as her enduring "without effort, explanation or excuse" (303). This strength of character, the ability to stand with full certainty, is one of Cordelia's main personality traits and functions. She is fully aware of her abilities and her own qualities, as she firmly states: "I am sure my love's / More ponderous than my tongue" (1.1.72-73). Cordelia's silent determination and faith in what she believes to be true give her the strength to remain constant to her principles of love and order.

The inception of a character such as Cordelia, whose nature is more prevalent than her words, and, as Elton notes, whose constancy to order is unwavering, creates a force which is directly opposed to the half-meanings and wild uncertainty of Lear (Elton, 75). Lear's words illustrate his selfish and confused personality as he remarks to Kent early in the play: "I loved her most, and thought to set my rest / On her kind nursery" (1.1.117-18). The real problem which Cordelia faces seems captured by Harry Berger's hypothesis that Cordelia embodies the young woman of virtue attempting to break away from the paternal bondage and filial duty that are exploited by Lear.[6] Her values suddenly come into conflict with Lear's "darker purpose" (1.1.31), which is illustrated by an image of confusion expressed by Gloucester: "but now in the division of the kingdom, it appears not which of the dukes he values most" (1.1.3-4). The aim for which Lear seems to be exploiting Cordelia is stated unequivocally when Lear expounds: "and 'tis our fast intent / To shake all cares and business from our age" (1.1.33-34). This introduces a grievous wound both to society and to order:

> Beneath the surface, then, his darker purpose seems to be to play on everyone's curiosity, stir up as much envy and contention as he can among the

"younger strengths" with the aim of dominating and dividing them, humbling and punishing them
(Berger, 355).

Lear's fear of weakness and need to dominate may lead to self-deception and reliance on the quantity of words rather than their quality. Regan and Goneril act as the dispensers of this excessive and formless language which offers much but provides little substance. It is in this vein of empty praise that Goneril states: "Sir, I love you more than word can wield the matter" (1.1.50). Regan reasserts these words, notably with her own version of Goneril's shadowy sentiment:

> I am made of that self-mettle as my sister
> And prize me at her worth. In my true heart
> I find she names my very deed of love.
> (1.1.64-66)

They are directly opposed to Cordelia, who avoids such formlessness and remains silent in truth.

Recent criticism has placed much emphasis on the Cordelia of the opening scenes as a speaker and performer of truth. Marion Perret rightly points out that "The opening scene asks us to balance good words and the deeds that should verify them [. . .]. The test of goodness becomes action."[7] Cordelia personifies the virtue that both action and truth form together. Her short and terse "Nothing, my lord" (1.1.82), which is repeated, answers Lear's demands for verbal opulence and self-justification. The nakedness of such a statement, compared with the utterances of Regan and Goneril, draws attention to itself and becomes a challenge for action on Lear's part. It goads Lear into making a choice between truth and self-deception. Cordelia's style of speech, operating as a challenge, emphasizes her rejection of the meaningless style her sisters use and Lear's insistence on quantity instead of quality.

In Lear's lack of judgement he insists on the quantity of language as he reverbalizes his demand for Cordelia's mended speech. The Folio version of the tragedy enhances this aspect of Lear with an added imperative: "What can you say to draw / A third more opulent than your sisters? Speak" (1.1.80-81). Further on he becomes insistent: "Nothing will come of nothing, speak again" (1.1.85). Finally he issues a threat to procure his need for quantity of speech: "How, how, Cordelia? Mend your speech a little, / Lest you may mar your fortunes" (1.1.88-89). In this way he demands an opulence of Cordelia which she is unwilling, and, according to Sophia Blaydes, is unable to provide: "She has not her sister's eloquence to express the nature and breadth of her love, but she is secure that Lear knows of her love; yet, she is puzzled at his request."[8] Cordelia's assurance of her position as speaker of truth never falters, even in reply to Lear's accusation: "So young, and so untender?" (1.1.100). She answers with another short reply typical of her character: "So young, my lord, and true" (1.1.101). This simple exchange embodies all that is contradictory between Lear's psychological bearing and Cordelia's certainty of mind and speech.

Lear recoils from Cordelia's certainty of mind like a wounded lion. Her certainty forces him to gaze at his own fears and weaknesses, which he is intent on denying. In epic proportions he renounces Cordelia in a speech which is self-damning as well as revealing:

> For by the sacred radiance of the sun,
> The mysteries of Hecate and the night,
> By all the operation of the orbs
> From whom we do exist and cease to be,
> Here I disclaim all my paternal care,
> Propinquity and property of blood,
> And as a stranger to my heart and me
> Hold thee from this forever. The barbarous Scythian,
> Or he that makes his generation messes
> To gorge his appetite, shall to my bosom
> Be as well neighboured, pitied, and relieved,
> As thou my sometime daughter.
> (1.1.103-14)

Lear's reaction to Cordelia's assurance in her role as the speaker of truth serves to portray his denial of guilt. His ironic use of the "barbarous Scythian" and the cannibalistic image which he advances only recoils upon himself. Lear goes to great lengths to deny his guilt throughout the play, which leads to a revealing process of self-exoneration. Berger sketches Lear's method of self-justification with insightful accuracy: "In the first scene, Lear seems on the verge of forcing others to make him acknowledge not so much what they really think about him, but what he has always thought about them, and therefore—by a kind of recoil—about himself." And as Berger also mentions, Lear will not let self-knowledge interfere with his false conception of self and "spends the rest of the play trying continually to regain the sleep of self-deception".[9] Lear spends most of the play denying the truth of his guilt in the "division of the kingdom", but Shakespeare gives King Lear a model of truth and self-knowledge to aspire to in the character of Cordelia. It is this choice of following Cordelia's model which serves as a crux for further development.

Lear's growth to self-knowledge is constantly based on his iamge of Cordelia, which changes as he changes. Lear first conceptualizes Cordelia as a creature who seemed substantial but, in fact, was nothing: "Sir, there she stands. / If aught within that little seeming substance" (1.1.191-92). He soon changes his thoughts after Goneril chastises him for the riotous behaviour of his knights:

> O most small fault,
> How ugly didst thou in Cordelia show!
> Which, like an engine, wrenched my frame of nature
> From the fixed place, drew from my heart all love,
> And added to the gall. O Lear, Lear, Lear!
> Beat at this gate that let thy folly in
> And thy dear judgment out.
>
> (1.4.221-27)

Lear's image of Cordelia is now further from the empty, hollow concept he had. He acknowledges that there is something in Cordelia which to him is ugly. In addition, he seems to separate the "small fault" and Cordelia by personifying the ugliness, giving it a separate existence outside of Cordelia.

In the storm scene Lear separates Cordelia even further from the cause of his anger. Raging against Regan and Goneril, he assigns to them the role of persecutors, yet forgets to mention Cordelia. In his growing madness he excludes Cordelia in an attempt to avoid his guilt over his denial of her:

> Here I stand your slave,
> A poor, infirm, weak, and despised old man;
> But yet I call you servile ministers,
> That will with two pernicious daughters join
> Your high-engendered battles 'gainst a head
> So old and white as this.
>
> (3.2.18-23)

His exclusion of Cordelia from his fury is a telling sign of his changing conception of Cordelia. This change comes at a crucial moment in Lear's development as he leaves selfish concern for a moment to tend to the fool: "Come on, my boy. How dost, my boy? Art cold? [. . .] Poor fool and knave, I have one part in my heart / That's sorry yet for thee" (3.2.66 and 70-71). Harvey Birenbaum remarks that in the fourth Act, Lear "finds relief from self-awareness but only by complete submission into the truth of his pain".[10] His own violence, deception and mortality are made clear to him. He can now see Cordelia in the role of victim as he states: "Take that of me, my friend, who have the power / To seal th'accuser's lips" (4.5.161-62). Lear's awareness of his own guilt expresses itself in his madness and reveals a soul tormented by his own denial of truth. Lear tells Gloucester:

> Get thee glass eyes,
> And, like a scurvy politician, seem
> To see the things thou dost not. Now, now, now, now.
> Pull off my boots. Harder, harder! So.
>
> (4.5.162-65)

Lear's removal of his boots—his "lendings"—symbolizes rejection, and perhaps the disgust and guilt Lear harbours in regard to his treatment of Cordelia. His view of Cordelia's silence has changed drastically from an ugly blemish to an abused strength. It is through this perception of Cordelia that Lear is able to make crucial changes in his character. He now understands his fault in relying on the quantity of language and not the unspoken truth. What remains to be discussed is whether or not Lear follows her example of constancy in the face of her uncertainty and despair of the "kind gods" (4.6.14) as she is removed from speech and action.

Cordelia's conception of truth lies beyond the realm of opulent speech and perhaps speech itself, as suggested by Anne Barton: "In Cordelia's case, the declaration of the inadequacy of language happens to express a true state of feeling. Her love for her father does indeed make her breath poor and speech unable."[11] Her resolve not to taint her love prompts her to remain taciturn: "What shall Cordelia speak? Love, and be silent" (1.1.57). Cordelia's conception of truth also lies in her pious and reverent belief in providence and divine justice, the "kind gods" (Elton, 76). This is certainly true of the beginning of the play, but does it remain true when civil war, the manifestation of the collapse of justice and order, breaks out?

The reappearance of Cordelia in Act 4 is substantially altered in the Folio version by the cutting of an entire scene from the Quarto. In the Quarto scene, a gentleman relates to Kent a dynamic and emotional Cordelia rather than the simply anxious leader of the Folio. When asked how Cordelia was moved by her father's fallen situation, the gentleman portrays a struggle between patience and sorrow in Cordelia, using contrary images:

> Not to a rage. Patience and sorrow strove
> Who should express her goodliest. You have seen
> Sunshine and rain at once; her smiles and tears
> Were like a better way; those happy smilets
> That played on her ripe lip seemed not to know
> What guests were in her eyes; which parted thence
> As pearls from diamonds dropped. In brief,
> Sorrow would be a rarity most beloved,
> If all could so become it.
>
> (Quarto, 4.3.13-21)

The gentleman's attempt to romanticize Cordelia's distress does not mask the struggle between the patience needed to accept fate and the sorrow of despair. This conflict alters Cordelia's attitude towards the "kind gods" and her behaviour. Indeed, the gentleman further relates that Cordelia's sorrow turns her terse, firm language into broken exclamations of deep doubt:

> Pantingly forth, as if it pressed her heart;
> Cried "Sisters, sisters! Shame of ladies! Sisters!
> Kent! Father! Sisters! What, i'th'storm? i'th'night?
> Let pity not be believed!" There she shook
> The holy water from her heavenly eyes,
> And, clamour-moistened. Then away she started
> To deal with grief alone.
>
> (Quarto, 4.3.24-30)

Cordelia's surprise and shock are not only confined to the actions of her sisters, but are extended towards the storm and the night, symbolic embodiments of the gods (Elton, 232). This is a crucial revelation for Cordelia, whose perceptions of justice and truth have thus far been based upon her faith in the "kind gods". This episode, according to Anne Barton, is similar to the opening scenes in that Cordelia cannot give linguistic shape to her intentions (Barton, 25). However, Cordelia's broken and panting words attempt to give shape to her shock and despair and emphasize a frightening rejection of pity and Cordelia's conception of the benevolent gods.

The strong and emotionally upset reaction of Cordelia in the gentleman's report may be the very reason why this scene is not included in the later Folio version of the play which is generally considered superior. Ian J. Kirby has noted the elusiveness with which Shakespeare wrote, agreeing "that in *King Lear* Shakespeare frequently frustrates his audience".[12] The Folio conforms to this elusiveness by removing the gentleman's careful observations and by presenting Cordelia as "much more the active exponent of her father's rights".[13] The inner struggle, which is so prominent in the Quarto version, is modified to appear less obvious, more evasive. This allows Cordelia a more self-confident re-entrance to the play, and thus a stronger effect is achieved once Cordelia begins to doubt the benevolence of fate. Her few lines in Act 4, scene 3 echo the shock found in the Quarto concerning the fate of King Lear: "Alack, 'tis he: why, he was met even now, / As mad as the vexed sea, singing aloud" (4.3.1-2). She questions not only her own but also mankind's ability to cope with Lear's madness: "What can man's wisdom / In the restoring his bereavèd sense?" (4.3.8-9). The elements of doubt are present in the Folio as they are in the Quarto, but are made less potent by the omission of the gentleman's remarks.

In either case, Cordelia's prayer becomes far more than a plea for Lear's good health:

> O you kind gods,
> Cure this great breach in his abusèd nature;
> Th'untuned and jarring senses O wind up
> Of this child-changèd father!
>
> (4.6.14-17)

This prayer becomes a final wish for the gods to remain kind, a hope for divine justice. Her gods confound her by remaining, as they have ever been, silent.

The result of the confusion in Cordelia's mind concerning her faith in the benevolent gods leads to a striking manifestation of despair and consequently to her removal from the world of *King Lear*. Her very last lines are uttered in captivity:

> We are not the first
> Who with best meaning have incurred the worst.
> For thee, oppressèd king, I am cast down,
> Myself could else outfrown false fortune's frown.
> Shall we not see these daughters and these sisters?
>
> (5.3.3-7)

Cordelia's "best meaning" intentions are devalued horribly by her having "incurred the worst". The awareness that the gods' justice is not based on the merit of the individual, reveals a changed Cordelia. The devaluation of divine justice may be an indication that Cordelia is bitter. In coldly addressing Lear as "oppressèd king" rather than "father" or "dear Lord"—a mode of address to which she is accustomed—she gives her last speech an accusing tone which shows the strained imbalance in her character. It is also unlike her to view fate, fortune, and the effects of time in negative terms. Yet, she says: "Myself could outfrown false fortune's frown" (5.3.6). Earlier Cordelia saw a positive view of time and fate: "Time shall unfold what plighted cunning hides; / Who covers faults, at last with shame derides" (1.1.274-75). Her last line further illustrates an attitude of despair with a powerless wish on Cordelia's part to see her sisters. It is perhaps feelings of distressing isolation which prompt her to call for the sight of her tormentors. Cordelia ends her life with these words, which are strange, unstable and bitter.

Like Cordelia, the Fool is also removed from speech and action at a crucial point. In a Folio addition, the Fool's last line, "And I'll go to bed at noon" (3.6.41), expresses his despair in watching his master succumb to the seeming madness of the heath. Lear's preceding utterance emphasizes the inversion of values in his world: "We'll go to supper i'th' morning" (3.6.40). The Fool echoes this sentiment with the surrender of his final line. Uttering in despair of common sense his anguish over the deflation of a King to a madman, the Fool complains: "This cold night will turn us all to fools and madmen" (3.4.72). His final silence serves the play's action by illuminating the polarity between reason and madness in Lear. The Fool attempts to provide, unsuccessfully, a support for Lear with his replies of common sense:

> O nuncle, court holy water in a dry house is better than this rain-water out o'door. Good nuncle, in ask thy daughters blessing. Here's a night pities neither wise men nor fools.
>
> (3.2.10-12)

In his delusion, Lear ignores the advice and common sense of the Fool and goes on to voice a frightening hatred aimed at Goneril and Regan. His madness is so powerful that Edgar remarks: "My tears begin to take his part so much / They mar my counterfeiting" (3.6.18-19). The Fool becomes so overwhelmed by Lear's madness that he imposes a self-induced silence, effectively suppressing common sense and truth.

The Fool, in his privileged role as Lear's verbal antagonist, is very like Cordelia in regard to the unspoken truth. The Fool presents the truth much like Cordelia, in precise terms but with all the problems of speaking truth in the deceptive world of *King Lear*. The Fool's first discussion with Lear points directly to Lear's denial of truth, but in allegory: "Truth's a dog must to kennel. He must be whipped out, when the Lady Brach may stand by th'fire and stink" (1.4.97-98). Arthur Davis remarks that: "The fool is of no practical help to the King, and his value as a companion is severely limited by the nature of his running commentary."[14] If Lear were able to accept his denial of the truth, the Fool would indeed become a valuable companion. However, Lear's denial and his stubborn lack of common sense deny him the Fool's unique rarity as a speaker of truth. In fact, according to John Kerrigan, the Folio additions to the text enhance this distance between the two characters:

> Still more strikingly, F emphasizes the Fool's hard-headedness. The new lines resemble the 1.4 quips about unfee'd lawyers and rent. Only whereas such observations were then to the point, they now seem distressingly irrelevant. The Fool's first few jokes may not have helped Lear recover his kingdom, but they did make him "See better" what he had done when he gave his crown away. At TLN 1322-7, by contrast, the Fool's sallies are disengaged from the king. The two characters no longer speak the same language, because Lear is losing touch with the way things are (220).

To buttress his theme of irresolution further, Shakespeare forbids Lear the common sense of the Fool. The Fool's silence seems self-imposed but this is more because Lear has gone beyond his help. As a result, the Fool despairs of his own common sense and succumbs to the topsy-turvy values of Lear's madness in his last line: "And I'll go to bed at noon" (3.6.41). The Fool completes his action and speech in the play much like Cordelia, in opposition to his perceived values. The sense of uncertainty, however, is far more prevalent in the Fool's case because his confusion is mirrored in the disorientation of Lear's madness.

When Shakespeare imposes a silence on both Cordelia and the Fool, these two characters are in despair of their personal views of the world. The Fool despairs of common sense while Cordelia surrenders to feelings of bitterness. Shakespeare purposely does this to allow for a lack of dramatic fulfilment or resolution for Lear. Through doubt of their own principles, Lear is denied the Fool's common sense and Cordelia's pristine goodness as vehicles for fulfilment. Lear's denial of truth is finally acknowledged late in the play, but even this has a tone of misunderstanding. Lear still does not fathom Cordelia's love for him: "If you have poison for me, I will drink it. / I know you do not love me" (4.6.70-71). Even near the end of his play, Shakespeare denies the audience any form of completion.

The irresolution of the final scene is the conclusion of Shakespeare's tragic vision in *King Lear*. The Folio again enhances the already elusive Quarto in terms of dramatic completion and points in the direction Shakespeare was exploring.[15] The debate over whether or not Lear dies happily or in anguish testifies to Shakespeare's ability to leave in question the meaning of his play. If we take into consideration the role of the Fool and Cordelia as discussed, we can see a definite pattern of refusal of any form of resolution in the play. Uncertainty on the part of Cordelia and the Fool creates a rich substructure of shifting values, attitudes and hopes. The spoken truth becomes just as uncertain as Cordelia's "Nothing", as Lear realizes too late. He demonstrates his grief with howling:

> Howl, howl, howl, howl! O, you are men of stones.
> Had I your tongues and eyes, I'd use them so,
> That heaven's vault should crack.
>
> (5.3.231-33)

Anne Barton states: "At the very end, entering with Cordelia dead in his arms, Lear will find that the howl of an animal is the only possible response to the situation" (27). Lear's howls are the closest he comes to any form of resolution between himself and the spoken truth, and they are cries of inarticulate disorder. He is denied dramatic union with the Fool because of his madness, and Cordelia's doubt and death leave him to face his own death and spiritual fulfilment or non-fulfilment alone.

Notes

[1] *The Tragedy of King Lear,* ed. Jay L. Halio, New Cambridge Shakespeare, Cambridge, 1992, 5.3.164.

Philip McGuire, *Speechless Dialect: Shakespeare's Open Silences,* Berkeley, 1985, 151.

[2] John Kerrigan, "Revision, Adaption, and the Fool in *King Lear*", in *The Division of the Kingdoms: Shakespeare's Two Versions of King Lear,* eds Gary Taylor and Michael Warren, Oxford, 1983, 229.

[3] John Danby, *Shakespeare's Doctrine of Nature: A Study of King Lear,* London, 1969, 114.

[4] Harley Granville-Barker, *Prefaces to Shakespeare,* Princeton: N. J., 1946, 303.

[5] William Elton, *"King Lear" and the Gods,* San Marino: Calif., 1966, 77.

[6] Harry Berger, Jr., "*King Lear:* The Lear Family Romance", *The Centennial Review,* 23 (1979), 368.

[7] Marion D. Perret, "Lear's Good Old Man", *Shakespeare Studies,* 17 (1985), 89.

[8] "Cordelia: Loss of Insolence", *Studies in the Humanities,* V/2 (1976), 15.

[9] Harry Berger, "*King Lear:* The Lear Family Romance", 358.

[10] Harvey Birenbaum, "The Art of Our Necessities: The Softness of *King Lear*", *The Yale Review,* LXXII/4 (1983), 591.

[11] Anne Barton, "Shakespeare and the Limits of Language", *Shakespeare Survey,* 24 (1971), 24-25.

[12] Ian J. Kirby, "The Passing of King Lear", *Shakespeare Survey,* 41 (1989), 147.

[13] Jay L. Halio, *King Lear,* 4.3, note to SD *"Enter . . . CORDELIA"*.

[14] Arthur G. Davis, *The Royalty of Lear,* New York, 1974, 85.

[15] Thomas Clayton, "'Is this the promis'd end?': Revision in the Role of the King", in *The Division of the Kingdoms,* 129.

THE FAMILY

Thomas McFarland (essay date 1978/79)

SOURCE: "The Image of the Family in *King Lear*," in *On King Lear,* edited by Lawrence Danson, Princeton University Press, 1981, pp. 91-118.

[*In the following essay, originally presented at Princeton University in 1978/79, McFarland maintains that the play focuses not on King Lear's personal suffering, but on "the agony of the family." The play's tragic situation, the critic argues, stems from the tension between Lear's role as king and his role as father.*]

King Lear develops its action along a pattern supplied simultaneously by poetic fantasy and by historical reality. In the main plot, the relationship between Lear and his daughters is prefigured in the record of a distressed family situation of the late Elizabethan period. Brian Annesley, who for many years had been a gentleman pensioner to Queen Elizabeth, had three daughters. As he grew old, Annesley's mind began to give way, and two of his daughters, Christian, who was the wife of Lord Sandys of the Essex Rebellion, and Lady Grace Wildgoose, petitioned to have the old man declared insane and his estate placed in the care of Lady Wildgoose's husband. Annesley's third daughter, who was named Cordell or Cordelia, opposed the action and in October 1603 sent a letter to Cecil on behalf of her "poor aged and daily dying father." History does not inform us of the ending of this family turbulence, other than that, when Annesley died in 1604, Lady Wildgoose unsuccessfully challenged his will. Some scholars think that when the Fool comments on the alliance of Regan and Goneril in the second act of the play, he is obliquely alluding to the Annesley affair in the line "Winter's not gone yet, if the wild geese fly that way" (2.4.45).

To this prototype for the main plot of *King Lear* drawn from the quotidian reality of family life in Shakespeare's milieu we may add a fictional prototype for the subplot, drawn from the furthest reaches of Elizabethan familial fantasy. For the story of Gloucester and his two sons is taken from what Sidney called "this idle worke of mine," "this child, which I am loath to father," this "trifle, and that triflinglie handled," that is, *The Arcadia*. Here, in 1590, in the tenth chapter of the second book, we read of

> an aged man, and a young, scarcely come to the age of a man, both poorely arayed, extreamely weather-beaten; the olde man blinde, the young man leading him: and yet through all those miseries, in both these seemed to appear a kind of noblenesse, not sutable to that affliction. But the first words they heard, were these of the old man. . . . feare not, my miserie cannot be greater than it is, & nothing doth become me but miserie; feare not the danger of my blind steps, I cannot fall worse than I am. And doo not I pray thee, do not obstinately continue to infect thee with my wretchedness.

The young man then tells the observers how this doleful scene came about:

This old man (whom I leade) was lately rightfull Prince of this countrie of *Paphlagonia*, by the hard-harted ungratefulnes of a sonne of his, deprived, not onely of his kingdome (whereof no forraine forces were ever able to spoyle him) but of his sight, the riches which Nature graûts to the poorest creatures. Whereby, & by other his unnaturall dealings, he hath bin driven to such griefe, as even now he would have had me to have led him to the toppe of this rocke, thêce to cast himselfe headlong to death: and so would have made me (who received my life of him) to be the worker of his destruction.

The "toppe of this rocke" in this passage becomes, in Shakespeare's imaginative expansion, the powerful evocation by which Edgar deludes his blinded father (and more than one modern critic) into thinking he stands on the cliffs of Dover:

Come on, sir; here's the place: stand still.
  How fearful
And dizzy 'tis to cast one's eyes so low!

. . . . .

       Half way down
Hangs one that gathers sampire, dreadful
  trade!
Methinks he seems no bigger than his head.
The fishermen that walk upon the beach
Appear like mice; and yond tall anchoring
  bark
Diminished to her cock; her cock, a buoy
Almost too small for sight. The murmuring
  surge
That on th' unnumb'red idle pebble chafes
Cannot be heard so high.
                (4.6.11-22)

Shakespeare's conception of what Edgar immediately afterward calls "the extreme verge" is thus directly linked to Sidney's fantasy, as we can see again in the play's expansion of the blind king's lament as formulated by Sidney: "my miserie cannot be greater than it is, & nothing doth become me but miserie. . . . I cannot fall worse than I am." For Edgar in effect supplies a commentary: "Who is't can say, 'I am at the worst'? / I am worse than e'er I was. . . . And worse I may be yet: the worst is not / So long as we can say, 'This is the worst'" (4.1.25-28).

King Lear, to take up Edgar's rhetoric of descent, is both a drama of "the extreme verge" and an extended trope of things getting worse. We might indeed say of its depiction of life that "This is the worst," except that to say so would be to turn us to Edgar's wisdom and make us realize that *Hamlet* may descend beyond even that description. Certainly over both plays there broods Hamlet's disbelieving realization "That it should come to this." In this statement, the sense of moving from hope to horror is accentuated by the stunning virtuosity of Shakespeare's rendering of happy past and terrible present by the pain-blurred pronouns of "it" and "this."

Both plays augment their pain by fostering it in the matrix of family life. After this initial congruence, however, the familial similarities diminish. The family situation in *Hamlet* follows the model of Senecan tragedy, which in its turn had its eye upon Greek tragedy, especially the familial horrors of the house of Atreus. Seneca, who is a much more considerable dramatist than is at present fashionable to believe (Scaliger, who did not take these things lightly, ranked him with Euripides), considered human life to be hell on earth.[1] In this line of genesis, the family situation in *Hamlet,* to adopt a modern perspective, can be not inappropriately summed up in the vision of R. D. Laing: "A family can act as gangsters, offering each other mutual protection against each other's violence. It is a reciprocal terrorism." Or again:

From the moment of birth, when the Stone Age baby confronts the twentieth-century mother, the baby is subjected to those forces of violence, called love, as its mother and father . . . have been. These forces are mainly concerned with destroying most of its potentialities, and on the whole this enterprise is successful. By the time the new human being is fifteen or so, we are left with a being like ourselves, a half-crazed creature more or less adjusted to a mad world.[2]

The latter part of Laing's formula for modern youth, "a half-crazed creature more or less adjusted to a mad world," might serve as a rough description of the situation of Hamlet himself.

The model of the family in *King Lear* is different. The play itself might be seen as an exalted version of the "domestic tragedy" of the period—as an elevated form of such structures as *A Woman Killed with Kindness* or even *Arden of Feversham.* The situation in *Hamlet,* by contrast, is almost flamboyant; it has the specialness of things that happen only once, in the realm of the hypothetical, and to others than ourselves. It is significant that the play has been approached through such pairings as "Hamlet and Orestes" and "Hamlet and Oedipus." When Freud first discerned the outline of the Oedipus complex, which he was forced to see as a flaw at the very root of human nature, he immediately illustrated it by reference to Hamlet. And the form of our contemplation of such shattering familial pain as that represented by Orestes and Oedipus is the aesthetic distancing described by Kant, whereby we take pleasure in catastrophic events such as hurricanes and erupting volcanoes provided we are simultaneously secure from their consequences. A shipwreck happens to others, not to us; and Oedipus, Orestes, and Hamlet find themselves in unthinkable situations that accentuate our own security as spectators. In this same context, we may note that of all Freud's insights into human nature, none has more fiercely engaged our protective mechanisms of resistance and denial than has his formulation of the Oedipus complex. It was not merely Malinowski who professed to find no such complex in the primitive societies he studied; almost every soi-disant rectifier of Freud begins by denying the universality of the Oedipus complex. It is as though we think it suitable for Oedipus, but not for us. We are not Prince Hamlet, nor were we meant to be.

The situation in *King Lear* involves a different model of experience, an image of family life that is neither flamboyant nor unique. On the contrary, it is in significant respects almost commonplace. Lear's pain and outrage are larger versions of the pain and outrage that almost all parents at some point and to some degree experience because of their offspring. Lear's agonized realization that "Age is unnecessary" is encountered again and again by aging parents and grandparents faced with loss of prestige and function, and possibly with transportation to homes for the elderly. Goneril's impatience with Lear's residing in her own domicile is an immensely larger version of a commonplace experience, that of the strains resulting when an aged parent takes up residence with a married child. "Let me not stay a jot for dinner; go, get it ready" (1.4.8-9), orders Lear imperiously, after the audience has just been informed of Goneril's instructions to "prepare for dinner" (1.3.27). This embryonic family clash, the experience of untold numbers of housewives and aging parents writ large, is the antipode of the poison coursing like quicksilver through the porches of ears that we find in Hamlet's context. "By day and night he wrongs me," flashes Goneril, her very accents being those of the harried and hateful, but by the same token those of the commonplace and oft-repeated:

> I'll not endure it.
> His knights grow riotous, and himself
>   upbraids us
> On every trifle. When he returns from
>   hunting,
> I will not speak with him. Say I am sick.
> If you come slack of former services,
> You shall do well; the fault of it I'll answer.
>   (1.3.6-11)

The same tone of quotidian exasperation permeates Goneril's spiteful references to her father's Fool:

> Not only, sir, this your all-licensed Fool,
> But other of your insolent retinue
> Do hourly carp and quarrel, breaking forth
> In rank and not-to-be-endurèd riots.
>   (1.4.201-204)

Unlovable though she is, Goneril here speaks in tones with which many with numerous and long-staying guests can sympathize, and we do remember that previously she has taken care to ascertain at least one of the facts: "Did my father strike my gentleman for chiding of his Fool?" "Ay, madam," comes the answer (1.3.1-3). Moreover, in the early part of the play's action she speaks in tones that at least attempt to justify her conduct:

> I do beseech you
> To understand my purposes aright.
> As you are old and reverend, should be
>   wise.
> Here do you keep a hundred knights and
>   squires,
> Men so disordered, so deboshed, and bold,
> That this our court, infected with their
>   manners,
> Shows like a riotous inn. Epicurism and lust
> Makes it more like a tavern or a brothel
> Than a gracèd palace.
>   (1.4.239-247)

Lear reacts like many a parent, and entirely like his own self-indulgent early self; we do not here have his later "O, I have ta'en / Too little care of this," but rather instant righteousness and thunderbolts:

> Darkness and devils!
> Saddle my horses; call my train together.
> Degenerate bastard, I'll not trouble thee:
> Yet have I left a daughter.
>   (1.4.253-256)

In this instance, Lear's manipulation of the dynamics of family favoritism, which repeats the fatuity with which he had offered Cordelia "a third more opulent than your sisters" (1.1.86), elicits from Goneril the shrill and wonderful rejoinder—wonderful because it endures in the common situations of human experience:

> You strike my people, and your disordered
>   rabble
> Make servants of their betters.
>   (1.4.257-258)

It is because of the repeated projection of such exquisitely nuanced appeals to the *sensus communis* (Kant says that "by the name *sensus communis* is to be understood the idea of a *public* sense, i.e. a critical faculty which in its reflective act takes account [*a priori*] of the mode of representation of every one else, in order, *as it were,* to weigh its judgment with the collective reason of mankind") that the situation between Lear and his daughters cannot rewardingly be described in terms of the rhetoric of good and evil. Thus Maynard Mack's reference, in his *King Lear in Our Time,* to "the unmitigated badness of Goneril and Regan" seems somewhat beside the point. Moreover, his belief that the two sisters represent "paradigms of evil" leads in my opinion to a subtle misconception of the play's meaning. In the rudimentary morality dramas that in some sense form an adumbrative basis of *King Lear,* such figures would indeed be paradigms of evil; in the two-dimensional fairy-tale motif of Lear's processional entrance at the beginning and his arbitrary dividing of his kingdom into three (an action of the same order as Old King Cole summoning his fiddlers three), Goneril and Regan do assume the roles of wicked elder sisters to the Cinderella-like good third sister. But these are lower layers and starting points, not the profound process of the play itself. In that process, as I have elsewhere urged, good and evil are conceptions with little purchase.[3]

If we persist in using the conventional rhetoric of good and evil, we should, of course, certainly have to stigmatize Goneril, Regan, and Edmund as evil. But by that same schematism we should also be forced to think of Lear and Gloucester as good. How unfitting this latter conception would be can perhaps be indicated in brief by returning to the source of the subplot. In *The Arcadia* the son who is helping his blind father says: "noble Gentlemen . . . if either of you have a father, and feele what deutifull affection is engraffed in a sonnes hart, let me intreate you to convey this afflicted Prince to some place of rest & securitie." What Sidney next writes should prompt our reflection on its probable function in Shakespeare's work: "But before they could make him answere his father began to speake, Ah my sonne (said he) how evill an Historian are you, that leave out the chief knotte of all the discourse? *my* wickednes, *my* wickednes."

In the movement of the play, as opposed to the source, the wickedness of the father is finally no more relevant than the evil of the child. What we are presented instead is an image of the family in dynamic interaction, an image intensified and underscored by being doubled into parallel plots. The process of things getting worse is coordinate with a process of progressive deterioration and dereliction in family relationships. After all, the source of the play found in Geoffrey of Monmouth specifically includes the allegedly evil Goneril and Regan in the original unity of love: "He was without Male Issue," says that source for *King Lear,* "but had three Daughters whose Names were Gonorilla, Regan, and Cordeilla, of whom he was doatingly fond, but especially of his youngest Cordeilla." It is hardly an exaggeration, indeed, to say that the subject of the play is, not the agony of the king, but the agony of the family; and in a very real sense the protagonist of the play is not Lear alone, nor even Lear and Gloucester in tandem, but the two fathers as the center of family relationships and the service relationships that pertain to them. Any impact on any strand of this web of relationships perturbs the whole;

when Gloucester suffers, a nameless serving man lays down his life in sympathetic response.

The protagonistic function is thus dispersed, and the dispersal is both welcome and in a sense necessary because of the unattractiveness of age. Although the fact that Lear is a man standing on the outer edge of existence—"O, sir, you are old," notes Regan, "Nature in you stands on the very verge / Of his confine" (2.4.143-145)—gives him immense tragic authenticity and the play immense leverage at the tragic intersection of being and nonbeing, by the same token, his standing at the verge of nature's confine makes it difficult for us to identify with him. For an aged man is but a paltry thing, and Lear's prospects on his very verge are as bleak as those of Gloucester on his own extreme verge. The motifs of "very verge" and "extreme verge," though emphasized by the aged fathers, actually pertain to all the characters and in truth to all human existence: in this life we all stand on the razor's edge, and death has a thousand doors. But it is Lear's definition as father that connects him with younger life and its attendant hope. His fatherhood draws him back into our common ken; his familial identity ropes him to the others as he teeters on the edge of the abyss.[4] Indeed, even Regan's heartless remark quoted above would not have been made were he not her father.

The tension between Lear's two roles in life, one as king with its patina of symbolic paternalism, the other as father to a specific family, generates the tragic situation that arises in the play. Or more exactly, it makes up the tragic abscissa that, along with the tragic ordinate constituted by being's straining against nonbeing, delimits *King Lear's* tragic space.

Lear pervasively assumes at the outset that his status as king and his status as father are the same, and this initial confusion leads him into the fallacious assumption that power and love are interchangeable.[5] It is not merely that he mistakenly believes that so much love can equal so much land, or that he carries the confusion between love and power into the further quantification of the hundred knights, appurtenances necessary to a king but irrelevant to a father. Rather, it is that he believes that the attributes he gives up as king are ones he can retain solely as father: "I do invest you jointly with my power, / Preeminence, and all the large effects / That troop with majesty," he says to Goneril and Regan and their husbands:

> Ourself, by monthly course,
> With reservation of an hundred knights,
> By you to be sustained, shall our abode
> Make with you by due turn. Only we shall
>   retain
> The name, and all th' addition to a king.
>   (1.1.130-136)

As Lawrence Stone observes, from a vantage ground atop a mass of sociohistorical data: "Shakespeare's interpretation of King Lear merely underscores the moral that a father who gives up real power, in the expectation of obtaining the love and attention of his children instead, is merely exhibiting a form of insanity. His inevitable disappointment would have come as no surprise to an Elizabethan audience."[6] Nor to a modern one either, we might append.

We see the same confusion of Lear's conception of himself as king and as father in his decision to divide his kingdom into three, a decision that violated the accumulated wisdom of Elizabethan statecraft. As Sir Thomas Elyot said in 1531, in *The Boke Named the Gouernour:*

> Lyke as to a castell or fortresse suffisethe one owner or soueraygne and where any mo be of like power and authoritie seldome cometh the warke to perfection.... In semblable wyse doth a publike weale that hath mo chiefe gouernours than one.

He goes on to say that "if any desireth to haue the gouernance of one persone proued by histories let him fyrste resorte to the holy scripture; where he shall fynde that almyghty god commanded Moses . . . gyuynge onely to hym that authoritie without appoyntynge to hym any other assistence of equall power or dignitie." After many examples of the ills attendant upon divided rule, he says,

> But what nede we to serche so ferre from vs sens we haue sufficient examples nere vnto us? . . . After that the Saxons by treason had expelled out of Englande the Britons whiche were the auncient inhabitantes: this realme was deuyded in to sondry regions or kyngdomes. O what mysery was the people then in: O howe this most noble Isle of the worlde was decerpt and rent in pieces.

Elyot's political admonitions find confirmation in 1561 in Sackville's and Norton's *Gorboduc,* where the choric counselor warns:

> To part your realm unto my lords, your sons,
> I think not good for you, ne yet for them,
> But worst of all for this our native land.
> Within one land one single rule is best.
> Divided reigns do make divided hearts,
> But peace preserves the country and the prince.
>
>   (1.2.256-261)

In 1599, finally, to trace the unanimity of opinion into Shakespeare's own day, King James VI wrote to his son in the *Basilikon Doron:*

> Make your eldest sonne ISAAC, leauing him all your Kingdomes, and prouide the rest with priuate possessiones: otherwayes by deuiding your Kingdomes, yee shall leaue the seede of diuisione and discorde among your posteritie.

Lear, in short, is behaving like a father and not like a king when he divides his kingdom. The inadequacy of his action purely as that of a father, as opposed to its patent folly as the decision of a king, is attendant, not upon the division as such, but rather upon the inequality of the division, that is, the doting promise to Cordelia to give her "a third more opulent than your sisters," a third that directly validates Goneril's once resentful but by now matter-of-fact realization that "he always loved our sister most" (1.1.290).

An even more damaging result of Lear's confusion of kingship and fatherhood is his feeling that, like a monarch, but not like a father, he can abrogate the ties of kinship. But the family has its deep-rooted sanctities. The original sin of this dark cosmos is constituted by Lear's denial of family relation in his rejection of Cordelia:

> Here I disclaim all my paternal care,
> Propinquity and property of blood,
> And as a stranger to my heart and me
> Hold thee from this for ever.
>
>   (1.1.113-116)

Thus Lear's action, not in becoming angry with Cordelia, who has herself acted with some of the old man's willfulness, but in disclaiming paternal care, propinquity, and property of blood, is, if we like the rhetoric of good and evil, the beginning of the evil in the play's progression of events; it is an action of the same order as those of Goneril and Regan. Lear's own violation is eventually redeemed, and its purgation begins with his dawning realization that "I did her wrong" (1.5.24); whereas Goneril and Regan cannot escape their own selves and eventually begin to prey upon each other, in Albany's phrase, "like monsters of the deep." Albany's terrifying image, which is the nadir of the play's animal references and alludes to the unspoken, dreaded boundary situation of possible descent from true human relation, is prefigured by Lear's violation at the beginning of the play. Thus France observes that Cordelia, as "the best, the dearest," could not "commit a thing so monstrous" (1.1.217) as Lear's reaction suggests; and he refers to her "offense" as being of "unnatural degree / That monsters it" (1.1.218-220) if Lear is to be thought justified. The same misconception and foreshadowing attend also on Gloucester's early self-indulgence: "He cannot be such a monster," he exclaims of Edgar; "Nor is not, sure," replies Edmund smoothly (1.2.97-98). Still again, the image is refocused when Lear speaks of Goneril's ingratitude as more hideous "in a child / Than the sea-monster!" (1.4.262-263).

Thus Lear's initial confusion as to what pertains to a king and what pertains to a father sets in motion the tragic descent. That he does confuse these roles points us to a truth about the structure of the family as presented in this play. That structure, as we have suggested, is fundamentally different from the Senecan flamboyance of the family in *Hamlet*. The tradition there is one in which Titus Andronicus can at the very outset of his play execute Tamora's son Alarbus ("Alarbus' limbs are lopped," report his sons matter-of-factly), despite her piteous pleas to spare him. Shortly thereafter Titus imperiously slays his own son Mutius. The play, adding the horrors of Ovid to those of Seneca, proceeds from this bloody beginning into a bizarre sequence of massacres along family lines. To reinvoke the phrase of R. D. Laing, this conception of the family exhibits on its face the contours of "reciprocal terrorism"; and it is this conception, though immensely refined, that obtains in *Hamlet*.

The family image in *King Lear* is much more like a different kind of ancient paradigm: that serene structure of mutual regard revealed in Plutarch's letter to his wife on the death of one of their children. Or to summon a modern reference to counterbalance Laing, the family image in *King Lear* is what in Christopher Lasch's rubric is termed "haven in a heartless world." It is to seek a haven that Lear gives up his crown:

> Know that we have divided
> In three our kingdom; and 'tis our fast intent
> To shake all cares and business from our age,
> Conferring them on younger strengths.
>
> (1.1.37-40)

"I loved her most," he says of Cordelia, "and thought to set my rest / On her kind nursery" (1.1.123-124).

That the family here is conceived of as a haven in a heartless world is not contradicted by the fact that the horrors later perpetrated within that family vie with and in certain senses even surpass those in *Hamlet*. For what we are talking about is, not the reality of family life, but merely the proffered image of the family. In truth, the conception of family as a haven in a heartless world can in certain respects lead to greater even though less visible destructions than can less affecting images, even as an explosion of dynamite is augmented if the explosive is covered. The offices of psychoanalysts are thronged with tormented patients who bear witness to this truth, and its dimensions are cogently revealed by the nineteenth-century diarist Amiel:

> Oh, the family! If the pious, traditional superstition with which we envelop this institution would let us tell the truth about the matter, what a reckoning it would have to settle! What numberless martyrdoms it has required, dissemblingly, inexorably! How many hearts have been stifled by it, lacerated and broken. . . . The family may be all that is best in this world, but too often it is all that is worst. . . . The truth is that the family relation exists only to put us to the proof and that it gives us infinitely more suffering than happiness.

In this context we see Goneril, Regan, and Edmund all as victims of the family situation. Their inadequate action is somewhat like that of Joseph's brothers, rendered envious and malicious by their father's favoritism, or even like that of another family victim named Cain.

Despite their differences in image and provenance, the family structures in *King Lear* and in *Hamlet* both generate tragic intensifications. In one way, moreover, the two structures are identical. For both are broken families at the outset, and broken in complementary ways. In *Hamlet* there is no father, in *King Lear* no mother. We think of correlates everywhere in Shakespeare, so quickly, indeed, that we are overwhelmed by the intuition that a very substantial portion of Shakespeare's literary energy was discharged through varying apprehensions of the dynamics of family structures. Almost all these families are also broken. We think of Bertram and his mother the Countess Rousillon, with their situation, as well as that of Helena, depending on a dead father. We think of Coriolanus and his mother, Volumnia, again with a dead father. We think yet again of Brabantio and Desdemona, with a dead mother, of Polonius and Ophelia, again with a dead mother, and, perhaps most compellingly of all and most germane to the situation in *King Lear*, of Prospero and Miranda, still again with a dead mother.

These relationships are for Shakespeare typically charged with the most electric emotions. It is perhaps not entirely accidental that his series of passionate sonnets to a young friend involves a recognition of the emotional bond between the youth and his mother, with apparently no father to consider: "Is it for fear to wet a widow's eye," he asks in the ninth sonnet, "That thou consum'st thyself in single life? / Ah, if thou issueless shalt hap to die, / The world will wail thee like a makeless wife; / The world will be thy widow and still weep." But possibly the most unmistakable index of the centrality of family kinesis in Shakespeare's concern is the scene in the fourth act of *King Lear* where Lear is reunited with Cordelia. Such a theme of reunion, and especially of the reunion of a family—or, as here, the living heart of a family—mines the deepest and richest lode of Shakespeare's affirmation of life; and that truth is apparent in other places than *King Lear*. In the vast tropes of reunion and reconciliation that conclude the action of Shakespeare's last comedies, the most intense themes of joy appear, and they are invariably generated by the resurgence of a family relationship.[7] Thus Leontes, having seemingly destroyed both his wife and his daughter, finds his daughter again in the lost Perdita and his wife again in the statue suddenly come to life. The language of joy in the familial reconstitution is almost overpowering; it is presented as a climax beyond even the reunion of friends as celebrated by the meeting of Leontes and Polixenes:

> Did you see the meeting of the two kings? . . . Then have you lost a sight which was to be seen, cannot be spoken of. There might you have beheld one joy crown another . . . their joy waded in tears. . . . Our king, being ready to leap out of himself for joy of his found daughter . . . then asks Bohemia forgiveness.
>
> (*The Winter's Tale*, 5.2.41-54)

As the almost orgiastic description continues, the final points of reference are familial. For the clown says:

> The king's son took me by the hand and called me brother; and then the two kings called my father brother; and then the prince, (my brother) and the princess (my sister) called my father father.
>
> (*The Winter's Tale*, 5.2.143-147)

This joy is confirmed and if possible even surpassed in the familial reconstitution of *Pericles*. First Pericles is reunited with his daughter Marina:

> O Helicanus, strike me, honored sir!
> Give me a gash, put me to present pain;
> Lest this great sea of joys rushing upon me
> O'erbear the shores of my mortality,
> And drown me with their sweetness. O, come hither,
> Thou that beget'st him that did thee beget;
> Thou that wast born at sea, buried at Tharsus,
> And found at sea again!
>
> (5.1.194-201)

>   I embrace you.
> Give me my robes. I am wild in my beholding.
> O heavens bless my girl!
>
> (5.1.225-227)

The reunion with the daughter Marina is followed by reunion with the wife Thaisa:

> This, this! No more. You gods, your present kindness
> Makes my past miseries sports. You shall do well
> That on the touching of her lips I may
> Melt and no more be seen.
>
> (5.3.39-42)

And yet not even in these outpourings of joy and wonder is the emotion as powerful as in the awesome reconciliation scene between Lear and Cordelia. Lear's awakening from madness into rationality is, on the literal plane, a moment of restoration, reconciliation, and reunion. But on the anagogical plane it is more; it is the reawakening of the dead into paradise. Lear's confused words on regaining consciousness reverberate with the sweetest *topoi* of Christian hope:

> You do me wrong to take me out o' th' grave.
> Thou art a soul in bliss.
>
> (4.7.45-46)

When Cordelia asks, "Sir, do you know me?" Lear's answer is "You are a spirit, I know. Where did you die?" (4.7.48-49). Shakespeare's astonishing evocation of the varieties of human tears in the remainder of the passage achieves a finality that suggests the supervening state of paradise, which, in the words of the Book of Revelation hauntingly taken up by Milton, will wipe the tears forever from our eyes. Lear first speaks of tears:

>   I am bound
> Upon a wheel of fire, that mine own tears
> Do scald like molten lead.
>
> (4.7.46-48)

The connection between scalding past and paradisal renewal is sealed by tears of watering restoration, as revealed by the virtuosity (never enough admired) of Cordelia's tear-choked replies "And so I am, I am," and "No cause, no cause":

> LEAR.   Do not laugh at me,
> For, as I am a man, I think this lady
> To be my child Cordelia.
> CORDELIA. And so I am, I am.
> LEAR. Be your tears wet? Yes, faith. I pray, weep not.
> If you have poison for me, I will drink it.
> I know you do not love me; for your sisters
> Have, as I do remember, done me wrong.
> You have some cause, they have not.
> CORDELIA. No cause, no cause.
>
> (4.7.68-75)

Art can hardly go beyond this. Both the literal and the anagogic planes are superintended by the Doctor, who naturally would stand by a sick man recovering consciousness (even though this doctor's sudden prominence is mysterious). But as I have elsewhere pointed out, this sudden figure takes up the function of the doctor from the English folk play or mummer's play, who, as E. K. Chambers records, abruptly appears to restore the slain duelist to life.

But doctors also assist at childbirth, and that additional function leads us to still another level of meaning in this supreme scene of reconciliation. For Lear is not merely the sick and confused man regaining consciousness and rationality. He is here not restricted even to the deeper motif of devastated mortal reborn to heaven's bliss. He is also, in palpable respects, the child entering the world for the first time; and Cordelia, hovering over his bed, is, in awesome psycho-dramatic recapitulation, the eternal mother brooding over the infant's crib. Earlier in the play age was equated with infancy in the statement "Old fools are babes again" (1.3.20), and just before the reconciliation scene there is insistent reference to our entrance into the world:

> We came crying hither:
> Thou know'st, the first time that we smell the air
> We wawl and cry. . . .
>
> . . . . .
>
> When we are born, we cry that we are come
> To this great stage of fools.
>   (4.6.178-183)

These images subliminally join with the tears of the restoration scene, for Lear's tears that scald like molten lead, though unforgettably part of the agony and guilt through which he has passed, are no more scalding than the infant's tears at birth. And the very indications by which we see Lear purged of his madness and spleen are also coordinate with the sense of infant joy and calm. The doctor informs us that "the great rage . . . is killed in him" (4.7.78-79). A "very foolish fond old man" who reiterates that "I am old and foolish," who asks others to "bear with me," to "forget and forgive" (4.7.60, 83-84), is a man who in essential respects resumes the relationships of his earliest life.

I have dwelt on this one supreme scene to make clear the enormous charge of emotion with which it is invested. Its recapitulation of the earliest family situation of mother and child, which receives additional emphasis from the absence of Cordelia's mother and Lear's wife throughout the play, leads us to understand how the scene can plumb such psychic depth. At the same time, we realize that the recreation of the child's union with the parent is precisely, in Freud's description, the impelling origin and ultimate goal in the sexual development of every human being.

This aperture of understanding provided by the third or recapitulative plane of the reconciliation scene reveals to us another aspect of the play's meaning as well. For it occurs to every careful critic that there is at least a surface anomaly in the play: *King Lear*, which is arguably the greatest of all human documents, largely dispenses with the sexual relationships of mankind. There is no proper vehicle here for love between the sexes. It is not simply that the nominal protagonist, Lear, is eighty years old; it is also that such interest seems deliberately to be evicted. The king of France, for instance, speaks in the idealistic language of Sonnet 116, paralleling its insistence that "love is not love / Which alters when it alteration finds" with "Love's not love / When it is mingled with regards that stands / Aloof from th' entire point" (1.1.238-240). But after thus displaying his own true understanding of love, the king of France withdraws to his own country, taking love with him. The possibilities for love thenceforth largely devolve on Edmund, and they become, not an index of idealistic intensification, but a grotesque badge of deterioration: "To both these sisters have I sworn my love; / Each jealous of the other, as the stung / Are of the adder" (5.1.56-58). This seething sexuality is further removed from the nobly human by Lear's searing hallucination:

> I pardon that man's life. What was thy cause?
> Adultery?
> Thou shalt not die: die for adultery! No:
> The wren goes to't, and the small gilded fly
> Does lecher in my sight.
> Let copulation thrive; for Gloucester's bastard son
> Was kinder to his father than my daughters
> Got 'tween the lawful sheets.
> To't, luxury, pell-mell! for I lack soldiers.
> Behold yond simp'ring dame,
> Whose face between her forks presages snow,
> That minces virtue, and does shake the head
> To hear of pleasure's name.
> The fitchew, nor the soilèd horse, goes to't
> With a more riotous appetite.
> Down from the waist they are Centaurs,
> Though women all above:
> But to the girdle do the gods inherit,
> Beneath is all the fiend's.
> There's hell, there's darkness, there is the sulphurous pit, burning, scalding, stench, consumption; fie, fie, fie! pah, pah! Give me an ounce of civet; good apothecary, sweeten my imagination.
>   (4.6.109-131)

And when Gloucester then comments, "O let me kiss that hand!" Lear's reply reverberates with sublime disgust: "Let me wipe it first; it smells of mortality."

The disgust with which the horizontal and procreative activities of man are here viewed tends to strengthen the urgency of the vertical and familial affections. The same disgust is expressed by Shakespeare in other places: in his Sonnet 129, for instance, or in the poisoned imaginations of Leontes and Othello; most of all, perhaps, in Hamlet's interview with his mother:

> Nay, but to live
> In the rank sweat of an enseamèd bed,
> Stewed in corruption, honeying and making love
> Over the nasty sty.
>
> (3.4.92-95)

And when Gertrude asks, "What shall I do?" Hamlet answers that she should not

> Let the bloat king tempt you again to bed,
> Pinch wanton on your cheek, call you his mouse,
> And let him, for a pair of reechy kisses,
> Or paddling in your neck with his damned fingers,
> Make you to ravel all this matter out,
> That I essentially am not in madness,
> But mad in craft.
>
> (3.4.183-189)

This vividly expressed sexual disgust functions in similar ways in both *Hamlet* and *King Lear;* it tends to displace Gertrude as paramour of Claudius and reinstate and emphasize Gertrude as wife of the father, as matron of the family, as mother of the son. The sexual disgust of *King Lear,* in the same way, should be seen as not merely a profound expression of something in the man Shakespeare himself, although I have no doubt that it is that as well, but also as a deliberate eviction from the play of the only force that in both common experience and psychological observation challenges the satisfactions and securities of the family. For whatever Shakespeare's idiosyncratic disgust with human sexuality (as we see, for instance, in Sonnet 94), he was also capable of depicting sexuality in the most radiant terms, as *Romeo and Juliet* and *Antony and Cleopatra* attest. We are reminded, nevertheless, that in both these plays the apotheosis of sexuality occurs explicitly at the expense of family solidarity. Yet by the same token, the fact that sexual disgust appears with jolting power in *King Lear* tends to reassert the primary importance of the ties of the family relationship.

If in *King Lear* the sexual interest largely devolves on Edmund and thereby becomes an insignia of deterioration, Edmund's position as bastard both threatens the normative structure of the family and reveals him as the initial legatee of family pain. He thereby becomes the leader, as it were, the first in line, of those who descend toward the disintegrative bleakness of the world of storm and night. But in his descent he is unable to purge himself and forge a new being. Hence Edmund also, like Goneril and Regan, is less rewardingly viewed as evil than as inadequate. Indeed, he is a figure invested with deep pathos.

Here again an examination of the two sources to which I referred at the beginning of this lecture is revealing. For the Annesley prototype differs from the other sources in that it alone presents the old man as infirm of mind (his daughter Cordell writes Cecil that her father's "many years service to our late dread Sovereign Mistress" deserved better than "at his last gasp to be recorded and registered a Lunatic"); it thereby enlists our universal or public sympathy with the plight of the old man and our outrage at the callousness of Lady Wildgoose. In the source for the subplot, however, something is absent rather than present; there is no bastard, and this fact paradoxically makes the figure of Edmund seem somehow more important in Shakespeare's design.

If, as I have been tacitly assuming and sometimes hinting, Shakespeare's almost obsessive preoccupation with dramatic structures of the family takes its enormous emotional force from his own family experience—however little the details of that experience may actually abide our question—then we will find interest in J. H. Padel's recent speculations about the relationship of the sonnets to the death of Shakespeare's son.[8] Whatever the truth may be, it is intriguing that Shakespeare had a brother named Edmund, who also became an actor, and who fathered a bastard son named Edward. This is one of a number of nagging similarities, such as that between the names Hamlet and Hamnet, or between the maiden name of Shakespeare's mother and the forest of Arden where all troubles are healed, or still again the rumor, reported by Rowe, of a gift of a thousand pounds from Southampton to Shakespeare, which Empson thinks must somehow pertain to the thousand pounds owed Falstaff by Prince Hal. These nagging similarities do not constitute evidence, but we are somehow reluctant to put them out of our minds. My visceral feeling is that the presence of Edmund and Edward, brother and bastard, in Shakespeare's familial awareness somehow pertains to his creation of Edmund and Edgar, brother and bastard, in his most familial play.

The figure of Edmund stands in starkest tension to the hegemony of the family in the play itself. If we think of the processional entry of Lear and his retainers at the beginning as having some of the formulaic depthlessness of royalty on playing cards, or perhaps even more appropriately as possessing the depthlessness of some grouped and resplendent representation of royal appearances on a late medieval tapestry, then we can think of Edmund as an unwanted thread dangling from that tapestry, a thread that, when tugged at by the play's action, comes out, not alone, but rather begins to unravel the frozen hierarchies of the tapestry itself. The pregnant encounter that opens the play establishes both the frozen hierarchies and the unwanted thread, for there we see two friends, who happen to be earls, exchanging courtesies from their hierarchical security, and one bastard, introduced with unintentional callousness and condescension. The bastard stands outside the haven represented by the family, apparently fully accepting the situation as laid down by his inattentive and carelessly joking father. But when we see the bastard alone, we understand how little those grouped hierarchies actually answer to the structure of human need.

Edmund's pathos lies in his exclusion from significant human attention. Nowhere is this more apparent than in a single line that, standing in the very midst of his plain-dealing villainy, nonetheless reverberates as a universal cry of agony. At the beginning of the second act, having involved Edgar in their father's suspicions, Edmund says, "I hear my father coming" (2.1.29). We pause at Edmund's use of the adjective "my." Edmund next tells Edgar to "draw, seem to defend yourself"; and then, as Edgar flees, Edmund says, "Some blood drawn on me would beget opinion / Of my more fierce endeavor." He next calls out (the words now beginning to reverberate beyond the immediate situation): "Father, fahter! / Stop, stop! No help?" Gloucester enters, the torches he brings with him ironically prefiguring not only the torch of the foul fiend Flibbertigibbet but also that darkness of the evolving situation in which no torch will avail him. By torchlight he sees nothing: "Now, Edmund, where's the villain?" The deprivation of a lifetime is in Edmund's answer: "Look, sir, I bleed" (2.1.42). But here, as elsewhere, Gloucester looks past his son into the miasma of self-preoccupation: "Where is the villain, Edmund?" is his only answer to the poignant cry. Small wonder, then, when he is blinded in act 4 and the Old Man says, "You cannot see your way," Gloucester's answer seems to be the voice of justice: "I have no way and therefore want no eyes; / I stumbled when I saw" (4.1.17-19).

The pathos of Edmund's "Look, sir, I bleed" constitutes an emotional nadir for the play, and it erupts from the family situation, as does an opposite but complementary emotional zenith: Lear's eulogy of the dead Cordelia: "Her voice was ever soft, / Gentle and low, an excellent thing in woman" (5.3.274-275). The power of the specification lies in its diminuendo of observation contrasted with its crescendo of emotion; but its substance comes from the repeated observations of family interaction, the attention paid to Cordelia by her father. And this attention is starkly opposed to Gloucester's inattention to Edmund.

In largest description, indeed, the opposites that generate the play's moral movement can be viewed as the struggle between attention and inattention ("O, I have ta'en / Too little care of this!"). The truth, both of the play and of human life, is that human inattention destroys the family as haven. But the family as haven, though it undergoes vicissitudes that reveal it to be largely illusion and absolutely so in terms of the insubstantial positings of the play's beginning, complements the idea of a heartless world. The bleakness of the *King Lear* cosmos stands in ironic tension to the posited security of family concern:

> No, I will weep no more. In such a night
> To shut me out! Pour on, I will endure.
> In such a night as this! O Regan, Goneril.
> (3.4.17-19)

The storm that harrows Lear compounds the irony of his familial illusion:

> Rumble thy bellyful. Spit, fire. Spout, rain!
> Nor rain, wind, thunder, fire are my daughters.
> I tax not you, you elements, with unkindness.
> I never gave you kingdom, called you children,
> You owe me no subscription.
> (3.2.14-18)

The storm is only the bleakest intensification of the idea of an uncaring cosmos, a heartless world. The play throughout exists in what I have elsewhere called "a nightmare corner of thought."

We may note, finally, that the mighty process by which familial haven is dissipated into heartless world results in the almost inconceivable power of the trial scene in the stormswept hovel, where the family is virtually turned inside out. The vast dialectical movement of the play's imagery and emotion is from insubstantial something toward and into nothing itself and out again to renewed and substantial something. The insubstantial something is the familial relationships and political and social hierarchies posited at the beginning; the nothing, brought alive by the repeated invocations of the word in the play's fabric of discourse and represented by repeated tropes of divestiture, from shelter to storm, from castle to hovel, from fine raiment to rags to nakedness itself, and, finally, from reason to madness, begins to reemerge as substantial something in the awesome trial scene. There the family situation is reversed. Cordelia is absent, having been replaced by the Fool. Goneril and Regan, the two other members of the family, are on trial on the mad but wonderful familial charge of having "kicked the poor king her father" (3.6.47-48). But Goneril and Regan are actually as "be-nothinged" as Cordelia, for Goneril is a joint stool, and Regan another, "whose warped looks proclaim / What store her heart is made on."

From this point the often noted wonder ensues. The worldly situation of Lear and Cordelia, except for the momentary calm of their reconciliation, grows worse and worse, but their spiritual situation becomes better and better, until it rises to the transcendent heights of gilded butterflies, purged to the ultimate relationship of "We two alone." All the sources concur in saying that Lear and Cordelia defeated their enemies and that Lear reigned once again over Britain. But in this play we have instead the choric cry of Edgar at the final battle: "King Lear hath lost, he and his daughter ta'en."

For worldly success would have worked against Shakespeare's final distillation of human meaning into the heavenly quintessence of family relationship. Father and daughter are more truly family than even husband and wife; and the familial nucleus of "We two alone" persists, in this greatest of Shakespeare's visions, beyond life into death itself.

Notes

[1] Commentators have said little on this matter, although the cumulative testimony of the plays is almost overwhelming. But compare a philosophical analyst's recent observation with respect to Seneca's statement that it is wrong to hate life too much: "The remark gives him away; his own view is based on a hatred of life.... Fundamentally Seneca's wise man is in love with death. He is looking out for a tolerable pretext to die." J. M. Rist, *Stoic Philosophy* (Cambridge: Cambridge Univ. Press, 1969), p. 249. For Scaliger's judgment of Seneca, see J. W. Cunliffe, *The Influence of Seneca on Elizabethan Tragedy* (1893; reprint ed., Hamden, Conn.: Archon Books, 1965), p. 7.

[2] *The Politics of Experience* (New York: Pantheon, 1967), pp. 59, 36. The reciprocal terrorism can be physical as well as mental, and it is certainly not limited to twentieth-century realities. Thus, for a single emphatic instance, Augustin Thierry records in his *Récits des temps mérovingiens* that, "in the year 561, after an expedition against one of his sons, whose rebellion he punished by having him burned at the stake together with his wife and children, Lothar, perfectly at ease in mind and conscience, returned to his house at Braine." (I have used the translation by M.F.O. Jenkins.)

[3] "Reduction and Renewal in *King Lear*," in *Tragic Meanings in Shakespeare* (New York: Random House, 1966).

[4] Compare, for example, William R. Elton: "Paralleled by Edgar's quest for identity, Lear demands his own identity of daughters, his retainers, his Fool, and himself.... From one point of view, indeed, Lear may be said sequentially to dissociate into his children, Goneril and Regan (selfish willfulness) and Cordelia (courageous adamancy), as Gloucester may be seen successively to dissolve into his components, Edmund (lust) and Edgar (pathos). Here, fatherhood, as in Dostoievsky's Karamazov family, involves not only the problem of identity but also that of identity in multiplicity. Thus, through self-alienation and division, characters generate proxies for themselves, as well as analogues of each other." *"King Lear" and the Gods* (San Marino, Calif.: Huntington Library, 1968), p. 280.

[5] Underlying the whole structure of Elizabethan attitudes about the nature of kingship was the implicit *analogia* of king with father (and of both with God). Thus, for instance, James VI composes his *Basilikon Doron* in the dual role of father counseling son and of king instructing subject (as we can see from the subtitle of the 1603 edition: *His Maiesties Instructions to his Dearest Sonne, Henry the Prince*). Furthermore, though the analogy of king and father was so taken for granted that explicit statements are infrequent, oblique alignments abound, e.g. "A good King (thinking his highest honour to consist in the due discharge of his calling) employeth all his studie and paines, to procure and mainteine (by the making and execution of good lawes) the well-fare and peace of his people, and (as their naturall father and kindly maister) thinketh his greatest contentment standeth in their prosperitie, and his greatest suretie in hauing their hearts." Or again: "Ye see nowe (my Sonne) how (for the zeale I beare to acquent you with the plain & single verity of al things) I haue not spared to playe the baird against all the estates of my kingdome: but I protest before God, I do it with the fatherly loue that I owe to them all, onely hating their vices, whereof there is a good number of honest men freed in euery estate." *Basilikon Doron,* reprint of 1599 edition, pp. 29 (sig. E3), 64 (sig. 14). But however much, under the most benign interpretation of their possibilities, the roles of king and father may be thought to coincide, in actual fact the absolute power of a king ill accords with the loving flexibility of a father. The dynamics of the contrast are existential, not historical or time-bound by Elizabethan convention. Thus a prominent modern psychiatrist prefaces a well-known study of the genesis of schizophrenia within a family by a description of the father that timelessly describes Lear's own preoccupation with his appurtenances as a king: "The father ... thought of himself as a great man and expected his family to support his narcissistic need for admiration. He was unable to recognize the needs of others or even realize that they viewed the world differently than he did." Theodore Lidz, Preface to *A Mingled Yarn: Chronicle of a Troubled Family,* by Beulah Parker (New Haven: Yale Univ. Press, 1972), p. xi. In this context, it is interesting to remind ourselves that James, unlike the Lear of the play's opening, insists that a king should be humble, because a king is simply an ordinary man called to eminence by God: "Foster true Humilitie in banishing pride," and "when ye ar there, remember the throne is Gods and not yours, that ye sit in." *Basilikon Doron,* pp. 115 (sig. Q2), 109-110 (sig. P3). In brief, whatever the identity of kingship and fatherhood in static conception, the formula that describes their functioning interaction is this: the more king, the less father; the more father, the less king.

[6] *The Family, Sex and Marriage in England, 1500-1800* (New York: Harper and Row, 1977), p. 97.

[7] Though Stanley Wells has pointed out that the joyous reconciliation scenes in the last comedies are pre-

figured by such scenes in the Greek romances that lie behind them, we may take it as an axiom of Shakespearean interpretation that what Shakespeare chooses to retain from his source materials is as truly representative of his intent as are themes created by his imagination ex nihilo.

[8] "Shakespeare's Sonnets—Sonnet 146," in *Times* (London) *Literary Supplement,* Oct. 21, 1977.

Harry Berger, Jr. (essay date 1979)

SOURCE: "*King Lear*: The Lear Family Romance," in *The Centennial Review,* Vol. XXIII, No. 4, Fall, 1979, pp. 348-76.

[*Below, Berger examines the relationship Lear has with his daughters by analyzing the psychological motivations for Lear's and his daughters' actions. Berger observes that the characters in the play tend to downplay their own contributions to their problems while intensifying the role of others.*]

I

This reading of some aspects of King Lear's relationship to his daughters is one of a series of reinterpretations of Shakespeare motivated by an interest in returning to a modified character-and-action approach—the approach for which A. C. Bradley is famous or nefarious. The chief differences between my version and his are as follows:

1) I have no interest in, for example, how many children Lady Macbeth had. But I do have an interest in her interest in, and fear of, children as these affect and illuminate her relationship with Macbeth. And I have an interest in the abiding nature of that relationship as it reveals or betrays itself to us in the language they speak. That relationship antedates the opening of the play. When Lady Macbeth comes onstage reading Macbeth's letter and soliloquizing, we are asked to attend to the shifting nuances of a settled relationship, and asked at the same time to wonder whether it is, in this very moment, on the verge of being permanently unsettled. We are therefore expected to assume, and so to reconstruct, a generalized past as the locus of stable or settled relationships. We are asked to deduce and to evaluate these relationships at least in enough detail to enable us to respond both to their *contribution to* the present conflict and to the jeopardy with which *it* threatens *them.*

2) I look for themes and forms of action which are centrally psychological and ethical, and are so in a way that enables us to use the resources of the thought and experience of our time. At the same time I think it is important to avoid succumbing to system-bound language, to systematic terminology such as that of psychoanalysis, and to try for a mix between ordinary language and the terminological suggestions offered by the language of any particular play.

3) I look for those themes and forms of action not only in individual characters but in the community or "group" of the play as a whole. By "community" or "group" I mean not only an aggregate of individuals but also the structured social and political relationships in which they find themselves as members of families, dynasties, courts, age groups, sex groups, kingdoms, etc. I think the institutions and structured relationships depicted in any play compose into a coherent and identifiable image of an institutional order specific (but not necessarily unique) to that play.

4) Putting items 2 and 3 together indicates the general orientation of this enterprise: I want to examine the way Shakespeare depicts the interaction of psyche with society in order to explore questions of the following kind: What are the social resources available to self-deception? How do characters *use* the roles and relationships of love, courtship, and marriage, of family, court, and kingdom, of race, religion, and gender, to validate their pursuits of power or pleasure or pain or self-interest or love?

5) Behind the particular themes and questions instanced above lurks a more abstract or pervasive question. Do the plays dramatize the thesis that individuals are not passive victims or servants of traditional arrangements, or of a divine order, but that they actively conspire with their institutions to re-create their world and society? And a correlative thesis: in so conspiring, do they jeopardize basic "natural" relationships?—relationships between parent and child, sibling and sibling, king and subject, leader and follower, woman and man, lover and lover, friend and friend?

6) My central interest, and one that integrates the previous items, is in a theme which I call "redistributing complicities," and in the way Shakespeare's language carries the burden of redistribution. The ethical *donnée* of any play includes a range of characters from bad through mixed to good. Generally, characters come onstage displaying their particular ethical affiliation, after which two different kinds of things can happen. The characters may shift position on the ethical spectrum; and the play may offer the audience a model of the ethical range that differs from any particular character's version of it. It is the second of these with which I am especially concerned. Between the native's and the observer's models, the basic differences will be those of contrast and placement: the character's model will have more intense lights and darks than our model; and the character will tend to locate himself/herself closer to one pole or the other. This does not mean that the audience is asked to condone duplicity, betrayal, or murder. It only means that

the roots of such actions are not confined to the shallow plots of individual characters but spread down and out through the whole community or group of the play. Don John the Bastard, in *Much Ado About Nothing,* offers a paradigm case. His name is clearly Villain, or Trouble: his magnificent brother, the good Don Pedro, is wise enough to entrust him with a clog and muzzle and drag him along wherever he goes. "Never," says Leonato to Pedro, "never came trouble to my house in the likeness of your grace"; and that is because he comes in the likeness of Don John, who seems eager to claim even more culpability than he deserves. Such characters, like ethical vacuums, suck the guilt out of their social environment. But for the character labelled Villain to succeed, everyone has to collaborate in helping him on with his wickedness. And this is especially true of a figure like Don John, who can hardly twirl his moustache without scratching his eye; whose watchword might well be, "Thou, Bumbling, art my goddess."

At the ethical poles of *King Lear* are two scenarios: the mixed and good characters try to make others and themselves believe, "I am more sinned against than sinning." The bad characters try to make others and themselves believe, "I am more sinning than sinned against." My hypothesis about the play is that while any character pledges allegiance to one of these two scenarios, his language also betrays the presence of the second challenging the first. The language reveals the complementary pressures of a self-justifying function and a scapegoating function. It shows us that characters tend to avoid recognizing their own contributions to the difficulties they face, while magnifying the complicity of others. Their scenarios are frequently cast in the simplistic mode of folklore, fairy tale, or parable: for example, the Good and Bad Sibling, the Outcast and Usurping King, the Terrible Father and Helpless Child (or Helpless Father and Terrible Child). These parabolic conceptions often reinforce the character's sense of the inevitability of his/her plight, and they seem to have the effect which Freud ascribed to dreams in that their displacements and condensations enable the dreamer/character to go on sleeping, to delay re-entry into a world or knowledge or self whose reality is feared. Such themes and issues provide a background for my reading. I shall deal with some of them only incidentally and indirectly, but it will help to keep them in mind as we turn to the play's first scene and its first family.

II

The play opens with Kent and Gloucester showing mild surprise at the fact that although they always thought "the King had more affected the Duke of Albany than Cornwall, . . . now, in the division of the kingdom, it appears not which of the Dukes he values most." Then Gloucester utters a tortuous phrase which will bear looking at: "for equalities were so weigh'd that curiosity in neither can make choice of either's moiety." Kenneth Muir, the Arden editor, brings out the uneasiness in his paraphrase: "the most careful scrutiny of either share could not induce either of the dukes to prefer his fellow's portion to their own." The weight of the phrase falls on the word *curiosity,* which Muir glosses as "the most minute and scrupulous attention or examination." Edmund later speaks of the inheritance laws covering primogeniture and bastardy as "the curiosity of nations." And in I. iv Lear chooses to blame the "faint neglect" of Goneril's household on "mine own jealous curiosity." Here Steevens' gloss suggests the force of the term applied by Gloucester to the two Dukes: "a punctilious jealousy, resulting from a scrupulous watchfulness of his own dignity."

Gloucester's phrase implies that each duke is scrupulously on the lookout for the chance to have his sense of his own merit injured. But it implies more than that, because it states Lear's perception of the case and his intention regarding it. Lear assumes that both dukes are anticipating an unequal distribution and waiting to start something—against each other or against him. And he will frustrate that impulse, deny them the satisfaction of injured merit. We learn, of course, that Lear is wrong, that Albany is more loyal, and that Lear's affecting Albany may have something to do with Corn   wall's quick disaffection and Albany's weakness. We also learn that Gloucester appears to have been ognorant of Lear's darker purpose, to give the dukes equal thirds smaller than Cordelia's. But Gloucester's phrase prepares us to see that Lear views the political situation confronting him primarily under the aspect of a potential conflict which threatens his own future. And since he is about to give his youngest daughter more than the wives of the two dukes, there is no reason why he should not view it in this light.

When Lear addresses the dukes directly, his careful rhetoric betrays the same concern:

> Know that we have divided
> In three our kingdom; and 'tis our fast intent
> To shake all cares and business from our age,
> Conferring them on younger strengths, while we
> Unburthen'd crawl toward death.

Note the articulated tension between the vigor implied by "our fast intent to shake" and the exaggerated weariness of "unburthen'd crawl toward death." The former warns his auditors not to underestimate his manhood in spite of their younger strengths while the latter prepares them to indulge in the weaknesses of age. Lear continues:

> Our son of Cornwall.
> And you, our no less loving son of Albany,
> We have this hour a constant will to publish

Our daughters' several dowers, that future strife
May be prevented now. The Princes, France and Burgundy,
Great rivals in our youngest daughter's love,
Long in our court have made their amorous sojourn,
And here are to be answer'd.

Lear does not say, "no less beloved," but "no less loving"; not, "I love you both equally," but, "each of you loves me equally." This is a way of reminding them that they are—or should be—contending with each other in loving Lear. The epithet, "no less loving," is reserved for Albany as a qualifier which applies to Cornwall only retroactively, making the first vocative ("Our son of Cornwall") a little terse or brusque by contrast. Yet *as* a qualifier, it is only mildly commendatory ("not *less* loving" than Cornwall; but perhaps not more). Since we have been told Lear affects Albany more than Cornwall, we may feel that his difference of phrasing shows a bias in the very act of disclaiming it, and that both his language and strategy are working to set the dukes against each other even as he proclaims his intention to keep peace between them: strife now between duke and duke may indeed prevent future strife between the united dukes and Lear.

Lear's reference to France and Burgundy adds a new set of rivals. As the succeeding action shows, they are rivals not only with each other but also with him, *and*—so far as land is concerned—with the husbands of Goneril and Regan. There is a certain bite in the phrase "amorous sojourn" which reflects back on "no less loving." The old king divines that none of them is there for love of him, that the princes are probably not even there for love of the daughter he loves, and that they would deprive him of her for the land and power she symbolizes. But he can take pride in having kept them all waiting—the dukes for their doweries, the princes for his answer—until the moment when he can beat them at their own game, using their various desires and interests to effect his darker purpose. Part of this purpose seems to be to unburden himself of obligations by loading them on "the younger strengths" in this final burst of beneficence. He will show them once more how kind a father he is, how dear they are to him, by giving them all. I say "once more" because in subsequent scenes Lear's angry thoughts turn often to the gratitude owed a father merely as his children's genitor: to give them birth is automatically to be kind and literally to be generous in an absolute sense which establishes a permanent inequity in the relationship. His children must always be diligent in honoring their bond to their creator, must say "ay" and "no" to everything he says, and tell him he is everything (4.6.100, 106). He, on the other hand, can rest on his laurels as their only begetter, can maintain that first advantage at little cost to himself, though it may be useful to re-

Xuan Fraser as Lear's Attendant, Martha Burns as Regan, William Hutt as King Lear, Andrew Croft as Lear's Attendant, Colombe Demers as Cordelia, and Diane D'Aquila as Goneril in the Stratford Festival's 1996 production of King Lear.

mind them occasionally of the sacrifices he has made for them. This seems to be the sense of the paternal prerogative which Lear has carried with him through life and into the play. Now, as the play opens, he finds himself in the position of having to give them all more strenuously and conspicuously than usual. He inflicts his generosity upon them with a show of power which betrays his sense of the weakness of his position.

We can feel this in the tortuous politics of his darker purpose, and in the tactical impulse behind the words with which he calls into play a third set of rivals.

Tell me, my daughters,
(Since now we will divest us both of rule,
Interest of territory, cares of state)
Which of you shall we say doth love us most?
That we our largest bounty may extend
Where nature doth with merit challenge.

Not, "which of you doth say you love us most," but "which of you *shall we say* doth love us most?"—the judgment and the reward will be his to confer, and will be arbitrarily determined by what he decides to say. Furthermore, their expressions of love are compromised in advance by the nature of his request, since he is asking them to show how amorous they are, not so much for him as for his land. Again, the rivalry cuts two ways: his daughters are to compete with each other, and he is now competing with them. *If* they want to strip him of his power, they will have to pay for it by risking a humiliating posture—sitting up and begging, crowing for cheese. And the bargain he offers is so unequal—all that land and power for a little rhetorical fluff—that they will suffer the wound of his vigorous charity for years to come. The terms of his divestiture are therefore in the nature of a challenge thrown down to his children.

For Goneril and Regan the psychological outlook is more hopeless than for Cordelia, because Lear's challenge to them is more specious. Why are their doweries withheld until *after* their marriages, while Cordelia's is to be given *before* hers? Kittredge and the Cambridge *New Shakespeare* editors tell us this means the older daughters must have been recently married. This may be so, but later, when Lear says "I gave you all," Regan replies "and in good time you gave it" (2.4.252). Setting aside the Fool's favorite theme—the folly of giving away his land—the question posed by his preferential treatment is, why did he do it in this particular manner? On the face of it, his darker purpose was to give Cordelia the most opulent third of the kingdom and then, should that draw in exchange the vines of France or milk of Burgundy, move in with Cordelia so as to take advantage of his largest bounty combined with that of his new son-in-law: "I loved her most and thought to set my rest / On her kind nursery." Stanley Cavell suggests that part of Lear's strategy may have been "to put Cordelia into the position of being denied her dowry, so that he will not lose her in marriage."[1] But even if he cannot prevent her marrying, he can give her in such a way as to get her back again by competing with her husband for her attention, and conferring on her the offices of the nursery—becoming his own grandson, outwitting death, i.e., making her his mother during his second childhood. None of this, however, required the particular strategy unfolded during the first scene. Having flaunted his power by withholding their doweries, Lear with gratuitous cruelty plans to use, deceive, and humiliate Goneril and Regan in order to accentuate Cordelia's triumph and his partiality. Beneath the surface, then, his darker purpose seems to be to play on everyone's curiosity, stir up as much envy and contention as he can among the "younger strengths" with the aim of dominating and dividing them, humbling and punishing them.

Lear's behavior in this scene displays an ambivalence which is barely under control, and of which he can scarcely be unaware. Consider, for example, the words with which he reassigns Cordelia's portion to the other two sons-in-law:

> Cornwall and Albany,
> With my two daughters' dowers digest the third;
> Let pride, which she calls plainness, marry her.
> I do invest you jointly with my power,
> Pre-eminence, and all the large effects
> That troop with majesty. Ourself, by monthly course,
> With reservation of an hundred knights
> By you to be sustain'd, shall our abode
> Make with you by due turn. Only we shall retain
> The name and all th 'addition to a king; the sway,
> Revenue, execution of the rest,
> Beloved sons, be yours: which to confirm,
> This coronet part between you.

His act of giving quickly turns into a new imposition when the power and large effects that troop with majesty materialize in the next sentence as his hundred knights. What he bestows in one line he takes away in another. His beloved land-hungry sons are first invited to gorge their appetites on Cordelia's portion. At the end Lear invites them to part—and thus, no doubt, to fight over—the coronet.

In this scene, then, he formally renounces power and property primarily with the intention of keeping informal control over them. As if afraid that the slow crawl toward death will inevitably leave him helpless, he tries to divide others, and lay them under obligation, against the time when he will no longer be able to deploy the political and psychological resources of kingship and fatherhood. By diverting himself of power he can hope to forestall or inhibit the more absolute divestiture he fears at the hands of others.

III

Lear's darker purpose is complicated and confused by an unruly range of feelings, but Shakespeare does not let the truth of his situation escape the old king any more than it escapes us. There is a still darker purpose under Lear's arbitrary and willful behavior, dark even to him but certainly not absent from his consciousness. As I said, he can hardly be unaware of the implications of his behavior—unaware that his giving was a form of taking; his paternal kindness a form of hostility; his renunciation an effort to retain his power; his retention of power a response to the terror of the impotency of old age. Cavell observes that Lear felt unworthy of love, and S. L. Goldberg agrees that he "needs others' respect in order to respect himself," and that "the very urgency of this need betrays the fear behind it—which is a form not of self ignorance, but rather of self-mistrust, as if he cannot believe . . . in his mere self as *worth* the love and respect it needs."[2]

To this insight I add one qualification: the source of his fear and need must lie in patterns of feeling, behavior, and relationship that pre-date the opening scene of the play. This is implicit in Goldberg's fine appraisal of Goneril, though he does not make enough of it. When Goneril says "let me still take away the harms I fear, / Not fear still to be taken" (1.4.339-400), she may be merely rationalizing, but the confidential remarks she and Regan exchange at the end of the opening scene would support the thesis that in her case *apprehension* genuinely cuts both ways: apprehension as *the desire to take* (*ap-prehend*) is a function of apprehension as *the fear of being taken.* I agree with Goldberg that Goneril is more than "a hypocritical ingrate." She knows Lear's heart, he argues, "in the only terms in which he has given it to her," and his behavior partly justifies her fears. Her response to the world is primarily defensive: "the control visible in Goneril's speech is the kind necessary to keep the world at bay, as though she could not cope with her experience of it otherwise." She "can see personal relationships only as power-relationships" (pp. 104-106). Since he is describing Goneril's "moral outlook" and its expression in her speech patterns—in tone, imagery, and rhythm—Goldberg would seem to be dealing with relatively stable aspects of her character, which raises the question he never quite asks, "how did she get that way?", a question leading directly to Lear. For isn't her defensiveness ultimately the mirror and consequence of his? It must be an index to his *habitual,* not merely his *recent,* behavior; an index to a chronic rather than a critical problem of relationship. Goneril reveals Lear's basic approach to his children, to paternity and filiality, by her reflection of it. If he too has always treated "personal relationships . . . as power-relationships" from some basic fear, and has at the same time proclaimed his love and generosity, then he must be more the cause of her reaction to him than he is willing to admit. Where he differs from her is that the harm he fears comes as much from within *himself* as from others. "He has it in him so much nearer home, to scare himself with his own desert places," to paraphrase Robert Frost's description of the feeling. Even the weakest twinge of recognition, the dimmest sense of his complicity, could have brought home to him the reason for, the justness of, his suspicion that he was unloved—the sense, that is, that he had never truly loved his children, that he had always used his paternal authority to command, demand, tease, and humiliate, that the hypocrisy of Goneril and Regan only reflected his own ambivalence in wanting to be flattered while having no respect for, no trust in, the flatterers. I find him quite openly showing contempt for his daughters and behaving otherwise in a manner calculated to make his court and family despise him. I think that in hurting and punishing Cordelia he is trying to hurt and punish himself, as if he finds out too late that *he* is the one who should have studied deserving and who, if he is genuinely loved, is under an obligation he could never, given his paternal premises, repay. Some of these feelings, in all their confusion, press into the flamboyant statement with which he unfathers Cordelia at 1.1.116:

> The barbarous Scythian
> Or he that makes his generation messes
> To gorge his appetite, shall to my bosom
> Be as well neighbor'd, pitied, and reliev'd,
> As thou my sometime daughter.

Commentators point out that "generation" can mean either parents or children; both are potentially cannibalistic: in the Scythian mode of relationship each generation views the other apprehensively as a source of danger and of food. Against Lear's intention to liken Cordelia to the Scythian, the phrase likens the Scythian to Lear. It works as unintended self-caricature, and its hyperbolic quality measures the pressure of displacement. Doesn't Lear neighbor, pity, and relieve himself in doing and saying this to Cordelia? And doesn't he, equally, hate himself for it? In turning his hate outward toward Cordelia and the Scythian, he goes on doing precisely the thing that will feed self-mistrust, the suspicion of his own unworthiness.

In the first scene, Lear seems on the verge of forcing others to make him acknowledge not so much what they really think about him, but what he has always thought about them, and therefore—by a kind of recoil—about himself. The darkest purpose, the one he keeps deflecting outward, can only be called self-retribution and self-wounding; the impulse to suffer the pain he obscurely but deeply feels he deserves, to bring on himself the judgment which alone "can tell me who I am" (1.4.238). If successful, the urge to self-retribution would have made this scene an awakening toward genuine, though possibly unbearable self-knowledge. But Lear cannot let this happen, and he spends the rest of the play trying continually to regain (or remain in) the sleep of self-deception which the darkest purpose continually impels him to renounce. He cannot bring himself to be his own judge or to risk facing the punishment he feels he deserves. Suppose that in his confusion of darker purposes he sets up the scene with Cordelia partly to encourage self-wounding through mutual rejection. In the single act by which he could keep her from a husband and lose her himself, he would both prove his jealousy to himself and punish it. But when he commits his future to his other two daughters and their husbands, he shies away from the harder task of self-judgment to the easier task of self-justification. This provides what I think is a better alternative to the conventional reading, which accedes to Lear's perspective in viewing him as the foolish victim of his two cruel daughters.

Lear knows that it is safer to make Regan and Goneril his chastisers, than Cordelia. He can more easily goad them into treating him shabbily. At the same time he can evade arousing his guilty awareness of the extent to which he has already victimized them, and he can do this by making himself their victim and making them his scapegoats. We can, then, distinguish in his speech and behavior the working-out of two purposes additional to his own consciously proclaimed "darker purpose"—by which he means dark to the others but not to him. The two I have in mind are initially both dark to him, and I shall speak of them as darker and darkest: the darker purpose moves him to aggression against others; the darkest purpose moves him to aggression against himself. The darker purpose justifies itself according to the logic of the victim's formula, "more sinned against than sinning"; the darkest purpose justifies itself according to the logic of "more sinning than sinned against." Lear quickly discovers the presence within him of the darker purpose, and its usefulness; and he puts it to work. Among its uses are its effectiveness against the efforts of the darkest purpose to make itself known. It is the darker purpose, of course, which counsels madness. At the same time, to the degree that the darker purpose is effective in this policing function, it exacerbates the darkest purpose. Aggression against others, the projective distortion of guilt feelings, is the bad faith which creates, intensifies, and festers the darkest purpose. Finally, though the darker and the darkest are cross-purposes, they may lead to the same practical effect. In Acts One and Two, Lear is moved by both together to get himself locked out of doors.

We should note, especially in 1.4 and 2.4, the extent to which Lear provoked Goneril and Regan into their aggressive and mean behavior. Not that they are blameless—far from it—but that he shares in their complicity more than he seems willing to admit. From the beginning, he makes himself an unwelcome guest, flaunts his willfulness, and in all but words dares Goneril *not* to throw him out. When he inflicts himself prematurely on Regan, he specifies precisely the condition which he knows will make her balk: "I can stay with Regan, / I and my hundred knights" (2.4.323). They owe him all, and he is going to do his best to demonstrate that they can't and won't pay it back; by acting unreasonably he will test their gratitude and prove it inadequate. Being turned out in the storm becomes, for him, a triumph. His decision to reject their grudging hospitality ratifies their monstrous ingratitude: "No, rather I abjure all roofs, and choose / To wage against the enmity o' th' air" (2.4.210).

IV

In Lear's experiences on the heath and at Dover—in Acts Three and Four—the conflict of purposes grows keener, and its terms vary, as the darkest purpose presses against constraint and cries for justice. Both purposes increase their force by moving Lear to assimilate the storm to his torn state as a kind of metonymic amplifier. When Lear exhorts the great gods that run the thunderstorms to "find out their enemies now," we should try to imagine that he dimly conceives himself to be their true target, and that he is addressing himself:

> Tremble, thou wretch,
> That hast within thee the undivulged crimes,
> Unwhipp'd of Justice; hide thee, thou bloody hand,
> Thou perjur'd, and thou simular of virtue
> That art incestuous; caitiff, to pieces shake,
> That under covert and convenient seeming
> Has practis'd on man's life; close pent-up guilts,
> Rive your concealing continents, and cry
> These dreadful summoners grace. I am a man
> More sinn'd against than sinning.
>
> (3.2.51ff.)

This may be felt as a generalized apostrophe to such wretches as his daughters and sons-in-law, yet the details reflect Lear's own condition more accurately. The image is melodramatic, hyperbolic, and simplistic, reducing the figure of evil to an outright stage villain, but this is partly because Lear is displacing its reference from himself to the world at large. With that crude form, he can avoid too close a fit. It is, so to speak, a systematically distorted communication to himself, at once thrusting in and fending off the sharp sword of justice. Only the subterranean pressure of self-retribution pushing up through layers of self-avoidance can account for the magnificence, the volcanic power, of "close pent-up guilts, / Rive your concealing continents, and cry / These dreadful summoners grace." But the power spends itself, or he rushes from it in terror toward the safety of the victim's plight: "I am a man / More sinn'd against than sinning." In his next utterance, after saying "My wits begin to turn," he urges the Fool into the hovel, thinks of straw to avert the cold, and muses, "the art of our necessities is strange, / And can make vile things precious." I read this according to the logic of the darker purpose: the necessities are those of self-avoidance; the art by which we keep our guilts pent-up can make these vile or base (lower-class) discomforts important to us as diversions from more terrible thoughts. The stormy heath is the immediate provider of these diversions, but only as an extension of the monstrous ingratitude of Lear's daughters. For it is by targeting on their cruelty to him that he can divert himself from his cruelty to them.

This process continues in the second heath scene, 3.4. Kent has been badgering Lear to take shelter in the hovel, and Lear's responses initially betray a certain confusion in his attitude toward the meaning of the storm. First he protests that it does not bother him, "is scarce felt," and in fact provides a distraction from the "greater malady" of "filial ingratitude," the tempest in his mind that "doth from my senses take all feeling else." Weathering the storm is an alternative to this, the lesser of two evils: "if thy flight lay toward the roaring sea, / Thou 'ldst meet the bear i' th' mouth."

Yet even as he pauses to define filial ingratitude at line 15, his language betrays itself: "Is it not as this mouth should tear this hand / For lifting food to 't?" The immediate impulse of meaning comes from Lear's sense of himself as the victimized feeder. But the deeper impulse shapes an image in which feeder and fed are one, and thus in which filial ingratitude is the projected or displaced version of self-inflicted suffering. As if in response to this, the darker purpose pushes the punitive impulse outward:

> But I will punish home:
> No, I will weep no more. In such a night
> To shut me out? Pour on; I will endure.

Here the relation between inner and outer storms changes—they become functionally related complements rather than alternatives: since exposure to the storm is the result of his daughters' ingratitude, enduring the elements only intensifies his sense of their cruelty. The elements and his daughters converge; to brave the weather is to stand up to Regan and Goneril and prove to himself that they have not yet deprived him of manliness or potency. Yet this feeling is immediately challenged at line 19 by the self-image of the helpless undeserving victim:

> In such a night as this? O Regan, Goneril!
> Your kind old father, whose frank heart gave all,—
> O! that way madness lies; let me shun that;
> No more of that.

Madness will be induced by dwelling on his plight as victim and dotard rather than on his power and endurance, but in either case the tempest in the mind feeds on the physical storm. Hence Lear's confusion (and ours) takes still another turn when he refuses Kent's fourth prompting to "enter here" with

> Prithee, go in thyself; seek thine own ease:
> This tempest [the physical storm] will not give me leave to ponder
> On things would hurt me more. But I'll go in.

The storm deepens the wound caused by filial ingratitude. What things would hurt him more? The answer is not difficult, and Lear's next speech contains it in distorted form.

Lear delays entering the hovel, sends the Fool ahead of him, begins a meditation with a personifying apostrophe ("You houseless poverty,—"), and interrupts it to urge the Fool in, while he explains, "I'll pray, and then I'll sleep." This is his prayer:

> Poor naked wretches, whereso'er you are,
> That bide the pelting of this pitiless storm,
> How shall your houseless heads and unfed sides,
> Your loop'd and window'd raggedness, defend you
> From seasons such as these? O! I have ta'en
> Too little care of this. Take physic, Pomp;
> Expose thyself to feel what wretches feel,
> That thou mayst shake the superflux to them,
> And show the Heavens more just.

On the face of it, this is an attempt to shun the madness self-pity might bring on by abjuring the victim's role, converting wretchedness to fellow feeling, and imagining a scenario in which suffering will lead to wisdom and improvement when (presumably) the king regains his power. But the lines of connection between this scenario and Lear's past and future are tenuous in the extreme. We suddenly hear that Lear has neglected the poor, which has comically little to do with what has been going on since the play's opening; and we hear him making what sounds like a suggestion for better housing and other economic reforms. Except for the echo of the theme of land distribution, these reflections are conspicuously irrelevant, and also reductive—to define his problem in terms of poverty and bad weather makes it both impertinent and easy to deal with. Pomp and Poverty are personifications in a morality play which ends happily with the triumph of poetic and political justice. Does all this mean that Lear is only—as T. S. Eliot once said about Othello—cheering himself up? Does he really imagine *he* can reassume the power of Pomp and redistribute goods as energetically as he had tried to "shake all cares and business from our age"?

It may seem that Lear is losing his grip on reality, but in a certain sense he is tightening it, trying to keep reality under control and out of sight. If we ask ourselves what persons or situations in the play this "prayer" calls to mind, two candidates present themselves: the effects, invoked and desired by Lear, of his banishment of Cordelia and Kent. In its evasive manner the prayer takes account of sentiments and phrases uttered in the anger of the first scene, *e.g.:* "Here I disclaim all my paternal care" (114); "The barbarous Scythian . . . shall . . . be as well neighbor'd, pitied, and reliev'd" (116-19); "now her price is fallen" (197); "Dower'd with our curse and stranger'd with our oath" (204); "a wretch whom Nature is asham'd / Almost t'acknowledge hers" (212-13); also the epithets Lear heard France apply to Cordelia—*poor, forsaken, despis'd, cast away* (250-53).

With this scene in mind, the conspicuous irrelevance of Lear's prayer comes to seem more like conspicuous evasion. The prayer is a skewed reference to the plight he wished for Cordelia—to his "little care"—and a skewed acknowledgement that *he* is ultimately responsible for his own houselessness as well as hers; it is also a muffled expression of hope that, by inflicting a similar physical punishment on himself, he will somehow be in the position to undo the wrong, and redistribute his land according to his original plan. "Expose thyself to feel what wretches feel" may merely command a new view, *ex post facto*, a new rationalization of the lockout Lear goaded his other daughters into imposing on him. But the degree of distortion or displacement in the prayer is an index of the pressure of guilt. His apostrophe, with its pluralizing, generalizing, and personifying force, and his focus on *house*lessness rather than *home*lessness, register both the effort of avoidance and the self-accusing truth from which he flinches.

Lear tries by verbal magic to grasp the power he feels deprived of, yet at the same time, as additional insurance, he keeps open the option of stepping into the role of wretched victim. "Expose thyself to feel what wretches feel" can mean two things: either (1) expose yourself to the feelings of wretches, share their feelings, or (2) expose yourself to the storm in order to feel what wretches feel, i.e., stay out of doors and get pelted, a course of action which by occasioning wretchedness would sustain his wrath against his daughters and keep him from pondering on things which would hurt him more. And this is in fact the exposure he courts. He does not "pray, and then . . . sleep" in the sense of going into the hovel to retire. But his prayer seems figuratively to be an effort to put his guilt to sleep. His displacement of guilt with respect to Cordelia seems to me to be fairly obvious. Does he also feel uneasy about Regan and Goneril? H. A. Mason thinks we cannot be sure whether Lear in this scene "had begun to see himself as in some way responsible for their treatment of him."[3] Yet we should not rule out the possibility that the intensity and extraordinary richness of the rhetoric of displacement is meant to alert us to the continual regenerating of the darkest purpose—this is the boomerang or backlash effect. If in these scenes Lear is—in Mason's words—"play-acting humility," "enjoying the spectacle he imagines he is offering," "posturing" and "spouting" (p. 159), he must also be uncomfortably aware of this—aware of the pressure if not the nature of the darkest purpose of genuine self-condemnation beneath his facile, misdirected "I have ta'en / Too little care of this." "In a ghostly way," as Mason nicely puts it, "Lear's evil now begins to confess" (p. 159).

The evil, the darkest purpose, confesses in less ghostly fashion in 4.6. In his diatribes against hypocrisy, lechery, woman, authority, and justice, he re-aims once again from his own complicity to the corrupt world where an egregious good man like himself is the victim of usurers, cozeners, and flatterers. But self-reproach keeps pushing up toward the surface: "Ay, every inch a king" gives way to "a dog's obey'd in office." After having verbally whipped "yond simpering dame" for her "riotous appetite," he tells the "rascal beadle" to hold his hand: "Why dost thou lash that whore? Strip thine own back." Having re-cast its aggression in the form of cynical philosophizing, the darker purpose defends against such efforts at self-judgment by distorting them to self-pity (a dog in office), or merely by its generalizing context. "None does offend, none, I say, none; I'll able 'em" (4.6.170). Like the Savior, Lear in his crown of weeds will protect the adulteress (*John* viii.3-11) by daring sinners to throw the first stone. "Take that of me, my friend, who have the power / To seal th' accuser's lips." But his next words come dangerously close to being a critique of his own performance in this scene—a critique of the darker purpose which has made Lear the world's accuser: "Get thee glass eyes; / And, like a scurvy politician, seem / To see the things thou dost not." Extricated from its concealing continents, the sub-text would read something like this: "I cannot cast the first stone since, looking within myself, I know myself sinful; playing the critic, the savior, only magnifies the sin. Rather than be my own accuser, I would prefer to seal my lips and blind myself by pretending to see deep flaws in human nature and society. In this way I can escape from the conscience that hunts me down." Lear then says, "Now, now, now, now; / Pull off my boots; harder, harder; so." He goes on to offer Gloucester his eyes "if thou wilt weep my fortunes," and to preach the patience that comes from knowing the world is a place for tears, a "great stage of fools." "Pull off my boots" has been glossed as the command of one who imagines he has come from hunting, and it also echoes the impulse worded in 3.4 as "off, off, you lendings"—the impulse to strip himself of what he has borrowed and owes in order to free himself from his conscience. So, in the effort to stop hunting himself down, he offers Gloucester his glass eyes, solicits his sympathy, and advocates the patience needed to tolerate the sins and follies of others.

The effort, however, does not quite succeed:

> This' a good block!
> It were a delicate strategem to shoe
> A troop of horse with felt; I'll put 't in proof,
> And when I have stol'n upon these son-in-laws,
> Then, kill, kill, kill, kill, kill, kill!

"This' a good block!": "this is a good hat" is the commentators' first choice for an adequate translation, and their second is, "this is a good mounting block," that is, for a horse. He might want to put his boots back on so he can pursue his sons-in-law instead of himself, or keep them off so he can sneak up on them. But I think a third translation also makes sense here: "this is a good execution block." He takes off his crown of weeds to offer his head to the ax. The three blocks converge: he is, confusedly, the murderous avenger, the sacrificial victim of an unjust world, and—taking off his crown—the sinner acknowledging the justice of his punishment (a *good* block); and perhaps he also longs wearily to have done with it—"off, off, you lendings." But Cordelia's men intervene to rescue him from that escape. He is cut to the brains, but not dead. He is the prisoner of friends who are yet his enemies because they represent the accuser within ("Your most dear daughter"). Elbowed by a sovereign shame, he flinches toward the victim's role ("the natural fool of Fortune") and asks for help. He tries to diminish the threat Cordelia poses by imagining that she is capturing him simply to get ransom money—coming not to do him any kindness but to claim what is rightly hers, what he owes her and withheld. And if that is the case, he can at least use her surgeons to cure his cut brains and restore him to a stronger state of self-delusion.

This mutual exchange will free them both of obligation. But Cordelia's spokesman thwarts this game: "You shall have any thing"—she will give him all; and after he gave her nothing. "No seconds? all myself?"—an unequal fight. Let him die rather than live on in torturing self-accusation, the captivity imposed by Cordelia. Let him confront her, fight her, make her kill him. Let her be, not the daughter he has injured but the bride who comes to unman him, corrupt him, betray him, if he lives beyond the first night. Let him finish the ax-cut by dying in a manly act, a jovial incestuous attack that will flaunt his worthlessness. Cordelia's spokesman agrees—"we obey you"—and twists him forcibly back toward life and consciousness, denying him the accusation or the death he wants. Lear runs away to escape from Cordelia but runs away to make her capture him again; fleeing yet calling the hounds ("sa, sa, sa, sa"), he demands once more to be hunted down.

V

It is to be expected that when Lear faces Cordelia the darker purpose will recoil from its pole of aggression to the pole of helplessness in order to defend against the power of the darkest purpose which her presence energizes. In 4.7 the darker purpose tries to manage Cordelia's responses in this manner. "You do me wrong to take me out o' th' grave," he begins; "thou art a soul in bliss; but I am bound / Upon a wheel of fire": "I am already dead and being punished for my sins, while you are no longer suffering from the wrong I've done you." He continues to appeal to her pity for his precarious condition: "I am a very foolish fond old man"; "I fear I am not in my perfect mind." It is as if, fearing he deserves more stringent punishment, he shrinks away from it, tries to forestall it. On the verge of facing the truth and giving up all claims on his daughter, he divests himself of manhood and becomes the childish dotard so as to maintain or regain mastery of the relationship, to re-impose the bond which his action in 1.1 had canceled.

But what about Cordelia in this scene? Has she no darker purpose? Is she as pure a redemptive figure as those about her believe? Does she entirely escape the play of darker purposes circulating through the *Lear* community? I think not, and I approach her performance in the first scene with a purely speculative hypothesis. This is, that the thought of Lear's setting his rest on her kind nursery (a heavy phrase! a heavy rest!) must surely be oppressive to her, though she is not likely to admit it to herself; that she would like to break free of the parental bondage, get out from under, though she is not likely to admit that to herself either; that if she could find a way to do it which wouldn't jeopardize her self-respect and her sense of obligation to Lear, she would be likely to take it; and that she *does* find a way, and *does* take it.

Cordelia's first two speeches are interesting in that both are asides, and both reveal by their use of the third person that she self-consciously observes herself—possesses a strong theatrical sense of her image and role. After Goneril's speech "What shall Cordelia speak? Love, and be silent." And after Regan's:

> Then poor Cordelia!
> And yet not so; since I am sure my love's
> More ponderous than my tongue.

The first aside may be construed as a stage direction to herself: given this overblown rhetoric of Goneril's, how shall *I* respond. I shall do the opposite of Goneril, hide my love, and say nothing ("nothing, my lord"). The decision is made partly on competitive grounds. But something more clearly defined emerges after Regan's speech: "Then poor Cordelia." Already she senses the value of the victim's role. "And yet not so; since I am sure *my* love's / More ponderous than *my* tongue." In some better world than this, her virtue might be rewarded, but here it will have to be its own reward, her only riches, for Cinderella is sure to go unappreciated when Father listens to her wicked sisters. Glancing critically at Regan's heavy tongue, Cordelia displays a concern for style, and especially for her own style, her own presentation of self, in this difficult moment. She competes not only with her sisters—"unhappy that I am, I cannot heave / My heart into my mouth"—but also with her father: "I love your Majesty / According to my bond; no more nor less." And in exposing the extravagance of her sisters' answers she also exposes her father to ridicule.

Some of the pressure which works on her is apparent in the following remark:

> Happily, when I shall wed,
> That lord whose hand must take my *plight* shall carry
> Half my love with him, half my care and duty:
> Sure I shall never marry like my sisters,
> To love my father all.
> (1.1.100ff.)

Bradley observes that this statement "perverts the truth when it implies that to give love to a husband is to take it from a father."[4] But this tells us that Cordelia has somehow accepted her father's view. Even as she distinguishes the role of daughter from that of wife, she slips into the marriage formula. She acknowledges the father's right to compete with the husband but feels it oppressive and strains away from it; she will have to *wrest* her love away from her father. This is her plight.

From line 223 until the royal entourage leaves the stage, Cordelia is caught in a losing struggle to sustain her dignity. "Make known," she says to Lear, "publish the fact," that it is no "vicious blot," no wickedness, "that hath depriv'd me of your grace and favor, / But even for want of that for which I am richer, / A still-soliciting eye, and such a tongue / That I am glad I have not, though not to have it / Hath lost me in your liking." Lear's renouncing his paternity only proves to her how faulty his judgment is, and how genuine her virtue. He should have recognized that she is much better than her sisters, and she wants him to publish this truth, tell everyone he has undervalued her. Much later, at 4.4.16, there is a displaced echo that reminds me of this sentiment and suggests how deeply Cordelia has been troubled by Lear's failure to make her virtue known: "All you unpublish'd virtues of the earth, / Spring with my tears." She will be able, she hopes, to cure him, and with the very virtues he refused to acknowledge.

When Burgundy rejects Cordelia, she responds with spirit, and saves face by acting as if she had a choice in the matter; "Peace be with Burgundy! / Since that respect and fortunes are his love, / I shall not be his wife." But France immediately diminishes her by dwelling on his largesse and her good fortune, indulging nice antitheses at her expense: Cordelia is "most rich, being poor, most choice, forsaken, and most loved, despised." France will lawfully seize upon "what's cast away," no doubt invoking the law of salvage. We may feel that Cordelia has brought this on herself by her commitment to the victim's role; that like Lear she wants to renounce, without really renouncing, the name and additions of daughter. But surely France's condescension must rankle. This is what Lear has brought her to. And so, when she bids her sisters farewell, we not only feel an edge of bitterness, we also hear a trace of vindictiveness:

> I know you what you are;
> And like a sister am most loth to call
> Your faults as they are named. Love well our father:
> To your professed bosoms I commit him;
> But yet alas! stood I within his grace,
> I would prefer him to a better place.

In asserting her moral superiority Cordelia is not entirely accurate, for she has already, and publicly, called their faults as they are named: "that glib and oily art / To speak and purpose not," "A still-soliciting eye, and such a tongue / That I am glad I have not" (224ff). Knowing what her sisters are, Cordelia nevertheless commits her father to them. It is, after all, his own fault and folly that he has deprived himself of "a better place." And then she utters the couplet which I find all the more chilling for its aphoristic bite: "Time shall unfold what plighted cunning hides; / Who covers faults, at last with shame derides." Cordelia is predicting the inevitable results to follow from her sisters' evil dispositions. But the gnomic form of the statement generalizes it, and increases its sense of predictive certainty: whoever cover his own faults, refuses to acknowledge his complicity, is finally exposed and shamed—not only to and by others, but to and by himself: when he finally acknowledges his own guilt he will deride and hate himself, be ashamed. In generalized form this is applicable to Lear. And what Cordelia's words imply is that by their bad treatment her sisters will bring him to uncover his faults and be exposed to shame. Whatever she consciously intends, her action commits Lear to his other daughters for the punishment he deserves. Cordelia will ultimately be vindicated by the effects of their punishment, without herself having any hand in it. *They* will do the bad things that will bring Lear to realize how he has mistreated and misprized the daughter who loved him most.

As I read her performance in this scene, then, Cordelia, for reasons of her own—not all of them available to her—accepted Lear's challenge, asserted her merit over against his nature-in-her, and by her stonewalling helped him bring on her *plight*. At the same time she helped Lear commit himself to her sisters' professed bosoms, after which Lear (with Kent's aid) worked with Regan and Goneril to bring out the worst in them. Yet nowhere in the play does Cordelia—or do her words—show the slightest recognition of her complicity in this skewing of relationships. When she returns in the fourth act her language remains—unlike Lear's—pure of conflicting voices, although there may be a touch of uneasiness in the way she carefully rehearses her good intentions in 4.4.23: "O dear father! It is thy business that I go about . . . No blown ambition doth our arms incite, / But love, dear love, and our ag'd father's right." This seems to me to be part of her persistent habit of publishing her unpublished virtues, and I find it disarmingly ingenuous that she has to protest she was not blown across from France by political ambition. But I also find a touch of smugness in her echoing the words of Christ (my father's business), and this is of a piece with other indications in her Dover scenes that she is here as a merciful redeemer, one who was more sinned against than sinning but has forgiven her tormenters and now returns to restore them from their crimes and woes. She joins others in viewing herself this way, and she also joins Lear in harping on the violent wrongs her two sisters did by throwing him out of doors into the terrible storm. In blaming her sisters for their treatment of him, she effectively blames Lear for bringing his misery on himself by failing to acknowledge her unpublished virtues.

With this background, Cordelia's performance in 4.7 and 5.3 takes on a more complex quality. To begin with S. L. Goldberg's good insight about the partial nature of her response:

> However deeply moving and necessary is the truth of Cordelia's "no cause, no cause" . . . this is still not the whole of the truth . . . What happened in the first scene and has happened since is . . . also real. Lear has something to feel guilty about . . . Nor, for that matter, is he wholly a "poor *perdu,*" a victim, as Cordelia supposes. His face was not just "oppos'd against the warring winds," it was urging them on. (pp. 32-33)

In the speech Goldberg alludes to, Cordelia reviles her two sisters for the violent harms they have made in his reverence, and she does so in the most Lear-like language she uses:

> Had you not been their father, these white flakes
> Did challenge pity of them. Was this a face
> To be oppos'd against the warring winds?
> To stand against the deep dread-bolted thunder?
> In the most terrible and nimble stroke
> Of quick, cross-lightning? to watch—poor *perdu!*—
> With this thin helm? Mine enemy's dog,
> Though he had bit me, should have stood that night
> Against my fire.
>
> (4.7.30)

This speech forgets, or at some level denies "To your professed bosoms I commit him"; it shelters under the rhetoric which characterized Lear's aggressive darker purpose on the heath. A *sentinelle perdu,* according to G. K. Hunter, "was an especially daring soldier who was placed . . . so close to the enemy that he was considered lost."[5] If Regan and Goneril are the enemy, who placed him there? Lear, all by himself? I think 4.7 is so poignant partly because of Cordelia's moving concern for Lear, the love she shows him in her careful tendance of his "reverence." At the same time, I think she has triumphantly refined the victim's role to a Christ-like perfection, and she has done this by denying, by rising above, the cause: "I know you do not love me . . . You have some cause." "No cause, no cause." But she *did* have a share in the cause he gave her; ignoring what he did is ignoring what she did. And this may be the only way the reunion can take place—its condition; its cost. And in Act 5, her one brief speech indicates that the cause is not simply forgotten, but still there to be denied, for both of them.

VI

"The Final scene," writes Stanley Cavell, "opens with Lear and Cordelia repeating or completing their actions in the opening scene: again Lear abdicates, and again Cordelia loves and is silent."[6] Her words are oddly formal, aphoristic, remote—and these are her last words in the play.

> We are not the first
> Who, with best meaning, have incurr'd the worst.
> For thee, oppressed King, I am cast down;
> Myself could else out-frown false Fortune's frown.
> Shall we not see these daughters and these sisters?

She moves into couplets with the old consolation (more sinned against than sinning) but by now we may be able to hear the sub-text more clearly in the active shading of "incurr'd": "we aren't the first who have made the worst happen—brought it on ourselves and others—while intending the best." "Oppressed King" in the next line has the force of a tactful oxymoron—balancing his dignity against his plight—yet Cordelia's practice of addressing Lear only by his royal titles in the reunion scene seems less positive and affectionate here, a little too cool. She might have ventured something warmer, like "Dear Father." And the sentence *reverbs* an unintended sentiment. She means to say, "I'm sorrier for you than for myslf," but the phrase also incurs a worse meaning: "I have been cast down on your account, defeated and imprisoned because I came to relieve your oppression." And her question about seeing her sisters adds a specific sense to the previous line. She wants to outface her false sisters' frowns; she would remind the jewels of her father that she knows what they are, and that, as she predicted, time *did* unfold what plighted cunning hid. Her lines reveal the same competitive impulse we saw in 1.1, and we remember that she was competing then with

Lear as well as her sisters. Now, as Cavell suggests, she wants to repeat or complete that episode and bid her sisters a morally triumphant farewell before going once more into a kind of exile from the world.

Lear prevents this reunion and banishes her again, this time to the cell of the smug bridegroom, giving her a share in his latest renunciation. The oppressed king becomes oppressive, and imposes his old fantasy on her (Cavell, p. 297), but in a more constraining form, now that he has finally succeeded in displacing France: "We two alone will sing like birds i' th' cage," fulfills the hope expressed in "I lov'd her most, and thought to set my rest / On her kind nursery." (1.1.123). His touching description of the life he projects for them betrays his awareness of the life she'll be deprived of: we'll laugh "at gilded butterflies, and hear poor rogues / Talk of court news; and we'll talk with them too, / Who loses and who wins; who's in, who's out"; and thus, as God's spies, "we'll wear out . . . packs and sects of great ones." He promises to repeat the propitiating gesture of 4.7—kneeling and asking forgiveness—but that will only be part of the ritual by which he forgives himself for preempting her from life. "Upon such sacrifices, my Cordelia, / The Gods themselves throw incense. Have I caught thee? / He that parts us shall bring a brand from heaven, and fire us hence like foxes." Edmund had just said, "Take them away," but Lear's "He that parts us" embraces friend and foe indifferently, and by no means excludes France. The sacrifices he enjoins have been, are, and will be mostly hers. He has caught her by running away from himself and making her run after him. And he is still running away, yet still urging on the hounds of heaven.

We never learn how Cordelia feels about being caught. Edmund tells us that he ordered the captain to hang her and "lay the blame upon her own despair" (5.3.253), but this does not quite reassure us that though she didn't hang herself she was not in despair. When Lear comes onstage with Cordelia's body immediately after, all these considerations bear in on us, as they do on him. It has been said that in this final scene he is caught between his knowledge that she is dead and his inability to accept it. Yet this does not quite square with the fluctuations his words express, nor is it adequate to the complex weight of feeling and responsibility he must now be suffering under. What he does is to make sure she is dead before bringing her back to life; he controls her return, and he sends her back again to death:

> She's gone for ever.
> I know when one is dead, and when one
>   lives;
> She's dead as earth. Lend me a looking-glass;
> If that her breath will mist or stain the stone,
> Why, then she lives.
>
> . . . . .
>
> This feather stirs; she lives! if it be so,
> It is a chance which does redeem all sorrows
> That ever I have felt.
>
> . . . . .
>
> A plague upon you, murderers, traitors all!
> I might have sav'd her; now she's gone for
>   ever!
> Cordelia, Cordelia! stay a little. Ha!
> What is't thou say'st? Her voice was ever
>   soft,
> Gentle and low, an excellent thing in woman.
> I killed the slave that was a-hanging thee.

"She's gone for ever" looks back toward Lear's proscription in the first scene: "Thou hast her, France; let her be thine, for we / Have no such daughter, nor shall we ever see / That face of hers again" (1.1.262). To have banished her to France was the first step in her banishment from life, and to have caught her in prison was the second step. He forgets this for a brief instant to grasp at "a chance which does redeem all sorrows," but Kent's interruption brings him back to himself, and also back, confusedly, to the first scene to listen again to Cordelia's "nothing, my Lord." Now his defenses return, he curses the sinners who might have helped him save her, puts her back to death, and revives her just long enough to reinterpret, or misinterpet, her "nothing" with a tonally bizarre statement, a statement which is at once an evasive explanation of his failure to hear her, and a courtly epitaph: "Her voice was ever soft, / Gentle and low, an excellent thing in woman"—as if to say, "the reason I misunderstood her was that she spoke softly and gently when I was asking for loud and clear protestations of love, and she could have given me that, or you traitors could have helped save her by speaking up for her. But no; the blame is mine, not hers; an excellent thing in woman." This touch of connoisseurship returns him to the role of her manly protector, which dissolves at once into self-protection: "I killed the slave that was a-hanging thee"—partly a brag, but partly also a defensive response to the accusing presence he imagines: "I did the best I could, and if it wasn't good enough, it's because I'm old"—which evokes the "I am old and foolish" of 4.7. Lear cannot shake the presence off, as the third person gives way to the second, and the past tense to the present. He can exorcise her, consign her to oblivion, only by dying. "Thou'lt come no more, / Never, never, never, never, never": is it a cry of pained recognition? or is it a judgment, a doom, a command? "Pray you, undo this button." Hearing this I think of the smug and incestuous bridegroom, but also of Lear's earlier "off, off, you lendings. Come; unbutton here" (3.4.111); another terrible effort to disencumber himself and make his conscience free, to shake all cares from his age and crawl unburdened toward death. But she will not let him. "Do you see this? Look on her, look, her lips, / Look there, look there!" What if she should wake before he dies? And waking, speak? And speaking, accuse? "For thee, oppressed King, I am cast down." And so are we.

Notes

[1] "The Avoidance of Love: A Reading of *King Lear,*" in *Must We Mean What We Say?* (New York: Scribner's, 1969), p. 295.

[2] *An Essay on "King Lear"* (Cambridge: Cambridge University Press, 1974), p. 113.

[3] *King Lear* (II) Manipulating Our Sympathies," *Cambridge Quarterly,* 2 (1966-67), 160.

[4] *Shakespearian Tragedy,* 2nd edition (1905; rpt. New York: Macmillan, 1949), p. 321.

[5] *King Lear,* ed. G. K. Hunter (Harmondsworth: Penguin Books, 1972), p. 298.

[6] "Avoidance of Love," p. 296.

LEAR

Alexander Leggatt (essay date 1988)

SOURCE: "Lear," in *Harvester New Critical Introductions to Shakespeare: King Lear,* Harvester Wheatsheaf, 1988, pp. 69-95.

[*In the following essay, Leggatt focuses on Lear's death, contending that it is "the completion of life lived to the extreme," and examines the parallels in the experiences of Lear and Gloucester.*]

One of the principal ways in which critics have sought consolation for the ending of *King Lear* is to note that, however much Lear has suffered, he has also learnt. Walter Stein puts it succinctly: 'The world remains what it was, a merciless, heart-breaking world. Lear is broken by it, but he has learned to love and be loved'.[1] Lear in the storm, according to Robert Bechtold Heilman, 'feels compassion, acknowledges his own failures, and lessens himself in terms of divine justice; like Gloucester, he has come to a new insight'.[2] The idea of Lear's progress is given a religious dimension by A. C. Bradley's suggestion that 'this poem' might be renamed *'The Redemption of King Lear',*[3] by G. Wilson Knight's description of the play as 'purgatorial'[4] and by Irving Ribner's reference to Lear's 'spiritual rebirth'.[5] Other critics have resisted this view. In the storm sequence, where Heilman finds growing wisdom, Jonathan Dollimore hears 'demented mumbling interspersed with brief insight'. Passages that for some critics are prophetic wisdom are for Dollimore 'incoherent ramblings'.[6] Combatting the view that Lear learns selfessness, Barbara Everett refers to his 'love of the "pride of life" that is involved in his first mistake, and that never leaves him up to his death. He fights passionately, at his noblest, against . . . the death of self'.[7] In her reading, Lear is not so much reformed or redeemed as intensified. This question is bound up with the question of whether Lear's experience is the full experience of the play. In the heath scenes in particular, according to L. C. Knights, the voices of the other characters are 'part of the tormented consciousness of Lear'.[8] For S. L. Goldberg, on the other hand, 'although [Lear] is at the centre of the play, neither his consciousness nor his experience comprehends all of its meaning'.[9] If Lear's experience is redemptive, and is the experience of the play, we can read the play as a whole through his redemption, and take a more hopeful view of it. But if Goldberg is right, we need to remain aware of the limitations of Lear's experience, and this will prevent us from seeing even his most positive insights as the play's ultimate statements.

Shakespeare has given us a point of reference to guide our reading of Lear, in the character of Gloucester. The use of a fully developed subplot is one of the features *King Lear* shares with Shakespeare's comedies, and one that separates it from his other tragedies. The parallels in the experience of the two old men are obvious enough: each misjudges his children, and is betrayed where he placed his trust; each is cast out, left to wander, and finally tended by the rejected child. But Gloucester always seems to operate at a different level. While Lear, in his first scene, is guilty of 'hideous rashness' (I.i. 151), Gloucester reminisces in a jocular way about an ordinary sexual lapse. Lear grandly divides a map; Gloucester is fooled by a letter. In the confrontation between Lear and his daughters, Lear storms and rages while Gloucester tries, ineffectually, to temporise: 'I would have all well betwixt you' (II.ii. 291 [II.iv]). Under pressure his resistance to evil grows, as does Albany's; but at first there is an unstable mixture of genuine, dangerous loyalty and ordinary time-serving: 'These injuries the King now bears will be revenged home. There is part of a power already footed. We must incline to the King. . . . If I die for't—as no less is threatened me—the King my old master must be relieved' (III.iii. 11-18). We can hear his resolution growing in that speech, from the cautious 'incline' to the final 'must'. When he is tied to a chair, and set upon by Cornwall and Regan, he tries to temporise at first, then throws away his caution and attacks his tormentors with exciting courage:

> Because I would not see thy cruel nails
> Pluck out his poor old eyes, nor thy fierce
>   sister
> In his anointed flesh stick boarish fangs.
> . . . But I shall see
> The wingèd vengeance overtake such children.
>   (III.vii. 54-6, 63-4)

His own words give Cornwall his cue; Gloucester's reward for courage is to have his eyes plucked out. Even here, his experience is at a different level from Lear's. Both men suffer physical and mental torment, but the physical is uppermost in Gloucester's case, the mental in Lear's. Gloucester's mind is always clear, and once he is blind he sees a path ahead of him. For the rest of the play he seeks for death, a thought that never once enters the mind of Lear.

Gloucester himself clarifies, and moralises, his experience. In the first moments of his blindness he learns the truth about his two sons, and declares, 'O, my follies! Then Edgar was abused. / Kind gods, forgive me that, and prosper him!' (III.vii. 89-90). He is unquestionably learning, and the equation of blindness and insight could hardly be plainer. But it works, we note, at a fairly simple narrative level: he learns that Edmond has deceived him. Later, he generalises his experience as Lear does, but in a more flat and prosaic way:

> I stumbled when I saw. Full oft 'tis seen
> Our means secure us, and our mere defects
> Prove our commodities.
>   (IV.i. 19-21)

According to Northrop Frye, 'Gloucester's is a morally intelligible tragedy' in which 'Everything can be explained'. He adds, 'But the fact that Gloucester's tragedy is morally explicable goes along with the fact that Gloucester is not the main character of the play. If we apply such formulae to Lear they give us very little comfort.'[10] The deaths of the two characters are strikingly different. Lear's occurs on stage and, as we will see, none of the witnesses can think of anything adequate to say about it. Gloucester's is off stage, and Edgar can describe it in a neat paradox with no stage reality to contradict or complicate it:

>   his flawed heart—
> Alack, too weak the conflict to support—
> 'Twixt two extremes of passion, joy and grief,
> Burst smilingly.
>   (V.iii. 188-91)

Lear's death resists analysis, resists language itself. Gloucester's death exists for us *only* as an analysis, a formula created by Edgar's words.

In Gloucester, then, we see a tragedy that can be moralised, analysed, explained; and we see a figure who unquestionably learns, and who moves from blindness to pained insight and finally to joy.[11] Does Gloucester's experience give us a simple and clarified version of Lear's to guide us through its greater complexity, or is it there essentially as a contrast? Those who want to see the main story as Lear's redemption will prefer the former reading. But the contrasts are so striking, and so thoroughly sustained, that we should probably look to them for a key to the relationship of the plots, and guide our reading of Lear accordingly. From the beginning, Gloucester is passive, worked on by Edmond as he will later be by Edgar. Lear is active, and precipitates his fall on his own initiative. While we first see Gloucester in an amiable man-to-man chat with Kent, Lear is not just centrally placed on his throne but self-enclosed, self-absorbed. His 'Know that we have divided / In three our kingdom' (I.i. 37-8) is Lear's *fiat;* this is the voice of a man who is used to having his words create reality. The love-test has a superficial air of ceremony but, whereas in a true ceremony the values of a community are expressed in a recurring occasion and a set form of words, this 'ceremony' expresses the needs and desires of one old man, the occasion is unique, and the speeches have to be made up on the spot. The principles of ceremony, and the communal stability they imply, are violated by the demands of Lear's will. As in the deposition scene in *Richard II,* we see the instruments of the state being untuned by the King himself. His surrender of power, however, is more apparent than real. Harry Berger, Jr, has argued that the terms of his bargain with his daughters are so one-sided—'all that land and power for a little rhetorical fluff'—that they will feel in his debt for the rest of his life; and Cordelia will have the extra burden of being 'his mother during his second childhood'.[12] Lear wants, as Alan Sinfield has pointed out, something it is very difficult for an absolute monarch to have: the assurance 'that he matters *personally*'.[13] And he intends to matter politically as well. While the hero of *King Leir* imagines genuine retreat—'My selfe will sojorne with my sonne of Cornwall, / And take me to my prayers and my beades' (vi. 556-7)—Lear's train of a hundred knights will mean that he is always surrounded by an image of power. Even his division of the kingdom has been seen by Ralph Berry as a clever strategy of divide and conquer.[14]

From the beginning there is a tension in Lear between the desire to surrender—'while we / Unburdened crawl toward death' (I.i. 41-2)—and the desire to cling to power, authority and love. Yet in clinging to these things Lear violates them. Richard II gives away his office; Lear splits his down the middle, separating 'The name and all th'addition to a king' from 'The sway, / Revenue, execution' (I.i. 136-7). He is not, we should notice, abdicating. He will be a king without acting like one, leaving his sons-in-law to act like kings without being kings. He breaks the integrity of his office, not giving away his crown, like Richard, but ordering his sons-in-law, 'This crownet part between you' (I.i. 139), leaving us to wonder how such a symbol can be divided. And of course he violates the integrity of love by making it a matter of bargaining. Kingship and love both demand some capacity for surrender: of the man to the office, of the lover to the beloved. Lear, instead, demands to be king on his terms, and to be loved on his terms. Susan Snyder has compared Lear's development to the psychology of dying, which begins with denial: he 'is by no means psychologically ready to yield up power, whatever he says. . . . When he banishes Kent for defending Cordelia, he is exercising automatically, unconsciously, the royal authority he has just supposedly handed over to others'.[15] Even in his act of controlled surrender, Lear in the first scene gives the impression of massive, undisciplined power. But it will not quite do to see him as 'more a magnificent portent than a man'.[16] Beneath the titanic arrogance Lear is vulnerable, anxious, needing to be assured of his future, with the contradictory wants of a child: ease and power, love that is given and love that is secured by being bought. Behind his arrogance lies the simple human fear, Old Adam's fear in *As You Like It* of 'unregarded age in corners thrown' (II.iii. 43). And behind that in turn lies the fear of loneliness and neglect, a fear that can be felt at any age. Lear is not just a foolish old man with everything to learn: some things he knows already, though his way of reacting to that knowledge may be grotesque: that the world is a harsh place even for the powerful, that nature plays vile tricks even on kings, and that the answer is to be found in the nurture and support one gets from other people. Lear enacts, through his contrived drama of surrendering power and finding love, a grotesque parody of the experience he will undergo more seriously in the rest of the play. Monstrously foolish though it is in its context, Lear's question, 'Which of you shall we say doth love us most' (I.i. 51), is not an idle one, and the play will take some pains to give it a proper answer.

But Lear's phrasing is interesting: 'Which of you *shall we say* doth love us most'. The final appeal is to his own judgement. And he seems to have made up his mind already, for he expects Cordelia to give the best speech. The arithmetical logic of the first scene is that once Goneril and Regan's portions have been given out, Cordelia's is already determined. Cordelia's refusal to play the game is the first in a series of moments in which Lear's expectations are frustrated and he has a hard time finding the right reaction. Kent and France try to make him 'See better' (I.i. 158), but they fail. This remains a salient feature of Lear's character throughout: not his openness to new knowledge but his titanic resistance to it. The Leir of the older play is a gentle, mild old man: 'But he, the myrrour of mild patience, / Puts up all wrongs, and never gives reply' (viii. 755-6). When his older daughters turn against him he slips away quietly, unnoticed, in a manner very different from the stormy exits of Shakespeare's Lear. As Shakespeare seems to have created his play's theology (such as it is) by reacting against the sentimental piety of the earlier play, so he seems to have created his hero by reversing the earlier one. Lear's manner in the early scenes is tough and ironic. He appreciates the gruff, self-deprecating humour of the disguised Kent and matches it with his own: 'If thou be'st as poor for a subject as he's for a king, thou'rt poor enough' (I.iv. 21-2). The exchange between the two men displays a style of masculine plain dealing in which Lear is relaxed and self-assured. Above all, he seems to enjoy the *speed* of their exchange. He likes fast decisions, for he does not like to dwell on a subject. It is the slow oily politeness of Goneril that drives him frantic.

At first he simply refuses to see what is happening. The 'great abatement of kindness' his knight perceives becomes in Lear's mind 'a most faint neglect' (I.iv. 58, 66). When he cannot reinterpret, he denies. Confronted with the sight of Kent in the stocks, he refuses to believe it has happened: 'They durst not do't, / They could not, would not do't' (II.ii. 199-200 [II.iv]). In a variation on the play's own technique of visual contradiction, Lear simply refuses to believe what his eyes, and ours, see all too plainly. When he cannot deny the facts he still has trouble learning from them. The way Goneril and Regan have turned against him should have told him something about the quantifying of love that has brought him to this pass; but he will not learn. Trying to assure himself of Regan's love, he puts his clinching argument last:

> Thou better know'st
> The offices of nature, bond of childhood,
> Effects of courtesy, dues of gratitude.
> Thy half o'th' kingdom hast thou not forgot,
> Wherein I thee endowed.
>
> (II.ii. 350-4 [II.iv])

His first appeal is to the established and natural connections of the family, which Cordelia invoked in the first scene: 'I love your majesty / According to my bond' (I.i. 92-3). In this view, to violate family ties is to violate a fixed arrangement that should not depend on individual wills. But Lear, in the first scene, was not willing to let his daughters' love rest on that basis: he needed a guarantee he had devised himself. And it is to that guarantee, 'Thy half o'the kingdom', that he finally appeals. We see him not advancing towards insight but retreating from it. As he clings desperately to the quantifying, bargain-striking view of love, his expression of it becomes increasingly grotesque: 'Thy fifty yet doth double five and twenty, / And thou art twice her love' (II.ii. 43-4 [II.iv]). It is as though Lear is trying to prove to himself that his system works, by stating it in its most absurd form and continuing stubbornly to believe in it.

When he tries to debate with his daughters, Lear's argument breaks down just as it is approaching its climax:

> O, reason not the need! Our basest beggars
> Are in the poorest thing superfluous.
> Allow not nature more than nature needs,
> Man's life is cheap as beast's. Thou art a lady.
> If only to go warm were gorgeous,
> Why, nature needs not what thou, gorgeous, wear'st,
> Which scarcely keeps thee warm. But for true need—
> You heavens, give me that patience, patience I need.
>
> (II.ii. 438-45 [II.iv])

The first part of the speech moves confidently, but when Lear tries to define 'true need' he breaks off and veers away from his point. He is in fact defending the superfluity, the trappings that deck unaccommodated man, which he himself will reject when he sees Poor Tom. As he describes Regan's garments his actual contempt for this superfluity begins to show through, and he seems about to distinguish between material need and a need for something extra that is not frivolous, but runs deeper than the material. A need for what? Presumably something in relations between people: courtesy, love or respect. But his own thinking is still so bound by the material, so committed to measuring his daughters' love by how many knights they will allow him, that he cannot get this next stage of his argument organised; and so he breaks off and changes the subject, not to what he needs from Goneril and Regan but to what he needs from the heavens.

At times he hovers on the edge of absurdity:

> I have another daughter
> Who, I am sure, is kind and comfortable.
> When she shall hear this of thee, with her nails
> She'll flay thy wolvish visage.
>
> (I.iv. 285-8)

Lear defines kindness as kindness to him; he does not notice the incongruity this leads to. Rather than building a coherent train of thought, he tries out reactions moment by moment, and again this leads to incongruity:

> Thou art a boil,
> A plague-sore or embossèd carbuncle
> In my corrupted blood. But I'll not chide thee.
>
> (II.ii. 396-8 [II.iv])

Yet these moments of absurdity are shot through with moments of insight, some of which are powerfully simple: 'I did her wrong' (I.v. 25). Lear's mind, like the play itself, is constantly on the move, in a dynamic pattern of advance and retreat, surrender and resistance. It is as characteristic of him to fight his feelings as to express them directly.[17] Part of *King Lear*'s overall tension is that while the play as a whole is constantly moving towards new insights, new discoveries, the central character is fighting a tremendous battle *against* knowledge, a battle in which, paradoxically, every loss is an advance.

A related tension is that between Lear's awareness of the world around him and his preoccupation with himself. Goneril's treatment of him leads him to an ironic questioning of his own identity, and the phrasing of his question is revealing:

> Does any here know me? This is not Lear.
> Does Lear walk thus, speak thus? Where are his eyes?
> Either his notion weakens, his discernings
> Are lethargied—ha, waking? 'Tis not so.
> Who is it that can tell me who I am?
> *Fool* Lear's shadow.
>
> (I.iv. 208-13)

We have seen already how problematic identity is in this play, and how the Fool's reply alerts us to the problem. Lear's sense of his identity depends on how other people treat him. If Goneril is not behaving like Lear's daughter, then he must be someone other than Lear. His question is not, who am I, but who is it that can *tell me* who I am? Identity is socially constructed, depending not on oneself but on other people. If Lear is about to start a journey of self-discovery, as his question implies, it will of necessity involve the discovery of other people. And the process works two ways: Lear's view of the rest of the world will be bound up with his sense of himself. As we watch him over the next few scenes, we may wonder whether these two lines of investigation, of the self and of the world, are helping or hindering each other.

One of Lear's achievements is his sudden pity for the Fool in the middle of the storm:

> My wits begin to turn.
> (*To Fool*) Come on, my boy. How dost, my boy? Art cold?
> I am cold myself.—Where is this straw, my fellow?
> The art of our necessities is strange,
> And can make vile things precious. Come, your hovel.—
> Poor fool and knave, I have one part in my heart
> That's sorry yet for thee.
>
> (III.ii. 67-73)

This is the first time Lear has expressed this kind of feeling for the Fool, indeed the first time in the storm scene that he has noticed him at all. The language is touchingly simple, in stark contrast to the magnificent tirades that have preceded it. The moral he draws about learning to love vile things may refer to the Fool as well as to the hovel. But Lear has discovered pity for the Fool through noticing that he is cold himself, just as he later sympathises with houseless poverty because he himself is houseless, and with Poor Tom because, he insists, his daughters brought him to his pass. In fact, it was not 'Tom's' daughters who brought him to this pass; it was his father. Beneath Tom is Edgar, who has suffered the fate Lear wished on Cordelia. Lear is still better at seeing his sufferings than his offences. His pity for others is real, but it is also a projection of his pity for himself. By the same token, Lear's denunciation of the wickedness of man in the storm scene, though wide-ranging, is focused on one idea: 'all germens spill at once / That makes ingrateful man' (III.ii. 8-9); the centre of humanity's wickedness is what has been done to him. His view of the storm is erratic: he calls on it to aid his curses; he denounces it for joining with his daughters against him. The common factor is that he relates the storm to his own plight. And he can still declare, 'I am a man / More sinned against than sinning' (III.ii. 59-60). In what follows it is the sin of others that continues to preoccupy him.

The treatment he has suffered and the jolting image of humanity Poor Tom presents lead him to ask, as the play itself does, large questions about man and society. His scene with Gloucester is full of broken images of his royal function: we see the king reviewing his troops, receiving homage, dispensing justice. But beneath the trappings of society is the vulnerability Lear has proved in himself:

> When the rain came to wet me once, and the wind to make me chatter; when the thunder would not peace at my bidding, there I found 'em, there I smelt 'em out. Go to, they are not men o' their words. They told me I was everything; 'tis a lie, I am not ague-proof.
>
> (IV.v.100-5 [IV.vi])

In the face of this brute reality all offices are absurd: 'change places and, handy-dandy, which is the justice, which is the thief?' (IV.v. 149-50) [IV.vi]). In his attack on his daughters Lear could not quite bring himself to denounce the superficial trappings of society, for he depended on them himself. Now he sees those trappings not just as superfluous but as deceptive:

> Through tattered clothes great vices do appear;
> Robes and furred gowns hide all. Plate sin with gold,
> And the strong lance of justice hurtles breaks;
> Arm it in rags, a pygmy's straw does pierce it.
>
> (IV.v.160-3 [IV.vi])

Lear also recalls Edgar's interpretation of Poor Tom. The animal beneath the robes is not just vulnerable but wicked, and his wickedness is sexual. He begins with a half-recognition of Gloucester:

> I pardon that man's life. What was thy cause?
> Adultery? Thou shalt not die. Die for adultery!
> No, the wren goes to't, and the small gilded fly
> Does lecher in my sight. Let copulation thrive,
> For Gloucester's bastard son
> Was kinder to his father than my daughters
> Got 'tween the lawful sheets. To't, luxury, pell-mell,
> For I lack soldiers. Behold yon simp'ring dame,
> Whose face between her forks presages snow,
> That minces virtue, and does shake the head
> To hear of pleasure's name.
> The fitchew nor the soilèd horse goes to't
> With a more riotous appetite. Down from the waist
> They're centaurs, though women all above.
> But to the girdle do the gods inherit;
> Beneath is all the fiend's. There's hell, there's darkness, there is the sulphurous pit, burning, scalding, stench, consumption. Fie, fie, fie; pah, pah! Give me an ounce of civet, good apothecary, sweeten my imagination.
>
> (IV.v. 109-27 [IV.vi])

Gloucester's offence was adultery, and Lear begins with that. While Edgar will later see this as a crime deserving the punishment of blindness, Lear excuses it with ironic tolerance: man is simply doing what the animals do. Why should one expect him to be different? Besides, the world must be peopled; for one thing, Lear's supply of knights is low: 'I lack soldiers'. But then the thought of the animal in man produces a sudden wave of disgust, in the image of the simpering dame. Initially, her offence seems to be not sexuality but the desire to conceal it. Even that degree of tolerance breaks, as sexuality itself becomes disgusting. We may have no glimpse of heaven in this play, but we do have a glimpse of hell: it lies, in Lear's imagination, between a woman's legs. Then Lear seems to decide that the fault lies not in humanity, but in his way of looking at humanity: it is his imagination, not the body, that is corrupt. Gloucester the adulterer, who began this train of thought, becomes the apothecary who must end it by curing Lear's diseased imagination. Gloucester tries, not to cure Lear, but simply to honour him: 'O, let me kiss that hand!' The fact that the gesture is physical recalls Lear's insight that beneath the trappings of society is the reality of the body, and leads to his final statement of the body's corruption: 'Let me wipe it first; it smells of mortality' (IV.v. 128-9 [IV.iv]). We go from the stench of sex to the stench of death. The general impression of the speech is not of secure insight but of a restless probing, excited and urgent, attacking and recoiling, moving through a series of self-contradictions, as the mind shrinks from the unbearable, then dares itself to face it, then turns away again.

Lear's insights into the corruption of justice and the foulness of sexuality fuse into a single image:

> Thou rascal beadle, hold thy bloody hand.
> Why dost thou lash that whore? Strip thine
>   own back.
> Thou hotly lusts to use her in that kind
> For which thou whip'st her.
>   (IV.v. 156-9 [IV.vi])

In this, one of Lear's most dreadful images, lust and cruelty seem to operate not just beneath the system of justice but through it. Yet this leads Lear not to a universal denunciation of man, like the one heard in the storm scene, but to a universal tolerance: 'None does offend, none, I say none' (IV.v. 164 [IV.vi]). He has passed beyond his casual tolerance of sex as something the animals do, to a bitter equivalent of Cordelia's 'no cause, no cause'. This forgiveness comes not through wiping out offences but through seeing them as universal. None does offend, because all are equally guilty. From this wide general insight Lear's mind suddenly snaps back to the particular: he recognises the old man who is clumsily pulling off his boots and crying like a baby. As Gloucester has said to Edgar, 'Take my purse', Lear makes a more basic offer:

> If thou wilt weep my fortunes, take my eyes.
> I know thee well enough; thy name is
>   Gloucester.
> Thou must be patient. We came crying hither.
> Thou know's the first time that we smell the
>   air
> We waul and cry.
>   (IV.v. 172-6 [IV.vi])

Universal sin has become universal suffering; we are back from the wicked animal to the naked one. The first symptom of life is a cry. And as the image of the weeping old man fuses with that of the crying baby, the whole of human life becomes a circle of pain that closes in a moment.

In much of this Lear's mind seems to have gone well beyond his own personal misfortunes. He is looking out at the world. But he offers his eyes to Gloucester on condition: 'If thou wilt keep my fortunes, take my eyes'. He is still bargaining, and his bargains still have reference to himself. We may wonder why he is so concerned with sex, since—unlike Troilus or Othello—he has not suffered betrayal in this area of his life. The answer may lie back in the storm sequence: 'Judicious punishment: 'twas this flesh begot / Those pelican daughters' (III.iv. 70-1). As a king exiled in his own land, Lear sees through the systems of power and justice that he used to administer. As a betrayed father, he sees beneath parenthood the sulphurous pit from which we all spring. Broad though it is, his vision is finally bordered by what has happened to him. Throughout his scene with Gloucester, from 'every inch a king' to 'None does offend . . . I'll able 'em' (IV.v. 107, 164 [IV.vi]), Lear insists on his own authority. And his view of universal corruption, as I have already suggested, finds no place for what we see all round him: images of loyalty and love, a son helping a father, an old blind courtier trying to honour a fallen king, an army led by his daughter coming to his rescue. Lear himself participates in this kindness, showing that there is more to parenthood than propagated curse. Comforting the crying Gloucester, he is like a parent tending a child. As the two old men cling together, all Edgar can do is stand back and comment lamely, 'O, matter and impertinency mixed— / Reason in madness' (IV.v. 170-1 [IV.vi]), as though to emphasise that no commentary can do justice to this picture of the human bond. Yet this achievement is not fixed, any more than earlier ones have been. In a moment the old cursing, vengeful Lear is back: 'when I have stol'n upon these son-in-laws, / Then kill, kill, kill, kill, kill!' (IV.v. 182-3 [IV.vi]). We are right back to the Lear of the first two acts, who could think of nothing better to do than get even; and his vengeance is pointlessly misdirected, for one son-in-law is dead and the other is on his side.

It is at this point that Cordelia's attendants come to rescue him. Lear runs away from them. Waking in Cordelia's tent, he gets what he wanted in the first scene: 'I . . . thought to set my rest / On her kind nursery' (I.i. 123-4). Yet once again he resists, fighting off comfort as he had fought off knowledge. Cordelia addresses him with titles of respect, 'How does my royal lord? How fares your majesty?', to which he replies by trying to put as much distance between them as he can:

> You do me wrong to take me out o'th' grave.
> Thou art a soul in bliss, but I am bound
> Upon a wheel of fire, that mine own tears
> Do scald like molten lead.
>   (IV.vi. 37-41 [IV.vii])

What we see is a daughter tending a father, a basic image of human kindness that echoes Lear's comforting of Gloucester and the Fool, and Edgar's taking Gloucester by the hand. What Lear sees is the unbridgeable gulf between heaven and hell. And while he is offered new life, in images of restoration (music and fresh garments) that will be used again in Shakespeare's final romances, his first reaction is resentment at being brought out of the grave.[18] Even as he gropes to understand his new experience, old ways of thought cling to him. He still imagines a scheme of retribution, the difference being that he is the offender who must be punished: 'If you have poison for me, I will drink it' (IV.vi. 65 [IV.vii]). He seeks physical guarantees of the reality of this experience, and they are images of suffering: 'I feel this pin prick'; 'Be your tears wet? Yes, faith' (IV.vi. 49, 64 [IV.vii]). He cannot accept this experience as real unless there is some pain in it.

Cordelia has a moment of shyness at Lear's waking. As he sleeps she kisses him, and speaks eloquently of her pity and her desire to restore him. but when he wakes her first impulse is to ask her attendant to speak to him, and he has to tell her, 'Madam, do you; 'tis fittest' (IV.vi. 36 [IV.vii]). We go for a moment back to the first scene, to Cordelia's reluctance to speak, her fear that her language cannot match the occasion. But this time her presence—for when she speaks, her words are few and simple and Lear never replies to them directly—is enough to guide him out of the abyss. We return to the first scene in another respect: this time Lear really does give away his kingship. He refuses to acknowledge the titles she uses, and when told he is in his own kingdom replies, 'Do not abuse me' (IV.vi. 71 [IV.vii]). And he has, at last, an answer to his question, 'Which of you shall we say doth love us most'. He gropes for an answer to his other key question: 'Who is it that can tell me who I am?' His own attempts to establish his identity are fumbling. Having seen the body as the essential reality of man, he now finds his own body unfamiliar: 'I will not swear these are my hands' (IV.vi. 48 [IV.vii]). The body is not, perhaps, our final reality after all. The fresh clothes, which in Geoffrey of Monmouth and Holinshed are given to him so that he will make a respectable appearance before Cordelia's husband, and which here are images of restoration and new life, not designed to impress in a worldly way—these clothes are simply disorientating: 'all the skill I have / Remembers not these garments' (IV.vi. 59-60 [IV.vii]). As before, clothing seems unnatural; but while previously Lear could denounce it as superfluous or deceptive, now it is simply puzzling. In his earlier tirades, he was grandly unaware of his own absurdity. Now, with nothing absurd about him, he asks shyly, 'Pray do not mock'; 'Do not laugh at me' (IV.vi. 52, 61 [IV.vii]). The old self-assertiveness is gone.

The difficulty of fixing an identity, which is part of our experience of responding to the play, is now embodied in Lear, who seems to himself, perhaps for the first time, to be truly Lear's shadow. He never does succeed in naming himself. In fact, for the rest of the play he never speaks his own name. The identity he finds for himself is both a plain but generalised recognition of present reality and a startling change from the proud, raging Lear of the earlier scenes:

> I am a very foolish, fond old man.
> Fourscore and upward,
> Not an hour more nor less; and to deal plainly
> I fear I am not in my perfect mind.
> (IV.vi. 53-6 [IV.vii])

Shy and apologetic, trying to kneel before his daughter, he seems more the meek Leir of the earlier play than Shakespeare's hero. In his confrontation with Goneril he affected not to recognize her—'Your name, fair gentlewoman?' (I.iv. 214)—as part of his ironic questioning of his own identity. Now he is genuinely unsure of himself, and when he finally gropes to an act of recognition, of naming, it is not himself he names:

> Do not laugh at me,
> For as I am a man, I think this lady
> To be my child, Cordelia.
> (IV.vi. 61-3 [IV.vii])

From this point he remembers what has happened to him, and what he has done; and some of his old habits of mind, particularly his view of human relations as a matter of bargaining and exchange, begin to reassert themselves:

> I know you do not love me; for your sisters
> Have, as I do remember, done me wrong.
> You have some cause; they have not.
> (IV.vi. 66-8 [IV.vii])

'I know you do not love me' shows him in some danger of repeating his old mistake about Cordelia; but at least he is re-establishing some sense of his identity, not through counting up the number of knights he is allowed, or noting gestures of respect (he rejects those) but simply through an awareness that he has a relationship with Cordelia. In a tentative way, he learns something from her. His reply to her 'No cause, no cause' is a *non sequitur,* 'Am I in France?' (IV.vi. 68-9 [IV.vii]). But the idea of forgiveness has been planted in this mind, and he returns to it at the end of the scene, asking her to do what she has already done: 'You must bear with me. Pray you now, forget / And forgive. I am old and foolish' (IV.vi. 76-7 [IV.vii]).

In the way it seems to resolve questions raised in the first scene, and to give a true image of what was parodied there—Lear shedding his kingship, to be tended by his youngest daughter—Act 4 Scene 6 could be an ending. Lear's achievement of humility seems a final breakthrough. So does his critical awareness of himself, based on his recognition of Cordelia ('You have some cause') and leading to his simple plea for forgiveness. But this is not altogether a new Lear. Part of what makes the scene convincing, and therefore moving, is that Lear is still, as he has always been, a slow learner. He gropes reluctantly towards his new life, trying at first to cling to the old certainties of pain and punishment. His expressions of new insight are tentative and incomplete. This includes his insight into himself: 'old and foolish' does not quite sum up the character we have seen or the reasons he needs forgiveness. And from this point in the play his mind contracts as sharply as it had expanded. He ceases to care about kingship, justice or power. Only one thing matters: Cordelia. Not even love, as an idea, matters; simply Cordelia. He is beyond abstractions. His entire life now hinges on one person. And about her he has one thing left to learn.

In watching the reunion, we hardly notice the acute contraction of Lear's mind, for his new experience seems so complete in itself. But when he next appears we are bound to notice. Lear is quite happy to have lost the battle and to be sent to prison so long as Cordelia is with him:

> Come, let's away to prison.
> We two alone will sing like birds i'th' cage.
> When thou dost ask me blessing, I'll kneel down
> And ask of thee forgiveness; so we'll live,
> And pray, and sing, and tell old tales, and laugh
> At gilded butterflies, and hear poor rogues
> Talk of court news, and we'll talk with them too—
> Who loses and who wins, who's in, who's out,
> And take upon's the mystery of things
> As if we were God's spies; and we'll wear out
> In a walled prison packs and sects of great ones
> That ebb and flow by th'moon.
>
> (V.iii. 8-19)

Questions like 'Who loses and who wins, who's in, who's out' were once of vital importance to him, for he was in the thick of such action himself. Now, in line with his rejection of kingship in his previous scene, he views the whole of public life with detached amusement. Even the notion of being God's spy does not imply judgement or insight; merely the detachment of a god who finds his creatures laughable—not unlike Gloucester's gods, who kill men for their sport. Yet we know that Lear cannot live like this. Cordelia's question, 'Shall we not see these daughters and these sisters?' (V.iii. 7) shows her awareness of political reality; and that reality, in the form of Edmond and his army, is on stage with Lear even as he speaks, theatrically contradicting his words. Who loses and who wins is not an idle question, but a question of life and death: Edmond has announced his intention of having Lear and Cordelia killed if they lose the battle, and in a few moments he will give the order.

Barbara Everett has noted the childlike, unreal quality of Lear's vision,[19] and W. F. Blissett observes the irony that Lear 'has not resigned the joys of resignation'.[20] Perhaps the most insidious danger in the speech is the way Lear turns his own relations with Cordelia into a childlike game of make-believe, kneeling and forgiving as they did at their reunion. We cannot blame Lear for wanting to hold on to that scene, but the cost of repeating it instead of letting it go is to devalue and trivialise it. As so often, Lear wants to hold back while the play moves on. As he imagined the gods aiding his curses, he now imagines them giving their blessing to his life with Cordelia. But his own imagination starts to send out warning signals:

> Upon such sacrifices, my Cordelia,
> The gods themselves throw incense. Have I caught thee?
> He that parts us shall bring a brand from heaven
> And fire us hence like foxes.
>
> (V.iii. 20-3)

The reference to incense implies a sacrifice on an altar, Lear and Cordelia going through a kind of death. It is a sanctified death, in which they will go together to a new life. But one worry still haunts him: they could be parted. Picking up the image of the sacrifice on the altar, he insists that only fire from heaven could do it. For a moment we glimpse an image of frightened, tortured animals, taking us back to the play's middle scenes. Lear insists that he is describing an impossibility, something that cannot happen. Yet we see in a moment that it will not need fire from heaven to part them; it needs only Edmond giving an order to his captain. The ordinary world, that Lear finds so comically distant, closes in and destroys him.

And so we return to the death of Cordelia. Lear resists it, as he has always resisted new knowledge. He kills the captain who is hanging her, and throughout his last moments he alternates between stark recognition—

> She's gone forever.
> I know when one is dead and when one lives.
> She's dead as earth.
>
> (V.iii. 234-6)

—and refusal:

> This feather stirs. She lives. If it be so,
> It is a chance which does redeem all sorrows
> That ever I have felt.
>
> (V.iii. 240-2)

Whatever we may have felt about Lear's earlier resistance to knowledge, we are with him here. His struggle between acceptance and refusal of this unbearable fact is our struggle as well. Lear's knowledge has never been the full knowledge of the play: we have always been able to see more than he does. But Lear's experience, of struggling bewildered through shock after shock, has been like our experience of the play, and here we are close to being one with him. We have already seen how many readers have in their own ways refused to accept the death of Cordelia.

But we feel its inevitably, not just in the way the last scene echoes and completes the first, but in the way images from all over the play come crashing down on us in Lear's last speech:

> And my poor fool is hanged! No, no, no life?
> Why should a dog, a horse, a rat have life,
> And thou no breath at all? Thou'lt come no
>   more.
> Never, never, never, never, never.
> (*To Kent*) Pray you, undo this button. Thank
>   you, sir.
>
> (V.iii. 281-6)

The Fool, the animals of the middle scenes, Lear's attempts to strip, the service he gets from his attendants, all find echoes here. It is as though the whole play is bearing down on him, and on us. Yet Lear's actual death seems to have given Shakespeare trouble, for it is at this point that we have the most striking and significant change between the Quarto and the Folio. Here is the Quarto version:

> *Lear*   . . . Pray you, undo
> This button. Thank you, sir. O, O, O, O!
> *Edgar*   He faints. (*To Lear*) My lord, my
>   lord!
> *Lear*   Break, heart, I prithee break.
> *Edgar*   Look up, my lord.
> *Kent*   Vex not his ghost. O, let him pass.
>
> (Q.xxiv. 303-8)

Lear seems to will his heart—the 'rising heart' of his exchange with the Fool (II.ii. 292-6 [IV.iv])—to break. His death is centred on his own feeling, his own pain; he is terribly aware of that pain, and consciously uses it to bring on death. If this were the only version of the scene we had, we would accept its terrible logic as a fitting end for Lear. But the Folio goes beyond it:

> *Lear*   . . . Pray you, undo this button.
>   Thank you, sir.
> Do you see this? Look on her. Look, her lips.
> Look there, look there. *He dies.*
> *Edgar*   He faints. (*To Lear*) My lord, my
>   lord!
> *Kent*   (*to Lear*) Break, heart, I prithee break.
> *Edgar*   (*to Lear*)   Look up, my lord.
> *Kent*   Vex not his ghost. O, let him pass.
>
> (V.iii. 285-9)

Lear does not even know he is dying;[21] his focus is on Cordelia. Once again our experience corresponds to his: the death that preoccupies us in the last scene is not the death of the hero: it is Cordelia's death, to which he is 'hardly more than a needful afterthought'.[22] As he found his identity in her, he finds his death in hers. It is the play's last and most painful image of the human bond. Less directly than Edgar, but just as decisively, Cordelia has killed her father.

Yet this does affirm something about Cordelia, and about humanity. Certainly not in any hope of immortality; there is no suggestion of that.[23] Nor, I think, in Bradley's notion that Lear thinks he sees returning life on Cordelia's lips. If he dies of joy it is at best a merciful delusion, a cheat like Gloucester's fall. More to the point, we do not know what Lear sees on Cordelia's lips: we register instead the fact of his concentration on them. The range of his mind has narrowed all through the last scenes, from humanity to Cordelia, and now it contracts to a single intense point: Cordelia's lips. The lips that kissed him as he slept, from which he wanted eloquent words in the first scene, from which he now wants merely breath. We do not know whether he sees life or death there; it is the concentration that matters. An actor could play unbearable joy, or unbearable grief, and be true to the scene either way. Lear's commitment to Cordelia is so intense that it ends his life, demonstrating her value to him with terrible decisiveness, and countering Lear's savage view of man in the middle scenes. If man were just a bare forked animal or a wicked animal, it would not matter, as it so painfully does, that a dog, a horse or a rat should live and that Cordelia should die.[24] Lear has learnt not just how much Cordelia loves him but how much he loves her, and this knowledge kills him. If this is an affirmation, it is an affirmation that comes not in spite of pain, but through it.

The survivors try for other kinds of affirmation. Albany wants the Tate ending:

> What comfort to this great decay may come
> Shall be applied; for us, we will resign
> During the life of this old majesty
> To him our absolute power. . . .
>   All friends shall taste
> The wages of their virtue, and all foes
> The cup of their deservings.—O see, see!
>
> (V.iii. 273-80)

Albany's words break off as he confronts the sight of Lear with the dead Cordelia; it is as though he can make this speech only by turning away from the reality on which our own eyes are fixed, and when he turns back he breaks down. Edgar's 'Look up, my lord' (V.iii. 288) recalls his attempt to comfort Gloucester at Dover, and earns Kent's rebuke. Comfort is not just irrelevant but cruel; Lear needs to die. And the play's last speeches are shaken, feeble, deliberately inadequate, as though in the end 'language as literature, therefore language at the top of its bent, declares itself inadequate for the task it has just performed':[25]

> *Albany* . . . Friends of my soul, you twain
> Rule in this realm, and the gored state sustain.
> *Kent* I have a journey, sir, shortly to go:
> My master calls me; I must not say no.
> *Edgar* The weight of this sad time we must obey,
> Speak what we feel, not what we ought to say.
> The oldest hath borne most. We that are young
> Shall never see so much, nor live so long.
>   (V.iii. 295-302)

There is no Fortinbras or Malcolm here to order the state and see that life goes on. The kingdom that Lear grandly sliced in three, and then in two, now lies in ruin, and no one feels like picking through the rubble. Albany wants no part of worldly power; Kent wants no part of life. Edgar seems prepared to confront only the present experience, feels that something ought to be at least *said* about it, but does not know what to say. He ends the play with what sounds like a lame tribute to the endurance and longevity of the old, and a fear that his own life may be shorter. (This may touch on the belief current in Shakespeare's time that the world was in its last days, one evidence for this being that modern men did not live as long as the patriarchs.) But what Edgar's halting words really convey, through their sheer inarticulateness, is an admission that Lear's experience, and to a lesser extent Gloucester's, have been larger and deeper than his own thoughts can compass. We cannot, finally, cope with this ending through discursive language any more than Edgar can. We have to face instead the thing itself, embodied in the stage picture of Lear with the dead Cordelia.

Lear is not so much a character who has been saved or educated as a character who has been through an intense experience, one that has presented him—and us—with basic images of the human condition, hurled at us with brutal speed and impact: the naked madman, the crying baby, the soul in bliss, the dead child. His death is the completion of a life lived at the extreme. That sense of extremity has been created by collisions between language and experience, as the characters confront an intractable world. If Lear seems the grandest of them, it is because he puts up the most titanic resistance to that world. But this final experience, Cordelia's death, is so intense that it kills him. For us that experience is the play's final reality, after which the efforts of language fade and die. But the image, as stubborn and intractable as Lear himself, survives to haunt us. Asserting his power over his own life, Lear began the play by asking his daughters to say how much they loved him. He ends by demonstrating his own love, and our mortal helplessness, in a manner beyond words.

Notes

[1] *Criticism as Dialogue* (Cambridge University Press, Cambridge, 1969), p. 113.

[2] *This Great Stage: Image and Structure in King Lear* (reprint University of Washington Press, Seattle, 1963), p. 270.

[3] *Shakespearean Tragedy* (Reprint Macmillan, London, 1957), p. 235.

[4] *The Wheel of Fire,* 4th edition (reprint Methuen, London, 1960), p. 179.

[5] *Patterns in Shakespearean Tragedy* (Methuen, London, 1960), p. 116.

[6] *Radical Tragedy* (Brighton, Harvester; and Chicago, University of Chicago Press, 1984), pp. 193, 195.

[7] 'The New King Lear', *Critical Quarterly* 2 (1960) 325-39 (p. 335).

[8] *Some Shakespearean Themes* (reprint Penguin, Harmondsworth, 1966), p. 80.

[9] *An Essay on King Lear* (Cambridge University Press, Cambridge, 1974), p. 68.

[10] *Fools of Time: Studies in Shakespearean Tragedy* (University of Toronto Press, Toronto, Buffalo and London, 1967), pp. 113-14.

[11] On the relationship between the two plots, see Bridget Gellert Lyons, 'The Subplot as Simplification in *King Lear*', in *Some Facets of King Lear: Essay in Prismatic Criticisim,* edited by Rosalie L. Colie and F.T. Flahiff (University of Toronto Press, Toronto and Buffalo, 1974), pp. 23-38.

[12] '*King Lear:* The Lear Family Romance', *Centennial Review* 23 (1979) 348-76 (pp. 354, 355).

[13] 'Lear and Laing', *Essays in Criticism* 26 (1976) 1-16 (p. 3).

[14] 'Lear's System', *Shakespeare Quarterly* 35 (1984) 421-9 (pp. 422-6).

[15] '*King Lear* and the Psychology of Dying', *Shakespeare Quarterly* 3 (1982) 449-60 (p. 455).

[16] Harley Granville-Barker, *Prefaces to Shakespeare,* I (reprint Princeton University Press, Princeton, 1952), p. 285.

[17] See Michael Goldman, *Acting and Action in Shakespearean Tragedy* (Princeton University Press, Princeton, 1985), p. 77.

[18] Marvin Rosenberg, in *The Masks of King Lear* (University of California Press, Berkeley, Los Angeles and London, 1972), reports John Gielgud's playing of this scene: he 'was bewildered, troubled, he was fretful—even at first 'a bit sulky,' as per Granville-Barker's direction' (p. 286).

[19] 'The New King Lear', p. 332-3.

[20] 'Recognition in *King Lear*', in *Some Facets,* pp. 103-16 (p. 113).

[21] See F.T. Flahiff, 'Edgar: Once and Future King', in *Some Facets,* pp. 221-37 (p.232).

[22] Maynard Mack, *King Lear in Our Time* (University of California Press, Berkeley and Los Angeles, 1965), p. 84.

[23] See William R. Elton, *King Lear and the Gods* (Huntington Library, San Marino, 1966), pp. 54-5.

[24] See Paul A. Jorgensen, *Lear's Self-Discovery* (University of California Press, Berkeley and Los Angeles; and Cambridge University Press, Cambridge, 1967), p. 124.

[25] Sheldon P. Zitner, '*King Lear* and Its Language', in *Some Facets,* pp. 3-22 (p. 4).

Phoebe S. Spinrad (essay date 1991)

SOURCE: "Dramatic 'Pity' and the Death of Lear," in *Renascence: Essays on Values in Literature,* Vol. XLIII, No. 4, Summer, 1991, pp. 231-40.

[*In the essay below, Spinrad analyzes the death of Lear, contending that this event resists explanation by dramatic or philosophical theories and fails to provide the audience with a sense of closure.*]

Despite centuries of the keenest critical analysis, there has been no real consensus on whether the death of King Lear is cathartic in the classical sense, redemptive in the medieval sense, retributive in the Renaissance sense, or futile in the modern sense. Audiences in the theater, however, reach a fairly simple consensus: they cry. Indeed, many of us may have experienced this anomaly at a performance of *Lear:* if not crying ourselves, then at least hearing the surreptitious sniffles of people around us—some of whom may just have spent a hard day in the classroom or at the keyboard examining the death of Lear as an academic exercise. In this essay I examine those academic exercises; and in seeming to dismantle each of them, I hope to show that they may be valid for other parts of the play, but not for what we cry over; that Shakespeare has denied us our expected forms of closure so that we may reach a kind of catharsis not covered by our standard dramatic theories.

Here I should note that when I speak of dramatic theories, I am addressing the elemental explanations that we normally use as teachers of and commentators on *Lear* itself: those theories, in other words, that may be heard in almost any classroom or read in any review. Indeed, if I am correct in my interpretation of what is happening in the play, analysis in terms of formal critical theory is counterproductive, since even modern theories of "indefinition" or lack of closure do not apply to a play that confirms and upsets several forms of expectation at once. As in Shakespeare's other great tragedies, there is always a "yes, but" to anything we can say about *Lear,* including the fact that there is always a "yes, but."

No matter which dramatic or philosophical theory we attempt to explain the play by, we will find that we must discard part of the play in order to make the theory fit. In the classic Aristotelian formulation, for example, we expect to see a man like ourselves, a mixture of good and bad, make a tragic mistake, gradually come to *anagnorisis* (self-knowledge), and die or at least undergo a symbolic maiming and exile in a kind of expiation of his error. Note that I have used the term "tragic mistake" rather than "tragic flaw." Aristotle himself puts it this way:

> [P]ity is aroused by someone who undeservedly falls into misfortune, and fear is evoked by our recognizing that it is someone like ourselves who encounters this misfortune. . . . This would be a person who is neither perfect in virtue or justice, nor one who falls into misfortune through vice and depravity; but rather, one who succumbs through miscalculation. (*Poetics,* xiii, 21-22)

In this sense, as O. B. Hardison points out, *katharsis* itself may be translated as "clarification" as well as "purgation" (*Poetics,* vi, 116). In the Renaissance, of course, this meaning was often overlooked, and the tragic hero was seen to have a flaw in the generally accepted sense (Montano, 55-56, 73). Whatever the translation of *hamartia,* however, Aristotelian "pity" is predicated on the hero's *anagnorisis;* and we all too often give King Lear credit for more enlightenment than is justified by the text, in order to justify the "pity" of the audience.

Does King Lear learn anything? Maybe—but he quickly forgets it again if he does. The moments put forth by Aristotelian critics as Lear's enlightenment are usually his remarks about his subjects during the storm, his concern for Kent's and the Fool's well-being at the doorway to the hovel, and his reconciliation with Cordelia. W.F. Blissett, indeed, refers to Lear's "charitable concern for the Fool as fellow creature" as a "heavenl[y] alchemy," suggesting a more than natural transformation pleasing to the gods (see Blissett 109 and Andresen 145-68). And Lear's words about his subjects seem to carry this transformation from the private to the public sphere as well:

> Poor naked wretches . . .
> How shall your houseless heads and unfed
>   sides,
> Your looped and windowed raggedness,
>   defend you
> From seasons such as these? O, I have ta'en
> Too little care of this!
>
> (3.4.28-33)

His words to Cordelia, too, "Pray you now, forget and forgive. I am old and foolish" (4.7.84), seem to acknowledge his fault and accept forgiveness. But these are, in truth, isolated incidents, and even in their own contexts may not be as unequivocal as we try to make them.

Certainly, Act 3, scene 4 (the scene of the "poor naked wretches") is the *only* time Lear evinces any sympathy with the unfortunate. By the time he meets the blinded Gloucester in 4.6, he is more callous than when he began, making horrifying jokes about Gloucester's empty eye-sockets: "I remember thine eyes well enough. Dost thou squiny at me? No, do thy worst, blind Cupid; I'll not love" (4.6.135-37). The pity we feel in this scene is for *both* old men, each blind in his own way—and the pity is fostered by the horror at what Lear is saying. Although it is true that Lear uses the images of blindness as an introduction to his satire on the moral blindness of a badly governed society, the satire neither invites Gloucester to participate in it nor implicates Lear in the bad governance. Furthermore, the references to adultery, whores, and tattered clothes in the satire are perhaps too pointed toward Gloucester's background and present condition to give him comfort. In short, this scene rather undercuts than supports any idea about Lear's new compassion for his subjects; Gloucester, after all, is one of those subjects, and in fact has come to his sorry condition partly because of the division of loyalties forced by Lear's only nominal abdication. Whatever self-knowledge Lear seemed to have before, it is gone now.

As for Lear's reconciliation with Cordelia, we must remember that each time he has left one daughter, he has tried to see more good in the next; he glosses over Regan's flaws after he has cursed Goneril, and he may very well be following a pattern of increasing attempts to see good in any one of his daughters who will protect him from the others. What we may be seeing, in other words, is more wish-fulfillment than real recognition. But at any rate, his impulse toward reconciliation does not survive this scene. At his death, there is no recognition of anything—not the fact of Cordelia's death, not his own faults, not even poor Kent, who has undergone so many hardships for his old master. Twice people try to tell Lear that his faithful servant Caius is his equally faithful servant Kent; and twice Lear ignores them. He does not ask Kent's forgiveness as he asked Cordelia's; he does not thank Kent for his help; he simply does not register Kent's existence at all.

In response to critics of the pessimist school, who see in this dual and final lack of recognition the futility of a blind universe[2] Maynard Mack points out that self-delusion in the face of loss is one of nature's palliatives to pain:

> Lear's joy in thinking that his daughter lives (if this is what his words imply) is illusory, but it is one we need not begrudge him on his deathbed, as we do not begrudge it to a dying man in hospital whose family has just been wiped out. Nor need we draw elaborate inferences from its illusoriness about the imbecility of our world; in a similar instance among our acquaintances, we would regard the illusion as a godsend. (Mack, 69)

But no matter how many excuses we may make for Lear in his final grief and madness, the fact remains that there is no classic "recognition" here in any sense of the word. The Aristotelian formula simply does not hold up.

Purists may object that Renaissance authors did not follow the classic formula, that in fact Othello (say) and Macbeth do not know themselves any more than Lear does at the end. To a certain extent, this is true. But in the Renaissance formula, the death of the tragic hero takes on a retributive note, with other characters describing the faults of the hero in explanation of why he must die. And in the concluding lines, order is carefully restored to the society that has been torn asunder by the mistake or flaw of the protagonist. Does this happen in *Lear?* Again, not really. The surrounding characters make no mention of Lear's original errors, and although Albany claims that "All friends shall taste / The wages of their virtue, and all foes / The cup of their deserving" (5.3.303-05), the surviving good people on whom the restoration of order must devolve seem curiously unwilling to take on the responsibility. Kent declines, hinting that he soon must die in order to follow his master; and Edgar gives a short speech odd in more ways than one:

> The weight of this sad time we must obey,
> Speak what we feel, not what we ought to
>   say.
> The oldest hath borne most; we that are
>   young
> Shall never see so much, nor live so long.
>   (5.3.324-27)

Looked at objectively, this is an equivocating speech, neither accepting nor rejecting the call to duty; following as it does on Kent's refusal, it implies a second unwilling ruler; and the fact that it is given to Edgar rather than to Albany in most editions, flies in the face of the Renaissance convention of having the highest ranking person give the final words. Furthermore, what Albany has just proposed ("Friends of my soul, you twain / Rule in this realm, and the gored state sustain" [5.3.320-21]) is exactly the kind of divided rule that caused all the trouble in the first place. The only real restoration has been that all the worst villains are dead; the hope for the future, in terms of Renaissance dramatic convention, is rather undercut than stated—although the hope is there.

Some critics who seek closure in Renaissance dramatic terms try to brush away this uncertain ending, either by ignoring the second split of the country or by giving the last speech to Albany and insisting that it says more than it really does. Others try to minimize the nature of Lear's original mistake so that reconciliation is not required here, having been accomplished earlier. Rocco Montano, for example, sees Lear as "a generous, impulsive person" whose breaking up of the kingdom would not have been perceived as all that bad, and whose misfortunes come entirely from the evil of his daughters rather than his own faults (ch. 11). What such a view does (and perhaps Montano's is more extreme than others in the group but is certainly representative) is to move the retribution and recognition back into previous scenes, so that the villains' deaths and the reconciliation of Gloucester and Edgar carry out the expected closure. Lear's death, then, becomes a sort of epilogue to the real ending.

But this will not do. If closure has been achieved before Lear's death, in dramatic terms we should not be required to cry at an epilogue. Furthermore, Lear's relative guiltlessness can be defended only if we look solely at his folkloric casting off of Cordelia. But there is more to Lear's fault than harsh treatment of a daughter. Renaissance audiences, *contra* Montano, would probably have been just as horrified to see Lear dividing the map of Britain and breaking his crown in half at the beginning of this play as they were during similar scenes in other plays—for example, Hotspur dividing up the kingdom in *1 Henry IV* or the tug of war over the crown in *Richard II*. And it cannot be denied that this division of the kingdom causes many of Gloucester's problems as well as Lear's. The blinding of Gloucester, we must remember, stems from the dilemma of conflicting loyalties that he is thrown into by the divided rule of his land. So the Renaissance formula will not work either.

Shall we try, next, to fit the ending into a Christian formula?—the redemptive death that atones for everyone's sins and brings on the providential restoration of order? We have already seen that order has not been restored with the usual closure; but more to the point, what does Lear's death add to what has already happened? Long before Lear dies, the villains have destroyed themselves; and Edmund has undergone a deathbed repentance that would be more dramatically effective if his dying words had managed to save Cordelia after all. Furthermore, in order to maintain the pattern of the innocent who dies for everyone else's sins, Cordelia rather than Lear must be the victim— and sad to say, neither we nor the on-stage audience focus on Cordelia's dead body in the last scene, but rather on what effect that dead body has on Lear. Her death certainly does not redeem *him;* as we have seen, he breaks down into denial and despair over it rather than coming to recognition and repentance through it. So the Christian formula does not entirely work either.

But now, I have seemingly dismantled every attempt that critics have made to bring some closure to an excruciatingly painful scene. The assumption must be that I agree with those moderns who see the world of *Lear* as a futile and meaningless one, whose every good impulse is destined for disaster, and whose every note of hope is undercut by futility. Unfortunately, pessimistic critics must leave out just as many parts of the play as must the optimistic ones.

Despite my quibbles over the restoration of order at the end of the play, the fact remains that the villains *are* dead; that Edmund *has* repented; that at least Albany *will* be left to rule, with Edgar as his good counselor. And as Rolf Soellner points out, "Edgar's general capacity for feeling and his strength to translate it into sympathetic action make him the most conspicuous learner and teacher" (Soellner 298. See also Calderwood 12).[3] But there is more to look at hopefully than the physical defeat of evil and the physical survival of a few good men. Something very important has been happening to people on stage throughout the play, something that is supposed to happen as well to the off-stage audience at the end of it.

Critics often note the action of the nameless servant who leaps to Gloucester's defense during the blinding scene; Kenneth Muir, indeed, sees this action as "the turning point of the play. The killing of Cornwall brings into the open the sex-rivalry of Goneril and Regan and so leads to their destruction and that of their lover" (120). But there is more import to the servant's action than the turning of the plot, and he is not the only servant who takes action. Notably, directors who want to emphasize the supposed absurdity of *Lear's* universe almost uniformly omit one short but significant scene: the aftermath of Gloucester's blinding, when the two remaining servants "fetch some flax and whites of eggs / To apply to his bleeding face" (3.7.106-07). Without this scene, despite the first servant's act of heroism, we bridge directly from the act of cruelty into Edgar's plunge from what he thinks the worst into still worse—the sight of his blinded father: "The worst is not / So long as we can say 'This is the worst'" (4.1.27-28). Gloucester's despair, then, seems natural; aside from the rash act of a servant who may be an anomaly in this dark world, the world contains nothing but oppressors and victims. And if Cornwall is dying (a fact that the audience does not know yet), the man who has wounded him is dead as well, and has not kept him from gouging out Gloucester's other eye.

True, the two servants who assist the blinded Gloucester are absent from the First Folio as well as from pessimistic productions of the play. However, the scene is generally accepted by most modern editors as one of the genuine Shakespearean passages in the two Quarto editions and is accordingly included in the text of the play (albeit in square brackets) rather than in appendices of variants or corruptions. At any rate, choosing a version of a scene can be as much of an ideological decision as making a deliberate omission, addition, or transposition; and modern directors can hardly be termed slavish followers of the text, whether Folio or Quarto. The point is that in order to maintain a predominantly pessimistic atmosphere in *King Lear*, the scene with the two servants must be omitted.

Unless such an omission is deliberately chosen, then, there *are* those other two servants between the blinding and the meeting with Edgar, the servants who, if they cannot save Gloucester, will at least try to help him in his pain. Like the First Servant, they have probably gone along with miscellaneous cruelties for years—perhaps out of fear for their lives, perhaps out of fear for their jobs, or perhaps, like too many of us, out of the thoughtlessness about such things that being around them all the time leads to. And yet they act at this point, at no profit and some danger to themselves, to help a wounded man. Where such impulses exist, the world cannot be utterly lost. What those impulses are, I will address in a moment.

It is probably fruitless, and counterproductive as well, to try to impose dramatic closure on the scene of Lear's death, even if the closure we impose is a statement about absurdity. Not only do all the attempts belie the text, but they also belie the very *un*closed pain that we feel in the theater. (Remember, people cry.) Nor, for that matter, should we categorically deny the play any closure at all, a denial which is an absolute itself and therefore a form of closure. We do have conventional forms of closure provided for us, but they are provided for other parts of the play. Gloucester is the Aristotelian hero who errs, undergoes suffering for his error, comes to *anagnorisis,* and dies reconciled (also see Perret 89-102). Edgar is the Christian hero who is taught and strengthened by suffering, and who then both saves and is saved by his father, whose redemptive death he narrates almost like a homily. Renaissance retribution overtakes Goneril, Regan, Cornwall, Oswald, and Edmund, whose very evil is shown to be self-defeating—with the added Christian hope that even the most evil (Edmund) may repent at the end. And the example of Cordelia shows that it is possible to remain good, even when provoked by evil. But the old King wanders through the play in contrast to all these proper workings-out of dramatic convention, and when he dies, we are left, dramatically speaking, with nothing. Will nothing come of nothing? Or is something left after all, something so conventional indeed that we have forgotten the convention?

To answer this question, let us go back to the blinding of Gloucester, and specifically to the two servants who lead Gloucester offstage and try to ease his pain. Significantly, these are not Gloucester's servants but Cornwall's, as we learn from the First Servant's cry to Cornwall:

> Hold your hand, my lord!
> I have served you ever since I was a child;
> But better service have I never done you
> Than now to bid you hold.
> (3.7.72-75)

They are not defending their master in helping Gloucester, nor are they seeing Cornwall's character for the first time; in fact, as Cornwall's servants, they may indeed view Gloucester's actions as treasonable. It should be noted, too, that they are taking risks in helping Gloucester—the same risks that Gloucester took in helping Lear. They are, in fact, as heroic as their partner who tried to stop Cornwall, if perhaps with a different kind of heroism. What, then, prompts such moral outrage in them that they risk their lives for a virtual stranger? I should like to suggest that their initial emotion is something nobler than pity; it is compassion—the sorrow we feel even for someone who does not deserve it, simply because he is in pain. Pity may lead us to shake our heads sadly; it may cause us to moralize on the cruelty of the world or the retribution that people bring down upon themselves; but compassion makes us want to *do* something, whether the person for whom we are doing it deserves it or not.

And there is a suggestion later in the play that even these servants are not anomalous in this supposedly cruel universe; in 4.5, Regan's reason for wanting to find Gloucester and have him killed is not simply gratuitous malice; it is a recognition that people are indeed capable of compassion:

> It was great ignorance, Gloucester's eyes
>   being out,
> To let him live. Where he arrives he moves
> All hearts against us.
>
>   (4.5.9-11)

Will all these hearts that are moved have any bearing on the outcome of the last battle between the forces of good and evil in the play? Maybe; maybe not. We do not know whether any of them join Cordelia's forces, and at any rate Cordelia's forces are defeated. But what we do know is that they are having the same reaction to Gloucester's suffering that the servants of Act 3 have had; and *they* were moved to heroism of one kind or another.

This, then, is why we must leave Lear's death alone, as his friends do on stage, and as we do off stage in the theater. To explain it away by dramatic convention is to falsify it and to deny ourselves the new kind of catharsis that it provides. Whether we see the disappointments and futilities at the end of the play as the sign of an absurd universe that annihilates all our efforts, a call to action in despite of a cruel universe because only the virtues work to ameliorate that universe in any way (Colie, "Energies" 119, Muir, 139), a stoic hardening of ourselves to give up even the "joys of resignation" in order to find perfect resignation to pain,[4] or a Christian reaffirmation of the survival of the good—whatever we choose to find is essentially a circular argument: the thing we were prepared to find in the first place. As Derek Peat points out, "the decision we make about [the final scene] finally determines the 'direction of the whole movement' of the play," and few of those decisions actually inform our behavior in the theater. Audiences do not behave with optimism, pessimism, resignation, or even "relative detachment" (45-46). As we have had occasion to note before, audiences cry. No explanations we may bring to bear on the play change that observable fact.

And yet, we cannot blame ourselves for wanting an explanation; the sight of suffering makes us, like the on-stage audience, want to *do* something about someone's pain. We cannot and perhaps would not draw a sword and jump to Lear's defense, as the First Servant does for Gloucester; we cannot and perhaps would not even risk our lives to bring him medicine, as the other two servants do for Gloucester; we do not need, I hope, to have our hearts hardened against evil as those citizens do who watch the passage of the blinded Gloucester. But perhaps we need to be shaken out of our dramatic expectations at the end; to weep for a poor, bare, forked creature who has not earned our tears; to weep without explaining our tears. If we can do that, we do have closure. We have learned a new kind of heroism so old that we have perhaps forgotten it: love not just for friends, but for enemies, and for the battered stranger at the side of the road: the heroism of compassion.

Notes

[1] Rocco Montano claims that Renaissance playwrights had only a limited sense of Aristotle, as filtered in a secondary descent from Euripides through Seneca, and that Elizabethan theater "developed on bases of its own . . . very distant from the Aristotelian system." I think it closer to the observable truth to say that the Aristotelian system was *incorporated* into those other systems than to assume it was tacked on or misappropriated.

[2] William R. Elton is part of this school, and cites Stoll, Orwell, Leech, G. B. Harrison, Holloway, Kott, and others as being in agreement with him; for a complete summary, see ch. 1, pp. 6-8.

[3] James Calderwood thinks slightly less of Edgar: "Edgar will not create a new order or discover the previously unapprehended relations of things, but he will keep the world intact for one more day." Despite his low opinion of Edgar's lack of aesthetic perception and heroism, the fact remains that when the world is falling apart, we need people to hold it together, even if only "for one more day."

[4] An idea advanced by Blissett in what I am tempted to call the euthanasia school of criticism. As Blissett describes Lear's "captivity" speech to Cordelia, "Lear has one last, hidden attachment to life: it is detachment, contentment of mind. He has not resigned the joys of resignation"—and so has to go through the horror of the death scene to accept lack of resignation as the ultimate resignation.

Works Cited

Adelman, Janet, ed. *Twentieth Century Interpretations of King Lear*. Englewood Cliffs, N.J.: Prentice-Hall, 1978.

Andresen, Martha. "'Ripeness Is All': Sententiae and Commonplaces in King Lear." Colie and Flahiff 145-68.

Blissett, W. F. "Recognition in King Lear." Colie and Flahiff 101-116.

Calderwood, James L. "Creative Uncreation in *King Lear*." *Shakespeare Quarterly* 37 (1986): 5-19.

Colie, Rosalie L., and F. T. Flahiff, ed. *Some Facets of King Lear: Essays in Prismatic Criticism.* Toronto: U of Toronto P, 1974.

Colie, Rosalie L. "The Energies of Endurance: Biblical Echo in *King Lear*." Colie and Flahiff 117-44.

Mack, Maynard. *The World of King Lear.* Exerpted in Adelman 56-69.

Montano, Rocco. *Shakespeare's Concept of Tragedy: The Bard as Anti-Elizabethan.* Chicago: Gateway Editions, 1985.

Muir, Kenneth. *Shakespeare's Tragic Sequence.* New York: Barnes & Noble, 1979.

Peat, Derek. "'And That's True Too'" 'King Lear' and the Tension of Uncertainty." *Shakespeare Survey* 33 (1980): 43-53.

Perret, Marion D. "*Lear*'s Good Old Man." *Shakespeare Studies* 17 (1985): 89-102.

Soellner, Rolf. *Shakespeare's Patterns of Self-Knowledge.* Columbus: Ohio State UP, 1972.

POLITICS AND THE LAW

Margot Heinemann (essay date 1992)

SOURCE: "'Demystifying the Mystery of State': *King Lear* and the World Upside Down," in *Shakespeare Survey: An Annual Survey of Shakespeare Studies and Production,* Vol. 44, 1992, pp. 75-83.

[*In the following essay, Heinemann argues that* King Lear *is a play as much concerned with government and politics as it is with personal, familial issues. The critic stresses that the play should be interpreted in terms of a personal loss of power and as the collapse of social and political structures. Additionally, Heinemann suggests ways in which the political implications of* King Lear *might be related to the politics of England under King James I.*]

King Lear is very much a political play—that is a play concerned with power and government in the state, with public and civil life, and not solely with private relationships and passions. Of course it is not *only* political; but it seems necessary to restate the point because recent productions so often try to make it a *purely* personal, familial, and psychological drama (much in the manner of A. C. Bradley, though a Bradley who has read Freud, Laing, and Foucault). However, even if this is intended to render the play acceptable to modern audiences (who are assumed to be very simple-minded), it is still a distortion, and makes much of the action unintelligible. As Peter Brook put it, the fact that the play is called *King Lear* does not mean that it is primarily the story of one individual[1]—or, one may add, of one family. Shakespeare himself, by introducing the Gloucester parallel plot from quite another source, seems concerned to generalize the issues, to show that Lear's personal psychology or 'character' is not the only force at work.

There was a period, of course, when an exclusively timeless, ahistorical way of reading was more or less taken for granted. It was a great illumination for me, then, to read studies like John Danby's *Shakespeare's Doctrine of Nature* (1949), and the chapters by Kenneth Muir and Arnold Kettle in *Shakespeare in a Changing World* (1964), which attempted to read the play in the light of its contemporary historical and political significance, whatever reservations one may now have about some of their particular interpretations. Many years later, when my own highly intelligent and dominating mother reached the age of eighty-six, my sister and I discovered in ourselves marked Goneril and Regan tendencies. In one sense, as Goethe has it, 'an old man is always a King Lear'. The frustrations of old age ('I will do such things / What they are yet I know not, but they shall be / The terrors of the earth!'); the pain of confusion and weakness, are superbly given. The play needs inescapably to be seen *both* as an individual's loss of power and control *and* as the breakdown of a social and political system: that is indeed its point.

Why, for instance, some critics ask, does not Cordelia humour her old father, in the opening scene, by telling him what he wants and expects to hear—that she loves him above everything? If he were *only* her father, that could perhaps be a reputable argument. But he is also the King, he wields absolute power in the state, and for Cordelia to join in the public competition of flattery and cadging would be to collude with the corruption of absolute power—a matter which preoccupied many of James I's most politically thoughtful subjects in 1604-7. This she cannot do, as Kent cannot do it, and we admire their courage, come what will. If we take it only as a personal story (which the legendary history of course does not), it becomes plausible to imagine Cordelia as culpably stubborn, opinionated, self-righteous and selfish, the inherited mirror-image of Lear's personal failings. But one cannot play it like this without destroying the force of the legendary narrative and the interaction in the theatre.

Demystifying the Mystery of State

The main political thrust is not, of course, to propound an ideal, simplified, harmonious solution for conflicts and contradictions that were genuinely insoluble in the society of the time. Shakespeare is not writing Agitprop. School pupils and students who ask: 'What is Shakespeare putting over?' can be given only a negative answer—some things he is clearly not putting over.

The political effect is, rather, sharply to represent the complex conflicts of interest and ideology in his own world; to dramatize them as human conflicts and actions, not ordained by fate; to present images of kings and queens, statesmen and counsellors as simultaneously holders of sacred office and fallible human beings who may be weak, stupid, greedy or cruel (in itself a central contradiction). Hence the drama empowers ordinary people in the audience to think and judge for themselves of matters usually considered 'mysteries of state' in which no one but the 'natural rulers'—the nobility and gentry and professional élites—should be allowed to meddle. Sir Henry Wotton commented after seeing *Henry VIII* at the Globe that it was 'sufficient in truth within a while to make greatness very familiar, if not ridiculous'. If this was what he thought about *Henry VIII*, the most spectacular and ceremonious of Shakespeare's history plays, what would he have said of *King Lear*, which produces this effect in its extremest form?

Reinforcing Dominant Ideology?

It has been argued that the dramatists necessarily reinforce the dominant ideology which holds the society together, within which institutions such as the theatre function and provide them with a living, so that on balance criticism is safely 'contained'. In the early seventeenth century, however, it becomes increasingly evident that no single dominant ideology or consensus is capable of holding the society together. The existence of different ideologies and of deep ideological and political conflicts over the nature and limits of monarchic power and prerogative, and the rights and liberties of subjects (however masked by the pervasive censorship), has been clearly demonstrated and documented for the years 1603-40 by younger historians, notably J. P. Sommerville, Richard Cust, and Peter Lake.[2] The Essex circle, where so many contesting ideological viewpoints were articulated and discussed in the 1590s, was a marvellous seedbed for Shakespeare's multivocal historical and political drama. But that complex clash of ideologies—bastard-feudal, politique, scientific-Machiavellian, republican, radical-Puritan crusading and anti-clerical—ended in the disaster of the Essex revolt. In the drama, optimistic confidence in political and military action to fulfil national destiny gave place to a sense of history as tragedy, and modern English history became for the time being a banned subject.

What the Politics of King Lear Cannot Be

The politics of the play cannot then be the assertion of absolute monarchal power, prerogative, and magnifi-

William Hutt as King Lear in the Stratford Festival's 1996 production of King Lear.

cence against mean-spirited Parliamentary attacks on royal expenditure and pleasures, symbolized allegorically in Goneril and Regan, though this has been seriously argued. The Parliament of 1604 was certainly no flatterer of the monarch. Neither does the play show that any interference with or diminution of the King's absolute power is unnatural and must lead to chaos: for it is Lear's refusal to listen to wise counsel, his insistence on his own will as paramount and absolute, that opens the way to chaos and disintegration. The patriarchalist view of monarchy, that equates kingly power with the power of the father within the family, is strongly present in the play, above all in the mind of Lear himself. Patriarchalism does not, however, necessarily entail an absolutist view of kingly power; the importance of paternal power was supported by many anti-absolutist and even some revolutionary and Leveller political thinkers.[3] Yet Cordelia, who challenges her father's use of absolute power, retains the audience's sympathy in so doing. To read the play as unequivocally patriarchalist is to read against the grain.

The assertion of the traditional and necessary rights and privileges of Parliament against government by royal prerogative was not something invented in the 1620s and 1630s, just in time for the Civil War, but goes back to the moment of *King Lear* and beyond it. James I was confused and annoyed by the institution of Parliament as he found it in his new kingdom, and the loyal Commons tried to explain to him that their right to be consulted and to criticize Crown policies did not imply disloyalty. The 'Apology of the Commons' in 1604 expressed their fears, based on what was happening to elected assemblies elsewhere in Europe:

> What cause your poor Commons have to watch over our privileges is manifest in itself to all men. The prerogatives of princes may easily and do daily grow: the privileges of subjects are for the most part at an everlasting stand. They may be by providence and good care preserved, but being once lost are not recovered but with much disquiet.[4]

The Apology itself (never finally passed through parliament or officially presented) was drafted by Sir Edwin Sandys, MP, thereafter a close associate of Shakespeare's former patron the Earl of Southampton, with other surviving Essexians (such as Sir Thomas Ridgway) taking an important part. Sandys himself, one of the foremost exponents of anti-absolutist thinking in Jacobean times, claimed that the King's power had originally been introduced by popular consent; he declared in Parliament that now 'it is come to be almost a tyrannical government in England'.[5] The tension between King and Parliament was indeed to continue throughout James's reign.

We do not know very much about Shakespeare's later connections with Southampton and his circle, but there is no evidence that they were broken off. Shakespeare apparently celebrated his former patron's release from the Tower with a congratulatory sonnet (No. 107), and continuing links with his circle are demonstrated by G. P. Akrigg.[6] *The Tempest*, begun around the time when Southampton (with Sandys) helped to found the Virginia Company, shows continuing cross-fertilization, and revolves (though sceptically) the colonialists' dream of creating a juster empire in the New World.[7]

In the context, it seems that Goneril, Regan, and Edmund were likely to be identified by the audience not with the Parliamentary oppositionists, but with what they saw as contemporary flatterers, cadgers, and upstarts at the Jacobean court, who were being rewarded for their obsequiousness with land, monopolies, offices and gifts—people like James's unpopular Scottish favourites. The land and the peasants who live on it are given away by Lear as if they were his private property. The decay of the old social order, with an alternative not yet ready to be born, gives rise to such morbid growths—as Gramsci expresses it.

Nature of the Political Interest

The heart of the political interest is not in the division of the kingdom or the issue of unification with Scotland, though there may well be allusions to this. The *division* as such does not in fact cause the war and barbarity that we see. The sole rule of Goneril, the eldest, would scarcely make for peace and harmony, and the single rule of Cordelia could only be secured if primogeniture were ignored. The causes of disaster lie deeper than that. The central focus is on the horror of a society divided between extremes of rich and poor, greed and starvation, the powerful and the powerless, robes and rags, and the impossibility of real justice and security in such a world. Lear himself, like the faithful Gloucester, discovers this only when his own world is turned upside down, when he himself is destitute and mad, and at last sees authority with the eyes of the dispossessed. Central to the language as well as the stage images is the opposition between 'looped and window'd raggedness', utter poverty, and the 'robes and furred gowns' that hide nakedness and crimes. All the difference lies in clothes and ceremony: 'a dog's obeyed in office'.

This crazy world is directly the responsibility of the King and of the rich and powerful in general, and the verse continually underlines this: 'You houseless poverty', cries Lear on the heath,

> O, I have ta'en
> Too little care of this. Take physic, pomp,
> Expose thyself to feel what wretches feel,
> That thou mayst shake the superflux to them
> And show the heavens more just.
> (3.4.32-6)

And Gloucester, blind and helpless, echoes this conclusion:

> Heavens deal so still!
> Let the superfluous and lust-dieted man
> That slaves your ordinance, that will not see
> Because he does not feel, feel your power quickly.
> So distribution should undo excess,
> And each man have enough.
> (4.1.60-5)

This is a note not struck in the earlier Histories, and certainly not in the other 'deposition play', *Richard II*.

The indictment is still, for us, very direct and near the bone. Audiences going to the South Bank to see in 1990 *King Lear* at the National Theatre passed by Cardboard City, the modern equivalent of Edgar's hovel, where the homeless shelter in cardboard boxes on the pavement. Mother Teresa of Calcutta, visiting London, said on television that she had seen such sights in the Third World, but in a rich country like Britain she could not understand it. Many of those sleeping rough are the mentally disturbed and the old, made homeless by the closing of mental hospitals and old people's homes, the cuts in home helps, the lack of funds for care in the community. Lear bitterly tells Goneril, 'Age is unnecessary'. It still is.[8]

This interest, and the rôle-reversal of riches and poverty, power and powerlessness, is stressed in Quarto and Folio alike, despite the many alterations. Nor is it just our modern prejudice that leads us to focus on this as a central concern. It is surely significant that so many of what are now widely believed to be Shakespeare's own revisions relate to this aspect of the play—the inverted world, the counterposing of king and clown, wisdom and madness, insight and fooling. Clearly he was particularly anxious to get this right. He has two goes at presenting the 'upside-down' view of monarchy and absolute power. Once this appears as a powerful stage image, the 'mock-trial' of the Quarto text, in which the very possibility of securing justice in such an anjust and unequal society is parodied and mocked. This scene can be much more effective on the stage than it looks on the page (*pace* Roger Warren),[9] since the parallel with Lear dispensing 'justice' from his throne in the opening scene can be made visually much sharper and more shocking.

In the Folio text the upside-down view of justice is presented purely in language, in the extended speech of Lear to Gloucester, which, after the brilliant images (already in Quarto) of the dog obeyed in office and the beadle lashing the whore he lusts for, adds the explicit general moral:

> Plate sin with gold,
> And the strong lance of justice hurtless breaks;
> Arm it in rags, a pygmy's straw does pierce it.
> None does offend, none, I say none. I'll able 'em.
> Take that of me, my friend, who have the power
> To seal th'accuser's lips.
>
> (4.5.161-6)

The 'upside-downness' is emphasized and made more explicit verbally in Folio—*extended* from Quarto but not *amended*. 'None does offend' suggests that no one has the right to accuse or judge since all are sinners, or that no one will dare to accuse if the king opposes it and has the power to silence the accusers and pardon the offenders. But there may also be an echo of antinomian discourse, implying that our categories of right and wrong, sin and righteousness, are meaningless and evil. The dreams of persecuted underground Familist groups at the time when *King Lear* was written surface again in the revolutionary years in the antinomian vision of Abiezer Coppe:

> Sin and transgression is finished and ended . . .
> Be no longer so horribly, hellishly, impudently, arrogantly wicked, as to judge what is sin, what not.[10]

Although I understand Roger Warren's point about the difficulty of staging the 'mock-trial', which *may* have prompted the revision, it has (as he concedes) been successfully done, for example in our time by Peter Brook, and it is difficult to accept that by cutting it Shakespeare made a better play. For the 'mock-trial' vividly makes the case not against a particular legal injustice or the corruption of individual judges (as Middleton does in, say, *The Phoenix*), but against the whole intrinsically ridiculous pretence of justice in an unjust society.

Warren criticizes the scene as ineffective on the grounds that the Fool and Edgar as Poor Tom, seated on the farmhouse bench alongside Lear, fail to keep to the legal-satirical point, though Lear himself does so.[11] But this is surely the essence. The entire set up is absurd—the rich and respectable are no more qualified to dispense justice than the whores and thieves, or the fools and madmen. To make this strike home and shake our complacency, the speech of madness and folly at this moment needs to sound truly mad, wild and disorganized, not the coherently composed discourse of a satirist in disguise. The image flashes on us as a moment of dreadful insight—enough, one might say, to drive the beholder mad.

Christopher Hill perceptively notes that many prophets of the upside-down world in the seventeenth century were thought by contemporaries to be mad, and some probably were—the vision was too much for their sanity.[12] But in some cases madness was a useful protection for the expression of opinions dangerous to the social order. There can be no doubt that the Ranter Thomas Webbe was being prudent when he called himself Mad Tom in a pamphlet foretelling the downfall of Charles II in 1660.[13]

This reversal of degree finds no easy resolution in the play. Edgar's final speech provides no strongly felt reassurance that the world is now once more firmly the right way up. It is deliberately quiet and bleak.

Resistance Upside Down

The resistance to evil too has an 'upside-down' dimension, coming first from the weak, the oppressed lower orders, the peasants and servants. This is highlighted in the first violent check to tyranny, when the Nazi-type brute Cornwall, about to put out the other eye of Gloucester, is defied and wounded by his own servant. In the few lines he speaks this unnamed man declares himself a lifelong servant of the Duke, not a casual hireling; but the bonds of feudal loyalty and rank cannot hold in face of such dishonourable cruelty:

> I have served you ever since I was a child,
> But better service have I never done you
> Than now to bid you hold.
>
> (3.7.71-3)

This echoes Kent's justification of his insubordination to Lear. A 'villein' of Cornwall's draws on his lord as an equal, and Regan screams out the indignation of the 'natural rulers':

> A *peasant* stand up thus!
>
> (3.7.77)

She kills him, running at him from behind. But the resistance has started, and Cornwall will not be there to help crush it.

For the audience, this action—quite unprepared—by one of the stage 'extras' is startling, and evidently meant to be so. It is followed, in Quarto, by the sympathy and indignation of the horrified servants, who despite their terror do their best to help Gloucester and bandage his wounds. This first tentative rallying of humane forces against the tyrants was cut in the Folio text, and also in a famous production by Peter Brook, who said he wished to prevent reassurance being given to the audience. One wonders why. The reassurance provided in these depths of agony hardly seems excessive. Was the suggestion of a justified *popular* rising against despotic power perhaps felt to be going too far? However that may be, Edgar when he kills Oswald is disguised as a peasant, wearing the 'best 'parel' provided by the honest old man, Gloucester's tenant, and talking stage country dialect. His peasant cudgel beats down the gentleman's sword and his fancy fencing:

> I's' try whether your costard or my baton be the harder . . .' Chill pick your teeth, sir. Come, no matter vor your foins.
>
> (4.5.240-4)

Ordinary countrymen were of course forbidden to wear a sword, which was the exclusive privilege of gentlemen.[14] Hence this victory must register in the theatre as symbolic of the common people defeating the hangers-on of court and wealth, though since Edgar is really a nobleman in disguise, and the audience knows this, the effect is less subversive than it might be. However, if we compare this fight with the concluding duels between Hamlet and Laertes, Prince Hal and Hotspur, or Coriolanus and Aufidius, this image is strikingly a contest of social unequals, in which the plain but righteous man wins against the odds. It may also have suggested a further symbolic meaning for some in the audience. The Surrey group of Familists, whose pacifist principles forbade them to bear arms, found that this made them too conspicuous, and therefore compromised by carrying staves (cudgels).[15]

Lear's Fool is of course the most obvious source of upside-downness in both texts, speaking wisdom in the proverbial idiom of the people, often coarsely, in contrast to the hypocrisy and folly of formal and ceremonial utterance by the great. (The distinction that has been suggested between a 'natural' Fool in Quarto and an 'artificial', skilful courtier-Fool in Folio has to my mind been greatly overstated.) The Fool's jokes and aphorisms are consistently in the irreverent upside-down style, often literally so, and some as old as Aesop:

> e'er since thou madest thy daughters thy mothers . . .
> and puttest down thine own breeches . . .
>
> (1.4.153-4)

> May not an ass know when the cart draws the horse?
>
> (1.4.206)

> When thou clovest thy crown i'th' middle and gavest away both parts, thou borest thine ass o'th' back o'er the dirt.
>
> (1.4.142-4)

This echoes the images of the topsy-turvy world in scores of songs and broadsides,[16] such as the popular ballad, 'Who's the fool now', favoured by James's own provocative Fool Archy Armstrong (and still in use at folksong festivals to this day). Textual revision has not substantially changed this effect. The King himself reduced to a fool is a key image in both texts. The main difference may be in the greater emphasis given to it in the Quarto:

> LEAR Dost thou call me fool, boy?
> FOOL All thy other titles thou hast given away.
> That thou wast born with.
>
> (Q.4.143-5)

And one may note also the obviousness of the topical application in Quarto, which it is suggested the censor may have jibbed at.[17] Among the lines excised is the Fool's jingle:

> That lord that counselled thee
> To give away thy land,
> Come, place him here by me;
> Do thou for him stand.
> The sweet and bitter fool

> Will presently appear,
> The one in motley here,
> The other found out there.
>
> (Q.4.135-142)

So too is the Fool's complaint that he has failed to secure a monopoly of folly, because:

> lords and great men will not let me. If I had a monopoly out, they would have part on't, and ladies too, they will not let me have all the fool to myself—they'll be snatching.
>
> (Q.4.147-50)

There is indeed a double topical reference here (1) to the land given away by the King to his favourites, and (2) to anti-monopoly pressure by the Commons, culminating in the Apology of 1604.

The Fool stands in a direct theatrical tradition from Tarlton, appearing as Simplicity in the 'medley' plays of the 1580s. Even his jokes are traditional.[18] The clown as prophet appears in *The Cobbler's Prophecy* (printed 1594) where the poor cobbler, endowed with prophetic gifts by the gods, denounces the rich and foresees the world turned upside down at the Day of Judgement, when widows and starving children will be avenged. The most direct analogy, however, is with Rowley's comic-historical presentation in 1605 of Henry VIII and his famous jester Will Summers, who in this rendering is an iconoclastic, egalitarian, anti-Popish clown and a champion of the poor. It would be better, he says, if Henry had their prayers rather than the Pope's, for the Pope is at best St Peter's deputy, 'but the poor present Christ, and so should be something better regarded'—an old anti-clerical aphovism traceable back to the Lollards.[19]

Not Only 'Carnivalesque'

The upside-down discourse here is not simply 'carnivalesque', if by that we mean providing a recognized safety-valve for the release of tensions in a repressive society—a temporary holiday from hierarchy which enables it to be reimposed more effectively afterwards, as we see in the Feast of Fools, the Lords of Misrule, or the iconoclastic Christmas entertainments customary to this day in the London teaching hospitals.

The deriding of accepted categories of sin, adultery, property and officially enforced law echoes Utopian ideas which survived in a serious and organized form, more or less underground, in late-Elizabethan and Jacobean times, among radical religious sects such as the Family of Love, and were to surface again forty to fifty years later in the revolutionary years, first with the Levellers, and after their defeat with Ranters and Seekers. A Presbyterian divine, denouncing the sect under Elizabeth, had emphasized the 'topsy-turvy' aspect of Henry Niclaes' teaching as especially subversive of order:

> To be brief in this matter of doctrine, H.N. turneth religion upside down, and buildeth heaven here upon earth: maketh God, man; and man, God; heaven, hell; and hell, heaven.[20]

The existence of such ideas was topical knowledge about the time when *King Lear* was first produced. In *Basilikon Doron* King James had particularly attacked Familists as an example of *dangerous* Puritanism:

> their humours . . . agreeing with the general rule of all Anabaptists, in the contempt of the civil magistrate, and in leaning to their own dreams and revelations.[21]

The Familists, replying to this, petitioned King James for toleration, disavowing any intent to overthrow the magistrate and place themselves in his seat: an appeal almost certainly drafted by Robert Seale, one of a group of Familists in the royal Guard.[22] They, did not obtain the toleration they sought. In 1606 a confutation of their *Supplication* was printed (together with the text) and thereafter little is known about the sect as such. The ideas, however, were in the air, and theatre people could have picked up their acquaintance with them around the court as well as in artisan circles (often no doubt in distorted form).

Not Mad From the Beginning

The 'world upside down' effect in the play is easily destroyed, though, if the King is played (as has happened in some recent productions) as deranged, undignified and in senile dementia from his first entrance. Dramatically, no fall or reversal is then possible, and 'Let me not be mad, not mad, sweet heaven!' loses all its agonizing force. No moral or political point can then be made, except perhaps that kings ought to be retired early, so that they can be replaced by sane people like Goneril and Regan.

It is not a question of the sacred untouchability of the text. As Brecht once said, 'I think we can alter Shakespeare if we can alter him'; but wrong alterations will 'mobilise all Shakespeare's excellences against us'. This particular one seems to me the kind of alteration that distorts the original to the point where the chemistry of the play no longer works. A successful production has to convince us that a King, however grand and mighty he has been, is a fool anyway, and mortal anyway. Lear's fearful experience makes him and the audience aware of this. Hence the need of any king for wise and courageous advisers prepared to tell him the truth and set limits to his power—the role played by Kent here, and in the contemporary political context, unevenly but increasingly, in their own mind at least, by some opposition elements in Parliament.

Censorship and the Reception of the Play

Direct censorship (as distinct from cautious self-censorship) has been argued as possibly accounting for some of the differences between the two texts—notably the omission of several of the Fool's speeches in Scene 4. It was a tricky moment to write in this tone about a *British* Court and Crown, even if legendary ones. But it may just have been that the bitter jokes against royalty did not please, and some were therefore cut by the dramatist and the players in a revised acting version. That, however, may not have been enough. No London revival of *Lear* after 1606, which might have used a revised text, is actually known, though there were many repeats, at court and elsewhere, of *Othello, Hamlet, Richard II,* and the late romances. The chances are that this play, directly representing a King as foolish, the rich as culpable, and the poor as victims, may have been felt as altogether too disturbing and subversive.

There is indeed evidence that the company was in political trouble with the Court around this time. The King's Men had, it seems, displeased James by a play performed 'in their theatre' reported to him as containing many 'galls', 'dark sentences / Pleasing to factious brains,' with 'every otherwhere a jest / Whose high abuse shall more torment than blows'. The company made their peace with a Court performance of the old romantic-heroic popular favourite *Mucedorus*, including a specially rewritten Epilogue, in which the characters appealed on their knees to the 'glorious and wise Arch-Caesar on this earth' to pardon 'our unwitting error'.[23] The references to the offending play in this Epilogue (attributed by several scholars to Shakespeare) sound more appropriate to *King Lear* than to anything else recently performed by the King's Men. However that may be, the company had certainly been warned; and the marked change of tone in Shakespeare's later plays—*Pericles* and *Winter's Tale, Cymbeline* and *Tempest*—may in part reflect this.

Notes

[1] Peter Brook, *The Empty Space* (London, 1968), p. 91.

[2] See in particular the chapters by these authors in *Conflict in Early Stuart England,* ed. R. Cust and A. Hughes (London, 1989); and J. P. Sommerville, *Politics and Ideology in England, 1603-1640* (London, 1989).

[3] Sommerville, *Politics and Ideology,* pp. 28-32.

[4] From 'A Form of Apology and Satisfaction', drawn up at the end of the 1604 session by a Committee of the House. Cited Conrad Russell, *The Crisis of Parliaments* (London, 1971), p. 270.

[5] Cited Derek Hirst, *Authority and Conflict in England 1603-1648* (London, 1986), p. 117.

[6] G. P. Akrigg, *Shakespeare and the Earl of Southampton* (London, 1968), pp. 264ff.

[7] Other links with Parliamentarian circles can be traced through the Digges brothers, who are connected in various ways with Shakespeare and later with anti-absolutist opposition trends. Their stepfather, Thomas Russell, was overseer of Shakespeare's will. Leonard Digges published eulogies of Shakespeare in 1623 and 1640. (*Shakespeare, Complete Works* (Oxford, 1986), pp. xlvi and xlviii). Dudley Digges, who is believed to have shown Strachey's confidential report on the state of Virginia to Shakespeare (see *The Tempest,* ed. Frank Kermode (London, 1964), pp. xxvii-xxviii) was a prominent anti-absolutist MP, and in 1629 drafted the Petition of Right.

[8] During the year to October 1990 London local authorities had to place over 31,000 families in temporary accommodation (a new high), and 8,000 in bed and breakfast accommodation. (Chairman of Association of Local Authorities Housing Committee, the *Guardian,* 12 October 1990). Even in prosperous Cambridge, 307 homeless families had to be rehoused in the year 1990-1, an increase of 44 on the previous year and the highest number on record. For England as a whole official statistics show homeless households have increased by 131 per cent in 1979-89 to a total of 122,680: recent research (by Professor John Greve) shows that in 1990 some 170,000 households were accepted as homeless by Local Authorities, amounting to about half a million people. Estimates of single homeless (who are not entitled to be rehoused) in London vary between 65,000 and 125,000: according to the housing charity *Shelter,* about 3,000 are currently sleeping rough in London.

[9] Roger Warren, 'The Folio Omission of the Mock Trial: Motives and Consequences', in Gary Taylor and Michael Warren, eds., *The Division of the Kingdoms* (Oxford, 1983), pp. 45ff.

[10] Abiezer Coppe, *A Fiery Flying Roll,* pt 1, ch. 8 (London, 1649).

[11] R. Warren, p. 46.

[12] Christopher Hill, *The World Turned Upside Down* (London, 1972), p. 224. The whole chapter 'The Island of Great Bedlam' is illuminating on the relation between lower-class prophecy and accusations of madness.

[13] Hill, p. 227.

[14] Oswald, as Kent points out earlier, while technically allowed to wear a sword, is too dishonourable to have a right to it.

[15] See Janet E. Halley, 'The Case of the English Family of Love', in *Representing the English Renaissance,* ed. Stephen Greenblatt (London, 1988), pp. 319-20. See also John Rogers, *The displaying of an horrible sect of gross and wicked heretics* (London, 1578).

[16] See Peter Burke, *Popular Culture in Early Modern Europe* (London, 1978), especially the illustrated broadsides of the mice burning the cat; the woman with the gun and the man with the distaff; and the peasant riding on the nobleman's back (between pp. 98 and 99).

[17] See Gary Taylor in *The Division of the Kingdoms,* pp. 104-9.

[18] The Fool's joke about the cockney's brother who, 'in pure kindness to his horse, buttered his hay' (*Lear* 2.4) is anticipated by Tarlton's story about the inn where they greased the horses' teeth to prevent them eating, and so saved the cost of the fodder (*Three Ladies of London,* Dodsley's Old Plays (London, 1874), vol. 6, p. 255).

[19] Samuel Rowley, *When You See Me You Know Me* (London, 1605) (Malone Society Reprint, 1952, line 1568).

[20] John Knewstub, *A Confutation of Monstrous and Horrible Heresies* (London, 1579). Preface.

[21] Cited by Halley.

[22] Seale was briefly imprisoned on suspicion of Familism in 1580, but was still in a position of trust at court as clerk of the Cheque of the Guard in 1599, a position which he continued to hold in 1606. In the reply confuting the Familists' Supplication (which includes their text) the editor refers (p. 18) to leading Familists 'receiving yearly both countenance and maintenance from her princely coffers, being her household servants': and on p. 28 states that the Elizabethan Familists are 'yet living and in Court', with 'their children in right ancient place about his majesty'. The Familists included both an educated élite and an organized popular following, mainly of artisans, in such areas as Wisbech, Surrey, Suffolk, and Cambridge. See Alastair Hamilton, *The Family of Love* (1981), especially Chapter 6 on the Family in England.

[23] I am grateful to Richard Proudfoot for drawing my attention to the *Mucedorus* Epilogue and its significance. The revised Epilogue, first printed in the 1610 edition, is included in *The Shakespeare Apocrypha,* ed. C. Tucker Brooke (1908), from which all the above phrases are quoted. The matter is discussed in *The Comedy of Mucedorus,* ed. K. Warnke and Ludwig Proeschold (1878); and by R. Simpson in *Academy,* (29 April 1876). The play is described in the Epilogue as a 'comedy' but this does not rule out a reference to *Lear:* Hamlet, after all, referred to *The Murder of Gonzago* as a 'comedy'.

Janet M. Green (essay date 1995)

SOURCE: "Earthy Doom and Heavenly Thunder: Judgement in *King Lear,*" in *The University of Dayton Review,* Vol. 23, No. 2, Spring, 1995, pp. 63-73.

[*In the essay that follows, Green studies the references to both secular and divine law and judgement in* King Lear, *arguing that through such intimations, Shakespeare heightens the experiences of cruelty, hopelessness, and pain in the play as well as intensifies the force of the play's final tragic scene. Green examines in particular how Shakespeare's audiences may have perceived such dramatic events.*]

In *King Lear* (1605-1606) Shakespeare refers to the law and to judgment, both secular and divine, again and again, heightening the pressure and force of the tragic outcome. The repeated legal situations, rather than offering hope of a fair judicial decision or a merciful reprieve, intensify and mirror the characters' experiences of heavenly wrath, human cruelty, and hopeless pain.

It is illuminating to recapitulate as much as possible the ways in which Shakespeare's audience might have perceived these situations, concentrating on what Shakespeare might reasonably have expected the ordinary playgoer to know and understand. Almost certainly this ordinary playgoer had not read all the contemporary materials which modern critics have perused—nor, one suspects, had Shakespeare—yet we can posit a certain community of knowledge of some legal situations and terms that occur and re-occur in *Lear*. These can be grouped under two kinds of judgment: secular doom and divine thunder—jacobean law courts and the Christian Last Judgment.[1]

Shakespeare's choice of legal situations demonstrates that the play's most powerful single dimension for spectators is "the nature and significance of human society" (Mack, *King Lear in Our Time*), for people's relations and responsibilities are set forth clearly in the law. Kiernan Ryan, while acknowledging that it is obvious Shakespeare's plays "have their historical basis in the social reality of his age," reminds us that more important is "ascertaining *how* that reality is perceived by the play, and *how we* are induced to perceive the play's representation of that reality" (26-27).

One of the realities is the highly litigious nature of Shakespeare's time. Going to law was common and frequent, as Shakespeare, and his father too, themselves demonstrated. An elaborate system of secular courts and legal entities with wide purposes and powers rendered judgments, not only to protect life and property, but to preserve the ranked structure of society and to encourage uniformity (Williams 217; Powell and Cook 41). Punishments were brutal, the range of felonies was wide, it was easy to bring prosecutions, and malicious litigation was widespread (Williams 248, 252).

Shakespeare's audience, like Lear himself, would condemn many things in such a legal system. Local justice was mostly in the hands of the much-criticized Justices of the Peace, who had both great responsibilities and great powers to enforce the law, which they did not always use with integrity. Sometimes, they might advocate clemency (as Lear does in the mock trial scene of 3.6 where he acts as a justice). Trial juries were known to be capricious, the attitude towards evidence often arbitrary, corruption and bribery prevalent, and haste could mar all procedure (Williams 231). A person could be—and often was—convicted one day and executed the next. Even the condemned ones making their farewells from the scaffold might be bidden by officials to make haste. The speed of resolutions in tragic drama resulting in the rapid heaping up of corpses which often seems artificial to us would not, perhaps, seem as contrived to Jacobeans.

Even more disliked than the secular courts, officials, and processes, were their ecclesiastical counterparts, which handled most matters of morality. Their autocratic approach and financial exactions "were resented and even hated by laymen" (Powell and Cook 86).

There was much to resent, fear and hate in both of these Jacobean legal systems, yet surely Shakespeare's audiences must have found the many highly dramatic renderings of judgment as fascinating as we do. The news-loving, lively Jacobeans were intensely interested in secular and religious trials, judgments and punishments, especially those with bizarre or gruesome details, or those involving the sad—perhaps satisfying—fall of great ones. John Foxe's *Book of Martyrs* still helped to feed the insatiable human appetite for gore, holy or otherwise. Accounts of trials were often printed for sale. Judgments (and their more interesting punishments) were enacted in the theatre. Public executions were common, often preceded by the condemned person's agreement with the judgment that had brought him (or her) to that dismal place. Secular judgment was a powerful reality to Shakespeare's audiences.

We see this consciousness in other works of Shakespeare, for example, *Measure for Measure, Much Ado About Nothing,* and *The Merchant of Venice*. It is most intensely mirrored and repeated in *King Lear*. In this tragedy, as in Jacobean life, legal terms and situations abound. In fact, they form an important framework for the action, from Lear's willful disposition of his kingdom in the first scene—that "trial of love"—until the end (Mack, *Everybody's Shakespeare* 162). When Lear summons his three daughters, it is to testify in a courtroom atmosphere.[2] In this scene, the royal judge metes out rewards and punishments like an overblown, arbitrary, powerful Jacobean magistrate, a character which would have been familiar to the audience. They would also have been aware of how contemporary laws of inheritance were violated by both Lear and Gloucester, and of how greed was threatening family ties (Kenneth Muir, *The Great Tragedies* 26). Many also would know the sensational story of Sir Brian Annesley. In 1603 when his eldest daughter and her husband sought to get him declared mad so they could gain his estate, Cordell, his youngest daughter, appealed to Sir Robert Cecil on his behalf.[3]

Other matters relating to law occur throughout *Lear,* almost too many to recount. For example, successful flight to avoid prosecution was then common (Williams 232) and, in 4.6 we see Lear running off to be pursued on the heath by Cordelia's people. Some allusions to legal matters in the drama are almost glancing, like Goneril's arrogant pronouncement to her disgusted husband Albany that "the laws are mine, not thine" (5.3.158-59).

However, it is fitting that the most powerful, sustained, and effective images of judgment should center on the doomed king. The legal situations progress from the ceremonial disposition scene which opens the play, in which King Lear has all the power, and none of the understanding, to the mock trial scene (3.6) in which mad Lear has no real power but much better understanding. In this scene, he sets up his "courtroom" with Edgar (as poor Tom), the Fool, Kent and himself as justices. Cued by the Fool, Lear opens the proceedings:

> Fool: He's mad that trusts in the tameness of a wolf, a horse's health, a boy's love, or a whore's oath.
>
> Lear: It shall be done; I will arraign them straight
>
> (18-20)

So he does, arraigning Goneril, represented by a joint stool, on charges that she kicked him. "Let us deal justly," the Fool remarks (41).

This exhibition of the demented King presiding over a mad, surrealistic legal system must have pleased the original audiences, many of whom we can safely assume had had direct experiences with secular or ecclesiastical law and, very probably, not happy ones. Though the King in the play is insane, the arbitrariness and inconsistency of his legal pronouncements ring true. The apparent reversion to some kind of order in this scene—the structure of a law trial—is really a reversion to chaos and insanity, a point the audience could well appreciate. The mirror image effect not only increases the impression of Lear's weakening capacities, but reveals the marred nature and impaired truth of society itself. By all his incisive and telling words, Lear describes not only problems which the characters in the play face but problems in Jacobean life where legal judgment, like the fates of the drama's characters, could be arbitrary, inconsistent, brutally swift or hideously slow, crooked, unjust. The play's setting disguises the contemporary references somewhat, and the privilege of madness has allowed Lear, like Hamlet, to criticize the corrupt Jacobean social system without incurring punishment from the drama's other characters—or stimulating punishment of the playwright by authorities.

As the play goes on, the images of judgment become even more serious. As Lear goes increasingly mad, he becomes increasingly cogent as a social critic. Shakespeare skillfully enables us to recognize both states but trust the latter more. Lear, wandering about, continues to discourse in a seemingly disjointed manner but with penetrating acumen on injustice (4.6). Like George Eliot's famous pierglass image in *Middlemarch* (182), his egoism begins to organize random memories and experiences into a pattern of awareness, as a candle held close organizes the meaningless scratches on a metal pierglass into concentric circles. When Lear characterizes a barking dog who makes a beggar run away as the "great image of Authority: / A dog's obey'd in office" (4.6.160-61), we think of his own misused authority, as evidently he does also.

His scope widens to include other wrongs besides his own, but he characterizes the officer of the law (the punisher) as the real sinner, once again a reflection of his own crucial fault in disposing of his kingdom. The "rascal beadle," though he lusts for the whore, nevertheless lashes her back. The usurer, a magistrate guilty of lending money at usurious rates, hangs the cozener, only a petty cheater (Muir 180n; 4.6.162-65). Money protects the sinful from discovery and prosecution, and rich clothes disarm justice:

> Plate sin with gold,
> And the strong lance of justice hurtless
>   breaks;
> Arm it in rags, a pigmy's straw does pierce it
>   (167-69)

The audience must have realized, as Maynard Mack points out, "that it was listening to an indictment far more relevant to its own social experience than to any this king of ancient Britain could be imagined to have had." Lear, a king of the realm like their own King James, had "registered for all to hear the bankruptcy of the very body politic (and body moral) of which he was representative and head. . . . Even the most casual playgoer, who had looked about him reflectively in Jacobean England, must have experienced a shudder of self-recognition as Lear's 'sermon' proceeded" (107-08).

After indicting hypocrisy, Lear imitates an impossibly ideal magistrate, or perhaps the hoped-for merciful Christ at the Last Judgment, when he says, "None does offend, none, I say, none: I'll able 'em ("vouch for them"; 170). (He seems to revert to his old arrogance, however, when he adds the sinister reminder that he has "the power / To seal th' accuser's lips" (171-72)). But he has reversed the procedure usual in any court of judgment—in fact, destroyed its basis—by pardoning an offense before he knows what it is. Human mercy can do no more, nor can divine.[4]

Once Lear is reunited with Cordelia, the madman's judging ceases. The action quickens. The King, now restored to his wits but weak, and his adored Cordelia must suffer Edmund's unjust and extreme judgment upon them. Before this comes to pass, Lear, reunited with his darling, has one last happy moment. His eloquent address to her, "Come, let's away to prison," (5.3.8-19) may sound fanciful to us—and has had, like almost every passage in *Lear*, myriad interpretations—but the audience might have found it not a piece of deluded, senile, or symbolic imagination, but an anachronistic reflection of possibility. The legal system often granted surprising leniency to prisoners in Shakespeare's time, even to "traitors," if of high rank. Lear does not live to enjoy the kind of imprisonment with Cordelia he describes, but it was not unreasonable for a king to expect it.

Shakespeare's use of such frequent allusions to secular judgment and to the legal systems must have deepened the playgoer's understanding of the tragedy and widened its meaning to include not only awareness of pagan Britain but of Jacobean England. And perhaps of life itself, for earthly judgments prefigured and mirrored in part God's final one.

Now we find in *Lear* more allusions to the judgment of the law than to Christianity's Last Judgment, even though religion was more pervasive in Jacobean daily life, but these Doomsday references reverberate powerfully, like the sounds of approaching thunder. They are fewer, of course, partly because *Lear* has a pagan setting, but also, it is likely, because overt references to religion could be dangerous. Prudent writers did not allude to religious matters except with great circumspection. The situation in Shakespeare's time resembled somewhat the circumstances surrounding the composition of most apocalyptic literature. Because it was often seditious and contemporary references dangerous, it was cryptic—as is Shakespeare's resolution of *Lear*. The consequences of offending the authorities could be severe. We cannot assume that Shakespeare stood aloof from the state religion of his time, for had he not conformed, S. Schoenbaum convincingly argues, he would have been noticed by authorities who were already hostile to the theatre on religious grounds (59-60).

The concept of the Last Judgment was one of the important ideas of Shakespeare's time (Weittrich 91). Queen Elizabeth had movingly referred to it in her Golden Speech in 1601.[5] King James, fascinated by theology, was obsessed with the Book of Revelation and his meditations on it were published in 1588 and 1603. Revelation pertained to the last age and would be fulfilled "in very short space," he wrote. Inspired by the King's concern, his subjects studied the subject enthusiastically (Weittrich 29-31). Besides the common verbal allusions to the Last Judgment were the common visual representations, like the paintings in churches (Lascelles 59-60). It seems reasonable to assume that the concept of the Last Judgment was as familiar to the ordinary playgoer as the creation of the world or the life of Jesus.

In church, sermons were preached on the Last Judgment, and in the liturgy Jacobeans heard and uttered references to it again and again. Church attendance was not optional, and the order of service, the creeds, and Scriptural readings were fixed. The use of and worship according to the *Book of Common Prayer* was enforced by statue, "and offenders were punishable by law," as described in "An Act for Uniformity of Common Prayer" (BCP 6-13; 372). The vision of judgment in all its scarifying power was set before Shakespeare's contemporaries frequently in the Scriptural selections appointed to be read in particular Morning and Evening Prayer services and in the less frequent Holy Communion service (such as Matthew 13:47-50 and 25; and Luke 21).[6]

Judgment appears also in the Apostles' Creed used in Morning Prayer (and said in common by the whole congregation), and the Nicene Creed: "And He shall come again to judge both the quick and the dead." The Athanasian Creed which was said in common at the end of Evening Prayer on selected high feast days describes the Last Judgment in more detail: ". . . he shall come to judge the quick and the dead. / At whose coming all men shall rise again with their bodies: and they shall give account for their own works. / And they that have done good, shall go into life everlasting: and they that have done evil, into everlasting fire. / This is the catholic faith: which except a man believe faithfully, he cannot be saved" (64-67). The Apostles' Creed was used in Baptism (273) and several other services, and references to the Last Judgment appear in many places, even in the marriage ceremony: "I require and charge you (as you will answer at the dreadful day of judgment, when the secrets of all hearts shall be disclosed) . . ." (291). And of course the concept appears frequently in the Order for the Burial of the Dead, along with hope of mercy (309-13).

Many briefer, but still relentless, reminders of the same cataclysmic final day were contained in other portions of the church services. Two of the most important seasons of the church year, Advent and Lent, emphasized the individual's preparation for the fulfillment of God's ordinances.

There are not only reflections in *King Lear* of the general assumption that everyone knew about the Last Judgment, but there are echoes in it of the *Book of Common Prayer*. One service even reads like program notes for the villains in *Lear*. In the colorful and dramatic Office of Commination Against Sinners . . ."To Be Used Divers Times in the year," drawn chiefly from Deut. 27, the minister leads the congregation in denouncing various kinds of sinners (*BCP* 316-23). These kinds could describe characters in *Lear*.

> Cursed is he:
> "that curseth his father"
>   (a description fitting Edmund);
> "that lieth with his neighbor's wife"
>   (Edmund);
> "that smiteth his neighbor secretly"
>   (Edmund, Goneril the poisoner);
> "that taketh reward to slay the soul of innocent blood"
>   (the Captain-hangman, Oswald);
> "that maketh the blind to go out of his way"
>   (Cornwall, Regan);
> "Cursed are the unmerciful"
> (fits Edmund, Goneril, Regan, Cornwall, Cornwall's servants, and Oswald. Gloucester and Lear, also, begin without the quality of mercy but advance towards it).

In this service of Commination, after the minister exhorts the congregation to return to God, "remembering the dreadful judgment hanging over our heads, and being always at hand," he reads a bloodcurdling description of that final day of wrath and vengeance, which it might have done even Edmund some good to hear.

It is well to remember in this discussion, though, that the Christian God is not possessed entirely by flaming judgmental wrath. It is also His property to have mercy. Mercy like the mercy Lear showed in the mock trial scene (3.6) when he forgave the sin before he knew the crime.[7] It was certain God accepted the repentance of the dying. So Shakespeare's audience might well have felt a sense of completion, of satisfaction, of justice, when even the villainous Edmund acknowledges a power greater than his own. Dying, he says, "I pant for life; some good I mean to do / Despite of mine own nature" (5.3.243-44).

The belief that God judges people on earth but also finally and dramatically—and not without mercy—in the life to come is so enshrined in the key protestations of Christian faith and Scripture that it must have affected the way in which Shakespeare's audience beheld their lives and his plays. What Joseph Weittrich terms "the apocalyptic myth" appears in other works, for example, *Anthony and Cleopatra* and *Macbeth* (6; Lascelles 56), and the comic murderers jest about Doomsday with perfect familiarity in *Richard III* (1.4. 101ff). But it is in *Lear* that the concept is used most powerfully. The resemblances of *Lear*'s world to the world of Shakespeare's audiences were obvious. They would see more easily what modern critics so often quote, Keats's "fierce dispute betwixt damnation and impassioned clay" (380, lines 5-6). David Kranz writes that Shakespeare and his audience, "being Christian, would clearly see the pagan tragedy and the hidden Christian insights more easily than we do," though the insights are perhaps not so hidden as that statement implies (140). Even in a play with an undoubtedly pagan setting, says Bruce Young, "Shakespeare draws freely on the Christian idea of the Apocalypse, the era of tribulation and judgment that will accompany the end of this fallen world" (103).

Shakespeare knew the Geneva Bible, which with the *Book of Common Prayer* and the Homilies "profoundly nourished his imagination," concludes S. Schoenbaum (57). René Fortin goes further: "an ear attuned to Scripture would discern in Lear's ordeal resonances of the Book of Revelation" (119). In *Lear* Shakespeare is particularly obsessed with the Doomsday idea (Weittrich 9-10). He seems to have before him, not the brief, flat statements of the Apostles' and Nicene Creeds, but the more terrifying vision of the Athanasian Creed (*BCP* 67):

> At whose coming all men shall rise again with their bodies: and shall give account for their own works.
>
> And they that have done good, shall go into life everlasting: and they that have done evil, into everlasting fire [the second death].

Apocalyptic events (as just described, and in Revelation and Daniel) take place, like the major events of *King Lear*, in a certain kind of time. Ordinary measured time ("chronos") is replaced by a period of massive change and danger, in which the sense of time is concentrated, quickened, and heightened because of the dramatic and important events that happen within it. This "chairos" (related to our term "crisis") brings change, good or bad, but always it brings anxiety and fear. In *Lear* we experience as the play progresses a growing sense of urgency, change, danger, and fear in which time is indeed heightened and rushes with unusual speed and force to the final destruction.

The effect is achieved not only by plot events but by the general atmosphere and by specific references. The quality of apocalyptic finality has occurred throughout the play—in trumpets, in thunders, in tempest. The hideous din of wind and rain on the heath seems to be at war "as if it were indeed Armageddon. . . . And everywhere "run tides of doomsday passion that seem to use up and wear away people, codes, expectations, all stable points of reference, till only a profound sense remains that an epoch, in fact a whole dispensation, has forever closed" (Mack, *King Lear* 85-86). In Keats's "vale of soul-making," the characters must make final choices, and in noise, chaos, madness, flight and battle their fates come upon them swiftly. "The wheel is come full circle," Edmund says. "I am here" (5.3.174).

Reference to another wheel has already brought to mind specific last things—Hell and punishment following Judgment. Lear seems to refer to a medieval torment in Purgatory (which the Protestants had abolished) when he wakes from his madness to behold above him the face of Cordelia:

> Thou art a soul in bliss; but I am bound
> Upon a wheel of fire, that mine own tears
> Do scald like molten lead
>
> (4.7.46-48)

Though the Established Church had rejected the doctrine of Purgatory, it could still linger in the minds of the audience and in the poetry of the playwright. Cordelia has bent above her suffering father in one pietà; now at the end he bends above her in another (Barber 119).

The most obvious specific indication of the Last Judgment occurs at the end of the drama after Lear has expired over Cordelia's body. Commentators still dispute whether the ending is "Christian" or not, whether Lear is redeemed by his suffering or dies uselessly, and they variously interpret Lear's last words, "Look on her, look, her lips, / Look there, look there!" (5.3.310-11). Some say Lear actually thinks Cordelia revives, and his heart, like Gloucester's, bursts in joy, not anguish. Even if he dies in this happy belief, we know he is horribly mistaken and our pity is not diminished. Perhaps it is even increased. The reversal of the happier ending in the old Lear story could itself be authorized by the implications of Apocalypse (Weittrich 12). But whatever the interpretation, the deliberately evoked resonances of Doomsday, our sense of "chairos," magnify the sorrow of the scene. The audience's understanding of apocalyptic possibilities makes the deaths of Lear and his Cordelia more believable, more horrible.

The comments of the three remaining "good" characters seem to refer to a Christian Last Judgment:

Kent: Is this the promised end?
Edgar: Or image of that horror?
Albany: Fall and cease
(5.3.263-64).

Albany's enigmatic imperatives have been interpreted as "let heavens fall and all things cease" (Bevington 132n).

However, the above lines could also refer to the end of time ("eschaton"), which encompasses cataclysmic events like warning signs and disasters, the destruction of the world, the Last Judgment, and the final defeat of evil and death. Thus the possibility that Lear and Cordelia's tragic fate may be a sign that this end of time is near (is beginning?) makes Edgar ask, "Or image of that horror?"[8]

The final reference in the tragedy to a legal system returns to secular law. The meaning of Lear's suffering deepens into almost unbearable intensity when Kent uses the word "rack" as a figure for his sufferings. When Edgar tries to revive the dead King with "Look up, my Lord," Kent protests (as we do):

> Vex not his ghost: O! let him pass; he hates him
> That would upon the rack of this tough world
> Stretch him out longer
> (5.3.313-15).

The infamous rack connoted pain and suffering which must be endured, sometimes relieved only by death. It was known that the state used routine unwarranted, sometimes enthusiastic torture to get information, to ensure the veracity of the victim as a later witness whether yet brought to trial or not, to serve on occasion "to the example of others" (Williams 393). It was used to punish *and* to gain a confession—sometimes in that order.

Who would disagree with Kent's passionate plea, "O! let him pass"? The rack of Lear's sufferings has done too much to him. His mind has been dislocated as the rack might have maimed his body. In fact, in Caroline Spurgeon's famous words, through verbs and metaphors the drama's references to violence and bodily agony have finally created the image "of a human body in anguished movement, tugged, wrenched, beaten, pierced, stung, scourged, dislocated, flayed, gashed, scalded, tortured and finally broken on the rack" (339). Lear's pain has, it is true, yielded him greater compassion for his fellow beings and greater understanding of himself. He had long ago confessed his chief error—"I did her wrong," he had said flatly about Cordelia (1.5.24). But the price of gaining such knowledge has been too high. There can be no recompense. Kent says, "If Fortune brag of two she lov'd and hated, / One of them we behold" (5.3.280-81). Lear's increased sensitivity does show in his courteous dying request, "Pray you, undo this button: thank you, Sir" (5.3.309). Still it cannot redeem his suffering which had made him like a condemned soul to roam the earth in mad anguish. At the end, he is like a corpse tied to the gibbet for warning. True, Kent, Albany, and Edgar remain alive at the end of the play, but their virtue is pale and insufficient comfort for the sorrow and evil the audience has seen, the judgments—just and unjust—that have been implied and given.[9]

The unspoken connotative meanings of these judgments must have increased the powerful impression of the drama. As the audience left Shakespeare's theatre, their impression of the entire tragedy must have been undergirded by their knowledge, perhaps fear, of secular law, and as they dispersed, the thunder of the Last Judgment must have resonated in their minds.

Notes

[1] In this paper, acts, scenes, and line numbers refer to The Arden Shakespeare edited by Kenneth Muir, Methuen, 1963. The terms "Last Judgment," "Day of Judgment," and "Doomsday" (Old English "doom" meant "judgment") were in Shakespeare's time more or less synonymous and referred to a time when all people, the living and the dead, would be judged by God, after the world is destroyed and before a New Kingdom is created.

[2] René Girard in *A Theatre of Envy* says what Cordelia rejects in this scene is "mimetic rivalry" with her sisters (182). This is an interesting point, since rivalry so often precedes violence. Rivalry is also the essence of litigation.

[3] Annesley died not long after Cordell's appeal, and the eldest daughter contested his will. Mack, *King Lear In Our Time* (45-47) and Muir in his edition of *King Lear* (xliii) summarize the details.

[4] A frequent New Testament idea is that sin and law reinforce each other, as in "for by the law is the knowledge of sin" (Rom. 3:20); "the strength of sin is the law" (1 Cor. 15:56); and "sin is not imputed when there is no law" (Rom. 5:13).

[5] To members of Parliament Elizabeth said: "I have ever used to set the Last-Judgment Day before mine eyes, and so to rule as I shall be judged to answer before a higher Judge, to whose judgment seat I do appeal, that never thought was cherished in my heart that tended not unto my people's good" (Neale 390).

[6] The 1559 edition of the *Book of Common Prayer* (hereafter *BCP*) was in constant use until 1604, when minor changes only were made. Further changes were

not made until 1661-1662 (Booty, "History of the 1559 Book of Common Prayer" in *BCP* 329).

Some of the appointed Scriptural readings which included descriptions of the Last Judgment were: Acts 17:31; 2 Peter 3:9-13; 2 Cor. 5:10; 1 Cor. 4:4-5; 2 Thess. 1:7-10; and Jude 1:6-8 ("Proper Lessons To Be Read" and "An Almanac for Thirty Years," *BCP* 27-47).

[7] Cordelia, like Edgar, embodies Christian constancy; she gives especially eloquent voice to the doctrine of mercy when she hears how her deadly sisters had locked their doors against their father in the apocalyptic storm: "Mine enemy's dog, / Though he had bit me, should have stood that night / Against my fire" (4.7.36-38). The shining thread of mercy is interwoven in *Lear* with the harsh poetic justice described in these famous lines: "The Gods are just, and of our pleasant vices / Make instruments to plague us" (5.3.170-71).

[8] Yet another reading of these much discussed lines concludes that the three characters may refer to death itself. Kent laments the death of good people like Lear and Cordelia in such terrible circumstances ("Is this the promis'd end?"). Edgar adds that the horrible scene they behold is the first of many deaths ("Or image of that horror?"). Albany's remark reinforces that despair; once you die, there is nothing more ("Fall and cease"). For this interpretation I am indebted to Pastor Elizabeth Eaton and Father Conrad Selnick of Ashtabula, Ohio.

[9] Eaton and Selnick have conjectured that several apparently Christian references in the last scene may not be chance occurrences; Shakespeare may have deliberately chosen them to soften the bleakness of the final events. (A pre-Christian setting did not require exact theology.) Edmund repents, providing the audience with a sense of resolution. Albany promises punishment and reward like the Christian God of the Last Judgment, thus providing a sense of justice and completion.

Some vocabulary has rich Christian connotations. Referring to the dead Goneril and Regan, Albany says, "*This judgment of the heavens*, that makes us tremble, / Touches us not with pity" (5.3.231-32). Lear says that if Cordelia lives, "It is a chance which does *redeem* all sorrows / That ever I have felt" (266-67). And Kent speaks of his imminent death as a journey he must undertake: "*My master calls me*" (322. Above italics mine).

Works Cited

Barber, C. L. "On Christianity and the Family: Tragedy of the Sacred." *Twentieth Century Interpretations of King Lear: A Collection of Critical Essays*. Ed. Janet Adelman. Englewood, NJ: Prentice-Hall, 1978. 117-19.

The Book of Common Prayer, 1559: The Elizabethan Prayer Book. Ed. John E. Booty. Folger Documents of Tudor and Stuart Civilization 22. Washington: Folger Shakespeare Library, 1976.

Eliot, George. *Middlemarch*. 1871-72. Ed. Bert G. Hornback. New York: Norton, 1977.

Fortin, René. "Hermeneutical Circularity and Christian Interpretations of 'King Lear,'" *Shakespeare Studies: An Annual Gathering of Research, Criticism and Reviews* 12 (1979): 113-25.

Girard, René. *A Theater of Envy: William Shakespeare*. New York: Oxford UP, 1991.

Keats, John. "On Sitting Down to Read *King Lear* Once Again" (sonnet). *Poetical Works*. Ed. H. W. Garrod. London: Oxford UP, 1969.

Krantz, David L. "'Is This the Promis'd End?': Teaching the Play's Conclusion." Approaches to Teaching World Literature 12 (*King Lear*). Ed. Robert H. Ray. 1986. New York: MLA, 1992. 136-141.

Lascelles, Mary. "*King Lear* and Doomsday." *Aspects of King Lear: Articles Reprinted from Shakespeare Survey*. Eds. Kenneth Muir and Stanley Wells. Cambridge: Cambridge UP, 1982. 55-65.

Mack, Maynard. *Everybody's Shakespeare: Reflections Chiefly on the Tragedies*. Lincoln, NE: UP of Nebraska, 1993. Chapter 8 ("We Came Crying Hither: *King Lear*") uses material published earlier in his *King Lear in Our Time*.)

———. *King Lear In Our Time*. Berkeley: UP of California, 1965.

Muir, Kenneth. *The Great Tragedies*. 1961. London: Longmans Green, 1963. 25-32.

Neale, John E. *Elizabeth I and Her Parliaments: 1584-1601*. 1958. New York: Norton, 1966.

Powell, Ken and Chris Cook. *English Historical Facts: 1485-1603*. London: Macmillan, 1977.

Ryan, Kiernan. *Shakespeare*. Atlantic Highlands, NJ: Humanities P Intl., 1989.

Schoenbaum, S. *William Shakespeare: A Compact Documentary Life*. New York: Oxford UP, 1977.

Shakespeare, William. *King Lear*. Ed. David Bevington et al. 1980. New York: Bantam, 1988.

———. *King Lear*. Ed. Kenneth Muir. The Arden Shakespeare. London: Methuen, 1963.

Spurgeon, Caroline F. E. *Shakespeare's Imagery and What It Tells Us*. 1935. Cambridge: Cambridge UP, 1966.

Weittrich, Joseph. *"Image of that Horror": History, Prophecy, and Apocalypse in King Lear*. San Marino, CA: Huntington Library, 1984.

Williams, Penry. *The Tudor Regime*. 1979. Oxford: Clarendon P, 1983.

Young, Bruce W. "Shakespearean Tragedy in a Renaissance Context: *King Lear* and Hooker's *Of the Laws of Ecclesiastical Polity*." Approaches to Teaching World Literature 12 (*King Lear*). Ed. Robert H. Ray. 1986. New York: MLA, 1992. 98-104.

FURTHER READING

Alfar, Cristina Leon. "King Lear's 'Immoral' Daughters and the Politics of Kingship." *Exemplaria* VIII, No. 2 (Fall 1996): 375-400.

　Argues that Goneril and Regan are not innately "evil" but rather that their deeds are reactions to the "patrilinial structure of power relations in which they live and to which they must accommodate themselves."

Asp, Carolyn. "'The Clamor of Eros': Freud, Aging, and *King Lear*." In *Memory and Desire: Aging—Literature—Psychoanalysis,* edited by Kathleen Woodward and Murray M. Schwartz, pp. 192-204. Bloomington: Indiana University Press, 1986.

　Analyzes the relationship between Lear and his daughters using Freud's conception of family obligation.

Boehrer, Bruce Thomas. "*King Lear* and the Royal Progress: Social Display in Shakespearean Tragedy." *Disorder and the Drama. Renaissance Drama,* New Series, edited by Mary Beth Rose, Vol. XXI, pp. 243-61. Evanston: Northwestern University Press and The Newberry Library for Renaissance Studies, 1990.

　Maintains that the concept of "royal progress" (the extended entertaining of a monarch undertaken by visiting castle after castle) underlies the structure of *King Lear,* and that the tragedy ensues when Lear presumes to separate this royal privilege from his role as king.

Brown, John Russell. Introduction to *King Lear,* by William Shakespeare, edited by John Russell Brown, pp. viii-xx. New York: Applause, 1996.

　Offers an overview of the play, discussing early performances, plot, later theatrical history and criticism.

Cox, Catherine S. "'An excellent thing in woman': Virgo and Viragos in *King Lear*." *Modern Philology* 96, No. 2 (November 1998): 143-57.

　Studies issues of gender identity in *King Lear,* examining in particular the ambiguous characterization of Lear's daughters. Cox maintains that the play both "valorizes" and "denigrates" women and that ultimately it rejects what it considers to be "'unnatural' gender."

Foakes, R. A. "Textual Revision and the Fool in *King Lear*." In *Lear from Study to Stage,* edited by James Ogden and Arthur H. Scouten, pp. 109-22. Madison: Fairleigh Dickinson University Press, 1997. Reprinted from *Trivium* 20 (1985).

　Explores contradictory interpretations of the Fool based on differences between the Fool's role in the Quarto and Folio versions of the play.

Gardner, Helen. "*King Lear* (1967)." In *King Lear: Critical Essays,* edited by Kenneth Muir, Garland Publishing, Inc., 1984, pp. 251-74.

　Emphasizes the unity of action, characterization, and language of *King Lear* and notes the qualities of the play that distinguish it from Shakespeare's other tragedies.

Matz, Robert. "Speaking What We Feel: Torture and Political Authority in *King Lear*." *Exemplaria* VI, No. 1 (Spring 1994): 223-41.

　Maintains that throughout the entire play, *King Lear* presents the audience with images of torture, both literal and figurative. Matz suggests the link between these scenes of torture and the fears of treason and torture during the end of Queen Elizabeth's reign.

McAlindon, Tom. "Tragedy, *King Lear*, and the Politics of the Heart." *Shakespeare Survey: An Annual Survey of Shakespeare Studies and Production* 44 (1992): 85-90.

　Examines the image of the heart in *King Lear*, arguing that the play "appeals more profoundly both to the heart and the mind than any other play of Shakespeare's."

McEwan, Neil. "The Lost Childhood of Lear's Fool." *Essays in Criticism* 26 (1976): 209-17.

　Studies references in *King Lear* to the Fool in order to determine the Fool's age and suggests that the part might appropriately be played by a youth.

Oyama, Toshiko. "The World of Lear's Fool—The Dramatic Mode of His Speech," in *Shakespeare Studies,* Vol. 2, 1963, pp.10-30.

　Studies the language and rhetorical style of the Fool, arguing that the Fool's use of logical argumentation and his dialogue with Lear heightens the tragic mood of the play and intensifies the ambiguity of Lear's situation.

Reid, Stephen. "In Defense of Goneril and Regan." *American Imago* 27 (1970): 226-44.

>Argues that Goneril and Regan accurately appraise Lear's condition at the beginning of the play as weak and feeble and demonstrate a normal (as opposed to evil) reaction to Lear's favoring of Cordelia. Reid demonstrates that only through the course of the play are the two sisters corrupted by power.

Smith, Donald M. "'And I'll go to bed at noon': The Fool in *King Lear*." *Essays in Arts and Sciences* V, No. I (May 1976): 37-45.

>Reviews the role of the Fool in *King Lear* in order to determine the Fool's effects upon the play.

Stern, Jeffrey. "*King Lear*: The Transference of the Kingdom." *Shakespeare Quarterly* 41, No. 3 (Fall 1990): 299-308.

>Explores the psychological and personal motivations for Lear's division of his kingdom, arguing that the public and political implications of this division are less crucial.

Whitehead, Frank. "The Gods in *King Lear*." *Essays in Criticism: A Quarterly Journal of Literary Criticism* XLII, No. 3 (July 1992): 196-220.

>Analyzes references to superhuman powers in *King Lear*, arguing that the characters in *King Lear* seem to accept that no such forces control the world or human destiny.

Willeford, William. "The Sovereign Fool: *The Tragedy of King Lear*." In *The Fool and His Scepter: A Study of Clowns and Jesters and Their Audience,* pp. 208-25. Chicago: Northwestern University Press, 1969.

>Maintains that the Fool highlights the disintegration of Lear's kingdom and that other elements of "clowning," such as Lear's mock trial, point to this disintegration as well.

Twelfth Night

For further information on the critical and stage history of *Twelfth Night,* see *SC* Volumes 1, 26, and 34.

INTRODUCTION

For nearly two hundred years, commentators have generally agreed that *Twelfth Night* represents the culmination of Elizabethan romantic comedy. By reshaping circumstances, dramatic conventions, and character types he had employed in earlier comedies, Shakespeare created a paragon of this genre—and then turned to other dramatic forms. Many twentieth-century scholars have noted that the play contains elements of the problem comedies and the romances that followed *Twelfth Night*. Over the past three decades, feminist, new historicist, Marxist, and materialist critics have emphasized these elements, raising questions about the play's depiction of love and gender relations, the treatment of Malvolio, and Feste's role in the punishment of Olivia's steward as well as in the work as a whole.

Over the past twenty years, many critics have looked closely at Shakespeare's portrayal of the principal characters in *Twelfth Night*. Offering what he has described as an "anti-romantic" interpretation of the play, Richard A. Levin (1979) has assessed Viola as a cunning young woman who intentionally charms and misleads Olivia as part of her overall strategy. In Levin's estimation, Viola is determined from the outset to marry Orsino, and her deceptions reflect the prevailing values of the play. René Girard (1990) has focused on Olivia and Orsino, viewing both of them as obsessed by self-love and desperately in need of a sense of superiority in their relations with the opposite sex. This kind of narcissism, he has argued, places a priority on desire rather than pleasure. Also evaluating the meaning of sexuality in *Twelfth Night,* John Astington (1994) has remarked that Malvolio is depicted as unsuited for marriage because of his spiritual impotence. The public mockery of Malvolio's lust for Olivia, the critic has maintained, exposes the steward's inadequate understanding of the true responsibilities of heterosexual love. Feste's role in the gulling of Malvolio has intrigued several recent commentators. Joan Hartwig (1973) has regarded it as mean-spirited, severe, and abusive. Feste's concept of justice, she has contended, is the legal equivalent of revenge, and the absence of forgiveness in the conclusion of the subplot leaves readers and audiences uneasy. Hartwig also has noted, however, that the clown offers other characters, including Malvolio, different perspectives from which to view themselves, and that he is particularly concerned with calling attention to human folly. Robert Wilcher (1982) has compared Feste with other Shakespearean clowns, particularly the type known as "the domestic fool." Wilcher stresses Feste's vulnerability—his precarious situation in Olivia's household and his shortcomings as a professional jester—and has argued that the fool's verbal agility is inadequate to fill the role assigned to him. Karen Greif (1988) has termed Feste as enigmatic and inscrutable, but also as a character who serves as "a unifying presence." Reviewing twentieth-century theatrical renditions of *Twelfth Night*'s fool, she has demonstrated that since Harley Granville-Barker's innovative staging of the play in 1912, Feste has become the personification of its melancholy undertone: a poignant mediator between the illusions of romantic comedy and the realities of human existence. Greif also has pointed out the connection between modern critical appreciation of the play's darker elements—stage productions that emphasize its bittersweet tonalities, and late twentieth-century philosophical concerns with issues of identity and alienation. In contrast to Wilcher, Bente A. Videbæk (1996) has recently rated Feste's linguistic abilities highly, noting in particular the different verbal manipulations the fool employs with aristocrats on one hand and with menials on the other. From this critic's point of view, Feste's paramount quality is his aloofness from the intrigues of the dramatic action. But Videbæk also has maintained that Feste's role as mediator between the audience and the on-stage characters, his talent for adjusting his clowning to different situations, and his capacity to show up Olivia's and Orsino's sentimental notions of love are vital to our understanding of *Twelfth Night*.

Aside from analyses of the play's principal characters, late twentieth-century criticism of Shakespeare's last romantic comedy is dominated by consideration of gender issues. Cristina Malcolmson (1991) has explored the relationship between gender and status in *Twelfth Night* and has argued that although the play questions the traditional social order, in which men are regarded as inherently superior to women, it also betrays a deep anxiety about independent and upwardly mobile females. In Malcolmson's judgment, Shakespeare resolves this tension and preserves harmonious social relations by portraying Viola as gracious, deferential, and motivated by love for Orsino—not by any interest in improving her rank in society. Douglas E. Green (1991) has also evaluated questions of love and gender in *Twelfth Night,* and, like Malcolmson, discerns there a repressed fear of strong-willed women. He further has claimed that while on the surface the play suggests that men and women are equally capable of being faithful or erratic in their love, the subtext endorses the value of homosexual rather than heterosexual love. Irene G. Dash (1997) has similarly examined the question of independent, headstrong women in *Twelfth Night*. In contrast to Malcolmson and Green, however, Dash has asserted that Shakespeare treats the subject with "humor and insight." From her perspective, though Olivia and Viola initially challenge traditional notions of female dependency, eventually their erotic desires lead them to yield their independence and then gracefully conform to the social and sexual norms of a patriarchal world. Clearly there is no general consensus among contemporary critics regarding Shakespeare's depiction in *Twelfth Night* of human love and gender relations, and it appears likely that these topics will continue to draw the attention of scholars and commentators well into the next century.

OVERVIEWS

Elizabeth Story Donno (essay date 1985)

SOURCE: "Critical Commentary," in *Twelfth Night or What You Will*, edited by Elizabeth Story Donno, Cambridge University Press, 1985, pp. 8-23.

[*In the excerpt below, Donno traces the progress of the play's dramatic action and discusses the principal characters. Although she acknowledges some discrepancies and inconsistencies in the story, she applauds Shakespeare's treatment of the complicated plot.*]

After the theatres reopened in 1660, Pepys saw *Twelfth Night* on three occasions—in 1661, 1663 and 1668. Despite such familiarity, he seems to have missed the evocative and allusive quality of Shakespeare's alternative title, noting in his diary after the 1663 performance that this 'silly' play did not relate 'at all' to the name or to the day. Even for Shakespeare's contemporary audience its most memorable element was the character of the proud, self-loving steward Malvolio—witness a performance presented at court by Shakespeare's company in 1623 (again on Candlemas Day) under the title *Malvolio*. Leonard Digges, who had contributed commendatory verses to the First Folio, observed in a later and longer tribute:

> loe in a trice
> The Cockpit Galleries, Boxes, all are full
> To hear Malvoglio that cross-garter'd gull.
> (Shakespeare's *Poems,* 1640)

Some time in 1632 (or later) King Charles inscribed 'Malvolio' against the printed title in his copy of the Second Folio. One may conclude that, so far as contemporary (and later) stage popularity was concerned, the whirligig of time did bring in the revenge on the 'whole pack' of the other characters that the discomfited steward promises as he exits in the final act.

But it is Sir Toby Belch, the Countess Olivia's perennially tipsy kinsman, who has the most lines to speak and who, despite his earlier 'fruitless pranks', contrives the means both to complicate the plot and to resolve it. From the outset the convivial Sir Toby is hard put to understand the countess's vow to abjure both the sight and the company of men in order to mourn her brother's death for seven long summers. This desire to cloister herself for so extended a period reveals, as John Russell Brown observes, that Olivia must be very young indeed;[1] so, too, if one judges from their emotional predispositions and actions, all the characters must be, except perhaps for Feste—the Lady Olivia's father having taken much delight in him—and, possibly, the sprightly Sir Toby, though modern productions do not always take such evidence into account.

Shakespeare, in fact, is fairly specific in indicating the ages of the two pairs of lovers. The twins were thirteen when their father died (5.1.228-9, 232); the disguised Viola is described by Malvolio as 'not yet old enough for a man, nor young enough for a boy' (1.5.130) and an 'apple cleft in two' is not more like than the pair of them (5.1.207-8). Though obviously beardless, Sebastian is a skilful swordsman (even if Viola is not). Orsino is described as of 'fresh and stainless youth' though he has a beard (1.5.214, 3.1.38-9); since he believes that a husband should be older than his wife (2.4.27-8), he may be assumed to be a little older than both Olivia and Viola. Whether or not he is as young as the four lovers, Sir Toby, like Touchstone in *As You Like It* (5.4.55-6), pressing in among the 'country copulatives', anticipates the dénouement by taking the 'little villain' Maria as his wife, an action presaged in the jesting remarks of Feste at 1.5.22-4 and of Sir Toby himself at 2.5.150, and performed, it would seem, as early as 4.2, as line 57 suggests. Convinced, on any count, that 'care's an enemy to life', he has brought in a suitor for Olivia, even if it is the fatuous Sir Andrew Aguecheek. As incorrigible a 'gull-catcher' as Maria, Sir Toby also uses him as his own 'dear manikin' from whom he can extract a steady supply of money.

Sentiment, which motivates Olivia's desire to become a weeping recluse (though Feste soon prompts her to laugh again, and she is without a veil when Cesario arrives at her gate), is also characteristic of the moody Orsino, the duke or perhaps simply a count of Illyria—Shakespeare seems to have wavered in his conception.[2] Having loved the image of Olivia for a month before the play opens, he continues to protest his love for three more months even before he has a chance to speak to her directly.³ Like Romeo infatuated with fair Rosaline, he is obsessed with the idea of being in love. His inconstancy of mood is emphasised in the first seven lines of the play when, calling for an excess of music in order that his appetite for it may sicken, he at once demands that the musicians repeat one particular strain because of its 'dying fall', but before he has spoken three more lines his appetite has already sickened, and he orders them to desist altogether.⁴ At the end of this opening speech he foreshadows the hasty replacement of the initial object of his affection that will occur in Act 5 by acknowledging here the capricious quality of love: whatever is held of greatest worth may 'fall into abatement and low price'. Yet as a result of the homage and solicitude of his young page, who bravely masks her own emotions in order to woo Olivia on his behalf, he comes by the end of the last act to recognise the value of the devotion she has tendered to him.

With Olivia and her o'erhasty marriage to Sebastian, the case is different. Shakespeare explains it with a metaphorical reference to bowling; in her case, 'nature in her bias drew in that'. Although it may be Olivia's own tendency to sentiment that prompts her to become so quickly enamoured of the disguised Cesario, her counter-wooing has the function of predisposing her to love Sebastian in accord with nature's bias. The rationale behind this quite absurd situation is, Porter Williams notes, much like that of the lover in Donne's 'The Good-morrow':

> If ever any beauty I did see,
> Which I desired and got, 'twas but a dream
>   of thee.⁵

Still, Olivia remains sufficiently cool-headed to take the wondering but infinitely pliable Sebastian-supposed-Cesario to a nearby chantry to plight their troth before a holy man.

Contrasting with the sentimental Orsino and Olivia is Viola, the charming but quite practical flotsam of the sea who quickly sets about improving her situation. Informed that she cannot serve Olivia, she at once determines to disguise herself as a page and serve the noble Orsino, known to her father and, fortuitously it seems, still a bachelor. Within three days she has endeared herself to him, so much so that he has unclasped to her the book even of his 'secret soul'. In the exchanges with Olivia and the 'lighter members' of her household, she conducts herself with great verbal skill, exhibiting a remarkable range of emotional responses, at times saucy, florid or outspoken, but in some situations she remains quite surprisingly taciturn. Though Antonio, having rescued her from the farcical duel with Sir Andrew, addresses her as Sebastian, she says nothing to interfere with his arrest as a pirate or to question him about the fate of her brother. She simply allows herself to hope that he is indeed alive. Her actions throughout can be said to be predicated on her view that time will untangle all things (2.2.37-8), this in accord with the commonplace doctrine (*topos*) that truth is the daughter of time (*veritas filia temporis*). Even in the final scene, when Orsino asks to take her hand and to see her in her woman's weeds, she says nothing more than that the captain who has them has been imprisoned at Malvolio's suit. When some forty lines later he again gives her his hand and declares that from this time on she is to be her 'master's mistress', she utters not a word. Nor does she say anything more for the remainder of the action. Yet underlying her variable responses and her taciturnity is an emotional constancy, well evoked in the lines beginning 'My father had a daughter loved a man' and culminating in the moving self-portrait of the figure of Patience smiling at grief (2.4.110-11).⁶

The clown Feste, mediating between the courtly milieu and Sir Toby's, is an irresistible figure. This results in large part from the fact that, actively engaged in both worlds, he distances himself from each by means of his witty and facetious comments. It is now accepted that Shakespeare's projection of the role of professional wit who wears the dress of the fool but does not wear motley in the brain, was the result of Robert Armin's entry into the Chamberlain's Company (probably in 1599). Early apprenticed to a goldsmith, Armin was also for some years a writer of ephemeral pamphlets and entertainments; these include an account of six 'natural' fools and a play exploiting the art of impersonation, in which he was adept. Two of the pamphlets he signed 'Clunnico del Curtanio Snuffe' and 'Clunnico del Mondo Snuffe', that is, Snuff, Clown of the Curtain Theatre and Snuff, Clown of the Globe. He was included in the list of actors in Jonson's *The Alchemist* in 1610, so at that date he was still a member of the King's Men, the title given to the Lord Chamberlain's Company on the accession of James I. He died five years later.⁷ The following lines, addressed to 'Honest, gamesom Robin Armine', attest to his skill and echo Viola's comment on Feste: 'This fellow is wise enough to play the fool' (3.1.50):

> So play thy part, be honest still with mirth,
> Then, when th'art in the tiring-house of earth;
> Thou being his servant whom all kings do
>   serve,
> Mayest for thy part well-played like praise
>   deserve:
> For in that tiring-house when either be,
> Y'are one man's men and equal in degree;
> So thou in sport the happiest men dost school
> To do as thou dost—wisely play the fool.
>   (John Davies, *Scourge of Folly* (1611))

Four years Shakespeare's junior, Armin would have been thirty or so when *Twelfth Night* was written, and the slightly wry speeches Feste is given seem intended to reflect a maturity of outlook that holds no illusions about the durable nature either of emotional situations or of practical circumstances. Hence his incorrigible begging and hence his stress both in words and in song on the transitory: youth is a stuff—a material thing—that will not endure; beauty is but a flower; present love is justified by present laughter since 'what's to come is still [i.e. always] unsure'. His wit is both corrective and apt. He uses his good fooling to remedy Olivia's displeasure at his truancy from her household and to persuade her of the folly of mourning a brother's soul which, after all, she *knows* is in heaven, and he pointedly remarks that Orsino's tailor should make him a doublet of changeable taffeta to accord with his changeable mind.

All in all, Feste seems to present through his nonsense a no-nonsense point of view. Accosting Cesario—though, ironically, it is in fact Sebastian—he speaks to him in his own highly ironic fashion:

> No, I do not know you, nor I am not sent to you by my lady to bid you come speak with her; nor your name is not Master Cesario; nor this is not my nose neither. Nothing that is so is so.
>
> (4.1.4-7)

In the next scene, as he impersonates Sir Topas the curate come to visit Malvolio the lunatic, he observes of his disguise:

> 'That that is, is', so I, being Master Parson, am Master Parson; for what is 'that' but 'that' and 'is' but 'is'?

Yet Cesario has declared to Olivia, in all truth, 'I am not what I am'; Sir Toby has said to Sir Andrew, with some truth, that 'not to be abed after midnight is to be up betimes'; even the dénouement of the play seems to go contrary to Feste's claim. When the twins are seen together, they seem so like that it is as if there were but one face, one voice and one manner of dress—that is, the *same* face, voice and dress but still two flesh-and-blood persons. To the others, struck with wonder at the sight, the identical appearance of the twins is declared to be, in the words of Orsino, 'A natural perspective, that is and is not!' Yet in so far as theatrical illusion has been achieved, the dénouement gives substance to Feste's claim, 'That that is, is', at least in Illyria.

The dissembling of one's true nature (conscious with Viola and Feste, unconscious with Orsino and Olivia) is highlighted in the figure of the steward Malvolio. The chief officer in Olivia's household—and one that she would not have miscarry for half of her dowry—he takes to his duties with seriousness and some pomposity. That these responsibilities would have included the preserving of discipline is shown by the rules for his household which a young nobleman, Anthony Browne, the second Viscount Montague, set down in 1595, at the age of twenty-one. The steward should 'in civil sort' reprehend and correct 'negligent and disordered persons', reforming them by his 'grave admonitions and vigilant eye', among these the 'riotous, the contentious, and quarrelous persons of any degree' as well as 'the frequenters of tabling, carding, and dicing in corners and at untimely hours and seasons'.[8]

But when Malvolio breaks in on the carousing Sir Toby, Sir Andrew and Feste, called to do so, it seems, by the countess herself as Maria has forewarned, he cannot be said to chide them 'in civil sort'. Rather he accuses the two knights of gabbling like tinkers, squeaking out—this of the mellifluous-voiced Feste—cobblers' catches as if they were in an ale-house. Such a rebuke by a social inferior is enough to set off Sir Toby and he rounds on him, 'Art any more than a steward?'; he then follows this up with one of the most quoted lines in the play, incorporating in it what Hazlitt termed an 'unanswerable answer':

> Does thou think because thou art virtuous there shall be no more cakes and ale?

Maria is also angered by his charge that she is at fault in providing the means for this 'uncivil rule', and she sums up for the others Malvolio's unpleasant qualities: he is a 'kind' of a puritan, that is, censorious, but one who is inconstantly so. He is, moreover, a time-server, an affected ass who imitates the behaviour of his betters, and is 'so crammed', she says, 'with his own excellencies' that he conceives of himself as worthy of the love of all. On these grounds she contrives the device of forging a love letter from the countess enjoining him to assume ridiculous behaviour and garb in order to secure her favour, a device which feeds his aspiration to become 'Count Malvolio'. Although Feste is not in the group which observes Malvolio's absurd response to the letter, he justifies his share in the 'interlude' on the grounds of Malvolio's having disparaged his ability as a jester, while Fabian justifies his on the grounds that Malvolio has brought him out of favour with his lady about a bear-baiting. The last of his officious actions, noted this time by Viola, is to have the kindly captain who has rescued her imprisoned on some unspecified charge. There is then in Malvolio's 'stubborn and uncourteous parts' sufficient motivation to justify Maria's trick. Intended 'to pluck on laughter', it begins to get out of hand with the confining of Malvolio in a dark room as a madman; at one moment, even Sir Toby wishes they were well rid of their knavery.

Yet Malvolio's lubricious self-projection, cunningly revealed in a day-dream-like soliloquy, is splendidly comic. He imagines himself as three months married to Olivia, now wearing a velvet gown and sitting in a chair of state, having just come from a day-bed where he has left her sleeping; he imagines how he will have 'seven' of his servants summon Sir Toby to his presence and how, after quenching his 'familiar smile' and saying, 'Cousin Toby, my fortunes having cast me on your niece', he will direct him to amend his ways. This fantasy on Malvolio's part is put into perspective when he appears before Olivia wearing yellow stockings and cross-garters, his face crimped into myriad lines by his incessant smiling. Even more startling to her than his dress is the 'ridiculous boldness' of his talk. Tipped off as she is by Maria's charge that he is 'for sure' tainted in his wits, she accepts his strange words as evidence that something is wrong and solicitously asks, 'Wilt thou go to bed, Malvolio?' Taking this in seriousness, since it accords with his secret desires, he responds, 'To bed? Ay, sweetheart, and I'll come to thee.'[9] The audacity of his response is further highlighted by Shakespeare's establishing the time-scheme by means of adroit references. At the end of the preceding scene (2.5), when Maria alerts the conspirators to hide in (or behind) a box-tree to spy on Malvolio, it is probably early morning since she comments that he has been 'yonder i'the sun practising behaviour to his own shadow this half hour'. In the exchange between Viola and the fool that opens this scene, Feste comments that foolery like the sun shines everywhere, which suggests that it is now midday. Thus Malvolio's avidity to go to bed at noon (as the Fool in *Lear* puts it) strikes an even more lubricious note.[10] From Shakespeare's time until the mid eighteenth century, the 'sportful malice' prompting the treatment of Malvolio seemed a just matter of comedy, but for Romantic and Victorian interpreters, as well as for some in the twentieth century, the ill-used steward came to seem a victim not of sport but of social discrimination.[11]

If Shakespeare's characterisation of Malvolio has stimulated a mixed reaction, so, too, has the structure of the play, some critics finding in it signs of hasty composition, though not so many as to distract a viewing audience. One discrepancy is the rank of Orsino, who is consistently called 'duke' in stage directions and speech headings and during two scenes of the first act but is otherwise called 'count'. In his careful analysis of the text, Robert K. Turner suggests that Shakespeare's conception of the character of Orsino changed during composition and that he decided to make him less of a figure of authority (such as Duke Theseus in *A Midsummer Night's Dream*) and more of a lover (like Count Claudio in *Much Ado about Nothing*).[12]

There are other inconsistencies and loose ends. On Viola's first entrance, when she resolves to serve Orsino, she gives as a qualification her ability to sing and to speak to him in many sorts of music, but when a song is required in the second act, it is Feste who performs. This has led some, including Dover Wilson, to postulate revision, a more radical explanation than is required in view of the favours Orsino has extended to Cesario, which have elevated him above the status of a mere performer: within three days' time (1.4.1-3) he is no longer a stranger to Orsino who has, within that short span, divulged to him his inmost sentiments (1.4.12-13).

Again one notes that it is Fabian who makes a 'third' in the espial of Malvolio's antics, rather than Feste as Maria had specified; yet at the end of Act 5, Feste is able to quote from the letter as if he, too, had been one of the eavesdroppers on Malvolio. In fact, what Maria first declares she intends for him—'some obscure epistles of love, wherein by the colour of his beard, the shape of his leg, the manner of his gait, the expressure of his eye, forehead, and complexion, he shall find himself most feelingly personated' (2.3.131-4)—does not concur with the letter that Malvolio reads aloud two scenes later—except, that is, for its amatory suggestiveness. One small inconsistency is in the two accounts of Antonio's sea fight with Orsino's galleys: for his part, Antonio denies (3.3.30) that it was of a 'bloody nature' whereas Orsino (5.1.45) speaks of the 'scathful grapple' directed against the finest of their ships, though the speech is also intended to acknowledge Antonio's valour even as a pirate. Finally, the appearance of Sir Andrew and Sir Toby with bleeding heads must be the result of a second encounter with Sebastian-supposed-Cesario (see Commentary and stage direction at 5.1.160), but this is not provided for in the text.

In spite of these inconsistencies and loose ends, there is much subtlety in Shakespeare's handling of his complex plot which is particularly evident when an attitude or an action or situation relating to one character is duplicated by another. This creates a 'twinning' effect that reinforces the central situation brought about by a pair of identical twins.[13] It is as if—to adapt Ulysses' words in *Troilus and Cressida*—many touches of nature make the whole world kin.

Despite the difference in the situation of the two heroines there is a similarity: both have lost their fathers and both, it would appear, have recently lost their brothers, but whereas Olivia would extravagantly mourn (even as Orsino would extravagantly love), Viola, trusting to her own escape as a promise of Sebastian's, reacts practically. Yet in the matter of falling in love the two heroines act alike, in that Viola freely extends her affection to Orsino without invitation on his part, even as Olivia extends hers to Cesario without any invitation except that suggested by her role as surrogate wooer. This makes for a slight touch of irony at the end of the first wooing scene, for when Cesario says 'Love make his heart of flint that you shall love', Viola does not know that she herself will turn out to be the inadvertent object of Olivia's love. The wish is also ironically cancelled with Sebastian's arrival in Illyria and the stunning alacrity with which he assents to a betrothal.

The two heroines are alike in their personal orientation. Viola's conviction that time will 'untangle' all things (*veritas filia temporis,* or, as the English proverb has it, 'time brings the truth to light' (Tilley T324)) is comparable to Olivia's (and Malvolio's) belief in 'fate' which is commented on below. The two are also alike in possessing the virtue of constancy, Viola in her devotion to Orsino, Olivia in her refusal to accept his suit. To Orsino's query in Act 5, 'Still so cruel?', she responds, 'Still so constant'. The emotional impact the twins make is, quite expectedly, alike; Olivia terms it an 'enchantment', Antonio a 'witchcraft'; the harsh denunciation he levels at Cesario-supposed-Sebastian for his seeming ingratitude is paralleled by that which Orsino levels at Cesario for the seeming betrayal of his trust.

Perhaps the most ingenious duplication is that between Olivia and Malvolio. She herself acknowledges their similarity of deportment: he is 'sad and civil', a kind of behaviour that she feels suits well with her own fortunes in love. When Maria informs her that he is surely tainted in his wits since he does nothing but smile, she confesses:

> I am as mad as he
> If sad and merry madness equal be.

And later she alludes to her own 'extracting frenzy', which has made her forget about his. Moreover, such sad and merry madness typifies the deportment of the other characters, whether it be the moody Orsino or the mad-brained Sir Toby; this is finely pinpointed in 4.1 when, out of the blue, Sir Andrew attacks Sebastian, who wonders incredulously: Are *all* the people mad? Again, in 4.3, Sebastian 'wrangles' with his reason, speculating in soliloquy whether it is he himself or Olivia who is mad. From the confines of the dark room Malvolio's words thus have special point when he asserts to Feste: 'I tell thee, I am as well in my wits as any man in Illyria.'

Malvolio also emphasises the similarity of his deportment to Olivia's when he writes assuring her that he has the benefit of his senses as well as she. But his assurance is comically belated; by the time Olivia hears the letter, read madly at first by Feste impersonating the 'mad' Malvolio and then straightforwardly by Fabian, she (like Orsino) has met with a happy corrective, first to her predisposition to grief and then to her infatuation with Cesario. In view of the psychological misrule prevailing in Illyria, it is not surprising that the word 'mad', together with its cognates (madness, madmen, madly), is used more frequently in this play than in any other in the canon, with *The Comedy of Errors,* and its double set of twins, a close rival.

Another point of likeness between Olivia and Malvolio is their willingness to justify their own desires by readily ascribing them to a power outside themselves called either 'fate' or 'fortune'. In the soliloquies following on Cesario's first visit, Olivia ponders how quickly she has caught the plague, questions her actions, and concludes:

> Fate, show thy force; ourselves we do not owe.
> What is decreed must be; and be this so.
> (1.5.265-6)

In writing to Malvolio, Maria simulates not only Olivia's hand but also this point of view when she specifies, 'Thy fates open their hands.' To Malvolio, willingly deluded by the letter's confirmation of his own desires, 'it is Jove's doing, and Jove make me thankful', a point he reiterates with supreme confidence after Olivia believes him to be mad:

> What can be said? Nothing that can be can come between me and the full prospect of my hopes. Well, Jove, not I, is the doer of this, and he is to be thanked![14]
> (3.4.71-3)

Even before Maria drops the letter, Malvolio prefaces his rationalising hope that Olivia might indeed love him, by saying ''Tis but fortune; all is fortune.' When Olivia pleads with Cesario-supposed-Sebastian to admit their betrothal, she echoes this point of view, urging him 'Fear not, Cesario, take thy fortunes up.'

This is, of course, what all the central characters do. If somewhat bewildered by the fortuitous opportunity to marry Olivia after the earlier 'malignancy' of his fate, Sebastian at once accepts 'this accident and flood of fortune', an acceptance that twins with Viola's attitude when, resolved to serve Orsino, she awaits whatever may be the outcome: 'What else may hap, to time I will commit.' The untangling of circumstances by the passage of time and the reliance on fortune and fate create, for characters 'of fresh and stainless youth', the sense of wonder that is proper to the ending of romantic comedy. For the lovers, the result, as it was earlier for Maria and Sir Toby, is to be marriage when 'golden time convents'. For Antonio and Sir Andrew, what's to come is still unsure. For Malvolio, the whirligig of time having also brought in its revenges, there is the hint that he may be entreated to a peace. For Feste, there is still the pleasure he takes in singing.

And, fittingly, in place of an epilogue, he is given a final song. This, while promising that the actors for their part will strive each day to please their audience, also provides a somewhat cryptic ending to the dramatic action. Commentators have ranged widely in their response to it. Eighteenth-century editors, followed by Dover Wilson and others in this century, reacted strongly to its seeming lack of relevance to the play or to the character of Feste; more recent commentators extract a bawdy and sexual import,[15] while still others find a strain of melancholy that harkens back to the potential within the play for violence and unhappiness—the arrest of Antonio, the (short-lived) anger of Orsino towards Olivia and Viola, perhaps even Sir Toby's harsh dismissal of the 'thin-faced knave' Sir Andrew. But since this potential is never actualised, Feste's song is perhaps more properly viewed as a means of breaking away from the Illyrian world of illusions with a return to the real world where it may—or it may not—rain every day. The song's cryptic nature, with its catch-phrase 'that's all one', may be particularly appropriate for the ending of a play with the subtitle 'What You Will'. . . .

Notes

[1] *Shakespeare and His Comedies*, pp. 176-7 n. Elsewhere ('Directions for *Twelfth Night*', *Shakespeare's Plays in Performance*, 1967, pp. 207-19, and reprinted in Palmer, *Casebook*, pp. 188-203) John Russell Brown presents a more elastic charting of the characters' ages.

[2] See p. 16 below and n. 4, and Textual Analysis, p. 153.

[3] As in other of Shakespeare's plays, there is a double-time scheme: the action requires three months for its fulfilment, but two consecutive days serve for the sequence of scenes. See Brown, 'Directions for *Twelfth Night*', where he correlates the references to time with the action.

[4] See Commentary (1.1.4) for Joseph H. Summers's suggestion of some comic stage business here.

[5] 'Mistakes in *Twelfth Night* and their resolution', p. 181, in Palmer, *Casebook*, originally published *PMLA* 76 (1961).

[6] Viola's taciturnity in the later part of Act 5 can, of course, be accounted for by the exigencies of the plot. Like his heroine earlier on, Shakespeare has a great many knots to untie. Having given her this moving speech when it applied so aptly to her emotional situation, he can assume (with the audience) that with its happy resolution, words are unnecessary.

[7] For a biographical account of Armin, see Jane Belfield, 'Robert Armin, citizen and goldsmith of London', *Notes and Queries* 225 (1980), 158-9, and M. C. Bradbrook, 'Robert Armin and *Twelfth Night*', in Palmer, *Casebook*, pp. 222-43 (originally published in *Shakespeare the Craftsman*, 1969).

[8] 'Booke of orders and rules', quoted by Muriel St Clare Byrne, 'The social background', in *A Companion to Shakespeare Studies,* ed. Granville-Barker and Harrison, pp. 204-5.

[9] For a reference in *A Transcript of the Registers of the Company of Stationers, 1554-1640,* ed. Edward Arber. 5 vols., 1875-94 to a ballad entitled 'goo to bed swete harte', see Commentary at 3.4.28.

[10] See Brown, 'Directions for *Twelfth Night*'.

[11] For an account of the theatrical history of the part of Malvolio see pp. 28-33 below.

[12] 'The text of *Twelfth Night*', pp. 128-38. Turner explains the consistency of stage directions and speech headings as a scribal normalising of foul papers. See Textual Analysis, pp. 152-4 below.

[13] See L. G. Salingar's detailed and perceptive account of this aspect of the play or what he calls 'points of contact' among the characters, 'The design of *Twelfth Night*', pp. 117-39.

[14] The frequency of references to Jove in a play not having a classical setting is often accounted for by the Act of Abuses (against profanity), but as Turner has pointed out ('Text of *Twelfth Night*', p. 136) 'God' appears about twice as often as the supposed substitute; this scarcely supports the notion of expurgation. See also Commentary at 2.5.142.

[15] See Hotson, pp. 167-72, for example, and John Hollander, '*Twelfth Night* and the morality of indulgence', *Sewanee Review* 67 (1959), 220-38.

J. A. Bryant, Jr. (essay date 1986)

SOURCE: "*Twelfth Night*," in *Shakespeare and the Uses of Comedy,* The University Press of Kentucky, 1986, pp. 165-78.

[*In the following essay, Bryant asserts that* Twelfth Night *is an iconoclastic work that challenges the reassuring conventions of romantic comedy.*]

Ever since the time of the Romantics, high praise for *Twelfth Night* has been one of the commonplaces of Shakespeare criticism. In our own time Leo Salingar has called it the "crowning achievement in one branch of his art";[1] and J. Dover Wilson, implicitly replying to Samuel Johnson, who complained that the latter half of the play "exhibits no just picture of life,"[2] has gone even farther: "That gem of his comic art, that condensation of life and (for those who know how to taste it rightly) elixir of life," were Wilson's superlatives; then he added, "He could never better this—and he never attempted to. He broke the mold—and passed on."[3] Other commentators have been more specific. Kenneth Muir, by way of introducing his comments on *Twelfth Night,* cites Barrett Wendell's characterization of the play as a masterpiece of recapitulation and goes on to note that it combines, among other things, the device of mistaken identity that has proved so successful in *The Comedy of Errors* (making the look-alike pair brother and sister, however, as in numerous Italian comedies); the use of the disguised heroine as emissary, "from the man she loves to the woman he loves," from *The Two Gentlemen of Verona;* the theme of friendship from *The Merchant of Venice;* the singing fool (a combination of Amiens and Touchstone); a Falstaffian character in Sir Toby; and a half-witted suitor from *The Merry Wives of Windsor.*[4] T. W. Baldwin has demonstrated that all this variety fits harmoniously into a frame that may well have been derived from Terence's *Andria;*[5] and both Salingar and C. L. Barber have attributed at least part of its unity of tone to a pervasive spirit of saturnalia, Barber adding that the play goes well beyond this in its "exhibition of the use and abuse of social liberty."[6] More recently Carolyn G. Heilbrun has touched briefly but persuasively upon the play as a celebration of androgyny;[7] and Walter N. King, in his introduction to a collection of essays on the play, has provided an able discussion of the subtly changing perspectives that threaten to bring most of its characters to complete bewilderment and frustration but, in the manner of similar perspectives in a metaphysical poem, ultimately find resolution.[8]

What many of these critics have been praising in *Twelfth Night* is the convention of romantic comedy—or rather the romantic version of Italianate comedy—which for Shakespeare's generation served, as it has for most generations since, to reassure audiences about civilized society's ability to renew itself. Joseph Summers, himself an admirer of *Twelfth Night,* finds the resolution of the play and hence its presumably implicit reassurances less than convincing. *Twelfth Night* is the climax of Shakespeare's early achievement, he writes, but at the same time it comes close to proclaiming the limitations of that achievement: "More obvious miracles are needed," he concludes, "for comedy to exist in a world in which evil also exists, not merely incipiently but with power."[9] Summers's reservation here also has to do with the convention of romantic comedy, which he understandably considers inadequate to represent real life. The details of his diagnosis are questionable, but not the insight that has prompted it: in Shakespearean comedy neither the dramatic convention nor the plot—nor even the special occasion if there is one—is ever more than incidentally determinative. Such things point not to the play but to the expectations that we in our habitual inattention to the complex way in which the world really works bring to the play and to other fictions, and in many cases to life itself.

The patterns of comedy that Shakespeare inherited, like patterns in other traditional forms of art, symbolized communal responses that his world still considered natural and valid—in particular, those responses involving the preservation of stability and order in a society which like its constituents was necessarily forever perishing. For the most part, we today are comfortable with those same responses and expect comic art to confirm their adequacy; thus Shakespeare's comedies still give most of us at least part of what we have always expected from comedy generally. Art, however, is not always the complaisant handmaiden of society. It is her nature, especially when endowed with the vitality of someone like Shakespeare, to deny as well as to confirm, to generate new responses to perennially recurring situations, and sometimes in the process to break as many icons as it preserves. As we have seen, even in such early and relatively conventional plays as *The Comedy of Errors* and *The Two Gentlemen of Verona* Shakespeare gave indications of the iconoclastic character that comic dramatic art was to assume under his hand. In *Love's Labor's Lost* and *The Merchant of Venice* he raised questions about human suffering, cruelty, and mortality that writers in fulfilling comedy's responsibility to entertain had traditionally elected to ignore. In *Much Ado about Nothing,* he challenged the propriety of comedy's traditional ending. In *As You Like It* he dared to suggest that the mold itself of comedy might ultimately be irrelevant. In short, hints about the limitations of conventional comedy had been lurking at the fringes of Shakespeare's vision all along, and the situation in *Twelfth Night* was calculated to make audiences uneasy almost from the outset.

To begin with, as Summers notes, there are no parents or their equivalent in *Twelfth Night,* and the young people are therefore free to make their own way. "According to the strictly romantic formula," Summers writes, "the happy ending should be already achieved at the beginning of the play."[10] Just the reverse is true, of course; and the reasons for that, though conspicuous, have apparently not been obvious to the play's admirers. First, Shakespeare at the beginning has provided no visible means of balancing the equation of lover and beloved that he has set before us. Olivia occupies the role of marriageable female in *Twelfth Night,* but she has no suitor that is both acceptable and available to her—no Fenton, no Orlando, no Ferdinand—until the beginning of Act IV, when Sebastian, who she thinks is the Cesario she knows, glides ready and able into her view. She could have Duke Orsino, but she will not. She would have Viola-Cesario, but cannot—for reasons that Viola, Antonio the sea captain, and we alone know. Thus for three acts the Duke pursues Olivia, Olivia pursues Viola, and Viola yearns for the Duke—a merry-go-round chase, a three-way stalemate, that has no prospect of resolution in matches until a fourth person arrives to turn Olivia out of the circle and make it possible for the other two to confront one another as pursuer and pursued.

Second, the absence of parents is not an unmixed blessing for any of the lovers in *Twelfth Night,* but it is an especially unfortunate circumstance for Olivia. In the normal course of a comic action, those filling the role of *senex* have subtle positive functions to perform as well as the more spectacular negative ones; and Olivia's parents and elder brother, all dead as the play begins, would have been expected at least to foster the idea of a good marriage for the girl and more than likely in the end to have come round to her way of thinking about an appropriate candidate. By convention they would have been faulty in their initial judgments about her best interests, but as sponsors distinguished by good will and protective instincts they would have been entitled to seats of honor at the prenuptial feast. As it is, Shakespeare's Olivia stands defenseless in a world that with the death of her brother has suddenly turned threatening. Orsino, whom she does not and apparently cannot love, relentlessly presses his suit, undoubtedly in part because he finds the love-game amusing but also in part because by marriage he would annex Olivia's estate. He has rivals in the latter objective. Commoner Malvolio, taking advantage of a social revolution that has recently made it possible for "the Lady of the Strachy" to marry her yeoman of the wardrobe (II.v.39-40), seeks to rise in the world from steward's quarters to his lady's chamber; and Sir Toby Belch, Olivia's sottish uncle and her next of kin, has presumed to stand *in loco parentis* and promote a suitor of his own.[11] We see no other suitors, but these are quite enough to show the dangerous situation of a landed and wealthy young female in Shakespeare's world, where authority over land and wealth was expected to be vested ultimately in a suitable male. Hence Olivia assumes a mask of grief, not necessarily out of self-love or whimsy (as has been commonly assumed by critics and producers of the play) and perhaps not even out of genuine grief, but out of an urgent need to protect her own interests. Despite her declared intention to mourn for an improbable seven years, the convention of mourning can serve at best as a temporary stay; but that convention is the only protection she has. Into this strained situation Viola enters to become unwittingly a fourth suitor for Olivia's hand—in Olivia's eyes the only suitor, and in the eyes of others, including eventually even Orsino, an impudent interloper to be dealt with contemptuously and with appropriate violence.

One might argue, especially in this last quarter of the twentieth century, that Olivia's need to be rescued by a strong male is to her discredit—that her position is only as parlous as she herself chooses to let it be. So it is; and so can it be considered in the world that Shakespeare creates in his plays, for repeatedly these invite approval for the threatened female who seizes the male role in a male-dominated society and triumphs over the disadvantages that society has imposed on her own sex. The fact remains, however, that Shakespeare lived in and depicted a society in which the woman who does not escape by extraordinary means must settle for being either an ornament or a slave. Moreover, even those who resort to extraordinary means may escape only temporarily—witness Julia, Portia, and Rosalind, all of whom presumably put off their masculine garments and return to live ever after in the subservient role that society has assigned to them. Angry Kate's ironic note, for all we know, was not detected until fairly recently. And Beatrice's concluding remark to Benedick is as follows: "I would not deny you, but by this good day, I yield upon great persuasion, and partly to save your life, for I was told you were in a consumption" (V.iv.94-97). To this, editors since the eighteenth century would have us believe, Benedick replies with a mouth-stopping kiss.[12] Shakespeare, however, apparently gave the quieting to an embarrassed Leonato, who told his irreverent niece, "Peace, I will stop your mouth," and perhaps applied a gesture of a different sort.

In Illyria, consensus about the natural dependency of women seems to be fairly solid. Malvolio is convinced that his mistress is secretly yearning for an appropriate man to take charge, and so when Maria applies the bait to his vanity, he is apt to believe he is that very man. Duke Orsino, denied admittance by the conventions of mourning, continues to make advances through his messengers and tells the last of these, Viola disguised as Cesario, that the problem with Olivia is her woman's inability to comprehend the depth and seriousness of the passion that men may feel:

> Alas, their love [i.e., women's] may be called appetite,
> No motion of the liver, but the palate,
> That suffer surfeit, cloyment, and revolt,
> But mine is all as hungry as the sea,
> And can digest as much. Make no compare
> Between that love a woman can bear me
> And that I owe Olivia.
>
> [II.iv.97-103]

Even Sir Andrew Aguecheek assumes that Olivia is ready for appropriate male advances and recoils in something between indignation and disgust when he spies her making what he believes to be overtures to the Duke's messenger: "No, faith, I'll not stay a jot longer. . . . Marry, I saw your niece do more favors to the Count's servingman than ever she bestow'd upon me. I saw't i' th' orchard" (III.ii.1-7). Sir Toby moves quickly to disabuse him, but Toby is clearly of like mind about women. He resents Olivia's declared state of mourning as a feminine frivolity that interferes with his more serious plans. "What a plague means my niece to take the death of her brother thus?" he fumes to

Maria (I.iii.1-2); and in the exchange that follows he details Sir Andrew's qualifications as a lover and thereby further reveals his obtuseness where Olivia's predilections are concerned. Fortunately for her, Sir Toby's implementation of his plans is as inefficient as his judgments about women are erroneous. The proposed duel between Sir Andrew and Cesario backfires upon the head, literally, of its perpetrator, though one should recognize here that but for the lucky presence of Sebastian on the scene to take the challenge intended for Cesario, that duel and the action of the play might have ended quite differently. Unseen by all these watchful males, however, is a clever Olivia driven to extraordinary means of her own, who will abandon proprieties and confound definitions by pursuing forthrightly and then marrying on the spot a young man of no station whatever.

In more ways than one Viola is a counterpart to Olivia. She too is parentless; she has also lost a brother, or thinks she has; and she has put on a pretense for essentially the same reason as Olivia—to protect herself against such predators as may be at large in the presumably civilized world of Illyria. The device Viola has chosen, however, has placed her in an awkward situation. No sooner has she put on male attire and enlisted in the Duke's service than she falls in love with her master, who requires her to advance his cause with a lady manifestly amenable to being woed by someone—though not by the Duke, either directly or indirectly.

This improbable situation is the source for several aspects of the play that have charmed modern audiences—most of these being touches of pathos rather than of comedy. Viola's best speeches are cases in point. For example, she tells Olivia at their first meeting that if she were Duke Orsino she would

> Make me a willow cabin at your gate,
> And call upon my soul within the house;
> Write loyal cantons of contemned love,
> And sing them loud even in the dead of night;
> Hallow your name to the reverberate hills,
> And make the babbling gossip of the air
> Cry out "Olivia!"
>
> [I.v.268-74]

Her language here speaks of a more intense experience than brief infatuation would warrant. Some critics have postulated a justification for it in Marsilian-Platonist terms,[13] but one is probably nearer the spirit of the play to see it as something quaintly amusing, the mysterious attraction of a scarcely grown moth for an unresponsive star. Nevertheless, Viola's argument here has the power of a nascent but very real love for the Duke; and the same bittersweet passion of young love informs the account she gives to him of the depth of women's affection as demonstrated by the unspoken adoration of her "father's daughter":

> . . . she never told her love
> But let concealment like a worm in th' bud
> Feed on her damask cheek; she pin'd in thought,
> And with a green and yellow melancholy
> She sate like Patience on a monument,
> Smiling at grief.
>
> [II.iv.110-15]

Because she is apt to feel such stirrings as no longer trouble the Duke, which indeed the Duke for all his declarations about masculine love can no longer even recall, Viola moves in company with Euphrasia-Bellario of Beaumont and Fletcher's *Philaster* (1608-10), the determined Helena of *All's Well That Ends Well*, and the Imogen of *Cymbeline*. Like these, Viola is genuinely and, to speak literally, hopelessly in love; but the special irony of the situation that develops in Act I is that Olivia is no less genuinely in love and in her misapplied affection exhibits to Viola precisely the kind of intense feeling that Viola chides her for not rendering to the Duke.

If we were not dealing with characters whom Shakespeare has endowed with flesh and blood, we might say that Viola is the love-in-idleness in this second play that Shakespeare wrote about "midsummer madness" (III.iv.56). Before her coming, there was no genuine love in Illyria. Her arrival there set all in motion, activating Olivia's suitors to an intensity that had previously seemed unwarranted and, more important, pushing the hitherto diffident Olivia out from behind her façade of grief to discover possibilities in the world that she had not dreamed of. Her newly found love, though it has some of the aspects of the ultimately divine fixation that Marsilio Ficino, Castiglione, and countless sonneteers have written about, is no more Neoplatonic than Viola's equally sudden love for the Duke. One might better say that the love manifested by these two women has an agapeic quality in that it prompts one of them, denied of her station and even of her sex, to offer services and devotion to a duke who barely notices her as anything more than a servant, and prompts the other, a lady of acknowledged station, to spurn suitors at all appropriate levels—duke, knight, and competent steward—to throw herself shamelessly upon a page boy.

Where Olivia is concerned, however, it is important to note that Shakespeare in presenting her initial awakening to the universal call of the flesh depicts it as an unconscious appreciation of that androgynous ideal which is normally conceived in youth and subsequently suppressed in adulthood, here beautifully portrayed by Viola as woman-man and reinforced subliminally for the Elizabethan audience by the boy-actors who were portraying both female characters on the stage. Regardless of how one tries to explain this love, there is much in it that remains inexplicable; and Shakespeare's portrayal continues to succeed with readers and audiences undoubtedly in part because most people subconsciously want something like it to be true and are delighted when Shakespeare's art can bring their wishes to a semblance of reality. Unfortunately, our latter-day conventions, translated into expectations, encourage us to discredit the genuine and innocent warmth present here and in similar situations in other Shakespearean plays and thus prevent our acknowledgment of emotional tremors which even now we hasten to dismiss as inchoate feelings, childish preludes to adult emotions that are presumably more stable and lasting, and in any case more respectable.

Nevertheless, regardless of how seriously one takes the suggestions of agapeic or androgynous attachments in *Twelfth Night,* one should never lose sight of the heterosexual grounding that is essential to the comic resolution achieved in the play. All the lovers here ultimately demand for satisfaction the physical possession of a member of the opposite sex. Olivia could not have been happy with Viola indefinitely, for all the beauty of Viola's face and form; and Orsino, attuned to practical considerations, finds it possible to disregard Viola's charms until he recognizes that they are as feminine in fact as they appear to be. Moreover, sexual attraction is all that really matters. Rank apparently has nothing to do with love and loving in *Twelfth Night*. In spite of the outrage Toby expresses at the thought of a steward's aspiring to take the hand of his niece, he does not hesitate to marry Maria, Olivia's diminutive gentlewoman ("the youngest wren of nine"), whom he mockingly dubs Penthesilea and repeatedly calls "wench." Olivia herself has no compunction about marrying someone she takes to be a serving-man; and even after the unveiling in Act V neither she nor the Duke gains any substantial knowledge about the pedigree of the twins they are linking permanently to their fortunes. One looks in vain here for some hint of what is clearly set forth in Barnaby Riche's *Apolonius and Silla:* that the two were actually children of another illustrious duke, Pontus of Cyprus, and worthy to mate with nobility anywhere.[14] In short, practical and even spiritual motives for love ultimately give way in Shakespeare's *Twelfth Night* to elemental sex, and thus the ancient order of society as understood by commentators—political, ecclesiastical, and otherwise—painfully maintained over the centuries and presumably divinely ordained, is here challenged by the basic animal impulses that are the reason, often unacknowledged, why society is essentially not an institution at all but a process.

This reduction of comedy in *Twelfth Night* to the ground of its being intensifies an ironic dimension in the gulling of Malvolio that is often overlooked in modern readings and productions, which persist in ignoring the complex effects of the play. To begin with, Malvolio is not a mere appendage to the plot; nor is he the insensitive killjoy and social climber that Sir Toby sees or the "time pleaser" Maria would have him be. As one critic has observed, Malvolio's part is structurally at the center of the plot and his gulling is symbolic of the challenge to order that persists throughout the play.[15] There is truth in both observations. The setting of Shakespeare's comedies, regardless of designation, is invariably English; and as Shakespeare and his contemporaries knew, the ranks of the English gentry included more than a few families that had achieved their status relatively recently. Lady Olivia's all but defunct family has the marks of being one of these; at the very least, Sir Toby, the one surviving elder member of the family, still has the class-consciousness of the newly arrived and the tavern manners of a serving-man. Malvolio, by contrast, has the marks of a belated aspirant, quite as class-conscious as Toby but awkwardly so, and as zealously committed as any newly arrived neophyte to the preservation of order, precedence, and propriety. Charles Lamb's view of him is not currently popular, but it is closer to the truth and infinitely preferable to the farcical Malvolio that simpers and prances on some stages. Consider this passage from Lamb's essay:

> His quality is at the best unlovely, but neither buffoon nor contemptible. His bearing is lofty, a little above his station, but probably not much above his deserts. . . . We must not confound him with the eternal old, low steward of comedy. He is master of the household to a great Princess, a dignity probably conferred upon him for other respects than age or length of service. . . . His rebuke to the knight, and his sottish revelers, is sensible and spirited; and when we take into consideration the unprotected condition of his mistress, and the strict regard with which her state of real or dissembled mourning would draw the eyes of the world upon her house affairs, Malvolio might feel the honor of the family in some sort in his keeping; as it appears not that Olivia had any more brothers, or kinsmen, to look to it—for Sir Toby had dropped all such nice respects at the buttery hatch.[16]

This is a Malvolio who makes the tactical error of forthrightly confronting one who is technically his superior for indulging in a form of gaiety that has in it no real love of life (Maria calls it "caterwauling") and certainly no consideration for others, and thus finds himself both rebuked by that superior and caught in a mill devised by a fellow servant (again Maria) who also aspires to a higher station no less than he, though with far less warrant. Malvolio is right to regard all of his tormentors with contempt. Maria's ingenuity probably makes her the best of the lot. Sir Toby is a bore as well as a boor. Fabian is an insensitive servingman, whom Malvolio has properly rebuked for staging a bear-baiting on the estate (II.v.7-11), Feste is at best (except for the actual gulling scene) a second-rate clown, and Sir Andrew is a fool. Fabian observes at the end that their mischief has been such as "may rather pluck on laughter than revenge, / If that the injuries be justly weigh'd / That have on both sides pass'd"; but Fabian the bear-baiter is hardly one to give a reliable opinion. Malvolio may be deficient in humor, and he is certainly naive; but he has injured no one, and he has every cause to be angry. Moreover, the gulling that destroys him destroys the last conscious defender of the graceful world to which he would aspire.

Mark Van Doren, who also considered Malvolio central to *Twelfth Night,* concluded his essay on the play with the following sentence: "The drama is between his [Malvolio's] mind and the music of old manners."[17] This is true, but perhaps not quite in the way Van Doren intended. For Van Doren the important thing about the play was its courtly decor, lyrics that could be set to appealing music, carefree roistering belowstairs, expressions of romantic love followed by appropriate matings. Considered solely in the light of these things, *Twelfth Night* appears to be a triumph of sophistication and wit and a reaffirmation of the values of conventional Italianate comedy. Actually it is nothing of the sort.

As has already been noted, *Twelfth Night* presents a world in which the opportunity for undertaking a comic action and pursuing it to the conventional conclusion has collapsed. Control of the social unit that occupies the center of our attention, Lady Olivia's estate, has passed for the moment to that lady's keeping; and because she is young, female, and unprotected, the wolves are circling. Wit characteristic of the old order is still present: for all her pretense of grief, Olivia has a large measure of it, and Viola brings in still more; but in the empty corridors where these two meet, its sparkle has more poignancy than brilliance. Music is still present, at least on the periphery of the main action, but music in *Twelfth Night* no longer symbolizes the harmony and order that comedy would achieve or restore. Of the two memorable lyrics in the play, the one that celebrates young love in its immediacy, "O mistress mine," is caterwauled by the aging Sir Toby and company. The other is a lament for a dead love that cannot be revived: "Come away, come away, Death." A number of older critics—F. G. Fleay, Richmond Noble, and J. Dover Wilson—suggested that this sophisticated piece of melancholy replaced the "old and antique song" that the text calls for (II.iv.3) when Robert Armin, a clown with a trained voice, performed the singing function originally intended for a singing boy who would play the part of Viola posing as a eunuch (I.ii.62). S. L. Bethell, after summarizing the whole argument, pointed out sensibly that it is sufficient the song be "romantically suggestive of antiquity," as indeed it is.[18] Orsino in asking for the song notes that it differs sharply from the "light airs and recollected terms / Of these brisk and giddy-paced times" (II.iv.5-6) and thus makes the point of the play: that the old times are beyond recall; the old order is dead. He speaks with more truth than he knows or would like to believe. No amount of music can bring back the world in which courtship of the kind he would pursue can exist. Maria knows this. Olivia shows by her actions that she knows it too. Viola, but for her infatuation with Orsino and her loyalty to him, would know it sooner than she does. Malvolio, who has been outside the magic circle all his life, does not know it and thus is apt to be tricked by a spurious invitation to join in the (to him) unfamiliar dance. Still inexperienced in spite of his years, he has no way of recognizing that the show of courtly manners he is urged to assume can only be an inadvertent parody and a reaffirmation of his incompetence to participate in a game that people are no longer playing. His incorrigible loneliness is merely accentuated by the folly that a heartless anarchy has thrust upon him.

A production of *Twelfth Night* at Stratford-upon-Avon some years ago solved the problem of Malvolio by playing him for laughs and reducing him to little more than a stick figure with the diminished humanity of a Keystone Cop from the early cinema. The gulling thus became a harmless trick perpetrated on one who had neither dignity nor the capacity to feel. What was left in that production, however, was hardly the graceful apotheosis of Italianate comedy for which Shakespeare "broke the mold—and passed on." Even Shakespeare's language, which was largely uncut, was insufficient to prevent the general charges by London critics of prosiness and farce; the balance had been disrupted, and the illusion dispelled. The glitter was tinsel.[19] One production, of course, proves nothing about a Shakespeare play; but *Twelfth Night* may best be regarded as an elaborate *trompe l'oeil.* Superficially it resembles Italianate comedy, but actually it is the apotheosis of a development that Shakespeare had been anticipating ever since he portrayed the French ladies at the court of Navarre. It is already a part of the era in which a Helena and a Mariana would resort to bed tricks to snare reluctant males, an Imogen put off her sex to go after a husband who had rejected her, a Hermione retire for sixteen years, freeze a kingdom, and take her man at the end by a trick, and an innocent and uninstructed Miranda out-woo and out-argue a prince who most likely would have preferred a casual seduction. Dr. Johnson was understandably disturbed by the ending of *Twelfth Night,* but he was wrong to say that it exhibits no just picture of life. Like most of his contemporaries, he was guided by expectations that are essentially inapplicable to this play except by way of ironic contrast. For him it exhibited no picture of life that he could comfortably accept, but one suspects he saw well enough what was there.

Notes

[1] Leo Salingar, "The Design of *Twelfth Night,*" *Shakespeare Quarterly,* 9 (1958), 117.

[2] In Johnson's edition of *The Plays of William Shakespeare* (London, 1765); see *Johnson as Critic,* ed. John Wain (London & Boston: Routledge & Kegan Paul, 1973), pp. 188-89.

[3] J. Dover Wilson, *Shakespeare's Happy Comedies* (Evanston, Ill.: Northwestern Univ. Press), p. 181.

[4] Kenneth Muir, *The Sources of Shakespeare's Plays* (New Haven, Conn.: Yale Univ. Press, 1977), p. 132.

[5] T.W. Baldwin, *William Shakespere's Five-Act Structure* (Urbana: Univ. of Illinois Press, 1947), p. 715.

[6] Salingar, *Shakespeare and the Traditions of Comedy* (Cambridge: Cambridge Univ. Press, 1974), pp. 8-19; Barber, *Shakespeare's Festive Comedy* (Princeton, N.J.: Princeton Univ. Press, 1959), pp. 248ff.

[7] Carolyn G. Heilbrun, *Toward a Recognition of Androgyny* (New York: Knopf, 1973), pp. 36-37.

[8] Walter N. King, ed., *Twentieth Century Interpretations of "Twelfth Night"* (Englewood Cliffs, N.J.: Prentice-Hall, 1968), pp. 5-12.

[9] Joseph Summers, "The Masks of *Twelfth Night*," *The University of Kansas City Review,* 22 (Autumn 1955), 30-32.

[10] Ibid., p. 24.

[11] Some critics see in Sir Toby's advocacy of Sir Andrew Aguecheek merely a device to bilk the fool of his money; see Van Doren, *Shakespeare* (Garden City, N.Y.: Anchor-Doubleday, 1953), p. 139. This does not quite account, however, for Sir Toby's eagerness to press for a duel with Cesario-Viola once he has detected a hint of real rivalry in that quarter.

[12] According to *The Riverside Shakespeare* ed. G. Blakemore Evans (Boston: Houghton Mifflin, 1974), p. 364, the attribution of the speech to Benedick and the stage direction about kissing originated with Styan Thirlby and Lewis Theobald, respectively.

[13] See John Vyvyan, *Shakespeare and Platonic Beauty* (London: Chatto & Windus, 1961), pp. 33-62.

[14] See the text in Geoffrey Bullough, *Narrative and Dramatic Sources of Shakespeare* (London: Routledge & Kegan Paul, 1957), II, 346.

[15] See the essay by Milton Crane, "*Twelfth Night* and Shakespearian Comedy," *Shakespeare Quarterly,* 6 (1955), 1-8.

[16] Charles Lamb, "On Some of the Old Actors," in *Elia. Essays which have appeared under the signature in The London Magazine* (London: Taylor & Hessey, 1823); quoted in Herschel Baker, ed., *Twelfth Night* (New York: New American Library, 1965), pp. 172-73.

[17] Van Doren, *Shakespeare,* p. 143.

[18] S. L. Bethell, *Shakespeare and the Popular Dramatic Tradition* (Durham, N.C.: Duke Univ. Press, 1944), p. 178.

[19] This was a summer production of 1966. Sir Andrew Aguecheek was given unusual prominence, with David Warner in the role.

FESTE

Joan Hartwig (essay date 1973)

SOURCE: "Feste's 'Whirligig' and the Comic Providence of *Twelfth Night*," in *ELH,* Vol. 40, No. 4, Winter, 1973, pp. 501-13.

[*In the essay that follows, Hartwig contends that Feste helps illuminate the discrepancy between human will and Providence in* Twelfth Night *and proposes that Feste's enigmatic final song emphasizes the ambiguities of human experience—which is neither as grim as the clown's pessimistic verses nor as blissful as romantic comedy.*]

Shakespeare's plays frequently counterpose the powers of human and of suprahuman will, and the antithesis usually generates a definition of natures, both human and suprahuman. These definitions vary, however, according to the play. For instance, Hamlet's "providence" does not seem the same as the darker, equivocating power that encourages Macbeth to pit his will against a larger order; and these controls differ from Diana and Apollo in the later plays, *Pericles* and *The Winter's Tale*. Furthermore, Hamlet's submission and Macbeth's submission to non-human controls (if indeed they do submit their individual wills) cannot be understood as the same action or even to imply the same kind of human vision.

Many of the conflicts of *Twelfth Night* seem to be concerned with the contest between human will and suprahuman control; yet, the latter manifests itself in various ways and is called different names by the characters themselves.[1] As each contest between the human will and another designer works itself out, the involved characters recognize that their will is fulfilled, but not according to their planning. The individual's will is finally secondary to a design that benevolently, but unpredictably, accords with what he truly desires.² For example, when Olivia, at the end of Act I, implores Fate to accord with her will in allowing her love for Cesario to flourish, she has no idea that her will must be circumvented for her own happiness. Yet the substitution of Sebastian for Cesario in her love fulfills her wishes more appropriately than her own design could have done. Inversely, when Duke Orsino says in the opening scene that he expects to replace Olivia's brother in her "debt of love," he doesn't realize that literally he will become her "brother" (I.i.34-40). As the closing moments of the play bring Olivia and the Duke together on the stage for the only time, she says to him, "think me as well a sister as a wife" (V.i.307); and the Duke responds in kind: "Madam, I am most apt t' embrace your offer," and a bit later, "Meantime, sweet sister, / We will not part from hence" (V.i.310, 373-74). The Duke had not understood the literal force of his prediction, but his early statement of his hope plants a subtle suggestion for the audience. When the play's action accords with Duke Orsino's "will," the discrepancy between intention and fulfillment is a delightful irony which points again to the fact that "what you will" may be realized, but under conditions which the human will cannot manipulate. Orsino's desire to love and be loved, on the other hand, is fulfilled by his fancy's true queen, Viola, more appropriately than his design for Olivia would have allowed.

The one character whose true desires are not fulfilled in the play is Malvolio. His hope to gain Olivia in marriage results in public humiliation at the hands of Feste, who takes obvious satisfaction in being able to throw Malvolio's former haughty words back at him under their new context of Malvolio's demonstrated foolishness:

> Why, 'some are born great, some achieve greatness, and some have greatness thrown upon them.' I was one, sir, in this interlude, one Sir Topas, sir; but that's all one. 'By the Lord, fool, I am not mad!' But do you remember, 'Madam, why laugh you at such a barren rascal? An you smile not, he's gagged'? And thus the whirligig of time brings in his revenges.
>
> (V.i.360-66)

Feste's assertion that the "whirligig of time" has brought this revenge upon Malvolio neglects the fact that Maria has been the instigator and Feste the enforcer of the plot to harass Malvolio. Time's design, insofar as Malvolio is concerned, depends upon Maria's and Feste's will, which differs significantly from a central point that the main plot makes—that human will is not the controller of events. The characters in the main plot learn from the play's confusing action that human designs are frequently inadequate for securing "what you will," and that a design outside their control brings fulfillment in unexpected ways. Feste's fallacy, of course, makes the results of the subplot *seem* to be the same as the results of the main plot, but Time's revenges on Malvolio are primarily human revenges, and this particular measure for measure is thoroughly within human control.³ Feste's justice allows no mitigation for missing the mark in human action; and the incipient cruelty that his precise justice manifests is felt, apparently, by other characters in the play.

When Olivia and her company hear Malvolio's case, she responds with compassion: "Alas, poor fool, how have they baffled thee! . . . He hath been most notoriously abused" (V.i.359, 368). Duke Orsino, upon hearing Malvolio's letter of explanation, comments, "This savors not much of distraction" (V.i.304). And even Sir Toby has become uneasy about the harsh treatment of Malvolio in the imprisonment scene: "I would we were well rid of this knavery. If he may be conveniently delivered, I would he were; for I am now so far in offense with my niece that I cannot pursue with any safety this sport to the upshot" (IV.ii.66-70). Actually, to place the responses into this sequence reverses the play's order; and we should consider the fact that Shakespeare builds *toward* a compassionate comment, with Olivia's statement climaxing an unwillingness to condone the actions of Feste and Maria in gulling Malvolio—at least in its last phase. Feste's exact form of justice without mercy has always characterized revenge, and even the word "revenge" is stressed by several of the characters in the subplot. When Maria voices her apparently spontaneous plot to gull Malvolio, she says:

> The devil a Puritan that he is . . . the best persuaded of himself; so crammed, as he thinks, with excellencies that it is his grounds of faith that all that look on him love him; and on that vice in him will my revenge find notable cause to work.
>
> (II.iii.134-40)

Maria's successful implementation of her "revenge" elicits Sir Toby's total admiration. At the end of II.v, he exclaims, "I could marry this wench for this device" (168), and when Maria appears soon thereafter, he asks, "Wilt thou set thy foot o' my neck?" (174). The battlefield image of the victor and the victim is mock-heroic, of course; but in the final scene Fabian testifies to its literal fruition: "Maria writ / The letter, at Sir Toby's great importance, / In recompense whereof he hath married her" (V.i.352-54). Sir Toby's submission to Maria's will is a comic parallel for two actions: the pairing off of lovers, and the submission of the individual's will to a design other than his own. Yet the inclusion of a parodic version of marriage-harmony in the subplot does not fully ease the discomfort of the subplot's conclusion. Fabian tries to smooth it away when he suggests that the "sportful malice" of gulling Malvolio "may rather pluck on laughter than revenge" (V.i.355-58).⁴ Neither Feste nor Malvolio seems to be convinced, however. Feste's "whirligig of time brings in his revenges," and Malvolio quits the stage with, "I'll be revenged on the whole pack of you!" (V.i.366-67). The forgiveness that should conclude the comic pattern is "notoriously" missing from the subplot and cannot be absorbed successfully by the Duke's line, "Pursue him and entreat him to a peace." Malvolio seems unlikely to return. The major differences between the subplot and the main plot is clearest at this dramatic moment: revenge is a human action that destroys; love, graced by the sanction of a higher providence, creates a "golden time."

Feste's "whirligig" seems to be a parody of Fortune's wheel in its inevitable turning, particularly with its suggestions of giddy swiftness and change.[5] It provides a perfect image for the wild but symmetrical comic conclusion of the play's action. Feste's speech which includes it gives the appearance of completion to a mad cycle of events over which no human had much control. Only in Malvolio's case was human control of events evident. In her forged letter, Maria caters to Malvolio's "will" and, by encouraging him to accept his own interpretation of circumstances as his desire dictates,[6] she leads him not only into foolishness, but also into a defense of his sanity. The discrepancy between Malvolio's assumption that fortune is leading him on his way and the fact that Maria is in charge of his fate manifests itself clearly in the juxtaposition of her directions to the revelers (as she leaves the stage) with Malvolio's lines as he enters:

> MARIA Get ye all three into the box tree. . . .
> Observe him, for the love of mockery; for I know this letter will make a contemplative idiot of him. Close, in the name of jesting. [*The others hide.*] Lie thou there [*throws down a letter*]; for here comes the trout that must be caught with tickling. *Exit.*
>
> *Enter Malvolio.*
> MALVOLIO 'Tis but fortune; all is fortune. Maria once told me she [Olivia] did affect me.
>
> (II.v.13-22)

The gulling of Malvolio which follows is hilariously funny, partly because Malvolio brings it all on himself. Even before he finds the letter, his assumptions of rank and his plans for putting Sir Toby in his place elicit volatile responses from the box tree. And after he finds the forged letter, Malvolio's self-aggrandizing interpretations of the often cryptic statements evoke howls of glee mixed with the already disdainful laughter. The comedy of this scene is simple in its objective exploitation of Malvolio's self-love, and Malvolio becomes an appropriately comic butt. The audience's hilarity is probably more controlled than Sir Toby's and the box tree audience's excessive laughter; still, we are united in laughing at Malvolio's foolishness. And when Malvolio appears in his yellow stockings and cross-garters, the visual comedy encourages a total release in the fun of the game—Malvolio is gulled and we need not feel the least bit guilty, because he is marvelously unaware of his own foolishness. Oblivious to any reality but his own, Malvolio thinks he is irresistibly appealing with his repugnant dress and his continuous smiles—so contrary to his usual solemnity—and Olivia concludes that he has gone mad. "Why, this is very midsummer madness," she says, and, then, as she is leaving to receive Cesario, she commends Malvolio to Maria's care.[7]

> Good Maria, let this fellow be looked to. Where's my cousin Toby? Let some of my people have a special care of him. I would not have him miscarry for the half of my dowry.
>
> (III.iv.55-58)

Malvolio misconstrues Olivia's generous concern as amorous passion and he thanks Jove for contriving circumstances so appropriately:

> I have limed her; but it is Jove's doing, and Jove make me thankful. . . . Nothing that can be can come between me and the full prospect of my hopes. Well, Jove, not I, is the doer of this, and he is to be thanked.
>
> (III.iv.68-77)

Malvolio's scrupulous praise of a higher designer than himself is a parodic echo of Olivia's earlier submission to Fate after she has begun to love Cesario: "What is decreed must be—and be this so!" (I.v.297). The impulses underlying Malvolio's speech (and to some extent, Olivia's speech as well) exert opposite pulls: Malvolio wants to attribute control of circumstances to Jove at the same time he wants divine identity. He attempts to simulate foreknowledge through predictive assertion: "Nothing that can be can come between me and the full prospect of my hopes." As long as events are in the hands of a non-human control, man cannot destroy or divert the predetermined order. But Malvolio cannot foresee the vindictive wit of Maria (often pronounced "Moriah"), nor can Olivia foresee the necessary substitution of Sebastian for Viola-Cesario. Each must learn that he, like the characters he wishes to control, is subject to an unpredictable will not his own. Precisely at this moment—when the character is forced to see a discrepancy between what he "wills" and what "is"—the possibility that he is mad confronts him.

Feste seems to adopt the disguise of Sir Topas to convince Malvolio that he is mad,[8] and the imprisonment scene evokes a different response than the letter that exploits Malvolio by encouraging him to wear yellow stockings and cross-garters. In the earlier phase of the gulling, Malvolio is a comic butt after the fashion of Sir Andrew Aguecheek, unaware of his foolishness; however, imprisoned, Malvolio is a helpless victim, fully aware that he is being abused. With Olivia, his extraordinary costume and perpetual smiles make him a visible clown, and, as a result, he even seems good-humored. But with Maria and Feste in the imprisonment scene, he is not visible; we only hear him and his protestations of abuse. These different visual presentations produce a notable difference in comic effect because visual comedy often changes a serious tone in the dialogue.[9]

In the imprisonment scene, Sir Topas keeps insisting that things are not as Malvolio perceives them; but Malvolio refuses to admit a discrepancy between what he perceives and reality. Accordingly, Malvolio insists that he is not mad.

> *Malvolio within.*
> MALVOLIO Who calls there?
> CLOWN Sir Topas the curate, who comes to visit Malvolio the lunatic. . . .
> MALVOLIO Sir Topas, never was man thus wronged. Good Sir Topas, do not think I am mad. They have laid me here in hideous darkness.
> CLOWN Fie, thou dishonest Satan. I call thee by the most modest terms, for I am one of those gentle ones that will use the devil himself with courtesy. Say'st thou that house is dark?
> MALVOLIO As hell, Sir Topas.
> CLOWN Why, it hath bay windows transparent as barricadoes, and the clerestories toward the south north are as lustrous as ebony; and yet complainest thou of obstruction?
> MALVOLIO I am not mad, Sir Topas. I say to you this house is dark.
> CLOWN Madman, thou errest. I say there is no darkness but ignorance, in which thou art more puzzled than the Egyptians in their fog.
> MALVOLIO I say this house is as dark as ignorance, though ignorance were as dark as hell; and I say there was never man thus abused. I am no more mad than you are.
> (IV.ii.20-48)

In the darkness of his prison, Malvolio literally is unable to see, and Feste makes the most of the symbolic implications of Malvolio's blindness. The audience perceives with Feste that the house is not dark (that hypothetical Globe audience would have been able to see the literal daylight in the playhouse), yet the audience also knows that Malvolio is being "abused" because he cannot see the light. The audience is therefore led to a double awareness of values in this scene: we are able to absorb the emblematic significance of Malvolio's separation from good-humored sanity and to know at the same time that Malvolio is not mad in the literal way that Feste, Maria, and Sir Toby insist.

Although the literal action engenders the emblematic awareness, the literal action does not necessarily support the emblematic meaning. This pull in two opposite directions occurs simultaneously and places the audience in a slightly uncomfortable position. We prefer to move in one direction or in the other. Yet it seems that here Shakespeare asks us to forgo the either-or alternatives and to hold contradictory impressions together. Malvolio cannot be dismissed as a simple comic butt when his trial in the dark has such severe implications.[10]

The ambiguities of his situation are clear to everyone except Malvolio, but he rigidly maintains his single point of view. Because he refuses to allow more than his own narrowed focus, he is *emblematically* an appropriate butt for the harsh comic action that blots out his power to see as well as to act. He must ultimately depend upon the fool to bring him "ink, paper, and light" so that he may extricate himself from his prison, a situation which would have seemed to Malvolio earlier in the play "mad" indeed. Feste thus does force Malvolio to act against his will in submitting to the fool, but Malvolio fails to change his attitudes.[11] Malvolio remains a literalist—Feste's visual disguise is for the audience so that we can see as well as hear the ambiguities of his performance, a point that Maria brings into focus when she says "Thou mightest have done this without thy beard and gown. He sees thee not" (IV.ii.63-64).

In the very next scene, Sebastian presents a contrast which delineates even more clearly the narrowness of Malvolio's response to an uncontrollable situation. Sebastian, too, confronts the possibility that he is mad: his situation in Illyria is anything but under his control.

> This is the air; that is the glorious sun;
> This pearl she gave me, I do feel't and see't;
> And *though* 'tis wonder that enwraps me thus,
> *Yet* 'tis not madness. . . .
> For *though* my soul disputes well with my sense
> That this may be some error, *but* no madness,
> *Yet* doth this accident and flood of fortune
> So far exceed all instance, all discourse,
> That I am ready to distrust mine eyes
> And wrangle with my reason that persuades me
> To any other trust *but* that I am mad,
> *Or else* the lady's mad.
> (IV.iii.1-16: my italics)

Sebastian's pile of contrasting conjunctions ("though," "yet," "but") underlines his hesitance to form a final judgment, unlike Malvolio, whose point of view never changes despite the onslaught of unmanageable circumstances. The contradictions of his sensory perceptions lead Sebastian to a state of "wonder" in which he is able to suspend reason and delay judgment, and this signifies a flexibility of perception which Malvolio cannot attain. Malvolio is not stirred by the discrepancies of experience to consider that appearances may not be reality; but Sebastian can appreciate the undefinable workings of a power beyond the evident. Sebastian's ability to sense the "wonder" in a world where cause and effect have been severed gives him a stature that Malvolio cannot achieve.[12] Yet the difference between them is due to the source of their manipulation as well as to their response. Sebastian is manipulated by Fate or by Fortune; Malvolio, by Maria and Feste. Human manipulators parody suprahuman control and because they do, Maria and Feste define both levels of action.

Feste, Maria, and Sir Toby are all in a set and predictable world of sporting gullery, and the rules for their games are known. Feste's "whirligig" associates Time with a toy (perhaps even with an instrument of torture) and limits Time to human terms of punishment. On the other hand, the Time that Viola addresses does untie her problematic knot of disguise. Feste's attribution of revenge to this "whirligig of Time" points up the difference between the two controls. The whirligig becomes a parodic substitute for the larger providence that other characters talk about under other titles: Time, Jove, Fate, Fortune, or Chance. Significantly, Malvolio's humiliation is the only humanly designed action that fulfills itself as planned. The subplot performs its parody in many other ways,[13] but in Feste's summary "whirligig" it displays the double vision that Shakespearean parody typically provides. The foibles of the romantics in Illyria are seen in their reduced terms through Sir Toby, Maria, and Sir Andrew, but the limitations of the parodic characters also heighten by contrast the expansive and expanding world of the play. Love, not revenge, is celebrated.

But even Feste's whirligig takes another spin and does not stop at revenge: in the play's final song the playwright extends an embrace to his audience. Feste's song creates an ambiguity of perspective which fuses the actual world with an ideal one: "the rain it raineth every day" is hardly the world described by the play. Romantic Illyria seems to have little to do with such realistic intrusions. Yet, the recognition of continuous rain is in itself an excess—it does not rain every day in the actual world, at least not in the same place.[14] Thus, the pessimistic excess of the song balances the optimistic excesses of the romance world of Illyria; neither excess accurately reflects the actual world. Despite the apparent progress the song describes of a man's growing from infancy to maturity and to old age, it remains something of an enigma.[15] The ambiguities of the first four stanzas build to a contrast of direct statements in the final stanza.

> A great while ago the world begun,
>   With hey, ho, the wind and the rain;
> But that's all one, our play is done,
>   And we'll strive to please you every day.

The first line of this stanza seems to imply that the world has its own, independent design;[16] and it also suggests that man's actions must take their place and find meaning within this larger and older pattern. The specific meaning of that larger design, however, remains concealed within the previous ambiguities of Feste's song. His philosophic pretensions to explain that design are comically vague and he knows it. He tosses them aside to speak directly to the audience: "But that's all one, our play is done." This is the same phrase Feste uses with Malvolio in his summary speech in Act V: "I was one, sir, in this interlude, one Sir Topas, sir; but that's all one." In both cases, Feste avoids an explanation.

Turning to the audience and shattering the dramatic illusion is typical in epilogues, but Feste's inclusion of the audience into his consciousness of the play as a metaphor for actual experience has a special significance here. Throughout *Twelfth Night,* Feste has engaged various characters in dialogues of self-determination. In one game of wit, he points out that Olivia is a fool "to mourn for your brother's soul, being in heaven" (I.v.65-66). By his irrefutable logic, he wins Olivia's favor and her tacit agreement that her mourning has been overdone. The Duke also is subject to Feste's evaluation in two scenes. Following his performance, upon the Duke's request, of a sad song of unrequited love, Feste leaves a paradoxical benediction:

> Now the melancholy god protect thee, and the tailor make thy doublet of changeable taffeta, for thy mind is a very opal. I would have men of such constancy put to sea, that their business might be everything, and their intent everywhere; for that's it that always makes a good voyage of nothing.
>
> (II.iv.72-77)

And later, when the Duke is approaching Olivia's house, Feste encounters him with one of his typically unique and audaciously applied truisms:

> DUKE I know thee well. How dost thou, my good fellow?
> CLOWN Truly, sir, the better for my foes, and the worse for my friends.
> DUKE Just the contrary: the better for thy friends.
> CLOWN No, sir, the worse.
> DUKE How can that be?
> CLOWN Marry, sir, they praise me and make an ass of me. Now my foes tell me plainly I am an ass; so that by my foes, sir, I profit in the knowledge of myself, and by my

friends I am abused; so that, conclusions to be as kisses, if your four negatives make your two affirmatives, why then, the worse for my friends, and the better for my foes.

(V.i.9-20)

The Duke has in fact lacked some knowledge of himself, and Feste's pointed remark makes it clear that he is using his role as fool to point up the true foolishness of others. In the prison scene with Malvolio, Feste provides a confusing game of switching identities from the Clown to Sir Topas. In each situation, Feste provides the other person with a different perspective for seeing himself. Thus, it is more than merely appropriate that at the end of the play Feste engages the audience in its own definition of self. By asking them to look at their participation in the dramatic illusion, Feste is requesting them to recognize their own desire for humanly willed happiness.[17]

The playwright, like the comic providence in the play, has understood "what we will" and has led us to a pleasurable fulfillment of our desires, but in ways which we could not have foreseen or controlled. The substitution of the final line, "And we'll strive to please you every day," for the refrain, "For the rain it raineth every day," is a crucial change. Like the incremental repetition in the folk ballad, this pessimistic refrain has built a dynamic tension which is released in the recognition that the play is an actual experience in the lives of the audience, even though it is enacted in an imagined world. The players, and the playwright who arranges them, are engaged in an ongoing effort to please the audience. The providential design remains incomplete within the play's action and only promises a "golden time"; similarly, the playwright promises further delightful experiences for his audience. The subplot's action, on the other hand, is limited within the framework of revenge: the revenge of the subplot characters elicits Malvolio's cry for revenge.

Malvolio is the only one who refuses to see himself in a subservient position to a larger design. And possibly because that design is too small, we cannot feel that his abuse and final exclusion from the happy community of lovers and friends allows the golden time to be fulfilled within the play. Feste's manipulation of Malvolio resembles the playwright's manipulation of his audience's will, but in such a reduced way that we cannot avoid seeing the difference between merely human revenge and the larger benevolence that controls the play's design.

Notes

[1] Viola's Captain calls this power "chance" (I. ii. 6, 8); Viola submits herself to "Time" (I. ii. 60; II. ii. 39); Olivia and Sebastian refer to "Fate" (I. v. 296; II. i. 4); Malvolio speaks of Jove's control (II. v. 158, 164; III. iv. 68-77); and the forged letter names "the stars," "the Fates," and "Fortune" (II. v. 131-146). Citations of the plays are from *William Shakespeare: The Complete Works,* ed. Alfred Harbage (Baltimore, Md.: Penguin Books, 1969).

[2] S. Nagarajan, "'What You Will': A Suggestion," *Shakespeare Quarterly,* 10 (1959), 61-67, employs Thomistic categories to discuss the function of human will in the play.

[3] Notice the similarity between Feste's description of events and Iago's prediction as he encourages Roderigo to join him in his revenge against Othello: "There are many events in the womb of time which will be delivered" (I. iii. 366). Iago implies that he is merely an agent bringing about time's inevitable retributions.

[4] Fabian's participation in the gulling of Malvolio has a vengeful motive, because, as he says to Sir Toby, Malvolio has at some previous time "brought me out o' favor with my lady about a bear-baiting here" (II. v. 4-7).

[5] The *OED* cites Feste's line as an example under "circling course, revolution (of time or events)," but other uses of the term cited there are also important in the force of the word in *Twelfth Night:* "whirligig" is the name of various toys which are whirled, twirled, or spun around; the term was also used to signify "an instrument of punishment"; and the word suggests fickleness, inconstancy, giddiness, or flightiness.

[6] Maria indicates her "foreknowledge" of Malvolio's certain response (II. iii. 137-40), and Malvolio's comments fulfill her prediction (II. v. 110-12, 150-52).

[7] Olivia has drawn a similar conclusion about herself in the opening lines of this scene: "I am as mad as he, / If sad and merry madness equal be" (III. iv. 13-14). Because Olivia concurs with Maria in classifying Malvolio's peculiar behavior as "madness," she inadvertently begets the subplotters plan for imprisoning Malvolio. We have Rosalind's word for it in *As You Like It* that the typical treatment for lunatics in the sixteenth centry was imprisonment:

> Love is merely a madness, and, I tell you, deserves as well a dark house and a whip as madmen do; and the reason why they are not so punished and cured is that the lunacy is so ordinary that the whippers are in love too.
>
> (III. ii. 376-80).

[8] Cf. Julian Markels, "Shakespeare's Confluence of Tragedy and Comedy: *Twelfth Night* and *King Lear,*" in *Shakespeare 400,* ed. James G. McManaway (New York: Holt, Rinehart, and Winston, 1964), pp. 85-86, for a similar observation. Feste makes evident his as-

sumption that Malvolio is "possessed" by associating carnal sexual interests with Malvolio's request that Sir Topas "go to my lady" (cf. Leslie Hotson, *The First Night of Twelfth Night* [New York: Macmillan, 1954], pp. 108-09). Feste replies:

> Out, hyperbolical fiend! How vexest thou this man! Talkest thou nothing but of ladies?
>
> (IV.ii.25-26)

Obsessive interest in sexual lust seems to have been a commonplace shorthand to indicate madness for Renaissance dramatists: for examples, see Ophelia's mad songs in *Hamlet* (IV.v); Edgar's speech to King Lear as poor Tom o' Bedlam (III.iv.); and the masque of madmen in *The Duchess of Malfi* (IV.ii.). Feste is also following Vice's typical role of teasing and tormenting the Devil when he berates Malvolio, who (Feste asserts) is possessed by the fiend—a point that Feste's song at the end of IV.ii reiterates.

[9] The two productions of *Twelfth Night* that I have seen both chose to emphasize visual comedy. One was the Royal Shakespeare Company's performance at Stratford-Upon-Avon in August 1971. During the scene, Malvolio kept popping his head up through a left-front trap door, and Feste responded with a swift stomp of his foot, closing the trap according to his whim. In this case, Malvolio was not allowed to see Feste, but the audience was allowed to see Malvolio. A performance in the fall of 1971, by Florida's Asolo Theater, had Feste roll onstage a wheeled cage with a small barred window on the upper left, covered by a flap. A sign reading "Beware the Lunatic" covered most of the visible side of the cage and evoked a large laugh from the audience. Throughout the scene, Feste was able to lift or lower the flap covering the bars, so that Malvolio was exposed to the audience and to Feste according to Feste's whim. In both of these instances, the visual comedy was heightened at the expense of the text and its suggested visual effects: Malvolio neither sees anyone nor is seen by anyone in the darkness of his prison. An illustration of this scene from Nicholas Rowe's edition of 1709 shows Malvolio separated from the others by a center stage partition, which would allow the audience to witness both situations simultaneously. This is closer to stage directions in the text, but, of course, would not have been probable for Shakespeare's staging of the scene. See "Plate 9 (c)," W. Moelwyn Merchant, *Shakespeare and the Artist* (London: Oxford University Press, 1959), between pp. 48, 49.

[10] The problem of whether to sympathize with or to reject and ridicule Malvolio is an old one. Charles Lamb probably opened this Pandora's box when he praised Malvolio as what Lamb thought he should have been—"brave, honourable, accomplished": from "On Some of the Old Actors," *The London Magazine,* 1822, reprinted in *Shakespeare's Twelfth Night,* ed. Leonard F. Dean and James A. S. McPeek (Boston: Allyn and Bacon, 1965), p. 150. Many arguments have been advanced against Malvolio's "humanity" as realized in the play. Two of the more interesting are by S. L. Bethell, *Shakespeare and the Popular Dramatic Tradition* (London: Kings and Staples, 1944), pp. 77-78, and Barbara K. Lewalski, "Thematic Patterns in *Twelfth Night*," *Shakespeare Studies,* 1 (1965), 168-81.

[11] Julian Markels, "Shakespeare's Confluence of Tragedy and Comedy," p. 84, and Barbara Lewalski, "Thematic Patterns in *Twelfth Night*," discuss the regenerative potentials of madness. Both discussions are pertinent to the emblematic values presented in this scene.

[12] Cf. Harold Jenkins, "Shakespeare's *Twelfth Night*," in *Shakespeare: The Comedies,* ed. Kenneth Muir (Englewood Cliffs, N. J.: Prentice-Hall, 1965), p. 76.

[13] L. G. Salingar discusses some of the other parodic functions of the subplot in "The Design of *Twelfth Night*," *Shakespeare Quarterly,* 9 (1958), 119-39.

[14] Joseph H. Summers makes a similar point, "The Masks of *Twelfth Night*," *The University of Kansas City Review,* 22 (1955), 31. In contrast, the song becomes an appropriate description of the play's world in *King Lear* (III. ii. 64-77).

[15] I disagree with John A. Hart's opinion that Feste's song "is not hard to fathom": "Foolery Shines Everywhere: The Fool's Function in the Romantic Comedies," *Starre of Poets, Carnegie Series in English,* 10 (Pittsburg: Carnegie Institute of Technology, 1966), p. 47. Hart's own reading of the song's "general meaning" differs in several major points from other readings. One of the most generally held readings is by John Weiss, *Wit, Humour, and Shakespeare* (Boston, 1876), p. 204. It is impossible to list every variant, but worth noting by contrast is Leslie Hotson, *The First Night of Twelfth Night,* pp. 168-71, who centers his discussion of the song on the sexual innuendoes that proceed from reading "thing" as male genitalia.

[16] Leslie Hotson, *ibid.,* p. 171, n. 2, points out that this line "recalls the Elizabethan euphemism for coition, 'To dance The Beginning of the World!'" Without discounting that allusion, I suggest that a much more general pattern of action is implied.

[17] Cf. Joseph Summers, "The Masks of *Twelfth Night*," pp. 31-32.

Robert Wilcher (essay date 1982)

SOURCE: "The Art of the Comic Duologue in Three Plays by Shakespeare," in *Shakespeare Survey: An*

Annual Survey of Shakespeare Studies and Production, Vol. 35, 1982, pp. 87-97.

[*In the following excerpt, Wilcher asserts that, in contrast to the more conventional clowns of Shakespeare's earlier comedies, Feste is a more fully human character.*]

I

Since Francis Douce's pioneering study of the 'clowns and fools' of the Elizabethan stage, a good deal of scholarly scrutiny and critical interpretation has been directed towards Shakespeare's use of his inheritance from popular drama in general and from traditions of fooling in particular.[1] But compared with the detailed studies that have been devoted to the serious dramatic functions that Shakespeare developed for the solo-turn exemplified by Launce's monologues in *The Two Gentlemen of Verona* and the porter scene in *Macbeth,*[2] that other familiar routine of popular comedy—the double-act—has been somewhat neglected. William Willeford traces the origins of the 'knockabout fool pair' to the interplay between the Devil and the Vice in the Tudor moralities;[3] and Austin Gray identifies the comic personalities of the actors Will Kemp and Dick Cowley behind the long line of Shakespearian double-acts, from Launce and Speed to the grave-diggers in *Hamlet,* offering this account of the relationship between the stooge and the lead comedian:

> This old fellow is a mere shadow to his wiser gossip. It is his business to ask simple-minded questions or to listen in simple-minded wonder to the dogmatic wisdom of his friend. In short, his main duty is to be the cause that wit and comicality express themselves through the mouth of his friend.[4]

The fullest account of the nature and function of the double-act is by J. A. B. Somerset who, in the course of tracing the history and significance of the comic turn in Renaissance English drama, spends some time on 'the "vaudeville" interchange in which the master acts the role of straight-man to the fooling of his servant or jester, while realizing that he is doing so'.[5] It is the purpose of the present paper to examine the use of comic duologues in *As You Like It, Twelfth Night,* and *Hamlet,* in order to indicate the variety of Shakespeare's artistic response to Dogberry's observation that 'an two men ride of a horse, one must ride behind' (*Much Ado About Nothing,* 3.5.35-6).[6]

Some preliminary attention must be given, however, to the early comedies, because they establish in simple form the materials which Shakespeare was to manipulate later in more complex ways and also offer glimpses of those insights into human behaviour which he perceived in the very nature of the double-act. Three variations can be distinguished, involving both the status of the participants and the kind of humorous exchange that takes place between them. First there is the Kemp-Cowley type of set-piece described by Gray, in which the lead clown and the stooge share the same low social class. The comedy resides in the ability of the dominant partner to outwit his slower companion, either by confusing him or by trapping him into an absurd situation by verbal trickery. A crude example occurs in *The Taming of the Shrew,* in the scene where Grumio thwarts his fellow-servant's eager desire for news of their master's marriage for some thirty lines and then clinches his comic superiority in a more material way:

> *Grumio.* First know my horse is tired; my master and mistress fall'n out.
> *Curtis.* How?
> *Grumio.* Out of their saddles into the dirt; and thereby hangs a tale.
> *Curtis.* Let's ha't, good Grumio.
> *Grumio.* Lend thine ear.
> *Curtis.* Here.
> *Grumio.* There. [*Striking him.*
> *Curtis.* This 'tis to feel a tale, not to hear a tale.
> *Grumio.* And therefore 'tis called a sensible tale; and this cuff was but to knock at your ear and beseech list'ning.
>
> (4.1.46-58)

Launcelot Gobbo's determination to 'try confusions' with his sand-blind father in *The Merchant of Venice* (2.2.28 ff.) is in a similar vein. In *The Two Gentlemen of Verona,* the servants Launce and Speed are more equally matched intellectually, but in each of their encounters Launce is given the upper hand in the verbal sparring and Speed is relegated to the stooge's role:

> *Speed.* How now, Signior Launce! What news with your mastership?
> *Launce.* With my master's ship? Why, it is at sea.
> *Speed.* Well, your old vice still: mistake the word. What news, then, in your paper?
> *Launce.* The black'st news that ever thou heard'st.
> *Speed.* Why, man? how black?
> *Launce.* Why, as black as ink.
>
> (3.1.276-83)

This exchange opens into the long sequence in which Speed 'feeds' Launce by reading items from a paper detailing the qualities of Launce's mistress, thus allowing the lead clown all the witty punch-lines.

In each of these cases, the double-act interrupts the progress of the plot and is clearly designed to display the talents of the company's clowns in an interlude of low comedy. At the other end of the social scale

Ben Kingsley as Feste in Trevor Nunn's 1996 film adaptation of Twelfth Night.

are the duologues between characters from the main plot. *The Two Gentlemen of Verona* opens with a witty scene of parting between Valentine and Proteus, which will serve to exhibit the distinctive features of this second kind of exchange:

> *Proteus.*
>   Upon some book of love I'll pray for thee.
> *Valentine.*
>   That's on some shallow story of deep love:
>   How young Leander cross'd the Hellespont.
> *Proteus.*
>   That's a deep story of a deeper love;
>   For he was more than over shoes in love.
> *Valentine.*
>   'Tis true; for you are over boots in love,
>   And yet you never swum the Hellespont.
> *Proteus.*
>   Over the boots! Nay, give me not the boots.
> *Valentine.*
>   No, I will not, for it boots thee not.
>
> (1.1.20-8)

Here, in contrast to the previous examples, there is no dominant partner. Each holds his own in a mutual display of verbal cleverness. The puns proliferate in the game of keeping the ball of wit in the air. It is more common for this kind of game to be played while other characters are present, and then it takes on the air of a contest, with the spectators frequently commenting on the expertise of the players. *Love's Labour's Lost* furnishes an example:

> *Katharine.*
>   She might 'a been a grandam ere she died.
>   And so may you; for a light heart lives
>   long.
> *Rosaline.*
>   What's your dark meaning, mouse, of this
>   light word?
> *Katharine.*
>   A light condition in a beauty dark.
> *Rosaline.*
>   We need more light to find your meaning
>   out.

> *Katharine.*
> You'll mar the light by taking it in snuff;
> Therefore I'll darkly end the argument.
> *Rosaline.*
> Look what you do, you do it still i' th' dark.
> *Katharine.*
> So do not you; for you are a light wench.
> *Rosaline.*
> Indeed, I weigh not you; and therefore light.
> *Katharine.*
> You weigh me not? O, that's you care not for me.
> *Rosaline.*
> Great reason; for 'past cure is still past care'.
> *Princess.*
> Well bandied both; a set of wit well play'd.
>
> (5.2.17-29)

The Princess's image indicates the holiday nature of this kind of repartee, having no other purpose than to exercise the participants and entertain their companions. In a scene from *The Two Gentlemen of Verona,* however, the sport is given an edge of seriousness when Valentine is challenged by Thurio, his rival for the hand of Silvia:

> *Silvia.* Servant, you are sad.
> *Valentine.* Indeed, madam, I seem so.
> *Thurio.* Seem you that you are not?

A needling interchange ensues, until Valentine catches Thurio on the raw by proving him a fool:

> *Silvia.* What, angry, Sir Thurio! Do you change colour?
> *Valentine.* Give him leave, madam; he is a kind of chameleon.
> *Thurio.* That hath more mind to feed on your blood than live in your air.
> *Valentine.* You have said, sir.
> *Thurio.* Ay, sir, and done too, for this time.
> *Valentine.* I know it well, sir; you always end ere you begin.
> *Silvia.* A fine volley of words, gentlemen, and quickly shot off.
>
> (2.4.8-31)

Silvia's two interventions suggest that Thurio, by taking up Valentine's initial 'I seem so' in a malicious sense and then becoming heated as the exchange develops to his disadvantage, is breaking the rules of this kind of social badinage. When personalities and the rivalries of real life become engaged in the verbal contest, the delicate mechanisms of social decorum are endangered. Silvia's concluding attempt to bring the uncomfortable situation back within the bounds of the courtly game is appropriately expressed in an image of warfare rather than sport. Already, thus early in his career, Shakespeare demonstrates how the witty duologue may be exploited dramatically to expose psychological and social tensions among characters.

The third type of comic duologue is that discussed by Somerset, in which a character of high status consents to play straight-man to a socially inferior comedian. In the early comedies, the comic actor had been accommodated in the fictional world of the play as a servant. This figure, as Robert Weimann has demonstrated in his analysis of Launce's contribution to *The Two Gentlemen of Verona,* moves between the real-life situation of a clown confronting a theatre audience and the dramatic situation of a character relating to other characters:

> The real performance of the actor and the imaginative role of the servant interact, and they achieve a new and very subtle kind of unity. Within this unity, the character's relations to the playworld begin to dominate, but the comic ease and flexibility of these relations are still enriched by some traditional connexion between the clowning actor and the laughing spectator.[7]

It is in monologues and asides, and with his dull companion in the low-comedy double-act, that the clown asserts his function as entertainer of the audience and maintains his semi-independence of the playworld. When he becomes involved in the third kind of duologue, he withdraws into the fiction and exerts his wit to entertain not us, directly, but his employer. The difference between the master-servant conversation and the low-comedy turn is indicated by Antipholus of Syracuse's description of his relationship with Dromio in *The Comedy of Errors:*

> A trusty villain, sir, that very oft,
> When I am dull with care and melancholy,
> Lightens my humour with his merry jests.
>
> (1.2.19-21)

Launcelot and Grumio play at fooling their social equals and intellectual inferiors, Old Gobbo and Curtis, for the delight of the audience; Dromio and his successors Touchstone and Feste are allowed to amuse their social superiors within the world of the drama.

On two occasions in *The Comedy of Errors,* Antipholus agrees to indulge Dromio, feeding him in act 2, scene 2 with such lines as 'Your reason?', 'Let's hear it', 'For what reason?', 'Name them'; and in act 3, scene 2 playing up to his conceit of the amorous kitchen-wench as 'a globe' by asking him to locate different countries on her anatomy. These two extended duologues are as much formal double-acts interrupting the plot as the Grumio-Curtis sequence, but the style of comedy is quite different, as we enjoy the inventiveness of Dromio's replies rather than the lower humour of one fool outwitting another. When Launcelot engages *his* superiors in witty conversation, another feature of this mode of comedy comes to light. He harps upon Jessica's Jewishness and her conversion to Christianity, asserting that she will be damned for her father's sins and complaining that 'this making of Christians will raise the price of hogs' (*The Merchant of Venice*, 3.5.20). These jokes are typical of the later professional fools' habit of telling home-truths and handling taboo subjects. Jessica is in no way offended or disconcerted, and seems to enjoy the chance to treat these disturbing personal matters in a mood of playfulness. As Olivia says, when Feste makes light of her brother's death: 'There is no slander in an allow'd fool' (*Twelfth Night*, 1.5.88). . . .

III

In *Twelfth Night*, Shakespeare uses the technique of the double-act to conduct his most penetrating psychological study of the domestic fool. The character and personal predicament of the early comic servants had never been the focus of dramatic attention. Launce's parting from his family and affection for his dog, and Launcelot's hard life in Shylock's household, had been used simply as the basis for comic turns. Touchstone's behaviour in the Forest of Arden had provided insights into social manners, but had not involved us in the clown's predicament as a unique individual. He was introduced, we remember, with a philosophical discussion about wit and folly, and it was his functioning as a jester not his character as a man that Shakespeare was interested in. The duologue routine which brings Feste before us for the first time immediately establishes the difference of approach in *Twelfth Night*:

> *Maria.* Nay, either tell me where thou hast been, or I will not open my lips so wide as a bristle may enter in way of thy excuse; my lady will hang thee for thy absence.
> *Clown.* Let her hang me. He that is well hang'd in this world needs to fear no colours.
> *Maria.* Make that good.
> *Clown.* He shall see none to fear.
> *Maria.* A good lenten answer. I can tell thee where that saying was born, of 'I fear no colours'.
> *Clown.* Where, good Mistress Mary?
> *Maria.* In the wars; and that may you be bold to say in your foolery.
> *Clown.* Well, God give them wisdom that have it; and those that are fools, let them use their talents.
> *Maria.* Yet you will be hang'd for being so long absent; or to be turn'd away—is not that as good as a hanging to you?
> *Clown.* Many a good hanging prevents a bad marriage; and for turning away, let summer bear it out.
> *Maria.* You are resolute, then?
> *Clown.* Not so, neither; but I am resolv'd on two points.
> *Maria.* That if one break, the other will hold; or if both break, your gaskins fall.
> *Clown.* Apt, in good faith, very apt!
>
> (1.5.1-24)

Feste is a hired man, dependent on his fooling for his living. Whatever licence he may have to speak, he is not free to be absent without his employer's permission, and the threat of being 'turn'd away' hangs over his position in the social microcosm of Olivia's household. The progress of the duologue illustrates just how precarious that position is. He begins with a rather feeble pun on 'colours' and 'collars', and when Maria 'feeds' him with the line, 'Make that good', he collapses into the even feebler conclusion: 'He shall see none to fear.' Maria registers the poorness of this 'lenten answer', and then takes over as dominant partner in the comic routine, with Feste dropping into the role of straight-man: 'Where, good Mistress Mary?' His reply, with its comment 'those that are fools, let them use their talents', is a resigned admission that *his* 'talents' in the field of fooling are small. A few lines later, after offering a threadbare proverb in response to Maria's repeated warning about hanging, he launches into another joke with an intended pun on 'points'. But Maria is too quick for him, and instead of playing straight-man steals his punch-line. 'Apt', says Feste, crestfallen, 'in good faith, very apt!': the kind of remark that one expects to hear from the impressed audience of the clown, not from the clown himself.

Feste's aside, as Olivia and Malvolio approach, is different in kind from the asides of clowns like Speed or Thersites, which register a critical attitude towards the antics of the other characters. It is more of an overheard thought (a silent prayer for help) than a wink at the audience, and it reveals Feste's critical awareness of his own shortcomings rather than the folly of others:

> Wit, an't be thy will, put me into good fooling! Those wits that think they have thee do very oft prove fools; and I that am sure I lack thee may pass for a wise man.
>
> (1.5.29-32)

His uneasiness is quite justified, since Olivia is evidently displeased with him and tired of his predictable brand of humour:

> *Olivia.* Take the fool away.
> *Clown.* Do you not hear, fellows? Take away the lady.

Olivia. Go to, y'are a dry fool. I'll no more of you. Besides, you grow dishonest.

(ll. 35-8)

He desperately produces a lengthy syllogistic proof that Olivia is a fool, to be met not with applause, but with a blocking speech: 'Sir, I bade them take away you.' The mock dignity of his assertion that 'I wear not motley in my brain' only half conceals his resentment at the role in which he has been cast by Fortune rather than by Nature, and he appeals for one more chance to demonstrate that he can perform adequately: 'Good madonna, give me leave to prove you a fool.'[10] Olivia relents, and agrees to play her part in the comic duologue with her dubious 'Can you do it?' and the feed line: 'Make your proof.' This opens the way for a comic catechism, which wins Olivia over: 'What think you of this fool, Malvolio? Doth he not mend?' The ensuing dialogue, in which Malvolio castigates 'these set kind of fools' and gets uncomfortably near the truth about Feste's limitations—'unless you laugh and minister occasion to him, he is gagg'd'—adds further detail to Shakespeare's study of this particular clown's predicament. He is caught up in the below-stairs rivalries of a great household, and it is easy to understand why he tries to avoid anything that would aggravate Olivia's displeasure—keeping in the background when Sir Toby and Maria hatch the plot against Malvolio, and only allowing himself to be drawn in somewhat diffidently at a late stage in the proceedings, when Sir Toby is looking for a way to be 'well rid of this knavery'.

He seems to be more valued by Orsino for his ability to sing than for his skill in fooling, and it is noticeable that he plays second fiddle to Sir Toby in the great merry-making scene, and that praise for his wit comes from the foolish Sir Andrew, who enjoys such jokes as 'I did impeticos thy gratillity' and 'I shall never begin if I hold my peace.' In the Sir Topas episode, Feste exhibits a skill in mimicry, not in verbal brilliance. His wit is at its most inventive when he is begging money from Orsino and Viola. Warde characterizes Feste's performances as a jester accurately as lacking in both the 'spontaneous humor' and the 'sententious wisdom' we expect from a fool. His wit, he continues, 'is at times labored, frequently forced, and seldom free from obvious effort. It is professional foolery, rather than intuitive fun.'[11] And Bradley gets closer to the heart of his mystery in recognizing that the lot of such a man, who is 'more than Shakespeare's other fools, superior in mind to his superiors in rank', must be 'more or less hard, if not of necessity degrading'.[12]

Apart from his opening exchanges with Maria and Olivia and the Sir Topas episode, Feste's lengthiest involvement in duologue is with Viola. In substance, this scene is as much a comic interlude as the letter-reading turn between Speed and Launce: it contributes nothing to the plot. It does, however, substantiate Warde's and Bradley's insights into Feste's character and raise issues that are of thematic importance in the play:

Viola. Save thee, friend, and thy music! Dost thou live by thy tabor?

Clown. No, sir, I live by the church.

Viola. Art thou a churchman?

Clown. No such matter, sir: I do live by the church; for I do live at my house, and my house doth stand by the church.

Viola. So thou mayst say the king lies by a beggar, if a beggar dwell near him; or the church stands by thy tabor, if thy tabor stand by the church.

Clown. You have said, sir. To see this age! A sentence is but a chev'ril glove to a good wit. How quickly the wrong side may be turn'd outward!

Viola. Nay, that's certain; they that dally nicely with words may quickly make them wanton.

(3.1.1-14)

Formally, this is a duologue that belongs to the Launce-Speed type, since both participants are supposedly of the servant class. Viola makes a good-natured approach, calling him 'friend', but Feste, with a mixture of resentment and insolence, underlines his own inferior position in the servant hierarchy by addressing the up-and-coming favourite, 'Cesario', in all but one of his thirteen replies with the mock-subservient 'sir'. In these opening moments of the encounter, the familiar double-act relationships fail to be established. Viola does not take up either of the conventional roles: that of stooge or that of straight-man. She attempts to engage the clown in a conversation between social and intellectual equals. C. L. Barber has pointed out that Feste's exasperation at the abuse of language in the interests of wit comes unexpectedly from the fool's mouth—in *The Merchant of Venice,* 'it was the gentlefolk who commented "How every fool can play upon the word!" '[13] Two further points need to be made: firstly, Feste is not, as far as he knows, addressing more than a fellow-employee of the gentlefolk, for although 'Cesario's' parentage is 'above my fortunes' (1.5.262), 'he' is a dependant in Orsino's household; and secondly, it is in line with what we have seen of Feste's character that he should be contemptuous of the very art on which he must rely for his living. After all, it was he, not 'Cesario', who began the riddling conversation by turning the phrase 'live by' inside out. One might dig deeper, and suggest that his dallying with Viola's words is triggered by his bitterness at being forced by necessity to 'live by' his profession as jester-minstrel.

As the duologue continues, subtle adjustments are made in the relationship between the two participants:

> *Clown.* I would, therefore, my sister had had no name, sir.
>
> *Viola.* Why, man?
>
> *Clown.* Why, sir, her name's a word; and to dally with that word might make my sister wanton. But indeed words are very rascals since bonds disgrac'd them.
>
> *Viola.* Thy reason, man?
>
> *Clown.* Troth, sir, I can yield you none without words, and words are grown so false I am loath to prove reason with them.
>
> (3.1.15-23)

Viola's control of both the sexual and the social aspects of her disguise as a male servant wavers in the face of Feste's refusal to respond straightforwardly to her greeting. This is delicately registered in the shift from 'friend' to the would-be hearty 'man' in her mode of address to the clown and in her assumption of the socially superior role as 'feed'—more appropriate to her real status—with the questions 'Why, man?' and 'Thy reason, man?'

The crisis of the scene occurs in the next few speeches, as Viola unwittingly nettles Feste and brings his submerged hostility into the open:

> *Viola.* I warrant thou art a merry fellow and car'st for nothing.
>
> *Clown.* Not so, sir; I do care for something; but in my conscience, sir, I do not care for you. If that be to care for nothing, sir, I would it would make you invisible.
>
> *Viola.* Art not thou the Lady Olivia's fool?
>
> *Clown.* No indeed, sir; the Lady Olivia has no folly; she will keep no fool, sir, till she be married; and fools are as like husbands as pilchers are to herrings—the husband's the bigger. I am indeed not her fool, but her corrupter of words.
>
> (ll. 24-34)

Viola compounds the error of her patronizing tone in 'I warrant thou art a merry fellow' by using the title which Feste resents because of its implications. We remember that he even bridled when Olivia hinted that his jester's garb extended from his office to his nature: 'I wear not motley in my brain.' Viola tries to change this prickly subject, but Feste will not be placated and she breaks off the conversation in a way that places her firmly above him in the social hierarchy:

> *Viola.* I saw thee late at the Count Orsino's.
>
> *Clown.* Foolery, sir, does walk about the orb like the sun—it shines everywhere. I would be sorry, sir, but the fool should be as oft with your master as with my mistress: I think I saw your wisdom there.
>
> *Viola.* Nay, an thou pass upon me, I'll no more with thee. Hold, there's expenses for thee. [*giving a coin.*]
>
> (ll. 35-41)

Having refused Viola's initial overtures of friendly equality, and resented her assumption of superiority, Feste now tries to turn her into his butt by calling her Orsino's fool. Viola's tip leads him into his routine of begging, but does not stem his insolence. In the very act of wheedling more money out of his antagonist, he is artfully implying that though 'Cesario' may not be a fool, he is nonetheless a hired man, and what is more, a pander:

> *Clown.* I would play Lord Pandarus of Phrygia, sir, to bring a Cressida to this Troilus.
>
> *Viola.* I understand you, sir; 'tis well begg'd. [*giving another coin.*
>
> *Clown.* The matter, I hope, is not great, sir, begging but a beggar: Cressida was a beggar. My lady is within, sir. I will conster to them whence you come.
>
> (ll. 49-54)

When he is gone, Viola gives her famous assessment of Feste and his art:

> This fellow is wise enough to play the fool;
> And to do that well craves a kind of wit.
> He must observe their mood on whom he jests,
> The quality of persons, and the time;
> And, like the haggard, check at every feather
> That comes before his eye. This is a practice
> As full of labour as a wise man's art.
>
> (ll. 57-63)

As Joseph H. Summers points out, most of the characters in the play are wearing masks, and 'Feste is the one professional among a crowd of amateurs.'[14] Unlike everyone else but Viola, however, Feste *knows* he is wearing a mask—that of fool—and must 'labour' to maintain it. This is why it is difficult to accept Roger Ellis's view that Feste 'covers his tracks so completely that we never see what he stands for, but only the folly and affectation which he ridicules in all around him', and that we never do find out what he does wear in his brain.[15] Feste may be 'wise enough to play the fool'—with an effort—but he resents the fact that Fortune has made it necessary for him to practise an art which he knows is not natural to him; and in the scenes with Maria and Olivia in act 1 and with Viola in act 3, the routines of the comic duologue are deliberately manipulated by Shakespeare to *un*cover his tracks, rather than to cover them. Touchstone was unconsciously trapped in his role; Feste is trapped in his, but with a full and painful awareness. It is typical of him that on the rare occasion when his wit rather than his singing is praised by Orsino—'Why, this is excellent'—Feste replies ruefully, 'By my troth, sir, no; though it please you to be one of my friends', and proceeds to beg for money. . . .

Notes

[1] See, for example, Francis Douce, 'A Dissertation on the Clowns and Fools of Shakespeare', in *Illustrations of Shakespeare, and of Ancient Manners* (1807), vol. 2, pp. 299-332; Olive Mary Busby, *Studies in the Development of the Fool in the Elizabethan Drama* (1923); Enid Welsford, *The Fool: His Social and Literary History* (1935); Leslie Hotson, *Shakespeare's Motley* (1952); Robert Hillis Goldsmith, *Wise Fools in Shakespeare* (Liverpool, 1958); William Willeford, *The Fool and His Sceptre: A Study in Clowns and Jesters and their Audience* (1969); Victor Bourgy, *Le Bouffon sur la scène anglaise au 16e siècle (c. 1495-1594)* (Paris, 1969); Robert Weimann, *Shakespeare and the Popular Tradition in the Theatre,* ed. Robert Schwartz (Baltimore and London, 1978).

[2] See Harold F. Brooks, 'Two Clowns in a Comedy (to say nothing of the Dog): Speed, Launce (and Crab) in "The Two Gentlemen of Verona"', *Essays and Studies,* 16 (1963), 91-100; John B. Harcourt, ' "I Pray You, Remember the Porter" ', *Shakespeare Quarterly,* 22 (1961), 393-402.

[3] Willeford, *The Fool and his Sceptre,* p. 123.

[4] Austin K. Gray, 'Robert Armine, The Foole', *PMLA,* 42 (1927), 673-85, p. 673. See Busby (pp. 70-1) and Ludwig Borinski ('Shakespeare's Comic Prose', *Shakespeare Survey 8* (Cambridge, 1955), pp. 57-68, p. 63) for brief accounts of some of the clown's duologue techniques.

[5] J. A. B. Somerset, 'The Comic Turn in English Drama, 1470-1616' (unpublished Ph.D. thesis, The Shakespeare Institute, University of Birmingham, 1966), pp. 619-26.

[6] All quotations from Shakespeare's plays are taken from Peter Alexander's text of the *Complete Works* (1951).

[7] Robert Weimann, 'Laughing with the Audience: "The Two Gentlemen of Verona" and the Popular Tradition of Comedy', *Shakespeare Survey 22* (1969), pp. 35-42; p. 40. . . .

[10] Feste wants to prove his own skill at fooling by inventing ingenious proof that his mistress is a fool—one of the traditional ploys of the jester.

[11] Frederick Warde, *The Fools of Shakespeare* (1915), p. 78.

[12] A. C. Bradley, 'Feste the Jester', in *A Miscellany* (1929), p. 213.

[13] C. L. Barber, *Shakespeare's Festive Comedy* (Princeton, 1959), p. 253.

[14] Joseph H. Summers, 'The Masks of *Twelfth Night,*' *University of Kansas City Review,* 22 (1955), reprinted in the Casebook on *Twelfth Night,* ed. D.J. Palmer (1972), p. 92.

[15] Roger Ellis, 'The Fool in Shakespeare: A Study in Alienation', *Critical Quarterly,* 10 (1968), 245-68, p. 260.

Karen Greif (essay date 1988)

SOURCE: "A Star is Born: Feste on the Modern Stage," in *Shakespeare Quarterly,* Vol. 39, No. 1, Spring, 1988, pp. 61-78.

[*In the essay below, Greif traces the evolution of Feste in twentieth-century productions of* Twelfth Night. *She contends that Feste has become an alienated figure, who is profoundly aware of human frailty and the transience of human existence.*]

All the characters in *Twelfth Night* are masqueraders—all imposters, self-deceivers, and counterfeiters, and all beguiled, to some degree, by the game of charades whirling around them. Only Feste the jester keeps his mask from slipping.[1] He alone remains inscrutable, a quality that has made his character particularly fascinating to our century. We are intrigued by ambiguities, obsessed with ironies, and bewitched by paradoxes. So it is natural that the modern theatre has drawn attention to Feste, and in him we have discovered our own key to *Twelfth Night.* Just as the Romantics found near-tragic pathos in Malvolio's misadventures, or as the Victorians transformed Viola into a model of womanly devotion,[2] we have searched for our own answers in the play's mirror; and the image cast back has been that of a wryly smiling, somewhat weary jester, one of life's privileged spies into the mystery of things.

I

That Feste has not always commanded respect in the theatre is clear from even a quick look at the play's stage history. To past audiences Feste was not compellingly enigmatic. He was simply baffling and all too often tiresome. His addiction to wordplay and witty jests, his oblique mockery, his delight in improvisation, his angling after coins, and his nebulous social rank all seemed alien to playgoers or actors who had lost touch with the Renaissance tradition of the "artificial" fool. Many of his jokes had become obscure and his ironic stance was hard to fathom. From the Restoration on, the standard practice was to play the hijinks in the comic plot for laughs while underlining the sentimental aspects of the romantic tangle, and Feste was odd man out in either simplified context. As a result, his part was invariably edited—sometimes emasculated—in performance. Not until this century has the fool moved from the periphery of the drama into its very heart.

A look at Bell's *Shakespeare* (London, 1773), an acting edition based on promptbooks used at Drury Lane and Covent Garden, reveals how dispensable Feste was once thought to be. Both of his love songs ("O mistress mine" and "Come away, death") were cut, along with the accompanying dialogue. The change in the revels scene (II.iii) kept the fun high-spirited and sped up the confrontation with the killjoy steward, but it also erased the rueful counterpoint the song provides by reminding us of time's passing. Similarly, the second abridgement (II.iv) showcased Viola's selfless devotion at the cost of the fool's deft parody of Orsino's love-melancholy. Other cuts also weakened Feste's part. His banter with Cesario in III.i was sharply trimmed, as was his mock inquisition of Malvolio (IV.ii). These alterations were eventually codified by John Philip Kemble, who published an acting edition of *Twelfth Night* in 1810 that became (whether in its own stead or in Oxberry's virtually identical text) the standard theatrical version during the nineteenth century.[3] Kemble adopted the cuts in Bell's edition and incorporated new ones of his own, including a few more slices from Feste's lines. Equally important, he re-aligned the scene order so that each act comprised a defined block of action, usually with strong opening and closing scenes that centered attention on Viola or Malvolio, the two leads. Such formal clarity was in line with Kemble's neoclassical standards, but it also broke the original dramatic structure. And in a theatre whether a linear plot was favored over a contrapuntal pattern, Feste's role in linking the story lines was easily ignored.

Of course, there were some managers who substituted their own versions for Kemble's, or who varied his formula, but they showed even less interest in the fool. For instance, one curious anomaly in *Twelfth Night*'s stage history was the "operatic" version concocted by Frederick Reynolds for Covent Garden in 1820. Reynolds specialized in lavishly staged musical adaptations of Shakespeare, which he devised by ransacking the canon for graftable lyrics. Yet oddly enough, in revamping *Twelfth Night*, he cut all the original music except for the familiar epilogue song. As one might guess, the fool played a very minor role in this mutilated songfest. Some years later, in 1884, Henry Irving presented a more orthodox version at the Lyceum Theatre. Still remembered for Irving's pseudo-tragic Malvolio and for Ellen Terry's sparkling Viola, this star-oriented production gave scant attention to the supporting cast. Dully played by a faltering comedian, Feste won small response from Lyceum patrons.

The growth of the star-system—like Kemble's disentangling of the plot strands—inevitably sapped Feste's role. Once the spotlight was aimed at the heroine and the gull, the other major characters automatically became "second-string" parts. Just as Olivia turned into a stately contralto because she was so often played by aging ingenues, or Orsino was relegated to the rising—or falling—matinee idol in the company, Feste usually went to whichever actor could muster a decent singing voice and take the obligatory pratfalls. In Augustin Daly's opulent and immensely successful revival, presented in New York in 1893 and the following year in London, Ada Rehan dominated the stage as Viola. The fool—stripped of over half his lines—dwindled away to an inconsequential zany, trotted out to sing a few tunes and crack an occasional jest, but serving mostly as a sidekick to Sir Toby and Sir Andrew. The hapless steward also suffered from Daly's scissors-and-paste approach to the text; but the two worst incisions (the abridgement—later the omission—of the prison scene and Malvolio's disappearance from the last act) also seriously diminished Feste, who normally plays a crucial part in these episodes.[4] However, this troubled few playgoers, to judge from the reviews.

Most of the later revivals presented under the actor-manager regimes did little to enhance Feste's prestige. Yet in one of history's small perversities, an early hint of the changes in store came from a most unlikely theatrical quarter. At the turn of the century, just after Queen Victoria's death in 1901, Herbert Beerbohm Tree produced a sumptuous staging of *Twelfth Night* at His Majesty's Theatre. In most respects, this was the usual Tree spectacular. There were extravagant sets, most conspicuously an awe-inspiring garden that seemed to stretch for acres, lavish costumes, and ebullient clowning by Tree as a vainglorious Malvolio. But Tree had decided to mount a joyously festive comedy, and he took as his motto Feste's line: "Foolery, sir, doth walk about the orb—like the sun, it shines everywhere." Tree's staging reserved center stage for the steward—here played as a fantastic grandee—but it also shed new light upon the fool. Set down in an Illyria dedicated to laughter, Feste became the "presiding genius" of the place, impishly serving as the "connecting link of stories otherwise disparate" who alerted everyone that the play's "swooning amorism no less than its roistering fun is 'high fantastical'" (*The Times*, 6 February 1901). In keeping with the show's sunny spirits, the jester's wit was more whimsical than sharp, and Courtice Pounds acted him as a genial humorist playing his pranks with cheeky nonchalance. "This Feste," Max Beerbohm wrote, "was as constant and as indispensable as punctuation"; and Tree himself called him "the all-pervading spirit of Twelfth Night."[5] But while Tree took advantage of the fool's unifying presence to improve the coherence of the heavily cut acting version employed, Feste himself, in a production so relentlessly keyed to merry laughter, remained an uncomplicated figure, a waggish Lord of Misrule overseeing the holiday fun.

It was not until Harley Granville-Barker staged his brilliant *Twelfth Night* at the Savoy Theatre in 1912 that Feste was anointed as the spokesman for the comedy's bittersweet undertones. Barker's viewpoint, expressed in his preface to the acting edition, was that the fool should not be played as a blithe spirit, flitting gaily through Illyria:

> Feste, I feel, is not a young man. . . . There runs through all he says and does that vein of irony by which we may so often mark one of life's self-acknowledged failures. We gather that in those days, for a man of parts without character and with more wit than sense, there was a kindly refuge from the world's struggles as an allowed fool.[6]

This portrait hints at several traits subsequent directors and actors would fasten on: the fool's ironic, faintly cynical detachment from his companions; his poignant, almost melancholy awareness of time's passage; and his use of wit as a shield against despair.

Sometimes these qualities have been magnified to the point of distortion, but in Barker's production Feste carried his mantle of irony lightly. He shared with his cohorts a delight in fellowship tempered by a keener sense that "present mirth" may vanish by tomorrow. As a member of Olivia's household he could enjoy his pleasures—and, like Sir Toby and Maria, he had a vested interest in protecting that refuge from Malvolio's stringent reforms. But he also showed a rueful awareness that for some listeners his fooling had indeed grown old. Because his part was not whittled down, as traditionally it had been, the full complexities of his nature were preserved. And by casting C. Hayden Coffin, a veteran of musical comedies, as Feste, and restoring all of the songs (set to authentic Elizabethan airs), Barker ensured that the musical interludes would not be slighted. He was careful not to distract attention from Feste during the songs, keeping the listeners onstage absorbed and still while Coffin sang the lyrics with quiet simplicity.

In the closing moments, Feste's role as mediator between the worlds of illusion and everyday reality was subtly evoked when the lovers passed through an arched gateway into the secluded garden, while the fool sang the epilogue verses from the forestage. As the gates closed upon the lovers and their fantasy world, the curtain slowly descended, leaving Feste alone on the apron. Then he, too, vanished through the curtains on the last notes: "But that's all one, our play is done, / And we'll strive to please you every day."[7] That farewell, critic John Palmer wrote, brought the enchantment to a graceful close: "We had wandered in Elia's fairyland, but the time had come for magic to be locked away. The spell, at last, was broken; and, thereafter, with hey ho, the wind and the rain, we must tumble forth into the crowd."[8]

Significantly, the Savoy *Twelfth Night* was the first revival to include virtually the full text (only about twenty lines were cut), with the scenes kept in their original sequence.[9] Combined with continuous staging that allowed only minimal breaks in the action and balanced ensemble playing from the cast, this reform enabled Barker to capitalize on the intricacy of *Twelfth Night*'s design. The rediscovery in the theatre of Shakespeare's interlacing dramatic structure, which the best contemporary directors have preserved, gave a healthy boost to the fool's long-devalued role. As the one character who encounters all the other major players, in a series of meetings spread over the action, Feste helps to weave together the assorted plot strands. Moreover, in his aspect as observer-cum-sooth-sayer, Feste gives voice to many of the play's thematic motifs. By restoring the comedy's original form, Barker gave Feste both a greater stake in the action and a more rounded, fully human personality.

II

Although he had demonstrated how much an expertly realized Feste could contribute to *Twelfth Night* in performance, Barker's cue was not at once picked up by subsequent producers. Most of the *Twelfth Night*s staged in the next few decades were lightweight affairs—sometimes drawing carefree laughter with *élan* and sometimes merely going through the motions, but seldom breaking free of the conventional expectation that it be played as a happy golden comedy. The fools in these productions were usually of the cavorting variety—sprightly, gay, always ready with a joke or a song—and little mention was made of such standardized clowns in most reviews.

There were, nonetheless, a few productions that pointed the way toward the present emphasis. Tyrone Guthrie was one director who experimented with a more serious approach. He directed *Twelfth Night* in 1933, for his first season in charge of the Old Vic, with Morland Graham cast as the fool. This was a fast-paced, rollicking version that reflected Guthrie's concern to liberate the comedy from its stodgier traditions. In place of scenic backdrops, he substituted an architectural setting intended to approximate the openness and depth of the Elizabethan stage. Caroline costumes broke with the rule of sixteenth-century dress. A flippant and skittish Olivia, acted with a disconcerting Russian accent by Lydia Lopokova, replaced the standard regal matron. And a deliberately discordant note was injected by making Feste a white-haired old man. He was still full of fun, but the suggestion that "clowns grow old like other people"[10] silently mocked the laughs. There was only muted appreciation from the critics for such innovations; but in his next outing with *Twelfth Night* for the Old Vic, in 1937, Guthrie once more gave Feste a touch of melancholy. This time playgoers were more receptive to his approach. *The Evening Standard* (24 November 1937) described the performance as a mellow blend of wit and beauty shadowed by "devouring time," calling particular attention to the nocturnal party when

> it is as though the revellers are drinking not for conviviality but to stiffen their hearts against the shadow of death. . . . And the clown, glancing at one and then the other, sings his song of sad mortality while the darkness deepens behind them. This is brilliantly done by Mr. Marius Goring, whose clown appears like a spirit from another world, commenting with bitter humour on the follies of mankind.

Some years later Alec Guinness, who had played Sir Andrew Aguecheek in Guthrie's 1937 production, staged his own revival of *Twelfth Night* for the Old Vic (1948). Having transposed Viola's shipwrecked arrival to the opening scene, Guinness began and ended the performance in thundery darkness. The intervening scenes presented, in J. C. Trewin's words, "a gentle summer-world with an odd tinge of pensive autumn in its sunlight"[11]—and Feste, played by Robert Eddison, served as the chief reminder of that nip in the air. Skeptical critics dismissed him as a refugee from Lear's heath or as a gaunt *memento mori*: "white-haired, hollow-eyed, obviously tubercular . . . [his] doomed voice and haunted countenance dominate the Illyrian scene."[12] Other viewers, however, were moved by the portrayal, which made Feste a more intriguing character than the stereotypical "fidget in cap-and-bells."[13] For example, Audrey Williamson, in a sympathetic, although not totally approving, account of Eddison's performance, remembered him as a sad-gay

> figure of haunted melancholy: a Pagliacci clown, mournful and elongated, with whitened hair and lines of age on his face, moving among the sad cypresses like a man, not with a load of mischief, but of sorrow.[14]

Perhaps it was the experience of the war and the frustrations of its peace that brought this melancholy conception into practice. The same impulses that nurtured such dramatists as Beckett, Osborne, and Pinter may also have fostered the modern tendency to shift *Twelfth Night*'s colors from midsummer brightness to autumnal shadings. Certainly, by the end of the 1950s, the bittersweet interpretation of the comedy had fully matured.

In 1957 Tyrone Guthrie re-staged *Twelfth Night* for the Stratford Festival Theatre in Ontario. Twenty years since his last Old Vic revival had only confirmed Guthrie's impression of darkness within the farcical intrigue: the hints that merriment may spill into madness, that love may turn sour, and earthly pleasures fade. In his program notes, Guthrie argued that, although the story belongs to the vernal season of blossoming exuberance, it should not be taken as a "sentimental Springtime Rhapsody." Rather, he believed that

> as always in the work of great masters, the laughter is not far from tears, behind the sunshine there is a hint of storm. The lyric poetry, some of it the loveliest ever written, . . . carries echoes and overtones of winter and death; we are never allowed to forget that soon, too soon, the garland is withered and the burgeoning tree will wave gaunt arms in the tempest engulfing King Lear.[15]

Despite this impassioned rhetoric, the laughter was not forgotten—indeed, the promptbook in the Festival archives shows that the comic business was both acrobatic and inventive—but the fragility of "present mirth" was keenly felt. Walter Kerr, who deeply admired the performance, reported that "from the outset of the evening an undercurrent of ingrained sadness, of rueful longing for a time when gaiety came easier, serves as a contrast and counterpoint to the abandoned horseplay."[16]

At the heart of this interpretation was Bruno Gerussi's Feste—a played-out entertainer whose songs had "all fallen into a minor key."[17] He was an elderly grizzled fellow, clad in rough homespun, no longer sure of his bearings but ready to improvise his way through the confusion. A Toronto critic remarked that the director's lens had pulled into focus the usually elusive jester:

> Dr. Guthrie has probed this strange misfit and found a figure of strange sadness, an aging professional clown, his place in Olivia's household held on sufferance, his jokes as shabby as his clothes, at odds with the world and finding expression only in song.[18]

In all three of Guthrie's *Twelfth Night* productions, an aging and saddened Feste was the spokesman for the darker truths that underpin the dreams and revelry. Yet what had seemed to most a daring experiment in the '30s had, by 1957, become an "authentic" reading. Not only had his vision mellowed with time and experience, but Guthrie's audience was now more willing to embrace it.

The following season in England brought two new productions, one at the Old Vic directed by Michael Benthall and the other staged at Stratford's Memorial Theatre by Peter Hall. A twilight mood, often brightened with sportive comedy, permeated the Old Vic *Twelfth Night,* set in a ruined garden dominated by a trellised pavilion and colored in hues of russet and gold. Derek Godfrey, as Feste, was handy at playing the local games; but he also conveyed that this was a fool with a history. He suggested to Harold Hobson a man too often "bruised by the world" and now in retreat; when Orsino tried to pay him for his song, he gravely refused the proffered coins—"No pains, I take pleasure in singing"—as if tired of having a price tagged to his art.[19] By hinting at the sensibility usually camouflaged by Feste's drollery, the actor could expand the dimensions of the jester's personality. Mary Clarke, in her overview of the Old Vic season, not only placed Feste at the center of the play as the "character who holds all parts together," but she also observed, in accord with the widening consensus that his foolery hides an injured soul:

> There is indeed an aching sadness at the very heart of his character, something much more pathetically, vulnerably human than can be suggested by the conventional white face of a clown. The secret of Derek Godfrey's success was that he allowed the humanity to shine through.[20]

Such efforts to find a subtext to Feste's lines are common in modern productions, especially those that give him a pivotal role. Robert Eddison, for example, had implied a motive for Feste's revenge against Malvolio by suggesting that the fool concealed an unrequited love for Olivia that made him jealous of her attentive steward. And in the 1954 Old Vic production, the director Hugh Hunt had supplied his Feste (Leo McKern), a middle-aged jester dressed in faded motely, with a younger rival by turning Fabian into an up-and-coming fool.[21] It is as if, by constructing a human face for the creature behind the jester's mask, the actor hopes to let us penetrate Feste's cryptic nature. If pushed too far, such Hamlet-like efforts to "glean what afflicts him" only undercut Feste's credibility as Illyria's resident truth-teller by making his motives transparently personal. But when handled subtly these glimpses into his secret mind can secure our trust that he speaks out of the lessons of heartfelt experience as much as from shrewd observation.

An effort to show a Feste who nurses a bitter knowledge of life without cracking the enigma was brilliantly—if sometimes unevenly—realized in the second of the 1958 productions, Peter Hall's staging for the Royal Shakespeare Company (revived in 1960). In a short essay on the play, written for the Folio Society edition, Hall characterized *Twelfth Night* as "complex, ambiguous, and heartbreakingly funny." He saw it as a "transitional play" bridging the gulf between the earlier romantic comedies and the disquieting complexities of the problem plays and the tragedies: "There is something of bitterness in its comedy. But the comedy is rich, because there is darkness and disturbance."[22] To dramatize this vision, Hall made Feste his presenter. This "allowed" fool, a self-proclaimed "corrupter of words," possessed a unique knowledge of life's inequities and its transience that tinged with irony the other characters' dreams of perpetual happiness—just as the Cavalier setting, evocative of Caroline extravagance and Puritan denial, hinted that history, in due course, would bring in *its* revenges.

As directed by Hall—and as played by Cyril Luckham and later Max Adrian—Feste was unusually astringent. This was a "dry fool" rather than a melancholy weeper, a man who knew too much and who shared his secrets only in oblique jests and songs. Hall described him as

> bitter, insecure, singing the old half-forgotten songs to the Duke . . . his jokes now tarnished and not very successful. He is the creation of a professional entertainer, and we may perhaps relate him to John Osborne's Archie Rice, or to that fearful misanthropy which overtakes most comics when they begin to despise their audiences. He is suffered by all, and liked by few. He is the most perceptive and formidable character in the play.[23]

Hall detected behind the jokes and the impostures an idealist embittered by experience, a loner made sharply conscious of human folly by the sting of his own failures: "Feste is the critical centre of the play, the Thersites, the Jacques without eloquence, the malcontent, the man who sees all and says little, the cynic. It takes an idealist to be such a cynic."[24]

The performance began with a theatrical metaphor for Feste's role as go-between: not only in the sense that he makes the rounds of all the unwitting fools residing in Illyria, but also in that he serves as mediator between the real-life audience and the illusions of the stage. When the audience entered the theatre, the stage was screened by a gauze drop-curtain showing the image of a fool wearing an ass-eared cap and holding his bauble. A silvery nimbus shimmered around this central figure, about which could be seen the faces of the other characters, faintly touched by his radiance. Then a spotlight illuminated the image until, as music sounded, the stage lights came up—making the gauze transparent—to reveal Orsino luxuriating in his melancholy in the company of his retainers.

Gauzes were used throughout the performance, along with lighting effects, to give Illyria the atmosphere of "a country of dream that, at the last, melts again into dream."[25] Through this mirage world, richly colored in earth tints reminiscent of Rembrandt and Van Dyck, the characters played out their fantasies, wryly observed by Feste, who alone seemed to know that "Youth's a stuff will not endure."

This was a world in which comedy and romance were inextricably mixed, where the clowns had their moments of dignity and the Countess was "a coquettish *poseuse* who seemed to have escaped from a columbarium for slightly cracked doves."[26] But it was also one in which the mirth, however zestful, was always on the brink of dissipating, and the lyricism, however lovely, of falling into decadence. The other players, rapt in their dreams of living "happily ever after," might ignore the hints of mortality in store, but Feste was there to remind the audience with a bemused shake of his head at Sir Toby's and Sir Andrew's idiocies, a caustic poke at Orsino's fickleness, or a flash of triumph at Malvolio's humiliation. His first scene (I.v) intimated that the snubbed jester was all too sensible of "infirmity that decays the wise," as when he turned away at Malvolio's taunt that his skills were failing, and again when word of the young messenger drew Olivia's attention away from him. Later on, finding himself accosted by the new favorite of both lord and lady (III.i), Feste treated Cesario with studied indifference. Distance from his "fellows"—whether real or feigned—was also implicit in the ending given the midnight party (II.iii) to close the First Act. Once Maria began to hatch the plot against the peevish steward, the fool apparently slumbered until, as the pranksters crept out, he raised his head and gazed thoughtfully after them. A more acid humor sometimes entered into his reactions. For example, Orsino's failure to applaud his song added bite to the warning that "pleasure will be paid, one time or another" (II.vi); and his mock inquisition of Malvolio (IV.ii) was deliberately harsh, capped by the fool dancing on the trapdoor above the "madman."[27] Such antics also exposed the human frailties of this disillusioned seer. Isolated from the rest of the characters by his bitterness no less than his prescience, Feste drifted through Illyria, a companion to all, but an intimate to none.

At the same time, other aspects of the production—its visual beauty and rich coloring, its inventive humor, and its lyrical moments—gave romantic love and all the other temptations of the flesh a compelling charm. The audience was left with the thought that to be the possessor of tragic wisdom, especially within the milieu of romantic comedy, might be a terrible burden. This reminder was poignantly enacted in the play's conclusion, eloquently described here by Roy Walker:

> . . . the play ended as it began, with music, all the romantic and comic characters, except Malvolio, dancing together in a golden distance behind a gauze curtain in love's now triumphant harmony, with Feste . . . seated on the fore-stage in the gathering dusk, sadly remembering how the world began. Now it was their light that just touched his figure, forlorn at the thought that there was no more for him to do in this world. Even a god who plays the wise fool may be left lonely at the dance of human love.[28]

With this ending the opening sequence was now reversed. The audience, having been drawn through Feste's agency into the illusory world of *Twelfth Night*, were at last thrust back out of the golden dreamworld into the reality of "the wind and the rain," still accompanied by their guide, the sadly privileged fool.

III

These three productions—the Guthrie, the Benthall, and the Hall—consolidated Feste's position both as the messenger for *Twelfth Night*'s darker tonalities and as a keystone to its dramatic structure. In particular, Guthrie's and Hall's versions have had profound effects on subsequent interpreters, sometimes to the point where the plaintive undertones these two directors tried to sound have usurped the melody. Surveying the *Twelfth Nights* staged since 1960, on both sides of the Atlantic, one uncovers a host of eccentric, heartsick, grouchy, and decaying Festes. The novelty has by now become the convention, even a worn cliché.

At Ontario, Guthrie's precedent has been adopted in several variations by his successors. Eric Christmas, under David Williams's direction in 1966, was made the eldest member of an otherwise youthful and perky cast, appearing to a visiting critic from *The New York Times* (10 June) "as an oldster . . . who putters about like a damp rustic wit in an Illyrian country-store." He was "as careworn and philosophic a clown," said *The Toronto Globe and Mail* (9 June), "as the fashion warrants, which is considerable in these gloomy times." A more austere impression of a man at odds with the world, and dissatisfied with fooling, was given, in David Jones's 1975 revival, by "Tom Kneebone's harsh and metallic clown, burnished by wit, but unhappy. This was a tough professional Feste, his eyes quizzical and disenchanted, his distaste for his fellow men beginning with himself."[29] By 1980 Feste had mellowed considerably. Robin Phillips's elegant Georgian *Twelfth Night* had no need of a cranky malcontent to dispel its already low-keyed mirth. Instead, William Hutt portrayed "a warm-hearted retainer who . . . shuffles about in comfortable slippers" (*Southern News*, 10 June 1980), a wise old fool domesticated to a well-fed and affluent household and in no hurry to venture out into the wind and the rain. Ready to share a companionable chat with Olivia, to indulge Orsino's affectations, or to give a rueful shrug for Malvolio, this Feste injected a compassionate tolerance into the vicissitudes of Illyrian fortunes. There was no mockery of the sentiment in his songs. Rather he moved his listeners with heartfelt pleasure. At the end, the others passed out of view while Feste sang his sad, sweet tune, until he alone was left on stage.[30] Much of the edge was lost in this characterization—indeed, some critics found the production as a whole overly genteel—but in compensation Feste gained a heart for sorrows other than his own.

Meanwhile, the traditional happy-go-lucky fool has proved remarkably hardy in America, where he still often surfaces in regional productions of the comedy. But the modern diagnosis that he suffers from *ennui*, complicated by mid-life syndrome, has attracted some notable converts. Morris Carnovsky, a tragedian of solid credentials, played "a grey and seedy Feste" (*New York Herald Tribune*, 9 June 1960) at Stratford, Connecticut in 1960. "Tradition having given us a lineage of youthful, prancing, gay fools," Claire McGlinchee commented, "it was difficult to adjust to Morris Carnovsky's interpretation of Feste as a kind of lamenting Deor" even though he acted it with characteristic skill.[31] A less gracious critic dismissed this gloomy fool as "a broken-down, seamed and moss-hung jester, a creaking wit . . . on his last legs" (*The Morning Telegraph*, 10 June). One severe disadvantage to the actor attempting this pensive mode for Feste was that he was plopped down in a gimmicky production set *à la H.M.S. Pinafore* in a Regency seaside resort.

Such incongruity has its drawbacks, as does the alternative extreme of muting the contrast between saturnalia and sobriety. When Ellis Rabb staged the play at Lincoln Center in 1972, Feste (George Pentecost) was again a sad-faced clown "happier commiserating with himself in song than he is in his profession of fooling" (*The Saturday Review*, 25 March 1972); but this time he resided in an Illyria geared to the sadder aspects of the comedy. Set on a vast stage swathed in midnight-blue, with exotic "Arabian Nights" props and costumes, the performance afforded enough visual beauty to lull many critics. Walter Kerr, however, who had so admired Tyrone Guthrie's fusion of "sad and merry madness," complained that Rabb and his actors had overplayed the heartache (*New York Times*, 12 March):

> Feste has always been a faintly weary clown, uncertain that his muse will sustain him through another bout of wordplay, and Feste's mood, as much as anyone's, lurks behind the prankish deceptions of the evening. But that is an undertone, one that can be beautifully exploited so long as it has a grinning surface to mock. Mr. Rabb has made it the whole tone, almost as though the company were singing a requiem for a comedy recently dead.

Kerr's remarks point up a weakness in the modern penchant for brooding Festes. When the hints of mortality and temporal urgency that give resonance to *Twelfth Night*'s celebration of life are diffused throughout, the fool's deft reminders of time's exigencies are apt to become an insistent blare. Then the comedy itself, rather than shimmering with light and shadow, will turn enervating—as it did in the 1974 American Shakespeare Theatre production. Commemorated as the "underwater" *Twelfth Night* for its aquarium-like setting as well as its listless style, this production culminated in an *anagnorisis* full of "aching pauses between beats, unnecessary exits that left the lonely principals trying to be cheery in a void, and a visible draining of energy from the actors."[32] Feste was a glum hanger-on, singing dirges to his fellow mopers. And in case anyone missed the point that Malvolio was "most notoriously abused," in the prison scene the poor man was strapped down under a spotlight while his inquisitor grilled him from the shadows.

A more playful mood was struck the same year at the Oregon Shakespeare Festival in Ashland. There Feste (Jeff Brooks) was restored to his tenure as humorist, and his presiding role as Master of the Revels was given a clever twist:

> Feste walked through the play like a stage manager. He oversaw Viola's landing in Illyria. The lighting obeyed the gestures of his hand. In short, he transcended reality and heightened the comic spirit of make-believe.[33]

Viola's affinity with the fool who wears no motley in his brain was signalled by allowing her to learn the same trick, while for his antagonist, Malvolio, "the lights were less obliging." Though potentially hokey, this method was an imaginative way of evincing Feste's centrality; and by allowing him to be genuinely amusing, the director (Jim Edmondson) kept the pacing nimble and the lessons diverting. Less happily, Feste's role was enhanced in Gerald Freeman's 1978 American Shakespeare Theatre *Twelfth Night* by subsuming Fabian's lines into the fool's part. Worse yet, in 1980 the jester's deadpan wit was trivialized by rigging him out as a chino-clad, Kool-smoking leftover from "a Bing-Crosby-as-middle-aged-frosh movie" (*The Village Voice*, 17 December 1980) in David Mamet's campy rendition with New York's Circle Repertory.

The vogue for world-weary Festes has spread as far afield as Paris—where Jean Anouilh cast him as "sad and obsequious, like the romanticized Pierrot," in a mannered 1961 production[34]—and Stockholm, where Ingmar Bergman staged a headily erotic *Twelfth Night* (1975) watched over by a timeworn Feste. The Swedish production impressed a visiting American critic as a more robust version of Bergman's own *Smiles of a Summer Night*, with the choric office of Madame Armfeldt, "that wise old woman who stands outside love's mysteries and comments on them," given to Feste and Fabian, here played as two canny old family retainers for whom "love is only a faded memory."[35]

But of all the places where *Twelfth Night* holds the stage, the bittersweet mode has been most persistent in Britain, where Hall's example and the Guthrie/Guinness Old Vic legacy have substantially recast the older notion of Feste. This is less true of amateur players, who often remain faithful to the tradition of flippant wits, but even so there are exceptions. One semiprofessional case was Jonathan Miller's staging for the Oxford and Cambridge Shakespeare Company

(1969). Vowing to dispense with "the capering ninnies of convention," the director promised instead "a clapped out clown with a bottle nose who knows he is scraping the bottom of the barrel to make his lady laugh."[36] The resulting gruff, acerbic fool was described, with less enthusiasm, by Sprague and Trewin (p. 131n.) as "a vinegary and unmusical hack." Perhaps the best symbol for the resilience of the weather-beaten Feste in the English theatre was Robert Eddison's reprise of his sad-gay fool for the Old Vic in 1978, thirty years after he had undertaken the role at the same house. If his nostalgia for better days, his threadbare outfit, and his forlorn visage gave Eddison something of the look of a retired flower child, this was still a memorable Feste: beautifully spoken and gallant in the face of sorrow.

But then he had some need of gallantry, since the fool, in this sometimes overblown production, was so achingly conscious of his own mortality. A typical instance came when, stricken by Olivia's gentle reproach—"Now you do see, sir, how your fooling grows old, and people dislike it?"—he buried his head sadly in her lap. For B. A. Young this was "a magical moment."[37] Yet, though truly affecting, it was also as hopelessly sentimental as any of the touching moments for Viola, or tormented histrionics for Malvolio, that the actor-managers had once devised. Unless Feste takes his own heartaches, as much as his pleasures, with a grain of salt, he is apt to turn maudlin. Just as important, his license to puncture the egocentric follies of others—like Justice Overdo's warrant or Gregers Werle's summons to the ideal—will be thrown in doubt if his own frailties are too much in view. Eddison's acting skill made Feste's troubles genuinely moving, in this case, but the voice of doom did rumble a bit naggingly. As well as demonstrating the tenacity of the sorrowful Feste in the theatre, this incarnation warned how easily he might slip into decadence.

IV

Nowhere has the serious interpretation of *Twelfth Night* made a deeper imprint than at Stratford's Royal Shakespeare Theatre. This is only natural in a company so responsive—in terms both of influence and reaction—to its own traditions; and Peter Hall's production was outstanding. It was also one that aged exceptionally well in memory. Despite the doubts about Hall's methods and intentions voiced in notices at the time, subsequent allusions reveal how durably this *Twelfth Night* stood as a measure for alternative visions. Of course, many aspects of Hall's interpretation—including his vision of Feste—were challenged, or else modified, by other RSC directors. Yet Stratford's Feste, although he has come in varying shapes and sizes, has kept with remarkable constancy both his ironic perspective on the masquerade at hand and his fund of privileged knowledge. C. L. Barber, writing at about the same time that Hall directed *Twelfth Night,* surmised that Feste "has been over the garden wall into some such world as the Vienna of *Measure for Measure.*"[38] And we might say that at Stratford he has remained a traveller still, bringing back to Illyria memories from less happy realms beyond its borders.

This was true even in the 1966 production directed by Clifford Williams, which marked the sharpest break with the modern accent on the comedy's darker colors. As demonstrated through the plentiful allusions to carnival and saturnalia splashed across the playbill pages, the 1966 interpretation was a deliberate reversal of Hall's seriocomic approach. Played as a high comedy romp "firmly steeled against pathos and poetry" (*The Times,* 17 June 1966), Williams's *Twelfth Night* demoted Feste, acted by Norman Rodway, from the key spot Hall had granted him back to the supporting ranks. He remained, nevertheless, an aloof and unfunny fool "with more of dark, brittle realism than wistful charm" (*The Glasgow Herald,* 18 June). Curiously, even in a production as determinedly vivacious as this one, Feste sustained his air of knowing more than anyone else, and of finding in such intuitions some cause for bitterness or sorrow. This was a trait, here only roughly sketched, that the next three productions would delineate in richer detail.

Feste was once again a major figure in John Barton's 1969 *Twelfth Night* (revived at the Aldwych in 1970 with several cast changes), one of the finest of the RSC versions. Intelligently and beautifully staged, this *Twelfth Night* was widely admired for its imagination and sensitive emotional shadings. Among its many virtues was the strength of the ensemble. The characters were fleshed-out, complex personalities, defined in good measure by the relationships—past and present, actual and desired—that joined them: "Mostly, the production simply explores the half-stated relationships and crannies of the play, loading them with feeling. . . . Everyone is connected to everyone else, with a sympathy which never confuses sentiment with the sentimentality that is the subject of the comedy" (*The Observer,* 24 August 1969). No single character, therefore, dominated the stage; but the knowing fool did much to set the tone, one of grave lyricism and of laughter shot through with sadness.

According to Robert Speaight, Feste "was quietly in command—seeing everything and through everything, and singing with delicate accomplishment about many of the things he saw."[39] Emrys James played him as a wryly compassionate fool, whose experience had earned him wisdom but not bitterness. A white-haired clown long in service to the family, he treated Olivia with affectionate concern and joked familiarly with her uncle. To Maria, who longed to marry the reluctant Toby, he gave quiet sympathy, and a smile to the ever-hopeful, though ever-thwarted, Sir Andrew. As a musician he was a welcome visitor to Orsino's court. Yet he remained detached, never forgetting his status as hired entertainer. Only with Viola, another independent spirit, did he find a momentary kinship when, in their brief interlude, "cross-talk gives way to music and unspoken communication, as the two characters sprawl out together ruefully surveying the human scene from some other plane" (*The Times,* 22 August 1969). Playing against the wrangling notes in this wit-contest, the actors brought out a shared understanding and respect between these two who play with words, just as they juggle roles, without losing their balance. It was even intimated that he had seen through her disguise when the fool crossed to her "as if [he] realized who [she] is" on the line "Who you are and what you would are out of my welkin."[40]

But more even than Viola, who at last joins the charmed circle of lovers insulated from loss or care, Feste was attuned to the hard realities of life, especially the sad fact that "Youth's a stuff will not endure." Awareness of time, which brings to a close all lovely things—youth, beauty, pleasure, even the play itself—was his special wisdom; and this gave the fool a crucial role in a production deeply concerned with the passing of time. From the reminders of transience and decay that sound in the lines, to the sundial upon the stage, time was felt as the untangling power that brought fulfillment to some, disillusionment to others, but irreversible change to all. Anne Barton, in the program note she wrote for the production, related the antics and revelry, sometimes bordering on madness, to the topsy-turvy holiday of Twelfth Night—but she emphasized that celebration must have an end. For a privileged few in Illyria the dream is left unbroken ("Viola and Orsino, Olivia and Sebastian remain, by the special dispensation of art, in a romance world that never falters"), but the others must face the "cold light of day." As the audience faces its own "jolt into reality," its guide is Feste:

> Left alone on the stage, Feste sings his song about the ages of man.... The reality of wind and rain wins out, the monotony of everyday. The passing of time is painful, may even seem unendurable, but there is nothing for it but resignation, the wise acceptance of the Fool. All holidays come to an end. All revels wind down at last. Only in the theatre can some people be left in Illyria.[41]

These were truths the fool had known all along. One way that this was pointed in performance was to have Feste give snatches of his songs from time to time as counterpoint to the dialogue. He made his first entrance whistling "Hey, Robin, jolly Robin"—the song of fickle love he later sings as he nears the confined steward—and he repeated the same tune in other scenes. For that more poignant lament of unsatisfied desire, "Come away, death," Feste had underlined the oblique parody of Orsino's melancholy by caricaturing a heart-sick lover—languidly circling the duke and pressing a hand to his brow—as he sang the second verse; later on, he hummed it again as Olivia pressed her favors on Cesario. Most telling, though, were the reprises of "O mistress mine." At the end of the revels scene, Maria returned and tried to lead Sir Toby off. When he resisted ("'Tis too late to go to bed now") and left her, Sir Andrew kissed her hand and Feste closed the scene with a pensive strain of "Youth's a stuff will not endure." He sang the same words to point another touching moment, when outside Malvolio's cell a subdued Sir Toby slipped his ring onto Maria's finger and said, "Come by and by to my chamber."[42]

These last two instances of invented business exemplify the pensive tinge Barton gave to the comedy's intimations of mortality. In his detailed account of the staging in *Royal Shakespeare,* Stanley Wells described how sensitively Barton integrated humor with the pathos. Still, he conceded that in such wistful moments the director "was reducing the spectrum," employing effects that were masterly but that "deprived the play of some of its brighter colors."[43] Many reviewers noted this rueful undertone. The critic for *The Daily Telegraph* (22 August 1969) judged that "what has interested John Barton in directing this revival is the melancholy that hangs over a play festive in spirit but concerned with people who misuse time, [who are] sadly deceived themselves and [are] deceived in each other." Others wrote of "the muted gold [light] of a winter garden" and of "the autumnal, sea-wrecked emotion which surged through" the play.[44]

This plangent strain was not, it should be emphasized, the sole mood expressed. Barton himself stated that his object was to do justice to the play's complexity: "The text contains an enormous range of emotions and moods and most productions seem to select one—farce or bitterness or romance—and emphasize it throughout. I wanted to sound all the notes that are there" (*Plays and Players,* November 1969). Like Hall before him, Barton sought to harmonize the elements of comedy and romance, of present delight and the regretful hints that "what's to come is still unsure," but without making the swings of feeling too broad. Still, the bittersweet nuances were felt. In an interview given a few years after directing *Twelfth Night,* Barton described Shakespeare's attitude in this play as "on the whole wry, tolerant and accepting," but with a "very conscious split between the 'happy-ever-after' world of romantic comedy and his sense of what life and people are really like."[45] His staging concentrated on the yearnings for satisfaction and security the characters all feel, but with the full knowledge that as many fantasies are shattered as are fulfilled, as many friendships damaged as upheld, as many courtships brought to nothing as to marriage. Sir Andrew carried with him a little bunch of golden primroses to give Olivia until he heard, to his dismay, that she detested anything yellow; Sir Toby spurned Sir Andrew's well-meant assistance, at the end, with "wintry" contempt; Antonio was left alone onstage, after the lovers had swept off, to make a solitary exit; and throughout the performance the distant sound of gulls and the restless sea reminded the audience of a reality circumscribing the Illyrian dreamworld.[46] Even Sebastian's trust that Olivia's proposal was a happy stroke of fortune and not some lunacy was given an ironic cast by punctuating his reverie with the offstage cries of the confined "madman," Malvolio.[47]

One notices, too, in looking through the reviews, how often this reflective sadness was associated with Feste. *The Times*, for example, recalled the original production as "Feste's *Twelfth Night:* a shifting perspective of romantic ardour and romantic folly seen through the eyes of the Fool against an ever present sense of the effects of time" (7 August 1970). "Emrys James's exquisite Feste sets the tone," stated *The Daily Telegraph* (22 August 1969): "This courtly jester . . . brings a Watteau-like dreaminess . . . to the very air we breathe in Illyria." In his lyrics and his word-games Feste reminds us of the rules that festive comedy can only temporarily suspend, but without the rancor or self-importance of a killjoy like Malvolio. And as James played him, the fool's perspective closely resembled the one Barton ascribed to his creator: realistic but "on the whole wry, tolerant and accepting." So it is not surprising that Feste seemed, to some viewers, to be at the play's heart, especially given his involvement with its deep concerns. The limits of fellowship, the problems of love, the fine line separating wisdom from folly or imagination from madness, the inconstancy of words and people, and the confounding of identity endemic to a world of quick-change artists—all these are spoken of or acted out by Feste. In licensing the fool as his truth-teller, Barton followed Hall. But he replaced the earlier embittered veteran with a more resilient, more forbearing clown. What Stanley Wells underlined, in summing up his memories of Barton's *Twelfth Night,* was its "beauty of communication, of sympathy, understanding, and compassion. It had a Chekhovian quality. . . . Shot through with sadness though the production was, its ultimate effect was a happy one."[48] The Feste was very much in keeping with this generosity. Some sharpness was lost and some brightness muted, but the acceptance of frailty and mutability that infuses this last festive comedy was shown without breaking its harmonies or transforming it into a problem play.

Some dissonance, of course, is often wanted in the modern theatre. That vein of bitterness in the fool's utterances was by no means mined out yet. If Cyril Luckham and later Max Adrian, under Hall's direction, had portrayed Feste as a worn-out entertainer in the mold of Osborne's Archie Rice, then Ron Pember—in Peter Gill's 1974 *Twelfth Night*—carried this idea one step further with his "savage, sardonic teeth-bearing Feste rasping out his songs as if it were 'The Three Penny Opera'" (*The Guardian,* 23 August 1974). This "unshaven malcontent" (*The Times,* 23 August) brimmed with contempt for his listeners—and for himself, no less, for pandering to them. Interestingly, whereas prelapsarian *Twelfth Nights* had often glossed over Feste's money-grubbing, by compressing the dialogue or tossing it off lightly, this production made much of these episodes, thereby underlining both the entertainer's dependence on his audience and his disdain for their limitations. Gill encapsulated this ambivalence, for example, when Sir Toby casually tossed a coin to Feste in anticipation of some music and then Sir Andrew held up his own small offering—which Feste promptly took out of his hand. He delivered the song ("O mistress mine") directly to the audience while the two knights sat at their cups behind him. His stance and gritty voice conveyed that even if the onstage celebrants were too rapt in the present to bother with "what's to come," he knew full well their bills were coming due—and that the listeners out front should heed his meaning and not just wallow in the sentiment. Similarly, his attitude toward Orsino, even as he palmed his fee for a fine lyric or a well-turned jest, was daringly caustic—the more so because his noble auditor so clearly missed the ironic applications to his own foibles; and his encounter with Cesario in Act III stressed the abrasive undertones to their exchange.[49]

Feste's isolation from his employers—and his cronies—was sociological no less than aesthetic. Peter Thomson incisively described this fallen but still testy class-warrior:

> Ron Pember spoke like a Londoner, dressed like a faded Harlequin now reduced to busking, and hinted always at a radical's distaste for the antics of privilege. He despised the effeteness of Orsino's court, and his angry assumption that Viola considered him a beggar had all the spikiness of class pride. . . . He was a working man among the leisured classes, deeply critical of their behavior and bitterly dissatisfied with his own.[50]

In an illuminating aside, Thomson reported that another member of the audience had compared this fool "with Bosola, another joker who declines to laugh at his own jokes." That to these viewers Feste resembled Webster's grimly sardonic outsider is a helpful gloss on Pember's acting. But that both critic and ordinary playgoer so casually accepted a kinsman to Bosola (however distantly related) as a lawful citizen of Illyria is an even more revealing sign of the preconceptions brought to a modern staging of *Twelfth Night.* Some reviewers found Pember's saturnine loner a bit eccentric—just as others thought the interpretation brashly original—but few dismissed him as a strange aberration in a festive comedy.

True, Pember's hard-boiled Feste gave a needed edge to an Illyria surfeiting on narcissism and sexual desire. His bitter dependence on patrons and their coins brought to new light all those other reminders of the economic realities that underpin holiday and romance: Orsino's "great estate" and Olivia's "quantity of dirty lands"; his counted-out "bounty" and her "inventoried charms"; Sir Toby sponging off Sir Andrew till the overextended pigeon "hadst need send for more money"; Malvolio dreaming of "some rich jewel" as he idly fondles his chain of office; Antonio's unlucky purse; Maria's "dowry" and Sir Toby's reluctant "recompense"; and all the many warnings that the piper must be paid, "one time or another."

The fool's unconvivial temperament also revealed an unexpected resemblance to another servant in the household: the steward Malvolio. In some ways, Feste was no less a "puritan" than his antagonist. He viewed the daily Illyrian carnival with the same disdainful glance Malvolio gave the impromptu late-night party. He set as high a value on his own opinions as the smug steward, even if they were formed by a keener intelligence. He was sensitive to class differences and monetary considerations. And he set himself apart from his fellows with equal insistence. Such a reading perhaps lays undue emphasis on connections that should only be hinted at. But Illyria is indeed a land where human beings are all mirrors to each other, casting back reflections—whether identical, reversed, or absurdly distorted—that most fail to recognize as images of themselves, so we should expect some correspondences between two fools.[51] Nonetheless, linking Feste with Malvolio, like comparing him with Bosola, is an idea only modern audiences would countenance. The irony implicit in seeing Feste as an "ill-wisher" is simply more than we can resist. Today the expectation that every silver lining must have its cloud is so strong that an out-of-sorts or even downright grumpy Feste comes as no surprise to us.

Nor are we likely to be startled when Feste's role is built up, any more than erstwhile audiences were overly dismayed when he was shoved into the wings so that Malvolio or Viola or Sir Toby could reign undisturbed. A case in point was Terry Hands's direction of *Twelfth Night* for the RSC in 1979, with Geoffrey Hutchings as Feste. The best word for this fool was "ubiquitous." Onstage virtually every moment, Feste observed the other characters act out their fantasies—or meet their rude awakenings—from the sidelines, whenever he was not involved in the action. From the first minute of the performance, when a hooded figure (shortly revealed, minus *cucullum,* as the fool) piped the notes that so engrossed the lovelorn duke, to the last strummed chords of the epilogue song, Feste was at hand: sometimes watching from the margins of the stage, or closer by, behind a box-tree, sometimes eyeing his own onlookers as he sang or joked for them, and sometimes catching a word or gesture his companions were too fatuous or self-absorbed to mark—but always poised not to miss a thing worth noting.[52] The possibilities for tongue-in-cheek dramatic irony, with this framework imposed, were naturally many. Since Feste had witnessed her arrival, Viola's disguise was occasion for wry glances rather than confusion; and his inside-track gave his encounter with Sebastian (IV.i) an almost farcical twist. As Roger Warren noted:

> "Your name is not Master Cesario; nor this is not my nose neither" had to be made to mean the reverse of what it in fact does mean, to the extent of Feste actually removing a *false* nose to emphasize knowingly that "nothing is so that is so."[53]

Feste's spying also gave him a ringside seat for Malvolio's reactions to the letter and his cross-gartered transformation—scenes from which the fool is textually excluded—so that his amused scrutiny added another circle of awareness to the side-show in motion, enveloping both the gullers and the gull.

In the later version of the staging, Feste even helped to dress the set. The scene throughout was an orchard of several trees planted in box-tubs. At the outset the landscape was wintry and bare, a bleak mirror to the men and women who ventured there, but as the sap began to rise in these repressed, barren, or somehow thwarted creatures, daffodils began to bloom in the tubs—each one planted by Feste, as the signs of warmth, release, and new growth appeared. Several marked the vows of heartfelt love soon proliferating; still more the late-night festivities and the deepening rapport between Viola and Orsino; and more yet Malvolio's headlong plunge into romance. By the time the steward reappeared, after the interval, decked out in yellow stockings, the trees had sprouted new leaves, more daffodils had flowered, and the midwinter chill had warmed into sunshine. The stagehands, of course, produced the greater miracle, but the fool's small plantings led the way into springtime.[54]

The direction of the role was, in some ways, an extension of Hall's idea of the fool's centrality, but softened by the more generous tone set by Barton. As before, Feste was a penetrating clown who knew more of the truth than anyone else, although in this case he was inclined to smile at what he had discerned. And once again he served as a kind of presenter, a mediator stationed midway between his fellow players and the spectators beyond the stage, but this time as a "showman" of another sort—not so much flagging entertainer as note-taking impresario. To Gareth Lloyd Evans he even seemed in charge of orchestrating the story: "He is on stage virtually all the time, not as the usual wry observer but as a kind of conductor of the action. You feel they dance to his tune, and he dispenses destiny."[55]

What saved this directorial imposition from heavy-handedness was, in large measure, Geoffrey Hutchings's self-effacing Feste. A small and quirky fellow, with a gnomish face that peered out of faded patchwork, his fascinated interest in the antics and revelations going on before him was seldom obtrusive, and he kept a light touch in his meetings with the other characters. Well aware of his own role-playing, he could smile at the poses that so absorbed the pretenders in his company—as when he snatched away Olivia's veil to show the girlish mirth hidden by her affected mourning or when, in the final scene, he maneuvered Orsino and Viola closer together[56]—but he kept his own secrets to himself. As a fool who had learned to live without illusions, he watched the human comedy spin itself out before his bemused eyes, relishing its ironies and accepting its pangs with equal humor. When at the last he sang of life's vicissitudes, a pensive tableau was formed around him: behind him, the quartet of lovers drifting slowly upstage, and off to the sides, sitting under the trees, those chastened by experience—"the wounded Aguecheek, head in hands, the isolated Antonio, and the sobered Maria and Toby, separated and facing away from each other."[57]

V

In his staging, Terry Hands carried to its practical limits the modern image of Feste as critic and chorus: the knowing observer who stands somewhere between the illusory fools upon the stage and their counterparts in the audience. Such an emphasis on Feste, like the ground bass of sadness that so often accompanies it, is a reflection of our time, our mindset. Isolation, problems of identity, and broken dreams pervade modern drama. Similarly, Shakespearean performers gravitate toward the uncertainties and the hints of disturbance ingrained in even the brightest of his plays. Illyria has turned to an unstable world where the enigmatic Feste reigns as master of the revels winding down. Sometimes the fool's ubiquity or his weary wisdom can become mere tricks of habit. Yet, if done intelligently, serious treatment of Feste can still yield stimulating results.

The versions staged by the Royal Shakespeare Company exemplify the modern tradition's potential richness. These Festes, whatever their imperfections, are imaginative enough to transcend convention. His traits remain fairly constant. He is usually an aging fool, unattached but alert to what goes on. Whether cynical or compassionate, he is deeply conscious of infirmity—in himself and others—and of mutability. He is a role-player who keeps his own mask in place, and at the same time a spectator able to see through others' charades. He is a paid entertainer, something of a misfit, and a realist. Yet within the basic formula Stratford actors and directors have ingeniously given new dimensions to the role. The familiar convention is thus revitalized. Moreover, the company's ensemble skills promote strong casting and encourage the actors to test out new balances, new tensions in the relationships they create.

Conversely, some of the examples I have shown illustrate the less attractive features of the jester's modern stage identity. Too-sad Festes can turn maudlin, thereby blunting the comedy. Hack Festes make bad entertainers. Fools whose thoughts have soured or whose failings are too obvious cannot make convincing ironists, and dreary ones are worse. Gimmicky productions trivialize the fool's wisdom. Criticism-conscious productions puff him up unduly. Lastly, monotone productions that take their cue entirely from Feste's saddest utterances, or farcical versions weighed down with a malcontent clown, too often blast the comedy's delicate harmonies.

These are dangers even the finest directors must skirt with some care. A Peter Hall or Tyrone Guthrie may "do it with a better grace," but if carried too far the bittersweetness will turn to Jan Kott's desolate perception that fools like "Feste and Touchstone are not clowns any more; their jokes have ceased to be funny. . . . They live in a bare world, bereft of myths, reduced to knowledge without illusions."[58] No doubt, somewhere, *Twelfth Night* has been or will be played in such a barren lunar landscape—with an unsmiling clown in the foreground—but this is no less a distortion than the winsome, laugh-strewn versions once popular. *Twelfth Night* celebrates life and heartfelt emotion. The reminders that such things are fleeting, sometimes elusive, even riddled with absurdity, may pierce us. But the poignance is meant to endorse life's value, not deny it. Feste may stand at the garden gates, ready to usher us out of the sheltered world of romantic comedy, but he must not be exiled from its precincts. A Feste without sympathy for love and the good life, however keen his sense of their caprices, cannot open our eyes to that fuller vision of earthly life.

The whirligig of time brings in its revenges as surely in the theatre as in any other human sphere, so we should expect future transformations in Feste. But the odds are that those changes will not be too radical so long as we keep the perceptions and the biases our century has nurtured. Feste has long been seen as a professional entertainer, a shrewd wit, a loner with few, if any, attachments of affection. What has intensified is our sense that he is entrapped, or at the very least defined, by his role—a hired clown who sports his mask because it is the only sanctioned outlet for his insights. His self-containment is now a sign of alienation; his knowledge of human nature the hard-earned wisdom of a social misfit. At best he wins some freedom by hiding his "real" behind his pretended face, but this is necessarily a limited release.

Such problems of identity are a longstanding preoccupation of the modern theatre. From Pirandello's mindgames and Beckett's mock rituals through Sam Shepard's image-locked rock stars and would-be desperadoes, modern playwrights have wrestled with the actor's relationship to his role. Feste's awareness of his roleplaying and the limits it imposes is therefore very much in keeping with our cultural milieu. His pessimism is no less an expression of the times. If romantic aspirations have not been completely extinguished in our drama, they have been searchingly, often achingly, questioned. Our archetypal clowns are Samuel Beckett's Vladimir and Estragon, doing their vaudeville turns to the echoes of "all the dead voices." Feste may be more sophisticated than these poor tramps, but his fooling, too, makes us doubt the promises of happy endings, makes us remember that "the rain it raineth every day." Whether he takes the form of a disenchanted joker or a dreamer gone to seed, Feste tells us that Twelfth Night, the last night of the Christmas season, marks the end to feasting. Even when a warmhearted mood is set, granting holiday and love their pleasures, he sees beyond the passing moment. That blend of irony and compassion in John Barton's *Twelfth Night* that generated instants when "Shakespeare touches hands with Chekhov" (*The Times*, 22 August 1969) owed much to the presence of Feste, the wise observer of human folly.

Today a major *Twelfth Night* without a worthy fool would be unthinkable. This honor has a license from no less an authority than Sir Arthur Quiller-Couch, who over fifty years ago affirmed: "We must hold and insist on holding Feste, Master of the Revels, to be the master-mind and controller of *Twelfth Night*, its comic spirit and president."[59] Viola may still win our hearts. Malvolio may grandstand all he pleases. The lovers and the merrymakers may take their turns as well. But the wily jester, inscrutable to the last, remains our chosen guide—deftly pointing our way through the comic maze and calling us back, at the end, to the waiting world outside the theatre's walls.

Notes

All *Twelfth Night* citations are from *The Riverside Shakespeare*, ed. G. B. Evans (Boston: Houghton Mifflin, 1974).

[1] This article focuses on Feste's theatrical metamorphosis; but, as most readers will be aware, much the same process has taken place in the criticism. As scholarly interpreters (like their theatrical counterparts) have stressed the play's darker, more ironic tones, they have more and more looked to Feste as its key. For anyone interested in comparing Feste's critical image with the stage version shown here, the following studies are representative: C. L. Barber, *Shakespeare's Festive Comedy* (Princeton: Princeton Univ. Press, 1959); Anne Barton, "*As You Like It* and *Twelfth Night:* Shakespeare's Sense of an Ending," in *Shakespearian Comedy,* Stratford-upon-Avon Studies, 14, eds. Malcolm Bradbury and David Palmer (London: Edward Arnold, 1972); A. C. Bradley, "Feste the Jester" in *A Book of Homage to Shakespeare* (1916; rpt. in *A Miscellany* [London: Macmillan, 1929]); Roger Ellis, "The Fool in Shakespeare: A Study in Alienation," *Critical Quarterly,* 10 (1968), 245-68; Gareth Lloyd Evans, "Shakespeare's Fools: The Shadow and the Substance of Drama," in *Shakespearian Comedy;* Robert Hillis Goldsmith, *Wise Fools in Shakespeare* (Liverpool: Liverpool Univ. Press, 1958); Joan Hartwig, "Feste's Whirligig and the Comic Providence of *Twelfth Night,*" *English Literary History,* 40 (1973), 501-13; Leslie Hotson, *Shakespeare's Motley* (London: Rupert Hart-Davis, 1952); Clifford Leech, *Twelfth Night and Shakespearian Comedy* (Toronto: Univ. of Toronto Press, 1965); Julian Markels, "Shakespeare's Confluence of Tragedy and Comedy: *Twelfth Night* and *King Lear,*" *Shakespeare Quarterly,* 15 (1964), 75-88; Leo Salingar, "The Design of *Twelfth Night,*" *SQ,* 9 (1958), 117-39; Joseph Summers, "The Masks of *Twelfth Night,*" *University of Kansas Review,* 22 (1955), 25-32; Enid Welsford, *The Fool: His Social and Literary History* (London: Faber and Faber, 1935); Robert Wilcher, "The Art of the Comic Duologue in Three Plays by Shakespeare," *Shakespeare Survey,* 35 (1982), 87-97.

[2] See Sylvan Barnet, "Charles Lamb and the Tragic Malvolio," *Philological Quarterly,* 23 (1954), 179-88; Joan Coldwell, "The Playgoer as Critic: Charles Lamb on Shakespeare's Characters," *SQ,* 26 (1975), 184-95; and Russell Jackson, "'Perfect Types of Womanhood': Rosalind, Beatrice and Viola in Victorian Criticism and Performance," *ShS,* 32 (1979), 15-26.

[3] *Shakespeare's "Twelfth Night: or, What You Will."* A Comedy Revised by J. P. Kemble: And Now First Published As It Is Acted at the Theatre Royal in Covent Garden (London: Printed for the Theatre, 1810; rpt. London: Cornmarket Press, 1971).

[4] *Twelfe Night, Or what you will.* By William Shakespeare, Arranged to be played in four acts, By Augustin Daly. Printed from the Prompt Book, and as produced at Daly's Theatre, February 21st, 1883 (Privately Printed, 1893).

[5] *The Saturday Review,* 9 February 1901; Preface to the Souvenir Program for *Twelfth Night,* 5 February 1901, His Majesty's Theatre, Harvard Theatre Collection.

[6] Preface to *Twelfth Night* (London: Heinemann, 1912), p. viii.

[7] Harley Granville-Barker's promptbook for *Twelfth Night* (1912), The University of Michigan, Shattuck, *TN*, No. 80; supplemented with theatrical reviews in the Harvard Theatre Collection.

[8] *The Saturday Review,* 23 November 1912. "Elia's fairyland" is an allusion to Charles Lamb's famous essay, "On Some of the Old Actors," in *The Works of Charles and Mary Lamb,* ed. E. V. Lucas (1903; rpt. New York, AMS Press, 1968), Vol. I, 132-41.

[9] William Poel had restored the original scene order, and earlier Samuel Phelps had come very close; but both producers had cut the text substantially. See Poel's promptbook for *Twelfth Night* (1897), The Victoria and Albert Museum, Shattuck, *TN,* No. 43; and Phelps's promptbook (1848), The Folger Shakespeare Library, Shattuck, *TN,* No. 11.

[10] *The Manchester Guardian,* 19 September 1933.

[11] *The Observer,* 24 September 1948.

[12] *The New Statesman and Nation,* 2 October 1948.

[13] Arthur Colby Sprague and J. C. Trewin, *Shakespeare's Plays Today: Customs and Conventions of the Stage* (Columbia: Univ. of South Carolina Press, 1970), p. 96.

[14] Audrey Williamson, *Old Vic Drama 2: 1947-1957* (London: Rockliff, 1957), p. 14.

[15] Tyrone Guthrie, Program for *Twelfth Night* (1957), Stratford Festival Archives.

[16] *New York Herald Tribune,* 4 July 1957.

[17] *New York Herald Tribune,* 7 July 1957.

[18] *Toronto Globe and Mail,* 3 July 1957.

[19] *The Sunday Times,* 6 April 1958.

[20] Mary Clarke, *Shakespeare at the Old Vic* (London: Hamish Hamilton, 1958).

[21] See Hugh Hunt, *Old Vic Prefaces: Shakespeare and the Producer* (London: Routledge and Kegan Paul, 1954), pp. 70-72, 76-79. Hunt ascribed a personal bitterness to Feste's last song, in which the discredited fool acknowledges that "not only has he lost his place, but his successor has probably already been found" (p. 78).

[22] *Twelfth Night* (London: The Folio Society, 1966), p. 3. Cf. C. L. Barber's verdict that Feste "has an air of knowing more of life than anyone else—too much, in fact. . . . His part does not darken the bright colors of the play; but it gives them a dark outline, suggesting that the whole bright revel emerges from shadow" (*Shakespeare's Festive Comedy* [Princeton: Princeton Univ. Press, 1959], p. 259).

[23] Folio Society edition, p. 5. Clifford Leech draws a similar analogy, but without Hall's emphasis on Feste's bitter cynicism, when he notes that Feste "has amused us, and enriched our transient Illyria, but will not let us go without claiming a common humanity with us. He is a player as well as an imaginary character: we can meet him outside the theatre when the performance is over, and the life-conditions that we know belong to him too. He has a descendant in the Archie Rice of John Osborne's *The Entertainer,* who ended the play by asking us to let him know where we were working tomorrow: he was ready to exchange roles and to come and watch us" (*Twelfth Night and Shakespearian Comedy,* p. 54).

[24] Folio Society edition, pp. 5-6. Surprisingly, the only sizable cuts in the text were made in Feste's scenes (the mock indictment of wordplay in III.i [ll. 11-25] and about thirty lines from the prison scene [IV.ii]). Apparently most of these lines were restored, however, in the later version (Peter Hall's promptbooks for *Twelfth Night* [1958 and 1960], The Shakespeare Centre Library).

[25] *The Birmingham Post,* 23 April 1958.

[26] J. C. Trewin, *Going to Shakespeare* (London: George Allen & Unwin, 1978), p. 163.

[27] Peter Hall's promptbook for *Twelfth Night* (1958), Shattuck, *TN,* No. 98, Shakespeare Centre Library. Hall remarks in his Introduction to the Folio Society edition that Feste "cruelly tortures the imprisoned Malvolio" (p. 5), and his speculation that the fool might have been a failed priest (p. 6) may help explain the caustic treatment of the Sir Topas scene in his staging. According to a review of the 1960 revival in *The Evening News* (18 May 1960), Feste—epitomized as an "ageing clown . . . endlessly cracking his stale jokes in a desperate attempt to win brief smiles"—took "a terrible revenge on Malvolio" in the prison scene and danced "a savage saraband" over his enemy.

[28] Roy Walker, "The Whirligig of Time: A Review of Recent Productions," *ShS,* 12 (1959), 122-30, esp. p. 128.

[29] Berners W. Jackson, "Shakespeare at Stratford, Ontario, 1975," *SQ,* 27 (1976), 24-32, esp. p. 29.

[30] Phillips's promptbook for *Twelfth Night* (1980), Festival Archives, Stratford, Ontario; supplemented by the videotape of the production in the archives, and by theatrical reviews.

[31] Claire McGlinchee, "Stratford, Connecticut, Shakespeare Festival, 1960," *SQ,* 11 (1960), 469-72, esp. p. 470.

[32] Peter Saccio, "American Shakespeare Theatre, Stratford, Connecticut, 1974," *SQ,* 25 (1974), 401-4, esp. p. 404.

[33] Robin B. Carey, "Oregon Shakespeare Festival, 1974," *SQ,* 25 (1974), 419-21, esp. p. 420.

[34] Alan S. Downer, "For Jesus' Sake Forbear: Shakespare vs. the Modern Theatre," *SQ,* 13 (1962), 219-30, esp. p. 227.

[35] Henry Popkin, *The New York Times,* 7 September 1975.

[36] Jonathan Miller, "Director's Notes," Program for *Twelfth Night* (Oxford and Cambridge Shakespeare Company, 1969), Harvard Theatre Collection.

[37] *The Financial Times,* 25 April 1978.

[38] Barber, *Shakespeare's Festive Comedy,* p. 259.

[39] Robert Speaight, "Shakespeare in Britain," *SQ,* 20 (1969), 435-41, esp. p. 438.

[40] John Barton's promptbook for *Twelfth Night* (1970), Shakespeare Centre Library. The promptbook for the original production is missing; the one consulted here was used at the Aldwych revival.

[41] Anne Barton, program note in *Twelfth Night* playbill (1969), Shakespeare Centre Library. A fuller reading can be found in Barton's essay "*As You Like It* and *Twelfth Night:* Shakespeare's Sense of an Ending" (cited in note 1, above).

[42] Barton's promptbook.

[43] *Royal Shakespeare: Four Major Productions at Stratford-upon-Avon.* Furman Studies (Manchester Univ. Press, 1976), p. 57.

[44] *Stratford-upon-Avon Herald,* 29 August 1969; *The Observer,* 9 August 1970.

[45] "Directing Problem Plays: John Barton Talks to Gareth Lloyd Evans," *ShS,* 25 (1972), 63-71, esp. p. 63. Here Barton echoes Hall's view, shared by many modern critics, that *Twelfth Night* is a transitional play bridging the mature comedies and the problem plays. The repertory for the 1969 season also linked *Twelfth Night* with the final romances. In her program note, Anne Barton wrote that the play "crowns" the preceding run of comedies and "prefigures the final romances."

[46] *The Glasgow Herald,* 25 August; *The Times,* 22 August; and the promptbook.

[47] Barton's promptbook.

[48] Wells (note 43, above), p. 61.

[49] Peter Gill's promptbook for *Twelfth Night* (1974), Shakespeare Centre Library; augmented by critical notices and my own recollections of the production.

[50] Peter Thomson, "The Smallest Season: The Royal Shakespeare Company at Stratford, 1974," *ShS,* 28 (1975), 137-48, esp. pp. 145-46.

[51] Appropriately, the back wall of the stage presented a picture of Narcissus gazing down at his own reflection in a pool of water. The director may have meant this to suggest the more obvious theme of self-love, but it was still an apt symbol for this pattern of "unreflecting reflectors."

[52] Terry Hands's promptbook for *Twelfth Night* (1979), Shakespeare Centre Library, Stratford-upon-Avon; supplemented with my recollections of the performance.

[53] Roger Warren, "Shakespeare at Stratford and the National Theatre," *ShS,* 33 (1980), 169-80, esp. p. 170.

[54] Hands's promptbook.

[55] *Stratford-upon-Avon Herald,* 22 June 1979.

[56] Hands's promptbook.

[57] Warren, p. 170.

[58] Jan Kott, *Shakespeare Our Contemporary,* trans. Boleslaw Taborski (New York: W. W. Norton, 1964), p. 285.

[59] A. Quiller-Couch, "Introduction" to *Twelfth Night. The New Shakespeare* (1930; rpt. Cambridge: Cambridge Univ. Press, 1949), p. xxvi.

CHARACTERIZATION

Richard A. Levin (essay date 1979)

SOURCE: "Viola: Dr. Johnson's 'Excellent Schemer'," in *Durham University Journal,* Vol. LXXI, No. 2, June, 1979, pp. 213-22.

[*In the following essay, Levin maintains that Viola has an unromantic view of love, a remarkable ability to handle crises, and a willingness to manipulate both Olivia and Orsino to achieve her goals.*]

Viola, the heroine of *Twelfth Night,* is widely admired as an example of 'selfless fidelity' in love.[1] She is praised by critics with divergent interpretations of the play itself. She appeals to those who regard *Twelfth Night* as a 'festive play', in the course of which characters overcome their illusions, grow in self-knowledge, and gain a sense of community. She is regarded as the one character who is not misled about herself, and who therefore can 'teach others the true meaning of love'.[2] Viola appeals just as strongly to critics who puncture the romantic surface of the play, and find excesses in Illyria that cannot be purged as a mere product of a 'holiday' atmosphere. For these critics, Viola stands above her environment. She has been called the single 'reality figure' among characters lost in a variety of illusions about themselves and others.[3] Another writer finds it a shame that so wonderful a girl as Viola should marry 'such a spineless figure as the Duke'.[4] Finally, Viola is also praised by critics occupying a moderate position. They qualify the generally cheerful tone of comedy by speaking of 'a silvery undertone of sadness', or 'a nostalgic, elegiac' note.[5] With this reading, Viola becomes 'the constant and unchanging heart at the centre of several shifting and unstable attachments'. Viola, it would seem, is worthy of the highest admiration.

This essay will argue that she has not been scrutinized with sufficient care, and that there is an important element of calculation in her personality. My purpose is to strengthen the anti-romantic reading of *Twelfth Night,* which, although it has had very able proponents, has yet to discover the 'worm i' th' bud' at the heart of the play (II. iv. 111).[6] In the latter nineteenth century, dissatisfaction with Illyria centered on the mistreatment of Malvolio. Our century has taken more interest in Feste's profound disillusionment and in the aristocratic malaise of Orsino, and, to a lesser extent, Olivia. It is time to move from the periphery to the supposed romantic center of the play, and to find there a young woman with a distinctly unromantic attitude towards love. I begin with a key to Viola's personality provided by Dr Johnson in two succinct footnotes he wrote for Act I, scene ii of the play.

Viola, having come ashore after a shipwreck, determines from a sea captain that she is in Illyria, a land ruled by a bachelor, Duke Orsino, who woos the Countess Olivia. Viola decides: 'O that I serv'd that lady, / And might not be delivered *to the world* / Till I had made mine own occasion mellow / What my estate is' (41-44; italics added). Dr Johnson paraphrased the lines and offered a gloss:

> I wish I might not be 'made publick' to the world, with regard to the 'state' of my birth and fortune, till I have gained a 'ripe opportunity' for my design.

> Viola seems to have formed a very deep design with very little premeditation: she is thrown by shipwreck on an unknown coast, hears that the prince is a batchelor, and resolves to supplant the lady whom he courts.[7]

Dr Johnson's reason for concluding that these particular lines illustrate Viola's desire to wed the Duke may not be obvious but we should recall that in editing another play, Johnson suggested that the idiom to go 'to the world' meant marriage.[8] In any event, Johnson is undoubtedly considering the lines in context, and he thinks that Viola's general intention is clear. A little later in the scene, Viola, on learning that Olivia is in mourning, changes her course of action. Dr Johnson commented: 'Viola is an excellent schemer, never at a loss; if she cannot serve the lady, she will serve the Duke'.[9] Johnson, in effect, suggests that Shakespeare quickly shows that Viola is not introduced as an idealized romantic heroine. He might have said, more cautiously, that Shakespeare provides equivocal details so that we will prepare ourselves to watch Viola and make some very careful judgments. In any event, Johnson's successors, rather than taking up his lead, have been busy to eliminate any suggestion of duplicity on Viola's part. In 1790, Malone explained her quick moves on the basis of a source for the play, *Riche His Farewell to Militarie Profession:* Viola sailed for Illyria in search of Orsino, who is the man she loves.[10] In 1821, James Boswell, the son of a more famous father, added to Malone's account: 'It would have been inconsistent with Viola's delicacy to have made an open confession of her love for the Duke to the Captain'.[11] Later still (1854), R. G. White dismissed the whole controversy with great irony:

> If there ever were an ingenuous, unsophisticated, unselfish character portrayed, it is this very Viola,— Dr Johnson's 'excellent schemer', who, wretched and in want, forms that 'very deep design' of supplanting a high-born beauty, of whom she had never heard, in the affections of a man of princely rank, whom she has never seen.[12]

White read both Johnson and the text in a very literal-minded way and was baffled by what seemed an outrageous accusation. Spedding (1865) subsequently gave an eloquent defense of Viola as a romantic heroine who, in very trying circumstances after a shipwreck, does nothing inappropriate 'for a lady of her birth and breeding'.[13]

This account of Viola's activity has remained intact in our own century. C. L. Barber, for example, writes that 'the shipwreck is made the occasion for Viola to exhibit an undaunted, aristocratic mastery of adversity'; and the New Arden *Twelfth Night* emphatically declares that Viola's 'disguise appears a natural step and neither a deep laid scheme nor an irresponsible

Imogen Stubbs as Viola/Cesario and Helena Bonham Carter as Olivia in Trevor Nunn's 1996 film adaptation of Twelfth Night.

caprice'.[14] If Johnson is nevertheless right, then the whole character of the play has been misunderstood, even by critics who put an anti-romantic case. As Spedding pointed out in well-chosen words: 'Our conception of Viola's very nature, and with it the spirit of every scene in which she subsequently appears, and the complexion of the whole play, depends on' a correct determination of the issue.[15] I am prepared to defend the essence of Johnson's analysis of Act I, scene ii, and to demonstrate Viola's subsequent 'scheming'.

Although Viola is safely ashore, the captain and the sailors (from the latter we hear nothing) are still her lifeline, and she treats them with calculation, beginning with the pretense of camaraderie: 'What country, friends, is this?' (1). The captain replies: 'This is Illyria, lady'. Viola then puns: 'And what should I do in *Illyria*? / My brother he is in *Elysium*' (italics added). Viola wittily suggests that a confusion of sounds has caused her to miss her proper destination. She now expeditiously sets about soliciting grounds for hoping that the mistake will in due course be corrected: 'Perchance he is not drown'd—what think you, sailors?' (5). The captain takes his cue and cheers her, and she thanks him with gold (17). This gesture requires scrutiny. Not every romantic heroine has gold in her purse (especially after a shipwreck), nor takes gold out to thank a man for spiritual solace. But Viola, it may be, has a design. She perhaps wishes to demonstrate that she has money, and that she knows how to reward favors. Viola is ready to see if there is more help she can get from the captain.

And, as it turns out, he knows Illyria well, having been born and bred there (22-23). 'Who governs here?' is her immediate response, and when the captain replies 'A noble duke, in nature as in name' she wants only hard fact, not speculation about the duke's character: 'What is his name?' (26). Upon hearing the name, Viola's memory, sharp on critical detail, recalls: 'Orsino! I have heard my father name him. / He was a bachelor then' (28-29). It seems fair to infer that Viola shows immediate interest in establishing herself well in the dukedom, and a royal marriage is entertained as a possibility. She hesitates momentarily, for she is not one to risk unnecessary danger, and thinks of biding her time in the safety of Olivia's court. But when the captain tells her that Olivia will entertain no kind of 'suit' (45), the word catches Viola's attention, and the captain nods in confirmation, adding, 'No, not the Duke's'. Viola's path is now clear to her; her approach to the captain characteristically indirect.

She first addresses him with a compliment that incidentally reveals her knowledgeable in the ways of the world:

> There is fair behaviour in thee, captain,
> And though that nature with a beauteous wall
> Doth oft close in pollution, yet of thee
> I will believe thou hast a mind that suits
> With this thy fair and outward character.
>
> (47-51)

She then proposes to disguise herself and enter the duke's court as a eunuch. 'I'll pay thee bounteously', she goes on to promise (52), and promptly urges: 'It may be worth thy pains; for I can sing / And speak to [the Duke] in many sorts of music' (57-58). Since music is 'the food of love' (I, i. 1), the direction of Viola's thoughts is plain enough. She may even exchange a smile with the captain when she blandly concludes: 'What else may hap, to time I will commit, / Only shape thou thy silence to my wit' (112-13). Only the least suspicious in the audience will be unprepared for Viola's contrivances at court.

The court, in English Renaissance drama, is a place where one seeks fortune, and where one's success—not to say life—depends upon pleasing a monarch. When Act I, scene iv, opens, Viola has disguised herself as Cesario, a male page. We may ask, why not a eunuch, as she had planned? Perhaps she has decided that a sexual identity, even if not her own, is still an asset. She has been at court 'three days', has already 'advanc'd', and is likely to advance further, if, as Valentine points out, 'the Duke continue these favors towards you' (1-4). Valentine is talking from bitter experience, for Cesario is replacing him at court. In Act i, scene i, Valentine, as Orsino's ambassador to Olivia, failed to gain entrance; Cesario is his successor. The duke enters, asks Valentine to stand aside (12), and gives Cesario 'his' instructions. Viola is most reluctant to accept the mission, for two very good reasons. First, she has her own designs on the duke. I say designs, for there has been no evidence yet, nor, I believe, is there reliable evidence subsequently, that Viola actually loves the duke. Second, while the duke mentions only the 'fortunes' that will be hers if she succeeds with Olivia (40), in fact, if she fails she will suffer Valentine's fate. The duke, however, is not to be refused, and Viola undertakes the task, in good faith, apparently.

She listens carefully as the duke urges her on her way. He tells Cesario 'to act my woes' (26), and that to do so 'shall become thee well . . . / [Olivia] will attend it better in thy youth / Than in a nuntio's of more grave aspect' (26-28)—with a stare for Valentine, no doubt. The duke goes on to describe why Cesario will appeal to Olivia, and in doing so reveals that he himself dotes on Cesario's lovely feminine features:

> They shall yet belie thy happy years,
> That say thou art a man. Diana's lip
> Is not more smooth and rubious; thy small pipe
> Is as the maiden's organ; shrill and sound,
> And all is semblative a woman's part.
>
> (30-34)

Viola can see that the duke is attracted to her; perhaps she also wonders whether the duke is right, and her combination of masculine and feminine characteristics has novelty even among the women of a jaded Illyrian aristocracy. A course of action becomes clear to her. She will do no more than the duke instructs if she 'acts' a role and emphasizes her youthful appearance. Meanwhile, she can cultivate the duke's own interest in her.

The setting now shifts to Olivia's household, and details are soon provided which prove pertinent to our inquiry. Feste, Olivia's jester, is returning after an unexplained absence, and Maria, the lady in waiting, expects that he will have difficulty getting back into Olivia's favor. Nevertheless, he concentrates his skill—'Wit, and't be thy will, put me into good fooling' (I. v. 32-33)—and in a few short lines achieves his end. As Viola is about to enter and achieve comparable success, it behooves us to see whether the two employ parallel means. Feste sees past Olivia's initial reluctance to listen to him. He assumes that a person in mourning for an extended period of time is in need of amusement, and that a young woman has special needs. Therefore, in his introductory move, he disports his colorful wit before Olivia, much as a serpentine Satan plays before Eve in the garden. Feste knows that Maria wants a husband (27-28), and so does Olivia, for 'beauty's a flower' (52). Olivia is soon telling him that, 'for want of other idleness', she will let him 'prove' her a 'fool'. Olivia has a positive desire to be proved a fool—to the good fortune of both Feste and, as it turns out, Viola as well. With a performance requiring minimal skill, Feste soon has Olivia laughing at herself and indulging him.

At this point, Sir Toby enters with the information that a gentleman has come to call upon Olivia. It is immediately apparent that her mourning is little more than a polite way of saying 'no' to the duke, for she issues the instruction: 'If it be a suit *from the Count*, I am sick, or not at home' (108-09; italics added). But

Cesario has cleverly declined to mention whose messenger 'he' is; Olivia is curious, and her curiosity becomes intolerable when Malvolio's description emphasizes Cesario's very youthful appearance: 'One would think his mother's milk were scarce out of him' (161-62). Olivia agrees to see Cesario; as we know, the latter has already been advised, by the duke, of Olivia's predilections.

Within just a little over a hundred lines of Cesario's entrance, Olivia has fallen in love with 'him'. It has been very widely assumed that Olivia does so in spite of Cesario's sincere attempt to woo for Orsino. To take two illustrations from the critics. Harold C. Goddard can usually see through anyone and anything, but he nevertheless says of Viola that 'she never toys with [the] possibility for a moment' of manipulating Olivia's emotions for her own ends. Alexander Leggatt finds that Viola urges the suit 'with the generosity that is part of her nature'.[16] Two other critics offer a more qualified account. Herbert Howarth begins very firmly: Cesario 'urges his entreaties on Olivia as no previous messenger has dared'. But towards the end of his discussion, he muses: Viola ' "unconsciously" wills Olivia to fall in love with her'. Even E. C. Pettet, writing on Shakespeare's 'detachment from romance', ventures no further than to suggest that in Viola's 'fine love speeches' to Olivia, there is sometimes 'a suggestion of parody'.[17] In spite of the weight of critical opinion, and the fact that Olivia is certainly an easy victim, I believe we can discover a systematic effort on Viola's part to awaken romantic affection. Viola, on her entrance, does not invoke 'wit', as we have seen Feste do, but she is a self-proclaimed believer in wit (I. ii. 61) and there is no reason to suppose that in her secretive way she has not gone about making calculations of her own. These should accord with Feste's but Viola has an additional advantage: 'she' is a handsome young man. What, then, if she offered herself as a suitor? To do so has many real advantages, and as many dangers. If Olivia loved her, Viola could be sure of a reception at her court, and Orsino would therefore remain satisfied with his ambassador. However, if the duke were to hear a word of what she were up to, she would be in serious trouble indeed. Hence Viola will have to seduce Olivia without the latter being aware that she does; Viola must appear to refuse and to serve her lord loyally, while Olivia herself can trip head over heels in love. Viola's apparent coolness to the suit would also serve to prolong the wooing, and hence give the patient Viola time to work on the duke.

When Viola enters the room, she begins a dull, stylized address, only to interrupt herself to ask with apparent nervousness, 'if this be the lady of the house?' (171-72). It is improbable that Viola is really in doubt as to Olivia's identity, for only one of the women is veiled and Viola knows Olivia to be in mourning.[18] Viola is presenting herself as an awkward and shy youth, who has carefully memorized lines, but who fears 'scorn' (175) and may easily be put out of a 'part' (179). She wishes to suggest that, behind the actor with not very interesting lines, lies a real person with a depth of feeling that Olivia might well wish to explore. Olivia is indeed interested, but Viola has yet to perfect her act, and Olivia's first guess at the person behind the mask is all too accurate: 'Are you a comedian?' she asks (182). Viola answers with a comic touch that she conceals from Olivia, whom she falsely reassures: 'No; . . . and yet (*by the very fangs of malice* I swear) I am not that I play' (183-84; italics added). Viola hints to the audience that she does not 'play' at all; she is in terrible earnest.[19]

Olivia now shows an interest in engaging Viola in 'skipping' (201) dialogue, for she answers her question, 'Are you the lady of the house?' with 'If I do not usurp myself, I am' (184-86). Viola, like Feste, now reminds her that a young woman should marry: 'What is yours to bestow is not yours to reserve' (188-89). Olivia is flattered. Viola goes on to suggest that beyond the introduction to the speech she has memorized lies 'the heart of my message' (190-91). She realizes, therefore, that Olivia, in asking her to come to the point, is not requesting that she leave, as Maria seems to think. Viola quickly asks Olivia to silence Maria: 'Some mollification for your giant, sweet lady' (204). Johnson provides a pertinent footnote: 'Ladies, in romance, are guarded by giants, who repel *all improper or troublesome advances*' (italics added).[20] Olivia is not wise enough to take a hint and allows Viola to ask twice for a private audience, the second time with a suggestion of the seductive: 'What I am, and what I would, are as secret as maidenhead: to your ears, divinity; to any other's, profanation' (215-17). Olivia replies: 'We will hear this divinity', and accedes to Viola's request (218-19).

Olivia and Viola alone together, the latter soon gives the conversation an intimate turn: 'Good madam, let me see your face' (230). Olivia picks up the implication and comments: 'Have you any commission from your lord to negotiate with my face? You are now out of your text; but we will draw the curtain'. Olivia waits for Viola's response. Viola looks at her face and says: 'Excellently done, if God did it all'. This is a little light bantering, and, of course, an incidental crack at a rival. Viola then gets down to business, praising Olivia's beauty in lavish terms (239-43). Leggatt describes the ensuing interaction perfectly, but misses Viola's underlying strategy: Olivia 'keeps her defences up with conventional anti-Petrarchan jokes. Viola will have none of this, and persists'.[21] Not realizing quite how vulnerable Olivia is at the moment, Viola urges Orsino's suit, rather than hinting at her own love. When Olivia quickly shuts to hear more, Viola replies with the most awful Petrarchanisms, and Olivia quickly shuts her up. Viola now makes the decisive move:

> *If I did love you* in my master's flame,
> With such a suff'ring, such a deadly life,
> In your denial I would find no sense,
> I would not understand it.
>
> (264-67; italics added)

Breathless, Olivia responds: 'Why, what would you?' and then Viola, with lyric passions, describes how fervently she would love, in famous lines beginning, 'Make me a willow cabin at your gate'. We have evidence (II. ii. 19-21) that from this point on Olivia speaks 'in starts distractedly'. 'You might do much', she says, and inquires of Cesario's parentage. 'Above my fortunes', is his obliging reply (278), thus reassuring her that he might not be an altogether unsuitable match. Olivia, greatly moved, breaks off the conference, instructing Cesario to give her refusal to his master, but for himself to come again, ostensibly to report the duke's reaction. Viola gone, Olivia comments, more truly than she knows, that Cesario 'with an invisible and subtle stealth' has crept 'in at mine eyes' (297-98).[22] Olivia then self-indulgently submits—'Well, let it be'—and sends Malvolio after Cesario to return a ring that Olivia alleges Cesario has brought from Orsino.

Upon overtaking Cesario, Malvolio offers the ring and reports Olivia's request that Cesario visit her again. So quickly does Viola fall in with the deceit, that critics have questioned the text. Malone suggested an emendation: 'She took *no* ring of me'. But Stevens, and, more fully, Spedding, explained that Viola tells a white lie:

> Though taken quite by surprise, and not knowing at first what it exactly meant, she saw at once thus much,—that the message contained a secret of some kind which had not been confided to the messenger; and *with her quick wit and sympathetic delicacy* suppressed the surprise which might have betrayed it. (Italics added).[23]

Among modern editions of the play, the New Cambridge quotes this passage approvingly, and the New Arden is in essential agreement; Kittredge, however, insists that Viola 'has not failed to understand Olivia's words and manner in their recent interview'.[24] To be even more cynical about Viola's motives, we can say that the return of the ring, along with Olivia's request, are clear signs to Viola that her plot has worked. She is not greatly surprised, and has long ago concluded on the need for secrecy; hence, she replies to Malvolio with perfect composure.[25] The accuracy of this interpretation, and my general approach to Viola's character, are most fully tested by the speech she gives after Malvolio's exit.

The Folio text follows:

> I left no Ring with her: what meanes this Lady? 17
> Fortune forbid my out-side have not charm'd her:
> She made good view of me, indeed so much,
> That me thought her eyes had lost her tongue, 20
> For she did speake in starts distractedly.
> She loves me sure, the cunning of her passion
> Invites me in this churlish messenger:
> None of my Lords Ring? Why he sent her none;
> I am the man, if it be so, as tis, 25
> Poore Lady, she were better love a dreame:
> Disguise, I see thou art a wickednesse,
> Wherein the pregnant enemie does much.
> How easie is it, for the proper false
> In womens waxen hearts to set their formes: 30
> Alas, O frailtie is the cause, not wee, 31
> For such as we are made, if such we bee: 32
> [Riverside text: 'Alas, our frailty is the cause, not we, (31)
> For such as we are made of, such we be.'] (32)
> How will this fadge? My master loves her deerely,
> And I (poore monster) fond asmuch on him:
> And she (mistaken) seemes to dote on me: 35
> What will become of this? As I am man,
> My state is desperate for my maisters love:
> As I am woman (now alas the day)
> What thriftlesse sighes shall poore Olivia breath?
> O time, thou must untangle this, not I, 40
> It is too hard a knot for me t'unty.

Undoubtedly many actresses have, like Ellen Terry, depicted Viola as pleased when she realizes that Olivia has fallen in love with her.[26] I would go further, and call Viola's mood triumphant. However, as is her practice, she does not admit her guilt outright, but lets those in the audience who will appreciate her irony. She begins by pointing out that she has just concurred in a statement that is palpably untrue: in fact, she 'left no Ring' with Olivia. Viola now asks the audience whether it is wondering, 'What meanes this Lady?' She gives the answer in the following line. While in Elizabethan English 'not' frequently follows a verbal negation without yielding a positive meaning, Viola is intentionally equivocal. *Her* 'fortune' depends on her 'charming' Olivia—and she has succeeded. Viola promptly exhibits the evidence supporting her conclusions, and suggests that she has *already* drawn the necessary inferences (19-21). She ends with the confident assertion: 'She loves me sure' (22), and adds that Malvolio's message is a final incontrovertible piece of evidence (22-24). We should not be misled by the apparent tentativeness of 'if it be so' for by finishing the line with 'as tis', she contradicts her false modesty (25). Viola follows with one line of mock sympathy for Olivia (26), and four of mock lament for the way evil flourishes in the world (27-30). In line 28, many editors from Johnson on have identified the 'pregnant enemy' as the devil, but Luce, in the original Arden edition, provides an alternative: 'This may be Satan, *or any designing foe*' (italics added).[27] The editor further defines 'pregnant': 'resourceful, ever ready with wiles'. The enemy, then, can be Viola, working silently with 'fangs of malice'. Rather than feeling sorrow on account of the evil in the world, she exults as one of those 'proper false' who have found it 'easie' to seduce women (29-30).

The next two lines are invariably emended much as they are in the Riverside *Shakespeare* (see insert in the Folio text above). The assumption is that Viola, as a woman, identifies with women, and excuses the frailty commonly associated with their nature. However, in the preceding lines, Viola has identified not with other women, but with the men who seduce them. Therefore, the Folio text is correct, although the emendations undoubtedly catch what may be carelessly heard in the lines. In point of fact, Viola starts off with a sympathetic 'alas', and then promptly excuses the 'frailtie' of seducers. To round off her offense, she teasingly adds, 'if such we be', as if to deny all she has seemed to be admitting about herself.

The passage closes with Viola looking over the damage she had done, and portraying herself as a poor helpless female caught in a terrible web. The couplet embodies this sentiment epigrammatically. That Viola does not know how to 'unty' the knot is perfectly true. The wise, however, will conclude that Viola is already looking around her, and will do all in her power to 'unty', as she tied, the knot, for her advantage. Another Shakespearean heroine who cloaks herself in the garb of patient Griselde is Helena, in Shakespeare's next comedy, *All's Well That Ends Well*. Critics have been far more willing to see an element of calculation in her. We may think that, like Viola, even in soliloquy she is not candid, so that when she claims she is leaving France to oblige Bertram, she in fact has a new plan to claim her reluctant husband (III. ii. 99-129). When Helena next appears, waiting on a street in Florence where Bertram is soon to pass, we should ask whether chance or design has brought her to the right place at the right time. Let us use equal caution on Viola's subsequent entrance, in scene iv.

When the duke enters, he draws Cesario to him, but his attention shifts in mid-line: 'Now, good Cesario, but that piece of song, / That old and antique song we heard last night' (2-3). Viola concludes from this interruption that she must compete with the Duke's sentimental interest in music, and therefore, when the duke calls her to him again, and asks 'How dost thou like this tune?' she responds in an intensely lyrical vein (20-22). The duke, visibly moved, says 'Thou dost speak masterly', and becomes interested in Cesario's love-life. It turns out that Cesario has loved one of the duke's 'favor' (25), 'complexion' (26), and 'years' (28). But the duke either misses Cesario's implications, or shies away from them. Perhaps he feels protective of Cesario, or perhaps he simply cannot help giving expert advice on love. He warns Cesario against taking a woman older than himself, and Viola, for the moment, is stymied.

After Feste's song, she pulls out all the stops by inventing a famous narrative. She tells the Duke: 'My father had a daughter lov'd a man / As it might be perhaps, were I a woman, / I should your lordship' (107-09). The duke of course wants to know more, and Viola tells him that the girl 'never told her love' and 'pin'd in thought' (110, 112). The story deeply impresses the duke, and he asks breathlessly, 'But died thy sister of her love, my boy?' Viola now has her chance, and she thinks of taking it:

> I am all the daughters of my father's house,
> And all the brothers too—and yet I know not.
> Sir, shall I to this lady?
>
> (120-22)

At the last moment, Viola decides against trusting the changeable duke, and quickly brings his attention back to the 'suit' at hand. She has resigned herself to further waiting.

Viola's strategy with Olivia remains unchanged in two subsequent interviews, which can therefore be passed over quickly. Viola of course needs to do very little to precipitate Olivia's outpourings, but that little she does. For example, in Act III, scene i, she greets Olivia in public with a stiff formal compliment, and then asks for a private interview, and gets it (84-85, 88-89, 92-93). Viola promptly introduces herself as Olivia's 'servant' (97, 102). The language of courtly love is sufficient provocation for Olivia, who replies with an outpouring of emotion. Later in the Act, Cesario returns once again—indication of 'his' interest, Olivia presumes—and in the midst of his adamant denials, Olivia places a jewel with her picture around his neck—Cesario accepts the gift! (III. iv. 208-209). But Olivia is the least of Viola's problems.

Critics have noticed that Viola does not control events in the latter acts of the play, although they have not been as quick to notice her ability to handle unexpected situations.[28] The first crisis occurs when, after the interview mentioned at the end of the last paragraph, Sir Toby foments conflict by having Sir Andrew challenge Cesario to a duel. In these circumstances our strategist is not rendered entirely helpless. She knows herself too well to meet the male world with a pale imitation of its 'macho'. Instead, she frankly admits that 'I am one that had rather go with sir priest than sir knight' (III. iv. 270-71), and quickly puts her cunning to work. She tries to extricate herself, first working on Sir Toby, and then, when he goes to Sir Andrew, by approaching Fabian in like manner. Finally, when Antonio enters and diverts the attention of the others, she quietly talks Sir Andrew out of both the duel and his horse (321-24)! But Antonio's presence solves one problem only by creating another.

When he identifies her as Sebastian and accuses her of lack of faith, Viola must shape a careful reply. If she repudiates Antonio sharply, she will provoke his anger, and also forego any chance that, should the occasion arise, he could be made her ally. On the other hand, to treat him kindly and settle his confusion would invite an immediate search for Sebastian, with unforeseeable consequences for herself at the duke's court. Viola's temporary solution is to give Antonio 'half' her purse—so she claims, anyway (346-47)—but not to explain his confusion. After Antonio leaves, under arrest, she reflects on what has happened. Taken at her word, she is still in doubt as to whether her brother has survived: 'Prove true, imagination, O prove true' (376). But she may be far from ingenuous. Not only must the mistake in identity lead to the natural conclusion that her brother survives, but Antonio actually names 'Sebastian' (366) and recalls rescuing him (360). And Viola herself admits that she looks exactly like her brother for 'him I imitate' (383). Viola therefore passes off on whoever will listen an excuse for not seeking her brother, and for not giving real aid to his friend, Antonio. She insists upon waiting until she can make 'occasion mellow' (I. ii. 43).[29]

Viola is not on stage in Act IV, but an event takes place which could have grave consequences for her. She has brilliantly succeeded in appearing to reject Olivia's advances, and she therefore need not fear direct communication between the Duke and Olivia. However, Olivia now comes upon Sebastian, takes him for Cesario, woos him with new success, and quickly marries him. Therefore Viola, unbeknownst to herself, has a new problem at the beginning of Act V, and, to make matters worse, the Duke has decided to go to Olivia's court himself. As he and Cesario arrive, Antonio is brought before the duke. Fortunately, Viola has already decided how to handle this eventuality, and immediately tells the duke that Antonio has been kind to her, but is mad (66-68). Luck is on her side because Antonio happens to say that he has kept Cesario company for the last 'three months . . . both day and night' (94, 96). The duke quickly adopts Viola's explanation, saying to Antonio: 'Thy words are madness' (98). At this moment, Olivia enters.

She naturally thinks Cesario is her husband, and though she has promised him to keep the marriage secret, she knows no restraint and throws him longing glances. Viola rebukes her in order to show the duke that she is loyal to him, but Orsino seems to have been harboring suspicions, and quickly concludes that Cesario has betrayed him. The duke expresses a cruel intention, and Viola seems to submit:

> *Duke.* Come, boy, with me, my thoughts are ripe in mischief.
> I'll sacrifice the lamb that I do love,
> To spite a raven's heart within a dove.
> *Viola.* And I most jocund, apt, and willingly,
> To do you rest, a thousand deaths would die.
> (129-33)

This has been called 'Viola's supreme moment of self-sacrifice',[30] but her lines are susceptible to more than one interpretation. As always, she has her wits about her. She has heard the duke finally accept Olivia's refusal: 'Live you the marble-breasted tyrant still' (124); and although Orsino seems to have turned his anger on Cesario, he has nevertheless inadvertently declared his love in the lines just quoted (see also l.126). And so, Viola has given voice to concealed exuberance. The 'thousand deaths' for which she is 'apt', and which she will die 'willingly', are—sexual deaths.[31] Viola once again shares her irony only with the audience; on stage she remains perfectly composed, for she has now to manage the dénouement.

In a moment, the situation actually appears to worsen. As Viola starts to follow Orsino off stage, all the while protesting her love for him, Olivia blurts out: 'Cesario, husband, stay' (143). Orsino turns to Cesario accusingly, and says: 'Her husband, sirrah?' Viola's response is knowing: 'No, my lord, *not I*' (145; italics added). All the parts of the puzzle are now clear to Viola, and she awaits the appearance of her twin brother. Sebastian enters. The duke speaks, and Antonio, and Olivia, but not Viola. Finally, an incredulous Sebastian turns to Cesario and remarks: 'I never had a brother . . . I had a sister' (226, 228). He goes on to inquire, 'What kin are you to me? / What countryman? What name? What parentage?' (230-31). Viola conceals from him her masculine disguise and instead contrives to perform a duet with her brother. Finally, at the emotional climax, she admits the deception.

Her delay in doing so is the most famous crux of the play. One critic has explained that Shakespeare wishes to freeze the action 'in the contemplation of a miracle'. Another that he is 'fumbling with the details of the . . . plot'. Still another that Shakespeare has created an 'intensely moving' but obviously theatrical moment.[32] The best explanation is a good deal simpler than these. Viola's goal has been to win the duke. A hundred-odd lines back, in his allusion to Heliodorus' *Ethiopica* (117-19), Orsino revealed himself as an avid reader of romances. Therefore Viola has now seized 'occasion', as she promised she would, to fashion a sentimental and melodramtic reunion with her brother. Her calculation, as always, is accurate. The duke speaks up immediately:

> I shall have share in this most happy wrack.
> Boy, thou has said to me a thousand times
> Thou never shouldst love woman like to me.
>   (266-68)

He looks forward to a wedding 'when golden time convents' (382). Viola is to be 'Orsino's mistress, and his fancy's queen' (388). He will go on living life as in a romance, and Viola will rule Orsino—and a dukedom.

The significance of the foregoing argument for interpretation of *Twelfth Night* may now be briefly explored, although a full discussion is beyond the scope of this essay.[33] That a generation of critics concerned with the theme of appearance and reality in Shakespeare should nevertheless have failed to penetrate Viola's disguise indicates that we still have a great deal to learn about the play. Shakespeare himself is very nearly explicit about the kind of discernment needed. In Act I, scene v, while Feste and Maria are conversing together, he suddenly says to her: 'If Sir Toby would leave drinking, thou wert as witty a piece of flesh as any in Illyria' (27-28). This comment perfectly explains Maria's efforts to reform Sir Toby in an earlier scene, and the truth of Feste's observation is confirmed by Maria's quick effort to hush him. Feste is unromantic, or realistic, call it 'what you will' about Maria's activity. In another scene, Feste looks Viola over, observes that she scurries as quickly as he does between Orsino's court and Olivia's, and, after begging money of Viola, seems to suggest that she is as much a 'beggar' as he is (III. i. 54-55). It is really Maria and Viola who have most in common, because Feste is of a divided mind about currying favor. Maria and Viola both use their 'wit' to execute a careful plot; they channel their energies in the service of men of superior social rank and inferior abilities. Both are patient, and both prevail. We might conclude, therefore, by saying that in a hierarchical social system, or in any social system, for that matter, there is competition for rewards. Fools like Malvolio and Sir Andrew reveal their motives and fall on their faces; but an intricate web of deception is the norm, and he who would understand, must look beneath the glitter in a romantic comedy like *Twelfth Night.*

Notes

[1] D. J. Palmer, 'Art and Nature in *Twelfth Night*' *Critical Quarterly,* IX, 3 (1967); reprinted in D. J. Palmer, ed., *Shakespeare:* Twelfth Night, *A Casebook* (London: Macmillan, 1972), p. 212.

[2] Porter Williams, Jr., 'Mistakes in *Twelfth Night* and Their Resolution', *PMLA,* LXXVI (1961); reprinted in Palmer, p. 180. The most influential argument of this kind is made by C. L. Barber in *Shakespeare's Festive Comedy: A Study of Dramatic Form and its Relation to Social Custom* (Princeton: Princeton University Press, 1959), pp. 240-61.

[3] Ralph Berry, *Shakespeare's Comedies: Explorations in Form* (Princeton: Princeton University Press, 1972), p. 199.

[4] H. C. Goddard, *The Meaning of Shakespeare* (Chicago: University of Chicago Press, 1960), I, 304.

[5] The first quotation is from John Middleton Murry, *Shakespeare* (London: Jonathan Cape, 1936), p. 225; the second quotation, and the one in the following sentence, is from Palmer, reprinted in his critical anthology, pp. 216 and 219. Peter G. Phialas, in *Shakespeare's Romantic Comedies: The Development of Their Form and Meaning* (Chapel Hill: University of North Carolina Press, 1966) finds: 'A sense of melancholy characteristic of the general mood of the play' (p. 266).

[6] Unless otherwise noted, all quotations from *Twelfth Night* are from *The Riverside Shakespeare,* ed. G. Blackemore Evans (Boston: Houghton Mifflin, 1974). Among the anti-romantic critics, two have already been mentioned: Berry and Goddard. See also W. H. Auden, 'Music in Shakespeare', *Encounter,* IX (1957), reprinted in *The Dyer's Hand and Other Essays* (New York: Vintage, 1962), pp. 520-22; John W. Draper, *The Twelfth Night of Shakespeare's Audience* (Stanford: Stanford University Press, 1950); and Jan Kott, *Shakespeare Our Contemporary* (Garden City, New York: Anchor, 1966), pp. 305-14.

[7] *Johnson on Shakespeare,* ed. Arthur Sherbo, Yale Edition of the Works of Samuel Johnson, Volume 7 (New Haven: Yale University Press, 1968), p. 312.

[8] *Ibid.* p. 365.

[9] *Ibid.* p. 312.

[10] Edmond Malone, *The Plays and Poems of William Shakespeare;* cited in *Twelfth Night,* ed. Horace Howard Furness (1901; reprinted New York: Dover, 1964), I. ii. 45-47n.

[11] James Boswell, *The Plays and Poems of William Shakespeare* (London, 1821), XI, 347 (n. 2); also in Furness, I. ii. 45-47n.

[12] Richard G. White, *Shakespeare's Scholar* (New York, 1854), p. 282; quoted in Furness, I. ii. 45-47n.

[13] James Spedding, *Fraser's Magazine,* August 1865; quoted in Furness, I. ii. 59n.

[14] Barber, p. 241; The New Arden *Twelfth Night,* eds. J. M. Lothian and T. W. Craik (London: Methuen,

[15] 1975), p. lxiii. Both Barber and Spedding (n. 13) give Viola an aristocratic birth. I believe that there is no evidence in the play justifying this assumption, and certainly no evidence that in plotting for a duke she is not aspiring beyond her class. In Shakespeare's London theatre, Viola's accent would have given the audience a precise indication of her social rank (unless she spoke with an ambiguous foreign accent). All Shakespeare criticism suffers from the absence of a direct dramatic tradition surviving from the dramatist's day; we should not make matters worse by inventing biographies out of whole cloth.

[15] Spedding, in Furness, I. ii. 59n.

[16] Goddard, I. 304; Alexander Leggatt, *Shakespeare's Comedy of Love* (London: Methuen, 1974), p. 233.

[17] Herbert Howarth, *The Tiger's Heart* (London: Chatto & Windus, 1970), pp. 96-98; E. C. Pettet, *Shakespeare and the Romance Tradition* (London: Staples Press, 1949), p. 127.

[18] See I. ii. 36-41 and 45; I. iv. 18-20.

[19] At Act III, scene i. lines 123-25, Viola first tells Olivia that she pities her, and when Olivia answers 'That's a degree to love', Viola's revealing comment is 'No, not a grize; for 'tis a vulgar proof / That very oft we pity *enemies*' (italics added). Olivia, naturally, does not get the point, but we should.

[20] *Johnson on Shakespeare,* p. 313.

[21] Leggatt, p. 233.

[22] In two subsequent passages, Olivia uses language which can be taken to suggest that she has an unconscious suspicion of what Viola is up to. Olivia blames Viola in the following lines: 'Have you not set mine honor at the stake, / And baited it with all th' unmuzzled thoughts / That tyrannous heart can think?' (III. i. 118-20). Later still, Olivia tells Viola that 'A fiend like thee might bear my soul to hell' (III. iv. 217).

[23] Spedding in Furness, II. ii. 14n.

[24] *Twelfth Night,* eds. Arthur Quiller-Couch and John Dover Wilson (Cambridge, England: Cambridge, 1968), II. ii. 12n (p. 124); New Arden *Twelfth Night,* p. lxvii; *Twelfth Night,* ed. George Lyman Kittredge (New York: Ginn, 1941), II. ii. 13 (pp. 108-09).

[25] Our interpretation of Viola's character will survive speculation (were it to occur) concerning her motive for not accepting the ring, and then, when Malvolio has thrown it on the ground, for leaving it there while he is present. No one will ever be able to say that Viola took the gift, but Olivia can think that Viola accepted it covertly. As we will see, Olivia subsequently places a jewel on Viola (III. iv. 208-09), and later still (IV. ii. 2), we learn that she has given a 'pearl' to Sebastian, whom she mistakes for Cesario.

[26] See Furness, II. ii. 27n and pp. 393-94. This is also the interpretation given to the passage by Anne Swift in a recent production of the play at the Berkeley Repertory Theatre, California.

[27] *Twelfth Night,* ed. Morton Luce (London: Methuen, 1929), II. ii. 29n.

[28] L. G. Salingar, 'The Design of *Twelfth Night*', SQ, IX (1958), rpt. in *Twentieth Century Interpretations of Twelfth Night,* ed. Walter N. King (Englewood Cliffs, N.J.: Prentice-Hall, 1968), p. 30. See also Leech, pp. 36-37.

[29] Bertrand Evans, in *Shakespeare's Comedies* (Oxford, England: Oxford University Press, 1960) comes to similar conclusions about Viola's discoveries, but his assessment of her motives is entirely different, pp. 140-43. Viola also compromises her moral standing by allowing the captain she promised to help to remain in jail (V. i. 274-77).

[30] New Arden *Twelfth Night,* p. lxxvi. See also Porter Williams, Jr, in Palmer, p. 184: 'Comedy here touches for a fleeting moment the pathos of tragedy'.

[31] Sexual puns on 'death' and 'will' are too common to need documentation. Partridge, in *Shakespeare's Bawdy* (New York: Dutton, 1969), gives instances where 'apt' means 'sexually apt'; see also *Twelfth Night,* I. v. 26-28.

[32] The three critics, in order, are: Leggatt, p. 247; Patrick Swinden, *An Introduction to Shakespeare's Comedies* (London: Macmillan, 1973), p. 130; Anne Barton, ' "As You Like It" and "Twelfth Night": Shakespeare's Sense of an Ending', in *Shakespearean Comedy,* Stratford-Upon-Avon Studies 14 (London: Edward Arnold, 1972).

[33] I am presently completing a book with a chapter on *Twelfth Night*.

René Girard (essay date 1990)

SOURCE: "''Tis Not So Sweet as It Was Before': Orsino and Olivia in *Twelfth Night*," in *Stanford Literature Review,* Vol. 7, Nos. 1&2, Spring-Fall, 1990, pp. 123-32.

[*In the essay below, Girard evaluates Orsino's and Olivia's notions of human love and characterizes both characters as pseudo-narcissists. The critic maintains that in their twin obsessions with mimetic desire, they are identical personalities, each pursuing an inaccessible object and thus avoiding the disenchantment that must occur when desire is satisfied.*]

Orsino and Olivia are complex and refined characters. The duke has artistic and intellectual pretensions; before the curtain is raised, at the beginning of *Twelfth Night,* his musicians are playing a piece of music which Orsino greatly enjoys and, when it is over, he wants to hear it again. "Give me excess of it," he says:

> that surfeiting,
> The appetite may sicken, and so die.

Once again, the music is heard and Orsino does indeed find it less beautiful than the first time. In a single instant, as he himself had predicted, his appetite has sickened and died:

> Enough, no more,
> 'Tis not sweet now as it was before.

"Surfeiting" suggests our modern nausea, a compulsive disgust, a revulsion so extreme and definitive that the word is a little shocking in the context of art. If we read on, however, we soon find that Orsino is not exclusively interested in esthetics. In the experience he describes, the erotic life looms larger than the arts. The "spirit of love" dies in the embrace of its objects, regardless of their nature:

> Spirit of love, how quick and fresh art thou,
> That notwithstanding thy capacity
> Receiveth as the sea, nought enters there,
> Of what validity and pitch soe'er,
> But falls into abatement and low price
> Even in a minute. So full of shapes is fancy
> That it alone is high fantastical.
> (I.i.1015)

It is traditional to compare the course of desire with physical appetite and its satiety. But a healthy individual, even when no longer hungry, does not find good food disgusting, unless, of course, he abuses it. Orsino's experience resembles indigestion and Anne Barton rightly observes: "This love is a kind of glutton that devours dainties only to vomit them up."[1]

The ups and downs of *normal* hunger are less extreme than what Orsino describes. His language evokes a pathological version of the natural process. The slant of the duke's metaphor suggests a human nature wounded by original sin.

This man who says that desire never outlives possession is nevertheless in love. During the rest of the play, he never utters more than two sentences in a row without mentioning Olivia, but Olivia is inexplicably absent from his speech on *the spirit of love.* Olivia is the one permanent goal, the only fixed point in an existence that would be empty and incoherent without her. Orsino's sense of self visibly depends on the unflagging intensity of his desire for Olivia. But he argues that there is no such thing as an unflagging desire once its object is won. If Olivia belonged to the duke, would she lose her charm as quickly as the piece of music? The question never comes up explicitly.

One of the duke's attendants, Curio, interrupts his meditation on desire:

> Will you go hunt, my lord?
> DUKE. What, Curio?
> CUR. The hart.
> DUKE. Why, so I do, the noblest that I have.
> O, when mine eyes did see Olivia first,
> Methought she purg'd the air of pestilence!
> That instant what I turn'd into a hart,
> And my desires, like fell and cruel hounds,
> E'er since pursue me.
> (I.i.16-22)

As soon as the conversation shifts away from desire, the duke remembers Olivia. It takes a hackneyed pun to remind him of his beloved. Orsino's passion seems more at ease among literary clichés than in the context of a serious debate about the life and death of desire.

Orsino's first tirade on the subject is part of a musical prelude to the whole play, but it is more than a decorative hors-d'oeuvre; it is essential to our understanding of the comedy. It must be interpreted in the light of what follows; what it leaves unsaid is just as important as what it actually says.

Like many disillusioned romantics, Orsino speaks cynically about desire in general but he will go on desiring romantically until the end of his life. His cynicism about the past is not really independent from his current passion but the connection is paradoxical and Orsino himself never makes it completely explicit. We must rely on indirect clues that Shakespeare provides for this very purpose; we can and we must uncover the truth that his character never fully acknowledges.

Before we have time to forget Orsino's first speech, he gives the second, so different from the first in some ways that it seems to demand a different author, and yet so similar in other ways that the author cannot fail to be the same:

> DUKE. There is no woman's sides
> Can bide the beating of so strong a passion
> As love doth give my heart; no woman's heart
> So big, to hold so much; they lack retention.

> Alas, their love may be called appetite,
> No motion of the liver, but the palate,
> That suffers surfeit, cloyment, and revolt,
> But mine is all as hungry as the sea,
> And can digest as much. Make no compare
> Between that love a woman can bear me
> And that I owe Olivia.
>
> (II.iv.93-103)

According to this second speech, the only desires afflicted with the infirmities earlier described by Orsino as *his own* are feminine desires in general and those of Olivia in particular. Only women "suffer surfeit, cloyment and revolt." To make the contradiction even more blatant, Orsino suggests that these same infirmities are uncharacteristic of men and especially of himself. He opposes the weakness and fickleness of feminine desire to the undying strength of his virile desire for Olivia.

Once again, desire is as hungry as the sea and it can "digest" whatever it devours. The metaphor sounds just as ominous as the first time; in the first tirade, however, the maritime digestion expressed a pathetic contrast between the *before* and the *after* of all desires, their apparent inexhaustibility before possession is achieved, their instant death as soon as it is achieved. This time, there is no *after,* no surfeit for Orsino himself, and we can easily understand why: the passion for Olivia is an eternal *before.*

Olivia must be the first woman who ever had the upper hand with Orsino, and Orsino realizes that she has for him the eyes that he himself has always had for the other women in his life, the women that he ruthlessly discarded, no doubt, after possessing them.

Whenever Orsino occupies in relation to women the position that Olivia now occupies in relation to him, he feels the same "surfeit" that he now detects in her. He reacts in the very manner that he denounces as specifically feminine when it is *her* reaction to *him personally.* The phenomenon is the same but its ethical connotation has shifted from neutral in the case of Orsino to negative in the case of Olivia and of women in general.

To Olivia the story of Orsino's love sounds like a piece of music repeated too many times. Orsino is the one, this time, who has fallen into "abatement and low price." Olivia is sincerely bored with his sempiternal passion. Who wants to make love to an already digested man? It would be a misunderstanding to suppose that Orsino and Olivia have been physically intimate and that he disappointed her as a lover. Orsino is the defeated partner in a battle of pseudo-narcissism. It just happened that Olivia did not respond to his advances and this is how her victory was achieved. This is the only way in which a woman can durably fascinate such a man as Orsino. Were Orsino in Olivia's place, he would feel and behave with her exactly as she now feels and behaves with him. If she gave up the type of superiority they both crave in their relations with the other sex, immediately, he would cease to love her. At a deeper level, Orsino realizes that he and Olivia are very much alike. The spectacular disharmony between them does not stem from a conflict of personalities or from some other intrinsic difference but from the very reverse, an almost perfect identity. When Olivia entered his life, Orsino for the first time lost a mimetic and metaphysical battle that he had always won with everyone else.

Shakespeare wants us to compare the two speeches of Orsino; proof of this lies in the conclusion of the second one: "Make no compare . . ." When we hear this kind of warning from such a man, we should know that a comparison is in order.

Even very intelligent people can be so obsessed with their mimetic rivals that they talk like Orsino on occasions when it would be better for them to keep silent. We always marvel at the naive compulsion that forces these people to divulge the very truth they are trying to hide, but we ourselves will make the same mistake at the first opportunity.

All individuals beset by mimetic desire are easily fooled into believing that the entire world shares their obsession with their current rival. Like all people caught in a mimetic spiral, Orsino wants to convince himself that he is enormously different from his "beloved enemy," whereas in reality there is no difference, and something in him obscurely knows this. The anti-Olivia "propaganda" of the second speech is really an extrapolation of the self-knowledge demonstrated in the first speech.

Orsino thinks that he understands Olivia's desire and he certainly does, but not because of what he says, not because Olivia is one more exemplar of the archetypal woman whom all frustrated men ritually execrate. The sexist cliché is really a mask for a science of desire that does not want to acknowledge its real source. Orsino recognizes in Olivia the successful pseudo-narcissist that he used to be but is no longer, because of Olivia.

Orsino rightly interprets his relationship to this particular woman as a reversal of his habitual experience with the other sex. His banal anti-feminism is an effort to hide the true nature of this reversal and the origin of his insight into Olivia.

The idea that the desire of women for men can be weakened by a specifically feminine self-centeredness has always been popular with men. Men still love to portray as narcissistic in an absolute and non-mimetic sense the women who spurn their sexual advances. Freud gave a new lease on life to that myth with his definition of "narcissism" as a genuine self-centeredness that would be primarily feminine. Freud claimed that he had diagnosed a specifically "feminine" inability to respond to the real "object-love" of genuinely masculine men. But, quite significantly, the genuinely masculine men have a regrettable penchant for squandering their precious object-love on the women who deserve it least, narcissistic women, of course.

This is exactly Orsino's illusion; his second speech seems patterned on Freud's *Introduction to Narcissism* and as soon as we compare the two speeches, the radical critique that Shakespeare intended emerges. When placed side by side, the two speeches suggest a deconstruction of Elizabethan self-love that really amounts to a deconstruction of the Freudian concept *avant la lettre*. The words change and the myth of a specifically feminine self-centeredness remains.

The metaphoric continuity of the two speeches indicates that Orsino *projects* upon Olivia his own experience of the dominant erotic position, the position that Olivia now occupies with him. The fact that his insight is projective does not mean that it is worthless. Our perspicacity in such matters is always rooted in self-criticism; mimetic desire is the same in all human beings, regardless of age, gender, race, culture, etc.

Being projected upon its own mimetic replica, Orsino's insight into himself (the first speech) generates some real knowledge of Olivia's behavior (the second speech), but the duke cannot acknowledge its source without acknowledging his kinship with his mimetic *double*, thus undermining his resentment against an attitude that he, himself, would have adopted with Olivia, had the opportunity presented itself.

Mimetic *doubles* are sharp-sighted in regard to one another but their vision is distorted by the need they all feel to abolish the reciprocity in which their perspicacity is rooted. They must indignantly deny that they have anything in common with their rivals and yet, the only possible basis for their remarkable "psychological acumen" is this mimetic desire that divides them *because they share it:*

> Therefore thou art inexcusable, O man, whosoever thou art that judgest; for wherein thou judgest another, thou condemnest thyself; for thou that judgest doest the same things.
>
> (Romans 2: 1)

Orsino slanders women not because he truly believes in the masculine superiority that he claims but because he feels inferior as the mimetic *double* whose desire is enslaved by the successful narcissism of his partner. The indifference that he disparages as feminine insubstantiality is really the source of the *metaphysical* prestige that Olivia would not enjoy for very long in his eyes, if she yielded to his desire.

Like all romantic thinkers, Orsino sees desire as an object/subject relationship exclusively; he systematically short-circuits the third dimension, the mimetic model/obstacle/rival that makes everything intelligible. This is an especially tempting illusion in cases of pseudo-narcissism, when all roles are played by the same individual. To Orsino, Olivia is simultaneously object, model, obstacle, and rival.

The view of desire as a subject/object relation is false even in the case of art, which esthetes love to bring up because it seems to prove the existence of the solipsistic desire in which they want to believe. In reality, the most powerful component of esthetic emotion is a godlike *otherness* in the admired work, a quality that too much familiarity may weaken or even destroy, as witnessed by the experiment of Orsino, the two successive performances of the same musical piece.

Like all divinities, beauty eludes the impurity of human contact and the illusion of unmediated desire is shattered. If this desire were truly unmediated, it would not be diminished by the continuous enjoyment of its object; it would survive the ordeal of possession and fulfillment would not turn to ashes. Unlike the romantics, Shakespeare rejects the theatrics of esthetic fetichism and this is part of his greatness.

The Orsino of the second speech is a frustrated lover dominated by the voice of his frustrated desire. The contradiction of the two speeches verifies the law that Orsino himself has formulated in the first: desire *seems* eternal and inexhaustible as long as it remains unsatisfied, and not one minute longer. The second speech is consistently inconsistent with the first because it is the voice of famished desire, the desire for Olivia, whereas the first is the voice of surfeit. From Olivia's standpoint, to surrender to Orsino's desire would be a bad idea.

The language and behavior of Orsino suggest that he is aware, more or less, of his own pseudo-narcissism and of everything we have just said about him. In spite of his own involvement, he is as lucid about it as Rosalind in *As You Like It;* he really understands what only outside observers understood in the earlier comedies. He embodies a more "advanced" version of the pseudo-narcissistic configuration.

He knows very well that his daily humiliations at the hands of Olivia are self-defeating. If he really wanted to seduce this woman, he would resort to the strategy outlined by Rosalind, feigned indifference, but he never does. What is the reason for Orsino's theatrically "romantic" behavior?

The duke knows that no desired object can fall into his hands and retain its appeal for very long. Only a victorious rival can invigorate desire; desire is irrevocably self-defeating. The only radical solution to its endless tyranny is total renunciation.

This policy is what all great religions recommend, all great ethical systems, all traditional wisdom. It is Hamlet's advice to Ophelia: *get thee to a nunnery.* Had she followed it, she would not have died the wretched death that she did.

Fortunately for desire, a rational loophole exists which enables the crafty *spirit of love* not to draw the correct lesson from its perpetual failures. Experience teaches us the unsatisfactory nature of all objects that can be possessed; it has nothing to say, strictly speaking, about objects that *cannot be possessed.* If we are punctiliously experimental about this matter, we can always claim that, as long as we do not possess these objects, we do not have enough information to dismiss them out of hand.

On the basis of a myopically interpreted experience, the absurdity of desire can never be demonstrated satisfactorily. A sophistic abuse of methodical doubt permits desire to reason as follows: "Since all objects that can be possessed prove valueless, I will renounce them once and for all in favor of *those objects that cannot be possessed.*"

In *Twelfth Night,* this solution has a name, Olivia. She seems so impregnable that the duke can sincerely lament the fragility of all desire and yet remain supremely confident in the eternal duration of his desire for her.

The ocean of indifference that engulfs all other desires will never devour this particular one, Orsino thinks, for the very reason that *it will never be satisfied.* Olivia will remain forever inaccessible, not to Orsino alone but to all men. This creed remains obscure and Orsino avoids facing and formulating it explicitly, but it governs his life.

For the man who proclaims the bankruptcy of all desires, it still makes sense to desire Olivia. Orsino seems "irrational" as long as his real priority remains invisible. The real priority is not pleasure but desire at any price.

It is wrong to assume that, at all stages in its history, desire is seeking positive rewards. This was true perhaps in the initial phases, the ones portrayed in the early comedies. Orsino has reached a stage when, under the pressure of perpetual disenchantment, desire itself moves *beyond the pleasure principle.* Desire gives up pleasure in order to preserve itself as desire. Orsino is the first but not the last example of this desperate strategy.

The duke's desire for Olivia arises from the depth of his disenchantment and not *in spite* of it. A "rational" connection exists, but of such a nature that Orsino will never make it explicit, even to himself; we must deduce it from our comparison of the two speeches. In spite of his cynicism, Orsino is a man with a vast capacity for self-delusion.

To say that desire cannot survive the model's defeat is the same as saying that it cannot survive its own victory. The more desire learns about its own operation, the more intractable the dilemma becomes. Since desire dies of its own fulfillment, the road to eternal desire can only lie in the selection of a forever inaccessible object.

Orsino is the embodiment of this desire. The mimetic process takes time to unfold and, on this "historical" trajectory, Orsino belongs to a phase posterior to that of previous Shakespearean heroes. The chronological order of the comedies corresponds to a diachronic development of desire that leads from bad to worse. Orsino is not the end of the process, but he is not far from it.

His "hopeless" passion, I suggested, is a desperate move in a strategy of desire itself, a strategy of self-preservation. This is certainly true and yet a little misleading at the same time because this strategy demands no calculation, no planning of any sort and, in a sense, it does not deserve the name; it results from the normal drift of desire. All it takes to get there is a little too much success with women and then, all of a sudden, a little failure, the chance encounter of an Olivia. The quest for the perfect passion is hardly distinguishable from what happens to a blasé consumerist if and when he finally stumbles upon the forever indigestible dish, the unconquerable object, the only object to which he can become durably attached.

By refusing to love him, Olivia renders a great service to the duke; she gives stability to his life. Deep down, the duke feels rather lucky; he is eager to perpetuate his sentimental deadlock with Olivia. When he and she finally come face to face in Act 5, the only words these strange accomplices exchange sound like a discreet acknowledgment of their negative partnership:

> DUKE.   Still so cruel?
> OLIVIA. Still so constant, lord?
> (v.i.110-11)

Orsino is confident that he can keep Olivia cruel forever. Since his desire is the model for her self-love, all he has to do, he thinks, to freeze the situation permanently in his favor, is to keep desiring her: she will keep rejecting not only him but all possible lovers; she will be the eternal prisoner of her monumental self-love, Orsino's personal gift to her. Even though he has fallen into "abatement and low price," Orsino feels that his prestige as a handsome young man and as a duke makes him superior to all potential suitors, so that Olivia will be forced to keep her part of the bargain; what she refuses to him she will never grant to any other man.

Orsino makes the usual mistake of "enslaved narcissists"; he has too much faith in the objective strength of his idol. This mistake is fatal. When he learns that Olivia has already betrayed him, he flies into a dreadful rage. Olivia is in love, and with whom? With Orsino's own ambassador! The irony of this is that, if something besides Olivia's narcissism is responsible for her falling in love, it is Orsino's behavior. He dispatched Cesario to his beloved because of the young man's personal charm, hoping that it would operate on Olivia as it did on him, and it certainly has; the duke's expectations are fulfilled beyond his wildest dream.

This plot is one more variation, of course, on the great Shakespearean theme of self-defeating mimetic lovers, who advertise the charms of their lovers to their rivals and the charms of their rivals to their lovers. The refined and subtle Orsino belongs to the same mimetic family as Valentine and Collatine. For a while, after he learns what has happened, he turns into a raving maniac. Olivia has fallen in love through Orsino's own mediation.

Notes

This essay is forthcoming as part of my book, *A Theater of Envy, William Shakespeare* to appear at Oxford University Press in 1991.

[1] *The Riverside Shakespeare,* ed. G. Blakemore Evans (New York: Houghton Mifflin, 1974) 408.

John Astington (essay date 1994)

SOURCE: "Malvolio and the Eunuchs: Text and Revels in *Twelfth Night,*" in *Shakespeare Survey: An Annual Survey of Shakespeare Studies and Production,* Vol. 46, 1994, pp. 23-34.

[*In the following essay, Astington explores the characterization of Malvolio in terms of the tension between paganism, Puritanism, and traditional Christian viewpoints in* Twelfth Night. *The critic compares Malvolio's humiliation to the mockery, exposure, and punishment of lust that was frequently a focus of traditional English folk festivals.*]

> . . . a good practise in it to make the steward beleeue his Lady widdowe was in Loue wth him by counterfayting a left^r
>
> John Manningham

> He that is unmarried careth for the things that belong to the Lord, how he may please the Lord: But he that is married careth for the things that are of the world, how he may please his wife.
>
> *1 Corinthians,* 7, 32-3

> Now she that is a widow indeed, and desolate, trusteth in God, and continueth in supplications and prayers night and day.

> But she that liveth in pleasure is dead while she liveth.
>
> *1 Timothy,* 5, 5-6

Fashionably enough, the central farcical scene of *Twelfth Night* concerns an act of reading. What Malvolio reads and how he reads it have significant connections both with other events in the play, and with the wider world of seventeenth-century English society. The letter he finds invites him to join the festive rituals of love—to disguise himself, to smile, and to become a wooer, on the expectation of ending the revelling with epithalamium and marriage. This model for human conduct—the argument of romantic comedy—is in fact endorsed by a secondary text hidden within the first, as we shall see. But Malvolio, reading the words eagerly in the light of his predisposition, sees no subtleties, let alone the gaping trap. The festival in which he has already begun to take part is not the affirmative and sustaining one he imagines, but a punitive, defaming, mocking ritual aimed at him, his pride, pretensions, and authority. His reading—or misreading—marks his entry to a festive world, and festivals, like texts, are ambiguous. Particularly his treatment at the hands of the plotters forms a suggestive inverse ritual to set against those patterns which are traced by the energies of misplaced and baffled erotic desire, eventually untangled and fulfilled.

In the last scene of the play Feste finally delivers Malvolio's letter, excusing himself with the observation that 'madman's epistles are no gospels'. One could say that Malvolio's mistake has been to fall into the trap of taking a mad epistle for gospel, but here Olivia is not to be diverted by Feste's attempt to superimpose a theatrical style on plain sense: Orsino's recognition that 'This savours not much of distraction' echoes her own. Earlier in the play, Toby has pre-empted another plain reader, Viola, by rewriting Sir Andrew's challenge and by avoiding committing it to paper: 'this letter, being so excellently ignorant, will breed no terror in the youth. He will find it comes from a clodpoll'. In the course of the play we have, then, two epistles which are gospels, in so far as their sense, or lack of it, is revealed in their style, and one which is dressed as a dish of poison, devilish and heretical.

Malvolio, if he is indeed a 'kind of puritan', should have had some experience in the interpretation of difficult or ambiguous writings, but he capitulates so absolutely to the apparent sense of a text that even Maria is amazed at his extreme folly: 'Yon gull Malvolio is turned heathen, a very renegado, for there is no Christian that means to be saved by believing rightly can ever believe such impossible passages of grossness.' Something has been wrong, clearly, with Malvolio's Puritan discipline, if he can fall so easily for 'some obscure epistles of love', taking the shadow for the substance in such an unguarded manner. In doing so, of course, he is unconsciously aping his betters, and it is the deluded Olivia who is readiest to understand and forgive him, pointedly comparing his case with hers twice in the play. Not that she is aware of her own delusion, however. She confidently assumes she is an accomplished reader of texts, and of bodies as texts, when she dismisses the first chapter of Orsino's heart, which Viola proposes as *her* gospel: 'O, I have read it. It is heresy.'

The revenge of foolery and holiday on Malvolio is motivated by his repressive and humourless sense of order, and by his self-conceit, but the terms of his humiliation are very deliberately chosen: not only is he made to transgress class barriers, but he is translated into a lover, about which role there is something deeply and fundamentally inappropriate. Malvolio's initial rule over the celibate, mourning household of Olivia is sterile and deathly. Sad and civil, he is customarily dressed in suits of solemn black, and he marks himself all too clearly as an enemy to the life of comic energy: his first line in the play invokes the pangs of death. Olivia's own brooding on death, however affected it may be, aligns her sympathetically with Malvolio's gloomy order: the entirely imaginary affection that Maria invents has at least a germ of plausibility about it. But Malvolio is valued by Olivia as a servant precisely because he appears to be passionless, 'Unmovèd, cold, and to temptation slow', a defender not only of wit, manners, and honesty, but of honesty in its sexual sense, a symbolic guardian at Olivia's gates. As a classically constructed blocking character, Malvolio *inamorato* is punished by the passion he apparently denies.

By the beginning of the box-tree scene, the treasons have already been planted in his mind, which is running on marriage: 'Having been three months married to her, sitting in my state— . . . Calling my officers about me, in my branched velvet gown, having come from a day-bed where I have left Olivia sleeping.' Dreams of power and luxury, therefore, accompany the relatively sober, yet preposterous 'married to her'; indeed the fantasy of high social rank runs slightly ahead of dreams of sexual indulgence. Married in his mind, he encounters the fateful epistle, the very letters of which drip with concupiscence.[1] The style of the text he reads is a clever mixture of obliquity and directness, fustian riddles, grandiloquence, and minor rhetorical flourishes with a rather dated air. The prose begins with a clear warning—'If this fall into thy hand, revolve'—and immediately passes to an apparently clear statement—'In my stars I am above thee'—followed by a fugal development on the theme of greatness, which Malvolio is naturally disposed to hear with pleasure. Within the famous tripartite clause, thrice repeated in the course of the play, there lurks, perhaps, another warning for the truly virtuous. That is to say that the construction of this part of the epistle is remarkably close to gospel. In the nineteenth chapter of the Gospel according to St Matthew, Christ has been drawn by the Pharisees into a discussion of divorce and marriage. The complexities of morality and law lead the disciples to think that perhaps 'it is not good to marry'. In the King James Bible, Christ replies as follows:

> 11 But hee said vnto them, All men cannot receiue this saying saue they to whom it is giuen.
>
> 12 For there are some Eunuches, which were so borne from their mothers wombe: and there are some Eunuches, which were made Eunuches of men: and there be Eunuches, which haue made themselues Eunuches for the kingdome of heauens sake. He that is able to receiue it, let him receiue it.

Christ's words, he twice warns, are not to be understood by everyone, and the terms of his analogy are in many respects puzzling, but the evident centre of his meaning is that true greatness is not of this world, and that sexuality may be a bar to finding it. If Maria has intended this gospel text to serve as an allusive reflection beneath the surface of her epistle, the sense of the phrases begins to shimmer with opposites and distinctions: physical loss and spiritual gain, greatness and littleness (deficiency), fertility and sterility.

Malvolio has been offered an oblique warning about the futility of his marriage, if not a veiled insult, but fails to catch either. He would not, however, have known the gospel in the Authorized Version, and any kind of Puritan would have been most likely to be familiar with the Geneva Bible. The 1560 text translates the crucial verse in Matthew in a slightly different way:

> For there are some chaste, which were so borne of (their) mothers bellie: and there be some chaste, which be made chaste by men: and there be some chaste, which haue made them selues chaste for the kingdome of heauen.[2]

The effect of 'chaste' is a good deal blander, and implies choice rather than compulsion or accident, although the second clause becomes puzzling in this respect. But the marginal glosses, a chief feature of the Calvinist bibles, leave the reader in no doubt over the sense in the first instance: 'the worde signifieth (gelded) and they were so made because they shuld, kepe the chambers of noble women: for they were iudged chaste.' Malvolio, keeper of the chamber to Olivia, certainly wishes to be judged chaste, but is far from deeming himself unable to marry, from recognizing his own incapacity. The gloss on those that make themselves chaste, or who achieve chasteness, might we say, explains the phrase as a positive effect of grace, and of an effort of free will rather than negative self-abnegation or mutilation: Christ's phrase refers to those 'Which haue the gift of cōtinēce, & vse it to serue God with more free libertie.' And perhaps because the connection between chastity and godliness has an unfortunately Papist slant, the final sentence of the verse, Christ's second *caveat,* receives the following gloss: 'This gift is not commune for all men, but is verie rare, and givē to fewe: therefore men may not rashly absteine from marriage.' The Puritan reading of the text, finally, is to endorse the argument of comedy. This is made particularly clear in Calvin's own commentary on these verses. Speaking of the disciples' uncertainty, he writes, perhaps rather surprisingly:

> But why do they not think on their side how hard was the bondage of their wives? Simply because they are thinking only of themselves and their own convenience and are not motivated by the mind of the flesh that they forget others and want only themselves to be considered. Their ungodly ingratitude betrays itself that they reject this wonderful gift of God out of fear of one inconvenience or out of boredom. According to them it would be better to flee marriage altogether than to tie oneself to a perpetual bond of fellowship. But if God instituted marriage for the common welfare of the human race, it is not to be rejected because it carries with it some things which are less agreeable.[3]

The world must be peopled, and the will of God followed. Malvolio may therefore have some sense of the buried text, but without necessarily reading it as being directed against marriage; God, or 'Jove', as he may have more innocuously become by the time of the Folio text, seems to be overseeing the whole affair, including the interpretative spirit with which the sense of the words is received. Malvolio's reading of the letter, which he imagines to be free of 'imagination', could therefore be said to be a parody of the tendency of Puritan interpretation to read ambiguous texts in the direction of a theological programme, or to invoke the will of God to endorse personal predilections.

Godliness may render a man unfit for marriage, but the Geneva glosses also warn that 'Some by nature are vnable to marie, and some by arte'; 'The worde Eunuche is a generall word, and hath diuers kindes under it, as gelded men and bursten men.' By extension, one might say that the metaphoric application of physiological circumstances, Christ's starting point, hath divers kinds under it.[4] Malvolio's spiritual sterility renders him unfit for comic marriage, whatever his physical potency may be. More importantly to the rituals of comedy, the gulling which is initiated in the box-tree scene is an extended episode of humiliation. Induced to declare himself no eunuch by nature, Malvolio then puts himself at risk of being made one by art. His self-exposure, capture, imprisonment, and binding—the entire course of his 'bafflement'—is not only the well-recognized expulsion of repressive order from festival and holiday, but an act of sexual degradation—a displaced gelding, through which Malvolio is emasculated by the laughter of the sexually united pairs:

> Maria writ
> The letter, at Sir Toby's great importance,
> In recompense whereof he hath married her.
> *(Twelfth Night,* 5.1.359-61)

Yet however absurd the holy duty of marriage may seem in Malvolio's case—and it is not so much that the world has no need of more Malvolios as that he is contemplating marriage with the wrong person and for entirely the wrong reasons—it is extremely important to the play as a whole. 'If anyone imagines', says Calvin, 'that it is to his advantage to be without a wife and so without further consideration decides to be celibate, he is very much in error. For God, who declared that it was good that the woman should be the help meet for the man, will exact punishment for contempt of his ordinance. Men arrogate too much to themselves when they try to exempt themselves from their heavenly calling.'[5] The solemnity of God's punishment may be out of place in a comedy, as may the name of God itself, but the sense of 'heavenly calling' in sexual union is precisely in key with the magical happiness towards which the romantic comedies move. Resistance against this movement, or surprised acquiescence in it, is generally expressed with reference to purely natural or pagan forces, as when Viola speaks to Olivia about her beauty.

> Lady, you are the cruell'st she alive
> If you will lead these graces to the grave
> And leave the world no copy.
> (1.5.230-2)

Or when, at the end of the same scene, Olivia gives in to something beyond her own power to resist:

> Fate, show thy force. Our selves we do not owe.
> What is decreed must be; and be this so.
> (1.5.300-1)

It is Olivia who most resists her obligation to marry by taking on a vow to what she imagines are higher things. Her withdrawal from the world is cast in the language of religious observance.

> . . . like a cloistress she will velièd walk,
> And water once a day her chamber round
> With eye-offending brine—
>
> (1.1.27-9)

But the form of the observance, as Feste points out, is really without a religious object, an empty fetish like that of abjuring the sight and company of men, 'as if celibacy contained some meritorious service—just as the Papists imagine it is an angelic state. But all Christ intended', Calvin says of making oneself a eunuch for the kingdom of heaven's sake, 'was that the unmarried should set the aim before them of being more ready for the exercises of religion if they are freed from all cares. It is foolish to imagine that celibacy is a virtue, for this is no more pleasing to God in itself than fasting is, nor does it deserve to be reckoned among the duties required of us.'[6] The 'divinity' the disguised Viola brings to Olivia shows her the vanity of withdrawing from the world. False and true divinity continue to pursue each other, with ironic effect, throughout the play. Immediately following the scene in which a false priest catechizes the desperate Malvolio, Olivia marries the dream she has loved since the fifth scene of Act I.

> If you mean well
> Now go with me, and with this holy man,
> Into the chantry by. There before him,
> And underneath that consecrated roof,
> Plight me the full assurance of your faith,
> That my most jealous and too doubtful soul
> May live at peace.
>
> (4.3.22-8)

The wonderful gift of God is celebrated in a religious ceremony which the seemingly arbitrary forces of nature, imagination, and sheer chance have helped bring about. The 'peace' Olivia looks forward to is precisely what has eluded Malvolio at the end of the play—but his symbolic and structural roles are very different from hers.

Viola's loss of a brother does not lead *her* to a cloistered withdrawal from the world, but she does pursue concealment, and specifically proposes a disguise which will remove her from the responsibilities of sexuality: 'Thou shalt present me as an eunuch to him.' She makes herself a eunuch not for the kingdom of heaven's sake but to gain some advantage over the forces of time and occasion, both of which eventually give her the peace they give Olivia. The exotic nature of Viola's proposed role, however, is unlikely to render her unobtrusive: in a Christian climate the eunuch was both freakish and foreign, specifically Turkish, as the Captain recognizes in his acknowledgment of Viola's request. Eunuchs might be fascinating in themselves as human types, but certainly by virtue of being involved in the mythologized fantasy world of Turkish sexuality. No more is made of the oddity of Viola's disguise—she is no Castrucchio, as Orsino's Illyria is not Volpone's Venice—but she retains a troublingly provocative physical presence, constantly drawing attention to her appearance from Orsino, Malvolio, Feste, and chiefly from Olivia. Disguise, and hence denial of sexual identity in her case, is a 'wickedness' as much as it is creative and liberating. It liberates, in fact, only for so long, and time first draws the knot of confusions tighter before untangling it. Olivia's claim on her as a husband, which she is able to corroborate with priestly authority, threatens first Viola's death and then the loss of the man she loves. So, once the appearance of Sebastian has begun to resolve the paradoxes, we have Viola's insistence, echoed by Orsino, that she resume her own clothes: 'Do not embrace me' she tells her brother, and the prohibition is implicitly extended to her future husband. As she is a man—or a eunuch—she is not ready to give herself to anyone.

Viola's superfluous disguise in Act 5 is matched by that of the humiliated Malvolio, still wearing the ludicrous costume he has been gulled into assuming by his reading of the letter—point devise, the very man. The 'notable shame' he has undergone has included his parading in the clothes and demeanour of an aspiring lover—a sexual role quite out of keeping with his peevish, repressed, sterile self-regard. One of the roles of festival customs, modern social historians agree, was to enforce communal order as much as temporarily to subvert it. David Underdown has described the clash in seventeenth-century English society between the cohesive function of festival and the godly order of those with a new vision of and programme for social organization:

> The division in the English body politic which erupted in civil war in 1642 can be traced in part to the earlier emergence of two quite different constellations of social, political, and cultural forces, involving diametrically opposite responses to the problems of the time. On the one side stood those who put their trust in the traditional conception of the harmonious, vertically integrated society—a society in which the old bonds of paternalism, deference, and good neighbourliness were expressed in familiar religious and communal rituals—and wished to strengthen and preserve it. On the other stood those—mostly among the gentry and middling sort of the new parish élites—who wished to emphasize the moral and cultural distinctions which marked them off from their poorer, less disciplined neighbours, and to use their power to reform society according to their own principles of order and godliness.[7]

The church ale—at which cakes and ale were the traditional fare—was one typical site of this conflict. An ancient parish tradition—a kind of communal picnic with drinking, as well as piping, dancing, and some-

Helena Bonham Carter as Olivia and Nigel Hawthorne as Malvolio in Trevor Nunn's 1996 film adaptation of Twelfth Night.

times dramatic activity—its function was to bring the parishioners together in a festive money-raising activity to support the parish's charitable works. To the Puritan eye this praiseworthy end was entirely vitiated by the displays of unrighteousness the feast gave rise to. From about the time of *Twelfth Night* onwards there are numerous instances from across the country of festal customs being used against local Malvolios, in the course of which the representatives of authority were both mocked and, in extreme cases, physically assaulted.

Violence is in fact an entirely traditional ingredient of many forms of game and festival, and hence could give further cause to the godly to suppress festive customs. The liminal and group-bonding functions of football games with neighbouring villages, for example, are noted by Underdown: ''Tis no festival unless there be some fightings' is a contemporary saying he quotes (p. 96). Personal or communal rivalries and disputes could therefore be sorted out—more or less symbolically—under the cover of festival licence. In *Twelfth Night* it is Sir Toby who is the lord of *violent* misrule, and he is perhaps not uncharacteristic of enthusiastic seventeenth-century revellers in that during his final appearance in the play he is both drunk and bleeding. The particular contest he has just lost, begun in jest and ended in earnest, is with a young stranger over his apparent sexual invasion into territory Toby may regard as his to defend, if not to bestow. However ironically, he has promised Olivia to Sir Andrew, and his oath to his gull earlier in the play is made on the physical manifestations of his own manliness: 'If thou hast her not i'th' end, call me cut' (2.3.180-1). Once Cesario shows some fighting spirit, male prowess is at stake: 'Come, my young soldier, put up your iron. You are well fleshed . . . Nay then, I must have an ounce or two of this malapert blood from you' (4.1.37-43).

Malvolio's heated imaginings about Olivia in the letter scene give rise to a string of violent stage-whispers from the box-tree—'O for a stone-bow to hit him in the eye!'; 'Fire and brimstone!'; 'Bolts and shackles!'

(a premonition of Malvolio's punishment); 'Shall this fellow live?'; '. . . does not Toby take you a blow o' the lips, then?'; 'Out scab'; 'Marry, hang thee brock'; '. . . I'll cudgel him, and make him cry "O!"' After this, Malvolio is perhaps lucky to undergo the relatively lenient treatment he gets, although it is certainly a fairly frequent tendency in modern stagings of the play to emphasize the physical punishment in the revellers' teasing of him in 3.4, and since the eighteenth century the pain and privation of the dark house scene have often been stressed, to the degree that Malvolio has seemed on the edge of being mad indeed. His binding—promised by Sir Toby in 3.4—is not usually seen. He leaves the stage free, and while on Shakespeare's stage he may have been entirely invisible in 4.2, these days we tend to see an anguished face and beseeching, clutching hands as he pleads with Sir Topas and Feste. In any event, in fictional terms he must be free enough to write his letter, and when he re-emerges into the world of light he doesn't usually bear about him signs of his bondage (the far commoner stage tradition is for him to have straw sticking to his hair and clothes). Yet he is still dressed in his lover's garb, as I noted above, usually sadly muddied and ripped in performance, to signal the trials of constancy. The absurd costume, Maria's fantastical invention, includes the restricting bonds of the cross garters, which soon after he has put them on are already making him 'sad':

> This does make some obstruction in the blood, this cross-gartering, but what of that?
> (3.4.19-21)

The Grocer's Wife from *The Knight of the Burning Pestle* could tell him; there are dangers in putting on silly costumes: 'I'll see no more else indeed, la: and I pray you let the youths understand so much by word of mouth; for I tell you truly, I'm afraid o' my boy. Come, come, George, let's be merry and wise. The child's a fatherless child; and say they should put him into a strait pair of gaskins, 'twere worse than knotgrass; he would never grow after it' (2.92-8).[8] The innocently lubricious sense of 'grow', typical of the Wife's chatter, alerts us to one element of Malvolio's shaming: his binding is a symbolic sign of his impotence, of his having been made a festival eunuch. I think he should keep his cross garters obediently tied until he finally hobbles off to seek revenge.

I want to return to the rituals of sexual humiliation, but first to explore a second violent festive practice which has frequently been noted in commentary on the play, as seeming in some way to stand for the treatment of Malvolio. The previously unannounced Fabian enters the play in 2.5 as a further resentful victim of Malvolio's war on holiday pastimes: he has been 'brought . . . out o' favour with my lady about a bear-baiting here'. 'To anger him', Toby replies, 'we'll have the bear again, and we will fool him black and blue'. Once again the promised violence happens only symbolically—Malvolio is not beaten up as is Captain Otter (as bear) by his wife (as dog) in Jonson's *Epicoene*—but we are reminded at this moment of the strong connections between festival and brutal punishment, and the evident need to give vent to disruptive and aggressive tendencies even in the midst of celebrations which affirmed the strength and mutual support of the community. Malvolio's bearishness remains in that he sees his tormentors as a 'pack'—hounds rather than people—at the end of the play.[9] The violent accompaniments of festive activity are everywhere apparent in the social world surveyed by David Underdown: bear and bull baitings are the invariable entertainments at church ales. While one may have been attendant on feasting—the bull was baited before being butchered—the other patently was not. That the actual torturing of animals, whatever symbolic function it may have been recognized to carry, could itself take a symbolic form in festival is proved by an intriguing reference Underdown cites from Somerset in 1603, involving some trouble while someone was 'playing Christmas sports in a bear's skin' (p. 60). Such a winter-time activity—very reminiscent of Lanthorn Leatherhead's reported feats in *Bartholomew Fair* (3.4. 126-28)—may have as much to do with *The Winter's Tale* as with *Twelfth Night,* but the ritualized hunting that is expressed in animal baiting, and the deliberate arousal, in the case of cock-fighting, for example, of competitive sexual aggression in the animals, reveal an ambivalent fascination with purely physical power and instinctive drive as forces which must be celebrated, yet punished.[10] Jonson, once again, more directly incorporates festive baitings and huntings into his comic structure, and his plays are to that extent crueller than Shakespeare's. Volpone's direct address to the audience following his sentence by the court—'This is called mortifying of a fox'—reminds us of the festive custom of hunting a fox or other small animal indoors, within the hall at a feast, frequently involving killing it by driving it into the fire. One of the fox's sins in *Volpone,* of course, is lust. The totemic sexual rituals associated with hunting and killing the stag, however, are clear enough in Shakespeare's work. The festive song in *As You Like It* is an anthem of male prowess and anxiety—the lusty horn is given to the victor as a sign that he is a potential victim of forces which lie outside his direct control. Falstaff's ritual punishment for lust at the end of *The Merry Wives of Windsor* is suffered in the disguise of a male deer—he is symbolically pinched and burnt, rather than actually butchered and cooked. Falstaff's dis-horning, George Turberville tells us, exactly follows the English practice of dismembering the stag after the kill; following the removal of one sign of the deer's maleness, 'before that you go about to take off his skynne, the fyrst thing that must be taken from him, are his stones which hunters call his doulcettes'. These form part of 'the dayntie morsells which appertayne to the

Prince or chief personage on field'.[11] In Beaumont and Fletcher's *Philaster* the cowardly and lustful Pharamond has paid the woodmen for the dowcets and head of a slain deer (4.2)—that he evidently needs them as aphrodisiacs hardly commends his unassisted sexual powers. Following the scenes of actual hunting in the fourth act, Pharamond becomes the human quarry of a popular riot in the fifth, when the citizens, like Laertes' Danish supporters, mutiny to reinstate Philaster. The language with which they threaten him deliberately recalls the hunting terms of Act 4, and his proposed punishment mockingly strips him of manhood.

> PHARAMOND
> Gods keep me from these hell-hounds.
> 1 CITIZEN
> Shall's geld him, Captain?
> CAPTAIN
> No, you shall spare his dowcets, my dear donsels; as you respect the ladies let them flourish. The curses of a longing woman kills as speedy as a plague, boys.
> 1 CITIZEN
> I'll have a leg, that's certain.
> 2 CITIZEN
> I'll have an arm.
>
> . . . . .
>
> 2 CITIZEN
> He had no horns, sir, had he?
> CAPTAIN
> No, sir, he's a pollard; what wouldst thou do with horns?
> 2 CITIZEN
> O, if he had, I would have made rare hafts and
> whistles of 'em; but his shin bones if they be sound
> shall serve me.
>
> (5.4.53-74)[12]

Symbolic hunting therefore carries within it a potential for sexual shaming and degradation. Pharamond and Falstaff are both punished for lust by public exposure, and Malvolio's treatment clearly has something of a similar purpose, although it certainly lacks the direct physical violence the two former figures suffer. At least this is so in the text; there is a *theatrical* tradition of varying degrees of physical torture of Malvolio by Feste in 4.2. Malvolio's punishment is to be 'propertied', but largely to be forgotten, removed, and 'baffled' until his incandescent entry into Act 5. He is certainly punished for excess, but punished by deprivation, and his physical powerlessness in the dark house is perhaps to remind him of his unsuitability for the preposterous role he has taken on. A born eunuch, in Christ's terms, he is absurdly unfitted for the position of comic wooer and bridegroom.

The impotent lover, in body, mind, and social conduct, is a stock figure of erotic comedy. The absurdly enamoured father, the old man, the stupid heir, the pretentious braggart, the rake, all are variant threats to the union of the true lovers, and they must be outwitted, exposed, or otherwise removed in the course of the plot. In Jonson's *Bartholomew Fair* the egregious ninny Cokes, the contracted bridegroom of the witty but powerless Grace Wellborn, loses his fiancée to Quarlous in the liberating chaos of a festival atmosphere. He also loses his money, but in having his purse cut—twice—he is symbolically gelded of the manhood he so ineptly represents. He half recognizes what has happened to him in the words he addresses—mistakenly—to Overdo: 'Cannot a man's purse be at quiet for you, i' the master's pocket, but you must entice it forth, and debauch it?' (3.5.213-14), while Wasp scornfully tells his charge 'now you ha' got the trick of losing, you'd lose your breech, an't 'twere loose' (ibid. 221-3).[13] Cokes, though he hardly cares in the regressively childish festive world he has entered, is symbolically shamed and neutered. His fascination with the puppets, babies, and trash is a complete identification—he, like the puppet Dionysius, has no sex. It is Jonson's disciple Richard Brome who writes the frankest version of what appears to be a submerged theme of festival and comedy when in his 1639-40 play *The Court Beggar* a doctor is held down across a table and threatened with castration at the hands of a 'Sowgelder' (4.2). His protests remind the audience of the dangerous uproar of popular holidays:

> You dare not use this violence upon me
> More rude than rage of Prentices.[14]

The gelding turns out to be a 'counterfeit plot'—partly a deliberate degradation in revenge for the doctor's prior actions, and partly to scare him into confessing that the patient he is attending is, like Antonio in *The Changeling*, a sham madman. The scene could therefore be taken simply as a particularly risqué piece of farce used to enliven a rather creakily episodic plot, yet the larger question remains of why this particular action may have occurred to Brome as being suitable to a comedy filled with spurious and defective wooers.[15]

Nothing quite so specifically humiliating or violent turns up in the court records of pre-Restoration England, although there is a good deal of material connected with disorders and outrages arising from popular rituals of sexual control.[16] The usual individual target for the community to direct its displeasure over aberrant sexual conduct was likely to be a woman; the whore, the adultress, the scold, all suffered ritual mockery, exposure, and varyingly violent degrees of punishment. Yet the ceremonies which marked such disapproval—ridings, parades, rhymes, lampoons, duckings, and so forth—were by no means directed at women alone. The man who suffered himself to be cuckolded or beaten was likely to be a target of mockery as an unmanly man, a man who couldn't wear the breeches. One particularly widespread custom, which has a literary record that stretches at least from Samuel Butler to Thomas Hardy, was the skimmington, a wild processional ride involving disguise, rough music, and, as Martin Ingram has written, 'mocking laughter, sometimes light-hearted, but often taking the form of hostile derision which could, on occasion, escalate into physical violence'.[17] The ritual is clearly related to symbolic hunting, and indeed could feature participants dressed in horns or animal skins. If the custom arose to mock unconventional sexuality or deviant behaviour within a marriage its scope could be far wider, as Ingram explains:

> While female domination and immorality were the characteristic pretexts for ridings, there were other occasions. A simple form of riding was sometimes used in a holiday context in 'trick or treat' games, and to punish people who refused to join in the festivities or who in other ways offended the holiday spirit. At Chichester in 1586, a game of 'tables' on New Year's Eve was rudely interrupted when 'William Brunne who then played the part of a lord of misrule came in . . . and said that that game was no Christmas game and so perforce took [one of the players] . . . from thence and made him ride on a staff to the High Cross.' The use of ridings to punish people who would not give money to Lords of Misrule on holidays was denounced by Philip Stubbes. Unfortunately, when refusal to take part in festivities (or, worse still, attempts to suppress such festivities) were based on Puritan principles, such ridings were apt to become distinctly less lighthearted and more elaborate. John Hole, the Puritan constable of Wells, discovered this to his cost in 1607. Hole and his associates tried to suppress the city's May games, which had been organised on a particularly grand scale that year in order to raise money for the repair of St Cuthbert's church. Hole's interference raised a storm of opposition, and he and his friends were savagely derided in a series of spectacular ridings performed before thousands of people.
>
> (Ingram, pp. 170-1)

The John Hole case, which was surveyed by C. J. Sisson in *Lost Plays of Shakespeare's Age* as long ago as 1936, is particularly suggestive about the treatment given Malvolio by the revellers of *Twelfth Night*. Hole, like Malvolio, set out to oppose holiday revels on principle; the revellers' revenge was character assassination, as Hole was accused of adultery with another godly objector to the festival, the delightfully named Mrs Yard. None of the surviving lampooning verses make what one would think to be the obvious jokes about hole and yard (suitably inverted in good festival fashion), but Hole *is* simultaneously accused of lechery and impotence, like Malvolio doubly mocked for sexual ambition and incapacity. Particularly the exposure of the Wells killjoys by theatricalizing them—staging them in disguises and caricatured paintings—by making them join, in effigy at least, the very celebrations they have tried to stop, reveals a direct relationship between festive rituals and the comic structure of such plays as *Twelfth Night*. In the play Malvolio is more subtly tricked into staging himself as a parodic festival figure—a grotesquely inept embodiment of the energy celebrated in holidays, and as such a betsy, a guy, a Jack-a-Lent, a cockshot man, at whom people can hardly forbear hurling things. Death, darkness, sterility, and ill luck are heaped on his back, and laughed out of the play.

His scapegoat function has frequently been remarked on, but one theoretical defence of festive customs, presumably including the shaming rituals, was that they were restorative and socially cohesive. The exhibition of conflict or aberrance under the special conditions of holiday licence would lead, with luck, to resolution and rehabilitation. Thus those accused as rioters at Rangeworthy near Bristol in 1611 defended themselves by pointing out that communal feasting was for 'the refreshing of the minds and spirits of the country people, being inured and tired with husbandry and continual labour . . . for preservation of mutual amity, acquaintance, and love . . . and allaying of strifes, discords and debates between neighbour and neighbour'. This sounds remarkably like the spirit of Fabian's plea to Olivia not to let retributive justice inappropriately be applied to holiday jests:

> Good madam, hear me speak,
> And let no quarrel nor no brawl to come
> Taint the condition of this present hour,
> Which I have wondered at. In hope it shall not,
> Most freely I confess myself and Toby
> Set this device against Malvolio here
>
> . . . . .
>
> How with a sportful malice it was followed
> May rather pluck on laughter than revenge
> If that the injuries be justly weighed
> That have on both sides passed.
>
> (5.1.352-65).

But the victims of the Rangeworthy riot, a Puritan constable and his followers who were beaten when they tried to arrest musicians and dancers, did pursue their case through the courts, and hence we happen to know about the incident. David Underdown holds up this obscure rural scuffle as an emblem of a changing world: 'The Rangeworthy revel is thus a classic example of Jacobean cultural conflict. Rituals appropriate to a traditional society, enshrining ancient values of custom and good neighbourhood, were attacked by people in authority who put individual piety, sobriety, and hard work above the older co-operative virtues' (p. 63).

Malvolio refuses Fabian's open hand. He has, after all, been most notoriously abused, and excluded from achieving greatness in any sense. Donald Sinden's entertaining account of playing the part ends with his invocation of the bitterness of Malvolio's humiliation and disappointment. There is nothing for him following his exit, Sinden suggests, save suicide.[18] Yet surely only a particularly sensitive, late-Romantic Malvolio would be snuffed out by a device. I think the seventeenth-century man is heading for his lawyer, and Star Chamber.

To return, finally, to texts, it is worth noting that mock preaching was a recurrent element in popular revels, particularly those with a satiric thrust against a local community figure. Such was the play which Sir Edward Dymock had performed at his house in Kyme, Lincolnshire, in August 1601, and which guyed Henry, Earl of Lincoln. Following the play proper one John Cradock preached a mock sermon in a black gown and cap; a witness said that he wore 'A counterfeat beard, and standing in a pulpitt fixed to the maypole on kyme greene, haveinge a pott of ale or beare haninge by him in steade of a hower glasse.' The costume sounds remarkably like that of Sir Topas, but the performance was evidently a good deal more elaborate, though entirely in key with Feste's excellent fooling. Cradock 'did represent the person of a Minister or Priests, and did . . . utter . . . "The Marcie of Musterd Seed and the blessing of Bullbeefe and the peace of Pottelucke be with you all. Amen."'[19] Cradock's spoof text for the sermon, from 'The 22 chapter of the book of Hitroclites', led to a series of improbable romance tales and jests, possibly with further parodic reference to the formulae of the liturgy and scripture. Some years later in Wiltshire a drunken revel included the preaching from the pulpit within the parish church of a mock sermon on the text of 'the one and twentieth chapter of Maud Butcher and the seventh verse' (Ingram, p. 166). Mockery of ecclesiastical authority and liturgical frameworks for mock heroics may be thought particularly Rabelaisian revels, but they were evidently equally English, and survived to the years when they might be employed to deride Puritan earnestness. If they did not appear overtly in plays licensed for the public stage, that should not surprise us. The subtler parodic text Maria includes in the spurious letter is at once a test of Malvolio's reading, a word to the wary, and a libel on his sexuality; as such it lies entirely within the English festival tradition.

Notes

[1] A further interpretation of Malvolio's chosen letters has been suggested by Leah Scragg: ' "Her C's, her U's, and her T's: Why That?": A New Reply for Sir Andrew Aguecheek', *RES* 42 (1991), 1-16. Her suggestion that the line may have some reference to cutpurses has an interesting incidental bearing on my argument in this essay: see below.

[2] This translation is superseded by the 1582 (*et seq.*) Geneva New Testament, which gives the word as 'eunuches', and in every other respect is very close to the King James version. The Bishops' Bible (1568) uses 'chaste'.

[3] *A Harmony of the Gospels Matthew, Mark and Luke*, trans. T. H. L. Parker (Edinburgh, 1972), p. 248.

[4] That the text was read literally as well as metaphorically is demonstrated by its citation in the discussions over the Essex divorce case in 1614. George Abbot, Archbishop of Canterbury, quoted the passage as clear 'warrant' for annulment of marriage. King James, arguing against too narrow a definition of 'inability', denied that Christ's categories of male impotence were prescriptive. See *The Narrative History of King James* (London, 1651), pp. 95, 102. I am grateful to Professor Leslie Thomson for drawing my attention to this material.

[5] *Harmony*, p. 249.

[6] *Harmony*, p. 249.

[7] *Revel, Riot and Revolution* (Oxford, 1985), p. 40.

[8] Francis Beaumont, *The Knight of the Burning Pestle*, ed. S. P. Zitner (Manchester, 1984).

[9] See, e.g., Ralph Berry, ' "Twelfth Night": The Experience of the Audience', *Shakespeare Survey 34* (1981), 111-19.

[10] See François Laroque, *Shakespeare's Festive World* (Cambridge, 1991), pp. 47-8.

[11] *The Noble Arte of Venerie* (London, 1575), p. 127.

[12] Francis Beaumont and John Fletcher, *Philaster*, ed. A. Gurr (London, 1969).

[13] Ben Jonson, *Bartholomew Fair*, ed. E. A. Horsman (London, 1960).

[14] *The Dramatic Works of Richard Brome*, 3 vols. (London, 1873), vol. 1.

[15] For a political reading of the play see Martin Butler, *Theatre and Crisis 1632-1642* (Cambridge, 1984), pp. 220-8. The aberrant sexual behaviour in the play might be said to be a further manifestation of the madness and corruption Butler locates as its organizing themes.

[16] An incident related in a letter by Robert Gell to Sir Martin Stuteville in July 1628 concerns violent revenge for rape at the siege of La Rochelle. Ten men of the town dressed up as women to lure the guilty

soldiers of the besieging army, who then 'were so received that all to save their lives yielded unto yᵉ young men, and went into the town, where, beeing most severely and barbarously punished, they were sent back to glory in the camp of their exploit, for which they were never again fitted'. *The Autobiography and Correspondence of Sir Simonds D'Ewes, Bart.,* ed. J. O. Halliwell, 2 vols. (London, 1845), vol. 2, p. 201.

[17] 'Ridings, Rough Music and Mocking Rhymes in Early Modern England', in *Popular Culture in Seventeenth-Century England,* ed. B. Reay (London, 1985), pp. 166-97: p. 168.

[18] *Players of Shakespeare,* ed. P. Brockbank (Cambridge, 1985), p. 66.

[19] N. J. O'Conor, *Godes Peace and the Queenes* (Cambridge, Mass., 1934), pp. 108-26: pp. 119-20. The Dymock episode is discussed at length by C. L. Barber: *Shakespeare's Festive Comedy* (Princeton, 1959), chapter 3.

GENDER ISSUES

Cristina Malcolmson (essay date 1991)

SOURCE: "'What You Will': Social Mobility and Gender in *Twelfth Night,*" in *The Matter of Difference: Materialist Feminist Criticism of Shakespeare,* edited by Valerie Wayne, Harvester Wheatsheaf, 1991, pp. 29-57.

[*In the essay below, Malcolmson explores the links between gender and social class in* Twelfth Night.]

When Sebastian enters the last scene of *Twelfth Night* and begins to untangle the various intricacies of the plot, Duke Orsino describes his vision of Sebastian and Viola together in these words:

> One face, one voice, one habit, and two persons—
> A natural perspective that is and is not.

Orsino refers to a set of Renaissance artifacts, including complicated mirrors, which highlighted the effect of perspective on human vision. With some of these 'perspectives', a confusion of images would resolve themselves into clarity if viewed from one indirect position. In others, like Holbein's famous painting of 'The Ambassadors', two images could only be seen clearly from two entirely different points of view. Orsino's reference to a 'natural perspective that is and is not' implies not only that he thinks nature has produced before him what is usually the work of art by bringing two mirroring figures on the stage at once; he also suggests that one of these figures, Viola or Sebastian, is a confusion to the eye, and if one took the proper point of view, the confusion would be cleared. But the play reveals that things are more complicated than he would like: there is no view from which Viola will blend into Sebastian; the play proves that Orsino must learn to accept the confusion or the deeper clarity of two, equally viable, points of view.[1]

Orsino's reference to the 'perspective' reproduces the problem of gender in the play (are women and men twins in their mental and emotional abilities? do they have fundamentally different perspectives?). But it also evokes the play's twin issue: the relationship between gender and status. The play in fact treats these issues as reflections of each other: Viola's relationship to Orsino includes both that of woman to man and that of servant to master. More complexly, Viola's relationship to Orsino mirrors Malvolio's relationship to Olivia: both servants want to marry their masters; both men in these pairs are self-obsessed; both women seem far more intelligent than their male counterparts. Shakespeare considers the compatibility of servants and masters as he considers the comparability of men and women. When Orsino recognises the 'impropriety' of Viola's service to him, he puts it in terms of gender and status:

> So much against the mettle of your sex,
> So far beneath your soft and tender breeding.
> (V, i, 322-3)

The artful rather than natural perspective of the play moves us to compare men and women, servants and masters, gender and status, and to ask if one can ever get all these issues clearly into view, while respecting their differences and understanding their connections.

The questions evoked by Orsino's reference to the 'perspective' are remarkably similar to those posed by the historian Joan Kelly in her article on gender and class, called 'The doubled vision of feminist theory'. Kelly urges feminist historians to recognise that a *'woman's place is not a separate sphere or domain of existence but a position within social existence generally.'* She claims that feminists can see 'the relations of the sexes as formed by both socio-economic and sexual-familial structures *in their systematic connectedness*'. She posits a critical method which would acknowledge the differences of feminism and Marxism, and yet recognise that the issues of gender and class can only be clearly understood in their relation to each other: 'From this perspective, our personal, social and historical experience is seen to be shaped by *the simultaneous operation* of relations of work and sex; relations that are systematically bound to each other—and always have been so bound.'[2]

Twelfth Night was written during a period before a woman's place was imagined as a separate sphere, since, for the Renaissance, a woman was considered to be analogous to other social inferiors in a hierarchical society. The Anglican homily on obedience substantiates its political claims through a mirroring set of obligations: 'some are in high degree, some in low, some Kings and Princes, some inferiors and subjects, Priests and laymen, Maisters and servauntes, Fathers and children, Husbands and Wives.' English society linked gender and status in its own, Renaissance version of Kelly's 'systematic connectedness'. The homily on marriage teaches wives to 'cease from commanding, and performe subjection' by using the same set of analogies: 'For when we ourselves doe teach our children to obey us as their parents, or when we reforme our servants, and tell them that they should obey their masters . . . If they should tell us againe our dueties, we should not thinke it well done.'[3] The homilies testify to the flexibility of this system of correspondences, since women can be included as parents when it serves the purpose (in the homily on marriage) but excluded when it does not: the homily on obedience prefers 'Fathers and children'. Shakespeare, and other authors, constructed literary representations of these mirroring social estates sometimes to reinforce the ideology preached in the homilies, sometimes to challenge it, but primarily by evoking and manipulating what amounted to a cultural language of the analogies of subordination.

Kelly's article suggests that we need to include a historical perspective of both gender and class in our analysis of literature. My thesis is a development of hers: we can understand how gender operates in Renaissance literature only if we consider its relationship to status or class, and only through focused historical research about socio-economic structures, as Kelly puts it, as well as sexual-familial structures. We have to uncover, first, how representations of gender and status in a particular work operate within the Renaissance language of interconnection, and, second, how these representations express or elide actual conditions. Materialist feminists and, actually, all literary historicists have to create a 'perspective' of their own, in which gender and status, literature and history can be perceived in a modern account of their 'systematic connectedness'.[4]

Twelfth Night dramatises the issue of social mobility through women who, though servants, are as capable as their male masters, and who rise out of their role as servants to become their master's mistresses. Our problem is to tease out the ideological significance inherent in the play's version of the cultural mirroring process, a version which links women and aspiring servants, marriage and social mobility. *Twelfth Night* considers advancement in terms of a marriage market which in the play is much more open to personal choice and status exogamy than it is in traditional society, and which also firmly closes down at particular moments. In the play, both men and women improve their lot through this open market, but the play explicitly compares the success of its women to the failure of particular men, who are excluded from the gifts of fortune for reasons which are culturally significant. Not only are female triumphs compared to male inadequacies; the proper attitude towards marriage becomes the mirroring reflection of the proper attitude towards social advancement.[5] The play therefore transfers anxieties about fluid social relations onto gender relations, and solves the problem through its ideal of marriage. I will argue that the play dramatises the superiority of women to men in order to call into question the rigid structures of the traditional order, and, in the process, to validate certain forms of social mobility. Nevertheless, such questioning is contained through the play's model of marriage, which requires a 'loving' commitment to others. The ideology of the play resides in its formulation of love, which includes both dominant, traditional notions of interdependence, and newly emerging attitudes towards individual choice and personal desire, or, as the play puts it, 'will'.[6]

As all critics of the play have noticed, desire or 'what you will' is the motivating force in the play, but this will or appetite is often hungry not only for music, drink or love, but for an improved social position. Maria's forged letter of love from Olivia to Malvolio, which promises him that 'thou art made, if thou desir'st to be so', is a jesting version of the projects of the other characters (II, v, 150-1). Sir Toby Belch seeks to better Sir Andrew Aguecheek's estate and his own by marrying Sir Andrew to his niece, Olivia. After Olivia marries Sebastian, and meets the unknowing Cesario in Act V, Olivia says:

> Fear not, Cesario; take thy fortunes up,
> Be that thou know'st thou art, and then thou art
> As great as that thou fearest.
>
> (V, i, 147-9)

Olivia points out the social distinction between Cesario and Duke Orsino, but exhorts the servant to embrace his new position as her husband, an estate which makes him as 'great' as his master. Marriage may be the goal of desire in the play, but these marriages can also elevate one of the partners to a higher social estate. Love and desire participate in the process of social mobility made most visible in Cesario's association with the Duke. Valentine says, 'If the Duke continue these favours towards you, Cesario, you are like to be much advanced' (I, iv, 1-2). Orsino says:

> Prosper well in this,
> And thou shalt live as freely as thy lord
> To call his fortunes thine.
>
> (I, iv, 38-40)

Viola herself has explicitly chosen her place in the play: 'I'll serve this Duke' (I, ii, 55); her marriage to him at the end of the play turns Cesario's advancement into a love-match.

The notion that one's social estate could be subject to one's will or a matter of desire underlies the play's simultaneous consideration of the relation of man to woman, and of master to servant. When Viola woos Olivia for Orsino, but wins her heart for herself, the wonder of it lies not only in that a woman has been mistaken for a man, but that a woman has been mistaken for a gentleman. When alone, Olivia repeats to herself her questioning of Cesario, and reveals her attraction to what she takes to be his 'gentility':

> 'What is your parentage?'
> 'Above my fortunes, yet my state is well.
> I am a gentleman.' I'll be sworn thou art.
> Thy tongue, thy face, thy limbs, actions, and spirit
> Do give you fivefold blazon. Not so fast; soft, soft,
> Unless the master were the man. How now?
> Even so quickly may one catch the plague?
> Methinks I feel this youth's perfections
> With an invisible and subtle stealth
> To creep in at mine eyes.
>
> (I, v, 287-96)

Olivia feels the inappropriateness of falling in love with a servant, but we see that she has in fact fallen for a cleverly created illusion, Viola's capable representation of the attributes of an upper-class young man, with his tongue, face, limbs, actions and spirit. As Sir Andrew puts it, 'That youth's a rare courtier' (III, i, 88). The argument of some critics that Viola's nobility shines through her disguise must be qualified by the emphasis that the play puts on manipulating illusions and fashioning appearances.[7] Viola's success at this task is measured by Sir Andrew Aguecheek's failure; he is both male and knight, but his inadequate wit and verbal awkwardness ensure that he will be 'put down' by both Maria and Sir Toby (I, iii, 79).

In the play, a gentleman is 'made' and made loveable not by his title or blood, but by his (or her) will. Olivia makes it quite clear that she cannot love Duke Orsino simply for his aristocratic blood, though he is 'noble' and of 'great estate', 'a gracious person' both 'in dimension and the shape of nature' (I, v, 255-60). Cesario instead wins Olivia's heart when he plays the wilful lover:

> Viola If I did love you in my master's flame,
> With such a suff'ring, such a deadly life,
> In your denial I would find no sense;
> I would not understand it.
> Olivia   Why, what would you?
> Viola Make me a willow cabin at your gate
> And call upon my soul within the house;
> Write loyal cantons of contemned love
> And sing them loud even in the dead of night;
> Hallo your name to the reverberate hills
> And make the babbling gossip of the air
> Cry out 'Olivia!' O, you should not rest
> Between the elements of air and earth
> But you should pity me.
> Olivia   You might do much. What is your parentage?
>
> (I, v, 262-75)

Viola's reference to and demonstration of her verbal talents reveal that a gentleman's 'tongue' and 'spirit' are the result of intelligence and will, rather than gender or the 'great estate' that supports Orsino. Olivia in fact only becomes interested in Cesario's parentage after she is impressed with his linguistic potency. Viola is as able as the clown, whom she commands for the skills that she, he and a successful courtier share:

> He must observe their mood on whom he jests,
> The quality of persons and the time.
>
> (III, i, 63-4)

A good wit can turn a sentence inside out, like a 'chev'ril glove' (III, i, 12); he can turn a woman into a man or a servant into a master. Viola and Maria are twinned in the play because, whereas Viola can produce the appearance of a man, Maria can produce the appearance of her mistress, not only through the similarity of their handwriting, but through the use of language that convinces Malvolio that this is indeed 'my Lady's hand' (I, v, 84). The skilful intelligence of Viola and Maria wins for them marriages which improve their social estate: clearly for Maria, whose role as a gentlewoman-in-waiting places her beneath Sir Toby, kinsman to Olivia; and mostly likely for Viola, whose father's noble position is never precisely identified, and is probably beneath the rank of Duke Orsino.[8] When Sir Toby marries Maria in recompense for her 'device', the play represents through the advancement of a woman by marriage what was occurring for ambitious men in society: verbal agility could turn a servant into a master, make a gentleman into a peer or send a commoner into the ranks of the upper classes.

Commentators on the social order speak frequently and heatedly during this period about a fluidity in the status structure which they take to be common knowledge and objective fact. William Harrison claims that merchants 'often change estate with gentlemen, as gentlemen do with them, by a mutual conversion of the one into the other'. According to Harrison, many obtain gentility through attending the Inns of Court or the University, gaining the money and leisure to 'bear the port, charge, and countenance of a gentleman', and purchasing a coat of arms from the heralds; by this process, they, 'being made so good cheap, bee called master . . . and reputed for a gentleman ever after'. Thomas Smith agrees with Harrison on this point, comments that the prince can 'make' gentlemen, esquires or peers, and, in a section entitled 'Whether the maner of England in making gentlemen so easily is to be allowed', decides that such changes of status are good for the realm, especially for the treasury. He also considers quite sympathetically the yeomen who 'doe come to such wealth, that they are able and daily doe buy the landes of unthriftie gentlemen'. By sending their sons to school and freeing them from manual labour, yeomen 'doe make their saide sonnes by these meanes gentlemen'. Thomas Wilson concurs that gentlemen have been 'overreched' by yeomen, and adds that city lawyers are in pursuit of a country seat: 'they undoe the country people and buy up all the lands that are to be sold.' Smith is less sympathetic to the phenomenon, as are a multitude of preachers and satirists. However, even a churchman like Robert Sanderson, middle-of-the-road Anglican minister, could in 1621 announce that such fluidity was not only the status quo, but to be preferred to a closed system of rank. In a sermon on vocation, Sanderson urges idle 'gallants' to find their own work:

> observe by what steps your worthy Progenitors raised their houses to the height of *Gentry,* or *Nobility.* Scarce shall you find a man of them, that gave an accession, or brought any noted Eminency to his house; but either serving in the *Camp,* or sweating at the *Bar,* or waiting at the *Court,* or adventuring on the *Seas,* or trucking in his *Shop,* or some other way industriously bestirring himself in some settled Calling and Course of Life.

Only by equal labours can these young heirs merit 'those Ensigns of *Honor* and *Gentry* which [their ancestors] by industry atchieved.'[9]

Modern historians who study social mobility agree in general with these views, but argue that the movement actually taking place was far less extensive than these comments imply. In his original account of the situation, Lawrence Stone represented the social mobility of the period as 'a seismic upheaval of unprecedented magnitude', and his figures suggest as much: between 1500 and 1700, the number of the upper classes trebled during a time when the population doubled; the number of peers rose from 60 to 160, of knights from 500 to 1,400, and of armigerous gentry from 'perhaps 5,000 to 15,000'.[10] In his later work, Stone severely restricts his earlier assessment by claiming that newcomers were largely younger sons of the gentry, who, through the professions or trade, re-established their gentility. Nevertheless, he does admit to 'the influx of mercantile wealth into land in the late sixteenth and early seventeenth century'.[11] Keith Wrightson states that 'social mobility was a constant phenomenon in English society', since gentility was based on 'the acquisition and retention of landed wealth' rather than birth. He also claims that the later sixteenth and seventeenth centuries 'produced a quickened pace of upward and downward social mobility'. He cites a study of Lancashire where 278 families lost their place among the gentry between 1600 and 1642, and 210 families (and perhaps 79 more) moved up into it. The rising families were in part those of wealthy townsmen, which Wrightson argues were largely younger sons of the gentry; nevertheless, by far the majority of newcomers were prosperous yeomen.[12] Although Stone had originally defined marriage as 'the easiest road to riches', Wrightson concludes, as does Stone elsewhere, that very few marriages took place across status lines. There were, however, some connections made between those in positions close to each other in rank or wealth: the peerage intermarried with the upper gentry, rich merchants and lawyers; the gentry with mercantile or yeoman families.[13] Both of these historians agree that there was significant movement between ranks; they also believe that contemporary accounts of its range and frequency were exaggerated.

In *Twelfth Night,* Shakespeare creates a unique version of the age's Commentary about social mobility, since the play represents as primarily a female achievement the advancement noted by his contemporaries. One would like to classify this as pure myth; on the other hand, there is very little historical evidence about the social mobility of women. According to David Cressy:

> widows and women who were heads of households were the only women assumed to have any independence, but the polity was normally assumed to exclude women of all sorts . . . While a wife in England was accorded the rank or status of her man, she was, nonetheless *'de jure* but the best of servants'.[14]

The analogies of English social theory were quite inaccurate in their identification of wives with male children or male servants, since women were prohibited from most avenues for advancement. There is evidence that some daughters of rich merchants married into the gentry or peerage, but most marriages occurred within particular status groups.[15] It is clear that studies of social mobility are severely lacking in evidence on women; more work needs to be done to investigate whether or not women improved their position through marriage or through trade. We can assume, however, that the play's representation of the mobility of its society through women is historically inaccurate, and curiously and significantly skewed in a way unlike the exaggerations of commentators.

Twelfth Night sets free a fluidity between the roles of man and woman, and master and servant in the case of Viola and Maria, but limits it severely and abruptly in the case of Malvolio. In *A Marxist Study of Shakespeare's Comedies,* Elliot Krieger argues that Malvolio's aspirations are ridiculed and exorcised by the play not in order to preserve the true 'liberty' of saturnalia, but 'to allow the aristocracy to achieve social consolidation.' He claims that whereas identity is generally mutable in the play, Malvolio's attempt to cross the line between servant and master is condemned as transgressive. Whereas Viola's enactment of gentility is rendered legitimate by our discovery at the end of the play of her 'noble' blood, Malvolio's inferior status ensures that his ambition will be viewed as presumption.[16]

Krieger is quite right to point out that the play balances the freedom of Viola's fluid identity against the strictures on Malvolio, and that such strictures finally reinforce class prejudice. But in this play such prejudice is more complex than Krieger suggests. The play includes a tentative but radical disruption of conventional categories of identity which is checked but not erased by its ending, and checked in a complicated way. Reducing Viola's astute role-playing to an expression of her nobility ignores the part she plays in this limited but tangible disruption as well as in its containment. Viola's performance as a courtier wins her prestige and potential financial rewards from Orsino and a proposal of marriage from Olivia; her noble breeding may make such success more likely, but her female gender makes it remarkable. Viola is never simply a noble person masquerading as a gentle person without wealth; her rendition of masculine gentility subtly suggests that all social roles can be impersonated. The play treats Viola very differently from Perdita in *Winter's Tale,* since *Twelfth Night* emphasises Viola's performative talent rather than her 'authentic' nobility. We may be convinced in Viola's first scene that she is no commoner: she speaks to the Captain and his sailors with authority, they defer to her, she pays them 'bounteously' (I, ii, 52). Yet the scene raises questions about whether Orsino's 'name' accurately represents his 'nature', or whether the Captain's 'outward character', either as behaviour or title, is related to his 'mind' (25, 50-1). These questions prepare us for Viola's experiments with appearance, partially because she has to negotiate in a world where titles may not be trustworthy, and partially because she herself will manipulate the relationship between seeming and being. The scene does not explicitly define Viola's status as either noble or gentle; rather, her rank is veiled from us just as Viola veils it from the people she will meet. Such masking has a purpose: we, and the characters, will know her through her role-playing and her 'intent':

>O that I served that lady,
>And might not be delivered to the world,
>Till I had made mine own occasion mellow,
>What my estate is . . .
>Conceal me what I am, and be my aid
>For such disguise as haply shall become
>The form of my intent.
>
>(41-4, 53-5)

In these passages, to will or choose her way allows Viola to disrupt conventional definitions of identity: 'my estate', 'what I am.' Not to be 'delivered to the world' is to withhold the details of one's family origins, gender and present situation until one can give birth to oneself at the most propitious moment. Such a self-protective delay replaces birth and status with a flexible identity, since not only can outer appearance be subject to one's will, but this will can also be influenced by the practice of acting: Viola's disguise 'haply shall become / The form of my intent.' The word 'form' reproduces the riddles about inner and outer identity that pervade the scene, and the word 'become' increases the dilemma: will the disguise 'become' or be used as the outward form of her inward intent? Will the 'matter' of her external costume represent decorously the inner structuring 'form' or principle of her willed purpose? Will this disguise itself become or begin to dictate her desires? To what extent do clothes make the man? Not only is rank replaced by intent in Viola's plot, but also the focus of the scene on a correspondence between outer and inner quality is complicated by the suggestion that external forms can determine internal states. When her estate is 'delivered' to us in the last act, it is only after we have seen to what an extent her skilful use of disguise becomes her.

Malvolio also does not fit within Krieger's rigid schema. The play manipulates Malvolio's status titles for dramatic purposes: when Malvolio is to appear presumptuous in his disciplining of Sir Toby, Toby cries, 'Art thou more than a steward?' (II, iii, 113). When we are to recoil and laugh at Malvolio's desire to wed Olivia, his analogy tricks us into overestimating the lowliness of his rank: 'There is example for't. The Lady of the strachy married the yeoman of the wardrobe' (II, v, 39-40). We find out only in the late prison scene, when our sympathy is needed, that Malvolio is in fact not a commoner but a gentleman (IV, ii, 85; see also V, i, 277, 280). He is therefore not disenfranchised in any technical sense; he has already crossed over the most significant boundary line in the society, and is already a legitimate member of the ruling classes. It is true that a marriage between Malvolio and the Countess Olivia would be viewed as unconventional—it would be analogous to the marriage between the Duchess of Malfi and her steward Antonio.[17] But Malvolio's dream of marrying Olivia is in principle no more socially disruptive than Olivia's dream of marrying what she takes to be the gentleman Cesario. Shakespeare seems less intent on stigmatising characters for behaviour outside their rank than on emphasising status differences at particular moments for particular purposes. The play veils and manipulates the rank of Malvolio and Viola in order to encourage the audience to compare their relative success at winning their desired marriages. When their status is identified, it seems unlikely that the ideological point would be that women of undefined noble blood can marry dukes, whereas gentlemen cannot marry countesses. We must search more deeply for Malvolio's offending characteristic.

The play presents the problem most forcefully in two conjoining scenes: Act II, scene iv, in which the Duke and Cesario debate whether or not a woman's love is equal to a man's, and scene v, in which Malvolio imagines himself to be equal to Olivia and superior to Sir Toby through the marriage that would make him 'Count Malvolio'. It is here that the play's interest in twin characters and twin issues becomes most complex: Cesario is like Malvolio because both are servants who wish to marry their masters; Viola is like Maria because both use language and counterfeited appearances to manage their chosen male subjects; Malvolio is like Orsino because both are self-absorbed men for whom mastery consists in the exercise of power and the exclusion of any consideration of the perspectives of others. The play calls attention to its twin issues by repeating lines: when the Duke asks Cesario what sort of woman he has fallen in love with, Cesario replies, 'Of your complexion' (II, iv, 26). When Malvolio imagines Olivia's love for him, he remembers Olivia's previous remark that, should she love, 'it should be one of my complexion' (II, v, 23-4). The play invites us to consider love from two angles: Viola's self-abnegating, amorous desire and Malvolio's self-deluded dream of power. It also encourages us to consider Orsino's inadequate sense of women in terms of Malvolio's more explicitly identified 'self-love'. It is in the simultaneous exploration of the worthiness of women and the inadequacy of Malvolio that we find the play's ideological bias: the desire of an inferior to be matched with a superior is acceptable as long as it is motivated by love; to the extent that desire is self-interested, it is foolish and dangerous. In the world of the play, Malvolio represents ill will or bad will (*mal:* evil; *voglio:* I will or desire). He pursues his ends for the wrong reasons rather than the right. Viola's name, on the other hand, suggests a female, positive version of Malvolio, one whose will has become, let us say, musical, and capable of harmonising society rather than disrupting it. In this play, desire replaces reverence as the basis of the bond that links master and servant, man and woman; we could say that loving and erotic desire mediates the issue of social mobility in the play, since loving desire acknowledges choice and human will, but it also ensures devotion or a commitment to others. In *Twelfth Night,* ambition is acceptable, as long as it is the ambition to love. Our question is, why is such devoted desire identified with a woman rather than a man? What does such an identification make possible for the play and what does it obscure?

In *Twelfth Night,* the current and popular controversy over women mediates the dilemmas about social mobility. This allows the play to question quite fully the traditional ideology that those who rule are mentally or morally superior to those who are ruled, but it holds such questioning in check through an ideal of marriage and a model of marital contract which guards against the dangers of personal independence. The romantic love in the play acknowledges the power of desire, but ensures that such desire will flow into the channels of traditional, socially instituted bonds.

Act II, scene iv, allows Viola to confront the Duke with the value and power of female intelligence, but such intelligence is only discussed in terms of a woman's capacity to love.[18] The erotic power of this scene consists not only in the Duke's ignorance that his man-to-man talk with Cesario about love finally allows Viola to express what she feels, but also in the fact that the scene stages between two potential lovers the debate about women which usually took place within the confines of contemporary treatises. Shakespeare stages the debate with a bias: Viola's concealed identity and love for Orsino ensure our sympathy for her point of view. The Duke claims that women cannot love as deeply as he does, but the scene suggests that his love for Olivia is superficial, inconstant and finally repressive, since he seems unwilling to imagine or believe that a woman could initiate a love of her own. The Duke's 'self-love' has already been revealed in the first scene of the play, when he proclaims that, after Olivia's grief over her brother dies out, the Duke himself will take his place as the new male sovereign, the 'one self king' reigning in Olivia's affections (I, i, 40). In their conversation in Act II, scene iv, Viola reminds the Duke that he may not be so successful, and offers him the possibility of seeing things from a woman's point of view:

> Viola   Say that some Lady, as perhaps there is,
> Hath for your love as great a pang of heart
> As you have for Olivia. You cannot love her.
> You tell her so. Must she not then be answered?
> Duke   There is no woman's sides
> Can bide the beating of so strong a passion
> As love doth give my heart; no woman's heart
> So big to hold so much; they lack retention.
> (II, iv, 89-96)

The Duke refuses to imagine that a woman could initiate desire as he does, and so he loses the point of the scene communicated to us: a woman, viola, loves as deeply as a man, and recognises that she cannot control her beloved's point of view.

The debate about love in this scene is a submerged exploration of the extent to which Renaissance masculinity depends on denying women a will of their own, and the independent perspective that goes with it. Viola deflates this masculine conceit by her words and her presence:

> Duke   Make no compare
> Between that love a woman can bear me
> And that I owe Olivia.
> Viola   Ay, but I know—
> Duke   What dost thou know?
> Viola   Too well what love women to men
>   may owe.
> In faith, they are as true of heart as we.
>
> (101-6)

When Viola interrupts the Duke's masculine and mastering order, 'Make no compare', she asserts that her knowledge and experience constitute an identity comparable to his own: 'Ay, but I know.' But what she knows is her erotic attachment to the Duke, 'what love women to men may owe', an attachment that ensures her willing participation in a marital system which fears more deeply the unattached woman than the brilliant wife. Viola's debate with the Duke exposes as masculine tyranny his desire to be Olivia's 'one self king', but protects him and the audience against the play's deeper fear of female independence, expressed in the Duke's reference to the story of Diana and Actaeon:

> O, when mine eyes did see Olivia first,
> Methought she purged the air of pestilence,
> That instant was I turned into a hart,
> And my desires, like fell and cruel hounds,
> E'er since pursue me.
>
> (I, i, 20-4)

The Duke speaks in the fanciful language of a poetic love, but his words reveal that he already fears rejection, since Olivia, like Diana, might refuse to be married; such a fear must be repressed because it would result in the dismemberment of a sense of masculinity which depends on female subservience. Again, the play questions Orsino's association of masculinity and power, but provides a new protection against the dangers of Diana: women will marry because they want to. When Sir Toby praises Maria for her victory over Malvolio, he calls her 'Penthesilea', the Amazon warrior with whom Achilles fell in love just before he killed her. These dangerous extremes of female independence and masculine tyranny are modified by Toby's affirmation that Maria is 'one that adores me' (II, iii, 176-9).

Viola's response to Orsino in their debate about love is similar to that of Jane Anger in the treatise 'Her Protection for Women' (1589), which answers a lost pamphlet by 'the surfeiting lover'. These two treatises took part in a series of exchanges which fuelled the controversy about women during the period.[19] Like Viola, 'Her Protection for Women' declares that women should be recognised for their 'trueness of love' (p. 181), but the difference between the treatise and the play is registered in the difference between the name Jane Anger and that of Viola. Like Viola, Anger counters male views of female love, but less as a preface to marriage than as a reproof of men, uttered, as she says, in a 'choleric vein' (p. 173). Answering an opponent whose treatise seems to have renounced love and women as well, Anger uses the author's term for himself as 'surfeiting' to consider the destructive effects on women of defining male desire as an appetite. Orsino proclaims his inability to 'suffer surfeit' in his appetite for love, since he 'is all as hungry as the sea / and can digest as much' (II, iv, 100-1), but Anger points out the problem with the metaphor: men 'become ravenous hawks, who do not only seize upon us, but devour us' (p. 178). Her treatise clarifies the contradictory nature of Orsino's love, which he describes as both 'so strong a passion' that 'no woman's heart' is 'so big to hold so much', and as 'more longing, wavering, sooner lost and worn, / Than women's are' (II, iv, 94-6, 33-4). His desire for Olivia is described as infinite, like the sea, but he uses words which suggest that marriage itself would be no solution:

> Nought enters there,
> Of what validity and pitch so ever,
> But falls into abatement and low price
> Even in a minute.
>
> (I, i, 11-14)

The Duke's description of desire implies that whether the lover surfeits or never surfeits, the fate of his wife will be the same:

> For women are as roses, whose fair flow'r,
> Being once displayed, doth fall that very hour.

Viola's reply is full of pathos:

> And so they are; alas, that they are so;
> To die, even when they to perfection grow.
>
> (II, v, 38-42)

Such a reply is quite different from Jane Anger's comment on the subject:

> men's eyes are so curious, as be not all women equal with Venus for beauty, they cannot abide the sight of them; their stomachs so queasy, as do they taste but twice of one dish they straight surfeit, and needs must a new diet be provided for them.
>
> (p. 178)

Viola's careful and caring instruction of the Duke as well as our sympathy for her concealed love prepare us for the harmony of their betrothal in the last scene of the play, but keep us from considering what their marriage will finally be like.

Jane Anger's treatise is unusual in its lack of interest in the subject of matrimony, since most pamphlet-writers defending women during this period praised them most highly for their capacity to be able companions to men. Nicholas Breton in 'The Praise of Vertuous Ladies' (1597) claims that a man should see a great part of a woman in himself, since Eve was made out of Adam, and this proves that a woman is 'no other substance but another himself'. For every excellent man, there is an excellent woman, who is 'everie waies his match'. The treatise soon turns to the match it most prizes, that of marriage, but here the equality of women stressed by the treatise becomes a threat. The best companion to a wise man is a witty woman, but 'it is wisdom for a man to take heed that a woman be not wiser than himself.' Finally, the treatise states with a jesting tone, but a serious purpose that the only worthy 'wit' of a maid is to choose a husband well; of a married woman, to love none other; and of a widow, to provide for her children. This treatise suggests that the faculties which made women 'everie waies' a man's 'match' could only usefully be exercised within the institution of marriage, and that even in marriage these capacities had to be restrained.[20]

A woman's love was essential to a successful marriage, according to the manuals of the period, which prized marriage as a form of companionship rather than simply as a necessity for lawful procreation. For William Perkins, the creation of Eve proved that a woman should not rule her husband, since she did not come out of his head, nor be his slave, since she did not come out of his feet, but, since she came out of his side, 'man should take her as his mate.'[21] But the equality that this notion of companionship seems to promise is quickly qualified by the manuals, and the love of a wife for her husband begins to appear as another form of masculine control. Edmund Tilney's *Flower of Friendshippe* (1568) states:

> equalitie is principally to be considered in thys matrimoniall amitie, as well of yeares, as of the gifts of nature, and fortune. For equalnesse herein, maketh friendliness . . . In this long and troublesome journey of matrimonie, the wise man maye not be contented onely with his spouses virginitie, but by little and little must gently procure that he maye also steale away her private will, and appetite, so that of two bodies there may be made one onely hart, which she will soone doe, if love raigne in her, and without this agreeable concord matrimonie hath but small pleasure . . . or none at all, and the man, that is not lyked, and loved of his mate, holdeth his lyfe in continuall perill, his goodes in great jeopardie, his good name in suspect, and his whole house in perdition.

John Dod and Richard Cleaver in *The Godly Form of a Household* (1598) use almost the same words as Tilney, but their sense of the relationship between love and possession has increased: 'The husband ought not to bee satisfied that, he hath robd his wife of her virginitie, but in that he hath possession and use of her will.' Dod and Cleaver recognise the tension between the requirements that men rule and that women love: 'For although the husband shall have power to his wife, to feare and obey him, yet he shall never have strength to force her to love him.'[22]

The marriage manuals emphasise the importance of personal choice and consent by the marriage partners, and such choice includes women as well as men, but the equality of choice does not extend much farther than the original decision. The literature on marriage during this period as well as current historical studies suggest that individual desire did influence marriage negotiations much more than we previously believed: Keith Wrightson has shown that Lawrence Stone overemphasised the capacity of aristocratic parents to determine marriages for their children, and ignored the extent to which lower-class marriages were initiated by the partners. Marriage manuals consistently acknowledge the fact of individual choice in their very structure, at the same time that they insist on parental approval. These manuals include chapters on consent and on the contractual nature of marriage, in order to stress the extent to which the marriage must be a matter of free will. It may finally be the case that marriage manuals were written for the children of the gentry or the middling sort' rather than for the aristocracy, whose marriages were more consistently determined by issues of status and wealth rather than personal choice. It is clear that they were written more often for men than for women. The voluntary nature of the marriage vow, in which the promise 'must not come from the lippes alone, but from the wel-liking and consent of the heart', nevertheless preceded a relationship in which a woman's love had to be matched by submission and obedience to her husband's will. Many marriage manuals suggest, in fact, that the only real choice appropriate for a woman after marriage was to choose to love her husband. In Tilney's *The Flower of Friendshippe,* which celebrates 'perfite love' that 'knitteth loving heartes, in an insoluable knot of amitie', the female speaker, Lady Julia, urges women to apply themselves to their duty, not only to revere their husbands, but to love them:

> The first thing, therefore, which the married woman must labour to intende, the first thing which she must with all her force, applie her whole minde unto, and the first thing which she must hartily put in execution, is to lyke, and love well. For reason doth bind us to love them, with whom we must eate, and drinke.[23]

The fear of unloving wives in the marriage manuals is like the fear of female independence in *Twelfth Night*: in both cases, women refuse to authorise as mutually beneficial and as benevolent the form of social control inherent in the Renaissance institution of marriage. But this fear of the independent woman in *Twelfth Night* and the celebration of a romantic love that impels one to choose to be dependent on another mediates and controls the play's twin issue: the danger of self-interested rather than devoted servants. The play and its various literary and social sources testify to a society searching to articulate a new social bond between 'master' and 'servant', one which would acknowledge choice and ensure a new kind of dependability', based on contract rather than feudal obligation.[24]

In Act II, scene v, which directly follows the debate about love between Orsino and Viola, Malvolio imagines his new estate as 'Count Malvolio', and the play reveals that such self-interest has always motivated his government within the house. It is clear that Malvolio does not pursue Olivia with the poetic abandon of the other lovers in the play; he sees her as his ticket to a higher social position. His desire for Olivia as well as his ethical severity is a mask for a will-to-power:

> Fabian   O, peace! Now he's deeply in. Look how imagination blows him.
> Malvolio   Having been three months married to her, sitting in my state –
> Toby   O for a stone bow, to hit him in the eye!
> Malvolio   Calling my officers about me, in my branched velvet gown; having come from a day-bed, where I have left Olivia sleeping— . . . And then to have the humour of state; and after a demure travel of regard, telling them I know my place, as I would they should do theirs, to ask for my kinsman Toby— . . . Saying, 'Cousin Toby, my fortunes having cast me on your niece, give me this prerogative of speech.'
> Toby   What, what?
> Malvolio   'You must amend your drunkenness'.
>
> (II, v, 40-71)

Malvolio's fantasy reveals that his disciplinary zeal is impelled by a desire to dominate, unlike Viola's gracious deference. His imagined reproof, 'You must amend your drunkeness', is, like his branched velvet gown and his imperious looks, only another means by which he demonstrates his new position of power within the household. Malvolio's imagined reproof of Sir Toby is to be compared to the kindly correction of Orsino by Viola: their motives, according to the play, establish their difference. Malvolio's crime is not that he, as a gentleman, wants to marry a countess, or even that a steward wants to marry his mistress; it is that he will use his new position to disrupt traditional customs and rituals, and that such use of his 'prerogative' will be motivated by an ambition to establish his superiority and to impose his will on others. His sense of being virtuous is actually a desire for supremacy; for this reason, there will be no more cakes and ale, as Toby puts it (II, iii, 116-17). We find during the play that Malvolio has brought Fabian 'out o' favour with my lady' Olivia for bearbaiting, and put Viola's benevolent captain into jail for some unidentified crime (II, v, 6-7; V, i, 275-6). Although Maria calls Malvolio only 'a kind of Puritan', Malvolio's fantasy of power constitutes the play's critique of London disciplinarians, those Puritan aldermen who were perhaps gentlemen but had originally been merchants, who condemned holiday revelry, bearbaiting and the theatre: such a concern for civil rule, according to the play, masks a self-interested desire to govern, an unwillingness to accept traditional social bonds, and a willingness to disrupt rather than harmonise the social order. London Puritans and Malvolio are like the 'politicians' and 'Brownists' that Sir Andrew fears (III, ii, 30-1): each is a type of 'separatist', one who does not respect the bonds that tie the community together, bonds which may be flexible and fluid, but which must continue to hold if society is to survive.

In 'Pierce Pennilesse: His Supplication to the Divell' (1592), Thomas Nash, Gent., attacks those newly rich men who have no respect for the 'noble' virtue of liberality, which he feels is the main source of income for struggling writers. The contempt for tradition on the part of these 'new men' is the result of a frenetic upward movement of tradesmen and lawyers, who dress 'as brave as any . . . Nobleman'. He makes it clear that he does not oppose social mobility *per se*, but only that worthy men are left impoverished, whereas the undeserving obtain higher estates through 'delicious gold' or are unjustly promoted like 'some such obscure upstart gallants, as without desert or service are raised from the plough, to be checkmate with Princes'. Indeed, such social advancement would be appropriate if granted to writers whose talents make them superior to their patrons: 'This is the lamentable condition of our Times, that men of Arte must seeke almes of Cormorants, and those that deserve best, be kept under by Dunces.' Like *Twelfth Night*, Nash questions the traditional notion that social superiors are necessarily better than those they govern, but he also attacks merchants and tradesmen who have no respect for the traditional nobility and no respect for the theatre. 'Pierce' claims that the ethical severity of those citizens who condemn playgoing only masks a desire to usurp the place of the traditional nobility:

> I will defend [the theatre] against any Collier or clubfooted Usurer of them all, there is no immortalitie, can be given a man on earth like unto Playes. What talke I to them of immortalitie, that

are the only underminers of Honour, and doe envie any man that is not sprung up by base Brokerie like themselves. They care not if all the ancient houses were rooted out, so that like the Burgomasters of the Low-Countries they might share the government amongst them as States, and be quarter-maisters of our Monarchie . . . [They respect] neither the right of Fame that is due to true Nobilitie deceased, nor what hopes of eternitie are to be proposed to adventurous mindes, to encourage them forward, but only their execrable luker, and filthie unquenchable avarice.

Social advancement is appropriate for 'adventurous mindes' and 'men of Arte', but not for those who seek to mount upward for the wrong reasons: a hunger for money and power over others. Such as these not only have no respect for the ancient houses of nobility, they want to cast society into a different form, so that, like the 'Burgomasters of the Low-Countries', they will be 'quarter-maisters of our Monarchie'. According to the treatise, this disruption of the social order is caused by the devil himself, 'Nicalao Malevolo . . . the great mister maister of hell'.[25]

In 'Pierce Pennilesse', Nash reacts against Puritan attacks on the theatres and against the influence of the London city government on the Privy Council. *Twelfth Night* (1602) was produced only a few years after the office of the Master of the Revels had affirmed its capacity to license theatrical companies and restrict the days of their performances, as well as the bearbaiting that occurred nearby. Such courtly and civic control over theatrical revelry mirrored the repression of holiday pastimes in the Countryside in places like Shakespeare's Stratford. Local Puritan elites were prohibiting many village festivities, including the church ales, in the name of a more thorough 'civil rule' (II, iii, 122).[26]

Nash's pamphlet illuminates one of the most important contexts for *Twelfth Night*: urban satire, including the Harvey-Nash quarrel, in which 'Pierce Pennilesse' figures, but also including the war of the theatres, occurring during this period and referring at times to this play. *What You Will* is one of John Marston's volleys in the war, and its connections to *Twelfth Night, or What You Will* clarify that, for these playwrights, the intersection between disguise and the problem of fluid social relations is commonplace. In a society where status categories are flexible, apparel becomes a 'god', and opinion, or 'what you will', according to Marston, determines all social value, including personal rank and identity. One of the central characters in Marston's play, Albano, is a merchant who for a time loses his wife, his property and his name because people assume that he is dead and the living person standing before them is an imposter. Whether *What You Will* appeared before or after *Twelfth Night,* the attributes they share suggest that *Twelfth Night* was not only about revelry or carnival, but about the difficulties of estimating the value of individuals when the externals of identity, including rank and gender, are so easily imitated. It is therefore relevant that Shakespeare's play and probably Marston's were put on before an Inns of Court audience, incipient lawyers, well versed in urban satire and preparing for the successes and dangers of social advancement in the city. 'What you will' for Marston refers to opinion, and for Shakespeare to desire, but both playwrights testify to a world in which individually initiated attitudes and acts have replaced a shared consensus about appropriate behaviour and the rules for evaluating it. Both plays fear such a world, in which every man and woman can be a phoenix; *Twelfth Night* offers us women and servants who exchange their independence for a willing desire for another and so preserve 'all relation'.[27]

Malvolio may be a kind of Puritan, but he is also the conventional butt of urban satire, the social climber who becomes obsessed with the externals of rank, 'the habit of some sir of note' (III, iv, 77-8), without a sense of 'true' worth and its significance for the community. Viola's decision to trust the Captain at the beginning of the play takes on new importance in this context, because she, like all members of society, must learn to accept and analyse a difference between external appearance and internal value:

> There is a fair behaviour in thee, captain,
> And though that nature with a beauteous wall
> Doth oft close in pollution, yet of thee
> I will believe thou hast a mind that suits
> With this thy fair and outward character.
> (I, i, 47-51)

Viola's trust in the Captain is a matter of judgement and of will, an opinion not a fact. The problems of disguise in *Twelfth Night* take the play into the world of Ben Jonson's exploration of character and the ambiguous relationship in his plays between inner worth and social rank.

For Jonson, the nobility are to be revered, but only if they

> Study the native frame of a true heart,
> An inward comeliness of bountie, knowledge,
> And spirit that may conforme them actually
> To *God's* high figures.[28]

In *Cynthia's Revels, Or the Fountayne of self-love* (1600), the Jonsonian surrogate Crites unmasks the narcissism that motivates decadent aristocrats as well as ambitious courtiers; the play uses terms that look forward to Shakespeare's presentation of the Duke and Malvolio. But unlike Shakespeare, Jonson proceeds to define a positive version of self-love, which transforms narcissism into an honourable method of establishing publicly one's inner value: 'allowable Self-love' quickens 'minds in the pursuit of honour', and impels individuals to reach a social position which will justly match 'that true measure of one's self' (V, vii, 26-35). In the play, Cynthia the Queen singles out for promotion her playwright Crites, whom she describes as one 'whom learning, virtue, and our favour last / Exempteth from the gloomy multitude' (V, viii, 32-3).

In *Twelfth Night,* Shakespeare pokes fun at a notion of 'allowable self-love' which results in the preferment of its author. He associates such self-love with the colour yellow theatrically attributed to it in *Cynthia's Revels,* and with an overly pretentious, censorious steward, who is convinced that his lady will thrust greatness upon him.[29] Malvolio's 'self-love' satirises Jonson's version of individual value not only as self-indulgent but as socially divisive, because it privileges censuring the faults of others and praising the self over the more difficult task of preserving the harmony of social relations. *Twelfth Night* suggests that Jonson's version of merit is just as 'separatist' as the Puritans he derides in his comedies. The 'railing' that Viola's social music tames is not only that of the Puritans but that of the satirists.

Shakespeare is as interested as Jonson in the relationship between the 'name' and 'nature' of nobility, but he explores the issue through 'Viola' rather than 'Crites'. The name of the Duke, Orsino (or 'the little bear'), indicates that the Duke as well as Malvolio is the subject of the play's bearbaiting. Marston's Duke in *What You Will* is blatantly frivolous and sensual; audiences must have understood that Orsino's attitude towards love and women was not presented uncritically by *Twelfth Night.* But such criticism never becomes biting satire in Shakespeare's play: 'there is no railing in a known discreet man, though he do nothing but reprove' (I, v, 95-6).[30]

In *Twelfth Night,* Shakespeare celebrates the social arts, very like his own, which can turn a servant into a master, a glove-maker's son into a gentleman, a woman into a man, a man into a woman. Nevertheless, he reproves those who would use this social fluidity for their own benefit or as an opportunity to reorder the traditional structure according to new ethical and political principles. Such ethical and political blueprints, he suggests, are simply fantasies of power, which exchange the community good for private profit.

The play links the issues of gender and status in order to make marriage, with its inclusion of desire and its commitment to permanence, the model of all social bonds. The Priest's description of Olivia's marriage betrothal to Sebastian represents the play's dream of a perpetual community, in which each member willingly takes his or her place:

> A contract of eternal bond of love
> Confirmed by mutual joinder of your hands,
> Attested by the holy close of lips,
> Strengthened by interchangment of your rings.
> (V, i, 156-9)

It is not a coincidence that in the last act, as the cases of mistaken identity mount up, willing service is coordinated with the contract of marriage, and the dangers of infidelity to such a contract are considered: Olivia's sense of her husband Cesario's betrayal is followed by Antonio's sense of his master Sebastian's betrayal, and then by Orsino's sense of his servant Cesario's betrayal. Antonio, of course, is the model for the new servant imagined by the play, since his service is based on desire rather than duty or reverence:

> I could not stay behind you. My desire
> (More sharp than filed steel) did spur me forth;
> ... My willing love ... Set forth in your pursuit.
> (III, iii, 4-5, 11-13)[31]

The marriage bonds that certify the socially acceptable 'willing love' of man and woman are forged by the 'true' priest in the play, who is opposed dramatically to the 'false' priest-fool, Sir Topas, who baits Malvolio. This carnivalesque figure reproaches others in society who have 'dissembled in such a gown' (IV, ii, 5-6), but also members of the aristocracy, who, like Chaucer's Sir Thopas, provide only an empty image of aristocratic superiority. Such an image becomes ridiculous when engendered by a non-aristocratic author-fool, like the narrator of the *Canterbury Tales,* who cannot get a tale of nobility quite right, but also when manipulated by a Sir Toby, whose name is so close to the Sir Topas he concocts that he becomes implicated in his own critique. Such satirists as Sir Toby miss the point when they bait Malvolio: blood is not the issue, but rather some mysterious quality of inner nobility which Sir Toby himself does not possess.

Viola's 'courtesy' is evidence not only of this inner nobility, but of her willingness to use her performative talent for unselfish purposes, to spin out the modes of social behaviour that can preserve the ties that bind. Orsino and Olivia think nostalgically about 'the old age' or the 'merry world' before true love and loyal servants were replaced by 'these most brisk and giddy-paced times' (II, iv, 6, 48; II, i, 100-1). *Twelfth Night* is plagued by a fear that when the witty whirl that is its surface and its plot shuts down, no trustworthy social order will remain: 'with hey, ho, the wind and the rain' (V, i, 391ff).

Perhaps this is one reason why the play so relentlessly excludes the figure of the merchant, although in the sources, the father of Viola and Sebastian is almost always a merchant, and frequently the father of Olivia is so as well.[32] In Marston's play, Albano the merchant most forcefully represents the fragility of an identity based on fortune or chance, since he has achieved his status in the community through the power of wealth rather than the tradition of family lineage. In *Twelfth Night,* a play that is filled with imagery of the sea, merchants are never mentioned, although the play does refer to a new map of the world which includes the West Indies, and which is used to describe the lines on Malvolio's smiling face as he pursues his hopes with Olivia (III, ii, 76-8). The play evokes the sense of treasure that can be obtained from the sea, as well as the riches that can satisfy a desire which is as infinite as the sea. But the treasure from the ocean in this play is Viola and Sebastian; like aspirations for social ascent, commercial interests are turned into romantic appetites.

The play cannot afford the figure of the merchant because such a social role does not fit clearly enough into the traditional hierarchical order of servant and master. The relations of the commercial classes to the classes above them could not easily be described in terms of feudal norms—they are not mentioned in the homily on obedience—since they were constituted more by monetary exchange than by the traditional ideals of reverence and duty. Shakespeare has to consider Malvolio as 'a kind of Puritan'; a real Calvinist merchant would upset the delicate balance of a play which explores the issue of social mobility through the lens of willing servants rather than successful entrepreneurs.[33]

The play solves the problem of self-interested desire through Viola's harmonious social bonding, and so projects anxieties about status relations onto gender relations. The play's fear of independent women is implicated in its fear of independent servants, since Viola's dependence is constituted in opposition to Malvolio's self-interest. Therefore sexual-familial structures are linked rather explicitly to socio-economic structures, as Kelly puts it, in such a way as to suggest that Viola's attitude to her labour as a servant to the Duke is praiseworthy because it partakes of her attitude towards her beloved, Orsino. As such, loving male-female relations mediate master-servant relations: both partners may be quite equal in intelligence and moral capacity, or indeed the subordinate may be superior to his or her master; nevertheless, an appreciative love should tie both together. Such a formula redefines traditional hierarchical bonds as more flexible in themselves, but also turns anything but the most loving commitment to one's superiors into 'self-love'.

The play's superimposition of labour relations onto marital relations results in a model of 'willing service' formed in the image of the 'mutual consent' required in the marriage contract. The history of the various kinds of contract during this period demonstrates that Shakespeare's model of contract is a selective one, since such an agreement could act as either a conservative or a disruptive force. At the time that the play was produced, changes in the law were eroding traditional restraints on business contracts, and strengthening the individual's control over these transactions. Such agreements required voluntary and mutual consent at the cost of feudal models of obligation, since deference to status was replaced with an interest in the market and personal profit. But such 'freedom' was not extended to labouring individuals, whose tendency to move throughout the country in pursuit of work had resulted in the passing of the Statute of Artificers (1563), which prohibited the sudden termination of contracts between employer and employed, and made illegal a horizontal mobility of workers responsive to new commercial developments. Through its labour-contract clauses, the Statute sought to place labourers under the firm control of a 'master', and often within the structure of the employer's family and paternal authority. *Twelfth Night* also mediates between a status and a market society through marriage and the family: it dramatises voluntary consent and 'free' will as mitigating the rigidity of the master-servant relationship, but also as preserving this traditional bond at a time when market forces were wearing away its feudal foundations. Shakespeare may have taken his cue from the marriage manuals of the period, which employ the language of contractual 'freedom', but nevertheless hedge it about with a concern for status and authority: 'consent' includes parental agreement and 'equality' requires likeness in rank; both consent and equality fade quickly away before the customary necessities of male authority and female submission. Like the manuals and marital law during this period, Shakespeare attempts to negotiate between individual interests and those of traditional society. He follows Perkins by making marriage the model for 'the commonwealth'.[34]

Twelfth Night imagines a world in which one's social estate is a matter of desire or will rather than birth or title. Such desire is innocent and successful to the extent that it moves one to be bound unselfishly to another. Shakespeare divides and conquers in his play not only by praising Viola and condemning Malvolio, but also by obscuring what Viola and Malvolio share in the play's various literary and social sources: a connection with a commercial class whose access to money has the power to upset the traditional link between high birth, wealth and status. The ideal that is set before women, servants and merchants in the play is that of loving and willing service, a Viola who chooses her man, but who also chooses to correct gently rather than dethrone the tyrant who will rule over her in the future. We might imagine a play about Mal-Viola (or Jane Anger), who does not wish the Duke well and says so, and whose female desire cannot so easily be presented as 'good will'. Just as Jonson in *Cynthia's Revels* presents himself in Crites,

Shakespeare in *Twelfth Night* presents himself in Viola, that figure so well versed in the 'arts' of social behaviour, far more intelligent than her superiors, who elects to preserve the social harmony rather than 'put down' her masters.

Notes

[1] I am grateful for the comments and suggestions made by the participants of the seminar 'Materialist feminist criticism of Shakespeare' held at the 1989 meeting of the Shakespeare Association of America. I would particularly like to thank Catherine Belsey, Barbara Bono, Mihoko Suzuki, Valerie Wayne and Marion Wynne-Davies. 'Perspectives' are discussed in Jurgis Baltrusaitis, *Anamorphic Act,* trans. W.L. Strachan (New York: Harry N. Abrams, 1977), pp. 11-18, 91-114. Orsino's comment on the perspective appears in *Twelfth Night,* V, i, 215-16 in *The Complete Signet Classic Shakespeare,* ed. Sylvan Barnet (New York: Harcourt Brace Jovanich, 1972). Subsequent citations will refer to this edition and appear in the text of the essay.

[2] Joan Kelly, 'The doubled vision of feminist theory', in Judith L. Newton, Mary P. Ryan and Judith R. Walkowitz, eds., *Sex and Class in Women's History* (London: Routledge and Kegan Paul, 1983), pp. 264, 265, 266. The emphasis is Kelly's own.

[3] 'An exhortation concerning good order, and obedience to rulers and magistrates,' and 'An homilie of the state of matrimonie', in *Certaine Sermons or Homilies appointed by the Queenes Majestie, to be declared and read by all Parsons, Vicars, and Curates . . .* (London, 1595), 13 and Gg7.

[4] Of course, several Renaissance critics have already discussed quite successfully the relationship of gender and status in Renaissance drama. Frank Whigham's 'Sexual and social mobility in *The Duchess of Malfi*' (*PMLA,* 100 [1985], pp. 167-86) is the best of this sort, and I am indebted to his discussion of social mobility. Nevertheless, in his essay, the gender issues tend to collapse into the status issues: 'the duchess's enterprise is not primarily private and romantic: it is, rather, a socially adaptive action that extends to the zone of gender conflict a maneuver actively in play in the arena of class conflict' (p. 171). Whigham's quotation from Kenneth Burke on *Venus and Adonis* at the beginning of the essay clarifies this: 'The real subject is not primarily sexual lewdness at all, but "social lewdness" mythically expressed in sexual terms.' If feminist writers in the 1970s ignored problems of class (Paula Berggren, 'The woman's part: female sexuality as power in Shakespeare's plays', and Clara Claiborne Park, 'As we like it: how a girl can be smart and still popular', both in Carolyn Lenz, Gayle Greene and Carol Neely, eds., *The Woman's Part: Feminist criticism of Shakespeare* [Urbana: University of Illinois Press, 1980], pp. 17-34, 100-16), then new historicists and cultural materialists in the 1980s often reduced gender concerns into a symbolic means of articulating what is 'the real subject': status, or issues of power in general. See Leonard Tennenhouse, *Power on Display: The politics of Shakespeare's genres* (New York and London: Methuen, 1986) for a fascinating discussion of 'Staging carnival', which attends to the role of women and Queen Elizabeth in the process of inheritance, but which finally defines the comedies and Petrarchan literature as 'presenting us with a political crisis which must be understood and resolved in sexual terms' (p. 19). This is the problem, I think, with focusing exclusively on Queen Elizabeth in discussing these issues: the sexual-familial questions can too easily disappear before the political or socio-economic concerns. Jean Howard avoids this difficulty in 'Crossdressing, the theatre, and gender struggle in early modern England', (*SQ,* 39 [1988], pp. 418-40), in which she discusses the 'various manifestations of crossdressing' as 'an interlocking grid through which we can read aspects of class and gender struggle in the period', and the particularity with which she does so is enlightening and refreshing. She interprets *Twelfth Night* quite differently from the way I do, however, because she sees Viola's crossdressing as 'in no way adopted to protest gender inequities' (p. 431).

[5] In an essay in this collection, 'The world turned upside down: inversion, gender and the state', Peter Stallybrass argues that 'there is no *intrinsic* connection between inversions of class [and] gender . . . Politics is precisely the work of *making* such connections.' I argue in this essay that *Twelfth Night* performs such work by coordinating the interests of women and servants, and by making female 'good will' the model for socially ambitious men.

[6] It is not a coincidence that the centrality of 'will' to the play reproduces the role of 'will' in the sonnets, in which Shakespeare represents his own peculiar linking of love and the potential rewards of patronage. For a largely psychoanalytic account of will in the sonnets, see Joel Fineman, *Shakespeare's Perjured Eye* (Berkeley: University of California Press, 1988). My analysis of traditional and emergent attitudes in the play is indebted to Raymond Williams' discussion of his terms 'dominant', 'emergent' and 'residual' in *Problems in Materialism and Culture* (London: Verso, 1980), pp. 31-49, and in *Marxism and Literature* (Oxford: Oxford University Press, 1977), pp. 121-8.

[7] I disagree with those critics who diagnose and/or dismiss Viola's successes in this play as the result of her noble rank (Tennenhouse, *Power on Display,* p. 66; Elliot Krieger, *A Marxist Study of Shakespeare's Comedies* [London: Macmillan Press, 1979], pp. 105-30).

⁸ As with several other characters, the play confuses us about the status of Maria: she is represented by Sir Toby as 'my niece's chambermaid' (I, iii, 50), but is identified by Olivia as 'my gentlewoman' (I, v, 162). But the play continually groups her with the 'lighter people', as Malvolio puts it (V, i, 341). In her forged letter to Malvolio, Maria herself delineates the line she will eventually cross: 'Be opposite with a kinsman, surly with servants' (II, v, 149-50).

⁹ William Harrison, 'A description of England' (1577), in F.J. Furnivall, ed., *Elizabethan England* (London: Walter Scott, 1902), pp. 7, 9; Thomas Smith, *De Republica Anglorum* (London, 1583), pp. 27-30; Thomas Wilson, *The State of England Anno-dom. 1600,* ed. F.J. Fisher (London: Camden Miscellany xvi, 3rd series lii, 1936), pp. 25, 38; Robert Sanderson, 'Ad populum; the fourth sermon . . . London, Nov. 4, 1621' in *XXXXVI Sermons* (London, 1986), p. 212.

¹⁰ Lawrence Stone, 'Social mobility in England, 1500-1700', *Past and Present,* 33 (1966), pp. 16, 23-24; see also David Cressy, 'Describing the social order of Elizabethan and Stuart England,' *Literature and History,* 3 (1976), pp. 29-44.

¹¹ Lawrence Stone, *An Open Elite? England 1540-1880* (Oxford: Clarendon Press, 1984), pp. 399-400; 405-6.

¹² Keith Wrightson, *English Society 1580-1680* (London: Hutchinson, 1982), pp. 26-30, 140.

¹³ Stone, 'Social mobility', p. 38; Wrightson, p. 86, cites Vivien Brodsky Elliott, 'Mobility and marriage in pre-industrial England' (unpubl. Ph.D. thesis, University of Cambridge, 1978), pt. 1, ch. 4; pt. 3, ch. 3. See also Elliott, 'Single women in the London marriage market: age, status, mobility, 1598-1619', in R.B. Outhwaite, ed., *Marriage and Society: Studies in the social history of marriage* (London: Europa Publications, 1981), pp. 81-100; and Stone, *The Family, Sex and Marriage in England, 1500-1800* (London: Weidenfeld and Nicolson, 1977), pp. 60-1, 491.

¹⁴ Cressy, 'Describing the social order', pp. 34-5.

¹⁵ Stone, 'Social mobility', p. 38; Lawrence Manley, *London in the Age of Shakespeare: An anthology* (London: Croom Helm, 1986), pp. 77-8.

¹⁶ Krieger, *A Marxist Study,* pp. 100-1, and throughout.

¹⁷ See Whigham, 'Sexual and social mobility in *The Duchess of Malfi*'.

¹⁸ See Catherine Belsey's illuminating and convincing reading of this scene in 'Disrupting sexual difference: meaning and gender in the comedies', in John Drakakis, ed., *Alternative Shakespeares* (London: Methuen, 1985), pp. 166-90. Belsey argues that Viola-as-Cesario calls 'into question that set of relations between terms which proposes as inevitable an antithesis between masculine and feminine, men and women' (p. 167). I am arguing that the difference between the categories of servant and master are also questioned by the play, and that Viola's success and 'good will' in disrupting these differences in scene iv are compared to Malvolio's failure in scene v. Viola's noble rank, like her role as a wife, is affirmed at the end of the play, and, as Belsey says, closes off 'the glimpsed transgression . . . But the plays are more than their endings' (pp. 187-8).

¹⁹ The full title of Anger's treatise is 'Jane Anger her Protection for Women. To defend them against the Scandalous Reportes of a late Surfeiting Lover, and all other like Venerians that complaine so to bee overcloyed with womens kindness' (London: Richard Jones, 1589). See the abridged text in Katherine Henderson and Barbara McManus, eds., *Half Humankind: Contexts and texts of the controversy about women in England, 1540-1640* (Urbana and Chicago: University of Illinois Press, 1985). Page numbers from this edition will appear in the text of the essay. For commentary on the controversy about women and lists of texts, see Henderson and McManus, *Half Humankind;* Edmund Tilney, *'The Flower of Friendshippe:' A Renaissance Dialogue Contesting Marriage,* ed., Valerie Wayne, forthcoming from Cornell University Press; Linda Woodhouse, *Women and the English Renaissance: Literature and the nature of womankind, 1540-1620* (Urbana: University of Chicago Press, 1984), pp. 139-51; and Louis B. Wright, *Middle-Class Culture in Elizabethan England* (Chapel Hill: University of North Carolina Press, 1935), pp. 481-502. For a discussion of the intersection of the controversy and later drama, see Sandra Clark, '*Hic Mulier, Haec Vir* and the controversy over masculine women', *Studies in Philology,* 82 (1985), pp. 157-83; and Mary Beth Rose, 'Women in men's clothing: apparel and social stability in *The Roaring Girl*', *English Literary Renaissance,* 14 (1984), pp. 139-51.

²⁰ Nicholas Breton, 'The Praise of Vertuous Ladies' in *The Wil of Wit, Wits Will, or Wils Wit, chuse you whether. Containing five discourses.* (London: Thomas Creede, 1597), pp. 65, 69, 67, 70-1.

²¹ William Perkins, *Christian Oeconomy,* trans. T. Pickering (London: E. Weaver, 1609), p. 125. The first occurrence of this representation of companionship is found in Bullinger, *Christen State of Matrimony* (1541), sig. A4v.

²² Tilney, 'A Brief and Pleasant Discourse of Duties in Marriage, called the Flower of Friendshippe' (Lon-

don: Henrie Denham, 1568), B2, B6. John Dod and Richard Cleaver include passages from 'The Flower' in *A Godly Form of Householde Government* (London: Thomas Creede, 1598), pp. 167, 165.

[23] For discussions on individual choice in marriage, see Stone, *The Family, Sex and Marriage in England, 1500-1800,* pp. 85-93, 117, 178-95, 270-95; Wrightson, *English Society 1580-1680,* pp. 70-88; Susan Dwyer Amussen, *An Ordered Society: Gender and Class in Early Modern England* (Oxford: Basil Blackwell, 1988), pp. 70-6, 105-8; and William and Malleville Haller, 'The Puritan art of love', *Huntington Library Quarterly,* 5 (1941-2), pp. 254-6, 265. Cleaver insists on the 'consent of the heart' (p. 115) and includes discussions on choice, consent, and contract (pp. 96-129). Perkins includes chapters entitled 'Of the Contract', 'Of the choice of persons fit for marriage' and 'Of consent in the Contract' (pp. 18, 23, 68). See Tilney, D4, for Lady Julia's advice on the choice of husbands and the practicality of love after the marriage has occurred.

[24] Howard discusses the emerging idea of contractual relations in 'Crossdressing', p. 428. Don Wayne applies it to Jonson's *Bartholomew Fair* in '*Drama and Society in the Age of Jonson:* an alternative view', *Renaissance Drama,* N.S. 13 (1982), pp. 103-29. See Gordon Schochet, *Patriarchalism in Political Thought: The authoritarian family and political speculation and attitudes* (Oxford: Basil Blackwell, 1975) for a consideration of the idea of contract in political relations, although not in socio-economic relations.

[25] Thomas Nash, 'Pierce Penilesse: His Supplication to the Divell' (London, 1592), A2, C4, F3.

[26] E.K. Chambers, *The Elizabethan Stage,* 4 vols. (Oxford: Clarendon Press, 1923), vol. I, pp. 298-302; vol. II, pp. 355-6, 471; David Underdown, *Revel, Riot and Rebellion: Popular politics and culture in England, 1603-1660* (Oxford: Oxford University Press, 1987), pp. 56-7.

[27] For the Nash-Harvey exchange, see Donald McGinn, *Thomas Nashe* (Boston: Twayne Publishers, 1981), pp. 104-51; for the war of the theatres, see Roscoe Small, *The Stage Quarrel between Ben Jonson and the So-Called Poetasters* (Breslau: M. & H. Marcus, 1899), pp. 101-14; and R. W. Ingram, *John Marston* (Boston: Twayne Publishers, 1978), pp. 43-54. For the exploration of the fluidity of social relations in the drama of the period, see Jean-Christophe Agnew, *Worlds Apart: The market and the theatre in Anglo-American thought, 1550-1750* (Cambridge: Cambridge University Press, 1986), especially pp. 57-148; L.C. Knights, *Drama and Society in the Age of Jonson* (London: Chatto and Windus, 1937); Manley, *London in the Age of Shakespeare,* pp. 75-81, 285-90; and Wayne, '*Drama and Society in the Age of Jonson:* an alternative view'. The date usually attributed to Marston's *What You Will* is 1601, one year before *Twelfth Night,* but this is just conjecture, as Philip Finkelpearl points out in *John Marston of the Middle Temple* (Cambridge, Mass.: Harvard University Press, 1969), pp. 162-3. Donne speaks of the disruption of traditional social bonds in 'An Anatomy of the World: The First Anniversary'.

[28] *Cynthia's Revels, Or the Fountayne of self-love* in *Ben Jonson,* eds. C.H. Herford and Percy Simpson, 11 vols. (Oxford: Clarendon Press, 1932), vol. 4, pp. 1-183, V, iv, 643-6. On Jonson's analysis of what constitutes 'nobility,' see Don Wayne, *Penshurst: The semiotics of place and the poetics of history* (Madison: The University of Wisconsin Press, 1984), pp. 129-73.

[29] I am not the first to entertain the notion that Malvolio may represent Jonson; John Hollander considers the possibility for reasons quite different from my own in his insightful and informative essay, '*Twelfth Night* and the morality of indulgence', *The Sewanee Review,* 68 (1959), pp. 220-38. Hollander dismisses the possibility, but reminds us that Marston's *What You Will* 'devotes much effort to lampooning Jonson' (p. 238). See V, vii, 26-35 in *Cynthia's Revels* for the yellow colour of 'allowable self-love', which later turns up as Malvolio's stockings.

[30] As Hollander points out, the Duke's name and nature are affirmed as equally 'noble' (I, ii, 25), but the name 'Orsino' suggests quite another character. Jean Howard offers a different interpretation of Shakespeare's treatment of Orsino in her article 'Crossdressing' (p. 432).

[31] Antonio is also the character left without a clear social position at the end of the play, since Sebastian never explicitly claims him as his man, nor frees him from Orsino's indictment. The play's tentative sympathy for this homoerotic relationship cannot save it from an exclusion from the community produced at the end of the play and most literally from the social legitimacy of marital bonds. Like that of the other characters, the 'desire' of Antonio for Sebastian begins by flowing into the traditional bonds of master and servant; therefore accounts of its homoeroticism have to be historicised. Nevertheless, Antonio is left at the end of the play a 'masterless' man.

[32] Emanuel Forde, *The Famous History of Parismus* (1578); *The Novels of Matteo Bandello,* trans. John Payne, 4 vols. (London: Villon Society, 1890), vol. 4, pp. 121-61 (part II, no. 28); *Gl'Ingannati* (1537), ed. and abridged T.L. Peacock (London: Chapman and Hall, 1862). See also the useful Morton Luce, ed., *Rich's 'Apolonius and Silla', An Original of Shakespeare's Twelfth Night* (New York: Duffield and Co., 1912), which discusses all the sources.

[33] Manley, *London in the Age of Shakespeare,* pp. 75-81; Ruth Mohl, *The Three Estates in Medieval and Renaissance Literature* (New York: F. Ungar, 1962).

[34] On changes in contract law, see David Little, *Religion, Order and Law* (New York: Harper & Row, 1969) pp. 204-5. On the Statute of Artificers and its relation to market influences, see F.J. Fisher, 'Commercial trends and policy in the sixteenth century', *Economic History Review,* 10 (1940), pp. 110-13; and Bernard Supple, *Commercial Crisis and Change in England, 1600-1642* (Cambridge: Cambridge University Press, 1959), p. 251. Martin Ingram comments on the implicit use of the family as a 'little commonwealth' in the Statute in *Church Courts, Sex and Marriage in England, 1570-1640* (Cambridge: Cambridge University Press, 1987), p. 126. Ingram also describes the mediation between individual and family interests in the courts (pp. 200-5). Consent was nothing new to the marriage contract; there were in fact some efforts made during this period to increase family control over individual decisions; see Ingram, pp. 135-6. On the contrast between a status and a market society, see C.B. Macpherson, *The Political Theory of Possessive Individualism, Hobbes to Locke* (London: Oxford University Press, 1962), pp. 46-70. Perkins described marriage as a 'seminary to church and commonwealth' in *Christian Oeconomy,* chapter 6. Also interesting on this subject is David Zaret, *The Heavenly Contract: Ideology and organization in pre-revolutionary Puritanism* (Chicago: University of Chicago, 1985), who comments that 'by modifying Calvinism with ideas about a heavenly contract, Puritan clerics provided greater scope for individual initiative in religion, but they channeled this initiative in ways that maintained their authority' (p. 129).

Douglas E. Green (essay date 1992)

SOURCE: "Shakespeare's Violation: 'One Face, One Voice, One Habit, and Two Persons'," in *Reconsidering the Renaissance: Papers from the Twenty-First Annual Conference,* edited by Mario A. Di Cesare, Medieval & Renaissance Texts & Studies, 1992, pp. 327-38.

[*In the following essay, Green discusses the portrayal of love and gender in* Twelfth Night, *maintaining that while the play exposes the narcissism and self-centeredness of masculine love, its ending—with Viola still costumed as Cesario—reinforces the idea that men are the only trustworthy objects of desire.*]

However much we may argue about Shakespearean texts, we never doubt that they mean something—and they do, although not quite in the way the old introductory Shakespeare course descriptions once implied. Because "Shakespeare is," according to Alan Sinfield, "one of the places where ideology is made,"[1] we have lately had a proliferation of multiply explicated Shakespeares, deconstructing and deconstructed Shakespeares, Marxist Shakespeares, psychoanalytic Shakespeares, new historicist Shakespeares, and feminist Shakespeares.[2] In her book *The Social Production of Art,* the Marxist-feminist theorist Janet Wolff discusses the implications of this sort of "interpretation as re-creation": "What is far more important than the fact that, as a literary critical exercise, we may attempt to recover an author's meaning, is the fact that this meaning is effectively dead. What an author intended, or even meant to his or her contemporary public and first readers, is only of interest insofar as that original meaning has historically informed the present reading of the text."[3] For many Shakespeareans that is a particularly bitter pill.[4] But as much recent feminist and new historical criticism has shown, the various constructions of gender in Shakespeare's plays do not transcend their historical determinants.[5] In connection with *Twelfth Night,* the kind of romantic comedy still admired for the pluck of its heroine, I shall suggest at least one of the dangers of persisting in the myth of a transcendent Shakespeare.

The construction of gender in *Twelfth Night* raises special issues for the modern reader or audience, which the mere insertion of women into roles originally written with boy-actors in mind does not eradicate, but further complicates. Stephen Greenblatt has recently argued that "licit sexuality in *Twelfth Night*—the only craving that the play can represent as capable of finding satisfaction—depends upon a [natural] movement that deviates from the desired object straight in one's path toward a marginal object, a body one scarcely knows." Thus, fortunately for Olivia and Viola, Sebastian and Orsino (or rather Antonio?), this deviating "nature is," according to Greenblatt, "an *unbalancing* act."[6] But even if we endorse wholeheartedly Greenblatt's intertextual conjunction of Renaissance medical discourse and *Twelfth Night*'s construction of gender and identity, we modern readers still face our own problematic transcription of the text's construction of gender: how do our diverse re-constitutions of the women's roles, usually without regard to the textual residue of the original mode of production, affect the representation of women on the stage, not to mention their place in the world? The question reminds us that, for feminist critics as well as others, interpretation has present, as well as past, historical and political import. In her provocative psychoanalytic account of gender and genre in Shakespeare, Linda Bamber has claimed that, even in the comedies, "insofar as the Self is within drama and human, it counts itself a member of the dominant social group," whereas "the feminine is Other to society's rules and regulations, to its hierarchies of power, and to the impersonality of its systems and sanctions."[7] But if, as Luce Irigaray asserts, "any theory of the subject has always been appropriated by the 'masculine,'"[8] then Shakespeare's *Twelfth Night*, insofar as it aims to represent versions of woman as desiring subject, not only suggests anxiety about feminine identity and desire, but ultimately denies any Other consciousness at all—that is, any consciousness not constituted in masculine terms. Thus, unlike her literary cousin Rosalind, Viola never returns from boyhood to even the illusion of womanhood; instead she remains Cesario—a colony of that "little Caesar," the *boy-actor inscribed in the text,* sign of the masculine as prototype of subjectivity.

Twelfth Night essentially exiles all but traditionally deceptive and erratic images of women from the stage; the puckish Maria, weaver of Toby's beloved "device," is the rule, not the exception. Her deceptive letter to Malvolio replicates various postures and disguises of Olivia and Viola, but with a difference: it exposes the dangers of feminine wiles and desire, as do Maria's appeal to Sir Toby and her own attraction to him. On the one hand, as her handwriting indicates, Maria is her mistress's diminutive double; as such, she suggests problems with Olivia's rule over the house and indirectly implicates her mistress in the deception of Malvolio. Though her household seems to respect and even fear Olivia, the chaos of the subplot undermines the illusion of her governance. And since Maria uses her mistress's "being addicted to a melancholy" as part of the ruse,[9] Olivia's own excesses are at least tangentially linked to Malvolio's cruelly comic imprisonment.

On the other hand, like Viola, Maria masquerades, albeit in the written word only. As in the obvious anagrammatic play among the names Viola, Olivia, and Malvolio, there is in Maria's writing a material illustration of the slipperiness of words that Viola and Feste note and employ in witty quibbles:

Viola. Thy reason, man?
Clown. Troth, sir, I can yield you none
without words, and words are grown so
false, I am loath to prove reason with them.
(3.1.22-25)

Furthermore, like Viola but with greater impetus, Maria maneuvers her way into marriage through her clever deception. True, she *uses* a "device" (2.5.182), whereas Viola merely *assumes* a disguise. Still, the audience's sense of Viola's cleverness derives at least in part from her convincing masquerade; subliminally, Viola's clever deception belies her virginal innocence, which has to be reintroduced through the duel *manque* with Sir Andrew. Finally, the anti-romantic marriage between Maria and Toby exposes many of the artificial conventions of *Twelfth Night*'s romantic main plot—both its chaotic courtships and its protean marital resolutions. Though I do not wish to overstate the importance of Maria, I do want to unmask the disguised implications of the subplot for issues of gender in the main.

Needless to say, the subplot's innuendoes hardly tell us everything we need to know about characters in the main plot; in particular, they seem to cast but a shadow of a doubt on Olivia, that remarkable characterization of a woman in love. Olivia recognizes and, unlike Orsino, takes responsibility for the swiftness and instability of her own passion and acknowledges that under its influence "ourselves we do not owe" (1.5.296). From her first encounter with Cesario, Olivia recognizes the pitfalls of the path down which she is headed: "I do not know what, and fear to find / Mine eye too great a flatterer for my mind" (312-13). In each successive encounter, she articulates her own precarious position as a female suitor and yet persists in her desires: "Under your hard construction must I sit, / To force that on you in a shameful cunning / Which you knew none of yours. What might you think?" (3.1.117-19). Like Viola, she submits to her fate as an unrequited lover (1.5.314-15); but, unlike the disguised female orphan and rather like Maria, she exercises her powers—feminine (she unveils her face [1.5.237]) and aristocratic (she arranges the betrothal [4.3] and later calls the priest as witness [5.1])—to get what she wants. Olivia is adept both at disguise and deferral—just why has she adopted that excessive posture of mourning that she so readily discards when the right love comes along?[10]—and at assertive forthright action—her most effective commands to Toby and his cohorts occur when having mistaken the besieged Sebastian for Cesario, she defends her beloved: "Rudesby, be gone!" (4.1.50).

But repressed anxiety about such headstrong women surfaces in the text. Finally, Olivia's attraction to the gentlemanly but impoverished Cesario also indicates a desire to retain the kind of authority in marriage that union with Orsino, a social superior, precludes; as Sir Toby remarks, "She'll none o' the' Count; she'll not match above her degree, neither in estate, years, nor wit; I have heard her swear't" (1.3.106-8). Olivia's superior social standing seems to guarantee, if not an equal place in the marriage she wants (Sebastian does, after all, beat her kinsman [5.1.207]), at least a better place than most married women could hope for.[11] As we shall see, though this nearer equality between husband and wife is offered as an ideal,[12] the final scene casts some doubt on its extra-theatrical efficacy and, from the masculine perspective of one such as Orsino, even on its desirability.

The debate between Viola and Orsino addresses the issue of difference between feminine and masculine desire. As a lover, Orsino claims at times an imaginative capaciousness and mutability as great as the "sea" (1.1.9-15; 2.4.101-2), an image whose feminine associations many critics have noted.[13] If Olivia has to adopt the uncharacteristic role of female suitor, Orsino often speaks of being in love as a feminine disposition: "Our fancies are more giddy and unfirm, / More longing, wavering sooner lost and worn / Than women's are" (2.4.33-35). By universalizing aspects of the love experience traditionally associated with one or the other gender, Shakespeare seems to eradicate the difference between men and women in love. What Viola, in a moment of solitary candor, says of the smitten Olivia applies equally to the masculine fancy of Orsino: "How easy it is for the proper false / In women's waxen hearts to set their forms!" (2.2.28-29). In this instance, both man and woman are erratic, unstable, unpredictable—in other words, conventionally feminine.

But Viola's remark is only half the story; it belies her later claim, in the person of Cesario, that women "are as true of heart as we [men]" (2.4.105). Though the play suggests that men in love are as erratic as women—we should note that Orsino, like many another Renaissance misogynist, considers fickleness essential to women whether or not they are in love—Shakespeare is also claiming in turn that women can be as faithful as men: "She [Cesario's fictive sister] sat like Patience on a monument, / Smiling at grief. Was not this love indeed?" (2.4.115-16). By conjuring up the Patient Griselda—that feminine prototype of steadfastness—Viola-Cesario and Shakespeare undercut the masculinist sentiments of Orsino.[14] In this way, virtue in love is extended to women; love's transforming power is made universal. The fact that the contradictory statements about women's faith and fickleness in comparison to men's come from the girl-boy Viola-Cesario helps to create the illusion that, at least in matters of the heart, men and women are more or less on an equal footing. Through the boy-actor masquerading as a woman imitating a man, Shakespeare attempts to erase sexual difference: "I am all the daughters of my father's house, / And all the brothers too" (2.4.121-22).

But because this illusion of universality requires the skills of a boy-actor, the mode of production itself accords the masculine a peculiar privilege. Here we see a very basic sense in which "any theory of the subject has always been appropriated by the 'masculine'"; in this Elizabethan script, subjective experience is constituted in masculine terms by men.[15] Thus, afflicted with his own version of Malvolio's self-love, Orsino too claims the "trick of singularity" in love (2.5.151), by defining himself as lover in the very manner that men in patriarchal society have defined themselves, the self, and subjectivity itself—as not feminine.[16] Indeed, in the key exchange with Cesario, cited earlier, Orsino predicates the depth of his desire and his very being on his difference from the woman, the mere object of desire.[17] In contrast to Olivia's, Orsino's passion makes him more himself: "Make no compare / Between that love a woman can bear me / And that I owe Olivia" (2.4.100-102).

Of course, it is not quite so simple; as we have seen, Orsino likes to have it both ways. Even his appropriation of the oceanic capacity of the feminine exposes the extent to which this "man is the measure of all things," including femininity. There is no lack of self-possession here, but a fruitless attempt to possess or appropriate all through the imaginative capacity (often for role-playing or at least posturing) that love occasions. Unfortunately for Orsino, who seems to believe his protestations at least as much as he presumably believes that Olivia is the only socially suitable match in town (5.1.110 ff.), his love's fancy does not extend much beyond the Petrarchan conceits and conventional courtly attitudes of the masculine, lover.[18] Moreover, since Orsino's various declarations, unlike Olivia's or for that matter Viola's, are made *in absentia* and in isolation or in company supposedly of his own sex, they underscore masculine self-absorption and self-affirmation in love.[19]

Certainly, given Orsino's rather sudden change of heart at the end, Viola's comment on women's being "as true of heart as we [men]" (2.4.105) suggests the instability of all desiring subjects, masculine as well as feminine. But it is through the image of woman that Shakespeare figures this lack of control, as we see in Orsino's long-awaited confrontation with Olivia in the final scene. Only when he has been repeatedly and undeniably thwarted, does he come in person and then prove the depth of his unrequited love by the will to murder—not the unfaithful woman herself but the object of ostensibly feminine desire: "But this your minion, whom I know you love, / And whom, by heaven, I swear I tender dearly, / Him will I tear out of that cruel eye / Where he sits crowned in his master's spite" (5.1.123-26). Orsino's violent verbal attack on Olivia and his threat against Cesario reveal almost as much as the play's omission of Cesario's transformation back into Viola. Most obviously, they cast all responsibility for his troubles on women, actual or disguised. They expose, furthermore, what Coppélia Kahn calls "his fear of losing himself in passion." That fear—particularly masculine, as I see it—is underscored by the threat against Cesario, the annihilation of Orsino's own ambiguous object of desire; Orsino unmasks once again his need to "defend against Eros as a threat to the integrity and stability of the self."[20] Whereas Olivia hauls forth a priest to declare and ratify the love relation she wants (a marital one both we and undoubtedly Queen Elizabeth might question),[21] Orsino's anti-social behavior, which culminates in the threat of violence against the boy-girl he loves, exposes masculine paranoia about the loss of self in love and about the indefinition of his own desire. Indeed, the indeterminacy of his own desire is suggested by Cesario (the boy playing a girl playing a boy), the target standing in for Olivia—who by the way is also played by a boy. Though the play certainly exposes many of the inconsistencies and contradictions of masculine love like Orsino's, the Shakespearean solution, the play's resolution, is nonetheless problematic, especially from a modern perspective.

Imogen Stubbs as Viola/Cesario, Peter Gunn as Fabian, Mel Smith as Sir Toby Belch, and Richard E. Grant as Sir Andrew Aguecheek in Trevor Nunn's 1996 film adapation of Twelfth Night.

The problems derive in large part from the comedy's mode of production; the boy-actor who plays Viola-Cesario remains a boy even after Orsino has declared his "share in this most happy wrack" (5.1.258). I cannot quite agree with Coppélia Kahn about "what Viola herself never forgets: that no matter how the duke and countess see her, she is not androgynous but irreducibly a woman."[22] In fact, Viola's witty disclaimer—"a little thing would make me tell them how much I lack of a man" (3.4.307-9)—is a two-edged sword, not only undercutting the female character's masculine bravado but also underscoring the boy-actor's irreducible, or at least incipient, manhood.[23] Though Orsino seems to deny it in his last lines, he finds his "mistress and his fancy's queen" in the boy Cesario, and not in Viola (5.1.377)—at least in terms of the visual tableau, a fact somewhat obscured in Phyllis Rackin's excellent article.[24] The theatrical presence of the boy-actor as a boy manifests what, in *The Daughter's Seduction,* Jane Gallop calls "homosexuality" or the "sexuality of sames"—precisely the effect that Lisa Jardine claims the boy-players generally evoked, according to Renaissance commentators, both homophobic and otherwise.[25] The dramatic resolution of the sexual play and the sexual tensions belies any acceptance of an Other by Orsino; it still relies on what Peter Erickson sees in *As You Like It* as the "security of male bodies mirroring and confirming a common physical identity."[26] Oddly enough, by having Orsino accept his lover untransformed (in some ways a radical move compared to *As You Like It*'s conservative ritualism and mystification of marriage),[27] Shakespeare replicates the very narcissism and self-absorption of masculine love that the play supposedly unmasks. In this sense, the self-expulsion of the ill-willed, vengeful, self-loving Malvolio is the text's greatest deception.

Furthermore, Erickson's claim that the comedies' narcissistic mirroring "depends precisely on relief from the specifically genital demand associated with the opposite sex" is especially applicable to *Twelfth Night,* where the appearance of Viola's male twin Sebastian underscores the all-male mode of production.[28] According to Kahn, "In *Twelfth Night* . . . the twin and other doubles function at first as projections of emotional obstacles to identity and then, in Viola and Sebastian, as the fulfillment of a wish for a way around the obstacles."[29] But the all-male Elizabethan production and its textual inscription in Orsino's remarks—that in Cesario "all is semblative a woman's part" (1.5.34) and that only "other habits" make the woman (5.1.386)—complicate the fulfillment of Viola's, the play's, and the critic-reader's wish that "imagination . . . prove true" (3.4.384). As Phyllis Rackin explains, "without the illusion (Viola's disguise as a boy), the right characters would not have fallen in love; without the reality, they could not have married. In the figure of Sebastian, gender and sex correspond, both within the play world and between the play and the audience."[30] Sebastian apparently resolves the play's problems because in him theatrical and actual sexual identity are one and the same; for the same reason, I maintain, the object of Orsino's transferred affections never transforms himself from Cesario back to that theatrical illusion—the girl Viola. Even though the transformation only requires the boy-actor's resumption of his "woman's weeds" (5.1.271), there is in a meta-dramatic sense more truth in the undisguised Viola's remaining Cesario, in her showing herself—like Sebastian, but in another way—both "maid and man" (5.1.261).

The uneasy Renaissance conflation of two "contradictory accounts of the origin of gender" that Greenblatt outlines in his discussion of the play may underlie some of the "slippage" in identities. In one version, the domination of male or female seed determines identity; "a double nature becomes single." In the other theory, "the unitary genital structure," conceived as essentially male, "divides into two distinct forms, internal [female] and external [male]"; "a single nature becomes double."[31] But how do we explain the relative values the play assigns to and by gender? Along with Malvolio's accusations of "Notorious wrong" by Olivia (5.1.327-28), who is at the end the one theatrically disguised boy remaining on stage, the image of Orsino with Cesario corroborates the traditional privilege the text accords to masculinity, as well as its imputation of duplicity to femininity. The bias of the text in this case is not nature's "bias" (5.1.258), but the culture's—akin to men's age-old wish for a single-sex utopia, a world without women.[32] The minor Sebastian-Antonio plot exposes this sub-text. Antonio's homoerotic infatuation with Sebastian, his "willing love" (3.3.11), is an unmasked version of Orsino's attraction to Cesario and, again, given the mode of production, even of the relationship between Sebastian and Olivia. In fact, it brings to the fore the all-male mode of production. When Antonio mistakes Viola-Cesario for the adored Sebastian, the error involves an indictment not only of beauty without virtue, but also of the disjunction between exterior and interior—in other words, of Viola's masquerade as "unkind" or unnatural: "Thou hast, Sebastian, done good feature shame. / In nature there's no blemish but the mind; / None can be call'd deform'd but the unkind" (3.4.375-77, 377n). Is it an accident that Antonio directs his accusations at a female character, who has already acknowledged her disguise "a wickedness" and herself a "monster"?[33]

The moment recalls Viola's own words to the Captain in act 1, words that conjure up the traditional masculine suspicion of feminine beauty: "There is a fair behaviour in thee, Captain; / And though that nature with a beauteous wall / Doth oft close in pollution, yet of thee / I will believe thou hast a mind that suits / With this thy fair and outward character" (1.3.47-51). Indeed, the proof that Viola is a virtuous woman, that she is worthy to be loved, and that she is everything she claims and seems to be requires not only her reunion with the brother she imitates to the life (3.4.389-93), but also her conforming to the masculine standards of truth reiterated by Antonio—an absolute correspondence between interior and exterior, spirit and body, even word and thing. Is it then an accident that Antonio, whose very presence exposes the inability of the theatrical illusion to achieve such a correspondence, "is left out in the cold," displaced by a second boy-actor masquerading as a woman, the Lady Olivia, without any authority calling to "entreat *him* to a peace" (5.1.379; emphasis mine)?[34] The ultimate corroboration of social order and expectations through the mediation of laws conceived as natural or providential makes this text's intersection with our own culture a problematic one. Though the "pleasure" of the play is less concerned with "truth of identity" than the "titillation" aroused by the "dangers that follow from the disruption of sexual difference,"[35] this comedy also closes down the possibilities implicit in Viola-Cesario's admission of sexual indeterminacy—"I am not what I am" (3.1.143)—and in Antonio's undisguised and unresolved homoerotic attraction.

Why then has Shakespeare refused to return to the initial illusion in which boy plays girl, the illusion that corroborates the traditional social union of male and female in marriage? I propose that, although other Shakespearean comedies may also manifest uneasiness toward their feisty heroines, *Twelfth Night* exiles its heroine—perhaps more thoroughly than it exiles Malvolio himself. Herein lies the danger of a supposedly transcendant Shakespeare, and herein lies as well the problem for the modern reader (or viewer or performer), who wishes to avoid complicity in this text's "bias." Ultimately there is not even the pretense of a sovereign female consciousness. Viola remains in masculine guise because that is the sign of her truth; Orsino can trust her only insofar as she is "masculine." Indeed, in the end, we realize that the play's model for true love is not heterosexual, but rather "homosexual" in Gallop's sense—the love of Antonio for Sebastian and, by a comforting displacement, of Orsino for Cesario *nee* Viola. In contrast to the androgynous epilogue of *As You Like It,* the last of Shakespeare's high comedies elevates the heroine by eradicating her, by letting her be absorbed into the masculine; for as Viola herself says, and as the play's dramatic illusion underscores, women "die, even as they to perfection grow" (2.4.40).

Notes

[1] Alan Sinfield, "Introduction: Reproductions, Interventions," in *Political Shakespeare,* ed. Jonathan Dollimore and Alan Sinfield (Ithaca: Cornell Univ. Press, 1985), 132.

[2] See the excellent bibliographies—and commentaries—in Edward Pechter's "The New Historicism and Its Discontents: Politicizing Renaissance Drama," *PMLA* 102 (1987): 292-303, and in Phyllis Rackin's "Androgyny, Mimesis, and the Marriage of the Boy Heroine on the English Renaissance Stage," *PMLA* 102 (1987): 29-41.

[3] Janet Wolff, *The Social Production of Art* (New York: New York Univ. Press, 1984), 95, 102.

[4] See Pechter, passim.

[5] See, for instance, Lisa Jardine's *Still Harping on Daughters: Women and Drama in the Age of Shakespeare* (New Jersey: Barnes and Noble, 1983); Leah Marcus's "Shakespeare's Comic Heroines, Elizabeth I, and the Political Uses of Androgyny," in *Women in the Middle Ages and the Renaissance,* ed. Mary Beth Rose (Syracuse: Syracuse Univ. Press, 1986), 135-53; and such essays by Adrian Louis Montrose as "*A Midsummer Night's Dream* and the Shaping Fantasies of Elizabethan Culture: Gender, Power, Form," in *Rewriting the Renaissance: The Discourses of Sexual Difference in Early Modern Europe,* ed. Margaret Ferguson, Maureen Quilligan, and Nancy J. Vickers (Chicago: Chicago Univ. Press, 1986), 65-87, 329-34, and "'The Place of a Brother' in *As You Like It:* Social Process and Comic Form," *Shakespeare Quarterly* 32 (1981): 28-54. Jean Howard's excellent article "Crossdressing, the Theater, and Gender Struggle in Early Modern England," *Shakespeare Quarterly* 39 (1988): 418-40, an early version of which was delivered at the 1987 CEMERS conference, rigorously discusses from a feminist-historicist perspective several issues addressed here.

[6] Stephen Greenblatt, *Shakespearean Negotiations: The Circulation of Social Energy in Renaissance England* (Berkeley: Univ. of California Press, 1988), 68. Not long after I had presented the original version of this paper at the CEMERS conference (October 1987), Greenblatt's controversial essay on "Fiction and Friction" appeared in the foregoing collection of essays (66-93, 175-84) and has since become the center of a debate among feminist and new historical critics of *Twelfth Night,* not least for the authority it grants Renaissance medical discourse on gender and for the effect its general acceptance might have on political and, in particular, feminist criticism. (See, for instance, Jean Howard, 422-23.) Therefore, since I am addressing concerns relevant to the current debate, it seems appropriate to note some points of agreement and disagreement between Greenblatt's views and mine.

[7] Linda Bamber, *Comic Women, Tragic Men* (Stanford: Stanford Univ. Press, 1982), 27-28.

[8] Luce Irigaray, *Speculum of the Other Woman,* trans. Gillian C. Gill (Ithaca: Cornell Univ. Press, 1985), 133.

[9] William Shakespeare, *Twelfth Night,* ed. J. M. Lothian and T. W. Craik, Arden Edition (London: Methuen, 1975), 2.5.202-3 (p. 73). All further references to this work appear in the text.

[10] For an answer to the question, see Coppélia Kahn's "The Providential Tempest and the Shakespearean Family," in *Representing Shakespeare: New Psychoanalytic Essays,* ed. Murray M. Schwartz and Coppélia Kahn (Baltimore: Johns Hopkins Univ. Press, 1980), 226.

[11] Marilyn L. Williamson, *The Patriarchy of Shakespeare's Comedies* (Detroit: Wayne State Univ. Press, 1986), 38-41.

[12] Marianne L. Novy discusses this view in *Love's Argument: Gender Relations in Shakespeare* (Chapel Hill: Univ. of North Carolina Press, 1984), 32-44.

[13] E.g., Kahn, 225.

[14] For the reference to Patient Griselda and further implications of this image, see Catherine Belsey's "Disrupting Sexual Difference: Meaning and Gender in the Comedies," in *Alternative Shakespeares,* ed. John Drakakis (New York: Methuen, 1985), 186-87.

[15] Notable among the treatments of masculine appropriation are such diverse ones as those by Peter Erickson in *Patriarchal Structures in Shakespeare's Drama* (Berkeley: Univ. of California Press, 1985), 1-13; by Lisa Jardine, 9-36; by Phyllis Rackin, 31-32; and by Linda Woodbridge in *Women and the English Renaissance: Literature and the Nature of Womankind, 1540-1620* (Urbana and Chicago: Univ. of Illinois Press, 1984), 152-56.

[16] Greenblatt notes that "if a crucial step in male individuation is separation from the female, this separation is enacted inversely in the rites of cross-dressing; characters like Rosalind and Viola pass through the state of being men in order to become women. Shakespearean women are in this sense the representation of Shakespearean men, the projected mirror images of masculine self-differentiation" (92). But when is Viola seen as a woman *again?* Whereas she remains Cesario, the boy-actor has undergone the passage through femininity to masculinity—and in this case, he never closes the circle by re-appearing in female guise. At the end of *Twelfth Night* the boy-actor remains true to himself; indeed, even in developing the heroine, the text manifests an unconscious association between individuation and maleness.

[17] Relevant to this point is Toril Moi's discussion of Kristevan "positionality" in *Sexual / Textual Politics: Feminist Literary Theory* (New York: Methuen, 1985), 166-67.

[18] Williamson, 35.

[19] Kahn, 226-27.

[20] Ibid.

[21] On the issue of Elizabeth and marriage, see Marcus, passim, as well as Greenblatt, 68-69.

[22] Kahn, 228.

[23] In contrast, Rackin notes the boy-player's economic dependency, an extra-dramatic extension of the feminine role, which underscores the indeterminacy of the boy-heroine both on and off the stage (33).

[24] Rackin, 38.

[25] On "homosexuality" in this sense, see Jane Gallop's "Impertinent Questions," in *Psychoanalysis and Feminism: The Daughter's Seduction* (Ithaca: Cornell Univ. Press, 1982), 80-91, especially 84. On the matter of the erotic effect of the boy-players, see Lisa Jardine's provocative argument (9-36).

[26] Peter Erickson, 5.

[27] Regarding the ending of *As You Like It* and that play's quite different construction of gender, see my article on "The 'Unexpressive She': Is There Really a Rosalind?," *Journal of Dramatic Theory and Criticism* 2, no. 2 (1988): 41-52.

[28] Peter Erickson, 5. Erickson's insightful comments have meta-dramatic significance that he suggests but often does not discuss in detail.

[29] Kahn, 225.

[30] Rackin, 38.

[31] Greenblatt, 84.

[32] See Greenblatt's explanation of the "metaphor from the game of bowls" and nature's bias; heterosexuality is conceived as a normal, "happy swerving" (68). Greenblatt's argument is fascinating, and the pattern he describes does indeed resemble the plot of a Shakespearean comedy (86). But unlike Greenblatt I would argue that, however problematic the Renaissance accounts of gender, the valuation of the genders is less so; at the very least the second theory of gender—with its play upon the male organ, the latter's inward or outward, hidden or open, disposition—is less ambiguous about the primacy of male nature and hence of masculinity. Indeed, if one combines this view of sexuality with Viola's and Antonio's talk about truth, the correspondence between interior and exterior, one finds that women are never quite themselves. *Twelfth Night*, as well as the context that gave rise to it, tends to promote the truth that shows itself—in Sebastian and in Viola-Cesario, emblem of the theater of boys and men that represents the world of women and men. For a provocative historicist reading that differs from Greenblatt's, see Howard, 430-33.

[33] Rackin, 37.

[34] Greenblatt notes that, though Renaissance church and state sanctioned only the heterosexual consummation of desire, "it did not follow that desire was inherently heterosexual. The delicious confusions of *Twelfth Night* depend on the mobility of desire. And if poor Antonio is left out in the cold, Orsino does in a sense get his Cesario" (93). But though Greenblatt mentions also the way in which the all-male cast of Shakespeare's theater embodies a double-sided Renaissance view of gender, he eschews the implications, for us, of the inscription in the text of this mode of production and this construction of gender. What values are inherent in these "delicious confusions," this "set of exchanges and transformations"? To formulate the matter at its most extreme, do the play's exile of the explicitly homosexual and the enforced masquerade of woman within marriage (or, in another sense, the absence of women altogether) recommend themselves, as immediately and unequivocally as Greenblatt implies, to the modern reader? What does it mean to accept Greenblatt's brilliant "corollary" theory about the play—"that men love women precisely *as representations,* a love the original performances of these plays literalized in the person of the boy actor" (93)? Pleasurable, "delicious confusions" perhaps—but not neutral ones, not ones without present ideological efficacy, given the place of Shakespeare in our culture.

[35] Belsey, 185.

Irene G. Dash (essay date 1997)

SOURCE: "Challenging Conventions: *Twelfth Night*," in *Women's Worlds in Shakespeare's Plays*, University of Delaware Press, 1997, pp. 211-44.

[*In the essay below, Dash stresses the similarities between Viola and Olivia as young, single, upper-class women who, for a brief period, challenge patriarchal restraints on female independence. She also calls attention to the textual alternations put in place by generations of theatrical directors which have minimized the difficulties Viola and Olivia face as they try to resolve the tension between erotic desire and the norms of society.*]

> "But if she cannot love you, sir?"
> "I cannot be so answer'd."
>
> (II.iv.87-88)

Endowed with wealth, their lives graced by neither fathers, brothers, husbands, nor lovers, the two major women characters of *Twelfth Night* briefly challenge patterns of patriarchy. Not revolutionaries, but merely young women grasping at suddenly available freedom, each would taste independence in her own way. One retreats behind the garb of mourning for her dead brother while the other, also turning to her supposedly dead brother—her twin—for support, retreats into his persona, adopting his clothes and his pose. Although at the play's end, neither woman achieves her goal, defeated by contemporary conventions surrounding love and matrimony, the dramatist, here, raises questions about women, wealth, power, and conformity, and teases his audience with contradictory evidence.

Shakespeare takes the contemporary debate about women's attire, for example, holds it lightly in his hand, turns it like a multifaceted prism, reflecting and refracting the light, then puts it down, revealing the larger issue that it illuminates: women's independence.[1] With humor and insight, he asks how important is conformity in dress in defining an acceptable woman? Is the woman in breeches really a monster as some of the tracts of the period proclaim because the blurring of fashion could lead to "confusion . . . something that can't be accommodated, a monster" (Shepherd, 1-2)? Or is she related to the tradition of the warrior woman who, like Britomart in Spenser's *Faerie Queene,* fights for virtuous ends (Shepherd, 67)? Denying these extremes and laughing at the debate, the dramatist offers another answer in *Twelfth Night.* In the mode of the modern social scientist, he presents a case and a control, revealing that whether dressed in her own garments—those proper to her sex—or in the borrowed clothes of the other sex, a single woman when young and wealthy faces problems in a patriarchal society, especially if she dares to fall in love and opt for marriage.

Although the play's two major women characters, Viola and Olivia, often have been presented on stage as exact opposites because one wears skirts, the other, breeches, the dramatist has carefully sculpted their roles as parallels—not the wealthy, self-confident, or arrogant Countess in skirts compared with the poor, clever, girl-disguised-as-a-page in breeches, but two bright, literate, young women, each with a sense of herself, each in her own way trying to cope, and each believing she has power. Economic independence and the absence of male authority figures in their families seem to promise self-sovereignty. The play explores the options each woman chooses, the resulting interaction between the two women, and the impact of sexual drives and patriarchal mores on their lives.

And here their difference in attire leads the women into unexpected situations and deflects them on their road to freedom. Disguised as the youth Cesario, Viola wins the heart of the independent Olivia but also, in this disguise, loses her heart to the Duke Orsino. Clothes, rather than freeing her, confine her to silence. In contrast, the woman in skirts forthrightly expresses her desire, overtly pursuing the "youth" Cesario.

As a result, Olivia suffers both in criticism and staging. Since patriarchal values favor the compliant woman over the aggressive one, Viola's breeches, ironically, appear far less threatening than Olivia's decision-making and husband-wooing. By endowing the young women with so many similar attributes with the potential for independence, the dramatist not only explores the limits on that independence for women, but also illuminates what is acceptable and unacceptable in women's behavior.

Even in the twentieth century, acceptable behavior for a young woman has been linked with her loss of independence. According to Simone de Beauvoir, women's "erotic urges" in a male-dominated society cause the problem. She writes of the decision women reach at maturity after having struggled during adolescence with the choice between self as primary and self as "Other." Using the term *subject* to refer to a person's perception of herself as central, or primary, de Beauvoir writes: "For the young woman, . . . there is a contradiction. . . . A conflict breaks out between her original claim to be subject, active, free," and the pressure of "her erotic urges" which dictates that she "accept herself as passive object" (314).[2] In *Twelfth Night* Shakespeare lightly dramatizes the shift in goals for both women. Because this is a comedy, the painfulness of the dilemma is not stressed as it is, for example, in a tragedy such as *Romeo and Juliet,* where Juliet has not yet recognized the necessity to "accept herself as passive object" and struggles to retain her self-sovereignty even while expressing her "erotic urges."[3] Here, in the comedy, Viola says merely, "O time, thou must untangle this, not I, / It is too hard a knot for me t' untie" (II.ii.40-41). But the dramatist's choice of opposite-sex twins, the weakness of Viola's argument for donning disguise, the basic social equality between the two women, and the subsequent hasty desire of each to discard the protective pose she has chosen suggest the applicability of de Beauvoir's comment.

The difference, however, in the ways the two women react to their "erotic urges" explains their "acceptability" in the eyes of critics, directors, and audiences. Unlike Viola, Olivia refuses to perceive herself as "Other," seeking instead to solve her problems by aggressively taking charge. After having claimed fealty to her dead brother's memory and adopting a vow of seven years of mourning, a period meant to discourage all the suitors who do not appeal to her, she then changes her mind about marriage when an attractive young "male" arrives at her door. Still retaining that sense of self as "subject, active, free," she nevertheless pursues Cesario, the disguised Viola. Thus in some ways, Olivia resembles Helena of *All's Well That Ends Well*. But Shakespeare has not only endowed Olivia with freedom, wealth, and power, he has also created an alternative double to her in Viola. Unlike Viola, however, Olivia refuses to leave everything for time "to untangle." Thus, while partially illustrating de Beauvoir's thesis—of the effect of "erotic urges" on women's decision-making—Olivia fails to conform to the properly acceptable behavior for a woman.

Behavior is ultimately more important for society than appearance: the debate on women's dress withers before that larger issue of woman's forwardness. Stage productions and criticism of *Twelfth Night* attack Olivia's violation of conformity in a variety of ways. First, they blur or ignore the many similarities between the women, magnifying Viola's role as a servant, and excising lines indicating her wealth and class. Thus, she becomes the "poor servant girl" as contrasted with the wealthy, aggressive Countess. In criticism, a blatant example of bias appears in William Winter's introduction to Augustin Daly's large souvenir promptbook of the 1893 production of the play. Winter writes that "Viola is Shakespeare's ideal of the patient idolatry and devoted, silent self-sacrifice of perfect love" (5). In contrast, Olivia draws the following comment:

> The poet has emphasized his meaning, furthermore, by the expedient of contrast between the two women. Olivia—self-absorbed, ostentatious in her mourning, acquisitive and voracious in her love, self-willed in her conduct, conventional in her character, physically very beautiful but spiritually insignificant—while she is precisely the sort of woman for whom men go wild, serves but to throw the immeasurable superiority of Viola into stronger relief.
>
> (6)

This hardly defines the Olivia whom we meet in the play—the young woman who graciously speaks of Orsino's virtues although she "cannot love him" (I.v.257); who good-naturedly accepts the criticism of her fool; and who even apologizes to the disguised Viola.

Although extreme in its language, Winter's reaction is not isolated. It had both predecessors and successors. Mrs. Inchbald's edition (1808), for example, faults Olivia for another aspect of her behavior, citing the "impudence of women in placing their affections, their happiness, on men younger than themselves" (4). For Inchbald the text itself warns against this in the Duke's words to Viola:

> Let stil the woman take
> An elder than herself; so wears she to him
> So sways she level in her husband's heart, & C
>
> (4-5)

Unfortunately, the editor lifts the speech out of context—a humorous context. The lines occur during a conversation between Duke Orsino and Cesario. Attempting to express herself as a man, Viola describes the person she loves (the Duke) as one "About your years, my lord" (II.iv.28). This leads to his swift reply that Cesario should choose a woman younger than "himself." The humor of the exchange is apparently lost on the indignant editor who even censures Olivia's treatment of her glum steward, the egocentric, puritanical Malvolio. He, like the Duke, has dreams of marrying her. Misreading his role in the play, Inchbald recommends him:

> It might nevertheless be asked by a partizan (sic) of Malvolio's, whether this credulous steward was much deceived, in imputing a degraded taste, in the sentiments of love, to his fair Lady Olivia as she actually did fall in love with a domestic; and one who, from his extreme youth, was perhaps a greater reproach to her discretion, than had she cast a tender regard upon her old and faithful servant.
>
> (4)

Prejudice against a strong woman who fails to conform to accepted societal patterns leads the editor astray. She forgets that Cesario is not a youthful domestic but a young woman whose background very much resembles Olivia's, as the dramatist subtly informs us.

Using a sophisticated theatrical methodology, Shakespeare introduces each woman in a different way—playing upon potential audience bias even while revealing the similarities between the women. Shipwrecked in a foreign land, Viola strides ashore, speaks in her own voice, paints a picture of her misfortunes, and quickly decides how to deal with them. During her first appearance, in scene 2, she also reveals her background. In contrast, hearsay precedes Olivia's entrance. In scene after scene a variety of characters evaluate her decision to mourn her brother's death for seven years. Some of these characters also raise questions about the proper behavior for a young countess. Through this technique, the dramatist employs a series of incomplete vignettes by others to suggest the obstacles confronting her.

Critics and actor-managers—or directors—often fall into the trap. They accept the hearsay about Olivia then find the lovesick Duke Orsino—whom we meet in the opening scene—just as irrational as the woman he so passionately wants to marry but who emphatically rejects him. Herschel Baker, for example, calls them "a pair of high-born lovers [who] indulge a set of attitudes untested by experience" (xxiv) and writes of "Orsino's egomania" and "Olivia's silly posture of bereavement" (xxx). Geoffrey Bullough, too, observes that "by the end of the first scene we know by Olivia's oath to spend seven years grieving indoors that she is akin to [the Duke] in sensibility" (2:278). Actually, we never see Olivia weeping or miserable; the closest she comes to discussing her mourning is in her opening scene when her clown berates her, and she responds by commending his cleverness. Hearsay, primarily, reveals her "silly posture of bereavement." On the other hand, Orsino exhibits his foolishness through his own actions and words in the play's opening scene although many of his lines are frequently cut from productions to make him seem less silly.[4]

That opening scene appears to have a purpose—to establish the world of Illyria, a mythic, ancient, unavailable world. Again we witness the dramatist's skill. For while he offers realistic reasons to suggest the kinds of options available to women who might freely move in society as equals of men, he quickly withdraws those options by creating this world. Though not inhabited by otherworldly creatures, this land of Illyria derives its magic from the sequential arrangement of scenes, keynoted by Orsino at the start. Unlike Hippolyta and Theseus, who provide a frame through which we, the audience, move into the enchanted wood on a midsummer's night, or the weird sisters who set the mood for *Macbeth,* here the lovesick Duke sets the distinctive tone and establishes the particularities of place.

The opening scene not only immerses us in that unrecognizable and slightly skewed world of Illyria but also provides the first glimpse of Olivia through the eyes of the Duke. In love with love as well as the Countess, he seeks solace in music. "That strain again," the Duke commands, noting, "it had a dying fall" (I.i.4). And then abruptly, three lines later, "Enough, no more, / 'Tis not so sweet now as it was before" (7-8). He stops the instrumentalist then continues, his lines a mockery of the Petrarchan sonneteer's lyric to his love. Although the comedy later ranges between low, raucous farce and sophisticated verbal jousting, this opening scene carries the audience to that mythical land where both women seek to understand the meaning of freedom.

Recounting how he lost his heart, including a pun on the word *hart,* the Duke speaks in labored metaphors.[5] Languishing in adoration of Olivia, he offers a portrait of the lover according to the most exaggerated sonnet conventions:

> O, when mine eyes did see Olivia first,
> Methought she purg'd the air of pestilence!
> That instant was I turn'd into a hart,
> And my desires, like fell and cruel hounds,
> E'er since pursue me.
>
> (I.i.18-22)

Poor Orsino, transformed into a hart, has been pursued by his desires. Enhancing the otherworldly quality of this scene, Shakespeare dubs the courier "Valentine." He, too, contributes to the portrait of Olivia by admitting his failure to deliver Orsino's message. Denied an audience, Valentine reports on Olivia:

> The element itself, till seven years' heat,
> Shall not behold her face at ample view;
>
> (25-26)

Since the message was conveyed by Olivia's "handmaid," whom we later discover to be Maria, a woman with a tendency to trickery and a love of giving instructions, we cannot be certain whether Valentine's language and delivery characterize the speech patterns in Illyria, or whether they belong specifically to Valentine, Maria, or Olivia. The message has been sifted through two messengers; thus we are twice-removed from Olivia. Valentine continues his report:

> . . . like a cloistress she will veiled walk,
> And water once a day her chamber round
> With eye-offending brine;
>
> (27-29)

Once again an overblown metaphor colors the speech as the reporter describes a woman constantly weeping, a condition never to be witnessed by the audience. Shakespeare has begun the portrait that he will develop in each succeeding scene. Here, indeed, we might agree with Baker's evaluation, until we meet the young Countess.

In this dual portrait—of Orsino as well as Olivia—our sympathies hardly go out to the fatuous Duke even while we wonder what sort of woman would make such a vow. Shakespeare's audience may have recognized the satire on the Renaissance courtier—as we do not; however, Orsino's method of wooing proved as unconvincing to the young Countess as it does to us today. As for her seven-year vow, while it seems an extreme measure, it certainly should have discouraged this persistent wooer. Like the women of *Love's Labour's Lost* and Queen Elizabeth herself, Olivia chooses to postpone marriage. Unlike the women of the earlier play, whose one-year wait may imply later acceptance, Olivia's drastic seven-year postponement should prove sufficiently discouraging to send all her suitors elsewhere.

Ironically, at this early moment in the play, Orsino admires her decision even while wondering how she will respond when she does fall in love:

> O, she that hath a heart of that fine frame
> To pay this debt of love but to a brother,
> How will she love when the rich golden shaft
> Hath kill'd the flock of all affections else
> That live in her.
>
> (32-36)

Despite the awkwardness of this metaphor, as critics have noted, Orsino's shaft hits the mark. Olivia will soon offer love, gifts, and marriage to Viola disguised as the Duke's page, Cesario.

Lyrical, musical, with a touch of melancholy as well as humor, this first scene, with its shimmering surface, quickly dissolves before the next in which we hear the simplicity and directness of Viola's language. Differing in style and tone from Orsino, she tramps ashore and immediately questions the sea captain who has rescued her from shipwreck: "What country, friends, is this?" (I.ii.1) "This is Illyria, lady" (2), he replies. This is the land where she is unknown, where the Duke Orsino rules, and the young Countess Olivia rejects his advances. This is the land where Viola, herself, will seek new identity. In language revealing her skill with words and sensitivity to puns, she continues: "And what should I do in Illyria? / My brother he is in Elysium" (3-4). Even while she captures the resonances in language between "Illyria" and "Elysium"—between life and death—she attempts to sum up her own situation at this moment. We may be in the distant land of Illyria, but we are listening to a realistic young woman with practical wisdom, an ear for words, and a sense of the ludicrous in contrasting Illyria with Elysium.

This short exchange reveals a good deal about her: her concern for her brother, her obvious upper-class background and education through her reference to "Elysium," and her positive attitude: "Perchance he is not drown'd—what think you, sailors?" (5). In five lines, she poses three questions. And when the captain suggests that her brother may also have survived—tied "To a strong mast that liv'd upon the sea," (11-14)—Viola answers with the directness already evident:

> For saying so, there's gold.
>
> (18)

This first impetuous offer of gold springs from her reaction to his words of hope. She will reward his reassurance with money, a learned pattern, indicating her upper-class background. Later, a second, more considered promise grows from her resolve to conceal her true, female identity and pose as a eunuch. "I'll pay thee bounteously" (52), she vows.

Viola's social status emerges again when, in seeking to convince the captain to recommend her (in her disguise) to the Duke, she lists her musical skills.

> . . . For I can sing
> And speak to him in many sorts of music
> That will allow me very worth his service.
>
> (57-59)

Critics have noted that she never does sing in the play. They therefore cite this as one of the many inconsistencies that tend to thwart audience expectations. M. M. Mahood writes in an otherwise perceptive analysis: "A further puzzle created by the second scene is that it leads us to expect Viola will sing to the Duke, but she never does so" (17). Nor is Mahood alone. Others, including W. W. Greg in his bibliographical and textual study *The Shakespeare First Folio,* had earlier seemed to establish this expectation as a fact:

> It is almost certain from the insistence on Viola's musical accomplishments at I.ii.57-58 that she was meant to be a singer, and from the awkward opening of II.iv that the song "Come away, come away death" has been transferred from her to Feste.
>
> (297)

More likely the insistence on musical training was meant to strengthen her class identification. As Warnicke points out, at this time upper-class young women frequently received a limited musical education (117 and passim). Nor would such an education qualify Viola as a professional—the role of Feste in this play. Rather she is providing one of her several "job qualifications" even if she does not use them once she is employed.

Scene 2 must be understood as Shakespeare's swift, frank introduction of Viola—one that will not be repeated. Rather than anticipating specific later actions, it sketches in her upper-class background. Not only her offers of money and reference to Elysium, but her indication of a musical education, would have been familiar clues to contemporary audiences. In addition, despite its ambiguity, her quick response to the captain's mention of Orsino, "I have heard my father name him" (I.ii.28), followed by the delightful specific, "He was a bachelor then" (29)—leading audiences to believe that the Duke and her father knew one another (never actually confirmed in the text)—seems to reinforce the class connection.[6] Not until the play's closing moments does she refer to her earlier life again, except in momentary lapses, such as her lines:

> My father had a daughter lov'd a man
> As it might be perhaps, were I a woman,
> I should your lordship.
>
> (II.iv.107-9)

Or it surfaces in her boast of her parentage to Olivia: "Above my fortunes, yet my state is well: / I am a gentleman" (I.v.278-79). In that instance, however, the gender shift masks her identity. But at this point in the play, scene 2 prepares the audience for the combat of wits that will ensue between the two women of similar backgrounds when they finally confront one another three scenes later.

Yet societal values and accepted stereotypes about women blur those similarities and stress the women's differences. As I pointed out earlier, hostility to the young woman who would defy conventions creeps into the criticism just as sympathy for Viola, who suffers in silence, develops. Like the critics, editors and actor-managers, too, prefer to sharpen the contrast between this shipwrecked young woman soon to masquerade in breeches and the wealthy young Countess Olivia who exercises nonconformist attitudes towards men.

To strengthen the difference between the women, staged versions help reshape Viola by excising her line "For saying so, there's gold" (I.ii.18) and deemphasizing her class through costuming. The excision has persisted from the eighteenth century into the twentieth. The Bell edition (1773), for example, which claims to record the play "As Performed at the Theatres-Royal," jettisons Viola's offer of gold to the captain, suggesting what audiences saw at Drury Lane and Covent Garden after 1741.[7] Mrs. Inchbald (1808), as we have seen, refers to Olivia's falling in love "with a domestic" (4-5) and John Philip Kemble, whose acting version, first published in 1810, becomes the standard for theatrical productions for close to a century, also excises the reference to gold.[8] By the end of the nineteenth century, Henry Irving creates his own version, one which stresses his role of Malvolio. Nevertheless, Irving adopts many of Kemble's excisions, including Viola's offer of a reward.[9] In the twentieth century, Herbert Beerbohm Tree, among others, also excises the line, perhaps thinking it unseemly for a young woman to be so comfortable with money. More likely, Tree is following a tradition both in text and attitude towards Viola.

As well as introducing her, scene 2 further develops the portrait of Olivia through hearsay. The captain narrates and Viola listens. A down-to-earth and non-involved spectator, he responds to Viola's query about Orsino's bachelorhood with uncertainty, assuring her only that a month earlier, before the captain left, Orsino was seeking Olivia's hand:

> And then 'twas fresh in murmur (as you know
> What great ones do, the less will prattle of)
> That he did seek the love of fair Olivia.
>
> (I.ii.32-34)

In scene 1, Orsino had provided the emotional background; in scene 2, the captain fills in many of the publicly known details about the young woman. A "virtuous maid," the phrase identifying her youth and unmarried status, she is also:

> . . . the daughter of a count
> That died some twelvemonth since, then leaving her
> In the protection of his son, her brother,
> Who shortly also died;
>
> (36-39)

Alone and wealthy, Olivia has much in common with the young woman listening. Malcolmson makes a similar point although she leaves Viola's exact status in doubt: "The scene does not explicitly define Viola's status as either noble or gentle; rather, her rank is veiled from us just as Viola veils it from the people she will meet. . . . [W]e, and the characters, will know her through her role-playing and her 'intent" (37). Although staging tends to obscure Viola's status, I believe that the dramatist offers sufficient clues both in her speeches and her actions to indicate her upper-class background.

As the captain continues, he also helps identify Illyria's social system, one that places an unmarried woman under the governance of a male in the family.[10] Finally, the captain speaks of the Countess's actions now that her brother's protection has ceased. In deference to the love she bore him: "They say, she hath abjur'd the company / And sight of men" (40-41). Omitting any reference to the seven-year limit on the mourning period, relayed by Orsino's messenger in scene 1, the captain's "they say" confirms his general reliance on hearsay and his distance from Olivia. When, therefore, Viola resolves to serve this countess, the captain quickly discourages her:

> That were hard to compass,
> Because she will admit no kind of suit,
> No, not the Duke's.
>
> (44-46)

Obviously, if the Duke has failed, Viola should not even consider such an option. Accepting the captain's advice, she quickly shifts her objective and decides on wearing breeches: "I'll serve this duke; / Thou shalt present me as a eunuch to him" (55-56).

Critics have questioned the ease with which Viola changes her mind, considering her later persistence and success in meeting Olivia. As Ruth Nevo observes, although Viola, upon hearing of Olivia's loss, exclaims, "O that I served that lady," she "does not fly to the Countess Olivia for succour, woman to woman, despite her sympathy for a fellow-mourner. Instead she chooses to be adventurously epicene in the Duke's entourage" (205). Nevo believes that Viola makes a sacrifice here by asking to be presented as a eunuch, a rational explanation for her high voice and feminine appearance. More importantly, the young woman's transformation permits her to enjoy the freedom of action allowed her twin brother, and formerly denied her because of her sex. The speed of her decision also leads C. L. Barber to comment that "the shipwreck is made the occasion for Viola to exhibit an undaunted, aristocratic mastery of adversity—she settles what she shall do next almost as though picking out a costume for a masquerade" (241). He is less concerned with the reason for her choice than with her free and easy manner, her language in making the decision. Unlike these modern critics, Samuel Johnson expresses disdain for Viola's actions and considers this a plot weakness:

> Viola seems to have formed a very deep design with very little premeditation: she is thrown by shipwreck on an unknown coast, hears that the prince is a batchelor, and resolves to supplant the lady whom he courts.
>
> (7:312)

The play, however, refutes this theory, as we discover later on when Viola, having fallen in love with the Duke, bemoans the limitations placed on her by disguise then courts the Countess for him.

Differing from Johnson, most actor-managers and directors, as well as critics, favor Viola over Olivia. To focus more sharply on the disguised young woman, these men often transpose the first and second scenes. Again Kemble's influential version dominates. It opens with noise, thunder, and lightning, heralding Viola's arrival on the shores of Illyria. Beerbohm Tree, in 1901, dramatizes Viola's weakness on arrival although the text offers no such suggestion. Sailors bring her ashore "as if insensible. She is put reclining on the steps. Wet dress. Sailors with chest and bundles." Winthrop Ames, in 1906, also has the sailors "supporting a woman, then carrying in a child" (a character added for pathos, I suspect). Augustin Daly, the famous American manager at the end of the nineteenth century, goes even further. He opens the play with the arrival of Viola's brother on the shores of Illyria, eliminating all suspense as to whether or not her twin has survived.

Despite Daly's more radical alteration of sequence, it was only a temporary aberration whereas Kemble's pattern has persisted. As recently as the summer of 1986, New York audiences were treated to a Kemble format under the aegis of Joseph Papp, the production opening with Viola's arrival in Illyria. Possibly the drive for realism and interest in plot development contributed to the decision to open with the second scene. More likely, however, the uncreased emphasis on the heroic Viola in contrast to the foolish Olivia was responsible.

Unfortunately, that transposition sacrifices the airy, wistful tone of the first scene with all its implications and resonances—a scene as important to the play as the three witches who open *Macbeth* or the ghost on the ramparts who chills the air with foreboding in *Hamlet*. In Shakespeare's sequence, Orsino's impassioned pleas and posing in the first scene add credibility to Olivia's decision whereas when the play opens with scene 2, she sounds arbitrary and unreasonable since the sea captain warns Viola of the impossibility of meeting this woman.

Shakespeare's scene sequence (as Clifford Leech observed) has its own specific validity and dictates a pattern of relationships (36-37). The patterns in the plays usually affect and often heighten the impact of the work on the audience. Shakespeare's method resembles that of the painter who establishes positive and negative areas of a painting, each helping to illuminate the other while through both he weaves color, line, and design that unify the whole. In *Twelfth Night*, Orsino's opening scene provides the background (or negative) area—of fantasy—against which Viola's realistic approach proves refreshing. Woven through both is the slowly developing character of Olivia.

Scene 3 intensifies the portrait of the Countess. This time the dramatist takes us closer to her world, introducing us to the ebullient and varied characters who inhabit her home. There, the multidimensional, and skewed, characterization continues to grow as others' words fill in the blank spaces of the sketch first begun by Orsino. The robustious, roaring, frequently drunk Sir Toby, identified in the cast list as "uncle to Olivia," introduces us to the comic characters even while he stews, "What a plague means my niece to take the death of her brother thus? I am sure care's an enemy to life" (I.iii.1-3). Maria, the serving woman, rather than answering, sharply reprimands, "Your cousin, my lady, takes great exceptions to your ill hours" (5-6), bearing witness to a more dynamic Olivia than thus far promised by either Orsino or the sea captain. With these two speeches, Shakespeare has catapulted us into Olivia's household and established the firmness of the mistress's control. She has accepted the obligations of her position. A life of mourning has led neither to a retreat from reality nor to an abdication of responsibility, merely an affirmation of the single life.

Challenges to that single life, however, seem endless. Suitors spring up everywhere. Even Sir Toby has a candidate—his drinking companion, the foolish Sir Andrew Aguecheek, a gull easily separated from his money. Nevertheless, Sir Andrew, skeptical of his chances, would withdraw from the field, admitting, "Your niece will not be seen, or if she be, it's four to one she'll none of me. The Count himself here hard by woos her" (I.iii.106-8). For the third time, we hear of the Count's persistent wooing. Anxious to prevent the departure of his wealthy drinking mate, Sir Toby confidently insists, "She'll none o' th' Count. She'll not match above her degree, neither in estate, years, nor wit" (109-10). Although his motive is suspect, Sir Toby, while he ultimately will prove wrong about the "degree" of Olivia's intelligence, or wit, is correct about her rejection of the Count and probably about her youthful age. Sir Andrew does not contradict him.

Interestingly, critics, too, have wrestled with the question of her age while directors have indicated their opinion through dress, make-up, and stage movement. They usually decide in favor of seniority, thus emphasizing the ways in which an older woman can be bested by a younger, more conventional one. The hostility to the older, aggressive woman on stage remains; she is a subject for laughter and audience mockery. And here the language of the text may inadvertently contribute to this misreading, for whereas Olivia is acting herself, a young single woman, Viola, playing a man's role, is described as "not yet old enough for a man, nor young enough for a boy" (I.v.156-57). Leo Salingar in 1958, for example, considers the Countess, "psychologically an elder sister to Viola" (125).[11] Although not censorious, as was Mrs. Inchbald in 1808, Salingar resembles Inchbald in stressing an age differential between the two women. However nowhere, neither in the language nor actions, does the text indicate an Olivia chronologically older or more psychologically mature than Viola. On the contrary, perhaps because of her disguise and the challenges it poses, Viola reveals keen insights into both her condition and Olivia's, insights unavailable to the deceived Countess.

In fact, Sir Toby's comment supports the notion that the two young women were approximately of the same age, thus reinforcing the similarities introduced at the start. Only later, when trapped in a comic relationship and engaged in wit combats built on disguise does confusion arise as to their respective ages. This, however, may result from costuming and staging. For example, an illustration of an older Olivia actually appears in the pages of costume designs in an Augustin Daly souvenir promptbook. Her face looks a bit pinched as well as haughty, in contrast with the illustration for Viola, who, with blonde, curly hair worn in a version of a wide pageboy, has an innocent, inquiring, friendly look on her face and stands in a deferential pose.[12] Although both illustrations seem to have provided the basis for the women's costumes, they must also reflect perceptions of the characters in the nineteenth century.[13]

Occasionally, of course, some independent thinking occurs and we read in a promptbook, "Olivia's youth should be emphasized in every way possible to make her love affair with so callow a strippling as Viola convincing" (Ames prompt, facing I.v.294-95). The comment is sparked by Olivia's soliloquy at the close of the scene where she first meets Viola. Again in a 1988 production at Stratford, Ontario, Olivia's youthfulness was stressed when she giggled with delight at discovering this new young "man," then subsequently discarded her black dress for a pink one.

As the play moves towards this moment when the two women meet, their divergent introductions continue: Olivia's through hearsay, Viola's through direct presentation. In scene 4 Orsino describes his passionate love for the incomparable Olivia, meanwhile confessing to his new page, the disguised Viola, "I have unclasp'd / To thee the book even of my secret soul" (I.iv.13-14). Incredibly, she has won her way into his confidence in a mere three days. Despite her brief period of service, Orsino is revealing all his innermost thoughts to her. The ease with which she accomplishes this suggests that she had no trouble being accepted in an aristocratic household because she could draw on the mores of her upper-class background to adjust to her new situation. But Viola has lost her heart to him even as he is entrusting her with his most precious errand, the wooing of Olivia. Shakespeare thus presents the first challenge to a wealthy young woman who would gain freedom from her sexual identity by donning male attire. Breeches have their drawbacks; but so do skirts, as Olivia too will soon discover.

When she finally sweeps onto the stage in scene 5, in all her grandeur or loneliness, certainty or uncertainty, age or youth, arrogance or self-confidence, she has been thoroughly characterized by the conflicting impressions passed on by others. John Russell Brown writes of the silences in the play—the moments when words are not spoken but audience attention is riveted to a character (28). Surely audiences are waiting to see just what she looks like, how she carries herself, and how she behaves. But the tendency to tamper with the text again changes the portrait. Just as the transposition of the play's first two scenes combined with the omission of many of the Duke's foolish self-pitying lines alter audiences' perceptions of him, and excision of Viola's reference to gold masks her upper-class background, so standard cuts in scene 5—some going back to the early nineteenth century—affect our first impression of Olivia.

Although the scene opens with twenty-five lines of teasing conversation between Maria and the Clown—lines preparing the audience for the Countess's annoyance with him—they seldom reach the stage. Henry Irving, John Philip Kemble, Augustin Daly, and Herbert Beerbohm Tree, among others, chopped off some or all of the exchange.[14] As a result, Olivia usually sounds arbitrary and arrogant at her entrance. To the Clown's "God bless thee, lady!" (I.v.36-37), she replies, "Take the fool away" (38). Nor does his "Do you not hear, fellows? Take away the lady," (39-40) amuse her. Olivia angrily charges, "Go to, y' are a dry fool; I'll no more of you. Besides, you grow dishonest" (41-42). In the conversation usually omitted, however, Shakespeare provides an explanation for this behavior. Officiously acting as her mistress's surrogate, Maria reprimands the Clown for his several absences. In their exchange lies the rational basis for Olivia's opening speeches, particularly her anger at the Clown. The excision contributes to a one-sided and distorted impression of her.

In fact, in the full text, she proves a tolerant manager of this conglomerate household. We glimpse her reasonable governance particularly when she allows the Fool his famous argument against mourning for her brother. "I think his soul is in hell, madonna" (68), he begins, quickly contradicted by her, "I know his soul is in heaven, fool" (69), leading to his conclusion, "The more fool, madonna, to mourn for your brother's soul, being in heaven" (70-71). The reasoning wins her admiration. "What think you of this fool, Malvolio? doth he not mend?" (73-74), she laughingly concedes. But her steward, a somber man with a great sense of self-importance, is not amused. Olivia then criticizes him, offering astute character analysis in her reprimand: "O, you are sick of self-love, Malvolio, and taste with a distemper'd appetite. To be generous, guiltless, and of free disposition, is to take those things for bird-bolts that you deem cannon-bullets" (90-93). Shakespeare has endowed her with a directness of language that matches Viola's. But in some promptbooks, such as those based on the Daly edition (p. 16, *TN* 21; p. 22, *TN* 10), the second sentence, with its analogy to "bird-bolts" and "cannon-bullets," has been excised. As written, the full text reveals Olivia's strengths. During the brief time that she is on stage, she appears neither unintelligent, intolerant, nor humorless. Nor does she exhibit any extremes of grief.

Rather, the young Countess appears well qualified for the battle of wits that will follow between her and Viola—two women who have, in their own ways, built their independent personas on the death (or seeming death) of their brothers, one through mourning, the other through disguise. The equality of their verbal gifts emerges at their first meeting. Sent to woo Olivia for Orsino, Viola combines flattery with insolence. "Most radiant, exquisite, and unmatchable beauty—I pray you tell me if this be the lady of the house. . . . I would be loath to cast away my speech; for besides that it is excellently well penn'd, I have taken great pains to con it" (I.v.170-74), she complains. When Olivia answers only "Whence came you, sir?" (177), Viola persists in her emphasis on the prepared speech being spoken to the properly identified Olivia: "I can say little more than I have studied, and that question's out of my part" (178-79).

Seeming to be aware of what Viola is doing, Olivia queries next, "Are you a comedian?" (182). To this Viola somewhat saucily responds, "No, my profound heart; and yet (by the very fangs of malice I swear) I am not that I play" (183-84). Why the expression "by the very fangs of malice"? What is its relevance? Does it have an underlying message or reveal her envy of Olivia? For surely, a suitor would not be using the "fangs of malice" to support an argument. Rather while the phrase may suggest an arrogance and a pose of self-confidence on Viola's part, it may also reflect her attempt to simulate male assertiveness first by swearing and then by calling up this strange phrase, perhaps a substitute for "by the devil." In closing, she repeats her request, "Are you the lady of the house?" (184-85). Finally Olivia gives an almost direct answer—although still equivocating—"If I do not usurp myself, I am" (186). But Viola responds in kind. "Most certain, if you are she, you do usurp yourself" (187-88). And then once more she refers to her memorized speech "in praise" of Olivia, the suggestion being that not Olivia herself, but the conventions of love are responsible for this praise.

This short exchange is usually reduced on the stage. Since drama is built on the interaction between characters—in other words, since dialogue helps define personality—the omissions alter the portraits of the women. The section leading to Olivia's question "Are you a comedian?" and Viola's mixed answer with its "fangs of malice" are frequently excised. What remains is Olivia's simple "If I do not usurp myself, I am."[15] Nor do audiences usually hear Olivia's sardonic admonition to Viola to "Come to what is important in't. I forgive you the praise" (192-93), indicating her sense of humor and awareness of the verbal battle under way. In the subsequent conversation, the cuts in Olivia's lines are rather curious. "Speak your office" (207) is all that remains of a speech that includes "Sure you have some hideous matter to deliver, when the courtesy of it is so fearful" (206-7). Eliminated too is the contretemps touched off by Viola's "I hold the olive in my hand" (209-10)—an offer she finds difficult to sustain after Olivia's simple observation "Yet you began rudely" (212). Viola immediately takes up the challenge, "The rudeness that hath appear'd in me have I learn'd from my entertainment" (214-15).

Their verbal combat continues, intensified by Viola's request that Olivia raise her veil although as the Countess notes, "You are now out of your text" (232). Nevertheless, she agrees to "draw the curtain, and show . . . the picture" (233), challenging, "Is't not well done?" (235) A too-quick response springs from the woman in breeches, "Excellently done, if God did all" (236). Just as sharply, however, Olivia retorts, "'Tis in grain, sir, 'twill endure wind and weather" (237-38). But much of this verbal jousting disappears from the stage, and Viola's speech begins instead with the flattering, "'Tis beauty truly blent" (239).

Consider too, the exchange triggered by Olivia's wonderful speech outlining the "divers schedules" of her beauty:

> It shall be inventoried, and every particle and utensil labell'd to my will: as, *item,* two lips, indifferent red; *item,* two grey eyes, with lids to them; *item,* one neck, one chin, and so forth. Were you sent hither to praise me?
>
> (I.v.245-49)

Undaunted, the page Cesario/Viola disapprovingly comments: "I see what you are; you are too proud; / But if you were the devil, you are fair" (250-51). And then, as if remembering her mission, she jumps from critical direct address to her major subject, "My lord and master loves you" (252). Promptbooks, reflecting stage productions, tend to retain only the last line, omitting Olivia's "schedule" of her beauty as well as Viola's accusation of pride. Thus the text, mocking the ideal of courtly love, emphasizes pertness and honesty over flattery. These excisions rob the portrait of Viola of irony and reduce Olivia to a stolid, unimaginative woman.

Finally, cut too is her gracious observation:

> Your lord does know my mind, I cannot love him,
> Yet I suppose him virtuous, know him noble,
> Of great estate, of fresh and stainless youth;
> In voices well divulg'd, free, learn'd, and valiant,
> And in dimension, and the shape of nature,
> A gracious person. But yet I cannot love him.
>
> (257-62)

The speech indicates Olivia's sensitivity as she lists his specific strengths. It is a remarkable statement to give to a young woman, since it suggests less an emotional reaction than a thoughtful evaluation of the man she rejects. She mentions none of his weaknesses but bases her decision only on her own taste: "I cannot love him," implying also that nothing in the future will change her mind. Adamant in her insistence that she will never love Orsino, the Countess repeats the words yet again near the scene's close. Viola understands and later attempts, unsuccessfully, to explain Olivia's point of view to Orsino.

Historically, most of the speech disappears from the stage. Kemble's version, setting the pattern for those to follow, combines the single opening line with the speech's closing, resulting in the cryptic, abbreviated message: "Your lord does know my mind, I cannot love him: / He might have took his answer long ago" (Kemble, 1810, p. 19). Conforming to the developing portrait of her in criticism, an arbitrary Olivia emerges here. Other acting texts follow Kemble's lead. Beerbohm Tree (1901) retains the first line of the speech. Augustin Daly (1893), Henry Irving (1884), and others retain its first three lines. These productions span almost an entire century and surely must have affected criticism.

In fact, in 1865, decrying this omission, Spedding writes:

> These lines are left out in the acting, which is surely a great mistake. As addressed by Olivia to Viola, they have a peculiar and pathetic meaning, and it is strange that the mixed emotions which they must have excited in her should not have been made one of the "points" in the play.
>
> (*Fraser's Magazine;* quoted in *Variorum Twelfth Night,* 90)

The lines not only affect Viola, who herself would like to "be his wife" (I.iv.42) but also illuminate the character of Olivia. She knows her own heart and mind; she can recognize virtue in others, even someone who is a bit foolish, like Orsino. Of course, she has only seen that side of him which is tangled in the conventions of wooing. Viola, on the other hand, hears a more relaxed man confiding his ideas not only about wooing and women but also about life generally. Employed as his page, she has also found him generous and trusting, having given her, an unknown youth, a position and quickly taken her into his confidence. Like Hermia and Helena, who encounter two different aspects of Demetrius in the early scenes of *A Midsummer Night's Dream,* Viola and Olivia encounter two different Orsinos.

Unmoved by the Orsino she knows, Olivia is captivated by his envoy, Viola. In this disguised woman of comparable background and wit, Olivia finds the perfect wooer—the one who verbalizes her own dream of what wooing should be: a challenging wit exchange between equals; honesty; and an absence of posing. Direct language can open a path to the heart. In scene 5, Viola adopts this method. Without realizing it, she once again departs from her "text" (232). This time she delivers an impassioned love lyric. Though meant to win Olivia for Orsino, it also reveals something of Viola's own feelings for the Duke: "If I did love you in my master's flame, / . . . I would. . . . / Make me a willow cabin at your gate, / . . . Hallo your name to the reverberate hills, / And make the babbling gossip of the air / Cry out 'Olivia'" (264-74).

The speech overwhelms the young Countess as it does the audience. Here are lines that differ from Orsino's flowery words; familiar images flood the language. One need not search for hidden meanings, merely visualize the youth standing before a simple cabin and hear him hallowing the name "Olivia." The air and the hills echo the name; the speaker captivates the listener, who admits in soliloquy after the young page leaves:

> How now?
> Even so quickly may one catch the plague?
> Methinks I feel this youth's perfections
> With an invisible and subtle stealth
> To creep in at mine eyes.[16] Well, let it be.
> (294-98)

But she doesn't "let it be." Instead, Olivia immediately sends Malvolio on a false errand, to return to the young Cesario a ring he never gave her. Each woman has been caught in an emotional response that will alter her self-perception and her desire for anonymity or privacy. No longer thinking of the brother she was mourning, Olivia seeks only to assure a return visit from Orsino's youthful page.

Perhaps squeamish about the possible impact of individual lines or simply choosing to cut at this point, actor-managers excised and revised. Charles Kean, the mid-nineteenth-century manager, for example, crossed out some of Olivia's speech above, specifically those lines expressing admiration for "this youth" (296-98). The intention was probably to remove any suggestion of Olivia's being homosexually attracted to Viola. In this comedy of mistaken identity, however, Shakespeare, not only suggests such an attachment, but then, through the sequential arrangement of scenes quickly offers an alternative possibility.

Olivia's startling emotional discovery precipitates an immediate scene change to the lost Sebastian, Viola's twin brother, who has survived the shipwreck. Derrida argues that the meanings of words are constantly being modified by the next signifier (Moi, 105-7). Building on Derrida's insight, I propose that meaning in drama derives not only from verbal signifiers, particularly the interaction of characters as they speak on stage, but also from the sequence of scenes as they unfold. This arrangement affects both our first, immediate response as well as the modification of that response. Moreover, because theater differs from the written text in at least one significant detail, it addresses a captive audience who must listen and react as the play progresses, this "deferral of meaning" occurs to a far larger extent with drama than with written literature since a reader may put down a book and stop reading.

The young Countess's comment about the disguised youth now takes on a different perspective with the introduction of Sebastian. His presence holds the promise of a possible new pairing, although audiences will have to wait to see when, and if, Sebastian meets Olivia and how that meeting will develop. The striking physical similarity between the twins will eventually resolve Olivia's dilemma. She will later woo Sebastian as Cesario although, as Heilbrun points out, Shakespeare, himself the father of opposite sex twins, surely knew such an indistinguishable resemblance to be impossible (37).

Similarities do, however, exist. Like Viola, Sebastian is first introduced with a sea captain, Antonio, who rescued him. Also like her, Viola's brother arouses intense feelings of affection, in his case from Antonio, who would serve the youth. And again like her, Sebastian stubbornly resists. "If you will not undo what you have done, that is, kill him whom you have recover'd, desire it not" (II.i.37-39), the young man insists before departing. Left alone on stage, Antonio, in soliloquy, first blesses the youth: "The gentleness of all the gods go with thee!" then reveals the intensity of his feelings.

> I have many enemies in Orsino's court,
> Else would I very shortly see thee there.
> But come what may, I do adore thee so
> That danger shall seem sport, and I will go.
> (II.i.44-48)

The speech suggests a strong, even if one-sided, affection. The captain will risk capture for the pleasure of following Sebastian.

Brother, like sister, rejects an implied homosexual relationship. Unlike Viola, however, Sebastian is not suffering from a misreading of his sexual identity since no disguise exists. And so the soliloquy is seldom heard on stage. The Bell version retains only a form of the first line, "The gentleness of the Gods go with thee!" (335), after which the two men "exeunt severally" (335). Kemble's text, followed by the French edition (*TN* 18) and others, transforms Antonio's first line into part of a brief dialogue, Sebastian answering with an invented line, "Fare ye well."

This first scene between Sebastian and Antonio often changes not only its shape, but also its place in the sequence. Despite its importance in the pattern of alternating scenes that illuminate the development of the two principal women characters, actor-managers and directors have often reshuffled the text—sometimes to simplify plot, sometimes to stress Malvolio's role (although it is shorter than those of Viola and Olivia), and sometimes to sustain a contrast between the women, favoring the disguised youth in breeches. Again Kemble's text set the example, transposing the Folio sequence by placing Malvolio's scene with Viola immediately after Olivia's order to "return the ring," although the introduction of Sebastian interferes with such a smooth narrative sequence.[17] Other directors, such as Irving, who played Malvolio, have withheld Sebastian's surprise appearance until later in the play.[18] Focusing on his own role, Irving also abbreviated the women's lines.[19] Other actor-managers tended to fall into similar patterns, sometimes stripping the scene of most of its intense lines with their homoerotic implications, sometimes transposing the sequence, and often doing both.

Occasionally, as in the Sothern and Marlowe production at the beginning of the twentieth century, the scene was even merged with the second brief Sebastian-Antonio scene even though each of these functions differently. The first creates that happy shock of recognition of the physical resemblances between the twins; it also introduces the relationship between the two men. The second adds important plot elements: the captain decides to remain in Illyria, despite the hazards, then lends his purse to Sebastian, later seeking to retrieve it from Sebastian's double, Viola. The scene also testifies to the intensity of Antonio's affection for the youth. Sequentially, the second scene separates Maria's description of Malvolio in yellow garters from his actual appearance on stage.

In contrast, the Sothern-Marlowe merged scene (II.ii. in typescript—*TN* 31) retains only the factual information necessary for the plot's later development. It begins with the opening of Shakespeare's second of the two scenes (III.iii.1-15) where Antonio reveals his decision to accompany the young man, but it excises specific references to his love for Sebastian. Next follows the youth's disclosure of his identity, plucked from the earlier scene (II.i), thus confirming as well Viola's upper-class background. Finally, returning to the later scene, this new mongrel concludes with Antonio giving his purse to Sebastian. Sequentially, it follows Malvolio's outburst to the drunken Sir Toby and Sir Andrew (II.iii) and precedes Viola's debate with Orsino on love (II.iv). Although in many ways the Sothern-Marlowe version defeats the purposes of the two separate scenes, it does not subvert the play's ability to construct strong parallels between two wealthy, young, single women who have lost father and brother. That was Daly's contribution and he achieved it by opening the play with Sebastian's arrival in Illyria. This assured audiences that the relationship between Olivia and Viola was just a game and that Viola's early quest for independence had no reality since her brother lived.

Shakespeare, however, not only raises this issue of independence but also further develops it in Viola's retort to Malvolio when he delivers the ring. For the dramatist here offers a significant example of women bonding. Knowing she never gave Olivia a ring, the disguised page nevertheless answers the steward: "She took the ring of me, I'll none of it" (12). Although the line has puzzled some editors, it seems consistent with Viola's constant makeshift attempts both to conceal her disguise and to reveal her insights as a woman into another woman's actions. This will occur again two scenes later when she attempts to explain to the Duke Olivia's feelings for him, but instead nearly trips over her own identity. Clearly in her scene with Malvolio, Viola understands what has occurred, as her soliloquy, following his brusque departure, indicates: "I left no ring with her. . . . / Fortune forbid my outside have not charm'd her" (II.ii.17-18). Indeed it has. But Sebastian's arrival may promise a "happy ending," even while the play continues to explore the women's struggles, whether in breeches or skirts, to assert their sense of self.

In the scenes that follow, Olivia's struggle once more comes to the fore, again through hearsay and inference as Shakespeare thrusts us ever more intimately into the dynamics of her household. Again the challenge to her independence grows out of her position as a marriageable, wealthy young woman. When the drunken Sir Toby and Sir Andrew wobble in, raucously singing, Maria first reprimands them, invoking the name of her mistress, but then later joins them. Less flexible, Malvolio, awakened from sleep by this boisterous crew, more vehemently chastises them, again invoking Olivia's name:

> My lady bade me tell you, that though she harbors you as her kinsman, she's nothing allied to your disorders. If you can separate yourself and your misdemeanors, you are welcome to the house; if not, and it would please you to take leave of her, she is very willing to bid you farewell.
>
> (II.iii.95-101)

Since he never carries out the threat but is himself bested, his lines indicate his misreading of Olivia, exhibiting his lust for power and his method of exercising it. Betraying his ambition as well as his vulnerability to the gulling he will later suffer, his speech illuminates the extent and intensiveness of another of Olivia's pursuers. He will readily adopt cross-garters and attempt to smile in his effort to win her hand and, with it, permanent power as her husband. Little disappears from this comic scene in staged versions—only the songs. First omitted from the Bell edition, they are later excised by Kemble and Irving who substitute other, briefer drinking songs.

A far different fate on stage meets the scene which follows: the debate between Viola and Orsino on men's and women's capacity for love. The scene loses much of its substance through cutting. It is full of inconsistencies and contradictions in Orsino's arguments while stressing at the same time the complexity of Viola's position as she strives to convey to the Duke something of a woman's point of view. Filled with humor and further mockery of the conventions of the Petrarchan lover, it continues the portrait of Orsino begun in the first scene—a silly lover drowning in self-pity. Again, his desire for music opens the scene:

> that piece of song,
> That old and antique song we heard last
>   night;
> Methought it did relieve my passion much,
> More than light airs and recollected terms
> Of these most brisk and giddy-paced times.
>
> (II.iv.2-6)

Still seeking to "relieve" his passion, Orsino sounds very much like the melancholy character we met earlier. But this request for music does not appear in the Bell edition, the Kemble edition, or the French edition, basically covering a century of staging. Instead, in those editions, the scene opens with Orsino attempting to warn his page of what to expect from love. "Come hither boy," the Duke instructs, "If ever thou shalt love, / In the sweet pangs of it remember me" (15-16). Observing Cesario/Viola's downcast expression, her master quizzes her about her beloved's appearance: "Of your complexion" and "about your years" (26, 28), confesses the disguised woman.

Her lines trigger Orsino's first dissertation on love, which will eventually be contradicted by his second. "[H]owever we do praise ourselves, / Our fancies are more giddy . . . Than women's are" (32-35), he claims, advising Cesario to choose a woman younger than himself. Later, however, when describing his own love for Olivia, the Duke contradicts himself, insisting, "no woman's heart / So big, to hold so much; they lack retention" (95-96). He also compares a woman's love which "may be call'd appetite" (97) with his own, which is "all as hungry as the sea" (100). Kemble and Bell omit the first assertion and Kemble, Bell, Irving, Daly, and Sothern and Marlowe omit its contradiction. As a result of these excisions, the Duke sounds consistent, a quality that Shakespeare denies him. The elimination of both groups of quotes by Bell and Kemble alters the scene's emphasis, losing much of its irony.

In these editions, reflecting stage performances, not only do the contradictions disappear, but also Orsino turns into a fairly direct, attractive man. Reduced, the text's long lecture on love becomes merely a brief comment to Viola/Cesario on her beloved, "too old, by heaven" (29), followed immediately by the direction: "Get thee to yond same sovereign cruelty" (80), Olivia. Covering a mere two pages in the Kemble text, the scene fails to develop the portrait of a melancholy and self-pitying Orsino resembling Shakespeare's Duke. Instead, it becomes a brief interlude of disagreement between the disguised page and the man she loves in which she stumbles when trying to fictionalize her love for him.

Juxtaposing the young page's clearly reasoned defense of Olivia against the Duke's confused and contradictory comments on men's and women's capacity to love, Shakespeare in this scene once again illustrates women bonding and also gives Viola rational arguments favoring a woman's right to free choice. Furthermore, the scene reaffirms Viola's sense of her own identity; she is always emotionally and intellectually clearly a woman. Attempting to deliver Olivia's message and sensitive to its intention, Viola tries to convince Orsino of its finality, transposing Olivia's words. "But if she *cannot love* you, sir?" (II.iv.87, emphasis added here and throughout this paragraph). In response, the Duke retains only the original "cannot." "I *cannot* be so answer'd" (88), he insists. Viola then cites the parallel of an imaginary woman (herself) in love with him. Suppose "*You* cannot love *her*" (91). The pronouns have shifted from that first expression by Olivia but the body of the line has been restored. The debate surrounding a woman's right to express or reject love on a plane equal to a man's is given clear expression through Viola as Cesario, the young lad, while the refusal of the man, Orsino, to respect Olivia's wishes resonates through the text.

In this scene, Viola seems torn between revealing her identity and maintaining her disguise. Earlier she had decided, "Time, thou must untangle this, not I" (II.ii.40). But here that resolve weakens, when, in trying to convince the Duke, she says, "My father had a daughter lov'd a man / As it might be perhaps, were I a woman, / I should your lordship" (II.iv.107-9). "And what's her history?" (109) the Duke quickly asks. Surely her answer, "I am all the daughters of my father's house, / And all the brothers too" (120-21), should have led to a full revelation. But the Duke is so self-absorbed in his own feelings that his ear is not keyed to Viola's words. And so she continues in her role as his messenger.

Having chosen her disguise almost whimsically, she finds its advantages quickly fading. First, her success in winning a place with the Duke has led to her appointment as his surrogate wooer although she confesses, in soliloquy: "Whoe'er I woo, myself would be his wife" (I.iv.42). Then her enchantment of Olivia further intensifies Viola's problem. Next, when she tries to explain the other woman's position to the Duke, he refuses to listen. Later, despite her protests, Sir Andrew challenges her to a duel for Olivia's hand, leading Viola to muse to herself: "A little thing would make me tell them how much I lack of a man" (III.iv.302-3). And finally, she must confront the issue of a dual identity, having become embroiled in the circle of pursued and pursuer. The problems Viola faces caused by her disguise are, if less life threatening, more subtle and emotionally complex than those that confront Shakespeare's other women in breeches: Rosalind of *As You Like It,* Imogen of *Cymbeline,* and Jessica of *The Merchant of Venice,* who choose disguise to evade pursuit; Julia of *The Two Gentlemen of Verona*, who concealed herself to pursue her lover; or Portia and Nerissa, who dress as lawyer and law clerk to save their husbands' friend.

If, however, Shakespeare were less interested in realistic reasons for the disguise than in the larger concept—the relationship of sexuality to women's economic independence—the silliness of the breeches controversy would be exposed by the similarities between the women's plights. Although differently dressed, both must revise their self-perceptions, modifying them to accommodate erotic urges as these affect women's lives in such a society. Viola's choice of disguise, like Olivia's choice of mourning, tests the limits of self-sovereignty when supported by economic independence.

Thus their new erotic interests conflict with their development of independence. Nevertheless, both women persevere in their chosen direction. Viola remains in service to Orsino, wooing Olivia, while she, in turn, continues her forthright pursuit of Cesario. Two other brief exchanges mark the women's time alone together. In the earlier one (III.i.93-164), Olivia apologizes for sending the false message and the ring and quite directly declares her love. In the second (III.iv.201-17), an exchange of less than twenty lines within a much longer scene, she acknowledges having compromised herself:

> I have said too much unto a heart of stone,
> And laid mine honor too unchary on't.
> There's something in me that reproves my fault;
> But such a headstrong potent fault it is
> That it but mocks reproof.
>
> (201-5)

Recognition but not retraction leads to her next speech, "Here, wear this jewel for me, 'tis my picture" (208), promising Viola, "it hath no tongue to vex you" (209). Olivia is ready to embark on what appears to be a cross-class marriage to a young page. Is she using her wealth to lure a husband, who, in fact has the virtues of a woman and is, perhaps, therefore attractive? In the text, ambiguity then prevails. Does Viola accept the jewel? No hint appears in the language. Her response, like so many of her answers to Olivia, evades the subject, asking instead, "your true love for my master" (213).

Further evasion appears in promptbooks, many of which excise this brief moment between the disguised woman and the lady who openly vows her love. For example, the encounter is crossed out by Charles Kean, who used a Kemble text (*TN* 14). And the Irving version retains only the last four lines of the women's conversation. Their brief moment is then over: no apologies for having declared her love, and no giving Viola "this jewel" that contains Olivia's picture (*TN* 15, p. 52). Was Viola's behavior not exemplary enough for the adaptors? Was the intensity of Olivia's passion, directed as it was to a woman, embarrassing? Probably both. In the text, the exchange amplifies their portraits, which have been acquiring dimension with each new scene.

Like a juggler, Shakespeare keeps aloft the atmosphere of romance as well as the realities of drunks and duels and always, whether directly or through hearsay, he illuminates the challenges facing the two women. Perhaps nowhere more clearly than in the middle section of the play are we witness to this balancing act. Act 3, scene 2 includes the conning of Sir Andrew (into penning a challenge to Cesario) and the report on Malvolio's appearance (wearing yellow cross-garters)—both men wishing to win Olivia through their actions.

Opening in her garden, scene 4 of act 3 shows the Countess ranging from one interest to another in quick succession.

> I have sent after him; he says he'll come.
> How shall I feast him? What bestow of him?
> For youth is bought more oft than begg'd or borrow'd.
> I speak too loud.
>
> (1-4)

The excitement generated within this speech, even including the suggestion that it is spoken in a whisper reveals an altered Olivia—one neither disinterested nor in mourning. The Bell edition contains a footnote on her appearance: "Olivia should possess beauty of countenance, elegance of figure, grace of deportment, and sensibility of speech" [bottom, p. 357, vol. 5, of Bell edition]. The edition also records a seemingly slight alteration in the opening line, but one which changes the idea. It reads: "I have sent after him; *say he will come,* / How shall I feast him? What bestow on him?" (emphasis added, p. 357). The conditional here contradicts the straight assertion in the Folio. Her lines reflect her excitement.

She then changes the subject, "Where's Malvolio?" (5).[20] Asking for him and commenting that his sad state suits her well, Olivia learns from Maria that he is as one "possessed." When he appears before her in yellow garters and smiling, she attempts to understand this sudden change, but the arrival of Cesario cuts short the interview, leading Olivia to assign Malvolio to Maria and Sir Toby—thus asking his gullers to be his handlers. After the steward's triumphant soliloquy celebrating what he believes to be his new status—the prospective husband to Olivia—the scene moves without a pause to Sir Andrew's timidly worded letter of challenge to Cesario. Here both Viola and Olivia are the subjects—the one's problems created by her disguise, the other's by her lack of disguise, but clearly her marriageability. Thus both illuminate challenges to the women's pursuit of their own independence. The brief interlude between the two women follows.

The focus then shifts to Viola. Suddenly her resemblance to her brother fades as she faces the "terror," Sir Andrew, an equally reluctant adversary. Their swords at the ready, both participants back off from one another, even as Antonio, mistaking Viola for Sebastian, interrupts their duel, finds himself under arrest by officers, requests his purse of "Sebastian," and denied, offers Viola her first inkling that her brother lives.

> He nam'd Sebastian. I my brother know
> Yet living in my glass; even such and so
> In favor was my brother, and he went
> Still in this fashion, color, ornament,
> For him I imitate.
>
> (379-83)

We discover how completely Viola has mimicked her brother and are prepared for the confusion that will result.

The dramatist next adds depth and shading to the design, for the following scene has the cinematic quality of a "double take." "Will you make me believe that I am not sent for you?" (IV.i.1-2), challenges the Clown to Cesario's double, Sebastian. But we have already witnessed the interview between Viola and Olivia. Replaying an earlier moment, the Clown's confrontational attack seems to precede the previous scene. But the take is skewed. The line is addressed to Sebastian, not Viola/Cesario, and the outcome differs from the expected. We are caught in Shakespeare's double time as he confirms, through witnesses, the extraordinary resemblance between the twins. Sir Andrew and Sir Toby provide the next testimony. Again challenging the character they assume to be Orsino's page, they little realize they are encountering a different adversary. Finally, Olivia rushes out to save one she believes to be Cesario, but instead overwhelms Sebastian: "Let fancy still my sense in Lethe steep; / If it be thus to dream, still let me sleep!" (IV.i.62-63). Brother, like sister, uses a classical allusion. Just as a painter places small dabs of similar colors strategically throughout his painting to orchestrate its parts and help unify it, the writer paints resemblances through language and literary references.

Culminating in Olivia's "Would thou'dst be rul'd by me!" (64), this scene has carried the accidental disguise motif to its climax, when Sebastian replies, "Madam, I will," and Olivia joyously exclaims, "O, say so, and so be!" (65) and departs to plan a wedding. In contrast, a scene of intentional disguise follows, its darkness contrasting with the light of the previous scene as well as the subsequent one. Both literally and figuratively, darkness prevails as Sir Toby, Maria, and the Clown seek to frustrate Malvolio and convince him he is mad while keeping him imprisoned in darkness and calling it light. Again, Olivia, though absent is present: hearsay and hope, Malvolio's hope of marriage, keep her in the audience's consciousness.

Darkness then gives way to light. "This is the air, that is the glorious sun" (IV.iii.1), Sebastian marvels in soliloquy at Olivia's gifts, then later follows her to church to exchange vows. The soliloquy wanders over several topics, but always with Olivia at its core. Wondering what has happened to Antonio and wishing for his advice, the youth speculates,

> For though my soul disputes well with my
>   sense,
> That this may be some error, but no
>   madness,
> Yet doth this accident and flood of fortune
> So far exceed all instance, all discourse,
> That I am ready to distrust mine eyes,
> And wrangle with my reason that persuades
>   me
> To any other trust but that I am mad,
> Or else the lady's mad.
>
> (9-16)

Debating with himself as to whether she is mad, he concludes this to be impossible—else she could not run her house, command her followers, and manage her affairs with such skill and "stable bearing" (19). Here in the testimony of a stranger who has observed the lady in action we are told of her ability.

But again the glorification of Olivia falls before the actor-manager's or director's pen. Since she is here challenging patterns of patriarchy, these producers of the play seem to assert that her more positive features need not be emphasized. Cuts in Sebastian's soliloquy appear in early promptbooks or acting versions and continue well into the twentieth century although they outline her skills. Clearly, the lines testify to her never having left this world, but merely having divorced herself from availability to suitors. And so, acting texts excise.[21] Kemble omits the lines as do the Oxberry and the French texts (*TN* 9). By the time we reach the Sothern-Marlowe version the soliloquy has been reduced to its first four lines, followed by its last two. With only its skeleton remaining, this abbreviated scene is then attached to the beginning of the closing scene (V.i) without a break.

Meanwhile, Viola is confronting the clear possibility that her brother lives. Although a joyous prospect, it will end her adventure into independence just as Olivia's decision to marry will end hers. In the single scene in act 5, Shakespeare, for the last time, presents the challenges the two single young women face and weaves together fact and fantasy, for this is Illyria.

Maria, too, has won her objective. Although she does not appear in the scene, we learn that through her successful plot to ensnare Malvolio "at Sir Toby's" wish, he hath "In recompense . . . married her" (363-64). A strong character, Maria differs from the other two women, having persistently sought marriage. Viola and Olivia, however, have had a momentary chance at self-ownership.

The conflict between the qualities referred to by de Beauvoir—the sense of the self being primary, and the "erotic urges and social pressures" to conform— is dramatized. By refusing to sacrifice the sense of self being primary, Olivia wins a husband; but he is only a facsimile of the "man" she pursued. However, because Sebastian's easy compliance to Olivia's proposal of marriage sharply contrasts with the passion of his rejection of Antonio earlier, one must question its reality. It is almost as if the dramatist were sending a signal to the audience to observe the character of the twin so as to realize the challenge to realism in the ending.

Critics have noted the weakness of this ending—its basic disregard for logic.[22] Anne Barton, for example, observes that in *Twelfth Night* "Shakespeare began to unbuild his own comic form at its point of greatest vulnerability: the ending" (171). The brief scene between Antonio and Sebastian at the beginning of act 2 contributes to the absence of logic in the ending. In the earlier scene, the youth exhibits qualities clearly out of character with his impulsive actions near the comedy's close. One need only compare the attitude of Bertram to Helena with that of Sebastian to Olivia, a total stranger who asks him to marry her thinking he is Cesario, to see Shakespeare's lack of interest in a realistic ending. Nor do audiences react negatively to this strange and speedy marriage where the characters do not know one another. Because this is a comedy and because the young man himself does not object, we accept the convention of marriage as the outcome and delight that here in Illyria, Viola's twin brother shows up at just the right moment.

We also realize that the relationship between the two people to be married is inconsequential in this play, as is the need for a realistic reason for Viola's decision to disguise. Rather, the comedy seems to concentrate more closely on the changes in the women's self-perception from "primary" to "other" as they accept their identities as sexual beings in a male-dominated world. Attire, whether breeches or skirts, fades in importance as the dramatist explores the potential for independence by single women with wealth when unhampered by brothers or fathers.

Notes

[1] Louis B. Wright, 491-507 and passim. Juliet Dusinberre ascribes the debates on women's rights in the late sixteenth century to the rise of Puritanism, which encouraged mutual respect between husband and wife. See especially the introduction and 231-40. Linda T. Fitz, although less optimistic about women's achieving new rights, believes that the magnitude of the literature dictating what women should do indicates that they were not following prescribed paths: "the irrepressible spirit of those Renaissance English women . . . made sober treatises necessary" (18). Preceding the earliest production of *Twelfth Night,* works such as Jane Anger's (1589) appeared and, as late as 1620, the John Chamberlain letter records the king's "express commandment . . . to inveigh vehemently against the insolencie of . . . women." See Edward Phillips Statham, 182-83. See also Lisa Jardine, 9-36, where she also discusses the censuring of boys playing women's roles. She also quotes a letter of John Rainoldes in 1592 citing Scripture that says: "a woman shall not weare that which pertaineth to a man, nether shall a man put on womans raiment: for all that do so are abhomination to the lord thy god" (14).

As Linda Woodbridge writes:

> In 1620, a controversy about women which had been simmering for nearly fifty years came to a boil in two essays, "Hic Mulier," an attack on women who wear masculine clothing, and "Haec-Vir," an answering defense which attacks male foppishness. In the unpromising context of fashion, the two essays really joined combat on the nature of the sexes. . . . The transvestite controversy began, as nearly as we can tell, in about the 1570s, when some women began adopting masculine attire.
>
> (139)

Woodbridge then cites George Gascoigne's satire *The Steele Glas,* 1576; Phillip Stubbes's *Anatomy of Abuses,* 1583; and William Averell's *A mervailous combat of contrarieties,* 1588 (Woodbridge, 140). She concludes that because the movement received no attention in the 1590s and early 1600s it "was apparently quiescent," comments not arising again until 1606 when Henry Parrot's *The Mous Trap* and Richard Niccols's *The Cuckow* appeared. According to Woodbridge, the movement then gained momentum, "climaxing between 1615 and 1620" (141). This supposes that because we have no literature during the intervening years, either none existed or women suddenly gave up this attire only to don it again around 1615 when Swetnam's *Arraignment of Lewd, Idle, Froward and Unconstant Women* appeared, followed by the anonymous *Hic Mulier; or, The Man-Woman: Being a Medicine to cure the Coltish Disease of the Staggers in the Masculine-Feminines of our Times,* 1620, and the anonymous response a week later, *Haec-Vir; or, The Womanish Man: Being an Answere to the late Booke intituled Hic-Mulier. Exprest in a briefe Dialogue between Haec-Vir the Womanish Man, and Hic-Mulier the Man-Woman* (Woodbridge, 142-46).

[2] Although some critics use the terms *self* and *other* to describe Shakespeare's relationship to, or perception of, his male and female characters, my reference is to de Beauvoir's use of these terms as they describe the self-perceptions of men and women.

[3] See the chapter "Growing Up," on *Romeo and Juliet*, in *Wooing, Wedding, and Power*.

[4] Aside from the scene transposition, which I discuss later, the following lines are excised in these works: the Bell edition; the Kemble edition and those deriving from it; the Irving edition where the scene is compressed with the later scene 4; the French edition; *TN* 21 (listed as "Ada Rehan's" but using the French text, not that of Augustin Daly, her manager); and the Southern-Marlowe typescript—among others:

> O spirit of love, how quick and fresh art thou,
> That notwithstanding thy capacity
> Receiveth as the sea, nought enters there,
> Of what validity and pitch soe'er,
> But falls into abatement and low price
> Even in a minute. So full of shapes is fancy
> That it alone is high fantastical.
>
> (I.i.9-15)

Also frequently cut are the scene's closing lines also spoken by the Duke:

> Away before me to sweet beds of flow'rs,
> Love-thoughts lie rich when canopied with
>   bow'rs.
>
> (39-40)

[5] See Stephen Booth's article ("*Twelfth Night:* 1.1") on the verbal incongruities in this scene and the ways in which these incongruities prepare us for the rest of the play.

[6] Robert Kimbrough, in an excellent article on androgyny, theorizes that Viola adopts male disguise to prevent being sent home immediately by the Duke (her father's friend) if she appear at his palace in her own attire ("Androgyny," 29).

[7] Several versions that barely resembled Shakespeare's were presented during the seventeenth and early eighteenth centuries. However, no acting edition of the play appeared before 1750 although Hogan records productions, referring to several of these as "the original" (I:545-57). I suspect, however, that the Bell edition recorded what had been performed during the 1740s, prior to its publication. Odell notes only that: "both the Clown's songs, 'O Mistress mine,' and 'Come away, come away, Death,' with their surrounding context are omitted, more's the pity, but nothing of importance, otherwise, is cast aside" (II.29). Obviously, to Odell, Viola's reference to gold was unimportant; to paraphrase Odell, "more's the pity."

[8] As well as productions that used Kemble editions of 1810, 1811, and 1815 into the late 1850s, the Modern Standard Drama edition published by William Taylor and Company with Samuel French as general agent includes many of the same inserts and textual changes as do the Kemble editions. Because the French publications hardly ever bear a date, one must usually date them by the cast list for a particular production, which is printed in the edition. Among the books I have seen are those of William Burton, 1852, and Miss Neilson, dated 2/78. Thomas Hailes Lacy (1867) also followed Kemble's format. Charles Kean altered Kemble's 1811 edition of *Twelfth Night*, for the performance of 28 September 1850. See also Folger prompts *TN* 16, *TN* 17, *TN* 4, *TN* 5, *TN* 3, *TN* 18; also Shattuck, 469-89.

[9] While Henry Irving's adaptation differs somewhat from Kemble's, it contains many of the same excisions and follows Kemble by beginning at scene 2. Irving, however, does not introduce scene 1 until after I.iv.7. Thus Viola is present during his mooning for Olivia although the scene itself is much abbreviated, containing only lines 1 to 8 and 16 to 38. See Folger promptbooks *TN* 13, *TN* 15.

[10] See Schochet, 65-66, for a discussion of the hierarchical structure in the patriarchal family in Renaissance England. Obviously the dramatist was drawing on generally accepted patterns in his society. In this play, however, both Viola and Olivia have temporarily been freed from this pattern.

[11] Salingar's article has many fine insights, particularly where he compares Shakespeare's play with his sources. As a matter of fact, Salingar may have made this statement because he was transferring the identity of a source character for Olivia to Shakespeare's Olivia.

[12] The illustration is taken from Cassell, Petter & Galpin (G. Greatbach, Sculpt. [i.e. engraver]; C. Green, Pinxt [this word means he drew the original illustration]). Greatbach flourished in mid nineteenth century.

[13] Daly's illustrations of the performance have a warmer and younger looking Olivia than appears in the designs for the role.

[14] Folger prompts: 16, 17 (Kemble); 15 (Irving); 10, 21, 29 (Daly). University of Bristol: HBT 138 (Tree).

[15] Excised by Irving (*TN* 15).

[16] Although some critics have read this phrase as an indication that she has formerly been weeping and now her eyes are tearing for joy, I believe that she is referring to the image of Cesario that is creeping into her heart through her eyes. The language is ambiguous.

[17] Daly, Irving, Tree, and others followed Kemble's lead although often slightly altering the exact sequential revision. Henry Irving, after first adopting Kemble's opening with Viola's I.ii, then moved immediately to "Court-yard of Olivia's house" (11), with Sir Toby's line "What a plague means my niece, to take the death of her brother thus?" Since Irving played Malvolio, the play was reshaped to emphasize the comedic scenes, while yet retaining Viola's role, played by Ellen Terry. Orsino's Palace, the setting of the third scene, opens as does I.iv., where Viola as Cesario has already won her way into the Duke's favor. Only after having established this time sequence, does Irving insert Shakespeare's opening lines, "If music be the food of love, play on" (15), continuing with abbreviated material from that first scene, and then moving on to Orsino's conversation with Cesario and his assignment to her to woo Olivia.

[18] It follows the second interlude between Viola and the Duke (II.iv), where she almost discloses her identity (III.ii in Irving's version—*TN* 15).

[19] According to the *Concordance*, Viola has 13.0 percent of the speeches, 13.0 percent of the lines and 13.2 percent of the words; Olivia has 12.7 percent of the speeches, 12.0 percent of the lines and 11.8 percent of the words. Actually the longest role belongs to Sir Toby who has 16.5 percent of the speeches, 14.0 percent of the lines, and 13.8 percent of the words, whereas Malvolio trails with 9.4 percent of the speeches, 11.0 percent of the lines, and 11.4 percent of the words. However Malvolio's role has frequently been taken by a lead actor since it allows for great antics and hamming. Spevack, *Concordance* 1:1162-1213.

[20] Irving begins his scene here, eliminating the earlier reference to Cesario. Sothern-Marlowe too delete the reference although it clearly anticipates the later intense interview between the two young women. Rather, in the Sothern-Marlowe typescript Maria's description of Malvolio (in the text's III.ii) immediately precedes his actual appearance (in the text's III.iv) without a break.

[21] Acknowledging the foolishness of excising the last six lines (16-21), the editor of the Bell edition even comments, "Why omit these lines? to us they seem necessary" (338), then prints them in small type at the bottom of the page. Daly also omits them. The entire soliloquy is crossed out in the Irving prompt, while Charles Kean (*TN* 14) cuts the entire scene.

[22] Several critics have recently written on the importance of the impact of the full text rather than of the ending, noting an overemphasis on closure. See, for example, Belsey, 187-88, and Jensen, 99-117.

Bibliography

Ames, Winthrop. Typescript of production of William Shakespeare's *Twelfth Night*. With notes on interpretations by critics. Billy Rose Theatre Collection, New York Public Library. *NCP+1906.

Anger, Jane. *Protection for Women*. 1589.

Baker, Herschel, ed. *Twelfth Night* by William Shakespeare. New York: Signet, 1965.

Barber, C. L. *Shakespeare's Festive Comedy*. Princeton: Princeton University Press, 1959. (*FC*)

Barton, Anne. "*As You Like It* and *Twelfth Night*: Shakespeare's Sense of an Ending." In Bradbury, 160-80.

Beauvoir, Simone de. *The Second Sex*. Translated and edited by H. M. Parshley. New York: Alfred A. Knopf, 1953. Reprint. Bantam Books, 1961.

Belsey, Catherine. "Disrupting Sexual Difference: Meaning and Gender in the Comedies." *Alternative Shakespeares*. Edited by John Drakakis, 166-90. London and New York: Methuen, 1985.

Booth, Stephen. "*Twelfth Night:* 1.1: The Audience as Malvolio." In *Shakespeare's Rough Magic*, edited by Peter Erickson and Coppélia Kahn, 149-67. Newark: University of Delaware Press; London and Toronto: Associated University Press, 1985.

Bradbury, Malcolm, and David Palmer, eds. *Shakespearian Comedy: Stratford-Upon-Avon Studies* 14. London: Edward Arnold Ltd., 1972.

Brown, John Russell. "The Presentation of Comedy: The First Ten Plays." In Bradbury, 9-30.

Bullough, Geoffrey, ed. *Narrative and Dramatic Sources of Shakespeare*. 8 vols. New York: Columbia University Press, 1957-75.

Cowl, Jane. *Twelfth Night* promptbook. New York Public Library. *NCP+1930.

[Daly, Augustin.] *Twelfe Night, or what you will*, by William Shakespere. Arranged to be played in four acts by Augustin Daly. Printed from the Prompt Book, and as produced at Daly's Theatre, 21 February 1893. With an Introductory Word by William Winter, Esq. Privately Printed for Augustin Daly, 1893. Folger Prompts *TN* 29, *TN* 10, *TN* 11.

Dash, Irene G. *Wooing, Wedding, and Power: Women in Shakespeare's Plays*. New York: Columbia University Press, 1981.

Dusinberre, Juliet. *Shakespeare and the Nature of Women*. London: Macmillan, 1975.

Fitz, L. T. "'What Says the Married Woman?': Marriage Theory and Feminism in the English Renaissance," *Mosaic* 13, no. 2 (1980): 1-22.

Furness, Horace Howard, ed. *A New Variorum Edition of Shakespeare*. Vol. 13. *Twelfe Night, or What you will*. Philadelphia: J. B. Lippincott Co., 1901.

Greg, W. W. *The Shakespeare First Folio*. 1955. Reprint. London: Oxford University Press, 1969.

Hogan, Charles Beecher. *Shakespeare in the Theatre, 1701-1800*. 2 vols. London: Oxford University Press, 1952-57.

[Irving, Henry]. *Twelfth Night* by William Shakespeare. London: George Bell and Sons, 1882. Folger Prompt TN 13.

———. *Twelfth Night* by William Shakespeare, As Arranged for the Stage by Henry Irving and presented at the Lyceum theatre on 8 July 1884. London: Chiswick Press, 1884. Folger Prompt TN 15.

James VI of Scotland, I of England. *Daemonologie, in forme of a Dialogue, Divided into three Bookes*. Edinburgh: Printed by Robert Walde-grave Printer to the Kings Majestie. An.1597.

Jardine, Lisa. *Still Harping on Daughters*. Totowa, N.J.: Barnes & Noble Books, 1983.

Jensen, Ejner J., *Shakespeare and the Ends of Comedy*. Drama and Performance Studies Series. Bloomington and Indianapolis: Indiana University Press, 1991.

Johnson, Samuel. *Johnson on Shakespeare*. Edited by Arthur Sherbo. Vols. 7 and 8 of *Works of Samuel Johnson*. New Haven: Yale University Press, 1968.

[Kemble, J. P.] *Twelfth Night; or What you will*. A Comedy. Revised by J. P. Kemble; & now first published as it is acted at the Theatre Royal in Covent Garden. London: Printed for the theatre, 1810 Folger prompts *TN* 16 (ms. cast list for 1818; bookplate and autograph of Walter Lacy; bookplate of Sir Henry Irving).

———. No t.p. 1810 or 1811. "Mr. Charles Kean. Prompt Copy" (embossed on cover). Charles Kean altered this edition of *Twelfth Night*, for the performance of 28 September 1850. Souvenir promptbook made in 1859 by T. W. Edmonds, the prompter. Folger prompt *TN* 14.

———. *Twelfth Night; or, What you will*. A comedy. Revised by J. P. Kemble; & now first published as it is acted at the Theatre Royal in Covent Garden. London: Printed for the Theatre. 1811 "Operatic version" by Frederick Reynolds, 1820 at Covent Garden. Folger prompt *TN* 17.

———. *Twelfth Night; or What you will*: a comedy. Revised by J. P. Kemble; and now published as it is performed at the Theatres Royal. London: Printed for John Miller, and sold in the theatres, 1815. Folger prompts *TN* 4 (in ink at top of p. 5: "Mr. J. B. Buckstone . . . 1859." ms. cast list for "July 2d 1856 Haymarket"), TN 6.

Kimbrough, Robert. "Androgyny Seen Through Shakespeare's Disguise." *Shakespeare Quarterly* 33 (1982): 17-33.

Leech, Clifford. *Twelfth Night and Shakespearian Comedy*. Toronto: Dalhousie University Press and University of Toronto, 1935.

Lothian, J.M., and T. W. Craik, eds. *Twelfth Night*. The Arden Shakespeare. London: Methuen, 1975.

Mahood, M. M., ed. *Twelfth Night* by William Shakespeare. Middlesex, England: Penguin Books, 1981.

Malcolmson, Cristina. "'What You Will': Social Mobility and Gender in *Twelfth Night*." In *The Matter of Difference: Materialist Feminist Criticism of Shakespeare*, edited by Valerie Wayne, 29-57. Ithaca: Cornell University Press, 1991.

Marsh, Ngaio. "A Note on a Production of *Twelfth Night*." *Shakespeare Survey* 8 (1955): 69-80.

Moi, Toril. *Sexual/Textual Politics: Feminist Literary Theory*. London and New York: Methuen, 1985.

Nevo, Ruth. *Comic Transformations in Shakespeare*. London and New York: Methuen, 1980.

Odell, George C. D. *Shakespeare from Betterton to Irving*. 2 vols. 1920. Reprint. New York: Dover, 1966.

Salingar, L. G. "The Design of *Twelfth Night*." *Shakespeare Quarterly* 9 (1958). Reprint in *Dramatic Form in Shakespeare and the Jacobeans*. Essays by Leo Salingar. London and New York: Cambridge University Press, 1986.

Schochet, Gordon J. *Patriarchalism in Political Thought*. New York: Basic Books, 1975.

Shakespeare, William. *Twelfth Night*. As Performed at the Theatres-Royal. London: John Bell, 1773.

———. *Twelfth Night or What You Will;* a comedy in five acts. As performed at the Theatres Royal, Drury Lane and Covent Garden. Printed under the authority of the managers, from the promptbook. With remarks by Mrs. Inchbald. London: Longman, Hurst, Rees, and Orme, 1808.

———. *Twelfth Night; or What You Will:* A comedy. With prefatory Remarks. The only edition existing which is faithfully marked with the stage business and stage directions; as it is performed at the Theatres Royal. by W. Oxberry, Comedian. London. Published for the proprietors, by W. Simpkin, and R. Marshall, stationers' Court, Ludgate-street; and C. Chapple, 59, Pall-mall. 1821. Folger prompt *TN* 20 (marked by Samuel Phelps and W. C. Williams, also reference to 1857 production on p. 69) (Shattuck dates this 1848).

———. *Twelfth Night; or What You Will:* A Comedy, In five Acts. London: Samuel French, publisher 89 Strand. New York: Samuel French & Son, publishers, 122 Nassau street. [n.d.]. (Autograph on front cover "Arranged by Miss Neilson 2/78"). Folger prompt *TN* 18.

———. *Twelfth Night; or What You Will:* A Comedy in five acts. With the stage business. New York: Wm. Taylor & Co. Modern Standard Drama no. 58. S. French, general agent. 151 Nassau Street. [n.d.]. [Folger prompt *TN* 5 (In ink on front paper cover, "Prompt Book Twelfth Night Burton's Theatre." In the hand of John Moore. According to Shattuck, the production was March 1852). Prompt *TN* 9 (cut and paste in a notebook: on cover in autograph "Twelfth Night Prompt Book Augustin Daly")].

———. *Twelfth Night; or What you will:* a comedy, in five acts. London, Thomas Hailes Lacy. [n.d.]. Folger prompt *TN* 3 (on first page: J. B. Buckstone . . . Theatre Royal, Haymarket, 1867).

———. *Twelfth Night*. Herbert Beerbohm Tree workbook, 1901. University of Bristol Collection.

———. *Twelfth Night; or What you will*. London, Edinburgh, & New York: Thomas Nelson and Sons. [n.d.]. P.359-428 from vol. 2 of *Dramatic Works*. Folger prompt *TN* 1, Viola Allen preparation copy for 1904 production.

———. *Twelfth Night*. Typescript of Winthrop Ames's production. *NCP+1906.

———. *Twelfth Night*. Published playscript. With producer's preface of Harley Granville-Barker. Produced at the Savoy Theatre, London. Opened 15 November 1912. London: William Heinemann, 1912.

———. *Twelfth Night*. As presented by Sothern-Marlowe [n.p., n.d]. Typescript (some notes refer to 1923 production). Folger prompt *TN* 31.

———. *Twelfth Night*. Joseph Papp, presents. New York Shakespeare Festival. Wilford Leach, director. Delacorte Theatre, Central Park, Summer 1986.

———. *Twelfth Night*. Stratford, Canada. 2-8 August 1988.

Shattuck, Charles H. *The Shakespeare Promptbooks*. Urbana and London: University of Illinois Press, 1965.

Shepherd, Simon. *Amazons and Warrior Women: Varieties of Feminism in Seventeenth-Century Drama*. Brighton, Sussex: Harvester Press, 1981.

Spevack, Marvin. *A Complete Concordance to the Works of Shakespeare*. 6 vols. Hildesheim, Germany: George Olms, 1968-70.

Statham, Edward Phillips. *A Jacobean Letter-Writer: The Life and Times of John Chamberlain*. London: 1920.

Tree, Herbert Beerbohm. *Twelfth Night* promptbook, 1901. Tree collection, University of Bristol, HBT 138.

Warnicke, Retha M. *Women of the English Renaissance and Reformation*. Westport, Conn.: Greenwood Press, 1983.

Woodbridge, Linda. *Women and the English Renaissance: Literature and the Nature of Womankind, 1540-1620*. Urbana and Chicago: University of Illinois Press, 1984.

Wright, Louis B. *Middle Class Culture in Elizabethan England*. Chapel Hill: University of North Carolina Press, 1935.

FURTHER READING

Bellringer, Alan W. "*Twelfth Night: or What You Will*: Alternatives." *Durham University Journal* LXXIV, No. 1, n.s. XLIII, No. 1 (December 1981): 1-13.

Evaluates the characters in *Twelfth Night* with reference to the theme of constancy versus flexibility. On one hand, Bellringer contends, Sir Toby and the other members of Olivia's household are each ruled by a single passion; by contrast, Orsino, Feste, Sebastian, and Viola demonstrate a willingness to modify their behavior and adapt to changing circumstances.

Breuer, Horst. "Shakespeare's Signior Fabian." *English Studies* 74, No. 5 (October 1993): 441-44.

Offers textual evidence to support the notion that Fabian is a member of the landed gentry, not one of Olivia's serving men. Brewer sees Fabian as a dramatic type or stock character—a humorous older gentleman who is contemptuous of parvenus and social climbers.

Cahill, Edward. "The Problem of Malvolio." *College Literature* 23, No. 2 (June 1996): 62-82.

A psychoanalytic evaluation of Olivia's steward and his connection to the main plot. From Cahill's perspective, Malvolio's confusion of identity and desire reflects the principal characters' search for love and selfhood.

Callaghan, Dympna. "'And all is semblative a woman's part': Body Politics and *Twelfth Night*." *Textual Practice* 7, No. 3 (Winter 1993): 428-52.

A feminist reading of the play's representations of the female body. Focusing on the scene in which Malvolio parses the forged letter, Callaghan asserts that both here and throughout *Twelfth Night*, the female body—as well as men who try to improve their social status—are ridiculed and disciplined because they threaten the patriarchal system.

Carroll, William C. "To Be and Not to Be: *The Comedy of Errors* and *Twelfth Night*." In *The Metamorphoses of Shakespearean Comedy*, pp. 63-102. Princeton: Princeton University Press, 1985.

Analyzes the linguistic and dramatic expressions of double perspectives in *Twelfth Night*. Carroll compares the characters who rigidly resist change with those whose capacity for self-transformation permits them to achieve redemption. His discussion of *Twelfth Night* appears on pp. 80-102 of this chapter.

Cave, Terence. "Recognition and the Reader." In *Comparative Criticism: A Yearbook* 2, edited by Elinor Shaffer, pp. 49-69. Cambridge: Cambridge University Press, 1980.

Assesses the application of the Aristotelian concept of anagnorisis to modern European dramatic theory—specifically to literary analyses of Corneille's *Héraclius* and Shakespeare's *Twelfth Night*. Translating anagnorisis as "recognition," Cave reads *Twelfth Night* as a comedy that both exploits and exposes rhetorical tricks, creating cognitive confusion of form and meaning.

Craik, T. W. "Critical Analysis by Acts and Scenes." In *Twelfth Night*, by William Shakespeare, edited by J. M. Lothian and T. W. Craik, pp. lxi-lxxix. Arden Edition. London: Routledge, 1975.

Traces the structural development of the principal and secondary plots as well as Shakespeare's elaboration on the theme of love.

Davies, Stevie. "A Note on Fools." In *Twelfth Night*, by William Shakespeare, edited by Stevie Davies, pp. 62-68. London: Penguin Books, 1993.

Discusses Feste as an emblem of the humanist tradition of Folly, which satirized human pretension and self-delusion. As Feste points out the affectations of all the other characters on stage, Davies notes, he implicitly mocks the audience's own hypocrises and poses.

Elam, Keir. "The Fertile Eunuch: *Twelfth Night*, Early Modern Intercourse, and the Fruits of Castration." *Shakespeare Quarterly* 47, No. 1 (Spring 1996): 1-36.

Argues that Viola's fleeting reference to emasculation—"present me as an eunuch" (I.ii.56)—is rich in significance for the play as a whole. Elam lays out the long tradition of the theme of castration—from Terence to Italian Renaissance *commedia* to post-Reformation English comedy—which Shakespeare drew on and reworked.

Freund, Elizabeth. "*Twelfth Night* and the Tyranny of Interpretation." *ELH* 53, No. 3 (Fall 1986): 471-89.

Uses *Twelfth Night* to compare semiotic and mimetic approaches to literary criticism. In Freund's judgment, the play illustrates the indeterminacy of language and is a perfect example of the challenge of recovering meaning from a text.

Hasler, Jörg. "The Dramaturgy of the Ending of *Twelfth Night*." In *Twelfth Night: Critical Essays*, edited by Stanley Wells, pp. 279-302. New York: Garland Publishing, 1986.

An analysis of the direct and indirect theatrical notation that governs the gestures, grouping, and movement of characters in the play's final scene. Hasler calls attention to the series of entrances that culminate in the appearance of Sebastian; the jarring interlude with Malvolio; and, most importantly, the way Cesario/Viola remains the focus of attention despite the fact that she is given few lines to speak.

Hunt, Maurice. "The Religion of *Twelfth Night*." *CLA Journal: Official Quarterly Publication of the College of Language Association* XXXVII, No. 2 (December 1993): 189-203.

Evaluates allusions in the play to Christian and other religious doctrines. In Hunt's view, the play satirizes the Puritan notion that Providence can be relied on to operate directly in human affairs and instead demonstrates that Providence works obliquely, through such natural agents as Time and Fortune.

Jardine, Lisa. "Twins and Travesties: Gender, Dependency and Sexual Availability in *Twelfth Night*." In *Erotic Politics: Desire on the Renaissance Stage*, edited by Susan Zimmerman, pp. 27-38.

Discerns in *Twelfth Night* a reflection of the sexual vulnerability of boys and young women in early modern England. The financial dependence of Viola and Sebastian leads each of them into household service, Jardine notes, and because of their subservient status both are objects of general erotic desire until they are safely married.

Muir, Kenneth. "*Twelfth Night.*" In *Shakespeare's Comic Sequence,* pp. 91-101. Liverpool: Liverpool University Press, 1979.

Praises *Twelfth Night* as the capstone of Shakespearean romantic comedy and comments particularly on its fully rounded characterization, the play's uniquely lyrical atmosphere, and the masterful way in which various plot strands are instigated.

Priest, Dale G. "'Or else this is a dream': Ambivalence and Madness in *Twelfth Night.*" *CLA Journal: Official Quarterly Publication of the College Language Association* XXXIV, No. 3 (March 1991): 371-83.

Focuses on the "darkhouse" scene—Feste's badgering of the imprisoned Malvolio—and the play's ambiguous treatment of comic madness. Priest claims that *Twelfth Night* demonstrates that madness can be a carnivalesque release from social decorum, a psychological delusion, or a perceptive vision of the illogical nature of human existence.

Scragg, Leah. "'Her C's, her U's, and her T's: why that?': A New Reply for Sir Andrew Aguecheek." *Review of English Studies: A Quarterly Journal of English Literature and the English Language* XLII, No. 165 (February 1991): 1-16.

Assesses the significance of Malvolio's repetition of "C...U...T... P" as he reads the forged missive in II. v. Elizabethan audiences would have enjoyed the bawdy implications of these initials, she remarks—"cut" was a vulgarism for the vagina, and "p" a slang abbreviation for "piss"—but this sequence of letters would also remind them to safeguard their wallets against *cut*purses and pickpockets, who found golden opportunities in theatrical playhouses.

Shapiro, Michael. "Anxieties of Intimacy: *Twelfth Night.*" In *Gender and Play on the Shakespearean Stage: Boy Heroines and Female Pages,* pp. 143-72. Ann Arbor: University of Michigan Press, 1996.

Compares *Twelfth Night*'s depiction of Cesario/Viola with other English plays of the Elizabethan and Jacobean eras that also feature a heroine disguised as a male. Shapiro contends that Shakespeare's treatment of the homoerotic possibilities inherent in this role is both fresh and subtle.

Slights, Camille. "The Principle of Recompense in *Twelfth Night.*" *Modern Language Review* 77, No. 3 (July 1982): 537-46.

Suggests that the design of *Twelfth Night* is governed by the principle of reciprocity—the continuing process of give-and-take that binds individuals together in a healthy community. Slights asserts that the action of the play moves from isolation and self-absorption toward each character's recognition of the necessity for mutual obligation and dependency in human society.

Smidt, Kristian. "Or, What You Will." In *Unconformities in Shakespeare's Later Comedies,* pp. 62-75. New York: St. Martin's Press, 1993.

Theorizes that Shakespeare heavily revised *Twelfth Night* after its completion and early staging. Smidt believes that the role of Feste is an interpolation, written to bring the famous Elizabethan stage clown Robert Armin into the cast, and that when Shakespeare added this character he overlooked the resulting textual anomalies—especially the mix-up of parts between Fabian and Feste.

Tromly, F. B. "*Twelfth Night:* Folly's Talents and the Ethics of Shakespearean Comedy." *Mosaic* VII, No. 3 (Spring 1974): 53-68.

Maintains that in this play Shakespeare shows folly as a positive value, indeed the principal means of coming to terms with human frailty and the harshness of the world. Tromly points out that it is delusion itself, created by Viola's disguise, that liberates Orsino and Olivia from their self-absorption and draws them into human society.

Videbæk, Bente A. "Feste in *Twelfth Night.*" In *The Stage Clown in Shakespeare's Theatre,* Greenwood Press, 1996, pp. 95-109.

Remarks on the nature of Feste's foolery, calling attention to the differences between Feste and Shakespeare's other court jester clowns.

Warren, Roger, and Stanley Wells. Introduction to *Twelfth Night, or What You Will,* by William Shakespeare, edited by Roger Warren and Stanley Wells, pp. 1-76. Oxford Shakespeare. Oxford: Clarendon Press, 1994.

An extensive overview of the play. The editors discuss a variety of issues, including *Twelfth Night*'s stage history, its Latin and Italian models, its complex presentation of romantic love, its characterization, and its dramatic structure.

Weiss, Theodore. "A Dying Fall: *Twelfth Night.*" In *The Breath of Clowns and Kings: Shakespeare's Early Comedies and Histories,* pp. 298-330. New York: Atheneum, 1971.

Views *Twelfth Night* as Shakespeare's most graceful and mellow comedy, but acknowledges an undertone of poignancy as well. Emphasizing Shakespeare's mature artistry Weiss proceeds through the play scene by scene to demonstrate its author's sure-handed control of tone, characterization, and dramatic effects.

Westerweel, Bart. "The Dialogic Imagination: The European Discovery of Time and Shakespeare's Mature Comedies." In *Renaissance Culture in Context: Theory and Practice,* edited by Jean R. Brink and William F. Gentrup, pp. 54-74. Aldershot, England: Scolar Press, 1993.

>Examines the paradoxical nature of time in *Twelfth Night* and *As You Like It.* Westerweel argues that each character in these two comedies inhabits a different and distinctive world of time; in the case of *Twelfth Night,* he calls particular attention to Orsino's fanciful image of a pastoral golden age, Feste's solid footing in the present, and Viola's belief in providential time.

Westlund, Joseph. "*Twelfth Night:* Idealization as an Issue." In *Shakespeare's Reparative Comedies: A Psychoanalytic View of the Middle Plays,* pp. 93-119. Chicago: University of Chicago Press, 1984.

>Finds consistency in the characterization of Orsino and Olivia, and contends that the apparently sudden shifts in their affections in the final scene are psychologically plausible. Westlund proposes that Orsino and Olivia are initially narcissistic and lack self-confidence, but Viola's receptivity to their needs helps them gain less idealistic appraisals of themselves, so they can recognize appropriate objects of desire.

Willbern, David. "Malvolio's Fall." *Shakespeare Quarterly* 29, No. 1 (Winter 1978): 85-90.

>Analyzes the gulling of Malvolio in relation to both the prevailing theme of festivity and the underlying tone of melancholy in *Twelfth Night.* In Willbern's judgment, the steward is punished for three reasons: his rationality, his social-climbing, and his latent desire to sleep with Olivia.

Guide to *Shakespearean Criticism* Series

VOLUMES 1-10	Provides an historical overview of the critical response to each Shakespearean work. Includes criticism from the seventeenth century to the present.
VOLUMES 11, 12, 14, 15, 17, 18, 20, 21, 23, 24, 26	Examines the performance history of Shakespeare's plays on the stage and screen through eyewitness reviews and retrospective evaluations of individual productions. Also provides comparisons of major interpretations and discusses staging issues.
VOLUMES 27, 29-31, 33-36, 38-41, 43, 44-46	Focuses on criticism published after 1960. Each volume is ordered around a theme, such as politics, religion, or sexuality, with a topic entry that introduces the volume and several entries devoted to individual works.
Yearbooks: **VOLUMES 13, 16, 19, 22, 25, 28, 32, 37, 42**	Compiled annually beginning in 1989. Includes the most noteworthy essays of the year published on Shakespeare as recommended by an international advisory board of distinguished Shakespearean scholars.

Cumulative Character Index

The Cumulative Character Index identifies the principal characters of discussion in the criticism of each play and non-dramatic poem. The characters are arranged alphabetically. Page references indicate the beginning page number of each essay containing substantial commentary on that character.

Aaron
Titus Andronicus **4**: 632, 637, 650, 651, 653, 668, 672, 675; **27**: 255; **28**: 249, 330; **43**: 176

Adonis
Venus and Adonis **10**: 411, 420, 424, 427, 429, 434, 439, 442, 451, 454, 459, 466, 473, 489; **25**: 305, 328; **28**: 355; **33**: 309, 321, 330, 347, 352, 357, 363, 370, 377

Adriana
The Comedy of Errors **16**: 3; **34**: 211, 220, 238

Albany
King Lear **32**: 308

Alcibiades
Timon of Athens **25**: 198; **27**: 191

Angelo
Measure for Measure
    anxiety **16**: 114
    authoritarian portrayal of **23**: 307
    characterization **2**: 388, 390, 397, 402, 418, 427, 432, 434, 463, 484, 495, 503, 511; **13**: 84; **23**: 297; **32**: 81; **33**: 77
    hypocrisy **2**: 396, 399, 402, 406, 414, 421; **23**: 345, 358, 362
    repentance or pardon **2**: 388, 390, 397, 402, 434, 463, 511, 524

Anne (Anne Boleyn)
Henry VIII See **Boleyn**

Anne (Anne Page)
The Merry Wives of Windsor See **Page**

Antigonus
The Winter's Tale
    characterization **7**: 394, 451, 464
    death (Act III, scene iii) **7**: 377, 414, 464, 483; **15**: 518, 532; **19**: 366

Antonio
The Merchant of Venice
    excessive or destructive love **4**: 279, 284, 336, 344; **12**: 54; **37**: 86
    love for Bassanio **40**: 156
    melancholy **4**: 221, 238, 279, 284, 300, 321, 328; **22**: 69; **25**: 22
    pitiless **4**: 254
    as pivotal figure **12**: 25, 129
Twelfth Night **22**: 69

Antonio and Sebastian
The Tempest **8**: 295, 299, 304, 328, 370, 396, 429, 454; **13**: 440; **29**: 278, 297, 343, 362, 368, 377; **45**: 200

Antony
Antony and Cleopatra
    characterization **6**: 22, 23, 24, 31, 38, 41, 172, 181, 211; **16**: 342; **19**: 270; **22**: 217; **27**: 117
    Cleopatra, relationship with **6**: 25, 27, 37, 39, 48, 52, 53, 62, 67, 71, 76, 85, 100, 125, 131, 133, 136, 142, 151, 161, 163, 165, 180, 192; **27**: 82
    death scene **25**: 245
    dotage **6**: 22, 23, 38, 41, 48, 52, 62, 107, 136, 146, 175; **17**: 28
    nobility **6**: 22, 24, 33, 48, 94, 103, 136, 142, 159, 172, 202; **25**: 245
    political conduct **6**: 33, 38, 53, 107, 111, 146, 181
    public vs. private personae **6**: 165
    self-knowledge **6**: 120, 131, 175, 181, 192
    as superhuman figure **6**: 37, 51, 71, 92, 94, 178, 192; **27**: 110
    as tragic hero **6**: 38, 39, 52, 53, 60, 104, 120, 151, 155, 165, 178, 192, 202, 211; **22**: 217; **27**: 90
Julius Caesar
    characterization **7**: 160, 179, 189, 221, 233, 284, 320, 333; **17**: 269, 271, 272, 284, 298, 306, 313, 315, 358, 398; **25**: 272; **30**: 316
    funeral oration **7**: 148, 154, 159, 204, 210, 221, 238, 259, 350; **25**: 280; **30**: 316, 333, 362

Apemantus
Timon of Athens **1**: 453, 467, 483; **20**: 476, 493; **25**: 198; **27**: 166, 223, 235

Arcite
The Two Noble Kinsmen See **Palamon and Arcite**

Ariel
The Tempest **8**: 289, 293, 294, 295, 297, 304, 307, 315, 320, 326, 328, 336, 340, 345, 356, 364, 420, 458; **22**: 302; **29**: 278, 297, 362, 368, 377

Armado
Love's Labour's Lost **23:** 207

Arthur
King John **9:** 215, 216, 218, 219, 229, 240, 267, 275; **22:** 120; **25:** 98; **41:** 251, 277

Arviragus
Cymbeline See **Guiderius and Arviragus**

Audrey
As You Like It **46:** 122

Aufidius
Coriolanus **9:** 9, 12, 17, 19, 53, 121, 148, 153, 157, 169, 180, 193; **19:** 287; **25:** 263, 296; **30:** 58, 67, 89, 96, 133

Autolycus
The Winter's Tale **7:** 375, 380, 382, 387, 389, 395, 396, 414; **15:** 524; **22:** 302; **37:** 31; **45:** 333; **46:** 14, 33

Banquo
Macbeth **3:** 183, 199, 208, 213, 278, 289; **20:** 279, 283, 406, 413; **25:** 235; **28:** 339

Baptista
The Taming of the Shrew **9:** 325, 344, 345, 375, 386, 393, 413

Barnardine
Measure for Measure **13:** 112

Bassanio
The Merchant of Venice **25:** 257; **37:** 86; **40:** 156

the Bastard
King John See **Faulconbridge (Philip) the Bastard**

Beatrice and Benedick
Much Ado about Nothing
    Beatrice's femininity **8:** 14, 16, 17, 24, 29, 38, 41, 91; **31:** 222, 245
    Beatrice's request to "kill Claudio" (Act IV, scene i) **8:** 14, 17, 33, 41, 55, 63, 75, 79, 91, 108, 115; **18:** 119, 120, 136, 161, 245, 257
    Benedick's challenge of Claudio (Act V, scene i) **8:** 48, 63, 79, 91; **31:** 231
    Claudio and Hero, compared with **8:** 19, 28, 29, 75, 82, 115; **31:** 171, 216
    marriage and the opposite sex, attitudes toward **8:** 9, 13, 14, 16, 19, 29, 36, 48, 63, 77, 91, 95, 115, 121; **16:** 45; **31:**216
    mutual attraction **8:** 13, 14, 19, 24, 29, 33, 41, 75
    nobility **8:** 13, 19, 24, 29, 36, 39, 41, 47, 82, 91, 108
    popularity **8:** 13, 38, 41, 53, 79
    transformed by love **8:** 19, 29, 36, 48, 75, 91, 95, 115; **31:** 209, 216
    unconventionality **8:** 48, 91, 95, 108, 115, 121
    vulgarity **8:** 11, 12, 33, 38, 41, 47
    wit and charm **8:** 9, 12, 13, 14, 19, 24, 27, 28, 29, 33, 36, 38, 41, 47, 55, 69, 95, 108, 115; **31:** 241

Belarius
Cymbeline **4:** 48, 89, 141

Benedick
Much Ado about Nothing See **Beatrice and Benedick**

Berowne
Love's Labour's Lost **2:** 308, 324, 327; **22:** 12; **23:** 184, 187; **38:** 194

Bertram
All's Well That Ends Well
    characterization **7:** 15, 27, 29, 32, 39, 41, 43, 98, 113; **26:** 48; **26:** 117
    conduct **7:** 9, 10, 12, 16, 19, 21, 51, 62, 104
    physical desire **22:** 78
    transformation or redemption **7:** 10, 19, 21, 26, 29, 32, 54, 62, 81, 90, 93, 98, 109, 113, 116, 126; **13:** 84

Bianca
The Taming of the Shrew **9:** 325, 342, 344, 345, 360, 362, 370, 375
    Bianca-Lucentio subplot **9:** 365, 370, 375, 390, 393, 401, 407, 413, 430; **16:** 13; **31:** 339

the boar
Venus and Adonis **10:** 416, 451, 454, 466, 473; **33:** 339, 347, 370

Boleyn (Anne Boleyn)
Henry VIII **2:** 21, 24, 31; **41:** 180

Bolingbroke
Richard II See **Henry (King Henry IV, previously known as Bolingbroke)**

Borachio and Conrade
Much Ado about Nothing **8:** 24, 69, 82, 88, 111, 115

Bottom
A Midsummer Night's Dream
    awakening speech (Act IV, scene i) **3:** 406, 412, 450, 457, 486, 516; **16:** 34
    folly of **46:** 1, 14, 29, 60
    imagination **3:** 376, 393, 406, 432, 486; **29:** 175, 190; **45:** 147
    self-possession **3:** 365, 376, 395, 402, 406, 480; **45:** 158
    Titania, relationship with **3:** 377, 406, 441, 445, 450, 457, 491, 497; **16:** 34; **19:** 21; **22:** 93; **29:** 216; **45:** 160
    transformation **3:** 365, 377, 432; **13:** 27; **22:** 93; **29:** 216; **45:** 147, 160

Brabantio
Othello **25:** 189

Brutus
Coriolanus See **the tribunes**
Julius Caesar
    arrogance **7:** 160, 169, 204, 207, 264, 277, 292, 350; **25:** 280; **30:** 351
    as chief protagonist or tragic hero **7:** 152, 159, 189, 191, 200, 204, 242, 250, 253, 264, 268, 279, 284, 298, 333; **17:** 272, 372, 387
    citizenship **25:** 272
    funeral oration **7:** 154, 155, 204, 210, 350
    motives **7:** 150, 156, 161, 179, 191, 200, 221, 227, 233, 245, 292, 303, 310, 320, 333, 350; **25:** 272; **30:** 321, 358
    nobility or idealism **7:** 150, 152, 156, 159, 161, 179, 189, 191, 200, 221, 242, 250, 253, 259, 264, 277, 303, 320; **17:** 269, 271, 273, 279, 280, 284, 306, 308, 321, 323, 324, 345, 358; **25:** 272, 280; **30:** 351, 362
    political ineptitude or lack of judgment **7:** 169, 188, 200, 205, 221, 245, 252, 264, 277, 282, 310, 316, 331, 333, 343; **17:** 323, 358, 375, 380
    self-knowledge or self-deception **7:** 191, 200, 221, 242, 259, 264, 268, 279, 310, 333, 336, 350; **25:** 272; **30:** 316
    soliloquy (Act II, scene i) **7:** 156, 160, 161, 191, 221, 245, 250, 253, 264, 268, 279, 282, 292, 303, 343, 350; **25:** 280; **30:** 333
The Rape of Lucrece **10:** 96, 106, 109, 116, 121, 125, 128, 135

Buckingham
Henry VIII **22:** 182; **24:** 129, 140; **37:** 109

Cade (Jack [John] Cade)
Henry VI, Parts 1, 2, and 3 **3:** 35, 67, 92, 97, 109; **16:** 183; **22:** 156; **25:** 102; **28:** 112; **37:** 97; **39:** 160, 196, 205

Caesar
Julius Caesar
    ambiguous nature **7:** 191, 233, 242, 250, 272, 298, 316, 320
    arrogance **7:** 160, 207, 218, 253, 272, 279, 298; **25:** 280
    idolatry **22:** 137
    leadership qualities **7:** 161, 179, 189, 191, 200, 207, 233, 245, 253, 257, 264, 272, 279, 284, 298, 310, 333; **17:** 317, 358; **22:** 280; **30:** 316, 326
    as tragic hero **7:** 152, 200, 221, 279; **17:** 321, 377, 384
    weakness **7:** 161, 167, 169, 179, 187, 188, 191, 207, 218, 221, 233, 250, 253, 298; **17:** 358; **25:** 280

Caliban
The Tempest **8:** 286, 287, 289, 292, 294, 295, 297, 302, 304, 307, 309, 315, 326, 328, 336, 353, 364, 370, 380, 390, 396, 401, 414, 420, 423, 429, 435, 454; **13:** 424, 440; **15:** 189, 312, 322, 374, 379; **22:** 302; **25:** 382; **28:** 249; **29:** 278, 292, 297, 343, 368, 377, 396; **32:** 367; **45:** 211, 219, 226, 259

Calphurnia
Julius Caesar
    Calphurnia's dream **45:** 10

Cambridge
Henry V See **traitors**

Canterbury and the churchmen
Henry V **5:** 193, 203, 205, 213, 219, 225, 252, 260; **22:** 137; **30:** 215, 262

Cardinal Wolsey
Henry VIII See **Wolsey**

Cassio
Othello **25:** 189

Cassius
Julius Caesar **7:** 156, 159, 160, 161, 169, 179, 189, 221, 233, 303, 310, 320, 333, 343; **17:** 272, 282, 284, 344, 345, 358; **25:** 272, 280; **30:** 351; **37:** 203

Celia
As You Like It **46:** 94

Chorus
Henry V
role of **5:** 186, 192, 226, 228, 230, 252, 264, 269, 281, 293; **14:** 301, 319, 336; **19:** 133; **25:** 116, 131; **30:** 163, 202, 220

the churchmen
Henry V See **Canterbury and the churchmen**

Claudio
Much Ado about Nothing
boorish behavior **8:** 9, 24, 33, 36, 39, 44, 48, 63, 79, 82, 95, 100, 111, 115; **31:** 209
credulity **8:** 9, 17, 19, 24, 29, 36, 41, 47, 58, 63, 75, 77, 82, 95, 100, 104, 111, 115, 121; **31:** 241
mercenary traits **8:** 24, 44, 58, 82, 91, 95
noble qualities **8:** 17, 19, 29, 41, 44, 58, 75
reconciliation with Hero **8:** 33, 36, 39, 44, 47, 82, 95, 100, 111, 115, 121
repentance **8:** 33, 63, 82, 95, 100, 111, 115, 121; **31:** 245
sexual insecurities **8:** 75, 100, 111, 115, 121

Claudius
Hamlet **13:** 502; **16** 246; **21:** 259, 347, 361, 371; **28:** 232, 290; **35:** 104, 182; **44:** 119, 241

Cleopatra
Antony and Cleopatra
Antony, relationship with **6:** 25, 27, 37, 39, 48, 52, 53, 62, 67, 71, 76, 85, 100, 125, 131, 133, 136, 142, 151, 161, 163, 165, 180, 192; **25:** 257; **27:** 82
contradictory or inconsistent nature **6:** 23, 24, 27, 67, 76, 100, 104, 115, 136, 151, 159, 202; **17:** 94, 113; **27:** 135
costume **17:** 94
creativity **6:** 197
death **6:** 23, 25, 27, 41, 43, 52, 60, 64, 76, 94, 100, 103, 120, 131, 133, 136, 140, 146, 161, 165, 180, 181, 192, 197, 208; **13:** 383; **17:** 48, 94; **25:** 245; **27:** 135
personal attraction of **6:** 24, 38, 40, 43, 48, 53, 76, 104, 115, 155; **17:** 113
staging issues **17:** 94, 113
as subverter of social order **6:** 146, 165
as superhuman figure **6:** 37, 51, 71, 92, 94, 178, 192; **27:** 110

as tragic heroine **6:** 53, 120, 151, 192, 208; **27:** 144
as voluptuary or courtesan **6:** 21, 22, 25, 41, 43, 52, 53, 62, 64, 67, 76, 146, 161

Cloten
Cymbeline **4:** 20, 116, 127, 155; **22:** 302, 365; **25:** 245; **36:** 99, 125, 142, 155

Collatine
The Rape of Lucrece **10:** 98, 131; **43:** 102

Cominius
Coriolanus **25:** 245

Conrade
Much Ado about Nothing See **Borachio and Conrade**

Constance
King John **9:** 208, 210, 211, 215, 219, 220, 224, 229, 240, 251, 254; **16:** 161; **24:** 177, 184, 196

Cordelia
King Lear
attack on Britain **25:** 202
characterization **2:** 110, 116, 125, 170; **16:** 311; **25:** 218; **28:** 223, 325; **31:** 117, 149, 155, 162; **46:** 218, 225, 231, 242
as Christ figure **2:** 116, 170, 179, 188, 222, 286
rebelliousness **13:** 352; **25:** 202
on stage **11:** 158
transcendent power **2:** 137, 207, 218, 265, 269, 273

Corin
As You Like It See **pastoral characters**

Coriolanus
Coriolanus
anger or passion **9:** 19, 26, 45, 80, 92, 157, 164, 177, 189; **30:** 79, 96
as complementary figure to Aufidius **19:** 287
death scene (Act V, scene vi) **9:** 12, 80, 100, 117, 125, 144, 164, 198; **25:** 245, 263
as epic hero **9:** 130, 164, 177; **25:** 245
immaturity **9:** 62, 80, 84, 110, 117, 142; **30:** 140
inhuman attributes **9:** 65, 73, 139, 157, 164, 169, 189, 198; **25:** 263
internal struggle **9:** 31, 43, 45, 53, 72, 117, 121, 130; **44:** 93
introspection or self-knowledge, lack of **9:** 53, 80, 84, 112, 117, 130; **25:** 296; **30:** 133
isolation or autonomy **9:** 53, 65, 142, 144, 153, 157, 164, 180, 183, 189, 198; **30:** 58, 89, 111
manipulation by others **9:** 33, 45, 62, 80; **25:** 296
modesty **9:** 8, 12, 19, 26, 53, 78, 92, 117, 121, 144, 183; **25:** 296; **30:** 79, 96, 129, 133, 149
narcissism **30:** 111
noble or aristocratic attributes **9:** 15, 18, 19, 26, 31, 33, 52, 53, 62, 65, 84, 92, 100, 121, 148, 157, 169; **25:** 263; **30:** 67, 74, 96

pride or arrogance **9:** 8, 11, 12, 19, 26, 31, 33, 43, 45, 65, 78, 92, 121, 148, 153, 177; **30:** 58, 67, 74, 89, 96, 129
reconciliation with society **9:** 33, 43, 45, 65, 139, 169; **25:** 296
as socially destructive force **9:** 62, 65, 73, 78, 110, 142, 144, 153; **25:** 296
soliloquy (Act IV, scene iv) **9:** 84, 112, 117, 130
as tragic figure **9:** 8, 12, 13, 18, 25, 45, 52, 53, 72, 80, 92, 106, 112, 117, 130, 148, 164, 169, 177; **25:** 296; **30:** 67, 74, 79, 96, 111, 129; **37:** 283
traitorous actions **9:** 9, 12, 19, 45, 84, 92, 148; **25:** 296; **30:** 133
as unsympathetic character **9:** 12, 13, 62, 78, 80, 84, 112, 130, 157

the courser and the jennet
Venus and Adonis **10:** 418, 439, 466; **33:** 309, 339, 347, 352

Cranmer
Henry VIII
prophesy of **2:** 25, 31, 46, 56, 64, 68, 72; **24:** 146; **32:** 148; **41:** 120, 190

Cressida
Troilus and Cressida
as ambiguous figure **43:** 305
inconsistency **3:** 538; **13:** 53; **16:** 70; **22:** 339; **27:** 362
individual will vs. social values **3:** 549, 561, 571, 590, 604, 617, 626; **13:** 53; **27:** 396
infidelity **3:** 536, 537, 544, 554, 555; **18:** 277, 284, 286; **22:** 58, 339; **27:** 400; **43:** 298
lack of punishment **3:** 536, 537
as mother figure **22:** 339
objectification of **43:** 329
as sympathetic figure **3:** 557, 560, 604, 609; **18:** 284, 423; **22:** 58; **27:** 396, 400; **43:** 305

Dark Lady
Sonnets **10:** 161, 167, 176, 216, 217, 218, 226, 240, 302, 342, 377, 394; **25:** 374; **37:** 374; **40:** 273

the Dauphin
Henry V See **French aristocrats and the Dauphin**

Desdemona
Othello
as Christ figure **4:** 506, 525, 573; **35:** 360
culpability **4:** 408, 415, 422, 427; **13:** 313; **19:** 253, 276; **35:** 265, 352, 380
innocence **35:** 360; **43:** 32
as mother figure **22:** 339; **35:** 282
passivity **4:** 402, 406, 421, 440, 457, 470, 582, 587; **25:** 189; **35:** 380
spiritual nature of her love **4:** 462, 530, 559
staging issues **11:** 350, 354, 359; **13:** 327; **32:** 201

Diana
Pericles
as symbol of nature **22:** 315; **36:** 233

Dogberry and the Watch
Much Ado about Nothing **8**: 9, 12, 13, 17, 24, 28, 29, 33, 39, 48, 55, 69, 79, 82, 88, 95, 104, 108, 115; **18**: 138, 152, 205, 208, 210, 213, 231; **22**: 85; **31**: 171, 229; **46**: 60

Don John
Much Ado about Nothing See **John (Don John)**

Don Pedro
Much Ado about Nothing See **Pedro (Don Pedro)**

Dromio Brothers
Comedy of Errors **42**: 80

Duke
Measure for Measure
as authoritarian figure **23**: 314, 317, 347; **33**: 85
characterization **2**: 388, 395, 402, 406, 411, 421, 429, 456, 466, 470, 498, 511; **13**: 84, 94, 104; **23**: 363, 416; **32**: 81; **42**: 1; **44**: 89
as dramatic failure **2**: 420, 429, 441, 479, 495, 505, 514, 522
godlike portrayal of **23**: 320
noble portrayal of **23**: 301
speech on death (Act III, scene i) **2**: 390, 391, 395
Othello **25**: 189

Edgar
King Lear **28**: 223; **32**: 212; **32**: 308; **37**: 295
Edgar-Edmund duel **22**: 365

Edmund
King Lear **25**: 218; **28**: 223
Edmund's forged letter **16**: 372

Edmund of Langley, Duke of York
Richard II See **York**

Elbow
Measure for Measure **22**: 85; **25**: 12

Elbow (Mistress Elbow)
Measure for Measure **33**: 90

elder characters
All's Well That Ends Well **7**: 9, 37, 39, 43, 45, 54, 62, 104

Elizabeth I
Love's Labour's Lost **38**: 239

Emilia
Othello **4**: 386, 391, 392, 415, 587; **35**: 352, 380; **43**: 32
The Two Noble Kinsmen **9**: 460, 470, 471, 479, 481; **19**: 394; **41**: 372, 385; **42**: 361

Enobarbus
Antony and Cleopatra **6**: 22, 23, 27, 43, 94, 120, 142; **16**: 342; **17**: 36; **22**: 217; **27**: 135

fairies
A Midsummer Night's Dream **3**: 361, 362, 372, 377, 395, 400, 423, 450, 459, 486; **12**: 287, 291, 294, 295; **19**: 21; **29**: 183, 190; **45**: 147

Falstaff
Henry IV, Parts 1 and 2
characterization **1**: 287, 298, 312, 333; **25**: 245; **28**: 203; **39**: 72, 134, 137, 143
as comic figure **1**: 287, 311, 327, 344, 351, 354, 357, 410, 434; **39**: 89; **46**: 1, 48, 52
as coward or rogue **1**: 285, 290, 296, 298, 306, 307, 313, 317, 323, 336, 337, 338, 342, 354, 366, 374, 391, 396, 401, 433; **14**: 7, 111, 125, 130, 133; **32**: 166
dual personality **1**: 397, 401, 406, 434
female attributes **13**: 183; **44**: 44
Iago, compared with **1**: 341, 351
Marxist interpretation **1**: 358, 361
as parody of the historical plot **1**: 314, 354, 359; **39**: 143
as positive character **1**: 286, 287, 290, 296, 298, 311, 312, 321, 325, 333, 344, 355, 357, 389, 401, 408, 434
rejection by Hal **1**: 286, 287, 290, 312, 314, 317, 324, 333, 338, 344, 357, 366, 372, 374, 379, 380, 389, 414; **13**: 183; **25**: 109; **39**: 72, 89
as satire of feudal society **1**: 314, 328, 361; **32**: 103
as scapegoat **1**: 389, 414
stage interpretations **14**: 4, 6, 7, 9, 15, 116, 130, 146
as subversive figure **16**: 183; **25**: 109
as Vice figure **1**: 342, 361, 366, 374
Henry V **5**: 185, 186, 187, 189, 192, 195, 198, 210, 226, 257, 269, 271, 276, 293, 299; **28**: 146; **46**: 48
The Merry Wives of Windsor
characterization in *1* and *2 Henry IV*, compared with **5**: 333, 335, 336, 337, 339, 346, 347, 348, 350, 373, 400; **18**: 5, 7, 75, 86; **22**: 93
diminishing powers **5**: 337, 339, 343, 347, 350, 351, 392
as Herne the Hunter **38**: 256, 286
incapability of love **5**: 335, 336, 339, 346, 348; **22**: 93
personification of comic principle or Vice figure **5**: 332, 338, 369, 400; **38**: 273
recognition and repentance of follies **5**: 338, 341, 343, 348, 369, 374, 376, 397
sensuality **5**: 339, 343, 353, 369, 392
shrewdness **5**: 332, 336, 346, 355
threat to community **5**: 343, 369, 379, 392, 395, 400; **38**: 297
vanity **5**: 332, 339
victimization **5**: 336, 338, 341, 347, 348, 353, 355, 360, 369, 373, 374, 376, 392, 397, 400

Faulconbridge, (Philip) the Bastard
King John **41**: 205, 228, 251, 260, 277
as chorus or commentator **9**: 212, 218, 229, 248, 251, 260, 271, 284, 297, 300; **22**: 120
as comic figure **9**: 219, 271, 297
development **9**: 216, 224, 229, 248, 263, 271, 275, 280, 297; **13**: 158, 163
as embodiment of England **9**: 222, 224, 240, 244, 248, 271
heroic qualities **9**: 208, 245, 248, 254, 263, 271, 275; **25**: 98
political conduct **9**: 224, 240, 250, 260, 280, 297; **13**: 147, 158; **22**: 120

Fenton
The Merry Wives of Windsor
Anne Page-Fenton plot **5**: 334, 336, 343, 353, 376, 390, 395, 402; **22**: 93

Ferdinand
The Tempest **8**: 328, 336, 359, 454; **19**: 357; **22**: 302; **29**: 362, 339, 377

Feste
Twelfth Night
characterization **1**: 558, 655, 658; **26**: 233, 364; **46**: 1, 14, 18, 33, 52, 60, 303, 310
role in play **1**: 546, 551, 553, 566, 570, 571, 579, 635, 658; **46**: 297, 303, 310
song **1**: 543, 548, 561, 563, 566, 570, 572, 603, 620, 642; **46**: 297
gender issues **19**: 78; **34**: 344; **37**: 59

Fluellen
Henry V **30**: 278; **37**: 105

Fool
King Lear **2**: 108, 112, 125, 156, 162, 245, 278, 284; **11**: 17, 158, 169; **22**: 227; **25**: 202; **28**: 223; **46**: 1, 14, 18, 24, 33, 52, 191, 205, 210, 218, 225

Ford
The Merry Wives of Windsor **5**: 332, 334, 343, 355, 363, 374, 379, 390; **38**: 273

Fortinbras
Hamlet **21**: 136, 347; **28**: 290

French aristocrats and the Dauphin
Henry V **5**: 188, 191, 199, 205, 213, 281; **22**: 137; **28**: 121

Friar
Much Ado about Nothing **8**: 24, 29, 41, 55, 63, 79, 111

Friar John
Romeo and Juliet See **John (Friar John)**

Friar Lawrence
Romeo and Juliet See **Lawrence (Friar Lawrence)**

the Friend
Sonnets **10**: 279, 302, 309, 379, 385, 391, 394

Gardiner (Stephen Gardiner)
Henry VIII **24**: 129

Gaunt
Richard II **6**: 255, 287, 374, 388, 402, 414; **24**: 274, 322, 325, 414, 423; **39**: 263, 279

Gertrude
Hamlet **21**: 259, 347, 392; **28**: 311; **32**: 238; **35**: 182, 204, 229; **43**: 12; **44**: 119, 160, 189, 195, 237, 247

Ghost
Hamlet **1**: 75, 76, 84, 85, 128, 134, 138, 154, 171, 218, 231, 254; **16**: 246; **21**: 17, 44, 112,

151, 334, 371, 377, 392; **25:** 288; **35:** 152, 157, 174, 237; **44:** 119

Gloucester
King Lear **46:** 254

Gobbo, Launcelot
The Merchant of Venice **46:** 24, 60

Goneril
King Lear **31:** 151; **46:** 231, 242

Gonzalo
The Tempest **22:** 302; **29:** 278, 343, 362, 368; **45:** 280

Gower chorus
Pericles **2:** 548, 575; **15:** 134, 141, 143, 145, 149, 152, 177; **36:** 279; **42:** 352

Grey
Henry V See **traitors**

Guiderius and Arviragus
Cymbeline **4:** 21, 22, 89, 129, 141, 148; **25:** 319; **36:** 125, 158

Hal
See **Henry (King Henry V, formerly known as Prince Henry [Hal] of Wales)**

Hamlet
Hamlet
  as a fool **46:** 1, 29, 52, 74
  delay **1:** 76, 83, 88, 90, 94, 98, 102, 103, 106, 114, 115, 116, 119, 120, 148, 151, 166, 171, 179, 188, 191, 194, 198, 221, 268; **13:** 296, 502; **21:** 81; **25:** 209, 288; **28:** 223; **35:** 82, 174, 212, 215, 237; **44:** 180, 209, 219, 229
  divided nature **16:** 246; **28:** 223; **32:** 288; **35:** 182, 215; **37:** 241
  elocution of the character's speeches **21:** 96, 104, 112, 127, 132, 172, 177, 179, 194, 245, 254, 257
  madness **1:** 76, 81, 83, 95, 102, 106, 128, 144, 154, 160, 234; **21:** 35, 50, 72, 81, 99, 112, 311, 339, 355, 361, 371, 377, 384; **35:** 117, 132, 134, 140, 144, 212; **44:** 107, 119, 152, 209, 219, 229
  melancholy **21:** 99, 112, 177, 194; **35:** 82, 95, 117; **44:** 209, 219
  as negative character **1:** 86, 92, 111, 171, 218; **21:** 386; **25:** 209; **35:** 167
  reaction to his father's death **22:** 339; **35:** 104, 174; **44:** 133, 160, 180, 189
  reaction to Gertrude's marriage **1:** 74, 120, 154, 179; **16:** 259; **21:** 371; **22:** 339; **35:** 104, 117; **44:** 133, 160, 189, 195
  romantic aspects of the character **21:** 96; **44:** 198
  as scourge or purifying figure **1:** 144, 209, 242; **25:** 288; **35:** 157
  sentimentality vs. intellectuality **1:** 75, 83, 88, 91, 93, 94, 96, 102, 103, 115, 116, 120, 166, 191; **13:** 296; **21:** 35, 41, 44, 72, 81, 89, 99, 129, 132, 136, 172, 213, 225, 339, 355, 361, 371, 377, 379, 381, 386; **25:** 209; **44:** 198

soliloquies **1:** 76, 82, 83, 148, 166, 169, 176, 191; **21:** 17, 31, 44, 53, 89, 112, 268, 311, 334, 347, 361, 384, 392; **25:** 209; **28:** 223; **44:** 107, 119, 229
theatrical interpretations **21:** 11, 31, 78, 101, 104, 107, 160, 177, 179, 182, 183, 192, 194, 197, 202, 203, 208, 213, 225, 232, 237, 249, 253, 254, 257, 259, 274, 311, 339, 347, 355, 361, 371, 377, 380; **44:** 198
virility **21:** 213, 301, 355

Helena
All's Well That Ends Well
  as agent of reconciliation, renewal, or grace **7:** 67, 76, 81, 90, 93, 98, 109, 116
  as dualistic or enigmatic character **7:** 15, 27, 29, 39, 54, 58, 62, 67, 76, 81, 98, 113, 126; **13:** 66; **22:** 78; **26:** 117
  as "female achiever" **19:** 113; **38:** 89
  desire **38:** 96; **44:** 35
  pursuit of Bertram **7:** 9, 12, 15, 16, 19, 21, 26, 27, 29, 32, 43, 54, 76, 116; **13:** 77; **22:** 78
  virginity **38:** 65
  virtue and nobility **7:** 9, 10, 12, 16, 19, 21, 27, 32, 41, 51, 58, 67, 76, 86, 126; **13:** 77
A Midsummer Night's Dream **29:** 269

Henry (King Henry IV, previously known as Bolingbroke)
Henry IV, Parts 1 and 2 **39:** 123, 137
Richard II
  Bolingbroke and Richard as opposites **24:** 423
  Bolingbroke-Mowbray dispute **22:** 137
  comic elements **28:** 134
  guilt **24:** 423; **39:** 279
  language and imagery **6:** 310, 315, 331, 347, 374, 381, 397; **32:** 189
  as Machiavellian figure **6:** 305, 307, 315, 331, 347, 388, 393, 397; **24:** 428
  as politician **6:** 255, 263, 264, 272, 277, 294, 364, 368, 391; **24:** 330, 333, 405, 414, 423, 428; **39:** 256
  Richard, compared with **6:** 307, 315, 347, 374, 391, 393, 409; **24:** 346, 349, 351, 352, 356, 395, 419, 423, 428
  his silence **24:** 423
  structure, compared with **39:** 235
  usurpation of crown, nature of **6:** 255, 272, 289, 307, 310, 347, 354, 359, 381, 385, 393; **13:** 172; **24:** 322, 356, 383, 419; **28:** 178

Henry (King Henry V, formerly known as Prince Henry [Hal] of Wales)
Henry IV, Parts 1 and 2
  as the central character **1:** 286, 290, 314, 317, 326, 338, 354, 366, 374, 396; **39:** 72, 100
  dual personality **1:** 397, 406; **25:** 109, 151
  as Everyman **1:** 342, 366, 374
  fall from humanity **1:** 379, 380, 383
  general assessment **1:** 286, 287, 289, 290, 314, 317, 326, 327, 332, 357, 397; **25:** 245; **32:** 212; **39:** 134
  as ideal ruler **1:** 289, 309, 317, 321, 326, 337, 342, 344, 374, 389, 391, 434; **25:** 109; **39:** 123
  as a negative character **1:** 312, 332, 333, 357; **32:** 212

Richard II, compared with **1:** 332, 337; **39:** 72
Henry V
  brutality and cunning **5:** 193, 203, 209, 210, 213, 219, 233, 239, 252, 260, 271, 287, 293, 302, 304; **30:** 159; **43:** 24
  characterization in *1* and *2 Henry IV* contrasted **5:** 189, 190, 241, 304, 310; **19:** 133; **25:** 131; **32:** 157
  chivalry **37:** 187
  courage **5:** 191, 195, 210, 213, 228, 246, 257, 267
  disguise **30:** 169, 259
  education **5:** 246, 267, 271, 289; **14:** 297, 328, 342; **30:** 259
  emotion, lack of **5:** 209, 212, 233, 244, 264, 267, 287, 293, 310
  as heroic figure **5:** 192, 205, 209, 223, 244, 252, 257, 260, 269, 271, 299, 304; **28:** 121, 146; **30:** 237, 244, 252; **37:** 187
  humor **5:** 189, 191, 212, 217, 239, 240, 276
  intellectual and social limitations **5:** 189, 191, 203, 209, 210, 225, 226, 230, 293; **30:** 220
  interpersonal relations **5:** 209, 233, 267, 269, 276, 287, 293, 302, 318; **19:** 133; **28:** 146
  mercy **5:** 213, 267, 289, 293
  mixture of good and bad qualities **5:** 199, 205, 209, 210, 213, 244, 260, 304, 314; **30:** 262, 273
  piety **5:** 191, 199, 209, 217, 223, 239, 257, 260, 271, 289, 310, 318; **30:** 244; **32:** 126
  public vs. private selves **22:** 137; **30:** 169, 207
  self-doubt **5:** 281, 310
  slaughter of prisoners **5:** 189, 205, 246, 293, 318; **28:** 146
  speech **5:** 212, 230, 233, 246, 264, 276, 287, 302; **28:** 146; **30:** 163, 227

Henry (King Henry VI)
Henry VI, Parts 1, 2, and 3
  characterization **3:** 64, 77, 151; **39:** 160, 177
  source of social disorder **3:** 25, 31, 41, 115; **39:** 154, 187
  as sympathetic figure **3:** 73, 143, 154; **24:** 32

Henry (King Henry VIII)
Henry VIII
  as agent of divine retribution **2:** 49
  characterization **2:** 23, 39, 51, 58, 60, 65, 66, 75; **28:** 184; **37:** 109
  incomplete portrait **2:** 15, 16, 19, 35; **41:** 120
  as realistic figure **2:** 21, 22, 23, 25, 32

Henry (Prince Henry)
King John **41:** 277

Hermia
A Midsummer Night's Dream **29:** 225, 269; **45:** 117

Hermione
The Winter's Tale
  characterization **7:** 385, 395, 402, 412, 414, 506; **15:** 495, 532; **22:** 302, 324; **25:** 347; **32:** 388; **36:** 311
  restoration (Act V, scene iii) **7:** 377, 379, 384, 385, 387, 389, 394, 396, 412, 425, 436, 451,

452, 456, 464, 483, 501; **15:** 411, 412, 413, 518, 528, 532
supposed death **25:** 339

Hero
Much Ado about Nothing **8:** 13, 14, 16, 19, 28, 29, 44, 48, 53, 55, 82, 95, 104, 111, 115, 121; **31:** 231, 245

Holofernes
Love's Labour's Lost **23:** 207

Horatio
Hamlet **44:** 189

Hotspur
Henry IV, Parts 1 and 2 **25:** 151; **28:** 101; **39:** 72, 134, 137; **42:** 99
Henry V **5:** 189, 199, 228, 271, 302

Humphrey
Henry VI, Parts 1, 2, and 3 **13:** 131

Iachimo
Cymbeline **25:** 245, 319; **36:** 166

Iago
Othello
affinity with Othello **4:** 400, 427, 468, 470, 477, 500, 506; **25:** 189; **44:** 57
as conventional dramatic villain **4:** 440, 527, 545, 582
as homosexual **4:** 503
Machiavellian elements **4:** 440, 455, 457, 517, 545; **35:** 336, 347
motives **4:** 389, 390, 397, 399, 402, 409, 423, 424, 427, 434, 451, 462, 545, 564; **13:** 304; **25:** 189; **28:** 344; **32:** 201; **35:** 265, 276, 310, 336, 347; **42:** 273
revenge scheme **4:** 392, 409, 424, 451
as scapegoat **4:** 506
as victim **4:** 402, 409, 434, 451, 457, 470

Imogen
Cymbeline **4:** 21, 22, 24, 29, 37, 45, 46, 52, 56, 78, 89, 108; **15:** 23, 32, 105, 121; **19:** 411; **25:** 245, 319; **28:** 398; **32:** 373; **36:** 129, 142, 148
reawakening of (Act IV, scene ii) **4:** 37, 56, 89, 103, 108, 116, 150; **15:** 23; **25:** 245

Isabella
Measure for Measure **2:** 388, 390, 395, 396, 397, 401, 402, 406, 409, 410, 411, 418, 420, 421, 432, 437, 441, 466, 475, 491, 495, 524; **16:** 114; **23:** 278, 279, 280, 281, 282, 296, 344, 357, 363, 405; **28:** 102; **33:** 77, 85

Jack [John] Cade
Henry VI, Parts 1, 2, and 3 See **Cade**

the jailer's daughter
The Two Noble Kinsmen **9:** 457, 460, 479, 481, 486, 502; **41:** 340

Jaques
As You Like It
love-theme, relation to **5:** 103; **23:** 7, 37, 118, 128

as malcontent **5:** 59, 70, 84
melancholy **5:** 20, 28, 32, 36, 39, 43, 50, 59, 63, 68, 77, 82, 86, 135; **23:** 20, 26, 103, 104, 107, 109; **34:** 85; **46:** 88, 94
pastoral convention, relation to **5:** 61, 63, 65, 79, 93, 98, 114, 118
Seven Ages of Man speech (Act II, scene vii) **5:** 28, 52, 156; **23:** 48, 103, 105, 126, 138, 152; **46:** 88, 156, 164, 169
Shakespeare, relation to **5:** 35, 50, 154
as superficial critic **5:** 28, 30, 43, 54, 55, 63, 65, 68, 75, 77, 82, 86, 88, 98, 138; **34:** 85

the jennet
Venus and Adonis See **the courser and the jennet**

Jessica
The Merchant of Venice **4:** 196, 200, 228, 293, 342

Joan of Arc
Henry VI, Parts 1, 2, and 3 **16:** 131; **32:** 212

John (Don John)
Much Ado about Nothing **8:** 9, 12, 16, 17, 19, 28, 29, 36, 39, 41, 47, 48, 55, 58, 63, 82, 104, 108, 111, 121

John (Friar John)
Romeo and Juliet
detention of **5:** 448, 467, 470

John (King John)
King John **41:** 205, 260
death **9:** 212, 215, 216, 240
decline **9:** 224, 235, 240, 263, 275
Hubert, scene with (Act III, scene iii) **9:** 210, 212, 216, 218, 219, 280
moral insensibility **13:** 147, 163
negative qualities **9:** 209, 212, 218, 219, 229, 234, 235, 244, 245, 246, 250, 254, 275, 280, 297
positive qualities **9:** 209, 224, 235, 240, 244, 245, 263

Julia
The Two Gentlemen of Verona **6:** 450, 453, 458, 476, 494, 499, 516, 519, 549, 564; **40:** 312, 327, 374

Juliet
Romeo and Juliet See **Romeo and Juliet**

Launcelot Gobbo
The Merchant of Venice See **Gobbo**

Kate
The Taming of the Shrew
characterization **32:** 1; **43:** 61
final speech (Act V, scene ii) **9:** 318, 319, 329, 330, 338, 340, 341, 345, 347, 353, 355, 360, 365, 381, 386, 401, 404, 413, 426, 430; **19:** 3; **22:** 48
love for Petruchio **9:** 338, 340, 353, 430; **12:** 435
portrayals of **31:** 282
shrewishness **9:** 322, 323, 325, 332, 344, 345, 360, 365, 370, 375, 386, 393, 398, 404, 413

transformation **9:** 323, 341, 355, 370, 386, 393, 401, 404, 407, 419, 424, 426, 430; **16:** 13; **19:** 34; **22:** 48; **31:** 288, 295, 339, 351

Katherine
Henry V **5:** 186, 188, 189, 190, 192, 260, 269, 299, 302; **13:** 183; **19:** 217; **30:** 278; **44:** 44
Henry VIII
characterization **2:** 18, 19, 23, 24, 38; **24:** 129; **37:** 109; **41:** 180
Hermione, compared with **2:** 24, 51, 58, 76
politeness strategies **22:** 182
religious discourse **22:** 182
as tragic figure **2:** 16, 18

Kent
King Lear **25:** 202; **28:** 223; **32:** 212

King
All's Well That Ends Well **38:** 150

King Richard II
Richard II See **Richard**

King Richard III, formerly Richard, Duke of Gloucester
Richard III See **Richard**

Lady Macbeth
Macbeth See **Macbeth (Lady Macbeth)**

Laertes
Hamlet **21:** 347, 386; **28:** 290; **35:** 182

Launce and Speed
The Two Gentlemen of Verona
comic function of **6:** 438, 439, 442, 456, 458, 460, 462, 472, 476, 478, 484, 502, 504, 507, 509, 516, 519, 549; **40:** 312, 320

Lavatch
All's Well That Ends Well **26:** 64; **46:** 33, 52, 68

Lavinia
Titus Andronicus **27:** 266; **28:** 249; **32:** 212; **43:** 1, 170, 239, 247, 255, 262

Lawrence (Friar Lawrence)
Romeo and Juliet
contribution to catastrophe **5:** 437, 444, 470; **33:** 300
philosophy of moderation **5:** 427, 431, 437, 438, 443, 444, 445, 458, 467, 479, 505, 538
as Shakespeare's spokesman **5:** 427, 431, 437, 458, 467

Lear
King Lear
curse on Goneril **11:** 5, 7, 12, 114, 116
love-test and division of kingdom **2:** 100, 106, 111, 124, 131, 137, 147, 149, 151, 168, 186, 208, 216, 281; **16:** 351; **25:** 202; **31:** 84, 92, 107, 117, 149, 155; **46:** 231, 242
madness **2:** 94, 95, 98, 99, 100, 101, 102, 103, 111, 116, 120, 124, 125, 149, 156, 191, 208, 216, 281; **46:** 264
as scapegoat **2:** 241, 253

self-knowledge **2:** 103, 151, 188, 191, 213, 218, 222, 241, 249, 262; **25:** 218; **37:** 213; **46:** 191, 205, 225, 254, 264

Leontes
The Winter's Tale
characterization **19:** 431; **43:** 39; **45:** 366
jealousy **7:** 377, 379, 382, 383, 384, 387, 389, 394, 395, 402, 407, 412, 414, 425, 429, 432, 436, 464, 480, 483, 497; **15:** 514, 518, 532; **22:** 324; **25:** 339; **36:** 334, 344, 349; **44:** 66; **45:** 295, 297, 344, 358
Othello, compared with **7:** 383, 390, 412; **15:** 514; **36:** 334; **44:** 66
repentance **7:** 381, 389, 394, 396, 402, 414, 497; **36:** 318, 362; **44:** 66

Lucentio
The Taming of the Shrew **9:** 325, 342, 362, 375, 393

Lucio
Measure for Measure **13:** 104

Lucrece
The Rape of Lucrece
chastity **33:** 131, 138; **43:** 92
as example of Renaissance *virtù* **22:** 289; **43:** 148
heroic **10:** 84, 93, 109, 121, 128
patriarchal woman, model of **10:** 109, 131; **33:** 169, 200
self-responsibility **10:** 89, 96, 98, 106, 125; **33:** 195; **43:** 85, 92, 158
unrealistic **10:** 64, 65, 66, 121
verbose **10:** 64, 81, 116; **25:** 305; **33:** 169
as victim **22:** 294; **25:** 305; **32:** 321; **33:** 131, 195; **43:** 102, 158

Macbeth
Macbeth
ambition **44:** 284, 324
characterization **20:** 20, 42, 73, 107, 113, 130, 146, 151, 279, 283, 312, 338, 343, 379, 406, 413; **29:** 139, 152, 155, 165; **44:** 289
courage **3:** 172, 177, 181, 182, 183, 186, 234, 312, 333; **20:** 107; **44:** 315
disposition **3:** 173, 175, 177, 182, 186; **20:** 245, 376
imagination **3:** 196, 208, 213, 250, 312, 345; **20:** 245, 376; **44:** 351
as "inauthentic" king **3:** 245, 302, 321, 345
inconsistencies **3:** 202
as Machiavellian villain **3:** 280
manliness **20:** 113; **29:** 127, 133; **44:** 315
psychoanalytic interpretations **20:** 42, 73, 238, 376; **44:** 284, 289, 297, 324; **45:** 48, 58
Richard III, compared with **3:** 177, 182, 186, 345; **20:** 86, 92; **22:** 365; **44:** 269
as Satan figure **3:** 229, 269, 275, 289, 318
self-awareness **3:** 312, 329, 338; **16:** 317; **44:** 361
as sympathetic figure **3:** 229, 306, 314, 338; **29:** 139, 152; **44:** 269, 306, 337
as tragic hero **44:** 269, 306, 315, 324, 337

Macbeth (Lady Macbeth)
Macbeth
ambition **3:** 185, 219; **20:** 279, 345
characterization **20:** 56, 60, 65, 73, 140, 148, 151, 241, 279, 283, 338, 350, 406, 413; **29:** 109, 146
childlessness **3:** 219, 223
good and evil, combined traits of **3:** 173, 191, 213; **20:** 60, 107
inconsistencies **3:** 202; **20:** 54, 137
influence on Macbeth **3:** 171, 185, 191, 193, 199, 262, 289, 312, 318; **13:** 502; **20:** 345; **25:** 235; **29:** 133
psychoanalytic interpretations **20:** 345; **44:** 289, 297; **45:** 58
sleepwalking scene **44:** 261
as sympathetic figure **3:** 191, 193, 203

Macduff
Macbeth **3:** 226, 231, 253, 262,; **25:** 235; **29:** 127, 133, 155

MacMorris
Henry V **22:** 103; **28:** 159; **30:** 278

Malcolm
Macbeth **25:** 235

Malvolio
Twelfth Night
characterization **1:** 540, 544, 545, 548, 550, 554, 558, 567, 575, 577, 615; **26:** 207, 233, 273; **46:** 286
forged letter **16:** 372; **28:** 1
punishment **1:** 539, 544, 548, 549, 554, 555, 558, 563, 577, 590, 632, 645; **46:** 291, 297, 338
as Puritan **1:** 549, 551, 555, 558, 561, 563; **25:** 47
role in play **1:** 545, 548, 549, 553, 555, 563, 567, 575, 577, 588, 610, 615, 632, 645; **26:** 337, 374; **46:** 347

Mamillius
The Winter's Tale **7:** 394, 396, 451; **22:** 324

Margaret
Henry VI, Parts 1, 2, and 3
characterization **3:** 18, 26, 35, 51, 103, 109, 140, 157; **24:** 48
Suffolk, relationship with **3:** 18, 24, 26, 157; **39:** 213
Richard III **8:** 153, 154, 159, 162, 163, 170, 193, 201, 206, 210, 218, 223, 228, 243, 248, 262; **39:** 345

Marina
Pericles **37:** 361

Menenius
Coriolanus **9:** 8, 9, 11, 14, 19, 26, 78, 80, 106, 148, 157; **25:** 263, 296; **30:** 67, 79, 89, 96, 111, 133

Mercutio
Romeo and Juliet
bawdy **5:** 463, 525, 550, 575
death **5:** 415, 418, 419, 547; **33:** 290

as worldly counterpart to Romeo **5:** 425, 464, 542; **33:** 290

minor characters
Richard III **8:** 154, 159, 162, 163, 168, 170, 177, 184, 186, 201, 206, 210, 218, 223, 228, 232, 239, 248, 262, 267

Miranda
The Tempest **8:** 289, 301, 304, 328, 336, 370, 454; **19:** 357; **22:** 302; **28:** 249; **29:** 278, 297, 362, 368, 377, 396

Mistress Elbow
Measure for Measure See **Elbow (Mistress Elbow)**

Mistress Quickly
Henry V See **Quickly**

Mortimer
Henry IV, Parts 1 and 2 **25:** 151

Norfolk
Henry VIII **22:** 182

Northumberland
Richard II **24:** 423

Nurse
Romeo and Juliet **5:** 419, 425, 463, 464, 575; **33:** 294

Oberon
A Midsummer Night's Dream
as controlling force **3:** 434, 459, 477, 502; **29:** 175

Octavius
Antony and Cleopatra **6:** 22, 24, 31, 38, 43, 53, 62, 107, 125, 146, 178, 181, 219; **25:** 257
Julius Caesar **30:** 316

Olivia
Twelfth Night **1:** 540, 543, 545; **46:** 286, 324, 369

Ophelia
Hamlet **1:** 73, 76, 81, 82, 91, 96, 97, 154, 166, 169, 171, 218, 270; **13:** 268; **16:** 246; **19:** 330; **21:** 17, 41, 44, 72, 81,101, 104, 107, 112, 136, 203, 259, 347, 381, 386, 392, 416; **28:** 232, 325; **35:** 104, 126, 140, 144, 182, 238; **44:** 189, 195, 248

Orlando
As You Like It
as ideal man **5:** 32, 36, 39, 162; **34:** 161; **46:** 94
as younger brother **5:** 66, 158; **46:** 94

Orsino
Twelfth Night **46:** 286, 333

Othello
Othello
affinity with Iago **4:** 400, 427, 468, 470, 477, 500, 506; **25:** 189; **35:** 276, 320, 327

as conventional "blameless hero" **4:** 445, 486, 500
credulity **4:** 384, 385, 388, 390, 396, 402, 434, 440, 455; **13:** 327; **32:** 302
Desdemona, relationship with **22:** 339; **35:** 301, 317; **37:** 269; **43:** 32
divided nature **4:** 400, 412, 462, 470, 477, 493, 500, 582, 592; **16:** 293; **19:** 276; **25:** 189; **35:** 320
egotism **4:** 427, 470, 477, 493, 522, 536, 541, 573, 597; **13:** 304; **35:** 247, 253
self-destructive anger **16:** 283
self-dramatizing or self-deluding **4:** 454, 457, 477, 592; **13:** 313; **16:** 293; **35:** 317
self-knowledge **4:** 462, 470, 477, 483, 508, 522, 530, 564, 580, 591, 596; **13:** 304, 313; **16:** 283; **28:** 243; **35:** 253, 317
spiritual state **4:** 483, 488, 517, 525, 527, 544, 559, 564, 573; **28:** 243; **35:** 253

Page (Anne Page)
The Merry Wives of Windsor
Anne Page-Fenton plot **5:** 334, 336, 343, 353, 376, 390, 395, 402; **22:** 93

Painter
Timon of Athens See **Poet and Painter**

Palamon and Arcite
The Two Noble Kinsmen **9:** 474, 481, 490, 492, 502

Parolles
All's Well That Ends Well
characterization **7:** 8, 9, 43, 76, 81, 98, 109, 113, 116, 126; **22:** 78; **26:** 48, 73, 97; **26:** 117; **46:** 68
exposure **7:** 9, 27, 81, 98, 109, 113, 116, 121, 126
Falstaff, compared with **7:** 8, 9, 16

pastoral characters (Silvius, Phebe, and Corin)
As You Like It **23:** 37, 97, 98, 99, 108, 110, 118, 122, 138; **34:** 147

Paulina
The Winter's Tale **7:** 385, 412, 506; **15:** 528; **22:** 324; **25:** 339; **36:** 311

Pedro (Don Pedro)
Much Ado about Nothing **8:** 17, 19, 48, 58, 63, 82, 111, 121

Perdita
The Winter's Tale
characterization **7:** 395, 412, 414, 419, 429, 432, 452, 506; **22:** 324; **25:** 339; **36:** 328; **43:** 39
reunion with Leontes (Act V, scene ii) **7:** 377, 379, 381, 390, 432, 464, 480

Pericles
Pericles
characterization **36:** 251; **37:** 361
patience **2:** 572, 573, 578, 579
suit of Antiochus's daughter **2:** 547, 565, 578, 579
Ulysses, compared with **2:** 551

Petruchio
The Taming of the Shrew
admirable qualities **9:** 320, 332, 341, 344, 345, 370, 375, 386
audacity or vigor **9:** 325, 337, 355, 375, 386, 404
characterization **32:** 1
coarseness or brutality **9:** 325, 329, 365, 390, 393, 398, 407; **19:** 122; **43:** 61
as lord of misrule **9:** 393
love for Kate **9:** 338, 340, 343, 344, 386; **12:** 435
portrayals of **31:** 282
pragmatism **9:** 329, 334, 375, 398, 424; **13:** 3; **31:** 345, 351
taming method **9:** 320, 323, 329, 340, 341, 343, 345, 355, 369, 370, 375, 390, 398, 407, 413, 419, 424; **19:** 3, 12, 21 **31:** 269, 295, 326, 335, 339

Phebe
As You Like It See **pastoral characters**

Pistol
Henry V **28:** 146

plebeians
Coriolanus **9:** 8, 9, 11, 12, 15, 18, 19, 26, 33, 39, 53, 92, 125, 153, 183, 189; **25:** 296; **30:** 58, 79, 96, 111

Poet and Painter
Timon of Athens **25:** 198

the poets
Julius Caesar **7:** 179, 320, 350

Polonius
Hamlet **21:** 259, 334, 347, 386, 416; **35:** 182

Porter
Henry VIII **24:** 155
Macbeth **3:** 173, 175, 184, 190, 196, 203, 205, 225, 260, 271, 297, 300; **20:** 283

Portia
The Merchant of Venice **4:** 194, 195, 196, 215, 254, 263, 336, 356; **12:** 104, 107, 114; **13:** 37; **22:** 3, 69; **25:** 22; **32:** 294; **37:** 86; **40:** 142, 156, 197, 208

Posthumus
Cymbeline **4:** 24, 30, 53, 78, 116, 127, 141, 155, 159, 167; **15:** 89; **19:** 411; **25:** 245, 319; **36:** 142; **44:** 28; **45:** 67, 75

Prince Henry
King John See **Henry (Prince Henry)**

Prospero
The Tempest
characterization **8:** 312, 348, 370, 458; **16:** 442; **22:** 302; **45:** 188, 272
as God or Providence **8:** 311, 328, 364, 380, 429, 435
magic, nature of **8:** 301, 340, 356, 396, 414, 423, 458; **25:** 382; **28:** 391; **29:** 278, 292, 368, 377, 396; **32:** 338, 343

psychoanalytic interpretation **45:** 259
redemptive powers **8:** 302, 320, 353, 370, 390, 429, 439, 447; **29:** 297
as ruler **8:** 304, 308, 309, 420, 423; **13:** 424; **22:** 302; **29:** 278, 362, 377, 396
self-control **8:** 312, 414, 420; **22:** 302; **44:** 11
self-knowledge **16:** 442; **22:** 302; **29:** 278, 292, 362, 377, 396
as Shakespeare or creative artist **8:** 299, 302, 308, 312, 320, 324, 353, 364, 435, 447
as tragic hero **8:** 359, 370, 464; **29:** 292

Proteus
The Two Gentlemen of Verona **6:** 439, 450, 458, 480, 490, 511; **40:** 312, 327, 330, 335, 359; **42:** 18

Puck
A Midsummer Night's Dream **45:** 96, 158

Quickly (Mistress Quickly)
Henry V **5:** 186, 187, 210, 276, 293; **30:** 278

Regan
King Lear **31:** 151; **46:** 231, 242

Richard (King Richard II)
Richard II
artistic temperament **6:** 264, 267, 270, 272, 277, 292, 294, 298, 315, 331, 334, 347, 368, 374, 393, 409; **24:** 298, 301, 304, 315, 322, 390, 405, 408, 411, 414, 419; **39:** 289
Bolingbroke, compared with **24:** 346, 349, 351, 352, 356, 419; **39:** 256
characterization **6:** 250, 252, 253, 254, 255, 258, 262, 263, 267, 270, 272, 282, 283, 304, 343, 347, 364, 368; **24:** 262, 263, 267, 269, 270, 271, 272, 273, 274, 278, 280, 315, 322, 325, 330, 333, 390, 395, 402, 405, 423; **28:** 134; **39:** 279, 289
dangerous aspects **24:** 405
delusion **6:** 267, 298, 334, 368, 409; **24:** 329, 336, 405
homosexuality **24:** 405
kingship **6:** 253, 254, 263, 272, 327, 331, 334, 338, 364, 402, 414; **24:** 278, 295, 336, 337, 339, 356, 419; **28:** 134, 178; **39:** 256, 263
loss of identity **6:** 267, 338, 368, 374, 381, 388, 391, 409; **24:** 298, 414, 428
as martyr-king **6:** 289, 307, 321; **19:** 209; **24:** 289, 291; **28:** 134
nobility **6:** 255, 258, 259, 262, 263, 391; **24:** 260, 263, 274, 280, 289, 291, 402, 408, 411
political acumen **6:** 263, 264, 272, 292, 310, 327, 334, 364, 368, 374, 388, 391, 397, 402, 409; **24:** 405; **39:** 256
private vs. public persona **6:** 317, 327, 364, 368, 391, 409; **24:** 428
role-playing **24:** 419, 423; **28:** 178
seizure of Gaunt's estate **6:** 250, 338, 388
self-dramatization **6:** 264, 267, 307, 310, 315, 317, 331, 334, 368, 393, 409; **24:** 339; **28:** 178
self-hatred **13:** 172; **24:** 383; **39:** 289
self-knowledge **6:** 255, 267, 331, 334, 338, 352, 354, 368, 388, 391; **24:** 273, 289, 411, 414; **39:** 263, 289

spiritual redemption **6:** 255, 267, 331, 334, 338, 352, 354, 368, 388, 391; **24:** 273, 289, 411, 414

Richard (King Richard III, formerly Richard, Duke of Gloucester)

Henry VI, Parts 1, 2, and 3
characterization **3:** 35, 48, 57, 64, 77, 143, 151; **22:** 193; **39:** 160, 177
as revenger **22:** 193
soliloquy (*3 Henry VI*, Act III, scene ii) **3:** 17, 48

Richard III
ambition **8:** 148, 154, 165, 168, 170, 177, 182, 213, 218, 228, 232, 239, 252, 258, 267; **39:** 308, 341, 360, 370, 383
attractive qualities **8:** 145, 148, 152, 154, 159, 161, 162, 165, 168, 170, 181, 182, 184, 185, 197, 201, 206, 213, 228, 243, 252, 258; **16:** 150; **39:** 370, 383
credibility, question of **8:** 145, 147, 154, 159, 165, 193; **13:** 142
death **8:** 145, 148, 154, 159, 165, 168, 170, 177, 182, 197, 210, 223, 228, 232, 243, 248, 252, 258, 267
deformity as symbol **8:** 146, 147, 148, 152, 154, 159, 161, 165, 170, 177, 184, 185, 193, 218, 248, 252, 267; **19:** 164
inversion of moral order **8:** 159, 168, 177, 182, 184, 185, 197, 201, 213, 218, 223, 232, 239, 243, 248, 252, 258, 262, 267; **39:** 360
as Machiavellian villain **8:** 165, 182, 190, 201, 218, 232, 239, 243, 248; **39:** 308, 326, 360, 387
as monster or symbol of diabolic **8:** 145, 147, 159, 162, 168, 170, 177, 182, 193, 197, 201, 228, 239, 248, 258; **13:** 142; **37:** 144; **39:** 326, 349
other literary villains, compared with **8:** 148, 161, 162, 165, 181, 182, 206, 213, 239, 267
role-playing, hypocrisy, and dissimulation **8:** 145, 148, 154, 159, 162, 165, 168, 170, 182, 190, 206, 213, 218, 228, 239, 243, 252, 258, 267; **25:** 141, 164, 245; **39:** 335, 341, 387
as scourge or instrument of God **8:** 163, 177, 193, 201, 218, 228, 248, 267; **39:** 308
as Vice figure **8:** 190, 201, 213, 228, 243, 248, 252; **16:** 150; **39:** 383, 387

Richard Plantagenet, Duke of York

Henry VI, Parts 1, 2, and 3 See **York**

Richmond

Richard III **8:** 154, 158, 163, 168, 177, 182, 193, 210, 218, 223, 228, 243, 248, 252; **13:** 142; **25:** 141; **39:** 349

the Rival Poet

Sonnets **10:** 169, 233, 334, 337, 385

Roman citizenry

Julius Caesar
portrayal of **7:** 169, 179, 210, 221, 245, 279, 282, 310, 320, 333; **17:** 271, 279, 288, 291, 292, 298, 323, 334, 351, 367, 374, 375, 378; **22:** 280; **30:** 285, 297, 316, 321, 374, 379; **37:** 229

Romeo and Juliet

Romeo and Juliet
death-wish **5:** 431, 489, 505, 528, 530, 538, 542, 550, 566, 571, 575; **32:** 212
immortality **5:** 536
Juliet's epithalamium speech (Act III, scene ii) **5:** 431, 477, 492
Juliet's innocence **5:** 421, 423, 450, 454; **33:** 257
maturation **5:** 437, 454, 467, 493, 498, 509, 520, 565; **33:** 249, 257
rebellion **25:** 257
reckless passion **5:** 419, 427, 431, 438, 443, 444, 448, 467, 479, 485, 505, 533, 538, 542; **33:** 241
Romeo's dream (Act V, scene i) **5:** 513, 536, 556; **45:** 40
Rosaline, Romeo's relationship with **5:** 419, 423, 425, 427, 438, 498, 542, 575

Rosalind

As You Like It **46:** 94, 122
Beatrice, compared with **5:** 26, 36, 50, 75
charm **5:** 55, 75; **23:** 17, 18, 20, 41, 89, 111
disguise, role of **5:** 75, 107, 118, 122, 128, 130, 133, 138, 141, 146, 148, 164, 168; **13:** 502; **23:** 35, 42, 106, 119, 123, 146; **34:** 130; **46:** 127, 134, 142
femininity **5:** 26, 36, 52, 75; **23:** 24, 29, 46, 54, 103, 108, 121, 146
love-theme, relation to **5:** 79, 88, 103, 116, 122, 138, 141; **23:** 114, 115; **34:** 85, 177

rustic characters

As You Like It **5:** 24, 60, 72, 84; **23:** 127; **34:** 78, 161
A Midsummer Night's Dream **3:** 376, 397, 432; **12:** 291, 293; **45:** 147, 160

Scroop

Henry V See **traitors**

Sebastian

The Tempest See **Antonio and Sebastian**

Shylock

The Merchant of Venice
alienation **4:** 279, 312; **40:** 175
ambiguity **4:** 247, 254, 315, 319, 331; **12:** 31, 35, 36, 50, 51, 52, 56, 81, 124; **40:** 175
forced conversion **4:** 209, 252, 268, 282, 289, 321
Jewishness **4:** 193, 194, 195, 200, 201, 213, 214, 279; **22:** 69; **25:** 257; **40:** 142, 175, 181
motives in making the bond **4:** 252, 263, 266, 268; **22:** 69; **25:** 22
as Puritan **40:** 127, 166
as scapegoat figure **4:** 254, 300; **40:** 166
as traditional comic villain **4:** 230, 243, 261, 263, 315; **12:** 40, 62, 124; **40:** 175
as tragic figure **12:** 6, 9, 10, 16, 21, 23, 25, 40, 44, 66, 67, 81, 97; **40:** 175

Sicinius

Coriolanus See **the tribunes**

Silvia

The Two Gentlemen of Verona **6:** 450, 453, 458, 476, 494, 499, 516, 519, 549, 564; **40:** 312, 327, 374

Silvius

As You Like It See **pastoral characters**

Sly

The Taming of the Shrew **9:** 320, 322, 350, 370, 381, 390, 398, 430; **12:** 316, 335, 416, 427, 441; **16:** 13; **19:** 34, 122; **22:** 48; **37:** 31

soldiers

Henry V **5:** 203, 239, 267, 276, 281, 287, 293, 318; **28:** 146; **30:** 169,

Speed

The Two Gentlemen of Verona See **Launce and Speed**

Stephano and Trinculo

The Tempest
comic subplot of **8:** 292, 297, 299, 304, 309, 324, 328, 353, 370; **25:** 382; **29:** 377; **46:** 14, 33

Stephen Gardiner

Henry VIII See **Gardiner**

Talbot

Henry VI, Parts 1, 2, and 3 **39:** 160, 213, 222

Tamora

Titus Andronicus **4:** 632, 662, 672, 675; **27:** 266; **43:** 170

Tarquin

The Rape of Lucrece **10:** 80, 93, 98, 116, 125; **22:** 294; **25:** 305; **32:** 321; **33:** 190; **43:** 102

Thersites

Troilus and Cressida **13:** 53; **25:** 56; **27:** 381

Theseus

A Midsummer Night's Dream
characterization **3:** 363
Hippolyta, relationship with **3:** 381, 412, 421, 423, 450, 468, 520; **29:** 175, 216, 243, 256; **45:** 84
as ideal **3:** 379, 391
"lovers, lunatics, and poets" speech (Act V, scene i) **3:** 365, 371, 379, 381, 391, 402, 411, 412, 421, 423, 441, 498, 506; **29:** 175
as representative of institutional life **3:** 381, 403

Time-Chorus

The Winter's Tale **7:** 377, 380, 412, 464, 476, 501; **15:** 518

Timon

Timon of Athens
comic traits **25:** 198
as flawed hero **1:** 456, 459, 462, 472, 495, 503, 507, 515; **16:** 351; **20:** 429, 433, 476; **25:** 198; **27:** 157, 161

misanthropy **13**: 392; **20**: 431, 464, 476, 481, 491, 492, 493; **27**: 161, 175, 184, 196; **37**: 222
as noble figure **1**: 467, 473, 483, 499; **20**: 493; **27**: 212

Titania
A Midsummer Night's Dream **29**: 243

Titus
Titus Andronicus **4**: 632, 637, 640, 644, 647, 653, 656, 662; **25**: 245; **27**: 255

Touchstone
As You Like It
callousness **5**: 88
comic and farcical elements **46**: 117
as philosopher-fool **5**: 24, 28, 30, 32, 36, 63, 75, 98; **23**: 152; **34**: 85; **46**: 1, 14, 18, 24, 33, 52, 60, 88, 105
relation to pastoral convention **5**: 54, 61, 63, 72, 75, 77, 79, 84, 86, 93, 98, 114, 118, 135, 138, 166; **34**: 72, 147, 161
satire or parody of pastoral conventions **46**: 122
selflessness **5**: 30, 36, 39, 76

traitors (Scroop, Grey, and Cambridge)
Henry V **16**: 202; **30**: 220, 278

the tribunes (Brutus and Sicinius)
Coriolanus **9**: 9, 11, 14, 19, 33, 169, 180

Trinculo
The Tempest See **Stephano and Trinculo**

Troilus
Troilus and Cressida
contradictory behavior **3**: 596, 602, 635; **27**: 362
Cressida, relationship with **3**: 594, 596, 606; **22**: 58
integrity **3**: 617
opposition to Ulysses **3**: 561, 584, 590
as unsympathetic figure **18**: 423; **22**: 58, 339; **43**: 317
as warrior **3**: 596; **22**: 339

Ulysses
Troilus and Cressida
speech on degree (Act I, scene iii) **3**: 549, 599, 609, 642; **27**: 396

Venetians
The Merchant of Venice **4**: 195, 200, 228, 254, 273, 300, 321, 331

Venus
Venus and Adonis **10**: 427, 429, 434, 439, 442, 448, 449, 451, 454, 466, 473, 480, 486, 489; **16**: 452; **25**: 305, 328; **28**: 355; **33**: 309, 321, 330, 347, 352, 357, 363, 370, 377

Viola
Twelfth Night **26**: 308; **46**: 286, 324, 347, 369

Virgilia
Coriolanus **9**: 11, 19, 26, 33, 58, 100, 121, 125; **25**: 263; **30**: 79, 96, 133

Volumnia
Coriolanus
Coriolanus's subservience to **9**: 16, 26, 33, 53, 62, 80, 92, 100, 117, 125, 142, 177, 183; **30**: 140, 149; **44**: 79
influence on Coriolanus **9**: 45, 62, 65, 78, 92, 100, 110, 117, 121, 125, 130, 148, 157, 183, 189, 193; **25**: 263, 296; **30**: 79, 96, 125, 133, 140, 142, 149; **44**: 93
as noble Roman matron **9**: 16, 19, 26, 31, 33
personification of Rome **9**: 125, 183

Wat the hare
Venus and Adonis **10**: 424, 451

the Watch
Much Ado about Nothing See **Dogberry and the Watch**

Williams
Henry V **13**: 502; **16**: 183; **28**: 146; **30**: 169, 259, 278

witches
Macbeth
and supernaturalism **3**: 171, 172, 173, 175, 177, 182, 183, 184, 185, 194, 196, 198, 202, 207, 208, 213, 219, 229, 239; **16**: 317; **19**: 245; **20**: 92, 175, 213, 279, 283, 374, 387, 406, 413; **25**: 235; **28**: 339; **29**: 91, 101, 109, 120

Wolsey (Cardinal Wolsey)
Henry VIII **2**: 15, 18, 19, 23, 24, 38; **22**: 182; **24**: 80, 91, 112, 113, 129, 140; **37**: 109; **41**: 129

York (Edmund of Langley, Duke of York)
Richard II **6**: 287, 364, 368, 388, 402, 414; **24**: 263, 320, 322, 364, 395, 414; **39**: 243, 279

York (Richard Plantagenet, Duke of York)
Henry VI, Parts 1, 2, and 3
death of **13**: 131

Cumulative Critic Index

Abel, Lionel
 Hamlet **1**: 237

Abrams, Richard
 Authorship Controversy (topic entry) **41**: 98
 King Lear **46**: 218
 The Two Noble Kinsmen **41**: 385

Adams, Howard C.
 Troilus and Cressida **27**: 400

Adams, John C.
 Romeo and Juliet **11**: 507
 The Tempest **15**: 346

Adams, John F.
 All's Well That Ends Well **7**: 86

Adams, John Quincy
 Othello **4**: 408
 Romeo and Juliet **5**: 426

Adams, Joseph Quincy
 The Phoenix and Turtle **10**: 16

Adams, Robert M.
 The Tempest **29**: 303

Adamson, Jane
 Othello **4**: 591

Adamson, W. D.
 Othello **35**: 360

Addenbrooke, David
 Macbeth **20**: 263

Addison, Joseph
 Hamlet **1**: 75
 Henry IV, 1 and 2 **1**: 287
 King Lear **2**: 93

Adelman, Janet
 All's Well That Ends Well **13**: 84
 Antony and Cleopatra **6**: 211; **27**: 110
 Coriolanus **9**: 183
 Hamlet **44**: 160
 Measure for Measure **13**: 84
 Othello **22**: 339; **42**: 198
 Psychoanalytic Interpretations (topic entry) **44**: 79
 Troilus and Cressida **22**: 339

Adler, Doris
 Antony and Cleopatra **17**: 94

Agate, James
 Coriolanus **17**: 157
 Hamlet **21**: 155, 167, 169, 177, 194
 Henry IV, 1 and 2 **14**: 25
 King Lear **11**: 46, 51
 Macbeth **20**: 182, 184
 Othello **11**: 262, 266
 Richard II **24**: 298
 Romeo and Juliet **11**: 444
 Troilus and Cressida **18**: 300
 The Two Noble Kinsmen **9**: 462

Agee, James
 Henry V **14**: 213, 214

Aichinger, C. P.
 Hamlet **35**: 212

Aire, Sally
 As You Like It **23**: 131
 The Merry Wives of Windsor **18**: 56
 A Midsummer Night's Dream **12**: 271
 Pericles **15**: 165
 Twelfth Night **26**: 294

Akrigg, G. P. V.
 Henry V **30**: 252

Alden, Barbara
 Othello **11**: 212

Alden, Raymond Macdonald
 Sonnets **10**: 247

Aldus, P. J.
 Hamlet **35**: 134

Alexander, Bill
 The Merry Wives of Windsor **18**: 64

Alexander, Peter
 Henry VIII **2**: 43

Alger, William Rounseville
 Othello **11**: 208

Allen, Don Cameron
 The Rape of Lucrece **10**: 89
 Venus and Adonis **10**: 451

Allen, John A.
 A Midsummer Night's Dream **3**: 457

Allen, Shirley
 Pericles **15**: 135

Allen, Shirley S.
 Antony and Cleopatra **17**: 20
 A Midsummer Night's Dream **12**: 175
 The Winter's Tale **15**: 419

Alleva, Richard
 Hamlet **21**: 321

Alleyn, Henry
 Cymbeline **15**: 50

Almeida, Barbara Heliodora C. de M. F. de
 Troilus and Cressida **3**: 604

Alpert, Hollis
 Hamlet **21**: 160

Altemus, Jameson Torr
 As You Like It **23**: 41

Altick, Richard D.
 Richard II **6**: 298

Altieri, Joanne
 Henry V **5**: 314

Altman, Joel B.
 Henry V **19**: 133

Alulis, Joseph
 As You Like It **46**: 94

Alvarez, A.
 All's Well That Ends Well **26**: 26

Coriolanus **17:** 166
Hamlet **21:** 268
King Lear **11:** 74
The Merchant of Venice **12:** 66
Othello **11:** 286
The Phoenix and Turtle **10:** 31
The Taming of the Shrew **12:** 356
Troilus and Cressida **18:** 322
Twelfth Night **26:** 253
The Two Gentlemen of Verona **12:** 473

Alvis, John
Politics and Power (topic entry) **30:** 11

Amhurst, Nicholas
Henry VIII **2:** 15

Amory, Mark
All's Well That Ends Well **26:** 58
Macbeth **20:** 309

Anderson, Linda
The Merry Wives of Windsor **38:** 264

Anderson, Mary
The Winter's Tale **15:** 443

Andreasen, Nancy J. C.
Madness (topic entry) **35:** 34

Andres, Michael Cameron
Hamlet **35:** 167

Andrews, Nigel
The Tempest **15:** 294

Anson, John
Julius Caesar **7:** 324

Ansorge, Peter
All's Well That Ends Well **26:** 46
Coriolanus **17:** 193
Cymbeline **15:** 75
Julius Caesar **17:** 382
The Merchant of Venice **12:** 74
A Midsummer Night's Dream **12:** 259
Richard II **24:** 349
The Tempest **15:** 280

Anstey, Edgar
Henry V **14:** 202

Anthony, Earl of Shaftesbury
Hamlet **1:** 75

Appleton, William W.
Macbeth **20:** 48

Archer, William
All's Well That Ends Well **26:** 8
Henry IV, 1 and 2 **14:** 16, 20, 21
Measure for Measure **23:** 284
A Midsummer Night's Dream **12:** 196
Richard III **14:** 400
The Tempest **15:** 222
Twelfth Night **1:** 558; **26:** 201, 216
The Winter's Tale **15:** 437

Arden, John
Henry V **14:** 336

Arditti, Michael
Macbeth **20:** 315

Armstrong, William A.
Hamlet **21:** 136

Arnold, Aerol
Richard III **8:** 210

Aronson, Alex
Appearance vs. Reality (topic entry) **34:** 12

Arthos, John
All's Well That Ends Well **7:** 58
Macbeth **3:** 250
Othello **4:** 541
The Phoenix and Turtle **10:** 50
Shakespeare and Classical Civilization (topic entry) **27:** 1
The Two Gentlemen of Verona **6:** 532
The Tempest **45:** 247

Ashcroft, Peggy
Antony and Cleopatra **17:** 113
Romeo and Juliet **11:** 516

Asnani, Shyam M.
Clowns and Fools (topic entry) **46:** 14

Asp, Carolyn
Love's Labour's Lost **38:** 200
Macbeth **29:** 133
Psychoanalytic Interpretations (topic entry) **44:** 35
Troilus and Cressida **27:** 396

Asquith, Ros
Richard III **14:** 490
Troilus and Cressida **18:** 382

Astington, John
Twelfth Night **28:** 1; **46:** 338

Aston, Anthony
Hamlet **21:** 10

Atkinson, Brooks
As You Like It **23:** 72, 75
Hamlet **21:** 219
Henry IV, 1 and 2 **14:** 60, 63, 64
Julius Caesar **17:** 318
King John **24:** 209
King Lear **11:** 58
Macbeth **20:** 200, 224, 232, 240
The Merchant of Venice **12:** 53
A Midsummer Night's Dream **12:** 209, 239
Much Ado about Nothing **18:** 171, 172, 175
The Taming of the Shrew **12:** 341, 345, 348
Troilus and Cressida **18:** 313
Twelfth Night **26:** 246

Auberlen, Eckhard
Henry VIII **2:** 78

Auden, W. H.
Henry IV, 1 and 2 **1:** 410
Much Ado about Nothing **8:** 77
Sonnets **10:** 325
Twelfth Night **1:** 599

Austin, L. F.
The Merry Wives of Windsor **18:** 26

Axton, Marie
The Phoenix and Turtle **38:** 378

Bache, William B.
Fathers and Daughters (topic entry) **36:** 51

Bacon, Lord Francis
Richard II **6:** 250

Baddeley, V. C. Clinton
Troilus and Cressida **18:** 394

Badeau, Adam
Hamlet **21:** 62

Bagebot, Walter
Measure for Measure **2:** 406

Baildon, H. Bellyse
Titus Andronicus **4:** 632

Baines, Barbara J.
Henry IV, 1 and 2 **39:** 123

Baker, David J.
Henry V **22:** 103

Baker, Donald
As You Like It **23:** 132

Baker, Felix
Antony and Cleopatra **17:** 26

Baker, George Pierce
Romeo and Juliet **5:** 448

Baker, H. Barton
Romeo and Juliet **11:** 378, 399, 422

Baker, Harry T.
Henry IV, 1 and 2 **1:** 347

Baker, Herschel
Macbeth **20:** 64

Baker, Nick
Pericles **15:** 173

Baker, Susan
Appearance vs. Reality (topic entry) **34:** 45

Baldwin, Thomas Whitfield
The Comedy of Errors **1:** 21; **34:** 215

Balk, Wes
The Taming of the Shrew **12:** 366

Bamber, Linda
Gender Identity (topic entry) **40:** 15

Bamford, Karen
Cymbeline **36:** 148

Banks-Smith, Nancy
Richard II **24:** 364

Barber, C. L.
As You Like It **5:** 79
The Comedy of Errors **34:** 190
Hamlet **44:** 152
Henry IV, 1 and 2 **1:** 414
Love's Labour's Lost **2:** 335
The Merchant of Venice **4:** 273
A Midsummer Night's Dream **3:** 427
Pericles **2:** 582
Sonnets **10:** 302
Twelfth Night **1:** 620
The Winter's Tale **7:** 480

Barish, Jonas
As You Like It **28:** 9
Measure for Measure **28:** 9
The Merchant of Venice **28:** 9
The Merry Wives of Windsor **28:** 9
A Midsummer Night's Dream **28:** 9
Violence in Shakespeare's Works (topic entry) **43:** 1

Barkan, Leonard
Titus Andronicus **43:** 203

Barker, Frank Granville
Coriolanus **17:** 168
Hamlet **21:** 216

Barker, Kathleen M. D.
Richard II **24:** 402

Barker, Ronald
Twelfth Night **26:** 245

Barnaby, Andrew
As You Like It **34:** 120; **37:** 1

Barnes, Clive
As You Like It **23:** 101
The Comedy of Errors **26:** 154
Hamlet **21:** 231, 269
Measure for Measure **23:** 330
The Merchant of Venice **12:** 80
A Midsummer Night's Dream **12:** 252
Pericles **15:** 158
Twelfth Night **26:** 290
The Winter's Tale **15:** 482

Barnes, Howard
King Lear **11:** 56

Barnes, Thomas
Hamlet **21:** 40

Barnet, Sylvan
As You Like It **5:** 125
Twelfth Night **1:** 588

Barnfield, Richard
Venus and Adonis **10:** 410

Barnstorff, D.
Sonnets **10:** 190

Barry, Gerald
A Midsummer Night's Dream **12:** 249

Bartels, Emily C.
Hamlet **28:** 223
King Lear **28:** 223
Titus Andronicus **43:** 176

Bartholomeusz, Dennis
The Winter's Tale **15:** 401, 465, 503, 507

Barton, Anne
Antony and Cleopatra **6:** 208
The Comedy of Errors **1:** 61
Henry V **30:** 169
The Merry Wives of Windsor **5:** 400
Twelfth Night **1:** 656

Barton, John
All's Well That Ends Well **26:** 48
Troilus and Cressida **18:** 403

Baskervill, Charles Read
The Merchant of Venice **4:** 226

Bate, Jonathan
Shakespeare and Classical Civilization (topic entry) **27:** 46
Sonnets **16:** 472
Venus and Adonis **25:** 305

Bates, Ronald
The Phoenix and Turtle **10:** 27

Bateson, F. W.
Sonnets **10:** 277

Battenhouse, Roy W.
Antony and Cleopatra **6:** 192
Henry IV, 1 and 2 **1:** 434
Henry V **5:** 260
King Lear **31:** 149
Macbeth **3:** 269
Measure for Measure **2:** 466
Othello **4:** 573
The Rape of Lucrece **10:** 98
Richard II **6:** 402
Romeo and Juliet **5:** 542

Baumlin, Tita French
Venus and Adonis **16:** 452

Bawcutt, N. W.
Measure for Measure **23:** 400
The Two Noble Kinsmen **9:** 492

Baxter, John
Cymbeline **25:** 319

Bayley, John
Coriolanus **30:** 133
King Lear **31:** 162
Othello **4:** 552
Timon of Athens **27:** 175
Troilus and Cressida **3:** 634; **27:** 381

Bayley, P. C.
Henry VI, 1, 2, and 3 **24:** 25

Bean, John C.
The Taming of the Shrew **9:** 426

Beauchamp, Gorman
Henry V **14:** 242

Beaufort, John
As You Like It **23:** 73
Measure for Measure **23:** 352
Much Ado about Nothing **18:** 219
Richard III **14:** 480
The Taming of the Shrew **12:** 347
Twelfth Night **26:** 313

Beauman, Sally
As You Like It **23:** 66
Henry V **14:** 287, 295, 297, 301
Love's Labour's Lost **23:** 186
Macbeth **20:** 197
Pericles **15:** 138
Titus Andronicus **17:** 459
Troilus and Cressida **18:** 292

Beaurline, L. A.
King John **41:** 228

Beckman, Margaret Boerner
As You Like It **34:** 172

Beckwith, Sarah
Macbeth **19:** 245

Beerbohm, Max
Hamlet **21:** 140
King John **24:** 201
Macbeth **20:** 164
A Midsummer Night's Dream **12:** 203
Much Ado about Nothing **18:** 145

Belsey, Catherine
Desire (topic entry) **38:** 19
The Merchant of Venice **22:** 3
A Midsummer Night's Dream **28:** 15
Romeo and Juliet **25:** 181
Shakespeare's Representation of Women (topic entry) **31:** 43

Bennett, H. S.
Pericles **15:** 139
Romeo and Juliet **11:** 458

Bennett, Josephine Waters
All's Well That Ends Well **7:** 104

Bennetts, Leslie
Much Ado about Nothing **18:** 223

Benson, Frank
Twelfth Night **26:** 207

Benson, John
Sonnets **10:** 153

Benston, Alice N.
The Merchant of Venice **4:** 336

Bentley, Eric
Julius Caesar **17:** 350

Berek, Peter
The Taming of the Shrew **31:** 276

Berge, Mark
King Lear **46:** 225

Berger, Harry, Jr.
General Commentary **13:** 457
Henry IV, 1 and 2 **28:** 101; **42:** 99
King Lear **46:** 242
Macbeth **3:** 340
Much Ado about Nothing **8:** 121
Othello **35:** 380
Richard II **13:** 172
The Tempest **29:** 278

Berger, Thomas L.
Henry V **13:** 183

Bergeron, David M.
Cymbeline **4:** 170
Henry IV, 1 and 2 **19:** 157; **39:** 143
Henry VI, 1, 2, and 3 **3:** 149
Richard II **19:** 151

Berggren, Paula S.
Gender Identity (topic entry) **40:** 1
The Two Noble Kinsmen **9:** 502

Berkeley, David S.
All's Well That Ends Well **38:** 155

Berkowitz, Gerald M.
Antony and Cleopatra **17:** 82
Hamlet **21:** 301
Much Ado about Nothing **18:** 211

Berlin, Normand
Macbeth **20:** 279

Berman, Ronald
Henry VI, 1, 2, and 3 **3:** 89
Love's Labour's Lost **2:** 348
Measure for Measure **33:** 52

Bermann, Sandra L.
Sonnets **40:** 303

Bernard, John
Othello **11:** 190; **32:** 201

Berry, Edward
Othello **16:** 293

Berry, Edward I.
Henry V **30:** 220
Henry VI, 1, 2, and 3 **39:** 177
Henry VIII **41:** 120

Berry, Philippa
Hamlet **42:** 212
The Rape of Lucrece **22:** 289

Berry, Ralph
All's Well That Ends Well **26:** 114
As You Like It **23:** 118; **34:** 72
Coriolanus **9:** 174; **17:** 248
Hamlet **21:** 361
Henry V **14:** 328
Julius Caesar **7:** 356; **17:** 317, 421
Love's Labour's Lost **2:** 348
Measure for Measure **23:** 335, 375; **33:** 69
The Merchant of Venice **12:** 48

The Merry Wives of Windsor **5:** 373; **18:** 52, 64
A Midsummer Night's Dream **12:** 207
Much Ado about Nothing **31:** 184
The Taming of the Shrew **9:** 401
The Tempest **15:** 338
Timon of Athens **20:** 470
Titus Andronicus **17:** 472
Troilus and Cressida **18:** 406
Twelfth Night **26:** 342, 374
The Two Gentlemen of Verona **6:** 529; **12:** 488

Bertin, Michael
Twelfth Night **26:** 299

Bertram, Joseph L.
King Lear **11:** 93
Much Ado about Nothing **18:** 182

Bertram, Paul
Henry VIII **2:** 60

Bethell, S. L.
Antony and Cleopatra **6:** 115
Henry VI, 1, 2, and 3 **3:** 67
Othello **4:** 517
The Winter's Tale **7:** 446

Bethell, Tom
Authorship Controversy (topic entry) **41:** 48, 61

Bevington, David
Antony and Cleopatra **17:** 101
Love's Labour's Lost **16:** 17; **38:** 209
The Merry Wives of Windsor **18:** 71
Politics and Power (topic entry) **30:** 29
The Winter's Tale **45:** 295

Bevington, David M.
Henry VI, 1, 2, and 3 **3:** 103
A Midsummer Night's Dream **3:** 491

Bickerstaff, Isaac
See also Steele, Sir Richard
Julius Caesar **7:** 152

Bickersteth, Geoffrey L.
King Lear **2:** 179

Billington, Michael
All's Well That Ends Well **26:** 57
Antony and Cleopatra **17:** 40, 54
As You Like It **23:** 103, 120, 145
The Comedy of Errors **26:** 149, 157, 158
Cymbeline **15:** 60
Hamlet **21:** 323, 329
Henry V **14:** 307
Julius Caesar **17:** 372, 382
King John **24:** 215, 221, 236
Love's Labour's Lost **23:** 207, 231
Macbeth **20:** 298, 317
The Merchant of Venice **12:** 82
The Merry Wives of Windsor **18:** 49, 54
Pericles **15:** 174, 176

Richard II **24:** 336, 337, 380
The Tempest **15:** 271
Titus Andronicus **17:** 465
Twelfth Night **26:** 282, 346
The Winter's Tale **15:** 474

Bingham, Madeleine
Julius Caesar **17:** 315

Bishop, T. G.
The Comedy of Errors **37:** 12
The Winter's Tale **45:** 297

Black, James
Henry IV, 1 and 2 **14:** 150; **39:** 89
Measure for Measure **2:** 519
The Tempest **19:** 357

Blackmur, R. P.
Sonnets **10:** 315

Paula Blank
Richard II **42:** 118

Blau, Herbert
King Lear **11:** 154

Bliss, Lee
Henry VIII **2:** 72

Bloom, Allan
Julius Caesar **7:** 310
Politics and Power (topic entry) **30:** 1

Bloom, Harold
A Midsummer Night's Dream **45:** 158

Bluestone, Max
Henry IV, 1 and 2 **14:** 67
Troilus and Cressida **18:** 338

Blumenthal, Eileen
Antony and Cleopatra **17:** 67

Bly, Mary
All's Well That Ends Well **38:** 118

Boaden, James
Hamlet **21:** 31
Henry V **14:** 180
Henry VIII **24:** 68
King John **24:** 175, 176
Macbeth **20:** 59
Sonnets **10:** 169

Boas, Frederick S.
As You Like It **5:** 54
King John **9:** 240
Measure for Measure **2:** 416
The Merry Wives of Windsor **5:** 347
A Midsummer Night's Dream **3:** 391
The Phoenix and Turtle **10:** 8
The Rape of Lucrece **10:** 68
Romeo and Juliet **5:** 443
Timon of Athens **1:** 476
Titus Andronicus **4:** 631
Troilus and Cressida **3:** 555
The Two Gentlemen of Verona **6:** 451

Bodenstedt, Friedrich
Othello **4:** 422

Bodkin, Maud
Othello **4:** 468

Bogard, Travis
Richard II **6:** 317

Bolton, Joseph S. G.
Titus Andronicus **4:** 635

Bonaventure, Sister Mary
The Phoenix and Turtle **38:** 326

Bonazza, Blaze Odell
The Comedy of Errors **1:** 50

Bond, R. Warwick
Cymbeline **15:** 36
The Two Gentlemen of Verona **6:** 46

Bond, Ronald B.
Romeo and Juliet **33:** 241

Bonheim, Helmut
Richard II **6:** 385

Bonheim, Jean
Richard II **6:** 385

Bonjour, Adrien
Julius Caesar **7:** 284
King John **9:** 263; **41:** 260
The Winter's Tale **7:** 456

Bonnard, George A.
A Midsummer Night's Dream **3:** 42
The Phoenix and Turtle **10:** 17
Richard II **6:** 310

Bono, Barbara J.
Gender Identity (topic entry) **40:** 90

Boose, Lynda E.
As You Like It **19:** 3
The Comedy of Errors **19:** 3
Fathers and Daughters (topic entry) **36:** 78
The Merchant of Venice **13:** 37
The Merry Wives of Windsor **19:** 3
The Taming of the Shrew **19:** 3; **28:** 24; **31:** 351

Booth, Michael R.
Henry VIII **24:** 91

Booth, Stephen
Hamlet **44:** 107
Macbeth **3:** 349
Sonnets **10:** 349

Booth, Wayne
Macbeth **3:** 306

Boothroyd, Basil
Richard II **24:** 331
Troilus and Cressida **18:** 346, 347

Boothroyd, J. B.
Measure for Measure **23:** 309
The Tempest **15:** 258
Titus Andronicus **17:** 440

Borot, Luc
Titus Andronicus **17:** 481

Bost, James S.
The Taming of the Shrew **12:** 396

Boswell, James
King Lear **11:** 6
Sonnets **10:** 166

Bowers, A. Robin
Rape of Lucrece **43:** 148

Bowers, Fredson Thayer
Hamlet **1:** 209
Titus Andronicus **4:** 637

Bowman, James
Hamlet **21:** 322

Boxer, Setphen
Julius Caesar **17:** 407

Boxill, Roger
All's Well That Ends Well **26:** 62
Richard III **14:** 484

Boyd, Brian
King John **32:** 93; **41:** 251

Bradbrook, M. C.
Appearance vs. Reality (topic entry) **34:** 1
Timon of Athens **20:** 492; **27:** 203

Bradbrook, Muriel C.
All's Well That Ends Well **7:** 51
Henry IV, 1 and 2 **1:** 418
Henry VI, 1, 2, and 3 **3:** 75
Love's Labour's Lost **2:** 321, 330
Measure for Measure **2:** 443
The Merchant of Venice **4:** 261
The Merry Wives of Windsor **5:** 366; **18:** 44
The Rape of Lucrece **10:** 78
Romeo and Juliet **5:** 479; **11:** 488
The Taming of the Shrew **9:** 355
Titus Andronicus **4:** 646
Twelfth Night **1:** 655
The Two Gentlemen of Verona **6:** 486
The Two Noble Kinsmen **9:** 490

Bradby, G. F.
As You Like It **5:** 65

Braddock, M. C.
Romeo and Juliet **11:** 488

Bradley, A. C.
Antony and Cleopatra **6:** 53
Coriolanus **9:** 43, 53
Hamlet **1:** 120
Henry IV, 1 and 2 **1:** 333
Henry V **5:** 209
Julius Caesar **7:** 188
King Lear **2:** 137; **11:** 137
Macbeth **3:** 213

The Merry Wives of Windsor **5:** 348
Othello **4:** 434
Sonnets **10:** 238
Twelfth Night **1:** 566

Bradshaw, Graham
Othello **22:** 207; **25:** 189
Sonnets **25:** 189

Brady, Owen E.
Macbeth **20:** 308
The Merry Wives of Windsor **18:** 35

Brahms, Caryl
Julius Caesar **17:** 368
King Lear **11:** 76
Measure for Measure **23:** 317
Othello **11:** 292
The Taming of the Shrew **12:** 361
The Tempest **15:** 263
Timon of Athens **20:** 448
Titus Andronicus **17:** 447
Troilus and Cressida **18:** 325
Twelfth Night **26:** 254
The Two Gentlemen of Verona **12:** 463, 475

Brandes, George
As You Like It **5:** 50
Coriolanus **9:** 39
Hamlet **1:** 116
Henry IV, 1 and 2 **1:** 329
King Lear **2:** 136
Love's Labour's Lost **2:** 315
Measure for Measure **2:** 414
The Merry Wives of Windsor **5:** 346
A Midsummer Night's Dream **3:** 389
Much Ado about Nothing **8:** 36
Pericles **2:** 551
Timon of Athens **1:** 474
Troilus and Cressida **3:** 554
The Two Gentlemen of Verona **6:** 456
The Two Noble Kinsmen **9:** 460

Brathwait, Richard
Venus and Adonis **10:** 411

Braunmuller, A. R.
King John **24:** 245; **41:** 243

Bredbeck, Gregory W.
Sonnets **40:** 268

Breight, Curt
The Tempest **16:** 426

Breitenberg, Mark
Love's Labour's Lost **22:** 12

Brewer, Derek
The Merry Wives of Windsor **38:** 278

Brewster, Dorothy
Henry V **14:** 177

Bridie, James
Othello **11:** 268

Brien, Alan
  All's Well That Ends Well **26**: 25
  Coriolanus **17**: 165
  Hamlet **21**: 223
  King Lear **11**: 73, 91
  The Merchant of Venice **12**: 65
  Much Ado about Nothing **18**: 184
  Othello **11**: 283
  Pericles **15**: 141
  The Taming of the Shrew **12**: 356
  Troilus and Cressida **18**: 320
  Twelfth Night **26**: 250
  The Two Gentlemen of Verona **12**: 472

Briggs, Julia
  All's Well That Ends Well **28**: 38
  Measure for Measure **28**: 38

Brigham, A.
  King Lear **2**: 116

Brill, Lesley W.
  Timon of Athens **1**: 526

Brink, Bernhard Ten
  Antony and Cleopatra **6**: 52

Brink, Jean R.
  Shakespeare's Representation of Women (topic entry) **31**: 53

Brissenden, Alan
  A Midsummer Night's Dream **3**: 513

Bristol, Michael D.
  The Winter's Tale **19**: 366

Brittin, Norman A.
  Twelfth Night **1**: 594

Broadbent, J. B.
  Sonnets **10**: 322

Brockbank, Philip
  All's Well That Ends Well **26**: 87
  Coriolanus **17**: 227
  General Commentary **13**: 476
  Henry VIII **24**: 118
  Julius Caesar **13**: 252
  Troilus and Cressida **13**: 53

Brodwin, Leonora Leet
  Romeo and Juliet **33**: 233

Bromley, John C.
  Richard III **39**: 341

Bromley, Laura G.
  Rape of Lucrece **43**: 85

Bronson, Bertrand H.
  Love's Labour's Lost **2**: 326

Brook, Peter
  Antony and Cleopatra **17**: 65
  As You Like It **23**: 173
  King Lear **11**: 84
  A Midsummer Night's Dream **12**: 254, 259
  Romeo and Juliet **11**: 459
  The Winter's Tale **15**: 528

Brooke, C. F. Tucker
  Henry IV, 1 and 2 **1**: 337, 341
  Othello **4**: 451
  Troilus and Cressida **3**: 560
  The Two Noble Kinsmen **9**: 461

Brooke, Nicholas
  All's Well That Ends Well **7**: 121
  Richard III **8**: 243
  Romeo and Juliet **5**: 528
  Titus Andronicus **27**: 246

Brooke, Stopford A.
  As You Like It **5**: 57
  Henry V **5**: 213
  Julius Caesar **7**: 205
  King Lear **2**: 149
  Othello **4**: 444
  Romeo and Juliet **5**: 447

Brooks, Charles
  The Taming of the Shrew **9**: 360

Brooks, Cleanth
  Henry IV, 1 and 2 **1**: 380
  Macbeth **3**: 253

Brooks, Harold F.
  The Comedy of Errors **1**: 40
  The Two Gentlemen of Verona **6**: 504

Brooks, Jeremy
  Romeo and Juliet **11**: 462
  The Winter's Tale **15**: 470

Broude, Ronald
  Titus Andronicus **4**: 680; **27**: 282

Broun, Heywood
  Julius Caesar **17**: 324

Brower, Reuben Arthur
  Coriolanus **9**: 164
  Hamlet **1**: 259
  The Tempest **8**: 384

Brown, Carolyn E.
  The Taming of the Shrew **32**: 1
  Measure for Measure **42**: 1

Brown, Charles Armitage
  Sonnets **10**: 176
  The Two Gentlemen of Verona **6**: 439

Brown, Constance A.
  Richard III **14**: 435

Brown, Ivor
  All's Well That Ends Well **26**: 13
  As You Like It **23**: 78, 87
  Hamlet **21**: 156, 178, 196, 218
  Henry IV, 1 and 2 **14**: 29
  King John **24**: 203
  King Lear **11**: 48
  Macbeth **20**: 232, 244
  The Merchant of Venice **12**: 47, 52
  Much Ado about Nothing **18**: 159
  Richard III **14**: 409
  Romeo and Juliet **11**: 443
  The Taming of the Shrew **12**: 351

Titus Andronicus **17**: 445
The Two Gentlemen of Verona **12**: 459

Brown, Jane K.
  A Midsummer Night's Dream **45**: 126

Brown, Jeffrey
  Othello **35**: 276

Brown, John Mason
  As You Like It **23**: 76
  Julius Caesar **17**: 319
  Macbeth **20**: 227
  The Tempest **15**: 242

Brown, John Russell
  All's Well That Ends Well **26**: 34
  As You Like It **5**: 103
  The Comedy of Errors **1**: 36
  Cymbeline **4**: 113; **15**: 70, 122
  Hamlet **21**: 217
  Macbeth **20**: 254, 265
  Measure for Measure **23**: 312
  The Merchant of Venice **4**: 270; **12**: 67
  The Merry Wives of Windsor **5**: 354
  A Midsummer Night's Dream **3**: 425 **12**: 244, 262
  Much Ado about Nothing **8**: 75; **18**: 261
  Othello **11**: 305
  Richard II **24**: 414
  Romeo and Juliet **11**: 466
  The Taming of the Shrew **9**: 353; **12**: 363
  The Tempest **15**: 193
  Troilus and Cressida **18**: 329
  Twelfth Night **1**: 600; **26**: 366, 371
  The Two Gentlemen of Verona **12**: 478
  The Winter's Tale **7**: 469; **15**: 524

Browne, Junius Henri
  Othello **11**: 323

Browne, Martin E.
  Coriolanus **17**: 182

Brownell, Arthur
  Measure for Measure **23**: 280

Browning, I. R.
  Coriolanus **9**: 117

Browning, Robert
  Sonnets **10**: 213

Brownlow, F. W.
  The Two Noble Kinsmen **9**: 498

Brubaker, Edward S.
  King John **24**: 249

Bruce, Brenda
  Romeo and Juliet **11**: 519

Brucher, Richard T.
  Titus Andronicus **27**: 255

Brustein, Robert
  The Comedy of Errors **26**: 176

Coriolanus **17**: 180, 221
Henry IV, 1 and 2 **14**: 66
Much Ado about Nothing **18**: 228
Othello **11**: 321

Bruster, Douglas
  The Two Noble Kinsmen **41**: 340

Bryan, George B.
  Richard II **24**: 291

Bryant, J. A., Jr.
  Cymbeline **4**: 105
  The Merry Wives of Windsor **5**: 376
  Twelfth Night **46**: 291
  Richard II **6**: 323

Bryant, James C.
  Romeo and Juliet **33**: 300

Bryden, Ronald
  Hamlet **21**: 253
  Henry IV, 1 and 2 **14**: 72, 81
  Henry V **14**: 277
  King John **24**: 221
  The Merry Wives of Windsor **18**: 38
  Othello **11**: 296

Buckle, Richard
  King Lear **11**: 63
  The Merry Wives of Windsor **18**: 33
  Much Ado about Nothing **18**: 162

Buckmann-de Villegas, Sabine
  Julius Caesar **17**: 411

Bucknill, John Charles
  King Lear **2**: 120

Buhler, Stephen M.
  Julius Caesar **37**: 203

Bullen, A. H.
  Titus Andronicus **4**: 631

Bullogh, Geoffrey
  King John **41**: 234

Bulthaupt, Heinrich
  The Winter's Tale **7**: 396

Burckhardt, Sigurd
  Henry IV, 1 and 2 **1**: 421
  Julius Caesar **7**: 331
  King John **9**: 284
  King Lear **2**: 257
  The Merchant of Venice **4**: 293

Burke, Kenneth
  Coriolanus **9**: 148; **30**: 67
  Julius Caesar **7**: 238
  Othello **4**: 506

Burkhardt, Louis
  Measure for Measure **32**: 16

Burnett, Mark Thornton
  Hamlet **28**: 232
  Love's Labour's Lost **25**: 1

Burnim, Kalman
Macbeth **20**: 32

Burrows, Jill
The Comedy of Errors **26**: 164
Measure for Measure **23**: 347

Burt, Richard A.
The Taming of the Shrew **31**: 269

Burton, Richard
Hamlet **21**: 245

Bush, Douglas
The Rape of Lucrece **10**: 73
Venus and Adonis **10**: 424

Bush, Geoffrey
As You Like It **5**: 102
King Lear **2**: 207

Bushnell, Nelson Sherwin
The Tempest **8**: 340

Butler, Francelia
Timon of Athens **20**: 433

Butler, Guy
As You Like It **46**: 117

Buxton, John
The Phoenix and Turtle **38**: 329

Byles, Joanna Montgomery
Hamlet **44**: 180

Byrne, Muriel St. Clare
All's Well That Ends Well **26**: 28
As You Like It **23**: 85
Cymbeline **15**: 100
Henry VIII **24**: 106
Othello **11**: 287
Pericles **15**: 145
The Tempest **15**: 261
Timon of Athens **20**: 449
The Two Gentlemen of Verona **12**: 464

Calderwood, James L.
All's Well That Ends Well **7**: 93; **38**: 65
Coriolanus **9**: 144, 198
Hamlet **35**: 215
Henry IV, 1 and 2 **39**: 117
Henry V **5**: 310; **30**: 181
Henry VI, 1, 2, and 3 **3**: 105
King John **9**: 275; **41**: 269
Love's Labour's Lost **2**: 356; **38**: 219
A Midsummer Night's Dream **3**: 477; **19**: 21; **22**: 23
Othello **13**: 304
Romeo and Juliet **5**: 550
Titus Andronicus **4**: 664

Callaghan, Dympna
Henry IV, 1 and 2 **25**: 89
Richard II **25**: 89

Camden, Carroll
Hamlet **35**: 126

Campbell, K. T. S.
The Phoenix and Turtle **10**: 42

Campbell, Mrs. Patrick
Macbeth **20**: 165

Campbell, Oscar James
As You Like It **5**: 70
Coriolanus **9**: 80
King Lear **2**: 188
Measure for Measure **2**: 456
The Tempest **15**: 247
Troilus and Cressida **3**: 574
Twelfth Night **1**: 577
The Two Gentlemen of Verona **6**: 468

Campbell, Thomas
Coriolanus **17**: 131
Hamlet **1**: 97
King John **24**: 177
Much Ado about Nothing **8**: 16
The Tempest **8**: 302
The Winter's Tale **7**: 387; **15**: 400

Candido, Joseph
The Comedy of Errors **16**: 3; **34**: 220
Henry VI, 1, 2, and 3 **39**: 213
King John **13**: 147

Cantor, Paul A.
King Lear **37**: 213

Capell, Edward
Henry VI, 1, 2, and 3 **3**: 20
Henry VIII **2**: 21
Love's Labour's Lost **2**: 300
Measure for Measure **2**: 394
Richard III **8**: 153
The Taming of the Shrew **9**: 318
Titus Andronicus **4**: 614

Carducci, Jane S.
Titus Andronicus **43**: 222

Carlisle, Carol J.
As You Like It **23**: 28
Cymbeline **15**: 11
King Lear **11**: 158
Romeo and Juliet **11**: 407
Two Gentlemen of Verona **42**: 18

Carlson, Harry
Coriolanus **17**: 183

Carlson, Marvin
Othello **11**: 235

Carlson, Susan
As You Like It **34**: 177

Carlyle, Thomas
Henry V **5**: 197

Carr, Joan
Cymbeline **36**: 142

Carroll, Lewis
Henry VIII **24**: 76
The Tempest **15**: 205

Carroll, William C.
Love's Labour's Lost **2**: 367
The Merry Wives of Windsor **5**: 379

Richard III **19**: 164
Sexuality (topic entry) **33**: 28
The Taming of the Shrew **9**: 430; **37**: 31
The Winter's Tale **37**: 31

Cartelli, Thomas
All's Well That Ends Well **38**: 142
Henry VI, 1, 2, and 3 **28**: 112
Macbeth **20**: 406

Carter, Albert Howard
All's Well That Ends Well **7**: 62

Carter, Stephen
The Rape of Lucrece **32**: 321

Case, Arthur E.
All's Well That Ends Well **26**: 94

Case, R. H.
Antony and Cleopatra **6**: 60

Cavell, Stanley
Coriolanus **30**: 111
King Lear **31**: 155
Macbeth **29**: 91

Cazemian, Louis
Henry IV, 1 and 2 **1**: 355

Cecil, David
Antony and Cleopatra **6**: 111

Cerasano, S. P.
Richard III **14**: 490

Cespedes, Frank V.
Henry VIII **2**: 81

Chaillet, Ned
The Comedy of Errors **26**: 158
Hamlet **21**: 308
Richard III **14**: 474
The Two Gentlemen of Verona **12**: 490

Challinor, A. M.
Authorship Controversy (topic entry) **41**: 42

Chalmers, George
Measure for Measure **2**: 394
Sonnets **10**: 156, 158

Chambers, Colin
Richard III **14**: 475

Chambers, E. K.
All's Well That Ends Well **7**: 27
Antony and Cleopatra **6**: 64
As You Like It **5**: 55
The Comedy of Errors **1**: 16
Coriolanus **9**: 43
Cymbeline **4**: 46
Henry IV, 1 and 2 **1**: 336
Henry V **5**: 210
Henry VIII **2**: 42
Julius Caesar **7**: 189
King John **9**: 244
King Lear **2**: 143
Love's Labour's Lost **2**: 316
The Merchant of Venice **4**: 221

The Merry Wives of Windsor **5**: 350
A Midsummer Night's Dream **3**: 395
Much Ado about Nothing **8**: 39
Othello **4**: 440
Pericles **2**: 554
Richard II **6**: 277
Richard III **8**: 182
Romeo and Juliet **5**: 445
The Taming of the Shrew **9**: 330
The Tempest **8**: 326
Timon of Athens **1**: 478
Troilus and Cressida **3**: 557
Twelfth Night **1**: 561
The Two Gentlemen of Verona **6**: 460
The Winter's Tale **7**: 410

Chambers, R. W.
King Lear **2**: 170
Measure for Measure **2**: 437

Champion, Larry S.
The Comedy of Errors **1**: 56
Henry V **30**: 227
Henry VI, 1, 2, and 3 **3**: 154; **39**: 187
King John **13**: 152
Much Ado about Nothing **31**: 216
Othello **35**: 253
Titus Andronicus **4**: 662

Chaney, Joseph
Love's Labour's Lost **38**: 172

Chapman, John
King Lear **11**: 55

Charles, Casey
Twelfth Night **42**: 32

Charlton, H. B.
All's Well That Ends Well **7**: 37
The Comedy of Errors **1**: 23
Hamlet **1**: 166
Henry IV, 1 and 2 **1**: 357
Henry V **5**: 225
Julius Caesar **7**: 218
Love's Labour's Lost **2**: 322
Measure for Measure **2**: 434
The Merry Wives of Windsor **5**: 350
A Midsummer Night's Dream **3**: 402
Richard II **6**: 304
Richard III **8**: 197
Romeo and Juliet **5**: 464
The Taming of the Shrew **9**: 334
Titus Andronicus **4**: 640
Troilus and Cressida **3**: 571
Twelfth Night **1**: 573
The Two Gentlemen of Verona **6**: 472

Charnes, Linda
Troilus and Cressida **43**: 340

Charney, Hanna
Madness (topic entry) **35**: 49

Charney, Maurice
Antony and Cleopatra **6**: 155, 161

Coriolanus **9**: 136
Henry V **14**: 303
Julius Caesar **7**: 296
King John **25**: 98
Madness (topic entry) **35**: 49
Timon of Athens **25**: 198
Titus Andronicus **16**: 225
Troilus and Cressida **27**: 366

Chateaubriand
Romeo and Juliet **5**: 420

Chaudhuri, Sukanta
Kingship (topic entry) **39**: 20

Cheney, Donald
The Rape of Lucrece **10**: 125

Chesterton, C. K.
A Midsummer Night's Dream **3**: 393

Child, Harold
All's Well That Ends Well **26**: 72
The Comedy of Errors **26**: 182
Coriolanus **17**: 34
Henry IV, 1 and 2 **14**: 120
The Merry Wives of Windsor **18**: 67
A Midsummer Night's Dream **12**: 282
Much Ado about Nothing **18**: 232
Richard II **24**: 390
The Winter's Tale **15**: 500

Chillington, Carol A.
Coriolanus **17**: 194
Henry VI, 1, 2, and 3 **24**: 38

Chinoy, Helen Krich
The Merchant of Venice **12**: 91

Christensen, Ann C.
Coriolanus **42**: 218

Church, Tony
Hamlet **21**: 416

Cibber, Colley
Hamlet **21**: 19
King John **9**: 209

Cibber, Theophilius
King Lear **11**: 114
Romeo and Juliet **11**: 379

Cirillo, Albert R.
As You Like It **5**: 130
Romeo and Juliet **11**: 475

Clapp, Henry A.
As You Like It **5**: 44
A Midsummer Night's Dream **3**: 380

Clark, Cumberland
A Midsummer Night's Dream **3**: 400

Clarke, Asia Booth
Hamlet **21**: 70

Clarke, Charles Cowden
As You Like It **5**: 36

Henry IV, 1 and 2 **1**: 321
King John **9**: 229; **24**: 186
A Midsummer Night's Dream **3**: 376
Much Ado about Nothing **8**: 24
Romeo and Juliet **11**: 400
The Tempest **8**: 308

Clarke, Mary
All's Well That Ends Well **26**: 37
Cymbeline **15**: 51
Henry V **14**: 260
King John **24**: 203
Othello **11**: 280
Timon of Athens **20**: 450
Troilus and Cressida **18**: 314
The Two Gentlemen of Verona **12**: 465

Clarke, Mary Cowden
Romeo and Juliet **11**: 400

Clayton, Thomas
Othello **28**: 243

Clemen, Wolfgang H.
Hamlet **1**: 188
Henry VI, 1, 2, and 3 **3**: 71
King Lear **2**: 199
Richard III **8**: 206
Romeo and Juliet **5**: 477
Titus Andronicus **4**: 644

Clements, John
The Tempest **15**: 366

Clurman, Harold
All's Well That Ends Well **26**: 27
King Lear **11**: 92, 103
The Merchant of Venice **12**: 78
A Midsummer Night's Dream **12**: 240
The Two Gentlemen of Verona **12**: 471

Coates, John
Antony and Cleopatra **27**: 117

Cochrane, Claire
Timon of Athens **20**: 475

Coddon, Karin S.
Madness (topic entry) **35**: 68
Macbeth **13**: 361
Twelfth Night **34**: 330

Coffey, Denise
Much Ado about Nothing **18**: 254

Coghill, Nevill
Measure for Measure **2**: 491
The Merchant of Venice **4**: 250
The Taming of the Shrew **9**: 344
The Winter's Tale **7**: 464; **15**: 518

Cohen, D. M.
The Merchant of Venice **40**: 175

Cohen, Derek
Henry VI, 1, 2, and 3 **25**: 102, 109
King Lear **25**: 202
Titus Andronicus **43**: 255
Violence in Shakespeare's Works (topic entry) **43**: 24

Cohn, Ruby
Coriolanus **17**: 188

Cole, Douglas
Troilus and Cressida **27**: 376

Cole, John William
Henry V **14**: 186
King John **24**: 196
A Midsummer Night's Dream **12**: 185
Richard II **24**: 280
The Tempest **15**: 210

Coleman, John
As You Like It **23**: 18
Hamlet **21**: 59
Macbeth **20**: 105
The Taming of the Shrew **12**: 371

Coleman, Robert
The Two Gentlemen of Verona **12**: 467

Coleridge, Hartley
Antony and Cleopatra **6**: 32
The Merry Wives of Windsor **5**: 339
Much Ado about Nothing **8**: 19
The Two Noble Kinsmen **9**: 455
The Winter's Tale **7**: 389

Coleridge, Samuel Taylor
All's Well That Ends Well **7**: 15
Antony and Cleopatra **6**: 25
As You Like It **5**: 23
The Comedy of Errors **1**: 14
Coriolanus **9**: 17
Hamlet **1**: 94, 95
Henry IV, 1 and 2 **1**: 310, 311
Henry VI, 1, 2, and 3 **3**: 27
Julius Caesar **7**: 160
King Lear **2**: 106
Love's Labour's Lost **2**: 302
Macbeth **3**: 184
Measure for Measure **2**: 397
A Midsummer Night's Dream **3**: 365
Much Ado about Nothing **8**: 16
Othello **4**: 399, 402, 405, 406
Pericles **2**: 544
Richard II **6**: 255, 262
Richard III **8**: 161
Romeo and Juliet **5**: 425
Sonnets **10**: 159, 173
The Tempest **8**: 295, 299
Timon of Athens **1**: 459
Titus Andronicus **4**: 617
Troilus and Cressida **3**: 541
The Two Noble Kinsmen **9**: 447
Venus and Adonis **10**: 414
The Winter's Tale **7**: 383, 387

Colie, Rosalie L.
As You Like It **34**: 147
Cymbeline **4**: 148
King Lear **31**: 92
Romeo and Juliet **5**: 559
Sonnets **40**: 247
Troilus and Cressida **43**: 293

Collier, Jeremy
See also Steevens, George; Hic et Ubique; Longinus; and Lorenzo
Hamlet **1**: 73
Henry IV, 1 and 2 **1**: 286

Henry V **5**: 185
Timon of Athens **1**: 456

Collins, A. S.
Timon of Athens **1**: 492

Collins, Glenn
The Comedy of Errors **26**: 172
Julius Caesar **17**: 398

Colman, E. A. M.
Cymbeline **36**: 155
Sexuality (topic entry) **33**: 1

Colman, George
King Lear **2**: 102
The Merchant of Venice **4**: 192

Colvin, Clare
Julius Caesar **17**: 394
Richard III **14**: 473

Conklin, Paul
Hamlet **21**: 339

Conrad, Hermann
Sonnets **10**: 214

Cook, Ann Jennalie
The Merchant of Venice **12**: 95

Cook, Carol
Much Ado about Nothing **31**: 245
Troilus and Cressida **43**: 329

Cook, Dorothy
Henry V **5**: 289

Cook, Dutton
The Merchant of Venice **12**: 16
Othello **11**: 244
Richard III **14**: 397
The Tempest **15**: 217

Cook, Judith
Antony and Cleopatra **17**: 113
Julius Caesar **17**: 387
Macbeth **20**: 294
Much Ado about Nothing **18**: 235, 236
Richard III **14**: 511

Cooke, William
The Merchant of Venice **12**: 4
Othello **11**: 189

Cookman, A. V.
Romeo and Juliet **11**: 447

Cope, Walter
Love's Labour's Lost **2**: 299

Copland, Murray
The Phoenix and Turtle **10**: 40

Corballis, Richard
Madness (topic entry) **35**: 7

Corbet, Richard
Richard III **8**: 144

Corfield, Coano
The Tempest **8**: 458

Coriat, Isador H.
  Macbeth **3**: 219
  Romeo and Juliet **5**: 425

Corliss, Richard
  Much Ado about Nothing **18**: 221

Cornwallis, Sir William
  Richard III **8**: 144

Cottrell, John
  Coriolanus **17**: 161
  Hamlet **21**: 203
  Henry V **14**: 232
  The Merchant of Venice **12**: 90
  Othello **11**: 311

Coursen, H. R.
  Hamlet **44**: 133
  Macbeth **44**: 289
  Much Ado about Nothing **18**: 201

Coursen, Herbert R., Jr.
  Macbeth **3**: 318
  The Tempest **8**: 429

Courthope, W. J.
  The Two Gentlemen of Verona **6**: 460

Courtney, W. L.
  A Midsummer Night's Dream **12**: 206

Cousins, A. D.
  Venus and Adonis **28**: 355

Coveney, Michael
  All's Well That Ends Well **26**: 71
  As You Like It **23**: 139, 146
  Hamlet **21**: 292, 326
  Henry IV, 1 and 2 **14**: 88
  Henry VIII **24**: 126
  King Lear **11**: 111
  Love's Labour's Lost **23**: 230
  Macbeth **20**: 291
  Much Ado about Nothing **18**: 208
  Twelfth Night **26**: 285, 329, 337
  The Winter's Tale **15**: 488

Cox, Catherine I.
  Clowns and Fools (topic entry) **46**: 78

Cox, Francis
  Troilus and Cressida **18**: 353

Cox, Frank
  Henry VI, 1, 2, and 3 **24**: 27

Cox, J. F.
  Much Ado about Nothing **18**: 257

Cox, John D.
  All's Well That Ends Well **13**: 66
  Henry V **30**: 215
  Henry VI, 1, 2, and 3 **3**: 151; **13**: 131
  Richard III **13**: 131

Cox, Majore Kolb
  Romeo and Juliet **33**: 249

Cox, Roger L.
  The Comedy of Errors **19**: 34
  Henry IV, 1 and 2 **1**: 438
  The Taming of the Shrew **19**: 34
  The Two Gentlemen of Verona **19**: 34

Craig, Edward
  Much Ado about Nothing **18**: 147

Craig, H. A. L.
  Much Ado about Nothing **18**: 178

Craig, Hardin
  The Comedy of Errors **1**: 31
  Coriolanus **30**: 74
  Pericles **2**: 564
  The Taming of the Shrew **9**: 341

Craik, T. W.
  Much Ado about Nothing **8**: 63
  Twelfth Night **26**: 337

Cran, Mrs. George
  The Merry Wives of Windsor **18**: 26
  Much Ado about Nothing **18**: 156

Crane, Milton
  As You Like It **5**: 92
  Twelfth Night **1**: 590

Crewe, Jonathan
  Rape of Lucrece **43**: 158

Crick, Bernard
  Antony and Cleopatra **17**: 61
  Twelfth Night **26**: 286

Crist, Judith
  The Merchant of Venice **12**: 69

Crockett, Bryan
  The Tempest **45**: 211

Crosman, Robert
  Sonnets **16**: 461

Crowley, Richard C.
  Coriolanus **9**: 177

Crowne, John
  Henry VI, 1, 2, and 3 **3**: 16

Crowther, Bosley
  Henry V **14**: 209, 211
  Macbeth **20**: 199

Cruttwell, Patrick
  Hamlet **1**: 234

Csengeri, Karen
  Pericles **16**: 391

Cumberland, Richard
  Henry IV, 1 and 2 **1**: 305
  Henry V **5**: 192

Cummings, Peter
  Sexuality (topic entry) **33**: 12

Cunliffe, John William
  Henry V **5**: 217

Cunningham, James
  Hamlet **42**: 229
  King Lear **42**: 229
  Macbeth **42**: 229
  Othello **42**: 229

Cunningham, John
  Macbeth **44**: 337

Cunningham, J. V.
  The Phoenix and Turtle **10**: 24

Cunningham, Karen
  Titus Andronicus **43**: 247

Curry, Walter Clyde
  Macbeth **3**: 239
  The Tempest **8**: 356

Curtis, Anthony
  The Comedy of Errors **26**: 160
  The Winter's Tale **15**: 484

Curtis, Jared R.
  Othello **4**: 580

Curtis, Nick
  Macbeth **20**: 315

Cusack, Sinead
  The Merchant of Venice **12**: 104

Cushman, Robert
  The Comedy of Errors **26**: 162
  Henry IV, 1 and 2 **14**: 101
  Macbeth **20**: 301
  Measure for Measure **23**: 344
  A Midsummer Night's Dream **12**: 269, 274
  Twelfth Night **26**: 268
  The Two Gentlemen of Verona **12**: 481

Cutts, John P.
  The Comedy of Errors **34**: 211
  The Two Gentlemen of Verona **40**: 327

Daigle, Lennett J.
  Venus and Adonis **33**: 330

Daly, Joseph Francis
  As You Like It **23**: 52
  The Merry Wives of Windsor **18**: 19

D'Amico, Jack
  Madness (topic entry) **35**: 62
  Politics and Power (topic entry) **30**: 49

Danby, David
  Hamlet **21**: 319

Danby, John F.
  Antony and Cleopatra **6**: 125
  Henry IV, 1 and 2 **1**: 391
  Pericles **2**: 573
  The Two Gentlemen of Verona **6**: 492

Daniel, George
  As You Like It **5**: 25

Daniell, David
  Coriolanus **17**: 201

Danson, Lawrence
  Desire (topic entry) **38**: 48
  Hamlet **44**: 198
  The Merchant of Venice **4**: 328
  Titus Andronicus **27**: 318

Darlington, W. A.
  Cymbeline **15**: 59
  King Lear **11**: 53
  The Merchant of Venice **12**: 65
  Othello **11**: 284
  The Taming of the Shrew **12**: 354

Dash, Irene G.
  A Midsummer Night's Dream **42**: 46
  Othello **35**: 369
  Romeo and Juliet **33**: 257
  Shakespeare's Representation of Women (topic entry) **31**: 1
  Twelfth Night **46**: 369

David, Richard
  All's Well That Ends Well **26**: 40
  As You Like It **23**: 109
  Cymbeline **15**: 83
  Hamlet **21**: 355
  Henry IV, 1 and 2 **14**: 49
  Henry V **14**: 259
  Julius Caesar **17**: 384
  King John **24**: 206, 228
  Love's Labour's Lost **23**: 191, 207
  Macbeth **20**: 302, 318
  Measure for Measure **23**: 299
  Richard II **24**: 325, 419
  The Taming of the Shrew **12**: 352
  Titus Andronicus **17**: 448
  Troilus and Cressida **18**: 307, 314
  Twelfth Night **26**: 231
  The Winter's Tale **15**: 490

Davidson, Clifford
  Timon of Athens **27**: 196

Davidson, Frank
  The Tempest **8**: 420

Davies, John
  Henry VIII **24**: 127
  Venus and Adonis **10**: 411

Davies, Robertson
  Henry V **14**: 263
  The Merchant of Venice **12**: 56

Davies, Thomas
  All's Well That Ends Well **26**: 92
  Antony and Cleopatra **6**: 23; **17**: 5
  Hamlet **21**: 21, 29, 334
  Henry IV, 1 and 2 **14**: 111
  Julius Caesar **7**: 159
  King John **9**: 216; **24**: 162, 167, 168
  King Lear **11**: 116
  Macbeth **3**: 181; **20**: 12, 25, 22
  Richard III **14**: 365
  Romeo and Juliet **11**: 377
  The Taming of the Shrew **12**: 309
  Troilus and Cressida **18**: 278
  The Winter's Tale **15**: 396

Davis, Lloyd
Appearance vs. Reality (topic entry) **34:** 23
Desire (topic entry) **38:** 31

Davis, Michael
Macbeth **44:** 315

Dawes, James
Sonnets **32:** 327

Dawson, Anthony B.
As You Like It **23:** 162
Hamlet **21:** 371
Henry IV, 1 and 2 **14:** 160
Henry V **14:** 342
Julius Caesar **17:** 426
Macbeth **20:** 413
Measure for Measure **23:** 395
Richard II **24:** 428
The Tempest **15:** 385
The Winter's Tale **15:** 532

Dawson, Helen
Love's Labour's Lost **23:** 201
A Midsummer Night's Dream **12:** 256

de Grazia, Margareta
General Commentary **13:** 487
Sonnets **28:** 363; **40:** 273

de Jongh, Nicholas
As You Like It **23:** 141, 148
King John **24:** 239
Twelfth Night **26:** 334

de Sousa, Geraldo U.
Henry VI, 1, 2, and 3 **37:** 97

De Quincey, Thomas
Macbeth **3:** 190
The Two Noble Kinsmen **9:** 447

Dean, Leonard F.
Henry IV, 1 and 2 **1:** 370
Richard II **6:** 315

Dean, Paul
General Commentary **13:** 481

Deats, Sara Munson
Violence in Shakespeare's Works (topic entry) **43:** 32

Deighton, K.
Pericles **2:** 553

Dench, Judi
Antony and Cleopatra **17:** 82

Dennis, John
Coriolanus **9:** 9
Julius Caesar **7:** 151
The Merry Wives of Windsor **5:** 333; **18:** 5, 7

Dent, Alan
All's Well That Ends Well **26:** 13
As You Like It **23:** 69
Julius Caesar **17:** 370
Macbeth **20:** 166
Richard II **24:** 329

Dent, R. W.
A Midsummer Night's Dream **3:** 441

Derrick, Patty S.
The Two Gentlemen of Verona **42:** 18

Desai, R. W.
The Winter's Tale **37:** 305

Desmet, Christy
Appearance vs. Reality (topic entry) **34:** 54

Dessen, Allan C.
As You Like It **32:** 212
Henry IV, 1 and 2 **32:** 212
King Lear **32:** 212
Macbeth **32:** 212
Romeo and Juliet **32:** 212
Titus Andronicus **17:** 483, 492

Detmer, Emily
Violence in Shakespeare's Works (topic entry) **43:** 61

DeVine, Lawrence
Titus Andronicus **17:** 473

DeWilde, G. J.
Macbeth **20:** 89

Dexter, John
As You Like It **23:** 124

Di Biase, Carmine
Cymbeline **28:** 373

Dibdin, Charles
Richard II **6:** 255
Romeo and Juliet **5:** 419
The Two Gentlemen of Verona **6:** 438

Dick Bernard F.
Julius Caesar **17:** 364

Dickey, Franklin M.
Romeo and Juliet **5:** 485
Troilus and Cressida **3:** 594
Venus and Adonis **10:** 449

Dickey, Stephen
Pericles **36:** 279
Twelfth Night **19:** 42

DiGangi, Mario
Measure for Measure **25:** 12; **33:** 90; **46:** 142

Digges, Leonard
Julius Caesar **7:** 149
Twelfth Night **1:** 539

Dillon, Janette
Sonnets **10:** 372

Disch, Thomas M.
Julius Caesar **17:** 403
Love's Labour's Lost **23:** 228

Dithmar, E. A.
The Merry Wives of Windsor **18:** 16

Twelfth Night **26:** 214

Dodds, W. M. T.
Measure for Measure **2:** 463

Dodsworth, Martin
All's Well That Ends Well **26:** 72
Hamlet **21:** 334
Julius Caesar **17:** 389
Love's Labour's Lost **23:** 215

Doebler, John
Venus and Adonis **10:** 486

Dolan, Frances E.
Violence in Shakespeare's Works (topic entry) **43:** 39

Donaldson, E. Talbot
Troilus and Cressida **43:** 305

Donaldson, Ian
All's Well That Ends Well **38:** 123
The Rape of Lucrece **33:** 131

Donnellan, Declan
The Tempest **15:** 338

Donno, Elizabeth Story
Twelfth Night **46:** 286

Donohue, Joseph
Macbeth **20:** 376

Donohue, Joseph W., Jr.
Macbeth **20:** 32, 70, 73

Doone, Rupert
Richard III **14:** 420

Doran, John
The Merchant of Venice **12:** 6

Doran, Madeleine
Antony and Cleopatra **27:** 96

Dorsch, T. S.
The Comedy of Errors **26:** 142, 186
Julius Caesar **7:** 277

Dowden, Edward
All's Well That Ends Well **7:** 26
Antony and Cleopatra **6:** 41
As You Like It **5:** 43
The Comedy of Errors **1:** 16
Coriolanus **9:** 31
Hamlet **1:** 115
Henry IV, 1 and 2 **1:** 326
Henry VI, 1, 2, and 3 **3:** 41
Julius Caesar **7:** 174
King John **9:** 234
King Lear **2:** 131
Love's Labour's Lost **2:** 308
Macbeth **3:** 207
Measure for Measure **2:** 410
A Midsummer Night's Dream **3:** 379
Much Ado about Nothing **8:** 28
Pericles **2:** 549
The Phoenix and Turtle **10:** 9
The Rape of Lucrece **10:** 68

Richard II **6:** 267
Richard III **8:** 168
Romeo and Juliet **5:** 437
Sonnets **10:** 215
The Taming of the Shrew **9:** 325
The Tempest **8:** 312
Timon of Athens **1:** 470
Titus Andronicus **4:** 625
Troilus and Cressida **3:** 548
Twelfth Night **1:** 561
The Two Gentlemen of Verona **6:** 449
The Two Noble Kinsmen **9:** 456
Venus and Adonis **10:** 419
The Winter's Tale **7:** 395

Dowling, Ellen
The Taming of the Shrew **12:** 441

Downer, Alan S.
Macbeth **20:** 107
Romeo and Juliet **11:** 463

Downes, John
Hamlet **21:** 9
Macbeth **20:** 12
A Midsummer Night's Dream **12:** 144
Romeo and Juliet **11:** 377
The Tempest **15:** 195

Downs-Gamble, Margaret
The Taming of the Shrew **31:** 339

Drake, James
Hamlet **1:** 73

Drake, Nathan
Richard II **6:** 259
Richard III **8:** 162
Sonnets **10:** 158, 161
Venus and Adonis **10:** 416

Draper, John W.
As You Like It **5:** 66
King Lear **2:** 168
Shakespeare's Representation of Women (topic entry) **31:** 12
Timon of Athens **1:** 487, 489
Twelfth Night **1:** 581

Draper, R. P.
Richard II **39:** 289

Dreher, Diane Elizabeth
Fathers and Daughters (topic entry) **36:** 12

Drew, John
Richard II **24:** 291
The Taming of the Shrew **12:** 330

Driver, Tom F.
King Lear **11:** 97
Macbeth **3:** 293
Richard III **8:** 223
Romeo and Juliet **5:** 518

Dromey, Mary Jane Scholtes
Coriolanus **17:** 148

Dronke, Peter
  The Phoenix and Turtle **38:** 367

Drury, Alan
  As You Like It **23:** 129
  The Merry Wives of Windsor **18:** 54
  Pericles **15:** 164

Dryden, John
  Henry IV, 1 and 2 **1:** 285
  Julius Caesar **7:** 149
  Macbeth **3:** 170
  The Merry Wives of Windsor **5:** 332
  A Midsummer Night's Dream **3:** 361
  Pericles **2:** 537
  Richard II **6:** 250
  Romeo and Juliet **5:** 415
  The Tempest **8:** 286; **15:** 189, 343
  Troilus and Cressida **3:** 536; **18:** 276, 277
  The Winter's Tale **7:** 376

Dubrow, Heather
  The Rape of Lucrece **10:** 135
  Sonnets **10:** 367; **40:** 238

Duff, William
  A Midsummer Night's Dream **3:** 362

Dukes, Ashley
  Richard II **24:** 302
  Romeo and Juliet **11:** 447

Dunbar, Mary Judith
  Pericles **36:** 251

Duncan-Jones, Katherine
  Authorship Controversy (topic entry) **41:** 110
  Richard II **24:** 382
  Sonnets **42:** 296
  Venus and Adonis **25:** 328

Dundas, Judith
  Rape of Lucrece **10:** 128

Dunkel, Wilbur
  Henry VIII **24:** 80

Dunkley, Chris
  The Taming of the Shrew **12:** 397

Dunn, Allen
  A Midsummer Night's Dream **13:** 19

Dunn, Esther Cloudman
  The Rape of Lucrece **10:** 74

Dusinberre, Juliet
  As You Like It **28:** 46
  Gender Identity (topic entry) **40:** 51
  King John **16:** 161
  The Taming of the Shrew **31:** 307

Duthie, George Ian
  Romeo and Juliet **5:** 480
  The Taming of the Shrew **9:** 347

Dyboski, Roman
  Coriolanus **9:** 62

Dyson, H. V. D.
  Henry VI, 1, 2, and 3 **3:** 64

Dyson, J. P.
  Macbeth **3:** 302

Eagleton, Terence
  Coriolanus **9:** 153
  Macbeth **3:** 321
  Measure for Measure **2:** 507
  Troilus and Cressida **3:** 617
  Twelfth Night **34:** 293

Edelman, Charles
  Cymbeline **22:** 365
  King Lear **22:** 365
  Macbeth **22:** 365

Eder, Richard
  Antony and Cleopatra **17:** 71
  As You Like It **23:** 119
  Henry V **14:** 325
  Macbeth **20:** 306
  Richard III **14:** 468

Edinborough, Arnold
  Antony and Cleopatra **17:** 47
  Hamlet **21:** 222
  Henry V **14:** 265, 269
  Much Ado about Nothing **18:** 176
  The Taming of the Shrew **12:** 368
  Timon of Athens **20:** 458
  Twelfth Night **26:** 248

Edwards, Christopher
  As You Like It **23:** 138
  Coriolanus **17:** 212
  Hamlet **21:** 314, 315
  Henry VI, 1, 2, and 3 **24:** 48
  Love's Labour's Lost **23:** 216
  The Taming of the Shrew **12:** 409
  Troilus and Cressida **18:** 385, 390
  Twelfth Night **26:** 305, 330
  The Two Gentlemen of Verona **12:** 493

Edwards, Philip
  Hamlet **44:** 119
  Pericles **2:** 586
  Romeo and Juliet **33:** 272
  Sonnets **10:** 342
  Twelfth Night **1:** 654
  The Two Noble Kinsmen **9:** 481

Egan, Robert
  The Tempest **8:** 435

Eggert, Katherine
  Henry V **28:** 121

Eliot, T. S.
  Coriolanus **9:** 58
  Hamlet **1:** 142
  Othello **4:** 454

Ellen, Terry
  Henry VIII **24:** 82
  Much Ado about Nothing **18:** 133

Elliot, John R., Jr.
  Richard II **39:** 235

Elliott, G. R.
  The Comedy of Errors **1:** 27
  Macbeth **3:** 286
  Othello **4:** 470, 522

Elliott, Michael
  The Winter's Tale **15:** 449

Ellis, David
  Clowns and Fools (topic entry) **46:** 68

Ellis, Roger
  Clowns and Fools (topic entry) **46:** 1

Ellis-Fermor, Una
  Coriolanus **9:** 121
  Henry IV, 1 and 2 **1:** 379
  Henry V **5:** 244
  Julius Caesar **7:** 252
  Measure for Measure **2:** 432
  Timon of Athens **1:** 490
  Troilus and Cressida **3:** 578; **18:** 412

Ellrodt, Robert
  The Phoenix and Turtle **38:** 350
  Sonnets **28:** 380

Elsom, John
  All's Well That Ends Well **26:** 54
  Antony and Cleopatra **17:** 66
  As You Like It **23:** 112, 122
  Henry IV, 1 and 2 **14:** 86
  King John **24:** 220
  Measure for Measure **23:** 338
  A Midsummer Night's Dream **12:** 271
  Pericles **15:** 159
  Richard II **24:** 345, 371
  The Taming of the Shrew **12:** 389
  The Tempest **15:** 279
  Troilus and Cressida **18:** 357
  The Two Gentlemen of Verona **12:** 491

Elze, Karl
  All's Well That Ends Well **7:** 21
  Henry VIII **2:** 35
  The Merchant of Venice **4:** 209

Emerson, Ralph Waldo
  The Phoenix and Turtle **10:** 7

Emerson, Sally
  The Comedy of Errors **26:** 157
  Henry VI, 1, 2, and 3 **24:** 34

Empson, William
  Hamlet **1:** 202
  Henry IV, 1 and 2 **1:** 359
  Measure for Measure **2:** 486
  The Rape of Lucrece **10:** 96
  Sonnets **10:** 256
  Troilus and Cressida **3:** 569

Engle, Lars
  The Merchant of Venice **25:** 22; **40:** 197
  Sonnets **13:** 445

Enright, D. J.
  Coriolanus **9:** 112

Enterline, Lynn
  The Winter's Tale **42:** 301

Erickson, Peter
  As You Like It **5:** 168
  Hamlet **44:** 189
  King Lear **31:** 137
  Love's Labour's Lost **38:** 232
  The Merry Wives of Windsor **5:** 402

Erskine, John
  Romeo and Juliet **5:** 450

Ervine, St. John
  The Two Gentlemen of Verona **12:** 459

Esslin, Martin
  As You Like It **23:** 98
  The Winter's Tale **15:** 480

Ettin, Andrew V.
  Titus Andronicus **27:** 275

Evans, B. Ifor
  The Merchant of Venice **4:** 267
  A Midsummer Night's Dream **3:** 415

Evans, Bertrand
  All's Well That Ends Well **7:** 81
  As You Like It **5:** 107
  The Comedy of Errors **1:** 37
  Love's Labour's Lost **2:** 338
  Macbeth **3:** 338
  Measure for Measure **2:** 498
  The Merry Wives of Windsor **5:** 355
  A Midsummer Night's Dream **3:** 434
  Much Ado about Nothing **8:** 82
  Pericles **2:** 575
  Romeo and Juliet **5:** 470
  Twelfth Night **1:** 625
  The Two Gentlemen of Verona **6:** 499

Evans, G. Blakemore
  Romeo and Juliet **11:** 517; **33:** 210

Evans, Gareth Lloyd
  All's Well That Ends Well **26:** 48
  As You Like It **23:** 132
  Clowns and Fools (topic entry) **46:** 52
  Henry IV, 1 and 2 **14:** 81
  King Lear **11:** 112
  Macbeth **20:** 262, 296, 329, 379
  The Merry Wives of Windsor **18:** 46
  A Midsummer Night's Dream **12:** 276
  Richard III **14:** 490
  The Taming of the Shrew **12:** 358
  Troilus and Cressida **18:** 349, 403
  Twelfth Night **26:** 272
  The Two Gentlemen of Verona **12:** 480

Evans, Malcolm
  Love's Labour's Lost **2**: 365

Evans, Peter
  The Merry Wives of Windsor **18**: 90

Evans, Robert O.
  Romeo and Juliet **5**: 530

Everett, Barbara
  Antony and Cleopatra **17**: 79
  Hamlet **1**: 268
  King Lear **2**: 229
  Much Ado about Nothing **8**: 91; **28**: 56
  Romeo and Juliet **33**: 294
  Sonnets **28**: 385
  Troilus and Cressida **27**: 347

Ewbank, Inga-Stina
  Hamlet **1**: 270
  The Tempest **19**: 379
  The Two Gentlemen of Verona **6**: 541
  The Winter's Tale **7**: 476; **13**: 409

Eyres, Harry
  Richard II **24**: 385

Faber, M. D.
  A Midsummer Night's Dream **3**: 483
  Othello **35**: 282
  Romeo and Juliet **5**: 556

Fairchild, Arthur H. R.
  The Phoenix and Turtle **10**: 9

Fairchild, Hoxie N.
  Measure for Measure **2**: 427

Falk, Florence
  A Midsummer Night's Dream **3**: 502

Farber, Manny
  Henry V **14**: 212

Farber, Stephen
  The Taming of the Shrew **12**: 373

Farjeon, Herbert
  All's Well That Ends Well **26**: 14
  As You Like It **23**: 68
  Henry IV, 1 and 2 **14**: 28
  King Lear **11**: 47, 52
  A Midsummer Night's Dream **12**: 235, 294
  Othello **11**: 264
  Richard II **24**: 300, 303
  Richard III **14**: 410
  The Tempest **15**: 233
  Twelfth Night **26**: 359

Farley-Hills, David
  The Taming of the Shrew **31**: 261
  Timon of Athens **16**: 351

Farmer, Richard
  Henry V **5**: 190
  Pericles **2**: 538

Farnham, Willard
  Antony and Cleopatra **6**: 136
  Coriolanus **9**: 92

Farrah
  Henry V **14**: 295

Farrell, Kirby
  Fathers and Daughters (topic entry) **36**: 25
  Romeo and Juliet **13**: 235
  Venus and Adonis **33**: 370

Faucit, Helena (Lady Martin)
  As You Like It **5**: 44
  Cymbeline **4**: 37
  Hamlet **21**: 386
  Othello **11**: 334
  The Winter's Tale **15**: 413

Fawcett, Mary Laughlin
  Titus Andronicus **43**: 239

Fehrenbach, Robert J.
  Henry IV, 1 and 2 **39**: 137

Feingold, Michael
  Measure for Measure **23**: 353
  Much Ado about Nothing **18**: 222
  Richard III **14**: 483

Felheim, Marvin
  The Merry Wives of Windsor **18**: 21; **38**: 313
  A Midsummer Night's Dream **12**: 198
  The Taming of the Shrew **12**: 331
  The Two Gentlemen of Verona **12**: 456; **40**: 330

Felperin, Howard
  Henry VIII **2**: 66
  Macbeth **44**: 341
  Pericles **2**: 581

Feltham, Owen
  Pericles **2**: 537

Felton, Felix
  A Midsummer Night's Dream **12**: 213

Felver, Charles
  Clowns and Fools (topic entry) **46**: 33

Fender, Stephen
  A Midsummer Night's Dream **3**: 459

Fenton, James
  The Comedy of Errors **26**: 162
  Much Ado about Nothing **18**: 211
  Twelfth Night **26**: 302

Fenwick, Henry
  Richard II **24**: 364

Ferber, Michael
  The Merchant of Venice **40**: 127

Ferguson, Otis
  A Midsummer Night's Dream **12**: 212

Fergusson, Francis
  The Comedy of Errors **1**: 35
  Hamlet **1**: 184
  Macbeth **3**: 267
  Richard III **39**: 305
  Troilus and Cressida **18**: 298

Ferry, Anne
  Sonnets **40**: 292

Fichter, Andrew
  Antony and Cleopatra **6**: 224

Fiedler, Leslie A.
  Henry VI, 1, 2, and 3 **3**: 140

Field, Kate
  Hamlet **21**: 81

Fielding, Henry
  Hamlet **21**: 15

Fienberg, Nona
  Pericles **2**: 590; **36**: 274

Figes, Eva
  Kingship (topic entry) **39**: 62

Findlater, Richard
  Antony and Cleopatra **17**: 37
  The Comedy of Errors **26**: 164
  Henry IV, 1 and 2 **14**: 37
  The Taming of the Shrew **12**: 358
  Twelfth Night **26**: 304
  The Two Gentlemen of Verona **12**: 476
  The Winter's Tale **15**: 469

Findlay, Alison
  Hamlet **35**: 144

Fineman, Joel
  Rape of Lucrece **43**: 113

Fink, Joel G.
  The Comedy of Errors **26**: 171

Fink, Z. S.
  As You Like It **5**: 68

Finkelpearl, Philip J.
  The Two Noble Kinsmen **37**: 312

Fisher, James E.
  Othello **11**: 306

Fisher, Sandra K.
  Henry IV, 1 and 2 **13**: 213
  Henry V **13**: 213
  Richard II **13**: 213

Fitz, L. T.
  Antony and Cleopatra **27**: 144

Fitzgerald, Percy
  Henry VIII **24**: 70
  A Midsummer Night's Dream **12**: 287
  Othello **11**: 253
  The Tempest **15**: 343

Fitzpatrick, Thomas
  King Lear **2**: 99

Fitzsimons, Raymond
  The Merchant of Venice **12**: 14

Flathe, J. L. F.
  Macbeth **3**: 199

Fleming, Peter
  Antony and Cleopatra **17**: 30
  As You Like It **23**: 79, 83
  Macbeth **20**: 188
  Measure for Measure **23**: 297
  The Merchant of Venice **12**: 52
  Othello **11**: 275
  Richard II **24**: 319
  Romeo and Juliet **11**: 446
  Twelfth Night **26**: 243
  The Winter's Tale **15**: 461

Flesy, F. G.
  Measure for Measure **2**: 548
  Timon of Athens **1**: 469

Fletcher, George
  King John **24**: 184

Flint, Stella
  The Taming of the Shrew **12**: 408

Fly, Richard D.
  King Lear **2**: 271
  Timon of Athens **1**: 522
  Troilus and Cressida **3**: 630; **27**: 354

Foakes, R. A.
  The Comedy of Errors **26**: 183; **34**: 208
  Cymbeline **4**: 134
  Hamlet **25**: 209
  Henry VIII **2**: 51
  King Lear **25**: 218
  Measure for Measure **2**: 516
  The Tempest **45**: 188
  Troilus and Cressida **27**: 341

Folland, Harold F.
  Richard II **6**: 393

Foote, Samuel
  King Lear **11**: 5

Forbes-Robinson, John
  King Lear **11**: 21

Ford-Davies, Oliver
  Coriolanus **17**: 195

Forker, Charles R.
  Henry VI, 1, 2, and 3 **3**: 97

Forman, Simon
  Cymbeline **4**: 17
  The Winter's Tale **7**: 375

Forster, John
  Hamlet **21**: 22, 51
  King Lear **11**: 17
  Macbeth **20**: 98

Fortin, Rene E.
  Julius Caesar **7**: 336
  King Lear **2**: 286
  The Merchant of Venice **4**: 324

Foster, Charles J.
  Henry IV, 1 and 2 **14**: 4
  The Merry Wives of Windsor **18**: 12

Foster, Donald W.
  Authorship Controversy (topic entry) **41**: 85

Foster, Verna A.
  The Winter's Tale **25**: 339

Foulkes, Richard
  The Merchant of Venice **12**: 43, 107
  A Midsummer Night's Dream **12**: 172
  Richard II **24**: 283

Fowler, Alastair
  The Winter's Tale **36**: 362

Fowler, William Warde
  Julius Caesar **7**: 200

Fox-Good, Jacquelyn
  The Tempest **37**: 320

Frail, David
  As You Like It **46**: 105

France, Richard
  Julius Caesar **17**: 334
  Macbeth **20**: 213

Fraser, Russell
  All's Well That Ends Well **26**: 87

Freedman, Barbara
  The Comedy of Errors **19**: 54
  The Merry Wives of Windsor **5**: 392

Freedman, Gerald
  Titus Andronicus **17**: 463

Freer, Coburn
  Cymbeline **36**: 166

French, A. L.
  Antony and Cleopatra **6**: 202
  Richard II **6**: 359

French, Marilyn
  Henry VI, 1, 2, and 3 **3**: 157
  Macbeth **3**: 333
  The Merry Wives of Windsor **5**: 395
  Othello **35**: 327

French, Philip
  Henry V **14**: 308
  Julius Caesar **17**: 372
  The Merry Wives of Windsor **18**: 41
  Romeo and Juliet **11**: 473

Frenzel, Karl
  Antony and Cleopatra **6**: 39

Freud, Sigmund
  Hamlet **1**: 119
  King Lear **2**: 147

Macbeth **3**: 223
Richard III **8**: 185

Frey, Charles
  Fathers and Daughters (topic entry) **36**: 37
  The Tempest **29**: 373
  The Two Gentlemen of Verona **12**: 488
  The Winter's Tale **7**: 497

Friedman, Michael D.
  Much Ado about Nothing **16**: 45; **31**: 222

Fripp, Edgar I.
  Henry VIII **2**: 46

Frost, William
  King Lear **2**: 216

Frye, Northrop
  Antony and Cleopatra **6**: 178
  The Comedy of Errors **1**: 32
  Coriolanus **9**: 142
  Cymbeline **4**: 115
  Henry V **5**: 269
  Henry VIII **2**: 65
  King Lear **2**: 253
  The Merry Wives of Windsor **5**: 353
  Pericles **2**: 580
  Romeo and Juliet **5**: 575
  Sonnets **10**: 309
  The Tempest **8**: 401
  Timon of Athens **1**: 512
  Troilus and Cressida **3**: 642
  The Winter's Tale **7**: 479; **36**: 289

Fuchs, Barbara
  The Tempest **42**: 320

Fujimura, Thomas H.
  The Merchant of Venice **4**: 308

Fuller, Edward
  Measure for Measure **23**: 279

Fuller, Thomas
  Henry IV, 1 and 2 **1**: 285

Funke, Lewis
  The Two Gentlemen of Verona **12**: 470

Furness, Horace Howard
  Antony and Cleopatra **6**: 62
  As You Like It **5**: 45
  Cymbeline **4**: 48
  A Midsummer Night's Dream **3**: 386

Furness, Horace Howard, Jr.
  Hamlet **21**: 151

Furnivall, F. J.
  Sonnets **10**: 213
  Twelfth Night **1**: 557

Furse, Roger
  Richard III **14**: 515

Fuxier, J.
  A Midsummer Night's Dream **12**: 272

Much Ado about Nothing **18**: 215
Richard III **14**: 489

Gajowski, Evelyn
  Othello **19**: 253

Gallenca, Christiane
  The Merry Wives of Windsor **38**: 256

Ganz, Arthur
  All's Well That Ends Well **26**: 62
  Richard III **14**: 484

Garber, Marjorie
  Antony and Cleopatra **45**: 28
  Hamlet **45**: 28
  A Midsummer Night's Dream **45**: 96
  Romeo and Juliet **33**: 246
  The Tempest **45**: 236
  The Winter's Tale **45**: 366

Gardiner, Judith Kegan
  Sonnets **10**: 379

Gardner, Helen
  As You Like It **5**: 98
  Hamlet **1**: 224

Gardner, Lyn
  Antony and Cleopatra **17**: 82

Garebian, Keith
  Macbeth **20**: 307
  The Merry Wives of Windsor **18**: 51

Garland, Robert
  King Lear **11**: 56

Garner, Stanton B., Jr.
  The Tempest **8**: 454
  The Winter's Tale **36**: 301; **45**: 374

Garnett, Edward
  Troilus and Cressida **18**: 286

Garnett, Richard
  The Two Gentlemen of Verona **6**: 464

Garrick, David
  Romeo and Juliet **5**: 378; **11**: 382

Gascoigne, Bamber
  As You Like It **23**: 89
  Cymbeline **15**: 65
  King Lear **11**: 87
  Macbeth **20**: 251
  Measure for Measure **23**: 316
  Much Ado about Nothing **18**: 179
  Othello **11**: 290
  Richard III **14**: 454
  The Taming of the Shrew **12**: 360

Gaw, Allison
  The Comedy of Errors **1**: 19

Geduld, Harry M.
  Henry V **14**: 225

Gelb, Arthur
  The Merchant of Venice **12**: 70

Gelb, Hal
  Measure for Measure **2**: 514

Geller, Lila
  Cymbeline **36**: 158

Gellert, Roger
  Hamlet **21**: 229
  Henry VI, 1, 2, and 3 **24**: 20
  Julius Caesar **17**: 368
  King Lear **11**: 87
  Measure for Measure **23**: 315
  A Midsummer Night's Dream **12**: 248

Genster, Julia
  Othello **16**: 272

Gent, Lucy
  Venus and Adonis **33**: 357

Gentleman, Francis
  Antony and Cleopatra **6**: 22
  As You Like It **5**: 19
  Coriolanus **9**: 12
  Cymbeline **15**: 94
  Hamlet **21**: 16
  Henry IV, 1 and 2 **1**: 295
  Henry V **5**: 190
  Henry VI, 1, 2, and 3 **3**: 21
  Julius Caesar **5**: 158
  King John **9**: 212; **24**: 167
  Love's Labour's Lost **2**: 301
  Macbeth **3**: 175; **20**: 21
  The Merchant of Venice **12**: 4
  A Midsummer Night's Dream **3**: 363
  Much Ado about Nothing **18**: 230
  Richard II **6**: 253
  Romeo and Juliet **11**: 384, 495
  Titus Andronicus **4**: 615
  Troilus and Cressida **3**: 538

Gerard, Albert
  Troilus and Cressida **3**: 596
  Twelfth Night **1**: 638

Gerard, Alexander
  Measure for Measure **2**: 394

Gervinus, G. G.
  All's Well That Ends Well **7**: 19; **26**: 93
  Antony and Cleopatra **6**: 33
  As You Like It **5**: 32
  Coriolanus **9**: 19
  Cymbeline **4**: 29
  Hamlet **1**: 103
  Henry IV, 1 and 2 **1**: 317
  Henry V **5**: 199
  Henry VI, 1, 2, and 3 **3**: 31
  Henry VIII **2**: 31
  Julius Caesar **7**: 161
  King John **9**: 224
  King Lear **2**: 116
  Love's Labour's Lost **2**: 305
  Macbeth **3**: 196
  Measure for Measure **2**: 402
  The Merchant of Venice **4**: 204
  The Merry Wives of Windsor **5**: 339
  A Midsummer Night's Dream **3**: 372

Much Ado about Nothing **8:** 19
Othello **4:** 415
Pericles **2:** 546
The Rape of Lucrece **10:** 66
Richard II **6:** 264
Richard III **8:** 165
Romeo and Juliet **5:** 431
Sonnets **10:** 185
The Taming of the Shrew **9:** 323
The Tempest **8:** 304
Timon of Athens **1:** 467
Titus Andronicus **4:** 623
Troilus and Cressida **3:** 544
Twelfth Night **1:** 551
The Two Gentlemen of Verona **6:** 445
The Two Noble Kinsmen **9:** 455
Venus and Adonis **10:** 418
The Winter's Tale **7:** 390

Ghose, Zulfikar
Macbeth **25:** 235

Gibbons, Brian
Coriolanus **25:** 245
Henry VI, 1, 2, and 3 **25:** 245
Richard III **25:** 245
Romeo and Juliet **25:** 245
The Tempest **28:** 391
Titus Andronicus **25:** 245

Gibson, H. N.
Authorship Controversy (topic entry) **41:** 66

Gibbs, Patrick
All's Well That Ends Well **26:** 24

Gibbs, Wolcott
As You Like It **23:** 73
King Lear **11:** 71
Macbeth **20:** 225, 226
The Tempest **15:** 240

Gibson, Joy Leslie
Richard II **24:** 339

Gielgud, John
Hamlet **21:** 182, 192, 237
Julius Caesar **17:** 344, 356
King Lear **11:** 50
Much Ado about Nothing **18:** 168, 170
Othello **11:** 295
Richard II **24:** 411
Romeo and Juliet **11:** 448
The Tempest **15:** 311

Gilbert, Miriam
Richard II **24:** 423

Gilbert, W. Stephen
Henry IV, 1 and 2 **14:** 85
Henry V **14:** 283

Gilder, Jeanette
As You Like It **23:** 40, 46
Twelfth Night **26:** 215

Gilder, Rosamond
Hamlet **21:** 172
Macbeth **20:** 230
Othello **11:** 272

Richard III **14:** 413
The Tempest **15:** 246
Twelfth Night **26:** 226

Gildon, Charles
All's Well That Ends Well **7:** 8
Antony and Cleopatra **6:** 20
As You Like It **5:** 18
The Comedy of Errors **1:** 13
Coriolanus **9:** 8
Cymbeline **4:** 17
Hamlet **1:** 75, 76
Henry IV, 1 and 2 **1:** 286
Henry V **5:** 186
Henry VI, 1, 2, and 3 **3:** 17
Julius Caesar **7:** 152
King John **9:** 208
King Lear **2:** 93
Love's Labour's Lost **2:** 299
Macbeth **3:** 171
Measure for Measure **2:** 387
The Merchant of Venice **4:** 192
The Merry Wives of Windsor **5:** 334
A Midsummer Night's Dream **3:** 362
Much Ado about Nothing **8:** 9
Othello **4:** 380, 384
The Rape of Lucrece **10:** 64
Richard II **6:** 252
Richard III **8:** 145
Romeo and Juliet **5:** 416
Sonnets **10:** 153
The Taming of the Shrew **9:** 318
The Tempest **8:** 287
Timon of Athens **1:** 454
Titus Andronicus **4:** 613
Troilus and Cressida **18:** 277
Twelfth Night **1:** 539
The Two Gentlemen of Verona **6:** 435
The Winter's Tale **7:** 377

Gilliatt, Penelope
Much Ado about Nothing **18:** 188

Gillies, John
Antony and Cleopatra **28:** 249
Othello **28:** 249
The Tempest **29:** 343
Titus Andronicus **28:** 249

Girard, René
The Merchant of Venice **4:** 331
A Midsummer Night's Dream **29:** 234; **45:** 147
Troilus and Cressida **43:** 317
Twelfth Night **46:** 333
The Two Gentlemen of Verona **13:** 12; **40:** 335
The Winter's Tale **36:** 334

Giroux, Robert
Love's Labour's Lost **23:** 224

Glavin, John
Romeo and Juliet **19:** 261

Glaz, A. Andre
Othello **35:** 265

Glazov-Corrigan, Elena
Cymbeline **28:** 398; **36:** 186
Pericles **19:** 387

Glick, Claris
Hamlet **21:** 347

Glover, Julian
Coriolanus **17:** 195

Goddard, Harold C.
As You Like It **5:** 88
Coriolanus **9:** 100
Cymbeline **4:** 89
Hamlet **1:** 194
Henry IV, 1 and 2 **1:** 397
Henry V **5:** 252
Henry VI, 1, 2, and 3 **3:** 73
The Merchant of Venice **4:** 254
A Midsummer Night's Dream **3:** 412
Much Ado about Nothing **8:** 55
The Taming of the Shrew **9:** 345
The Two Gentlemen of Verona **6:** 484

Godfrey, D. R.
Othello **35:** 310

Godshalk, William Leigh
All's Well That Ends Well **7:** 113
Henry V **30:** 273
Measure for Measure **33:** 61
The Merry Wives of Windsor **5:** 374
The Two Gentlemen of Verona **6:** 526

Godwin, William
Troilus and Cressida **3:** 539

Goethe, Johann Wolfgang von
Hamlet **1:** 91; **21:** 379
Henry IV, 1 and 2 **1:** 311
Troilus and Cressida **3:** 541

Goldberg, Jonathan
Henry IV, 1 and 2 **22:** 114

Goldman, Michael
Henry V **30:** 163
Othello **11:** 362

Goldstein, Neal L.
Love's Labour's Lost **38:** 185

Gollanez, Sir Israel
The Merchant of Venice **4:** 224

Gomme, Andor
Timon of Athens **1:** 503

Gordon, D. J.
Coriolanus **30:** 58

Gordon, Giles
Julius Caesar **17:** 390
Measure for Measure **23:** 344
Pericles **15:** 173
Richard III **14:** 487, 488

Gorfain, Phyllis
Pericles **2:** 588

Gottfried, Martin
As You Like It **23:** 101
Love's Labour's Lost **23:** 206

Gould, Gerald
Henry V **5:** 219

Gould, Robert
Timon of Athens **1:** 453

Gourlay, Patricia Southard
The Winter's Tale **36:** 311

Gow, Gordon
As You Like It **23:** 124

Goy-Blanquet, Dominique
Henry VI, 1, 2, and 3 **24:** 48
Julius Caesar **17:** 393

Grady, Hugh
As You Like It **37:** 43

Graham, Virginia
Richard III **14:** 422

Grangier, Derek
Measure for Measure **23:** 307

Granville-Barker, F.
As You Like It **23:** 84

Granville-Barker, Harley
Antony and Cleopatra **6:** 80; **17:** 104
Coriolanus **9:** 84
Cymbeline **4:** 56; **15:** 111
Hamlet **1:** 160
Henry V **5:** 226
Julius Caesar **7:** 210; **17:** 416
King Lear **2:** 154; **11:** 145
Love's Labour's Lost **2:** 317; **23:** 237
Macbeth **20:** 353
The Merchant of Venice **4:** 232; **12:** 115
A Midsummer Night's Dream **12:** 291
Othello **4:** 488
Richard II **24:** 301
Romeo and Juliet **5:** 454; **11:** 505
Twelfth Night **1:** 562; **26:** 357
The Winter's Tale **7:** 412; **15:** 514

Gray, Henry David
Pericles **2:** 558

Gray, Simon
Twelfth Night **26:** 265

Grebanier, Bernard
Hamlet **35:** 182

Green, Andrew J.
Hamlet **1:** 207

Green, Brian
The Phoenix and Turtle **38:** 345

Green, Douglas E.
Twelfth Night **46:** 362
Titus Andronicus **43:** 170

Green, Harris
Much Ado about Nothing **18:** 197

Green, Janet M.
King Lear **46:** 276

Green, London
Richard III **14:** 383, 390

Greenblatt, Stephen
King Lear **31:** 107

Greene, Gayle
Julius Caesar **7:** 350; **30:** 333
Othello **4:** 587
Troilus and Cressida **43:** 298

Greene, Robert
Henry VI, 1, 2, and 3 **3:** 16

Greene, Thomas M.
Love's Labour's Lost **2:** 351
Sonnets **10:** 385

Greenfield, Thelma Nelson
The Taming of the Shrew **9:** 350

Greg, Walter W.
As You Like It **5:** 60
Hamlet **1:** 134

Greif, Karen
Twelfth Night **34:** 316; **46:** 310

Grene, Nicholas
Antony and Cleopatra **22:** 217
Coriolanus **30:** 79

Grennan, Eamon
As You Like It **34:** 155
The Comedy of Errors **34:** 238
Henry V **30:** 202

Grey, Zachary
The Tempest **8:** 292

Griffin, Alice
Macbeth **20:** 234
The Merchant of Venice **12:** 55, 64, 72
Richard III **14:** 426

Griffith, Elizabeth
Antony and Cleopatra **6:** 22
As You Like It **5:** 20
Coriolanus **9:** 12
Henry IV, 1 and 2 **1:** 296
Henry V **5:** 191
Henry VIII **2:** 19
Richard II **6:** 254
Richard III **8:** 152
Romeo and Juliet **5:** 418
The Taming of the Shrew **9:** 319
Titus Andronicus **4:** 615
Troilus and Cressida **3:** 538
The Two Gentlemen of Verona **6:** 438
The Winter's Tale **7:** 381

Griffiths, G. S.
Antony and Cleopatra **6:** 120

Griffiths, L. M.
Titus Andronicus **4:** 626

Griffiths, Trevor R.
The Tempest **15:** 312

Grindon, Mrs. Rosa Leo
The Merry Wives of Windsor **5:** 349

Gross, Gerard J.
All's Well That Ends Well **38:** 132

Gross, John
Henry VIII **24:** 126

Gross, Kenneth
Othello **13:** 313

Guinness, Alec
Richard II **24:** 318

Guizot, M.
Romeo and Juliet **5:** 436

Gunderode, Freiherr von
Hamlet **21:** 17

Gurr, Andrew
General Commentary **13:** 494
Hamlet **44:** 241
Henry V **30:** 234
Sonnets **10:** 358

Gussow, Mel
Henry IV, 1 and 2 **14:** 87
King John **24:** 237
Love's Labour's Lost **23:** 226
Macbeth **20:** 312
Much Ado about Nothing **18:** 191, 214
Pericles **15:** 162
Timon of Athens **20:** 468
Titus Andronicus **17:** 473, 480
Twelfth Night **26:** 297, 313

Guthrie, Tyrone
All's Well That Ends Well **26:** 15, 19
The Merchant of Venice **12:** 129
The Tempest **15:** 364

Guthrie, William
Hamlet **1:** 79

Gutierrez, Nancy A.
Henry VI, 1, 2, and 3 **16:** 131

Hackett, James Henry
Hamlet **21:** 53
Henry IV, 1 and 2 **14:** 4

Hager, Alan
The Taming of the Shrew **16:** 13

Hale, David George
Coriolanus **30:** 105

Hale, Lionel
Love's Labour's Lost **23:** 187

Hales, John W.
Macbeth **3:** 205

Halio, Jay L.
As You Like It **5:** 112
Coriolanus **9:** 169
A Midsummer Night's Dream **29:** 263; **45:** 169

Hall, Joan Lord
Antony and Cleopatra **19:** 270

Hall, Jonathan
Desire (topic entry) **38:** 56
Henry IV, 1 and 2 **32:** 103

Hall, Peter
Hamlet **21:** 251
Macbeth **20:** 265
The Tempest **15:** 274, 338
Twelfth Night **26:** 257

Hallam, Henry
Hamlet **1:** 98
King Lear **2:** 111
Romeo and Juliet **5:** 426
Sonnets **10:** 175

Hallinan, Tim
The Taming of the Shrew **12:** 400

Halliwell-Phillipps, J. O.
Love's Labour's Lost **2:** 307
A Midsummer Night's Dream **3:** 370
The Phoenix and Turtle **10:** 7
Sonnets **10:** 217

Halmstrom, John
Othello **11:** 300

Halpern, Richard
The Tempest **45:** 280

Halverson, John
Richard II **28:** 134; **39:** 243

Hamilton, A. C.
Henry VI, 1, 2, and 3 **3:** 83
Titus Andronicus **4:** 659; **43:** 195
Venus and Adonis **10:** 454

Hamilton, Donna B.
King John **22:** 120
The Winter's Tale **25:** 347

Hamlin, William M.
The Tempest **45:** 226

Hammersmith, James P.
Richard III **13:** 142

Hammond, Gerald
Sonnets **40:** 228

Handelman, Susan
Timon of Athens **1:** 529

Hands, Terry
Coriolanus **17:** 190
Henry V **14:** 293

Hankey, Julie
Richard II **24:** 371

Hankin, St. John
Julius Caesar **17:** 308

Hanmer, Sir Thomas
Hamlet **1:** 76
Henry V **5:** 188

Hapgood, Norman
Henry V **14:** 199

Hapgood, Robert
General Commentary **13:** 502
King Lear **13:** 343
Othello **11:** 332; **35:** 247

Harbage, Alfred
King Lear **11:** 101

Harcourt, John B.
Macbeth **3:** 297

Hardin, Richard F.
Henry V **22:** 137
Julius Caesar **22:** 137
Kingship (topic entry) **39:** 45
The Merry Wives of Windsor **5:** 390
Richard II **22:** 137

Harding, D. W.
Shakespeare's Representation of Women (topic entry) **31:** 16

Haring-Smith, Tori
The Taming of the Shrew **12:** 416

Harrier, Richard C.
Troilus and Cressida **3:** 602

Harris, Anthony
Magic and the Supernatural (topic entry) **29:** 65

Harris, Arthur J.
Measure for Measure **23:** 291

Harris, Bernard
Henry VIII **2:** 67

Harris, Diana
The Tempest **42:** 332

Harris, Frank
The Comedy of Errors **1:** 18
Pericles **2:** 555
Richard II **6:** 279
Sonnets **10:** 240
Timon of Athens **1:** 480

Harrison, Carey
The Taming of the Shrew **12:** 372

Harrison, G. B.
Timon of Athens **1:** 499

Harrison, W. A.
Sonnets **10:** 216

Harron, Mary
Titus Andronicus **17:** 477

Hart, John
The Tempest **37:** 335

Hart, John A.
As You Like It **34:** 78
Clowns and Fools (topic entry) **46:** 60
Fathers and Daughters (topic entry) **36:** 32

Hart, Jonathan
 The Rape of Lucrece **22:** 294
 Venus and Adonis **33:** 363

Hart, Lynda
 Henry IV, 1 and 2 **14:** 109

Hart-Davis, Rupert
 A Midsummer Night's Dream **12:** 210

Hartley, Anthony
 King Lear **11:** 64

Hartsock, Mildred E.
 Julius Caesar **7:** 320

Hartwig, Joan
 Cymbeline **36:** 99
 The Taming of the Shrew **31:** 335
 Twelfth Night **1:** 658; **46:** 297

Harvey, Gabriel
 The Rape of Lucrece **10:** 63
 Venus and Adonis **10:** 410

Harvey, John Martin
 The Taming of the Shrew **12:** 335

Harwood, Ellen Aprill
 Venus and Adonis **33:** 339

Hassel, R. Chris
 As You Like It **34:** 85

Hassel, R. Chris, Jr.
 The Merchant of Venice **4:** 321
 A Midsummer Night's Dream **3:** 506
 Richard III **14:** 497

Hassell, Graham
 Hamlet **21:** 328

Hatch, Robert
 Hamlet **21:** 200
 The Merchant of Venice **12:** 70
 Richard III **14:** 424

Hatlen, Burton
 Coriolanus **42:** 243

Hattaway, Michael
 Henry VI, 1, 2, and 3 **39:** 222
 Sexuality (topic entry) **33:** 39

Hatton, Joseph
 The Merchant of Venice **12:** 31

Hawkes, Terence
 Love's Labour's Lost **2:** 359
 Richard II **6:** 374

Hawkins, C. Halford
 Julius Caesar **17:** 289

Hawkins, F. W.
 King John **24:** 179
 Macbeth **20:** 92
 Richard II **24:** 267
 Romeo and Juliet **11:** 397

Hawkins, Harriet
 Antony and Cleopatra **25:** 257
 Othello **25:** 257
 Romeo and Juliet **25:** 257

Hawkins, Sherman H.
 Henry IV, 1 and 2 **39:** 100

Hawkins, William
 Cymbeline **4:** 19

Hayes, Richard
 Much Ado about Nothing **18:** 166

Hayles, Nancy K.
 Appearance vs. Reality (topic entry) **34:** 5
 As You Like It **5:** 146
 Cymbeline **4:** 162

Hayman, Ronald
 Hamlet **21:** 183
 Julius Caesar **17:** 357
 King Lear **11:** 67
 A Midsummer Night's Dream **12:** 254
 Othello **11:** 295
 Romeo and Juliet **11:** 474

Hays, Janice
 Much Ado about Nothing **8:** 111

Hazlitt, William
 All's Well That Ends Well **7:** 9
 Antony and Cleopatra **6:** 25
 As You Like It **5:** 24
 The Comedy of Errors **1:** 14
 Coriolanus **9:** 15; **17:** 129
 Cymbeline **4:** 22
 Hamlet **1:** 96; **21:** 30, 41
 Henry IV, 1 and 2 **1:** 312
 Henry V **5:** 193
 Henry VI, 1, 2, and 3 **3:** 25
 Henry VIII **2:** 23
 Julius Caesar **17:** 273
 King John **9:** 219; **24:** 174
 King Lear **2:** 108; **11:** 12, 16
 Love's Labour's Lost **2:** 303
 Macbeth **3:** 185; **20:** 58, 59, 86
 Measure for Measure **2:** 396
 The Merchant of Venice **4:** 195; **12:** 9, 10, 11
 The Merry Wives of Windsor **5:** 337
 A Midsummer Night's Dream **3:** 364; **12:** 152
 Much Ado about Nothing **8:** 13
 Othello **4:** 402; **11:** 191, 195, 196, 197, 198
 Pericles **2:** 544
 The Rape of Lucrece **10:** 65
 Richard II **6:** 258; **24:** 267
 Richard III **8:** 161, **14:** 376, 377, 380
 Romeo and Juliet **5:** 421; **11:** 393, 395
 Sonnets **10:** 160
 The Taming of the Shrew **9:** 320
 The Tempest **8:** 297
 Timon of Athens **1:** 460
 Titus Andronicus **4:** 617
 Troilus and Cressida **3:** 540
 Twelfth Night **1:** 544
 The Two Gentlemen of Verona **6:** 439
 Venus and Adonis **10:** 415
 The Winter's Tale **7:** 384

Heath, Benjamin
 The Tempest **8:** 292
 Titus Andronicus **4:** 614

Hecht, Anthony
 Sonnets **37:** 346

Hecht, Anthony B.
 The Tempest **25:** 357

Heffernan, Carol F.
 The Taming of the Shrew **31:** 345

Heilbrun, Carolyn G.
 Hamlet **44:** 237

Heilman, Robert
 Politics and Power (topic entry) **30:** 22

Heilman, Robert Bechtold
 Antony and Cleopatra **6:** 175
 Henry IV, 1 and 2 **1:** 380
 King Lear **2:** 191
 Macbeth **3:** 312, 314; **29:** 139; **44:** 306
 Othello **4:** 508, 530
 Richard III **8:** 239
 The Taming of the Shrew **9:** 386

Heine, Heinrich
 The Merchant of Venice **4:** 200
 Richard III **8:** 164
 Troilus and Cressida **3:** 542

Heinemann, Margot
 King Lear **22:** 227; **46:** 269

Helgerson, Richard
 Henry VI, 1, 2, and 3 **22:** 156

Helms, Lorraine
 Gender Identity (topic entry) **40:** 27
 Shakespeare's Representation of Women (topic entry) **31:** 68
 Troilus and Cressida **43:** 357

Hemingway, Samuel B.
 Henry IV, 1 and 2 **1:** 401; **14:** 130
 A Midsummer Night's Dream **3:** 396

Henneman, John Bell
 Henry VI, 1, 2, and 3 **3:** 46

Henze, Richard
 The Comedy of Errors **1:** 57
 Julius Caesar **30:** 321
 The Taming of the Shrew **9:** 398
 Twelfth Night **34:** 287

Heraud, J. A.
 Antony and Cleopatra **6:** 37
 Othello **4:** 421
 Sonnets **10:** 191

Herbert, T. Walter
 A Midsummer Night's Dream **3:** 447

Herford, C. H.
 Antony and Cleopatra **6:** 76
 The Phoenix and Turtle **10:** 16

Herring, Robert
 Cymbeline **15:** 46
 Henry VIII **24:** 105

Hethmon, Robert H.
 Measure for Measure **23:** 407

Hewes, Henry
 Antony and Cleopatra **17:** 43
 Hamlet **21:** 232, 239, 288
 King John **24:** 210
 King Lear **11:** 72, 89, 103
 The Merchant of Venice **12:** 54, 62, 71, 79
 A Midsummer Night's Dream **12:** 240
 Much Ado about Nothing **18:** 173
 Othello **11:** 314
 The Taming of the Shrew **12:** 365
 Timon of Athens **20:** 456
 Troilus and Cressida **18:** 337
 Twelfth Night **26:** 247

Hewison, Robert
 Coriolanus **17:** 208
 A Midsummer Night's Dream **12:** 274
 Twelfth Night **26:** 316

Heyse, Paul
 Antony and Cleopatra **6:** 38

Hibbard, George R.
 Antony and Cleopatra **27:** 105
 Love's Labour's Lost **23:** 233
 Othello **4:** 569
 The Taming of the Shrew **9:** 375

Hic et Ubique
 See also Steevens, George; Collier, Jeremy; Longinus, and Lorenzo
 Hamlet **1:** 87
 Twelfth Night **1:** 542

Hieatt, A. Kent
 Cymbeline **13:** 401

Hieatt, Charles W.
 The Winter's Tale **36:** 374

Higgins, John
 Antony and Cleopatra **17:** 65
 Coriolanus **17:** 190
 The Merry Wives of Windsor **18:** 42
 The Taming of the Shrew **12:** 386
 The Two Gentlemen of Verona **12:** 490

Hignett, Sean
 Richard III **14:** 473

Hill, Aaron
 Hamlet **1:** 76; **21:** 377

Hill, Errol G.
The Tempest **15:** 322

Hill, R. F.
Richard II **6:** 347
Romeo and Juliet **5:** 492

Hill, Sir John
Antony and Cleopatra **6:** 21
Romeo and Juliet **11:** 494

Hill, William
Henry V **14:** 174

Hillebrand, Harold Newcomb
Richard II **24:** 272

Hillman, David
Troilus and Cressida **42:** 66

Hillman, Richard
Hamlet **44:** 219
Henry IV, 1 and 2 **19:** 170
Henry V **19:** 170
Measure for Measure **22:** 302
Richard II **19:** 170
The Tempest **8:** 464; **22:** 302
The Two Noble Kinsmen **19:** 394; **41:** 301
The Winter's Tale **22:** 302

Hinely, Jan Lawson
The Merry Wives of Windsor **5:** 397
A Midsummer Night's Dream **45:** 107

Hinman, Charlton
Timon of Athens **1:** 518

Hirsch, Foster
Richard III **14:** 447

Hirsh, James
Othello **19:** 276

Hirst, David L.
The Tempest **15:** 327

Hirvela, David P.
King John **24:** 241

Hobday, C. H.
Henry V **30:** 159
The Two Noble Kinsmen **41:** 317

Hobson, Harold
Antony and Cleopatra **17:** 33
Henry IV, 1 and 2 **14:** 54, 84
Henry V **14:** 281
Much Ado about Nothing **18:** 205
Troilus and Cressida **18:** 362
The Winter's Tale **15:** 486

Hoby, Sir Edward
Richard II **6:** 249

Hockey, Dorothy C.
Much Ado about Nothing **8:** 73

Hodgdon, Barbara
King John **19:** 182
Romeo and Juliet **13:** 243
Troilus and Cressida **16:** 70

Hodgson, Moira
Measure for Measure **23:** 354

Hoeniger, F. David
Cymbeline **4:** 103
Pericles **2:** 576, 578
The Winter's Tale **7:** 452

Hofling, Charles K.
Coriolanus **9:** 125
Cymbeline **36:** 134

Holden, Anthony
Coriolanus **17:** 163
Hamlet **21:** 213

Holden, Stephen
The Tempest **15:** 288

Holderness, Graham
Henry V **14:** 247
King Lear **31:** 84
Richard II **6:** 414
The Taming of the Shrew **12:** 404
The Winter's Tale **16:** 410

Holding, Edith
As You Like It **23:** 10

Hole, Richard
Othello **4:** 397

Holland, Norman N.
A Midsummer Night's Dream **29:** 225
Psychoanalytic Interpretations (topic entry) **44:** 11
Romeo and Juliet **5:** 513, 525

Holland, Peter
As You Like It **23:** 151
Measure for Measure **23:** 362
A Midsummer Night's Dream **29:** 216; **45:** 117
The Tempest **32:** 334

Hollander, John
Twelfth Night **1:** 596, 615

Holleran, James V.
Hamlet **13:** 268

Holloway, John
Coriolanus **9:** 139
King Lear **2:** 241

Holmer, Joan Ozark
Romeo and Juliet **32:** 222; **45:** 40

Holmes, Martin
Henry IV, 1 and 2 **14:** 146
The Merry Wives of Windsor **18:** 86

Holmstrom, John
Othello **11:** 300

Holt, John
The Comedy of Errors **1:** 13

Homan, Sidney
Henry V **30:** 207
The Merry Wives of Windsor **18:** 95

Homan, Sidney R.
The Comedy of Errors **34:** 194
A Midsummer Night's Dream **3:** 466
Richard II **6:** 391

Home, Henry, Lord Kames
Romeo and Juliet **5:** 418

Honigmann, E. A. J.
All's Well That Ends Well **13:** 77; **38:** 89
Julius Caesar **30:** 342
Macbeth **29:** 146
Timon of Athens **1:** 507

Hope, John Francis
All's Well That Ends Well **26:** 11

Hope-Wallace, Philip
As You Like It **23:** 80, 81
Cymbeline **15:** 47
Hamlet **21:** 181
Henry VI, 1, 2, and 3 **24:** 16
Julius Caesar **17:** 343
King John **24:** 214
Macbeth **20:** 221
Richard III **14:** 461
Troilus and Cressida **18:** 305
The Two Gentlemen of Verona **12:** 462

Hopkins, Lisa
Henry V **37:** 105
Macbeth **42:** 258

Horn, Franz
Coriolanus **9:** 16
Macbeth **3:** 190
Romeo and Juliet **5:** 423

Hornby, Richard
Julius Caesar **17:** 403

Horwich, Richard
The Merchant of Venice **4:** 326

Hosley, Richard
Othello **11:** 359

Hotson, Leslie
Sonnets **10:** 270

Houseman, John
Julius Caesar **17:** 326, 347, 348
King John **24:** 211

Houston, Penelope
Romeo and Juliet **11:** 472
The Taming of the Shrew **12:** 372

Howard, Alan
Coriolanus **17:** 195
Henry V **14:** 297

Howard, Jean E.
Gender Identity (topic entry) **40:** 61

Howard, Skiles
A Midsummer Night's Dream **25:** 36

Hoy, Cyrus
Fathers and Daughters (topic entry) **36:** 45
Timon of Athens **1:** 523
The Two Noble Kinsmen **41:** 308

Hoyle, Martin
The Comedy of Errors **26:** 168
Julius Caesar **17:** 391
Troilus and Cressida **18:** 389
Twelfth Night **26:** 322

Hubert, Judd D.
Much Ado about Nothing **19:** 68

Hubler, Edward
Othello **4:** 544
Sonnets **10:** 279

Hudson, Rev. H. N.
As You Like It **5:** 39
Coriolanus **9:** 26
Henry VI, 1 and 2 **1:** 323, 324
Henry VI, 1, 2, and 3 **3:** 35
Henry VIII **2:** 32
Julius Caesar **7:** 167
King Lear **2:** 125
Macbeth **3:** 203
Measure for Measure **2:** 406
The Merry Wives of Windsor **5:** 341
A Midsummer Night's Dream **3:** 377
Twelfth Night **1:** 555

Huebert, Ronald
The Merry Wives of Windsor **5:** 385

Hughes, Alan
Coriolanus **17:** 144
Hamlet **21:** 112
Macbeth **20:** 151
Much Ado about Nothing **18:** 138
Othello **11:** 259
Richard III **14:** 405

Hughes, John
Othello **4:** 384

Hugo, Francois-Victor
Coriolanus **9:** 25

Hugo, Victor
Antony and Cleopatra **6:** 37
Henry IV, 1 and 2 **1:** 323
King Lear **2:** 124
Othello **4:** 421
The Winter's Tale **7:** 394

Hulse, Clark
The Rape of Lucrece **10:** 121
Venus and Adonis **10:** 480

Hulse, S. Clark
Titus Andronicus **27:** 325

Humphreys, A. R.
Henry IV, 1 and 2 **1:** 419

Humphreys, Arthur
Julius Caesar **30**: 297

Hunt, Hugh
Julius Caesar **17**: 418
The Merchant of Venice **12**: 119
The Merry Wives of Windsor **18**: 75
Twelfth Night **26**: 233

Hunt, Leigh
Hamlet **21**: 50
Julius Caesar **17**: 272
King John **24**: 180
King Lear **11**: 10, 136
Much Ado about Nothing **18**: 231
Othello **11**: 198
Richard III **14**: 379, 389
Timon of Athens **1**: 460; **20**: 439

Hunt, Maurice
Comedy of Errors **42**: 80
Coriolanus **19**: 287
Cymbeline **36**: 115
Henry VIII **41**: 190
Love's Labour's Lost **38**: 239
A Midsummer Night's Dream **22**: 39
Richard III **39**: 349; **42**: 130
Titus Andronicus **27**: 299
Twelfth Night **25**: 47
The Two Gentlemen of Verona **6**: 564

Hunter, G. K.
All's Well That Ends Well **7**: 76; **26**: 52
As You Like It **5**: 116
Henry IV, 1 and 2 **1**: 402
Henry V **16**: 217
Henry VI, 1, 2, and 3 **16**: 217; **24**: 55
King Lear **16**: 217
Politics and Power (topic entry) **30**: 39
Richard II **16**: 217
Richard III **16**: 217
Shakespeare and Classical Civilization (topic entry) **27**: 21
Sonnets **10**: 283
The Taming of the Shrew **16**: 217
Troilus and Cressida **16**: 217
Twelfth Night **1**: 635

Hunter, Joseph
Twelfth Night **1**: 549

Hunter, Mark
Julius Caesar **7**: 221

Hunter, Robert Grams
All's Well That Ends Well **7**: 98
Cymbeline **4**: 116
Macbeth **44**: 351
Othello **4**: 582
The Two Gentlemen of Verona **6**: 514

Hurd, Richard
As You Like It **5**: 18

Hurdis, James
Coriolanus **9**: 13

Hurrell, John D.
The Merchant of Venice **4**: 284

Hurren, Kenneth
Antony and Cleopatra **17**: 56
As You Like It **23**: 106
Hamlet **21**: 298
Love's Labour's Lost **23**: 204
A Midsummer Night's Dream **12**: 251
Much Ado about Nothing **18**: 206
Titus Andronicus **17**: 467
Troilus and Cressida **18**: 357
Twelfth Night **26**: 326
The Winter's Tale **15**: 487

Huston, J. Dennis
Love's Labour's Lost **2**: 375
A Midsummer Night's Dream **3**: 516
The Taming of the Shrew **9**: 419

Hutchings, Geoffrey
All's Well That Ends Well **26**: 64

Hutson, Lorna
Twelfth Night **34**: 344; **37**: 59

Hyde, Mary Crapo
As You Like It **23**: 71

Hyland, Peter
As You Like It **34**: 130
Troilus and Cressida **25**: 56

Hyman, Lawrence W.
Measure for Measure **2**: 524

Hynes, Sam
The Rape of Lucrece **10**: 80

Ide, Richard S.
Measure for Measure **13**: 94

Ihering, Rudolf von
The Merchant of Venice **4**: 213

Inchbald, Elizabeth
Henry IV, 1 and 2 **1**: 309
Much Ado about Nothing **8**: 12

Inglis, Brian
Troilus and Cressida **18**: 311

Irving, Henry
Hamlet **21**: 381

Irving, Laurence
Henry VIII **24**: 87
Much Ado about Nothing **18**: 136
Othello **11**: 255
Twelfth Night **26**: 210

Isaacs, Edith J. R.
Richard II **24**: 308

Isaacs, Hermine Rich
The Taming of the Shrew **12**: 346
The Tempest **15**: 237

Iser, Wolfgang
As You Like It **34**: 131

Itzin, Catherine
Macbeth **20**: 17

Jackson, Barry
Henry VI, 1, 2, and 3 **24**: 12

Jackson, Berners W.
Pericles **15**: 155, 158
The Taming of the Shrew **12**: 485
Twelfth Night **26**: 292

Jackson, Glenda
Antony and Cleopatra **17**: 113

Jackson, MacDonald
The Tempest **42**: 332

Jackson, Russell
All's Well That Ends Well **26**: 58
As You Like It **23**: 158
Love's Labour's Lost **23**: 217
Richard II **24**: 373

Jackson, T. A.
Henry IV, 1 and 2 **1**: 361

Jacobson, Gerald F.
A Midsummer Night's Dream **3**: 44

Jaffa, Harry V.
King Lear **2**: 208
Measure for Measure **33**: 101

Jahn, J. D.
Venus and Adonis **10**: 466

James, D. G.
Hamlet **1**: 191
King Lear **2**: 201
Pericles **2**: 561
The Tempest **8**: 423

James, Emrys
Henry IV, 1 and 2 **14**: 92
Henry V **14**: 301

James, Heather
Titus Andronicus **27**: 306

James, Henry
Cymbeline **15**: 41
Henry V **14**: 194
Henry VIII **24**: 77
King Lear **11**: 27
Macbeth **20**: 135
The Merchant of Venice **12**: 29
The Merry Wives of Windsor **18**: 25
Othello **11**: 225
Richard III **14**: 405
Romeo and Juliet **11**: 424, 426

James, John
Antony and Cleopatra **17**: 80
The Comedy of Errors **26**: 161

Jameson, Anna Brownell
All's Well That Ends Well **7**: 12
Antony and Cleopatra **6**: 27
As You Like It **5**: 26
Coriolanus **9**: 16
Cymbeline **4**: 24

Henry VI, 1, 2, and 3 **3**: 26
Henry VIII **2**: 24
King John **9**: 220
King Lear **2**: 110
Macbeth **3**: 191
Measure for Measure **2**: 397
The Merchant of Venice **4**: 196
Much Ado about Nothing **8**: 14
Othello **4**: 406
Romeo and Juliet **5**: 423
Sonnets **10**: 167
The Tempest **8**: 301
Twelfth Night **1**: 545
The Winter's Tale **7**: 385

Jamieson, Michael
As You Like It **23**: 176
Shakespeare's Representation of Women (topic entry) **31**: 60

Janakiram, A.
The Rape of Lucrece **33**: 195

Jarman, Derik
The Tempest **15**: 299

Jayne, Sears
The Taming of the Shrew **9**: 381

Jefford, Barbara
Antony and Cleopatra **17**: 113

Jekels, Ludwig
Macbeth **3**: 226

Jenkins, Harold
As You Like It **5**: 93
Hamlet **44**: 229
Henry VI, 1 and 2 **1**: 404
Twelfth Night **1**: 610

Jenkins, Peter
The Taming of the Shrew **12**: 394

Jennings, H. J.
King Lear **11**: 39

Jennings, Richard
Othello **11**: 264

Jensen, Ejner J.
Love's Labour's Lost **28**: 63
The Merchant of Venice **28**: 63
The Merry Wives of Windsor **28**: 63
Much Ado about Nothing **28**: 63

Joffee, Linda
Henry V **14**: 312

John, Lord Chedworth
Measure for Measure **2**: 395

Johnson, Robert Carl
Romeo and Juliet **33**: 290

Johnson, Samuel
All's Well That Ends Well **7**: 8
Antony and Cleopatra **6**: 21
As You Like It **5**: 19
Coriolanus **9**: 11
Cymbeline **4**: 20
Hamlet **1**: 83

Henry IV, 1 and 2 **1:** 290
Henry V **5:** 189
Henry VI, 1, 2, and 3 **3:** 19
Henry VIII **2:** 18
Julius Caesar **7:** 156
King John **9:** 211
King Lear **2:** 101
Love's Labour's Lost **2:** 300
Macbeth **3:** 171, 172
Measure for Measure **2:** 390
The Merchant of Venice **4:** 193
The Merry Wives of Windsor **5:** 335
Othello **4:** 390
Richard II **6:** 253
Richard III **8:** 146
Romeo and Juliet **5:** 418
The Taming of the Shrew **9:** 318
The Tempest **8:** 292
Timon of Athens **1:** 454
Titus Andronicus **4:** 614
Troilus and Cressida **3:** 538
Twelfth Night **1:** 542
The Two Gentlemen of Verona **6:** 437
The Winter's Tale **7:** 380

Jones, D. A. N.
  King John **24:** 216
  Macbeth **20:** 258
  Measure for Measure **23:** 320
  The Merry Wives of Windsor **18:** 43
  Pericles **15:** 151
  Richard III **14:** 463
  Troilus and Cressida **18:** 342

Jones, David E.
  Henry IV, 1 and 2 **14:** 78
  Timon of Athens **20:** 458

Jones, Emrys
  Measure for Measure **23:** 345
  Much Ado about Nothing **18:** 212
  Titus Andronicus **27:** 285

Jones, Ernest
  Hamlet **1:** 179

Jones, Gemma
  The Winter's Tale **15:** 495

Jones, Gordon P.
  Love's Labour's Lost **23:** 223

Jones, James Earl
  Othello **11:** 319

Jones, Robert C.
  Richard II **39:** 263

Jonson, Ben
  Julius Caesar **7:** 148
  Pericles **5:** 536
  Titus Andronicus **4:** 612
  The Winter's Tale **7:** 376

Jorgens, Jack
  Richard II **24:** 379

Jorgens, Jack J.
  Hamlet **21:** 208
  Henry V **14:** 238

Julius Caesar **17:** 358
Macbeth **20:** 283
Pericles **15:** 163
Richard III **14:** 443
The Taming of the Shrew **12:** 374

Jorgensen, Paul A.
  The Comedy of Errors **1:** 55
  Hamlet **35:** 117
  King Lear **2:** 262; **31:** 133
  Macbeth **3:** 327

Joseph, Bertram L.
  Cymbeline **15:** 67

Joseph, Sister Miriam, C.S.C.
  Hamlet **1:** 231

Jump, John
  Julius Caesar **30:** 369

Kael, Pauline
  Macbeth **20:** 276

Kahn, Coppelia
  Coriolanus **30:** 149
  Gender Identity (topic entry) **40:** 33
  The Merchant of Venice **40:** 151
  The Rape of Lucrece **10:** 109; **33:** 200
  Romeo and Juliet **5:** 566
  The Taming of the Shrew **9:** 413
  Timon of Athens **27:** 212
  Venus and Adonis **10:** 473

Kaison, Albert E.
  Richard III **14:** 358

Kaiser, Walter
  Clowns and Fools (topic entry) **46:** 48

Kalem, T. E.
  Richard III **14:** 482

Kalson, Albert E.
  The Comedy of Errors **26:** 170

Kaminsky, Judith
  Rape of Lucrece **43:** 141

Kamps, Ivo
  Henry VIII **37:** 109

Kantorowicz, Ernst H.
  Richard II **6:** 327

Karhl, George M.
  Much Ado about Nothing **18:** 116
  Richard III **14:** 366

Kastan, David Scott
  Antony and Cleopatra **17:** 101
  Henry IV, 1 and 2 **19:** 195
  The Merry Wives of Windsor **18:** 71

Katz, Leslie S.
  The Merry Wives of Windsor **32:** 31

Kauffman, Stanley
  Hamlet **21:** 321

Henry V **14:** 291, 313
Much Ado about Nothing **18:** 195
Othello **11:** 322

Kaufman, Gerald
  The Taming of the Shrew **12:** 371

Kaufmann, R. J.
  Troilus and Cressida **3:** 611

Kautsky, Karl
  The Merry Wives of Windsor **5:** 343

Kay, Carol McGinnis
  Henry VI, 1, 2, and 3 **3:** 131
  Othello **4:** 596

Keach, William
  Desire (topic entry) **38:** 1

Kean, Charles
  A Midsummer Night's Dream **12:** 184
  Richard II **24:** 279

Keatman, Martin
  Authorship Controversy (topic entry) **41:** 76

Keats, John
  King Lear **2:** 109
  Sonnets **10:** 160

Kee, Robert
  Henry VI, 1, 2, and 3 **24:** 29

Keesee, Donald
  All's Well That Ends Well **38:** 155

Kegl, Rosemary
  The Merry Wives of Windsor **28:** 69

Kehler, Dorothea
  The Comedy of Errors **34:** 251
  Hamlet **32:** 238

Keith, W. J.
  Henry V **14:** 270

Kellaway, Kate
  Twelfth Night **26:** 324

Kelly, Henry Ansgar
  Henry IV, 1 and 2 **1:** 429

Kelly, Hugh
  Richard III **14:** 364

Kelly, Katherine E.
  The Two Gentlemen of Verona **16:** 122

Kemble, Frances Anne
  Henry VIII **2:** 38
  Othello **11:** 227
  Romeo and Juliet **11:** 401

Kemble, John Philip
  Macbeth **3:** 186

Kemp, Peter
  As You Like It **23:** 147

King John **24:** 231
Love's Labour's Lost **23:** 221
Twelfth Night **26:** 323

Kemp, T. C.
  Henry V **14:** 259
  Henry VI, 1, 2, and 3 **24:** 15
  Henry VIII **24:** 112
  Julius Caesar **17:** 344
  The Taming of the Shrew **12:** 350

Kendall, Gillian Murray
  Titus Andronicus **13:** 225

Kendall, Paul M.
  Troilus and Cressida **3:** 587

Kennedy, Dennis
  Antony and Cleopatra **17:** 73
  A Midsummer Night's Dream **12:** 231
  The Winter's Tale **15:** 454

Kenny, Thomas
  Cymbeline **4:** 35
  Hamlet **1:** 113
  Twelfth Night **1:** 554

Kenrick, William
  Measure for Measure **2:** 391
  Much Ado about Nothing **8:** 11
  Othello **4:** 392
  The Winter's Tale **7:** 380

Keown, Eric
  Antony and Cleopatra **17:** 32, 36
  As You Like It **23:** 80, 89
  Cymbeline **15:** 55, 65
  Henry IV, 1 and 2 **14:** 58
  King John **24:** 215
  Macbeth **20:** 189, 222, 251
  Measure for Measure **23:** 315
  The Merry Wives of Windsor **18:** 34
  Much Ado about Nothing **18:** 160, 163, 179, 185
  Othello **11:** 277
  The Taming of the Shrew **12:** 355
  Troilus and Cressida **18:** 305, 324, 331
  Twelfth Night **26:** 242, 253
  The Two Gentlemen of Verona **12:** 474

Keown, Roger
  All's Well That Ends Well **26:** 37

Kermode, Frank
  Cymbeline **15:** 75
  Henry VIII **2:** 49
  King Lear **11:** 104
  The Tempest **8:** 396; **15:** 295
  The Two Noble Kinsmen **9:** 480

Kernan, Alvin
  Measure for Measure **33:** 58
  The Tempest **32:** 343
  Timon of Athens **27:** 155

Kernan, Alvin B.
  Henry IV, 1 and 2 **1:** 427
  Henry V **5:** 287
  Henry VI, 1, 2, and 3 **3:** 76

King Lear **2:** 255
The Taming of the Shrew **9:** 424

Kernodle, George R.
King Lear **2:** 177

Kerr, Heather B.
Titus Andronicus **43:** 186

Kerr, Walter
Antony and Cleopatra **17:** 23, 45
The Merchant of Venice **12:** 124
Much Ado about Nothing **18:** 192; 219
Othello **11:** 315
Richard III **14:** 469
The Taming of the Shrew **12:** 364
The Two Gentlemen of Verona **12:** 469

Kerrigan, John
Henry IV, 1 and 2 **16:** 161
Sonnets **10:** 394; **28:** 407

Kerrigan, William
As You Like It **34:** 109
General Commentary **13:** 523
Hamlet **28:** 280

Keyishian, Harry
Hamlet **35:** 174
Othello **35:** 261

Kiasashvili, Nico
Richard III **14:** 477

Kiberd, Declan
Shakespeare's Representation of Women (topic entry) **31:** 8

Kiefer, Frederick
Pericles **22:** 315; **36:** 233
Romeo and Juliet **5:** 573

Kierkegaard, Soren
See Taciturnus, Frater

Kiernan, Pauline
Sonnets **32:** 352
Venus and Adonis **32:** 352; **33:** 377

Kiernan, Thomas
Coriolanus **17:** 162

Kiernan, Victor
Timon of Athens **37:** 222

Kilbourne, Frederick W.
As You Like It **23:** 6
Henry VI, 1, 2, and 3 **24:** 3
King John **24:** 163
Measure for Measure **23:** 267, 274
The Merry Wives of Windsor **18:** 8
Much Ado about Nothing **18:** 112
Pericles **15:** 129
Richard II **24:** 261
The Tempest **15:** 190
Troilus and Cressida **18:** 278

Kimbrough, Robert
As You Like It **5:** 164
Cymbeline **16:** 442
Macbeth **29:** 127

Pericles **16:** 442
The Tempest **16:** 442
Troilus and Cressida **27:** 374
The Winter's Tale **16:** 442

King, Bruce
Coriolanus **30:** 140

King, Walter N.
Much Ado about Nothing **8:** 95
Twelfth Night **34:** 301

Kingston, Jeremy
As You Like It **23:** 105
The Comedy of Errors **26:** 149, 150
Cymbeline **15:** 18
Hamlet **21:** 281, 324
Henry VI, 1, 2, and 3 **24:** 50
Julius Caesar **17:** 375
Macbeth **20:** 257
The Merry Wives of Windsor **18:** 37, 41, 61
Pericles **15:** 150
Richard III **14:** 463
The Taming of the Shrew **12:** 384
Timon of Athens **20:** 474
Titus Andronicus **17:** 469
Troilus and Cressida **18:** 392
Twelfth Night **26:** 262, 267
The Two Gentlemen of Verona **12:** 482
The Winter's Tale **15:** 479

Kinney, Arthur F.
The Comedy of Errors **34:** 258

Kirk, John Foster
Hamlet **21:** 58

Kirkman, Francis
A Midsummer Night's Dream **3:** 361

Kirkman, Rev. J.
King Lear **2:** 129

Kirsch, Arthur
Hamlet **16:** 381; **35:** 85; **44:** 209
Macbeth **16:** 381
Othello **16:** 381
The Tempest **42:** 339

Kirsch, Arthur C.
All's Well That Ends Well **7:** 109
Cymbeline **4:** 138
Macbeth **44:** 324
Much Ado about Nothing **8:** 115

Kirschbaum, Leo
Julius Caesar **7:** 255
Macbeth **3:** 278
The Merchant of Venice **40:** 166

Kirstein, Lincoln
A Midsummer Night's Dream **12:** 295

Kitchin, Laurence
Coriolanus **17:** 169

Kitto, H. D. F.
Hamlet **1:** 212

Kittredge, George Lyman
Macbeth **3:** 225

Kleinstuck, Johannes
Troilus and Cressida **3:** 599

Kliman, Bernice W.
Hamlet **21:** 311

Kline, Herbert W.
The Merchant of Venice **12:** 40

Knapp, Jeffrey
Henry V **25:** 116
Henry VI, 1, 2, and 3 **25:** 116

Knapp, Margaret
The Comedy of Errors **26:** 138

Knight, Charles
All's Well That Ends Well **7:** 16
Henry V **5:** 198
Henry VI, 1, 2 and 3 **3:** 29
Henry VIII **2:** 27
Love's Labour's Lost **2:** 304
Measure for Measure **2:** 401
A Midsummer Night's Dream **3:** 371
Sonnets **10:** 182
Timon of Athens **1:** 464
Titus Andronicus **4:** 619
Twelfth Night **1:** 548
The Two Gentlemen of Verona **6:** 442

Knight, G. Wilson
All's Well That Ends Well **7:** 67
Antony and Cleopatra **6:** 85
The Comedy of Errors **1:** 25
Coriolanus **9:** 65
Cymbeline **4:** 78
Hamlet **1:** 144
Henry VIII **2:** 51
Julius Caesar **7:** 227, 233
King Lear **2:** 156; **11:** 127, 130, 150
Macbeth **3:** 231, 234
Measure for Measure **2:** 421
The Merchant of Venice **12:** 117
A Midsummer Night's Dream **3:** 401
Much Ado about Nothing **8:** 43
Othello **4:** 462; **11:** 339
Pericles **2:** 559, 565
Romeo and Juliet **11:** 509
Sonnets **10:** 290
The Tempest **8:** 364
Timon of Athens **1:** 483, 499
Troilus and Cressida **3:** 561
Twelfth Night **1:** 570
Venus and Adonis **10:** 428
The Winter's Tale **7:** 417, 436

Knight, Joseph
The Merchant of Venice **12:** 21
Othello **11:** 223, 245
Richard III **14:** 398
Romeo and Juliet **11:** 421, 422

Knights, L. C.
Antony and Cleopatra **6:** 131
Coriolanus **9:** 110
Hamlet **1:** 221

Henry IV, 1 and 2 **1:** 354, 411
Julius Caesar **7:** 262
King Lear **2:** 222
Macbeth **3:** 241
Measure for Measure **2:** 446
Sonnets **10:** 251
The Tempest **29:** 292
Timon of Athens **1:** 515
Troilus and Cressida **3:** 584
The Winter's Tale **7:** 493

Knoepflmacher, U. C.
Henry IV, 1 and 2 **1:** 413

Knowles, James Sheridan
Romeo and Juliet **11:** 413

Kobialka, Michael
The Comedy of Errors **26:** 138

Kolin, Philip C.
Titus Andronicus **32:** 249

Koller, Ann Marie
Julius Caesar **17:** 302

Komisarjevsky, Theodore
Macbeth **20:** 192

Kott, Jan
As You Like It **5:** 118
Gender Identity (topic entry) **40:** 65
Hamlet **1:** 247
Henry IV, 1 and 2 **1:** 418
King Lear **2:** 245; **11:** 151
Macbeth **3:** 309
A Midsummer Night's Dream **3:** 445
Richard II **6:** 354
Richard III **8:** 232; **39:** 308
The Tempest **8:** 408; **15:** 361; **29:** 368
Titus Andronicus **17:** 449
Troilus and Cressida **3:** 609
Twelfth Night **1:** 639

Kowsar, Mohammad
Richard III **14:** 477

Kramer, Jerome A.
Rape of Lucrece **43:** 141

Kramer, Mimi
Coriolanus **17:** 220
Much Ado about Nothing **18:** 227

Kreider, P. V.
As You Like It **5:** 72

Krempel, Daniel
Henry V **14:** 222

Kreyssig, Friedrich
King Lear **2:** 124
The Merchant of Venice **4:** 208
Twelfth Night **1:** 553

Krieger, Elliot
As You Like It **5:** 148
Much Ado about Nothing **31:** 191

Krieger, Murray
Measure for Measure **2:** 482

Richard III **8:** 218
Sonnets **10:** 329; **40:** 284

Kroll, Jack
Antony and Cleopatra **17:** 68
As You Like It **23:** 121
Othello **11:** 316
Richard III **14:** 471

Kronenfeld, Judy
King Lear **22:** 233

Kronenfeld, Judy Z.
As You Like It **34:** 161

Krutch, Joseph Wood
Hamlet **21:** 171
Julius Caesar **17:** 321
Macbeth **20:** 229
Richard III **14:** 411
The Taming of the Shrew **12:** 344
The Tempest **15:** 241
Troilus and Cressida **18:** 297
Twelfth Night **26:** 223

Kuhl, Ernest P.
The Taming of the Shrew **12:** 427

Kuner, Mildred C.
Titus Andronicus **17:** 462

Kurland, Stuart M.
Hamlet **28:** 290
Pericles **37:** 360
The Winter's Tale **19:** 401

Kurtz, Martha
Henry IV, 1 and 2 **37:** 122
Henry V **37:** 122
Henry VI, 1, 2, and 3 **37:** 122
Richard II **37:** 122
Richard III **37:** 122

Kyle, Howard
Henry VIII **24:** 85

Lady Martin
See Faucit, Helena

LaGuardia, Eric
All's Well That Ends Well **7:** 90

Laird, David
Romeo and Juliet **5:** 520

Lamb, Charles
Hamlet **1:** 93
King Lear **2:** 106; **11:** 136
Macbeth **3:** 184
Othello **4:** 401; **11:** 334
Richard III **8:** 159; **14:** 368, 369
Timon of Athens **1:** 459
Twelfth Night **1:** 545
The Two Noble Kinsmen **9:** 446

Lamb, Margaret
Antony and Cleopatra **17:** 12, 84

Lamb, Mary Ellen
Measure for Measure **13:** 104
A Midsummer Night's Dream **3:** 498

Lambert, J. W.
Antony and Cleopatra **17:** 58
As You Like It **23:** 99, 105
Hamlet **21:** 293
Love's Labour's Lost **23:** 202, 210
Macbeth **20:** 293
The Merchant of Venice **12:** 93
Richard II **24:** 355
The Taming of the Shrew **12:** 393
The Tempest **15:** 272
Troilus and Cressida **18:** 356
Twelfth Night **26:** 283

Lamont, Rosette
The Tempest **15:** 292

Lamont, Rosette C.
The Tempest **15:** 287

Lancashire, Anne
Timon of Athens **1:** 518

Lancaster, Osbert
All's Well That Ends Well **26:** 95

Landor, Walter Savage
Sonnets **10:** 167

Landry, D. E.
Cymbeline **4:** 167; **45:** 67

Landstone, Charles
King Lear **11:** 124

Lane, John Francis
The Tempest **15:** 285

Lane, Robert
Henry V **28:** 146
King John **32:** 114

Lang, Andrew
Much Ado about Nothing **8:** 33

Lang, David Marshall
Richard III **14:** 476

Langbaine, Gerard
Antony and Cleopatra **6:** 20
Cymbeline **4:** 17
Henry V **5:** 185
Henry VI, 1, 2, and 3 **3:** 17
The Merry Wives of Windsor **5:** 332
Much Ado about Nothing **8:** 9
Pericles **2:** 538

Langbaum, Robert
Henry IV, 1 and 2 **1:** 408

Langham, Michael
Antony and Cleopatra **17:** 48

Langton, Robert Gore
Antony and Cleopatra **17:** 74

Lanham, Richard A.
The Rape of Lucrece **10:** 116; **33:** 190
Sonnets **40:** 221

Lanier, Douglas
The Comedy of Errors **25:** 63; **34:** 201

Lanier, Sidney
The Phoenix and Turtle **10:** 7

Lardner, James
Hamlet **21:** 309

Laroque, Francois
Henry VI, 1, 2, and 3 **39:** 205
Macbeth **29:** 109
The Merry Wives of Windsor **18:** 56
Romeo and Juliet **32:** 256
Titus Andronicus **17:** 481
Twelfth Night **26:** 318

Larson, Orville K.
Richard III **14:** 516

Latham, Grace
The Two Gentlemen of Verona **6:** 453

Laver, James
Macbeth **20:** 52

Law, Robert Adger
Henry IV, 1 and 2 **1:** 348

Lawlor, John
Romeo and Juliet **5:** 509

Lawrence, W. J.
Henry VIII **24:** 150
The Tempest **15:** 196

Lawrence, William Witherle
All's Well That Ends Well **7:** 32
Cymbeline **4:** 53
Measure for Measure **2:** 429
Troilus and Cressida **3:** 566

Leavis, F. R.
Cymbeline **4:** 77
Measure for Measure **2:** 449
Othello **4:** 477
The Winter's Tale **7:** 436

Lecter-Siegal Amy
Measure for Measure **33:** 85

Lee, Jane
Henry VI, 1, 2, and 3 **3:** 39

Lee, Sidney
Henry V **14:** 334
Pericles **2:** 553
The Phoenix and Turtle **10:** 8
The Rape of Lucrece **10:** 69
Sonnets **10:** 233

Leech, Clifford
All's Well That Ends Well **7:** 54
Antony and Cleopatra **17:** 34
Henry IV, 1 and 2 **1:** 393
Henry VIII **2:** 64
Macbeth **29:** 152
Measure for Measure **2:** 479
Pericles **2:** 571
Romeo and Juliet **5:** 562
Shakespeare and Classical Civilization (topic entry) **27:** 60
The Taming of the Shrew **12:** 350
The Tempest **8:** 380

Twelfth Night **1:** 645
The Two Noble Kinsmen **9:** 479, 486

Leggatt, Alexander
As You Like It **5:** 141; **46:** 254
The Comedy of Errors **1:** 63
Cymbeline **4:** 159
Henry VI, 1, 2, and 3 **39:** 160
King John **41:** 205
Love's Labour's Lost **2:** 362
Pericles **36:** 257
The Taming of the Shrew **9:** 407
Twelfth Night **1:** 660
The Two Gentlemen of Verona **6:** 549

Lejeune, C. A.
Henry V **14:** 204

Lelyveld, Toby
The Merchant of Venice **12:** 6

Lemmon, Jeremy
Macbeth **20:** 382

Lennox, Charlotte
Cymbeline **4:** 18
Hamlet **1:** 81
Henry IV, 1 and 2 **1:** 289
Henry V **5:** 188
Henry VI, 1, 2, and 3 **3:** 18
Henry VIII **2:** 16
King Lear **2:** 100
Macbeth **3:** 172
Measure for Measure **2:** 388
Much Ado about Nothing **8:** 9
Othello **4:** 386
Richard II **6:** 252
Richard III **8:** 145
Romeo and Juliet **5:** 416
Troilus and Cressida **3:** 537
Twelfth Night **1:** 540
The Two Gentlemen of Verona **6:** 436
The Winter's Tale **7:** 377

Lenz, Joseph M.
The Winter's Tale **36:** 380

Leonard, Hugh
Henry V **14:** 278
Twelfth Night **26:** 262

Lesser, Simon O.
Macbeth **45:** 48

Lessing, Gotthold Ephraim
Hamlet **1:** 84

Levenson, Jill L.
Romeo and Juliet **11:** 451

Lever, J. W.
Measure for Measure **2:** 505
The Merchant of Venice **4:** 263
Sonnets **10:** 293

Levett, Karl
Much Ado about Nothing **18:** 229

Levin, Bernard
As You Like It **23:** 89, 115, 120

Cymbeline **15**: 62
Henry VI, 1, 2, and 3 **24**: 31
King Lear **11**: 110
A Midsummer Night's Dream **12**: 270
Twelfth Night **26**: 330

Levin, Harry
Hamlet **1**: 227
Macbeth **44**: 261
Othello **4**: 562
Romeo and Juliet **5**: 496
Timon of Athens **1**: 520

Levin, Richard
The Rape of Lucrece **33**: 138

Levin, Richard A.
Julius Caesar **30**: 362
Twelfth Night **46**: 324

Levine, Nina S.
Richard III **39**: 345

Lewalski, B. K.
Much Ado about Nothing **31**: 209

Lewalski, Barbara K.
The Merchant of Venice **4**: 289
Twelfth Night **1**: 642

Lewes, George Henry
Hamlet **21**: 384
Othello **11**: 201, 219

Lewis, Anthony J.
Pericles **36**: 264

Lewis, C. S.
The Phoenix and Turtle **10**: 20
The Rape of Lucrece **10**: 77
Sonnets **10**: 287
Venus and Adonis **10**: 448

Lewis, Chariton M.
Hamlet **1**: 125

Lewis, Cynthia
Cymbeline **19**: 411

Lewis, Wyndham
Coriolanus **9**: 62
Henry VI, 1 and 2 **1**: 351
Othello **4**: 455
Timon of Athens **1**: 481

Lewsen, Charles
Antony and Cleopatra **17**: 55
Henry V **14**: 280
Pericles **15**: 161

Lezra, Jacques
Measure for Measure **13**: 112

Lictenberg, Georg Christoph
Hamlet **21**: 17

Lidz, Theodore
Hamlet **35**: 132

Lieber, Naomi Conn
Titus Andronicus **32**: 265

Lief, Madelon
The Two Noble Kinsmen **41**: 326

Lillo, George
Pericles **2**: 538

Lindenbaum, Peter
The Two Gentlemen of Verona **6**: 555

Lindheim, Nancy
Venus and Adonis **10**: 489

Linville, Susan E.
King Lear **16**: 311

Liston, William T.
A Midsummer Night's Dream **45**: 143

Littledale, Harold
The Two Noble Kinsmen **9**: 457

Lloyd, William Watkiss
Henry V **5**: 203
Pericles **2**: 547
The Two Gentlemen of Verona **6**: 447

Lockridge, Richard
Romeo and Juliet **11**: 418

Loewenstein, Joseph
Hamlet **13**: 282

Loggins, Vernon P.
Troilus and Cressida **43**: 377

Lolleran, James V.
Hamlet **13**: 268

Londre, Felicia Hardison
Coriolanus **17**: 151

Loney, Glenn
As You Like It **23**: 117

Long, John H.
A Midsummer Night's Dream **3**: 418

Long, Michael
Antony and Cleopatra **6**: 219

Longinus
See also Steevens, George; Collier, Jeremy; Hic et Ubique; Lorenzo
Hamlet **1**: 86

Longstaffe, Steve
King John **37**: 132

Lorenzo
See also Steevens, George; Collier, Jeremy; Hic et Ubique; Longinus
Othello **4**: 391
Richard III **8**: 147

Lowe, Lisa
Coriolanus **30**: 125

Lowell, James Russell
The Tempest **8**: 308

Lowenthal, David
King Lear **46**: 177

Lubbock, Tom
Pericles **15**: 174

Lucas, Walter
The Taming of the Shrew **12**: 369

Lucking, David
The Merchant of Venice **13**: 43
Romeo and Juliet **32**: 276; **42**: 266

Luders, Charles Henry
The Winter's Tale **15**: 440

Lusardi, James P.
King Lear **19**: 295

Lustig, Vera
Julius Caesar **17**: 406

Lyons, Charles R.
A Midsummer Night's Dream **3**: 474

Mabie, Hamilton Wright
Antony and Cleopatra **6**: 53

Mac Liammoir, Micheal
Othello **11**: 285

Macauly, Alastair
Twelfth Night **26**: 335

MacCallum, M. W.
Coriolanus **9**: 45
Julius Caesar **7**: 191

MacCarthy, Desmond
Hamlet **21**: 157, 179
A Midsummer Night's Dream **12**: 223
Richard III **14**: 416
Troilus and Cressida **18**: 302

MacCary, W. Thomas
Love's Labour's Lost **38**: 194
Much Ado about Nothing **31**: 241
The Two Gentlemen of Verona **40**: 365

Macdonald, Dwight
Hamlet **21**: 242

MacDonald, Jan
The Taming of the Shrew **12**: 338

MacDonald, Joyce Green
The Rape of Lucrece **33**: 155

MacDonald, Ronald R.
Antony and Cleopatra **6**: 228
Measure for Measure **16**: 114
A Midsummer Night's Dream **29**: 210

Mack, Maynard
Antony and Cleopatra **6**: 163; **27**: 90
Hamlet **1**: 198
Julius Caesar **7**: 298
King Lear **2**: 249; **11**: 132
The Taming of the Shrew **9**: 369

Mack, Maynard, Jr.
Hamlet **1**: 264
Macbeth **29**: 155

Mackail, J. W.
Sonnets **10**: 243

Mackenzie, Henry
Hamlet **1**: 88
Henry IV, 1 and 2 **1**: 304

Mackenzie, Suzie
As You Like It **23**: 142

Macklin, Charles
Othello **11**: 185

MacLeish, Archibald
Julius Caesar **17**: 323

Macready, William Charles
King John **24**: 181
King Lear **11**: 15
Macbeth **20**: 100, 101, 103
Romeo and Juliet **11**: 398

Madariaga, Salvador de
Hamlet **1**: 171

Maginn, William
As You Like It **5**: 28
Macbeth **3**: 193
A Midsummer Night's Dream **3**: 365
Othello **4**: 409

Magnusson, Lynne A.
Henry VIII **22**: 182
Othello **42**: 273

Maguin, J. M.
Henry V **14**: 284
Henry VI, 1, 2, and 3 **24**: 36
Julius Caesar **17**: 396
King John **24**: 238
Much Ado about Nothing **18**: 215
Pericles **15**: 166
The Taming of the Shrew **12**: 410
Titus Andronicus **17**: 481

Maguin, Jean Marie
Julius Caesar **30**: 293
The Merry Wives of Windsor **18**: 60
The Tempest **32**: 367

Mahood, M. M.
Macbeth **3**: 283
Richard II **6**: 331
Romeo and Juliet **5**: 489
Sonnets **10**: 296
The Winter's Tale **7**: 460

Mairowitz, David Zane
Troilus and Cressida **18**: 359

Majors, G. W.
The Rape of Lucrece **10**: 106

Malcolm, Donald
Henry IV, 1 and 2 **14**: 62, 65

Malcolmson, Cristina
Twelfth Night **19**: 78; **46**: 347

Mallett, Phillip
Richard III **39:** 387

Mallin, Eric S.
Troilus and Cressida **16:** 84; **43:** 365

Malone, Edmond
Henry VI, 1, 2, and 3 **3:** 21
Henry VIII **2:** 19
King John **9:** 218
A Midsummer Night's Dream **3:** 363
Pericles **2:** 538, 543
The Rape of Lucrece **10:** 64
Richard III **8:** 158
Sonnets **10:** 155, 156
Titus Andronicus **4:** 616
Venus and Adonis **10:** 412

Manheim, Leonard F.
Twelfth Night **34:** 338

Manheim, Michael
Henry VI, 1, 2, and 3 **3:** 143
King John **9:** 297; **13:** 158

Manningham, John
Richard III **8:** 144
Twelfth Night **1:** 539

Mantel, Hilary
Henry V **14:** 309

Manvell, Roger
Henry V **14:** 203
Macbeth **20:** 148, 203
A Midsummer Night's Dream **12:** 214
Richard III **14:** 442

Manzoni, Alessandro
Richard II **6:** 260

Marchitello, Howard
The Merchant of Venice **32:** 41

Marcus, Frank
As You Like It **23:** 99
The Taming of the Shrew **12:** 387

Marcus, Leah
The Taming of the Shrew **22:** 48

Marcus, Mordecai
A Midsummer Night's Dream **3:** 511

Marder, Louis
Authorship Controversy (topic entry) **41:** 5

Mares, F. H.
Much Ado about Nothing **18:** 239

Margeson, John
Henry VIII **24:** 146; **41:** 129

Markels, Julian
Antony and Cleopatra **6:** 181; **27:** 121

Marowitz, Charles
Hamlet **21:** 256
King Lear **11:** 78
Love's Labour's Lost **23:** 200

Marriott, J. A. R.
Henry VI, 1, 2, and 3 **3:** 51

Marsh, Derick R. C.
Romeo and Juliet **5:** 565

Marsh, Henry
A Midsummer Night's Dream **3:** 361

Marsh, Ngaio
Twelfth Night **26:** 364

Marshall, David
A Midsummer Night's Dream **3:** 520

Marshall, Margaret
Hamlet **21:** 201
Othello **11:** 268

Marston, Westland
King Lear **11:** 18
Romeo and Juliet **11:** 404

Martin, Theodore
As You Like It **23:** 47
The Merchant of Venice **12:** 25

Martindale, Charles
Shakespeare and Classical Civilization (topic entry) **27:** 67

Martindale, Michelle
Shakespeare and Classical Civilization (topic entry) **27:** 67

Marx, Joan C.
Cymbeline **36:** 125

Marx, Karl
Timon of Athens **1:** 466

Marx, Leo
The Tempest **8:** 404

Marx, Steven
Henry V **32:** 126

Masefield, John
Coriolanus **9:** 52
Henry V **5:** 212
King John **9:** 245
Macbeth **20:** 363
The Phoenix and Turtle **10:** 14
Richard III **8:** 184

Mason, John Monck
Sonnets **10:** 156

Massey, Daniel
Measure for Measure **23:** 416

Massey, Gerald
Sonnets **10:** 196
Titus Andronicus **4:** 624

Masters, Anthony
A Midsummer Night's Dream **12:** 277

Timon of Athens **20:** 471

Matchett, William H.
King John **41:** 277
The Phoenix and Turtle **38:** 357
The Winter's Tale **7:** 483

Matheson, Mark
Hamlet **32:** 284
Othello **32:** 294

Matthews, Brander
Cymbeline **4:** 52
Henry V **5:** 213
Julius Caesar **7:** 204; **17:** 296
Romeo and Juliet **5:** 448

Matthews, C. M.
Othello **4:** 564

Matthews, Harold
As You Like It **23:** 85
Coriolanus **17:** 167
Henry VI, 1, 2, and 3 **24:** 24
King Lear **11:** 75
Love's Labour's Lost **23:** 197
Measure for Measure **23:** 311, 317
Much Ado about Nothing **18:** 180
Othello **11:** 294
Richard III **14:** 460

Matthews, Harold G.
Troilus and Cressida **18:** 307, 323

Matthews, William
Love's Labour's Lost **2:** 345

Matus, Irvin
Authorship Controversy (topic entry) **41:** 57, 63

Maus, Katharine Eisaman
Love's Labour's Lost **19:** 92
Measure for Measure **33:** 112
The Rape of Lucrece **33:** 144

Maxwell, Baldwin
Hamlet **35:** 204

Maxwell, J. C.
Timon of Athens **1:** 495

Mayer, Jean-Christophe
Henry IV, Parts 1 and 2 **42:** 141
Henry V **42:** 141

Mazer, Cary M.
Much Ado about Nothing **18:** 148
The Taming of the Shrew **12:** 337

McAleer, John J.
Henry IV, and 1 and 2 **14:** 13

McAlindon, T.
Hamlet **1:** 249
Richard II **6:** 397
Troilus and Cressida **3:** 624

McAlindon, Tom
Antony and Cleopatra **19:** 304
Coriolanus **25:** 263
Henry IV, 1 and 2 **32:** 136

McBride, Tom
Henry VIII **2:** 75
Measure for Measure **2:** 522

McCarten, John
Hamlet **21:** 199
Henry V **14:** 210

McClain, John
The Two Gentlemen of Verona **12:** 469

McCloskey, John C.
Henry V **5:** 239

McCollom, William G.
Much Ado about Nothing **31:** 178

McConnell, Stanlie
Henry V **14:** 219

McCourt, James
The Tempest **15:** 298

McCoy, Richard C.
Kingship (topic entry) **39:** 34

McCreadie, Marsha
Henry V **14:** 326

McDonald, Jan
The Taming of the Shrew **12:** 317

McDonald, Russ
The Tempest **19:** 421

McElroy, Bernard
King Lear **2:** 273
Macbeth **3:** 329

McEwan, Ian
As You Like It **23:** 123

McFarland, Thomas
King Lear **46:** 231

McGlinchee, Claire
The Merchant of Venice **12:** 63
A Midsummer Night's Dream **12:** 241
Much Ado about Nothing **18:** 174
Troilus and Cressida **18:** 338

McGrath, John
Macbeth **20:** 259

McGuire, Philip C.
A Midsummer Night's Dream **29:** 256
The Tempest **45:** 200

McKellan, Ian
Richard II **24:** 337

McKenzie, Stanley D.
Coriolanus **9:** 193

McLaughlin, John J.
Richard III **39:** 383

McLaughlin, John
Hamlet **21:** 249

McLuhan, Herbert Marshall
Henry IV, 1 and 2 **1**: 385

McLuskie, Kathleen
King Lear **31**: 123
Shakespeare's Representation of Women (topic entry) **31**: 35

McMullan, Gordon
Henry VIII **32**: 148

McMullen, Glenys
Clowns and Fools (topic entry) **46**: 18

McPeek, James A. S.
Much Ado about Nothing **8**: 88
Richard II **6**: 334

Meadowcroft, J. R. W.
King Lear **11**: 165

Mebane, John S.
Magic and the Supernatural (topic entry) **29**: 12

Mehl, Dieter
Macbeth **44**: 269

Merchant, Moelwyn W.
Henry VIII **24**: 71

Merchant, W. M.
Timon of Athens **1**: 500

Meres, Francis
The Rape of Lucrece **10**: 63
Sonnets **10**: 153
Venus and Adonis **10**: 410

Merryn, Anthony
Measure for Measure **23**: 312

Meryman, Richard
Othello **11**: 297

Meszaros, Patricia K.
Coriolanus **9**: 180

Mezieres, Alfred J. F.
Macbeth **3**: 198
Romeo and Juliet **5**: 437

Micheli, Linda McJ.
Henry VIII **24**: 101; **41**: 180

Michell, John
Authorship Controversy (topic entry) **41**: 2

Michener, Charles
Othello **11**: 321
Pericles **15**: 162

Midgley, Graham
The Merchant of Venice **4**: 279

Mikalachki, Jodi
Cymbeline **32**: 373

Miko, Stephen J.
The Tempest **29**: 297
The Winter's Tale **13**: 417

Miles, Geoffrey
Julius Caesar **37**: 229

Millard, Barbara C.
Fathers and Daughters (topic entry) **36**: 60
King Lear **13**: 352

Miller, J. Hillis
Troilus and Cressida **3**: 635

Miller, Jonathan
The Merchant of Venice **12**: 92
The Taming of the Shrew **12**: 400, 402
The Tempest **15**: 338

Miller, Robert P.
Venus and Adonis **10**: 439

Miller, Ronald F.
King Lear **2**: 278
A Midsummer Night's Dream **3**: 486

Miller, Tice L.
The Taming of the Shrew **12**: 425

Mills, John A.
Hamlet **21**: 89, 44, 274

Milne, Tom
The Taming of the Shrew **12**: 359

Miola, Robert S.
Othello **16**: 283
Julius Caesar **30**: 326
Shakespeare and Classical Civilization (topic entry) **27**: 39
Titus Andronicus **43**: 206

Milton, John
Richard III **8**: 145

Mincoff, M.
The Two Noble Kinsmen **9**: 471

Mincoff, Marco
Henry VIII **41**: 158

Miner, Madonne M.
Richard III **8**: 262

Mizener, Arthur
Sonnets **10**: 265

Modjeska, Helena
As You Like It **23**: 42

Moffet, Robin
Cymbeline **4**: 108

Moglen, Helene
Twelfth Night **34**: 311

Moisan, Thomas
The Taming of the Shrew **32**: 56

Monsey, Derek
All's Well That Ends Well **26**: 36

Montagu, Elizabeth
Hamlet **1**: 85

Henry IV, 1 and 2 **1**: 293
Julius Caesar **7**: 156
Macbeth **3**: 173

Montague, C. E.
Measure for Measure **23**: 286
Richard II **24**: 408

Montegut, Emile
Love's Labour's Lost **2**: 306
Twelfth Night **1**: 554
The Winter's Tale **7**: 394

Montrose, Louis Adrian
As You Like It **5**: 158
Love's Labour's Lost **2**: 371
A Midsummer Night's Dream **29**: 243; **45**: 84

Moody, A. D.
The Merchant of Venice **4**: 300

Mooney, Michael E.
Antony and Cleopatra **16**: 342
Julius Caesar **19**: 321
Richard III **16**: 150

Moore, Dan
The Merchant of Venice **12**: 80

Moore, Don D.
Much Ado about Nothing **18**: 216

Moore, Edward M.
Measure for Measure **23**: 293
The Merchant of Venice **12**: 44

Moore, Hannah
Hamlet **21**: 20

Moore, Jeanie Grant
Richard II **39**: 295

Morgann, Maurice
Henry IV, 1 and 2 **1**: 298
The Tempest **8**: 293

Morley, Henry
As You Like It **23**: 26
Cymbeline **15**: 19, 20
Henry IV, 1 and 2 **14**: 15
King John **24**: 194
King Lear **11**: 20
Macbeth **20**: 121
A Midsummer Night's Dream **12**: 169, 183
Othello **11**: 217
Richard II **24**: 273
The Taming of the Shrew **12**: 323
Timon of Athens **20**: 444

Morley, Sheridan
All's Well That Ends Well **26**: 57
Coriolanus **17**: 213
Cymbeline **15**: 86
Hamlet **21**: 314, 333
Henry V **14**: 282
Henry VIII **24**: 123
Julius Caesar **17**: 388
The Merry Wives of Windsor **18**: 62
Much Ado about Nothing **18**: 207
Romeo and Juliet **11**: 483

The Taming of the Shrew **12**: 410
Titus Andronicus **17**: 485
Troilus and Cressida **18**: 363
Twelfth Night **26**: 293, 306, 317, 325
The Two Gentlemen of Verona **12**: 492
The Winter's Tale **15**: 488

Morris, Brian
Macbeth **3**: 345

Morris, Corbyn
Henry IV, 1 and 2 **1**: 287

Morris, Harry
As You Like It **46**: 164

Morris, Mowbray
Othello **11**: 249

Morrisey, LeRoy J.
As You Like It **23**: 9

Morse, Ruth
The Two Gentlemen of Verona **40**: 359

Morse, William R.
The Winter's Tale **19**: 431

Mortimer, Anthony
Venus and Adonis **42**: 347

Mortimer, Raymond
Hamlet **21**: 197
Othello **11**: 267

Morton, Richard
Timon of Athens **20**: 431

Mosdell, D.
Henry V **14**: 215

Moseley, Charles
Macbeth **44**: 361

Moulton, Ian Frederick
Richard III **37**: 144

Moulton, Richard G.
Henry VI, 1, 2, and 3 **3**: 48
Julius Caesar **7**: 179
Richard III **8**: 170
Romeo and Juliet **5**: 444
The Tempest **8**: 315
The Winter's Tale **7**: 407

Mowat, Barbara A.
Cymbeline **4**: 124
Shakespeare's Representation of Women (topic entry) **31**: 29
The Winter's Tale **45**: 333

Mueller, Martin
King Lear **28**: 301

Muir, Edwin
King Lear **2**: 183

Muir, Kenneth
As You Like It **5**: 154
Macbeth **3**: 300; **29**: 76

The Merchant of Venice **12:** 81
Pericles **2:** 568; **36:** 199
The Phoenix and Turtle **10:** 18
Shakespeare and Classical Civilization (topic entry) **27:** 15
Timon of Athens **1:** 495; **27:** 161
Troilus and Cressida **3:** 589
The Two Noble Kinsmen **9:** 474
Venus and Adonis **10:** 459

Mullaney, Steven
Hamlet **28:** 311

Muller, Wolfgang G.
Richard III **39:** 360

Mullin, Michael
Hamlet **21:** 270
Henry IV, 1 and 2 **14:** 92
Macbeth **20:** 175, 192, 210, 245, 324
A Midsummer Night's Dream **12:** 250

Mullini, Roberta
Clowns and Fools (topic entry) **46:** 24

Mulryne, J. R.
Coriolanus **17:** 195
Much Ado about Nothing **18:** 252
Pericles **15:** 167

Munoz, Marie-Christine
The Comedy of Errors **26:** 178

Murphy, Arthur
All's Well That Ends Well **7:** 8
Hamlet **1:** 82; **21:** 21
Henry IV, 1 and 2 **1:** 290
Henry VIII **2:** 17
King Lear **2:** 98
Macbeth **3:** 172; **20:** 23
Measure for Measure **2:** 390
Much Ado about Nothing **18:** 114
Richard III **14:** 364
Romeo and Juliet **11:** 382, 385
The Tempest **15:** 200
The Winter's Tale **7:** 379; **15:** 397

Murphy, Gerard
Henry IV, 1 and 2 **14:** 98

Murray, Gilbert
Hamlet **1:** 130

Murray, Peter B.
Hamlet **37:** 241

Murry, John Middleton
Antony and Cleopatra **6:** 94
Coriolanus **9:** 58
Henry IV, 1 and 2 **1:** 365
Henry VI, 1, 2, and 3 **3:** 55
King John **9:** 248
King Lear **2:** 165
The Merchant of Venice **4:** 247
The Phoenix and Turtle **10:** 14
Richard II **6:** 287
The Tempest **8:** 353
Twelfth Night **1:** 572
The Winter's Tale **7:** 419

Myrick, Kenneth O.
Othello **4:** 483

Nagarajan, S.
Twelfth Night **1:** 609

Nagler, A. M.
Romeo and Juliet **11:** 514
The Tempest **15:** 303

Nardo, Anna K.
Hamlet **35:** 104
Romeo and Juliet **33:** 255

Naremore, James
Macbeth **20:** 206

Nashe, Thomas
Henry VI, 1, 2, and 3 **3:** 16

Nathan, George Jean
Henry VIII **24:** 100
Macbeth **20:** 222
Richard III **14:** 414
The Tempest **15:** 251

Nathan, Norman
The Merchant of Venice **4:** 252, 266

Nechkina, M.
Henry IV, 1 and 2 **1:** 358

Neely, Carol Thomas
All's Well That Ends Well **38:** 99
Gender Identity (topic entry) **40:** 75
Hamlet **19:** 330
King Lear **19:** 330
Macbeth **19:** 330
Madness (topic entry) **35:** 8
Much Ado about Nothing **31:** 231
The Winter's Tale **7:** 506

Neill, Kerby
Much Ado about Nothing **8:** 58

Neill, Michael
Henry IV, 1 and 2 **28:** 159
Henry V **28:** 159
Henry VI, 1, 2, and 3 **28:** 159
Othello **13:** 327
Richard II **28:** 159

Nemerov, Howard
A Midsummer Night's Dream **3:** 421
The Two Gentlemen of Verona **6:** 509

Nemirovich-Danchenko, V. I.
Julius Caesar **17:** 295

Nesbitt, Cathleen
The Winter's Tale **15:** 449

Nevo, Ruth
The Comedy of Errors **34:** 245
Pericles **36:** 214
The Two Gentlemen of Verona **6:** 560
The Winter's Tale **45:** 344

Newlin, Jeanne T.
Troilus and Cressida **18:** 395, 437

Newman, Karen
Henry V **19:** 203
The Merchant of Venice **40:** 208

Nice, David
Troilus and Cressida **18:** 387

Nicholls, Graham
Measure for Measure **23:** 379

Nichols, Lewis
The Tempest **15:** 237, 240

Nicoll, Allardyce
Othello **4:** 457

Nietzsche, Friedrich
Hamlet **1:** 114
Julius Caesar **7:** 179

Nightingale, Benedict
All's Well That Ends Well **26:** 55, 71
Antony and Cleopatra **17:** 57
As You Like It **23:** 128, 148
The Comedy of Errors **26:** 150
Coriolanus **17:** 192, 207
Cymbeline **15:** 73
Hamlet **21:** 267, 297, 330
Henry IV, 1 and 2 **14:** 90
Henry V **14:** 282
Henry VI, 1, 2, and 3 **24:** 32
Henry VIII **24:** 115, 124
Julius Caesar **17:** 380
King John **24:** 216
King Lear **11:** 109
Macbeth **20:** 289, 314
Measure for Measure **23:** 321, 327, 339, 355
The Merchant of Venice **12:** 95
The Merry Wives of Windsor **18:** 55
A Midsummer Night's Dream **12:** 257, 275
Much Ado about Nothing **18:** 205
Pericles **15:** 148, 160, 175
Richard II **24:** 345, 374, 381
Richard III **14:** 464
Romeo and Juliet **11:** 485
The Taming of the Shrew **12:** 389
The Tempest **15:** 269, 289
Titus Andronicus **17:** 466
Troilus and Cressida **18:** 343, 389
Twelfth Night **26:** 270, 327, 336
The Winter's Tale **15:** 477, 485, 486

Nilan, Mary M.
The Tempest **15:** 215, 305

Noble, James Ashcroft
Sonnets **10:** 214

Noble, Richmond
Love's Labour's Lost **2:** 316

Nokes, David
Troilus and Cressida **18:** 364

North, Richard
Much Ado about Nothing **18:** 200

Norton, Elliot
Antony and Cleopatra **17:** 52

Novick, Julius
Hamlet **21:** 287
Henry V **14:** 304
Measure for Measure **23:** 331
Titus Andronicus **17:** 461, 474

Novy, Marianne
Fathers and Daughters (topic entry) **36:** 54
Gender Identity (topic entry) **40:** 9
King Lear **31:** 117
The Merchant of Venice **40:** 142
Shakespeare's Representation of Women (topic entry) **31:** 3
Troilus and Cressida **27:** 362; **43:** 351

Novy, Marianne L.
The Taming of the Shrew **31:** 288

Nowottny, Winifred M. T.
King Lear **2:** 213, 235
Othello **4:** 512
Romeo and Juliet **5:** 522
Timon of Athens **1:** 505
Troilus and Cressida **3:** 590

Nunn, Trevor
Julius Caesar **17:** 421

Nuttail, A. D.
Measure for Measure **2:** 511
The Tempest **29:** 313
Timon of Athens **13:** 392; **27:** 184

O'Loughlin, Sean
The Phoenix and Turtle **10:** 18

Odell, George C. D.
Antony and Cleopatra **17:** 5
As You Like It **23:** 8, 19
Henry V **14:** 178, 182, 188, 189, 194, 195
Henry VI, 1, 2, and 3 **24:** 4
Henry VIII **24:** 70, 77, 84
King John **24:** 165
Measure for Measure **23:** 267
The Merry Wives of Windsor **18:** 9
A Midsummer Night's Dream **12:** 144, 146, 155, 180
Much Ado about Nothing **18:** 113
Pericles **15:** 130
Richard II **24:** 262, 271
The Tempest **15:** 199, 201
Timon of Athens **20:** 428, 442, 445
Troilus and Cressida **18:** 280
The Winter's Tale **15:** 397, 431, 444

Ogawa, Yasuhiro
Hamlet **42:** 279

Ogburn, Charlton
Authorship Controversy (topic entry) **41:** 32

Ogden, Dunbar H.
  The Comedy of Errors **26:** 154

Oliver, Edith
  The Comedy of Errors **26:** 175
  Hamlet **21:** 288
  Julius Caesar **17:** 401
  Othello **11:** 314
  Twelfth Night **26:** 299

Oliver, H. J.
  Coriolanus **30:** 129
  Timon of Athens **27:** 157

Olivier, Laurence
  Antony and Cleopatra **17:** 28
  Hamlet **21:** 202
  Henry V **14:** 252
  Othello **11:** 297

Ong, Walter J.
  The Phoenix and Turtle **10:** 31

Orgel, Stephen
  Sexuality (topic entry) **33:** 18
  The Tempest **29:** 396
  The Winter's Tale **19:** 441; **45:** 329

Orgel, Stephen Kitay
  The Tempest **8:** 414

Ormerod, David
  A Midsummer Night's Dream **3:** 497

Ornstein, Robert
  Hamlet **1:** 230
  Henry IV, 1 and 2 **1:** 431
  Henry V **5:** 293
  Henry VI, 1, 2, and 3 **3:** 136
  Henry VIII **2:** 68
  Julius Caesar **7:** 282
  King John **9:** 292
  King Lear **2:** 238
  Measure for Measure **2:** 495
  A Midsummer Night's Dream **29:** 175
  Troilus and Cressida **27:** 370
  The Two Gentlemen of Verona **40:** 312

Orwell, George
  King Lear **2:** 186

Osborne, Laurie
  Twelfth Night **37:** 78

Osborne, Laurie E.
  The Merry Wives of Windsor **38:** 273

Over, William
  Coriolanus **17:** 225

Overholser, Winfred
  Madness (topic entry) **35:** 24

Owens, Margaret E.
  Henry VI, 1, 2, and 3 **37:** 157

O'Connor, Garry
  Julius Caesar **17:** 394

King John **24:** 223
Love's Labour's Lost **23:** 204
Richard II **24:** 383
Titus Andronicus **17:** 479
Twelfth Night **26:** 318

O'Connor, John J.
  Hamlet **21:** 310
  King John **24:** 232
  Richard II **24:** 368
  Troilus and Cressida **18:** 370

O'Dair, Sharon
  Julius Caesar **25:** 272

O'Rourke, James
  Macbeth **44:** 366
  Troilus and Cressida **22:** 58

Pack, Robert
  Macbeth **3:** 275

Page, Malcolm
  Richard II **24:** 405

Page, Nadine
  Much Ado about Nothing **8:** 44

Palmer, D. J.
  As You Like It **5:** 128; **46:** 88
  Julius Caesar **7:** 343
  Macbeth **20:** 400
  The Merchant of Venice **40:** 106
  Titus Andronicus **4:** 668
  Twelfth Night **1:** 648

Palmer, Daryl W.
  The Winter's Tale **32:** 388

Palmer, John
  Coriolanus **17:** 147
  King John **9:** 260
  Love's Labour's Lost **2:** 324
  A Midsummer Night's Dream **3:** 406; **12:** 220
  The Taming of the Shrew **12:** 333
  Troilus and Cressida **18:** 284
  The Winter's Tale **15:** 446

Pansinetti, P. M.
  Julius Caesar **17:** 354

Panter-Downes, Mollie
  Richard II **24:** 331

Paolucci, Anne
  A Midsummer Night's Dream **3:** 494

Papp, Joseph
  Troilus and Cressida **18:** 423

Paris, Bernard J.
  Psychoanalytic Interpretations (topic entry) **44:** 89
  Richard II **19:** 209

Parker, A. A.
  Henry VIII **2:** 56

Parker, Barbara L.
  Julius Caesar **25:** 280

Parker, Brian
  Richard III **14:** 523

Parker, David
  Sonnets **10:** 346

Parker, Patricia
  General Commentary **22:** 378

Parker, R. B.
  All's Well That Ends Well **7:** 126
  King Lear **19:** 344

Parr, Wolstenholme
  Coriolanus **9:** 13
  Othello **4:** 396

Parrott, Thomas Marc
  As You Like It **5:** 84
  Love's Labour's Lost **2:** 327
  A Midsummer Night's Dream **3:** 410
  Timon of Athens **1:** 481
  The Two Gentlemen of Verona **6:** 476

Parsons, Philip
  Love's Labour's Lost **2:** 344

Parten, Anne
  The Merchant of Venice **4:** 356
  The Merry Wives of Windsor **38:** 300

Pasco, Richard
  Richard II **24:** 346
  Timon of Athens **20:** 494

Paster, Gail Kern
  Julius Caesar **13:** 260

Pater, Walter
  Love's Labour's Lost **2:** 308
  Measure for Measure **2:** 409
  Richard II **6:** 270

Patterson, Annabel
  Henry V **13:** 194
  A Midsummer Night's Dream **13:** 27

Paulin, Bernard
  Timon of Athens **1:** 510

Payne, Ben Iden
  Measure for Measure **23:** 294
  The Merchant of Venice **12:** 131

Payne, Michael
  The Tempest **45:** 272

Pearce, Edward
  Twelfth Night **26:** 320

Pearce, Frances M.
  All's Well That Ends Well **7:** 116

Pearce, G. M.
  All's Well That Ends Well **26:** 51
  Antony and Cleopatra **17:** 73
  As You Like It **23:** 116, 124
  Henry IV, 1 and 2 **14:** 104
  King John **24:** 233

Love's Labour's Lost **23:** 222
Richard II **24:** 370
The Taming of the Shrew **12:** 395
Timon of Athens **20:** 473
Troilus and Cressida **18:** 365, 369

Pearce, Jill
  Troilus and Cressida **18:** 388
  Twelfth Night **26:** 326

Pearlman, E.
  Henry V **32:** 157
  Henry VI, 1, 2, and 3 **22:** 193; **37:** 165; **42:** 153
  Richard III **22:** 193; **39:** 370
  Romeo and Juliet **33:** 287

Pearson, Lu Emily
  Venus and Adonis **10:** 427

Pearson, Norman Holmes
  Antony and Cleopatra **6:** 142

Pechter, Edward
  Henry IV, 1 and 2 **1:** 441
  Othello **37:** 269

Pedicord, Harry William
  King John **24:** 171

Pepys, Samuel
  Hamlet **21:** 9
  Henry VIII **2:** 15
  Macbeth **3:** 170; **20:** 11
  Measure for Measure **23:** 267
  The Merry Wives of Windsor **5:** 332
  A Midsummer Night's Dream **3:** 361; **12:** 144
  Romeo and Juliet **5:** 415; **11:** 377
  The Tempest **15:** 189

Pequigney, Joseph
  Desire (topic entry) **38:** 40
  The Merchant of Venice **22:** 69
  Sonnets **10:** 391
  Twelfth Night **22:** 69

Percival, John
  A Midsummer Night's Dream **12:** 250

Perret, Marion D.
  The Taming of the Shrew **31:** 295

Perry, Ruth
  Madness (topic entry) **35:** 1

Perry, Thomas A.
  The Two Gentlemen of Verona **6:** 490

Peter, John
  All's Well That Ends Well **26:** 44
  Antony and Cleopatra **17:** 76
  As You Like It **23:** 112
  The Comedy of Errors **26:** 177
  Hamlet **21:** 327
  Henry VI, 1, 2, and 3 **24:** 47
  Henry VIII **24:** 122
  Julius Caesar **17:** 392, 406
  King John **24:** 235
  Measure for Measure **23:** 356

The Merry Wives of Windsor **18**: 58
Much Ado about Nothing **18**: 209
Richard III **14**: 486
The Taming of the Shrew **12**: 387
Titus Andronicus **17**: 477
Troilus and Cressida **18**: 361, 382
Twelfth Night **26**: 329

Peterson, Douglas L.
Cymbeline **4**: 141
Romeo and Juliet **5**: 533
The Tempest **8**: 439

Petronella, Vincent
The Comedy of Errors **34**: 233
The Phoenix and Turtle **10**: 45

Pettet, E. C.
All's Well That Ends Well **7**: 43
King John **9**: 267
Measure for Measure **2**: 474
A Midsummer Night's Dream **3**: 408
Much Ado about Nothing **8**: 53
Romeo and Juliet **5**: 467
The Taming of the Shrew **9**: 342
Twelfth Night **1**: 580
The Two Gentlemen of Verona **6**: 478
The Two Noble Kinsmen **9**: 470

Pettigrew, John
The Comedy of Errors **26**: 155
Henry V **14**: 267
Measure for Measure **23**: 333
Pericles **15**: 156
Timon of Athens **20**: 459
Twelfth Night **26**: 290
The Two Gentlemen of Verona **12**: 486

Phelps, Samuel
As You Like It **23**: 18

Phelps, W. May
King Lear **11**: 21

Phialas, Peter G.
As You Like It **5**: 122
The Comedy of Errors **1**: 53
Henry V **5**: 267
Love's Labour's Lost **38**: 163
The Merchant of Venice **4**: 312
A Midsummer Night's Dream **3**: 450
Much Ado about Nothing **31**: 198
Richard II **6**: 352
Twelfth Night **34**: 270
The Two Gentlemen of Verona **6**: 516

Philip, Duke of Wharton
Henry V **14**: 175

Phillabaum, Corliss E.
Timon of Athens **20**: 446

Phillipps, Augustine
Richard II **6**: 249

Phillips, Graham
Authorship Controversy (topic entry) **41**: 76

Phillips, James E.
Julius Caesar **17**: 351

Phillips, James Emerson, Jr.
Antony and Cleopatra **6**: 107
Henry V **14**: 216
Julius Caesar **7**: 245
Richard III **14**: 429

Phillips, Robin
Measure for Measure **23**: 335

Pierce, Robert B.
Henry VI, 1, 2, and 3 **3**: 126
Richard II **6**: 388
Richard III **8**: 248

Pietscher, A.
The Merchant of Venice **4**: 214

Pilkington, Ace G.
Henry V **19**: 217

Piper, William Bowman
Sonnets **10**: 360

Pitcher, John
The Tempest **29**: 355

Pittenger, Elizabeth
The Merry Wives of Windsor **19**: 101

Planche, James Robinson
The Taming of the Shrew **12**: 316

Platt, Peter G.
Pericles **42**: 352

Playfair, Giles
Macbeth **20**: 95

Playfair, Nigel
As You Like It **23**: 60

Plotz, John
Coriolanus **37**: 283

Poel, William
Henry V **14**: 336
King Lear **11**: 142
Macbeth **20**: 350
Measure for Measure **23**: 405
The Merchant of Venice **12**: 111
Romeo and Juliet **11**: 499

Pollock, Lady
As You Like It **23**: 17
Hamlet **21**: 58

Poole, Adrian
Richard II **28**: 178

Poole, Kristen
Henry IV, 1 and 2 **32**: 166

Pope, Alexander
Cymbeline **4**: 17
Henry V **5**: 187
Richard II **6**: 252
Troilus and Cressida **3**: 536
The Two Gentlemen of Verona **6**: 435

The Two Noble Kinsmen **9**: 444
The Winter's Tale **7**: 377

Pope, Elizabeth Marie
Measure for Measure **2**: 470

Popkin, Henry
All's Well That Ends Well **26**: 48
Measure for Measure **23**: 332
Richard II **24**: 378
Timon of Athens **20**: 469

Porter, Joseph A.
Henry IV, 1 and 2 **1**: 439

Potter, John
Cymbeline **4**: 20
The Merchant of Venice **4**: 193
The Merry Wives of Windsor **5**: 335
Othello **4**: 390
Timon of Athens **1**: 455
Twelfth Night **1**: 543

Potter, Lois
Julius Caesar **17**: 405
Love's Labour's Lost **23**: 230
Timon of Athens **20**: 474

Potter, Nick
As You Like It **16**: 53
King Lear **31**: 84
Twelfth Night **16**: 53

Potter, Stephen
Henry IV, 1 and 2 **14**: 30, 36
Richard II **24**: 314

Powell, Raymond
Othello **32**: 302

Preston, Dennis R.
Twelfth Night **34**: 281

Price, Hereward T.
Henry VI, 1, 2, and 3 **3**: 69
Venus and Adonis **10**: 434

Price, Jonathan Reeve
King John **9**: 290

Price, Joseph G.
All's Well That Ends Well **26**: 73, 97; **38**: 72

Price, Thomas R.
Love's Labour's Lost **2**: 310
The Winter's Tale **7**: 399

Priestley, J. B.
As You Like It **5**: 63
Henry IV, 1 and 2 **1**: 344
Twelfth Night **1**: 567

Priestley, Joseph
King John **9**: 215

Prince, F. T.
The Phoenix and Turtle **10**: 35
The Rape of Lucrece **10**: 81

Prior, Moody E.
Henry V **5**: 299

Henry VI, 1, 2, and 3 **39**: 154

Pritchett, V. S.
Much Ado about Nothing **18**: 184
Richard III **14**: 453
The Taming of the Shrew **12**: 360

Procter, Bryan Waller
Hamlet **21**: 44
Macbeth **20**: 91
The Merchant of Venice **12**: 13
Othello **11**: 199
Romeo and Juliet **11**: 396

Prosser, Eleanor
Hamlet **1**: 254; **35**: 152

Proudfoot, Richard
A Midsummer Night's Dream **12**: 268

Prouse, Derek
Richard III **14**: 423

Prouty, Charles Tyler
Twelfth Night **34**: 323

Pryce-Jones, Alan
The Comedy of Errors **26**: 153
The Two Gentlemen of Verona **12**: 473

Pryce-Jones, David
Henry VI, 1, 2, and 3 **24**: 21
Othello **11**: 298

Puckler-Muskau, Prince
Macbeth **20**: 96

Pugliatti, Paolo
Henry V **25**: 131

Puknat, Elisabeth M.
Romeo and Juliet **11**: 414

Purdom, C. B.
Henry VIII **2**: 65

Pursell, Michael
The Taming of the Shrew **12**: 378

Pushkin, A. S.
Henry VI, 1 and 2 **1**: 313
Measure for Measure **2**: 399

Putney, Rufus
Venus and Adonis **10**: 442

Pye, Christopher
Henry V **16**: 202
King Lear **16**: 202
Macbeth **16**: 328
Richard II **16**: 202

Quayle, Anthony
Henry IV, 1 and 2 **14**: 38

Quiller-Couch, Sir Arthur
All's Well That Ends Well **7**: 29
Antony and Cleopatra **6**: 71
As You Like It **5**: 61
The Comedy of Errors **1**: 19
Cymbeline **15**: 105

Macbeth **3**: 229
Measure for Measure **2**: 420
The Merchant of Venice **4**: 228
Much Ado about Nothing **8**: 41
The Taming of the Shrew **9**: 332
The Tempest **8**: 334
Twelfth Night **1**: 569
The Two Gentlemen of Verona **6**: 466
The Winter's Tale **7**: 414

Quinn, Michael
Richard II **6**: 338

Rabkin, Leslie Y.
Othello **35**: 276

Rabkin, Norman
Antony and Cleopatra **6**: 180
Coriolanus **30**: 96
Henry V **5**: 304
Julius Caesar **7**: 316
The Merchant of Venice **4**: 350
Richard II **6**: 364
Romeo and Juliet **5**: 538
Troilus and Cressida **3**: 613
Venus and Adonis **10**: 462

Rackin, Phyllis
Antony and Cleopatra **6**: 197; **27**: 135
Coriolanus **9**: 189
Henry IV, 1 and 2 **16**: 183
Henry V **16**: 183
Henry VI, 1, 2, and 3 **16**: 183; **39**: 196
King John **9**: 303; **41**: 215
King Lear **2**: 269
Politics and Power (topic entry) **30**: 46
Richard III **25**: 141
Shakespeare's Representation of Women (topic entry) **31**: 48

Radel, Nicholas F.
The Two Noble Kinsmen **41**: 326

Raleigh, Walter
Cymbeline **4**: 48
Measure for Measure **2**: 417
Pericles **2**: 554
Rape of Lucrece **10**: 70
Timon of Athens **1**: 477
Venus and Adonis **10**: 423

Ramsey, Jarold W.
Timon of Athens **1**: 513

Ranald, Margaret Loftus
The Comedy of Errors **26**: 180
The Taming of the Shrew **31**: 282, 326

Ransley, Peter
Twelfth Night **26**: 284

Ransom, John Crowe
Sonnets **10**: 260

Ratcliffe, Michael
Antony and Cleopatra **17**: 78
As You Like It **23**: 138
Coriolanus **17**: 209

Henry VI, 1, 2, and 3 **24**: 45
Julius Caesar **17**: 392, 405
King John **24**: 235
Love's Labour's Lost **23**: 214
Pericles **15**: 175
Richard III **14**: 485
Romeo and Juliet **11**: 483
The Taming of the Shrew **12**: 398
Titus Andronicus **17**: 485
Twelfth Night **26**: 315

Ravenscroft, Edward
Titus Andronicus **4**: 613

Ravich, Robert A.
Psychoanalytic Interpretations (topic entry) **44**: 1

Ray, Robin
Antony and Cleopatra **17**: 78

Read, David
Henry IV, Parts 1 and 2 **42**: 162
Henry V **42**: 162

Rebhorn, Wayne A.
Henry IV, 1 and 2 **39**: 130
Julius Caesar **16**: 231; **30**: 379
Venus and Adonis **33**: 321

Rede, W. L.
The Merchant of Venice **12**: 12

Redfern, James
Hamlet **21**: 181

Redfern, Stephen
Henry IV, 1 and 2 **14**: 31

Redgrave, Michael
Antony and Cleopatra **17**: 38

Reed, Robert Rentoul, Jr.
Magic and the Supernatural (topic entry) **29**: 53

Rees, Roger
Cymbeline **15**: 88

Reese, Jack E.
Titus Andronicus **17**: 501

Reese, M. M.
Henry IV, 1 and 2 **39**: 134
Henry V **30**: 237
Henry VI, 1, 2, and 3 **3**: 77
King John **9**: 280
Richard III **8**: 228

Reibetanz, John
King Lear **2**: 281

Reid, B. L.
Hamlet **1**: 242

Reid, Stephen
Othello **35**: 301

Reik, Theodor
The Merchant of Venice **4**: 268

Reynolds, Frederick
Much Ado about Nothing **18**: 115

Reynolds, George F.
Hamlet **21**: 407

Reynolds, Sir Joshua
Macbeth **3**: 181

Ribner, Irving
Henry VI, 1, 2, and 3 **3**: 100
Julius Caesar **7**: 279
King Lear **2**: 218
Macbeth **3**: 289
Othello **4**: 527, 559
Richard II **6**: 305
Romeo and Juliet **5**: 493
The Taming of the Shrew **9**: 390
Titus Andronicus **4**: 656

Rice, Julian
Othello **35**: 352

Rich, Alan
Henry V **14**: 290

Rich, Frank
Coriolanus **17**: 217
Julius Caesar **17**: 401
Measure for Measure **23**: 351
Much Ado about Nothing **18**: 217
Othello **11**: 319
Richard II **24**: 375
Richard III **14**: 479

Richard, David
Henry V **14**: 337
Othello **11**: 317

Richardson, D. L.
Sonnets **10**: 174

Richardson, Ian
Richard II **24**: 346

Richardson, Jack
Richard III **14**: 471

Richardson, Ralph
A Midsummer Night's Dream **12**: 284

Richardson, William
As You Like It **5**: 20
Hamlet **1**: 88
Henry IV, 1 and 2 **1**: 307
King Lear **2**: 103
Richard III **8**: 154
Timon of Athens **1**: 456

Richman, David
Much Ado about Nothing **18**: 264

Richmond, H. M.
Henry VIII **41**: 171

Richmond, Hugh M.
As You Like It **5**: 133
Henry V **5**: 271
Henry VI, 1, 2, and 3 **3**: 109
Henry VIII **2**: 76; **28**: 184
Julius Caesar **7**: 333
A Midsummer Night's Dream **3**: 480
Richard II **39**: 256
Richard III **16**: 137

Ridley, M. R.
Antony and Cleopatra **6**: 140
King John **9**: 250
The Taming of the Shrew **9**: 337

Riemer, A. P.
Antony and Cleopatra **6**: 189
As You Like It **5**: 156
Love's Labour's Lost **2**: 374
Much Ado about Nothing **8**: 108

Riggs, David
Henry VI, 1, 2, and 3 **3**: 119
Richard III **39**: 335

Ripley, John
Coriolanus **17**: 232, 248
Julius Caesar **17**: 345

Riss, Arthur
Coriolanus **22**: 248

Rissik, Andrew
Antony and Cleopatra **17**: 80

Ristori, Adelaide
Macbeth **20**: 345

Ritchey, David
Richard III **14**: 527

Ritson, Joseph
Hamlet **1**: 90
Julius Caesar **7**: 158

Rives, Amelie
The Taming of the Shrew **12**: 325

Roberts, Jeanne Addison
The Merry Wives of Windsor **5**: 369; **38**: 297

Roberts, Josephine A.
Sonnets **37**: 373

Roberts, Peter
The Comedy of Errors **26**: 147
Cymbeline **15**: 60
Hamlet **21**: 283
Henry IV, 1 and 2 **14**: 74
Henry V **14**: 273
Henry VI, 1, 2, and 3 **24**: 22
Julius Caesar **17**: 375
King Lear **11**: 84, 97
Measure for Measure **23**: 347
The Merchant of Venice **12**: 67
The Merry Wives of Windsor **18**: 43
Much Ado about Nothing **18**: 179, 189, 213, 216
Othello **11**: 304
Pericles **15**: 152
Richard II **24**: 332, 338
Richard III **14**: 459, 465
The Taming of the Shrew **12**: 385
Troilus and Cressida **18**: 332
Twelfth Night **26**: 271
The Two Gentlemen of Verona **12**: 483
The Winter's Tale **15**: 473, 480

Robertson, John M.
The Rape of Lucrece **10**: 70

Robertson, W. Graham
The Merchant of Venice **12**: 35

Robinson, David
The Taming of the Shrew **12**: 370
The Tempest **15**: 294

Robinson, Henry Crabb
Hamlet **21**: 43
King Lear **11**: 12, 18
A Midsummer Night's Dream **12**: 153
Othello **11**: 193
Pericles **15**: 135
Richard II **24**: 269
The Taming of the Shrew **12**: 316
The Tempest **15**: 210
The Two Gentlemen of Verona **12**: 452

Robson, Flora
The Winter's Tale **15**: 528

Roche, Thomas P.
Sonnets **10**: 353

Roderick, Richard
Henry VIII **2**: 16

Roe, John
The Phoenix and Turtle **38**: 334
Rape of Lucrece **43**: 92

Roesen, Bobbyann
Love's Labour's Lost **2**: 331

Rogers, Paul
A Midsummer Night's Dream **12**: 238

Rogers, Robert
Othello **35**: 320

Rogoff, Gordon
Hamlet **21**: 240
Julius Caesar **17**: 402
Richard II **24**: 377

Ronk, Martha
Hamlet **44**: 248
Psychoanalytic Interpretations (topic entry) **44**: 66
The Winter's Tale **36**: 349

Rose, Mark
Julius Caesar **30**: 374

Rosen, William
Antony and Cleopatra **6**: 165

Rosenberg, Marvin
King Lear **11**: 161
Macbeth **20**: 297, 338, 387
Othello **11**: 344

Rosenfeld, Megan
Love's Labour's Lost **23**: 221

Rosenfeld, Sybil
Coriolanus **17**: 140
The Two Gentlemen of Verona **12**: 453

Ross, Daniel W.
Hamlet **13**: 296

Ross, Lawrence J.
Othello **11**: 354

Ross, T. A.
The Merchant of Venice **4**: 238

Rossi, Alfred
A Midsummer Night's Dream **12**: 238

Rossiter, A. P.
Coriolanus **9**: 106; **30**: 89
Henry V **30**: 193
Much Ado about Nothing **8**: 69
Richard II **6**: 343
Richard III **8**: 201

Rossky, William
The Two Gentlemen of Verona **40**: 354

Rostron, David
Henry V **14**: 180
Henry VIII **24**: 74
Julius Caesar **17**: 274

Rothschild, Herbert B., Jr.
Henry IV, 1 and 2 **1**: 433
Richard II **6**: 381

Rothwell, Kenneth
Henry V **14**: 315
The Taming of the Shrew **12**: 402

Rothwell, Kenneth S.
All's Well That Ends Well **26**: 51
Macbeth **20**: 277

Rougement, Denis de
Romeo and Juliet **5**: 484

Rowe, Katherine A.
Titus Andronicus **43**: 262

Rowe, Nicholas
Hamlet **1**: 74; **21**: 9
Henry IV, 1 and 2 **1**: 286
Henry V **5**: 186
Henry VI, 1, 2, and 3 **3**: 17
Henry VIII **2**: 15
The Merchant of Venice **4**: 191
The Merry Wives of Windsor **5**: 334
Romeo and Juliet **5**: 415
The Tempest **8**: 287
Timon of Athens **1**: 453
The Winter's Tale **7**: 376

Rowse, A. L.
Sonnets **10**: 377

Roy, Emil
Troilus and Cressida **43**: 287

Rubenstein, Frankie
Dreams in Shakespeare (topic entry) **45**: 1

Rudnytsky, Peter L.
Henry VIII **41**: 146

Ruskin, John
The Tempest **8**: 307

Russell, Edward R.
King Lear **11**: 42
The Tempest **8**: 311

Russell, Robert
The Taming of the Shrew **12**: 365

Rustin, Michael
Romeo and Juliet **33**: 225

Rutherford, Malcolm
All's Well That Ends Well **26**: 70
Hamlet **21**: 324, 331
Julius Caesar **17**: 369
Macbeth **20**: 314
Troilus and Cressida **18**: 391
Twelfth Night **26**: 328

Rutter, Carol
All's Well That Ends Well **19**: 113

Rylands, George
Antony and Cleopatra **17**: 24
Othello **11**: 295
Pericles **15**: 139
Romeo and Juliet **11**: 458

Rylands, George H. W.
The Rape of Lucrece **10**: 71
Sonnets **10**: 255

Rymer, Thomas
Julius Caesar **7**: 150
Othello **4**: 370

Sacharoff, Mark
Julius Caesar **30**: 358

Sage, Lorna
The Taming of the Shrew **12**: 390

Salgaudo, Gaumini
Magic and the Supernatural (topic entry) **29**: 46

Salingar, L. G.
Twelfth Night **1**: 603

Salinger, Leo
King Lear **31**: 77

Salkeld, Duncan
Hamlet **35**: 140

Salomon, Patricia P.
Henry V **32**: 185

Salvini, Tommaso
King Lear **11**: 29
Othello **11**: 229

Sampson, Martin W.
The Two Gentlemen of Verona **6**: 465

Sams, Eric
Twelfth Night **26**: 332

Sanders, Norman
Julius Caesar **30**: 316

The Two Gentlemen of Verona **6**: 519

Sanderson, James L.
The Comedy of Errors **1**: 66

Sanfield, Keith
Macbeth **20**: 315

Santayana, George
Hamlet **1**: 128

Sargent, Ralph M.
The Two Gentlemen of Verona **6**: 480

Sasayama, Takashi
Hamlet **28**: 325
King Lear **28**: 325

Saunders, J. G.
King Lear **37**: 295

Saunders, J. W.
Antony and Cleopatra **17**: 110
Henry VIII **24**: 155

Schalkwyk, David
The Winter's Tale **22**: 324

Schanzer, Ernest
Antony and Cleopatra **27**: 32
Julius Caesar **7**: 268, 272
Measure for Measure **2**: 503
A Midsummer Night's Dream **3**: 411
Pericles **2**: 579
The Winter's Tale **7**: 473

Schein, Harry
Richard III **14**: 432

Scheye, Thomas E.
The Two Gentlemen of Verona **6**: 547

Schiffhorst, Gerald J.
Pericles **36**: 244

Schlegel, August Wilhelm
All's Well That Ends Well **7**: 9
Antony and Cleopatra **6**: 24
As You Like It **5**: 24
The Comedy of Errors **1**: 13
Coriolanus **9**: 14
Cymbeline **4**: 21
Hamlet **1**: 92
Henry IV, 1 and 2 **1**: 309
Henry V **5**: 192
Henry VI, 1, 2, and 3 **3**: 24
Henry VIII **2**: 22
Julius Caesar **7**: 159
King John **9**: 218
King Lear **2**: 104
Love's Labour's Lost **2**: 301
Macbeth **3**: 183
Measure for Measure **2**: 395
The Merchant of Venice **4**: 194
The Merry Wives of Windsor **5**: 336
A Midsummer Night's Dream **3**: 364
Much Ado about Nothing **8**: 13

Othello **4**: 400
Richard II **6**: 255
Richard III **8**: 159
Romeo and Juliet **5**: 421
Sonnets **10**: 159
The Taming of the Shrew **9**: 320
The Tempest **8**: 294
Timon of Athens **1**: 459
Titus Andronicus **4**: 616
Troilus and Cressida **3**: 539
Twelfth Night **1**: 543
The Two Gentlemen of Verona **6**: 439
The Two Noble Kinsmen **9**: 446
The Winter's Tale **7**: 382

Schlegel, Frederick
Sonnets **10**: 160

Schlueter, June
King Lear **19**: 295

Schlueter, Kurt
The Two Gentlemen of Verona **40**: 320

Schmidt, Dana Adams
As You Like It **23**: 96

Schneider, Michael
A Midsummer Night's Dream **45**: 160

Schneider, Pierre
Timon of Athens **20**: 466

Schoen, Elin
Othello **11**: 319

Schoenbaum, S.
Authorship Controversy (topic entry) **41**: 18
Love's Labour's Lost **23**: 211
The Merchant of Venice **12**: 94
The Taming of the Shrew **12**: 393

Schucking, Levin L.
Antony and Cleopatra **6**: 67
Julius Caesar **7**: 207
King Lear **2**: 151
The Tempest **8**: 336

Schwartz, Elias
The Phoenix and Turtle **38**: 342

Scofield, Paul
Timon of Athens **20**: 464

Scott, Clement
Hamlet **21**: 96, 132
King Lear **11**: 34
Macbeth **20**: 130
The Merchant of Venice **12**: 17
Much Ado about Nothing **18**: 120
Othello **11**: 243
Romeo and Juliet **11**: 427

Scott, William O.
The Two Gentlemen of Verona **6**: 511

Scuro, Daniel
Titus Andronicus **17**: 452

Sedgwick, Eve Kosofsky
Sonnets **40**: 254

Sedulus
Much Ado about Nothing **18**: 198

Seelig, Sharon Cadman
Richard II **32**: 189; **39**: 279

Seiden, Melvin
King Lear **2**: 284
Twelfth Night **1**: 632

Seltzer, Daniel
Othello **11**: 350
The Phoenix and Turtle **10**: 37

Sen Gupta, S. C.
As You Like It **5**: 86
The Comedy of Errors **1**: 34
Henry VI, 1, 2, and 3 **3**: 92
Love's Labour's Lost **2**: 328
Troilus and Cressida **3**: 583

Sen, Sailendra Kumar
Coriolanus **9**: 130

Seoufos, Alice-Lyle
As You Like It **5**: 162

Seronsy, Cecil C.
The Taming of the Shrew **9**: 370

Sewall, Richard B.
King Lear **2**: 226

Seward, Thomas
Antony and Cleopatra **6**: 21

Sewell, Arthur
Henry IV, 1 and 2 **1**: 396
King Lear **2**: 197
Measure for Measure **2**: 484

Sewell, Elizabeth
A Midsummer Night's Dream **3**: 432

Sewell, George
Sonnets **10**: 154

Sexton, Joyce H.
Shakespeare's Representation of Women (topic entry) **31**: 34

Sexton, Joyce Hengerer
Much Ado about Nothing **8**: 104

Seymour, Alan
Othello **11**: 301

Shaaber, M. A.
Henry IV, 1 and 2 **1**: 387

Shabani, Ranjee G.
The Phoenix and Turtle **10**: 21

Shakespeare, William
Venus and Adonis **10**: 409

Shannon, Laurie J.
The Two Noble Kinsmen **41**: 372; **42**: 361

Shapiro, James
Henry IV, 1 and 2 **19**: 233
Henry V **19**: 233
The Merchant of Venice **32**: 66
Richard II **19**: 233

Shapiro, Michael
The Merchant of Venice **40**: 156
The Taming of the Shrew **31**: 315
The Two Gentlemen of Verona **40**: 374

Shapiro, Stephen A.
Othello **35**: 317
Romeo and Juliet **5**: 516

Sharp, Cecil
A Midsummer Night's Dream **12**: 289

Shattuck, Charles H.
Julius Caesar **17**: 277, 287
As You Like It **23**: 20, 54
Hamlet **21**: 72, 145
Henry V **14**: 200
King John **24**: 187
Measure for Measure **23**: 282
A Midsummer Night's Dream **12**: 199
The Merry Wives of Windsor **18**: 15, 22, 31
Othello **11**: 327
Twelfth Night **26**: 211, 219

Shaw, Bernard
Antony and Cleopatra **6**: 52
All's Well That Ends Well **26**: 9
As You Like It **5**: 52; **23**: 51
Coriolanus **9**: 42
Cymbeline **4**: 45; **15**: 23, 32
Hamlet **21**: 129, 154
Henry IV, 1 and 2 **1**: 328, 332; **14**: 24
Henry V **5**: 209
Julius Caesar **7**: 187, 188; **17**: 306
The Merchant of Venice **12**: 33
A Midsummer Night's Dream **12**: 194
Much Ado about Nothing **8**: 38; **18**: 146, 152
Othello **4**: 433, 442; **11**: 335
Richard III **8**: 181, 182, **14**: 402
Romeo and Juliet **11**: 438
The Taming of the Shrew **9**: 329
The Tempest **15**: 223
The Two Gentlemen of Verona **12**: 454

Shaw, Glen Byam
Julius Caesar **17**: 419
Macbeth **20**: 242

Shaw, William P.
Troilus and Cressida **18**: 332

Shebbeare, John
Othello **4**: 388

Shelley, Percy Bysshe
King Lear **2**: 110
The Two Noble Kinsmen **9**: 447

Sheppard, Samuel
Pericles **2**: 537

Sher, Antony
King Lear **11**: 169

Sheridan, Thomas
Hamlet **1**: 83

Shewey, Don
Coriolanus **17**: 238

Shickman, Allan R.
King Lear **46**: 205

Shindler, Robert
Sonnets **10**: 230

Shorter, Eric
As You Like It **23**: 141
Timon of Athens **20**: 466

Showalter, Elaine
Madness (topic entry) **35**: 54

Shrimpton, Nicholas
All's Well That Ends Well **26**: 63
As You Like It **23**: 143
The Comedy of Errors **26**: 169
Coriolanus **17**: 215
Hamlet **21**: 317
Henry IV, 1 and 2 **14**: 110
Henry VIII **24**: 124
King John **24**: 230
Love's Labour's Lost **23**: 220
Macbeth **20**: 312
Measure for Measure **23**: 350
The Merry Wives of Windsor **18**: 63
A Midsummer Night's Dream **12**: 275
Richard III **14**: 488
Romeo and Juliet **11**: 486
The Tempest **15**: 368
Troilus and Cressida **18**: 383
Twelfth Night **26**: 307

Shulman, Jeffrey
A Midsummer Night's Dream **45**: 136

Shumaker, Wayne
Magic and the Supernatural (topic entry) **29**: 28

Shurgot, Michael W.
The Taming of the Shrew **12**: 435
Troilus and Cressida **18**: 451

Shuttleworth, Betram
Macbeth **20**: 146

Siddons, Sarah
Macbeth **20**: 60
The Winter's Tale **15**: 400

Siegel, Paul N.
Hamlet **25**: 288
Macbeth **3**: 280
A Midsummer Night's Dream **3**: 417
Othello **4**: 525
Romeo and Juliet **5**: 505

Siemon, James Edward
Cymbeline **4:** 155
The Merchant of Venice **4:** 319

Sierz, Alex
Macbeth **20:** 318

Simeon, James R.
Richard II **28:** 188

Simmons, J. L.
Henry IV, 1 and 2 **25:** 151
Henry V **25:** 151
Henry VI, 1, 2, and 3 **25:** 151
The Two Gentlemen of Verona **40:** 343

Simon, Francesca
Henry IV, 1 and 2 **14:** 98

Simon, John
All's Well That Ends Well **26:** 59
The Comedy of Errors **26:** 175, 182
Coriolanus **17:** 219
Hamlet **21:** 243, 290
Henry V **14:** 292, 305
King Lear **11:** 106
Love's Labour's Lost **23:** 227
Measure for Measure **23:** 353
A Midsummer Night's Dream **12:** 298
Much Ado about Nothing **18:** 193, 221, 225
Richard II **24:** 354, 376
Richard III **14:** 480, **14:** 470
Twelfth Night **26:** 314

Simpson, Percy
Julius Caesar **17:** 311

Simpson, Richard
Sonnets **10:** 205

Sinclair, Andrew
The Taming of the Shrew **12:** 398

Sinden, Donald
King Lear **11:** 165
Twelfth Night **26:** 273

Sinfield, Alan
The Merchant of Venice **37:** 86

Singleton, Mary
King Lear **11:** 8

Sirluck, Katherine A.
The Taming of the Shrew **19:** 122

Sisk, John P.
The Merchant of Venice **4:** 317

Sisson, C. J.
The Taming of the Shrew **12:** 430

Sitwell, Edith
Macbeth **3:** 256

Skinner, Richard Dana
Troilus and Cressida **18:** 296

Skura, Meredith Anne
Clowns and Fools (topic entry) **46:** 29
Psychoanalytic Interpretations (topic entry) **44:** 28
Richard II **42:** 173
Richard III **25:** 164
The Tempest **13:** 425

Slater, Ann Pasternak
Twelfth Night **26:** 303

Slights, Camille Wells
The Merchant of Venice **4:** 342
Much Ado about Nothing **25:** 77
The Taming of the Shrew **13:** 3
The Two Gentlemen of Verona **6:** 568

Slights, William W. E.
Timon of Athens **1:** 525

Slulsky, Harold
Hamlet **35:** 157

Small, S. Asa
Henry IV, 1 and 2 **1:** 353

Smallwood, R. L.
Henry IV, 1 and 2 **14:** 105

Smallwood, Robert
As You Like It **23:** 149
Love's Labour's Lost **23:** 232
Measure for Measure **23:** 359
Pericles **15:** 177
Richard II **24:** 383
Troilus and Cressida **18:** 392

Smidt, Kristian
Hamlet **16:** 259
Pericles **25:** 365

Smith, Bruce R.
Sonnets **40:** 264

Smith, Gordon Ross
Henry V **30:** 262
Julius Caesar **7:** 292; **30:** 351

Smith, James
Much Ado about Nothing **8:** 48; **31:** 229

Smith, Lisa Gordon
The Taming of the Shrew **12:** 357

Smith, Marion Bodwell
The Comedy of Errors **1:** 49

Smith, Peter D.
The Taming of the Shrew **12:** 367

Smith, Peter J.
Twelfth Night **26:** 332

Smith, Rebecca
Hamlet **35:** 229

Smith, Warren D.
Romeo and Juliet **5:** 536

Smith, William
Julius Caesar **7:** 155

Smollett, Tobias
Hamlet **1:** 82

Snider, Denton J.
Antony and Cleopatra **6:** 43
As You Like It **5:** 46
Coriolanus **9:** 33
Cymbeline **4:** 38
Henry V **5:** 205
Henry VI, 1, 2, and 3 **3:** 42
Henry VIII **3:** 39
King John **9:** 235
King Lear **2:** 133
Love's Labour's Lost **2:** 312
Macbeth **3:** 208
Measure for Measure **2:** 411
The Merchant of Venice **4:** 215
The Merry Wives of Windsor **5:** 343
A Midsummer Night's Dream **3:** 381
Much Ado about Nothing **8:** 29
Othello **4:** 427
Richard II **6:** 272
Richard III **8:** 177
Romeo and Juliet **5:** 438
The Taming of the Shrew **9:** 325
The Tempest **8:** 320
Timon of Athens **1:** 472
Troilus and Cressida **3:** 549
The Two Gentlemen of Verona **6:** 450
The Winter's Tale **7:** 402

Snyder, Susan
All's Well That Ends Well **22:** 78
Macbeth **44:** 373
Othello **4:** 575
Romeo and Juliet **5:** 547

Soellner, Rolf
Timon of Athens **1:** 531; **27:** 191

Solomon, Alisa
Love's Labour's Lost **23:** 228
Much Ado about Nothing **18:** 226
The Tempest **15:** 290

Solway, Diane
Twelfth Night **26:** 312

Sommers, Alan
Titus Andronicus **4:** 653

Southall, Raymond
Troilus and Cressida **3:** 606

Spalding, William
The Two Noble Kinsmen **9:** 448

Spanabel, Robert R.
Henry V **14:** 189

Spargo, John Webster
Henry IV, 1 and 2 **1:** 342

Speaight, Robert
All's Well That Ends Well **26:** 47
Antony and Cleopatra **17:** 60
As You Like It **23:** 92, 107
The Comedy of Errors **26:** 148
Cymbeline **15:** 79
Hamlet **21:** 254, 257, 284
Henry IV, 1 and 2 **14:** 75, 79, 88
Henry V **14:** 274
Henry VIII **24:** 117
Julius Caesar **17:** 370, 378, 383
King Lear **11:** 77, 99
Love's Labour's Lost **23:** 198, 202
Macbeth **20:** 260, 294
Measure for Measure **23:** 287, 324, 328
Much Ado about Nothing **18:** 181, 190
Othello **11:** 304
Richard II **24:** 296, 333, 351
Richard III **14:** 455, 466
Romeo and Juliet **11:** 463
The Taming of the Shrew **12:** 357
The Tempest **8:** 390; **15:** 224, 273, 283
Timon of Athens **20:** 463
Troilus and Cressida **18:** 289, 327, 347
Twelfth Night **26:** 255, 263, 269, 284
The Two Gentlemen of Verona **12:** 457, 478, 484
The Winter's Tale **15:** 427, 482, 489

Speaight, Robert W.
Pericles **15:** 154

Spedding, James
Henry VIII **2:** 28

Spencer, Anthony
Richard III **14:** 357

Spencer, Benjamin T.
Antony and Cleopatra **6:** 159
Henry IV, 1 and 2 **1:** 372

Spencer, Hazelton
Henry IV, 1 and 2 **14:** 116
Henry VI, 1, 2, and 3 **24:** 6
Macbeth **20:** 12
Measure for Measure **23:** 269, 276
The Merry Wives of Windsor **18:** 10
Much Ado about Nothing **8:** 47
Richard II **24:** 263
Timon of Athens **20:** 429
Troilus and Cressida **18:** 281

Spencer, Janet M.
Henry V **37:** 175

Spencer, T. J. B.
Julius Caesar **30:** 285
Shakespeare and Classical Civilization (topic entry) **27:** 56

Spencer, Theodore
Hamlet **1:** 169
Henry IV, 1 and 2 **1:** 366
King Lear **2:** 174
Macbeth **3:** 248
Pericles **2:** 564
The Two Noble Kinsmen **9:** 463

Spender, Stephen
Macbeth **3:** 246

Spinrad, Phoebe S.
King Lear **46:** 264

Measure for Measure **22**: 85
Much Ado about Nothing **22**: 85

Spivack, Bernard
Othello **4**: 545
Richard III **8**: 213
Titus Andronicus **4**: 650

Sprague, Arthur Colby
Hamlet **21**: 11, 35, 392
Henry IV, 1 and 2 **14**: 10, 133
Henry V **14**: 319
Henry VI, 1, 2, and 3 **24**: 51
Henry VIII **24**: 140, 152
Macbeth **20**: 65, 113
The Merchant of Venice **12**: 36
The Merry Wives of Windsor **18**: 68
Othello **11**: 202, 257
Richard II **24**: 395
Richard III **14**: 517
Twelfth Night **26**: 360
The Winter's Tale **15**: 517

Sprengnether, Madelon
Antony and Cleopatra **13**: 368
Coriolanus **30**: 142
Psychoanalytic Interpretations (topic entry) **44**: 93

Sprigg, Douglas C.
Troilus and Cressida **18**: 442

Spurgeon, Caroline F. E.
Antony and Cleopatra **6**: 92
Coriolanus **9**: 64
Cymbeline **4**: 61
Hamlet **1**: 153
Henry IV, 1 and 2 **1**: 358
Henry VI, 1, 2, and 3 **3**: 52
Henry VIII **2**: 45
Julius Caesar **7**: 242
King John **9**: 246
King Lear **2**: 161
Love's Labour's Lost **2**: 320
Macbeth **3**: 245
Measure for Measure **2**: 431
The Merchant of Venice **4**: 241
Much Ado about Nothing **8**: 46
Pericles **2**: 560
Richard II **6**: 283
Richard III **8**: 186
Romeo and Juliet **5**: 456
The Taming of the Shrew **9**: 336
Timon of Athens **1**: 488
The Winter's Tale **7**: 418

Spurling, Hilary
All's Well That Ends Well **26**: 45
As You Like It **23**: 97
Hamlet **21**: 281
Henry VIII **24**: 116
Julius Caesar **17**: 372, 377
King John **24**: 217
Macbeth **20**: 259
Measure for Measure **23**: 323
The Merry Wives of Windsor **18**: 38
Pericles **15**: 149
The Tempest **15**: 270
Troilus and Cressida **18**: 344, 351
Twelfth Night **26**: 260, 267
The Winter's Tale **15**: 478

Squire, Jack Collings
Macbeth **20**: 172

Squire, Sir John
Henry VIII **2**: 44

St. George, Andrew
Love's Labour's Lost **23**: 229
Measure for Measure **23**: 356
Richard II **24**: 379

St. John, Christopher
The Merry Wives of Windsor **18**: 27

Stack, Rev. Richard
Henry IV, 1 and 2 **1**: 306

Staebler, Warren
As You Like It **5**: 82

Stallybrass, Peter
Macbeth **29**: 120

Stampfer, Judah
Julius Caesar **7**: 339
King Lear **2**: 231

Stanhope, Lord
Much Ado about Nothing **8**: 8

Stanislavski, Constantin
Othello **11**: 233

Stapfer, Paul
Julius Caesar **7**: 169

Stapleton, M. L.
Sonnets **25**: 374

Starkey, David
Henry VIII **24**: 120

Stauffer, Donald A.
Cymbeline **4**: 87
Julius Caesar **7**: 257
The Merry Wives of Windsor **5**: 353
Pericles **2**: 569
Romeo and Juliet **5**: 469
The Taming of the Shrew **9**: 343
The Two Gentlemen of Verona **6**: 479

Steadman, John M.
The Merry Wives of Windsor **38**: 286

Stedman, Jane W.
Pericles **15**: 161
The Tempest **15**: 283

Steele, Richard
Hamlet **21**: 9

Steele, Sir Richard
See also Bickerstaff, Isaac
Hamlet **1**: 74
Twelfth Night **1**: 540

Steevens, George
See also Collier, Jeremy; Hic et Ubique; Longinus; Lorenzo
Antony and Cleopatra **6**: 24
The Comedy of Errors **1**: 13
Cymbeline **4**: 20, 21
King Lear **11**: 7, 8
Macbeth **3**: 182
Measure for Measure **2**: 393
Much Ado about Nothing **8**: 12
Pericles **2**: 540
Richard III **8**: 159
Sonnets **10**: 155, 156
Titus Andronicus **4**: 616
Troilus and Cressida **3**: 538
Twelfth Night **1**: 543
The Two Noble Kinsmen **9**: 445
Venus and Adonis **10**: 411

Stein, Arnold
Macbeth **3**: 263
Troilus and Cressida **43**: 277

Stein, Rita
Richard II **24**: 353

Steinberg, Theodore L.
Venus and Adonis **33**: 352

Stempel, Daniel
Antony and Cleopatra **6**: 146
Othello **35**: 336

Stephenson, A. A., S.J.
Cymbeline **4**: 73

Stephenson, William E.
The Two Gentlemen of Verona **6**: 514

Sterne, Richard L.
Hamlet **21**: 237, 245

Sternroyd, Vincent
Much Ado about Nothing **18**: 134

Sterrit, David
The Taming of the Shrew **12**: 399

Stewart, J. I. M.
Henry IV, 1 and 2 **1**: 389
Julius Caesar **7**: 250
Othello **4**: 500

Stewart, Patrick
The Merchant of Venice **12**: 97

Still, Colin
The Tempest **8**: 328

Stirling, Brents
Antony and Cleopatra **6**: 151
Julius Caesar **7**: 259
Macbeth **3**: 271
Othello **4**: 486, 536
Richard II **6**: 307

Stockard, Emily E.
Sonnets **42**: 375

Stockholder, Kay
Macbeth **44**: 297; **45**: 58
The Merchant of Venice **45**: 17
The Winter's Tale **45**: 358

Stoker, Bram
Much Ado about Nothing **18**: 132
Romeo and Juliet **11**: 433

Stokes, Margaret
As You Like It **23**: 26
Romeo and Juliet **11**: 406

Stokes, Sewell
King Lear **11**: 53

Stoll, Elmer Edgar
All's Well That Ends Well **7**: 41
Antony and Cleopatra **6**: 76
As You Like It **5**: 59, 75
Coriolanus **9**: 72
Hamlet **1**: 151
Henry IV, 1 and 2 **1**: 338
Henry V **5**: 223
Measure for Measure **2**: 460
The Merchant of Venice **4**: 230, 445
Romeo and Juliet **5**: 458
The Tempest **8**: 345

Stone, George Winchester, Jr.
Antony and Cleopatra **17**: 6
Cymbeline **15**: 6
Hamlet **21**: 23
Macbeth **20**: 25
A Midsummer Night's Dream **12**: 147
Much Ado about Nothing **18**: 116
Othello **11**: 183
Richard III **14**: 366
Romeo and Juliet **11**: 386
The Tempest **15**: 203

Storey, Graham
Much Ado about Nothing **8**: 79

Strachey, Edward
Hamlet **1**: 102

Strachey, Lytton
The Tempest **8**: 324

Straumann, Heinrich
The Phoenix and Turtle **10**: 48

Strehler, Giorgio
The Tempest **15**: 338

Stribrny, Zdenek
Henry V **30**: 244

Stubbes, George
Hamlet **1**: 76

Styan, J. L.
All's Well That Ends Well **26**: 85, 117
As You Like It **23**: 64, 118
A Midsummer Night's Dream **12**: 215, 228, 264
The Winter's Tale **15**: 451

Suchet, David
The Tempest **15**: 374

Suddard, Mary, S.J.
Measure for Measure **2**: 418

Suhamy, Henri
Hamlet **35**: 241

Sullivan, Dan
Antony and Cleopatra **17**: 43
Titus Andronicus **17**: 460

Sullivan, Patrick
  The Merchant of Venice **12:** 83

Summers, Joseph H.
  Twelfth Night **1:** 591

Summers, Montague
  Troilus and Cressida **18:** 283

Sundelson, David
  Measure for Measure **2:** 528
  The Tempest **29:** 377

Suzman, Janet
  Antony and Cleopatra **17:** 113

Swan, Christopher
  King John **24:** 232

Swander, Homer
  A Midsummer Night's Dream **16:** 34

Swander, Homer D.
  Cymbeline **4:** 127

Sweeney, Louise
  Macbeth **20:** 273

Swinarski, Konrad
  All's Well That Ends Well **26:** 114

Swinburne, Algernon Charles
  Antony and Cleopatra **6:** 40
  As You Like It **5:** 42
  The Comedy of Errors **1:** 16
  Coriolanus **9:** 31
  Cymbeline **4:** 37
  Henry IV, 1 and 2 **1:** 325
  Henry V **5:** 205
  Henry VIII **2:** 36
  King Lear **2:** 129
  Love's Labour's Lost **2:** 307
  Much Ado about Nothing **8:** 28
  Othello **4:** 423
  Pericles **2:** 550
  The Rape of Lucrece **10:** 69
  Richard II **6:** 282
  Richard III **8:** 167
  Romeo and Juliet **5:** 437
  Troilus and Cressida **3:** 548
  The Two Gentlemen of Verona **6:** 449
  The Two Noble Kinsmen **9:** 456
  Venus and Adonis **10:** 419
  The Winter's Tale **7:** 396

Swinden, Patrick
  As You Like It **5:** 138

Sykes, H. Dugdale
  Pericles **2:** 556

Sylvester, Bickford
  The Rape of Lucrece **10:** 93

Symonds, John Addington
  Titus Andronicus **4:** 627

Symons, Arthur
  Antony and Cleopatra **6:** 48
  Coriolanus **17:** 140
  Titus Andronicus **4:** 628

Taciturnus, Frater (Kierkegaard, Seren)
  Hamlet **1:** 102

Taine, Nippolyte A.
  As You Like It **5:** 35
  Much Ado about Nothing **8:** 27

Talbert, Ernest William
  The Comedy of Errors **1:** 43

Tate, Nahum
  Julius Caesar **7:** 149
  King Lear **2:** 92
  Richard II **6:** 250; **24:** 260

Tatham, John
  Pericles **2:** 537

Tatlock, John S. P.
  Troilus and Cressida **3:** 558

Taubman, Howard
  The Comedy of Errors **26:** 153
  Cymbeline **15:** 62
  Hamlet **21:** 236
  Othello **11:** 313
  Timon of Athens **20:** 455
  Troilus and Cressida **18:** 336

Tave, Stuart M.
  A Midsummer Night's Dream **45:** 175

Tayler, Edward W.
  King Lear **16:** 301

Taylor, Anthony Brian
  A Midsummer Night's Dream **16:** 25

Taylor, Donn Ervin
  As You Like It **34:** 102

Taylor, Gary
  Henry V **30:** 278
  Authorship Controversy (topic entry) **41:** 81

Taylor, John Russell
  Macbeth **20:** 272
  Romeo and Juliet **11:** 471
  The Taming of the Shrew **12:** 369

Taylor, Mark
  Cymbeline **15:** 66
  Fathers and Daughters (topic entry) **36:** 1
  King Lear **16:** 372
  Macbeth **16:** 372
  A Midsummer Night's Dream **29:** 269
  The Tempest **25:** 382
  Twelfth Night **16:** 372

Taylor, Michael
  Cymbeline **4:** 172
  Pericles **36:** 226

Taylor, Paul
  Hamlet **21:** 325, 332
  Macbeth **20:** 316
  Richard II **24:** 381
  Twelfth Night **26:** 335

Teague, Frances
  Love's Labour's Lost **23:** 222

Tennenhouse, Leonard
  Kingship (topic entry) **39:** 1
  Violence in Shakespeare's Works (topic entry) **43:** 12

Tenschert, Joachim
  Coriolanus **17:** 185

Terry, Ellen
  Cymbeline **15:** 23
  Hamlet **21:** 107
  King John **24:** 198
  Macbeth **20:** 144
  The Merchant of Venice **12:** 34, 114
  The Merry Wives of Windsor **18:** 27
  A Midsummer Night's Dream **12:** 187
  Much Ado about Nothing **18:** 245
  Othello **11:** 336
  Romeo and Juliet **11:** 434
  The Winter's Tale **15:** 429

Thaler, Alwin
  The Two Gentlemen of Verona **6:** 471

Thatcher, David
  Measure for Measure **32:** 81; **33:** 117

Thayer, C. G.
  Henry V **5:** 318

Theobald, Lewis
  Henry V **5:** 187
  Henry VI, 1, 2, and 3 **3:** 18
  Julius Caesar **7:** 153
  King John **9:** 209
  King Lear **2:** 94
  Love's Labour's Lost **2:** 299
  Measure for Measure **2:** 388
  Othello **4:** 385
  Timon of Athens **1:** 454
  Titus Andronicus **4:** 613
  Troilus and Cressida **3:** 537
  Twelfth Night **1:** 540

Thomas, Ceridwen
  Measure for Measure **23:** 358

Thomas, Moy
  Hamlet **21:** 101

Thomas, Sidney
  King Lear **32:** 308
  Richard III **8:** 190

Thompson, Ann
  Comedy of Errors **42:** 93
  Cymbeline **36:** 129
  Love's Labour's Lost **42:** 93

Thompson, Karl F.
  Richard II **6:** 321
  Twelfth Night **1:** 587
  The Two Gentlemen of Verona **6:** 488

Thomson, Leslie
  Antony and Cleopatra **13:** 374

Thomson, Patricia
  Troilus and Cressida **27:** 332

Thomson, Peter
  Antony and Cleopatra **17:** 62
  As You Like It **23:** 108
  Cymbeline **15:** 81
  Hamlet **21:** 294
  Henry IV, 1 and 2 **14:** 91
  King John **24:** 218, 225
  Measure for Measure **23:** 328
  A Midsummer Night's Dream **12:** 260
  Richard III **14:** 467
  The Taming of the Shrew **12:** 484
  Twelfth Night **26:** 288

Thomson, Richard
  Richard II **24:** 352

Thomson, Virgil
  Much Ado about Nothing **18:** 249

Thorne, W. B.
  Cymbeline **4:** 129
  Pericles **2:** 584
  The Taming of the Shrew **9:** 393

Thorp, Joseph
  Macbeth **20:** 191

Thorpe, Thomas
  Sonnets **10:** 153

Tice, Terrence N.
  Julius Caesar **45:** 10

Tieck, Ludwig
  Hamlet **21:** 30

Tierney, Margaret
  Antony and Cleopatra **17:** 58

Tiffany, Grace
  The Merry Wives of Windsor **22:** 93; **38:** 319

Tilley, Morris P.
  Twelfth Night **1:** 563

Tillyard, E. M. W.
  All's Well That Ends Well **7:** 45
  Antony and Cleopatra **6:** 103
  The Comedy of Errors **1:** 46
  Cymbeline **4:** 68
  Hamlet **1:** 176
  Henry IV, 1 and 2 **1:** 378
  Henry V **5:** 241
  Henry VI, 1, 2, and 3 **3:** 59
  King John **9:** 254
  Love's Labour's Lost **2:** 340
  Measure for Measure **2:** 475
  The Merchant of Venice **4:** 282
  Othello **4:** 483
  Pericles **2:** 563
  Richard II **6:** 294
  Richard III **8:** 193
  The Taming of the Shrew **9:** 365
  The Tempest **8:** 359
  Titus Andronicus **4:** 639
  The Winter's Tale **7:** 429

Tinker, Jack
 As You Like It **23**: 140

Tinkler, F. C.
 Cymbeline **4**: 64
 The Winter's Tale **7**: 420

Tofte, Robert
 Love's Labour's Lost **2**: 299

Toliver, Harold
 Antony and Cleopatra **13**: 383

Tolstoy, Leo
 Henry IV, 1 and 2 **1**: 337
 King Lear **2**: 145

Tompkins, J. M. S.
 Pericles **2**: 572

Toole, William B.
 Richard III **8**: 252

Totten, Eileen
 Richard II **24**: 346

Tovey, Barbara
 The Merchant of Venice **4**: 344

Towse, John Ranken
 Hamlet **21**: 107
 Henry VIII **24**: 83
 King Lear **11**: 26, 31
 Measure for Measure **23**: 281
 The Merry Wives of Windsor **18**: 28
 Othello **11**: 231
 Richard II **24**: 291

Traci, Philip
 As You Like It **46**: 127
 The Merry Wives of Windsor **38**: 313
 The Two Gentlemen of Verona **40**: 330

Tracy, Robert
 Hamlet **35**: 163

Traister, Barbara Howard
 Kingship (topic entry) **39**: 16
 Magic and the Supernatural (topic entry) **29**: 1

Traub, Valerie
 Hamlet **44**: 195
 Henry IV, 1 and 2 **13**: 183
 Henry V **13**: 183
 Psychoanalytic Interpretations (topic entry) **44**: 44

Traversi, Derek A.
 Antony and Cleopatra **6**: 100
 The Comedy of Errors **1**: 39
 Coriolanus **9**: 73, 157
 Cymbeline **4**: 93
 Henry IV, 1 and 2 **1**: 383
 Henry V **5**: 233
 Julius Caesar **7**: 303
 Macbeth **3**: 323
 Measure for Measure **2**: 452
 The Merchant of Venice **4**: 315
 Othello **4**: 493

The Taming of the Shrew **9**: 362
The Tempest **8**: 370
Troilus and Cressida **3**: 621
The Two Gentlemen of Verona **6**: 502
The Winter's Tale **7**: 425

Tree, Herbert Beerbohm
 Henry IV, 1 and 2 **14**: 19
 Henry VIII **24**: 89
 Julius Caesar **17**: 310
 The Tempest **15**: 228

Tree, Maud
 Julius Caesar **17**: 313
 The Merry Wives of Windsor **18**: 30

Treglown, Jeremy
 All's Well That Ends Well **26**: 50
 Antony and Cleopatra **17**: 69
 As You Like It **23**: 129
 Cymbeline **15**: 87

Trench, Richard Chenevix
 Antony and Cleopatra **6**: 39

Trewin, J. C.
 All's Well That Ends Well **26**: 46
 Antony and Cleopatra **17**: 33, 70
 As You Like It **23**: 20, 70, 82, 91, 95, 114, 126, 135
 The Comedy of Errors **26**: 146
 Coriolanus **17**: 160
 Cymbeline **15**: 48, 57, 68, 77, 87
 Hamlet **21**: 216, 224, 230, 293, 300
 Henry IV, 1 and 2 **14**: 28, 58, 73
 Henry V **14**: 77, 318
 Henry VI, 1, 2, and 3 **24**: 11, 21, 41
 Henry VIII **24**: 91, 118
 Julius Caesar **17**: 374
 King Lear **11**: 61, 66, 88, 110
 Love's Labour's Lost **23**: 184, 212
 Macbeth **20**: 187, 241, 252, 292, 311
 Measure for Measure **23**: 301, 309, 316, 322
 A Midsummer Night's Dream **12**: 236, 242, 248, 258
 The Merry Wives of Windsor **18**: 34, 47, 70
 Much Ado about Nothing **18**: 160, 163
 Othello **11**: 285, 291, 300
 Pericles **15**: 136, 142, 152, 160
 Richard II **24**: 335, 372
 Richard III **14**: 416, 419, 455, 457
 Romeo and Juliet **11**: 441
 The Taming of the Shrew **12**: 355, 385
 The Tempest **15**: 259, 266, 267, 282
 Timon of Athens **20**: 462
 Titus Andronicus **17**: 442, 456, 469
 Troilus and Cressida **18**: 306, 331, 345, 352, 358
 Twelfth Night **26**: 230, 244, 261, 295
 The Two Gentlemen of Verona **12**: 461, 474, 482

The Winter's Tale **15**: 462, 464, 471

Tricomi, Albert H.
 Titus Andronicus **4**: 672; **27**: 313

Trotter, Stewart
 The Comedy of Errors **26**: 151

Truax, Elizabeth
 Rape of Lucrece **43**: 77

Turgenieff, Ivan
 Hamlet **1**: 111

Turner, Frederick
 As You Like It **46**: 156
 The Tempest **15**: 335

Turner, John
 Hamlet **16**: 246
 King Lear **31**: 84

Tyler, Thomas
 Sonnets **10**: 226

Tynan, Kenneth
 King John **24**: 213
 Measure for Measure **23**: 298
 The Merchant of Venice **12**: 50
 A Midsummer Night's Dream **12**: 247
 Othello **11**: 278, 288, 289
 Pericles **15**: 141
 Richard II **24**: 317
 Richard III **14**: 420
 Romeo and Juliet **11**: 460
 The Taming of the Shrew **12**: 354
 The Tempest **15**: 257
 Titus Andronicus **17**: 439

Ulrici, Hermann
 All's Well That Ends Well **7**: 15
 Antony and Cleopatra **6**: 31
 As You Like It **5**: 30
 The Comedy of Errors **1**: 14
 Coriolanus **9**: 18
 Cymbeline **4**: 28
 Hamlet **1**: 98
 Henry IV, 1 and 2 **1**: 314
 Henry V **5**: 195
 Henry VI, 1, 2, and 3 **3**: 27
 Henry VIII **2**: 25
 Julius Caesar **7**: 160
 King John **9**: 222
 King Lear **2**: 112
 Love's Labour's Lost **2**: 303
 Macbeth **3**: 194
 Measure for Measure **2**: 399
 The Merchant of Venice **4**: 201
 The Merry Wives of Windsor **5**: 338
 A Midsummer Night's Dream **3**: 368
 Much Ado about Nothing **8**: 17
 Othello **4**: 412
 Pericles **2**: 544
 Richard II **6**: 263
 Richard III **8**: 163
 Romeo and Juliet **5**: 427
 Sonnets **10**: 182
 The Taming of the Shrew **9**: 322
 The Tempest **8**: 302
 Timon of Athens **1**: 462

Titus Andronicus **4**: 618
Troilus and Cressida **3**: 543
Twelfth Night **1**: 546
The Two Gentlemen of Verona **6**: 442
The Winter's Tale **7**: 387

Unger, Leonard
 Henry IV, 1 and 2 **1**: 406

Uphaus, Robert W.
 The Winter's Tale **7**: 501

Upton, John
 Coriolanus **9**: 11
 Henry IV, 1 and 2 **1**: 289
 Julius Caesar **7**: 155
 Titus Andronicus **4**: 613
 The Two Gentlemen of Verona **6**: 436

Ure, Peter
 Timon of Athens **1**: 511

Vache, Jean
 Coriolanus **17**: 201

Valesio, Paolo
 Madness (topic entry) **35**: 40

Van de Water, Julia C.
 King John **9**: 271

Van Doren, Mark
 All's Well That Ends Well **7**: 39
 Antony and Cleopatra **6**: 104
 As You Like It **5**: 77
 The Comedy of Errors **1**: 30
 Coriolanus **9**: 78
 Cymbeline **4**: 70
 Henry IV, 1 and 2 **1**: 365
 Henry V **5**: 230
 Henry VI, 1, 2, and 3 **3**: 57
 Henry VIII **2**: 48
 Julius Caesar **7**: 242
 King John **9**: 251
 Measure for Measure **2**: 441
 The Merry Wives of Windsor **5**: 351
 Richard II **6**: 292
 Richard III **8**: 187
 Romeo and Juliet **5**: 463
 The Taming of the Shrew **9**: 338
 Timon of Athens **1**: 489
 Twelfth Night **1**: 575
 The Two Noble Kinsmen **9**: 469
 The Winter's Tale **7**: 432

Van Laan, Thomas F.
 Richard II **6**: 409
 Richard III **8**: 258

Vandenbroucke, Russell
 Cymbeline **15**: 78
 King John **24**: 224

Vandenhoff, George
 Romeo and Juliet **11**: 413

Vaughan, Alden T.
 The Tempest **45**: 219

Vaughan, James N.
 Richard III **14**: 411

Vaughan, Virgina Mason
King John **41**: 221
Othello **28**: 330
The Tempest **15**: 379; **45**: 219

Velie, Alan R.
Pericles **2**: 585

Velz, John W.
Julius Caesar **7**: 346
Shakespeare and Classical Civilization (topic entry) **27**: 9

Venezky, Alice
Henry VIII **24**: 112
King Lear **11**: 62
Much Ado about Nothing **18**: 157
The Winter's Tale **15**: 463

Vernon, Grenville
Julius Caesar **17**: 323
Richard II **24**: 306, 309
Twelfth Night **26**: 225

Verplanck, Gulian C.
Pericles **2**: 545
Timon of Athens **1**: 466
Twelfth Night **1**: 550

Vickers, Brian
Henry V **5**: 276
The Merry Wives of Windsor **5**: 363
Twelfth Night **1**: 650

Vickers, Nancy J.
The Rape of Lucrece **10**: 131; **43**: 102

Victor, Benjamin
The Two Gentlemen of Verona **6**: 437; **12**: 450

Vidal, Gore
Much Ado about Nothing **18**: 164

Videbaek, Bente A.
As You Like It **46**: 122, 210

Voltaire, Francois-Marie Arouet de
Hamlet **1**: 80
Julius Caesar **7**: 154

Von Rumelin, Gustav
Macbeth **3**: 202

Vyvyan, John
A Midsummer Night's Dream **3**: 437
Romeo and Juliet **5**: 498
The Two Gentlemen of Verona **6**: 494

Waddington, Raymond B.
The Merchant of Venice **40**: 117

Wade, Nicholas
Henry V **14**: 314

Wain, John
Much Ado about Nothing **8**: 100
Romeo and Juliet **5**: 524
Twelfth Night **26**: 249

Waith, Eugene M.
Antony and Cleopatra **6**: 172
Macbeth **3**: 262; **20**: 367
Titus Andronicus **4**: 647; **17**: 487; **27**: 261
The Two Noble Kinsmen **41**: 355

Walcutt, Charles C.
Hamlet **35**: 82

Waldock, A. J. A.
Hamlet **1**: 148

Walker, Roy
As You Like It **23**: 87
Henry V **14**: 266
King John **24**: 215
Macbeth **3**: 260
The Merchant of Venice **12**: 51
Timon of Athens **20**: 452
Twelfth Night **26**: 251

Walkley, A. B.
As You Like It **23**: 46
Much Ado about Nothing **18**: 151
The Two Gentlemen of Verona **12**: 457
The Winter's Tale **15**: 445

Wall, Stephen
Coriolanus **17**: 210
Henry IV, 1 and 2 **14**: 102
Macbeth **20**: 310
Measure for Measure **23**: 340, 357
Troilus and Cressida **18**: 384
The Winter's Tale **15**: 493

Wallace, John M.
Coriolanus **25**: 296
Timon of Athens **27**: 235

Walley, Harold R.
The Merchant of Venice **4**: 243
The Rape of Lucrece **10**: 84

Walpole, Horace
The Winter's Tale **7**: 381

Walter, J. H.
Henry V **5**: 257

Walwyn, B.
The Merchant of Venice **4**: 193

Wanamaker, Zoe
Twelfth Night **26**: 308

Wangh, Martin
Othello **4**: 503

Wapshott, Nicholas
Hamlet **21**: 232

Warburton, William
As You Like It **5**: 18
Henry IV, 1 and 2 **1**: 287
Julius Caesar **7**: 155
Love's Labour's Lost **2**: 300
Othello **4**: 386
The Tempest **8**: 289
The Two Noble Kinsmen **9**: 445

Ward, Adolphus William
Henry VI, 1, 2, and 3 **3**: 50

Ward, David
Hamlet **22**: 258

Ward, John Paul
As You Like It **46**: 134

Warde, Frederick
Henry V **14**: 195

Wardle, Irving
Antony and Cleopatra **17**: 76
As You Like It **23**: 96, 110, 114, 128, 137
The Comedy of Errors **26**: 157
Coriolanus **17**: 191
Cymbeline **15**: 72, 80
Hamlet **21**: 267, 280, 291, 296, 328, 330
Henry IV, 1 and 2 **14**: 84, 89, 101
Henry V **14**: 286
Henry VI, 1, 2, and 3 **24**: 45
Henry VIII **24**: 125
Julius Caesar **17**: 379, 405
King John **24**: 219, 234
King Lear **11**: 90, 108
Love's Labour's Lost **23**: 200, 203
Macbeth **20**: 256, 289, 299, 317
Measure for Measure **23**: 319, 326, 343
The Merchant of Venice **12**: 72
The Merry Wives of Windsor **18**: 48, 49
A Midsummer Night's Dream **12**: 253, 277
Much Ado about Nothing **18**: 177, 204
Richard II **24**: 335
Richard III **14**: 452, 462, 475
The Taming of the Shrew **12**: 384, 389, 409
The Tempest **15**: 269, 278
Titus Andronicus **17**: 465
Troilus and Cressida **18**: 341, 355, 350, 363, 381
Twelfth Night **26**: 265, 282, 301, 321, 336
The Two Gentlemen of Verona **12**: 481
The Winter's Tale **15**: 475, 492

Warner, Beverley E.
Henry IV, 1 and 2 **1**: 328

Warren, Roger
All's Well That Ends Well **26**: 61; **38**: 80
Antony and Cleopatra **17**: 81
As You Like It **23**: 115, 126, 136, 143
The Comedy of Errors **26**: 161, 167
Coriolanus **17**: 214
Cymbeline **4**: 150; **15**: 88
Hamlet **21**: 316
Henry IV, 1 and 2 **14**: 108
Henry VI, 1, 2, and 3 **24**: 42
Henry VIII **24**: 121
Julius Caesar **17**: 390
Love's Labour's Lost **23**: 212
Macbeth **20**: 299, 312

Measure for Measure **23**: 342, 348
The Merchant of Venice **12**: 96
The Merry Wives of Windsor **18**: 62
A Midsummer Night's Dream **12**: 273, 285
Much Ado about Nothing **18**: 210
Pericles **15**: 172, 180; **16**: 399
Romeo and Juliet **11**: 485
The Taming of the Shrew **12**: 396
Titus Andronicus **17**: 475
Troilus and Cressida **18**: 366, 386
Twelfth Night **26**: 295, 305
The Two Gentlemen of Verona **12**: 495
The Winter's Tale **15**: 494

Warton, Joseph
King Lear **2**: 95
The Tempest **8**: 289

Warton, Thomas
Romeo and Juliet **5**: 419

Wasson, John
Measure for Measure **23**: 413

Watkins, Ronald
Macbeth **20**: 382

Watkins, W. B. C.
Venus and Adonis **10**: 429

Watson, Donald G.
Venus and Adonis **33**: 309

Watson, Robert N.
Measure for Measure **16**: 102
Richard III **8**: 267
The Winter's Tale **36**: 318

Watt, David
Henry VI, 1, 2, and 3 **24**: 16
The Tempest **15**: 265

Watters, Tammie
Antony and Cleopatra **17**: 67

Watts, Richard, Jr.
As You Like It **23**: 72
King Lear **11**: 57

Waugh, Evelyn
Titus Andronicus **17**: 443

Weales, Gerald
The Comedy of Errors **26**: 177

Webster, Margaret
Cymbeline **15**: 121
Henry IV, 1 and 2 **14**: 118
Love's Labour's Lost **23**: 250
Macbeth **20**: 374
The Merry Wives of Windsor **18**: 74
A Midsummer Night's Dream **12**: 293
Much Ado about Nothing **18**: 247
Othello **11**: 273, 342
Richard II **24**: 310
Romeo and Juliet **11**: 512
The Taming of the Shrew **9**: 340
The Tempest **15**: 253
Timon of Athens **20**: 491

Wedmore, Frederick
King Lear 11: 33
Macbeth 20: 142
Othello 11: 222
Romeo and Juliet 11: 425

Weever, John
Julius Caesar 7: 148
Venus and Adonis 10: 410

Wehl, Feodor
A Midsummer Night's Dream 12: 167

Weightman, J. G.
Henry V 14: 264

Weightman, John
The Merchant of Venice 12: 76

Weil, Herbert S.
Measure for Measure 23: 301

Weimann, Robert
The Two Gentlemen of Verona 6: 524

Weiner, Albert B.
Macbeth 20: 123

Weinraub, Bernard
Macbeth 20: 273

Weinstein, Philip M.
The Winter's Tale 7: 490

Weiss, Theodore
The Comedy of Errors 1: 59

Wekwerth, Manfred
Coriolanus 17: 185

Weller, Barry
The Two Noble Kinsmen 41: 363

Wells, Charles
Antony and Cleopatra 27: 126
Shakespeare and Classical Civilization (topic entry) 27: 35

Wells, Robert Headlam
Henry V 37: 187
Politics and Power (topic entry) 30: 42

Wells, Stanley
All's Well That Ends Well 26: 56
Antony and Cleopatra 17: 83
The Comedy of Errors 26: 163; 179
Coriolanus 17: 172
Hamlet 21: 259
Julius Caesar 17: 397
King John 24: 235; 240
Macbeth 29: 101
Measure for Measure 23: 372
The Merry Wives of Windsor 18: 59
A Midsummer Night's Dream 12: 188; 29: 183
Richard II 24: 356
Richard III 14: 486
The Taming of the Shrew 12: 398

Timon of Athens 20: 472
Titus Andronicus 17: 486
Troilus and Cressida 18: 368
Twelfth Night 26: 317
The Two Gentlemen of Verona 6: 507; 12: 492

Wells, Stanley W.
The Tempest 28: 415

Welsford, Enid
As You Like It 5: 75
King Lear 2: 162
A Midsummer Night's Dream 3: 397
Twelfth Night 1: 571

Welsh, Andrew
Pericles 36: 205

Wendell, Barrett
Cymbeline 4: 43
Twelfth Night 1: 560

Wendlandt, Wilhelm
Timon of Athens 1: 473

Wentersdorf, Karl P.
The Taming of the Shrew 12: 431

Werder, Karl
Hamlet 1: 106

Wesley, Samuel
Antony and Cleopatra 6: 20

West, E. J.
Twelfth Night 1: 579

West, Fred
Othello 35: 347

West, Grace Starry
Titus Andronicus 27: 293

West, Michael
The Taming of the Shrew 9: 404

West, Rebecca
Hamlet 1: 218

West, Robert H.
King Lear 2: 265; 31: 129

West, Thomas G.
Troilus and Cressida 3: 638

Westlund, Joseph
All's Well That Ends Well 38: 96
Cymbeline 45: 75
The Tempest 32: 400

Whately, Thomas
Macbeth 3: 177
Richard III 8: 148

Wheeler, Richard P.
Fathers and Daughters (topic entry) 36: 70
Hamlet 44: 152
Psychoanalytic Interpretations (topic entry) 44: 18
Richard III 39: 326
The Tempest 45: 259

Whitaker, Virgil K.
Julius Caesar 7: 264

White, Antonia
The Taming of the Shrew 12: 349

White, Howard B.
Timon of Athens 27: 223

White, R. S.
The Merry Wives of Windsor 38: 307

White, Richard Grant
As You Like It 23: 167
Henry IV, 1 and 2 1: 327
Much Ado about Nothing 8: 23
Othello 4: 424

Whitebait, William
Hamlet 21: 198
Richard III 14: 422

Whitehead, Frank
King Lear 22: 271

Whitehead, Ted
Hamlet 21: 308

Whiter, Walter
As You Like It 5: 21

Whitney, Charles
Henry VIII 28: 203

Whittaker, Herbert
All's Well That Ends Well 26: 22
A Midsummer Night's Dream 12: 239

Whittier, Gayle
General Commentary 13: 530

Whitworth, C. W.
The Comedy of Errors 26: 165

Wickham, Glynn
The Tempest 29: 339
The Two Noble Kinsmen 41: 289

Wiess, Theodore
Henry IV, 1 and 2 39: 72

Wigston, W. F. C.
The Phoenix and Turtle 10: 7
The Winter's Tale 7: 397

Wilcher, Robert
Twelfth Night 46: 303

Willbern, David
The Rape of Lucrece 33: 179

Wilcher, Robert
As You Like It 5: 166

Wilcox, Helen
Gender Identity (topic entry) 40: 99

Wilde, Oscar
Sonnets 10: 218

Wilkes, Thomas
Macbeth 20: 20
Othello 4: 389
Richard III 14: 363

Willbern, David
Henry IV, Parts 1 and 2 42: 185
Titus Andronicus 4: 675

Willcock, Gladys Doidge
Love's Labour's Lost 2: 319

Willeford, William
Clowns and Fools (topic entry) 46: 74

William, David
The Merry Wives of Windsor 18: 84
The Tempest 15: 352

Williams, Charles
Henry V 5: 228
Troilus and Cressida 3: 568

Williams, Clifford
The Comedy of Errors 26: 188

Williams, Gary Jay
A Midsummer Night's Dream 12: 153, 161, 278
Timon of Athens 20: 481

Williams, George Walton
Macbeth 28: 339

Williams, Gordon
Macbeth 20: 343
Venus and Adonis 33: 347

Williams, Gwyn
The Comedy of Errors 1: 45; 34: 229

Williams, Harcourt
Macbeth 20: 186
Much Ado about Nothing 18: 134

Williams, John T.
Richard III 14: 528
The Tempest 15: 371

Williams, Mary C.
Much Ado about Nothing 8: 125

Williams, Simon
A Midsummer Night's Dream 12: 168

Williams, Stanley T.
Timon of Athens 20: 476

Williamson, Audrey
All's Well That Ends Well 26: 41
Coriolanus 17: 159
Henry IV, 1 and 2 14: 35
Henry VIII 24: 113
King John 24: 206
Macbeth 20: 186, 234
Othello 11: 279
Richard II 24: 304, 315
The Tempest 15: 234
Troilus and Cressida 18: 318

Williamson, Jane
  Measure for Measure **23**: 363

Williamson, Marilyn L.
  All's Well That Ends Well **38**: 99
  Henry V **5**: 302; **30**: 259
  Romeo and Juliet **5**: 571

Williamson, Nicol
  Hamlet **21**: 268

Willis, Deborah
  The Tempest **13**: 440

Willis, Susan
  Troilus and Cressida **18**: 371

Wills, Garry
  Coriolanus **17**: 223
  Hamlet **21**: 244

Wilmeth, Don B.
  Richard III **14**: 370

Wilson, Daniel
  The Tempest **8**: 309

Wilson, Edmund
  Henry IV, 1 and 2 **1**: 393

Wilson, Harold S.
  Measure for Measure **2**: 490
  Romeo and Juliet **5**: 487

Wilson, John Dover
  Antony and Cleopatra **6**: 133
  As You Like It **5**: 114
  Hamlet **1**: 138, 154
  Henry IV, 1 and 2 **1**: 125, 366, 373
  Henry V **5**: 246
  Henry VI, 1, 2, and 3 **3**: 66
  Julius Caesar **7**: 253
  King Lear **2**: 160
  Love's Labour's Lost **2**: 342; **23**: 252
  The Merry Wives of Windsor **5**: 360
  Much Ado about Nothing **31**: 171
  Richard II **6**: 289
  Sonnets **10**: 334
  The Tempest **8**: 348
  Titus Andronicus **4**: 642
  Venus and Adonis **10**: 427

Wilson, Milton
  Hamlet **21**: 220

Wilson, Rawdon R.
  As You Like It **46**: 169
  The Rape of Lucrece **33**: 169

Wilson, Richard
  Julius Caesar **22**: 280

Wilson, Rob
  Psychoanalytic Interpretations (topic entry) **44**: 57

Wincor, Richard
  Pericles **2**: 570
  The Winter's Tale **7**: 451

Wingate, Charles E. L.
  King Lear **11**: 119
  Macbeth **20**: 103
  Much Ado about Nothing **18**: 115
  The Taming of the Shrew **12**: 411

Winny, James
  Henry IV, 1 and 2 **1**: 424
  Henry V **5**: 281
  Henry VI, 1, 2, and 3 **3**: 115
  Richard II **6**: 368
  Sonnets **10**: 337

Winstanley, William
  Richard III **8**: 145

Winter, Jack
  The Taming of the Shrew **12**: 366

Winter, William
  Antony and Cleopatra **6**: 51
  As You Like It **23**: 27
  Coriolanus **17**: 132
  Cymbeline **15**: 21, 43, 96
  Hamlet **21**: 64, 143
  Henry IV, 1 and 2 **14**: 9
  Henry VIII **24**: 129
  Julius Caesar **17**: 284, 286
  King Lear **11**: 25
  Measure for Measure **23**: 281
  The Merry Wives of Windsor **18**: 14, 17, 18, 29, 66, 126
  A Midsummer Night's Dream **12**: 192, 225, 280
  Richard II **24**: 289
  Richard III **14**: 503
  Romeo and Juliet **11**: 416, 423
  The Taming of the Shrew **12**: 414
  Twelfth Night **26**: 207, 212
  The Winter's Tale **15**: 442

Winton, Calhoun
  Henry V **14**: 178

Wittenburg, Robert
  The Tempest **29**: 362

Witts, Noel
  As You Like It **23**: 113

Wixson, Douglas C.
  King John **9**: 300

Wofford, Susanne L.
  As You Like It **28**: 82

Wolf, Matt
  Antony and Cleopatra **17**: 81

Womersley, David
  King John **13**: 163

Wood, Glena D.
  King Lear **46**: 191

Wood, James O.
  Pericles **2**: 583

Wood, Robert E.
  The Comedy of Errors **26**: 190

Wood, Roger
  All's Well That Ends Well **26**: 37

Henry V **14**: 260
King John **24**: 203
Othello **11**: 280
Troilus and Cressida **18**: 314

Woodbridge, Linda
  Shakespeare's Representation of Women (topic entry) **31**: 41

Woods, George B.
  Hamlet **21**: 78

Woollcott, Alexander
  A Midsummer Night's Dream **12**: 224

Worden, Blair
  General Commentary **22**: 395

Wordsworth, William
  Sonnets **10**: 159, 160, 167

Worsley, T. C.
  Antony and Cleopatra **17**: 31
  As You Like It **23**: 94
  The Comedy of Errors **26**: 145
  Cymbeline **15**: 45, 58, 64
  Hamlet **21**: 225
  Henry IV, 1 and 2 **14**: 38, 39, 56
  Henry V **14**: 256
  Henry VI, 1, 2, and 3 **24**: 17
  Julius Caesar **17**: 366
  King Lear **11**: 58, 60, 65
  Macbeth **20**: 188, 221, 239
  Measure for Measure **23**: 297, 311, 313
  The Merchant of Venice **12**: 52
  The Merry Wives of Windsor **18**: 36
  Much Ado about Nothing **18**: 157, 177
  Othello **11**: 276
  Pericles **15**: 143
  Richard II **24**: 305, 320, 322
  The Taming of the Shrew **12**: 353
  Titus Andronicus **17**: 441
  Troilus and Cressida **18**: 313, 319, 330
  Twelfth Night **26**: 229, 245, 256

Wotton, Sir Henry
  Henry VIII **2**: 14

Woudhuysen, H. R.
  Titus Andronicus **17**: 478
  Twelfth Night **26**: 325

Wright, Abraham
  Othello **4**: 370

Wright, Laurence
  The Winter's Tale **36**: 344

Wright, Neil H.
  The Tempest **8**: 447

Wyatt, Euphemia Van Rensselaer
  Julius Caesar **17**: 325
  Macbeth **20**: 201, 230, 233
  The Merchant of Venice **12**: 63
  Much Ado about Nothing **18**: 174
  The Tempest **15**: 245
  Twelfth Night **26**: 228

The Two Gentlemen of Verona **12**: 471

Wylie, Betty Jane
  Pericles **15**: 181

Wyndham, George
  Sonnets **10**: 236
  Venus and Adonis **10**: 420

Wynne-David, Marion
  Titus Andronicus **27**: 266

Yates, Frances A.
  Henry VIII **2**: 71

Yearling, Elizabeth M.
  Twelfth Night **1**: 664

Yeats, W. B.
  Henry IV, 1 and 2 **1**: 332
  Henry V **5**: 210
  Richard II **6**: 277

Yoder, R. A.
  Troilus and Cressida **3**: 626

Young, B. A.
  All's Well That Ends Well **26**: 43
  Antony and Cleopatra **17**: 55
  As You Like It **23**: 104, 112, 121
  Hamlet **21**: 252
  Henry V **14**: 271, 275, 279
  Henry VI, 1, 2, and 3 **24**: 19, 30
  Julius Caesar **17**: 377, 379
  King John **24**: 220
  Love's Labour's Lost **23**: 196, 203, 207
  Macbeth **20**: 256, 292, 307
  Measure for Measure **23**: 319, 326
  The Merry Wives of Windsor **18**: 40, 46, 47
  Much Ado about Nothing **18**: 187, 203, 209
  Pericles **15**: 147
  Richard III **14**: 462
  The Taming of the Shrew **12**: 382, 388
  The Tempest **15**: 268
  Timon of Athens **20**: 461
  Titus Andronicus **17**: 464
  Troilus and Cressida **18**: 340, 354
  Twelfth Night **26**: 281

Young, Bruce W.
  The Winter's Tale **36**: 328

Young, C. B.
  Cymbeline **15**: 102
  Henry VIII **24**: 136
  Julius Caesar **17**: 408
  Pericles **15**: 178
  Richard III **14**: 507

Young, David
  As You Like It **23**: 102
  Macbeth **16**: 317
  The Tempest **29**: 323

Young, David P.
  As You Like It **5**: 135
  A Midsummer Night's Dream **3**: 453; **29**: 190

Young, Julian Charles
Coriolanus **17:** 132
Julius Caesar **17:** 273

Young, Stark
Hamlet **21:** 148
Julius Caesar **17:** 321
Othello **11:** 270

Richard II **24:** 307
Richard III **14:** 412
The Taming of the Shrew **12:** 344
Troilus and Cressida **18:** 295
Twelfth Night **26:** 224

Zarkin, Robert
The Tempest **15:** 297

Zender, Karl F.
Macbeth **3:** 336
Measure for Measure **28:** 92; **33:** 77
Othello **28:** 344

Zimbardo, Rose A.
Henry V **5:** 264

A Midsummer Night's Dream **3:** 468

Zinter, Sheldon P.
All's Well That Ends Well **26:** 91, 128; **38:** 150
Henry IV, 1 and 2 **14:** 156

Cumulative Topic Index

The Cumulative Topic Index identifies the principal topics of discussion in the criticism of each play and non-dramatic poem. The topics are arranged alphabetically. Page references indicate the beginning page number of each essay containing substantial commentary on that topic. A parenthetical reference after a topic indicates that the topic is extensively discussed in that volume.

absurdities, inconsistencies, and shortcomings
The Two Gentlemen of Verona **6**: 435, 436, 437, 439, 464, 507, 541, 560

accident or chance
Romeo and Juliet **5**: 418, 444, 448, 467, 470, 487, 573

acting and dissimulation
Richard II **6**: 264, 267, 307, 310, 315, 368, 393, 409; **24**: 339, 345, 346, 349, 352, 356

adolescence
Romeo and Juliet **33**: 249, 255, 257

adultery
The Comedy of Errors **34**: 215

aggression
Coriolanus **9**: 112, 142, 174, 183, 189, 198; **30**: 79, 111, 125, 142; **44**: 11, 79

alienation
Timon of Athens **1**: 523; **27**: 161

allegorical elements
King Lear **16**: 311
The Merchant of Venice **4**: 224, 250, 261, 268, 270, 273, 282, 289, 324, 336, 344, 350
The Phoenix and Turtle **10**: 7, 8, 9, 16, 17, 48; **38**: 334, 378
The Rape of Lucrece **10**: 89, 93
Richard II **6**: 264, 283, 323, 385
The Tempest **8**: 294, 295, 302, 307, 308, 312, 326, 328, 336, 345, 364; **42**: 320
Venus and Adonis **10**: 427, 434, 439, 449, 454, 462, 480; **28**: 355; **33**: 309, 330

ambiguity
Antony and Cleopatra **6**: 53, 111, 161, 163, 180, 189, 208, 211, 228; **13**: 368
Hamlet **1**: 92, 160, 198, 227, 230, 234, 247, 249; **21**: 72; **35**: 241
King John **13**: 152; **41**: 243
Measure for Measure **2**: 417, 420, 432, 446, 449, 452, 474, 479, 482, 486, 495, 505
A Midsummer Night's Dream **3**: 401, 459, 486; **45**: 169
Richard III **44**: 11
Sonnets **10**: 251, 256; **28**: 385; **40**: 221, 228, 268
Troilus and Cressida **3**: 544, 568, 583, 587, 589, 599, 611, 621; **27**: 400; **43**: 305
Twelfth Night **1**: 554, 639; **34**: 287, 316
Venus and Adonis **10**: 434, 454, 459, 462, 466, 473, 480, 486, 489; **33**: 352

ambition or pride
Henry VIII **2**: 15, 38, 67
Macbeth **44**: 284, 324

ambivalent or ironic elements
Henry VI, Parts 1, 2, and 3 **3**: 69, 151, 154; **39**: 160
Richard III **44**: 11
Troilus and Cressida **43**: 340

amorality, question of
The Two Noble Kinsmen **9**: 447, 460, 492

amour-passion or *Liebestod* myth
Romeo and Juliet **5**: 484, 489, 528, 530, 542, 550, 575; **32**: 256

anachronisms
Julius Caesar **7**: 331

androgyny
Antony and Cleopatra **13**: 530
As You Like It **23**: 98, 100, 122, 138, 143, 144; **34**: 172, 177; **46**: 134
Romeo and Juliet **13**: 530

anti-Catholic rhetoric
King John **22**: 120; **25**: 98

anti-romantic elements
As You Like It **34**: 72

antithetical or contradictory elements
Macbeth **3**: 185, 213, 271, 302; **25**: 235; **29**: 76, 127

anxiety
Romeo and Juliet **13**: 235

appearance, perception, and illusion
A Midsummer Night's Dream **3**: 368, 411, 425, 427, 434, 447, 459, 466, 474, 477, 486, 497, 516; **19**: 21; **22**: 39; **28**: 15; **29**: 175, 190; **45**: 136

Appearance versus Reality (Volume 34: 1, 5, 12, 23, 45, 54)
All's Well That Ends Well **7**: 37, 76, 93; **26**: 117
As You Like It **34**: 130, 131; **46**: 105
The Comedy of Errors **34**: 194, 201
Coriolanus **30**: 142
Cymbeline **4**: 87, 93, 103, 162; **36**: 99
Hamlet **1**: 95, 116, 166, 169, 198; **35**: 82, 126, 132, 144, 238; **44**: 248; **45**: 28
Macbeth **3**: 241, 248; **25**: 235
The Merchant of Venice **4**: 209, 261, 344; **12**: 65; **22**: 69

Much Ado about Nothing **8:** 17, 18, 48, 63, 69, 73, 75, 79, 88, 95, 115; **31:** 198, 209
The Taming of the Shrew **9:** 343, 350, 353, 365, 369, 370, 381, 390, 430; **12:** 416; **31:** 326
Timon of Athens **1:** 495, 500, 515, 523
The Two Gentlemen of Verona **6:** 494, 502, 511, 519, 529, 532, 549, 560
Twelfth Night **34:** 293, 301, 311, 316
The Winter's Tale **7:** 429, 446, 479

appetite
Twelfth Night **1:** 563, 596, 609, 615

archetypal or mythic elements
Macbeth **16:** 317

archetypal structure
Pericles **2:** 570, 580, 582, 584, 588; **25:** 365

aristocracy and aristocratic values
As You Like It **34:** 120
Hamlet **42:** 212
Julius Caesar **16:** 231; **22:** 280; **30:** 379

art and nature
See also **nature**
Pericles **22:** 315; **36:** 233
The Phoenix and Turtle **10:** 7, 42

art versus nature
See also **nature**
As You Like It **5:** 128, 130, 148; **34:** 147
The Tempest **8:** 396, 404; **29:** 278, 297, 362
The Winter's Tale **7:** 377, 381, 397, 419, 452; **36:** 289, 318; **45:** 329

artificial nature
Love's Labour's Lost **2:** 315, 317, 324, 330; **23:** 207, 233

Athens
Timon of Athens **27:** 223, 230

Athens and the forest, contrast between
A Midsummer Night's Dream **3:** 381, 427, 459, 466, 497, 502; **29:** 175

assassination
Julius Caesar **7:** 156, 161, 179, 191, 200, 221, 264, 272, 279, 284, 350; **25:** 272; **30:** 326

audience perception
The Comedy of Errors **1:** 37, 50, 56; **19:** 54; **34:** 258
King Lear **19:** 295; **28:** 325
Richard II **24:** 414, 423; **39:** 295
Pericles **42:** 352

audience perception, Shakespeare's manipulation of
The Winter's Tale **7:** 394, 429, 456, 483, 501; **13:** 417; **19:** 401, 431, 441; **25:** 339; **45:** 374

audience perspective
All's Well That Ends Well **7:** 81, 104, 109, 116, 121

audience response
Hamlet **28:** 325; **32:** 238; **35:** 167; **44:** 107
Julius Caesar **7:** 179, 238, 253, 255, 272, 316, 320, 336, 350; **19:** 321
Macbeth **20:** 17, 400, 406; **29:** 139, 146, 155, 165; **44:** 306

audience versus character perceptions
The Two Gentlemen of Verona **6:** 499, 519, 524

authenticity
The Phoenix and Turtle **10:** 7, 8, 16
Sonnets **10:** 153, 154, 230, 243

Authorship Controversy (Volume 41: 2, 5, 18, 32, 42, 48, 57, 61, 63, 66, 76, 81, 85, 98, 110)
Cymbeline **4:** 17, 21, 35, 48, 56, 78
Henry VI, Parts 1, 2, and 3 **3:** 16, 18, 19, 20, 21, 26, 27, 29, 31, 35, 39, 41, 55, 66; **24:** 51
Henry VIII **2:** 16, 18, 19, 22, 23, 27, 28, 31, 35, 36, 42, 43, 44, 46, 48, 51, 58, 64, 68; **41:** 129, 146, 158, 171
Love's Labour's Lost **2:** 299, 300; **32:** 308
Pericles **2:** 538, 540, 543, 544, 545, 546, 548, 550, 551, 553, 556, 558, 564, 565, 568, 576, 586; **15:** 132, 141, 148, 152; **16:** 391, 399; **25:** 365; **36:** 198, 244
Timon of Athens **1:** 464, 466, 467, 469, 474, 477, 478, 480, 490, 499, 507, 518; **16:** 351; **20:** 433
Titus Andronicus **4:** 613, 614, 615, 616, 617, 619, 623, 624, 625, 626, 628, 631, 632, 635, 642
The Two Gentlemen of Verona **6:** 435, 436, 437, 438, 439, 449, 466, 476
The Two Noble Kinsmen
 Shakespeare not a co-author **9:** 445, 447, 455, 461
 Shakespearean portions of the text **9:** 446, 447, 448, 455, 456, 457, 460, 462, 463, 471, 479, 486; **41:** 308, 317, 355
 Shakespeare's part in the overall conception or design **9:** 444, 446, 448, 456, 457, 460, 480, 481, 486, 490; **37:** 313; **41:** 326

autobiographical elements
As You Like It **5:** 25, 35, 43, 50, 55, 61
The Comedy of Errors **1:** 16, 18
Cymbeline **4:** 43, 46; **36:** 134
Hamlet **1:** 98, 115, 119; **13:** 487
Henry VI, Parts 1, 2, and 3 **3:** 41, 55
King John **9:** 209, 218, 245, 248, 260, 292
King Lear **2:** 131, 136, 149, 165
Measure for Measure **2:** 406, 410, 414, 431, 434, 437
A Midsummer Night's Dream **3:** 365, 371, 379, 381, 389, 391, 396, 402, 432
Othello **4:** 440, 444
Pericles **2:** 551, 554, 555, 563, 581
The Phoenix and Turtle **10:** 14, 18, 42, 48
Sonnets **10:** 159, 160, 166, 167, 175, 176, 182, 196, 205, 213, 215, 226, 233, 238, 240, 251, 279, 283, 302, 309, 325, 337, 377; **13:** 487; **16:** 461; **28:** 363, 385; **42:** 296
The Tempest **8:** 302, 308, 312, 324, 326, 345, 348, 353, 364, 380
Timon of Athens **1:** 462, 467, 470, 473, 474, 478, 480; **27:** 166, 175

Titus Andronicus **4:** 619, 624, 625, 664
Troilus and Cressida **3:** 548, 554, 557, 558, 574, 606, 630
Twelfth Night **1:** 557, 561, 599; **34:** 338
The Winter's Tale **7:** 395, 397, 410, 419

avarice
The Merry Wives of Windsor **5:** 335, 353, 369, 376, 390, 395, 402

battle of Agincourt
Henry V **5:** 197, 199, 213, 246, 257, 281, 287, 289, 293, 310, 318; **19:** 217; **30:** 181

battle of the sexes
Much Ado about Nothing **8:** 14, 16, 19, 48, 91, 95, 111, 121, 125; **31:** 231, 245

bawdy elements
As You Like It **46:** 122
Cymbeline **36:** 155

bear-baiting
Twelfth Night **19:** 42

beauty
Sonnets **10:** 247
Venus and Adonis **10:** 420, 423, 427, 434, 454, 480; **33:** 330, 352

bed-trick
All's Well That Ends Well **7:** 8, 26, 27, 29, 32, 41, 86, 93, 98, 113, 116, 126; **13:** 84; **26:** 117; **28:** 38; **38:** 65, 118
Measure for Measure **13:** 84

bird imagery
The Phoenix and Turtle **10:** 21, 27; **38:** 329, 350, 367

body, role of
Troilus and Cressida **42:** 66

body politic, metaphor of
Coriolanus **22:** 248; **30:** 67, 96, 105, 125

bonding
The Merchant of Venice **4:** 293, 317, 336; **13:** 37

British nationalism
See also **nationalism and patriotism**
Cymbeline **4:** 19, 78, 89, 93, 129, 141, 159, 167; **32:** 373; **36:** 129; **45:** 6

brutal elements
A Midsummer Night's Dream **3:** 445, 491, 497, 511; **12:** 259, 262, 298; **16:** 34; **19:** 21; **29:** 183, 225, 263, 269; **45:** 169

Caesarism
Julius Caesar **7:** 159, 160, 161, 167, 169, 174, 191, 205, 218, 253, 310; **30:** 316, 321

capriciousness of the young lovers
A Midsummer Night's Dream **3:** 372, 395, 402, 411, 423, 437, 441, 450, 497, 498; **29:** 175, 269; **45:** 107

caricature
The Merry Wives of Windsor **5**: 343, 347, 348, 350, 385, 397

carnival elements
Henry IV, Parts 1 and 2 **28**: 203; **32**: 103
Henry VI, Parts 1, 2, and 3 **22**: 156
Richard II **19**: 151; **39**: 273

censorship
Richard II **24**: 260, 261, 262, 263, 386; **42**: 118

ceremonies, rites, and rituals, importance of
See also **pageantry**
Coriolanus **9**: 139, 148, 169
Hamlet **13**: 268; **28**: 232
Julius Caesar **7**: 150, 210, 255, 259, 268, 284, 316, 331, 339, 356; **13**: 260; **22**: 137; **30**: 374
Richard II **6**: 270, 294, 315, 368, 381, 397, 409, 414; **24**: 274, 356, 411, 414, 419
Titus Andronicus **27**: 261; **32**: 265
The Two Noble Kinsmen **9**: 492, 498

change
Henry VIII **2**: 27, 65, 72, 81

characterization
As You Like It **5**: 19, 24, 25, 36, 39, 54, 82, 86, 116, 148; **34**: 72
The Comedy of Errors **1**: 13, 21, 31, 34, 46, 49, 50, 55, 56; **19**: 54; **25**: 63; **34**: 194, 201, 208, 245
Henry IV, Parts 1 and 2 **1**: 321, 328, 332, 333, 336, 344, 365, 383, 385, 389, 391, 397, 401; **19**: 195; **39**: 123, 137; **42**: 99, 162
Henry V **5**: 186, 189, 192, 193, 199, 219, 230, 233, 252, 276, 293; **30**: 227, 278; **42**: 162
Henry VI, Parts 1, 2, and 3 **3**: 18, 20, 24, 25, 31, 57, 64, 73, 77, 109, 119, 151; **24**: 22, 28, 38, 42, 45, 47; **39**: 160
Henry VIII **2**: 17, 23, 25, 32, 35, 39; **24**: 106
King John **9**: 222, 224, 229, 240, 250, 292; **41**: 205, 215
King Lear **2**: 108, 125, 145, 162, 191; **16**: 311; **28**: 223; **46**: 177, 210
Love's Labour's Lost **2**: 303, 310, 317, 322, 328, 342; **23**: 237, 250, 252; **38**: 232
Macbeth **20**: 12, 318, 324, 329, 353, 363, 367, 374, 387; **28**: 339; **29**: 101, 109, 146, 155, 165; **45**: 67
Measure for Measure **2**: 388, 390, 391, 396, 406, 420, 421, 446, 466, 475, 484, 505, 516, 524; **23**: 299, 405; **33**:
The Merry Wives of Windsor **5**: 332, 334, 335, 337, 338, 351, 360, 363, 366, 374, 379, 392; **18**: 74, 75; **38**: 264, 273, 313, 319
The Tempest **8**: 287, 289, 292, 294, 295, 308, 326, 334, 336; **28**: 415; **42**: 332; **45**: 219
Titus Andronicus **4**: 613, 628, 632, 635, 640, 644, 647, 650, 675; **27**: 293; **43**: 170, 176,
Troilus and Cressida **3**: 538, 539, 540, 541, 548, 566, 571, 604, 611, 621; **27**: 381, 391
Twelfth Night **5**: 539, 540, 543, 545, 550, 554, 581, 594; **26**: 257, 337, 342, 346, 364, 366, 371, 374; **34**: 281, 293, 311, 338; **46**: 286, 324
The Two Gentlemen of Verona **6**: 438, 442, 445,
447, 449, 458, 462, 560; **12**: 458; **40**: 312, 327, 330, 365
The Two Noble Kinsmen **9**: 457, 461, 471, 474; **41**: 340, 385

chastity
A Midsummer Night's Dream **45**: 143

Chaucer's Criseyde, compared with
Troilus and Cressida **43**: 305

chivalry, decline of
Troilus and Cressida **16**: 84; **27**: 370, 374

Christian elements
See also **religious, mythic, or spiritual content**
As You Like It **5**: 39, 98, 162
Coriolanus **30**: 111
King Lear **2**: 137, 170, 179, 188, 191, 197, 207, 218, 222, 226, 229, 238, 249, 265, 286; **22**: 233, 271; **25**: 218; **46**: 276
Macbeth **3**: 194, 239, 260, 269, 275, 286, 293, 297, 318; **20**: 203, 206, 210, 256, 262, 289, 291, 294; **44**: 341, 366
Measure for Measure **2**: 391, 394, 399, 421, 437, 449, 466, 479, 491, 511, 522
Much Ado about Nothing **8**: 17, 19, 29, 55, 95, 104, 111, 115; **31**: 209
The Phoenix and Turtle **10**: 21, 24, 31; **38**: 326
The Rape of Lucrece **10**: 77, 80, 89, 96, 98, 109
Sonnets **10**: 191, 256
Titus Andronicus **4**: 656, 680
Twelfth Night **46**: 338
The Two Gentlemen of Verona **6**: 438, 494, 514, 532, 555, 564
The Winter's Tale **7**: 381, 387, 402, 410, 417, 419, 425, 429, 436, 452, 460, 501; **36**: 318

church versus state
King John **9**: 209, 212, 222, 235, 240; **22**: 120

civilization versus barbarism
Titus Andronicus **4**: 653; **27**: 293; **28**: 249; **32**: 265

class distinctions, conflict, and relations
Henry V **28**: 146
Henry VI, Parts 1, 2, and 3 **37**: 97; **39**: 187
The Merry Wives of Windsor **5**: 338, 343, 346, 347, 366, 390, 395, 400, 402; **22**: 93; **28**: 69
A Midsummer Night's Dream **22**: 23; **25**: 36; **45**: 160
The Taming of the Shrew **31**: 300, 351

classical influence and sources
The Comedy of Errors **1**: 13, 14, 16, 31, 32, 43, 61
The Tempest **29**: 278, 343, 362, 368

Clowns and Fools (Volume 46: 1, 14, 18, 24, 29, 33, 48, 52, 60)
As You Like It **5**: 24, 28, 30, 32, 36, 39, 54, 61, 63, 72, 75, 76, 77, 79, 84, 86, 93, 98, 114, 118, 135, 138, 166; **23**: 152; **34**: 72, 85, 147, 161; **46**: 88, 105, 117, 122
King Lear **2**: 108, 112, 125, 156, 162, 245, 278, 284; **11**: 17, 158, 169; **22**: 227; **25**: 202; **28**: 223; **46**: 191, 205, 210, 218, 225
Twelfth Night **1**: 543, 548, 558, 561, 563, 566, 570, 572, 603, 620, 642, 655, 658; **26**: 233, 364; **46**: 297, 303, 310

colonialism
Henry V **22**: 103
The Tempest **13**: 424, 440; **15**: 228, 268, 269, 270, 271, 272, 273; **19**: 421; **25**: 357, 382; **28**: 249; **29**: 343, 368; **32**: 338, 367, 400; **42**: 320; **45**: 200, 280

combat
King Lear **22**: 365
Macbeth **22**: 365

comedy of affectation
Love's Labour's Lost **2**: 302, 303, 304; **23**: 191, 224, 226, 228, 233

comic and tragic elements, combination of
King Lear **2**: 108, 110, 112, 125, 156, 162, 245, 278, 284; **46**: 191
Measure for Measure **16**: 102
Romeo and Juliet **5**: 496, 524, 528, 547, 559; **46**: 78
Troilus and Cressida **43**: 351

comic and farcical elements
All's Well That Ends Well **26**: 97, 114
Antony and Cleopatra **6**: 52, 85, 104, 125, 131, 151, 192, 202, 219
The Comedy of Errors **1**: 14, 16, 19, 23, 30, 34, 35, 43, 46, 50, 55, 56, 59, 61; **19**: 54; **26**: 183, 186, 188, 190; **34**: 190, 245
Coriolanus **9**: 8, 9, 14, 53, 80, 106
Cymbeline **4**: 35, 56, 113, 141; **15**: 111, 122
Henry IV, Parts 1 and 2 **1**: 286, 290, 314, 327, 328, 336, 353; **19**: 195; **25**: 109; **39**: 72
Henry V **5**: 185, 188, 191, 192, 217, 230, 233, 241, 252, 260, 276; **19**: 217; **28**: 121; **30**: 193, 202
The Merry Wives of Windsor **5**: 336, 338, 346, 350, 360, 369, 373; **18**: 74, 75, 84
Richard II **24**: 262, 263, 395; **39**: 243
Twelfth Night **26**: 233, 257, 337, 342, 371
Venus and Adonis **10**: 429, 434, 439, 442, 459, 462, 489; **33**: 352

comic form
As You Like It **46**: 105
Measure for Measure **2**: 456, 460, 479, 482, 491, 514, 516; **13**: 94, 104; **23**: 309, 326, 327

comic resolution
Love's Labour's Lost **2**: 335, 340; **16**: 17; **19**: 92; **38**: 209

comic, tragic, and romantic elements, fusion of
The Winter's Tale **7**: 390, 394, 396, 399, 410, 412, 414, 429, 436, 479, 483, 490, 501; **13**: 417; **15**: 514, 524, 532; **25**: 339; **36**: 295, 380

commodity
King John **9**: 224, 229, 245, 260, 275, 280, 297; **19**: 182; **25**: 98; **41**: 228, 269

communication, failure of
Troilus and Cressida **43:** 277

compassion, theme of
The Tempest **42:** 339

complex or enigmatic nature
The Phoenix and Turtle **10:** 7, 14, 35, 42; **38:** 326, 357

composition date
The Comedy of Errors **1:** 18, 23, 34, 55
Henry VIII **2:** 19, 22, 35; **24:** 129
Pericles **2:** 537, 544
Sonnets **10:** 153, 154, 161, 166, 196, 217, 226, 270, 277; **28:** 363, 385
Twelfth Night **37:** 78

conclusion
All's Well That Ends Well **38:** 123, 132, 142
Love's Labour's Lost **38:** 172
Troilus and Cressida **3:** 538, 549, 558, 566, 574, 583, 594
    comedy vs. tragedy **43:** 351

conflict between Christianity and Judaism
The Merchant of Venice **4:** 224, 250, 268, 289, 324, 344; **12:** 67, 70, 72, 76; **22:** 69; **25:** 257 **40:** 117, 127, 166, 181

conscience
Richard III **8:** 148, 152, 162, 165, 190, 197, 201, 206, 210, 228, 232, 239, 243, 252, 258; **39:** 341

as consciously philosophical
The Phoenix and Turtle **10:** 7, 21, 24, 31, 48; **38:** 342, 378

conspiracy or treason
The Tempest **16:** 426; **19:** 357; **25:** 382; **29:** 377

constancy and faithfulness
The Phoenix and Turtle **10:** 18, 20, 21, 48; **38:** 329

construing the truth
Julius Caesar **7:** 320, 336, 343, 350; **37:** 229

consummation of marriage
Othello **22:** 207

contemptus mundi
Antony and Cleopatra **6:** 85, 133

contractual and economic relations
Henry IV, Parts 1 and 2 **13:** 213
Richard II **13:** 213

contradiction, paradox, and opposition
As You Like It **46:** 105
Romeo and Juliet **5:** 421, 427, 431, 496, 509, 513, 516, 520, 525, 528, 538; **33:** 287; **44:** 11
Troilus and Cressida **43:** 377

contrasting dramatic worlds
Henry IV, Parts 1 and 2 **14:** 56, 60, 61, 84, 105
The Merchant of Venice **44:** 11

contrasts and oppositions
Othello **4:** 421, 455, 457, 462, 508; **25:** 189

corruption in society
As You Like It **46:** 94
King John **9:** 222, 234, 280, 297

costume
As You Like It **46:** 117
Hamlet **21:** 81
Henry VIII **24:** 82, 87; **28:** 184
Richard II **24:** 274, 278, 291, 304, 325, 356, 364, 423
Romeo and Juliet **11:** 505, 509
Troilus and Cressida **18:** 289, 371, 406, 419

counsel
The Winter's Tale **19:** 401

Court of Love
The Phoenix and Turtle **10:** 9, 24, 50

court society
The Winter's Tale **16:** 410

courtly love
Troilus and Cressida **22:** 58

courtly love tradition, influence of
Romeo and Juliet **5:** 505, 542, 575; **33:** 233

courtship and marriage
See also **marriage**
As You Like It **34:** 109, 177
Much Ado about Nothing **8:** 29, 44, 48, 95, 115, 121, 125; **31:** 191, 231

credibility
Twelfth Night **1:** 540, 542, 543, 554, 562, 581, 587

critical history
Henry IV, Parts 1 and 2 **42:** 185

cynicism
Troilus and Cressida **43:** 298

dance
Henry VI, Parts 1, 2, and 3 **22:** 156

dance and patterned action
Love's Labour's Lost **2:** 308, 342; **23:** 191, 237

dark elements
All's Well That Ends Well **7:** 27, 37, 39, 43, 54, 109, 113, 116; **26:** 85
Twelfth Night **46:** 310

death, decay, nature's destructiveness
As You Like It **46:** 169
Hamlet **1:** 144, 153, 188, 198, 221, 242; **13:** 502; **28:** 280, 311; **35:** 241; **42:** 279
King Lear **2:** 93, 94, 101, 104, 106, 109, 112, 116, 129, 131, 137, 143, 147, 149, 156, 160, 170, 179, 188, 197, 207, 218, 222, 226, 231, 238, 241, 245, 249, 253, 265, 269, 273; **16:** 301; **25:** 202, 218; **31:** 77, 117, 137, 142; **46:** 264

Love's Labour's Lost **2:** 305, 331, 344, 348
Measure for Measure **2:** 394, 452, 516; **25:** 12
Venus and Adonis **10:** 419, 427, 434, 451, 454, 462, 466, 473, 480, 489; **25:** 305; **33:** 309, 321, 347, 352, 363, 370

decay of heroic ideals
Henry VI, Parts 1, 2, and 3 **3:** 119, 126

deception, disguise, and duplicity
As You Like It **46:** 134
Henry IV, Parts 1 and 2 **1:** 397, 406, 425; **42:** 99
The Merry Wives of Windsor **5:** 332, 334, 336, 354, 355, 379; **22:** 93
Much Ado about Nothing **8:** 29, 55, 63, 69, 79, 82, 88, 108, 115; **31:** 191, 198
Sonnets **25:** 374; **40:** 221
The Taming of the Shrew **12:** 416

deposition scene
Richard II **42:** 118

Desire (Volume 38: 1, 19, 31, 40, 48, 56)
All's Well That Ends Well **38:** 96, 99, 109, 118
As You Like It **37:** 43
Love's Labour's Lost **38:** 185, 194, 200, 209
The Merchant of Venice **22:** 3; **40:** 142; **45:** 17
The Merry Wives of Windsor **38:** 286, 297, 300
Troilus and Cressida **43:** 317, 329, 340,

discrepancy between prophetic ending and preceding action
Henry VIII **2:** 22, 25, 31, 46, 49, 56, 60, 65, 68, 75, 81; **32:** 148; **41:** 190

disillusioned or cynical tone
Troilus and Cressida **3:** 544, 548, 554, 557, 558, 571, 574, 630, 642; **18:** 284, 332, 403, 406, 423; **27:** 376

disorder
Troilus and Cressida **3:** 578, 589, 599, 604, 609; **18:** 332, 406, 412, 423; **27:** 366

disorder and civil dissension
Henry VI, Parts 1, 2, and 3 **3:** 59, 67, 76, 92, 103, 126; **13:** 131; **16:** 183; **24:** 11, 17, 28, 31, 47; **25:** 102; **28:** 112; **39:** 154, 177, 187, 196, 205

displacement
All's Well That Ends Well **22:** 78
Measure for Measure **22:** 78

divine will, role of
Romeo and Juliet **5:** 485, 493, 505, 533, 573

domestic elements
As You Like It **46:** 142
Coriolanus **42:** 218

double-plot
King Lear **2:** 94, 95, 100, 101, 104, 112, 116, 124, 131, 133, 156, 253, 257; **46:** 254
Troilus and Cressida **3:** 569, 613

doubling of roles
  Pericles **15:** 150, 152, 167, 173, 180

dramatic elements
  Sonnets **10:** 155, 182, 240, 251, 283, 367
  Venus and Adonis **10:** 459, 462, 486

dramatic shortcomings or failure
  As You Like It **5:** 19, 42, 52, 61, 65
  Love's Labour's Lost **2:** 299, 301, 303, 322
  Romeo and Juliet **5:** 416, 418, 420, 426, 436, 437, 448, 464, 467, 469, 480, 487, 524, 562

dramatic structure
  The Comedy of Errors **1:** 19, 27, 40, 43, 46, 50; **26:** 186, 190; **34:** 190, 229, 233; **37:** 12
  Cymbeline **4:** 17, 18, 19, 20, 21, 22, 24, 38, 43, 48, 53, 64, 68, 89, 116, 129, 141; **22:** 302, 365; **25:** 319; **36:** 115, 125
  Othello **4:** 370, 390, 399, 427, 488, 506, 517, 569; **22:** 207; **28:** 243
  The Winter's Tale **7:** 382, 390, 396, 399, 402, 407, 414, 429, 432, 473, 479, 493, 497, 501; **15:** 528; **25:** 339; **36:** 289, 295, 362, 380; **45:** 297, 344, 358, 366

as dream-play
  A Midsummer Night's Dream **3:** 365, 370, 372, 377, 389, 391; **29:** 190; **45:** 117

Dreams in Shakespeare (Volume 45: 1, 10, 17, 28, 40, 48, 58, 67, 75**)**
  Antony and Cleopatra **45:** 28
  Cymbeline **4:** 162, 167; **44:** 28; **45:** 67, 75
  Hamlet **45:** 28
  Julius Caesar **45:** 10
  A Midsummer Night's Dream **45:** 96, 107, 117
  Romeo and Juliet **45:** 40
  The Tempest **45:** 236, 247, 259

dualisms
  Antony and Cleopatra **19:** 304; **27:** 82
  Cymbeline **4:** 29, 64, 73

duration of time
  As You Like It **5:** 44, 45
  A Midsummer Night's Dream **3:** 362, 370, 380, 386, 494; **45:** 175

economic relations
  Henry V **13:** 213

economics and exchange
  The Merchant of Venice **40:** 197, 208

editorial and textual issues
  Sonnets **28:** 363; **40:** 273; **42:** 296

education
  All's Well That Ends Well **7:** 62, 86, 90, 93, 98, 104, 116, 126
  The Two Gentlemen of Verona **6:** 490, 494, 504, 526, 532, 555, 568

education or nurturing
  The Tempest **8:** 353, 370, 384, 396; **29:** 292, 368, 377

egotism or narcissism
  Much Ado about Nothing **8:** 19, 24, 28, 29, 55, 69, 95, 115

Elizabeth's influence
  The Merry Wives of Windsor **5:** 333, 334, 335, 336, 339, 346, 355, 366, 402; **18:** 5, 86; **38:** 278

Elizabethan and Jacobean politics, relation to
  Hamlet **28:** 232; **28:** 290, 311; **35:** 140

Elizabethan attitudes, influence of
  Richard II **6:** 287, 292, 294, 305, 321, 327, 364, 402, 414; **13:** 494; **24:** 325; **28:** 188; **39:** 273; **42:** 118

Elizabethan betrothal and marriage customs
  Measure for Measure **2:** 429, 437, 443, 503

Elizabethan culture, relation to
  As You Like It **5:** 21, 59, 66, 68, 70, 158; **16:** 53; **28:** 46; **34:** 120; **37:** 1; **46:** 142
  The Comedy of Errors **26:** 138, 142; **34:** 201, 215, 233, 238, 258; **42:** 80
  Hamlet **1:** 76, 148, 151, 154, 160, 166, 169, 171, 176, 184, 202, 209, 254; **13:** 282, 494; **19:** 330; **21:** 407, 416; **22:** 258
  Henry IV, Parts 1 and 2 **19:** 195
  Henry V **5:** 210, 213, 217, 223, 257, 299, 310; **16:** 202; **19:** 133, 233; **28:** 121, 159; **30:** 215, 262; **37:** 187
  Julius Caesar **16:** 231; **30:** 342, 379
  King Lear **2:** 168, 174, 177, 183, 226, 241; **19:** 330; **22:** 227, 233, 365; **25:** 218; **46:** 276
  Measure for Measure **2:** 394, 418, 429, 432, 437, 460, 470, 482, 503
  The Merchant of Venice **32:** 66; **40:** 117, 127, 142, 166, 181, 197, 208
  Much Ado about Nothing **8:** 23, 33, 44, 55, 58, 79, 88, 104, 111, 115
  The Rape of Lucrece **33:** 195; **43:** 77
  The Taming of the Shrew **31:** 288, 295, 300, 315, 326, 345, 351
  Timon of Athens **1:** 487, 489, 495, 500; **20:** 433; **27:** 203, 212, 230
  Titus Andronicus **27:** 282
  Troilus and Cressida **3:** 560, 574, 606; **25:** 56
  Twelfth Night **1:** 549, 553, 555, 563, 581, 587, 620; **16:** 53; **19:** 42, 78; **26:** 357; **28:** 1; **34:** 323, 330; **46:** 291

Elizabethan dramatic conventions
  Cymbeline **4:** 53, 124
  Henry VIII **24:** 155

Elizabethan literary influences
  Henry VI, Parts 1, 2, and 3 **3:** 75, 97, 100, 119, 143; **22:** 156; **28:** 112; **37:** 97

Elizabethan love poetry
  Love's Labour's Lost **38:** 232

Elizabethan poetics, influence of
  Romeo and Juliet **5:** 416, 520, 522, 528, 550, 559, 575

Elizabethan politics, relation to
  Henry IV, Parts 1 and 2 **22:** 395; **28:** 203
  Henry VIII **22:** 395; **24:** 115, 129, 140; **32:** 148
  Richard III **22:** 395; **25:** 141; **37:** 144; **39:** 345, 349; **42:** 130

Elizabethan setting
  The Two Gentlemen of Verona **12:** 463, 485

emulation or rivalry
  Julius Caesar **16:** 231

England and Rome, parallels between
  Coriolanus **9:** 39, 43, 106, 148, 180, 193; **25:** 296; **30:** 67, 105

English language and colonialism
  Henry V **22:** 103; **28:** 159

English Reformation, influence of
  Henry VIII **2:** 25, 35, 39, 51, 67; **24:** 89

epic elements
  Henry V **5:** 192, 197, 246, 257, 314; **30:** 181, 220, 237, 252

erotic elements
  A Midsummer Night's Dream **3:** 445, 491, 497, 511; **12:** 259, 262, 298; **16:** 34; **19:** 21; **29:** 183, 225, 269
  Venus and Adonis **10:** 410, 411, 418, 419, 427, 428, 429, 442, 448, 454, 459, 466, 473; **25:** 305, 328; **28:** 355; **33:** 321, 339, 347, 352, 363, 370

as experimental play
  Romeo and Juliet **5:** 464, 509, 528

Essex Rebellion, relation to
  Richard II **6:** 249, 250; **24:** 356

ethical or moral issues
  King John **9:** 212, 222, 224, 229, 235, 240, 263, 275, 280

ethnicity
  The Winter's Tale **37:** 306

Euripides, influence of
  Titus Andronicus **27:** 285

evil
  See also **good versus evil**
  Macbeth **3:** 194, 208, 231, 234, 239, 241, 267, 289; **20:** 203, 206, 210, 374
  Romeo and Juliet **5:** 485, 493, 505

excess
  King John **9:** 251

fame
  Coriolanus **30:** 58

family honor, structure, and inheritance
  Richard II **6:** 338, 368, 388, 397, 414; **39:** 263, 279
  Richard III **8:** 177, 248, 252, 263, 267; **25:** 141; **39:** 335, 341, 349, 370

family, theme of
  Cymbeline **44:** 28

fancy
  Twelfth Night **1:** 543, 546

as farce
  The Taming of the Shrew **9:** 330, 337, 338, 341, 342, 365, 381, 386, 413, 426

farcical elements
  See **comic and farcical elements**

fate
  Richard II **6:** 289, 294, 304, 352, 354, 385
  Romeo and Juliet **5:** 431, 444, 464, 469, 470, 479, 480, 485, 487, 493, 509, 530, 533, 562, 565, 571, 573; **33:** 249

Fathers and Daughters (Volume 36: 1, 12, 25, 32, 37, 45, 70, 78)
  As You Like It **46:** 94
  Cymbeline **34:** 134
  King Lear **34:** 51, 54, 60
    cruelty of daughters **2:** 101, 102, 106; **31:** 84, 123, 137, 142
  Pericles **34:** 226, 233
  The Winter's Tale **34:** 311, 318, 328

feminist criticism
  As You Like It **23:** 107, 108
  Comedy of Errors **42:** 93
  Love's Labour's Lost **42:** 93
  Measure for Measure **23:** 320

festive or folklore elements
  Twelfth Night **46:** 338

feud
  Romeo and Juliet **5:** 415, 419, 425, 447, 458, 464, 469, 479, 480, 493, 509, 522, 556, 565, 566, 571, 575; **25:** 181

fire and water
  Coriolanus **25:** 263

flattery
  Coriolanus **9:** 26, 45, 92, 100, 110, 121, 130, 144, 157, 183, 193; **25:** 296
  Henry IV, Parts 1 and 2 **22:** 395
  Henry VIII **22:** 395
  Richard III **22:** 395

folk drama, relation to
  The Winter's Tale **7:** 420, 451

folk elements
  The Taming of the Shrew **9:** 381, 393, 404, 426

folk rituals, elements and influence of
  Henry VI, Parts 1, 2, and 3 **39:** 205
  The Merry Wives of Windsor **5:** 353, 369, 376, 392, 397, 400; **38:** 256, 300

food, meaning of
  The Comedy of Errors **34:** 220
  Troilus and Cressida **43:** 298

forest
  The Two Gentlemen of Verona **6:** 450, 456, 492, 514, 547, 555, 564, 568

Forest of Arden
  As You Like It
    as "bitter" Arcadia **5:** 98, 118, 162; **23:** 97, 98, 99, 100, 122, 139
    Duke Frederick's court, contrast with **5:** 46, 102, 103, 112, 130, 156; **16:** 53; **23:** 126, 128, 129, 131, 134; **34:** 78, 102, 131; **46:** 164
    pastoral elements **5:** 18, 20, 24, 32, 35, 47, 50, 54, 55, 57, 60, 77, 128, 135, 156; **23:** 17, 20, 27, 46, 137; **34:** 78, 147; **46:** 88
    as patriarchal society **5:** 168; **23:** 150; **34:** 177
    as source of self-knowledge **5:** 98, 102, 103, 128, 130, 135, 148, 158, 162; **23:** 17; **34:** 102
    as timeless, mythical world **5:** 112, 130, 141; **23:** 132; **34:** 78; **37:** 43; **46:** 88
    theme of play **46:** 88

forgiveness or redemption
  The Winter's Tale **7:** 381, 389, 395, 402, 407, 436, 456, 460, 483; **36:** 318

free will versus fate
  Macbeth **3:** 177, 183, 184, 190, 196, 198, 202, 207, 208, 213; **13:** 361; **44:** 351, 361, , 366, 373
  The Two Noble Kinsmen **9:** 474, 481, 486, 492, 498

freedom and servitude
  The Tempest **8:** 304, 307, 312, 429; **22:** 302; **29:** 278, 368, 377; **37:** 336

French language, Shakespeare's use of
  Henry V **5:** 186, 188, 190; **25:** 131

Freudian analysis
  A Midsummer Night's Dream **44:** 1

friendship
  See also **love and friendship** *and* **love versus friendship**
  Coriolanus **30:** 125, 142
  Sonnets **10:** 185, 279; **28:** 380
  The Two Noble Kinsmen **9:** 448, 463, 470, 474, 479, 481, 486, 490; **19:** 394; **41:** 363, 372; **42:** 361

Gender Identity and Issues (Volume 40: 1, 9, 15, 27, 33, 51, 61, 65, 75, 90, 99)
  As You Like It **46:** 127, 134
  All's Well That Ends Well **7:** 9, 10, 67, 126; **13:** 77, 84; **19:** 113; **26:** 128; **38:** 89, 99, 118; **44:** 35
  Antony and Cleopatra **13:** 368; **25:** 257; **27:** 144
  The Comedy of Errors **34:** 215, 220
  Coriolanus **30:** 79, 125, 142; **44:** 93
  Hamlet **35:** 144; **44:** 189, 195, 198
  Henry IV, Parts 1 and 2 **13:** 183; **25:** 151; **44:** 44
  Henry V **13:** 183; **28:** 121, 146, 159; **44:** 44
  Julius Caesar **13:** 260

  The Merchant of Venice **40:** 142, 151, 156
  Othello **32:** 294; **35:** 327
  Richard II **25:** 89; **39:** 295
  Richard III **25:** 141; **37:** 144; **39:** 345
  Romeo and Juliet **32:** 256
  Sonnets **37:** 374; **40:** 238, 247, 254, 264, 268, 273
  The Taming of the Shrew **28:** 24 **31:** 261, 268, 276, 282, 288, 295, 300, 335, 351
  Twelfth Night **19:** 78; **34:** 344; **37:** 59; **42:** 32; **46:** 347, 362, 369
  The Two Gentlemen of Verona **40:** 374
  The Two Noble Kinsmen **42:** 361

genre
  As You Like It **5:** 46, 55, 79
  The Comedy of Errors **34:** 251, 258
  Coriolanus **9:** 42, 43, 53, 80, 106, 112, 117, 130, 164, 177; **30:** 67, 74, 79, 89, 111, 125
  Hamlet **1:** 176, 212, 237
  Love's Labour's Lost **38:** 163
  The Merchant of Venice **4:** 191, 200, 201, 209, 215, 221, 232, 238, 247; **12:** 48, 54, 62
  Much Ado about Nothing **8:** 9, 18, 19, 28, 29, 39, 41, 44, 53, 63, 69, 73, 79, 82, 95, 100, 104
  Richard III **8:** 181, 182, 197, 206, 218, 228, 239, 243, 252, 258; **13:** 142; **39:** 383
  The Taming of the Shrew **9:** 329, 334, 362, 375; **22:** 48; **31:** 261, 269, 276
  Timon of Athens **1:** 454, 456, 459, 460, 462, 483, 492, 499, 503, 509, 511, 512, 515, 518, 525, 531; **27:** 203
  Troilus and Cressida **3:** 541, 542, 549, 558, 566, 571, 574, 587, 594, 604, 630, 642; **27:** 366
  The Two Gentlemen of Verona **6:** 460, 468, 472, 516; **40:** 320

genres, mixture of
  Timon of Athens **16:** 351; **25:** 198

gift exchange
  Love's Labour's Lost **25:** 1

good versus evil
  See also **evil**
  Measure for Measure **2:** 432, 452, 524; **33:** 52, 61
  The Tempest **8:** 302, 311, 315, 370, 423, 439; **29:** 278; 297

grace
  The Winter's Tale **7:** 420, 425, 460, 493; **36:** 328

grace and civility
  Love's Labour's Lost **2:** 351

Greece
  Troilus and Cressida **43:** 287

grotesque or absurd elements
  Hamlet **42:** 279
  King Lear **2:** 136, 156, 245; **13:** 343

handkerchief, significance of
  Othello **4:** 370, 384, 385, 396, 503, 530, 562; **35:** 265, 282, 380

Hercules Furens (Seneca) as source
  Othello **16:** 283

Hippolytus, myth of
  A Midsummer Night's Dream **29:** 216; **45:** 84

historical accuracy
  Henry VI, Parts 1, 2, and 3 **3:** 18, 21, 35, 46, 51; **16:** 217; **24:** 16, 18, 25, 31, 45, 48
  Richard III **8:** 144, 145, 153, 159, 163, 165, 168, 213, 223, 228, 232; **39:** 305, 308, 326, 383

historical allegory
  The Winter's Tale **7:** 381; **15:** 528

historical and romantic elements, combination of
  Henry VIII **2:** 46, 49, 51, 75, 76, 78; **24:** 71, 80, 146; **41:** 129, 146, 180

historical content
  Henry IV, Parts 1 and 2 **1:** 310, 328, 365, 366, 370, 374, 380, 387, 421, 424, 427, 431; **16:** 172; **19:** 157; **25:** 151; **32:** 136; **39:** 143
  Henry V **5:** 185, 188, 190, 192, 193, 198, 246, 314; **13:** 201; **19:** 133; **25:** 131; **30:** 193, 202, 207, 215, 252
  King John **9:** 216, 219, 220, 222, 235, 240, 254, 284, 290, 292, 297, 300, 303; **13:** 163; **32:** 93, 114; **41:** 234, 243
  The Tempest **8:** 364, 408, 420; **16:** 426; **25:** 382; **29:** 278, 339, 343, 368; **45:** 226

historical determinism versus free will
  Julius Caesar **7:** 160, 298, 316, 333, 346, 356; **13:** 252

historical epic, as epilogue to Shakespeare's
  Henry VIII **2:** 22, 25, 27, 39, 51, 60, 65

historical epic, place in or relation to Shakespeare's
  Henry IV, Parts 1 and 2 **1:** 309, 314, 328, 374, 379, 424, 427
  Henry V **5:** 195, 198, 205, 212, 225, 241, 244, 287, 304, 310; **14:** 337, 342; **30:** 215
  Henry VI, Parts 1, 2, and 3 **3:** 24, 59; **24:** 51

historical principles
  Richard III **39:** 308, 326, 387

historical relativity, theme of **41: 146**

historical sources, compared with
  Richard II **6:** 252, 279, 343; **28:** 134; **39:** 235

historiography
  Henry VIII **37:** 109

homoerotic elements
  As You Like It **46:** 127, 142
  Henry V **16:** 202
  Sonnets **10:** 155, 156, 159, 161, 175, 213, 391; **16:** 461; **28:** 363, 380; **37:** 347; **40:** 254, 264, 273

homosexuality
  As You Like It **46:** 127, 142

Measure for Measure **42:** 1
The Merchant of Venice **22:** 3, 69; **37:** 86; **40:** 142, 156, 197
Twelfth Night **22:** 69; **42:** 32; **46:** 362

honor or integrity
  Coriolanus **9:** 43, 65, 73, 92, 106, 110, 121, 144, 153, 157, 164, 177, 183, 189; **30:** 89, 96, 133

hospitality
  The Winter's Tale **19:** 366

as humanistic play
  Henry VI, Parts 1, 2, and 3 **3:** 83, 92, 109, 115, 119, 131, 136, 143

hunt motif
  Venus and Adonis **10:** 434, 451, 466, 473; **33:** 357, 370

hypocrisy
  Henry V **5:** 203, 213, 219, 223, 233, 260, 271, 302

ideal love
  See also **love**
  Romeo and Juliet **5:** 421, 427, 431, 436, 437, 450, 463, 469, 498, 505, 575; **25:** 257; **33:** 210, 225, 272

idealism versus pragmatism
  Hamlet **16:** 246; **28:** 325

idealism versus realism
  See also **realism**
  Love's Labour's Lost **38:** 163
  Othello **4:** 457, 508, 517; **13:** 313; **25:** 189

identities of persons
  Sonnets **10:** 154, 155, 156, 161, 166, 167, 169, 173, 174, 175, 185, 190, 191, 196, 218, 226, 230, 233, 240; **40:** 238

identity
  The Comedy of Errors **34:** 201, 208, 211
  Coriolanus **42:** 243
  A Midsummer Night's Dream **29:** 269
  The Two Gentlemen of Verona **6:** 494, 511, 529, 532, 547, 560, 564, 568; **19:** 34

illusion
  The Comedy of Errors **1:** 13, 14, 27, 37, 40, 45, 59, 63; **26:** 188; **34:** 194, 211

illusion versus reality
  Love's Labour's Lost **2:** 303, 308, 331, 340, 344, 348, 356, 359, 367, 371, 375; **23:** 230, 231

imagery
  Venus and Adonis **10:** 414, 415, 416, 420, 429, 434, 449, 459, 466, 473, 480; **25:** 328; **28:** 355; **33:** 321, 339, 352, 363, 370, 377; **42:** 347

imagination and art
  A Midsummer Night's Dream **3:** 365, 371, 381,

402, 412, 417, 421, 423, 441, 459, 468, 506, 516, 520; **22:** 39; **45:** 96, 126, 136, 147

immortality
  Measure for Measure **16:** 102

imperialism
  Henry V **22:** 103; **28:** 159

implausibility of plot, characters, or events
  All's Well That Ends Well **7:** 8, 45
  King Lear **2:** 100, 136, 145, 278; **13:** 343
  The Merchant of Venice **4:** 191, 192, 193; **12:** 52, 56, 76, 119
  Much Ado about Nothing **8:** 9, 12, 16, 19, 33, 36, 39, 44, 53, 100, 104
  Othello **4:** 370, 380, 391, 442, 444

inaction
  Troilus and Cressida **3:** 587, 621; **27:** 347

incest, motif of
  Pericles **2:** 582, 588; **22:** 315; **36:** 257, 264

inconsistencies
  Henry VIII **2:** 16, 27, 28, 31, 60

inconsistency between first and second halves
  Measure for Measure **2:** 474, 475, 505, 514, 524

induction
  The Taming of the Shrew **9:** 320, 322, 332, 337, 345, 350, 362, 365, 369, 370, 381, 390, 393, 407, 419, 424, 430; **12:** 416, 427, 430, 431, 441; **19:** 34, 122; **22:** 48; **31:** 269, 315, 351

as inferior or flawed play
  Henry VI, Parts 1, 2, and 3 **3:** 20, 21, 25, 26, 35
  Pericles **2:** 537, 546, 553, 563, 564; **15:** 139, 143, 156, 167, 176; **36:** 198
  Timon of Athens **1:** 476, 481, 489, 499, 520; **20:** 433, 439, 491; **25:** 198; **27:** 157, 175

infidelity
  Troilus and Cressida **43:** 298

innocence
  Macbeth **3:** 234, 241, 327
  Pericles **36:** 226, 274

innocence to experience
  The Two Noble Kinsmen **9:** 481, 502; **19:** 394

Irish affairs
  Henry V **22:** 103; **28:** 159

ironic or parodic elements
  The Two Gentlemen of Verona **6:** 447, 472, 478, 484, 502, 504, 509, 516, 529, 549; **13:** 12
  Henry VIII **41:** 129

irony
  All's Well That Ends Well **7:** 27, 32, 58, 62, 67, 81, 86, 109, 116
  Antony and Cleopatra **6:** 53, 136, 146, 151, 159, 161, 189, 192, 211, 224
  As You Like It **5:** 30, 32, 154

Coriolanus **9:** 65, 73, 80, 92, 106, 153, 157, 164, 193; **30:** 67, 89, 133
Cymbeline **4:** 64, 77, 103
Henry V **5:** 192, 210, 213, 219, 223, 226, 233, 252, 260, 269, 281, 299, 304; **14:** 336; **30:** 159, 193
Julius Caesar **7:** 167, 257, 259, 262, 268, 282, 316, 320, 333, 336, 346, 350
The Merchant of Venice **4:** 254, 300, 321, 331, 350; **28:** 63
Much Ado about Nothing **8:** 14, 63, 79, 82; **28:** 63
The Rape of Lucrece **10:** 93, 98, 128
Richard II **6:** 270, 307, 364, 368, 391; **24:** 383; **28:** 188
Sonnets **10:** 256, 293, 334, 337, 346
The Taming of the Shrew **9:** 340, 375, 398, 407, 413; **13:** 3; **19:** 122
The Two Noble Kinsmen **9:** 463, 481, 486; **41:** 301
The Winter's Tale **7:** 419, 420

the island
The Tempest **8:** 308, 315, 447; **25:** 357, 382; **29:** 278, 343

Italian influences
Sonnets **28:** 407

Jacobean culture, relation to
Coriolanus **22:** 248
Macbeth **19:** 330; **22:** 365
Pericles **37:** 361
The Winter's Tale **19:** 366, 401, 431; **25:** 347; **32:** 388; **37:** 306

jealousy
The Merry Wives of Windsor **5:** 334, 339, 343, 353, 355, 363; **22:** 93; **38:** 273, 307
Othello **4:** 384, 488, 527; **35:** 253, 265, 282, 301, 310; **44:** 57, 66
The Winter's Tale **44:** 66

Jonsonian humors comedy, influence of
The Merry Wives of Windsor **38:** 319

judicial versus natural law
Measure for Measure **2:** 446, 507, 516, 519; **22:** 85; **33:** 58, 117

justice
As You Like It **46:** 94
Othello **35:** 247

justice and mercy
Measure for Measure **2:** 391, 395, 399, 402, 406, 409, 411, 416, 421, 437, 443, 463, 466, 470, 491, 495, 522, 524; **22:** 85; **33:** 52, 61, 101
The Merchant of Venice **4:** 213, 214, 224, 250, 261, 273, 282, 289, 336; **12:** 80, 129; **40:** 127
Much Ado about Nothing **22:** 85

juxtaposition of opposing perspectives
As You Like It **5:** 86, 93, 98, 141; **16:** 53; **23:** 119; **34:** 72, 78, 131

Kingship (Volume 39: 1, 16, 20, 34, 45, 62)
Henry IV, Parts 1 and 2 **1:** 314, 318, 337, 366, 370, 374, 379, 380, 383, 424; **16:** 172; **19:** 195; **28:** 101; **39:** 100, 116, 123, 130; **42:** 141
Henry V **5:** 205, 223, 225, 233, 239, 244, 257, 264, 267, 271, 287, 289, 299, 302, 304, 314, 318; **16:** 202; **22:** 137; **30:** 169, 202, 259, 273; **42:** 141
Henry VI, Parts 1, 2, and 3 **3:** 69, 73, 77, 109, 115, 136, 143; **24:** 32; **39:** 154, 177, 187
Henry VIII **2:** 49, 58, 60, 65, 75, 78; **24:** 113; **41:** 129, 171
King John **9:** 235, 254, 263, 275, 297; **13:** 158; **19:** 182; **22:** 120
Richard II **6:** 263, 264, 272, 277, 289, 294, 327, 354, 364, 381, 388, 391, 402, 409, 414; **19:** 151, 209; **24:** 260, 289, 291, 322, 325, 333, 339, 345, 346, 349, 351, 352, 356, 395, 408, 419, 428; **28:** 134; **39:** 235, 243, 256, 263, 273, 279, 289; **42:** 173
Richard III **39:** 335, 341, 345, 349

knighthood
The Merry Wives of Windsor **5:** 338, 343, 390, 397, 402

knowledge
Love's Labour's Lost **22:** 12

language and imagery
All's Well That Ends Well **7:** 12, 29, 45, 104, 109, 121; **38:** 132
Antony and Cleopatra **6:** 21, 25, 39, 64, 80, 85, 92, 94, 100, 104, 142, 146, 155, 159, 161, 165, 189, 192, 202, 211; **13:** 374, 383; **25:** 245, 257; **27:** 96, 105, 135
As You Like It **5:** 19, 21, 35, 52, 75, 82, 92, 138; **23:** 15, 21, 26; **28:** 9; **34:** 131; **37:** 43
The Comedy of Errors **1:** 16, 25, 39, 40, 43, 57, 59; **34:** 233
Coriolanus **9:** 8, 9, 13, 53, 64, 65, 73, 78, 84, 100, 112, 121, 136, 139, 142, 144, 153, 157, 174, 183, 193, 198; **22:** 248; **25:** 245, 263; **30:** 111, 125, 142; **37:** 283; **44:** 79
Cymbeline **4:** 43, 48, 61, 64, 70, 73, 93, 108; **13:** 401; **25:** 245; **28:** 373, 398; **36:** 115, 158, 166, 186
Hamlet **1:** 95, 144, 153, 154, 160, 188, 198, 221, 227, 249, 259, 270; **22:** 258, 378; **28:** 311; **35:** 144, 152, 238, 241; **42:** 212; **44:** 248
Henry IV, Parts 1 and 2 **13:** 213; **16:** 172; **25:** 245; **28:** 101; **39:** 116, 130; **42:** 153
Henry V **5:** 188, 230, 233, 241, 264, 276; **9:** 203; **19:** 203; **25:** 131; **30:** 159, 181, 207, 234
Henry VI, Parts 1, 2, and 3 **3:** 21, 50, 52, 55, 57, 66, 67, 71, 75, 76, 97, 105, 109, 119, 126, 131; **24:** 28; **37:** 157; **39:** 213, 222
Henry VIII **41:** 180, 190
Julius Caesar **7:** 148, 155, 159, 188, 204, 207, 227, 242, 250, 277, 296, 303, 324, 346, 350; **13:** 260; **17:** 347, 348, 350, 356, 358; **19:** 321; **22:** 280; **25:** 280; **30:** 333, 342
King Lear **2:** 129, 137, 161, 191, 199, 237, 257, 271; **16:** 301; **19:** 344; **22:** 233; **46:** 177
King John **9:** 212, 215, 220, 246, 251, 254, 267, 280, 284, 292, 297, 300; **13:** 147, 158; **22:** 120; **37:** 132
Love's Labour's Lost **2:** 301, 302, 303, 306, 307, 308, 315, 319, 320, 330, 335, 344, 345, 348, 356, 359, 362, 365, 371, 374, 375; **19:** 92; **22:** 12, 378; **23:** 184, 187, 196, 197, 202, 207, 211, 221, 227, 231, 233, 237, 252; **28:** 9, 63; **38:** 219, 226
Macbeth **3:** 170, 193, 213, 231, 234, 241, 245, 250, 253, 256, 263, 271, 283, 300, 302, 306, 323, 327, 338, 340, 349; **13:** 476; **16:** 317; **20:** 241, 279, 283, 367, 379, 400; **25:** 235; **28:** 339; **29:** 76, 91; **42:** 258; **44:** 366; **45:** 58
Measure for Measure **2:** 394, 421, 431, 466, 486, 505; **13:** 112; **28:** 9; **33:** 69
The Merry Wives of Windsor **5:** 335, 337, 343, 347, 351, 363, 374, 379; **19:** 101; **22:** 93, 378; **28:** 9, 69; **38:** 313, 319
The Merchant of Venice **4:** 241, 267, 293; **22:** 3; **25:** 257; **28:** 9, 63; **32:** 41; **40:** 106
A Midsummer Night's Dream **3:** 397, 401, 410, 412, 415, 432, 453, 459, 468, 494; **22:** 23, 39, 93, 378; **28:** 9; **29:** 263; **45:** 143, 169, 175
Much Ado about Nothing **8:** 9, 38, 43, 46, 55, 69, 73, 88, 95, 100, 115, 125; **19:** 68; **25:** 77; **28:** 63; **31:** 178, 184, 222, 241, 245
Othello **4:** 433, 442, 445, 462, 493, 508, 517, 552, 587, 596; **13:** 304; **16:** 272; **22:** 378; **25:** 189, 257; **28:** 243, 344; **42:** 273
Pericles **2:** 559, 560, 565, 583; **16:** 391; **19:** 387; **22:** 315; **36:** 198, 214, 233, 244, 251, 264
The Rape of Lucrece **10:** 64, 65, 66, 71, 78, 80, 89, 93, 116, 109, 125, 131; **22:** 289, 294; **25:** 305; **32:** 321; **33:** 144, 155, 179, 200; **43:** 102, 113, 141
Richard II **6:** 252, 282, 283, 294, 298, 315, 323, 331, 347, 368, 374, 381, 385, 397, 409; **13:** 213, 494; **24:** 269, 270, 298, 301, 304, 315, 325, 329, 333, 339, 356, 364, 395, 405, 408, 411, 414, 419; **28:** 134, 188; **39:** 243, 273, 289, 295; **42:** 173
Richard III **8:** 159, 161, 165, 167, 168, 170, 177, 182, 184, 186, 193, 197, 201, 206, 218, 223, 243, 248, 252, 258, 262, 267; **16:** 150; **25:** 141, 245; **39:** 360, 370, 383
Romeo and Juliet **5:** 420, 426, 431, 436, 437, 456, 477, 479, 489, 492, 496, 509, 520, 522, 528, 538, 542, 550, 559; **25:** 181, 245, 257; **32:** 276; **33:** 210, 272, 274, 287; **42:** 266
Sonnets **10:** 247, 251, 255, 256, 290, 353, 372, 385; **13:** 445; **28:** 380, 385; **32:** 327, 352; **40:** 228, 247, 284, 292, 303
The Taming of the Shrew **9:** 336, 338, 393, 401, 404, 407, 413; **22:** 378; **28:** 9; **31:** 261, 288, 300, 326, 335, 339; **32:** 56
The Tempest **8:** 324, 348, 384, 390, 404, 454; **19:** 421; **29:** 278; **29:** 297, 343, 368, 377
Timon of Athens **1:** 488; **13:** 392; **25:** 198; **27:** 166, 184, 235
Titus Andronicus **4:** 617, 624, 635, 642, 644, 646, 659, 664, 668, 672, 675; **13:** 225; **16:** 225; **25:** 245; **27:** 246, 293, 313, 318, 325; **43:** 186, 222, 227, 239, 247, 262
Troilus and Cressida **3:** 561, 569, 596, 599, 606, 624, 630, 635; **22:** 58, 339; **27:** 332; **366**; **42:** 66
Twelfth Night **1:** 570, 650, 664; **22:** 12; **28:** 9; **34:** 293; **37:** 59
The Two Gentlemen of Verona **6:** 437, 438, 439, 445, 449, 490, 504, 519, 529, 541; **28:** 9; **40:** 343

The Two Noble Kinsmen **9:** 445, 446, 447, 448, 456, 461, 462, 463, 469, 471, 498, 502; **41:** 289, 301, 308, 317, 326
The Winter's Tale **7:** 382, 384, 417, 418, 420, 425, 460, 506; **13:** 409; **19:** 431; **22:** 324; **25:** 347; **36:** 295; **42:** 301; **45:** 297, 344, 333

language versus action
Titus Andronicus **4:** 642, 644, 647, 664, 668; **13:** 225; **27:** 293, 313, 325; **43:** 186

law versus passion for freedom
Much Ado about Nothing **22:** 85

laws of nature, violation of
Macbeth **3:** 234, 241, 280, 323; **29:** 120

legal issues
King Lear **46:** 276

legitimacy
Henry VI, Parts 1, 2, and 3 **3:** 89, 157; **39:** 154
Henry VIII **37:** 109

legitimacy or inheritance
King John **9:** 224, 235, 254, 303; **13:** 147; **19:** 182; **37:** 132; **41:** 215

liberty versus tyranny
Julius Caesar **7:** 158, 179, 189, 205, 221, 253; **25:** 272

love
See also **ideal love**
All's Well That Ends Well **7:** 12, 15, 16, 51, 58, 67, 90, 93, 116; **38:** 80
As You Like It **5:** 24, 44, 46, 57, 79, 88, 103, 116, 122, 138, 141, 162; **28:** 46, 82; **34:** 85
King Lear **2:** 109, 112, 131, 160, 162, 170, 179, 188, 197, 218, 222, 238, 265; **25:** 202; **31:** 77, 149, 151, 155, 162
Love's Labour's Lost **2:** 312, 315, 340, 344; **22:** 12; **23:** 252; **38:** 194
The Merchant of Venice **4:** 221, 226, 270, 284, 312, 344; **22:** 3, 69; **25:** 257; **40:** 156
  sacrificial love **13:** 43; **22:** 69; **40:** 142
A Midsummer Night's Dream
  passionate or romantic love **3:** 372, 389, 395, 396, 402, 408, 411, 423, 441, 450, 480, 497, 498, 511; **29:** 175, 225, 263, 269; **45:** 126, 136
Much Ado about Nothing **8:** 24, 55, 75, 95, 111, 115; **28:** 56
Othello **4:** 412, 493, 506, 512, 530, 545, 552, 569, 570, 575, 580, 591; **19:** 253; **22:** 207; **25:** 257; **28:** 243, 344; **32:** 201; **35:** 261, 317
The Phoenix and Turtle **10:** 31, 37, 40, 50; **38:** 342, 345, 367
Sonnets **10:** 173, 247, 287, 290, 293, 302, 309, 322, 325, 329, 394; **28:** 380; **37:** 347
The Tempest **8:** 435, 439; **29:** 297, 339, 377, 396
Twelfth Night **1:** 543, 546, 573, 580, 587, 595, 600, 603, 610, 660; **19:** 78; **26:** 257, 364; **34:** 270, 293, 323; **46:** 291, 333, 347, 362
The Two Gentlemen of Verona **6:** 442, 445, 456, 479, 488, 492, 494, 502, 509, 516, 519, 549; **13:** 12; **40:** 327, 335, 343, 354, 365

The Two Noble Kinsmen **9:** 479, 481, 490, 498; **41:** 289, 301, 355, 363, 372, 385
The Winter's Tale **7:** 417, 425, 469, 490

love and friendship
See also **friendship**
Julius Caesar **7:** 233, 262, 268; **25:** 272

love and honor
Troilus and Cressida **3:** 555, 604; **27:** 370, 374

love and passion
Antony and Cleopatra **6:** 51, 64, 71, 80, 85, 100, 115, 159, 165, 180; **25:** 257; **27:** 126

love and reason
See also **reason**
Othello **4:** 512, 530, 580; **19:** 253

love, lechery, or rape
Troilus and Cressida **43:** 357

love versus fate
Romeo and Juliet **5:** 421, 437, 438, 443, 445, 458; **33:** 249

love versus friendship
See also **friendship**
The Two Gentlemen of Verona **6:** 439, 449, 450, 458, 460, 465, 468, 471, 476, 480; **40:** 354, 365

love versus lust
Venus and Adonis **10:** 418, 420, 427, 434, 439, 448, 449, 454, 462, 466, 473, 480, 489; **25:** 305; **28:** 355; **33:** 309, 330, 339, 347, 357, 363, 370

love versus reason
See also **reason**
Sonnets **10:** 329

love versus war
Troilus and Cressida **18:** 332, 371, 406, 423; **22:** 339; **27:** 376

Machiavellianism
Henry V **5:** 203, 225, 233, 252, 287, 304; **25:** 131; **30:** 273
Henry VI, Parts 1, 2, and 3 **22:** 193

Madness (Volume 35: 1, 7, 8, 24, 34, 49, 54, 62, 68)
Hamlet **19:** 330; **35:** 104, 117, 126, 132, 134, 140, 144
King Lear **19:** 330
Macbeth **19:** 330
Othello **35:** 265, 276, 282
Twelfth Night **1:** 554, 639, 656; **26:** 371

Magic and the Supernatural (Volume 29: 1, 12, 28, 46, 53, 65)
The Comedy of Errors **1:** 27, 30
Macbeth
  supernatural grace versus evil or chaos **3:** 241, 286, 323
  witchcraft and supernaturalism **3:** 171, 172, 173, 175, 177, 182, 183, 184, 185, 194, 196, 198, 202, 207, 208, 213, 219, 229, 239; **16:** 317; **19:** 245; **20:** 175, 213, 279, 283, 374, 387, 406, 413; **25:** 235; **28:** 339; **29:** 91, 101, 109, 120; **44:** 351, 373
A Midsummer Night's Dream **29:** 190, 201, 210, 216
The Tempest **8:** 287, 293, 304, 315, 340, 356, 396, 401, 404, 408, 435, 458; **28:** 391, 415; **29:** 297, 343, 377; **45:** 272
The Winter's Tale
  witchcraft **22:** 324

male discontent
The Merry Wives of Windsor **5:** 392, 402

male domination
Love's Labour's Lost **22:** 12
A Midsummer Night's Dream **3:** 483, 520; **13:** 19; **25:** 36; **29:** 216, 225, 243, 256, 269; **42:** 46; **45:** 84

male/female relationships
As You Like It **46:** 134
The Comedy of Errors **16:** 3
The Rape of Lucrece **10:** 109, 121, 131; **22:** 289; **25:** 305; **43:** 113, 141,
Troilus and Cressida **16:** 70; **22:** 339; **27:** 362

male sexual anxiety
Love's Labour's Lost **16:** 17

manhood
Macbeth **3:** 262, 309, 333; **29:** 127, 133

Marlowe's works, compared with
Richard II **42:** 173

marriage
See also **courtship and marriage**
The Comedy of Errors **34:** 251
Hamlet **22:** 339
Love's Labour's Lost **2:** 335, 340; **19:** 92; **38:** 209, 232
Measure for Measure **2:** 443, 507, 516, 519, 524, 528; **25:** 12; **33:** 61, 90
The Merry Wives of Windsor **5:** 343, 369, 376, 390, 392, 400, 407; **22:** 93; **38:** 297
A Midsummer Night's Dream **3:** 402, 423, 450, 483, 520; **29:** 243, 256; **45:** 136, 143
Othello **35:** 369
The Taming of the Shrew **9:** 322, 325, 329, 332, 329, 332, 334, 341, 342, 343, 344, 345, 347, 353, 360, 362, 375, 381, 390, 398, 401, 404, 413, 426, 430; **13:** 3; **19:** 3; **28:** 24; **31:** 288
Troilus and Cressida **22:** 339

Marxist criticism
Hamlet **42:** 229
King Lear **42:** 229
Macbeth **42:** 229
Othello **42:** 229

masque elements
The Two Noble Kinsmen **9:** 490
The Tempest **42:** 332

master-slave relationship
  Troilus and Cressida **22:** 58
mediation
  The Merry Wives of Windsor **5:** 343, 392
as medieval allegory or morality play
  Henry IV, Parts 1 and 2 **1:** 323, 324, 342, 361, 366, 373, 374; **32:** 166; **39:** 89
  Measure for Measure **2:** 409, 421, 443, 466, 475, 491, 505, 511, 522; **13:** 94
  Timon of Athens **1:** 492, 511, 518; **27:** 155
medieval chivalry
  Richard II **6:** 258, 277, 294, 327, 338, 388, 397, 414; **24:** 274, 278, 279, 280, 283; **39:** 256
  Troilus and Cressida **3:** 539, 543, 544, 555, 606; **27:** 376
medieval dramatic influence
  All's Well That Ends Well **7:** 29, 41, 51, 98, 113; **13:** 66
  King Lear **2:** 177, 188, 201; **25:** 218
  Othello **4:** 440, 527, 545, 559, 582
medieval homilies, influence of
  The Merchant of Venice **4:** 224, 250, 289
medieval influence
  Romeo and Juliet **5:** 480, 505, 509, 573
medieval literary influence
  Henry VI, Parts 1, 2, and 3 **3:** 59, 67, 75, 100, 109, 136, 151; **13:** 131
  Titus Andronicus **4:** 646, 650; **27:** 299
medieval mystery plays, relation to
  Macbeth **44:** 341
medieval physiology
  Julius Caesar **13:** 260
mercantilism and feudalism
  Richard II **13:** 213
merit versus rank
  All's Well That Ends Well **7:** 9, 10, 19, 37, 51, 76; **38:** 155
Messina
  Much Ado about Nothing **8:** 19, 29, 48, 69, 82, 91, 95, 108, 111, 121, 125; **31:** 191, 209, 229, 241, 245
metadramatic elements
  As You Like It **5:** 128, 130, 146; **34:** 130
  Henry V **13:** 194; **30:** 181
  Love's Labour's Lost **2:** 356, 359, 362
  Measure for Measure **13:** 104
  A Midsummer Night's Dream **3:** 427, 468, 477, 516, 520; **29:** 190, 225, 243
  The Taming of the Shrew **9:** 350, 419, 424; **31:** 300, 315
  The Winter's Tale **16:** 410
metamorphosis or transformation
  Much Ado about Nothing **8:** 88, 104, 111, 115
  The Taming of the Shrew **9:** 370, 430

metaphysical poem
  The Phoenix and Turtle **10:** 7, 8, 9, 20, 31, 35, 37, 40, 45, 50
Midlands Revolt, influence of
  Coriolanus **22:** 248; **30:** 79
military and sexual hierarchies
  Othello **16:** 272
mimetic rivalry
  The Two Gentlemen of Verona **13:** 12; **40:** 335
as "mingled yarn"
  All's Well That Ends Well **7:** 62, 93, 109, 126; **38:** 65
Minotaur, myth of
  A Midsummer Night's Dream **3:** 497, 498; **29:** 216
as miracle play
  Pericles **2:** 569, 581; **36:** 205
misgovernment
  Measure for Measure **2:** 401, 432, 511; **22:** 85
  Much Ado about Nothing **22:** 85
misogyny
  King Lear **31:** 123
  Measure for Measure **23:** 358
misperception
  Cymbeline **19:** 411; **36:** 99, 115
mistaken identity
  The Comedy of Errors **1:** 13, 14, 27, 37, 40, 45, 49, 55, 57, 61, 63; **19:** 34, 54; **25:** 63; **34:** 194
modernization
  Richard III **14:** 523
Montaigne's *Essais*, relation to
  Sonnets **42:** 375
  The Tempest **42:** 339
moral choice
  Julius Caesar **7:** 179, 264, 279, 343
moral corruption
  Troilus and Cressida **3:** 578, 589, 599, 604, 609; **18:** 332, 406, 412, 423; **27:** 366
moral corruption of English society
  Richard III **8:** 154, 163, 165, 177, 193, 201, 218, 228, 232, 243, 248, 252, 267; **39:** 308
moral inheritance
  Henry VI, Parts 1, 2, and 3 **3:** 89, 126
moral intent
  Henry VIII **2:** 15, 19, 25; **24:** 140
moral lesson
  Macbeth **20:** 23
moral relativism
  Antony and Cleopatra **22:** 217; **27:** 121

moral seriousness, question of
  Measure for Measure **2:** 387, 388, 396, 409, 417, 421, 452, 460, 495; **23:** 316, 321
morality
  Henry V **5:** 195, 203, 213, 223, 225, 239, 246, 260, 271, 293
  The Merry Wives of Windsor **5:** 335, 339, 347, 349, 353, 397
  The Two Gentlemen of Verona **6:** 438, 492, 494, 514, 532, 555, 564
  Venus and Adonis **10:** 411, 412, 414, 416, 418, 419, 420, 423, 427, 428, 439, 442, 448, 449, 454, 459, 466; **33:** 330
multiple perspectives of characters
  Henry VI, Parts 1, 2, and 3 **3:** 69, 154
music
  The Tempest **8:** 390, 404; **29:** 292; **37:** 321; **42:** 332
  Twelfth Night **1:** 543, 566, 596
music and dance
  A Midsummer Night's Dream **3:** 397, 400, 418, 513; **12:** 287, 289; **25:** 36
  Much Ado about Nothing **19:** 68; **31:** 222
mutability, theme of
  Sonnets **42:** 375
mythic elements
  See **religious, mythic, or spiritual content**
mythological allusions
  As You Like It **46:** 142
  Antony and Cleopatra **16:** 342; **19:** 304; **27:** 110, 117
naming, significance of
  Coriolanus **30:** 58, 96, 111, 125
narrative strategies
  The Rape of Lucrece **22:** 294
nationalism and patriotism
  See also **British nationalism**
  Henry V **5:** 198, 205, 209, 210, 213, 219, 223, 233, 246, 252, 257, 269, 299; **19:** 133, 217; **30:** 227, 262
  Henry VI, Parts 1, 2, and 3 **24:** 25, 45, 47
  King John **9:** 209, 218, 222, 224, 235, 240, 244, 275; **25:** 98; **37:** 132
  The Winter's Tale **32:** 388
nature
  See also **art and nature** *and* **art versus nature**
  As You Like It **46:** 94
  The Tempest **8:** 315, 370, 390, 408, 414; **29:** 343, 362, 368, 377
  The Winter's Tale **7:** 397, 418, 419, 420, 425, 432, 436, 451, 452, 473, 479; **19:** 366; **45:** 329
nature as book
  Pericles **22:** 315; **36:** 233
nature, philosophy of
  Coriolanus **30:** 74

negative appraisals
    Cymbeline **4:** 20, 35, 43, 45, 48, 53, 56, 68; **15:** 32, 105, 121
    Richard II **6:** 250, 252, 253, 255, 282, 307, 317, 343, 359
    Venus and Adonis **10:** 410, 411, 415, 418, 419, 424, 429

Neoclassical rules
    As You Like It **5:** 19, 20
    Henry IV, Parts 1 and 2 **1:** 286, 287, 290, 293
    Henry VI, Parts 1, 2, and 3 **3:** 17, 18
    King John **9:** 208, 209, 210, 212
    Love's Labour's Lost **2:** 299, 300
    Macbeth **3:** 170, 171, 173, 175; **20:** 17
    Measure for Measure **2:** 387, 388, 390, 394; **23:** 269
    The Merry Wives of Windsor **5:** 332, 334
    Romeo and Juliet **5:** 416, 418, 426
    The Tempest **8:** 287, 292, 293, 334; **25:** 357; **29:** 292; **45:** 200
    Troilus and Cressida **3:** 537, 538, **18:** 276, 278, 281
    The Winter's Tale **7:** 376, 377, 379, 380, 383, 410; **15:** 397

Neoplatonism
    The Phoenix and Turtle **10:** 7, 9, 21, 24, 40, 45, 50; **38:** 345, 350, 367
    Sonnets **10:** 191, 205

nightmarish quality
    Macbeth **3:** 231, 309; **20:** 210, 242; **44:** 261

nihilistic elements
    King Lear **2:** 130, 143, 149, 156, 165, 231, 238, 245, 253; **22:** 271; **25:** 218; **28:** 325
    Timon of Athens **1:** 481, 513, 529; **13:** 392; **20:** 481
    Troilus and Cressida **27:** 354

"nothing," significance of
    Much Ado about Nothing **8:** 17, 18, 23, 55, 73, 95; **19:** 68

nurturing or feeding
    Coriolanus **9:** 65, 73, 136, 183, 189; **30:** 111; **44:** 79

oaths, importance of
    Pericles **19:** 387

obscenity
    Henry V **5:** 188, 190, 260

omens
    Julius Caesar **22:** 137; **45:** 10

oppositions or dualisms
    King John **9:** 224, 240, 263, 275, 284, 290, 300

order
    Henry V **5:** 205, 257, 264, 310, 314; **30:** 193,
    Twelfth Night **1:** 563, 596; **34:** 330; **46:** 291, 347

order versus disintegration
    Titus Andronicus **4:** 618, 647; **43:** 186, 195

other sonnet writers, Shakespeare compared with
    Sonnets **42:** 296

Ovid, influence of
    A Midsummer Night's Dream **3:** 362, 427, 497, 498; **22:** 23; **29:** 175, 190, 216
    Titus Andronicus **4:** 647, 659, 664, 668; **13:** 225; **27:** 246, 275, 285, 293, 299, 306; **28:** 249; **43:** 195, 203, 206

Ovid's *Metamorphoses*, relation to
    The Winter's Tale **42:** 301
    Venus and Adonis **42:** 347

pagan elements
    King Lear **25:** 218

pageantry
    See also **ceremonies, rites, and rituals, importance of**
    Henry VIII **2:** 14, 15, 18, 51, 58; **24:** 77, 83, 84, 85, 89, 91, 106, 113, 118, 120, 126, 127, 140, 146, 150; **41:** 120, 129, 190

paradoxical elements
    Coriolanus **9:** 73, 92, 106, 121, 153, 157, 164, 169, 193

parent-child relations
    A Midsummer Night's Dream **13:** 19; **29:** 216, 225, 243

pastoral convention, parodies of
    As You Like It **5:** 54, 57, 72

pastoral convention, relation to
    As You Like It **5:** 72, 77, 122; **34:** 161; **37:** 1

patience
    Henry VIII **2:** 58, 76, 78
    Pericles **2:** 572, 573, 578, 579; **36:** 251

patriarchal claims
    Henry VI, Parts 1, 2, and 3 **16:** 131 **25:** 102

patriarchal or monarchical order
    King Lear **13:** 353, 457; **16:** 351; **22:** 227, 233; **25:** 218; **31:** 84, 92, 107, 117, 123, 137, 142; **46:** 269

patriarchy
    Cymbeline **32:** 373; **36:** 134
    Henry V **37:** 105; **44:** 44
    Troilus and Cressida **22:** 58

patriotism
    See **nationalism and patriotism**

Pauline doctrine
    A Midsummer Night's Dream **3:** 457, 486, 506

pedagogy
    Sonnets **37:** 374
    The Taming of the Shrew **19:** 122

perception
    Othello **19:** 276; **25:** 189, 257

performance history
    The Taming of the Shrew **31:** 282

performance issues
    See also **staging issues**
    King Lear **2:** 106, 137, 154, 160; **11:** 10, 20, 27, 56, 57, 132, 136, 137, 145, 150, 154; **19:** 295, 344; **25:** 218
    Much Ado about Nothing **18:** 173, 174, 183, 184, 185, 186, 187, 188, 189, 190, 191, 192, 193, 195, 197, 199, 201, 204, 206, 207, 208, 209, 210, 254
    The Taming of the Shrew **12:** 313, 314, 316, 317, 337, 338; **31:** 315

pessimistic elements
    Timon of Athens **1:** 462, 467, 470, 473, 478, 480; **20:** 433, 481; **27:** 155, 191

Petrarchan poetics, influence of
    Romeo and Juliet **5:** 416, 520, 522, 528, 550, 559, 575; **32:** 276

philosophical elements
    Julius Caesar **7:** 310, 324; **37:** 203
    Twelfth Night **1:** 560, 563, 596; **34:** 301, 316; **46:** 297

physical versus intellectual world
    Love's Labour's Lost **2:** 331, 348, 367

pictorial elements
    Venus and Adonis **10:** 414, 415, 419, 420, 423, 480; **33:** 339

Platonic elements
    A Midsummer Night's Dream **3:** 368, 437, 450, 497; **45:** 126

play-within-the-play, convention of
    Henry VI, Parts 1, 2, and 3 **3:** 75, 149
    The Merry Wives of Windsor **5:** 354, 355, 369, 402
    The Taming of the Shrew **12:** 416; **22:** 48

plot
    The Winter's Tale **7:** 376, 377, 379, 382, 387, 390, 396, 452; **13:** 417; **15:** 518; **45:** 374

plot and incident
    Richard III **8:** 146, 152, 159; **25:** 164

Plutarch and historical sources
    Coriolanus **9:** 8, 9, 13, 14, 16, 26, 39, 92, 106, 130, 142, 164; **30:** 74, 79, 105

poetic justice, question of
    King Lear **2:** 92, 93, 94, 101, 129, 137, 231, 245
    Othello **4:** 370, 412, 415, 427

poetic style
    Sonnets **10:** 153, 155, 156, 158, 159, 160, 161, 173, 175, 182, 214, 247, 251, 255, 260, 265, 283, 287, 296, 302, 315, 322, 325, 337, 346, 349, 360, 367, 385; **16:** 472; **40:** 221, 228

political and social disintegration
    Antony and Cleopatra **6:** 31, 43, 53, 60, 71,

80, 100, 107, 111, 146; 180, 197, 219; **22:** 217; **25:** 257; **27:** 121

political content
Titus Andronicus **43:** 262

Politics (Volume 30: 1, 4, 11, 22, 29, 39, 42, 46, 49)
Coriolanus **9:** 15, 17, 18, 19, 26, 33, 43, 53, 62, 65, 73, 80, 92, 106, 110, 112, 121, 144, 153, 157, 164, 180; **22:** 248; **25:** 296; **30:** 58, 67, 79, 89, 96, 105, 111, 125; **37:** 283; **42:** 218
Hamlet **44:** 241
Henry IV, Parts 1 and 2 **28:** 101; **39:** 130; **42:** 141
Henry VIII **2:** 39, 49, 51, 58, 60, 65, 67, 71, 72, 75, 78, 81; **24:** 74, 121, 124; **41:** 146
Julius Caesar **7:** 161, 169, 191, 205, 218, 221, 245, 262, 264, 279, 282, 310, 324, 333, 346; **17:** 317, 318, 321, 323, 334, 350, 351, 358, 378, 382, 394, 406; **22:** 137, 280; **25:** 272, 280; **30:** 285, 297, 316, 321, 342, 374, 379; **37:** 203
King John **9:** 218, 224, 260, 280; **13:** 163; **22:** 120; **37:** 132; **41:** 221, 228
King Lear **46:** 269
Measure for Measure **23:** 379
A Midsummer Night's Dream **29:** 243
Pericles **37:** 361
The Tempest **8:** 304, 307, 315, 353, 359, 364, 401, 408; **16:** 426; **19:** 421; **29:** 339; **37:** 336; **42:** 320; **45:** 272, 280
Timon of Athens **27:** 223, 230
Titus Andronicus **27:** 282
Troilus and Cressida **3:** 536, 560, 606; **16:** 84

popularity
Pericles **2:** 536, 538, 546; **37:** 361
Richard III **8:** 144, 146, 154, 158, 159, 162, 181, 228; **39:** 383
The Taming of the Shrew **9:** 318, 338, 404
Venus and Adonis **10:** 410, 412, 418, 427; **25:** 328

power
Henry V **37:** 175
Measure for Measure **13:** 112; **22:** 85; **23:** 327, 330, 339, 352; **33:** 85
A Midsummer Night's Dream **42:** 46; **45:** 84
Much Ado about Nothing **22:** 85; **25:** 77; **31:** 231, 245

pride and rightful self-esteem
Othello **4:** 522, 536, 541; **35:** 352

primitivism
Macbeth **20:** 206, 213; **45:** 48

primogeniture
As You Like It **5:** 66, 158; **34:** 109, 120

as "problem" plays
The Comedy of Errors **34:** 251
Julius Caesar **7:** 272, 320
Measure for Measure **2:** 416, 429, 434, 474, 475, 503, 514, 519; **16:** 102; **23:** 313, 328, 351

Troilus and Cressida **3:** 555, 566
lack of resolution **43:** 277

procreation
Sonnets **10:** 379, 385; **16:** 461
Venus and Adonis **10:** 439, 449, 466; **33:** 321, 377

providential order
King Lear **2:** 112, 116, 137, 168, 170, 174, 177, 218, 226, 241, 253; **22:** 271
Macbeth **3:** 208, 289, 329, 336

Psychoanalytic Interpretations of Shakespeare's Works (Volume 44: 1, 11, 18, 28, 35, 44, 57, 66, 79, 89, 93)
As You Like It **5:** 146, 158; **23:** 141, 142; **34:** 109
Coriolanus **44:** 93
Cymbeline **45:** 67, 75
Hamlet **1:** 119, 148, 154, 179, 202; **21:** 197, 213, 361; **25:** 209; **28:** 223; **35:** 95, 104, 134, 237; **37:** 241; **44:** 133, 152, 160, 180, 209, 219
Henry IV, Parts 1 and 2 **13:** 457; **28:** 101; **42:** 185; **44:** 44
Henry V **13:** 457; **44:** 44
Julius Caesar **45:** 10
Macbeth **3:** 219, 223, 226; **44:** 11, 284, 289, 297; **45:** 48, 58
Measure for Measure **23:** 331, 332, 333, 334, 335, 340, 355, 356, 359, 379, 395; **44:** 89
Merchant of Venice **45:** 17
A Midsummer Night's Dream **3:** 440, 483; **28:** 15; **29:** 225; **44:** 1; **45:** 107, 117
Othello **4:** 468, 503; **35:** 265, 276, 282, 301, 317, 320, 347; **42:** 198; **44:** 57
Romeo and Juliet **5:** 513, 556
The Tempest **45:** 259
Troilus and Cressida **43:** 287
Twelfth Night **46:** 333

psychological elements
Cymbeline **36:** 134; **44:** 28

public versus private principles
Julius Caesar **7:** 161, 179, 252, 262, 268, 284, 298; **13:** 252

public versus private speech
Love's Labour's Lost **2:** 356, 362, 371

public versus private worlds
As You Like It **46:** 164
Coriolanus **37:** 283; **42:** 218
Romeo and Juliet **5:** 520, 550; **25:** 181; **33:** 274

as "pure" poetry
The Phoenix and Turtle **10:** 14, 31, 35; **38:** 329

Puritanism
Measure for Measure **2:** 414, 418, 434
Twelfth Night **1:** 549, 553, 555, 632; **16:** 53; **25:** 47; **46:** 338

racial issues
Othello **4:** 370, 380, 384, 385, 392, 399, 401,

402, 408, 427, 564; **13:** 327; **16:** 293; **25:** 189, 257; **28:** 249, 330; **35:** 369; **42:** 198

rape
Titus Andronicus **43:** 227, 255

realism
See also **idealism versus realism**
The Merry Wives of Windsor **38:** 313
The Tempest **8:** 340, 359, 464
Troilus and Cressida **43:** 357

reality and illusion
The Tempest **8:** 287, 315, 359, 401, 435, 439, 447, 454; **22:** 302; **45:** 236, 247

reason
See also **love and reason** *and* **love versus reason**
Venus and Adonis **10:** 427, 439, 449, 459, 462, 466; **28:** 355; **33:** 309, 330

reason versus imagination
Antony and Cleopatra **6:** 107, 115, 142, 197, 228; **45:** 28
A Midsummer Night's Dream **3:** 381, 389, 423, 441, 466, 506; **22:** 23; **29:** 190; **45:** 96

rebellion
See also **usurpation**
Henry IV, Parts 1 and 2 **22:** 395; **28:** 101
Henry VIII **22:** 395
King John **9:** 218, 254, 263, 280, 297
Richard III **22:** 395

rebirth, regeneration, resurrection, or immortality
All's Well That Ends Well **7:** 90, 93, 98
Antony and Cleopatra **6:** 100, 103, 125, 131, 159, 181
Cymbeline **4:** 38, 64, 73, 93, 105, 113, 116, 129, 138, 141, 162, 170
Measure for Measure **13:** 84; **16:** 102, 114; **23:** 321, 327, 335, 340, 352; **25:** 12
Pericles **2:** 555, 564, 584, 586, 588; **36:** 205
The Tempest **8:** 302, 312, 320, 334, 348, 359, 370, 384, 401, 404, 414, 429, 439, 447, 454; **16:** 442; **22:** 302; **29:** 297; **37:** 336
The Winter's Tale **7:** 397, 414, 417, 419, 429, 436, 451, 452, 456, 480, 490, 497, 506; **25:** 339 452, 480, 490, 497, 506; **45:** 366

reconciliation
As You Like It **46:** 156
All's Well That Ends Well **7:** 90, 93, 98
Antony and Cleopatra **6:** 100, 103, 125, 131, 159, 181
Cymbeline **4:** 38, 64, 73, 93, 105, 113, 116, 129, 138, 141, 162, 170
The Merry Wives of Windsor **5:** 343, 369, 374, 397, 402
A Midsummer Night's Dream **3:** 412, 418, 437, 459, 468, 491, 497, 502, 513; **13:** 27; **29:** 190
Romeo and Juliet **5:** 415, 419, 427, 439, 447, 480, 487, 493, 505, 533, 536, 562
The Tempest **8:** 302, 312, 320, 334, 348, 359, 370, 384, 401, 404, 414, 429, 439, 447, 454; **16:** 442; **22:** 302; **29:** 297; **37:** 336; **45:** 236

reconciliation of opposites
As You Like It **5:** 79, 88, 103, 116, 122, 138; **23:** 127, 143; **34:** 161, 172; **46:** 156

redemption
The Comedy of Errors **19:** 54; **26:** 188

regicide
Macbeth **3:** 248, 275, 312; **16:** 317, 328

relationship to other Shakespearean plays
Twelfth Night **46:** 303
Henry IV, Parts 1 and 2 **42:** 99, 153

relationship between Parts 1 and 2
Henry IV, Parts 1 and 2 **32:** 136; **39:** 100

religious and theological issues
Macbeth **44:** 324, 341, 351, 361, 366, 373

religious, mythic, or spiritual content
See also **Christian elements**
All's Well That Ends Well **7:** 15, 45, 54, 67, 76, 98, 109, 116
Antony and Cleopatra **6:** 53, 94, 111, 115, 178, 192, 224
Cymbeline **4:** 22, 29, 78, 93, 105, 108, 115, 116, 127, 134, 138, 141, 159; **28:** 373; **36:** 142, 158, 186
Hamlet **1:** 98, 102, 130, 184, 191, 209, 212, 231, 234, 254; **21:** 361; **22:** 258; **28:** 280; **32:** 238; **35:** 134
Henry IV, Parts 1 and 2 **1:** 314, 374, 414, 421, 429, 431, 434; **32:** 103
Henry V **25:** 116; **32:** 126
Macbeth **3:** 208, 269, 275, 318; **29:** 109
Othello **4:** 483, 517, 522, 525, 559, 573; **22:** 207; **28:** 330
Pericles **2:** 559, 561, 565, 570, 580, 584, 588; **22:** 315; **25:** 365
The Tempest **8:** 328, 390, 423, 429, 435; **45:** 211, 247
Timon of Athens **1:** 505, 512, 513, 523; **20:** 493

repentance and forgiveness
Much Ado about Nothing **8:** 24, 29, 111
The Two Gentlemen of Verona **6:** 450, 514, 516, 555, 564
The Winter's Tale **44:** 66

resolution
Measure for Measure **2:** 449, 475, 495, 514, 516; **16:** 102, 114
The Merchant of Venice **4:** 263, 266, 300, 319, 321; **13:** 37
The Two Gentlemen of Verona **6:** 435, 436, 439, 445, 449, 453, 458, 460, 462, 465, 466, 468, 471, 476, 480, 486, 494, 509, 514, 516, 519, 529, 532, 541, 549; **19:** 34

retribution
Henry VI, Parts 1, 2, and 3 **3:** 27, 42, 51, 59, 77, 83, 92, 100, 109, 115, 119, 131, 136, 151
Julius Caesar **7:** 160, 167, 200
Macbeth **3:** 194, 208, 318

Richard III **8:** 163, 170, 177, 182, 184, 193, 197, 201, 206, 210, 218, 223, 228, 243, 248, 267

revenge
Hamlet **1:** 74, 194, 209, 224, 234, 254; **16:** 246; **22:** 258; **25:** 288; **28:** 280; **35:** 152, 157, 167, 174, 212; **44:** 180, 209, 219, 229
The Merry Wives of Windsor **5:** 349, 350, 392; **38:** 264, 307
Othello **35:** 261

revenge tragedy elements
Julius Caesar **7:** 316
Titus Andronicus **4:** 618, 627, 628, 636, 639, 644, 646, 664, 672, 680; **16:** 225; **27:** 275, 318

reversal
A Midsummer Night's Dream **29:** 225

rhetoric
Venus and Adonis **33:** 377
Romeo and Juliet **42:** 266

rhetoric of consolation
Sonnets **42:** 375

rhetoric of politeness
Henry VIII **22:** 182

rhetorical style
King Lear **16:** 301

riddle motif
Pericles **22:** 315; **36:** 205, 214

rightful succession
Titus Andronicus **4:** 638

rings episode
The Merchant of Venice **22:** 3; **40:** 106, 151, 156

role-playing
Julius Caesar **7:** 356; **37:** 229
The Taming of the Shrew **9:** 322, 353, 355, 360, 369, 370, 398, 401, 407, 413, 419, 424; **13:** 3; **31:** 288, 295, 315

as romance play
As You Like It **5:** 55, 79; **23:** 27, 28, 40, 43

romance or chivalric tradition, influence of
Much Ado about Nothing **8:** 53, 125

romance or folktale elements
All's Well That Ends Well **7:** 32, 41, 43, 45, 54, 76, 104, 116, 121; **26:** 117

romance or pastoral tradition, influence of
The Tempest **8:** 336, 348, 396, 404; **37:** 336

romantic and courtly conventions
The Two Gentlemen of Verona **6:** 438, 460, 472, 478, 484, 486, 488, 502, 507, 509, 529, 541, 549, 560, 568; **12:** 460, 462; **40:** 354, 374

romantic elements
The Comedy of Errors **1:** 13, 16, 19, 23, 25, 30, 31, 36, 39, 53
Cymbeline **4:** 17, 20, 46, 68, 77, 141, 148, 172; **15:** 111; **25:** 319; **28:** 373
King Lear **31:** 77, 84
The Taming of the Shrew **9:** 334, 342, 362, 375, 407

royalty
Antony and Cleopatra **6:** 94

Salic Law
Henry V **5:** 219, 252, 260; **28:** 121

as satire or parody
Love's Labour's Lost **2:** 300, 302, 303, 307, 308, 315, 321, 324, 327; **23:** 237, 252
The Merry Wives of Windsor **5:** 338, 350, 360, 385; **38:** 278, 319

satire or parody of pastoral conventions
As You Like It **5:** 46, 55, 60, 72, 77, 79, 84, 114, 118, 128, 130, 154

satirical elements
The Phoenix and Turtle **10:** 8, 16, 17, 27, 35, 40, 45, 48
Timon of Athens **27:** 155, 235
Troilus and Cressida **3:** 539, 543, 544, 555, 558, 574; **27:** 341

Saturnalian elements
Twelfth Night **1:** 554, 571, 603, 620, 642; **16:** 53

schemes and intrigues
The Merry Wives of Windsor **5:** 334, 336, 339, 341, 343, 349, 355, 379

Scholasticism
The Phoenix and Turtle **10:** 21, 24, 31

School of Night, allusions to
Love's Labour's Lost **2:** 321, 327, 328

self-conscious or artificial nature of play
Cymbeline **4:** 43, 52, 56, 68, 124, 134, 138; **36:** 99

self-deception
Twelfth Night **1:** 554, 561, 591, 625

self-indulgence
Twelfth Night **1:** 563, 615, 635

self-interest or expediency
Henry V **5:** 189, 193, 205, 213, 217, 233, 260, 287, 302, 304; **30:** 273

self-knowledge
As You Like It **5:** 32, 82, 102, 116, 122, 133, 164
Much Ado about Nothing **8:** 69, 95, 100
Timon of Athens **1:** 456, 459, 462, 495, 503, 507, 515, 518, 526; **20:** 493; **27:** 166

self-love
Sonnets **10:** 372; **25:** 374

Senecan or revenge tragedy elements
  Timon of Athens **27**: 235
  Titus Andronicus **4**: 618, 627, 628, 636, 639, 644, 646, 664, 672, 680; **16**: 225; **27**: 275, 318; **43**: 170, 206, 227

servitude
  See also **freedom and servitude**
  Comedy of Errors **42**: 80

setting
  Much Ado about Nothing **18**: 173, 174, 183, 184, 185, 186, 187, 188, 189, 190, 191, 192, 193, 195, 197, 199, 201, 204, 206, 207, 208, 209, 210, 254
  Richard III **14**: 516, 528
  The Two Gentlemen of Verona **12**: 463, 465, 485

sexual ambiguity and sexual deception
  As You Like It **46**: 134, 142
  Twelfth Night **1**: 540, 562, 620, 621, 639, 645; **22**: 69; **34**: 311, 344; **37**: 59; **42**: 32
  Troilus and Cressida **43**: 365

sexual anxiety
  Macbeth **16**: 328; **20**: 283

sexual politics
  The Merchant of Venice **22**: 3
  The Merry Wives of Windsor **19**: 101; **38**: 307

Sexuality in Shakespeare (Volume 33: 1, 12, 18, 28, 39)
  As You Like It **46**: 122, 127, 134, 142
  All's Well That Ends Well **7**: 67, 86, 90, 93, 98, 126; **13**: 84; **19**: 113; **22**: 78; **28**: 38; **44**: 35
  Coriolanus **9**: 112, 142, 174, 183, 189, 198; **30**: 79, 111, 125, 142
  Cymbeline **4**: 170, 172; **25**: 319; **32**: 373
  King Lear **25**: 202; **31**: 133, 137, 142
  Love's Labour's Lost **22**: 12
  Measure for Measure **13**: 84; **16**: 102, 114; **23**: 321, 327, 335, 340, 352; **25**: 12; **33**: 85, 90, 112
  A Midsummer Night's Dream **22**: 23, 93; **29**: 225, 243, 256, 269; **42**: 46; **45**: 107
  Othello **22**: 339; **28**: 330, 344; **35**: 352, 360; **37**: 269; **44**: 57, 66
  Romeo and Juliet **25**: 181; **33**: 225, 233, 241, 246, 274, 300
  Sonnets **25**: 374
  Troilus and Cressida **22**: 58, 339; **25**: 56; **27**: 362; **43**: 365

Shakespeare and Classical Civilization (Volume 27: 1, 9, 15, 21, 30, 35, 39, 46, 56, 60, 67)
  Antony and Cleopatra
    Egyptian versus Roman values **6**: 31, 33, 43, 53, 104, 111, 115, 125, 142, 155, 159, 178, 181, 211, 219; **17**: 48; **19**: 270; **27**: 82, 121, 126; **28**: 249
  The Rape of Lucrece
    Roman history, relation to **10**: 84, 89, 93, 96, 98, 109, 116, 125, 135; **22**: 289; **25**: 305; **33**: 155, 190
  Timon of Athens **27**: 223, 230, 325
  Titus Andronicus **27**: 275, 282, 293, 299, 306

Roman elements **43**: 206, 222
Troilus and Cressida
  Trojan versus Greek values **3**: 541, 561, 574, 584, 590, 596, 621, 638; **27**: 370

Shakespeare's artistic growth, *Richard III*'s contribution to
  Richard III **8**: 165, 167, 182, 193, 197, 206, 210, 228, 239, 267; **25**: 164; **39**: 305, 326, 370

Shakespeare's canon, place in
  Titus Andronicus **4**: 614, 616, 618, 619, 637, 639, 646, 659, 664, 668; **43**: 195
  Twelfth Night **1**: 543, 548, 557, 569, 575, 580, 621, 635, 638

Shakespeare's dramas, compared with
  The Rape of Lucrece **43**: 92

Shakespeare's moral judgment
  Antony and Cleopatra **6**: 33, 37, 38, 41, 48, 51, 64, 76, 111, 125, 136, 140, 146, 163, 175, 189, 202, 211, 228; **13**: 368, 523; **25**: 257

Shakespeare's political sympathies
  Coriolanus **9**: 8, 11, 15, 17, 19, 26, 39, 52, 53, 62, 80, 92, 142; **25**: 296; **30**: 74, 79, 89, 96, 105, 133
  Richard II **6**: 277, 279, 287, 347, 359, 364, 391, 393, 402
  Richard III **8**: 147, 163, 177, 193, 197, 201, 223, 228, 232, 243, 248, 267; **39**: 349; **42**: 130

Shakespeare's Representation of Women (Volume 31: 1, 3, 8, 12, 16, 21, 29, 34, 35, 41, 43, 48, 53, 60, 68)
  Henry VI, Parts 1, 2, and 3 **3**: 103, 109, 126, 140, 157; **16**: 183; **39**: 196
  King John **9**: 222, 303; **16**: 161; **19**: 182; **41**: 215, 221
  King Lear **31**: 117, 123, 133
  Love's Labour's Lost **19**: 92; **22**: 12; **23**: 215; **25**: 1
  The Merry Wives of Windsor **5**: 335, 341, 343, 349, 369, 379, 390, 392, 402; **19**: 101; **38**: 307
  Much Ado about Nothing **31**: 222, 231, 241, 245
  Othello **19**: 253; **28**: 344
  The Taming of the Shrew **31**: 288, 300, 307, 315
  The Winter's Tale **22**: 324; **36**: 311; **42**: 301

Shakespeare's romances, compared with
  Henry VIII **41**: 171

shame
  Coriolanus **42**: 243

sibling rivalry
  As You Like It **34**: 109
  Henry VI, Parts 1, 2, and 3 **22**: 193

slander or hearsay, importance of
  Much Ado about Nothing **8**: 58, 69, 82, 95, 104

social and moral corruption
  King Lear **2**: 116, 133, 174, 177, 241, 271; **22**: 227; **31**: 84, 92; **46**: 269

social and political context
  All's Well That Ends Well **13**: 66; **22**: 78; **38**: 99, 109, 150, 155

social aspects
  Measure for Measure **23**: 316, 375, 379, 395

social milieu
  The Merry Wives of Windsor **18**: 75, 84; **38**: 297, 300

social order
  As You Like It **37**: 1; **46**: 94
  The Comedy of Errors **34**: 238

society
  Coriolanus **9**: 15, 17, 18, 19, 26, 33, 43, 53, 62, 65, 73, 80, 92, 106, 110, 112, 121, 144, 153, 157, 164, 180; **22**: 248; **25**: 296; **30**: 58, 67, 79, 89, 96, 105, 111, 125
  Troilus and Cressida **43**: 298

songs, role of
  Love's Labour's Lost **2**: 303, 304, 316, 326, 335, 362, 367, 371, 375

sonnet arrangement
  Sonnets **10**: 174, 176, 182, 205, 226, 230, 236, 315, 353; **28**: 363; **40**: 238

sonnet form
  Sonnets **10**: 255, 325, 367; **37**: 347; **40**: 284, 303

source of tragic catastrophe
  Romeo and Juliet **5**: 418, 427, 431, 448, 458, 469, 479, 480, 485, 487, 493, 509, 522, 528, 530, 533, 542, 565, 571, 573; **33**: 210

sources
  Antony and Cleopatra **6**: 20, 39; **19**: 304; **27**: 96, 126; **28**: 249
  As You Like It **5**: 18, 32, 54, 59, 66, 84; **34**: 155; **46**: 117
  The Comedy of Errors **1**: 13, 14, 16, 19, 31, 32, 39; **16**: 3; **34**: 190, 215, 258
  Cymbeline **4**: 17, 18; **13**: 401; **28**: 373
  Hamlet **1**: 76, 81, 113, 125, 128, 130, 151, 191, 202, 224, 259
  Henry VI, Parts 1, 2, and 3 **3**: 18, 21, 29, 31, 35, 39, 46, 51; **13**: 131; **16**: 217; **39**: 196
  Henry VIII **2**: 16, 17; **24**: 71, 80
  Julius Caesar **7**: 149, 150, 156, 187, 200, 264, 272, 282, 284, 320; **30**: 285, 297, 326, 358
  King John **9**: 216, 222, 300; **32**: 93, 114; **41**: 234, 243, 251
  King Lear **2**: 94, 100, 143, 145, 170, 186; **13**: 352; **16**: 351; **28**: 301
  Love's Labour's Lost **16**: 17
  Measure for Measure **2**: 388, 393, 427, 429, 437, 475; **13**: 94
  The Merry Wives of Windsor **5**: 332, 350, 360, 366, 385; **32**: 31
  A Midsummer Night's Dream **29**: 216
  Much Ado about Nothing **8**: 9, 19, 53, 58, 104

Pericles **2**: 538, 568, 572, 575; **25**: 365; **36**: 198, 205
The Phoenix and Turtle **10**: 7, 9, 18, 24, 45; **38**: 326, 334, 350, 367
The Rape of Lucrece **10**: 63, 64, 65, 66, 68, 74, 77, 78, 89, 98, 109, 121, 125; **25**: 305; **33**: 155, 190; **43**: 77, 92, 148
Richard III
   chronicles **8**: 145, 165, 193, 197, 201, 206, 210, 213, 228, 232
   Marlowe, Christopher **8**: 167, 168, 182, 201, 206, 218
   morality plays **8**: 182, 190, 201, 213, 239
   Seneca, other classical writers **8**: 165, 190, 201, 206, 228, 248
Romeo and Juliet **5**: 416, 419, 423, 450; **32**: 222; **33**: 210; **45**: 40
Sonnets **10**: 153, 154, 156, 158, 233, 251, 255, 293, 353; **16**: 472; **28**: 407; **42**: 375
The Taming of the Shrew
   folk tales **9**: 332, 390, 393
   Old and New Comedy **9**: 419
   Ovid **9**: 318, 370, 430
   Plautus **9**: 334, 341, 342
   shrew tradition **9**: 355; **19**: 3; **32**: 1, 56
The Tempest **45**: 226
Timon of Athens **16**: 351; **27**: 191
Troilus and Cressida **3**: 537, 539, 540, 541, 544, 549, 558, 566, 574, 587; **27**: 376, 381, 391, 400
Twelfth Night **1**: 539, 540, 603; **34**: 301, 323, 344; **46**: 291
The Two Gentlemen of Verona **6**: 436, 460, 462, 468, 476, 480, 490, 511, 547; **19**: 34; **40**: 320
The Two Noble Kinsmen **19**: 394; **41**: 289, 301, 363, 385
Venus and Adonis **10**: 410, 412, 420, 424, 429, 434, 439, 451, 454, 466, 473, 480, 486, 489; **16**: 452; **25**: 305; **28**: 355; **33**: 309, 321, 330, 339, 347, 352, 357, 370, 377; **42**: 347

spectacle
Love's Labour's Lost **38**: 226
Macbeth **42**: 258
Pericles **42**: 352

spectacle versus simple staging
The Tempest **15**: 206, 207, 208, 210, 217, 219, 222, 223, 224, 225, 227, 228, 305, 352; **28**: 415

stage history
As You Like It **46**: 117
Antony and Cleopatra **17**: 84, 94, 101
The Merry Wives of Windsor **18**: 66, 67, 68, 70, 71

staging issues
See also **performance issues**
All's Well That Ends Well **19**: 113; **26**: 15, 19, 48, 52, 64, 73, 85, 92, 93, 94, 95, 97, 114, 117, 128
Antony and Cleopatra **17**: 6, 12, 84, 94, 101, 104, 110; **27**: 90
As You Like It **13**: 502; **23**: 7, 17, 19, 22, 58, 96, 97, 98, 99, 101, 110, 137; **28**: 82; **32**: 212
The Comedy of Errors **26**: 182, 183, 186, 188, 190

Coriolanus **17**: 172, 242, 248
Cymbeline **15**: 6, 23, 75, 105, 111, 121, 122; **22**: 365
Hamlet **13**: 494, 502; **21**: 11, 17, 31, 35, 41, 44, 50, 53, 78, 81, 89, 101, 112, 127, 139, 142, 145, 148, 151, 157, 160, 172, 182, 183, 202, 203, 208, 225, 232, 237, 242, 245, 249, 251, 259, 268, 270, 274, 283, 284, 301, 311, 334, 347, 355, 361, 371, 377, 379, 380, 381, 384, 386, 392, 407, 410, 416; **44**: 198
Henry IV, Parts 1 and 2 **32**: 212
Henry V **5**: 186, 189, 192, 193, 198, 205, 226, 230, 241, 281, 314; **13**: 194, 502; **14**: 293, 295, 297, 301, 310, 319, 328, 334, 336, 342; **19**: 217; **32**: 185
Henry VI, Parts 1, 2, and 3 **24**: 21, 22, 27, 31, 32, 36, 38, 41, 45, 48, 55; **32**: 212
Henry VIII **24**: 67, 70, 71, 75, 77, 83, 84, 85, 87, 89, 91, 101, 106, 113, 120, 127, 129, 136, 140, 146, 150, 152, 155; **28**: 184
King John **16**: 161; **19**: 182; **24**: 171, 187, 203, 206, 211, 225, 228, 241, 245, 249
King Lear **11**: 136, 137, 142, 145, 150, 151, 154, 158, 161, 165, 169; **32**: 212; **46**: 205, 218
Love's Labour's Lost **23**: 184, 187, 191, 196, 198, 200, 201, 202, 207, 212, 215, 216, 217, 229, 230, 232, 233, 237, 252
Macbeth **13**: 502; **20**: 12, 17, 32, 64, 65, 70, 73, 107, 113, 151, 175, 203, 206, 210, 213, 245, 279, 283, 312, 318, 324, 329, 343, 345, 350, 353, 363, 367, 374, 376, 379, 382, 387, 400, 406, 413; **22**: 365; **32**: 212
Measure for Measure **2**: 427, 429, 437, 441, 443, 456, 460, 482, 491, 519; **23**: 283, 284, 285, 286, 287, 291, 293, 294, 298, 299, 311, 315, 327, 338, 339, 340, 342, 344, 347, 363, 372, 375, 395, 400, 405, 406, 413; **32**: 16
The Merchant of Venice **12**: 111, 114, 115, 117, 119, 124, 129, 131
The Merry Wives of Windsor **18**: 74, 75, 84, 86, 90, 95
A Midsummer Night's Dream **3**: 364, 365, 371, 372, 377; **12**: 151, 152, 154, 158, 159, 280, 284, 291, 295; **16**: 34; **19**: 21; **29**: 183, 256
Much Ado about Nothing **8**: 18, 33, 41, 75, 79, 82, 108; **16**: 45; **18**: 245, 247, 249, 252, 254, 257, 261, 264; **28**: 63
Othello **11**: 273, 334, 335, 339, 342, 350, 354, 359, 362
Pericles **16**: 399
Richard II **13**: 494; **24**: 273, 274, 278, 279, 280, 283, 291, 295, 296, 301, 303, 304, 310, 315, 317, 320, 325, 333, 338, 346, 351, 352, 356, 364, 383, 386, 395, 402, 405, 411, 414, 419, 423, 428; **25**: 89
Richard III **14**: 515, 527, 528, 537; **16**: 137
Romeo and Juliet **11**: 499, 505, 507, 514, 517; **13**: 243; **25**: 181; **32**: 212
The Tempest **15**: 343, 346, 352, 361, 364, 366, 368, 371, 385; **28**: 391, 415; **29**: 339; **32**: 338, 343; **42**: 332; **45**: 200
Timon of Athens **20**: 445, 446, 481, 491, 492, 493
Titus Andronicus **17**: 449, 452, 456, 487; **25**: 245; **32**: 212, 249
Troilus and Cressida **16**: 70; **18**: 289, 332, 371, 395, 403, 406, 412, 419, 423, 442, 447, 451

Twelfth Night **26**: 219, 233, 257, 337, 342, 346, 357, 359, 360, 364, 366, 371, 374; **46**: 310, 369
The Two Gentlemen of Verona **12**: 457, 464; **42**: 18
The Winter's Tale **7**: 414, 425, 429, 446, 464, 480, 483, 497; **13**: 409; **15**: 518

structure
All's Well That Ends Well **7**: 21, 29, 32, 45, 51, 76, 81, 93, 98, 116; **22**: 78; **26**: 128; **38**: 72, 123, 142
As You Like It **5**: 19, 24, 25, 35, 44, 45, 46, 86, 93, 116, 138, 158; **23**: 7, 8, 9, 10, 11; **34**: 72, 78, 131, 147, 155
Coriolanus **9**: 8, 9, 11, 12, 13, 14, 16, 26, 33, 45, 53, 58, 72, 78, 80, 84, 92, 112, 139, 148; **25**: 263; **30**: 79, 96
Hamlet **22**: 378; **28**: 280, 325; **35**: 82, 104, 215; **44**: 152
Henry V **5**: 186, 189, 205, 213, 230, 241, 264, 289, 310, 314; **30**: 220, 227, 234, 244
Henry VI, Parts 1, 2, and 3 **3**: 31, 43, 46, 69, 83, 103, 109, 119, 136, 149, 154; **39**: 213
Henry VIII **2**: 16, 25, 27, 28, 31, 36, 44, 46, 51, 56, 68, 75; **24**: 106, 112, 113, 120
Julius Caesar **7**: 152, 155, 159, 160, 179, 200, 210, 238, 264, 284, 298, 316, 346; **13**: 252; **30**: 374
King John **9**: 208, 212, 222, 224, 229, 240, 244, 245, 254, 260, 263, 275, 284, 290, 292, 300; **24**: 228, 241; **41**: 260, 269, 277
King Lear **28**: 325; **32**: 308; **46**: 177
Love's Labour's Lost **22**: 378; **23**: 191, 237, 252; **38**: 163, 172
Macbeth **16**: 317; **20**: 12, 245
Measure for Measure **2**: 390, 411, 449, 456, 466, 474, 482, 490, 491; **33**: 69
The Merchant of Venice **4**: 201, 215, 230, 232, 243, 247, 254, 261, 263, 308, 321; **12**: 115; **28**: 63
The Merry Wives of Windsor **5**: 332, 333, 334, 335, 343, 349, 355, 369, 374; **18**: 86; **22**: 378
A Midsummer Night's Dream **3**: 364, 368, 381, 402, 406, 427, 450, 513; **13**: 19; **22**: 378; **29**: 175; **45**: 126, 175
Much Ado about Nothing **8**: 9, 16, 17, 19, 28, 29, 33, 39, 48, 63, 69, 73, 75, 79, 82, 115; **31**: 178, 184, 198, 231
Othello **22**: 378; **28**: 325
The Phoenix and Turtle **10**: 27, 31, 37, 45, 50; **38**: 342, 345, 357
The Rape of Lucrece **10**: 84, 89, 93, 98, 135; **22**: 294; **25**: 305; **43**: 102, 141
Richard II **6**: 282, 304, 317, 343, 352, 359, 364, 39; **24**: 307, 322, 325, 356, 395
Richard III **8**: 154, 161, 163, 167, 168, 170, 177, 184, 193, 197, 201, 206, 210, 218, 223, 228, 232, 243, 252, 262, 267; **16**: 150
Romeo and Juliet **5**: 438, 448, 464, 469, 470, 477, 480, 496, 518, 524, 525, 528, 547, 559; **33**: 210, 246
Sonnets **10**: 175, 176, 182, 205, 230, 260, 296, 302, 309, 315, 337, 349, 353; **40**: 238
The Taming of the Shrew **9**: 318, 322, 325, 332, 334, 341, 362, 370, 390, 426; **22**: 48, 378; **31**: 269
The Tempest **8**: 294, 295, 299, 320, 384, 439; **28**: 391, 415; **29**: 292, 297; **45**: 188

Timon of Athens **27**: 157, 175, 235
Titus Andronicus **4**: 618, 619, 624, 631, 635, 640, 644, 646, 647, 653, 656, 659, 662, 664, 668, 672; **27**: 246, 285
Troilus and Cressida **3**: 536, 538, 549, 568, 569, 578, 583, 589, 611, 613; **27**: 341, 347, 354, 391
Twelfth Night **1**: 539, 542, 543, 546, 551, 553, 563, 570, 571, 590, 600, 660; **26**: 374; **34**: 281, 287; **46**: 286
The Two Gentlemen of Verona **6**: 445, 450, 460, 462, 504, 526
The Two Noble Kinsmen **37**: 313
Venus and Adonis **10**: 434, 442, 480, 486, 489; **33**: 357, 377

style
Henry VIII **41**: 158
The Phoenix and Turtle **10**: 8, 20, 24, 27, 31, 35, 45, 50; **38**: 334, 345, 357
The Rape of Lucrece **10**: 64, 65, 66, 68, 69, 70, 71, 73, 74, 77, 78, 81, 84, 98, 116, 131, 135; **43**: 113, 158
Venus and Adonis **10**: 411, 412, 414, 415, 416, 418, 419, 420, 423, 424, 428, 429, 439, 442, 480, 486, 489; **16**: 452

subjectivity
Hamlet **45**: 28
Sonnets **37**: 374

substitution of identities
Measure for Measure **2**: 507, 511, 519; **13**: 112

subversiveness
Cymbeline **22**: 302
The Tempest **22**: 302
The Winter's Tale **22**: 302

suffering
King Lear **2**: 137, 160, 188, 201, 218, 222, 226, 231, 238, 241, 249, 265; **13**: 343; **22**: 271; **25**: 218
Pericles **2**: 546, 573, 578, 579; **25**: 365; **36**: 279

symbolism
The Winter's Tale **7**: 425, 429, 436, 452, 456, 469, 490, 493

textual arrangement
Henry VI, Parts 1, 2, and 3 **24**: 3, 4, 6, 12, 17, 18, 19, 20, 21, 24, 27, 42, 45; **37**: 165
Richard II **24**: 260, 261, 262, 263, 271, 273, 291, 296, 356, 390

textual issues
Henry IV, Parts 1 and 2 **22**: 114
King Lear **22**: 271; **37**: 295
A Midsummer Night's Dream **16**: 34; **29**: 216
The Taming of the Shrew **22**: 48; **31**: 261, 276; **31**: 276
The Winter's Tale **19**: 441; **45**: 333

textual problems
Henry V **5**: 187, 189, 190; **13**: 201

textual revisions
Pericles **15**: 129, 130, 132, 134, 135, 136, 138, 152, 155, 167, 181; **16**: 399; **25**: 365

textual variants
Hamlet **13**: 282; **16**: 259; **21**: 11, 23, 72, 101, 127, 129, 139, 140, 142, 145, 202, 208, 259, 270, 284, 347, 361, 384; **22**: 258; **32**: 238

theatrical viability
Henry VI, Parts 1, 2, and 3 **24**: 31, 32, 34

theatricality
Macbeth **16**: 328
Measure for Measure **23**: 285, 286, 294, 372, 406

thematic disparity
Henry VIII **2**: 25, 31, 56, 68, 75; **41**: 146

time
As You Like It **5**: 18, 82, 112, 141; **23**: 146, 150; **34**: 102; **46**: 88, 156, 164, 169
Macbeth **3**: 234, 246, 283, 293; **20**: 245
Richard II **22**: 137
Sonnets **10**: 265, 302, 309, 322, 329, 337, 360, 379; **13**: 445; **40**: 292
The Tempest **8**: 401, 439, 464; **25**: 357; **29**: 278, 292; **45**: 236
Troilus and Cressida **3**: 561, 571, 583, 584, 613, 621, 626, 634
Twelfth Night **37**: 78; **46**: 297
The Winter's Tale **7**: 397, 425, 436, 476, 490; **19**: 366; **36**: 301, 349; **45**: 297, 329, 366, 374

time and change, motif of
Henry IV, Parts 1 and 2 **1**: 372, 393, 411; **39**: 89
As You Like It **46**: 156, 164, 169

time scheme
Othello **4**: 370, 384, 390, 488; **22**: 207; **35**: 310

topical allusions or content
Hamlet **13**: 282
Henry V **5**: 185, 186; **13**: 201
Love's Labour's Lost **2**: 300, 303, 307, 315, 316, 317, 319, 321, 327, 328; **23**: 187, 191, 197, 203, 221, 233, 237, 252; **25**: 1
Macbeth **13**: 361; **20**: 17, 350; **29**: 101

traditional values
Richard III **39**: 335

tragedies of major characters
Henry VIII **2**: 16, 39, 46, 48, 49, 51, 56, 58, 68, 81; **41**: 120

tragic elements
The Comedy of Errors **1**: 16, 25, 27, 45, 50, 59; **34**: 229
Cymbeline **25**: 319; **28**: 373; **36**: 129
Henry V **5**: 228, 233, 267, 269, 271
King John **9**: 208, 209, 244
A Midsummer Night's Dream **3**: 393, 400, 401, 410, 445, 474, 480, 491, 498, 511; **29**: 175; **45**: 169

The Rape of Lucrece **10**: 78, 80, 81, 84, 98, 109; **43**: 85, 148
The Tempest **8**: 324, 348, 359, 370, 380, 408, 414, 439, 458, 464
Twelfth Night **1**: 557, 569, 572, 575, 580, 599, 621, 635, 638, 639, 645, 654, 656; **26**: 342

treachery
Coriolanus **30**: 89
King John **9**: 245

treason and punishment
Macbeth **13**: 361; **16**: 328

trickster, motif of
Cymbeline **22**: 302
The Tempest **22**: 302; **29**: 297
The Winter's Tale **22**: 302; **45**: 333

triumph over death or fate
Romeo and Juliet **5**: 421, 423, 427, 505, 509, 520, 530, 536, 565, 566

Trojan War
Troilus and Cressida as myth **43**: 293

The Troublesome Reign (anonymous), compared with
King John **41**: 205, 221, 260, 269

Troy
Troilus and Cressida **43**: 287

Troy passage
The Rape of Lucrece **43**: 77, 85

Tudor doctrine
King John **9**: 254, 284, 297; **41**: 221

Tudor myth
Henry VI, Parts 1, 2, and 3 **3**: 51, 59, 77, 92, 100, 109, 115, 119, 131; **39**: 222
Richard III **8**: 163, 165, 177, 184, 193, 201, 218, 228, 232, 243, 248, 252, 267; **39**: 305, 308, 326, 387; **42**: 130

Turkish elements
Henry IV, Parts 1 and 2 **19**: 170
Henry V **19**: 170

two fathers
Henry IV, Parts 1 and 2 **14**: 86, 101, 105, 108; **39**: 89, 100

tyranny
King John **9**: 218

unity
Antony and Cleopatra **6**: 20, 21, 22, 24, 25, 32, 33, 39, 43, 53, 60, 67, 111, 125, 146, 151, 165, 208, 211, 219; **13**: 374; **27**: 82, 90, 135
Hamlet **1**: 75, 76, 87, 103, 113, 125, 128, 142, 148, 160, 184, 188, 198, 264; **16**: 259; **35**: 82, 215
Henry VI, Parts 1, 2, and 3 **39**: 177, 222

A Midsummer Night's Dream **3**: 364, 368, 381, 402, 406, 427, 450, 513; **13**: 19; **22**: 378; **29**: 175, 263

unity of double plot
The Merchant of Venice **4**: 193, 194, 201, 232; **12**: 16, 67, 80, 115; **40**: 151

unnatural ordering
Hamlet **22**: 378
Love's Labour's Lost **22**: 378
The Merry Wives of Windsor **22**: 378
A Midsummer Night's Dream **22**: 378
Othello **22**: 378

as unsuccessful play
Measure for Measure **2**: 397, 441, 474, 482; **23**: 287

usurpation
See also **rebellion**
Richard II **6**: 263, 264, 272, 287, 289, 315, 323, 331, 343, 354, 364, 381, 388, 393, 397; **24**: 383
The Tempest **8**: 304, 370, 408, 420; **25**: 357, 382; **29**: 278, 362, 377; **37**: 336

utopia
The Tempest **45**: 280

value systems
Troilus and Cressida **3**: 578, 583, 589, 602, 613, 617; **13**: 53; **27**: 370, 396, 400

Venetian politics
Othello **32**: 294

Venice, Elizabethan perceptions of
The Merchant of Venice **28**: 249; **32**: 294; **40**: 127

Venus and Adonis
The Rape of Lucrece **43**: 148

Vergil, influence of
Titus Andronicus **27**: 306; **28**: 249

verisimilitude
As You Like It **5**: 18, 23, 28, 30, 32, 39, 125; **23**: 107

Verona society
Romeo and Juliet **5**: 556, 566; **13**: 235; **33**: 255

Violence in Shakespeare's Works (Volume 43: 1, 12, 24, 32, 39, 61)
Henry IV, Parts 1 and 2 **25**: 109
Henry VI, Parts 1, 2, and 3 **24**: 25, 31; **37**: 157
Love's Labour's Lost **22**: 12
Macbeth **20**: 273, 279, 283; **45**: 58
Othello **22**: 12
The Rape of Lucrece **43**: 148, 158
Titus Andronicus **13**: 225; **25**: 245; **27**: 255; **28**: 249; **32**: 249, 265; **43**: 186, 203, 227, 239, 247, 255, 262
Troilus and Cressida **43**: 329, 340, 351, 357, 365, 377

virginity or chastity, importance of
Much Ado about Nothing **8**: 44, 75, 95, 111, 121, 125; **31**: 222

visual arts, relation to
Sonnets **28**: 407

visual humor
Love's Labour's Lost **23**: 207, 217

war
Coriolanus **25**: 263; **30**: 79, 96, 125, 149
Henry V **5**: 193, 195, 197, 198, 210, 213, 219, 230, 233, 246, 281, 293; **28**: 121, 146; **30**: 262; **32**: 126; **37**: 175, 187; **42**: 141

Wars of the Roses
Richard III **8**: 163, 165, 177, 184, 193, 201, 218, 228, 232, 243, 248, 252, 267; **39**: 308

Watteau, influence on staging
Love's Labour's Lost **23**: 184, 186

wealth
The Merchant of Venice **4**: 209, 261, 270, 273, 317; **12**: 80, 117; **22**: 69; **25**: 22; **28**: 249; **40**: 117, 197, 208; **45**: 17

wealth and social class
Timon of Athens **1**: 466, 487, 495; **25**: 198; **27**: 184, 196, 212

wheel of fortune, motif of
Antony and Cleopatra **6**: 25, 178; **19**: 304
Henry VIII **2**: 27, 65, 72, 81

widowhood and remarriage, themes of
Hamlet **32**: 238

wisdom
King Lear **37**: 213; **46**: 210

wit
The Merry Wives of Windsor **5**: 335, 336, 337, 339, 343, 351
Much Ado about Nothing **8**: 27, 29, 38, 69, 79, 91, 95; **31**: 178, 191

witchcraft
See **Magic and the Supernatural**

women, role of
See **Shakespeare's Representation of Women**

wonder, dynamic of
The Comedy of Errors **37**: 12

wordplay
As You Like It **46**: 105
Romeo and Juliet **32**: 256

written versus oral communication
Love's Labour's Lost **2**: 359, 365; **28**: 63

youth
The Two Gentlemen of Verona **6**: 439, 450, 464, 514, 568

youth versus age
All's Well That Ends Well **7**: 9, 45, 58, 62, 76, 81, 86, 93, 98, 104, 116, 126; **26**: 117; **38**: 109

Cumulative Topic Index, by Play

The Cumulative Topic Index, by Play identifies the principal topics of discussion in the criticism of each play and non-dramatic poem. The topics are arranged alphabetically by play. Page references indicate the beginning page number of each essay containing substantial commentary on that topic. A parenthetical reference after a play indicates which volumes discuss the play extensively.

All's Well That Ends Well (Volumes 7, 26, 38)

   appearance versus reality **7**: 37, 76, 93; **26**: 117
   audience perspective **7**: 81, 104, 109, 116, 121
   bed-trick **7**: 8, 26, 27, 29, 32, 41, 86, 93, 98, 113, 116, 126; **13**: 84; **26**: 117; **28**: 38; **38**: 65, 118
   Bertram
      characterization **7**: 15, 27, 29, 32, 39, 41, 43, 98, 113; **26**: 48; **26**: 117
      conduct **7**: 9, 10, 12, 16, 19, 21, 51, 62, 104
      desire **22**: 78
      transformation or redemption **7**: 10, 19, 21, 26, 29, 32, 54, 62, 81, 90, 93, 98, 109, 113, 116, 126; **13**: 84
   comic elements **26**: 97, 114
   dark elements **7**: 27, 37, 39, 43, 54, 109, 113, 116; **26**: 85
   Decameron (Boccaccio), compared with **7**: 29, 43
   desire **38**: 99, 109, 118
   displacement **22**: 78
   education **7**: 62, 86, 90, 93, 98, 104, 116, 126
   elder characters **7**: 9, 37, 39, 43, 45, 54, 62, 104
   conclusion **38**: 123, 132, 142
   gender issues **7**: 9, 10, 67, 126; **13**: 77, 84; **19**: 113; **26**: 128; **38**: 89, 99, 118; **44**: 35
   Helena
      as agent of reconciliation, renewal, or grace **7**: 67, 76, 81, 90, 93, 98, 109, 116
      as dualistic or enigmatic character **7**: 15, 27, 29, 39, 54, 58, 62, 67, 76, 81, 98, 113, 126; **13**: 66; **22**: 78; **26**: 117
      as "female achiever" **19**: 113; **38**: 89
      desire **38**: 96; **44**: 35

      pursuit of Bertram **7**: 9, 12, 15, 16, 19, 21, 26, 27, 29, 32, 43, 54, 76, 116; **13**: 77; **22**: 78
   virginity **38**: 65
   virtue and nobility **7**: 9, 10, 12, 16, 19, 21, 27, 32, 41, 51, 58, 67, 76, 86, 126; **13**: 77
   implausibility of plot, characters, or events **7**: 8, 45
   irony, paradox, and ambiguity **7**: 27, 32, 58, 62, 67, 81, 86, 109, 116
   King **38**: 150
   language and imagery **7**: 12, 29, 45, 104, 109, 121; **38**: 132
   Lavatch **26**: 64; **46**: 33, 52, 68
   love **7**: 12, 15, 16, 51, 58, 67, 90, 93, 116; **38**: 80
   merit versus rank **7**: 9, 10, 19, 37, 51, 76; **38**: 155
   "mingled yarn" **7**: 62, 93, 109, 126; **38**: 65
   morality plays, influence of **7**: 29, 41, 51, 98, 113; **13**: 66
   Parolles
      characterization **7**: 8, 9, 43, 76, 81, 98, 109, 113, 116, 126; **22**: 78; **26**: 48, 73, 97; **26**: 117; **46**: 68
      exposure **7**: 9, 27, 81, 98, 109, 113, 116, 121, 126
      Falstaff, compared with **7**: 8, 9, 16
   reconciliation **7**: 90, 93, 98
   religious, mythic, or spiritual content **7**: 15, 45, 54, 67, 76, 98, 109, 116
   romance or folktale elements **7**: 32, 41, 43, 45, 54, 76, 104, 116, 121; **26**: 117
   sexuality **7**: 67, 86, 90, 93, 98, 126; **13**: 84; **19**: 113; **22**: 78; **28**: 38; **44**: 35
   social and political context **13**: 66; **22**: 78; **38**: 99, 109, 150, 155

   staging issues **19**: 113; **26**: 15, 19, 48, 52, 64, 73, 85, 92, 93, 94, 95, 97, 114, 117, 128
   structure **7**: 21, 29, 32, 45, 51, 76, 81, 93, 98, 116; **22**: 78; **26**: 128; **38**: 72, 123, 142
   youth versus age **7**: 9, 45, 58, 62, 76, 81, 86, 93, 98, 104, 116, 126; **26**: 117; **38**: 109

Antony and Cleopatra (Volumes 6, 17, 27)

   All for Love (John Dryden), compared with **6**: 20, 21; **17**: 12, 94, 101
   ambiguity **6**: 53, 111, 161, 163, 180, 189, 208, 211, 228; **13**: 368
   androgyny **13**: 530
   Antony
      characterization **6**: 22, 23, 24, 31, 38, 41, 172, 181, 211; **16**: 342; **19**: 270; **22**: 217; **27**: 117
      Cleopatra, relationship with **6**: 25, 27, 37, 39, 48, 52, 53, 62, 67, 71, 76, 85, 100, 125, 131, 133, 136, 142, 151, 161, 163, 165, 180, 192; **27**: 82
      death scene **25**: 245
      dotage **6**: 22, 23, 38, 41, 48, 52, 62, 107, 136, 146, 175; **17**: 28
      nobility **6**: 22, 24, 33, 48, 94, 103, 136, 142, 159, 172, 202; **25**: 245
      political conduct **6**: 33, 38, 53, 107, 111, 146, 181
      public versus private personae **6**: 165
      self-knowledge **6**: 120, 131, 175, 181, 192
      as superhuman figure **6**: 37, 51, 71, 92, 94, 178, 192; **27**: 110
      as tragic hero **6**: 38, 39, 52, 53, 60, 104, 120, 151, 155, 165, 178, 192, 202, 211; **22**: 217; **27**: 90

459

Cleopatra
- Antony, relationship with **6:** 25, 27, 37, 39, 48, 52, 53, 62, 67, 71, 76, 85, 100, 125, 131, 133, 136, 142, 151, 161, 163, 165, 180, 192; **25:** 257; **27:** 82
- contradictory or inconsistent nature **6:** 23, 24, 27, 67, 76, 100, 104, 115, 136, 151, 159, 202; **17:** 94, 113; **27:** 135
- costume **17:** 94
- creativity **6:** 197
- death, decay, and nature's destructiveness **6:** 23, 25, 27, 41, 43, 52, 60, 64, 76, 94, 100, 103, 120, 131, 133, 136, 140, 146, 161, 165, 180, 181, 192, 197, 208; **13:** 383; **17:** 48, 94; **25:** 245; **27:** 135
- personal attraction of **6:** 24, 38, 40, 43, 48, 53, 76, 104, 115, 155; **17:** 113
- staging issues **17:** 94, 113
- as subverter of social order **6:** 146, 165
- as superhuman figure **6:** 37, 51, 71, 92, 94, 178, 192; **27:** 110
- as tragic heroine **6:** 53, 120, 151, 192, 208; **27:** 144
- as voluptuary or courtesan **6:** 21, 22, 25, 41, 43, 52, 53, 62, 64, 67, 76, 146, 161

comic elements **6:** 52, 85, 104, 125, 131, 151, 192, 202, 219
contemptus mundi **6:** 85, 133
dreams **45:** 28
dualisms **19:** 304; **27:** 82
Egyptian versus Roman values **6:** 31, 33, 43, 53, 104, 111, 115, 125, 142, 155, 159, 178, 181, 211, 219; **17:** 48; **19:** 270; **27:** 82, 121, 126; **28:** 249
Enobarbus **6:** 22, 23, 27, 43, 94, 120, 142; **16:** 342; **17:** 36; **22:** 217; **27:** 135
gender issues **13:** 368; **25:** 257; **27:** 144
irony or paradox **6:** 53, 136, 146, 151, 159, 161, 189, 192, 211, 224
language and imagery **6:** 21, 25, 39, 64, 80, 85, 92, 94, 100, 104, 142, 146, 155, 159, 161, 165, 189, 192, 202, 211; **13:** 374, 383; **25:** 245, 257; **27:** 96, 105, 135
love and passion **6:** 51, 64, 71, 80, 85, 100, 115, 159, 165, 180; **25:** 257; **27:** 126
monument scene **13:** 374; **16:** 342; **17:** 104, 110; **22:** 217
moral relativism **22:** 217; **27:** 121
mythological allusions **16:** 342; **19:** 304; **27:** 110, 117
Octavius **6:** 22, 24, 31, 38, 43, 53, 62, 107, 125, 146, 178, 181, 219; **25:** 257
political and social disintegration **6:** 31, 43, 53, 60, 71, 80, 100, 107, 111, 146; 180, 197, 219; **22:** 217; **25:** 257; **27:** 121
reason versus imagination **6:** 107, 115, 142, 197, 228; **45:** 28
reconciliation **6:** 100, 103, 125, 131, 159, 181
religious, mythic, or spiritual content **6:** 53, 94, 111, 115, 178, 192, 224
royalty **6:** 94
Seleucus episode (Act V, scene ii) **6:** 39, 41, 62, 133, 140, 151; **27:** 135
Shakespeare's major tragedies, compared with **6:** 25, 53, 60, 71, 120, 181, 189, 202; **22:** 217
Shakespeare's moral judgment **6:** 33, 37, 38, 41, 48, 51, 64, 76, 111, 125, 136, 140, 146, 163, 175, 189, 202, 211, 228; **13:** 368, 523; **25:** 257
sources **6:** 20, 39; **19:** 304; **27:** 96, 126; **28:** 249
stage history **17:** 84, 94, 101
staging issues **17:** 6, 12, 84, 94, 101, 104, 110; **27:** 90
unity **6:** 20, 21, 22, 24, 25, 32, 33, 39, 43, 53, 60, 67, 111, 125, 146, 151, 165, 208, 211, 219; **13:** 374; **27:** 82, 90, 135
wheel of fortune, motif of **6:** 25, 178; **19:** 304

As You Like It (Volumes 5, 23, 34, 46)
Appearance versus Reality **46:** 105
androgyny **23:** 98, 100, 122, 138, 143, 144; **34:** 172, 177; **46:** 134
anti-romantic elements **34:** 72
aristocracy **34:** 120
art versus nature **5:** 128, 130, 148; **34:** 147
Audrey **46:** 122
autobiographical elements **5:** 25, 35, 43, 50, 55, 61
bawdy elements **46:** 122
Celia **46:** 94
characterization **5:** 19, 24, 25, 36, 39, 54, 82, 86, 116, 148; **34:** 72
Christian elements **5:** 39, 98, 162
contradiction, paradox, and opposition **46:** 105
comic form **46:** 105
corruption in society **46:** 94
costume **46:** 117
courtship and marriage **34:** 109, 177
death, decay, nature's destructiveness **46:** 169
deception, disguise, and duplicity **46:** 134
desire **37:** 43
domestic elements **46:** 142
dramatic shortcomings or failure **5:** 19, 42, 52, 61, 65
duration of time **5:** 44, 45
Elizabethan culture, relation to **5:** 21, 59, 66, 68, 70, 158; **16:** 53; **28:** 46; **34:** 120; **37:** 1; **46:** 142
Fathers and Daughters **46:** 94
feminism **23:** 107, 108
Forest of Arden
- as "bitter" Arcadia **5:** 98, 118, 162; **23:** 97, 98, 99, 100, 122, 139
- Duke Frederick's court, contrast with **5:** 46, 102, 103, 112, 130, 156; **16:** 53; **23:** 126, 128, 129, 131, 134; **34:** 78, 102, 131; **46:** 164
- pastoral elements **5:** 18, 20, 24, 32, 35, 47, 50, 54, 55, 57, 60, 77, 128, 135, 156; **23:** 17, 20, 27, 46, 137; **34:** 78, 147; **46:** 88
- as patriarchal society **5:** 168; **23:** 150; **34:** 177
- as source of self-knowledge **5:** 98, 102, 103, 128, 130, 135, 148, 158, 162; **23:** 17; **34:** 102
- as timeless, mythical world **5:** 112, 130, 141; **23:** 132; **34:** 78; **37:** 43; **46:** 88
- theme of play **46:** 88
gender identity **46:** 127, 134,
genre **5:** 46, 55, 79
homoerotic elements **46:** 127, 142
homosexuality **46:** 127, 142
Hymen episode **5:** 61, 116, 130; **23:** 22, 48, 54, 109, 111, 112, 113, 115, 146, 147

irony **5:** 30, 32, 154
Jaques
- love-theme, relation to **5:** 103; **23:** 7, 37, 118, 128
- as malcontent **5:** 59, 70, 84
- melancholy **5:** 20, 28, 32, 36, 39, 43, 50, 59, 63, 68, 77, 82, 86, 135; **23:** 20, 26, 103, 104, 107, 109; **34:** 85; **46:** 88, 94
- pastoral convention, relation to **5:** 61, 63, 65, 79, 93, 98, 114, 118
- Seven Ages of Man speech (Act II, scene vii) **5:** 28, 52, 156; **23:** 48, 103, 105, 126, 138, 152; **46:** 88, 156, 164, 169
- Shakespeare, relation to **5:** 35, 50, 154
- as superficial critic **5:** 28, 30, 43, 54, 55, 63, 65, 68, 75, 77, 82, 86, 88, 98, 138; **34:** 85
justice **46:** 94
juxtaposition of opposing perspectives **5:** 86, 93, 98, 141; **16:** 53; **23:** 119; **34:** 72, 78, 131
language and imagery **5:** 19, 21, 35, 52, 75, 82, 92, 138; **23:** 15, 21, 26; **28:** 9; **34:** 131; **37:** 43
love **5:** 24, 44, 46, 57, 79, 88, 103, 116, 122, 138, 141, 162; **28:** 46, 82; **34:** 85
Love in a Forest (Charles Johnson adaptation) **23:** 7, 8, 9, 10
male/female relationships
metadramatic elements **5:** 128, 130, 146; **34:** 130
mythological allusions **46:** 142
nature **46:** 94
Neoclassical rules **5:** 19, 20
Orlando
- as ideal man **5:** 32, 36, 39, 162; **34:** 161; **46:** 94
- as younger brother **5:** 66, 158; **46:** 94
pastoral characters (Silvius, Phebe, and Corin) **23:** 37, 97, 98, 99, 108, 110, 118, 122, 138; **34:** 147
pastoral convention, parodies of **5:** 54, 57, 72
pastoral convention, relation to **5:** 72, 77, 122; **34:** 161; **37:** 1
primogeniture **5:** 66, 158; **34:** 109, 120
psychoanalytic interpretation **5:** 146, 158; **23:** 141, 142; **34:** 109
public versus private worlds **46:** 164
reconciliation of opposites **5:** 79, 88, 103, 116, 122, 138; **23:** 127, 143; **34:** 161, 172; **46:** 156
as romance **5:** 55, 79; **23:** 27, 28, 40, 43
Rosalind **46:** 94, 122,
- Beatrice, compared with **5:** 26, 36, 50, 75
- charm **5:** 55, 75; **23:** 17, 18, 20, 41, 89, 111
- disguise, role of **5:** 75, 107, 118, 122, 128, 130, 133, 138, 141, 146, 148, 164, 168; **13:** 502; **23:** 35, 42, 106, 119, 123, 146; **34:** 130; **46:** 134
- femininity **5:** 26, 36, 52, 75; **23:** 24, 29, 46, 54, 103, 108, 121, 146
- as Ganymede **5:** 127, 142
- love-theme, relation to **5:** 79, 88, 103, 116, 122, 138, 141; **23:** 114, 115; **34:** 85, 177
rustic characters **5:** 24, 60, 72, 84; **23:** 127; **34:** 78, 161
sexual ambiguity and sexual deception **46:** 134, 142
Sexuality in Shakespeare **46:** 122, 127, 134, 142

as satire or parody of pastoral conventions **5**: 46, 55, 60, 72, 77, 79, 84, 114, 118, 128, 130, 154
self-knowledge **5**: 32, 82, 102, 116, 122, 133, 164
sibling rivalry **34**: 109
social order **37**: 1; **46**: 94
sources **5**: 18, 32, 54, 59, 66, 84; **34**: 155; **46**: 117
stage history **46**: 117
staging issues **13**: 502; **23**: 7, 17, 19, 22, 58, 96, 97, 98, 99, 101, 110, 137; **28**: 82; **32**: 212
structure **5**: 19, 24, 25, 35, 44, 45, 46, 86, 93, 116, 138, 158; **23**: 7, 8, 9, 10, 11; **34**: 72, 78, 131, 147, 155
time **5**: 18, 82, 112, 141; **23**: 146, 150; **34**: 102; **46**: 88, 156, 164, 169
Touchstone
   callousness **5**: 88
   comic and farcical elements **46**: 117
   as philosopher-fool **5**: 24, 28, 30, 32, 36, 63, 75, 98; **23**: 152; **34**: 85; **46**: 1, 14, 18, 24, 33, 52, 60, 88, 105,
   relation to pastoral convention **5**: 54, 61, 63, 72, 75, 77, 79, 84, 86, 93, 98, 114, 118, 135, 138, 166; **34**: 72, 147, 161
   selflessness **5**: 30, 36, 39, 76
verisimilitude **5**: 18, 23, 28, 30, 32, 39, 125; **23**: 107
wordplay **46**: 105

The Comedy of Errors (Volumes 1, 26, 34)

Adriana **16**: 3; **34**: 211, 220, 238
adultery **34**: 215
audience perception **1**: 37, 50, 56; **19**: 54; **34**: 258
autobiographical elements **1**: 16, 18
characterization **1**: 13, 21, 31, 34, 46, 49, 50, 55, 56; **19**: 54; **25**: 63; **34**: 194, 201, 208, 245
classical influence and sources **1**: 13, 14, 16, 31, 32, 43, 61
comic elements **1**: 43, 46, 55, 56, 59; **26**: 183, 186, 188, 190; **34**: 190, 245
composition date **1**: 18, 23, 34, 55
dramatic structure **1**: 19, 27, 40, 43, 46, 50; **26**: 186, 190; **34**: 190, 229, 233; **37**: 12
Elizabethan culture, relation to **26**: 138, 142; **34**: 201, 215, 233, 238, 258; **42**: 80
Dromio brothers **42**: 80
farcical elements **1**: 14, 16, 19, 23, 30, 34, 35, 46, 50, 59, 61; **19**: 54; **26**: 188, 190; **34**: 245
feminist criticism **42**: 93
food, meaning of **34**: 220
gender issues **34**: 215, 220
genre **34**: 251, 258
identity **34**: 201, 208, 211
illusion **1**: 13, 14, 27, 37, 40, 45, 59, 63; **26**: 188; **34**: 194, 211
language and imagery **1**: 16, 25, 39, 40, 43, 57, 59; **34**: 233
male/female relationships **16**: 3
marriage **34**: 251
mistaken identity **1**: 13, 14, 27, 37, 40, 45, 49, 55, 57, 61, 63; **19**: 34, 54; **25**: 63; **34**: 194
Plautus's works, compared with **1**: 13, 14, 16, 53, 61; **16**: 3; **19**: 34

problem comedy **34**: 251
redemption **19**: 54; **26**: 188
romantic elements **1**: 13, 16, 19, 23, 25, 30, 31, 36, 39, 53
servitude **42**: 80
social order **34**: 238
sources **1**: 13, 14, 16, 19, 31, 32, 39; **16**: 3; **34**: 190, 215, 258
staging issues **26**: 182, 183, 186, 188, 190
supernatural, role of **1**: 27, 30
tragic elements **1**: 16, 25, 27, 45, 50, 59; **34**: 229
wonder, dynamic of **37**: 12

Coriolanus (9, 17, 30)

aggression **9**: 112, 142, 174, 183, 189, 198; **30**: 79, 111, 125, 142; **44**: 11, 79
Anthony and Cleopatra, compared with **30**: 79, 96
appearance versus reality **30**: 142
Aufidius **9**: 9, 12, 17, 19, 53, 121, 148, 153, 157, 169, 180, 193; **19**: 287; **25**: 263, 296; **30**: 58, 67, 89, 96, 133
body politic, metaphor of **22**: 248; **30**: 67, 96, 105, 125
butterfly episode (Act I, scene iii) **9**: 19, 45, 62, 65, 73, 100, 125, 153, 157
capitulation scene (Act V, scene iii) **9**: 19, 26, 53, 65, 100, 117, 125, 130, 157, 164, 183
ceremonies, rites, and rituals, importance of **9**: 139, 148, 169
Christian elements **30**: 111
comic elements **9**: 8, 9, 14, 53, 80, 106
Cominius **25**: 245
Cominius's tribute (Act II, scene ii) **9**: 80, 100, 117, 125, 144, 164, 198; **25**: 296
Coriolanus
   anger or passion **9**: 19, 26, 45, 80, 92, 157, 164, 177, 189; **30**: 79, 96
   as complementary figure to Aufidius **19**: 287
   death scene (Act V, scene vi) **9**: 12, 80, 100, 117, 125, 144, 164, 198; **25**: 245, 263
   as epic hero **9**: 130, 164, 177; **25**: 245
   immaturity **9**: 62, 80, 84, 110, 117, 142; **30**: 140
   inhuman attributes **9**: 65, 73, 139, 157, 164, 169, 189, 198; **25**: 263
   internal struggle **9**: 31, 43, 45, 53, 72, 117, 121, 130; **44**: 93
   introspection or self-knowledge, lack of **9**: 53, 80, 84, 112, 117, 130; **25**: 296; **30**: 133
   isolation or autonomy **9**: 53, 65, 142, 144, 153, 157, 164, 180, 183, 189, 198; **30**: 58, 89, 111
   manipulation by others **9**: 33, 45, 62, 80; **25**: 296
   modesty **9**: 8, 12, 19, 26, 53, 78, 92, 117, 121, 144, 183; **25**: 296; **30**: 79, 96, 129, 133, 149
   narcissism **30**: 111
   noble or aristocratic attributes **9**: 15, 18, 19, 26, 31, 33, 52, 53, 62, 65, 84, 92, 100, 121, 148, 157, 169; **25**: 263; **30**: 67, 74, 96
   pride or arrogance **9**: 8, 11, 12, 19, 26, 31, 33, 43, 45, 65, 78, 92, 121, 148, 153, 177; **30**: 58, 67, 74, 89, 96, 129

   reconciliation with society **9**: 33, 43, 45, 65, 139, 169; **25**: 296
   as socially destructive force **9**: 62, 65, 73, 78, 110, 142, 144, 153; **25**: 296
   soliloquy (Act IV, scene iv) **9**: 84, 112, 117, 130
   as tragic figure **9**: 8, 12, 13, 18, 25, 45, 52, 53, 72, 80, 92, 106, 112, 117, 130, 148, 164, 169, 177; **25**: 296; **30**: 67, 74, 79, 96, 111, 129; **37**: 283
   traitorous actions **9**: 9, 12, 19, 45, 84, 92, 148; **25**: 296; **30**: 133
   as unsympathetic character **9**: 12, 13, 62, 78, 80, 84, 112, 130, 157
domestic elements **42**: 223
England and Rome, parallels between **9**: 39, 43, 106, 148, 180, 193; **25**: 296; **30**: 67, 105
fable of the belly (Act I, scene i) **9**: 8, 65, 73, 80, 136, 153, 157, 164, 180, 183, 189; **25**: 296; **30**: 79, 105, 111
fame **30**: 58
fire and water **25**: 263
flattery or dissimulation **9**: 26, 45, 92, 100, 110, 121, 130, 144, 157, 183, 193; **25**: 296
friendship **30**: 125, 142
gender issues **30**: 79, 125, 142; **44**: 93
genre **9**: 42, 43, 53, 80, 106, 112, 117, 130, 164, 177; **30**: 67, 74, 79, 89, 111, 125
honor or integrity **9**: 43, 65, 73, 92, 106, 110, 121, 144, 153, 157, 164, 177, 183, 189; **30**: 89, 96, 133
identity **42**: 248
irony or satire **9**: 65, 73, 80, 92, 106, 153, 157, 164, 193; **30**: 67, 89, 133
Jacobean culture, relation to **22**: 248
language and imagery **9**: 8, 9, 13, 53, 64, 65, 73, 78, 84, 100, 112, 121, 136, 139, 142, 144, 153, 157, 174, 183, 193, 198; **22**: 248; **25**: 245, 263; **30**: 111, 125, 142; **37**: 283; **44**: 79
Macbeth, compared with **30**: 79
Menenius **9**: 8, 9, 11, 14, 19, 26, 78, 80, 106, 148, 157; **25**: 263, 296; **30**: 67, 79, 89, 96, 111, 133
Midlands Revolt, influence of **22**: 248; **30**: 79
naming, significance of **30**: 58, 96, 111, 125
nature, philosophy of **30**: 74
nurturing or feeding **9**: 65, 73, 136, 183, 189; **30**: 111; **44**: 79
paradoxical elements **9**: 73, 92, 106, 121, 153, 157, 164, 169, 193
plebeians **9**: 8, 9, 11, 12, 15, 18, 19, 26, 33, 39, 53, 92, 125, 153, 183, 189; **25**: 296; **30**: 58, 79, 96, 111
Plutarch and historical sources **9**: 8, 9, 13, 14, 16, 26, 39, 92, 106, 130, 142, 164; **30**: 74, 79, 105
politics **9**: 15, 17, 18, 19, 26, 33, 43, 53, 62, 65, 73, 80, 92, 106, 110, 112, 121, 144, 153, 157, 164, 180; **22**: 248; **25**: 296; **30**: 58, 67, 79, 89, 96, 105, 111, 125; **37**: 283; **42**: 223
psychoanalytic interpretations **44**: 93
public versus private worlds **37**: 283; **42**: 223
sexuality **9**: 112, 142, 174, 183, 189, 198; **30**: 79, 111, 125, 142
shame **42**: 248
Shakespeare's political sympathies **9**: 8, 11, 15, 17, 19, 26, 39, 52, 53, 62, 80, 92, 142; **25**: 296; **30**: 74, 79, 89, 96, 105, 133

society **9:** 15, 17, 18, 19, 26, 33, 43, 53, 62, 65, 73, 80, 92, 106, 110, 112, 121, 144, 153, 157, 164, 180; **22:** 248; **25:** 296; **30:** 58, 67, 79, 89, 96, 105, 111, 125
staging issues **17:** 172, 242, 248
structure **9:** 8, 9, 11, 12, 13, 14, 16, 26, 33, 45, 53, 58, 72, 78, 80, 84, 92, 112, 139, 148; **25:** 263; **30:** 79, 96
treachery **30:** 89
the tribunes (Brutus and Sicinius) **9:** 9, 11, 14, 19, 33, 169, 180
Virgilia **9:** 11, 19, 26, 33, 58, 100, 121, 125; **25:** 263; **30:** 79, 96, 133
Volumnia
    Coriolanus's subservience to **9:** 16, 26, 33, 53, 62, 80, 92, 100, 117, 125, 142, 177, 183; **30:** 140, 149; **44:** 79
    influence on Coriolanus **9:** 45, 62, 65, 78, 92, 100, 110, 117, 121, 125, 130, 148, 157, 183, 189, 193; **25:** 263, 296; **30:** 79, 96, 125, 133, 140, 142, 149; **44:** 93
    as noble Roman matron **9:** 16, 19, 26, 31, 33
    personification of Rome **9:** 125, 183
war **25:** 263; **30:** 79, 96, 125, 149

Cymbeline (Volumes 4, 15, 36)

appearance versus reality **4:** 87, 93, 103, 162; **36:** 99
authorship controversy **4:** 17, 21, 35, 48, 56, 78
autobiographical elements **4:** 43, 46; **36:** 134
bawdy elements **36:** 155
Beaumont and Fletcher's romances, compared with **4:** 46, 52, 138
Belarius **4:** 48, 89, 141
British nationalism **4:** 19, 78, 89, 93, 129, 141, 159, 167; **32:** 373; **36:** 129; **45:** 67
Cloten **4:** 20, 116, 127, 155; **22:** 302, 365; **25:** 245; **36:** 99, 125, 142, 155
combat scenes **22:** 365
comic elements **4:** 35, 56, 113, 141; **15:** 111, 122
dramatic structure **4:** 17, 18, 19, 20, 21, 22, 24, 38, 43, 48, 53, 64, 68, 89, 116, 129, 141; **22:** 302, 365; **25:** 319; **36:** 115, 125
dreams **4:** 162, 167; **44:** 28; **45:** 67, 75
dualisms **4:** 29, 64, 73
Elizabethan dramatic conventions **4:** 53, 124
family, theme of **44:** 28
Guiderius and Arviragus **4:** 21, 22, 89, 129, 141, 148; **25:** 319; **36:** 125, 158
Iachimo **25:** 245, 319; **36:** 166
Imogen **4:** 21, 22, 24, 29, 37, 45, 46, 52, 56, 78, 89, 108; **15:** 23, 32, 105, 121; **19:** 411; **25:** 245, 319; **28:** 398; **32:** 373; **36:** 129, 142, 148
Imogen's reawakening (Act IV, scene ii) **4:** 37, 56, 89, 103, 108, 116, 150; **15:** 23; **25:** 245
irony **4:** 64, 77, 103
language and imagery **4:** 43, 48, 61, 64, 70, 73, 93, 108; **13:** 401; **25:** 245; **28:** 373, 398; **36:** 115, 158, 166, 186
Lucretia, analogies to **36:** 148
misperception **19:** 411; **36:** 99, 115
religious, mythic, or spiritual content **28:** 373; **36:** 142

negative appraisals **4:** 20, 35, 43, 45, 48, 53, 56, 68; **15:** 32, 105, 121
patriarchy **32:** 373; **36:** 134
Posthumus **4:** 24, 30, 53, 78, 116, 127, 141, 155, 159, 167; **15:** 89; **19:** 411; **25:** 245, 319; **36:** 142; **44:** 28; **45:** 67, 75
psychological elements **36:** 134; **44:** 28; **45:** 67, 75
reconciliation **4:** 38, 64, 73, 93, 105, 113, 116, 129, 138, 141, 162, 170
religious, mythical, or spiritual content **4:** 22, 29, 78, 93, 105, 108, 115, 116, 127, 134, 138, 141, 159; **36:** 158, 186
romantic elements **4:** 17, 20, 46, 68, 77, 141, 148, 172; **15:** 111; **25:** 319; **28:** 373
self-conscious or artificial nature of play **4:** 43, 52, 56, 68, 124, 134, 138; **36:** 99
sexuality **4:** 170, 172; **25:** 319; **32:** 373
Shakespeare's lyric poetry, compared with **13:** 401
sources **4:** 17, 18; **13:** 401; **28:** 373
staging issues **15:** 6, 23, 75, 105, 111, 121, 122; **22:** 365
subversiveness **22:** 302
tragic elements **25:** 319; **28:** 373; **36:** 129
trickster, motif of **22:** 302
vision scene (Act V, scene iv) **4:** 17, 21, 28, 29, 35, 38, 78, 105, 108, 134, 150, 167
wager plot **4:** 18, 24, 29, 53, 78, 155; **22:** 365; **25:** 319

Hamlet (1, 21, 35, 44)

ambiguity **1:** 92, 160, 198, 227, 230, 234, 247, 249; **21:** 72; **35:** 241
appearance versus reality **1:** 95, 116, 166, 169, 198; **35:** 82, 126, 132, 144, 238; **44:** 248; **45:** 28
aristocracy **42:** 217
audience response **28:** 325; **32:** 238; **35:** 167; **44:** 107
autobiographical elements **1:** 98, 115, 119; **13:** 487
classical Greek tragedies, compared with **1:** 74, 75, 130, 184, 212; **13:** 296; **22:** 339
Claudius **13:** 502; **16:** 246; **21:** 259, 347, 361, 371; **28:** 232, 290; **35:** 104, 182; **44:** 119, 241
closet scene (Act III, scene iv) **16:** 259; **21:** 151, 334, 392; **35:** 204, 229; **44:** 119, 237
costume **21:** 81
death, decay, and nature's destructiveness **1:** 144, 153, 188, 198, 221, 242; **13:** 502; **28:** 280, 311; **35:** 241; **42:** 284
dreams **45:** 28
dumbshow and play scene (Act III, scene ii) **1:** 76, 86, 134, 138, 154, 160, 207; **13:** 502; **21:** 392; **35:** 82; **44:** 241; **46:** 74
Elizabethan culture, relation to **1:** 76, 148, 151, 154, 160, 166, 169, 171, 176, 184, 202, 209, 254; **13:** 282, 494; **19:** 330; **21:** 407, 416; **22:** 258
Elizabethan and Jacobean politics, relation to **28:** 232; **28:** 290, 311; **35:** 140
fencing scene (Act V, scene ii) **21:** 392
Fortinbras **21:** 136, 347; **28:** 290
gender issues **35:** 144; **44:** 189, 195, 198
genre **1:** 176, 212, 237

Gertrude **21:** 259, 347, 392; **28:** 311; **32:** 238; **35:** 182, 204, 229; **44:** 119, 160, 189, 195, 237, 248
Ghost **1:** 75, 76, 84, 85, 128, 134, 138, 154, 171, 218, 231, 254; **16:** 246; **21:** 17, 44, 112, 151, 334, 371, 377, 392; **25:** 288; **35:** 152, 157, 174, 237; **44:** 119
gravedigger scene (Act V, scene i) **21:** 392; **28:** 280; **46:** 74
grotesque elements **42:** 284
Hamlet
    delay **1:** 76, 83, 88, 90, 94, 98, 102, 103, 106, 114, 115, 116, 119, 120, 148, 151, 166, 171, 179, 188, 191, 194, 198, 221, 268; **13:** 296, 502; **21:** 81; **25:** 209, 288; **28:** 223; **35:** 82, 174, 212, 215, 237; **44:** 180, 209, 219, 229
    divided nature **16:** 246; **28:** 223; **32:** 288; **35:** 182, 215; **37:** 241
    elocution of the character's speeches **21:** 96, 104, 112, 127, 132, 172, 177, 179, 194, 245, 254, 257
    as a fool **46:** 1, 29, 52, 74
    madness **1:** 76, 81, 83, 95, 102, 106, 128, 144, 154, 160, 234; **21:** 35, 50, 72, 81, 99, 112, 311, 339, 355, 361, 371, 377, 384; **35:** 117, 132, 134, 140, 144, 212; **44:** 107, 119, 152, 209, 219, 229
    melancholy **21:** 99, 112, 177, 194; **35:** 82, 95, 117; **44:** 209, 219
    as negative character **1:** 86, 92, 111, 171, 218; **21:** 386; **25:** 209; **35:** 167
    reaction to his father's death **22:** 339; **35:** 104, 174; **44:** 133, 160, 180, 189
    reaction to Gertrude's marriage **1:** 74, 120, 154, 179; **16:** 259; **21:** 371; **22:** 339; **35:** 104, 117; **44:** 133, 160, 189, 195
    romantic aspects of the character **21:** 96; **44:** 198
    as scourge or purifying figure **1:** 144, 209, 242; **25:** 288; **35:** 157
    sentimentality versus intellectuality **1:** 75, 83, 88, 91, 93, 94, 96, 102, 103, 115, 116, 120, 166, 191; **13:** 296; **21:** 35, 41, 44, 72, 81, 89, 99, 129, 132, 136, 172, 213, 225, 339, 355, 361, 371, 377, 379, 381, 386; **25:** 209; **44:** 198
    soliloquies **1:** 76, 82, 83, 148, 166, 169, 176, 191; **21:** 17, 31, 44, 53, 89, 112, 268, 311, 334, 347, 361, 384, 392; **25:** 209; **28:** 223; **44:** 107, 119, 229
    theatrical interpretations **21:** 11, 31, 78, 101, 104, 107, 160, 177, 179, 182, 183, 192, 194, 197, 202, 203, 208, 213, 225, 232, 237, 249, 253, 254, 257, 259, 274, 311, 339, 347, 355, 361, 371, 377, 380
    virility **21:** 213, 301, 355; **44:** 198
Hamlet with Alterations (David Garrick adaptation) **21:** 23, 334, 347
Horatio **44:** 189
idealism versus pragmatism **16:** 246; **28:** 325
Laertes **21:** 347, 386; **28:** 290; **35:** 182
language and imagery **1:** 95, 144, 153, 154, 160, 188, 198, 221, 227, 249, 259, 270; **22:** 258, 378; **28:** 311; **35:** 144, 152, 238, 241; **42:** 217; **44:** 248
madness **19:** 330; **35:** 104, 126, 134, 140, 144; **44:** 107, 119, 152, 209, 219, 229

marriage **22:** 339

Marxist criticism **42:** 234

nunnery scene (Act III, scene i) **21:** 157, 381, 410

Ophelia **1:** 73, 76, 81, 82, 91, 96, 97, 154, 166, 169, 171, 218, 270; **13:** 268; **16:** 246; **19:** 330; **21:** 17, 41, 44, 72, 81, 101, 104, 107, 112, 136, 203, 259, 347, 381, 386, 392, 416; **28:** 232, 325; **35:** 104, 126, 140, 144, 182, 238; **44:** 189, 195, 248

Polonius **21:** 259, 334, 347, 386, 416; **35:** 182

prayer scene (Act III, scene iii) **1:** 76, 106, 160, 212, 231; **44:** 119

psychoanalytic interpretations **1:** 119, 148, 154, 179, 202; **21:** 197, 213, 361; **25:** 209; **28:** 223; **35:** 95, 104, 134, 237; **37:** 241; **44:** 133, 152, 160, 180, 209, 219

religious, mythic, or spiritual content **1:** 98, 102, 130, 184, 191, 209, 212, 231, 234, 254; **21:** 361; **22:** 258; **28:** 280; **32:** 238; **35:** 134

revenge **1:** 74, 194, 209, 224, 234, 254; **16:** 246; **22:** 258; **25:** 288; **28:** 280; **35:** 152, 157, 167, 174, 212; **44:** 180, 209, 219, 229

Richard II, compared with **1:** 264

ceremonies, rites, and rituals, importance of **13:** 268; **28:** 232

sources **1:** 76, 81, 113, 125, 128, 130, 151, 191, 202, 224, 259

staging issues **13:** 494, 502; **21:** 11, 17, 31, 35, 41, 44, 50, 53, 78, 81, 89, 101, 112, 127, 139, 142, 145, 148, 151, 157, 160, 172, 182, 183, 202, 203, 208, 225, 232, 237, 242, 245, 249, 251, 259, 268, 270, 274, 283, 284, 301, 311, 334, 347, 355, 361, 371, 377, 379, 380, 381, 384, 386, 392, 407, 410, 416; **44:** 198

structure **22:** 378; **28:** 280, 325; **35:** 82, 104, 215; **44:** 152

subjectivity **45:** 28

textual variants **13:** 282; **16:** 259; **21:** 11, 23, 72, 101, 127, 129, 139, 140, 142, 145, 202, 208, 259, 270, 284, 347, 361, 384; **22:** 258; **32:** 238

topical allusions or content **13:** 282

unity **1:** 75, 76, 87, 103, 113, 125, 128, 142, 148, 160, 184, 188, 198, 264; **16:** 259; **35:** 82, 215

unnatural ordering **22:** 378

widowhood and remarriage, themes of **32:** 238

Henry IV, Parts 1 and 2 (Volumes 1, 14, 39)

carnival elements **28:** 203; **32:** 103

characterization **1:** 321, 328, 332, 333, 336, 344, 365, 383, 385, 389, 391, 397, 401; **19:** 195; **39:** 123, 137; **42:** 101, 164

comic elements **1:** 286, 290, 314, 327, 328, 336, 353; **19:** 195; **25:** 109; **39:** 72

contractual and economic relations **13:** 213

contrasting dramatic worlds **14:** 56, 60, 61, 84, 105

critical history **42:** 187

deception, disguise, and duplicity **1:** 397, 406, 425; **42:** 101

Elizabethan culture, relation to **19:** 195

Elizabethan politics, relation to **22:** 395; **28:** 203

Falstaff

characterization **1:** 287, 298, 312, 333; **25:** 245; **28:** 203; **39:** 72, 134, 137, 143

as comic figure **1:** 287, 311, 327, 344, 351, 354, 357, 410, 434; **39:** 89; **46:** 1, 48, 52

as coward or rogue **1:** 285, 290, 296, 298, 306, 307, 313, 317, 323, 336, 337, 338, 342, 354, 366, 374, 391, 396, 401, 433; **14:** 7, 111, 125, 130, 133; **32:** 166

dual personality **1:** 397, 401, 406, 434

female attributes **13:** 183; **44:** 44

Iago, compared with **1:** 341, 351

Marxist interpretation **1:** 358, 361

as parody of the historical plot **1:** 314, 354, 359; **39:** 143

as positive character **1:** 286, 287, 290, 296, 298, 311, 312, 321, 325, 333, 344, 355, 357, 389, 401, 408, 434

rejection by Hal **1:** 286, 287, 290, 312, 314, 317, 324, 333, 338, 344, 357, 366, 372, 374, 379, 380, 389, 414; **13:** 183; **25:** 109; **39:** 72, 89

as satire of feudal society **1:** 314, 328, 361; **32:** 103

as scapegoat **1:** 389, 414

stage interpretations **14:** 4, 6, 7, 9, 15, 116, 130, 146

as subversive figure **16:** 183; **25:** 109

as Vice figure **1:** 342, 361, 366, 374

flattery **22:** 395

gender issues **13:** 183; **25:** 151; **44:** 44

Hal

as the central character **1:** 286, 290, 314, 317, 326, 338, 354, 366, 374, 396; **39:** 72, 100

dual personality **1:** 397, 406; **25:** 109, 151

as Everyman **1:** 342, 366, 374

fall from humanity **1:** 379, 380, 383

general assessment **1:** 286, 287, 289, 290, 314, 317, 326, 327, 332, 357, 397; **25:** 245; **32:** 212; **39:** 134

as ideal ruler **1:** 289, 309, 317, 321, 326, 337, 342, 344, 374, 389, 391, 434; **25:** 109; **39:** 123

as a negative character **1:** 312, 332, 333, 357; **32:** 212

Richard II, compared with **1:** 332, 337; **39:** 72

Henry **39:** 123, 137

historical content **1:** 310, 328, 365, 366, 370, 374, 380, 387, 421, 424, 427, 431; **16:** 172; **19:** 157; **25:** 151; **32:** 136; **39:** 143

historical epic, place in or relation to Shakespeare's **1:** 309, 314, 328, 374, 379, 424, 427

Hotspur **25:** 151; **28:** 101; **39:** 72, 134, 137; **42:** 101

kingship **1:** 314, 318, 337, 366, 370, 374, 379, 380, 383, 424; **16:** 172; **19:** 195; **28:** 101; **39:** 100, 116, 123, 130; **42:** 143

language and imagery **13:** 213; **16:** 172; **25:** 245; **28:** 101; **39:** 116, 130; **42:** 155

as medieval allegory or morality play **1:** 323, 324, 342, 361, 366, 373, 374; **32:** 166; **39:** 89

Mortimer **25:** 151

Neoclassical rules **1:** 286, 287, 290, 293

Oldcastle, references to **22:** 114; **32:** 166

politics **28:** 101; **39:** 130; **42:** 143

psychoanalytic interpretations **13:** 457; **28:** 101; **42:** 187; **44:** 44

rebellion **22:** 395; **28:** 101

relationship to other Shakespearean plays **1:** 286, 290, 309, 329, 365, 396; **28:** 101; **42:** 101, 155

relationship of Parts 1 and 2 **32:** 136; **39:** 100

religious, mythic, or spiritual content **1:** 314, 374, 414, 421, 429, 431, 434; **32:** 103

as autonomous works **1:** 289, 337, 338, 347, 348, 373, 387, 393, 411, 418, 424

comparison **1:** 290, 295, 329, 348, 358, 393, 411, 419, 429, 431, 441

unity of both parts **1:** 286, 290, 309, 314, 317, 329, 365, 373, 374, 396, 402, 404, 419

staging issues **32:** 212

textual issues **22:** 114

time and change, motif of **1:** 372, 393, 411; **39:** 89

Turkish elements **19:** 170

two fathers **14:** 86, 101, 105, 108; **39:** 89, 100

violence **25:** 109

Henry V (Volumes 5, 14, 30)

battle of Agincourt **5:** 197, 199, 213, 246, 257, 281, 287, 289, 293, 310, 318; **19:** 217; **30:** 181

Canterbury and churchmen **5:** 193, 203, 205, 213, 219, 225, 252, 260; **22:** 137; **30:** 215, 262

characterization **5:** 186, 189, 192, 193, 199, 219, 230, 233, 252, 276, 293; **30:** 227, 278

Chorus, role of **5:** 186, 192, 226, 228, 230, 252, 264, 269, 281, 293; **14:** 301, 319, 336; **19:** 133; **25:** 116, 131; **30:** 163, 202, 220

class distinctions, conflict, and relations **28:** 146

colonialism **22:** 103

comic elements **5:** 185, 188, 191, 192, 217, 230, 233, 241, 252, 260, 276; **19:** 217; **28:** 121; **30:** 193, 202,

economic relations **13:** 213

Elizabethan culture, relation to **5:** 210, 213, 217, 223, 257, 299, 310; **16:** 202; **19:** 133, 233; **28:** 121, 159; **30:** 215, 262; **37:** 187

English language and colonialism **22:** 103; **28:** 159

epic elements **5:** 192, 197, 246, 257, 314; **30:** 181, 220, 237, 252

Falstaff **5:** 185, 186, 187, 189, 192, 195, 198, 210, 226, 257, 269, 271, 276, 293, 299; **28:** 146; **46:** 48

Fluellen **30:** 278; **37:** 105

French aristocrats and the Dauphin **5:** 188, 191, 199, 205, 213, 281; **22:** 137; **28:** 121

French language, Shakespeare's use of **5:** 186, 188, 190; **25:** 131

gender issues **13:** 183; **28:** 121, 146, 159; **44:** 44

Henry

brutality and cunning **5:** 193, 203, 209, 210, 213, 219, 233, 239, 252, 260, 271, 287, 293, 302, 304; **30:** 159

characterization in *1* and *2 Henry IV* contrasted **5:** 189, 190, 241, 304, 310; **19:** 133; **25:** 131; **32:** 157

chivalry **37:** 187

courage **5:** 191, 195, 210, 213, 228, 246, 257, 267
disguise **30:** 169, 259
education **5:** 246, 267, 271, 289; **14:** 297, 328, 342; **30:** 259
emotion, lack of **5:** 209, 212, 233, 244, 264, 267, 287, 293, 310
as heroic figure **5:** 192, 205, 209, 223, 244, 252, 257, 260, 269, 271, 299, 304; **28:** 121, 146; **30:** 237, 244, 252; **37:** 187
humor **5:** 189, 191, 212, 217, 239, 240, 276
intellectual and social limitations **5:** 189, 191, 203, 209, 210, 225, 226, 230, 293; **30:** 220
interpersonal relations **5:** 209, 233, 267, 269, 276, 287, 293, 302, 318; **19:** 133; **28:** 146
mercy **5:** 213, 267, 289, 293
mixture of good and bad qualities **5:** 199, 205, 209, 210, 213, 244, 260, 304, 314; **30:** 262, 273
piety **5:** 191, 199, 209, 217, 223, 239, 257, 260, 271, 289, 310, 318; **30:** 244; **32:** 126
public versus private selves **22:** 137; **30:** 169, 207
self-doubt **5:** 281, 310
slaughter of prisoners **5:** 189, 205, 246, 293, 318; **28:** 146
speech **5:** 212, 230, 233, 246, 264, 276, 287, 302; **28:** 146; **30:** 163, 227
historical content **5:** 185, 188, 190, 192, 193, 198, 246, 314; **13:** 201; **19:** 133; **25:** 131; **30:** 193, 202, 207, 215, 252
historical epic, place in or relation to Shakespeare's **5:** 195, 198, 205, 212, 225, 241, 244, 287, 304, 310; **14:** 337, 342; **30:** 215
homoerotic elements **16:** 202
Hotspur **5:** 189, 199, 228, 271, 302
hypocrisy **5:** 203, 213, 219, 223, 233, 260, 271, 302
imperialism **22:** 103; **28:** 159
Irish affairs **22:** 103; **28:** 159
irony **5:** 192, 210, 213, 219, 223, 226, 233, 252, 260, 269, 281, 299, 304; **14:** 336; **30:** 159, 193,
Katherine **5:** 186, 188, 189, 190, 192, 260, 269, 299, 302; **13:** 183; **19:** 217; **30:** 278; **44:** 44
kingship **5:** 205, 223, 225, 233, 239, 244, 257, 264, 267, 271, 287, 289, 299, 302, 304, 314, 318; **16:** 202; **22:** 137; **30:** 169, 202, 259, 273
language and imagery **5:** 188, 230, 233, 241, 264, 276; **19:** 203; **25:** 131; **30:** 159, 181, 207, 234
Machiavellianism **5:** 203, 225, 233, 252, 287, 304; **25:** 131; **30:** 273
MacMorris **22:** 103; **28:** 159; **30:** 278
Marlowe's works, compared with **19:** 233
metadramatic elements **13:** 194; **30:** 181
Mistress Quickly **5:** 186, 187, 210, 276, 293; **30:** 278
morality **5:** 195, 203, 213, 223, 225, 239, 246, 260, 271, 293
obscenity **5:** 188, 190, 260
order **5:** 205, 257, 264, 310, 314; **30:** 193,
patriarchy **37:** 105; **44:** 44
nationalism and patriotism **5:** 198, 205, 209, 210, 213, 219, 223, 233, 246, 252, 257, 269, 299; **19:** 133, 217; **30:** 227, 262

Pistol **28:** 146
power **37:** 175
psychoanalytic interpretations **13:** 457; **44:** 44
religious, mythic, or religious content **25:** 116; **32:** 126
Salic Law **5:** 219, 252, 260; **28:** 121
self-interest or expediency **5:** 189, 193, 205, 213, 217, 233, 260, 287, 302, 304; **30:** 273
soldiers **5:** 203, 239, 267, 276, 281, 287, 293, 318; **28:** 146; **30:** 169,
staging issues **5:** 186, 189, 192, 193, 198, 205, 226, 230, 241, 281, 314; **13:** 194, 502; **14:** 293, 295, 297, 301, 310, 319, 328, 334, 336, 342; **19:** 217; **32:** 185
structure **5:** 186, 189, 205, 213, 230, 241, 264, 289, 310, 314; **30:** 220, 227, 234, 244
textual problems **5:** 187, 189, 190; **13:** 201
topical allusions or content **5:** 185, 186; **13:** 201
tragic elements **5:** 228, 233, 267, 269, 271
traitors (Scroop, Grey, and Cambridge) **16:** 202; **30:** 220, 278
Turkish elements **19:** 170
violence **43:** 24
war **5:** 193, 195, 197, 198, 210, 213, 219, 230, 233, 246, 281, 293; **28:** 121, 146; **30:** 262; **32:** 126; **37:** 175, 187; **42:** 143
Williams **13:** 502; **16:** 183; **28:** 146; **30:** 169, 259, 278
wooing scene (Act V, scene ii) **5:** 186, 188, 189, 191, 193, 195, 260, 276, 299, 302; **14:** 297; **28:** 121, 159; **30:** 163, 207

Henry VI, Parts 1, 2, and 3 (Volumes 3, 24, 39)

ambivalent or ironic elements **3:** 69, 151, 154; **39:** 160
authorship controversy **3:** 16, 18, 19, 20, 21, 26, 27, 29, 31, 35, 39, 41, 55, 66; **24:** 51
autobiographical elements **3:** 41, 55
Bordeaux sequence **37:** 165
Cade scenes **3:** 35, 67, 92, 97, 109; **16:** 183; **22:** 156; **25:** 102; **28:** 112; **37:** 97; **39:** 160, 196, 205
carnival elements **22:** 156
characterization **3:** 18, 20, 24, 25, 31, 57, 64, 73, 77, 109, 119, 151; **24:** 22, 28, 38, 42, 45, 47; **39:** 160
class distinctions, conflict, and relations **37:** 97; **39:** 187
dance **22:** 156
decay of heroic ideals **3:** 119, 126
disorder and civil dissension **3:** 59, 67, 76, 92, 103, 126; **13:** 131; **16:** 183; **24:** 11, 17, 28, 31, 47; **25:** 102; **28:** 112; **39:** 154, 177, 187, 196, 205
Elizabethan literary and cultural influences **3:** 75, 97, 100, 119, 143; **22:** 156; **28:** 112; **37:** 97
Folk rituals, elements and influence of **39:** 205
Henry
  characterization **3:** 64, 77, 151; **39:** 160, 177
  source of social disorder **3:** 25, 31, 41, 115; **39:** 154, 187
  as sympathetic figure **3:** 73, 143, 154; **24:** 32
historical accuracy **3:** 18, 21, 35, 46, 51; **16:** 217; **24:** 16, 18, 25, 31, 45, 48
historical epic, place in or relation to Shakespeare's **3:** 24, 59; **24:** 51

as humanistic play **3:** 83, 92, 109, 115, 119, 131, 136, 143
Humphrey **13:** 131
as inferior or flawed plays **3:** 20, 21, 25, 26, 35
Joan of Arc **16:** 131; **32:** 212
kingship **3:** 69, 73, 77, 109, 115, 136, 143; **24:** 32; **39:** 154, 177, 187
language and imagery **3:** 21, 50, 52, 55, 57, 66, 67, 71, 75, 76, 97, 105, 109, 119, 126, 131; **24:** 28; **37:** 157; **39:** 213, 222
legitimacy **3:** 89, 157; **39:** 154,
Machiavellianism **22:** 193
Margaret
  characterization **3:** 18, 26, 35, 51, 103, 109, 140, 157; **24:** 48
  Suffolk, relationship with **3:** 18, 24, 26, 157; **39:** 213
Marlowe's works, compared with **19:** 233
medieval literary influence **3:** 59, 67, 75, 100, 109, 136, 151; **13:** 131
molehill scene (*3 Henry VI*, Act III, scene ii) **3:** 75, 97, 126, 149
moral inheritance **3:** 89, 126
multiple perspectives of characters **3:** 69, 154
Neoclassical rules **3:** 17, 18
patriarchal claims **16:** 131 **25:** 102
nationalism and patriotism **24:** 25, 45, 47
play-within-the-play, convention of **3:** 75, 149
retribution **3:** 27, 42, 51, 59, 77, 83, 92, 100, 109, 115, 119, 131, 136, 151
Richard of Gloucester
  characterization **3:** 35, 48, 57, 64, 77, 143, 151; **22:** 193; **39:** 160, 177
  as revenger **22:** 193
  soliloquy (*3 Henry VI*, Act III, scene ii) **3:** 17, 48
sibling rivalry **22:** 193
sources **3:** 18, 21, 29, 31, 35, 39, 46, 51; **13:** 131; **16:** 217; **39:** 196
staging issues **24:** 21, 22, 27, 31, 32, 36, 38, 41, 45, 48, 55; **32:** 212
structure **3:** 31, 43, 46, 69, 83, 103, 109, 119, 136, 149, 154; **39:** 213
Talbot **39:** 160, 213, 222
textual arrangement **24:** 3, 4, 6, 12, 17, 18, 19, 20, 21, 24, 27, 42, 45; **37:** 165
theatrical viability **24:** 31, 32, 34
Tudor myth **3:** 51, 59, 77, 92, 100, 109, 115, 119, 131; **39:** 222
Unity **39:** 177, 222
violence **24:** 25, 31; **37:** 157
women, role of **3:** 103, 109, 126, 140, 157; **16:** 183; **39:** 196
York's death **13:** 131

Henry VIII (Volumes 2, 24, 41)

ambition or pride **2:** 15, 38, 67
authorship controversy **2:** 16, 18, 19, 22, 23, 27, 28, 31, 35, 36, 42, 43, 44, 46, 48, 51, 58, 64, 68; **41:** 129, 146, 158, 171,
Anne Boleyn **2:** 21, 24, 31; **41:** 180
Buckingham **22:** 182; **24:** 129, 140; **37:** 109
change **2:** 27, 65, 72, 81
characterization **2:** 17, 23, 25, 32, 35, 39; **24:** 106
composition date **2:** 19, 22, 35; **24:** 129
costumes **24:** 82, 87; **28:** 184

Cranmer's prophecy **2:** 25, 31, 46, 56, 64, 68, 72; **24:** 146; **32:** 148; **41:** 120, 190
Cymbeline, compared with **2:** 67, 71
discrepancy between prophetic ending and preceding action **2:** 22, 25, 31, 46, 49, 56, 60, 65, 68, 75, 81; **32:** 148; **41:** 190
Elizabethan politics, relation to **22:** 395; **24:** 115, 129, 140; **32:** 148
Elizabethan dramatic conventions **24:** 155
English Reformation, influence of **2:** 25, 35, 39, 51, 67; **24:** 89
flattery **22:** 395
historical and romantic elements, combination of **41:** 129, 146, 180
historical epic, as epilogue to Shakespeare's **2:** 22, 25, 27, 39, 51, 60, 65
historical relativity, theme of **41:** 146
King Henry
    as agent of divine retribution **2:** 49
    characterization **2:** 23, 39, 51, 58, 60, 65, 66, 75; **28:** 184; **37:** 109
    incomplete portrait **2:** 15, 16, 19, 35; **41:** 120
    as realistic figure **2:** 21, 22, 23, 25, 32
historical and romantic elements, combination of **2:** 46, 49, 51, 75, 76, 78; **24:** 71, 80, 146
historiography **37:** 109
inconsistencies **2:** 16, 17, 28, 31, 60
ironic aspects **41:** 129
Katherine
    characterization **2:** 18, 19, 23, 24, 38; **24:** 129; **37:** 109; **41:** 180
    Hermione, compared with **2:** 24, 51, 58, 76
    politeness strategies **22:** 182
    religious discourse **22:** 182
    as tragic figure **2:** 16, 18
kingship **2:** 49, 58, 60, 65, 75, 78; **24:** 113; **41:** 129, 171
language and imagery **41:** 180, 190
legitimacy **37:** 109
moral intent **2:** 15, 19, 25; **24:** 140
Norfolk **22:** 182
pageantry **2:** 14, 15, 18, 51, 58; **24:** 77, 83, 84, 85, 89, 91, 106, 113, 118, 120, 126, 127, 140, 146, 150; **41:** 120, 129, 190
patience **2:** 58, 76, 78
politics **2:** 39, 49, 51, 58, 60, 65, 67, 71, 72, 75, 78, 81; **24:** 74, 121, 124; **41:** 146
Porter **24:** 155
rebellion **22:** 395
rhetoric of politeness **22:** 182
Shakespeare's romances, compared with **2:** 46, 51, 58, 66, 67, 71, 76; **41:** 171
sources **2:** 16, 17; **24:** 71, 80
staging issues **24:** 67, 70, 71, 75, 77, 83, 84, 85, 87, 89, 91, 101, 106, 113, 120, 127, 129, 136, 140, 146, 150, 152, 155; **28:** 184
Stephen Gardiner **24:** 129
structure **2:** 16, 25, 27, 28, 31, 36, 44, 46, 51, 56, 68, 75; **24:** 106, 112, 113, 120
style **41:** 158
thematic disparity **2:** 25, 31, 56, 68, 75; **41:** 146
tragedies of major characters **2:** 16, 39, 46, 48, 49, 51, 56, 58, 68, 81; **41:** 120
wheel of fortune, motif of **2:** 27, 65, 72, 81
Cardinal Wolsey **2:** 15, 18, 19, 23, 24, 38; **22:** 182; **24:** 80, 91, 112, 113, 129, 140; **37:** 109; **41:** 129

Julius Caesar (Volumes 7, 17, 30)

anachronisms **7:** 331
Antony
    characterization **7:** 160, 179, 189, 221, 233, 284, 320, 333; **17:** 269, 271, 272, 284, 298, 306, 313, 315, 358, 398; **25:** 272; **30:** 316
    funeral oration **7:** 148, 154, 159, 204, 210, 221, 238, 259, 350; **25:** 280; **30:** 316, 333, 362
aristocratic values **16:** 231; **22:** 280; **30:** 379
the assassination **7:** 156, 161, 179, 191, 200, 221, 264, 272, 279, 284, 350; **25:** 272; **30:** 326
audience response **7:** 179, 238, 253, 255, 272, 316, 320, 336, 350; **19:** 321
Brutus
    arrogance **7:** 160, 169, 204, 207, 264, 277, 292, 350; **25:** 280; **30:** 351
    as chief protagonist or tragic hero **7:** 152, 159, 189, 191, 200, 204, 242, 250, 253, 264, 268, 279, 284, 298, 333; **17:** 272, 372, 387
    citizenship **25:** 272
    funeral oration **7:** 154, 155, 204, 210, 350
    motives **7:** 150, 156, 161, 179, 191, 200, 221, 227, 233, 245, 292, 303, 310, 320, 333, 350; **25:** 272; **30:** 351, 358
    nobility or idealism **7:** 150, 152, 156, 159, 161, 179, 189, 191, 200, 221, 242, 250, 253, 259, 264, 277, 303, 320; **17:** 269, 271, 273, 279, 280, 284, 306, 308, 321, 323, 324, 345, 358; **25:** 272, 280; **30:** 351, 362
    political ineptitude or lack of judgment **7:** 169, 188, 200, 205, 221, 245, 252, 264, 277, 282, 310, 316, 331, 333, 343; **17:** 323, 358, 375, 380
    self-knowledge or self-deception **7:** 191, 200, 221, 242, 259, 264, 268, 279, 310, 333, 336, 350; **25:** 272; **30:** 316
    soliloquy (Act II, scene i) **7:** 156, 160, 161, 191, 221, 245, 250, 253, 264, 268, 279, 282, 292, 303, 343, 350; **25:** 280; **30:** 333
Caesar
    ambiguous nature **7:** 191, 233, 242, 250, 272, 298, 316, 320
    arrogance **7:** 160, 207, 218, 253, 272, 279, 298; **25:** 280
    idolatry **22:** 137
    leadership qualities **7:** 161, 179, 189, 191, 200, 207, 233, 245, 253, 257, 264, 272, 279, 284, 298, 310, 333; **17:** 317, 358; **22:** 280; **30:** 316, 326
    as tragic hero **7:** 152, 200, 221, 279; **17:** 321, 377, 384
    weakness **7:** 161, 167, 169, 179, 187, 188, 191, 207, 218, 221, 233, 250, 253, 298; **17:** 358; **25:** 280
Caesarism **7:** 159, 160, 161, 167, 169, 174, 191, 205, 218, 253, 310; **30:** 316, 321
Calphurnia
    dream **45:** 10
Cassius **7:** 156, 159, 160, 161, 169, 179, 189, 221, 233, 303, 310, 320, 333, 343; **17:** 272, 282, 284, 344, 345, 358; **25:** 272, 280; **30:** 351; **37:** 203
construing the truth **7:** 320, 336, 343, 350; **37:** 229
Elizabethan culture, relation to **16:** 231; **30:** 342, 379

emulation or rivalry **16:** 231
gender issues **13:** 260
historical determinism versus free will **7:** 160, 298, 316, 333, 346, 356; **13:** 252
irony or ambiguity **7:** 167, 257, 259, 262, 268, 282, 316, 320, 333, 336, 346, 350
language and imagery **7:** 148, 155, 159, 188, 204, 207, 227, 242, 250, 277, 296, 303, 324, 346, 350; **13:** 260; **17:** 347, 348, 350, 356, 358; **19:** 321; **22:** 280; **25:** 280; **30:** 333, 342
liberty versus tyranny **7:** 158, 179, 189, 205, 221, 253; **25:** 272
love and friendship **7:** 233, 262, 268; **25:** 272
medieval physiology **13:** 260
moral choice **7:** 179, 264, 279, 343
Octavius **30:** 316
omens **22:** 137; **45:** 10
philosophical elements **7:** 310, 324; **37:** 203
the poets **7:** 179, 320, 350
politics **7:** 161, 169, 191, 205, 218, 221, 245, 262, 264, 279, 282, 310, 324, 333, 346; **17:** 317, 318, 321, 323, 334, 350, 351, 358, 378, 382, 394, 406; **22:** 137, 280; **25:** 272, 280; **30:** 285, 297, 316, 321, 342, 374, 379; **37:** 203
as "problem play" **7:** 272, 320
psychoanalytic interpretation **45:** 10
public versus private principles **7:** 161, 179, 252, 262, 268, 284, 298; **13:** 252
quarrel scene (Act IV, scene iii) **7:** 149, 150, 152, 153, 155, 160, 169, 188, 191, 204, 268, 296, 303, 310
retribution **7:** 160, 167, 200
revenge tragedy elements **7:** 316
ceremonies, rites, and rituals, importance of **7:** 150, 210, 255, 259, 268, 284, 316, 331, 339, 356; **13:** 260; **22:** 137; **30:** 374
role-playing **7:** 356; **37:** 229
Roman citizenry, portrayal of **7:** 169, 179, 210, 221, 245, 279, 282, 310, 320, 333; **17:** 271, 279, 288, 291, 292, 298, 323, 334, 351, 367, 374, 375, 378; **22:** 280; **30:** 285, 297, 316, 321, 374, 379; **37:** 229
Senecan elements **37:** 229
Shakespeare's English history plays, compared with **7:** 161, 189, 218, 221, 252; **22:** 137; **30:** 369
Shakespeare's major tragedies, compared with **7:** 161, 188, 227, 242, 264, 268
sources **7:** 149, 150, 156, 187, 200, 264, 272, 282, 284, 320; **30:** 285, 297, 326, 358
structure **7:** 152, 155, 159, 160, 179, 200, 210, 238, 264, 284, 298, 316, 346; **13:** 252; **30:** 374

King John (Volumes 9, 24, 41)

ambiguity **13:** 152; **41:** 243
anti-catholic rhetoric **22:** 120; **25:** 98
Arthur **9:** 215, 216, 218, 219, 229, 240, 267, 275; **22:** 120; **25:** 98; **41:** 251, 277
autobiographical elements **9:** 209, 218, 245, 248, 260, 292
characterization **9:** 222, 224, 229, 240, 250, 292; **41:** 205, 215
church versus state **9:** 209, 212, 222, 235, 240; **22:** 120
commodity or self-interest **9:** 224, 229, 245, 260, 275, 280, 297; **19:** 182; **25:** 98; **41:** 228

commodity versus honor **41:** 269
Constance **9:** 208, 210, 211, 215, 219, 220, 224, 229, 240, 251, 254; **16:** 161; **24:** 177, 184, 196
corruption in society **9:** 222, 234, 280, 297
ethical or moral issues **9:** 212, 222, 224, 229, 235, 240, 263, 275, 280
excess **9:** 251
Faulconbridge, the Bastard **41:** 205, 228, 251, 260, 277
   as chorus or commentator **9:** 212, 218, 229, 248, 251, 260, 271, 284, 297, 300; **22:** 120
   as comic figure **9:** 219, 271, 297
   development **9:** 216, 224, 229, 248, 263, 271, 275, 280, 297; **13:** 158, 163
   as embodiment of England **9:** 222, 224, 240, 244, 248, 271
   heroic qualities **9:** 208, 245, 248, 254, 263, 271, 275; **25:** 98
   political conduct **9:** 224, 240, 250, 260, 280, 297; **13:** 147, 158; **22:** 120
Henry **41:** 277
historical content **9:** 216, 219, 220, 222, 235, 240, 254, 284, 290, 292, 297, 300, 303; **13:** 163; **32:** 93, 114; **41:** 234, 243
John **41:** 205, 260
   death, decay, and nature's destructiveness **9:** 212, 215, 216, 240
   decline **9:** 224, 235, 240, 263, 275
   Hubert, scene with (Act III, scene iii) **9:** 210, 212, 216, 218, 219, 280
   moral insensibility **13:** 147, 163
   negative qualities **9:** 209, 212, 218, 219, 229, 234, 235, 244, 245, 246, 250, 254, 275, 280, 297
   positive qualities **9:** 209, 224, 235, 240, 244, 245, 263
kingship **9:** 235, 254, 263, 275, 297; **13:** 158; **19:** 182; **22:** 120
language and imagery **9:** 212, 215, 220, 246, 251, 254, 267, 280, 284, 292, 297, 300; **13:** 147, 158; **22:** 120; **37:** 132
legitimacy or inheritance **9:** 224, 235, 254, 303; **13:** 147; **19:** 182; **37:** 132; **41:** 215
Neoclassical rules **9:** 208, 209, 210, 212
oppositions or dualisms **9:** 224, 240, 263, 275, 284, 290, 300
Papal Tyranny in the Reign of King John (Colley Cibber adaptation) **24:** 162, 163, 165
nationalism and patriotism **9:** 209, 218, 222, 224, 235, 240, 244, 275; **25:** 98; **37:** 132
politics **9:** 218, 224, 260, 280; **13:** 163; **22:** 120; **37:** 132; **41:** 221, 228
rebellion **9:** 218, 254, 263, 280, 297
Shakespeare's other history plays, compared with **9:** 218, 254; **13:** 152, 158; **25:** 98
sources **9:** 216, 222, 300; **32:** 93, 114; **41:** 234, 243, 251
staging issues **16:** 161; **19:** 182; **24:** 171, 187, 203, 206, 211, 225, 228, 241, 245, 249
structure **9:** 208, 212, 222, 224, 229, 240, 244, 245, 254, 260, 263, 275, 284, 290, 292, 300; **24:** 228, 241; **41:** 260, 269, 277
tragic elements **9:** 208, 209, 244
treachery **9:** 245
The Troublesome Reign (anonymous), compared with **9:** 216, 244, 260, 292; **22:** 120; **32:** 93; **41:** 205, 221, 260, 269

Tudor doctrine **9:** 254, 284, 297; **41:** 221
tyranny **9:** 218
women, role of **9:** 222, 303; **16:** 161; **19:** 182; **41:** 205, 221

King Lear (Volumes 2, 11, 31, 46)

Albany **32:** 308
allegorical elements **16:** 311
audience perception **19:** 295; **28:** 325
autobiographical elements **2:** 131, 136, 149, 165
characterization **2:** 108, 125, 145, 162, 191; **16:** 311; **28:** 223; **46:** 177, 210
Christian elements **2:** 137, 170, 179, 188, 191, 197, 207, 218, 222, 226, 229, 238, 249, 265, 286; **22:** 233, 271; **25:** 218; **46:** 276
combat scenes **22:** 365
comic and tragic elements, combination of **2:** 108, 110, 112, 125, 156, 162, 245, 278, 284; **46:** 191
Cordelia
   attack on Britain **25:** 202
   characterization **2:** 110, 116, 125, 170; **16:** 311; **25:** 218; **28:** 223, 325; **31:** 117, 149, 155, 162; **46:** 225, 231, 242
   as Christ figure **2:** 116, 170, 179, 188, 222, 286
   rebelliousness **13:** 352; **25:** 202
   self-knowledge **46:** 218
   on stage **11:** 158
   transcendent power **2:** 137, 207, 218, 265, 269, 273
cruelty of daughters **2:** 101, 102, 106; **31:** 84, 123, 137, 142
death, decay, and nature's destructiveness **2:** 93, 94, 101, 104, 106, 109, 112, 116, 129, 131, 137, 143, 147, 149, 156, 160, 170, 179, 188, 197, 207, 218, 222, 226, 231, 238, 241, 245, 249, 253, 265, 269, 273; **16:** 301; **25:** 202, 218; **31:** 77, 117, 137, 142; **46:** 264
double-plot **2:** 94, 95, 100, 101, 104, 112, 116, 124, 131, 133, 156, 253, 257; **46:** 254
Dover Cliff scene **2:** 156, 229, 255, 269; **11:** 8, 151
Edgar **28:** 223; **32:** 212; **32:** 308; **37:** 295
Edgar-Edmund duel **22:** 365
Edmund **25:** 218; **28:** 223
Edmund's forged letter **16:** 372
Elizabethan culture, relation to **2:** 168, 174, 177, 183, 226, 241; **19:** 330; **22:** 227, 233, 365; **25:** 218; **46:** 276
Fool **2:** 108, 112, 125, 156, 162, 245, 278, 284; **11:** 17, 158, 169; **22:** 227; **25:** 202; **28:** 223; **46:** 1, 14, 18, 24, 33, 52, 191, 205, 210, 218, 225
Gloucester **46:** 254
Goneril **31:** 151; **46:** 231, 242
grotesque or absurd elements **2:** 136, 156, 245; **13:** 343
implausibility or plot, characters, or events **2:** 100, 136, 145, 278; **13:** 343
Job, compared with **2:** 226, 241, 245; **25:** 218
Kent **25:** 202; **28:** 223; **32:** 212
language and imagery **2:** 129, 137, 161, 191, 199, 237, 257, 271; **16:** 301; **19:** 344; **22:** 233; **46:** 177

Lear
   curse on Goneril **11:** 5, 7, 12, 114, 116
   love-test and division of kingdom **2:** 100, 106, 111, 124, 131, 137, 147, 149, 151, 168, 186, 208, 216, 281; **16:** 351; **25:** 202; **31:** 84, 92, 107, 117, 149, 155; **46:** 231, 242
   madness **2:** 94, 95, 98, 99, 100, 101, 102, 103, 111, 116, 120, 124, 125, 149, 156, 191, 208, 216, 281; **46:** 264
   as scapegoat **2:** 241, 253
   self-knowledge **2:** 103, 151, 188, 191, 213, 218, 222, 241, 249, 262; **25:** 218; **37:** 213; **46:** 191, 205, 225, 254, 264,
legal issues **46:** 276
love **2:** 109, 112, 131, 160, 162, 170, 179, 188, 197, 218, 222, 238, 265; **25:** 202; **31:** 77, 149, 151, 155, 162
madness **19:** 330
Marxist criticism **42:** 234
medieval or morality drama, influence of **2:** 177, 188, 201; **25:** 218
misogyny **31:** 123
nihilistic or pessimistic vision **2:** 130, 143, 149, 156, 165, 231, 238, 245, 253; **22:** 271; **25:** 218; **28:** 325
pagan elements **25:** 218
patriarchal or monarchical order **13:** 353, 457; **16:** 351; **22:** 227, 233; **25:** 218; **31:** 84, 92, 107, 117, 123, 137, 142; **46:** 269
performance issues **2:** 106, 137, 154, 160; **11:** 10, 20, 27, 56, 57, 132, 136, 137, 145, 150, 154; **19:** 295, 344; **25:** 218
poetic justice, question of **2:** 92, 93, 94, 101, 129, 137, 231, 245
politics **46:** 269
providential order **2:** 112, 116, 137, 168, 170, 174, 177, 218, 226, 241, 253; **22:** 271
Regan **31:** 151; **46:** 231, 242
rhetorical style **16:** 301
romantic elements **31:** 77, 84
sexuality **25:** 202; **31:** 133, 137, 142
social and moral corruption **2:** 116, 133, 174, 177, 241, 271; **22:** 227; **31:** 84, 92; **46:** 269
sources **2:** 94, 100, 143, 145, 170, 186; **13:** 352; **16:** 351; **28:** 301
staging issues **11:** 1-178; **32:** 212; **46:** 205, 218
structure **28:** 325; **32:** 308; **46:** 177
suffering **2:** 137, 160, 188, 201, 218, 222, 226, 231, 238, 241, 249, 265; **13:** 343; **22:** 271; **25:** 218
Tate's adaptation **2:** 92, 93, 94, 101, 102, 104, 106, 110, 112, 116, 137; **11:** 10, 136; **25:** 218; **31:** 162
textual issues **22:** 271; **37:** 295
Timon of Athens, relation to **16:** 351
wisdom **37:** 213; **46:** 210

Love's Labour's Lost (Volumes 2, 23, 38)

Armado **23:** 207
artificial nature **2:** 315, 317, 324, 330; **23:** 207, 233
authorship controversy **2:** 299, 300; **32:** 308
Berowne **2:** 308, 324, 327; **22:** 12; **23:** 184, 187; **38:** 194
characterization **2:** 303, 310, 317, 322, 328, 342; **23:** 237, 250, 252; **38:** 232

as comedy of affectation **2:** 302, 303, 304; **23:** 191, 224, 226, 228, 233
comic resolution **2:** 335, 340; **16:** 17; **19:** 92; **38:** 209
conclusion **38:** 172
dance and patterned action **2:** 308, 342; **23:** 191, 237
death, decay, and nature's destructiveness **2:** 305, 331, 344, 348
desire **38:** 185, 194, 200, 209
dramatic shortcomings or failure **2:** 299, 301, 303, 322
Elizabeth I **38:** 239
Elizabethan love poetry **38:** 232
feminist criticism **42:** 93
genre **38:** 163
gift exchange **25:** 1
grace and civility **2:** 351
Holofernes **23:** 207
illusion versus reality **2:** 303, 308, 331, 340, 344, 348, 356, 359, 367, 371, 375; **23:** 230, 231
knowledge **22:** 12
language and imagery **2:** 301, 302, 303, 306, 307, 308, 315, 319, 320, 330, 335, 344, 345, 348, 356, 359, 362, 365, 371, 374, 375; **19:** 92; **22:** 12, 378; **23:** 184, 187, 196, 197, 202, 207, 211, 221, 227, 231, 233, 237, 252; **28:** 9, 63; **38:** 219, 226
love **2:** 312, 315, 340, 344; **22:** 12; **23:** 252; **38:** 194
male domination **22:** 12
male sexual anxiety **16:** 17
marriage **2:** 335, 340; **19:** 92; **38:** 209, 232
metadramatic elements **2:** 356, 359, 362
Neoclassical rules **2:** 299, 300
as satire or parody **2:** 300, 302, 303, 307, 308, 315, 321, 324, 327; **23:** 237, 252
physical versus intellectual world **2:** 331, 348, 367
public versus private speech **2:** 356, 362, 371
School of Night, allusions to **2:** 321, 327, 328
sexuality **22:** 12
songs, role of **2:** 303, 304, 316, 326, 335, 362, 367, 371, 375
sources **16:** 17
spectacle **38:** 226
staging issues **23:** 184, 187, 191, 196, 198, 200, 201, 202, 207, 212, 215, 216, 217, 229, 230, 232, 233, 237, 252
structure **22:** 378; **23:** 191, 237, 252; **38:** 163, 172
theme
idealism versus realism **38:** 163
topical allusions or content **2:** 300, 303, 307, 315, 316, 317, 319, 321, 327, 328; **23:** 187, 191, 197, 203, 221, 233, 237, 252; **25:** 1
unnatural ordering **22:** 378
violence **22:** 12
visual humor **23:** 207, 217
Watteau, influence on staging **23:** 184, 186
women, role of **19:** 92; **22:** 12; **23:** 215; **25:** 1
written versus oral communication **2:** 359, 365; **28:** 63

Macbeth (Volumes 3, 20, 29, 44)

antithetical or contradictory elements **3:** 185, 213, 271, 302; **25:** 235; **29:** 76, 127

appearance versus reality **3:** 241, 248; **25:** 235
archetypal or mythic elements **16:** 317
audience response **20:** 17, 400, 406; **29:** 139, 146, 155, 165; **44:** 306
banquet scene (Act III, scene iv) **20:** 22, 32, 175
Banquo **3:** 183, 199, 208, 213, 278, 289; **20:** 279, 283, 406, 413; **25:** 235; **28:** 339
characterization **20:** 12, 318, 324, 329, 353, 363, 367, 374, 387; **28:** 339; **29:** 101, 109, 146, 155, 165; **44:** 289
Christian elements **3:** 194, 239, 260, 269, 275, 286, 293, 297, 318; **20:** 203, 206, 210, 256, 262, 289, 291, 294; **44:** 341, 366
combat scenes **22:** 365
dagger scene (Act III, scene i), staging of **20:** 406
evil **3:** 194, 208, 231, 234, 239, 241, 267, 289; **20:** 203, 206, 210, 374
free will versus fate **3:** 177, 183, 184, 190, 196, 198, 202, 207, 208, 213; **13:** 361; **44:** 351, 361, 366, 373
innocence **3:** 234, 241, 327
Jacobean culture, relation to **19:** 330; **22:** 365
Lady Macbeth
ambition **3:** 185, 219; **20:** 279, 345
characterization **20:** 56, 60, 65, 73, 140, 148, 151, 241, 279, 283, 338, 350, 406, 413; **29:** 109, 146
childlessness **3:** 219, 223
good and evil, combined traits of **3:** 173, 191, 213; **20:** 60, 107
inconsistencies **3:** 202; **20:** 54, 137
influence on Macbeth **3:** 171, 185, 191, 193, 199, 262, 289, 312, 318; **13:** 502; **20:** 345; **25:** 235; **29:** 133
psychoanalytic interpretations **20:** 345; **44:** 289, 297, 324; **45:** 58
as sympathetic figure **3:** 191, 193, 203
language and imagery **3:** 170, 193, 213, 231, 234, 241, 245, 250, 253, 256, 263, 271, 283, 300, 302, 306, 323, 327, 338, 340, 349; **13:** 476; **16:** 317; **20:** 241, 279, 283, 367, 379, 400; **25:** 235; **28:** 339; **29:** 76, 91; **42:** 263; **44:** 366; **45:** 58
laws of nature, violation of **3:** 234, 241, 280, 323; **29:** 120
letter to Lady Macbeth **16:** 372; **20:** 345; **25:** 235
Macbeth
ambition **44:** 284, 324
characterization **20:** 20, 42, 73, 107, 113, 130, 146, 151, 279, 283, 312, 338, 343, 379, 406, 413; **29:** 139, 152, 155, 165; **44:** 289
courage **3:** 172, 177, 181, 182, 183, 186, 234, 312, 333; **20:** 107; **44:** 315
disposition **3:** 173, 175, 177, 182, 186; **20:** 245, 376
imagination **3:** 196, 208, 213, 250, 312, 345; **20:** 245, 376; **44:** 351
as "inauthentic" king **3:** 245, 302, 321, 345
inconsistencies **3:** 202
as Machiavellian villain **3:** 280
manliness **20:** 113; **29:** 127, 133; **44:** 315
psychoanalytic interpretations **20:** 42, 73, 238, 376; **44:** 284, 289, 297, 324; **45:** 48, 58
Richard III, compared with **3:** 177, 182, 186, 345; **20:** 86, 92; **22:** 365; **44:** 269
as Satan figure **3:** 229, 269, 275, 289, 318

self-awareness **3:** 312, 329, 338; **16:** 317; **44:** 361
as sympathetic figure **3:** 229, 306, 314, 338; **29:** 139, 152; **44:** 269, 306, 337
as tragic hero **44:** 269, 306, 315, 324, 337
Macduff **3:** 226, 231, 253, 262,; **25:** 235; **29:** 127, 133, 155
madness **19:** 330
major tragedies, relation to Shakespeare's other **3:** 171, 173, 213; **44:** 269
Malcolm **25:** 235
manhood **3:** 262, 309, 333; **29:** 127, 133
Marxist criticism **42:** 234
medieval mystery plays, relation to **44:** 341
moral lesson **20:** 23
murder scene (Act II, scene ii) **20:** 175
Neoclassical rules **3:** 170, 171, 173, 175; **20:** 17
nightmarish quality **3:** 231, 309; **20:** 210, 242; **44:** 261
Porter scene (Act II, scene iii) **3:** 173, 175, 184, 190, 196, 203, 205, 225, 260, 271, 297, 300; **20:** 283; **44:** 261; **46:** 29, 78
primitivism **20:** 206, 213; **45:** 48
providential order **3:** 208, 289, 329, 336
psychoanalytic interpretations **3:** 219, 223, 226; **44:** 11, 284, 289, 297
regicide **16:** 317, 328; **45:** 48 248, 275, 312
religious and theological issues **44:** 324, 341, 351, 361, 366, 373
religious, mythic, or spiritual content **3:** 208, 269, 275, 318; **29:** 109
retribution **3:** 194, 208, 318
sexual anxiety **16:** 328; **20:** 283
sleepwalking scene (Act V, scene i) **3:** 191, 203, 219; **20:** 175; **44:** 261
staging issues **13:** 502; **20:** 12, 17, 32, 64, 65, 70, 73, 107, 113, 151, 175, 203, 206, 210, 213, 245, 279, 283, 312, 318, 324, 329, 343, 345, 350, 353, 363, 367, 374, 376, 379, 382, 387, 400, 406, 413; **22:** 365; **32:** 212
structure **16:** 317; **20:** 12, 245
supernatural grace versus evil or chaos **3:** 241, 286, 323
theatricality **16:** 328
time **3:** 234, 246, 283, 293; **20:** 245
topical allusions or content **13:** 361; **20:** 17, 350; **29:** 101
treason and punishment **13:** 361; **16:** 328
violence **20:** 273, 279, 283; **45:** 58
witches and supernaturalism **3:** 171, 172, 173, 175, 177, 182, 183, 184, 185, 194, 196, 198, 202, 207, 208, 213, 219, 229, 239; **16:** 317; **19:** 245; **20:** 92, 175, 213, 279, 283, 374, 387, 406, 413; **25:** 235; **28:** 339; **29:** 91, 101, 109, 120; **44:** 351, 373,

Measure for Measure (Volumes 2, 23, 33)

ambiguity **2:** 417, 420, 432, 446, 449, 452, 474, 479, 482, 486, 495, 505
Angelo
anxiety **16:** 114
authoritarian portrayal of **23:** 307
characterization **2:** 388, 390, 397, 402, 418, 427, 432, 434, 463, 484, 495, 503, 511; **13:** 84; **23:** 297; **32:** 81; **33:** 77

hypocrisy **2**: 396, 399, 402, 406, 414, 421; **23**: 345, 358, 362
  repentance or pardon **2**: 388, 390, 397, 402, 434, 463, 511, 524
autobiographical elements **2**: 406, 410, 414, 431, 434, 437
Barnardine **13**: 112
bed-trick **13**: 84
characterization **2**: 388, 390, 391, 396, 406, 420, 421, 446, 466, 475, 484, 505, 516, 524; **23**: 299, 405; **33**: 77
Christian elements **2**: 391, 394, 399, 421, 437, 449, 466, 479, 491, 511, 522
comic form **2**: 456, 460, 479, 482, 491, 514, 516; **13**: 94, 104; **23**: 309, 326, 327
death, decay, and nature's destructiveness **2**: 394, 452, 516; **25**: 12
displacement **22**: 78
Duke
  as authoritarian figure **23**: 314, 317, 347; **33**: 85
  characterization **2**: 388, 395, 402, 406, 411, 421, 429, 456, 466, 470, 498, 511; **13**: 84, 94, 104; **23**: 363, 416; **32**: 81; **42**: 1; **44**: 89
  dramatic shortcomings or failure **2**: 420, 429, 441, 479, 495, 505, 514, 522
  godlike portrayal of **23**: 320
  noble portrayal of **23**: 301
  speech on death (Act III, scene i) **2**: 390, 391, 395
Elbow **22**: 85; **25**: 12
Elbow, Mistress **33**: 90
Elizabethan betrothal and marriage customs **2**: 429, 437, 443, 503
Elizabethan culture, relation to **2**: 394, 418, 429, 432, 437, 460, 470, 482, 503
feminist interpretation **23**: 320
good and evil **2**: 432, 452, 524; **33**: 52, 61
homosexuality **42**: 1
immortality **16**: 102
inconsistency between first and second halves **2**: 474, 475, 505, 514, 524
Isabella **2**: 388, 390, 395, 396, 397, 401, 402, 406, 409, 410, 411, 418, 420, 421, 432, 437, 441, 466, 475, 491, 495, 524; **16**: 114; **23**: 278, 279, 280, 281, 282, 296, 344, 357, 363, 405; **28**: 92; **33**: 77, 85
judicial versus natural law **2**: 446, 507, 516, 519; **22**: 85; **33**: 58, 117
justice and mercy **2**: 391, 395, 399, 402, 406, 409, 411, 416, 421, 437, 443, 463, 466, 470, 491, 495, 522, 524; **22**: 85; **33**: 52, 61, 101
language and imagery **2**: 394, 421, 431, 466, 486, 505; **13**: 112; **28**: 9; **33**: 69
Lucio **13**: 104
marriage **2**: 443, 507, 516, 519, 524, 528; **25**: 12; **33**: 61, 90
as medieval allegory or morality play **2**: 409, 421, 443, 466, 475, 491, 505, 511, 522; **13**: 94
metadramatic elements **13**: 104
misgovernment **2**: 401, 432, 511; **22**: 85
misogyny **23**: 358;
moral seriousness, question of **2**: 387, 388, 396, 409, 417, 421, 452, 460, 495; **23**: 316, 321
Neoclassical rules **2**: 387, 388, 390, 394; **23**: 269
politics **23**: 379
power **13**: 112; **22**: 85; **23**: 327, 330, 339, 352; **33**: 85

as "problem play" **2**: 416, 429, 434, 474, 475, 503, 514, 519; **16**: 102; **23**: 313, 328, 351
psychoanalytic interpretations **23**: 331, 332, 333, 334, 335, 340, 355, 356, 359, 379, 395; **44**: 79
Puritanism **2**: 414, 418, 434
rebirth, regeneration, resurrection, or immortality **13**: 84; **16**: 102, 114; **23**: 321, 327, 335, 340, 352; **25**: 12
resolution **2**: 449, 475, 495, 514, 516; **16**: 102, 114
sexuality **13**: 84; **16**: 102, 114; **23**: 321, 327, 335, 340, 352; **25**: 12; **33**: 85, 90, 112
social aspects **23**: 316, 375, 379, 395
sources **2**: 388, 393, 427, 429, 437, 475; **13**: 94
staging issues **2**: 427, 429, 437, 441, 443, 456, 460, 482, 491, 519; **23**: 283, 284, 285, 286, 287, 291, 293, 294, 298, 299, 311, 315, 327, 338, 339, 340, 342, 344, 347, 363, 372, 375, 395, 400, 405, 406, 413; **32**: 16
structure **2**: 390, 411, 449, 456, 466, 474, 482, 490, 491; **33**: 69
substitution of identities **2**: 507, 511, 519; **13**: 112
theatricality **23**: 285, 286, 294, 372, 406
comic and tragic elements, combination of **16**: 102
as unsuccessful play **2**: 397, 441, 474, 482; **23**: 287

The Merchant of Venice (Volumes 4, 12, 40)

Act V, relation to Acts I through IV **4**: 193, 194, 195, 196, 204, 232, 270, 273, 289, 300, 319, 321, 326, 336, 356
allegorical elements **4**: 224, 250, 261, 268, 270, 273, 282, 289, 324, 336, 344, 350
Antonio
  excessive or destructive love **4**: 279, 284, 336, 344; **12**: 54; **37**: 86
  love for Bassanio **40**: 156
  melancholy **4**: 221, 238, 279, 284, 300, 321, 328; **22**: 69; **25**: 22
  pitiless **4**: 254
  as pivotal figure **12**: 25, 129
appearance versus reality **4**: 209, 261, 344; **12**: 65; **22**: 69
Bassanio **25**: 257; **37**: 86; **40**: 156
bonding **4**: 293, 317, 336; **13**: 37
casket scenes **4**: 226, 241, 308, 344; **12**: 23, 46, 47, 65, 117; **13**: 43; **22**: 3; **40**: 106
contrasting dramatic worlds **44**: 11
conflict between Christianity and Judaism **4**: 224, 250, 268, 289, 324, 344; **12**: 67, 70, 72, 76; **22**: 69; **25**: 257; **40**: 117, 127, 166, 181
desire **22**: 3; **40**: 142; **45**: 17
Economics and exchange **40**: 197, 208
Elizabethan culture, relation to **32**: 66; **40**: 117, 127, 142, 166, 181, 197, 208
genre **4**: 191, 200, 201, 209, 215, 221, 232, 238, 247; **12**: 48, 54, 62
homosexuality **22**: 3, 69; **37**: 86; **40**: 142, 156, 197
implausibility of plot, characters, or events **4**: 191, 192, 193; **12**: 52, 56, 76, 119
irony **4**: 254, 300, 321, 331, 350; **28**: 63

Jessica **4**: 196, 200, 228, 293, 342
justice and mercy **4**: 213, 214, 224, 250, 261, 273, 282, 289, 336; **12**: 80, 129; **40**: 127
language and imagery **4**: 241, 267, 293; **22**: 3; **25**: 257; **28**: 9, 63; **32**: 41; **40**: 106
Launcelot Gobbo **46**: 24, 60
love **4**: 221, 226, 270, 284, 312, 344; **22**: 3, 69; **25**: 257; **40**: 156
medieval homilies, influence of **4**: 224, 250, 289
Portia **4**: 194, 195, 196, 215, 254, 263, 336, 356; **12**: 104, 107, 114; **13**: 37; **22**: 3, 69; **25**: 22; **32**: 294; **37**: 86; **40**: 142, 156, 197, 208
psychoanalytic interpretation **45**: 17
resolution **4**: 263, 266, 300, 319, 321; **13**: 37
rings episode **22**: 3; **40**: 106, 151, 156
sacrificial love **13**: 43; **22**: 69; **40**: 142
sexual politics **22**: 3
Shylock
  alienation **4**: 279, 312; **40**: 175
  ambiguity **4**: 247, 254, 315, 319, 331; **12**: 31, 35, 36, 50, 51, 52, 56, 81, 124; **40**: 175
  forced conversion **4**: 209, 252, 268, 282, 289, 321
  Jewishness **4**: 193, 194, 195, 200, 201, 213, 214, 279; **22**: 69; **25**: 257; **40**: 142, 175, 181
  motives in making the bond **4**: 252, 263, 266, 268; **22**: 69; **25**: 22
  as Puritan **40**: 127, 166
  as scapegoat figure **4**: 254, 300; **40**: 166
  as traditional comic villain **4**: 230, 243, 261, 263, 315; **12**: 40, 62, 124; **40**: 175
  as tragic figure **12**: 6, 9, 10, 16, 21, 23, 25, 40, 44, 66, 67, 81, 97; **40**: 175
staging issues **12**: 111, 114, 115, 117, 119, 124, 129, 131
structure **4**: 201, 215, 230, 232, 243, 247, 254, 261, 263, 308, 321; **12**: 115; **28**: 63
trial scene **13**: 43; **25**: 22; **40**: 106, 156
unity of double plot **4**: 193, 194, 201, 232; **12**: 16, 67, 80, 115; **40**: 151
Venetians **4**: 195, 200, 228, 254, 273, 300, 321, 331
Venice, Elizabethan perceptions of **28**: 249; **32**: 294; **40**: 127
wealth **4**: 209, 261, 270, 273, 317; **12**: 80, 117; **22**: 69; **25**: 22; **28**: 249; **40**: 117, 197, 208; **45**: 17

The Merry Wives of Windsor (Volumes 5, 18, 38)

Anne Page-Fenton plot **5**: 334, 336, 343, 353, 376, 390, 395, 402; **22**: 93
avarice **5**: 335, 353, 369, 376, 390, 395, 402
caricature **5**: 343, 347, 348, 350, 385, 397
characterization **5**: 332, 334, 335, 337, 338, 351, 360, 363, 366, 374, 379, 392; **18**: 74, 75; **38**: 264, 273, 313, 319
class distinctions, conflict, and relations **5**: 338, 343, 346, 347, 366, 390, 395, 400, 402; **22**: 93; **28**: 69
comic and farcical elements **5**: 336, 338, 346, 350, 360, 369, 373; **18**: 74, 75, 84
The Comical Gallant (John Dennis adaptation) **18**: 5, 7, 8, 9, 10
deception, disguise, and duplicity **5**: 332, 334, 336, 354, 355, 379; **22**: 93

desire **38:** 286, 297, 300
Elizabeth's influence **5:** 333, 334, 335, 336, 339, 346, 355, 366, 402; **18:** 5, 86; **38:** 278
Falstaff
    characterization in *1 and 2 Henry IV*, compared with **5:** 333, 335, 337, 339, 346, 347, 348, 350, 373, 400; **18:** 5, 7, 75, 86; **22:** 93
    diminishing powers **5:** 337, 339, 343, 347, 350, 351, 392
    as Herne the Hunter **38:** 256, 286
    incapability of love **5:** 335, 336, 339, 346, 348; **22:** 93
    personification of comic principle or Vice figure **5:** 332, 338, 369, 400; **38:** 273
    recognition and repentance of follies **5:** 338, 341, 343, 348, 369, 374, 376, 397
    sensuality **5:** 339, 343, 353, 369, 392
    shrewdness **5:** 332, 336, 346, 355
    threat to community **5:** 343, 369, 379, 392, 395, 400; **38:** 297
    vanity **5:** 332, 339
    victimization **5:** 336, 338, 341, 347, 348, 353, 355, 360, 369, 373, 374, 376, 392, 397, 400
folk rituals, elements and influence of **5:** 353, 369, 376, 392, 397, 400; **38:** 256, 300
Ford **5:** 332, 334, 343, 355, 363, 374, 379, 390; **38:** 273
jealousy **5:** 334, 339, 343, 353, 355, 363; **22:** 93; **38:** 273, 307
Jonsonian humors comedy, influence of **38:** 319
knighthood **5:** 338, 343, 390, 397, 402
language and imagery **5:** 335, 337, 343, 347, 351, 363, 374, 379; **19:** 101; **22:** 93, 378; **28:** 9, 69; **38:** 313, 319
male discontent **5:** 392, 402
marriage **5:** 343, 369, 376, 390, 392, 400; **22:** 93; **38:** 297
mediation **5:** 343, 392
morality **5:** 335, 339, 347, 349, 353, 397
Neoclassical rules **5:** 332, 334
play-within-the-play, convention of **5:** 354, 355, 369, 402
realism **38:** 313
reconciliation **5:** 343, 369, 374, 397, 402
revenge **5:** 349, 350, 392; **38:** 264, 307
as satire or parody **5:** 338, 350, 360, 385; **38:** 278, 319
schemes and intrigues **5:** 334, 336, 339, 341, 343, 349, 355, 379
sexual politics **19:** 101; **38:** 307
social milieu **18:** 75, 84; **38:** 297, 300
sources **5:** 332, 350, 360, 366, 385; **32:** 31
stage history **18:** 66, 67, 68, 70, 71
staging issues **18:** 74, 75, 84, 86, 90, 95
structure **5:** 332, 333, 334, 335, 343, 349, 355, 369, 374; **18:** 86; **22:** 378
unnatural ordering **22:** 378
wit **5:** 335, 336, 337, 339, 343, 351
women, role of **5:** 335, 341, 343, 349, 369, 379, 390, 392, 402; **19:** 101; **38:** 307

A Midsummer Night's Dream (Volumes 3, 12, 29, 45)

adaptations **12:** 144, 146, 147, 153, 280, 282
ambiguity **3:** 401, 459, 486; **45:** 169
appearance, perception, and illusion **3:** 368, 411, 425, 427, 434, 447, 459, 466, 474, 477, 486, 497, 516; **19:** 21; **22:** 39; **28:** 15; **29:** 175, 190; **45:** 136
Athens and the forest, contrast between **3:** 381, 427, 459, 466, 497, 502; **29:** 175
autobiographical elements **3:** 365, 371, 379, 381, 389, 391, 396, 402, 432
Bottom
    awakening speech (Act IV, scene i) **3:** 406, 412, 450, 457, 486, 516; **16:** 34
    folly of **46:** 1, 14, 29, 60
    imagination **3:** 376, 393, 406, 432, 486; **29:** 175, 190; **45:** 147
    self-possession **3:** 365, 376, 395, 402, 406, 480; **45:** 158
    Titania, relationship with **3:** 377, 406, 441, 445, 450, 457, 491, 497; **16:** 34; **19:** 21; **22:** 93; **29:** 216; **45:** 160
    transformation **3:** 365, 377, 432; **13:** 27; **22:** 93; **29:** 216; **45:** 147, 160
brutal elements **3:** 445, 491, 497, 511; **12:** 259, 262, 298; **16:** 34; **19:** 21; **29:** 183, 225, 263, 269; **45:** 169
capriciousness of the young lovers **3:** 372, 395, 402, 411, 423, 437, 441, 450, 497, 498; **29:** 175, 269; **45:** 107
chastity **45:** 143
class distinctions, conflict, and relations **22:** 23; **25:** 36; **45:** 160
as dream-play **3:** 365, 370, 372, 377, 389, 391; **29:** 190; **45:** 117
dreams **45:** 96, 107, 117
duration of time **3:** 362, 370, 380, 386, 494; **45:** 175
erotic elements **3:** 445, 491, 497, 511; **12:** 259, 262, 298; **16:** 34; **19:** 21; **29:** 183, 225, 269
fairies **3:** 361, 362, 372, 377, 395, 400, 423, 450, 459, 486; **12:** 287, 291, 294, 295; **19:** 21; **29:** 183, 190; **45:** 147
Helena **29:** 269
Hermia **29:** 225, 269; **45:** 117
Hippolytus, myth of **29:** 216; **45:** 84
identity **29:** 269
imagination and art **3:** 365, 371, 381, 402, 412, 417, 421, 423, 441, 459, 468, 506, 516, 520; **22:** 39
language and imagery **3:** 397, 401, 410, 412, 415, 432, 453, 459, 468, 494; **22:** 23, 39, 93, 378; **28:** 9; **29:** 263; **45:** 96, 126, 136, 147; **45:** 143, 169, 175
male domination **3:** 483, 520; **13:** 19; **25:** 36; **29:** 216, 225, 243, 256, 269; **42:** 46; **45:** 84
marriage **3:** 402, 423, 450, 483, 520; **29:** 243, 256; **45:** 136, 143
metadramatic elements **3:** 427, 468, 477, 516, 520; **29:** 190, 225, 243
Metamorphoses (Golding translation of Ovid) **16:** 25
Minotaur, myth of **3:** 497, 498; **29:** 216
music and dance **3:** 397, 400, 418, 513; **12:** 287, 289; **25:** 36
Oberon as controlling force **3:** 434, 459, 477, 502; **29:** 175
Ovid, influence of **3:** 362, 427, 497, 498; **22:** 23; **29:** 175, 190, 216
parent-child relations **13:** 19; **29:** 216, 225, 243
passionate or romantic love **3:** 372, 389, 395, 396, 402, 408, 411, 423, 441, 450, 480, 497, 498, 511; **29:** 175, 225, 263, 269; **45:** 126, 136
Pauline doctrine **3:** 457, 486, 506
Platonic elements **3:** 368, 437, 450, 497; **45:** 126
politics **29:** 243
power **42:** 46; **45:** 84
psychoanalytic interpretations **3:** 440, 483; **28:** 15; **29:** 225; **44:** 1; **45:** 107, 117
Puck **45:** 96, 158
Pyramus and Thisbe interlude **3:** 364, 368, 379, 381, 389, 391, 396, 408, 411, 412, 417, 425, 427, 433, 441, 447, 457, 468, 474, 511; **12:** 254; **13:** 27; **16:** 25; **22:** 23; **29:** 263; **45:** 107, 175
reason versus imagination **3:** 381, 389, 423, 441, 466, 506; **22:** 23; **29:** 190; **45:** 96
reconciliation **3:** 412, 418, 437, 459, 468, 491, 497, 502, 513; **13:** 27; **29:** 190
reversal **29:** 225
Romeo and Juliet, compared with **3:** 396, 480
rustic characters **3:** 376, 397, 432; **12:** 291, 293; **45:** 147, 160
sexuality **22:** 23, 93; **29:** 225, 243, 256, 269; **42:** 46; **45:** 107
sources **29:** 216
staging issues **3:** 364, 365, 371, 372, 377; **12:** 151, 152, 154, 158, 159, 280, 284, 291, 295; **16:** 34; **19:** 21; **29:** 183, 256
structure **3:** 364, 368, 381, 402, 406, 427, 450, 513; **13:** 19; **22:** 378; **29:** 175; **45:** 126, 175
textual issues **16:** 34; **29:** 216
Theseus
    characterization **3:** 363
    Hippolyta, relationship with **3:** 381, 412, 421, 423, 450, 468, 520; **29:** 175, 216, 243, 256; **45:** 84
    as ideal **3:** 379, 391
    "lovers, lunatics, and poets" speech (Act V, scene i) **3:** 365, 371, 379, 381, 391, 402, 411, 412, 421, 423, 441, 498, 506; **29:** 175
    as representative of institutional life **3:** 381, 403
Titania **29:** 243
tragic elements **3:** 393, 400, 401, 410, 445, 474, 480, 491, 498, 511; **29:** 175; **45:** 169
unity **3:** 364, 368, 381, 402, 406, 427, 450, 513; **13:** 19; **22:** 378; **29:** 175, 263
unnatural ordering **22:** 378

Much Ado about Nothing (Volumes 8, 18, 31)

appearance versus reality **8:** 17, 18, 48, 63, 69, 73, 75, 79, 88, 95, 115; **31:** 198, 209
battle of the sexes **8:** 14, 16, 19, 48, 91, 95, 111, 121, 125; **31:** 231, 245
Beatrice and Benedick
    Beatrice's femininity **8:** 14, 16, 17, 24, 29, 38, 41, 91; **31:** 222, 245
    Beatrice's request to "kill Claudio" (Act IV, scene i) **8:** 14, 17, 33, 41, 55, 63, 75, 79, 91, 108, 115; **18:** 119, 120, 136, 161, 245, 257
    Benedick's challenge of Claudio (Act V, scene i) **8:** 48, 63, 79, 91; **31:** 231
    Claudio and Hero, compared with **8:** 19, 28, 29, 75, 82, 115; **31:** 171, 216

marriage and the opposite sex, attitudes toward **8:** 9, 13, 14, 16, 19, 29, 36, 48, 63, 77, 91, 95, 115, 121; **16:** 45; **31:** 216
mutual attraction **8:** 13, 14, 19, 24, 29, 33, 41, 75
nobility **8:** 13, 19, 24, 29, 36, 39, 41, 47, 82, 91, 108
popularity **8:** 13, 38, 41, 53, 79
transformed by love **8:** 19, 29, 36, 48, 75, 91, 95, 115; **31:** 209, 216
unconventionality **8:** 48, 91, 95, 108, 115, 121
vulgarity **8:** 11, 12, 33, 38, 41, 47
wit and charm **8:** 9, 12, 13, 14, 19, 24, 27, 28, 29, 33, 36, 38, 41, 47, 55, 69, 95, 108, 115; **31:** 241
Borachio and Conrade **8:** 24, 69, 82, 88, 111, 115
Christian elements **8:** 17, 19, 29, 55, 95, 104, 111, 115; **31:** 209
church scene (Act IV, scene i) **8:** 13, 14, 16, 19, 33, 44, 47, 48, 58, 63, 69, 75, 79, 82, 91, 95, 100, 104, 111, 115; **18:** 120, 130, 138, 145, 146, 148, 192; **31:** 191, 198, 245
Claudio
 boorish behavior **8:** 9, 24, 33, 36, 39, 44, 48, 63, 79, 82, 95, 100, 111, 115; **31:** 209
 credulity **8:** 9, 17, 19, 24, 29, 36, 41, 47, 58, 63, 75, 77, 82, 95, 100, 104, 111, 115, 121; **31:** 241
 mercenary traits **8:** 24, 44, 58, 82, 91, 95
 noble qualities **8:** 17, 19, 29, 41, 44, 58, 75
 reconciliation with Hero **8:** 33, 36, 39, 44, 47, 82, 95, 100, 111, 115, 121
 repentance **8:** 33, 63, 82, 95, 100, 111, 115, 121; **31:** 245
 sexual insecurities **8:** 75, 100, 111, 115, 121
courtship and marriage **8:** 29, 44, 48, 95, 115, 121, 125; **31:** 191, 231
deception, disguise, and duplicity **8:** 29, 55, 63, 69, 79, 82, 88, 108, 115; **31:** 191, 198
Dogberry and the Watch **8:** 9, 12, 13, 17, 24, 28, 29, 33, 39, 48, 55, 69, 79, 82, 88, 95, 104, 108, 115; **18:** 138, 152, 205, 208, 210, 213, 231; **22:** 85; **31:** 171, 229; **46:** 60
Don John **8:** 9, 12, 16, 17, 19, 28, 29, 36, 39, 41, 47, 48, 55, 58, 63, 82, 104, 108, 111, 121
Don Pedro **8:** 17, 19, 48, 58, 63, 82, 111, 121
eavesdropping scenes (Act II, scene iii and Act III, scene i) **8:** 12, 13, 17, 19, 28, 29, 33, 36, 48, 55, 63, 73, 75, 82, 121; **18:** 120, 138, 208, 215, 245, 264; **31:** 171, 184
egotism or narcissism **8:** 19, 24, 28, 29, 55, 69, 95, 115
Elizabethan culture, relation to **8:** 23, 33, 44, 55, 58, 79, 88, 104, 111, 115
Friar **8:** 24, 29, 41, 55, 63, 79, 111
genre **8:** 9, 18, 19, 28, 29, 39, 41, 44, 53, 63, 69, 73, 79, 82, 95, 100, 104
Hero **8:** 13, 14, 16, 19, 28, 29, 44, 48, 53, 55, 82, 95, 104, 111, 115, 121; **31:** 231, 245
implausibility of plot, characters, or events **8:** 9, 12, 16, 19, 33, 36, 39, 44, 53, 100, 104
irony **8:** 14, 63, 79, 82; **28:** 63
justice and mercy **22:** 85
language and imagery **8:** 9, 38, 43, 46, 55, 69, 73, 88, 95, 100, 115, 125; **19:** 68; **25:** 77; **28:** 63; **31:** 178, 184, 222, 241, 245

law versus passion for freedom **22:** 85
love **8:** 24, 55, 75, 95, 111, 115; **28:** 56
Messina **8:** 19, 29, 48, 69, 82, 91, 95, 108, 111, 121, 125; **31:** 191, 209, 229, 241, 245
misgovernment **22:** 85
music and dance **19:** 68; **31:** 222
"nothing," significance of **8:** 17, 18, 23, 55, 73, 95; **19:** 68
performance issues **18:** 173, 174, 183, 184, 185, 186, 187, 188, 189, 190, 191, 192, 193, 195, 197, 199, 201, 204, 206, 207, 208, 209, 210, 254
power **22:** 85; **25:** 77; **31:** 231, 245
repentance or forgiveness **8:** 24, 29, 111
resurrection, metamorphosis, or transformation **8:** 88, 104, 111, 115
romance or chivalric tradition, influence of **8:** 53, 125
self-knowledge **8:** 69, 95, 100
setting **18:** 173, 174, 183, 184, 185, 186, 187, 188, 189, 190, 191, 192, 193, 195, 197, 199, 201, 204, 206, 207, 208, 209, 210, 254
slander or hearsay, importance of **8:** 58, 69, 82, 95, 104
sources **8:** 9, 19, 53, 58, 104
staging issues **8:** 18, 33, 41, 75, 79, 82, 108; **16:** 45; **18:** 245, 247, 249, 252, 254, 257, 261, 264; **28:** 63
structure **8:** 9, 16, 17, 19, 28, 29, 33, 39, 48, 63, 69, 73, 75, 79, 82, 115; **31:** 178, 184, 198, 231
virginity or chastity, importance of **8:** 44, 75, 95, 111, 121, 125; **31:** 222
wit **8:** 27, 29, 38, 69, 79, 91, 95; **31:** 178, 191
works by Shakespeare or other authors, compared with **8:** 16, 19, 27, 28, 33, 38, 39, 41, 53, 69, 79, 91, 104, 108; **31:** 231

Othello (Volumes 4, 11, 35)

autobiographical elements **4:** 440, 444
Brabantio **25:** 189
Cassio **25:** 189
consummation of marriage **22:** 207
contrasts and oppositions **4:** 421, 455, 457, 462, 508; **25:** 189
Desdemona
 as Christ figure **4:** 506, 525, 573; **35:** 360
 culpability **4:** 408, 415, 422, 427; **13:** 313; **19:** 253, 276; **35:** 265, 352, 380
 innocence **35:** 360
 as mother figure **22:** 339; **35:** 282
 passivity **4:** 402, 406, 421, 440, 457, 470, 582, 587; **25:** 189; **35:** 380
 spiritual nature of her love **4:** 462, 530, 559
 staging issues **11:** 350, 354, 359; **13:** 327; **32:** 201
dramatic structure **4:** 370, 390, 399, 427, 488, 506, 517, 569; **22:** 207; **28:** 243
Duke **25:** 189
Emilia **4:** 386, 391, 392, 415, 587; **35:** 352, 380
gender issues **32:** 294; **35:** 327
handkerchief, significance of **4:** 370, 384, 385, 396, 503, 530, 562; **35:** 265, 282, 380
Hercules Furens (Seneca) as source **16:** 283
Iago
 affinity with Othello **4:** 400, 427, 468, 470, 477, 500, 506; **25:** 189; **44:** 57

 as conventional dramatic villain **4:** 440, 527, 545, 582
 as homosexual **4:** 503
 Machiavellian elements **4:** 440, 455, 457, 517, 545; **35:** 336, 347
 motives **4:** 389, 390, 397, 399, 402, 409, 423, 424, 427, 434, 451, 462, 545, 564; **13:** 304; **25:** 189; **28:** 344; **32:** 201; **35:** 265, 276, 310, 336, 347; **42:** 278
 revenge scheme **4:** 392, 409, 424, 451
 as scapegoat **4:** 506
 as victim **4:** 402, 409, 434, 451, 457, 470
idealism versus realism **4:** 457, 508, 517; **13:** 313; **25:** 189
implausibility of plot, characters, or events **4:** 370, 380, 391, 442, 444
jealousy **4:** 384, 488, 527; **35:** 253, 265, 282, 301, 310; **44:** 57, 66
justice **35:** 247
language and imagery **4:** 433, 442, 445, 462, 493, 508, 517, 552, 587, 596; **13:** 304; **16:** 272; **22:** 378; **25:** 189, 257; **28:** 243, 344; **42:** 278
love **4:** 412, 493, 506, 512, 530, 545, 552, 569, 570, 575, 580, 591; **19:** 253; **22:** 207; **25:** 257; **28:** 243, 344; **32:** 201; **35:** 261, 317
love and reason **4:** 512, 530, 580; **19:** 253
madness **35:** 265, 276, 282
marriage **35:** 369
Marxist criticism **42:** 234
Measure for Measure, compared with **25:** 189
medieval dramatic conventions, influence of **4:** 440, 527, 545, 559, 582
military and sexual hierarchies **16:** 272
Othello
 affinity with Iago **4:** 400, 427, 468, 470, 477, 500, 506; **25:** 189; **35:** 276, 320, 327
 as conventional "blameless hero" **4:** 445, 486, 500
 credulity **4:** 384, 385, 388, 390, 396, 402, 434, 440, 455; **13:** 327; **32:** 302
 Desdemona, relationship with **22:** 339; **35:** 301, 317; **37:** 269
 divided nature **4:** 400, 412, 462, 470, 477, 493, 500, 582, 592; **16:** 293; **19:** 276; **25:** 189; **35:** 320
 egotism **4:** 427, 470, 477, 493, 522, 536, 541, 573, 597; **13:** 304; **35:** 247, 253
 self-destructive anger **16:** 283
 self-dramatizing or self-deluding **4:** 454, 457, 477, 592; **13:** 313; **16:** 293; **35:** 317
 self-knowledge **4:** 462, 470, 477, 483, 508, 522, 530, 564, 580, 591, 596; **13:** 304, 313; **16:** 283; **28:** 243; **35:** 253, 317
 spiritual state **4:** 483, 488, 517, 525, 527, 544, 559, 564, 573; **28:** 243; **35:** 253
perception **19:** 276; **25:** 189, 257
poetic justice, question of **4:** 370, 412, 415, 427
pride and rightful self-esteem **4:** 522, 536, 541; **35:** 352
psychoanalytic interpretations **4:** 468, 503; **35:** 265, 276, 282, 301, 317, 320, 347; **42:** 203; **44:** 57
racial issues **4:** 370, 380, 384, 385, 392, 399, 401, 402, 408, 427, 564; **13:** 327; **16:** 293; **25:** 189, 257; **28:** 249, 330; **35:** 369; **42:** 203
religious, mythic, or spiritual content **4:** 483, 517, 522, 525, 559, 573; **22:** 207; **28:** 330

revenge **35:** 261
Romeo and Juliet, compared with **32:** 302
sexuality **22:** 339; **28:** 330, 344; **35:** 352, 360; **37:** 269; **44:** 57, 66
sources **28:** 330
staging issues **11:** 273, 334, 335, 339, 342, 350, 354, 359, 362
structure **22:** 378; **28:** 325
time scheme **4:** 370, 384, 390, 488; **22:** 207; **35:** 310
'Tis Pity She's a Whore (John Ford), compared with
unnatural ordering **22:** 378
Venetian politics **32:** 294
violence **22:** 12; **43:** 32
The Winter's Tale, compared with **35:** 310
women, role of **19:** 253; **28:** 344

Pericles **(Volumes 2, 15, 36)**

archetypal structure **2:** 570, 580, 582, 584, 588; **25:** 365
art and nature **22:** 315; **36:** 233
audience perception **42:** 359
authorship controversy **2:** 538, 540, 543, 544, 545, 546, 548, 550, 551, 553, 556, 558, 564, 565, 568, 576, 586; **15:** 132, 141, 148, 152; **16:** 391, 399; **25:** 365; **36:** 198, 244
autobiographical elements **2:** 551, 554, 555, 563, 581
brothel scenes (Act IV, scenes ii and vi) **2:** 548, 550, 551, 553, 554, 586, 590; **15:** 134, 145, 154, 166, 172, 177; **36:** 274
composition date **2:** 537, 544
Diana, as symbol of nature **22:** 315; **36:** 233
doubling of roles **15:** 150, 152, 167, 173, 180
Gower chorus **2:** 548, 575; **15:** 134, 141, 143, 145, 149, 152, 177; **36:** 279; **42:** 359
incest, motif of **2:** 582, 588; **22:** 315; **36:** 257, 264
as inferior or flawed plays **2:** 537, 546, 553, 563, 564; **15:** 139, 143, 156, 167, 176; **36:** 198
innocence **36:** 226, 274
Jacobean culture, relation to **37:** 361
language and imagery **2:** 559, 560, 565, 583; **16:** 391; **19:** 387; **22:** 315; **36:** 198, 214, 233, 244, 251, 264
Marina **37:** 361
as miracle play **2:** 569, 581; **36:** 205
nature as book **22:** 315; **36:** 233
oaths, importance of **19:** 387
patience **2:** 572, 573, 578, 579; **36:** 251
Pericles
  characterization **36:** 251; **37:** 361
  patience **2:** 572, 573, 578, 579
  suit of Antiochus's daughter **2:** 547, 565, 578, 579
  Ulysses, compared with **2:** 551
politics **37:** 361
popularity **2:** 536, 538, 546; **37:** 361
recognition scene (Act V, scene i) **15:** 138, 139, 141, 145, 161, 162, 167, 172, 175
reconciliation **2:** 555, 564, 584, 586, 588; **36:** 205
religious, mythic, or spiritual content **2:** 559, 561, 565, 570, 580, 584, 588; **22:** 315; **25:** 365
riddle motif **22:** 315; **36:** 205, 214

Shakespeare's other romances, relation to **2:** 547, 549, 551, 559, 564, 570, 571, 584, 585; **15:** 139; **16:** 391, 399; **36:** 226, 257
spectacle **42:** 359
sources **2:** 538, 568, 572, 575; **25:** 365; **36:** 198, 205
staging issues **16:** 399
suffering **2:** 546, 573, 578, 579; **25:** 365; **36:** 279
textual revisions **15:** 129, 130, 132, 134, 135, 136, 138, 152, 155, 167, 181; **16:** 399; **25:** 365

The Phoenix and Turtle **(Volumes 10, 38)**

allegorical elements **10:** 7, 8, 9, 16, 17, 48; **38:** 334, 378
art and nature **10:** 7, 42
authenticity **10:** 7, 8, 16
autobiographical elements **10:** 14, 18, 42, 48
bird imagery **10:** 21, 27; **38:** 329, 350, 367
Christian elements **10:** 21, 24, 31; **38:** 326
complex or enigmatic nature **10:** 7, 14, 35, 42; **38:** 326, 357
consciously philosophical **10:** 7, 21, 24, 31, 48; **38:** 342, 378
constancy and faithfulness **10:** 18, 20, 21, 48; **38:** 329
Court of Love **10:** 9, 24, 50
Donne, John, compared with **10:** 20, 31, 35, 37, 40
satiric elements **10:** 8, 16, 17, 27, 35, 40, 45, 48
love **10:** 31, 37, 40, 50; **38:** 342, 345, 367
as metaphysical poem **10:** 7, 8, 9, 20, 31, 35, 37, 40, 45, 50
Neoplatonism **10:** 7, 9, 21, 24, 40, 45, 50; **38:** 345, 350, 367
as "pure" poetry **10:** 14, 31, 35; **38:** 329
Scholasticism **10:** 21, 24, 31
Shakespeare's dramas, compared with **10:** 9, 14, 17, 18, 20, 27, 37, 40, 42, 48; **38:** 342
sources **10:** 7, 9, 18, 24, 45; **38:** 326, 334, 350, 367
structure **10:** 27, 31, 37, 45, 50; **38:** 342, 345, 357
style **10:** 8, 20, 24, 27, 31, 35, 45, 50; **38:** 334, 345, 357

The Rape of Lucrece **(Volumes 10, 33, 43)**

allegorical elements **10:** 89, 93
Brutus **10:** 96, 106, 109, 116, 121, 125, 128, 135
Christian elements **10:** 77, 80, 89, 96, 98, 109
Collatine **10:** 98, 131; **43:** 102
Elizabethan culture, relation to **33:** 195; **43:** 77
irony or paradox **10:** 93, 98, 128
language and imagery **10:** 64, 65, 66, 71, 78, 80, 89, 93, 116, 109, 125, 131; **22:** 289, 294; **25:** 305; **32:** 321; **33:** 144, 155, 179, 200; **43:** 102, 113, 141
Lucrece
  chastity **33:** 131, 138; **43:** 92
  as example of Renaissance *virtù* **22:** 289; **43:** 148
  heroic **10:** 84, 93, 109, 121, 128
  patriarchal woman, model of **10:** 109, 131; **33:** 169, 200

self-responsibility **10:** 89, 96, 98, 106, 125; **33:** 195; **43:** 85, 92, 158
  unrealistic **10:** 64, 65, 66, 121
  verbose **10:** 64, 81, 116; **25:** 305; **33:** 169
  as victim **22:** 294; **25:** 305; **32:** 321; **33:** 131, 195; **43:** 102, 158
male/female relationships **10:** 109, 121, 131; **22:** 289; **25:** 305; **43:** 113, 141
narrative strategies **22:** 294
Roman history, relation to **10:** 84, 89, 93, 96, 98, 109, 116, 125, 135; **22:** 289; **25:** 305; **33:** 155, 190
Shakespeare's dramas, compared with **10:** 63, 64, 65, 66, 68, 71, 73, 74, 78, 80, 81, 84, 98, 116, 121, 125; **43:** 92
sources **10:** 63, 64, 65, 66, 68, 74, 77, 78, 98, 109, 121, 125; **25:** 305; **33:** 155, 190; **43:** 77, 92, 148,
structure **10:** 84, 89, 93, 98, 135; **22:** 294; **25:** 305, **43:** 102, 141
style **10:** 64, 65, 66, 68, 69, 70, 71, 73, 74, 77, 78, 81, 84, 98, 116, 131, 135; **43:** 113, 158
Tarquin **10:** 80, 93, 98, 116, 125; **22:** 294; **25:** 305; **32:** 321; **33:** 190; **43:** 102
tragic elements **10:** 78, 80, 81, 84, 98, 109; **43:** 85, 148
the Troy passage **10:** 74, 89, 98, 116, 121, 128; **22:** 289; **32:** 321; **33:** 144, 179; **43:** 77, 85
Venus and Adonis, compared with **10:** 63, 66, 68, 69, 70, 73, 81; **22:** 294; **43:** 148
violence **43:** 148, 158

Richard II **(Volumes 6, 24, 39)**

abdication scene (Act IV, scene i) **6:** 270, 307, 317, 327, 354, 359, 381, 393, 409; **13:** 172; **19:** 151; **24:** 274, 414
acting and dissimulation **6:** 264, 267, 307, 310, 315, 368, 393, 409; **24:** 339, 345, 346, 349, 352, 356
allegorical elements **6:** 264, 283, 323, 385
audience perception **24:** 414, 423; **39:** 295
Bolingbroke
  comic elements **28:** 134
  guilt **24:** 423; **39:** 279
  language and imagery **6:** 310, 315, 331, 347, 374, 381, 397; **32:** 189
  as Machiavellian figure **6:** 305, 307, 315, 331, 347, 388, 393, 397; **24:** 428
  as politician **6:** 255, 263, 264, 272, 277, 294, 364, 368, 391; **24:** 330, 333, 405, 414, 423, 428; **39:** 256
  Richard, compared with **6:** 307, 315, 347, 374, 391, 393, 409; **24:** 346, 349, 351, 352, 356, 395, 419, 423, 428
  his silence **24:** 423
  structure, compared with **39:** 235
  usurpation of crown, nature of **6:** 255, 272, 289, 307, 310, 347, 354, 359, 381, 385, 393; **13:** 172; **24:** 322, 356, 383, 419; **28:** 178
Bolingbroke and Richard as opposites **24:** 423
Bolingbroke-Mowbray dispute **22:** 137
carnival elements **19:** 151; **39:** 273
censorship **24:** 260, 261, 262, 263, 386; **42:** 120
ceremonies, rites, and rituals, importance of **6:** 270, 294, 315, 368, 381, 397, 409, 414; **24:** 274, 356, 411, 414, 419
comic elements **24:** 262, 263, 395; **39:** 243

contractual and economic relations **13:** 213
costumes **24:** 274, 278, 291, 304, 325, 356, 364, 423
deposition scene (Act III, scene iii) **24:** 298, 395, 423; **42:** 120
Elizabethan attitudes, influence of **6:** 287, 292, 294, 305, 321, 327, 364, 402, 414; **13:** 494; **24:** 325; **28:** 188; **39:** 273; **42:** 120
Essex Rebellion, relation to **6:** 249, 250; **24:** 356
family honor, structure, and inheritance **6:** 338, 368, 388, 397, 414; **39:** 263, 279
fate **6:** 289, 294, 304, 352, 354, 385
garden scene (Act III, scene iv) **6:** 264, 283, 323, 385; **24:** 307, 356, 414
Gaunt **6:** 255, 287, 374, 388, 402, 414; **24:** 274, 322, 325, 414, 423; **39:** 263, 279
gender issues **25:** 89; **39:** 295
historical sources, compared with **6:** 252, 279, 343; **28:** 134; **39:** 235
irony **6:** 270, 307, 364, 368, 391; **24:** 383; **28:** 188
King of Misrule **19:** 151; **39:** 273
kingship **6:** 263, 264, 272, 277, 289, 294, 327, 354, 364, 381, 388, 391, 402, 409, 414; **19:** 151, 209; **24:** 260, 289, 291, 322, 325, 333, 339, 345, 346, 349, 351, 352, 356, 395, 408, 419, 428; **28:** 134; **39:** 235, 243, 256, 273, 279, 289; **42:** 175
language and imagery **6:** 252, 282, 283, 294, 298, 315, 323, 331, 347, 368, 374, 381, 385, 397, 409; **13:** 213, 494; **24:** 269, 270, 298, 301, 304, 315, 325, 329, 333, 339, 356, 364, 395, 405, 408, 411, 414, 419; **28:** 134, 188; **39:** 243, 273, 289, 295; **42:** 175
Marlowe's works, compared with **19:** 233; **24:** 307, 336; **42:** 175
medievalism and chivalry, presentation of **6:** 258, 277, 294, 327, 338, 388, 397, 414; **24:** 274, 278, 279, 280, 283; **39:** 256
mercantilism and feudalism **13:** 213
mirror scene (Act IV, scene i) **6:** 317, 327, 374, 381, 393, 409; **24:** 267, 356, 408, 414, 419, 423; **28:** 134, 178; **39:** 295
negative assessments **6:** 250, 252, 253, 255, 282, 307, 317, 343, 359
Northumberland **24:** 423
Richard
  artistic temperament **6:** 264, 267, 270, 272, 277, 292, 294, 298, 315, 331, 334, 347, 368, 374, 393, 409; **24:** 298, 301, 304, 315, 322, 390, 405, 408, 411, 414, 419; **39:** 289
  Bolingbroke, compared with **24:** 346, 349, 351, 352, 356, 419; **39:** 256
  characterization **6:** 250, 252, 253, 254, 255, 258, 262, 263, 267, 270, 272, 282, 283, 304, 343, 347, 364, 368; **24:** 262, 263, 267, 269, 270, 271, 272, 273, 274, 278, 280, 315, 322, 325, 330, 333, 390, 395, 402, 405, 423; **28:** 134; **39:** 279, 289
  dangerous aspects **24:** 405
  delusion **6:** 267, 298, 334, 368, 409; **24:** 329, 336, 405
  homosexuality **24:** 405
  kingship **6:** 253, 254, 263, 272, 327, 331, 334, 338, 364, 402, 414; **24:** 278, 295, 336, 337, 339, 356, 419; **28:** 134, 178; **39:** 256, 263
  loss of identity **6:** 267, 338, 368, 374, 381, 388, 391, 409; **24:** 298, 414, 428

as martyr-king **6:** 289, 307, 321; **19:** 209; **24:** 289, 291; **28:** 134
nobility **6:** 255, 258, 259, 262, 263, 391; **24:** 260, 263, 274, 280, 289, 291, 402, 408, 411
political acumen **6:** 263, 264, 272, 292, 310, 327, 334, 364, 368, 374, 388, 391, 397, 402, 409; **24:** 405; **39:** 256
private versus public persona **6:** 317, 327, 364, 368, 391, 409; **24:** 428
role-playing **24:** 419, 423; **28:** 178
seizure of Gaunt's estate **6:** 250, 338, 388
self-dramatization **6:** 264, 267, 307, 310, 315, 317, 331, 334, 368, 393, 409; **24:** 339; **28:** 178
self-hatred **13:** 172; **24:** 383; **39:** 289
self-knowledge **6:** 255, 267, 331, 334, 338, 352, 354, 368, 388, 391; **24:** 273, 289, 414; **39:** 263, 289
spiritual redemption **6:** 255, 267, 331, 334, 338, 352, 354, 368, 388, 391; **24:** 273, 289, 411, 414
Shakespeare's other histories, compared with **6:** 255, 264, 272, 294, 304, 310, 317, 343, 354, 359; **24:** 320, 325, 330, 331, 332, 333; **28:** 178
Shakespeare's sympathies, question of **6:** 277, 279, 287, 347, 359, 364, 391, 393, 402
Sicilian Usurper (Nahum Tate adaptation) **24:** 260, 261, 262, 263, 386, 390
staging issues **13:** 494; **24:** 273, 274, 278, 279, 280, 283, 291, 295, 296, 301, 303, 304, 310, 315, 317, 320, 325, 333, 338, 346, 351, 352, 356, 364, 383, 386, 395, 402, 405, 411, 414, 419, 423, 428; **25:** 89
structure **6:** 282, 304, 317, 343, 352, 359, 364, 39; **24:** 307, 322, 325, 356, 395
textual arrangement **24:** 260, 261, 262, 263, 271, 273, 291, 296, 356, 390
time **22:** 137
usurpation **6:** 263, 264, 272, 287, 289, 315, 323, 331, 343, 354, 364, 381, 388, 393, 397; **24:** 383
York **6:** 287, 364, 368, 388, 402, 414; **24:** 263, 320, 322, 364, 395, 414; **39:** 243, 279

Richard III (Volumes 8, 14, 39)

ambivalence and abiguity **44:** 11
conscience **8:** 148, 152, 162, 165, 190, 197, 201, 206, 210, 228, 232, 239, 243, 252, 258; **39:** 341
Elizabethan politics, relation to **22:** 395; **25:** 141; **37:** 144; **39:** 345, 349; **42:** 132
family honor, structure and inheritance **8:** 177, 248, 252, 263, 267; **25:** 141; **39:** 335, 341, 349, 370
flattery **22:** 395
gender issues **25:** 141; **37:** 144; **39:** 345
genre **8:** 181, 182, 197, 206, 218, 228, 239, 243, 252, 258; **13:** 142; **39:** 383
ghost scene (Act V, scene iii) **8:** 152, 154, 159, 162, 163, 165, 170, 177, 193, 197, 210, 228, 239, 243, 252, 258, 267
Henry VI, relation to **8:** 159, 165, 177, 182, 193, 201, 210, 213, 218, 228, 243, 248, 252, 267; **25:** 164; **39:** 370

historical accuracy **8:** 144, 145, 153, 159, 163, 165, 168, 213, 223, 228, 232; **39:** 305, 308, 326, 383
historical principles **39:** 308, 326, 387
language and imagery **8:** 159, 161, 165, 167, 168, 170, 177, 182, 184, 186, 193, 197, 201, 206, 218, 223, 243, 248, 252, 258, 262, 267; **16:** 150; **25:** 141, 245; **39:** 360, 370, 383
Margaret **8:** 153, 154, 159, 162, 163, 170, 193, 201, 206, 210, 218, 223, 228, 243, 248, 262; **39:** 345
Christopher Marlowe's works, compared with **19:** 233
minor characters **8:** 154, 159, 162, 163, 168, 170, 177, 184, 186, 201, 206, 210, 218, 223, 228, 232, 239, 248, 262, 267
modernization **14:** 523
moral corruption of English society **8:** 154, 163, 165, 177, 193, 201, 218, 228, 232, 243, 248, 252, 267; **39:** 308
plot and incident **8:** 146, 152, 159; **25:** 164
popularity **8:** 144, 146, 154, 158, 159, 162, 181, 228; **39:** 383
rebellion **22:** 395
retribution **8:** 163, 170, 177, 182, 184, 193, 197, 201, 206, 210, 218, 223, 228, 243, 248, 267
Richard III
  ambition **8:** 148, 154, 165, 168, 170, 177, 182, 213, 218, 228, 232, 239, 252, 258, 267; **39:** 308, 341, 360, 370, 383
  attractive qualities **8:** 145, 148, 152, 154, 159, 161, 162, 165, 168, 170, 181, 182, 184, 185, 197, 201, 206, 213, 228, 243, 252, 258; **16:** 150; **39:** 370, 383
  credibility, question of **8:** 145, 147, 154, 159, 165, 193; **13:** 142
  death, decay, and nature's destructiveness **8:** 145, 148, 154, 159, 165, 168, 170, 177, 182, 197, 210, 223, 228, 232, 243, 248, 252, 258, 267
  deformity as symbol **8:** 146, 147, 148, 152, 154, 159, 161, 165, 170, 177, 184, 185, 193, 218, 248, 252, 267; **19:** 164
  inversion of moral order **8:** 159, 168, 177, 182, 184, 185, 197, 201, 213, 218, 223, 232, 239, 243, 248, 252, 258, 262, 267; **39:** 360
  as Machiavellian villain **8:** 165, 182, 190, 201, 218, 232, 239, 243, 248; **39:** 308, 326, 360, 387
  as monster or symbol of diabolic **8:** 145, 147, 159, 162, 168, 170, 177, 182, 193, 197, 201, 228, 239, 248, 258; **13:** 142; **37:** 144; **39:** 326, 349
  other literary villains, compared with **8:** 148, 161, 162, 165, 181, 182, 206, 213, 239, 267
  role-playing, hypocrisy, and dissimulation **8:** 145, 148, 154, 159, 162, 165, 168, 170, 182, 190, 206, 213, 218, 228, 239, 243, 252, 258, 267; **25:** 141, 164, 245; **39:** 335, 341, 387
  as scourge or instrument of God **8:** 163, 177, 193, 201, 218, 228, 248, 267; **39:** 308
  as Vice figure **8:** 190, 201, 213, 228, 243, 248, 252; **16:** 150; **39:** 383, 387
Richmond **8:** 154, 158, 163, 168, 177, 182, 193, 210, 218, 223, 228, 243, 248, 252; **13:** 142; **25:** 141; **39:** 349

settings **14:** 516, 528
Shakespeare's artistic growth, *Richard III*'s contribution to **8:** 165, 167, 182, 193, 197, 206, 210, 228, 239, 267; **25:** 164; **39:** 305, 326, 370
Shakespeare's political sympathies **8:** 147, 163, 177, 193, 197, 201, 223, 228, 232, 243, 248, 267; **39:** 349; **42:** 132
sources
   chronicles **8:** 145, 165, 193, 197, 201, 206, 210, 213, 228, 232
   Marlowe, Christopher **8:** 167, 168, 182, 201, 206, 218
   morality plays **8:** 182, 190, 201, 213, 239
   Seneca, other classical writers **8:** 165, 190, 201, 206, 228, 248
staging issues **14:** 515, 527, 528, 537; **16:** 137
structure **8:** 154, 161, 163, 167, 168, 170, 177, 184, 193, 197, 201, 206, 210, 218, 223, 228, 232, 243, 252, 262, 267; **16:** 150
The Tragical History of King Richard III (Colley Cibber adaptation), compared with **8:** 159, 161, 243
traditional values **39:** 335
Tudor myth **8:** 163, 165, 177, 184, 193, 201, 218, 228, 232, 243, 248, 252, 267; **39:** 305, 308, 326, 387; **42:** 132
Wars of the Roses **8:** 163, 165, 177, 184, 193, 201, 218, 228, 232, 243, 248, 252, 267; **39:** 308
wooing scenes (Act I, scene ii and Act IV, scene iv) **8:** 145, 147, 152, 153, 154, 159, 161, 164, 170, 190, 197, 206, 213, 218, 223, 232, 239, 243, 252, 258, 267; **16:** 150; **19:** 164; **25:** 141, 164; **39:** 308, 326, 360, 387

Romeo and Juliet (Volumes 5, 11, 33)

accident or chance **5:** 418, 444, 448, 467, 470, 487, 573
adolescence **33:** 249, 255, 257
amour-passion or *Liebestod* myth **5:** 484, 489, 528, 530, 542, 550, 575; **32:** 256
androgyny **13:** 530
anxiety **13:** 235
balcony scene **32:** 276
Caius Marius (Thomas Otway adaptation) **11:** 377, 378, 488, 495
comic and tragic elements, combination of **46:** 78
contradiction, paradox, and opposition **5:** 421, 427, 431, 496, 509, 513, 516, 520, 525, 528, 538; **33:** 287; **44:** 11
costuming **11:** 505, 509
courtly love tradition, influence of **5:** 505, 542, 575; **33:** 233
detention of Friar John **5:** 448, 467, 470
divine will, role of **5:** 485, 493, 505, 533, 573
dramatic shortcomings or failure **5:** 416, 418, 420, 426, 436, 437, 448, 464, 467, 469, 480, 487, 524, 562
Elizabethan poetics, influence of **5:** 416, 520, 522, 528, 550, 559, 575
evil **5:** 485, 493, 505
as experimental play **5:** 464, 509, 528
fate **5:** 431, 444, 464, 469, 470, 479, 480, 485, 487, 493, 509, 530, 533, 562, 565, 571, 573; **33:** 249
feud **5:** 415, 419, 425, 447, 458, 464, 469, 479, 480, 493, 509, 522, 556, 565, 566, 571, 575; **25:** 181
Friar Lawrence
   contribution to catastrophe **5:** 437, 444, 470; **33:** 300
   philosophy of moderation **5:** 427, 431, 437, 438, 443, 444, 445, 458, 467, 479, 505, 538
   as Shakespeare's spokesman **5:** 427, 431, 437, 458, 467
ideal love **5:** 421, 427, 431, 436, 437, 450, 463, 469, 498, 505, 575; **25:** 257; **33:** 210, 225, 272
gender issues **32:** 256
lamentation scene (Act IV, scene v) **5:** 425, 492, 538
language and imagery **5:** 420, 426, 431, 436, 437, 456, 477, 479, 489, 492, 496, 509, 520, 522, 528, 538, 542, 550, 559; **25:** 181, 245, 257; **32:** 276; **33:** 210, 272, 274, 287; **42:** 271
love versus fate **5:** 421, 437, 438, 443, 445, 458; **33:** 249
medieval influence **5:** 480, 505, 509, 573
Mercutio
   bawdy **5:** 463, 525, 550, 575
   death, decay, and nature's destructiveness **5:** 415, 418, 419, 547; **33:** 290
   as worldly counterpoint to Romeo **5:** 425, 464, 542; **33:** 290
comic and tragic elements, combination of **5:** 496, 524, 528, 547, 559
Neoclassical rules **5:** 416, 418, 426
Nurse **5:** 419, 425, 463, 464, 575; **33:** 294
Othello, compared with **32:** 302
Petrarchan poetics, influence of **5:** 416, 520, 522, 528, 550, 559, 575; **32:** 276
prose adaptations of Juliet's character **19:** 261
psychoanalytic interpretation **5:** 513, 556
public versus private worlds **5:** 520, 550; **25:** 181; **33:** 274
reconciliation **5:** 415, 419, 427, 439, 447, 480, 487, 493, 505, 533, 536, 562
rhetoric **42:** 271
rival productions **11:** 381, 382, 384, 385, 386, 487
Romeo and Juliet
   death-wish **5:** 431, 489, 505, 528, 530, 538, 542, 550, 566, 571, 575; **32:** 212
   Romeo's Dream **45:** 40
   immortality **5:** 536
   Juliet's epithalamium speech (Act III, scene ii) **5:** 431, 477, 492
   Juliet's innocence **5:** 421, 423, 450, 454; **33:** 257
   maturation **5:** 437, 454, 467, 493, 498, 509, 520, 565; **33:** 249, 257
   rebellion **25:** 257
   reckless passion **5:** 419, 427, 431, 438, 443, 444, 448, 467, 479, 485, 505, 533, 538, 542; **33:** 241
   Romeo's dream (Act V, scene i) **5:** 513, 536, 556
   Rosaline, Romeo's relationship with **5:** 419, 423, 425, 427, 438, 498, 542, 575
sexuality **25:** 181; **33:** 225, 233, 241, 246, 274, 300
source of tragic catastrophe **5:** 418, 427, 431, 448, 458, 469, 479, 480, 485, 487, 493, 509, 522, 528, 530, 533, 542, 565, 571, 573; **33:** 210
sources **5:** 416, 419, 423, 450; **32:** 222; **33:** 210; **45:** 40
staging issues **11:** 499, 505, 507, 514, 517; **13:** 243; **25:** 181; **32:** 212
structure **5:** 438, 448, 464, 469, 470, 477, 480, 496, 518, 524, 525, 528, 547, 559; **33:** 210, 246
tomb scene (Act V, scene iii) **5:** 416, 419, 423; **13:** 243; **25:** 181, 245
triumph over death or fate **5:** 421, 423, 427, 505, 509, 520, 530, 536, 565, 566
Verona society **5:** 556, 566; **13:** 235; **33:** 255
wordplay **32:** 256

Sonnets (Volumes 10, 40)

ambiguity **10:** 251, 256; **28:** 385; **40:** 221, 228, 268
authenticity **10:** 153, 154, 230, 243
autobiographical elements **10:** 159, 160, 166, 167, 175, 176, 182, 196, 205, 213, 215, 226, 233, 238, 240, 251, 279, 283, 302, 309, 325, 337, 377; **13:** 487; **16:** 461; **28:** 363, 385; **42:** 303
beauty **10:** 247
Christian elements **10:** 191, 256
composition date **10:** 153, 154, 161, 166, 196, 217, 226, 270, 277; **28:** 363, 385
Dark Lady **10:** 161, 167, 176, 216, 217, 218, 226, 240, 302, 342, 377, 394; **25:** 374; **37:** 374; **40:** 273
deception, disguise, and duplicity **25:** 374; **40:** 221
dramatic elements **10:** 155, 182, 240, 251, 283, 367
editorial and textual issues **28:** 363; **40:** 273; **42:** 303
the Friend **10:** 279, 302, 309, 379, 385, 391, 394
friendship **10:** 185, 279; **28:** 380
gender issues **37:** 374; **40:** 238, 247, 254, 264, 268, 273
homoerotic elements **10:** 155, 156, 159, 161, 175, 213, 391; **16:** 461; **28:** 363, 380; **37:** 347; **40:** 254, 264, 273
identities of persons **10:** 154, 155, 156, 161, 166, 167, 169, 173, 174, 175, 185, 190, 191, 196, 218, 226, 230, 233, 240; **40:** 238
irony or satire **10:** 256, 293, 334, 337, 346
Italian influences **28:** 407
language and imagery **10:** 247, 251, 255, 256, 290, 353, 372, 385; **13:** 445; **28:** 380, 385; **32:** 327, 352; **40:** 228, 247, 284, 292, 303
love **10:** 173, 247, 287, 290, 293, 302, 309, 322, 325, 329, 394; **28:** 380; **37:** 347
love versus reason **10:** 329
A Lover's Complaint (the Rival Poet) **10:** 243, 353
Mr. W. H. **10:** 153, 155, 161, 169, 174, 182, 190, 196, 217, 218, 377
Montaigne's *Essais*, relation to **42:** 382
mutability, theme of **42:** 382
Neoplatonism **10:** 191, 205
other sonnet writers, Shakespeare compared with **10:** 247, 260, 265, 283, 290, 293, 309, 353, 367; **28:** 380, 385, 407; **37:** 374; **40:** 247, 264, 303; **42:** 303

pedagogy 37: 374
poetic style 10: 153, 155, 156, 158, 159, 160, 161, 173, 175, 182, 214, 247, 251, 255, 260, 265, 283, 287, 296, 302, 315, 322, 325, 337, 346, 349, 360, 367, 385; 16: 472; 40: 221, 228
procreation 10: 379, 385; 16: 461
rhetoric of consolation 42: 382
the Rival Poet 10: 169, 233, 334, 337, 385
self-love 10: 372; 25: 374
sexuality 25: 374
sonnet arrangement 10: 174, 176, 182, 205, 226, 230, 236, 315, 353; 28: 363; 40: 238
sonnet form 10: 255, 325, 367; 37: 347; 40: 284, 303
sonnets (individual):
  3 10: 346
  12 10: 360
  15 40: 292
  18 40: 292
  20 10: 391; 13: 530
  21 32: 352
  26 10: 161
  30 10: 296
  35 10: 251
  49 10: 296
  53 10: 349; 32: 327, 352
  54 32: 352
  55 13: 445
  57 10: 296
  59 16: 472
  60 10: 296; 16: 472
  64 10: 329, 360
  65 10: 296; 40: 292
  66 10: 315
  68 32: 327
  71 10: 167
  73 10: 315, 353, 360
  76 10: 334
  79 32: 352
  82 32: 352
  86 32: 352
  87 10: 296; 40: 303
  93 13: 487
  94 10: 256, 296; 32: 327
  95 32: 327
  98 32: 352
  99 32: 352
  104 10: 360
  105 32: 327
  107 10: 270, 277
  116 10: 329, 379; 13: 445
  117 10: 337
  119 10: 337
  121 10: 346
  123 10: 270
  124 10: 265, 270, 329
  126 10: 161
  129 10: 353, 394; 22: 12
  130 10: 346
  138 10: 296
  144 10: 394
  145 10: 358; 40: 254
  146 10: 353
sonnets (groups):
  1-17 10: 296, 315, 379, 385; 16: 461; 40: 228
  1-21 40: 268
  1-26 10: 176
  1-126 10: 161, 176, 185, 191, 196, 205, 213, 226, 236, 279, 309, 315, 372
  18-22 10: 315
  18-126 10: 379
  23-40 10: 315
  27-55 10: 176
  33-9 10: 329
  56-77 10: 176
  76-86 10: 315
  78-80 10: 334, 385
  78-101 10: 176
  82-6 10: 334
  100-12 10: 337
  102-26 10: 176
  123-25 10: 385
  127-52 10: 293, 385
  127-54 10: 161, 176, 185, 190, 196, 213, 226, 236, 309, 315, 342, 394
  151-52 10: 315
sources 10: 153, 154, 156, 158, 233, 251, 255, 293, 353; 16: 472; 28: 407; 42: 382
structure 10: 175, 176, 182, 205, 230, 260, 296, 302, 309, 315, 337, 349, 353; 40: 238
subjectivity 37: 374
time 10: 265, 302, 309, 322, 329, 337, 360, 379; 13: 445; 40: 292
visual arts, relation to 28: 407

The Taming of the Shrew (Volumes 9, 12, 31)

appearance versus reality 9: 343, 350, 353, 365, 369, 370, 381, 390. 430; 12: 416; 31: 326
Baptista 9: 325, 344, 345, 375, 386, 393, 413
Bianca 9: 325, 342, 344, 345, 360, 362, 370, 375
Bianca-Lucentio subplot 9: 365, 370, 375, 390, 393, 401, 407, 413, 430; 16: 13; 31: 339
Catherine and Petruchio (David Garrick adaptation) 12: 309, 310, 311, 416
class distinctions, conflict, and relations 31: 300, 351
deception, disguise, and duplicity 12: 416
Elizabethan culture, relation to 31: 288, 295, 300, 315, 326, 345, 351
as farce 9: 330, 337, 338, 341, 342, 365, 381, 386, 413, 426
folk elements 9: 381, 393, 404, 426
gender issues 28: 24 31: 261, 268, 276, 282, 288, 295, 300, 335, 351
genre 9: 329, 334, 362, 375; 22: 48; 31: 261, 269, 276
induction 9: 320, 322, 332, 337, 345, 350, 362, 365, 369, 370, 381, 390, 393, 407, 419, 424, 430; 12: 416, 427, 430, 431, 441; 19: 34, 122; 22: 48; 31: 269, 315, 351
irony or satire 9: 340, 375, 398, 407, 413; 13: 3; 19: 122
Kate
  characterization 32: 1
  final speech (Act V, scene ii) 9: 318, 319, 329, 330, 338, 340, 341, 345, 347, 353, 355, 360, 365, 381, 386, 401, 404, 413, 426, 430; 19: 3; 22: 48
  love for Petruchio 9: 338, 340, 353, 430; 12: 435
  portrayals of 31: 282
  shrewishness 9: 322, 323, 325, 332, 344, 345, 360, 365, 370, 375, 386, 393, 398, 404, 413
  transformation 9: 323, 341, 355, 370, 386, 393, 401, 404, 407, 419, 424, 426, 430; 16: 13; 19: 34; 22: 48; 31: 288, 295, 339, 351
Kiss Me, Kate (Cole Porter adaptation) 31: 282
language and imagery 9: 336, 338, 393, 401, 404, 407, 413; 22: 378; 28: 9; 31: 261, 288, 300, 326, 335, 339; 32: 56
Lucentio 9: 325, 342, 362, 375, 393
marriage 9: 322, 325, 329, 332, 329, 332, 334, 341, 342, 343, 344, 345, 347, 353, 360, 362, 375, 381, 390, 398, 401, 404, 413, 426, 430; 13: 3; 19: 3; 28: 24; 31: 288
metadramatic elements 9: 350, 419, 424; 31: 300, 315
metamorphosis or transformation 9: 370, 430
pedagogy 19: 122
performance history 31: 282
performance issues 12: 313, 314, 316, 317, 337, 338; 31: 315
Petruchio
  admirable qualities 9: 320, 332, 341, 344, 345, 370, 375, 386
  audacity or vigor 9: 325, 337, 355, 375, 386, 404
  characterization 32: 1
  coarseness or brutality 9: 325, 329, 365, 390, 393, 398, 407; 19: 122
  as lord of misrule 9: 393
  love for Kate 9: 338, 340, 343, 344, 386; 12: 435
  portrayals of 31: 282
  pragmatism 9: 329, 334, 375, 398, 424; 13: 3; 31: 345, 351
  taming method 9: 320, 323, 329, 340, 341, 343, 345, 355, 369, 370, 375, 390, 398, 407, 413, 419, 424; 19: 3, 12, 21 31: 269, 295, 326, 335, 339
popularity 9: 318, 338, 404
role-playing 9: 322, 353, 355, 360, 369, 370, 398, 401, 407, 413, 419, 424; 13: 3; 31: 288, 295, 315
romantic elements 9: 334, 342, 362, 375, 407
Shakespeare's other plays, compared with 9: 334, 342, 360, 393, 426, 430; 31: 261
Sly 9: 320, 322, 350, 370, 381, 390, 398, 430; 12: 316, 335, 416, 427, 441; 16: 13; 19: 34, 122; 22: 48; 37: 31
sources
  Ariosto 9: 320, 334, 341, 342, 370
  folk tales 9: 332, 390, 393
  Gascoigne 9: 370, 390
  Old and New Comedy 9: 419
  Ovid 9: 318, 370, 430
  Plautus 9: 334, 341, 342
  shrew tradition 9: 355; 19: 3; 32: 1, 56
structure 9: 318, 322, 325, 332, 334, 341, 362, 370, 390, 426; 22: 48, 378; 31: 269
play-within-a-play 12: 416; 22: 48
The Taming of a Shrew (anonymous), compared with 9: 334, 350, 426; 12: 312; 22: 48; 31: 261, 276, 339
textual issues 22: 48; 31: 261, 276; 31: 276
violence 43: 61

The Tempest (Volumes 8, 15, 29, 45)

allegorical elements **8:** 294, 295, 302, 307, 308, 312, 326, 328, 336, 345, 364; **42:** 327
Antonio and Sebastian **8:** 295, 299, 304, 328, 370, 396, 429, 454; **13:** 440; **29:** 278, 297, 343, 362, 368, 377
Ariel **8:** 289, 293, 294, 295, 297, 304, 307, 315, 320, 326, 328, 336, 340, 345, 356, 364, 420, 458; **22:** 302; **29:** 278, 297, 362, 368, 377
art versus nature **8:** 396, 404; **29:** 278, 297, 362
autobiographical elements **8:** 302, 308, 312, 324, 326, 345, 348, 353, 364, 380
Caliban **8:** 286, 287, 289, 292, 294, 295, 297, 302, 304, 307, 309, 315, 326, 328, 336, 353, 364, 370, 380, 390, 396, 401, 414, 420, 423, 429, 435, 454; **13:** 424, 440; **15:** 189, 312, 322, 374, 379; **22:** 302; **25:** 382; **28:** 249; **29:** 278, 292, 297, 343, 368, 377, 396; **32:** 367; **45:** 211, 219, 226, 259
characterization **8:** 287, 289, 292, 294, 295, 308, 326, 334, 336; **28:** 415; **42:** 339; **45:** 219
classical influence and sources **29:** 278, 343, 362, 368
colonialism **13:** 424, 440; **15:** 228, 268, 269, 270, 271, 272, 273; **19:** 421; **25:** 357, 382; **28:** 249; **29:** 343, 368; **32:** 338, 367, 400; **42:** 327; **45:** 200, 280
compassion, theme of **42:** 346
conspiracy or treason **16:** 426; **19:** 357; **25:** 382; **29:** 377
dreams **45:** 236, 247, 259
education or nurturing **8:** 353, 370, 384, 396; **29:** 292, 368, 377
exposition scene (Act I, scene ii) **8:** 287, 289, 293, 299, 334
Ferdinand **8:** 328, 336, 359, 454; **19:** 357; **22:** 302; **29:** 362, 339, 377
freedom and servitude **8:** 304, 307, 312, 429; **22:** 302; **29:** 278, 368, 377; **37:** 336
Gonzalo **22:** 302; **29:** 278, 343, 362, 368
Gonzalo's commonwealth **8:** 312, 336, 370, 390, 396, 404; **19:** 357; **29:** 368; **45:** 280
good versus evil **8:** 302, 311, 315, 370, 423, 439; **29:** 278, 297
historical content **8:** 364, 408, 420; **16:** 426; **25:** 382; **29:** 278, 339, 343, 368; **45:** 226
the island **8:** 308, 315, 447; **25:** 357, 382; **29:** 278, 343
language and imagery **8:** 324, 348, 384, 390, 404, 454; **19:** 421; **29:** 278; **29:** 297, 343, 368, 377
love **8:** 435, 439; **29:** 297, 339, 377, 396
magic or supernatural elements **8:** 287, 293, 304, 315, 340, 356, 396, 401, 404, 408, 435, 458; **28:** 391, 415; **29:** 297, 343, 377; **45:** 272
the masque (Act IV, scene i) **8:** 404, 414, 423, 435, 439; **25:** 357; **28:** 391, 415; **29:** 278, 292, 339, 343, 368; **42:** 339; **45:** 188
Miranda **8:** 289, 301, 304, 328, 336, 370, 454; **19:** 357; **22:** 302; **28:** 249; **29:** 278, 297, 362, 368, 377, 396
Montaigne's *Essais*, relation to **42:** 346
music **8:** 390, 404; **29:** 292; **37:** 321; **42:** 339
nature **8:** 315, 370, 390, 408, 414; **29:** 343, 362, 368, 377
Neoclassical rules **8:** 287, 292, 293, 334; **25:** 357; **29:** 292; **45:** 200
politics **8:** 304, 307, 315, 353, 359, 364, 401, 408; **16:** 426; **19:** 421; **29:** 339; **37:** 336; **42:** 327; **45:** 272, 280
Prospero
  characterization **8:** 312, 348, 370, 458; **16:** 442; **22:** 302; **45:** 188, 272
  as God or Providence **8:** 311, 328, 364, 380, 429, 435
  magic, nature of **8:** 301, 340, 356, 396, 414, 423, 458; **25:** 382; **28:** 391; **29:** 278, 292, 368, 377, 396; **32:** 338, 343
  psychoanalytic interpretation **45:** 259
  redemptive powers **8:** 302, 320, 353, 370, 390, 429, 439, 447; **29:** 297
  as ruler **8:** 304, 308, 309, 420, 423; **13:** 424; **22:** 302; **29:** 278, 362, 377, 396
  self-control **8:** 312, 414, 420; **22:** 302; **44:** 11
  self-knowledge **16:** 442; **22:** 302; **29:** 278, 292, 362, 377, 396
  as Shakespeare or creative artist **8:** 299, 302, 308, 312, 320, 324, 353, 364, 435, 447
  as tragic hero **8:** 359, 370, 464; **29:** 292
realism **8:** 340, 359, 464
reality and illusion **8:** 287, 315, 359, 401, 435, 439, 447, 454; **22:** 302; **45:** 236, 247
reconciliation **8:** 302, 312, 320, 334, 348, 359, 370, 384, 401, 404, 414, 429, 439, 447, 454; **16:** 442; **22:** 302; **29:** 297; **37:** 336; **45:** 236
religious, mythic, or spiritual content **8:** 328, 390, 423, 429, 435; **45:** 211, 247
romance or pastoral tradition, influence of **8:** 336, 348, 396, 404; **37:** 336
Shakespeare's other plays, compared with **8:** 294, 302, 324, 326, 348, 353, 380, 401, 464; **13:** 424
spectacle versus simple staging **15:** 206, 207, 208, 210, 217, 219, 222, 223, 224, 225, 227, 228, 305, 352; **28:** 415
sources **45:** 226
staging issues **15:** 343, 346, 352, 361, 364, 366, 368, 371, 385; **28:** 391, 415; **29:** 339; **32:** 338, 343; **42:** 339; **45:** 200
Stephano and Trinculo, comic subplot of **8:** 292, 297, 299, 304, 309, 324, 328, 353, 370; **25:** 382; **29:** 377; **46:** 14, 33
structure **8:** 294, 295, 299, 320, 384, 439; **28:** 391, 415; **29:** 292, 297; **45:** 188
subversiveness **22:** 302
The Tempest; or, The Enchanted Island (William Davenant/John Dryden adaptation) **15:** 189, 190, 192, 193
The Tempest; or, The Enchanted Island (Thomas Shadwell adaptation) **15:** 195, 196, 199
time **8:** 401, 439, 464; **25:** 357; **29:** 278, 292; **45:** 236
tragic elements **8:** 324, 348, 359, 370, 380, 408, 414, 439, 458, 464
trickster, motif of **22:** 302; **29:** 297
usurpation or rebellion **8:** 304, 370, 408, 420; **25:** 357, 382; **29:** 278, 362, 377; **37:** 336
utopia **45:** 280

Timon of Athens (Volumes 1, 20, 27)

Alcibiades **25:** 198; **27:** 191
alienation **1:** 523; **27:** 161
Apemantus **1:** 453, 467, 483; **20:** 476, 493; **25:** 198; **27:** 166, 223, 235
appearance versus reality **1:** 495, 500, 515, 523
Athens **27:** 223, 230
authorship controversy **1:** 464, 466, 467, 469, 474, 477, 478, 480, 490, 499, 507, 518; **16:** 351; **20:** 433
autobiographical elements **1:** 462, 467, 470, 473, 474, 478, 480; **27:** 166, 175
Elizabethan culture, relation to **1:** 487, 489, 495, 500; **20:** 433; **27:** 203, 212, 230
as inferior or flawed plays **1:** 476, 481, 489, 499, 520; **20:** 433, 439, 491; **25:** 198; **27:** 157, 175
genre **1:** 454, 456, 459, 460, 462, 483, 492, 499, 503, 509, 511, 512, 515, 518, 525, 531; **27:** 203
King Lear, relation to **1:** 453, 459, 511; **16:** 351; **27:** 161; **37:** 222
language and imagery **1:** 488; **13:** 392; **25:** 198; **27:** 166, 184, 235
as medieval allegory or morality play **1:** 492, 511, 518; **27:** 155
mixture of genres **16:** 351; **25:** 198
nihilistic elements **1:** 481, 513, 529; **13:** 392; **20:** 481
pessimistic elements **1:** 462, 467, 470, 473, 478, 480; **20:** 433, 481; **27:** 155, 191
Poet and Painter **25:** 198
politics **27:** 223, 230
religious, mythic, or spiritual content **1:** 505, 512, 513, 523; **20:** 493
satirical elements **27:** 155, 235
self-knowledge **1:** 456, 459, 462, 495, 503, 507, 515, 518, 526; **20:** 493; **27:** 166
Senecan elements **27:** 235
Shakespeare's other tragedies, compared with **27:** 166
sources **16:** 351; **27:** 191
staging issues **20:** 445, 446, 481, 491, 492, 493
structure **27:** 157, 175, 235
Timon
  comic traits **25:** 198
  as flawed hero **1:** 456, 459, 462, 472, 495, 503, 507, 515; **16:** 351; **20:** 429, 433, 476; **25:** 198; **27:** 157, 161
  misanthropy **13:** 392; **20:** 431, 464, 476, 481, 491, 492, 493; **27:** 161, 175, 184, 196; **37:** 222
  as noble figure **1:** 467, 473, 483, 499; **20:** 493; **27:** 212
wealth and social class **1:** 466, 487, 495; **25:** 198; **27:** 184, 196, 212

Titus Andronicus (Volumes 4, 17, 27, 43)

Aaron **4:** 632, 637, 650, 651, 653, 668, 672, 675; **27:** 255; **28:** 249, 330; **43:** 176
authorship controversy **4:** 613, 614, 615, 616, 617, 619, 623, 624, 625, 626, 628, 631, 632, 635, 642
autobiographical elements **4:** 619, 624, 625, 664
banquet scene **25:** 245; **27:** 255; **32:** 212
ceremonies, rites, and rituals, importance of **27:** 261; **32:** 265
characterization **4:** 613, 628, 632, 635, 640, 644, 647, 650, 675; **27:** 293; **43:** 170, 176
Christian elements **4:** 656, 680

civilization versus barbarism **4:** 653; **27:** 293; **28:** 249; **32:** 265
Elizabethan culture, relation to **27:** 282
Euripides, influence of **27:** 285
language and imagery **4:** 617, 624, 635, 642, 644, 646, 659, 664, 668, 672, 675; **13:** 225; **16:** 225; **25:** 245; **27:** 246, 293, 313, 318, 325; **43:** 186, 222, 227, 239, 247, 262,
language versus action **4:** 642, 644, 647, 664, 668; **13:** 225; **27:** 293, 313, 325; **43:** 186
Lavinia **27:** 266; **28:** 249; **32:** 212; **43:** 170, 239, 247, 255, 262
medieval literary influence **4:** 646, 650; **27:** 299
order versus disintegration **4:** 618, 647; **43:** 186, 195
Ovid, influence of **4:** 647, 659, 664, 668; **13:** 225; **27:** 246, 275, 285, 293, 299, 306; **28:** 249; **43:** 195, 203, 206
political content **43:** 262
politics **27:** 282
rape **43:** 227, 255
rightful succession **4:** 638
Roman elements **43:** 206, 222
Romans versus Goths **27:** 282
Senecan or revenge tragedy elements **4:** 618, 627, 628, 636, 639, 644, 646, 664, 672, 680; **16:** 225; **27:** 275, 318; **43:** 170, 206, 227
Shakespeare's canon, place in **4:** 614, 616, 618, 619, 637, 639, 646, 659, 664, 668; **43:** 195
Shakespeare's other tragedies, compared with **16:** 225; **27:** 275, 325
staging issues **17:** 449, 452, 456, 487; **25:** 245; **32:** 212, 249
structure **4:** 618, 619, 624, 631, 635, 640, 644, 646, 647, 653, 656, 659, 662, 664, 668, 672; **27:** 246, 285
Tamora **4:** 632, 662, 672, 675; **27:** 266; **43:** 170
Titus **4:** 632, 637, 640, 644, 647, 653, 656, 662; **25:** 245; **27:** 255
Vergil, influence of **27:** 306; **28:** 249
violence **13:** 225; **25:** 245; **27:** 255; **28:** 249; **32:** 249, 265; **43:** 1, 186, 203, 227, 239, 247, 255, 262,

Troilus and Cressida (Volumes 3, 18, 27, 43)

ambiguity **3:** 544, 568, 583, 587, 589, 599, 611, 621; **27:** 400; **43:** 365
ambivalence **43:** 340
assignation scene (Act V, scene ii) **18:** 442, 451
autobiographical elements **3:** 548, 554, 557, 558, 574, 606, 630
body, role of **42:** 66
characterization **3:** 538, 539, 540, 541, 548, 566, 571, 604, 611, 621; **27:** 381, 391
Chaucer's Criseyde, compared with **43:** 305
chivalry, decline of **16:** 84; **27:** 370, 374
communication, failure of **43:** 277
conclusion **3:** 538, 549, 558, 566, 574, 583, 594
  comedy vs. tragedy **43:** 351
contradictions **43:** 377
costumes **18:** 289, 371, 406, 419
courtly love **22:** 58
Cressida
  as ambiguous figure **43:** 305
  inconsistency **3:** 538; **13:** 53; **16:** 70; **22:** 339; **27:** 362
  individual will versus social values **3:** 549, 561, 571, 590, 604, 617, 626; **13:** 53; **27:** 396
  infidelity **3:** 536, 537, 544, 554, 555; **18:** 277, 284, 286; **22:** 58, 339; **27:** 400; **43:** 298
  lack of punishment **3:** 536, 537
  as mother figure **22:** 339
  objectification of **43:** 329
  as sympathetic figure **3:** 557, 560, 604, 609; **18:** 284, 423; **22:** 58; **27:** 396, 400; **43:** 305
cynicism **43:** 298
desire **43:** 317, 329, 340
disillusioned or cynical tone **3:** 544, 548, 554, 557, 558, 571, 574, 630, 642; **18:** 284, 332, 403, 406, 423; **27:** 376
disorder **3:** 578, 589, 599, 604, 609; **18:** 332, 406, 412, 423; **27:** 366
double plot **3:** 569, 613
Elizabeth I
  waning power **43:** 365
Elizabethan culture, relation to **3:** 560, 574, 606; **25:** 56
food imagery **43:** 298
genre **3:** 541, 542, 549, 558, 566, 571, 574, 587, 594, 604, 630, 642; **27:** 366
Greece **43:** 287
inaction **3:** 587, 621; **27:** 347
language and imagery **3:** 561, 569, 596, 599, 606, 624, 630, 635; **22:** 58, 339; **27:** 332; 366; **42:** 66
love and honor **3:** 555, 604; **27:** 370, 374
love versus war **18:** 332, 371, 406, 423; **22:** 339; **27:** 376; **43:** 377
male/female relationships **16:** 70; **22:** 339; **27:** 362
marriage **22:** 339
master-slave relationship **22:** 58
medieval chivalry **3:** 539, 543, 544, 555, 606; **27:** 376
moral corruption **3:** 578, 589, 599, 604, 609; **18:** 332, 406, 412, 423; **27:** 366; **43:** 298
Neoclassical rules **3:** 537, 538; **18:** 276, 278, 281
nihilistic elements **27:** 354
patriarchy **22:** 58
politics **3:** 536, 560, 606; **16:** 84
as "problem play" **3:** 555, 566
  lack of resolution **43:** 277
psychoanalytical criticism **43:** 287
rape **43:** 357
satirical elements **3:** 539, 543, 544, 555, 558, 574; **27:** 341
sexuality **22:** 58, 339; **25:** 56; **27:** 362; **43:** 365
sources **3:** 537, 539, 540, 541, 544, 549, 558, 566, 574, 587; **27:** 376, 381, 391, 400
staging issues **16:** 70; **18:** 289, 332, 371, 395, 403, 406, 412, 419, 423, 442, 447, 451
structure **3:** 536, 538, 549, 568, 569, 578, 583, 589, 611, 613; **27:** 341, 347, 354, 391
Thersites **13:** 53; **25:** 56; **27:** 381
time **3:** 561, 571, 583, 584, 613, 621, 626, 634
Troilus
  contradictory behavior **3:** 596, 602, 635; **27:** 362
  Cressida, relationship with **3:** 594, 596, 606; **22:** 58
  integrity **3:** 617
  opposition to Ulysses **3:** 561, 584, 590
  as unsympathetic figure **18:** 423; **22:** 58, 339; **43:** 317
  as warrior **3:** 596; **22:** 339
Troilus and Cressida, or Truth Found too late (John Dryden adaptation) **18:** 276, 277, 278, 280, 281, 283
Trojan versus Greek values **3:** 541, 561, 574, 584, 590, 596, 621, 638; **27:** 370
Trojan War
  as myth **43:** 293
Troy **43:** 287
Ulysses's speech on degree (Act I, scene iii) **3:** 549, 599, 609, 642; **27:** 396
value systems **3:** 578, 583, 589, 602, 613, 617; **13:** 53; **27:** 370, 396, 400
violence **43:** 329, 351, 357, 365, 377
  through satire **43:** 293

Twelfth Night (Volumes 1, 26, 34, 46)

ambiguity **1:** 554, 639; **34:** 287, 316
Antonio **22:** 69
appetite **1:** 563, 596, 609, 615
autobiographical elements **1:** 557, 561, 599; **34:** 338
bear-baiting **19:** 42
characterization **1:** 539, 540, 543, 545, 550, 554, 581, 594; **26:** 257, 337, 342, 346, 364, 366, 371, 374; **34:** 281, 293, 311, 338; **46:** 286, 324
Christian elements **46:** 338
comic elements **26:** 233, 257, 337, 342, 371
composition date **37:** 78
credibility **1:** 540, 542, 543, 554, 562, 581, 587
dark or tragic elements **46:** 310
Elizabethan culture, relation to **1:** 549, 553, 555, 563, 581, 587, 620; **16:** 53; **19:** 42, 78; **26:** 357; **28:** 1; **34:** 323, 330; **46:** 291
fancy **1:** 543, 546
Feste
  characterization **1:** 558, 655, 658; **26:** 233, 364; **46:** 1, 14, 18, 33, 52, 60, 303, 310
  role in play **1:** 546, 551, 553, 566, 570, 571, 579, 635, 658; **46:** 297, 303, 310
  song **1:** 543, 548, 561, 563, 566, 570, 572, 603, 620, 642; **46:** 297
festive or folklore elements **46:** 338
gender issues **19:** 78; **34:** 344; **37:** 59; **42:** 32; **46:** 347, 362, 369
homosexuality **22:** 69; **42:** 32; **46:** 362
language and imagery **1:** 570, 650, 664; **22:** 12; **28:** 9; **34:** 293; **37:** 59
love **1:** 543, 546, 573, 580, 587, 595, 600, 603, 610, 660; **19:** 78; **26:** 257, 364; **34:** 270, 293, 323; **46:** 291, 333, 347, 362
madness **1:** 554, 639, 656; **26:** 371
Malvolio
  characterization **1:** 540, 544, 545, 548, 550, 554, 558, 567, 575, 577, 615; **26:** 207, 233, 273; **46:** 286

forged letter **16:** 372; **28:** 1
punishment **1:** 539, 544, 548, 549, 554, 555, 558, 563, 577, 590, 632, 645; **46:** 291, 297, 338
as Puritan **1:** 549, 551, 555, 558, 561, 563; **25:** 47
role in play **1:** 545, 548, 549, 553, 555, 563, 567, 575, 577, 588, 610, 615, 632, 645; **26:** 337, 374; **46:** 347
music **1:** 543, 566, 596
Olivia **1:** 540, 543, 545; **46:** 286, 333, 369
order **1:** 563, 596; **34:** 330; **46:** 291, 347
Orsino **46:** 286, 333
philosophical elements **1:** 560, 563, 596; **34:** 301, 316; **46:** 297
Puritanism **1:** 549, 553, 555, 632; **16:** 53; **25:** 47; **46:** 338
psychoanalytic criticism **46:** 333
Saturnalian elements **1:** 554, 571, 603, 620, 642; **16:** 53
self-deception **1:** 554, 561, 591, 625
self-indulgence **1:** 563, 615, 635
sexual ambiguity and sexual deception **1:** 540, 562, 620, 621, 639, 645; **22:** 69; **34:** 311, 344; **37:** 59; **42:** 32
Shakespeare's canon, place in **1:** 543, 548, 557, 569, 575, 580, 621, 635, 638
Shakespeare's other plays, relation to **34:** 270; **46:** 303
sources **1:** 539, 540, 603; **34:** 301, 323, 344; **46:** 291
staging issues **26:** 219, 233, 257, 337, 342, 346, 357, 359, 360, 364, 366, 371, 374; **46:** 310, 369
structure **1:** 539, 542, 543, 546, 551, 553, 563, 570, 571, 590, 600, 660; **26:** 374; **34:** 281, 287; **46:** 286
time **37:** 78; **46:** 297
tragic elements **1:** 557, 569, 572, 575, 580, 599, 621, 635, 638, 639, 645, 654, 656; **26:** 342
Viola **26:** 308; **46:** 286, 324, 347, 369

The Two Gentlemen of Verona (Volumes 6, 12, 40)

absurdities, inconsistencies, and shortcomings **6:** 435, 436, 437, 439, 464, 507, 541, 560
appearance versus reality **6:** 494, 502, 511, 519, 529, 532, 549, 560
audience versus character perceptions **6:** 499, 519, 524
authorship controversy **6:** 435, 436, 437, 438, 439, 449, 466, 476
characterization **6:** 438, 442, 445, 447, 449, 458, 462, 560; **12:** 458; **40:** 312, 327, 330, 365
Christian elements **6:** 438, 494, 514, 532, 555, 564
education **6:** 490, 494, 504, 526, 532, 555, 568
Elizabethan setting **12:** 463, 485
forest **6:** 450, 456, 492, 514, 547, 555, 564, 568
genre **6:** 460, 468, 472, 516; **40:** 320
identity **6:** 494, 511, 529, 532, 547, 560, 564, 568; **19:** 34
ironic or parodic elements **6:** 447, 472, 478, 484, 502, 504, 509, 516, 529, 549; **13:** 12

Julia or Silvia **6:** 450, 453, 458, 476, 494, 499, 516, 519, 549, 564; **40:** 312, 327, 374
language and imagery **6:** 437, 438, 439, 445, 449, 490, 504, 519, 529, 541; **28:** 9; **40:** 343
Launce and Speed, comic function of **6:** 438, 439, 442, 456, 458, 460, 462, 472, 476, 478, 484, 502, 504, 507, 509, 516, 519, 549; **40:** 312, 320
love **6:** 442, 445, 456, 479, 488, 492, 494, 502, 509, 516, 519, 549; **13:** 12; **40:** 327, 335, 343, 354, 365
love versus friendship **6:** 439, 449, 450, 458, 460, 465, 468, 471, 476, 480; **40:** 354, 359, 365
mimetic rivalry **13:** 12; **40:** 335
morality **6:** 438, 492, 494, 514, 532, 555, 564
Proteus **6:** 439, 450, 458, 480, 490, 511; **40:** 312, 327, 330, 335, 359; **42:** 18
repentance and forgiveness **6:** 450, 514, 516, 555, 564
resolution **6:** 435, 436, 439, 445, 449, 453, 458, 460, 462, 465, 466, 468, 471, 476, 480, 486, 494, 509, 514, 516, 519, 529, 532, 541, 549; **19:** 34
romantic and courtly conventions **6:** 438, 460, 472, 478, 484, 486, 488, 502, 507, 509, 529, 541, 549, 560, 568; **12:** 460, 462; **40:** 354, 374
setting **12:** 463, 465, 485
sources **6:** 436, 460, 462, 468, 476, 480, 490, 511, 547; **19:** 34; **40:** 320
staging issues **12:** 457, 464; **42:** 18
structure **6:** 445, 450, 460, 462, 504, 526
youth **6:** 439, 450, 464, 514, 568

The Two Noble Kinsmen (Volumes 9, 41)

amorality, question of **9:** 447, 460, 492
authorship controversy
Shakespeare not a co-author **9:** 445, 447, 455, 461
Shakespearean portions of the text **9:** 446, 447, 448, 455, 456, 457, 460, 462, 463, 471, 479, 486; **41:** 308, 317, 355
Shakespeare's part in the overall conception or design **9:** 444, 446, 448, 456, 457, 460, 480, 481, 486, 490; **37:** 313; **41:** 326
ceremonies, rites, and rituals, importance of **9:** 492, 498
characterization **9:** 457, 461, 471, 474; **41:** 340, 385
Emilia **9:** 460, 470, 471, 479, 481; **19:** 394; **41:** 372, 385; **42:** 368
free will versus fate **9:** 474, 481, 486, 492, 498
friendship **9:** 448, 463, 470, 474, 479, 481, 486, 490; **19:** 394; **41:** 355, 363, 372; **42:** 368
gender issues **42:** 368
innocence to experience **9:** 481, 502; **19:** 394
irony or satire **9:** 463, 481, 486; **41:** 301
the jailer's daughter **9:** 457, 460, 479, 481, 486, 502; **41:** 340
language and imagery **9:** 445, 446, 447, 448, 456, 461, 462, 463, 469, 471, 498, 502; **41:** 289, 301, 308, 317, 326
love **9:** 479, 481, 490, 498; **41:** 289, 355, 301, 363, 372, 385
masque elements **9:** 490

Palamon and Arcite **9:** 474, 481, 490, 492, 502
sources **19:** 394; **41:** 289, 301, 363, 385
structure **37:** 313

Venus and Adonis (Volumes 10, 33)

Adonis **10:** 411, 420, 424, 427, 429, 434, 439, 442, 451, 454, 459, 466, 473, 489; **25:** 305, 328; **28:** 355; **33:** 309, 321, 330, 347, 352, 357, 363, 370, 377
allegorical elements **10:** 427, 434, 439, 449, 454, 462, 480; **28:** 355; **33:** 309, 330
ambiguity **10:** 434, 454, 459, 462, 466, 473, 480, 486, 489; **33:** 352
beauty **10:** 420, 423, 427, 434, 454, 480; **33:** 330, 352
the boar **10:** 416, 451, 454, 466, 473; **33:** 339, 347, 370
the courser and the jennet **10:** 418, 439, 466; **33:** 309, 339, 347, 352
death, decay, and nature's destructiveness **10:** 419, 427, 434, 451, 454, 462, 466, 473, 480, 489; **25:** 305; **33:** 309, 321, 347, 352, 363, 370
dramatic elements **10:** 459, 462, 486
eroticism or sensuality **10:** 410, 411, 418, 419, 427, 428, 429, 442, 448, 454, 459, 466, 473; **25:** 305, 328; **28:** 355; **33:** 321, 339, 347, 352, 363, 370
Faerie Queene (Edmund Spenser), compared with **33:** 339
Hero and Leander (Christopher Marlowe), compared with **10:** 419, 424, 429; **33:** 309, 357
comic elements **10:** 429, 434, 439, 442, 459, 462, 489; **33:** 352
hunt motif **10:** 434, 451, 466, 473; **33:** 357, 370
imagery **10:** 414, 415, 416, 420, 429, 434, 449, 459, 466, 473, 480; **25:** 328; **28:** 355; **33:** 321, 339, 352, 363, 370, 377; **42:** 348
love versus lust **10:** 418, 420, 427, 434, 439, 448, 449, 454, 462, 466, 473, 480, 489; **25:** 305; **28:** 355; **33:** 309, 330, 339, 347, 357, 363, 370
morality **10:** 411, 412, 414, 416, 418, 419, 420, 423, 427, 428, 439, 442, 448, 449, 454, 459, 466; **33:** 330
negative appraisals **10:** 410, 411, 415, 418, 419, 424, 429
Ovid, compared with **32:** 352; **42:** 348
pictorial elements **10:** 414, 415, 419, 420, 423, 480; **33:** 339
popularity **10:** 410, 412, 418, 427; **25:** 328
procreation **10:** 439, 449, 466; **33:** 321, 377
reason **10:** 427, 439, 449, 459, 462, 466; **28:** 355; **33:** 309, 330
rhetoric **33:** 377
Shakespeare's plays, compared with **10:** 412, 414, 415, 434, 459, 462
Shakespeare's sonnets, compared with **33:** 377
sources **10:** 410, 412, 420, 424, 429, 434, 439, 451, 454, 466, 473, 480, 486, 489; **16:** 452; **25:** 305; **28:** 355; **33:** 309, 321, 330, 339, 347, 352, 357, 370, 377; **42:** 348
structure **10:** 434, 442, 480, 486, 489; **33:** 357, 377
style **10:** 411, 412, 414, 415, 416, 418, 419, 420, 423, 424, 428, 429, 439, 442, 480, 486, 489; **16:** 452

Venus **10:** 427, 429, 434, 439, 442, 448, 449, 451, 454, 466, 473, 480, 486, 489; **16:** 452; **25:** 305, 328; **28:** 355; **33:** 309, 321, 330, 347, 352, 357, 363, 370, 377
Wat the hare **10:** 424, 451

The Winter's Tale **(Volumes 7, 15, 36, 45)**

Antigonus
   characterization **7:** 394, 451, 464
   death scene (Act III, scene iii) **7:** 377, 414, 464, 483; **15:** 518, 532; **19:** 366
appearance versus reality **7:** 429, 446, 479
art versus nature **7:** 377, 381, 397, 419, 452; **36:** 289, 318; **45:** 329
audience perception, Shakespeare's manipulation of **7:** 394, 429, 456, 483, 501; **13:** 417; **19:** 401, 431, 441; **25:** 339; **45:** 374
autobiographical elements **7:** 395, 397, 410, 419
Autolycus **7:** 375, 380, 382, 387, 389, 395, 396, 414; **15:** 524; **22:** 302; **37:** 31; **45:** 333; **46:** 14, 33
Christian elements **7:** 381, 387, 402, 410, 417, 419, 425, 429, 436, 452, 460, 501; **36:** 318
counsel **19:** 401
court society **16:** 410
dramatic structure **7:** 382, 390, 396, 399, 402, 407, 414, 429, 432, 473, 479, 493, 497, 501; **15:** 528; **25:** 339; **36:** 289, 295, 362, 380; **45:** 297, 344, 358, 366
ethnicity **37:** 306
folk drama, relation to **7:** 420, 451
forgiveness or redemption **7:** 381, 389, 395, 402, 407, 436, 456, 460, 483; **36:** 318
fusion of comic, tragic, and romantic elements **7:** 390, 394, 396, 399, 410, 412, 414, 429, 436, 479, 483, 490, 501; **13:** 417; **15:** 514, 524, 532; **25:** 339; **36:** 295, 380; **45:** 295, 329

grace **7:** 420, 425, 460, 493; **36:** 328
Hermione
   characterization **7:** 385, 395, 402, 412, 414, 506; **15:** 495, 532; **22:** 302, 324; **25:** 347; **32:** 388; **36:** 311
   restoration (Act V, scene iii) **7:** 377, 379, 384, 385, 387, 389, 394, 396, 412, 425, 436, 451, 452, 456, 464, 483, 501; **15:** 411, 412, 413, 518, 528, 532
   supposed death **25:** 339
as historical allegory **7:** 381; **15:** 528
hospitality **19:** 366
irony **7:** 419, 420
Jacobean culture, relation to **19:** 366, 401, 431; **25:** 347; **32:** 388; **37:** 306
language and imagery **7:** 382, 384, 417, 418, 420, 425, 460, 506; **13:** 409; **19:** 431; **22:** 324; **25:** 347; **36:** 295; **42:** 308; **45:** 297, 333, 344
Leontes
   characterization **19:** 431; **45:** 366
   jealousy **7:** 377, 379, 382, 383, 384, 387, 389, 394, 395, 402, 407, 412, 414, 425, 429, 432, 436, 464, 480, 483, 497; **15:** 514, 518, 532; **22:** 324; **25:** 339; **36:** 334, 344, 349; **44:** 66; **45:** 295, 297, 344, 358
   Othello, compared with **7:** 383, 390, 412; **15:** 514; **36:** 334; **44:** 66
   repentance **7:** 381, 389, 394, 396, 402, 414, 497; **36:** 318, 362; **44:** 66
love **7:** 417, 425, 469, 490
Mamillius **7:** 394, 396, 451; **22:** 324
metadramatic elements **16:** 410
myth of Demeter and Persephone, relation to **7:** 397, 436
nationalism and patriotism **32:** 388
nature **7:** 397, 418, 419, 420, 425, 432, 436, 451, 452, 473, 479; **19:** 366; **45:** 329
Neoclassical rules **7:** 376, 377, 379, 380, 383, 410; **15:** 397

Ovid's *Metamorphoses*, relation to **42:** 308
Pandosto, compared with **7:** 376, 377, 390, 412, 446; **13:** 409; **25:** 347; **36:** 344, 374
Paulina **7:** 385, 412, 506; **15:** 528; **22:** 324; **25:** 339; **36:** 311
Perdita
   characterization **7:** 395, 412, 414, 419, 429, 432, 452, 506; **22:** 324; **25:** 339; **36:** 328
   reunion with Leontes (Act V, scene ii) **7:** 377, 379, 381, 390, 432, 464, 480
plot **7:** 376, 377, 379, 382, 387, 390, 396, 452; **13:** 417; **15:** 518; **45:** 374
rebirth, regeneration, resurrection, or immortality **7:** 397, 414, 417, 419, 429, 436, 451, 452, 456, 480, 490, 497, 506; **25:** 339 452, 480, 490, 497, 506; **45:** 366
sheep-shearing scene (Act IV, scene iv) **7:** 379, 387, 395, 396, 407, 410, 412, 419, 420, 429, 432, 436, 451, 479, 490; **16:** 410; **19:** 366; **25:** 339; **36:** 362, 374; **45:** 374
staging issues **7:** 414, 425, 429, 446, 464, 480, 483, 497; **13:** 409; **15:** 518
statue scene (Act V, scene iii) **7:** 377, 379, 384, 385, 387, 389, 394, 396, 412, 425, 436, 451, 456, 464, 483, 501; **15:** 411, 412, 518, 528, 532; **25:** 339, 347; **36:** 301
subversiveness **22:** 302
symbolism **7:** 425, 429, 436, 452, 456, 469, 490, 493
textual issues **19:** 441; **45:** 333
Time-Chorus **7:** 377, 380, 412, 464, 476, 501; **15:** 518
time **7:** 397, 425, 436, 476, 490; **19:** 366; **36:** 301, 349; **45:** 297, 329, 366, 374
trickster, motif of **22:** 302; **45:** 333
Union debate, relation to **25:** 347
violence **43:** 39
witchcraft **22:** 324
women, role of **22:** 324; **36:** 311; **42:** 308

ISBN 0-7876-2422-5

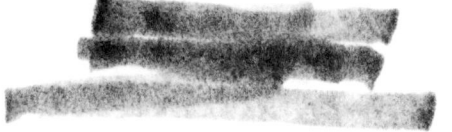

REFERENCE--NOT TO BE
TAKEN FROM THIS ROOM